McDougal Littell
CLASSZONE

Visit classzone.com and get connected.

ClassZone resources provide instruction, practice and learning support for students and parents.

Help with the Math

- @Home Tutor enables students to focus on the math and be more prepared for class, using animated examples and instruction.
- Extra examples similar to those in the book provide additional support.
- Hints and Homework Help offers assistance solving select homework exercises.

Practice, Practice, Practice

- eWorkbook includes interactive worksheets with additional practice problems.
- Problem of the Week features a new problem to solve every week.

Games and Activities

- Crossword puzzles, memory games, and other activities help students connect to essential math concepts.
- Math Vocabulary Flipcards are a fun way to learn math terminology.

Animated Math

- Engaging activities with animated problem-solving graphics support each lesson.

Access the online version of your textbook at classzone.com

Your complete text is available for immediate use!

McDougal Littell
Where Great Lessons Begin

CALIFORNIA

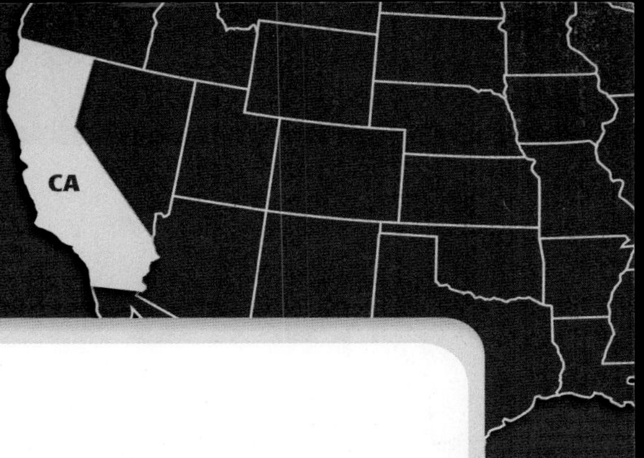

McDougal Littell

MATH
Course 2

Ron Larson
Laurie Boswell
Timothy D. Kanold
Lee Stiff

McDougal Littell
A DIVISION OF HOUGHTON MIFFLIN COMPANY
Evanston, Illinois • Boston • Dallas

About *California Math Course 2*

The content of *California Math Course 2* is organized around and offers complete coverage of California's Grade 7 Mathematics Content Standards. Mathematics standards from previous grades are reviewed to help with your understanding of the Grade 7 standards. Activities are provided to develop Grade 7 concepts. Each lesson has ample skill practice so that you can master the important mathematical processes taught in Grade 7. *California Math Course 2* also teaches you valuable techniques for solving purely mathematical as well as real-world problems. Throughout each chapter you will engage in error analysis and mathematical reasoning to build critical thinking skills and to construct logical arguments. *California Math Course 2* thus provides a balance between basic skills, conceptual understanding, and problem solving—all supported by mathematical reasoning.

In *California Math Course 2* you will have many opportunities to practice your understanding of the Grade 7 standards. At the end of each lesson are multiple choice exercises that review standards that you learned in previous lessons. Additionally, multiple choice exercises on chapter content appear in each lesson, on Mixed Review pages twice per chapter, and at the end of each chapter on the Multiple Choice Strategies and Multiple Choice Practice pages. Technology support for course content is available at classzone.com.

ISBN-13: 978-0-618-72651-6
ISBN-10: 0-618-72651-9   3 4 5 6 7 8 9-DWO-13 12 11 10 09 08

Internet Web Site: http://www.mcdougallittell.com

About the Authors

Ron Larson is a professor of mathematics at Penn State University at Erie, where he has taught since receiving his Ph.D. in mathematics from the University of Colorado. Dr. Larson is well known as the author of a comprehensive program for mathematics that spans middle school, high school, and college courses. Dr. Larson's numerous professional activities keep him in constant touch with the needs of teachers and supervisors. He closely follows developments in mathematics standards and assessment.

Laurie Boswell is a mathematics teacher at The Riverside School in Lyndonville, Vermont, and has taught mathematics at all levels, elementary through college. A recipient of the Presidential Award for Excellence in Mathematics Teaching, she was also a Tandy Technology Scholar. She served on the NCTM Board of Directors (2002–2005), and she speaks frequently at regional and national conferences on topics related to instructional strategies and course content.

Timothy D. Kanold is the superintendent of Adlai E. Stevenson High School District 125 in Lincolnshire, Illinois. Dr. Kanold served as a teacher and director of mathematics for 17 years prior to becoming superintendent. He is the recipient of the Presidential Award for Excellence in Mathematics and Science Teaching, and a past president of the Council for Presidential Awardees in Mathematics. Dr. Kanold is a frequent speaker at national and international mathematics meetings.

Lee Stiff is a professor of mathematics education in the College of Education and Psychology of North Carolina State University at Raleigh and has taught mathematics at the high school and middle school levels. He served on the NCTM Board of Directors and was elected President of NCTM for the years 2000–2002. He is a recipient of the W. W. Rankin Award for Excellence in Mathematics Education presented by the North Carolina Council of Teachers of Mathematics.

Advisers and Reviewers
McDougal Littell's *California Math* series

Program Advisory Panel

Rick Austin
Mathematics Teacher
Daniel Lewis Middle School
Paso Robles, CA

Gregory T. Miyata
EETT/IMaST II Lead
  Coach/Advisor
Robert Louis Stevenson
  Middle School
Los Angeles, CA

Karen Cliffe
Mathematics Curriculum
  Specialist
Sweetwater Union
  High School District
Chula Vista, CA

Yoshiko Okamoto
Mathematics Teacher,
  Department Chair
Hoover Middle School
Lakewood, CA

Stephanie Davis
Mathematics and Science
  Teacher
Jefferson Middle School
San Gabriel, CA

Jane Marie Smith
Mathematics Teacher
Hillview Middle School
Palmdale, CA

Barry Fox
Mathematics Teacher/
  Assistant Principal
Florence Nightingale Middle
  School
Los Angeles, CA

Gwendolyn Walker-Jennels
Mathematics Teacher
Ralph Waldo Emerson
  Middle School
Pomona, CA

Brent T. Kuykendall
Mathematics Teacher
Ridgecrest Intermediate School
Rancho Palos Verdes, CA

Joan Hairston
Mathematics Teacher
Francisco Bravo Medical Magnet
  School
Los Angeles, CA

Textbook Reviewers

José Aguilar
Mathematics Coach
Eagle Rock High School
Los Angeles, CA

Rick Austin
Mathematics Teacher
Daniel Lewis Middle School
Paso Robles, CA

Tamesha Carter
Mathematics Teacher
DeMille Middle School
Long Beach, CA

Gregory T. Miyata
EETT/IMaST II Lead
   Coach/Advisor
Robert Louis Stevenson
   Middle School
Los Angeles, CA

Mark Chavez
Mathematics Teacher
DeMille Middle School
Long Beach, CA

Yoshiko Okamoto
Mathematics Teacher,
   Department Chair
Hoover Middle School
Lakewood, CA

Karen Cliffe
Mathematics Curriculum
   Specialist
Sweetwater Union
   High School District
Chula Vista, CA

Mike Pacheco
Mathematics Teacher
David Wark Griffith Middle School
Los Angeles, CA

Ed Kohn
Professional Development
   Facilitator
Los Angeles Unified School
   District
Los Angeles, CA

Rudy Sass
Mathematics Teacher
Orangeview Junior High School
Anaheim, CA

Chris Martinez
Mathematics Teacher
Arden Middle School
Sacramento, CA

Teacher's Editions Advisory Panel

Edie Birbeck
Mathematics Teacher
William Hopkins Junior
  High School
Fremont, CA

Janet L. Bryson
Mathematics Coach,
TASEL-M
Orange, CA

Ellen Duffy
Mathematics Coach
TASEL-M
Fullerton, CA

Donna Krueger Phair
Mathematics Teacher,
  Department Chair
William Hopkins Junior
  High School
Fremont, CA

Frank Dong
Mathematics Teacher
Marina Middle School
San Francisco, CA

Diane Jacobs
Mathematics Teacher
Fitz Intermediate School
Santa Ana, CA

Ellen Fujii
7–12 Mathematics Program
  Facilitator
Garden Grove Unified
  School District
Garden Grove, CA

Shauna Poong
Mathematics Teacher
Marina Middle School
San Francisco, CA

Douglas Harik
Mathematics Teacher
Westborough Middle School South
San Francisco, CA

Jenita Whiting-Dandridge
Mathematics Teacher
Los Angeles Academy
  Middle School
Los Angeles, CA

Sheila Hernandez
Mathematics Teacher
Horner Junior High School
Fremont, CA

Overview
California Student Edition

Yosemite National Park

CHAPTER

1

Unit 1
Number Sense
with Mathematical Reasoning

California

Distributive Property, p. 51
$$a(b + c) = ab + ac$$

Integer Operations

Chapter 1 Highlights

⟲ TECHNOLOGY

At *classzone.com*:
- Animated Math, 5, 6, 7, 21, 53, 54
- California @Home Tutor, 4, 9, 15, 16, 22, 27, 34, 39, 44, 45, 51, 56, 57, 62
- Online Quiz, 10, 16, 23, 28, 35, 40, 45, 51, 58

STUDENT HELP

- Vocabulary and Reading, 4, 5, 7, 8, 12, 14, 18, 20, 24, 26, 28, 31, 33, 36, 38, 41, 43, 48, 50, 52, 53, 55, 62, 67
- Notetaking, 4, 14, 62
- Another Way, 13, 17, 20
- Avoid Errors, 5, 25, 31, 36
- Hints and Homework Help, 8, 14, 20, 26, 33, 38, 43, 50, 55

◆ ASSESSMENT

- Multiple choice examples and exercises, 8, 9, 15, 21, 22, 26, 27, 34, 37, 38, 39, 43, 44, 45, 50, 51, 54, 56, 57
- California Standards Spiral Review, 10, 16, 23, 28, 35, 40, 45, 51, 58
- Writing, Open-Ended, and Short Response, 8, 16, 20, 21, 26, 33, 35, 38, 39, 40, 43, 50, 55, 57

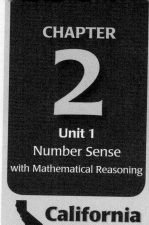

Adding Fractions and Mixed Numbers, p. 89
$$6\frac{1}{4} + \frac{1}{4}$$

Rational Number Operations

Chapter 2 Highlights

⚙ TECHNOLOGY

At *classzone.com*:
- Animated Math, 82
- California @Home Tutor, 74, 78, 83, 84, 88, 94, 103, 110, 116, 121
- Online Quiz, 79, 84, 89, 95, 104, 111, 117

STUDENT HELP

- Vocabulary and Reading, 74, 75, 77, 80, 82, 85, 87, 91, 93, 98, 101, 106, 107, 108, 113, 115, 116, 121, 125
- Notetaking, 74, 87, 121
- Another Way, 87, 100, 105, 114
- Avoid Errors, 86, 98
- Hints and Homework Help, 77, 82, 87, 93, 101, 108, 115

◆ ASSESSMENT

- Multiple choice examples and exercises, 78, 79, 81, 83, 86, 88, 93, 94, 99, 101, 102, 103, 109, 110, 115, 116
- California Standards Spiral Review, 79, 84, 89, 95, 104, 111, 117
- Writing, Open-Ended, and Short Response, 77, 79, 82, 93, 95, 101, 104, 108, 110, 115

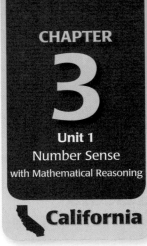

Finding Profit, p. 162
Profit = Income − Expenses

Decimals and Percents

Chapter 3 Highlights

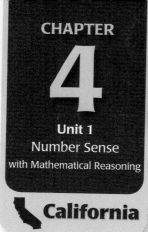

CHAPTER
4

Unit 1
Number Sense
with Mathematical Reasoning

California

Powers of Ten, p. 199
$5 \times 1000 = 5 \times 10^3$

Exponents and Irrational Numbers

Chapter 4 Highlights

🖉 TECHNOLOGY

At classzone.com:
- **Animated Math,** 225, 226
- **California @Home Tutor,** 194, 199, 204, 209, 217, 222, 229, 234
- **Online Quiz,** 200, 204, 210, 218, 223, 230

STUDENT HELP

- **Vocabulary and Reading,** 194, 196, 197, 198, 201, 203, 206, 208, 213, 216, 218, 219, 221, 225, 227, 234, 237
- **Notetaking,** 194, 216, 234
- **Another Way,** 198, 220, 224, 226
- **Avoid Errors,** 201, 207, 208
- **Hints and Homework Help,** 198, 203, 208, 216, 221, 227

◆ ASSESSMENT

- **Multiple choice examples and exercises,** 198, 199, 202, 203, 204, 208, 209, 210, 214, 216, 217, 222, 228, 229
- **California Standards Spiral Review,** 200, 204, 210, 218, 223, 230
- **Writing, Open-Ended, and Short Response,** 198, 203, 208, 221, 227, 229, 230

Unit 2
Algebra
and Functions
with Mathematical Reasoning

California

Simplifying Expressions, p. 253
$18.95n + 5n = 23.95n$

Solving Equations and Inequalities

Chapter 5 Highlights

⊘ TECHNOLOGY

At _classzone.com_:
- **Animated Math,** 258, 259, 278, 284, 293
- **California @Home Tutor,** 246, 250, 255, 261, 266, 267, 274, 280, 286, 291, 296, 302
- **Online Quiz,** 251, 255, 262, 267, 275, 281, 287, 292, 297

STUDENT HELP

- **Vocabulary and Reading,** 246, 247, 249, 251, 252, 254, 257, 260, 261, 263, 265, 270, 272, 277, 278, 279, 282, 284, 288, 289, 290, 293, 295, 302, 307
- **Notetaking,** 246, 254, 302
- **Another Way,** 271, 276, 277, 283
- **Avoid Errors,** 247, 294
- **Hints and Homework Help,** 249, 254, 260, 265, 272, 279, 284, 290, 295

◆ ASSESSMENT

- **Multiple choice examples and exercises,** 249, 250, 254, 255, 260, 261, 266, 267, 271, 273, 274, 279, 280, 285, 286, 290, 291, 294, 295, 296
- **California Standards Spiral Review,** 251, 255, 262, 267, 275, 281, 287, 292, 297
- **Writing, Open-Ended, and Short Response,** 249, 260, 261, 265, 272, 274, 275, 279, 284, 285, 286, 290, 295

CHAPTER

6

Unit 2
Algebra
and Functions
with Mathematical Reasoning

California

Finding Solutions, p. 316
$C = 10 + 7h$; $(1, 17)$

Linear Equations and Graphs

Chapter 6 Highlights

CHAPTER

7

Unit 2
Algebra
and Functions
with Mathematical Reasoning

California

Nonlinear Functions, p. 414
$$d = \frac{1}{2}at^2$$

Exponents and Nonlinear Functions

Chapter 7 Highlights

TECHNOLOGY

At *classzone.com*:
- Animated Math, 409
- California @Home Tutor, 384, 391, 397, 403, 411, 412, 418, 424
- Online Quiz, 391, 398, 404, 412, 419

STUDENT HELP

- Vocabulary and Reading, 384, 386, 389, 393, 396, 398, 399, 402, 407, 410, 413, 414, 417, 424, 427
- Notetaking, 384, 389, 424
- Another Way, 386, 405
- Avoid Errors, 393, 401
- Hints and Homework Help, 389, 396, 402, 410, 417

◆ **ASSESSMENT**

- Multiple choice examples and exercises, 390, 391, 396, 397, 402, 403, 408, 411, 416, 417, 418
- California Standards Spiral Review, 391, 398, 404, 412, 419
- Writing, Open-Ended, and Short Response, 387, 396, 397, 402, 410, 417

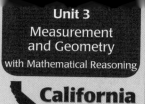

150 hours < 20 days

Measurements and Planar Figures

Chapter 8 Highlights

🖉 TECHNOLOGY

At classzone.com:
- Animated Math, 472, 479, 481, 491
- California @Home Tutor, 436, 441, 447, 452, 458, 467, 475, 485, 494, 502
- Online Quiz, 442, 448, 453, 458, 467, 476, 485, 495

STUDENT HELP

- Vocabulary and Reading, 436, 437, 440, 443, 445, 446, 449, 451, 454, 455, 456, 463, 464, 465, 471, 473, 474, 478, 481, 482, 489, 492, 494, 502, 507
- Notetaking, 436, 482, 502
- Another Way, 438, 481, 488
- Avoid Errors, 491, 492
- Hints and Homework Help, 440, 446, 451, 456, 465, 474, 482, 492

◆ ASSESSMENT

- Multiple choice examples and exercises, 440, 442, 444, 446, 447, 450, 451, 452, 457, 458, 466, 467, 472, 475, 483, 485, 490, 493, 494
- California Standards Spiral Review, 442, 448, 453, 458, 467, 476, 485, 495
- Writing, Open-Ended, and Short Response, 440, 442, 446, 451, 456, 465, 474, 482, 483, 492

CHAPTER

9

Unit 3
Measurement
and Geometry
with Mathematical Reasoning

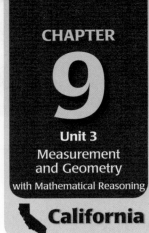

California

Reflections, p. 528
$(x, y) \rightarrow (x, -y)$

Congruence and Similarity

Chapter 9 Highlights

⤤ TECHNOLOGY

At *classzone.com*:
- Animated Math, 523, 530
- California @Home Tutor, 514, 520, 521, 526, 532, 544
- Online Quiz, 521, 526, 533, 539, 545

STUDENT HELP

- Vocabulary and Reading, 514, 516, 519, 522, 524, 528, 530, 537, 541, 543, 544, 550, 553
- Notetaking, 514, 524, 550
- Another Way, 541, 546
- Avoid Errors, 524, 528
- Hints and Homework Help, 519, 524, 530, 537, 543

◆ ASSESSMENT

- Multiple choice examples and exercises, 518, 519, 521, 522, 525, 526, 529, 531, 532, 537, 538, 542, 543, 544
- California Standards Spiral Review, 521, 526, 533, 539, 545
- Writing, Open-Ended, and Short Response, 519, 530, 537, 543, 544

CHAPTER

10

Unit 3
Measurement
and Geometry
with Mathematical Reasoning

California

Finding Surface Area, p. 579
$S = 2B + Ph$

Surface Area and Volume

Chapter 10 Highlights

TECHNOLOGY

At *classzone.com*:
* Animated Math, 566, 567, 568, 589, 600, 607
* California @Home Tutor, 560, 565, 570, 578, 585, 594, 602, 603, 609, 615
* Online Quiz, 565, 571, 579, 586, 596, 603, 611

STUDENT HELP

* **Vocabulary and Reading,** 560, 561, 563, 566, 568, 573, 576, 580, 583, 589, 591, 593, 598, 600, 605, 608, 610, 615, 619
* **Notetaking,** 560, 593, 615
* **Another Way,** 568, 572, 574
* **Avoid Errors,** 562, 589
* **Hints and Homework Help,** 563, 568, 576, 583, 593, 600, 608

◆ ASSESSMENT

* **Multiple choice examples and exercises,** 564, 565, 568, 569, 570, 576, 577, 578, 584, 585, 594, 595, 601, 602, 603, 607, 608, 609, 610
* **California Standards Spiral Review,** 565, 571, 579, 586, 596, 603, 611
* **Writing, Open-Ended, and Short Response,** 563, 568, 569, 576, 578, 579, 583, 586, 600, 608

CHAPTER 11

Unit 4 Statistics, Data Analysis, and Probability
with Mathematical Reasoning

California

Making Bar Graphs, p. 636
Bar height = Number of volcanoes

Data Displays

Chapter 11 Highlights

📡 TECHNOLOGY

At *classzone.com*:
- Animated Math, 636, 650, 655
- California @Home Tutor, 634, 641, 642, 647, 653, 658, 665, 674
- Online Quiz, 635, 642, 648, 654, 659, 667

STUDENT HELP

- Vocabulary and Reading, 628, 631, 633, 635, 636, 639, 643, 645, 650, 652, 655, 657, 660, 663, 674, 679
- Notetaking, 628, 645, 674
- Another Way, 660, 670
- Avoid Errors, 632, 639, 643, 651, 662
- Hints and Homework Help, 633, 639, 645, 652, 657, 663

◆ ASSESSMENT

- Multiple choice examples and exercises, 632, 633, 634, 640, 641, 642, 644, 646, 647, 652, 653, 657, 658, 664, 665
- California Standards Spiral Review, 635, 642, 648, 654, 659, 667
- Writing, Open-Ended, and Short Response, 633, 634, 639, 647, 652, 657, 663, 666

CHAPTER

12

Review
and
Preview

California

Evaluating Polynomials, p. 690
$-16t^2 + 80t + 2$

Polynomials:
Review and Preview

Chapter 12 Highlights

⚙ TECHNOLOGY

At *classzone.com*:
- Animated Math, 694, 704
- California @Home Tutor, 688, 692, 697, 702, 708
- Online Quiz, 692, 698, 702, 709

STUDENT HELP

- Vocabulary and Reading, 688, 689, 691, 693, 695, 697, 699, 701, 705, 707, 714, 717
- Notetaking, 688, 701, 714
- Another Way, 705, 710
- Avoid Errors, 689, 694, 695
- Hints and Homework Help, 691, 695, 701, 707

◆ ASSESSMENT

- Multiple choice examples and exercises, 691, 692, 696, 697, 700, 701, 702, 705, 707, 708
- California Standards Spiral Review, 692, 698, 702, 709
- Writing, Open-Ended, and Short Response, 691, 695, 707

Standards Review Handbook

Extra Practice for Chapters 1–12

Tables

English-Spanish Glossary

Index

Credits

Selected Answers

CALIFORNIA

CA

California Student Guide

Getting Started

The following pages will help you get started by providing a preview of the course and an introduction to your textbook.

California Standards Practice

Pages SG2 – SG23

Gives you an overview of the standards for this course. Lists all Grade 7 standards with multiple choice exercises for each standard.

California Pre-Course Test

Pages SG24 – SG25

Tests prerequisite skills for this course with page references to the Standards Review Handbook at the back of the book.

Scavenger Hunt

Pages SG26 – SG27

Provides an opportunity to explore student resources at the back of the book.

Yosemite National Park

CALIFORNIA STUDENT GUIDE

Standards Practice

As you answer each multiple choice question, you may want to turn to the page given in blue to study the mathematical concepts that the question is addressing. The symbol ● identifies the key seventh grade standards.

Grade 7 | Number Sense

NS 1.0 Students know the properties of, and compute with, rational numbers expressed in a variety of forms:

NS 1.1 Read, write, and compare rational numbers in scientific notation (positive and negative powers of 10), compare rational numbers in general.

1. Which of the following numbers is the greatest: -2.38, -2.4, $-\frac{5}{2}$, $-2\frac{21}{50}$? *(p. 133)*

   (A) -2.38 (B) -2.4

   (C) $-\frac{5}{2}$ (D) $-2\frac{21}{50}$

2. Which number is between 800 and 900? *(p. 201)*

   (A) 8.1×10^1 (B) 8.4×10^2

   (C) 9.8×10^2 (D) 9.2×10^3

NS 1.2 **Add, subtract, multiply, and divide rational numbers (integers, fractions, and terminating decimals) and take positive rational numbers to whole-number powers.**

3. What is $3\frac{1}{5} \div \left(\frac{4}{5}\right)^2$? *(p. 106)*

   (A) 0   (B) $\frac{1}{5}$

   (C) 5   (D) 125

4. You are buying notebooks for members of your science club. The notebooks cost $.75 each. You have $9.00 to spend. At most, how many notebooks can you buy? *(p. 144)*

   (A) 10   (B) 11

   (C) 12   (D) 13

NS 1.3 Convert fractions to decimals and percents and use these representations in estimations, computations, and applications.

5. San Luis Obispo, California, has about 285 mostly sunny days per year. About what percent of the days of the year are mostly sunny? *(p. 155)*

   (A) 29%   (B) 78%

   (C) 95%   (D) 128%

6. In the 2004–2005 season, the Sacramento Kings basketball team won about $\frac{3}{5}$ of the 82 games played. What expression can you use to estimate the number of games they won? *(p. 113)*

   (A) 0.3×80 (B) 0.35×80

   (C) 0.4×80 (D) 0.6×80

Grade 7 — Number Sense

NS 1.4 **Differentiate between rational and irrational numbers.**

7. Which is an irrational number? *(p. 225)*

    (A) −0.2

    (B) −1.7777...

    (C) $\sqrt{7}$

    (D) $\sqrt{25}$

8. Which is sometimes (but not always) a rational number? *(p. 225)*

    (A) A terminating decimal

    (B) A repeating decimal

    (C) A negative integer

    (D) The square root of a whole number

NS 1.5 **Know that every rational number is either a terminating or a repeating decimal and be able to convert terminating decimals into reduced fractions.**

9. What is the decimal 0.67 written as a fraction? *(p. 113)*

    (A) $\frac{2}{3}$

    (B) $\frac{67}{100}$

    (C) $\frac{67}{99}$

    (D) $\frac{6}{7}$

10. Willie Mays had a career batting average of 0.302. What is this decimal written as a fraction? *(p. 113)*

    (A) $\frac{151}{5000}$

    (B) $\frac{3}{10}$

    (C) $\frac{151}{500}$

    (D) $\frac{151}{50}$

NS 1.6 Calculate the percentage of increases and decreases of a quantity.

11. The price of a computer is reduced from $1240 to $1054. What is the percent of decrease? *(p. 168)*

    (A) 15%

    (B) 18%

    (C) 82%

    (D) 85%

12. The tax on the purchase of a $47 jacket adds 6.2% to the cost. What is the amount of the tax? *(p. 168)*

    (A) $2.82

    (B) $2.91

    (C) $29.14

    (D) $49.91

Go On ➡

Standards Practice

NS 1.7 Solve problems that involve discounts, markups, commissions, and profit and compute simple and compound interest.

13. How much interest would a $600 deposit earn in one year at a simple annual interest rate of 5%? *(p. 172)*

   Ⓐ $30   Ⓑ $60

   Ⓒ $600   Ⓓ $630

14. The wholesale price of a shirt is $24. A department store marks up the wholesale price by 80%. Laura buys the shirt at 30% off the retail price when it is on sale. What is the price Laura paid for the shirt? *(p. 160)*

   Ⓐ $12.96   Ⓑ $13.44

   Ⓒ $30.24   Ⓓ $56.16

NS 2.0 Students use exponents, powers, and roots and use exponents in working with fractions:

NS 2.1 Understand negative whole-number exponents. Multiply and divide expressions involving exponents with a common base.

15. Which of the following has the same value as $\dfrac{5^{-4} \times 5^2}{5^{-2}}$? *(p. 393)*

   Ⓐ $\dfrac{1}{5^6}$

   Ⓑ $\dfrac{1}{5^4}$

   Ⓒ 1

   Ⓓ 5^2

16. Which of the following has the same value as $(-2)^{-3} \times 16$? *(p. 206)*

   Ⓐ -128

   Ⓑ -2

   Ⓒ 2

   Ⓓ 128

NS 2.2 Add and subtract fractions by using factoring to find common denominators.

17. What is the simplified form of $\dfrac{1}{15} + \dfrac{7}{20}$? *(p. 91)*

   Ⓐ $\dfrac{7}{300}$

   Ⓑ $\dfrac{8}{35}$

   Ⓒ $\dfrac{23}{60}$

   Ⓓ $\dfrac{5}{12}$

18. What is the first step if you want to use the least common denominator to simplify the difference $\dfrac{7}{9} - \dfrac{1}{12}$? *(p. 91)*

   Ⓐ Multiply $\dfrac{7}{9}$ by $\dfrac{4}{4}$ and multiply $\dfrac{1}{12}$ by $\dfrac{3}{3}$.

   Ⓑ Multiply $\dfrac{7}{9}$ by $\dfrac{12}{12}$ and multiply $\dfrac{1}{12}$ by $\dfrac{9}{9}$.

   Ⓒ Subtract the numerators.

   Ⓓ Multiply the denominators.

Grade 7 | **Number Sense**

NS 2.3 Multiply, divide, and simplify rational numbers by using exponent rules.

19. What is the value of $\dfrac{4^3 \times (0.3)^4}{4 \times (0.3)^3}$? *(p. 393)*

(A) 0.3

(B) $(1.2)^2$

(C) $4^2 \times 0.3$

(D) $4^3 \times 0.3$

20. Which expression is equivalent to $-\left(\dfrac{2}{5}\right)^5 \cdot \left(\dfrac{2}{5}\right)^{-2}$? *(p. 393)*

(A) $-\left(\dfrac{2}{5}\right)^3$

(B) $\left(\dfrac{2}{5}\right)^3$

(C) $-\left(\dfrac{2}{5}\right)^{-10}$

(D) $\left(\dfrac{2}{5}\right)^{-10}$

NS 2.4 Use the inverse relationship between raising to a power and extracting the root of a perfect square integer; for an integer that is not square, determine without a calculator the two integers between which its square root lies and explain why.

21. Between which two integers does $\sqrt{89}$ lie? *(p. 213)*

(A) 7 and 8

(B) 8 and 9

(C) 9 and 10

(D) 10 and 11

22. A square has an area of 2.25 square inches. What is the length of a side of the square? *(p. 213)*

(A) 1.125 in.

(B) 1.5 in.

(C) 4.5 in.

(D) 225 in.

NS 2.5 Understand the meaning of the absolute value of a number; interpret the absolute value as the distance of the number from zero on a number line; and determine the absolute value of real numbers.

23. Maura conjectures that $|a + b| = |a| + |b|$ where a and b are real numbers. Which of the following is a true statement? *(p. 12)*

(A) The conjecture is true if a and b have the same sign.

(B) The conjecture is true if $a + b > 0$.

(C) The conjecture is true if a is positive and b is negative.

(D) The conjecture is true for any real numbers a and b.

24. Which expression has the greatest value? *(p. 12)*

(A) $|2 - 5|$

(B) $|-2 + 2|$

(C) $|-2|$

(D) $|-1(-1)|$

Go On ➡

AF 1.0 Students express quantitative relationships by using algebraic terminology, expressions, equations, inequalities, and graphs:

AF 1.1 Use variables and appropriate operations to write an expression, an equation, an inequality, or a system of equations or inequalities that represents a verbal description (e.g., three less than a number, half as large as area A).

25. Which of the following expressions represents the verbal phrase, "A number, n, multiplied by two subtracted from 10"? *(p. 270)*

Ⓐ $2n - 10$

Ⓑ $2(n - 10)$

Ⓒ $10 - 2n$

Ⓓ $10 - n$

26. When 3 is subtracted from a number x, the difference is less than twice x. Which mathematical statement shows this relationship? *(p. 293)*

Ⓐ $x - 3 < 2x$

Ⓑ $3 - x < 2x$

Ⓒ $x - 3 = x - 2$

Ⓓ $3 - x = x - 2$

AF 1.2 Use the correct order of operations to evaluate algebraic expressions such as $3(2x + 5)^2$.

27. What is the value of $x^2(1 - xy)$ when $x = -2$ and $y = 3$? *(p. 5)*

Ⓐ -28

Ⓑ -20

Ⓒ 20

Ⓓ 28

28. What is the value of $\dfrac{2r + rs}{r - 4}$ when $r = 6$ and $s = 8$? *(p. 5)*

Ⓐ 15

Ⓑ 16

Ⓒ 30

Ⓓ 60

AF 1.3 Simplify numerical expressions by applying properties of rational numbers (e.g., identity, inverse, distributive, associative, commutative) and justify the process used.

29. Which property is illustrated by the statement $1 \times ab = ab$? *(p. 48)*

Ⓐ Identity Property of Multiplication

Ⓑ Associative Property of Multiplication

Ⓒ Commutative Property of Multiplication

Ⓓ Distributive Property

30. Which expression is equivalent to $2(x - 1) + 2$? *(p. 252)*

Ⓐ 4

Ⓑ x

Ⓒ $2x$

Ⓓ $2x + 1$

Grade 7 — Algebra and Functions

AF 1.4 Use algebraic terminology (e.g., variable, equation, term, coefficient, inequality, expression, constant) correctly.

31. Which best describes $y + 2 \geq 5$? *(p. 282)*

   (A) An expression

   (B) An equation

   (C) An inequality

   (D) A variable

32. Which best describes 3 in the equation $3t + 1 = 7$? *(p. 252)*

   (A) A coefficient

   (B) A constant term

   (C) A variable

   (D) An exponent

AF 1.5 Represent quantitative relationships graphically and interpret the meaning of a specific part of a graph in the situation represented by the graph.

33. Your family buys tickets for a baseball game and later pays for parking.

Hours of parking	1	2	3	4
Total cost (dollars)	25	30	35	40

Which graph best represents the total cost of parking? *(p. 407)*

(A)
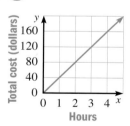

(B)
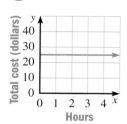

(C)
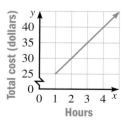

(D)
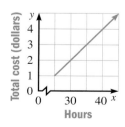

34. The graph shows the height (in feet) of a red oak tree for 5 years after it is planted.

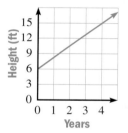

What does the *y*-intercept represent? *(p. 407)*

   (A) The rate at which the oak is growing each year

   (B) The height of the oak when it is planted

   (C) The height of the oak one year after it is planted

   (D) The number of years since the oak was planted

Go On

Standards Practice

AF 2.0 Students interpret and evaluate expressions involving integer powers and simple roots:

AF 2.1 Interpret positive whole-number powers as repeated multiplication and negative whole-number powers as repeated division or multiplication by the multiplicative inverse. Simplify and evaluate expressions that include exponents.

35. Which expression is equivalent to x^{-4}?
(p. 206)

  Ⓐ $\dfrac{1}{x \cdot x \cdot x \cdot x}$ Ⓑ $x \cdot x \cdot x \cdot x$

  Ⓒ $\dfrac{1}{4x}$ Ⓓ $\dfrac{4}{x}$

36. What is the value of $(4z)^3$ when $z = -2$?
(p. 31)

  Ⓐ -512 Ⓑ -24

  Ⓒ -8 Ⓓ 512

AF 2.2 Multiply and divide monomials; extend the process of taking powers and extracting roots to monomials when the latter results in a monomial with an integer exponent.

37. Which expression is equivalent to $5n^2 \cdot 2n^4$? *(p. 399)*

  Ⓐ $7n^6$ Ⓑ $10n^6$

  Ⓒ $7n^8$ Ⓓ $10n^8$

38. What is the simplified form of $\dfrac{a^4 b^{10}}{ab^2}$?
(p. 399)

  Ⓐ $a^3 b^8$ Ⓑ $a^4 b^5$

  Ⓒ $a^8 b^3$ Ⓓ $(ab)^{11}$

AF 3.0 Students graph and interpret linear and some nonlinear functions:

AF 3.1 Graph functions of the form $y = nx^2$ and $y = nx^3$ and use in solving problems.

39. Which graph shows $y = \dfrac{1}{2}x^2$? *(p. 413)*

  Ⓐ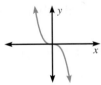

  Ⓑ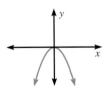

  Ⓒ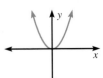

  Ⓓ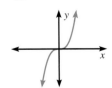

40. Use the graph below to find the *best* estimate of the edge length of a cube with a volume of 125 cubic inches.
(p. 413)

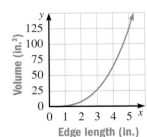

  Ⓐ 3 in.   Ⓑ 4 in.

  Ⓒ 5 in.   Ⓓ 25 in.

Grade 7 | Algebra and Functions

AF 3.2 Plot the values from the volumes of three-dimensional shapes for various values of the edge lengths (e.g., cubes with varying edge lengths or a triangle prism with a fixed height and an equilateral triangle base of varying lengths).

41. A rectangular prism with a square base has a height of 3 meters and a base edge of length *x*. Which graph *best* represents the volume of the prism as a function of *x*? *(p. 589)*

Ⓐ
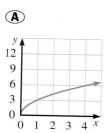

Ⓑ
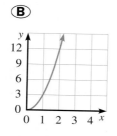

Ⓒ
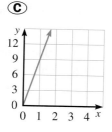

Ⓓ
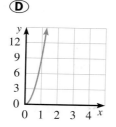

42. The radius *x* of a cylinder is the same as its height. Which graph *best* represents the volume of the cylinder as a function of *x*? *(p. 589)*

Ⓐ
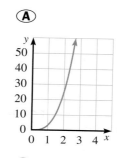

Ⓑ
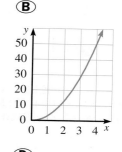

Ⓒ
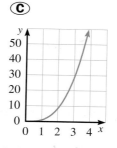

Ⓓ
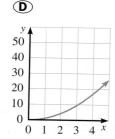

AF 3.3 Graph linear functions, noting that the vertical change (change in *y*-value) per unit of horizontal change (change in *x*-value) is always the same and know that the ratio ("rise over run") is called the slope of a graph.

43. Which statement is true about the line that is graphed at the right? *(p. 334)*

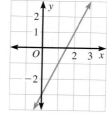

Ⓐ The slope of the line is 2.

Ⓑ The *x*-intercept is 1.

Ⓒ The *y*-intercept is −2.

Ⓓ The slope of the line increases as the value of *x* increases.

44. Which points lie on the graph of a linear function? *(p. 334)*

Ⓐ (2, 5), (0, 1), (−1, −2)

Ⓑ (−3, −4), (−2, 1), (0, 9)

Ⓒ (−4, 3), (−1, 1), (5, −3)

Ⓓ (3, −4), (1, −2), (−1, −3)

Go On

AF 3.4 Plot the values of quantities whose ratios are always the same (e.g., cost to the number of an item, feet to inches, circumference to diameter of a circle). Fit a line to the plot and understand that the slope of the line equals the ratio of the quantities.

45. Which graph shows the relationship between a number of gallons and the corresponding number of quarts? *(p. 348)*

Ⓐ
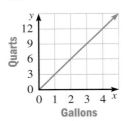

Ⓑ
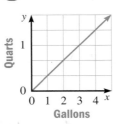

Ⓒ
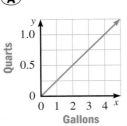

Ⓓ
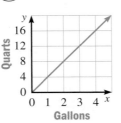

46. An Internet music site charges a fixed price of $.99 for each song downloaded. Suppose you create a graph to show the relationship between the number of songs you download and the total cost of the songs. Which statement about the graph is true? *(p. 348)*

Ⓐ The slope of the line is the cost for each song.

Ⓑ The slope of the line is the total amount you spent on songs.

Ⓒ The slope of the line increases as the number of songs downloaded increases.

Ⓓ The slope of the line is the number of songs you downloaded.

AF 4.0 Students solve simple linear equations and inequalities over the rational numbers:

AF 4.1 Solve two-step linear equations and inequalities in one variable over the rational numbers, interpret the solution or solutions in the context from which they arose, and verify the reasonableness of the results.

47. You have $55 to spend at a music store. You buy a pair of headphones for $13. Each CD at the music store costs $14. If the equation below shows this relationship, what is the number x of CDs you can buy? *(p. 270)*

$$14x + 13 = 55$$

Ⓐ 2 CDs   Ⓑ 3 CDs

Ⓒ 4 CDs   Ⓓ 5 CDs

48. What is the solution set to the inequality $2t - 5 < -9$? *(p. 293)*

Ⓐ $\{t: t < -7\}$

Ⓑ $\{t: t > -7\}$

Ⓒ $\{t: t < -2\}$

Ⓓ $\{t: t > -2\}$

Grade 7 | Algebra and Functions; Measurement and Geometry

AF 4.2 Solve multistep problems involving rate, average speed, distance, and time or a direct variation.

49. Luisa drove 20 miles in 0.5 hour and then drove another 18 miles in 0.3 hour. What was Luisa's average speed for the entire trip? *(p. 52)*

Ⓐ 40 mi/h

Ⓑ 47.5 mi/h

Ⓒ 50 mi/h

Ⓓ 52.5 mi/h

50. David earns a commission of $150 on furniture sales of $2500. At that rate, what commission would he earn on furniture sales of $4250? *(p. 160)*

Ⓐ $88.24

Ⓑ $255

Ⓒ $405

Ⓓ $708.33

MG 1.0 Students choose appropriate units of measure and use ratios to convert within and between measurement systems to solve problems:

MG 1.1 Compare weights, capacities, geometric measures, times, and temperatures within and between measurement systems (e.g., miles per hour and feet per second, cubic inches to cubic centimeters).

51. Keisha is 62 inches tall. How tall is Keisha in centimeters? *(p. 437)*

Ⓐ 20.67 cm

Ⓑ 24.41 cm

Ⓒ 157.48 cm

Ⓓ 186 cm

52. A car travels at a speed of about 50 feet per second. About how fast is this in miles per hour? *(p. 449)*

Ⓐ 0.6 mi/h

Ⓑ 34 mi/h

Ⓒ 50 mi/h

Ⓓ 73 mi/h

MG 1.2 Construct and read drawings and models made to scale.

53. A map of California is drawn with a scale of $\frac{5}{8}$ in. : 100 mi. If you measure the distance from San Francisco to Sacramento to be $\frac{1}{2}$ inch, what is the actual distance from San Francisco to Sacramento? *(p. 541)*

Ⓐ 40 mi   Ⓑ 60 mi

Ⓒ 80 mi   Ⓓ 100 mi

54. A blueprint of a room is drawn with a scale factor of 1 inch to 16 feet. Which is the *best* estimate of the perimeter of the actual room if the perimeter of the room in the blueprint is 6.25 inches? *(p. 541)*

Ⓐ 50 ft   Ⓑ 100 ft

Ⓒ 150 ft   Ⓓ 500 ft

Go On

Standards Practice

MG 1.3 Use measures expressed as rates (e.g., speed, density) and measures expressed as products (e.g., person-days) to solve problems; check the units of the solutions; and use dimensional analysis to check the reasonableness of the answer.

55. You estimate it will take 60 person-hours to paint the auditorium in the community center. If 3 people work with you and each of you works 5 hours per day, how many days will it take to paint the auditorium? *(p. 443)*

(A) 1 d   (B) 2 d   (C) 3 d   (D) 4 d

56. A miniature robot that is used to access pipes can travel 1 inch in 3 seconds. How many feet does the robot travel in 6 minutes? *(p. 443)*

(A) $1\frac{2}{3}$ ft   (B) 2 ft

(C) 10 ft   (D) 120 ft

MG 2.0 Students compute the perimeter, area, and volume of common geometric objects and use the results to find measures of less common objects. They know how perimeter, area, and volume are affected by changes of scale:

MG 2.1 Use formulas routinely for finding the perimeter and area of basic two-dimensional figures and the surface area and volume of basic three-dimensional figures, including rectangles, parallelograms, trapezoids, squares, triangles, circles, prisms, and cylinders.

57. What is the area of a right triangle with side lengths 8 centimeters, 15 centimeters, and 17 centimeters? *(p. 463)*

(A) 40 cm^2 (B) 60 cm^2

(C) 68 cm^2 (D) 127.5 cm^2

58. A cylinder has a radius of 4 feet and a height of 6 feet. What is the *best* estimate of its surface area? *(p. 573)*

(A) 151 ft^2 (B) 251 ft^2

(C) 302 ft^2 (D) 452 ft^2

MG 2.2 Estimate and compute the area of more complex or irregular two- and three-dimensional figures by breaking the figures down into more basic geometric objects.

59. What is the area of the shaded region? *(p. 478)*

(A) 40 ft^2
(B) 80 ft^2
(C) 92 ft^2
(D) 96 ft^2

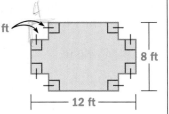

60. What is the *best* estimate of the surface area of the solid shown? *(p. 573)*

(A) 15 in.^{2}
(B) 38 in.^{2}
(C) 39 in.^{2}
(D) 40 in.^{2}

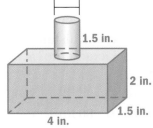

Grade 7 — Measurement and Geometry

MG 2.3 Compute the length of the perimeter, the surface area of the faces, and the volume of a three-dimensional object built from rectangular solids. Understand that when the lengths of all dimensions are multiplied by a scale factor, the surface area is multiplied by the square of the scale factor and the volume is multiplied by the cube of the scale factor.

61. Each dimension of a rectangular prism is multiplied by 3. Which statement is true? *(p. 605)*

Ⓐ The surface area is multiplied by 3.

Ⓑ The surface area is multiplied by 27.

Ⓒ The volume is multiplied by 9.

Ⓓ The volume is multiplied by 27.

62. What is the volume of the solid? *(p. 589)*

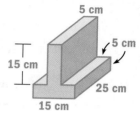

Ⓐ 2050 cm^3

Ⓑ 3000 cm^3

Ⓒ 3750 cm^3

Ⓓ 4100 cm^3

MG 2.4 Relate the changes in measurement with a change of scale to the units used (e.g., square inches, cubic feet) and to conversions between units (1 square foot = 144 square inches or $\lceil 1 \text{ ft.}^2 \rceil = \lceil 144 \text{ in.}^2 \rceil$; 1 cubic inch is approximately 16.38 cubic centimeters or $\lceil 1 \text{ in.}^3 \rceil = \lceil 16.38 \text{ cm}^3 \rceil$).

63. The concrete used for a tennis court is 100 feet long, 50 feet wide, and 6 inches thick. Approximately how many cubic meters of concrete are used? (1 cubic foot ≈ 0.0283 cubic meters) *(p. 589)*

Ⓐ 71 m^3

Ⓑ 849 m^3

Ⓒ 88,339 m^3

Ⓓ 1,060,071 m^3

64. A rectangle is 11 *feet* long and 2 *yards* wide. What is the area of the rectangle in *square feet?* *(p. 478)*

Ⓐ $7\frac{1}{3}$ ft^2

Ⓑ 22 ft^2

Ⓒ 34 ft^2

Ⓓ 66 ft^2

Go On ➡

MG 3.0 Students know the Pythagorean theorem and deepen their understanding of plane and solid geometric shapes by constructing figures that meet given conditions and by identifying attributes of figures:

MG 3.1 Identify and construct basic elements of geometric figures (e.g., altitudes, midpoints, diagonals, angle bisectors, and perpendicular bisectors; central angles, radii, diameters, and chords of circles) by using a compass and straightedge.

65. What is the name for a segment whose endpoints are on a circle? *(p. 489)*

  A Radius

  B Diameter

  C Median

  D Chord

66. What is the name for the perpendicular segment from a triangle's vertex to the opposite side or line containing the opposite side? *(p. 463)*

  A Angle bisector

  B Perpendicular bisector

  C Altitude

  D Median

MG 3.2 Understand and use coordinate graphs to plot simple figures, determine lengths and areas related to them, and determine their image under translations and reflections.

67. The point $(4, -2)$ is reflected in the x-axis. What is the image of the point? *(p. 528)*

  A $(4, 2)$ **B** $(-4, -2)$

  C $(-4, 2)$ **D** $(4, -2)$

68. What is the image of the point $(-7, -3)$ after the translation $(x, y) \rightarrow (x - 3, y + 4)$? *(p. 522)*

  A $(-10, -7)$ **B** $(-4, 1)$

  C $(10, 7)$ **D** $(-10, 1)$

MG 3.3 **Know and understand the Pythagorean theorem and its converse and use it to find the length of the missing side of a right triangle and the lengths of other line segments and, in some situations, empirically verify the Pythagorean theorem by direct measurement.**

69. In the figure below, point X is the midpoint of $\overline{RT}$, $\overline{SX}$ is perpendicular to $\overline{RT}$, and $\overline{RS} \cong \overline{ST}$.

What is the perimeter of triangle RST? *(p. 471)*

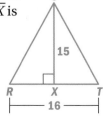

  A 17 units   **C** 48 units

  B 33 units   **D** 50 units

70. Which of the following could be the lengths of the sides of a right triangle? *(p. 471)*

  A 9 cm, 15 cm, 17 cm

  B 9 cm, 36 cm, 37 cm

  C 9 cm, 40 cm, 41 cm

  D 9 cm, 50 cm, 51 cm

Grade 7 | Measurement and Geometry

MG 3.4 Demonstrate an understanding of conditions that indicate two geometrical figures are congruent and what congruence means about the relationships between the sides and angles of the two figures.

71. $\triangle ABC \cong \triangle DEF$. Which statement *must* be true? *(p. 516)*

    A $\overline{AC} \cong \overline{DF}$

    B $\angle B \cong \angle F$

    C $\angle A \cong \angle E$

    D $\overline{AB} \cong \overline{EF}$

72. $ABCD \cong FGHJ$. Which statement *must* be true? *(p. 516)*

    A $ABCD$ and $FGHJ$ are not the same shape.

    B $ABCD$ and $FGHJ$ are the same size.

    C All of the angles in $ABCD$ are congruent.

    D All of the sides of $FGHJ$ are congruent.

MG 3.5 Construct two-dimensional patterns for three-dimensional models, such as cylinders, prisms, and cones.

73. Which of the following is the net for a cylinder? *(p. 566)*

    A

    B

    C

    D

74. What type of solid is formed by folding up the net shown below? *(p. 566)*

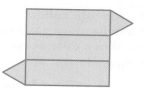

    A Pyramid

    B Prism

    C Cylinder

    D Cone

Standards Practice

Go On

MG 3.6 Identify elements of three-dimensional geometric objects (e.g., diagonals of rectangular solids) and describe how two or more objects are related in space (e.g., skew lines, the possible ways three planes might intersect).

75. Which statement is *false*? *(p. 561)*

A A line and a plane in three-dimensional space can intersect in exactly one point.

B A line and a plane in three-dimensional space can have no points in common.

C A line and a plane in three-dimensional space can intersect in exactly two points.

D A line and a plane in three-dimensional space can have an unlimited number of points in common.

76. Which statement is *true*? *(p. 561)*

A Two lines that intersect must be parallel.

B Two planes that intersect must intersect in exactly one point.

C Two lines that are parallel have many points in common.

D Two lines that are skew cannot intersect.

SDAP 1.0 Students collect, organize, and represent data sets that have one or more variables and identify relationships among variables within a data set by hand and through the use of an electronic spreadsheet software program:

SDAP 1.1 Know various forms of display for data sets, including a stem-and-leaf plot or box-and-whisker plot; use the forms to display a single set of data or to compare two sets of data.

77. The stem-and-leaf plot below shows the test scores of all the students in a math class.

```
 5 | 2 9
 6 | 6 7
 7 | 1 7 8 9
 8 | 0 1 3 4 5 5 9
 9 | 0 2 3 5
10 | 0            Key: 9 | 2 = 92
```

What is the median score? *(p. 650)*

A 80.3 **B** 81

C 82 **D** 85

78. The circle graph shows the number of each type of medal won by Great Britain in the 2004 Summer Olympics.

9 gold   9 silver   12 bronze

What percent of the medals won by Great Britain were gold or silver? *(p. 636)*

A 15% **B** 30%

C 60% **D** 70%

Grade 7 — Statistics, Data Analysis, and Probability

SDAP 1.2 Represent two numerical variables on a scatterplot and informally describe how the data points are distributed and any apparent relationship that exists between the two variables (e.g., between time spent on homework and grade level).

79. Which scatter plot shows approximately no correlation between the two quantities? *(p. 660)*

(A)
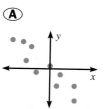

(B)
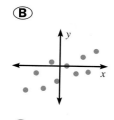

(C)
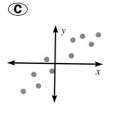

(D)
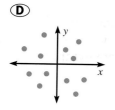

80. The scatter plot shows the time needed to roast turkeys of different weights.

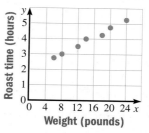

Which statement is *most strongly* suggested by the scatter plot? *(p. 660)*

(A) As the weight of a turkey increases, the roasting time decreases.

(B) Heavier turkeys tend to require more time to roast.

(C) The roasting time tends to remain constant as the weight of a turkey changes.

(D) There is no relationship between the weight of a turkey and the roasting time.

Standards Practice

Go On

SDAP 1.3 Understand the meaning of, and be able to compute, the minimum, the lower quartile, the median, the upper quartile, and the maximum of a data set.

81. The box-and-whisker plot below shows the average monthly temperature for San Diego, California.

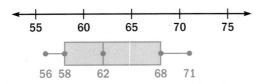

What is the lower quartile of the data? *(p. 655)*

(A) 15

(B) 58

(C) 62

(D) 71

82. The following statistics provide information from a survey about the ages of people watching a news report.

Minimum:	12
Lower quartile:	32
Median:	45
Upper quartile:	65
Maximum:	95

If there were 30 people in the survey who were 45 to 65 years old, give the *best* estimate of the total number of people in the survey. *(p. 655)*

(A) 60

(B) 90

(C) 120

(D) 150

MR 1.0 Students make decisions about how to approach problems:

MR 1.1 Analyze problems by identifying relationships, distinguishing relevant from irrelevant information, identifying missing information, sequencing and prioritizing information, and observing patterns.

83. A delivery service charges a fixed fee to deliver a package plus an extra charge for each pound the package weighs. A customer is billed $22.85 for shipping a 3-pound package. What additional information would allow you to find the cost per pound? *(p. 334)*

(A) The total cost for another package

(B) The weight of another package

(C) The total cost and weight of another package

(D) The contents of the package that was shipped

Grade 7 | Mathematical Reasoning

MR 1.2 Formulate and justify mathematical conjectures based on a general description of the mathematical question or problem posed.

84. If a and b are negative numbers, which of the following could be positive, negative, or zero? *(pp. 18, 24, 31, 36)*

Ⓐ $a \times b$

Ⓑ $a - b$

Ⓒ $a + b$

Ⓓ $a \div b$

MR 1.3 Determine when and how to break a problem into simpler parts.

85. What is the area of the figure shown? *(p. 478)*

Ⓐ 46 mi^2

Ⓑ 50 mi^2

Ⓒ 52 mi^2

Ⓓ 96 mi^2

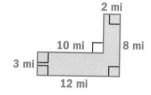

MR 2.0 Students use strategies, skills, and concepts in finding solutions:

MR 2.1 Use estimation to verify the reasonableness of calculated results.

86. At the beginning of May you had $68.73 in your savings account. You deposited a check for $23.49 and withdrew $25 twice during the month. Which expression gives the *best* estimate of your balance in dollars at the end of May? *(p. 137)*

Ⓐ $68 + 23 - 50$

Ⓑ $69 + 23 - 50$

Ⓒ $68 + 24 - 25$

Ⓓ $69 + 24 - 50$

Go On ➡

MR 2.2 Apply strategies and results from simpler problems to more complex problems.

87. You are cutting out numbers to sew onto jerseys. All of the numbers are to be double digits, so 01 represents 1. If you sew the numbers 01 through 99 onto jerseys, how many 5's will be needed? *(p. 52)*

(A) 18   **(B)** 19

(C) 20   **(D)** 21

MR 2.3 Estimate unknown quantities graphically and solve for them by using logical reasoning and arithmetic and algebraic techniques.

88. The scatter plot below shows the normal maximum heart rate for people of different ages.

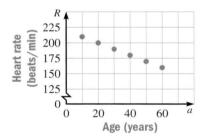

Use the graph to decide which is the *best* estimate of the normal maximum heart rate for a person who is 70 years old. *(p. 660)*

(A) 140   **(B)** 150

(C) 160   **(D)** 170

MR 2.4 Make and test conjectures by using both inductive and deductive reasoning.

89. The table shows values for x and corresponding values for y.

x	2	3	4
y	4	5	6

Which of the following represents the relationship between x and y? *(p. 407)*

(A) $y = 6x$ **(B)** $xy = 24$

(C) $y = x + 10$ **(D)** $y = x + 2$

Grade 7 | Mathematical Reasoning

MR 2.5 Use a variety of methods, such as words, numbers, symbols, charts, graphs, tables, diagrams, and models, to explain mathematical reasoning.

90. Which statement *best* describes the relationship between x and y in the chart below? *(p. 660)*

x	0	1	2	3
y	2	4	5	9

(A) The value of y decreases as the value of x increases.

(B) The value of y decreases as the value of x decreases.

(C) The value of x is constant.

(D) The value of y is constant.

MR 2.6 Express the solution clearly and logically by using the appropriate mathematical notation and terms and clear language; support solutions with evidence in both verbal and symbolic work.

91. The hypotenuse of a right triangle is 29 inches long and one leg is 21 inches long. What is the perimeter of the triangle? *(p. 471)*

(A) The third side of the triangle is 20 inches long, so the perimeter is $20 + 21 + 29 = 70$ inches.

(B) The third side of the triangle is 20 inches long, so the perimeter is $\frac{1}{2} \times 20 \times 21 = 210$ inches.

(C) The third side of the triangle is about 36 inches long, so the perimeter is about $36 + 21 + 29 = 86$ inches.

(D) The third side of the triangle is about 36 inches long, so the perimeter is about $\frac{1}{2} \times 36 \times 21 = 378$ inches.

MR 2.7 Indicate the relative advantages of exact and approximate solutions to problems and give answers to a specified degree of accuracy.

92. The front tire on a bicycle has a diameter of 26 inches. About how far will you travel when the tire makes 15 complete revolutions? *(p. 489)*

(A) 7 ft   (B) 82 ft

(C) 102 ft   (D) 1225 ft

Go On ➡

MR 2.8 Make precise calculations and check the validity of the results from the context of the problem.

93. The deposit on small cans and bottles is $.04 each. Your school is collecting small cans and bottles to earn $150 for three new basketballs. From the graph shown, you estimate that you will need 3800 small cans and bottles to earn enough money. Exactly how many small cans and bottles do you need to earn $150? *(p. 320)*

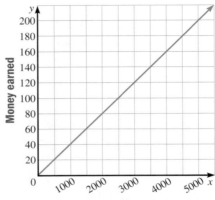

Number of small
cans and bottles

Ⓐ 3725   Ⓑ 3750

Ⓒ 3790   Ⓓ 3815

MR 3.0 Students determine a solution is complete and move beyond a particular problem by generalizing to other situations:

MR 3.1 Evaluate the reasonableness of the solution in the context of the original situation.

94. A health club charges $10 for a one-month trial membership. After the trial month, the regular membership fee is $45 per month. Let y be the total cost (in dollars) of being a member of the health club for x months. Which of the following points represents a solution in terms of the situation? *(p. 315)*

Ⓐ $(-1, -80)$

Ⓑ $(3, 145)$

Ⓒ $(4.5, 212.50)$

Ⓓ $(8, 325)$

Grade 7 **Mathematical Reasoning**

MR 3.2 Note the method of deriving the solution and demonstrate a conceptual understanding of the derivation by solving similar problems.

95. One way to solve an equation like $x^2 = 16$ is to graph $y = x^2$ and note that $y = 16$ when $x = 4$ and when $x = -4$.

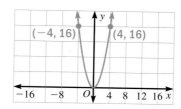

This shows that the equation $x^2 = 16$ has the solutions 4 and -4. How could you use this method to find the solutions of the equation $x^2 = 25$? *(p. 413)*

 Ⓐ Graph $y = x^2$ and find the y-intercept of the graph.

 Ⓑ Graph $y = x^2$ and find the x-coordinates of the points with a y-coordinate of 25.

 Ⓒ Graph $y = x^2$ and find the y-coordinate when $x = 25$.

 Ⓓ Graph $y = x^2$ and find the y-coordinates when $x = -25$ and when $x = 25$.

MR 3.3 Develop generalizations of the results obtained and the strategies used and apply them to new problem situations.

96. Marc used the following process to graph the linear equation $3x - 4y = 12$.

Step 1: The graph crosses the x-axis at $(4, 0)$, so plot $(4, 0)$.

Step 2: The graph crosses the y-axis at $(0, -3)$, so plot $(0, -3)$.

Step 3: Draw a line through the two plotted points.

According to Marc's method, which points are plotted to graph the equation $ax + by = c$ where $a \neq 0$ and $b \neq 0$? *(p. 327)*

 Ⓐ $(a, 0)$ and $(0, b)$

 Ⓑ $(b, 0)$ and $(0, a)$

 Ⓒ $\left(\dfrac{c}{a}, 0\right)$ and $\left(0, \dfrac{c}{b}\right)$

 Ⓓ $\left(\dfrac{a}{c}, 0\right)$ and $\left(0, \dfrac{b}{c}\right)$

Standards Practice

Pre-Course Test

Number Sense

Rounding, Factors, and Multiples *(pp. 723, 725–726)*

Round the number to the place value of the red digit.

1. 2234   **2.** 48,139   **3.** 4.566   **4.** 33.86

Find the greatest common factor and the least common multiple of the numbers.

5. 4, 20   **6.** 24, 196   **7.** 42, 18   **8.** 6, 15

Operations *(pp. 728–731)*

9. You bought 4 cans of tennis balls, each of which contains 3 balls. Use a verbal model to find the number of tennis balls you bought.

Estimate the sum or difference by rounding each number to the place of its leading digit.

10. $6845 + 2687$ **11.** $8999 + 3456$ **12.** $7356 - 4699$ **13.** $4567 - 3499$

Find a high and low estimate for the product or quotient using compatible numbers.

14. 44×18 **15.** 555×34 **16.** $333 \div 8$ **17.** $7656 \div 19$

Mixed Numbers, Improper Fractions, Ratios, and Rates *(pp. 727, 732)*

In Exercises 18–21, write the mixed number as an improper fraction or the improper fraction as a mixed number.

18. $4\frac{1}{2}$ **19.** $8\frac{4}{9}$ **20.** $\frac{12}{7}$ **21.** $\frac{21}{5}$

22. There are 21 boys and 23 girls in the chorus. Write the ratio of the number of boys to the number of girls in the chorus in three ways.

23. You drive at a constant speed of 48 miles per hour. How far do you travel in 2 hours?

Algebra and Functions

Inequalities *(p. 733)*

24. You can buy no more than 3 sale items. Write an inequality to represent the situation.

Coordinate Plane *(p. 734)*

Plot the point in a coordinate plane.

25. $A(4, 1)$ **26.** $B(2, -3)$ **27.** $C(-3, 0)$ **28.** $D(-2, -1)$

Measurement and Geometry

Two-Dimensional Figures (pp. 735–738, 740–742)

In Exercises 29–31, use the diagram.

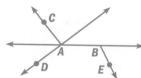

29. Name three points.

30. Name two rays.

31. Name a segment that has *D* as an endpoint.

Classify the angle as *acute, right, obtuse,* **or** *straight.*

32.

33.

34.

Use a protractor to draw an angle that has the given measure.

35. 56°

36. 125°

37. 140°

Classify the polygon and tell if it is regular. If it is regular, explain why.

38.

39.

40.

Find the perimeter and area of the rectangle or square.

41. 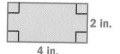 2 in. 4 in.

42. 3.5 cm 3.5 cm

43. 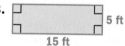 5 ft 15 ft

Statistics, Data Analysis, and Probability

Data Analysis (p. 743)

In Exercises 44 and 45, use the bar graph.

44. Which sale made the least money?

45. How much more money was made from the bake sale than the yard sale?

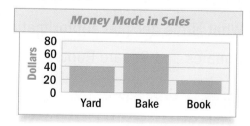

Mathematical Reasoning

Logical Reasoning and Problem Solving (pp. 744–745)

46. Amy calls a store to order a tote bag with her initials ABC embroidered on it. The store employee she talks to later forgets the order of the initials. How many bags would the employee have to make to be sure that one bag has the initials in the correct order?

Pre-Course Test

Textbook SCAVENGER HUNT

S

Practice using your textbook!

Use the student resources described on the next page to answer each question. Give page numbers to show where you found the answer to the question.

1 What is slope?

2 Tell what each of these symbols means: $\overleftrightarrow{AB}$, $a:b$, $\cong$.

3 How many millimeters are there in 1 meter?

4 On what page of the book are fractions first discussed?

5 What is a chord?

6 What is the decimal approximation of $\sqrt{54}$ according to the Table of Squares and Square Roots?

7 On what page can you review the skill of using divisibility tests?

8 On what page can you find selected answers for Lesson 1.1?

9 What formula can you use to find the area of a trapezoid?

Student Resources in Your Textbook

Your textbook contains many resources that you can use for reference when you are studying or doing your homework.

Standards Review Handbook Use the Standards Review Handbook on pages 723–746 to review material learned in previous courses.

Tables Refer to the tables on pages 759–765 if you need information about topics such as mathematical symbols, measures, formulas, and squares and square roots.

English-Spanish Glossary Use the English-Spanish Glossary on pages 767–794 to look up the meanings of math vocabulary terms in both English and Spanish. Each glossary entry also tells where in your book a term is covered in more detail.

Index Use the Index on pages 795–814 as a quick guide for finding out where a particular math topic is covered in the book.

Selected Answers Use the Selected Answers starting on page SA1 to check your work or to see whether you are on the right track in solving a problem.

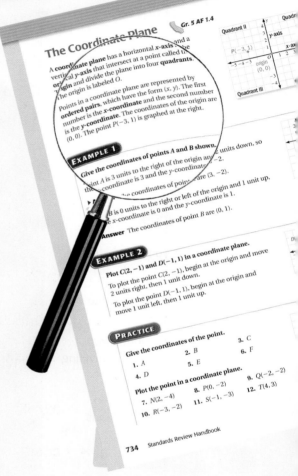

1 Integer Operations

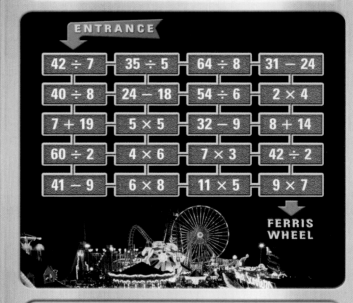

Get-Ready Games

Whole Number Ride

California Standards

Review operations with whole numbers. *Gr. 6 NS 2.3*
Prepare for operations with integers. *Gr. 7 NS 1.2*

ENTRANCE

42 ÷ 7	35 ÷ 5	64 ÷ 8	31 − 24
40 ÷ 8	24 − 18	54 ÷ 6	2 × 4
7 + 19	5 × 5	32 − 9	8 + 14
60 ÷ 2	4 × 6	7 × 3	42 ÷ 2
41 − 9	6 × 8	11 × 5	9 × 7

FERRIS WHEEL

How to Play
Find a path from the entrance to the Ferris wheel.

• Begin at the space marked *Entrance*. Find the sum, difference, product, or quotient. Then move one space along the path to a space that has a greater value.

Before

In previous courses, you learned the following skills, which you'll use in Chapter 1:

- Performing operations with whole numbers
- Comparing whole numbers
- Using a verbal model to solve a problem
- Using rates

Now

In Chapter 1 you'll study these **Big Ideas:**

1 Finding the absolute value of a number

2 Adding, subtracting, multiplying, and dividing integers

3 Using properties to simplify expressions

Why?

So you can solve real-world problems about . . .

- In-line skating, p. 10
- Aviation, p. 22
- Cycling, p. 22
- Miniature golf, p. 22
- Dinosaurs, p. 28
- Music, p. 39

Animated Math
at *classzone.com*

CALIFORNIA STANDARDS

- **Gr. 7 NS 2.5** Understand the meaning of the absolute value of a number; interpret the absolute value as the distance of the number from zero on a number line; and determine the absolute value of real numbers. *(Lesson 1.2)*

- **Gr. 7 AF 1.3** Simplify numerical expressions by applying properties of rational numbers (e.g., identity, inverse, distributive, associative, commutative) and justify the process used. *(Lessons 1.3, 1.5, 1.7, 1.8)*

BUMPER CARS

California Standards

Review operations with whole numbers. **Gr. 6 NS 2.3**
Prepare for operations with integers. **Gr. 7 NS 1.2**

How to Play

You and a partner each place a paper clip on a different number. The first player to bump the other player three times is the winner.

- Move one space to a new number. State one number fact using your old and new numbers and one of the operations $+$, $-$, $\times$, and $\div$.

- If the value of your number fact is the number where your partner's paper clip is located, bump your partner to another number.

Games Wrap-Up

Draw Conclusions

Complete these exercises after playing the games.

1. **WRITING** Suppose you want to move from the Ferris wheel to the Entrance in *Whole Number Ride*. How could you rewrite the rules of the game to make this possible?

2. **REASONING** List all of the number facts that you could make in *Bumper Cars* to bump your partner from car number nine.

Prerequisite Skills

California @HomeTutor

Prerequisite skills practice
at classzone.com

REVIEW VOCABULARY

- **sum,** *p. 728*
- **difference,** *p. 728*
- **product,** *p. 728*
- **quotient,** *p. 728*

VOCABULARY CHECK

Copy and complete using a review term from the list at the left.

1. When you add two numbers, the result is called the __?__ .

2. When you multiply two numbers, the result is called the __?__ .

3. When you split up an amount into equal parts, the result is called the __?__ . **n**

SKILL CHECK

Round the number to the place value of the red digit. *(p. 723)*

4. 26.80
5. 45.951
6. 139.07
7. 6.394

Find the sum, difference, product, or quotient. *(p. 728)*

8. $13 - 9$
9. $18 + 26$
10. $10 + 6$
11. $20 - 17$
12. 13×3
13. $96 \div 6$
14. $136 \div 17$
15. 5×23
16. 12×16

17. You are shopping for new clothes. If you have $75.00 and buy a pair of jeans for $38.00, how much money do you have left? *(p. 728)*

Notetaking Skills

NOW YOU TRY

Make a *definition and examples chart* for the word *rate*.

Focus on Graphic Organizers

You can use a *definition and examples chart* to organize examples that illustrate a vocabulary word, such as *ratio*.

Ratio: a comparison of two numbers using division — **Word and definition**

3 to 4 — Example

$\frac{3}{4}$ — Example

3:4 — Example

1.1 Expressions and Order of Operations

Standards **AF 1.2** Use the correct order of operations to evaluate algebraic expressions such as $3(2x + 5)^2$.

AF 1.4 Use algebraic terminology (e.g., **variable**, equation, term, coefficient, inequality, **expression**, constant) correctly.

Connect *Before* you performed simple arithmetic operations. *Now* you will evaluate expressions with powers.

Math and **SPORTS**
Ex. 69, p. 10

KEY VOCABULARY
- power
- numerical expression
- evaluate
- order of operations
- variable
- algebraic expression

A **power** is a way of writing repeated multiplication. The **exponent** tells how many times the **base** is being multiplied.

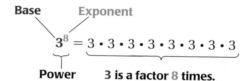

Base   Exponent

$$3^8 = 3 \cdot 3 \cdot 3 \cdot 3 \cdot 3 \cdot 3 \cdot 3 \cdot 3$$

Power   3 is a factor 8 times.

EXAMPLE 1 Writing Powers

Write the product as a power and describe it in words.

AVOID ERRORS
In part (a) of Example 1, make sure that you write 4^2 and not $4 \cdot 2$.

a. $4 \cdot 4 = 4^2$ 4 to the *second power*, or 4 *squared*

b. $9 \cdot 9 \cdot 9 = 9^3$ 9 to the *third power*, or 9 *cubed*

c. $2 \cdot 2 \cdot 2 \cdot 2 \cdot 2 = 2^5$ 2 to the *fifth power*

EXAMPLE 2 Finding the Value of a Power

Animated Math

For an interactive example of finding the value of a power, go to **classzone.com**.

Find the value of five cubed.

$$5^3 = 5 \cdot 5 \cdot 5 \qquad \text{Write 5 as a factor 3 times.}$$
$$= 125 \qquad \text{Multiply.}$$

 GUIDED PRACTICE for Examples 1 and 2

Write the product as a power and describe it in words.

1. $7 \times 7 \times 7 \times 7 \times 7 \times 7$ **2.** $10 \times 10 \times 10 \times 10$ **3.** 24×24

4. $1 \cdot 1 \cdot 1 \cdot 1 \cdot 1 \cdot 1 \cdot 1$ **5.** $8 \cdot 8 \cdot 8$ **6.** $9 \cdot 9 \cdot 9 \cdot 9 \cdot 9$

Find the value of the power.

7. 6^3 **8.** 2^5 **9.** 13^2 **10.** 3^1

EXPRESSIONS In Example 2, you found the value of 5^3, which is called a *numerical expression*. A **numerical expression** consists of numbers and operations. To find the value of a numerical expression is to **evaluate** it.

When a numerical expression has more than one operation, use a set of rules called the **order of operations** to evaluate the expression.

KEY CONCEPT   *For Your Notebook*

Order of Operations

1. Evaluate expressions inside grouping symbols.
2. Evaluate powers.
3. Multiply and divide from left to right.
4. Add and subtract from left to right.

EXAMPLE 3   **Using the Order of Operations**

Evaluate the expression.

a. $9 + 6 \div 3 \cdot 5 = 9 + 2 \cdot 5$ Divide 6 by 3.

$\qquad\qquad\qquad = 9 + 10$ Multiply 2 and 5.

$\qquad\qquad\qquad = 19$ Add 9 and 10.

RECOGNIZE GROUPING SYMBOLS

The most common grouping symbols are parentheses ( ), brackets [ ], and fraction bars.

b. $45 \div [63 \div (56 \div 8)] = 45 \div [63 \div 7]$ Divide inside the innermost set of grouping symbols.

$\qquad\qquad\qquad\qquad = 45 \div 9$ Divide inside brackets.

$\qquad\qquad\qquad\qquad = 5$ Divide.

c. $(7 - 4)^3 + 3 - 2^2 = 3^3 + 3 - 2^2$ Evaluate inside grouping symbols.

$\qquad\qquad\qquad\qquad = 27 + 3 - 4$ Evaluate powers.

$\qquad\qquad\qquad\qquad = 26$ Add and subtract from left to right.

Animated Math

For an interactive example of using the order of operations, go to **classzone.com**.

d. $\dfrac{9 \cdot 8}{4 + 8} = \dfrac{72}{4 + 8}$ Evaluate numerator.

$\qquad = \dfrac{72}{12}$ Evaluate denominator.

$\qquad = 6$ Divide.

✓ **GUIDED PRACTICE**   **for Example 3**

Evaluate the expression.

11. $20 - 7 \cdot 2 + 1$

12. $13 + 8 \cdot 5 \div 4$

13. $(5 - 2)^2 - 7 + 4^3$

14. $9 + [(6 - 4)^2]^3$

15. $\dfrac{17 - 5}{2 + 4}$

16. $\dfrac{20 - 5}{3 \cdot 5}$

VARIABLES A **variable** is a symbol, usually a letter, that represents one or more numbers. An **algebraic expression**, or *variable expression*, consists of numbers, variables, and operations. To evaluate an algebraic expression, substitute a number for each variable. Then find the value of the resulting numerical expression.

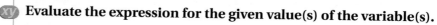

EXAMPLE 4 Evaluating Algebraic Expressions

Evaluate the expression for the given value(s) of the variable(s).

a. $3x + 4$, $x = 7$

b. $10s^3 - 3p^2$, $s = 2$, $p = 4$

READING
The product of a number and a variable is often written without a multiplication symbol. For instance, $3x$ means $3 \cdot x$.

SOLUTION

a. $3x + 4 = 3(7) + 4$ Substitute 7 for x.

            $= 21 + 4$ Multiply.

            $= 25$ Add.

b. $10s^3 - 3p^2 = 10(2)^3 - 3(4)^2$ Substitute 2 for s and 4 for p.

                 $= 10(8) - 3(16)$ Evaluate powers.

                 $= 80 - 48$ Multiply.

                 $= 32$ Subtract.

Animated Math

For an interactive example of evaluating an algebraic expression, go to **classzone.com**.

EXAMPLE 5 Evaluating a Real-Life Expression

WATERFALL A river carries a stone over a waterfall. The stone hits the water 5 seconds later. To find the height of the waterfall, use the expression $16t^2$, which gives the distance in feet that a dropped object falls in t seconds.

SOLUTION

$16t^2 = 16(5)^2$ Substitute 5 for t.

      $= 16(25)$ Evaluate the power.

      $= 400$ Multiply.

▶ **Answer** The waterfall is about 400 feet high.

✓ **GUIDED PRACTICE** for Examples 4 and 5

Evaluate the expression for the given value(s) of the variable(s).

17. $4r + 6$, $r = 5$ **18.** $3(y - 5)$, $y = 8$ **19.** $n^2 + q^3$, $n = 1$, $q = 2$

20. WHAT IF? In Example 5, suppose the stone hits the water after 2 seconds. Find the height of the waterfall.

1.1 EXERCISES

HOMEWORK KEY

◆ = **MULTIPLE CHOICE PRACTICE**
Exs. 42, 63, 67, 75–77

○ = **HINTS AND HOMEWORK HELP**
for Exs. 21, 51, 69 at classzone.com

SKILLS • PROBLEM SOLVING • REASONING

1. **VOCABULARY** Copy and complete: $3t - 4$ is a(n) __?__ expression and $5 + 13$ is a(n) __?__ expression.

2. **WRITING** *Describe* the steps you would take to evaluate the expression x^3 when $x = 4$.

SEE EXAMPLE 1
on p. 5
for Exs. 3–11

WRITING POWERS Write the product as a power and describe it in words.

3. $9 \cdot 9$

4. $3 \cdot 3 \cdot 3$

5. $7 \cdot 7 \cdot 7$

6. $4 \cdot 4 \cdot 4 \cdot 4 \cdot 4$

7. $10 \cdot 10 \cdot 10$

8. $6 \cdot 6 \cdot 6 \cdot 6$

9. $x \cdot x$

10. $m \cdot m \cdot m$

11. $a \cdot a \cdot a \cdot a \cdot a$

SEE EXAMPLE 2
on p. 5
for Exs. 12–23

EVALUATING POWERS Evaluate the power.

12. Three squared

13. Eleven cubed

14. One to the ninth

15. 2^6

16. 5^5

17. 0^7

18. 6^1

19. 11^2

20. 2^7

21. 10^3

22. 1^8

23. 20^2

SEE EXAMPLE 3
on p. 6
for Exs. 24–42

USING ORDER OF OPERATIONS Evaluate the expression.

24. $12 - 10 + 4$

25. $7 + 3 - 2 + 4$

26. $18 + 6 \div 3 \cdot 2$

27. $16 - 6 + 2 \cdot 4$

28. $26 - 15 + 8 \div 2$

29. $18 \div (8 + 4 - 9)$

30. $(2 + 1)^4 \div 9 - 4$

31. $48 \div (9 - 7)^3$

32. $(5 \cdot 3)^2 - 4$

33. $(2 \cdot 5)^2 + 9$

34. $500 \div (12 - 7)^1$

35. $6 \cdot 18 \div 3^2$

36. $\dfrac{8 + 2}{5 - 3}$

37. $\dfrac{16}{7 - 3}$

38. $3\left(\dfrac{7 + 1}{2}\right)$

39. $9 \div \left[3\left(\dfrac{5 + 4}{3}\right)\right]$

40. $4(12 - 5) + \dfrac{23 - 9}{7}$

41. $\dfrac{41 - 2(3 + 4)}{36 \div 4}$

42. ◆ **MULTIPLE CHOICE** In what order should the operations be performed to evaluate the expression $2 \times 4 - 6 \div 3 + 1$?

Ⓐ $\times, \div, -, +$　　Ⓑ $\times, -, \div, +$　　Ⓒ $\times, \div, +, -$　　Ⓓ $\times, +, -, \div$

ERROR ANALYSIS *Describe* and correct the error in evaluating the expression.

43.
$$7^2 = 7 \times 2$$
$$= 14$$ ✗

44.
$$\dfrac{4 + 8}{2 + 4} = 4 + 8 \div 2 + 4$$
$$= 4 + 4 + 4$$
$$= 12$$ ✗

SEE EXAMPLE 4
on p. 7
for Exs. 45–63

XY ALGEBRA Evaluate the expression when $g = 4$, $s = 8$, and $t = 6$.

45. $7g$

46. $3g - 12$

47. $6(s - 2)$

48. $2(15 - 3g)$

49. $g^4 \div 16$

50. $(s - 5)^3$

51. $7g + 2t^2$

52. $10(s + t - g)$

53. $4t - 2s - 4$

54. $8t \div s$

55. $2t^2 - s$

56. $s(t - g)^2$

XY ALGEBRA Evaluate the expression for the given value(s) of the variable(s).

57. $4x - 5$, $x = 7$

58. $3(c - d)$, $c = 12$, $d = 7$

59. $3x + y^2$, $x = 6$, $y = 3$

60. $r^3 - t^5 \div 2$, $r = 3$, $t = 2$

61. $\dfrac{d + 10}{c - d}$, $c = 14$, $d = 8$

62. $\dfrac{50 - r}{p + 3}$, $p = 6$, $r = 5$

63. ◆ MULTIPLE CHOICE Which values make the expression $x \cdot [4 + (y \div 5)]$ have a value of 18?

(A) $x = 10$, $y = 20$

(B) $x = 3$, $y = 30$

(C) $x = 2$, $y = 50$

(D) $x = 3$, $y = 10$

CONNECT SKILLS TO PROBLEM SOLVING Exercises 64–66 will help you prepare for problem solving.

64. You buy 3 notebooks for $2 each and 4 pens for $1 each. Evaluate the expression $3 \cdot 2 + 4 \cdot 1$ to find the total number of dollars you spend.

65. There are $100x$ sheets of paper in x packages. How many sheets of paper are there in 6 packages?

66. The area of a square is s^2 where s is the length of one side of the square. Find the area of a square that has a side length of 7 inches.

SEE EXAMPLE 5
on p. 7 for
Exs. 67, 70–71

67. ◆ MULTIPLE CHOICE The *volume* of a cube is s^3 where s is the length of one edge of the cube. A cube has an edge length of 14 centimeters. What is the volume of the cube in cubic centimeters?

(A) 42 cm^3

(B) 196 cm^3

(C) 1400 cm^3

(D) 2744 cm^3

California @HomeTutor for problem solving help at classzone.com

68. MULTI-STEP PROBLEM Zoe and Ty are making lasagna for a school fundraiser. The recipe they are using calls for one dozen noodles for each batch of lasagna. Zoe makes 4 batches, and Ty makes 3 batches .

a. Evaluate the expression $4 \cdot 12 + 3 \cdot 12$ to find how many noodles Zoe and Ty need.

b. One box of lasagna noodles contains 14 noodles. How many boxes of noodles do Zoe and Ty need?

California @HomeTutor for problem solving help at classzone.com

One dozen = 12

69. **IN-LINE SKATING** An in-line skater starts moving downhill. After 6 feet, the skater's speed is 3 miles per hour, and his speed doubles every 6 feet. After traveling 30 feet, the skater's speed is represented by the expression $3(2)(2)(2)(2)$. Rewrite this expression as the product of 3 and a power. Then evaluate the expression to find the skater's speed.

70. **POOL MEMBERSHIP** A neighborhood pool has a summer membership cost of $5 and a per visit cost of $2. Evaluate the expression $2n + 5$ when $n = 10$ to find the total cost of 10 visits to the pool.

71. **MULTI-STEP PROBLEM** In Acapulco, Mexico, divers jump from a cliff at heights of 85 to 115 feet above the water. After t seconds, a diver has fallen $16t^2$ feet.

a. Does a diver jumping from a height of 85 feet reach the surface of the water within 2 seconds? *Explain* your reasoning.

b. How much lower is the diver from part (a) after 2 seconds than after 1 second? *Explain.*

72. **REASONING** Some powers of 11 read the same forward and backward. For example, $11^1 = 11$ and $11^2 = 121$. What is the smallest value of n such that 11^n does *not* read the same forward and backward?

Acapulco, Mexico

73. **CHALLENGE** To make the statement true, copy and complete using one or more of the operators $\times$, $\div$, $-$, or $+$: $8 \underline{\ ?\ } 6 \underline{\ ?\ } 3 \underline{\ ?\ } 7 \underline{\ ?\ } 1 = 5$.

74. **CHALLENGE** The population of Amesville can be represented by $6800 - 120x$ and the population of Boomville can be represented by $4200 + 80x$, where x is the number of years since 2006. In what year will the population of the two towns be equal?

◆ CALIFORNIA STANDARDS SPIRAL REVIEW

Gr 6 NS 2.4

75. What is the greatest common divisor of 56, 48, and 12? *(p. 725)*

    (A) 4   **(B)** 6   **(C)** 8   **(D)** 12

Gr 5 NS 1.5

76. Which statement about the value of P is true? *(p. 733)*

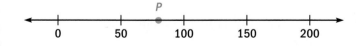

    (A) $P < 10$ **(B)** $P = 50$ **(C)** $P < 100$ **(D)** $P > 175$

Gr 5 NS 1.1

77. In 2005, the population of California was about 34,441,000. What is this value rounded to the nearest hundred thousand? *(p. 723)*

    (A) 34,000,000   **(B)** 34,400,000   **(C)** 34,440,000   **(D)** 34,500,000

1.1 Using Order of Operations

Standards

AF 1.2 Use the correct order of operations to evaluate algebraic expressions such as $3(2x + 5)^2$.

QUESTION How can you use a calculator to evaluate an algebraic expression?

EXAMPLE Evaluate an algebraic expression

Evaluate the expression $\dfrac{148 + 2x}{x - 3}$ when $x = 17$.

STEP 1 **Substitute** 17 for x in the algebraic expression.

$$\dfrac{148 + 2x}{x - 3} = \dfrac{148 + 2 \cdot 17}{17 - 3}$$

STEP 2 **Evaluate** the expression using the order of operations. Use parentheses to separate expressions that should be grouped together.

Keystrokes

(148 + 2 × 17) ÷ (17 − 3) =

Display

13

PRACTICE

Use a calculator to evaluate the expression.

1. $2x + 4$ when $x = 7$

2. $24 - x \div 3$ when $x = 6$

3. $238 \div x + x \div 7$ when $x = 14$

4. $21x + 6x \div 9$ when $x = 18$

5. $\dfrac{x + 5}{19 - x}$ when $x = 16$

6. $\dfrac{33 + 7x}{3x + 7}$ when $x = 6$

7. $\dfrac{2x - 9}{x - 1}$ when $x = 8$

8. $\dfrac{11 + 3x}{x + 8}$ when $x = 5$

9. AQUARIUM You are filling a 29-gallon aquarium with water at a rate of 4 gallons per minute. To determine how many minutes it takes to fill the aquarium, use the expression $(29 - x) \div 4$ where x is the number of gallons already in the aquarium. Evaluate the expression when $x = 5$.

10. BASKETBALL A basketball team scores a total of 79 points in a game. To find the number of foul shots (worth 1 point) made by the team, use the expression $79 - (2x + 3y)$ where x is the number of two-point baskets and y is the number of three-point baskets. Evaluate the expression when $x = 25$ and $y = 4$.

1.2 Integers and the Number Line

Standards   NS 1.1 Read, write, and compare rational numbers in scientific notation (positive and negative powers of 10), **compare rational numbers in general.**

NS 2.5 **Understand the meaning of the absolute value of a number; interpret the absolute value as the distance of the number from zero on a number line; and determine the absolute value of real numbers.**

Math and TECHNOLOGY
Ex. 44, p. 15

Connect   *Before* you studied whole numbers. *Now* you will study integers.

KEY VOCABULARY
- integers
- negative integers
- positive integers
- absolute value
- opposites

The following numbers are **integers**.

$$\ldots, -5, -4, -3, -2, -1, 0, 1, 2, 3, 4, 5, \ldots$$

Integers consist of the **negative integers**, which are less than 0, the **positive integers**, which are greater than 0, and 0. The negative integers lie *to the left* of 0 on a number line. The positive integers lie *to the right* of 0 on a number line. Zero is neither positive nor negative. Numbers increase as you move to the right on a number line.

Zero

Negative integers   Positive integers

$-4 \quad -3 \quad -2 \quad -1 \quad 0 \quad 1 \quad 2 \quad 3 \quad 4$

EXAMPLE 1   Ordering Integers Using a Number Line

Use a number line to order the following integers from least to greatest.

$$0, -1, 2, -3, 4, 5$$

About the Standards

You will learn more about comparing numbers (NS 1.1) in Lessons 2.2, 3.1, 4.1, and 4.2.

SOLUTION

Graph the integers on a number line. Then list the integers in the order (from left to right) that they appear on the number line.

▶ **Answer** The integers from least to greatest are $-3, -1, 0, 2, 4,$ and 5.

✓ GUIDED PRACTICE   for Example 1

Use a number line to order the integers from least to greatest.

1. $-7, 2, -1, 0, -2$

2. $9, -4, 8, -5, -1$

3. $0, -90, 40, -60, 10$

4. $8, -2, -5, 4, -3$

5. $-9, 5, -3, 2, -7$

6. $-6, -4, -1, -3, -8$

ABSOLUTE VALUE The **absolute value** of a number is the distance between the number and zero on a number line. The absolute value of a number n is written as $|n|$. The absolute value of 0 is 0.

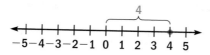

The distance between 4 and 0 is 4. So, $|4| = 4$.

The distance between -5 and 0 is 5. So, $|-5| = 5$.

EXAMPLE 2 **Finding Absolute Value**

EYEGLASSES An eyeglass prescription is given as a positive or negative number. A prescription for a person who is farsighted is positive. A prescription for a person who is nearsighted is negative. The greater the absolute value, the stronger the prescription. Which prescription is stronger, -3 or 2?

ANOTHER WAY

For an alternative method for solving the problem in Example 2, turn to page 17 for the **Problem Solving Workshop**.

SOLUTION

STEP 1 **Find** the absolute value of -3 using a number line.

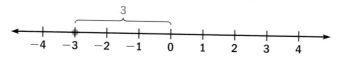

The distance between -3 and 0 is 3. So, $|-3| = 3$.

STEP 2 **Find** the absolute value of 2 using a number line.

The distance between 2 and 0 is 2. So, $|2| = 2$.

REVIEW INEQUALITY SYMBOLS

For help with inequality symbols, see p. 733.

▶**Answer** The prescription of -3 is stronger because $3 > 2$.

✓ **GUIDED PRACTICE** for Example 2

Identify the graphed number with the greater absolute value.

7.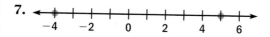

8.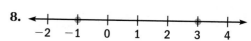

Find the absolute value of the integer using a number line.

9. -6 10. 3 11. -1 12. 0

13. 5 14. -2 15. 16 16. -14

17. **WHAT IF?** In Example 2, suppose you are comparing prescriptions of 4 and -5. Which of these prescriptions is stronger?

READING
The integer -2 can be read "negative 2" or "the opposite of 2."

OPPOSITES Two numbers are **opposites** if they have the same absolute value but different signs. Opposites are the same distance from 0 on a number line but are on opposite sides of 0. The opposite of 0 is 0.

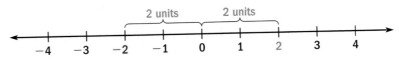

-2 and 2 are opposites.

EXAMPLE 3 Finding Opposites

Write the opposite of the integer.

a. 5   The opposite of 5 is -5.

b. -12 The opposite of -12 is 12.

c. $|-9|$ Because $|-9| = 9$, the opposite of $|-9|$ is -9.

✓ **GUIDED PRACTICE**   **for Example 3**

Write the opposite of the integer.

18. -9 **19.** 8   **20.** -100 **21.** $|5|$

1.2 EXERCISES

HOMEWORK KEY

◆ = **MULTIPLE CHOICE PRACTICE**
Exs. 17, 36, 44, 51–53

○ = **HINTS AND HOMEWORK HELP**
for Exs. 13, 21, 47 at classzone.com

SKILLS • PROBLEM SOLVING • REASONING

1. VOCABULARY Copy and complete: Two integers are __?__ if they have the same absolute value but different signs.

2. NOTETAKING SKILLS Make a *definition and examples chart* like the one on page 4 for *opposite*.

SEE EXAMPLE 1
on p. 12
for Exs. 3–19

COMPARING INTEGERS Copy and complete the statement with < or >.

3. $4 \underline{\ ?\ } -6$ **4.** $-12 \underline{\ ?\ } 1$ **5.** $-9 \underline{\ ?\ } -2$ **6.** $0 \underline{\ ?\ } -5$

7. $5 \underline{\ ?\ } -5$ **8.** $-17 \underline{\ ?\ } 2$ **9.** $34 \underline{\ ?\ } -29$ **10.** $-20 \underline{\ ?\ } -14$

ORDERING INTEGERS Use a number line to order the integers from least to greatest.

11. $5, -10, 4, -6, -2, 3$ **12.** $7, 4, 0, -5, 11, -1$

13. $-3, -7, -11, -2, -8, -5$ **14.** $6, -4, 9, -3, 8, 1$

15. $60, -10, 10, 50, -20, 40$ **16.** $270, 120, -300, 260, -150$

17. ◆ **MULTIPLE CHOICE** Which list orders the integers from least to greatest?

    A $-1, -6, -12, -34$ **B** $-1, -12, -34, -6$

    C $-34, -12, -6, -1$ **D** $-34, -6, -12, -1$

ERROR ANALYSIS *Describe* and correct the error in ordering the integers $3, 1, 0, -9, -2,$ and 5 from least to greatest.

18.

    $0, 1, -2, 3, 5, -9$ ✗

19.

    $-2, -9, 0, 1, 3, 5$ ✗

SEE EXAMPLES 2 AND 3 on pp. 13–14 for Exs. 20–36

ABSOLUTE VALUE AND OPPOSITES Write the absolute value and the opposite of the integer.

20. 19 **21.** -8 **22.** -7 **23.** 13

24. -4 **25.** 11 **26.** 25 **27.** -340

SIMPLIFYING EXPRESSIONS Simplify the expression.

28. $|-32|$ **29.** $-|9|$ **30.** $-|29|$ **31.** $-(-5)$

32. $-(-81)$ **33.** $-|-17|$ **34.** $-|-3|$ **35.** $-(-(-4))$

36. ◆ **MULTIPLE CHOICE** Which number has the greatest absolute value?

    A -12 **B** -3 **C** 0 **D** 7

ORDERING NUMBERS Order the numbers from least to greatest.

37. $-28, -(-73), |-65|, |95|, -|47|$ **38.** $|-19|, -74, -|12|, -(-56), -|-58|$

39. $-|6|, -8, -(-5), -14, |-1|$ **40.** $|38|, -37, -|-42|, -(-29), |-49|$

CONNECT SKILLS TO PROBLEM SOLVING Exercises 41–43 will help you prepare for problem solving.

Use the table that shows the elevations of five lakes in the United States.

41. Which lake is at a lower elevation, Gieselmann Lake or Silver Lake?

42. Which lake is at a higher elevation, Craigs Pond or Jones Lake?

43. Which lake has the lowest elevation?

Lake	Elevation (ft)
Jones Lake	−30
Silver Lake	90
Gieselmann Lake	−162
Seneca Lake	445
Craigs Pond	0

Seneca Lake, New York

SEE EXAMPLE 3 on p. 14 for Ex. 44

44. ◆ **MULTIPLE CHOICE** The Global Positioning System (GPS) uses satellites to determine elevations given relative to sea level. The elevation of sea level is 0. Which number represents 86 meters below sea level, the lowest elevation in the United States?

    A -86 **B** $-(-86)$ **C** $|-86|$ **D** $|86|$

California @HomeTutor for problem solving help at classzone.com

SEE EXAMPLE 1
on p. 12
for Ex. 45

45. **LAUNCH COUNTDOWN** Put the following activities for a shuttle launch in the order in which they occur. "T−5 minutes" means 5 minutes before liftoff.

Count	Activity
T−5 minutes	Pilot starts auxiliary power units.
T+7 seconds	Shuttle clears launch tower, and control switches to the Mission Control Center.
T−2 hours, 55 minutes	Flight crew departs for launch pad.
T−6 seconds	Main engine starts.
T−0	Liftoff.

California @HomeTutor for problem solving help at classzone.com

T minus 0: Liftoff

46. **REASONING** What numbers have opposites that are the same as their absolute values? What numbers have opposites that are different from their absolute values? Use examples to support your answer.

47. **WRITING** Suppose $|a| < |b|$ where a and b are negative integers. What is the possible relationship between a and b?

CHALLENGE In Exercises 48 and 49, tell whether the statement is *always*, *sometimes*, or *never* true. *Justify* your answer.

48. The absolute value of a number x is greater than or equal to x.

49. The opposite of a number y is greater than or equal to y.

50. **CHALLENGE** The table below shows the substances in a solution and their boiling points in degrees Celsius. Order the substances from lowest boiling point to highest boiling point. The boiling point is the temperature at which a substance changes to a gas. If you heat the solution until one substance remains, which substance would it be?

Substance	Ethanol	Water	Propanol	Methanol
Boiling point	$|{-78}|$	$-(-100)$	97	$|{-65}|$

◆ CALIFORNIA STANDARDS SPIRAL REVIEW

AF 1.2

51. What is the value of $4(2x - 3)^2$ when $x = 4$? *(p. 5)*

(A) 4   **(B)** 29   **(C)** 100   **(D)** 400

Gr 4 MG 3.5

52. What is the name of an angle that measures 90 degrees? *(p. 736)*

(A) Acute   **(B)** Obtuse   **(C)** Right   **(D)** Straight

Gr 6 AF 2.2

53. Alicia types 210 words in 5 minutes. At this rate, how many words can Alicia type in 15 minutes? *(p. 732)*

(A) 70   **(B)** 420   **(C)** 630   **(D)** 1050

Using ALTERNATIVE METHODS

Another Way to Solve Example 2, page 13

Standards
NS 2.5

In Example 2 on page 13, you used number lines to find the absolute values of two integers. You can also find the absolute values of integers by using a rule.

PROBLEM

EYEGLASSES An eyeglass prescription is given as a positive or negative number. A prescription for a person who is farsighted is positive. A prescription for a person who is nearsighted is negative. The greater the absolute value, the stronger the prescription. Which prescription is stronger, -3 or 2?

METHOD

Using a Rule You can find the absolute value of an integer by using the following rule: $|n| = n$ if $n \geq 0$ and $|n| = -n$ if $n < 0$.

STEP 1 **Find** the absolute value of each prescription by using the rule.

Because $-3 < 0$, $|-3| = -(-3) = 3$.
Because $2 \geq 0$, $|2| = 2$.

STEP 2 **Compare** the absolute values.

$3 > 2$

▶ **Answer** The eyeglass prescription of -3 is stronger than the prescription of 2.

PRACTICE

In Exercises 1–4, use a rule to find the absolute value of the integer.

1. -5 **2.** 9

3. 22 **4.** -116

5. LAKE LEVELS In seven consecutive months in 2004, the water level of Lake St. Clair, in the Great Lakes system, changed from the previous month's level by the following amounts in centimeters: 12, 3, -3, -5, -18, -7, and 4. *Compare* the absolute values of these data to determine the value that represents the greatest change.

6. ELEVATION The elevation at sea level is 0. The table shows the elevations relative to sea level of four locations in and around Death Valley. Which location is closest to sea level? Which is farthest from sea level? Order the locations from least to greatest elevation.

Location	Elevation (ft)
Badwater	-259
Dante's View	5384
Furnace Creek	-177
Telescope Peak	$11,049$

1.3 Adding Integers

Standards

NS 1.2 **Add**, subtract, multiply, and divide **rational numbers** (**integers**, fractions, and terminating decimals) and take positive rational numbers to whole-number powers.

AF 1.3 **Simplify numerical expressions by applying properties of rational numbers** (e.g., **identity, inverse**, distributive, associative, commutative) **and justify the process used.**

Math and **RECREATION**
Ex. 58, p. 22

Connect *Before* you added whole numbers. *Now* you will add integers.

KEY VOCABULARY
• **additive identity**
• **additive inverse**
• **integer,** *p. 12*
• **absolute value,** *p. 13*
• **sum,** *p. 728*

You can use a number line to add integers.

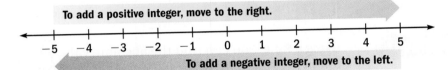

To add a positive integer, move to the right.

To add a negative integer, move to the left.

EXAMPLE 1 **Adding Integers Using a Number Line**

Use a number line to find the sum.

a. $-6 + 10$

b. $-4 + (-3)$

SOLUTION

a. Start at 0. Move **6** units to the left. Then move **10** units to the right.

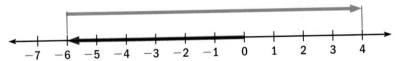

▶ **Answer** The final position is 4. So, $-6 + 10 = 4$.

b. Start at 0. Move **4** units to the left. Then move **3** units to the left.

▶ **Answer** The final position is -7. So, $-4 + (-3) = -7$.

✓ **GUIDED PRACTICE** for Example 1

Use a number line to find the sum.

1. $-8 + 4$

2. $-1 + (-6)$

3. $9 + (-3)$

For Your Notebook

Adding Integers

You can add integers without using a number line by following these rules.

Same sign

Add the absolute values and use the common sign.

Different signs

Subtract the lesser absolute value from the greater absolute value. Use the sign of the number with the greater absolute value.

EXAMPLE 2 Adding Integers

Find the sum $-12 + 4$.

$$-12 + 4 = -8$$

Different signs, so subtract $|4|$ from $|-12|$.

Use sign of number with greater absolute value.

CHECK You can use a number line to check your answer.

For Your Notebook

Addition Properties

Identity Property of Addition

Words   The sum of a number and the **additive identity**, 0, is the number.

Numbers $-3 + 0 = -3$ **Algebra** $a + 0 = a$

Inverse Property of Addition

Words   The sum of a number and its **additive inverse**, or opposite, is 0.

Numbers $5 + (-5) = 0$ **Algebra** $a + (-a) = 0$

Closure Property of Addition

The sum of two integers is an integer.

EXAMPLE 3 Using Addition Properties

About the Standards

You will learn more about properties (AF 1.3) in Lessons 1.5, 1.7, and 1.8.

Find the sum using the order of operations.

$$(-7 + 7) + (-8) + (-5) = \mathbf{0} + (-8) + (-5)$$ Inverse property of addition

$$= -8 + (-5)$$ Identity property of addition

$$= -13$$ Same sign, so sum has common sign

EXAMPLE 4 Adding More Than Two Integers

BANKING You have $50 in your checking account at the beginning of the month. The record below shows all of your account transactions during the month. How much money is in your account after these transactions?

RECORD ALL CREDITS AND CHARGES THAT AFFECT YOUR ACCOUNT

Check Number	Date	Transaction Description	Payment (−)	Deposit (+)
102	9/14	Team T-shirt	$12	
	9/15	Deposit		$20
103	9/21	Bus pass	$24	
	9/29	Deposit		$30

ANOTHER WAY
You can also add the numbers in order from left to right.

SOLUTION

Add the **positive amounts (the deposits)** and the **negative amounts (the payments)** to your beginning balance.

$$50 + 20 + 30 + (-12) + (-24) = 50 + 50 + (-36)$$
$$= 100 + (-36)$$
$$= 64$$

▶ **Answer** After the transactions shown, there is $64 in your account.

✓ **GUIDED PRACTICE** for Examples 2, 3, and 4

Find the sum. Identify any addition properties you use.

4. $-20 + (-15)$

5. $18 + (-18) + (-54)$

6. WHAT IF? In Example 4, suppose that the T-shirt costs $18 and the final deposit is $22. What is the balance of the account?

1.3 EXERCISES

HOMEWORK KEY

◆ = **MULTIPLE CHOICE PRACTICE**
Exs. 13, 29, 52, 61–63

○ = **HINTS AND HOMEWORK HELP**
for Exs. 5, 15, 53 at classzone.com

SKILLS • PROBLEM SOLVING • REASONING

1. **VOCABULARY** Copy and complete: To add two integers with the same sign, add their __?__ and use the common sign.

2. **WRITING** *Explain* how to find the additive inverse of 6.

SEE EXAMPLE 1
on p. 18
for Exs. 3–13

ADDING WITH A NUMBER LINE Use a number line to find the sum.

3. $-6 + 8$

4. $-3 + (-9)$

5. $5 + (-7)$

6. $-4 + 4$

7. $-2 + (-1)$

8. $-10 + (-9)$

9. $-3 + 7$

10. $7 + (-5)$

ERROR ANALYSIS *Describe* and correct the error in finding the sum.

11.

$\times$ $-8 + 5 = -13$

12.

$\times$ $-9 + (-7) + 6 = -16 + 6$
$\qquad\qquad\qquad\quad = 10$

13. ◆ **MULTIPLE CHOICE** What is the value of $-8 + 3$?

(A) -11 **(B)** -5 **(C)** 5 **(D)** 11

SEE EXAMPLES 2, 3, AND 4 on pp. 19–20 for Exs. 14–29

ADDING INTEGERS Find the sum. Identify any addition properties you use.

14. $42 + (-23)$ **15.** $-63 + (-49)$ **16.** $-93 + 16$

17. $-25 + 25$ **18.** $0 + (-82)$ **19.** $98 + (-128)$

20. $-9 + 9 + (-14)$ **21.** $-12 + 9 + (-5)$ **22.** $20 + (-15) + (-22)$

23. $-12 + (-25) + 8$ **24.** $-21 + (-15) + (-25)$ **25.** $-17 + 8 + 16$

26. $-7 + 15 + 4 + (-9)$ **27.** $11 + (-11) + 5 + (-8)$ **28.** $-4 + (-6) + 10 + 5$

Animated **Math** at classzone.com

29. ◆ **MULTIPLE CHOICE** Which equation shows the identity property of addition?

(A) $4 + 4 = 8$ **(B)** $4 + (-4) = 0$ **(C)** $4 - 4 = 0$ **(D)** $4 + 0 = 4$

XY **EVALUATING EXPRESSIONS** Evaluate when $a = -13, b = 24,$ and $c = -27$.

30. $a + b$ **31.** $-b + c$ **32.** $a + |c|$ **33.** $|a| + |c|$

34. $a + b + c$ **35.** $a + (-b) + c$ **36.** $|a| + b + c$ **37.** $|a| + b + |c|$

XY **ALGEBRA** Evaluate $x + (-478)$ using the given value of x.

38. $x = 806$ **39.** $x = -729$ **40.** $x = |-349|$ **41.** $x = -|-521|$

42. **OPEN-ENDED** Name two integers with the same sign that have a sum of -28. Name two integers with different signs that have a sum of -28.

REASONING Tell whether the sum of the two integers described is *always*, *sometimes*, or *never* negative. *Justify* your answer.

43. Two negative integers   **44.** Two positive integers

45. A positive integer and a negative integer   **46.** A negative integer and zero

CONNECT SKILLS TO PROBLEM SOLVING Exercises 47–50 will help you prepare for problem solving.

Use the following information: In chemistry, you will study *protons* and *electrons*. A proton has a charge of $+1$, and an electron has a charge of -1. Find the sum of the charges.

47. Sodium ion: 11 protons, 10 electrons   **48.** Argon: 18 protons, 18 electrons

49. Oxide ion: 8 protons, 10 electrons   **50.** Calcium ion: 20 protons, 18 electrons

SEE EXAMPLE 4
on p. 20 for
Exs. 51–52, 54,
56–58

51. ELEVATOR You enter an elevator on the sixth floor. The elevator goes up 3 floors and then down 5 floors, where you exit. Find the floor on which you exit.

California @HomeTutor for problem solving help at classzone.com

52. ◆ MULTIPLE CHOICE Your family begins a trip with 16 gallons of gasoline in the car. You use 9 gallons, and then put 7 more gallons in the tank. How many gallons of gasoline are now in the tank?

(A) 12 gal   **(B)** 14 gal   **(C)** 18 gal   **(D)** 23 gal

California @HomeTutor for problem solving help at classzone.com

53. REASONING You want to add a positive integer and a negative integer. How do you choose the sign of your answer? *Explain.*

54. AVIATION You are traveling in a jet at an altitude of 33,000 feet. Because of turbulence, the pilot decreases the altitude by 8000 feet. Thirty minutes later, the pilot increases the altitude by 12,500 feet. What is the jet's new altitude?

55. MULTI-STEP PROBLEM The classic Mexican period began around 200 B.C. and lasted for 1100 years. The classic Greek period began around 500 B.C. and lasted for 200 years.

   a. About what year did the classic Mexican period end?

   b. About what year did the classic Greek period end?

   c. About how many years after the classic Greek period ended did the classic Mexican period end?

Mask from classic Mexican period

56. FOOTBALL A football team gained 7 yards on the first play, lost 9 yards on the second play, and gained 6 yards on the third play. To get a first down, they must gain 10 yards in 4 plays. How many yards must they gain on the fourth play to get a first down? *Explain* your reasoning.

57. CYCLING You are at an elevation of 192 feet above sea level as you start a bicycle ride. During the ride, your elevation changes by the following amounts in feet: 270, −134, 58, −76, 245, −422, and 47. What is your elevation above sea level at the end of the ride?

58. MINIATURE GOLF In miniature golf, *par* is the number of strokes considered necessary to get the ball in the hole. A player's score for each hole is the number of strokes above par (a positive number) or below par (a negative number). The total score is the sum of the scores for each hole. Is Jill's total score for the first 9 holes *above par*, *below par*, or *at par*? *Explain* your reasoning.

HOLE	1	2	3	4	5	6	7	8	9	OUT
PAR	4	5	3	3	5	4	3	5	3	35
Jill	0	+1	−2	−1	0	+1	+2	+1	−1	?

59. CHALLENGE Does $|x + y| = |x| + |y|$ if x and y are both positive? both negative? What if x is positive and y is negative? *Explain*.

60. CHALLENGE A newspaper reports these changes in the price of a stock during a 5 month period: $-\$1$, $-\$8$, $+\$2$, $-\$4$, and $+\$6$. At the end of the fifth month, the stock price was $35. Use a number line to show the price of the stock at the beginning of the 5 month period.

◆ CALIFORNIA STANDARDS SPIRAL REVIEW

NS 1.2

61. What is the value of 5^4? *(p. 5)*

    Ⓐ 20   **Ⓑ** 125   **Ⓒ** 625   **Ⓓ** 50,000

NS 1.1

62. Which list of integers is written in order from least to greatest? *(p. 12)*

    Ⓐ $-3, -1, 0, 4, -6, 6$ **Ⓑ** $-6, -3, -1, 0, 4, 6$

    Ⓒ $0, -1, -3, 4, -6, 6$ **Ⓓ** $0, -1, -3, -6, 4, 6$

Gr 6 SDAP 2.5

63. The table shows the salaries of five coworkers in 2006. Which statement is valid about the salaries of these five workers? *(p. 743)*

    Ⓐ Worker E made $15,000 more than worker C.

    Ⓑ No worker made less than $40,000 in salary.

    Ⓒ No worker made more than $50,000 in salary.

    Ⓓ Workers B and E had the same salary.

2006 Salaries	
Worker	**Salary**
A	$40,000
B	$55,000
C	$35,000
D	$55,000
E	$50,000

QUIZ *for Lessons 1.1–1.3*

Evaluate the expression. *(p. 5)*

1. $25 + 8 \cdot 10 - 40$ **2.** $(3 + 1)^2 - 1^5$ **3.** $\dfrac{8 - 2}{18 - 4^2}$

Evaluate the expression for the given value(s) of the variable(s). *(p. 5)*

4. $5a - 3 + 7, a = 4$ **5.** $(9 - x)^5 \cdot y - 16, x = 7, y = 3$

Copy and complete the statement with < or >. *(p. 12)*

6. $-8 \underline{\ ?\ } 8$ **7.** $0 \underline{\ ?\ } -14$ **8.** $-20 \underline{\ ?\ } |-30|$ **9.** $|-7| \underline{\ ?\ } 5$

Find the sum. Identify any addition properties you use. *(p. 18)*

10. $-6 + 1$ **11.** $(-8 + 8) + (-12)$ **12.** $-9 + 11 + (-7)$

13. TEMPERATURE On Monday morning, the temperature is -5 degrees Fahrenheit. During the day, the temperature increases by 30 degrees. That night the temperature decreases by 15 degrees. What is the new temperature? *(p. 18)*

1.4 Subtracting Integers

Standards NS 1.2 **Add, subtract,** multiply, and divide **rational numbers (integers,** fractions, and terminating decimals) and take positive rational numbers to whole-number powers.

Connect *Before* you added integers. *Now* you will subtract integers.

Math and **SCIENCE**
Ex. 35, p. 28

KEY VOCABULARY
- **integer,** *p. 12*
- **opposite,** *p. 14*
- **difference,** *p. 728*

ACTIVITY

You can use patterns to describe a rule for subtracting integers.

STEP 1 **Copy** the table below. In the second column, write the answer to each subtraction problem. Use a pattern to find the differences involving negative integers.

STEP 2 **Complete** each addition problem in the third column so the sum is equal to the number in the difference column.

Subtraction problem	Difference	Addition problem
3 − 3	0	3 + (−3)
3 − 2	?	3 + ?
3 − 1	?	3 + ?
3 − 0	?	3 + ?
3 − (−1)	?	3 + ?
3 − (−2)	?	3 + ?
3 − (−3)	?	3 + ?

STEP 3 **Tell** how the second number in the addition problems relates to the second number in the subtraction problems.

STEP 4 **Describe** how to use addition to subtract integers.

About the Standards

You can formulate a conjecture (MR 1.2) about subtracting integers based on the table you complete in the activity.

When you subtract integers, you can first write the expression as an addition expression and then use the rules for adding integers.

KEY CONCEPT
For Your Notebook

Subtracting Integers

Words To subtract an integer, add its opposite.

Numbers $3 - 7 = 3 + (-7) = -4$
$2 - (-6) = 2 + 6 = 8$

Algebra $a - b = a + (-b)$
$a - (-b) = a + b$

EXAMPLE 1 **Subtracting Integers**

a. $-56 - (-9) = -56 + 9$ Add the opposite of -9.

$= -47$ Add.

b. $-14 - 21 = -14 + (-21)$ Add the opposite of 21.

$= -35$ Add.

c. $24 - (-15) = 24 + 15$ Add the opposite of -15.

$= 39$ Add.

EXAMPLE 2 **Evaluating an Algebraic Expression**

 Evaluate $15 - a - b$ when $a = 24$ and $b = -36$.

$15 - a - b = 15 - 24 - (-36)$ Substitute 24 for a and -36 for b.

$= 15 + (-24) + 36$ Add the opposite of 24 and of -36.

$= -9 + 36$ Add 15 and -24.

$= 27$ Add -9 and 36.

EXAMPLE 3 **Using Subtraction in Real Life**

OCEANOGRAPHY The SOFAR (*SO*und *F*ixing *A*nd *R*anging) channel is a layer of water in the oceans, as shown at the right, that allows sounds to travel extremely long distances. What is the vertical height of the SOFAR channel?

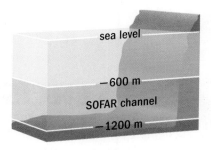

SOLUTION

The height is the difference of the upper and lower elevations.

Vertical height $= -600 - (-1200)$ Write subtraction statement.

$= -600 + 1200$ Add the opposite of -1200.

$= 600$ Add.

AVOID ERRORS
Make sure to subtract the lower elevation from the higher elevation when finding height so that you obtain a positive value.

▶ **Answer** The height of the SOFAR channel is 600 meters.

✓ **GUIDED PRACTICE**   for Examples 1, 2, and 3

Evaluate the expression.

1. $15 - 41$

2. $-16 - 8$

3. $a - b - (-6); a = 8, b = -15$

4. ELEVATION What is the difference in elevation between 4 feet above sea level and 30 feet below sea level?

DISTANCE BETWEEN NUMBERS On a number line, the distance between two numbers x and y is given by $|x - y|$.

EXAMPLE 4 ♦ **Multiple Choice Practice**

> **Which two numbers are closest together on a number line?**
>
> **A** 9 and -7 **B** -11 and 6   **C** -22 and -12 **D** 8 and -7

Find the distance between each pair of numbers.

$$\textbf{9 and } -\textbf{7: } |9 - (-7)| = |9 + 7| = |16| = 16$$
$$-\textbf{11 and 6: } |-11 - 6| = |-11 + (-6)| = |-17| = 17$$
$$-\textbf{22 and } -\textbf{12: } |-22 - (-12)| = |-22 + 12| = |-10| = 10$$
$$\textbf{8 and } -\textbf{7: } |8 - (-7)| = |8 + 7| = |15| = 15$$

The smallest distance, 10, is between -22 and -12.

▶ **Answer** The correct answer is C. Ⓐ Ⓑ ⓒ Ⓓ

✓ **GUIDED PRACTICE**   **for Example 4**

Find the distance between the two numbers on a number line.

5. 4 and -6 **6.** -7 and -5 **7.** -3 and 11   **8.** 1 and -14

1.4 **EXERCISES**

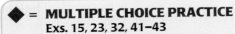

HOMEWORK KEY

♦ = **MULTIPLE CHOICE PRACTICE**
  Exs. 15, 23, 32, 41–43
○ = **HINTS AND HOMEWORK HELP**
  for Exs. 5, 25, 35 at classzone.com

SKILLS • PROBLEM SOLVING • REASONING

1. VOCABULARY Copy and complete: To subtract an integer, add its ? .

2. WRITING How can you find the distance between two numbers on a number line?

SEE EXAMPLE 1 on p. 25 for Exs. 3–18

SUBTRACTING INTEGERS **Find the difference.**

3. $5 - 12$ **4.** $6 - (-16)$ **⑤** $-11 - (-7)$

6. $-13 - 12$ **7.** $-14 - (-14)$ **8.** $-20 - 7$

9. $32 - 40$ **10.** $28 - (-16)$ **11.** $-39 - (-13)$

12. $-5 - (-5) - (-5)$ **13.** $8 - 2 - 6 - 10$ **14.** $-52 - (-18) - 37$

15. ♦ MULTIPLE CHOICE What is the value of $-15 - (-6)$?

  A -21 **B** -9 **C** 9   **D** 21

ERROR ANALYSIS *Describe* and correct the error in finding the difference.

16.

✗ $-12 - 5 = -7$

17.

✗ $3 - 5 - (-9) = 3 - 5 + 9$
$= 3 - 14$
$= -11$

18. OPEN-ENDED Give an example of two integers with the same sign that have a difference of -9.

SEE EXAMPLE 2
on p. 25
for Exs. 19–23

XY ALGEBRA **Evaluate the expression when** $a = -9$, $b = 18$, **and** $c = -4$.

19. $a - 6$ **20.** $b - c$ **21.** $14 - a - b$ **22.** $c - a + b$

23. ◆ MULTIPLE CHOICE What is the value of $-3 + 2(5) - a$ when $a = -9$?

(A) -2 (B) 4 (C) 16 (D) 22

SEE EXAMPLE 4
on p. 26
for Exs. 24–27

FINDING DISTANCE **Use absolute value to find the distance between the two numbers on a number line.**

24. -7 and 12 **25.** -14 and -19 **26.** 22 and -19 **27.** 1 and -10

28. REASONING Are the expressions $x - y$ and $y - x$ always opposites? *Explain* your reasoning.

CONNECT SKILLS TO PROBLEM SOLVING **Exercises 29–31 will help you prepare for problem solving.**

Use the following information: Jan is on a game show. Her score is -400 with one question left. Find Jan's score after the given scenario.

29. She answers the question incorrectly and loses 600 points.

30. She answers the question correctly and gains 600 points.

31. She answers the question incorrectly and loses 1150 points.

SEE EXAMPLE 3
on p. 25
for Exs. 32–34

32. ◆ MULTIPLE CHOICE A whale that is 660 feet below sea level rises up and breaches out of the water to a height of 32 feet above sea level. What is the vertical distance the whale travels?

(A) -628 ft   (B) 628 ft

(C) 660 ft   (D) 692 ft

California @HomeTutor for problem solving help at classzone.com

Whale breaching

TEMPERATURES **In Exercises 33 and 34, use the given table.**

33. How much colder is Alaska's coldest temperature than California's?

34. How much colder is California's coldest temperature than Mississippi's?

California @HomeTutor for problem solving help at classzone.com

Coldest Recorded Temperatures	
State	**Temperature**
Alaska	$-80°F$
California	$-45°F$
Mississippi	$-19°F$

35. **DINOSAURS** The table shows the ranges of three dinosaur periods during the Mesozoic Era. Which period lasted 64 million years? About what fraction of the three periods did that period last?

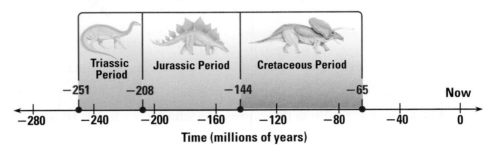

Time (millions of years)

READING *IN* MATH Read the information below for Exercises 36–38.

Lunar Temperatures Temperatures on the moon are extreme because there is no atmosphere. During the day, it can reach a high temperature of 265°F. At night, the temperature can reach a low of −170°F. In comparison, the highest temperature ever recorded on Earth is 136°F, and the lowest temperature recorded on Earth is −129°F.

Low temperature: −170°F

36. Compare What is the difference between the high temperatures on the moon and on Earth?

37. Compare What is the difference between the low temperatures on Earth and on the moon?

38. Interpret How does the range of temperatures on the moon compare with the range of temperatures on Earth?

39. CHALLENGE Is a negative number minus a negative number *always*, *sometimes*, or *never* positive? *Justify* your reasoning.

40. CHALLENGE Craig had $150 in his checking account on April 1. He wrote 3 checks in April. One check was for $47 and another check was for $63. On April 30, he received a statement stating that he overdrew his account by $23. What was the amount of the third check that he wrote?

◆ CALIFORNIA STANDARDS SPIRAL REVIEW

AF 1.3

41. What is the result of adding the additive identity to 3? *(p. 18)*

   A −3   **B** 0   **C** 3   **D** 6

AF 1.4

42. Which of the following is a numerical expression? *(p. 5)*

   A $3x^2 + 5(4)$ **B** $5 + 6 \cdot 3$ **C** $3x − 5$ **D** $x + 2$

NS 1.2

43. What is the change in the balance of a bank account after a $15 withdrawal and a $25 deposit? *(p. 18)*

   A −$40   **B** −$10   **C** $10   **D** $40

Multiple Choice Practice for Lessons 1.1–1.4

1. What is the value of the expression $x^2 - y^3$ when $x = 4$ and $y = 2$? **AF 1.2**

- **A** 4
- **B** 8
- **C** 16
- **D** 56

2. A moped is moving at a steady rate. It travels $20x$ feet every x seconds. How many feet does the moped travel in 40 seconds? **AF 1.2, MR 2.8**

- **A** 80 ft
- **B** 200 ft
- **C** 800 ft
- **D** 2000 ft

3. Which list of integers is ordered from least to greatest? **NS 1.1**

- **A** $-10, -6, -1, 0, 4, 12$
- **B** $-1, -6, -10, 0, 4, 12$
- **C** $0, -10, -6, -1, 4, 12$
- **D** $0, -1, 4, -6, -10, 12$

4. The table shows the low elevation in each of several countries.

Lowest Elevations	
Country	**Elevation (m)**
Canada	0
China	-154
Bolivia	90
Czech Republic	115

Which country has the lowest elevation?
NS 1.1

- **A** Canada
- **B** China
- **C** Bolivia
- **D** Czech Republic

5. What is the opposite of $|-7|$? **NS 2.5**

- **A** -7
- **B** 7
- **C** $|-(-7)|$
- **D** $|7|$

6. What is the value of the expression $b + |-c|$ when $b = -12$ and $c = -4$? **NS 1.2**

- **A** -16
- **B** -8
- **C** 4
- **D** 8

7. The table shows the earnings and expenses of a school theater club for one year.

Event	Earnings	Expenses
Fall play	$500	$800
Winter play	$800	$600
Musical	$1500	$900
Spring play	$600	$700

What was the theater club's total profit for the year? **NS 1.2, MR 1.3**

- **A** $-\$400$
- **B** $-\$200$
- **C** $\$400$
- **D** $\$800$

8. What is the value of $-23 - 12$? **NS 1.2**

- **A** -35
- **B** -11
- **C** 11
- **D** 35

9. The high and low temperatures for one day in Ellwood City, Pennsylvania, are shown.

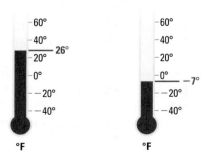

What is the difference in degrees between the high and low temperatures? **NS 1.2**

- **A** $7°F$
- **B** $19°F$
- **C** $26°F$
- **D** $33°F$

1.5 Integer Multiplication

MATERIALS · paper and pencil

Standards

NS 1.2 Add, subtract, **multiply**, and divide **rational numbers (integers**, fractions, and terminating decimals) and take positive rational numbers to whole-number powers.

QUESTION How can you use patterns to multiply integers?

You already know how to multiply positive integers. You can use patterns to describe rules for finding products involving negative integers.

EXPLORE Identify a pattern in the products of integers

STEP 1 **Copy** the following table. Identify a pattern in the products. Use the pattern to complete the table. Then make a conjecture about the product of two integers with different signs.

Expression	3(4)	3(3)	3(2)	3(1)	3(0)	3(−1)	3(−2)
Product	12	9	6	3	?	?	?

STEP 2 **Copy** the following table. Use your conjecture from Step 1 to find the first three products. Identify a pattern in those products and use the pattern to find the rest of the products.

Expression	3(−3)	2(−3)	1(−3)	0(−3)	−1(−3)	−2(−3)	−3(−3)
Product	?	?	?	?	?	?	?

DRAW CONCLUSIONS Use your observations to complete these exercises

1. Apply what you learned from the tables above to find the products $4(−7)$ and $−6(−4)$. *Explain* your reasoning.

2. **REASONING** Another way to understand the product of a positive integer and a negative integer is to think of the multiplication as repeated addition. For example, the product $3(−1)$ is equal to the sum $−1 + (−1) + (−1)$. Use this idea to justify the statements $5(−3) = −15$ and $4(−2) = −8$.

3. **REASONING** Suppose a and b are positive integers. Then $(−a)b = −ab$ and $a(−b) = −ab$. To find a rule for multiplying two negative integers, apply the first rule and then the second rule: $(−a)(−b) = −[a(−b)] = −(−ab)$. Notice that the last expression is the opposite of an opposite. Use what you know about opposites to copy and complete the rule in a simpler form: $(−a)(−b) = \underline{\quad?\quad}$.

1.5 Multiplying Integers

Math and SPORTS
Ex. 56, p. 34

Standards) **NS 1.2** Add, subtract, **multiply**, and divide **rational numbers (integers,** fractions, and terminating decimals) and **take positive rational numbers to whole-number powers.**

AF 1.3 Simplify numerical expressions by applying properties of rational numbers (e.g., **identity,** inverse, distributive, associative, commutative) **and justify the process used.**

Connect *Before* you added and subtracted integers. *Now* you will multiply integers.

KEY VOCABULARY
- **multiplicative identity**
- **integer,** *p. 10*
- **product,** *p. 728*

When you multiply integers, the sign of the product depends on the signs of the factors.

KEY CONCEPT *For Your Notebook*

Multiplying Integers

Words

Same Sign The product of two integers with the same sign is positive.

Different Signs The product of two integers with different signs is negative.

Numbers

$4(2) = 8$
$-3(-7) = 21$

$4(-2) = -8$
$-3(7) = -21$

EXAMPLE 1 Multiplying Integers

AVOID ERRORS
If a product has an even number of negative factors, it is positive. If a product has an odd number of negative factors, it is negative.

a. $3(-4) = -12$ — Different signs, so product is negative.

b. $-6(-3) = 18$ — Same sign, so product is positive.

c. $-4(2)(-3) = -8(-3)$ — Multiply from left to right.

$\qquad\qquad\quad = 24$ — Multiply.

EXAMPLE 2 Finding Powers of Integers

a. $(-3)^4 = (-3)(-3)(-3)(-3)$ — Write as a repeated product.

$\qquad = 9(-3)(-3)$ — Multiply from left to right.

$\qquad = -27(-3)$ — Multiply from left to right.

$\qquad = 81$ — Multiply.

b. $-3^4 = -(3^4)$ — Use order of operations.

$\qquad = -81$ — Evaluate power.

EXAMPLE 3 **Evaluating an Expression Involving Multiplication**

 MOVIES A stuntman working on a movie set falls from a building's roof 90 feet above an air cushion. The expression $-16t^2 + 90$ gives the stuntman's height (in feet) above the air cushion after t seconds. What is the height of the stuntman after 2 seconds?

90 ft

SOLUTION

Evaluate the expression for the height when $t = 2$.

$$-16t^2 + 90 = -16(2)^2 + 90 \quad \text{Substitute 2 for } t.$$
$$= -16(4) + 90 \quad \text{Evaluate the power.}$$
$$= -64 + 90 \quad \text{Multiply.}$$
$$= 26 \quad \text{Add.}$$

▶ **Answer** After 2 seconds, the stuntman is 26 feet above the air cushion.

✓ **GUIDED PRACTICE** | for Examples 1, 2, and 3

Find the product.

1. $-5(4)$ **2.** $6(-3)$ **3.** $-3(-7)$ **4.** $-2(-8)(5)$

Find the power.

5. $(-2)^2$ **6.** -2^2 **7.** -4^3 **8.** $(-4)^3$

9. MOVIES In Example 3, what is the height of the stuntman after 1 second?

KEY CONCEPT *For Your Notebook*

Multiplication Properties

Multiplication Property of Zero

Words The product of a number and 0 is 0.

Numbers $-4 \cdot 0 = 0$ **Algebra** For any value of a, $a \cdot 0 = 0$.

Identity Property of Multiplication

Words The product of a number and the **multiplicative identity**, 1, is the number.

Numbers $4 \cdot 1 = 4$ **Algebra** For any value of a, $a \cdot 1 = a$.

Closure Property of Multiplication

The product of two integers is an integer.

About the Standards

You will learn about the inverse property of multiplication (AF 1.3) in Lesson 2.5.

EXAMPLE 4 **Using Multiplication Properties**

Find the product.

a. $6(1)$

b. $-15(0)$

SOLUTION

a. $6(1) = 6$ Identity property of multiplication

b. $-15(0) = 0$ Multiplication property of zero

✓ **GUIDED PRACTICE**   for Example 4

Find the product. Identify any multiplication properties you use.

10. $4(0)$ **11.** $1(-4)$ **12.** $-3(0)$ **13.** $-11(1)$

1.5 **EXERCISES**

HOMEWORK KEY

◆ = **MULTIPLE CHOICE PRACTICE**
Exs. 53, 54, 61, 71–73

○ = **HINTS** AND **HOMEWORK HELP**
for Exs. 15, 27, 61 at classzone.com

SKILLS • PROBLEM SOLVING • REASONING

1. **VOCABULARY** Copy and complete: The product of the __?__, 1, and a number is the number.

2. **WRITING** *Describe* how to determine whether the product of two integers is positive or negative.

SEE EXAMPLES 1 AND 4
on pp. 31–33
for Exs. 3–23

MULTIPLYING INTEGERS Find the product. Identify any properties you use.

3. $-4(-7)$ **4.** $0(-9)$ **5.** $-3(6)$ **6.** $8(-5)$

7. $-17(1)$ **8.** $-6(7)$ **9.** $0(-13)$ **10.** $-4(-11)$

11. $9(-2)$ **12.** $3(-5)$ **13.** $-15(-12)$ **14.** $1(-32)$

15. $-1(-2)(-3)$ **16.** $2(-4)(5)$ **17.** $10(-9)(-3)$ **18.** $-7(-9)(-6)$

19. $-2(5)(-6)$ **20.** $6(-4)(12)$ **21.** $-8(-7)(-5)$ **22.** $12(0)(-45)$

ERROR ANALYSIS *Describe* and correct the error in evaluating the expression.

23.

$\times$ $-8(-12) = -96$

24.

$\times$ $(-2)^4 = -16$

SEE EXAMPLE 2
on p. 31
for Exs. 25–32

POWERS INVOLVING INTEGERS Evaluate the expression.

25. $(-3)^2$ **26.** $(-4)^2$ **27.** -2^4 **28.** -5^3

29. $2(-6)^3$ **30.** $-3(-7)^2$ **31.** $-5(4^4)$ **32.** $-3^2(-1)^3$

SEE EXAMPLE 3
on p. 32
for Exs. 33–44

ⓧⓨ ALGEBRA Evaluate the expression when $x = -9$, $y = -7$, and $z = -4$.

33. xy

34. y^2

35. $2xyz$

36. $-3z^2$

37. $-x(-x)$

38. $z(-y^2)$

39. $3xy - yz$

40. $x + 2y^2 - z$

41. $x^2 + y$

42. $z - y^2$

43. $[x + (-x)y]^2$

44. $xz^2 - (-y)^2z$

USING ABSOLUTE VALUE Find the product.

45. $-12 \cdot |11|$

46. $|-9| \cdot 5$

47. $-6 \cdot |-15|$

48. $10(-4) \cdot |13|$

49. $-7(-8) \cdot |-4|$

50. $15(9) \cdot |-2|$

51. $-3 \cdot |6| \cdot |-7|$

52. $|8| \cdot |-14| \cdot 3$

53. ◆ **MULTIPLE CHOICE** What is the value of the expression $-4(-8) \cdot |-3|$?

Ⓐ -96 **Ⓑ** -36 **Ⓒ** 12 **Ⓓ** 96

54. ◆ **MULTIPLE CHOICE** When you multiply an integer less than 1 and an integer less than -1, the product is which of the following?

Ⓐ Less than zero **Ⓑ** Greater than zero

Ⓒ Less than or equal to zero **Ⓓ** Greater than or equal to zero

---

CONNECT SKILLS TO PROBLEM SOLVING Exercises 55–58 will help you prepare for problem solving.

55. An airplane flies at a rate of 4 miles per minute. Evaluate $4t$ when $t = 10$ to find the distance traveled by the airplane in 10 minutes.

56. A diver swims downward from the surface of the water at a rate of 2 feet per second. Evaluate $-2t$ when $t = 11$ to find the diver's position relative to the surface after 11 seconds.

57. A hot air balloon rises from the ground at a rate of 50 feet per minute. Evaluate $50t$ when $t = 3$ to find the balloon's height after 3 minutes.

58. A hiker's elevation decreases at a rate of 46 feet per minute. Evaluate $-46t$ when $t = 9$ to find the hiker's change in elevation after 9 minutes.

SEE EXAMPLE 1
on p. 31
for Exs. 59–60

59. FINDING POSITION A coin is tossed off a boat into the ocean. The coin's position relative to the water's surface changes by -8 inches per second. Determine the position of the coin 12 seconds after it hits the water.

California @HomeTutor for problem solving help at classzone.com

60. BANKING You have $500 in a savings account. Over a 2 month period, you make 9 withdrawals of $30 each. What is your new balance?

California @HomeTutor for problem solving help at classzone.com

61. ◆ **MULTIPLE CHOICE** David is playing a video game. If he falls into a pit, he loses 125 points. He has 400 points before he falls into 5 pits. Which expression represents the number of points he has now?

Ⓐ $400 - 5(-125)$ **Ⓑ** $400 + 5(-125)$

Ⓒ $400 - 125 \div 5$ **Ⓓ** $400 + 125 \div 5$

SEE EXAMPLE 3
on p. 32
for Exs. 62–63

62. **FINDING HEIGHT** A coconut in a palm tree falls from a height of 27 feet above the ground. The expression $-16t^2 + 27$ gives the coconut's height (in feet) after t seconds. Evaluate the expression when t equals 1 and 2 seconds. Has the coconut hit the ground after 2 seconds? *Explain.*

63. **REASONING** Evaluate $(-10)^n$ for $n = 1, 2, 3, 4,$ and 5. How is the exponent related to the sign of the power?

64. **REASONING** When multiplying integers other than zero, explain why the product is negative when there is an odd number of negative factors. Why is the product positive when there is an even number of negative factors?

65. **OPEN-ENDED** Give an example of three integers that have the same sign, and when multiplied, result in a negative product.

66. **STOCK MARKET** Your uncle owns 25 shares of stock A, 45 shares of stock B, and 60 shares of stock C. The table shows one day's change in the price per share for each stock. Find the total change (in dollars) of the value of your uncle's stock.

Stock	A	B	C
Change in share price	+56¢	−$2	−56¢

CHALLENGE **What are the next three numbers in the list?** *Explain* your reasoning.

67. $-2, 4, -8, 16, \ldots$ 68. $5, -10, 20, -40, \ldots$ 69. $-3, 9, -27, 81, \ldots$

70. **CHALLENGE** The elevation at the top of Mount Everest is 8850 meters. The temperature falls at a rate of 1°C per 100 meters. The base of Mount Everest is at an elevation of 5400 meters and its temperature is −3°C. What is the temperature at the top of the mountain?

◆ CALIFORNIA STANDARDS SPIRAL REVIEW

NS 1.2

71. What is the value of $-9 - (-13)$? *(p. 24)*

Ⓐ −22   Ⓑ −4   Ⓒ 4   Ⓓ 22

NS 1.2

72. What is the quotient of 20 and 4? *(p. 728)*

Ⓐ 5   Ⓑ 16   Ⓒ 24   Ⓓ 80

NS 1.1

73. Six temperature sensors are in the water. The sensors are at the following positions (in feet): −22, 0, −16, −25, −12, and −8. Which list shows these positions in order from least to greatest? *(p. 12)*

Ⓐ −8, −12, −16, −22, −25, 0   Ⓑ 0, −8, −12, −16, −22, −25

Ⓒ 0, −25, −22, −16, −12, −8   Ⓓ −25, −22, −16, −12, −8, 0

1.6 Dividing Integers

Standards NS 1.2 Add, subtract, multiply, and **divide rational numbers (integers,** fractions, and terminating decimals) and take positive rational numbers to whole-number powers.

Connect *Before* you added, subtracted, and multiplied integers. *Now* you will divide integers.

KEY VOCABULARY
- data
- mean
- quotient, *p. 728*

The rules for dividing integers are similar to the rules for multiplying integers.

Math and **MUSIC**
Ex. 47, p. 39

KEY CONCEPT   *For Your Notebook*

Dividing Integers

Words   **Numbers**

Same Sign The quotient of two integers with the same sign is positive.
$$\frac{12}{6} = 2 \qquad \frac{-12}{-6} = 2$$

Different Signs The quotient of two integers with different signs is negative.
$$\frac{12}{-6} = -2 \qquad \frac{-12}{6} = -2$$

Zero The quotient of 0 and any nonzero integer is 0.
$$\frac{0}{12} = 0 \qquad \frac{0}{-12} = 0$$

EXAMPLE 1 Dividing Integers

a. $\dfrac{-40}{-8} = 5$ Same sign, so quotient is positive.

b. $\dfrac{-14}{2} = -7$ Different signs, so quotient is negative.

c. $\dfrac{36}{-9} = -4$ Different signs, so quotient is negative.

d. $\dfrac{0}{-7} = 0$ Dividend is 0 and divisor is nonzero, so quotient is 0.

AVOID ERRORS
You cannot divide a number by 0. The quotient of any number and 0 is *undefined*.

✓ **GUIDED PRACTICE**   for Example 1

Find the quotient, if possible.

1. $\dfrac{-33}{11}$ **2.** $\dfrac{56}{-8}$ **3.** $\dfrac{-25}{-5}$ **4.** $\dfrac{0}{-4}$

5. $\dfrac{72}{-9}$ **6.** $\dfrac{-36}{18}$ **7.** $\dfrac{-28}{0}$ **8.** $\dfrac{-54}{-6}$

MEAN OF A DATA SET **Data** are facts or numerical information. You can find the **mean** of a numerical set of data by dividing the sum of the values by the number of values.

$$\text{Mean} = \frac{\text{Sum of values}}{\text{Number of values}}$$

 EXAMPLE 2 ◆ **Multiple Choice Practice**

One of the coldest places on Earth is a Russian town located near the Arctic Circle. To the nearest degree, what is the mean of the average high temperatures shown in the table for winter in the Russian town?

Winter Temperatures				
Month	Dec	Jan	Feb	Mar
Average high	−41°F	−40°F	−48°F	−18°F

(A) −147°F **(B)** −48°F **(C)** −43°F **(D)** −37°F

SOLUTION

STEP 1 **Find** the sum of the temperatures.

$$-41 + (-40) + (-48) + (-18) = -147$$

STEP 2 **Divide** the sum by the number of temperatures.

$$\frac{-147}{4} = -36.75$$

To the nearest degree, the mean of the temperatures is −37°F.

▶ **Answer** The correct answer is D. Ⓐ Ⓑ Ⓒ ⬤

EXAMPLE 3 **Evaluating an Expression**

 Evaluate the expression $\frac{ab}{c}$ **when** $a = -24$, $b = 8$, **and** $c = -4$.

$$\frac{ab}{c} = \frac{-24(8)}{-4} \qquad \text{Substitute values.}$$

$$= \frac{-192}{-4} \qquad \text{Multiply.}$$

$$= 48 \qquad \text{Divide. Same sign, so quotient is positive.}$$

 GUIDED PRACTICE for Examples 2 and 3

Find the mean of the data.

9. −16, 17, 8, −23, −31

10. 0, −4, −10, 4, 11, −9, −13

11. Evaluate $\frac{a}{bc}$ when $a = -42$, $b = -3$, and $c = 7$.

1.6 EXERCISES

HOMEWORK KEY

◆ = **MULTIPLE CHOICE PRACTICE**
Exs. 31, 40, 46, 54–56

○ = **HINTS** AND **HOMEWORK HELP**
for Exs. 11, 17, 49 at classzone.com

SKILLS • PROBLEM SOLVING • REASONING

1. **VOCABULARY** Copy and complete: To find the __?__ of four numbers, add them and divide the sum by four.

2. **WRITING** *Describe* the two cases when the quotient of two integers a and b is not negative or positive.

SEE EXAMPLE 1
on p. 36
for Exs. 3–16

DIVIDING INTEGERS Find the quotient, if possible.

3. $\dfrac{-44}{4}$ 4. $\dfrac{0}{-7}$ 5. $\dfrac{-81}{-9}$ 6. $\dfrac{50}{-10}$

7. $\dfrac{-49}{-7}$ 8. $\dfrac{-28}{2}$ 9. $\dfrac{36}{-4}$ 10. $\dfrac{-19}{-1}$

11. $\dfrac{-66}{-11}$ 12. $\dfrac{-27}{0}$ 13. $\dfrac{-42}{6}$ 14. $\dfrac{-60}{-3}$

ERROR ANALYSIS *Describe* and correct the error in finding the quotient.

15. ✗ $\dfrac{0}{3} = 3$

16. ✗ $\dfrac{-20}{-10} = -2$

SEE EXAMPLE 2
on p. 37
for Exs. 17–22

FINDING A MEAN Find the mean of the data.

17. $-12, 5, -9, 10, 16, -8, -2, 8$

18. $4, -3, -8, 7, -1, 4, -2, -9, -1$

19. $-18, 14, 16, -24, 31, -8, -4$

20. $-38, 32, 41, -45, 39, -21, -22$

21. $65, -23, 58, -32, -12, 22$

22. $11, -21, -5, 4, -7, 9, -3, -12$

SEE EXAMPLE 3
on p. 37
for Exs. 23–31

XY ALGEBRA Evaluate the expression when $x = 18$, $y = -12$, and $z = -6$.

23. $\dfrac{y}{z}$ 24. $\dfrac{x}{z}$ 25. $\dfrac{xz}{y}$ 26. $\dfrac{z^2}{y}$

27. $\dfrac{x}{y+z}$ 28. $\dfrac{x-yz}{x}$ 29. $\dfrac{x^2+y}{z}$ 30. $\dfrac{y-z^2}{y}$

31. ◆ **MULTIPLE CHOICE** What is the value of $\dfrac{a}{b}$ when $a = -32$ and $b = 8$?

Ⓐ -8 Ⓑ -4 Ⓒ 4 Ⓓ 8

ORDER OF OPERATIONS Evaluate the expression.

32. $2 + 3(-4) \div 6$ 33. $5 + 6 \cdot 8 \div 4 - 3$ 34. $12 \div 3 + 3 \cdot (-4)$ 35. $16 + 8(-2) - 4$

36. $7 - 10 \div 2$ 37. $5 \cdot 6 - 2(6) \div 4$ 38. $-14 - 6 \div 2 + 7$ 39. $7 \cdot 3 - 12 \div 6$

40. ◆ **MULTIPLE CHOICE** You multiply the quotient of a negative integer and a positive integer by -1. Which word describes the product?

Ⓐ Negative Ⓑ Positive Ⓒ Zero Ⓓ Undefined

41. REASONING Suppose that $a > 0$ and $b > 0$. Which expression has a value that doesn't belong? *Explain* your reasoning.

    A. $-a \cdot (-b)$ **B.** $b \div (-a)$ **C.** $-ab$ **D.** $a \div (-b)$

CONNECT SKILLS TO PROBLEM SOLVING Exercises 42–45 will help you prepare for problem solving.

42. The profits for a used sporting goods store in June, July, and August were $-\$332$, $-\$118$, and $\$414$. Find the mean profit over these months.

43. A player has scores of 870, 700, -330, -450, and 200 through 5 rounds of a video game. Find the mean score for the 5 rounds.

44. A lake's water level is measured once each month. Over a 6 month period, the water level changed by -3, -5, -4, 0, -1, and -5 inches. Find the mean monthly change in water level.

45. Over a 4 year period, the annual changes in the number of students attending a school are -18, -23, 12, and -7. Find the mean annual change in the number of students over this period.

SEE EXAMPLE 2
on p. 37
for Exs. 46–48

46. ◆ **MULTIPLE CHOICE** Over a 6 month period, a bookstore has earnings of $\$400$, $-\$76$, $-\$139$, $\$526$, $\$650$, and $-\$17$. What is the mean of the monthly earnings for the 6 months?

    (A) $\$224$ **(B)** $\$268.80$ **(C)** $\$301.33$ **(D)** $\$361.60$

California @HomeTutor for problem solving help at classzone.com

47. MUSIC The table shows the profits earned by a jazz band in its first 3 months.

    a. What was the mean profit for the first 3 months?

    b. The band earned $\$605$ in January. What was the mean profit for the first 4 months?

Month	Profit
October	$-\$172$
November	$\$42$
December	$\$157$

California @HomeTutor for problem solving help at classzone.com

48. TEMPERATURE The table shows the daily high temperatures during a 5 day period in a city. What is the mean daily high temperature for the 5 days?

Day	Thu	Fri	Sat	Sun	Mon
Temperature	$-19°F$	$-14°F$	$-8°F$	$13°F$	$18°F$

49. REASONING The natural habitat of reindeer is the Arctic tundra. The mean temperature during the winter in the Arctic tundra is $-34°C$. Is it possible to determine the high and low winter temperatures by simply using this mean? *Explain* your reasoning.

50. WRITING Is the mean of a set of negative numbers *always*, *sometimes*, or *never* negative? *Explain* your reasoning, and include examples.

Reindeer

51. **SHORT RESPONSE** The table shows the temperatures in Fairbanks, Alaska, during a 5 day period. Find the mean. Suppose the temperature on Tuesday was 5°F lower than shown. How would this affect the mean? *Explain* your reasoning.

Day	Mon	Tues	Wed	Thu	Fri
Temperature	−8°F	−1°F	−6°F	−21°F	−31°F

52. **CHALLENGE** The mean of five daily high temperatures is −2°F. Four of the temperatures are −4°F, −6°F, 3°F, and −1°F. Find the fifth temperature.

53. **CHALLENGE** Use the number line shown to determine the sign of the quotient $\dfrac{a - b}{ab}$. *Explain* your reasoning.

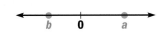

◆ CALIFORNIA STANDARDS SPIRAL REVIEW

NS 2.5

54. What is the value of $|7 - 5| - |8 - 12|$? *(p. 24)*

    Ⓐ −6   Ⓑ −4   Ⓒ −2   Ⓓ 4

AF 1.2

55. What is the value of the expression $x + x \div 3 + 6$ when $x = 9$? *(p. 5)*

    Ⓐ 2   Ⓑ 10   Ⓒ 12   Ⓓ 18

NS 1.2

56. You are one of three rock climbers on a rock face. Relative to your position, the elevations of the other climbers are 58 feet and −132 feet. What is the vertical distance between the other climbers? *(p. 24)*

    Ⓐ −74 ft   Ⓑ 32 ft   Ⓒ 74 ft   Ⓓ 190 ft

QUIZ *for Lessons 1.4–1.6*

Find the difference, product, or quotient.

1. $-4 - (-3)$ *(p. 24)*   2. $-11 - 8$ *(p. 24)*   3. $3(-5)$ *(p. 31)*   4. $-12(4)$ *(p. 31)*

5. $-6(-8)$ *(p. 31)*   6. $-20 \div (-2)$ *(p. 36)*   7. $\dfrac{-48}{-8}$ *(p. 36)*   8. $\dfrac{36}{-9}$ *(p. 36)*

Use absolute value to find the distance between the two integers. *(p. 24)*

9. −7 and 15   10. −4 and 3   11. −8 and 6   12. −2 and 13

Find the mean of the data. *(p. 36)*

13. −9, −15, 16, 4, 2, −10, 8, 20   14. −10, 6, −11, −6, −7, 3, −4, 1, 1

15. **GRAVITY** You drop a ball out of a window that is 144 feet above the ground. The expression $-16t^2 + 144$ gives the height (in feet) of the ball after t seconds. Find the height of the ball after 1, 2, and 3 seconds. After how many seconds does the ball hit the ground? *(p. 31)*

1.7 Number Properties

Math and **SPORTS**
Example 1, p. 41

Standards **AF 1.3** Simplify numerical expressions by applying properties of rational numbers (e.g., identity, inverse, distributive, **associative**, **commutative**) and justify the process used.

Connect *Before* you used order of operations to evaluate expressions. *Now* you will use properties to evaluate expressions.

KEY VOCABULARY
• **sum,** *p. 728*
• **product,** *p. 728*

You can use the commutative properties of addition and multiplication to more easily evaluate expressions using mental math.

KEY CONCEPT   *For Your Notebook*

Commutative Properties

	Addition	**Multiplication**
Words	You can add numbers in a sum in any order.	You can multiply factors in a product in any order.
Numbers	$3 + (-8) = -8 + 3$	$5(-6) = -6(5)$
Algebra	$a + b = b + a$	$ab = ba$

EXAMPLE 1   Using a Commutative Property

TOUR BIKING You are going on a 400 mile bike trip. You plan to cycle at an average speed of 12 miles per hour for 7 hours per day. Can you complete the trip in 5 days?

SOLUTION

REVIEW VERBAL MODELS
For help with verbal models, see p. 728.

Write a verbal model to find the total distance you can cycle in 5 days.

Total distance	=	Average speed	·	Hours per day	·	Number of days

$= 12 \cdot 7 \cdot 5$ **Substitute known values.**

$= 12 \cdot 5 \cdot 7$ **Commutative property of multiplication**

$= 60 \cdot 7$ **Multiply 12 and 5.**

$= 420$ **Multiply 60 and 7.**

▶ **Answer** Because 400 miles is less than the 420 miles you can cycle in 5 days, you can complete the trip in 5 days.

PROPERTIES AND SUBTRACTION Because subtracting a number is the same as adding its opposite, you can simplify a subtraction expression by first rewriting it in terms of addition and then using the commutative property of addition.

EXAMPLE 2 Using a Commutative Property

SIMPLIFY COMPUTATIONS
When deciding what numbers to add or multiply first, look for pairs whose sum or product ends in zero, because multiples of 10 are easier to work with.

$$-54 + 45 - 16 = -54 + 45 + (-16) \quad \text{Change subtraction to addition.}$$
$$= -54 + (-16) + 45 \quad \text{Commutative property of addition}$$
$$= -70 + 45 \quad \text{Add } -54 \text{ and } -16.$$
$$= -25 \quad \text{Add } -70 \text{ and } 45.$$

✓ GUIDED PRACTICE for Examples 1 and 2

1. **WHAT IF?** In Example 1, suppose you only want to bike for 6 hours a day at an average speed of 14 miles per hour. Can you complete the trip in 6 days?

Use a commutative property to evaluate the expression.

2. $4 \cdot (-9) \cdot 25$

3. $-13 + 34 - 7$

4. $27 + 64 - 37$

ASSOCIATIVE PROPERTIES You can also use the associative properties of addition and multiplication to evaluate expressions more easily using mental math.

KEY CONCEPT   *For Your Notebook*

Associative Properties

	Addition	**Multiplication**
Words	Changing the grouping of numbers will not change their sum.	Changing the grouping of factors will not change their product.
Numbers	$(2 + 3) + 4 = 2 + (3 + 4)$	$(7 \cdot 4) \cdot 5 = 7 \cdot (4 \cdot 5)$
Algebra	$(a + b) + c = a + (b + c)$	$(ab)c = a(bc)$

EXAMPLE 3 Using an Associative Property

$$24 + [(-44) + 58] = [24 + (-44)] + 58 \quad \text{Associative property of addition}$$
$$= -20 + 58 \quad \text{Add 24 and } -44.$$
$$= 38 \quad \text{Add } -20 \text{ and } 58.$$

EXAMPLE 4 Using an Associative Property

$$5 \cdot (11 \cdot 2) = 5 \cdot (2 \cdot 11) \qquad \text{Commutative property of multiplication}$$
$$= (5 \cdot 2) \cdot 11 \qquad \text{Associative property of multiplication}$$
$$= 10 \cdot 11 \qquad \text{Multiply 5 and 2.}$$
$$= 110 \qquad \text{Multiply 10 and 11.}$$

✓ **GUIDED PRACTICE** for Examples 3 and 4

Use an associative property to evaluate the expression.

5. $-8 + (8 + 17)$

6. $(15 + 11) - 11$

7. $(24 - 47) + 37$

8. $-20(5 \cdot 43)$

9. $25(2 \cdot 37)$

10. $(7 \cdot 4) \cdot 5$

1.7 EXERCISES

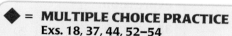

HOMEWORK KEY

◆ = **MULTIPLE CHOICE PRACTICE**
Exs. 18, 37, 44, 52–54

◯ = **HINTS** AND **HOMEWORK HELP**
for Exs. 3, 25, 45 at classzone.com

SKILLS • PROBLEM SOLVING • REASONING

1. **VOCABULARY** Copy and complete: You can change the order of the factors in a multiplication problem without affecting the product by using the __?__ property of multiplication.

2. **WRITING** Which property would you use to evaluate the expression $(29 + 33) + 7$? *Explain.*

SEE EXAMPLES 1, 2, 3, AND 4 on pp. 41–43 for Exs. 3–37

MENTAL MATH Evaluate the expression using mental math. Identify any properties you used.

3. $17 + 15 + 13$

4. $-27 + 42 - 13$

5. $5 \cdot (-29) \cdot 2$

6. $-53 + (-27 + 44)$

7. $(-39 + 48) + 12$

8. $-2(-9 \cdot 50)$

9. $[-4 \cdot (-7)](-5)$

10. $[25 \cdot (-7)](4)$

11. $(-20 \cdot 9) \cdot 5$

USING PROPERTIES Copy and complete the statement using the property indicated.

12. $28 + 65 = $ __?__ ; commutative

13. $54 \cdot 16 = $ __?__ ; commutative

14. $(7 \cdot 3)3 = $ __?__ ; associative

15. $4 + (6 + 19) = $ __?__ ; associative

16. $5(11 \cdot 2) = $ __?__ ; commutative

17. $(8 + 16) + 2 = $ __?__ ; commutative

18. ◆ **MULTIPLE CHOICE** Which expression is equivalent to $7 + 5 - 17$?

Ⓐ $7 + 17 - 5$
Ⓑ $17 - 7 + 5$
Ⓒ $7 - 17 + 5$
Ⓓ $7 - 5 + 17$

EVALUATING EXPRESSIONS Evaluate the expression. Show and justify each step.

19. $45 - (-68) - 44$

20. $-57 - 38 - (-57)$

21. $(-26 + 33) + (-4)$

22. $5(45 \cdot 2)$

23. $(16 + 8) + 44$

24. $(23 \cdot 8) \cdot 5$

(25.) $12 \cdot (7 \cdot 1 \cdot 5)$

26. $-2 \cdot (19 \cdot 15) \cdot 1$

27. $36 + 57 + (-36)$

28. $17 + 0 + (-19)$

29. $24 + (-12 - 8) + 6$

30. $5(7 \cdot 4)(5)$

31. $44 - 17 - 12 + 66 + 7$

32. $37 + 54 - 47 - 18 + 28$

33. $58 - 39 - 48 - 11 + 2$

34. $(4 \cdot 7)(15 \cdot 3)(-10)$

35. $16(5 \cdot 2)(15 \cdot 7)(10)$

36. $-5(14 \cdot 8)(5 \cdot 5)(-4)$

37. ◆ MULTIPLE CHOICE Which statement demonstrates the commutative property of addition?

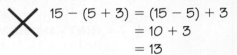

(A) $(x + y) + z = x + (y + z)$

(B) $x + y - z = x + z - y$

(C) $xyz = xzy$

(D) $x + y + z = y + x + z$

ERROR ANALYSIS *Describe* and correct the error in evaluating the expression.

38.

$\times$
$15 - (5 + 3) = (15 - 5) + 3$
$= 10 + 3$
$= 13$

39.

$\times$
$3 + (-8) = 8 + (-3)$
$= 5$

CONNECT SKILLS TO PROBLEM SOLVING Exercises 40–42 will help you prepare for problem solving.

40. The total revenue (in dollars) from a bake sale is $34 + 29 + 26$. What property can you use to rewrite this expression so that the sum of the first two numbers ends in zero?

41. The volume (in cubic inches) of a gift box is $25 \cdot 7 \cdot 4$. What property can you use to rewrite this expression so that the product of the first two numbers ends in zero?

42. The cost (in dollars) of a banquet dinner is $5(8 \cdot 13)$. What property can you use to rewrite this expression so that the first product you find ends in zero?

SEE EXAMPLE 1
on p. 41
for Ex. 43

43. PAYCHECK The table shows the hours you worked as a cashier during one week. You earn $8 per hour. Write a verbal model involving multiplication to find the amount you earned during the week. Then find the amount.

Time Card					
Day	Mon	Tues	Wed	Thu	Fri
Time in	4 P.M.	4 P.M.	4 P.M.	3 P.M.	3 P.M.
Time out	6 P.M.	6 P.M.	6 P.M.	5 P.M.	5 P.M.

Cashier: $8 per hour

California @HomeTutor for problem solving help at classzone.com

SEE EXAMPLE 2
on p. 42
for Exs. 44–46

44. ◆ **MULTIPLE CHOICE** You buy a portable CD player for $38, a CD for $17, and a carrying case for $12. What is the total cost?

(**A**) $47   (**B**) $57   (**C**) $67   (**D**) $77

California @HomeTutor   for problem solving help at classzone.com

45. **FOOTBALL** In a football game, six players on one team rushed the football for 92 yards, 22 yards, 15 yards, 5 yards, 3 yards, and −4 yards. What was the total number of rushing yards for the six players?

46. **REASONING** Is the expression $-15 + 34 - 44 - 19 + 51$ equivalent to the expression $34 - 19 + 15 - 44 + 51$? *Explain* your reasoning.

47. **PUZZLE PROBLEM** You need to find the sum of 52, 99, 65, 38, and 11. *Describe* how the commutative and associative properties of addition can help you find the sum using mental math.

48. **REASONING** Is division commutative? *Justify* your answer with an example.

49. **REASONING** *Explain* how a student used the properties of addition to go from the first expression to the second expression below. Use the same method to find the sum of the numbers from 1 to 19. *Describe* how to use this method to find the sum of the numbers from 1 to 99.

$$1 + 2 + 3 + 4 + 5 + 6 + 7 + 8 + 9 = 10 + 10 + 10 + 10 + 5$$
$$= 45$$

50. **CHALLENGE** The shortest side length of a four-sided figure is a feet. The second side is 4 feet longer than the shortest side. The third side is 8 feet longer than the second side. The fourth side is 6 feet shorter than the third side. Find the perimeter when $a = 6$ feet.

51. **CHALLENGE** Use the commutative properties of addition and multiplication to write three expressions equivalent to $4 \cdot 8 + 5$.

◆ CALIFORNIA STANDARDS SPIRAL REVIEW

AF 1.4 **52.** Which expression is an algebraic expression? *(p. 5)*

(**A**) $4(3 \cdot 2 - 1)$ (**B**) $6x + 2$ (**C**) $3(4) - 3^2$ (**D**) $10 + 4 \div 2$

NS 2.5 **53.** Which integer is closest to 0 on a number line? *(p. 12)*

(**A**) −12   (**B**) −9   (**C**) −6   (**D**) 5

Gr 6 NS 1.2 **54.** Barbara orders 55 blue shirts and 32 green shirts to sell for a fundraiser. What is the ratio of blue shirts to green shirts in her order? *(p. 732)*

(**A**) 55:32   (**B**) 32:55   (**C**) 55:87   (**D**) 87:32

1.8 Equivalent Expressions

MATERIALS · algebra tiles

Standards

AF 1.3 Simplify numerical expressions by applying properties of rational numbers (e.g., identity, inverse, **distributive**, associative, commutative) and justify the process used.

QUESTION How can you use algebra tiles to model equivalent expressions?

You can use algebra tiles to model simple algebraic expressions.

x-tile

An x-tile represents the variable x.

1-tile

A 1-tile represents positive 1.

EXPLORE 1 Use algebra tiles to model an expression

Use algebra tiles to model the expression $4x + 2$.

STEP 1 Collect four x-tiles and two 1-tiles.

STEP 2 Group the x-tiles together and the 1-tiles together.

EXPLORE 2 Write an expression modeled by algebra tiles

Write the algebraic expression that is modeled by the tiles.

STEP 1 Count the x-tiles and the 1-tiles.

Count 2 x-tiles.
Count 3 1-tiles.

STEP 2 Write an expression.

$2x + 3$

EXPLORE 3 Model equivalent expressions

Use algebra tiles to model the expressions $4x + 6$ and $2(2x + 3)$. Then explain whether the expressions are equivalent.

STEP 1 Model $4x + 6$.

STEP 2 Model $2(2x + 3)$ by modeling $2x + 3$ twice.

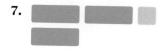

STEP 3 Count the tiles used in Step 1 and in Step 2. Because four x-tiles and six 1-tiles are used in each model, you can conclude that the expressions $4x + 6$ and $2(2x + 3)$ are equivalent.

DRAW CONCLUSIONS Use your observations to complete these exercises

Use algebra tiles to model the expression.

1. $2x + 1$

2. $4x + 7$

3. $3x + 9$

4. $x + 5$

5. $5x + 2$

6. $6x + 4$

Write the algebraic expression that is modeled by the tiles.

7.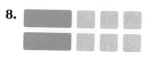

8.

9.

10.

11.

12.

13. Use algebra tiles to explain whether $2x + 8$ and $2(x + 4)$ are equivalent expressions.

14. Use algebra tiles to explain whether $2x + 3$ and $2(x + 3)$ are equivalent expressions.

15. **REASONING** Use what you have learned in this activity to rewrite the expression $2(x + 2)$ in an equivalent form without using algebra tiles.

1.8 The Distributive Property

Math and ART
Ex. 39, p. 51

Standards AF 1.3 Simplify numerical expressions by applying properties of rational numbers (e.g., identity, inverse, **distributive**, associative, commutative) and justify the process used.

Connect *Before* you used addition and multiplication properties. *Now* you will use the distributive property.

KEY VOCABULARY
• **equivalent expressions**

A replica of the Parthenon, a temple in ancient Greece, was built in Nashville, Tennessee, in 1897. The diagram below shows the approximate dimensions of two adjacent rooms inside the replica. You can find the total area of the rooms in two ways, as shown in Example 1.

EXAMPLE 1 Finding a Combined Area

ARCHITECTURE Two methods can be used to find the total area of the two rectangular rooms.

REVIEW AREA
For help with finding the area of a rectangle, see p. 742.

METHOD 1 Find the area of each room, and then add the two areas.

$$\text{Area} = 63(44) + 63(98)$$
$$= 2772 + 6174$$
$$= 8946 \text{ square feet}$$

METHOD 2 Find the total length, and then multiply by the common width.

$$\text{Area} = 63(44 + 98)$$
$$= 63(142)$$
$$= 8946 \text{ square feet}$$

63 ft
98 ft
44 ft

▶ **Answer** The total area of the two rooms is 8946 square feet.

Example 1 demonstrates the *distributive property*.

KEY CONCEPT   *For Your Notebook*

The Distributive Property

Words You can multiply a number and a sum by multiplying the number by each part of the sum and then adding these products. The same property applies to subtraction.

Algebra $a(b + c) = ab + ac$ **Numbers** $6(4 + 3) = 6(4) + 6(3)$
$a(b - c) = ab - ac$ $7(8 - 5) = 7(8) - 7(5)$

EQUIVALENT EXPRESSIONS You can apply the distributive property to expressions with a sum or difference of two or more numbers or algebraic expressions. Applying the distributive property produces an *equivalent expression*. **Equivalent expressions** are numerical expressions that are equal, or algebraic expressions that are equal for all values of the variable(s).

EXAMPLE 2 Using the Distributive Property

a. $-5(x + 10) = -5x + (-5)(10)$ **Distributive property**

$= -5x + (-50)$ **Multiply.**

$= -5x - 50$ **Simplify.**

b. $3[1 - 20 + (-5)] = 3(1) - 3(20) + 3(-5)$ **Distributive property**

$= 3 - 60 + (-15)$ **Multiply.**

$= -72$ **Add from left to right.**

✓ **GUIDED PRACTICE** for Examples 1 and 2

Use the distributive property to find the area of the rectangle.

1.

10 ft

12 ft   22 ft

2.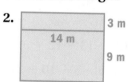

3 m

14 m

9 m

Evaluate the expression or write an equivalent expression.

3. $-2(5 + 12)$ **4.** $-4(-7 - 10)$ **5.** $2(w - 8)$ **6.** $-8(z + 25)$

CONCEPT SUMMARY *For Your Notebook*

Properties of Addition and Multiplication

Let a, b, and c be integers.

Property	Addition	Multiplication
Commutative Property (p. 41)	$a + b = b + a$	$ab = ba$
Associative Property (p. 42)	$(a + b) + c = a + (b + c)$	$(ab)c = a(bc)$
Identity Property (pp. 19, 32)	$a + 0 = a$	$a(1) = a$
Inverse Property of Addition (p. 19)	$a + (-a) = 0$	
Multiplication Property of Zero (p. 32)		$a \cdot 0 = 0$
Closure Property (pp. 19, 32)	$a + b$ is an integer	ab is an integer
Distributive Property (p. 48)	$a(b + c) = ab + ac$ and $a(b - c) = ab - ac$	

1.8 EXERCISES

HOMEWORK KEY

◆ = **MULTIPLE CHOICE PRACTICE**
Exs. 18, 28, 39, 42–44

○ = **HINTS AND HOMEWORK HELP**
for Exs. 11, 21, 39 at classzone.com

SKILLS • PROBLEM SOLVING • REASONING

VOCABULARY Match the equation with the property it illustrates.

1. $(x + 9) + 1 = x + (9 + 1)$

2. $12(1) = 12$

3. $2(3 + 6) = 2(3) + 2(6)$

4. $8a = a \cdot 8$

5. $-16 + 0 = -16$

6. $(5 \cdot 7)y = 5(7y)$

7. $-24 + a = a + (-24)$

A. Identity property of addition

B. Commutative property of multiplication

C. Commutative property of addition

D. Distributive property

E. Associative property of multiplication

F. Associative property of addition

G. Identity property of multiplication

8. WRITING *Explain* how to simplify $2(x + 5)$.

SEE EXAMPLE 2
on p. 49
for Exs. 9–34

WRITING EQUIVALENT EXPRESSIONS Use the distributive property to write an equivalent expression. Then evaluate the expression.

9. $4(7 + 8)$

10. $3(5 + 6)$

11. $-7(3 + 2)$

12. $-13(-12 + 9)$

13. $8(9 - 16)$

14. $-4(7 - 2)$

15. $6(-5 + 10 + 2)$

16. $-4(3 + 6 - 8)$

17. $-5[4 - 1 + (-9)]$

18. ◆ MULTIPLE CHOICE What is the value of $-5(-6 + 1 + 4)$?

Ⓐ -10 　　Ⓑ -5 　　Ⓒ 5 　　Ⓓ 10

USING PROPERTIES Use properties to simplify the expression.

19. $9(x - 3)$

20. $-8(5 - x)$

21. $-3(7 + x)$

22. $7(x + 8)$

23. $5(9 + 22 + y)$

24. $-12(4 + 5 + y)$

25. $19[7 + w + (-2)]$

26. $-34(z - 21 - 5)$

27. $-2[4 - x + (-7)]$

28. ◆ MULTIPLE CHOICE Which expression is equivalent to $-3(x + 4)$?

Ⓐ $-3x + 4$ 　　Ⓑ $-3x + 12$ 　　Ⓒ $-3x - 12$ 　　Ⓓ $-3x - 3$

REASONING Use the distributive property and mental math to find the product. *Explain* your reasoning.

29. $4(34)$

30. $9(19)$

31. $24(12)$

32. $50(24)$

ERROR ANALYSIS *Describe* and correct the error in simplifying the expression.

33. ✗ $6(x + 3) = 6x + 3$

34. ✗ $-2(x - 4) = -2x - 2(4)$
$= -2x - 8$

CONNECT SKILLS TO PROBLEM SOLVING Exercises 35–37 will help you prepare for problem solving.

> Write an expression of the form $a(b + c)$ for the total cost. Then use the distributive property to evaluate the expression.

35. You buy 2 shirts that cost $15 each and 2 hats that cost $8 each.

36. You buy 6 pencils that cost $.25 each and 2 erasers that cost $.25 each.

37. You buy 4 books that cost $12 each and 4 books that cost $11 each.

SEE EXAMPLE 1
on p. 48
for Exs. 38–39

38. HOME IMPROVEMENT A floor plan of a house is shown. You want to carpet the family room and the living room. The carpeting you want to use in these two rooms sells for $3 per square foot. How much will the carpet cost?

California **@HomeTutor** for problem solving help at classzone.com

39. ◆ **MULTIPLE CHOICE** Some students have been given permission to paint murals on 5 walls around your school. The murals are each 8 feet tall. The mural widths are 21 feet, 35 feet, 27 feet, 33 feet, and 22 feet. Which expression models the total area of the murals?

(**A**) $21 + 35 + 27 + 33 + 22$

(**B**) $5(21 + 35 + 27 + 33 + 22)$

(**C**) $8(21 + 35 + 27 + 33 + 22)$

(**D**) $40(21 + 35 + 27 + 33 + 22)$

California **@HomeTutor** for problem solving help at classzone.com

40. CHALLENGE You are ordering T-shirts with your school logo. Each T-shirt costs $7. There is a $25 setup fee for silk screening and a screening charge of $2 per shirt. What is the total cost for 170 T-shirts?

41. CHALLENGE Simplify the expression $7[6 - 2(x + 3)]$ using the order of operations. Show and justify each step. Then show how to get the same result by first distributing the 7.

◆ CALIFORNIA STANDARDS SPIRAL REVIEW

Gr 5 NS 1.1

42. What is 0.1659 rounded to the nearest hundredth? *(p. 723)*

(**A**) 0.1   (**B**) 0.166   (**C**) 0.17   (**D**) 0.2

AF 1.3

43. Which statement shows the identity property of multiplication? *(p. 31)*

(**A**) $ab = ba$ (**B**) $a(1) = a$ (**C**) $a(0) = 0$ (**D**) $a + b = b + a$

Gr 6 NS 2.3

44. A broker invested $1200 in the stock market on day 1. On day 2, the investment increased by $39. On day 3, the investment decreased by $112. How much is the investment worth at the end of day 3? *(p. 728)*

(**A**) $1049   (**B**) $1127   (**C**) $1273   (**D**) $1351

1.9 A Problem Solving Plan

Standards MR 1.0 Students make decisions about how to approach problems.

MR 2.0 Students use strategies, skills, and concepts in finding solutions.

MR 3.0 Students determine a solution is complete and move beyond a particular problem by generalizing to other situations.

Connect *Before* you used problem solving strategies to solve problems.
Now you will use a problem solving plan to solve problems.

Math and SPORTS
Example 1, p. 52

KEY VOCABULARY
• unit analysis

Mathematical reasoning is used throughout mathematics in many different situations. The Problem Solving Plan is a way to step through a problem using mathematical reasoning in order to answer the question asked.

EXAMPLE 1 Understanding and Planning

DUATHLON You and a friend decide to compete in a duathlon. You both bike 10,000 meters and run 4000 meters.

The table shows the biking and running speeds (in meters per minute) for both you and your friend. Who has the better total time?

	Biking (m/min)	Running (m/min)
You	410	170
Friend	430	160

To solve this problem, you need to make sure you understand the problem. Then make a plan for solving the problem.

READ AND UNDERSTAND

What do you know?

The table displays the speeds of you and your friend for biking and running.

You both bike 10,000 meters and run 4000 meters.

What do you want to find out?

Who has the better total time for biking and running?

MAKE A PLAN

How can you relate what you know to what you want to find out?

Find each of your biking and running times. You can organize this information in a table.

Find each of your total times and then compare these times.

You will solve the problem in Example 2.

EXAMPLE 2 Solving and Looking Back

DUATHLON Carry out the plan from Example 1 to solve the problem. Then, check your answer.

SOLVE THE PROBLEM

Use the formula $Time = \dfrac{Distance}{Rate}$.

	Biking	**Running**
You	$t = \dfrac{d}{r} = \dfrac{10{,}000}{410}$ ≈ 24.4 min	$t = \dfrac{d}{r} = \dfrac{4000}{170}$ ≈ 23.5 min
Friend	$t = \dfrac{d}{r} = \dfrac{10{,}000}{430}$ ≈ 23.3 min	$t = \dfrac{d}{r} = \dfrac{4000}{160}$ $= 25$ min

READING
The symbol $\approx$ means *is approximately equal to.*

Add to find the total times.

You $24.4 + 23.5 = 47.9$ min

Friend $23.3 + 25 = 48.3$ min

▶ **Answer** You have the better total time for the duathlon.

LOOK BACK

Does your answer make sense?

You bike more slowly than your friend, so your biking time should be greater. You run faster than your friend, so your running time should be less. Therefore, the calculations are reasonable.

AnimatedMath

For an interactive example of solving and looking back, go to **classzone.com.**

✓ **GUIDED PRACTICE**   for Examples 1 and 2

1. **WHAT IF?** In Examples 1 and 2, suppose that your friend bikes at a rate of 440 meters per minute. What is your friend's biking time? Who has the better total time in the duathlon?

UNIT ANALYSIS You can use **unit analysis**, also called *dimensional analysis*, to evaluate an expression involving units of measure and to check that your answer uses the correct units.

For example, when you find the product of a rate in meters per minute and time in minutes, the units for the product will be meters:

$$\frac{\text{meters}}{\text{minute}} \cdot \text{minutes} = \text{meters}$$

EXAMPLE 3 ◆ **Multiple Choice Practice**

In parts of New York City, the blocks between streets are called *short blocks*. There are 20 short blocks per mile. Blocks between avenues are called *long blocks*. There are 4 long blocks per mile. You walk 40 short blocks and 8 long blocks. How many miles do you walk?

Ⓐ 4 mi   **Ⓑ** 6 mi

Ⓒ 10.4 mi   **Ⓓ** 12.5 mi

REVIEW PROBLEM SOLVING STRATEGIES

For help with problem solving strategies, see p. 744.

SOLUTION

Read and Understand You walk 40 short blocks and 8 long blocks. There are 20 short blocks per mile and 4 long blocks per mile. You are asked to find how many miles you walk.

Make a Plan Convert short blocks to miles and long blocks to miles using unit analysis. Then add to find the total miles.

Solve the Problem Because 20 short blocks equal one mile, you can multiply the number of short blocks by $\frac{1 \text{ mile}}{20 \text{ short blocks}}$ to convert to miles.

$$40 \text{ short blocks} \times \frac{1 \text{ mile}}{20 \text{ short blocks}} = \frac{40}{20} \text{ miles} = 2 \text{ miles}$$

You can convert long blocks to miles by multiplying by $\frac{1 \text{ mile}}{4 \text{ long blocks}}$.

$$8 \text{ long blocks} \times \frac{1 \text{ mile}}{4 \text{ long blocks}} = \frac{8}{4} \text{ miles} = 2 \text{ miles}$$

You walk a total of $2 + 2 = 4$ miles.

▶ **Answer** The correct answer is A.   Ⓐ Ⓑ Ⓒ Ⓓ

Look Back Check your answer by drawing a diagram.

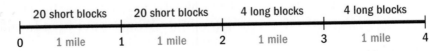

From the diagram you can see that 40 short blocks are 2 miles and 8 long blocks are 2 miles, which is a total of 4 miles. So, your answer checks.

Animated Math

For an interactive example of using a problem solving plan, go to **classzone.com**.

 GUIDED PRACTICE   for Example 3

2. **WHAT IF?** In Example 3, how many miles do you walk if you walk 60 short blocks and 16 long blocks?

A Problem Solving Plan

1. Read and understand the problem.
  • Distinguish between relevant and irrelevant information.
  • Identify missing information.
  • Sequence and prioritize information.

2. Make a plan.
  • Identify relationships.
  • Observe patterns.
  • Determine whether the problem can be broken into simpler parts.
  • Make conjectures.
  • Determine whether the answer needs to be exact or can be approximate.

3. Solve the problem.
  • Apply strategies/results from simpler problems.
  • Test/justify conjectures.
  • Use estimation, then make precise calculations and give the answer to an appropriate degree of accuracy.
  • Express the solution clearly; explain mathematical reasoning.

4. Look back.
  • Check the reasonableness of the solution using estimation and the context of the problem.
  • Generalize results.

1.9 EXERCISES

HOMEWORK
KEY

◆ = **MULTIPLE CHOICE PRACTICE**
  Exs. 6, 18, 21, 31–33

○ = **HINTS** AND **HOMEWORK HELP**
  for Exs. 3, 9, 19 at classzone.com

SKILLS • PROBLEM SOLVING • REASONING

1. VOCABULARY Copy and complete: When solving problems, you can use __?__ to evaluate expressions involving units of measure and to check that your answers use the correct units.

2. WRITING List the four steps of the problem solving plan.

SEE EXAMPLE 1
on p. 52
for Ex. 3

(3.) READ AND UNDERSTAND A customer buys a lunch that costs $3.99 and a drink that costs $.99. The customer pays with a $10 bill. You are the cashier. Identify what you know and what you need to find out.

SEE EXAMPLE 2
on p. 53
for Exs. 4–5

4. **LOOK BACK** The cost of a ticket to a baseball game is $10. The cost of a hot dog is $2. Matt goes to the game and eats 3 hot dogs. One of your friends says that Matt spent $16. *Explain* how to check the answer.

5. **ERROR ANALYSIS** Daniel can take 96 photos on a 5 day trip. He takes 45 photos in 2 days. He wants to take an equal number of photos each of the last 3 days. *Describe* and correct the error in finding the number of photos he can take each day.

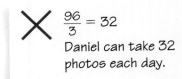

$$\frac{96}{3} = 32$$
Daniel can take 32 photos each day.

6. ◆ **MULTIPLE CHOICE** Which represents the 15th arrow in the pattern?

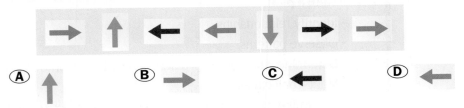

7. **REASONING** You buy 3 packs of pens for $12. Each pack of pens contains 12 pens. How much does each pack of pens cost? Identify the unnecessary information in this problem.

8. **MAKE A TABLE** You have a handful of quarters, nickels, and dimes that totals 75 cents. Make a table listing all possible combinations of coins.

LOOK FOR A PATTERN **Complete the pattern.**

9. $7x^2$, $15x^2$, $23x^2$, ___?___, ___?___

10. $81x$, $78x^2$, $75x^3$, $72x^4$, ___?___, ___?___

11. **ERROR ANALYSIS** You need to read 55 pages for English and 25 pages for History in 5 days. You read 20 pages on the first day. You want to read the same number of pages each of the remaining days. *Describe* and correct the error in the solution.

$$\frac{60}{5} = 12$$
You need to read 12 pages per day.

CONNECT SKILLS TO PROBLEM SOLVING **Exercises 12–15 will help you prepare for problem solving.**

Use the following question: You buy 4 tickets to a concert. Each ticket costs $15 and there is a $2 service charge for every ticket after the second one. What is the total cost?

12. Identify what you know and what you need to find out.

13. Make and describe a plan to solve the problem.

14. Carry out the plan and solve the problem.

15. Check that your answer is reasonable.

SEE EXAMPLE 3
on p. 54
for Exs. 16–22

16. **MONORAIL** A monorail ride at an amusement park has 5 cars in each train, and each car can hold 4 passengers. In one hour, 900 people can ride the monorail. How many trains run in one hour?

California @HomeTutor for problem solving help at classzone.com

◆ = **MULTIPLE CHOICE PRACTICE**   ○ = **HINTS AND HOMEWORK HELP** at classzone.com

17. MUSIC You practice drums for 50 minutes each weekday and for 40 minutes on each weekend day. How many hours per week do you practice?

Drums practice: 50 minutes each weekday

California @HomeTutor for problem solving help at classzone.com

18. ◆ MULTIPLE CHOICE You are trying to earn 4000 points in a computer game. In the first round you get 1540 points. In the next round you get 780 points. How many more points do you need?

A 760   **B** 1680   **C** 1760   **D** 2680

19. BICYCLE RACE A Tour de France bicycle race covered 3462 kilometers in 21 days. Riders traveled 3152 kilometers during the first 19 racing days and 160 kilometers the next day. How long was the ride on the last day?

20. SALES During a 4 week period, a salesperson at a photography studio wants to sell photography packages worth a total of $16,000. What does the sales amount need to be in week 4 to reach the $16,000 goal?

Week	1	2	3	4
Sales	$1240	$3720	$5980	?

21. ◆ MULTIPLE CHOICE You are making salad for 30 people. You need 4 tomatoes to make enough for 10 people. You have 8 tomatoes. How many more tomatoes do you need?

A 0   **B** 4   **C** 8   **D** 12

22. WRITING Is there enough information to answer the question? *Explain* how to solve the problem, or tell what information is needed.

Amanda has sold magazine subscriptions worth $330 for a school fundraiser. If she reaches a total of $500, she wins a gift certificate. How many more subscriptions does she need to sell to reach $500?

23. GUESS, CHECK, AND REVISE You know that you have 15 coins in your pocket, of which 5 are nickels and the rest are dimes and quarters. The total amount is $2.30. How many dimes and quarters do you have? Use the problem solving strategy guess, check, and revise.

24. MAKE A TABLE Your school talent show allows people to sign up for 3 minute or 5 minute acts. There is one minute between acts. The talent show has 15 acts and lasts for 79 minutes. How many 3 minute acts are there? Use the problem solving strategy make a table.

25. OPEN-ENDED *Describe* a real life situation that is modeled by the expression $5x + 3$.

26. PUZZLE PROBLEM The product of two numbers is 104. Their difference is 5. Find the two numbers.

27. USE A DIAGRAM John lives 2 miles west of the library, and his school is 1 mile east of the library on the same road. The distance between the school and the post office is twice the distance between John's home and the school. Use the diagram below to find the distance between John's home and the post office.

John's house   Library   School   Post office

2 mi   1 mi

CHALLENGE **What are the next three numbers?** *Describe* the rule.

28. 11, 7, 14, 10, 20, 16, . . .   **29.** 7, 20, 46, 98, 202, 410, . . .

30. CHALLENGE Bill's house is third in a row of 12 houses. There are 5 houses between Chris's house and Audrey's house, and 2 between Chris's house and Bill's house. How many houses are between Audrey's house and the first house? *Explain* how you found your answer.

◆ CALIFORNIA STANDARDS SPIRAL REVIEW

AF 1.3 | **31.** Which statement illustrates the distributive property? *(p. 48)*

    Ⓐ $a + (-a) = 0$ **Ⓑ** $(ab)c = a(bc)$

    Ⓒ $a + b = b + a$ **Ⓓ** $a(b - c) = ab - ac$

NS 1.2 | **32.** What is the value of -3^3? *(p. 31)*

    Ⓐ -27 **Ⓑ** -9 **Ⓒ** 9 **Ⓓ** 27

NS 1.2 | **33.** You spend $46 on a new shirt and two new sweaters. The shirt costs $12. How much is each sweater if they cost the same amount? *(p. 52)*

    Ⓐ $15   **Ⓑ** $17   **Ⓒ** $23   **Ⓓ** $34

QUIZ *for Lessons 1.7–1.9*

Evaluate the expression. Identify any properties you use. *(p. 41)*

  1. $19 + 33 + 11$ **2.** $(25 \cdot 16)(-4)$ **3.** $5(-4 \cdot 9)$

Use the distributive property to simplify the expression. *(p. 48)*

  4. $9(x + 9)$ **5.** $-2(z - 15)$ **6.** $-8(-2 - 3y)$

  7. EXERCISE You plan to exercise 200 minutes over 5 days. The first 4 days you exercise 45 minutes, 30 minutes, 20 minutes, and 1 hour. Use a problem solving plan to find the number of minutes you need to exercise on the fifth day to meet your goal. *(p. 52)*

MIXED REVIEW *of Skills and Problem Solving*

Multiple Choice Practice for Lessons 1.5–1.9

1. What is the value of $-12(-6)$? **NS 1.2**

   (A) -72 (B) -6

   (C) 18 (D) 72

2. The manager of an art gallery records the widths of 4 walls that need painting in the table shown.

Wall	1	2	3	4
Width (ft)	42	87	22	29

Each wall is 6 feet high. What is the total area of the 4 walls that need painting? **NS 1.2**

   (A) 180 ft^2 (B) 186 ft^2

   (C) 540 ft^2 (D) 1080 ft^2

3. You are planning a field trip to a museum. The cost for the bus is \$250. Admission is \$8 per person, and lunch is \$5 per person. Which expression shows the total cost in dollars if 20 students go on the trip? **AF 1.3, MR 1.0**

   (A) $250 + 20 \times 8 + 5$

   (B) $20(250 + 8 + 5)$

   (C) $250 + 8 + 5 \times 20$

   (D) $20(8 + 5) + 250$

4. What is the value of $-25(32)(4)$? Use properties and mental math. **AF 1.3**

   (A) -3200 (B) -320

   (C) 320 (D) 3200

5. Which expression is equivalent to $(8 + x) - 2$? **AF 1.3**

   (A) $x - 6$

   (B) $x + 6$

   (C) $x - 10$

   (D) $x + 10$

6. What is the mean monthly profit for the 3 months shown? **NS 1.2**

Month	Profit
Oct.	\$34,549
Nov.	\$38,325
Dec.	\$51,680

   (A) \$38,325   (B) \$41,518

   (C) \$43,115   (D) \$124,554

7. What is the value of $\dfrac{x^2 + y}{xz}$ when $x = 4$, $y = 8$, and $z = -3$? **NS 1.2**

   (A) -4 (B) -2

   (C) 2 (D) 6

8. You are selling printed shirts at a fair. Total expenses are \$12 per shirt. Which expression *cannot* be used to find the profit in dollars made by selling 50 shirts for \$20 each? **AF 1.3**

T-shirts
$20
per shirt

   (A) $8(50)$ (B) $20(50) - 12$

   (C) $50(20 - 12)$ (D) $20(50) - 12(50)$

9. The volume of a rectangular solid is the product of the length, width, and height. Volume is measured in cubic units. One ton of gravel will fill 16 cubic feet. You want to cover a driveway that is 12 feet wide and 60 feet long with 4 inches of gravel. How many tons of gravel should you buy? **NS 1.2, MR 2.0**

   (A) 15 tons   (B) 45 tons

   (C) 120 tons   (D) 180 tons

BIG IDEAS

For Your Notebook

Big Idea 1

Finding the Absolute Value of a Number

The absolute value of a number is the distance between the number and zero on a number line.

The distance between -2 and 0 is 2. So, $|-2| = 2$. The distance between 2 and 0 is 2. So, $|2| = 2$.

Big Idea 2

Adding, Subtracting, Multiplying, and Dividing Integers

You can use the following rules to perform operations on integers.

Expression	a and b have the same sign	a and b have different signs
$a + b$	Add $|a|$ and $|b|$. The sum has the same sign as a and b.	Subtract the lesser absolute value from the greater absolute value. The sum has the same sign as the integer with the greater absolute value.
$a - b$	To subtract b from a, add the opposite of b to a and use the addition rules.	
$a \cdot b$	The product is positive.	The product is negative.
$\dfrac{a}{b}$	The quotient is positive.	The quotient is negative.

Big Idea 3

Using Properties to Simplify Expressions

The properties in the table below are often useful for simplifying expressions. Let a, b, and c be integers.

Property	Addition	Multiplication
Commutative Property	$a + b = b + a$	$ab = ba$
Associative Property	$(a + b) + c = a + (b + c)$	$(ab)c = a(bc)$
Identity Property	$a + 0 = a$	$a(1) = a$
Inverse Property of Addition	$a + (-a) = 0$	
Multiplication Property of Zero		$a \cdot 0 = 0$
Closure Property	$a + b$ is an integer	ab is an integer
Distributive Property	$a(b + c) = ab + ac$ and $a(b - c) = ab - ac$	

Standards

NS 1.2, NS 2.5,
AF 1.3

APPLYING THE
BIG IDEAS

Big Idea 1
You find the absolute value of a number in **Step 3.**

Big Idea 2
You add and multiply integers in **Step 2.**

Big Idea 3
You use properties to simplify expressions in **Step 2.**

PROBLEM How can you use integer operations to plan a field trip?

STEP 1 Write a verbal model.

You are planning a class field trip. The table below shows the costs of admission and lunch for an individual for several different field trips. The cost of transportation for each of the field trips is $80. There will be 21 students and 1 teacher on the trip. Write a verbal model that can be used to find the total cost for any of the field trips.

Place	Admission	Lunch
History museum	$4	$5
Science center	$9	$6
State park	$2	$5
Theater	$7	$4
Art museum	$3	$6

STEP 2 Write and evaluate expressions.

Choose one of the field trips. Use the verbal model from Step 1 to write and evaluate an expression to find the total cost of the field trip. The class has a $300 budget for the field trip. Can the class go on the trip you chose? By what amount is the trip over budget or under budget?

STEP 3 Find absolute value.

Suppose your class is going to two destinations. You travel 12 miles directly north from school to reach your first destination. Then you travel 15 miles directly south to reach your second destination. Evaluate $12 + (-15)$ to find your position relative to school. Are you north or south of the school? Use absolute value to find your distance from school.

Extending the Problem

Use your results from the problem to complete the exercises.

1. The theater offers an admission discount of $1 and the science center offers an admission discount of $2. Write and evaluate expressions to find the total cost of taking a field trip to the theater or the science center. Can the class go on either of these trips with the discount?

2. Research admission costs to a museum or science center near you. Write and evaluate an expression to find the total cost of taking a field trip to the place you research if lunch is $5 per person. Would the class be able to go on this field trip?

REVIEW KEY VOCABULARY

- power, base, exponent, *p. 5*
- numerical expression, *p. 6*
- evaluate, *p. 6*
- order of operations, *p. 6*
- variable, *p. 7*
- algebraic expression, *p. 7*

- integer, *p. 12*
- negative integer, *p. 12*
- positive integer, *p. 12*
- absolute value, *p. 13*
- opposite, *p. 14*
- additive identity, *p. 19*

- additive inverse, *p. 19*
- multiplicative identity, *p. 32*
- data, *p. 37*
- mean, *p. 37*
- equivalent expressions, *p. 49*
- unit analysis, *p. 53*

VOCABULARY EXERCISES

In Exercises 1–3, copy and complete the statement.

1. The expression $3(4 - 2)$ is an example of a(n) __?__ expression.

2. In the expression $x - 2$, x is best described as a(n) __?__.

3. The __?__ of a data set is the sum of the values divided by the number of values.

4. How many integers have an absolute value of 15? List them.

5. **NOTETAKING SKILLS** Make a *definition and examples chart* like the one on page 4 for *absolute value*.

REVIEW EXAMPLES AND EXERCISES

1.1 Expressions and Order of Operations
pp. 5–10

AF 1.2 **EXAMPLE**

Evaluate $(x - 2)^2 + 7 - 2^2$ when $x = 5$.

$$(x - 2)^2 + 7 - 2^2 = (5 - 2)^2 + 7 - 2^2 \qquad \text{Substitute 5 for } x.$$
$$= 3^2 + 7 - 2^2 \qquad \text{Evaluate inside grouping symbols.}$$
$$= 9 + 7 - 4 \qquad \text{Evaluate powers.}$$
$$= 12 \qquad \text{Add and subtract from left to right.}$$

EXERCISES

**SEE EXAMPLES
2, 3, AND 5**
on pp. 5–7
for Exs. 6–9

Evaluate the expression.

6. $(5 + 4)^2 \div 3$

7. $5 \cdot (6 - 3)^5 + 45$

8. $[10 + (4 \cdot 2)^3] \div 2$

9. **ICICLES** An icicle falls from the roof of a building. It hits the ground in 3 seconds. To find the height of the building, use the expression $16t^2$, which gives the distance in feet that the icicle falls in t seconds.

1.2 Integers and the Number Line

pp. 12–16

NS 2.5 | **EXAMPLE**

Use a number line to order these integers from least to greatest: 2, −8, −6, 4, −1.

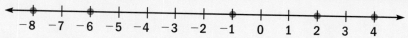

▶ **Answer** Integers ordered from least to greatest: −8, −6, −1, 2, 4

NS 1.1 | **EXAMPLE**

Find the absolute value of −5 using a number line.

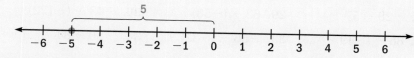

▶ **Answer** The distance between −5 and 0 is 5. So, $|-5| = 5$.

EXERCISES

**SEE EXAMPLES
1, 2, AND 3**
on pp. 12–14
for Exs. 10–19

Order the integers from least to greatest.

10. −4, 5, 8, −3, −5, 11, 7

11. −6, −10, 4, −9, 3, −1

Write the opposite and the absolute value of the integer.

12. 22

13. −13

14. −6

15. 10

16. −9

17. 7

18. 14

19. −25

1.3 Adding Integers

pp. 18–23

NS 1.2 | **EXAMPLE**

Find the sum −9 + 6.

$-9 + 6 = -3$ ◀— **Different signs, so subtract $|6|$ from $|-9|$.**

└── **Use sign of number with greater absolute value.**

EXERCISES

SEE EXAMPLE 2
on p. 19
for Exs. 20–27

Find the sum.

20. −81 + (−91)

21. 32 + (−79)

22. −32 + 50

23. −46 + (−19)

24. 75 + (−35)

25. −96 + (−11)

26. −24 + 19

27. −28 + (−59)

1.4 Subtracting Integers

pp. 24–28

NS 1.2 **EXAMPLE**

a. $-62 - (-8) = -62 + 8$ **Add the opposite of −8.**

$= -54$ **Add.**

b. $-12 - 43 = -12 + (-43)$ **Add the opposite of 43.**

$= -55$ **Add.**

EXERCISES

SEE EXAMPLE 1
on p. 25
for Exs. 28–35

Find the difference.

28. $-29 - 57$ **29.** $62 - (-58)$ **30.** $-43 - (-122)$ **31.** $31 - 108$

32. $88 - (-49)$ **33.** $-56 - (-32)$ **34.** $-50 - 84$ **35.** $61 - 28$

1.5 Multiplying Integers

pp. 31–35

NS 1.2 **EXAMPLE**

a. $-3(5) = -15$ **Different signs, so product is negative.**

b. $-6(-2) = 12$ **Same sign, so product is positive.**

c. $-22(0) = 0$ **Multiplication property of zero**

d. $5(-9)(-8) = -45(-8)$ **Multiply from left to right.**

$= 360$ **Multiply.**

EXERCISES

**SEE EXAMPLES
1 AND 3**
on pp. 31–32
for Exs. 36–52

Find the product.

36. $20(12)$ **37.** $31(-4)$ **38.** $-6(9)$ **39.** $-8(-14)$

40. $-7(1)(-18)$ **41.** $-9(-23)(0)$ **42.** $-2(-3)(6)(-8)$ **43.** $5(-9)(7)(-4)$

Evaluate the expression when $x = -6$, $y = -4$, and $z = -8$.

44. xyz **45.** $9z - 2x$ **46.** $11y - 2xz$ **47.** $2x + 3yz$

48. $2xy - z$ **49.** $3y + 4x$ **50.** $2yz + 3yz$ **51.** $9z - 4xy$

52. HOT AIR BALLOON A hot air balloon at an altitude of 218 feet drops 22 feet per minute for 3 minutes. Evaluate the expression $218 + 3(-22)$ to find the new altitude (in feet) of the balloon.

1.6 Dividing Integers

pp. 36–40

NS 1.2

EXAMPLE

a. $\dfrac{-96}{-16} = 6$ Same sign, so quotient is positive.

b. $\dfrac{-36}{4} = -9$ Different signs, so quotient is negative.

c. $\dfrac{0}{-4} = 0$ Dividend is 0 and divisor is nonzero, so quotient is 0.

EXERCISES

SEE EXAMPLES 1 AND 2
on pp. 36–37
for Exs. 53–66

Find the quotient.

53. $\dfrac{-26}{2}$ **54.** $\dfrac{-98}{-7}$ **55.** $\dfrac{-120}{-15}$ **56.** $\dfrac{63}{-7}$

57. $\dfrac{-56}{-14}$ **58.** $\dfrac{-84}{12}$ **59.** $\dfrac{0}{-9}$ **60.** $\dfrac{-48}{-16}$

Find the mean of the data.

61. $5, 7, -9, -2, -6, 8, -9, 6$

62. $15, -9, 6, -14, -18, 12, 7, 5, -2, 8$

63. $-11, 15, 26, 12, -8, 0, 1$

64. $24, -23, -17, -13, 27, 31, -44, -9$

65. $-6, 14, 34, 15, 2, 7, -10$

66. $-18, 4, -30, -9, 33, 37, -14, 5$

1.7 Number Properties

pp. 41–45

AF 1.3

EXAMPLE

$5 \cdot (13 \cdot 4) = 5 \cdot (4 \cdot 13)$ **Commutative property of multiplication**

$= (5 \cdot 4) \cdot 13$ **Associative property of multiplication**

$= 20 \cdot 13$ **Multiply 5 and 4.**

$= 260$ **Multiply 20 and 13.**

EXERCISES

SEE EXAMPLES 1, 2, 3, AND 4
on pp. 41–43
for Exs. 67–75

Evaluate the expression using mental math. Identify any properties you used.

67. $19 - (-58 - 81)$ **68.** $-28 + 85 + (-62)$ **69.** $-45 + (45 + 97)$

70. $4(25 \cdot 19)$ **71.** $[-54 \cdot (-56)] \cdot 0 \cdot (-17)$ **72.** $-20 \cdot (-15) \cdot 5$

73. $(-19 - 56) + 19$ **74.** $12 \cdot 96 \cdot 0 + 3$ **75.** $(-92 + 47) - (-92)$

AF 1.3 **EXAMPLE**

a. $3(5 + x) = 3(5) + 3x$ **Distributive property**

$= 15 + 3x$ **Multiply.**

b. $-2(5x - 8) = -2(5x) - (-2)(8)$ **Distributive property**

$= -10x - (-16)$ **Multiply.**

$= -10x + 16$ **Simplify.**

EXERCISES

SEE EXAMPLES 1 AND 2
on pp. 48–49
for Exs. 76–82

Use the distributive property to write an equivalent expression.

76. $5(12x - 20)$ **77.** $7(9 + 2y)$ **78.** $4(5z - 3)$

79. $12(6y - 4)$ **80.** $9(5 - 12t)$ **81.** $5(4r + 5)$

82. REAL ESTATE The figure shows the dimensions of two adjacent rooms. Use the distributive property to write two equivalent expressions for the total area of the rooms. Then evaluate the expressions.

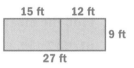

15 ft   12 ft   9 ft   27 ft

MR 2.0 **EXAMPLE**

It takes 3 trips with a full pitcher of water to fill a 5 gallon aquarium. If you use the same pitcher, how many trips will it take to fill a 55 gallon aquarium?

Read, Understand, and Make a Plan Use division to find how many smaller aquariums it would take to fill the larger aquarium. Then multiply that number by 3, because it takes 3 trips to fill the smaller aquarium.

Solve the Problem $\dfrac{55 \text{ gal}}{5 \text{ gal}} \cdot 3 \text{ trips} = 11 \cdot 3 \text{ trips} = 33 \text{ trips}$

▶ **Answer** You need 33 trips to fill the larger aquarium.

Look Back The larger aquarium has 11 times the capacity as the smaller aquarium, so it should take 11 times the number of trips. Your answer checks.

EXERCISES

SEE EXAMPLE 3
on p. 54
for Ex. 83

83. NUTRITION You like to add 3 tablespoons of granola to a 6 ounce container of yogurt. How many tablespoons of granola should you add to a 32 ounce container of yogurt?

VOCABULARY Copy and complete the statement.

1. A power has an exponent and a(n) __?__.

2. The additive identity is __?__.

Evaluate the expression.

3. $20 + 12 \div 4$

4. $6 \cdot 5 - 20 \div 2$

5. $(3 + 7) \div 5 + 10$

6. $(2 + 3)^4 \div 5$

7. $10^2 - 3^4 + 22$

8. $[(11 - 5)^3 - 12] \div 12$

Order the integers from least to greatest.

9. $-9, 5, 1, -11, 0, -1$

10. $2, 8, -5, -2, -1, 6$

11. $9, -3, 4, -1, -4$

Identify the graphed number with the greater absolute value.

12.

13.

Evaluate the expression for the given values of x.

14. $|x|$ when $x = 2$ and when $x = -4$

15. $-|x|$ when $x = 3$ and when $x = -5$

16. $-x$ when $x = -6$ and when $x = 8$

17. $-(-x)$ when $x = -1$ and when $x = 7$

Evaluate the expression.

18. $17 + (-9)$

19. $-8 + (-14)$

20. $10 - (-15)$

21. $-4 - 17$

22. $-5(14)$

23. $-12(-20)$

24. $\dfrac{-152}{-19}$

25. $\dfrac{-132}{6}$

Evaluate the expression. Identify any properties you used.

26. $17 - 35 + 13$

27. $16 + (14 - 12)$

28. $-2 \cdot (-17) \cdot 5$

29. $-2 \cdot (-5 \cdot 19)$

Use the distributive property to write an equivalent expression.

30. $4(x + 8)$

31. $-6(3x + 7)$

32. $-2(5x - 1)$

33. $7(2x - 9)$

34. **TENNIS** A tennis team bought a total of 72 cans of tennis balls during a season. Of these, 52 cans had 3 balls and 20 cans had 4 balls. Evaluate the expression $52x + 20y$ when $x = 3$ and $y = 4$ to determine the total number of tennis balls the team bought.

35. **SHIP DECKS** Relative to the water's surface, one deck of a ship is at -6 meters and another deck is at 12 meters. What is the vertical distance between the two decks?

36. **EVAPORATION** The water level of a swimming pool changes over 5 days by the following amounts (in inches): $-2, -3, -2, -1$, and -2. Find the mean daily change in the water level.

STRATEGIES YOU'LL USE:
- SOLVE DIRECTLY
- ELIMINATE CHOICES

📎 **Standards**

NS 1.2

If you have difficulty solving a multiple choice problem directly, you may be able to use another approach to eliminate incorrect answer choices and obtain the correct answer.

PROBLEM 1

You want to buy some new computer games. You earn $8 per hour at your job, and you worked 14 hours last weekend. What is the most you can spend with the money you earned last weekend?

(A) $8   (B) $80   (C) $112   (D) $300

Strategy 1 — SOLVE DIRECTLY

Use a verbal model to find the amount of money that you earned last weekend.

STEP 1 **Write** a verbal model. Your total income is the amount you earned per hour multiplied by the number of hours you worked.

Total income	=	Amount earned per hour	•	Number of hours

STEP 2 **Substitute** known values into the verbal model and simplify.

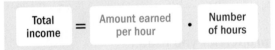

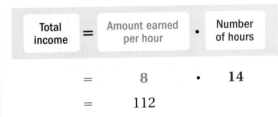

Your total income was $112. So, you can spend at most $112 on computer games.

The correct answer is C. (A) (B) (C) (D)

Strategy 2 — ELIMINATE CHOICES

In some cases, you can identify choices of a multiple choice question that can be eliminated.

Because you earned $8 per hour and you worked more than 1 hour, your total income will be more than $8. So, you can eliminate choice A.

To find your total income, you would multiply $8 by 14. Using the distributive property, you can rewrite the product of 8 and 14 as follows.

$$8 \cdot 14 = 8(10 + 4)$$
$$= 8 \cdot 10 + 8 \cdot 4$$
$$= 80 + 8 \cdot 4$$

You can see that your income was greater than $80. So, you can eliminate choice B.

Because your hourly wage is less than $10 and you worked fewer than 20 hours, your income must be less than $10 \cdot 20 = 200. So, you can eliminate choice D.

The correct answer is C. (A) (B) (C) (D)

PROBLEM 2

The numbers of points scored by a player in five basketball games are listed in the table. What is the player's mean number of points scored per game?

Game	1	2	3	4	5
Points	22	19	28	15	21

A −15   **B** 10   **C** 21   **D** 31

Strategy 1 SOLVE DIRECTLY

Recall that the mean of a data set is the sum of the values divided by the number of values.

STEP 1 **Find** the sum of the points scored in each game.

$22 + 19 + 28 + 15 + 21 = 105$

STEP 2 **Divide** the sum by the number of basketball games played.

$\frac{105}{5} = 21$

The mean number of points the player scored is 21.

The correct answer is C. **A** **B** **C** **D**

Strategy 2 ELIMINATE CHOICES

In some cases, you can identify choices of a multiple choice question that can be eliminated.

To find the mean number of points the player scored, divide the sum of the values by the number of values. Because both the numerator and denominator are positive, the quotient will be positive. So, choice A can be eliminated because it is negative.

The mean of a data set must be between the least and greatest values. So, choices B and D can be eliminated because choice B is less than 15 and choice D is greater than 28.

The correct answer is C. **A** **B** **C** **D**

STRATEGY PRACTICE

Explain why you can eliminate the highlighted answer choice.

1. What is the value of 4^3?

   A ✗ 0   **B** 12   **C** 32   **D** 64

2. Which expression is equivalent to $4 - 3 + 6$?

   A $4 - 6 + 3$ **B** ✗ $3 - 4 - 6$ **C** $6 - 4 + 3$ **D** $4 + 6 - 3$

3. What is the value of $-5x - 2$ when $x = 3$?

   A −17   **B** −12   **C** −5   **D** ✗ 13

4. You and a friend decide to go to the movies on Saturday afternoon. The price for admission is $4 and a large water costs $2. What is the total cost if you both see a movie and both buy a large water?

   A ✗ $3   **B** $8   **C** $10   **D** $12

1. Which of the following is a numerical expression? **AF 1.4**

   Ⓐ $7x$

   Ⓑ $7^2 + x^2$

   Ⓒ $8x - 5$

   Ⓓ $3(4 - 2)$

2. A customer presents the coupon below to buy 5 sandwiches and 2 salads.

   THE SEA BASS
   FISH HOUSE

   Any regular sandwich: **$3** (*limit 5*)

   Any regular salad: **$4** (*limit 2*)

   Prices good with coupon

   Find the total cost of the order by evaluating $3x + 4y$ when $x = 5$ and $y = 2$. **AF 1.2**

   Ⓐ $7

   Ⓑ $19

   Ⓒ $23

   Ⓓ $26

3. A bird flies at a height of 30 feet above the ground. The bird decreases its height by 7 feet per second for 3 seconds. What is the height of the bird now? **NS 1.2**

   Ⓐ 9 ft

   Ⓑ 20 ft

   Ⓒ 40 ft

   Ⓓ 51 ft

4. Which property is illustrated by the statement $-3 + 3 = 0$? **AF 1.3**

   Ⓐ Identity property of addition

   Ⓑ Inverse property of addition

   Ⓒ Distributive property

   Ⓓ Inverse property of multiplication

5. The bar graph shows the change in value of four vehicles in one year. Which statement is *not* supported by the graph? **NS 1.1, MR 2.5**

   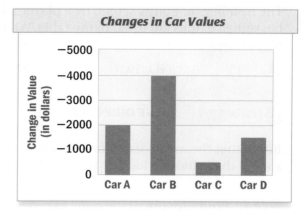

   Changes in Car Values

   Ⓐ Car A decreased the least in value.

   Ⓑ Car A decreased less in value than Car B.

   Ⓒ Car A decreased more in value than Car D.

   Ⓓ Car B decreased the most in value.

6. The bar graph shows the daily earnings at a store from Monday through Friday. What is the difference (in dollars) between the store's greatest and least daily earnings? **NS 1.2**

   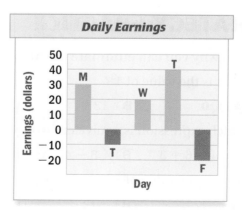

   Daily Earnings

   Ⓐ $30

   Ⓑ $60

   Ⓒ $70

   Ⓓ $80

7. Your school's science club started out the year with $60. The club had fundraisers where the members raised $100, $150, and $125. The club then spent $400 on a field trip. How much money does the science club have left after the field trip? **NS 1.2**

  (A) $25

  (B) $35

  (C) $50

  (D) $315

8. Luke completes the statement $|-6|$ __?__ $|5|$ with $<$. Why is his answer incorrect? **NS 2.5, MR 2.6**

  (A) Because -6 is to the left of 0 on a number line

  (B) Because -6 is greater than -5

  (C) Because 5 is to the right of -6 on a number line

  (D) Because the distance from -6 to 0 is greater than the distance from 5 to 0 on a number line

9. What is the distance on a number line between -12 and 27? **NS 2.5**

  (A) -39

  (B) -15

  (C) 15

  (D) 39

10. Which property is used to rewrite $54 + (-17) + 26$ as $54 + 26 + (-17)$? **AF 1.3**

  (A) Associative property of addition

  (B) Commutative property of addition

  (C) Associative property of multiplication

  (D) Distributive property

11. A person is rowing upstream on a river. The table below shows the distance traveled each minute by the rower. Positive distances indicate movement upstream. Negative distanced indicate movement downstream. What is the rower's net distance traveled upstream after 5 minutes? **NS 1.2**

Minute	1	2	3	4	5
Distance (ft)	20	12	8	-10	-15

  (A) 10 ft

  (B) 15 ft

  (C) 40 ft

  (D) 45 ft

12. Use the distributive property to find the area of the figure. **AF 1.3**

  (A) 80 ft^2

  (B) 120 ft^2

  (C) 168 ft^2

  (D) 216 ft^2

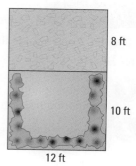

8 ft

10 ft

12 ft

13. Which equation illustrates the identity property of multiplication? **AF 1.3**

  (A) $-7 \cdot 0 = 0$

  (B) $-3 \cdot 1 = -3$

  (C) $4(x + 7) = 4x + 4(7)$

  (D) $3(5 - 2) = 15 - 6$

14. Eight scuba divers are below the ocean's surface at an elevation of -10 feet. Six other people are still on the boat at an elevation of 4 feet. What is the mean elevation (in feet) of all 14 people? **NS 1.2**

  (A) -14 ft

  (B) -6 ft

  (C) -4 ft

  (D) 2 ft

2 Rational Number Operations

Before

In previous chapters, you learned the following skills, which you'll use in Chapter 2:

- Using the distributive property
- Performing operations with integers
- Evaluating expressions
- Using the order of operations

Now

In Chapter 2 you'll study these

Big Ideas:

1 Simplifying and comparing fractions

2 Adding, subtracting, multiplying, and dividing fractions

3 Converting between fractions and decimals

Why?

So you can solve real-world problems about . . .

- Pets, p. 78
- Racing, p. 89
- Olympic sledding, p. 94
- Cooking, p. 103
- Exercising, p. 103
- Great Lakes, p. 116

Animated **Math**

at *classzone.com*

Get-Ready Games

GOING for GOLD

California Standards

Review operations with integers. *Gr. 7 NS 1.2*
Prepare for operations with fractions. *Gr. 7 NS 1.2*

Medals: 24, 18, 2, −12, −6, −4, 8, 12, −6

How to Play

Each athlete shown above can only win gold medals whose sum, difference, product, or quotient is equal to the athlete's number.

- Find the arrangement of medals that allows each athlete to win two medals. Each medal can be used only once.

CALIFORNIA STANDARDS

• **Gr. 7 NS 1.5** Know that every rational number is either a terminating or a repeating decimal and be able to convert terminating decimals into reduced fractions. *(Lesson 2.7)*

• **Gr. 7 NS 2.2** Add and subtract fractions by using factoring to find common denominators. *(Lesson 2.4)*

HEPTATHLON

California Standards

Review operations with integers. *Gr. 7 NS 1.2*
Prepare for operations with fractions. *Gr. 7 NS 1.2*

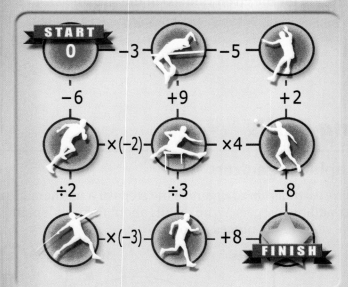

How to Play

In a heptathlon, athletes compete in seven events.

• Begin at Start with a value of 0. Move to an adjacent event. Perform the operation in the path using the value from your previous location. You may visit an event only once. You do not need to visit every event.

• Find the path to Finish with the greatest value.

Games Wrap-Up

Draw Conclusions

Complete these exercises after playing the games.

1. **WRITING** In *Going for Gold*, is there more than one way that the athletes can each win two gold medals? *Explain* why or why not.

2. **REASONING** Suppose you want to visit all of the events in *Heptathlon. Describe* two different paths from Start to Finish. Give the resulting value for each path.

Prerequisite Skills

California @HomeTutor

Prerequisite skills practice
at classzone.com

**REVIEW
VOCABULARY**

- **variable,** *p. 7*
- **integer,** *p. 12*
- **opposite,** *p. 14*
- **equivalent
  expressions,** *p. 49*

VOCABULARY CHECK

Copy and complete using a review term from the list at the left.

1. A symbol that represents one or more numbers is called a(n) __?__.

2. 5 is the __?__ of -5.

SKILL CHECK

Round the decimal to the nearest whole number. *(p. 723)*

3. 10.61   4. 134.7   5. 0.25   6. 12.86

Evaluate the expression. *(p. 5)*

7. $32 - 27 + 14$ 8. $4 \cdot 12 \div 6$ 9. $6 + 34 \div 2$

10. $5 \cdot 4 + 3^2$ 11. $\dfrac{38 - 4(3 + 2)}{3}$ 12. $7\left(\dfrac{9 + 5}{2}\right)$

Evaluate the expression for the given value(s) of the variable(s). *(pp. 31, 36)*

13. $7x + 3$, $x = -2$ 14. $5(c \div d)$, $c = 12$, $d = 4$

15. $\dfrac{r - 7}{2t}$, $r = -9$, $t = 8$ 16. $\dfrac{3w^3}{2y + 2}$, $w = -2$, $y = -4$

Notetaking Skills

NOW YOU TRY
Make a *process
diagram* for
multiplying integers.
You may want to use
colored pencils.

Focus on Graphic Organizers

You can use a *process diagram* to organize the steps of a mathematical
process, such as adding integers. Write details about the problem in
rectangles. Write steps of the process in ovals.

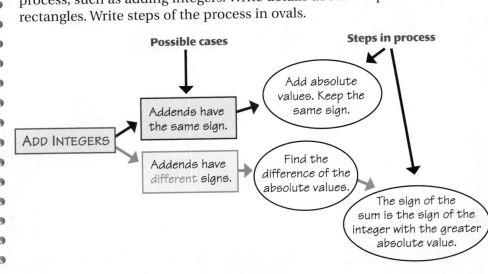

2.1 Simplifying Fractions

Math and **PETS**
Ex. 41, p. 78

Standards Preparation

Gr. 6 NS 2.4 **Determine** the least common multiple and **the greatest common divisor of whole numbers; use them to solve problems with fractions** (e.g., to find a common denominator to add two fractions or **to find the reduced form for a fraction**).

Connect

Before you found greatest common divisors of whole numbers.
Now you will simplify fractions to prepare for Grade 7 Standard NS 1.2.

KEY VOCABULARY

• fraction
• simplest form of a fraction
• equivalent fractions
• greatest common factor (GCF),
  p. 725

A **fraction** is a number of the form $\frac{a}{b}$ $(b \neq 0)$ where a is called the numerator and b is called the denominator. The **simplest form of a fraction** is when the numerator and denominator of a fraction have 1 as their greatest common factor (GCF).

Equivalent fractions represent the same number. They have the same simplest form.

EXAMPLE 1   Writing a Fraction in Simplest Form

HISTORY One of the Czech Republic's royal coronation jewels is decorated with 44 spinels, 30 emeralds, 22 pearls, 19 sapphires, and 1 ruby. Write the fraction of jewels in the crown that are emeralds in simplest form.

SOLUTION

Write the fraction of jewels in the crown that are emeralds. Then simplify.

$$\frac{\text{Number of emeralds}}{\text{Total number of jewels in the crown}} = \frac{30}{116}$$

About the Standards

The greatest common factor (GCF) is sometimes called the greatest common divisor (GCD).

METHOD 1   Find and use the GCF of 30 and 116.

$$30 = 2 \cdot 3 \cdot 5 \qquad 116 = 2^2 \cdot 29$$

The GCF of 30 and 116 is 2.

$$\frac{30}{116} = \frac{30 \div 2}{116 \div 2} \qquad \text{Divide numerator and denominator by GCF.}$$

$$= \frac{15}{58} \qquad \text{Simplify.}$$

REVIEW GCF

For help with finding GCFs, see p. 725.

METHOD 2   Use prime factorization.

$$\frac{30}{116} = \frac{2 \cdot 3 \cdot 5}{2 \cdot 2 \cdot 29} \qquad \text{Write prime factorizations.}$$

$$= \frac{\overset{1}{\cancel{2}} \cdot 3 \cdot 5}{\underset{1}{\cancel{2}} \cdot 2 \cdot 29} = \frac{15}{58} \qquad \text{Divide out common factor and simplify.}$$

▶ **Answer** The fraction of jewels that are emeralds is $\frac{15}{58}$.

Sapphire

Ruby

Pearl

Spinel

Emerald

EXAMPLE 2 Identifying Equivalent Fractions

Tell whether the fractions $\frac{3}{8}$ and $\frac{18}{48}$ are equivalent.

SOLUTION

Write each fraction in simplest form.

$\frac{3}{8}$ is in simplest form.

$$\frac{18}{48} = \frac{18 \div 6}{48 \div 6} = \frac{3}{8}$$

▶ **Answer** The fractions have the same simplest form, so they are equivalent.

EXAMPLE 3 Writing Equivalent Fractions

Write two fractions that are equivalent to $\frac{4}{10}$.

SOLUTION

Multiply or divide the numerator and denominator by the same nonzero number.

$$\frac{4}{10} = \frac{4 \times 3}{10 \times 3} = \frac{12}{30} \qquad \text{Multiply numerator and denominator by 3.}$$

$$\frac{4}{10} = \frac{4 \div 2}{10 \div 2} = \frac{2}{5} \qquad \begin{array}{l}\text{Divide numerator and denominator by 2,}\\ \text{a common factor of 4 and 10.}\end{array}$$

OTHER SOLUTIONS
Many other equivalent fractions can be found by multiplying the numerator and denominator by other numbers.

▶ **Answer** The fractions $\frac{12}{30}$ and $\frac{2}{5}$ are equivalent to $\frac{4}{10}$.

✓ **GUIDED PRACTICE**   for Examples 1, 2, and 3

Of your 25 classmates, 5 prefer apples, 7 prefer oranges, and 9 prefer bananas. Write the fraction of your classmates who prefer the given fruit in simplest form.

1. Apple   2. Orange   3. Banana   4. Other

Tell whether the fractions are equivalent.

5. $\frac{1}{6}, \frac{4}{24}$ 6. $\frac{3}{7}, \frac{10}{21}$ 7. $\frac{24}{30}, \frac{4}{6}$ 8. $\frac{15}{35}, \frac{3}{7}$

Write two fractions that are equivalent to the given fraction.

9. $\frac{8}{16}$ 10. $\frac{9}{15}$ 11. $\frac{10}{12}$ 12. $\frac{21}{24}$

ALGEBRAIC EXPRESSIONS You can use prime factorization to simplify fractions that contain algebraic expressions, as you will see in Example 4 at the top of the next page.

EXAMPLE 4 **Simplifying and Evaluating an Expression**

 Simplify the algebraic expression. Then evaluate when $x = 4$ and $y = -2$.

$$\frac{-4x^2y}{2xy^2} = \frac{-1 \cdot 2 \cdot 2 \cdot x \cdot x \cdot y}{2 \cdot x \cdot y \cdot y}$$ Factor numerator and denominator.

$$= \frac{-1 \cdot \overset{1}{\cancel{2}} \cdot 2 \cdot \overset{1}{\cancel{x}} \cdot x \cdot \overset{1}{\cancel{y}}}{\underset{1}{\cancel{2}} \cdot \underset{1}{\cancel{x}} \cdot \underset{1}{\cancel{y}} \cdot y}$$ Divide out common factors.

$$= \frac{-2x}{y}$$ Simplify.

$$= \frac{-2(4)}{-2}$$ Substitute 4 for x and -2 for y.

$$= 4$$ Simplify.

✓ **GUIDED PRACTICE**   for Example 4

Simplify the algebraic expression. Then evaluate when $x = -2$ and $y = 3$.

13. $\dfrac{4xy}{6x}$ **14.** $\dfrac{32x}{8xy}$ **15.** $\dfrac{2x^3y}{6x}$ **16.** $\dfrac{5x^2y}{10xy}$

2.1 EXERCISES

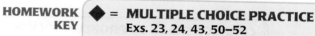
HOMEWORK KEY

◆ = **MULTIPLE CHOICE PRACTICE**
Exs. 23, 24, 43, 50–52

○ = **HINTS** AND **HOMEWORK HELP**
for Exs. 15, 31, 43 at classzone.com

SKILLS • PROBLEM SOLVING • REASONING

1. VOCABULARY Copy and complete: The GCF of the numerator and denominator of a fraction in __?__ is 1.

2. WRITING *Explain* how you can find a fraction that is equivalent to a given fraction.

SEE EXAMPLE 1
on p. 75
for Exs. 3–13

WRITING IN SIMPLEST FORM Write the fraction in simplest form.

3. $\dfrac{21}{49}$ **4.** $\dfrac{-9}{72}$ **5.** $\dfrac{10}{15}$ **6.** $\dfrac{16}{20}$ **7.** $\dfrac{-25}{40}$

8. $\dfrac{-36}{72}$ **9.** $\dfrac{39}{52}$ **10.** $\dfrac{18}{27}$ **11.** $\dfrac{-49}{56}$ **12.** $\dfrac{33}{121}$

ERROR ANALYSIS *Describe* and correct the error in the solution.

13. Simplify $\dfrac{42}{92}$.   **14.** Write a fraction equivalent to $\dfrac{3}{14}$.

$$✗\quad \frac{42}{92} = \frac{\cancel{2} \cdot 3 \cdot 7}{\cancel{2} \cdot \cancel{2} \cdot 23} = \frac{21}{23}$$

$$✗\quad \frac{3}{14} = \frac{3 + 2}{14 + 2} = \frac{5}{16}$$

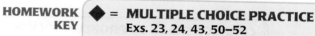

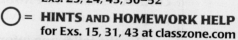

SEE EXAMPLE 2
on p. 76
for Exs. 15–24

EQUIVALENT FRACTIONS Tell whether the fractions are equivalent.

(15.) $\frac{4}{5}, \frac{20}{25}$

16. $\frac{21}{28}, \frac{1}{3}$

17. $\frac{24}{40}, \frac{30}{50}$

18. $\frac{30}{60}, \frac{27}{54}$

19. $\frac{30}{75}, \frac{75}{105}$

20. $\frac{45}{54}, \frac{90}{108}$

21. $\frac{54}{96}, \frac{144}{256}$

22. $\frac{84}{112}, \frac{168}{192}$

23. ◆ **MULTIPLE CHOICE** Which pair of fractions are equivalent?

(A) $\frac{6}{10}, \frac{9}{25}$

(B) $\frac{3}{8}, \frac{15}{35}$

(C) $\frac{14}{21}, \frac{12}{18}$

(D) $\frac{2}{5}, \frac{5}{20}$

24. ◆ **MULTIPLE CHOICE** Which fraction is *not* equivalent to $\frac{36}{64}$?

(A) $\frac{180}{320}$

(B) $\frac{9}{16}$

(C) $\frac{81}{144}$

(D) $\frac{14}{25}$

SEE EXAMPLE 3
on p. 76
for Exs. 25–28

WRITING FRACTIONS Write two fractions equivalent to the given fraction.

25. $\frac{45}{90}$

26. $\frac{36}{81}$

27. $\frac{24}{60}$

28. $\frac{48}{140}$

SEE EXAMPLE 4
on p. 77
for Exs. 29–36

ALGEBRA Simplify the algebraic expression. Then evaluate the simplified expression when $x = 3$ and $y = 5$.

29. $\frac{3x}{x^3}$

30. $\frac{2y^2}{-5y}$

(31.) $\frac{5y}{y^2}$

32. $\frac{4x^4}{24x^3}$

33. $\frac{-18x^2y}{24x}$

34. $\frac{35xy^2}{7x^2y^4}$

35. $\frac{6x^3y^2}{21xy^4}$

36. $\frac{-20x^2y}{8x^4y^3}$

CONNECT SKILLS TO PROBLEM SOLVING Exercises 37–40 will help you prepare for problem solving.

Use the following information: The U.S. Census Bureau divides the 50 states into 4 regions. Write the number of states in the region as a fraction of all the states. Write your answer in simplest form.

4 census regions

37. Northeast: 9

38. Midwest: 12

39. South: 16

40. West: 13

SEE EXAMPLE 1
on p. 75
for Exs. 41–44

41. PETS One hundred people were asked to name their favorite pet. The results are shown in the table. What fraction of people surveyed did not choose fish? Write your answer in simplest form.

Pet	Dog	Cat	Fish
Votes	60	25	15

California @HomeTutor for problem solving help at classzone.com

42. GROCERIES You buy two dozen eggs. In one carton, 1 egg is broken. In the other, 2 are broken. What fraction of all the eggs are broken? What fraction of all the eggs are unbroken? Write your answers in simplest form. *Explain* your reasoning.

California @HomeTutor for problem solving help at classzone.com

◆ = **MULTIPLE CHOICE PRACTICE**   ◯ = **HINTS AND HOMEWORK HELP** at classzone.com

43. ◆ **MULTIPLE CHOICE** Mr. Wilkens has attended 18 of his daughter's 24 basketball games. What fraction of the games has he *missed*?

    A $\frac{1}{4}$ **B** $\frac{2}{3}$ **C** $\frac{3}{4}$ **D** $\frac{4}{3}$

44. MULTI-STEP PROBLEM The table gives information about animals in Peru.

    a. Calculate Find the fraction of known species in each group (mammals, birds, and reptiles) that are threatened. Write your answers in simplest form.

    b. Estimate Round the number of known bird species to 1500 and the number of threatened bird species to 60. Approximately what fraction of bird species are threatened?

Peruvian Animal Species		
	Known	**Threatened**
Mammals	460	46
Birds	1541	64
Reptiles	360	9

45. FUNDRAISER Your class of 30 students votes on what type of fundraiser to have this year: a car wash, a fair, or a dance. Eight students choose a car wash and 12 students choose a fair. Find the fraction of students who choose to have a dance. Write your answer in simplest form. *Explain* how you found your answer.

46. OPEN-ENDED Write three equivalent fractions with different denominators that represent the fraction of students in your math class that are girls.

47. REASONING If you divide the numerator and denominator of a fraction by a common factor, will the resulting fraction always be in simplest form? *Explain* your reasoning and give an example to justify your answer.

48. CHALLENGE The product of the integers from n down to 1 is called *n factorial* and is written $n! = n \cdot (n - 1) \cdot (n - 2) \cdot \cdots \cdot 1$. Simplify the expression $\frac{12!}{3! \cdot 9!}$.

49. CHALLENGE Jason believes that if the numerator or the denominator of a fraction is prime, then the fraction is in simplest form. *Explain* why this is not always true.

◆ CALIFORNIA STANDARDS SPIRAL REVIEW

NS 1.1

50. Which list orders the integers from least to greatest? *(p. 12)*

    A $6, 2, -2, -6$ **B** $-2, 2, -6, 6$ **C** $-6, 6, -2, 2$ **D** $-6, -2, 2, 6$

NS 2.5

51. Which number has the least value? *(p. 12)*

    A $|2|$ **B** $|-17|$ **C** $|-30|$ **D** $|14|$

AF 1.2

52. Sara buys 2 shirts at $7 each and 4 scarves at $3 each. Evaluate the expression $2 \cdot 7 + 4 \cdot 3$ to find Sara's total cost. *(p. 5)*

    A $10   **B** $26   **C** $54   **D** $63

2.2 Comparing Fractions and Mixed Numbers

Standards NS 1.1 Read, write, and compare rational numbers in scientific notation (positive and negative powers of 10), **compare rational numbers in general.**

Connect *Before* you compared and ordered integers. *Now* you will compare and order fractions and mixed numbers.

Math and **SPORTS**
Ex. 50, p. 84

KEY VOCABULARY

- **least common denominator (LCD)**
- **improper fraction,** *p. 727*
- **least common multiple (LCM),** *p. 725*
- **mixed number,** *p. 727*

You can use models to compare the fractions $\frac{2}{3}$ and $\frac{3}{4}$. Represent both fractions with rectangular diagrams that are divided into the same number of parts.

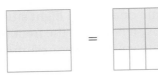   

$$\frac{2}{3} = \frac{2 \cdot 4}{3 \cdot 4} = \frac{8}{12} \qquad \frac{3}{4} = \frac{3 \cdot 3}{4 \cdot 3} = \frac{9}{12}$$

In the diagrams above, $\frac{8}{12} < \frac{9}{12}$, so $\frac{2}{3} < \frac{3}{4}$.

The **least common denominator (LCD)** of two or more fractions is the least common multiple (LCM) of the denominators. You can compare fractions by using the LCD to write equivalent fractions.

EXAMPLE 1 **Comparing Fractions**

a. Compare $\frac{1}{4}$ and $\frac{2}{5}$.

b. Compare $-\frac{3}{8}$ and $-\frac{5}{12}$.

SOLUTION

a. The LCM of 4 and 5 is 20, so the LCD is 20.

$$\frac{1}{4} = \frac{1 \cdot 5}{4 \cdot 5} = \frac{5}{20}$$

$$\frac{2}{5} = \frac{2 \cdot 4}{5 \cdot 4} = \frac{8}{20}$$

$5 < 8$, so $\frac{5}{20} < \frac{8}{20}$.

b. The LCM of 8 and 12 is 24, so the LCD is 24.

$$-\frac{3}{8} = \frac{-3 \cdot 3}{8 \cdot 3} = -\frac{9}{24}$$

$$-\frac{5}{12} = \frac{-5 \cdot 2}{12 \cdot 2} = -\frac{10}{24}$$

$-9 > -10$, so $-\frac{9}{24} > -\frac{10}{24}$.

INTERPRET FRACTIONS

A negative fraction can be written with a negative sign in either the numerator or the denominator. For example, $-\frac{3}{8}$ can be written as $\frac{-3}{8}$ or as $\frac{3}{-8}$.

▶ **Answer** $\frac{1}{4} < \frac{2}{5}$.

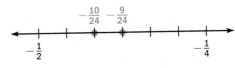

▶ **Answer** $-\frac{3}{8} > -\frac{5}{12}$.

EXAMPLE 2 ◆ **Multiple Choice Practice**

What is the order of $2, \frac{3}{8}, \frac{9}{5}$, and $|-1|$ from least to greatest?

A $|-1|, \frac{9}{5}, 2, \frac{3}{8}$ **B** $\frac{3}{8}, \frac{9}{5}, |-1|, 2$

C $|-1|, \frac{3}{8}, \frac{9}{5}, 2$ **D** $\frac{3}{8}, |-1|, \frac{9}{5}, 2$

ELIMINATE CHOICES
As a fraction with a numerator less than the denominator, $\frac{3}{8}$ is less than one. Therefore, choice A can be eliminated.

SOLUTION

STEP 1 **Find** the least common denominator of the fractions. The LCM of 8 and 5 is 40, so the LCD is 40.

STEP 2 **Use** the least common denominator to write equivalent fractions.

$$2 = \frac{2 \cdot 40}{40} = \frac{80}{40} \qquad\qquad \frac{3}{8} = \frac{3 \cdot 5}{8 \cdot 5} = \frac{15}{40}$$

$$\frac{9}{5} = \frac{9 \cdot 8}{5 \cdot 8} = \frac{72}{40} \qquad\qquad |-1| = 1 = \frac{40}{40}$$

STEP 3 **Compare** the numerators: $15 < 40$, $40 < 72$, and $72 < 80$. It follows that $\frac{15}{40} < \frac{40}{40}$, $\frac{40}{40} < \frac{72}{40}$, and $\frac{72}{40} < \frac{80}{40}$.

So, from least to greatest, the numbers are $\frac{3}{8}$, $|-1|$, $\frac{9}{5}$, and 2. This can be illustrated on a number line.

▶ **Answer** The correct answer is D. Ⓐ Ⓑ Ⓒ Ⓓ

✓ **GUIDED PRACTICE**   for Examples 1 and 2

Copy and complete the statement with < or >.

1. $\frac{2}{3} \underset{?}{\_} \frac{5}{8}$ **2.** $-\frac{2}{4} \underset{?}{\_} -\frac{15}{20}$ **3.** $\frac{3}{10} \underset{?}{\_} \frac{2}{4}$ **4.** $-\frac{9}{16} \underset{?}{\_} -\frac{11}{18}$

Order the numbers from least to greatest. Then graph the numbers on a number line.

5. $8, \frac{31}{3}, \frac{52}{9}$, and $|-7|$ **6.** $5, \frac{7}{2}, \frac{13}{3}, \frac{38}{8}$

REVIEW MIXED NUMBERS AND IMPROPER FRACTIONS
For help with mixed numbers and improper fractions, see p. 727.

MIXED NUMBERS To order a list of numbers that includes mixed numbers, first rewrite the mixed numbers as improper fractions.

When the whole parts of two positive mixed numbers are equal, you can just compare the fraction parts. Because $\frac{4}{7} > \frac{3}{8}$, $5\frac{4}{7} > 5\frac{3}{8}$.

EXAMPLE 3 **Comparing Mixed Numbers**

ORANGUTANS A female orangutan is about $3\frac{3}{7}$ feet tall. A male is about $3\frac{2}{5}$ feet tall. Which of the two orangutans is taller?

Orangutan

SOLUTION

STEP 1 Write equivalent fractions using the LCD, 35.

$$3\frac{3}{7} = \frac{24}{7} = \frac{24 \cdot 5}{7 \cdot 5} = \frac{120}{35} \qquad 3\frac{2}{5} = \frac{17}{5} = \frac{17 \cdot 7}{5 \cdot 7} = \frac{119}{35}$$

STEP 2 Compare the fractions: $\frac{120}{35} > \frac{119}{35}$, so $3\frac{3}{7} > 3\frac{2}{5}$.

▶ **Answer** The female orangutan is taller.

Animated Math

For an interactive example of comparing mixed numbers, go to **classzone.com.**

✓ **GUIDED PRACTICE** for Example 3

Copy and complete the statement with <, >, or =.

7. $\frac{16}{5}$? $3\frac{1}{3}$

8. $1\frac{4}{5}$? $\frac{21}{12}$

9. $2\frac{2}{3}$? $4\frac{5}{6}$

10. Order the numbers $2\frac{7}{9}$, $2\frac{5}{12}$, and $\frac{11}{4}$ from least to greatest.

2.2 EXERCISES

HOMEWORK KEY

◆ = **MULTIPLE CHOICE PRACTICE**
Exs. 26, 35, 43, 51–53

○ = **HINTS AND HOMEWORK HELP**
for Exs. 3, 17, 45 at classzone.com

SKILLS • PROBLEM SOLVING • REASONING

1. **VOCABULARY** Copy and complete: The least common denominator of two fractions is the __?__ of their denominators.

2. **WRITING** *Explain* how to compare fractions using the least common denominator.

**SEE EXAMPLES
1 AND 3**
on pp. 80–82
for Exs. 3–25

FINDING LCDS Find the least common denominator of the fractions.

3. $\frac{1}{2}, \frac{2}{3}$

4. $\frac{3}{4}, -\frac{7}{20}$

5. $\frac{11}{24}, \frac{5}{6}$

6. $-\frac{5}{12}, -\frac{7}{18}$

7. $\frac{1}{2}, \frac{3}{7}, \frac{3}{4}$

8. $\frac{1}{3}, \frac{5}{6}, \frac{3}{8}$

9. $\frac{17}{20}, \frac{13}{30}, \frac{9}{40}$

10. $\frac{1}{6}, \frac{5}{18}, \frac{11}{27}$

GRAPHING Graph the numbers on the same number line.

11. $\frac{5}{8}$

12. $-\frac{2}{4}$

13. $\frac{20}{16}$

14. $1\frac{7}{8}$

15. $-3\frac{3}{4}$

COMPARING NUMBERS Copy and complete the statement with <, >, or =.

16. $\frac{7}{18}$? $\frac{5}{9}$

17. $-\frac{24}{32}$? $-\frac{3}{4}$

18. $-\frac{5}{8}$? $\frac{9}{16}$

19. $\frac{165}{36}$? $4\frac{5}{12}$

20. $2\frac{4}{5}$? $\frac{7}{3}$

21. $\left|\frac{-31}{6}\right|$? $5\frac{2}{12}$

22. $-3\frac{1}{4}$? $-\frac{13}{14}$

23. $\left|\frac{-5}{9}\right|$? $\left|\frac{-16}{24}\right|$

ERROR ANALYSIS *Describe* and correct the error in the statement.

24. ✗ $-\frac{1}{3} < -\frac{2}{3}$ because $1 < 2$

25. ✗ $\frac{3}{5} < \frac{4}{7}$ because $3 < 4$

26. ◆ **MULTIPLE CHOICE** Which fraction has the least absolute value?

Ⓐ $\frac{7}{10}$

Ⓑ $-\frac{2}{3}$

Ⓒ $-\frac{12}{5}$

Ⓓ $\frac{2}{15}$

SEE EXAMPLE 2
on p. 81
for Exs. 27–35

ORDERING NUMBERS Order the numbers from least to greatest. Then graph the numbers on a number line.

27. $\frac{1}{2}, \frac{1}{8}, \frac{3}{4}, \frac{5}{16}$

28. $-1\frac{1}{2}, -\frac{5}{4}, -\frac{11}{6}$

29. $\frac{5}{3}, 1, 2\frac{2}{5}, \frac{15}{16}$

30. $-\frac{3}{4}, -\frac{5}{9}, -1\frac{1}{3}$

31. $\frac{19}{6}, 3\frac{1}{2}, -\frac{11}{4}$

32. $1\frac{3}{5}, \frac{7}{3}, 2\frac{1}{4}, |3|$

33. $\left|-\frac{34}{3}\right|, 11\frac{7}{12}, \frac{47}{4}$

34. $\frac{15}{4}, 3\frac{2}{3}, \frac{25}{7}$

35. ◆ **MULTIPLE CHOICE** Which list is in order from least to greatest?

Ⓐ $\frac{12}{18}, \frac{13}{30}, \frac{8}{15}$

Ⓑ $\frac{4}{18}, \frac{9}{15}, \frac{18}{27}$

Ⓒ $-\frac{4}{18}, -\frac{6}{10}, -1$

Ⓓ $|-2|, -\frac{7}{8}, 2\frac{3}{5}$

REASONING Copy and complete the statement with <, >, or = by first comparing each fraction to $\frac{1}{2}$ or $-\frac{1}{2}$.

36. $\frac{25}{50}$? $\frac{37}{74}$

37. $-\frac{10}{33}$? $-\frac{17}{30}$

38. $\frac{19}{36}$? $\frac{23}{100}$

39. $-\frac{105}{210}$? $-\frac{13}{27}$

CONNECT SKILLS TO PROBLEM SOLVING Exercises 40–42 will help you prepare for problem solving.

40. Sarah walks $\frac{2}{3}$ mile to school every day. Amy walks $\frac{5}{8}$ mile to school. Who walks the greater distance to school?

41. Jose has completed $\frac{5}{7}$ of his school project. Juan has completed $\frac{4}{5}$ of his school project. Who has completed more of the project?

42. Maria takes $\frac{8}{15}$ of an hour to finish her homework. Ann takes $\frac{3}{5}$ of an hour to finish her homework. Who takes less time to do her homework?

SEE EXAMPLE 1
on p. 80
for Ex. 43

43. ◆ **MULTIPLE CHOICE** In a class of 32 people, 28 were at school. Which fraction is *less* than the fraction of people in the class who were at school?

Ⓐ $\frac{27}{30}$

Ⓑ $\frac{24}{27}$

Ⓒ $\frac{21}{24}$

Ⓓ $\frac{24}{28}$

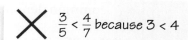 **California @HomeTutor** for problem solving help at classzone.com

44. GEOLOGY A geologist unearths two quartz crystals. Crystal A weighs $2\frac{5}{16}$ pounds and crystal B weighs $2\frac{1}{4}$ pounds? Which crystal is heavier?

California **@HomeTutor** for problem solving help at classzone.com

45. ELEPHANTS Which elephant's trunk represents a greater fraction of the elephant's weight? *Explain* how you can answer this question without writing the fractions with a common denominator.

Elephant	Trunk
10,200 lb	340 lb
15,050 lb	430 lb

CHALLENGE Copy and complete the statement with <, >, or = where $a > b$ and a and b are whole numbers. *Explain* your reasoning.

46. $\frac{a}{b}$? $\frac{1}{b}$ **47.** $\frac{1}{a}$? $\frac{1}{b}$ **48.** $\frac{a}{a+1}$? $\frac{b}{b+1}$ **49.** $\frac{a+1}{a}$? $\frac{b+1}{b}$

50. CHALLENGE Teams from California have played in the world championship game of the Little League World Series 20 times and won 5 times. Texas teams have appeared in 7 world championship games and won twice. Assuming California wins at every future appearance, what is the *least* number of future wins California needs in order to have won a *greater* fraction of their games? *Explain*.

◆ CALIFORNIA STANDARDS SPIRAL REVIEW

51. Which fraction is equivalent to $\frac{3}{4}$? *(p. 75)*

(A) $\frac{10}{12}$ **(B)** $\frac{6}{8}$ **(C)** $\frac{3}{5}$ **(D)** $\frac{4}{3}$

52. What is the value of $2xy - x$ when $x = 4$ and $y = 2$. *(p. 5)*

(A) -16 **(B)** 4 **(C)** 12 **(D)** 20

53. In a baseball game, an outfielder can throw the ball at a speed of 80 feet per second. Evaluate the expression $80t$ when $t = 2$ to find the horizontal distance that the ball travels in 2 seconds. *(p. 31)*

(A) 40 ft   **(B)** 120 ft   **(C)** 160 ft   **(D)** 240 ft

QUIZ for Lessons 2.1–2.2

Tell whether the fractions are equivalent. *(p. 75)*

1. $\frac{9}{27}, \frac{60}{180}$ **2.** $\frac{39}{91}, \frac{42}{56}$ **3.** $\frac{-40}{48}, \frac{-70}{84}$

Order the numbers from least to greatest. Then graph the numbers on a number line. *(p. 80)*

4. $\frac{3}{5}, -1, -\frac{3}{4}, \frac{7}{8}$ **5.** $1\frac{4}{7}, \left|-\frac{15}{9}\right|, 1\frac{5}{8}$ **6.** $\left|-5\right|, 4\frac{17}{18}, \frac{65}{14}$

7. BASKETBALL Team A won 16 out of 22 games. Team B won 19 out of 24 games. Which team won a greater fraction of games? *(p. 80)*

2.3 Adding and Subtracting Fractions

Standards

NS 1.2 Add, subtract, multiply, and divide **rational numbers** (integers, **fractions**, and terminating decimals) and take positive rational numbers to whole-number powers.

AF 1.3 Simplify numerical expressions by applying properties of rational numbers (e.g., identity, inverse, distributive, associative, commutative) and justify the process used.

Connect   *Before* you added and subtracted whole numbers and integers.
Now you will add and subtract fractions with common denominators.

Math and SPORTS
Ex. 38, p. 89

KEY VOCABULARY
• **order of operations,** *p. 6*
• **numerator,** *p. 727*
• **denominator,** *p. 727*

You may have used a model, such as the one below, to add or subtract fractions with common denominators.

$$\frac{2}{5} \quad + \quad \frac{1}{5} \quad = \quad \frac{3}{5}$$

The model illustrates the following rules for adding and subtracting fractions.

KEY CONCEPT   *For Your Notebook*

Adding and Subtracting Fractions

Words   To add fractions or subtract fractions with a common denominator, write the sum or difference of the numerators over the denominator.

Numbers $\frac{3}{9} + \frac{5}{9} = \frac{8}{9}$ **Algebra** $\frac{a}{c} + \frac{b}{c} = \frac{a+b}{c}$ $(c \neq 0)$

$\frac{3}{5} - \frac{2}{5} = \frac{1}{5}$ $\frac{a}{c} - \frac{b}{c} = \frac{a-b}{c}$ $(c \neq 0)$

EXAMPLE 1   **Adding and Subtracting Fractions**

INTERPRET FRACTIONS
In part (a) of Example 1, think of $-\frac{11}{13}$ as $\frac{-11}{13}$, and then apply the rule for adding fractions with a common denominator.

Find the sum or difference. Then simplify if possible.

a. $-\frac{11}{13} + \frac{8}{13} = \frac{-11 + 8}{13}$

$= \frac{-3}{13}$

$= -\frac{3}{13}$

b. $\frac{17}{20} - \frac{13}{20} = \frac{17 - 13}{20}$

$= \frac{4}{20}$

$= \frac{1}{5}$

2.3 Adding and Subtracting Fractions   **85**

EXAMPLE 2 ◆ **Multiple Choice Practice**

What is the value of $-5\frac{6}{7} + 3\frac{2}{7}$?

    A $-3\frac{3}{7}$ **B** $-2\frac{4}{7}$ **C** $2\frac{4}{7}$ **D** $3\frac{3}{7}$

ELIMINATE CHOICES

Because $|-5\frac{6}{7}| > |3\frac{2}{7}|$, the sum is less than zero, so you can eliminate choices C and D.

SOLUTION

$$-5\frac{6}{7} + 3\frac{2}{7} = \left(-5 - \frac{6}{7}\right) + \left(3 + \frac{2}{7}\right)$$ **Write mixed numbers in expanded form.**

$$= \left(-5 + 3\right) + \left(-\frac{6}{7} + \frac{2}{7}\right)$$ **Commutative property**

$$= -2 - \frac{4}{7}$$ **Add integers and fractions.**

$$= -2\frac{4}{7}$$ **Write as a mixed number.**

▶ **Answer** The correct answer is B. Ⓐ **Ⓑ** Ⓒ Ⓓ

✓ **GUIDED PRACTICE**   for Examples 1 and 2

1. What is the value of $-\frac{1}{3} - \frac{2}{3}$?

2. What is the value of $-2\frac{4}{5} + 2\frac{1}{5}$?

EXAMPLE 3 **Using Mixed Numbers in Real Life**

BIOLOGY A corn snake that is $14\frac{3}{4}$ inches long grows to a length of $27\frac{1}{4}$ inches. How much does it grow?

SOLUTION

Corn snake

AVOID ERRORS

When you subtract mixed numbers, compare their fraction parts. If you are subtracting a larger fraction from a smaller fraction, rename the mixed number before you subtract.

To find the amount of growth, subtract the original length from the current length.

$$27\frac{1}{4} - 14\frac{3}{4} = 26\frac{5}{4} - 14\frac{3}{4}$$ **Rename $27\frac{1}{4}$ so its fraction part is greater than $\frac{3}{4}$**

$$= \left(26 + \frac{5}{4}\right) - \left(14 + \frac{3}{4}\right)$$ **Write mixed numbers in expanded form.**

$$= 26 + \frac{5}{4} - 14 - \frac{3}{4}$$ **Distributive property**

$$= (26 - 14) + \left(\frac{5}{4} - \frac{3}{4}\right)$$ **Commutative property**

$$= 12 + \frac{2}{4}$$ **Subtract integers and fractions.**

$$= 12\frac{2}{4} = 12\frac{1}{2}$$ **Write as a mixed number and simplify.**

▶ **Answer** The snake grows $12\frac{1}{2}$ inches.

ORDER OF OPERATIONS The rules for adding and subtracting fractions can be applied to evaluate longer expressions. Remember to always use the order of operations.

EXAMPLE 4 **Evaluating Longer Expressions**

a. $\dfrac{2}{11} - \dfrac{5}{11} + \dfrac{9}{11} = \dfrac{2 - 5 + 9}{11}$ Write 2 − 5 + 9 over common denominator.

$= \dfrac{6}{11}$ Evaluate numerator from left to right.

ANOTHER WAY
You can also write the mixed numbers as improper fractions and then evaluate:

$3\dfrac{6}{7} - 2\dfrac{3}{7} + 4\dfrac{5}{7} =$

$\dfrac{27}{7} - \dfrac{17}{7} + \dfrac{33}{7} =$

$\dfrac{43}{7}$, or $6\dfrac{1}{7}$.

b. $3\dfrac{6}{7} - 2\dfrac{3}{7} + 4\dfrac{5}{7} = (3 - 2 + 4) + \left(\dfrac{6}{7} - \dfrac{3}{7} + \dfrac{5}{7}\right)$ Commutative property

$= 5\dfrac{8}{7}$ Evaluate inside parentheses.

$= 6\dfrac{1}{7}$ Rename.

✓ **GUIDED PRACTICE** for Examples 3 and 4

3. GARDENING A plant that is $5\dfrac{7}{8}$ inches high grows to a height of $8\dfrac{3}{8}$ inches. Find the amount of growth.

Evaluate. Then simplify if possible.

4. $\dfrac{3}{4} + \dfrac{7}{4} + \dfrac{5}{4}$

5. $\dfrac{15}{8} - \dfrac{7}{8} + \dfrac{3}{8}$

6. $2\dfrac{1}{3} - \dfrac{2}{3} + 3\dfrac{2}{3}$

2.3 EXERCISES

HOMEWORK KEY

◆ = **MULTIPLE CHOICE PRACTICE**
Exs. 15, 28, 34, 43–45

○ = **HINTS** AND **HOMEWORK HELP**
for Exs. 5, 21, 39 at classzone.com

SKILLS • PROBLEM SOLVING • REASONING

1. VOCABULARY Copy and complete: In the fraction $\dfrac{4}{9}$, 9 is the __?__ and 4 is the __?__.

2. NOTETAKING SKILLS Make a *process diagram* like the one on page 74 for adding fractions.

SEE EXAMPLES 1 AND 2
on pp. 85–86
for Exs. 3–15

FRACTION OPERATIONS Find the sum or difference. Then simplify if possible.

3. $\dfrac{5}{18} + \dfrac{7}{18}$

4. $\dfrac{5}{21} + \dfrac{2}{21}$

5. $\dfrac{3}{10} - \dfrac{7}{10}$

6. $\dfrac{7}{18} - \dfrac{5}{18}$

7. $\dfrac{4}{15} - \dfrac{1}{15}$

8. $1\dfrac{5}{9} + \dfrac{2}{9}$

9. $-4\dfrac{2}{7} - 4\dfrac{2}{7}$

10. $3\dfrac{1}{7} - 1\dfrac{5}{7}$

11. $-4\dfrac{9}{14} + 3\dfrac{5}{14}$

12. $2\dfrac{7}{9} + \dfrac{8}{9}$

13. $-7\dfrac{3}{5} - \dfrac{4}{5}$

14. $\dfrac{2}{3} - 1\dfrac{1}{3}$

15. ◆ **MULTIPLE CHOICE** What is the sum of $-\frac{5}{19}$ and $\frac{3}{19}$?

    A $-\frac{2}{19}$ **B** $-\frac{2}{18}$ **C** $\frac{2}{19}$ **D** $\frac{8}{19}$

SEE EXAMPLES 1, 2, 3, AND 4 on pp. 85–87 for Exs. 16–30

EVALUATING EXPRESSIONS **Evaluate. Then simplify if possible.**

16. $7\frac{1}{3} - 3\frac{2}{3}$ **17.** $19\frac{1}{4} - 17\frac{3}{4}$ **18.** $1\frac{4}{15} + \left(-\frac{11}{15}\right)$

19. $\frac{13}{18} + \frac{5}{18} + \frac{11}{18}$ **20.** $-\frac{4}{5} - \frac{1}{5} - \frac{2}{5}$ **21.** $4\frac{5}{12} - \left(\frac{11}{12} - \frac{7}{12}\right)$

22. $-5\frac{4}{15} - \left(3\frac{7}{15} + \frac{8}{15}\right)$ **23.** $-\frac{3}{16} - 2\frac{1}{16} - \frac{15}{16}$ **24.** $1\frac{3}{8} + \frac{5}{8} - 1\frac{7}{8}$

25. $-2\frac{1}{3} + 4\frac{2}{3} - 5\frac{1}{3} - 7\frac{2}{3}$ **26.** $6\frac{3}{7} + \frac{4}{7} - 2\frac{1}{7} + 1\frac{6}{7}$ **27.** $-4\frac{5}{12} - 1\frac{7}{12} + 2\frac{5}{12} - 3\frac{11}{12}$

28. ◆ **MULTIPLE CHOICE** What is the difference of $4\frac{4}{7}$ and $2\frac{1}{7}$?

    A $2\frac{3}{14}$ **B** $2\frac{5}{14}$ **C** $2\frac{3}{7}$ **D** $2\frac{5}{7}$

ERROR ANALYSIS *Describe* **and correct the error made.**

29.

    ✗ $\frac{2 - 5 + 9}{11} = \frac{-12}{11}$

30.

    ✗ $\frac{1}{3} + \frac{1}{3} = \frac{2}{6}$

CONNECT SKILLS TO PROBLEM SOLVING **Exercises 31–33 will help you prepare for problem solving.**

31. You knit $21\frac{3}{8}$ inches of a scarf. You have to shorten the scarf by $2\frac{5}{8}$ inches. How many inches of the scarf are left?

32. You have a piece of paper that is $8\frac{2}{4}$ inches wide. You cut off $\frac{3}{4}$ inch. What is the width of the paper now?

33. You study for $2\frac{1}{6}$ hours on Monday and $1\frac{5}{6}$ hours on Tuesday. What is the total number of hours you studied?

SEE EXAMPLE 3 on p. 86 for Exs. 34–35

34. ◆ **MULTIPLE CHOICE** You are fencing a rectangular plot of land. The plot and its dimensions are shown. How many feet of fencing do you need total?

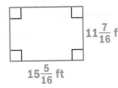
$11\frac{7}{16}$ ft
$15\frac{5}{16}$ ft

    A $26\frac{3}{4}$ feet   **B** $52\frac{1}{2}$ feet

    C $53\frac{1}{4}$ feet   **D** $53\frac{1}{2}$ feet

California @*HomeTutor* for problem solving help at classzone.com

35. EUROS A 2-euro coin is $25\frac{3}{4}$ millimeters wide. A 1-euro coin is $23\frac{1}{4}$ millimeters wide. How much wider is a 2-euro coin than a 1-euro coin?

California @*HomeTutor* for problem solving help at classzone.com

Euro coins

REASONING Two students evaluated $5\frac{2}{3} - 2\frac{1}{3}$ as shown. *Justify* each step.

36.

$$5\frac{2}{3} - 2\frac{1}{3} = \frac{17}{3} - \frac{7}{3}$$

$$= \frac{10}{3}$$

$$= \frac{3+3+3+1}{3}$$

$$= \frac{3}{3} + \frac{3}{3} + \frac{3}{3} + \frac{1}{3}$$

$$= 1 + 1 + 1 + \frac{1}{3}$$

$$= 3\frac{1}{3}$$

37.

$$5\frac{2}{3} - 2\frac{1}{3} = \left(5 + \frac{2}{3}\right) - \left(2 + \frac{1}{3}\right)$$

$$= 5 + \frac{2}{3} - 2 - \frac{1}{3}$$

$$= 5 - 2 + \frac{2}{3} - \frac{1}{3}$$

$$= (5 - 2) + \left(\frac{2}{3} - \frac{1}{3}\right)$$

$$= 3 + \frac{1}{3}$$

$$= 3\frac{1}{3}$$

38. RACING Some cars in a race were allowed to reduce the height of their rear spoilers by one fourth of an inch to reduce drag and increase speed. After the change, one car's spoiler was $6\frac{1}{4}$ inches tall. How tall was the spoiler before the change in height? *Justify* your answer.

← spoiler

39. LONG JUMP RECORD You want to match your school's long jump record of 17 feet $8\frac{1}{4}$ inches. Your best long jump so far is 15 feet $11\frac{3}{4}$ inches. How much farther do you need to jump to match the school record?

CHALLENGE Find the missing fraction.

40. $\frac{5}{11} + \frac{9}{11} - \underline{} = -\frac{2}{11}$

41. $\frac{7}{16} + \frac{9}{16} - \underline{} = \frac{5}{16}$

42. CHALLENGE Bill is 1 foot $3\frac{3}{8}$ inches taller than Hollie. Hollie is $6\frac{1}{8}$ inches taller than Chris. Amanda is $4\frac{7}{8}$ inches shorter than Chris. Amanda is 4 feet $2\frac{3}{8}$ inches tall. How tall are Bill, Hollie, and Chris in feet and inches?

◆ CALIFORNIA STANDARDS SPIRAL REVIEW

NS 2.5

43. What is the distance between -1 and 2 on a number line? *(p. 12)*

    A -3 **B** 0   **C** 2   **D** $|-3|$

AF 1.3

44. Which statement illustrates the associative property of multiplication? *(p. 41)*

    A $5 \cdot 0 = 0$ **B** $5 \cdot (3 \cdot 2) = (5 \cdot 3) \cdot 2$

    C $5 + (3 + 2) = (5 + 3) + 2$ **D** $5 \cdot (3 \cdot 2) = (3 \cdot 2) \cdot 5$

NS 1.2

45. The profits earned by a band fundraiser in three months were $225, $198, and $294. What was the mean monthly profit? *(p. 36)*

    A $225   **B** $239   **C** $300   **D** $717

2.4 Adding Fractions

MATERIALS · pencil and paper

Standards

NS 1.2 Add, subtract, multiply, and divide **rational numbers** (integers, **fractions**, and terminating decimals) and take positive rational numbers to whole-number powers.

QUESTION How can you add fractions with different denominators?

EXPLORE Add two fractions with different denominators

Find the sum of $\frac{1}{2} + \frac{1}{3}$.

STEP 1 **Find** a common denominator for the fractions. One common denominator is the product of the individual denominators: $2 \cdot 3 = 6$.

STEP 2 **Write** each fraction using the common denominator from Step 1.

$$\frac{1}{2} = \frac{1}{2} \cdot \frac{3}{3} = \frac{3}{6} \qquad \frac{1}{3} = \frac{1}{3} \cdot \frac{2}{2} = \frac{2}{6}$$

STEP 3 **Draw** a number line divided into intervals of $\frac{1}{6}$, since 6 is the common denominator from Step 1. Draw two adjacent line segments that represent the fractions from Step 2, as shown.

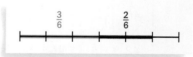

STEP 4 **Identify** the total length of the line segments from Step 3. The line segments cover 5 intervals on the number line, so their total length is $\frac{5}{6}$. So, $\frac{1}{2} + \frac{1}{3} = \frac{5}{6}$.

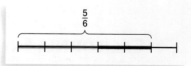

DRAW CONCLUSIONS Use your observations to complete these exercises

Use the method described in the steps above to find the sum.

1. $\frac{1}{3} + \frac{1}{4}$
2. $\frac{1}{4} + \frac{2}{5}$
3. $\frac{3}{2} + \frac{2}{3}$
4. $\frac{1}{2} + \frac{3}{4}$

5. In Exercise 4, explain why you may want to use a common denominator other than $2 \cdot 4 = 8$ to add the fractions.

6. **REASONING** Make a conjecture about how the sum $\frac{a}{b} + \frac{c}{d}$ can be written as a single fraction.

2.4 Using a Common Denominator

Standards

NS 1.2 Add, subtract, multiply, and divide **rational numbers** (integers, **fractions,** and terminating decimals) and take positive rational numbers to whole-number powers.

NS 2.2 Add and subtract fractions by using factoring to find common denominators.

AF 1.3 Simplify numerical expressions by applying properties of rational numbers (e.g., identity, **inverse**, distributive, associative, **commutative**) and justify the process used.

Math and **CARPENTRY** Example 3, p. 92

Connect *Before* you added and subtracted fractions with common denominators. *Now* you will add and subtract fractions with different denominators.

KEY VOCABULARY
- **least common denominator (LCD),** *p. 80*

To add or subtract fractions with different denominators, first rewrite the fractions so the denominators are the same using the least common denominator (LCD) of the fractions.

KEY CONCEPT
For Your Notebook

Adding and Subtracting Fractions

Words   If the fractions have different denominators, multiply the fractions by a fraction equivalent to 1 to make a common denominator.

Numbers $\dfrac{2}{5} + \dfrac{1}{3} = \dfrac{2 \cdot 3}{5 \cdot 3} + \dfrac{1 \cdot 5}{3 \cdot 5} = \dfrac{6}{15} + \dfrac{5}{15} = \dfrac{6+5}{15} = \dfrac{11}{15}$

$\dfrac{4}{7} - \dfrac{1}{2} = \dfrac{4 \cdot 2}{7 \cdot 2} - \dfrac{1 \cdot 7}{2 \cdot 7} = \dfrac{8}{14} - \dfrac{7}{14} = \dfrac{8-7}{14} = \dfrac{1}{14}$

Algebra $\dfrac{a}{b} + \dfrac{c}{d} = \dfrac{ad}{bd} + \dfrac{bc}{bd} = \dfrac{ad + bc}{bd}$ $\dfrac{a}{b} - \dfrac{c}{d} = \dfrac{ad}{bd} - \dfrac{bc}{bd} = \dfrac{ad - bc}{bd}$

EXAMPLE 1   Adding Fractions

FIND LCDS
Sometimes the LCD is the denominator of one of the fractions, as in part (a) of Example 1.

a. $\dfrac{2}{3} + \dfrac{1}{6}$

To find the LCD of the fractions, write the prime factorization of each denominator.

$3 = 3$

$6 = 2 \cdot 3$

So, the LCD is $2 \cdot 3 = 6$.

$\dfrac{2}{3} \cdot \dfrac{2}{2} = \dfrac{4}{6}$ $\dfrac{1}{6} \cdot \dfrac{1}{1} = \dfrac{1}{6}$

$\dfrac{4}{6} + \dfrac{1}{6} = \dfrac{4+1}{6} = \dfrac{5}{6}$

b. $\dfrac{7}{18} + \left(-\dfrac{5}{12}\right)$

To find the LCD of the fractions, write the prime factorization of each denominator.

$18 = 2 \cdot 3^2$

$12 = 2^2 \cdot 3$

So, the LCD is $2^2 \cdot 3^2 = 36$.

$\dfrac{7}{18} \cdot \dfrac{2}{2} = \dfrac{14}{36}$ $\dfrac{-5}{12} \cdot \dfrac{3}{3} = \dfrac{-15}{36}$

$\dfrac{14}{36} + \left(-\dfrac{15}{36}\right) = -\dfrac{1}{36}$

EXAMPLE 2 Subtracting Fractions

a. $\dfrac{3}{10} - \dfrac{5}{6}$

To find the LCD of the fractions, write the prime factorization of each denominator.

$$10 = 2 \cdot 5$$
$$6 = 2 \cdot 3$$

So, the LCD is $2 \cdot 3 \cdot 5 = 30$.

$$\dfrac{3}{10} \cdot \dfrac{\mathbf{3}}{\mathbf{3}} = \dfrac{9}{30} \qquad \dfrac{5}{6} \cdot \dfrac{\mathbf{5}}{\mathbf{5}} = \dfrac{25}{30}$$

$$\dfrac{9}{30} - \dfrac{25}{30} = -\dfrac{16}{30} = -\dfrac{8}{15}$$

b. $4 - \dfrac{7}{8}$

To find the LCD, write the prime factorization of each denominator.

$$1 = 1$$
$$8 = 2^3$$

So, the LCD is $2^3 = 8$.

$$\dfrac{4}{1} \cdot \dfrac{\mathbf{8}}{\mathbf{8}} = \dfrac{32}{8} \qquad \dfrac{7}{8} \cdot \dfrac{\mathbf{1}}{\mathbf{1}} = \dfrac{7}{8}$$

$$\dfrac{32}{8} - \dfrac{7}{8} = \dfrac{25}{8} = 3\dfrac{1}{8}$$

IDENTIFY DENOMINATORS

In part (b) of Example 2, note that the denominator of 4 is 1 because $4 = \dfrac{4}{1}$.

EXAMPLE 3 Modeling with Mixed Numbers

CARPENTRY A board is $36\dfrac{5}{8}$ inches long. You cut off a piece $12\dfrac{3}{4}$ inches long. The saw blade destroys an additional $\dfrac{1}{16}$ inch of wood, which is equal to the blade's width. What is the length of the remaining piece of wood?

Blade width = $\dfrac{1}{16}$ in.

$12\dfrac{3}{4}$ in.

SOLUTION

Remaining length	=	Original length	− (	Length cut off	+	Blade width	)

$$= 36\dfrac{5}{8} - \left(12\dfrac{3}{4} + \dfrac{1}{16}\right) \qquad \textbf{Write an algebraic model.}$$

$$= 36\dfrac{10}{16} - \left(12\dfrac{12}{16} + \dfrac{1}{16}\right) \qquad \textbf{Rewrite fractions using LCD of 16.}$$

$$= 36\dfrac{10}{16} - 12\dfrac{13}{16} \qquad \textbf{Add inside parentheses.}$$

$$= 35\dfrac{26}{16} - 12\dfrac{13}{16} \qquad \textbf{Rename } 36\dfrac{10}{16} \textbf{ as } 35\dfrac{26}{16}.$$

$$= (35 - 12) + \left(\dfrac{26}{16} - \dfrac{13}{16}\right) \qquad \begin{array}{l}\textbf{Write mixed numbers in expanded form}\\ \textbf{and use the commutative property.}\end{array}$$

$$= 23\dfrac{13}{16} \qquad \textbf{Subtract whole numbers and fractions.}$$

▶ **Answer** The remaining piece of wood is $23\dfrac{13}{16}$ inches long.

About the Standards

You can use estimation to check whether the sum or difference of mixed numbers is reasonable (MR 2.1). In Example 3,
$$36\dfrac{5}{8} - \left(12\dfrac{3}{4} + \dfrac{1}{16}\right) \approx$$
$$37 - 13 = 24.$$

Find the sum or difference. Then simplify if possible.

1. $-\dfrac{1}{3} + \dfrac{5}{9}$

2. $\dfrac{4}{5} + \dfrac{3}{10}$

3. $\dfrac{7}{12} + \dfrac{1}{4}$

4. $\dfrac{1}{3} - \dfrac{3}{8}$

5. $3 - \dfrac{9}{10}$

6. $\dfrac{5}{12} - \dfrac{7}{9}$

7. **WHAT IF?** In Example 3, suppose you cut $4\dfrac{5}{6}$ inches off the original piece of wood. What is the length of the remaining piece of wood?

2.4 EXERCISES

HOMEWORK
KEY

 = **MULTIPLE CHOICE PRACTICE**
Exs. 21, 22, 33, 43–45

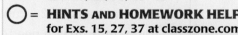 = **HINTS AND HOMEWORK HELP**
for Exs. 15, 27, 37 at classzone.com

SKILLS • PROBLEM SOLVING • REASONING

1. **VOCABULARY** Copy and complete: The ___?___ of $\dfrac{1}{8}$ and $\dfrac{1}{12}$ is 24.

2. **WRITING** *Describe* the procedure for adding two fractions that have different denominators.

**SEE EXAMPLES
1 AND 2**
on pp. 91–92
for Exs. 3–10

ADDING AND SUBTRACTING FRACTIONS **Find the sum or difference. Then simplify if possible.**

3. $\dfrac{1}{2} + \dfrac{1}{8}$

4. $\dfrac{7}{8} - \dfrac{1}{4}$

5. $\dfrac{1}{8} - 2$

6. $\dfrac{5}{18} + \dfrac{1}{6}$

7. $-\dfrac{7}{12} + \dfrac{4}{15}$

8. $-\dfrac{3}{8} + 1$

9. $\dfrac{5}{8} - \dfrac{2}{3}$

10. $\dfrac{1}{2} - \dfrac{7}{10}$

SEE EXAMPLE 3
on p. 92
for Exs. 11–18

11. $7\dfrac{4}{5} + 5\dfrac{3}{7}$

12. $12\dfrac{5}{18} - \dfrac{3}{4}$

13. $12 - 16\dfrac{3}{7}$

14. $-7\dfrac{3}{11} - (-8)$

15. $6\dfrac{2}{5} + 3\dfrac{2}{3}$

16. $3\dfrac{1}{7} - 6\dfrac{1}{4}$

17. $\dfrac{11}{12} - 2\dfrac{4}{5}$

18. $6\dfrac{2}{9} + 4\dfrac{5}{7}$

ERROR ANALYSIS *Describe* and correct the error in adding the fractions.

19.
✗ $\dfrac{1}{3} + \dfrac{1}{2} = \dfrac{1}{6} + \dfrac{1}{6}$
$= \dfrac{2}{6}$

20.
✗ $\dfrac{1}{5} + \dfrac{1}{2} = \dfrac{2}{10} + \dfrac{2}{10}$
$= \dfrac{4}{10}$

21. ◆ **MULTIPLE CHOICE** What is the value of $4 - 2\dfrac{3}{7}$?

Ⓐ $1\dfrac{3}{7}$ Ⓑ $1\dfrac{4}{7}$ Ⓒ $2\dfrac{3}{7}$ Ⓓ $2\dfrac{4}{7}$

22. ◆ **MULTIPLE CHOICE** What is the value of $\dfrac{5}{6} + \dfrac{1}{9} - \dfrac{2}{3}$?

Ⓐ $\dfrac{1}{6}$ Ⓑ $\dfrac{2}{9}$ Ⓒ $\dfrac{5}{18}$ Ⓓ $\dfrac{1}{3}$

REASONING Find the sum or difference. *Justify* each step.

23. $\frac{1}{4} - \frac{6}{7} + \frac{3}{14}$

24. $\frac{3}{4} + 2\frac{1}{2} - \frac{1}{4}$

25. $1\frac{1}{3} - \frac{2}{9} - \frac{5}{6}$

26. $\frac{4}{9} + \frac{7}{8} + \frac{1}{24}$

(27.) $3\frac{4}{9} - 1\frac{1}{2} - \frac{1}{3}$

28. $10\frac{7}{8} - 3\frac{1}{10} - 2\frac{1}{4}$

CONNECT SKILLS TO PROBLEM SOLVING Exercises 29–31 will help you prepare for problem solving.

29. The length of a stone wall will be 13 feet. You built $5\frac{3}{4}$ feet of the wall yesterday. How much of the wall do you have left to build?

30. You bike $1\frac{5}{8}$ miles from school to a store, and then you bike $2\frac{3}{4}$ miles from the store to your home. What is the total distance that you bike?

31. A recipe calls for $2\frac{2}{3}$ cups of milk. You only have $1\frac{1}{4}$ cups. How much more milk do you need?

SEE EXAMPLE 3
on p. 92
for Exs. 32–34

32. OLYMPIC SLEDDING What is the difference in the lengths of the skeleton sleds below?

$31\frac{1}{2}$ in. $47\frac{1}{4}$ in.

Skeleton sled

California **@HomeTutor** for problem solving help at classzone.com

33. ◆ **MULTIPLE CHOICE** A board $2\frac{1}{4}$ inches thick is placed on top of a board $\frac{5}{6}$ inch thick. What is the combined thickness of the boards?

(**A**) $1\frac{5}{12}$ in.   (**B**) $2\frac{1}{12}$ in.   (**C**) $2\frac{3}{5}$ in.   (**D**) $3\frac{1}{12}$ in.

California **@HomeTutor** for problem solving help at classzone.com

34. MULTI-STEP PROBLEM The table shows the results of an annual softball throwing contest. The player with the greatest combined distance wins.

a. Who won the contest?

b. What was the difference between the winner's combined distance and the third place player's combined distance?

	Distance Thrown (feet)		
	1st throw	**2nd throw**	**3rd throw**
Curtis	$151\frac{1}{3}$	$185\frac{1}{2}$	$180\frac{1}{4}$
Shane	$202\frac{1}{2}$	$154\frac{2}{3}$	$157\frac{3}{4}$
Dave	$171\frac{1}{3}$	$172\frac{3}{4}$	$167\frac{1}{6}$

c. What distance would the second place player need on his third throw to *tie* the winner's combined distance? *Explain* how you found your answer.

35. REASONING Is the sum of two mixed numbers always a mixed number? Give examples to justify your answer.

36. WRITING *Explain* how you could use improper fractions to find the length of the remaining piece of wood in Example 3.

37. EQUATOR The fractions in the diagram are fractions of the total distance around Earth on the equator.

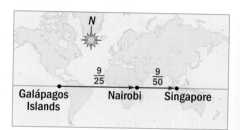

  a. What fraction of the equator do you cover if you travel east from the Galápagos Islands to Singapore?

  b. Is traveling from the Galápagos Islands to Singapore a shorter trip if you travel east or west? *Explain.*

38. PUZZLE PROBLEM You were assigned a research project to do in three weeks. In the first week, you completed $\frac{3}{7}$ of the project. In the second week, you completed $\frac{4}{9}$ of the project. How much of the project do you need to complete in the third week?

CHALLENGE *Describe* the pattern. Then write the next three fractions in the pattern.

39. $1\frac{7}{10}, 2, 2\frac{3}{10}, 2\frac{3}{5}, \ldots$ **40.** $5\frac{3}{4}, 4\frac{5}{8}, 3\frac{1}{2}, 2\frac{3}{8}, \ldots$ **41.** $\frac{11}{12}, \frac{19}{24}, \frac{2}{3}, \frac{13}{24}, \ldots$

42. CHALLENGE You put a cake in the oven to bake and notice that the hour hand on the oven's clock is broken. At the same time, you hear a radio announcer mention that it is 3:17 P.M. The minute hand on the clock makes $\frac{5}{8}$ revolution before you check the cake. The minute hand makes another $\frac{13}{24}$ revolution before you take the baked cake out of the oven. What time is it when the cake is done?

◆ CALIFORNIA STANDARDS SPIRAL REVIEW

NS 1.2 | **43.** What is the value of $-9(-7)(-2)$? *(p. 31)*

     (A) -126 **(B)** -18 **(C)** 81 **(D)** 126

NS 1.1 | **44.** Which list of fractions is in order from least to greatest? *(p. 80)*

     (A) $\frac{3}{5}, \frac{2}{3}, \frac{1}{2}$ **(B)** $-\frac{2}{9}, -\frac{3}{7}, -\frac{4}{5}$ **(C)** $\frac{1}{2}, \frac{4}{7}, \frac{11}{24}$ **(D)** $\frac{7}{10}, \frac{5}{7}, \frac{3}{4}$

NS 1.2 | **45.** Your friend has 2 pieces of ribbon, one measures $\frac{5}{8}$ feet and the other measures $\frac{3}{8}$ feet of ribbon. You have $\frac{7}{8}$ feet of ribbon. How many feet of ribbon do you have all together? *(p. 85)*

     (A) 1 ft   **(B)** $1\frac{2}{8}$ ft   **(C)** $1\frac{7}{8}$ ft   **(D)** $2\frac{1}{8}$ ft

MIXED REVIEW *of Skills and Problem Solving*

Multiple Choice Practice for Lessons 2.1–2.4

1. Which fraction is equivalent to $\frac{24}{42}$?
Gr. 6 NS 2.4

   (A) $\frac{3}{7}$ (B) $\frac{5}{9}$

   (C) $\frac{8}{14}$ (D) $\frac{32}{50}$

2. The Orb of 1661 is displayed in the Tower of London. It is set with 365 diamonds, 363 cultured pearls, 18 rubies, 9 emeralds, 9 sapphires, and 1 amethyst. What fraction of the jewels are emeralds? **Gr. 6 NS 2.4**

   (A) $\frac{1}{765}$ (B) $\frac{1}{85}$

   (C) $\frac{1}{9}$ (D) $\frac{9}{37}$

3. What is the value of $\frac{5}{7} + 1\frac{3}{7}$? **NS 1.2**

   (A) $1\frac{1}{7}$ (B) 2

   (C) $2\frac{1}{7}$ (D) $3\frac{1}{7}$

4. A fitness trail is broken into five segments, as shown below. You run the first segment of the trail, and walk the next. You continue to alternate between running and walking until you finish the trail.

How many miles did you run? **NS 2.2, MR 1.1**

   (A) $2\frac{1}{2}$ mi   (B) $3\frac{3}{4}$ mi

   (C) 4 mi   (D) 5 mi

5. The table shows the numbers of shots you made and attempted in five basketball games. In which game did you make the greatest fraction of your shots? **NS 1.1**

Game	1	2	3	4	5
Shots made	10	9	6	15	9
Attempts	22	12	18	25	18

   (A) 1   (B) 2

   (C) 4   (D) 5

6. What is the value of $\frac{1}{4} - \frac{2}{15}$? **NS 2.2**

   (A) $-\frac{1}{9}$ (B) $\frac{7}{60}$

   (C) $\frac{7}{15}$ (D) $\frac{13}{15}$

7. A dead tree is being cut down in three parts. The lengths of the first and second cuts are shown.

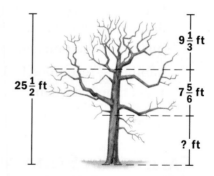

How many feet of the tree remain to be cut down? **NS 1.2, MR 2.3**

   (A) $8\frac{1}{3}$ ft   (B) $9\frac{1}{2}$ ft

   (C) $9\frac{2}{3}$ ft   (D) $10\frac{1}{6}$ ft

8. What is the value of $5 - \frac{3}{8}$? **NS 2.2**

   (A) $\frac{1}{4}$ (B) $4\frac{1}{4}$

   (C) $4\frac{1}{2}$ (D) $4\frac{5}{8}$

2.5 Modeling Fraction Multiplication

MATERIALS · paper · colored pencils

Standards

NS 1.2 Add, subtract, **multiply**, and divide **rational numbers** (integers, **fractions**, and terminating decimals) and take positive rational numbers to whole-number powers.

QUESTION How can you multiply two fractions?

You can use a paper-folding method to model two fractions so that you can determine their product.

EXPLORE Find the product $\frac{1}{2} \cdot \frac{1}{3}$

STEP 1 **Fold** a piece of paper in half horizontally. Unfold the paper and shade one of the halves red.

Fold. Open. Shade.

STEP 2 **Fold** the paper vertically into thirds. Unfold the paper and shade one of the thirds blue.

Fold. Open. Shade.

STEP 3 **Find** the product of the fractions. The product is represented by the portion shaded with both colors. Because this is one of six equal portions, $\frac{1}{2} \cdot \frac{1}{3} = \frac{1}{6}$.

DRAW CONCLUSIONS Use your observations to complete these exercises

1. Use the paper-folding method shown above to find the product.

   a. $\frac{1}{2} \cdot \frac{1}{4}$ **b.** $\frac{1}{3} \cdot \frac{2}{3}$ **c.** $\frac{2}{3} \cdot \frac{2}{3}$ **d.** $\frac{2}{3} \cdot \frac{3}{4}$

2. Look for a pattern in the products you have found using the paper folding method. Use the pattern to complete the following rule:

$$\frac{a}{b} \cdot \frac{c}{d} = \underline{\ ?\ }$$

3. **REASONING** Can the product of two fractions between 0 and 1 be greater than either of the two fractions? Use the paper-folding method to explain your answer.

2.5 Multiplying Fractions

Standards

NS 1.2 Add, subtract, **multiply**, and divide **rational numbers** (integers, **fractions**, and terminating decimals) and **take positive rational numbers to whole-number powers**.

AF 1.3 **Simplify numerical expressions by applying properties of rational numbers** (e.g., identity, **inverse**, distributive, associative, commutative) and justify the process used.

Math and
GRAPHIC DESIGN
Example 3, p. 100

Connect *Before* you added and subtracted fractions and mixed numbers. *Now* you will multiply fractions and mixed numbers.

KEY VOCABULARY
- **multiplicative inverse**
- **numerator,** *p. 727*
- **denominator,** *p. 727*

You can use the model at the right or the rule below to find the product of two fractions such as $\frac{5}{8}$ and $\frac{3}{4}$. The blue region of the model represents $\frac{5}{8}$. The red region represents $\frac{3}{4}$.

Because 15 of the 32 rectangles in the model are shaded both red and blue, the product is $\frac{15}{32}$.

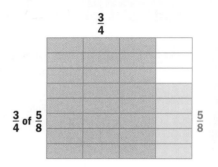

$\frac{3}{4}$ of $\frac{5}{8}$

KEY CONCEPT   *For Your Notebook*

Multiplying Fractions

Words   The product of two or more fractions is equal to the product of the numerators divided by the product of the denominators.

Numbers $\frac{3}{4} \cdot \frac{5}{8} = \frac{3 \cdot 5}{4 \cdot 8} = \frac{15}{32}$ **Algebra** $\frac{a}{b} \cdot \frac{c}{d} = \frac{a \cdot c}{b \cdot d} \ (b, d \neq 0)$

EXAMPLE 1   Multiplying Fractions

AVOID ERRORS
Remember that the product of two numbers with the same sign is positive. The product of two numbers with different signs is negative.

a. $-\frac{2}{5} \cdot \left(-\frac{2}{3}\right) = \frac{-2 \cdot (-2)}{5 \cdot 3}$ **Use rule for multiplying fractions.**

$= \frac{4}{15}$ **Evaluate numerator and denominator.**

b. $-\frac{3}{10} \cdot \frac{5}{6} = \frac{-3 \cdot 5}{10 \cdot 6}$ **Use rule for multiplying fractions.**

$= \frac{\overset{-1}{\cancel{-3}} \cdot \overset{1}{\cancel{5}}}{\underset{2}{\cancel{10}} \cdot \underset{2}{\cancel{6}}}$ **Divide out common factors.**

$= -\frac{1}{4}$ **Multiply.**

MULTIPLICATIVE INVERSES The **multiplicative inverse** of a nonzero number a is the number that, when multiplied by a, gives a product of 1. The multiplicative inverse of a can be written as $\frac{1}{a}$.

For example, 3 and $\frac{1}{3}$ are multiplicative inverses because $3 \cdot \frac{1}{3} = 1$. Zero does not have a multiplicative inverse because there is no number z for which $0 \cdot z = 1$.

KEY CONCEPT   *For Your Notebook*

Inverse Property of Multiplication

Words   The product of a nonzero number and its multiplicative inverse is 1.

Algebra $a \cdot \dfrac{1}{a} = \dfrac{1}{a} \cdot a = 1$, where $a \neq 0$

Example $8 \cdot \dfrac{1}{8} = \dfrac{1}{8} \cdot 8 = 1$

Note that fractions of the form $\frac{a}{b}$ and $\frac{b}{a}$ are multiplicative inverses where $a \neq 0$ and $b \neq 0$.

$$\frac{a}{b} \cdot \frac{b}{a} = \frac{\overset{1}{\cancel{a}} \cdot \overset{1}{\cancel{b}}}{\underset{1}{\cancel{b}} \cdot \underset{1}{\cancel{a}}} = 1$$

EXAMPLE 2   ◆ **Multiple Choice Practice**

> What is the value of $\dfrac{3}{4} \cdot \dfrac{1}{8} \cdot \dfrac{4}{3}$?
>
> **(A)** $\dfrac{1}{24}$ **(B)** $\dfrac{1}{8}$ **(C)** $\dfrac{3}{8}$ **(D)** 1

SOLUTION

$\dfrac{3}{4} \cdot \dfrac{1}{8} \cdot \dfrac{4}{3} = \dfrac{3}{4} \cdot \dfrac{4}{3} \cdot \dfrac{1}{8}$ **Commutative property of multiplication**

$= 1 \cdot \dfrac{1}{8}$ **Inverse property of multiplication**

$= \dfrac{1}{8}$ **Identity property of multiplication**

▶ **Answer** The correct answer is B. Ⓐ **Ⓑ** Ⓒ Ⓓ

✓ **GUIDED PRACTICE**   for Examples 1 and 2

Find the product. Simplify if possible.

1. $-\dfrac{5}{12} \cdot \dfrac{9}{10}$ **2.** $-\dfrac{5}{6} \cdot \left(-\dfrac{7}{9}\right)$ **3.** $\dfrac{4}{5} \cdot \dfrac{5}{4}$ **4.** $7 \cdot \dfrac{3}{5} \cdot \dfrac{1}{7}$

MIXED NUMBERS To multiply mixed numbers, first write them as improper fractions.

EXAMPLE 3 Multiplying Mixed Numbers

POSTCARDS A designer creates postcards that are $5\frac{1}{2}$ inches long and $3\frac{3}{4}$ inches wide. Find the area of the postcard.

$3\frac{3}{4}$ in.

FINDING AREA

For help with finding area, see p. 742.

SOLUTION

Area $=$ Length $\cdot$ Width	Write area formula.
$= 5\frac{1}{2} \cdot 3\frac{3}{4}$	Substitute values.
$= \frac{11}{2} \cdot \frac{15}{4}$	Write as improper fractions.
$= \frac{11 \cdot 15}{2 \cdot 4}$	Use rule for multiplying fractions.
$= \frac{165}{8}$	Multiply.
$= 20\frac{5}{8}$	Write as a mixed number.

$5\frac{1}{2}$ in.

▶ **Answer** The area of a postcard is $20\frac{5}{8}$ square inches.

EXAMPLE 4 Using an Algebraic Expression

COSTUMES You are making costumes for a school play. Each costume requires $2\frac{2}{9}$ yards of fabric. Evaluate $2\frac{2}{9} \cdot x$ when $x = 3$ to determine how many yards of fabric you need to make 3 costumes.

ANOTHER WAY

For an alternative method for solving the problem in Example 4, turn to page 105 for the **Problem Solving Workshop**.

SOLUTION

$2\frac{2}{9} \cdot x = 2\frac{2}{9} \cdot 3$	Substitute 3 for x.
$= \frac{20}{9} \cdot \frac{3}{1}$	Write as improper fractions.
$= \frac{20 \cdot 3}{9 \cdot 1}$	Use rule for multiplying fractions.
$= \frac{20 \cdot \overset{1}{\cancel{3}}}{\underset{3}{\cancel{9}} \cdot 1}$	Divide out common factors.
$= \frac{20}{3}$	Multiply.
$= 6\frac{2}{3}$	Write as a mixed number.

▶ **Answer** You need $6\frac{2}{3}$ yards of fabric to make 3 costumes.

EXAMPLE 5 **Evaluating an Algebraic Expression**

Evaluate x^2y when $x = -2\frac{1}{3}$ and $y = \frac{3}{4}$.

$$x^2y = \left(-2\frac{1}{3}\right)^2\left(\frac{3}{4}\right) \qquad \text{Substitute } -2\frac{1}{3} \text{ for } x \text{ and } \frac{3}{4} \text{ for } y.$$

$$= \left(-\frac{7}{3}\right)^2\left(\frac{3}{4}\right) \qquad \text{Write } -2\frac{1}{3} \text{ as an improper fraction.}$$

$$= \left(-\frac{7}{3}\right)\left(-\frac{7}{3}\right)\left(\frac{3}{4}\right) \qquad \text{Write } -\frac{7}{3} \text{ as a factor 2 times.}$$

$$= \frac{(-7) \cdot (-7) \cdot 3}{3 \cdot 3 \cdot 4} \qquad \text{Use rule for multiplying fractions.}$$

$$= \frac{(-7) \cdot (-7) \cdot \cancel{3}^{\,1}}{3 \cdot \cancel{3} \cdot 4}_{\,1} \qquad \text{Divide out common factors.}$$

$$= \frac{49}{12} \qquad \text{Multiply.}$$

$$= 4\frac{1}{12} \qquad \text{Write as a mixed number.}$$

✔ **GUIDED PRACTICE** for Examples 3, 4, and 5

Find the product. Simplify if possible.

5. $1\frac{2}{5} \cdot 3\frac{1}{2}$ **6.** $5\frac{1}{2} \cdot \left(-1\frac{5}{6}\right)$ **7.** $-5\frac{3}{4} \cdot 2\frac{3}{5}$ **8.** $-2\frac{1}{3} \cdot \left(-\frac{3}{4}\right)$

9. **WHAT IF?** In Example 4, how many yards of fabric would be needed to make 5 costumes?

Evaluate the expression when $x = -\frac{3}{4}$ and $y = 1\frac{5}{6}$.

10. $\frac{2}{3}x$ **11.** $2y$ **12.** xy **13.** xy^2

2.5 EXERCISES

HOMEWORK KEY

◆ = **MULTIPLE CHOICE PRACTICE**
Exs. 3, 16, 53, 63–65

○ = **HINTS AND HOMEWORK HELP**
for Exs. 9, 19, 55 at classzone.com

SKILLS • PROBLEM SOLVING • REASONING

1. VOCABULARY Copy and complete: The fraction $\frac{1}{8}$ is the __?__ of 8.

2. WRITING *Explain* how to multiply fractions.

SEE EXAMPLES
1 AND 2
....
on pp. 98–99
for Exs. 3–16

3. ◆ **MULTIPLE CHOICE** What is the value of $\frac{2}{7} \cdot \frac{9}{11}$?

(**A**) $\frac{14}{99}$ (**B**) $\frac{18}{77}$ (**C**) $\frac{22}{63}$ (**D**) $\frac{63}{22}$

MULTIPLYING FRACTIONS **Find the product. Simplify if possible.**

4. $\dfrac{5}{8} \cdot \dfrac{7}{16}$

5. $-\dfrac{9}{4} \cdot \dfrac{5}{6}$

6. $\dfrac{7}{11} \cdot \dfrac{5}{6}$

7. $\dfrac{3}{2} \cdot \dfrac{2}{3}$

8. $\dfrac{4}{5} \cdot \dfrac{3}{10}$

(9.) $-\dfrac{3}{4} \cdot \left(-\dfrac{2}{9}\right)$

10. $\dfrac{7}{8} \cdot \dfrac{8}{7}$

11. $-\dfrac{5}{6} \cdot \dfrac{5}{12}$

12. $4 \cdot \dfrac{5}{6} \cdot \dfrac{1}{4}$

13. $\dfrac{5}{7} \cdot \dfrac{2}{9} \cdot \dfrac{7}{5}$

14. $\dfrac{4}{3} \cdot \dfrac{3}{5} \cdot \dfrac{1}{2}$

15. $-\dfrac{4}{5} \cdot -\dfrac{3}{4} \cdot \dfrac{5}{4}$

16. ◆ **MULTIPLE CHOICE** Which operation with a nonzero number will always result in a value of 1?

    (A) Multiplying by the multiplicative inverse

    (B) Multiplying by 1

    (C) Multiplying by 0

    (D) Adding the additive inverse

SEE EXAMPLE 3
on p. 100
for Exs. 17–27

MULTIPLYING MIXED NUMBERS **Find the product. Simplify if possible.**

17. $-4 \cdot 2\dfrac{9}{16}$

18. $6\dfrac{3}{16} \cdot \left(-3\dfrac{1}{5}\right)$

(19.) $-9\dfrac{2}{7} \cdot 1\dfrac{2}{5}$

20. $5\dfrac{2}{3} \cdot (-6)$

21. $-4\dfrac{2}{7} \cdot \dfrac{3}{5}$

22. $4 \cdot 8\dfrac{1}{4}$

23. $1\dfrac{2}{9} \cdot \dfrac{3}{8}$

24. $-\dfrac{1}{9} \cdot 9\dfrac{3}{7}$

GEOMETRY **Find the area of the figure.**

25.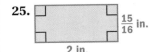

$\dfrac{15}{16}$ in.

2 in.

26.

$\dfrac{3}{4}$ ft

$1\dfrac{1}{2}$ ft

27.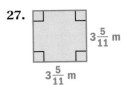

$3\dfrac{5}{11}$ m

$3\dfrac{5}{11}$ m

ERROR ANALYSIS *Describe* and correct the error in multiplying.

28.

✗ $\dfrac{2}{3} \cdot \dfrac{4}{5} = \dfrac{10}{12}$

    $= \dfrac{5}{6}$

29.

✗ $2\dfrac{2}{3} \cdot 3\dfrac{3}{4} = 2 \cdot 3 + \dfrac{2}{3} \cdot \dfrac{3}{4}$

    $= 6 + \dfrac{6}{12}$

    $= 6\dfrac{1}{2}$

SEE EXAMPLES 4 AND 5
on pp. 100–101
for Exs. 30–41

ALGEBRA **Evaluate the expression when** $a = \dfrac{5}{8}, b = -\dfrac{7}{6},$ **and** $c = -1\dfrac{1}{2}.$

30. ac

31. bc

32. ab^2

33. $16c^3$

34. ab

35. $36b^2$

36. abc

37. $16ac$

38. $a + b - c$

39. $4c + 2a$

40. $ab - c$

41. $7 - b$

EVALUATING EXPRESSIONS **Evaluate the expression.**

42. $\dfrac{2}{5} \cdot 1\dfrac{1}{5} \cdot \left(-4\dfrac{7}{12}\right)$

43. $-\dfrac{7}{8} + 5\dfrac{1}{2} \cdot \dfrac{11}{15}$

44. $\dfrac{5}{2} \cdot \left(\dfrac{8}{9} - \dfrac{5}{12}\right)$

45. $5 - \left(\dfrac{1}{3} + \dfrac{1}{6}\right)^2$

46. $4 - \left(\dfrac{1}{4} + \dfrac{7}{8}\right)^3$

47. $\dfrac{2}{3}\left(\dfrac{3}{5} - \dfrac{7}{12}\right)$

48. $\dfrac{-7}{16} + 8\dfrac{1}{3} \cdot \dfrac{3}{5}$

49. $\dfrac{2}{9}\left(-2\dfrac{1}{5}\right)\left(3\dfrac{3}{10}\right)$

◆ = **MULTIPLE CHOICE PRACTICE**   ○ = **HINTS AND HOMEWORK HELP** at classzone.com

CONNECT SKILLS TO PROBLEM SOLVING Exercises 50–52 will help you prepare for problem solving.

50. Moltke Crater is a crater on the moon that is 7 kilometers wide. Its depth is $\frac{1}{5}$ of its width. What is its depth?

51. Leisha hits a baseball 224 feet. Lamont hits a baseball $\frac{7}{8}$ as far. How far does Lamont hit the ball?

52. A tree that was $6\frac{1}{2}$ feet tall grows to $\frac{5}{4}$ of that height. How tall is it now?

SEE EXAMPLE 3
on p. 100
for Exs. 53–54

53. ◆ **MULTIPLE CHOICE** A poster measures $8\frac{1}{2}$ inches by 11 inches. You enlarge it by increasing each dimension by a factor of $1\frac{1}{2}$. What is the area of the new poster?

   (A) $93\frac{1}{2}$ in.²   (B) $140\frac{1}{4}$ in.²   (C) $210\frac{3}{8}$ in.²   (D) $280\frac{1}{2}$ in.²

California **@HomeTutor** for problem solving help at classzone.com

54. COOKING A recipe requires $\frac{3}{4}$ cup of sugar and $2\frac{1}{2}$ cups of flour. If you halve the recipe, how much sugar and flour do you need?

California **@HomeTutor** for problem solving help at classzone.com

55. COMPUTERS One of the first computers, the ENIAC, took $\frac{1}{5000}$ second to perform one operation. Use this fact to complete the table.

Number of operations	10,000	15,000	20,000
Time (seconds)	?	?	?

56. MULTI-STEP PROBLEM You are making a mosaic using square tiles that measure $\frac{2}{5}$ inch by $\frac{2}{5}$ inch.

  a. Find the area (in square inches) covered by one tile.

  b. Find the area (in square inches) covered by 1000 tiles.

  c. Multiply your answer to part (b) by $\frac{1}{144}$ to find the area in square feet covered by 1000 tiles.

57. PUZZLE PROBLEM Margie is $\frac{3}{4}$ as old as Rick. Four years ago, Rick was 12 years old. How old is Margie now?

58. EXERCISING You ride a bike three times per week for exercise. On Mondays and Tuesdays, you bike for $\frac{3}{4}$ hour, and on Thursdays you bike for $\frac{11}{4}$ hours. If you burn about 450 calories per biking hour, how many calories do you burn per week from biking?

Mosaic tiles

59. COMMUTING Only $\frac{1}{5}$ of employees who work downtown drive to work. Of those who do not drive, $\frac{3}{16}$ ride bicycles to work. What fraction of employees ride bicycles to work?

60. OPEN-ENDED *Describe* a real-life situation that can be modeled by the expression $\frac{1}{2}\left(\frac{4}{9}x\right)$.

61. CHALLENGE List the expressions, $-b^2 + 2ac$, $-a + 5c$, and a^2bc, in the order of their values from least to greatest when $a = 2\frac{3}{4}$, $b = \frac{2}{3}$, and $c = 3$.

62. CHALLENGE For a petition to be presented to the student council, $\frac{1}{8}$ of the student and teacher population of 1200 must sign the petition. Also, $\frac{1}{25}$ of the signatures must be from teachers. A petition currently has 150 signatures of which $\frac{73}{75}$ are student signatures. Can this petition be presented? *Explain.*

◆ CALIFORNIA STANDARDS SPIRAL REVIEW

AF 1.2

63. What is the value of $16 + (x - x \div 3) + 5$ when $x = 6$? *(p. 5)*

   (A) 14   **(B)** 17   **(C)** 21   **(D)** 25

AF 1.3

64. Which statement illustrates the distributive property? *(p. 48)*

   (A) $3 + (-3) = 0$ **(B)** $4 \cdot (25 \cdot 3) = (4 \cdot 25) \cdot 3$

   (C) $9(x - 4) = 9x - 36$ **(D)** $2(3 \cdot 4) = 3 \cdot 4 + 3 \cdot 4$

NS 1.2

65. The grass on a golf course fairway is $\frac{2}{3}$ inch high. It needs to be $\frac{3}{8}$ inch high. How much shorter does the grass need to be? *(p. 91)*

   (A) $\frac{1}{12}$ in.   **(B)** $\frac{5}{24}$ in.   **(C)** $\frac{1}{4}$ in.   **(D)** $\frac{7}{24}$ in.

QUIZ *for Lessons 2.3–2.5*

Find the sum or difference. Simplify if possible.

1. $\frac{5}{8} - \frac{7}{8}$ *(p. 85)*   **2.** $-\frac{4}{9} + \frac{5}{9}$ *(p. 85)*   **3.** $1\frac{5}{12} + \frac{11}{12}$ *(p. 85)*   **4.** $\frac{4}{9} - \frac{8}{9} + \frac{5}{9}$ *(p. 85)*

5. $\frac{2}{3} + \frac{3}{2}$ *(p. 91)*   **6.** $-\frac{3}{4} + \left(-\frac{5}{6}\right)$ *(p. 91)*   **7.** $-5\frac{3}{4} - 2\frac{1}{3}$ *(p. 91)*   **8.** $\frac{3}{10} + \frac{2}{5} - \frac{1}{2}$ *(p. 91)*

Find the product. Simplify if possible. *(p. 98)*

9. $\frac{7}{2} \cdot \frac{8}{21}$ **10.** $-\frac{11}{12} \cdot \left(-\frac{3}{10}\right)$ **11.** $-\frac{14}{5} \cdot 2\frac{6}{7}$ **12.** $1\frac{1}{8} \cdot (-3)$

13. RECIPE A recipe uses $4\frac{2}{3}$ cups of flour. You have 9 cups of flour. Do you have enough flour to double the recipe? *Explain.* *(p. 98)*

Using ALTERNATIVE METHODS

Another Way to Solve Example 4, page 100

Standards
NS 1.2, AF 1.3

Example 4 on page 100 was solved by first writing the mixed number and integer as improper fractions, and then multiplying. You can also solve this problem by using the distributive property.

PROBLEM

COSTUMES You are making costumes for a school play. Each costume requires $2\frac{2}{9}$ yards of fabric. Evaluate $2\frac{2}{9} \cdot x$ when $x = 3$ to determine how many yards of fabric you need to make 3 costumes.

METHOD

Using the Distributive Property You can use the distributive property to find the product of a whole number and a mixed number.

$$2\frac{2}{9} \cdot x = 2\frac{2}{9} \cdot 3 \qquad \text{Substitute 3 for } x.$$

$$= 3 \cdot 2\frac{2}{9} \qquad \text{Commutative property}$$

$$= 3\left(2 + \frac{2}{9}\right) \qquad \text{Rewrite mixed number.}$$

$$= 6 + \frac{6}{9} \qquad \text{Distributive property}$$

$$= 6 + \frac{2}{3} \qquad \text{Write } \frac{6}{9} \text{ in simplest form.}$$

$$= 6\frac{2}{3} \qquad \text{Add.}$$

▶ **Answer** You need $6\frac{2}{3}$ yards of fabric to make 3 costumes.

PRACTICE

MULTIPLYING FRACTIONS Use two methods to find the product.

1. $5 \cdot 4\frac{1}{8}$

2. $6 \cdot 4\frac{3}{10}$

3. $\frac{1}{2} \cdot 6\frac{1}{4}$

4. $\frac{3}{5} \cdot 2\frac{1}{8}$

5. **CANDLES** You are carrying a bag that holds 4 candles weighing $1\frac{1}{8}$ pounds each. What is the total weight of the candles? Solve this problem using two different methods.

6. **LANDSCAPING** You stack 6 rows of bricks to form a wall around a garden. Each row is $2\frac{2}{3}$ inches high. Use two different methods to find the height of the wall.

7. **TRUCK WEIGHT** A truck is carrying 5 new cars of the same model. The weight of each car is $1\frac{3}{4}$ tons. What is the total weight of the cars? If the truck weighs $17\frac{9}{20}$ tons, what is the total weight of the truck and the cars?

2.6 Dividing Fractions

Standards

NS 1.2 Add, subtract, multiply, and **divide rational numbers** (integers, **fractions,** and terminating decimals) and take positive rational numbers to whole-number powers.

AF 1.3 Simplify numerical expressions by applying properties of rational numbers (e.g., identity, **inverse**, distributive, associative, commutative) **and justify the process used.**

Connect   *Before* you added, subtracted, and multiplied fractions and mixed numbers. *Now* you will divide fractions and mixed numbers.

Math and ANIMAL CARE
Ex. 56, p. 110

KEY VOCABULARY
• reciprocal

ACTIVITY

You can use models to divide fractions.

STEP 1   **Model** $6 \div \frac{3}{4} = 8$ to show that $\frac{3}{4}$ is a part of 6 eight times.

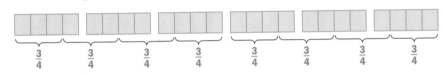

$$\frac{3}{4} \quad \frac{3}{4} \quad \frac{3}{4} \quad \frac{3}{4} \quad \frac{3}{4} \quad \frac{3}{4} \quad \frac{3}{4} \quad \frac{3}{4}$$

STEP 2   **Calculate** $6 \cdot \frac{4}{3}$. Compare the values of $6 \div \frac{3}{4}$ and $6 \cdot \frac{4}{3}$.

STEP 3   **Copy** and use the model below to evaluate $4 \div \frac{2}{5}$.

STEP 4   **Calculate** $4 \cdot \frac{5}{2}$. Compare the values of $4 \div \frac{2}{5}$ and $4 \cdot \frac{5}{2}$.

RECIPROCALS As the activity suggests, dividing a number by a fraction and multiplying the number by the fraction's multiplicative inverse give the same result. The multiplicative inverse of a number is also called the **reciprocal** of the number.

KEY CONCEPT   *For Your Notebook*

Dividing Fractions

Words   To divide by a fraction, multiply by its reciprocal.

Numbers $\frac{3}{10} \div \frac{4}{7} = \frac{3}{10} \cdot \frac{7}{4} = \frac{21}{40}$

Algebra $\frac{a}{b} \div \frac{c}{d} = \frac{a}{b} \cdot \frac{d}{c}$ $(b, c, d \neq 0)$

EXAMPLE 1 Dividing a Fraction by a Fraction

a. $\dfrac{5}{6} \div \dfrac{10}{21} = \dfrac{5}{6} \cdot \dfrac{21}{10}$

$= \dfrac{\overset{1}{\cancel{5}} \cdot \overset{7}{\cancel{21}}}{\underset{2}{\cancel{6}} \cdot \underset{2}{\cancel{10}}}$

$= \dfrac{7}{4},\ \text{or } 1\dfrac{3}{4}$

b. $\dfrac{9}{14} \div \dfrac{-2}{7} = \dfrac{9}{14} \cdot \dfrac{7}{-2}$

$= \dfrac{9 \cdot \overset{1}{\cancel{7}}}{\underset{2}{\cancel{14}} \cdot (-2)}$

$= \dfrac{9}{-4},\ \text{or } -2\dfrac{1}{4}$

EXAMPLE 2 Dividing a Fraction by an Integer

TRAIL MIX You are making 5 bag lunches. You have $\dfrac{3}{4}$ pound of trail mix to divide equally. How much mix should you put in each lunch?

SOLUTION

$\dfrac{3}{4} \div 5 = \dfrac{3}{4} \cdot \dfrac{1}{5}$ $5 \cdot \dfrac{1}{5} = 1$, so the reciprocal of 5 is $\dfrac{1}{5}$.

$\qquad\quad = \dfrac{3 \cdot 1}{4 \cdot 5}$ Use rule for multiplying fractions.

$\qquad\quad = \dfrac{3}{20}$ Multiply.

▶ **Answer** You should put $\dfrac{3}{20}$ pound of trail mix in each lunch.

✓ **GUIDED PRACTICE** for Examples 1 and 2

Find the quotient. Simplify if possible.

1. $\dfrac{5}{8} \div \left(-\dfrac{7}{10}\right)$ **2.** $\dfrac{2}{15} \div 8$ **3.** $-\dfrac{3}{4} \div \dfrac{-7}{12}$ **4.** $\dfrac{6}{7} \div 2$

5. **WHAT IF?** In Example 2, suppose you are making 6 bag lunches. How much mix should you put in each lunch?

EXAMPLE 3 Dividing Mixed Numbers

$6\dfrac{1}{3} \div \left(-2\dfrac{5}{6}\right) = \dfrac{19}{3} \div \left(-\dfrac{17}{6}\right)$ Write $6\dfrac{1}{3}$ and $-2\dfrac{5}{6}$ as improper fractions.

$\qquad\qquad\qquad = \dfrac{19}{3} \cdot \left(-\dfrac{6}{17}\right)$ Multiply by $-\dfrac{6}{17}$ the reciprocal of $-\dfrac{17}{6}$.

$\qquad\qquad\qquad = \dfrac{19 \cdot (-6)}{3 \cdot 17}$ Use rule for multiplying fractions.

$\qquad\qquad\qquad = \dfrac{19 \cdot \overset{-2}{\cancel{(-6)}}}{\underset{1}{\cancel{3}} \cdot 17}$ Divide out common factor.

$\qquad\qquad\qquad = -\dfrac{38}{17},\ \text{or } -2\dfrac{4}{17}$ Multiply.

EXAMPLE 4 Simplify an Expression with Fractions

$$\frac{\left(\frac{2}{3}\right)^2\left(\frac{1}{5}\right)}{\left(\frac{2}{7}\right)} = \frac{\left(\frac{4}{9}\right)\left(\frac{1}{5}\right)}{\left(\frac{2}{7}\right)}$$ Evaluate power.

$$= \frac{\left(\frac{4}{45}\right)}{\left(\frac{2}{7}\right)}$$ Multiply the fractions in the numerator.

$$= \frac{\overset{2}{\cancel{4}}}{45} \cdot \frac{7}{\underset{1}{\cancel{2}}}$$ Rewrite as a product. Divide out common factor.

$$= \frac{14}{45}$$ Multiply.

✓ **GUIDED PRACTICE**   for Examples 3 and 4

Find the quotient. Simplify if possible.

6. $6\frac{2}{7} \div 4$ **7.** $-12\frac{1}{4} \div 7$ **8.** $10 \div 3\frac{1}{3}$ **9.** $-15\frac{3}{4} \div 2\frac{5}{8}$

10. Simplify the expression $\dfrac{\left(\frac{1}{4}\right)\left(\frac{3}{5}\right)}{\left(\frac{5}{6}\right)}$.

2.6 EXERCISES

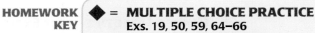

HOMEWORK
KEY

◆ = **MULTIPLE CHOICE PRACTICE**
    Exs. 19, 50, 59, 64–66

○ = **HINTS AND HOMEWORK HELP**
    for Exs. 9, 45, 59 at classzone.com

SKILLS • PROBLEM SOLVING • REASONING

1. VOCABULARY What is the reciprocal of $\frac{a}{b}$ if both a and b do not equal zero?

2. WRITING How are the reciprocal of a nonzero number and the multiplicative inverse of the number related?

RECIPROCALS Write the reciprocal of the number.

3. $\frac{1}{2}$ **4.** $\frac{4}{7}$ **5.** -8 **6.** $1\frac{1}{2}$

SEE EXAMPLES
1 AND 2
on p. 107
for Exs. 7–29

DIVIDING FRACTIONS Find the quotient. Simplify if possible.

7. $\frac{3}{4} \div \frac{1}{8}$ **8.** $\frac{11}{12} \div \frac{11}{16}$ **9.** $\frac{5}{6} \div \left(-\frac{1}{3}\right)$ **10.** $-\frac{7}{10} \div \frac{4}{5}$

11. $\frac{4}{9} \div \frac{4}{7}$ **12.** $-\frac{3}{8} \div \frac{7}{12}$ **13.** $\frac{9}{14} \div \left(-\frac{3}{26}\right)$ **14.** $-\frac{21}{22} \div \frac{-7}{11}$

15. $-\frac{5}{6} \div (-2)$ **16.** $\frac{2}{3} \div 3$ **17.** $\frac{3}{5} \div (-4)$ **18.** $-\frac{8}{5} \div 12$

19. ◆ **MULTIPLE CHOICE** What is the value of $\frac{2}{3} \div \frac{1}{8}$?

    (A) $\frac{1}{12}$ **(B)** $\frac{3}{16}$ **(C)** $1\frac{1}{2}$ **(D)** $5\frac{1}{3}$

ERROR ANALYSIS *Describe* and correct the error in dividing the fractions.

20.
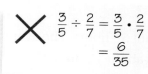
$$\frac{3}{5} \div \frac{2}{7} = \frac{3}{5} \cdot \frac{2}{7}$$
$$= \frac{6}{35}$$

21.
$$\frac{3}{10} \div \frac{4}{5} = \frac{\overset{2}{\cancel{10}}}{3} \cdot \frac{4}{\underset{1}{\cancel{5}}}$$
$$= \frac{8}{3}, \text{ or } 2\frac{2}{3}$$

MENTAL MATH Use mental math to find the quotient.

22. $\frac{1}{2} \div 3$ **23.** $4 \div \frac{1}{2}$ **24.** $1 \div \frac{4}{7}$ **25.** $\frac{2}{3} \div \frac{3}{2}$

26. $9 \div \frac{1}{3}$ **27.** $\frac{5}{6} \div \frac{6}{5}$ **28.** $6 \div \frac{2}{3}$ **29.** $10 \div \frac{1}{10}$

SEE EXAMPLE 3
on p. 107
for Exs. 30–41

DIVIDING MIXED NUMBERS Find the quotient. Simplify if possible.

30. $5\frac{1}{4} \div 2\frac{1}{3}$ **31.** $12\frac{1}{7} \div 5\frac{5}{6}$ **32.** $7\frac{7}{8} \div \left(-2\frac{1}{4}\right)$ **33.** $-22\frac{2}{3} \div 3\frac{1}{5}$

34. $-8 \div -9\frac{3}{5}$ **35.** $8\frac{4}{13} \div 6\frac{3}{4}$ **36.** $1\frac{5}{7} \div (-6)$ **37.** $15 \div 4\frac{1}{6}$

38. $2 \div 1\frac{1}{3}$ **39.** $6\frac{4}{7} \div (-4)$ **40.** $13\frac{1}{6} \div \frac{2}{5}$ **41.** $-9\frac{5}{6} \div 1\frac{2}{3}$

SEE EXAMPLE 4
on p. 108
for Exs. 42–49

SIMPLIFYING EXPRESSIONS Simplify the expression.

42. $\dfrac{\left(\frac{2}{5}\right)}{\left(\frac{4}{5}\right)}$ **43.** $\dfrac{\left(-\frac{3}{5}\right)}{\left(\frac{4}{5}\right)}$ **44.** $\dfrac{-\left(\frac{2}{3}\right)\left(\frac{3}{5}\right)}{\left(\frac{4}{5}\right)}$ **(45.)** $\dfrac{\left(\frac{2}{5}\right)^2}{\left(\frac{1}{4}\right)\left(\frac{3}{5}\right)}$

46. $\dfrac{\left(\frac{1}{3}\right)^2\left(\frac{2}{5}\right)}{\left(\frac{3}{7}\right)}$ **47.** $\dfrac{-\left(\frac{2}{7}\right)}{\left(\frac{2}{5}\right)\left(\frac{1}{2}\right)}$ **48.** $\dfrac{\left(\frac{3}{8}\right)\left(\frac{4}{5}\right)^2}{\left(\frac{2}{3}\right)}$ **49.** $\dfrac{\left(-\frac{1}{8}\right)\left(-\frac{4}{9}\right)}{\left(\frac{1}{5}\right)^2}$

50. ◆ **MULTIPLE CHOICE** By what do you multiply $\frac{5}{6}$ to get -15?

    (A) -18 **(B)** $-\frac{6}{5}$ **(C)** $\frac{6}{5}$ **(D)** 18

INTERPRETING MODELS Write and evaluate the division expression illustrated by the model.

51.
$\underbrace{\qquad}_{\frac{4}{5}} \underbrace{\qquad}_{\frac{4}{5}} \underbrace{\ }_{\frac{1}{2} \text{ of } \frac{4}{5}}$

52.
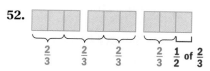
$\underbrace{\ }_{\frac{2}{3}} \underbrace{\ }_{\frac{2}{3}} \underbrace{\ }_{\frac{2}{3}} \underbrace{\ }_{\frac{2}{3}} {\scriptstyle\frac{1}{2} \text{ of } \frac{2}{3}}$

53. **REASONING** Juan says, "To divide a fraction by another fraction, rewrite the fractions with a common denominator. Then use the formula $\frac{a}{c} \div \frac{b}{c} = \frac{a}{b}$." Does Juan's method work? *Explain* your reasoning.

CONNECT SKILLS TO PROBLEM SOLVING Exercises 54–56 will help you prepare for problem solving.

Tell which operation you would use to solve the problem and why. Then solve the problem.

54. How many hamburgers can you make from 5 pounds of ground beef if you use $\frac{1}{4}$ pound of beef per hamburger?

55. A portable DVD player's battery lasts about $5\frac{1}{2}$ hours. The average length of the movies in your collection is about $1\frac{3}{4}$ hour. How many movies can you expect to watch if the battery is fully charged?

56. A horse eats about $4\frac{1}{2}$ pounds of feed per day. How many pounds of feed will a horse eat in a week?

SEE EXAMPLE 3
on p. 107
for Exs. 57–58

57. TRIPLE JUMP Jasmine did the triple jump in gym class. What was the mean distance she covered in her three jumps?

$9\frac{1}{3}$ ft $6\frac{3}{4}$ ft $9\frac{1}{2}$ ft

California @HomeTutor for problem solving help at classzone.com

58. MULTI-STEP PROBLEM Haley has a summer job at which she normally works $7\frac{1}{2}$ hours a day, 3 days per week. She plans to work for 7 weeks.

  a. Haley earns $180 per week. How much does she earn per hour?

  b. How much does she earn in 7 weeks?

  c. How much will Haley earn weekly if she works an extra 3 hour shift?

  d. How many extra 3 hour shifts does Haley need to work in order to earn a total of $1356 for the summer?

California @HomeTutor for problem solving help at classzone.com

59. ◆ **MULTIPLE CHOICE** The formula $C = (F - 32) \div \frac{9}{5}$ gives the Celsius temperature C that is equivalent to the Fahrenheit temperature F. What is 77°F in degrees Celsius?

  (A) 20°C   **(B)** 25°C   **(C)** 30°C   **(D)** 81°C

60. SHORT RESPONSE You are creating a board game. You want to cut square game pieces that measure $1\frac{1}{4}$ inches on each side from a piece of paper that measures $8\frac{1}{2}$ inches by 11 inches. How many game pieces can you cut from the paper? How many square inches of paper are left over? *Explain* how you found your answer.

61. REASONING You can use an area model to verify the rule for dividing fractions on page 106. Consider the rectangle shown at the right, which has length l, width $\frac{c}{d}$ and area $\frac{a}{b}$.

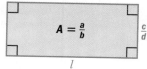

a. The rectangle's area equals its length times its width, so $\frac{a}{b} = l \cdot \frac{c}{d}$. This means that $l = \frac{a}{b} \div \frac{c}{d}$. Use the rule for dividing fractions to express l as a single fraction involving a, b, c, and d.

b. Multiply your expression from part (a) by the expression for the width of the rectangle. Simplify the result.

c. *Explain* why your answer to part (b) demonstrates that the rule for dividing fractions on page 106 is correct.

62. CHALLENGE Students were asked whether they preferred watching fall, winter, or spring school sports. Then they were asked to choose their favorite sport from their preferred season. One third of the students chose winter sports. Of those students, two sevenths chose basketball. One half of the students chose spring sports. Of those students, three fifths chose baseball. The number of students who chose baseball was how many times the number who chose basketball?

63. CHALLENGE Find the quotient of each expression below. Then go back and find the fraction whose numerator is the first numerator divided by the second numerator, and whose denominator is the first denominator divided by the second denominator. Make and prove a generalization based on the results.

a. $\frac{10}{21} \div \frac{2}{3}$ b. $\frac{9}{20} \div \frac{3}{4}$ c. $\frac{15}{16} \div \frac{5}{8}$ d. $\frac{24}{25} \div \frac{4}{5}$

◆ CALIFORNIA STANDARDS SPIRAL REVIEW

AF 1.2

64. What is the value of $3x^3$ when $x = -2$? *(p. 31)*

(A) -216 (B) -24 (C) 24 (D) 216

AF 1.3

65. Which property is used in the equation below? *(p. 48)*

$$4(x + 5) = 4x + 20$$

(A) Commutative Property of Multiplication   (B) Associative Property of Multiplication

(C) Distributive Property   (D) Identity Property of Addition

NS 1.2

66. The table shows scores for a dance contestant. What is the mean score for technical merit? *(p. 41)*

Judge	1	2	3	4	5
Technical merit	68	72	66	77	71
Choreography	74	79	71	79	78

(A) 66   (B) 70.8

(C) 76.2   (D) 354

2.6 Operations with Fractions

Standards

NS 1.2 Add, subtract, multiply, and divide rational numbers (integers, **fractions**, and terminating decimals) and take positive rational numbers to whole-number powers.

QUESTION How can you use a calculator to evaluate expressions with fractions?

First, set your calculator to display the answers as fractions or mixed numbers in simplest form.

Press **2nd** [FracMode]. Select $A \, \llcorner \, b/c$ and press **=** to set the calculator to mixed number mode.

Press **2nd** [FracMode]. Select *Auto* and press **=** to set the calculator to simplify fractions automatically.

EXAMPLE Use a calculator to evaluate expressions

		Keystrokes	Display	Answer
a.	$\frac{2}{3} - 4\frac{6}{7}$	**2** / **3** − **4** UNIT **6** / **7** =	$-4\llcorner4/21$	$-4\frac{4}{21}$
b.	$-\frac{5}{17} \cdot \left(-\frac{8}{35}\right)$	(−) **5** / **17** × (−) **8** / **35** =	$8/119$	$\frac{8}{119}$
c.	$\frac{3}{10} \div \left(-1\frac{4}{5}\right)$	**3** / **10** ÷ (−) **1** UNIT **4** / **5** =	$-1/6$	$-\frac{1}{6}$

PRACTICE

In Exercises 1–12, use a calculator to evaluate the expression.

1. $\frac{5}{11} + \frac{2}{5}$ **2.** $3\frac{1}{4} + \left(-\frac{6}{7}\right)$ **3.** $7\frac{1}{2} - 6\frac{5}{6}$ **4.** $\frac{2}{5} - \frac{2}{3}$

5. $\frac{7}{9} \cdot 1\frac{1}{3}$ **6.** $\frac{2}{5} \cdot \left(-\frac{3}{4}\right)$ **7.** $\frac{4}{7} \cdot \frac{1}{2}$ **8.** $2\frac{2}{3} \cdot \left(-\frac{1}{4}\right)$

9. $9\frac{4}{5} \div \frac{7}{8}$ **10.** $-10\frac{2}{13} \div \left(-3\frac{1}{3}\right)$ **11.** $1\frac{7}{9} \div \frac{1}{3}$ **12.** $\frac{5}{8} \div \left(-\frac{1}{7}\right)$

13. RECYCLING A community center's members are having a newspaper drive. They want to collect 1000 pounds of newspaper to be recycled. They already have $625\frac{3}{8}$ pounds. How many more pounds do they need?

14. CAR CARE Rosa's car needs $4\frac{1}{4}$ quarts of oil to run properly. It has only $\frac{3}{4}$ of that amount. How much oil should Rosa add?

2.7 Rational Numbers in Decimal Form

Standards **NS 1.3** Convert fractions to decimals and percents and use these representations in estimations, computations, and applications.

NS 1.5 Know that every rational number is either a terminating or a repeating decimal and be able to convert terminating decimals into reduced fractions.

Connect *Before* you divided fractions. *Now* you will write fractions as decimals and decimals as fractions.

Math and **NATURE**
Ex. 47, p. 116

KEY VOCABULARY
• rational number
• terminating decimal
• repeating decimal

A **rational number** is a number that can be written as a quotient $\frac{a}{b}$ where a and b are integers and $b \neq 0$. The diagram below shows how rational numbers, integers, and whole numbers are related.

Rational numbers include integers.

Integers include whole numbers.

Rational numbers

Integers
−3 −2
−1
3 1
Whole numbers
0 2

Numbers like 2, −6, −5$\frac{3}{5}$, and −8.73 are rational numbers.

About the Standards

You will learn more about converting fractions and decimals (NS 1.3) in Lesson 3.1.

To write any rational number $\frac{a}{b}$ as a decimal, divide a by b. If the quotient has a remainder of zero, the result is a **terminating decimal**. If the quotient has a digit or group of digits that repeats without end, the result is a **repeating decimal**. Every rational number can be written as either a terminating or a repeating decimal.

EXAMPLE 1 **Writing Fractions as Decimals**

Write the fraction as a decimal.

WRITE REPEATING DECIMALS
You can use an ellipsis (. . .) or an overbar to show that one or more digits repeat. For example, 0.333. . . = 0.$\overline{3}$.

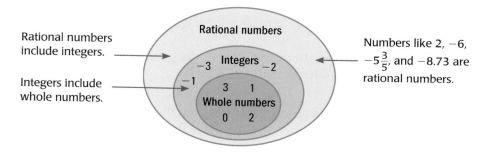

a. $\frac{5}{11}$ →
$$\begin{array}{r} 0.4545\ldots \\ 11\overline{)5.0000\ldots} \\ \underline{4\,4} \\ 60 \\ \underline{55} \\ 50 \\ \underline{44} \\ 60 \\ \underline{55} \end{array}$$
← Repeating decimal

b. $\frac{7}{20}$ →
$$\begin{array}{r} 0.35 \\ 20\overline{)7.00} \\ \underline{6\,0} \\ 1\,00 \\ \underline{1\,00} \\ 0 \end{array}$$
← Terminating decimal

▶ **Answer** $\frac{5}{11} = 0.4545\ldots = 0.\overline{45}$

▶ **Answer** $\frac{7}{20} = 0.35$

EXAMPLE 2 Writing Mixed Numbers as Decimals

BIOLOGY The table lists the mean lengths of four species of finches. Write the lengths as decimals.

Finch species	House finch	Indigo bunting	Lazuli bunting	Purple finch
Length (inches)	$5\frac{5}{8}$	$5\frac{1}{2}$	$5\frac{7}{16}$	$5\frac{3}{4}$

Indigo bunting

ANOTHER WAY
You can also convert a mixed number to a decimal by writing it as an improper fraction and then dividing the numerator by the denominator.

SOLUTION

Write each mixed number as the sum of a whole number and a fraction. Then convert the fraction to a decimal and add it to the whole number.

$$5\frac{5}{8} = 5 + \frac{5}{8} = 5 + 0.625 = 5.625 \qquad 5\frac{1}{2} = 5 + \frac{1}{2} = 5 + 0.5 = 5.5$$

$$5\frac{7}{16} = 5 + \frac{7}{16} = 5 + 0.4375 = 5.4375 \qquad 5\frac{3}{4} = 5 + \frac{3}{4} = 5 + 0.75 = 5.75$$

▶ **Answer** In decimal form, the lengths are 5.625 inches, 5.5 inches, 5.4375 inches, and 5.75 inches.

TERMINATING DECIMALS To write a terminating decimal as a fraction or mixed number, use the place value of the decimal's last digit as the denominator. For example, write 0.37 as $\frac{37}{100}$ because 7 is in the hundredths' place.

EXAMPLE 3 Writing Terminating Decimals as Fractions

Write the decimal as a fraction or mixed number in simplest form.

a. $0.4 = \frac{4}{10}$ ◄— 4 is in the tenths' place.

$= \frac{2}{5}$ Simplify.

b. $-1.905 = -1\frac{905}{1000}$ ◄— 5 is in the thousandths' place.

$= -1\frac{\overset{181}{\cancel{905}}}{\underset{200}{\cancel{1000}}}$

$= -1\frac{181}{200}$ Simplify.

✓ **GUIDED PRACTICE** for Examples 1, 2, and 3

Write the fraction or mixed number as a decimal.

1. $\frac{8}{25}$ **2.** $\frac{1}{6}$ **3.** $4\frac{2}{5}$ **4.** $-5\frac{1}{3}$

Write the decimal as a fraction or mixed number in simplest form.

5. Write 0.62 as a fraction.   **6.** Write -2.45 as a mixed number.

2.7 EXERCISES

HOMEWORK KEY

◆ = **MULTIPLE CHOICE PRACTICE**
Exs. 27, 42, 46, 55–57

◯ = **HINTS AND HOMEWORK HELP**
for Exs. 17, 31, 49 at classzone.com

SKILLS • PROBLEM SOLVING • REASONING

1. VOCABULARY Copy and complete: If you divide a fraction's numerator by its denominator and the quotient has a digit or group of digits that repeats without end, then the quotient is a(n) __?__ decimal.

2. WRITING How can you tell that a number is rational?

CLASSIFYING NUMBERS Tell whether the number is included in each of the following number sets: *rational numbers, integers, whole numbers.*

3. 0

4. 0.55

5. -14

6. $0.\overline{3}$

7. $-\dfrac{3}{4}$

8. $2\dfrac{3}{4}$

9. $-\dfrac{8}{2}$

10. $\dfrac{2}{0}$

SEE EXAMPLES 1 AND 2
on pp. 113–114
for Exs. 11–29

FRACTIONS AS DECIMALS Write the fraction or mixed number as a decimal.

11. $\dfrac{3}{5}$

12. $\dfrac{2}{3}$

13. $-\dfrac{7}{10}$

14. $\dfrac{5}{6}$

15. $\dfrac{3}{4}$

16. $-\dfrac{1}{9}$

17. $-\dfrac{12}{25}$

18. $\dfrac{7}{12}$

19. $-10\dfrac{4}{25}$

20. $\dfrac{27}{50}$

21. $3\dfrac{11}{16}$

22. $-4\dfrac{33}{80}$

23. $-\dfrac{14}{33}$

24. $5\dfrac{27}{44}$

25. $6\dfrac{8}{15}$

26. $-14\dfrac{7}{11}$

27. ◆ MULTIPLE CHOICE Which number is equivalent to $\dfrac{3}{2}$?

(**A**) 0.325

(**B**) 1.5

(**C**) 2.3

(**D**) 3.25

ERROR ANALYSIS *Describe* and correct the error in writing the mixed number as a decimal.

28.

$$\times \quad 2\dfrac{3}{10} = 2.03$$

29.

$$\times \quad 5\dfrac{1}{3} = \dfrac{5}{3} = 1.\overline{6}$$

SEE EXAMPLE 3
on p. 114
for Exs. 30–37

DECIMALS AS FRACTIONS Write the decimal as a fraction or mixed number in simplest form.

30. 0.6

31. -0.48

32. -3.2

33. -2.79

34. 0.365

35. 7.253

36. -5.0032

37. 0.0012

PERIOD OF A REPEATING DECIMAL The *period* of a repeating decimal is the number of digits that repeat. For instance, the period of $0.\overline{13}$ is 2. In Exercises 38–41, write the period of the repeating decimal.

38. 0.333. . .

39. $0.\overline{459}$

40. $0.2\overline{1}$

41. $0.2\overline{857}$. . .

42. ◆ **MULTIPLE CHOICE** Look back at the information in Exercises 38–41. What is the period of 6.273273. . . ?

(A) 1   **(B)** 2   **(C)** 3   **(D)** 6

CONNECT SKILLS TO PROBLEM SOLVING Exercises 43–45 will help you prepare for problem solving.

Use the following information: In 2001, the New York Stock Exchange switched its format for stock prices from fractions to decimals. Write the value in decimal form.

43. A stock has a value of $44\frac{1}{2}$ per share.

44. The value of a stock increases by $5\frac{1}{4}$ per share.

45. The value of a stock decreases by $3\frac{7}{16}$ per share.

SEE EXAMPLE 1
on p. 113
for Ex. 46

46. ◆ **MULTIPLE CHOICE** In a class, $\frac{22}{25}$ of the students are right-handed. What is another way to express this number?

(A) 0.22   **(B)** 0.25   **(C)** 0.47   **(D)** 0.88

California @HomeTutor for problem solving help at classzone.com

SEE EXAMPLE 2
on p. 114
for Ex. 47

47. CATERPILLARS Write the following lengths of caterpillars in decimal form.

$$1\frac{7}{8} \text{ inches,} \quad 1\frac{4}{5} \text{ inches,} \quad 2\frac{1}{9} \text{ inches,} \quad 2\frac{1}{12} \text{ inches}$$

California @HomeTutor for problem solving help at classzone.com

---

READING IN MATH   Read the information below for Exercises 48–50.

Great Lakes In the United States, water covers a surface area of about 182,000 square miles. Nearly one third of this area is in the Great Lakes. Lake Superior is the largest of the Great Lakes, but only about 21,000 of its 32,000 square miles lie within the United States. Lake Michigan is the third largest Great Lake, and it lies entirely within the United States. Lake Michigan is also the largest body of freshwater in the U.S.

Lake Superior

48. Interpret How is it possible that Lake Michigan is only the third largest Great Lake, but it is the largest body of fresh water in the U.S.?

49. Calculate What fraction of the surface area of water in the U.S. is in Lake Superior? Write this fraction as a decimal.

50. Estimation *Explain* how you can use estimation to check the decimal in Exercise 49.

51. REASONING Is the number 0.1010010001. . . a rational number? *Explain.*

52. MULTI-STEP PROBLEM In a survey, 1200 students were asked to name their favorite breakfast food. For each of several foods, the table shows the ratio (expressed as a decimal) of students who picked the food as their favorite to all students surveyed.

Breakfast food	Bagels	Bacon	Eggs	Cereal	Pancakes
Ratio of students	0.125	0.08	0.1875	0.25	0.12

 a. Write each decimal as a fraction.

 b. Multiply each fraction by 1200 to find the number of students who chose the food.

 c. Another school has 2500 students. Multiply each fraction in part (a) by 2500 to estimate the number of students in this school who would prefer each food.

53. CHALLENGE Find a rational number between $-\dfrac{1}{64}$ and $-\dfrac{1}{63}$. Write your answer as a decimal and as a fraction.

54. CHALLENGE At the end of a race, all of the runners' times are posted as decimals rounded to the nearest thousandth of an hour. Kim finished the race in 1 hour, 22 minutes, and 34 seconds. What was Kim's posted time? If no two runners finished at the same time, how many runners could have the same *posted* time as Kim? *Explain.*

◆ CALIFORNIA STANDARDS SPIRAL REVIEW

AF 1.3

55. Which statement shows the inverse property of multiplication? *(p. 98)*

 (A) $\dfrac{1}{6} \cdot 6 = 1$ (B) $-5 \cdot 0 = 0$ (C) $7 \cdot 1 = 7$ (D) $-1 \cdot 3 = -3$

NS 1.2

56. What is the value of $-7 + 4$? *(p. 18)*

 (A) -11 (B) -3 (C) 3 (D) 11

NS 1.2

57. How long is a $7\dfrac{5}{8}$ inch board after you cut $2\dfrac{7}{8}$ inches off the length? *(p. 85)*

 (A) $4\dfrac{1}{4}$ in. (B) $4\dfrac{3}{4}$ in. (C) $5\dfrac{1}{4}$ in. (D) $5\dfrac{3}{4}$ in.

QUIZ for Lessons 2.6–2.7

Find the quotient. *(p. 106)*

1. $\dfrac{1}{2} \div \dfrac{5}{6}$ **2.** $\dfrac{4}{9} \div 8$ **3.** $-\dfrac{4}{5} \div \dfrac{3}{2}$ **4.** $-1\dfrac{3}{4} \div \left(\dfrac{-7}{12}\right)$

Write the fraction as a decimal or the decimal as a fraction. *(p. 113)*

5. 4.25   **6.** $-\dfrac{4}{9}$ **7.** 0.58   **8.** $\dfrac{7}{15}$

9. BIOLOGY A human hair grows $1\dfrac{3}{4}$ inches in $3\dfrac{1}{2}$ months. What is the mean monthly growth of the hair? *(p. 106)*

Multiple Choice Practice for Lessons 2.5–2.7

1. In a survey, 800 students were asked to name their favorite type of movie. The table shows the ratio expressed as a decimal of students who picked the movie type as their favorite type of movie. What fraction of students favored action movies? **NS 1.5, MR 2.2**

Movie type	Comedy	Drama	Action
Ratio of students	0.4	0.224	0.3125

  A $\frac{5}{16}$ **B** $\frac{2}{5}$

  C $\frac{3}{8}$ **D** $\frac{5}{8}$

2. Anna takes $\frac{1}{6}$ of the 24 beads in a bowl. Then John takes $\frac{1}{10}$ of the remaining beads. What fraction of the original beads is left in the bowl? **NS 1.2**

  A $\frac{1}{6}$ **B** $\frac{1}{4}$

  C $\frac{7}{24}$ **D** $\frac{3}{4}$

3. The ruler shows the length of the baby turtle's shell. What is the length as a decimal? **NS 1.3**

  A 1.3 in.   **B** 1.625 in.

  C 1.9 in.   **D** 2.0 in.

4. What is the value of $\frac{2}{3} \cdot \frac{3}{2}$? **AF 1.3**

  A 0   **B** 1

  C 6   **D** 12

5. A mixed number multiplied by a fraction is less than 1. The mixed number divided by the fraction is less than 2. Which values are possible for the mixed number and the fraction? **NS 1.2, MR 1.2**

  A $1\frac{1}{4}$ and $\frac{1}{3}$ **B** $1\frac{1}{6}$ and $\frac{1}{4}$

  C $1\frac{1}{5}$ and $\frac{3}{4}$ **D** $1\frac{2}{5}$ and $\frac{5}{6}$

6. You want to decorate 5 gifts with ribbon around the gift and a bow on top. The amounts of ribbon that you use for each gift are shown below. How many yards of ribbon do you use for all 5 gifts? **NS 1.2**

 $2\frac{1}{6}$ yards $1\frac{1}{2}$ yards

  A $13\frac{1}{3}$ yd   **B** $16\frac{2}{3}$ yd

  C $18\frac{1}{3}$ yd   **D** $19\frac{1}{6}$ yd

7. What is the value of $17 \div 5\frac{2}{3}$? **NS 1.2**

  A $\frac{1}{3}$ **B** $2\frac{2}{3}$

  C 3   **D** 4

8. The weight of a backpack and its contents should be no more than $\frac{1}{5}$ of the carrier's bodyweight. Levi weighs 130 pounds. What is the heaviest total backpack weight he should carry? **NS 1.2**

  A 18 lb   **B** 22 lb

  C 23 lb   **D** 26 lb

9. What is the value of $-\dfrac{\left(\frac{2}{5}\right)\left(\frac{1}{6}\right)}{\left(\frac{4}{5}\right)}$? **NS 1.2**

  A −12   **B** $-\frac{1}{12}$

  C $\frac{1}{12}$ **D** 12

CHAPTER SUMMARY

BIG IDEAS

For Your Notebook

Big Idea 1

Simplifying and Comparing Fractions

Writing Equivalent Fractions	Multiply or divide the numerator and denominator of a fraction by the same nonzero number.	$\dfrac{3}{4} = \dfrac{3 \cdot 5}{4 \cdot 5} = \dfrac{15}{20}$ $\dfrac{10}{30} = \dfrac{10 \div 10}{30 \div 10} = \dfrac{1}{3}$
Simplifying Fractions	Use GCF of the numerator and denominator.	The GCF of 8 and 20 is 4. So $\dfrac{8}{20} = \dfrac{8 \div 4}{20 \div 4} = \dfrac{2}{5}$
Comparing Fractions	Use the LCD to write equivalent fractions.	$\dfrac{1}{3} = \dfrac{1 \cdot 5}{3 \cdot 5} = \dfrac{5}{15}$ and $\dfrac{2}{5} = \dfrac{2 \cdot 3}{5 \cdot 3} = \dfrac{6}{15}$. Since $\dfrac{5}{15} < \dfrac{6}{15}$, you know that $\dfrac{1}{3} < \dfrac{2}{5}$.

Big Idea 2

Adding, Subtracting, Multipying, and Dividing Fractions

To add or subtract two fractions with same denominator, add or subtract the numerators. To add or subtract fractions with different denominators, first use the LCD to write equivalent fractions with the same denominators.

$$\frac{3}{7} + \frac{2}{7} = \frac{3 + 2}{7} = \frac{5}{7} \qquad\qquad \frac{5}{9} - \frac{1}{6} = \frac{10}{18} - \frac{3}{18} = \frac{10 - 3}{18} = \frac{7}{18}$$

To multiply two fractions, multiply both the numerators and denominators. To divide by a fraction, multiply by its reciprocal.

$$\frac{2}{3} \cdot \frac{4}{5} = \frac{2 \cdot 4}{3 \cdot 5} = \frac{8}{15} \qquad\qquad \frac{2}{3} \div \frac{1}{4} = \frac{2}{3} \cdot \frac{4}{1} = \frac{8}{3} = 2\frac{2}{3}$$

Big Idea 3

Converting Between Fractions and Decimals

To write a fraction as a decimal, divide the numerator by the denominator. The result will be either a terminating decimal or a repeating decimal.

Terminating

$\dfrac{1}{2}$ becomes $2\overline{)1.0}$ with quotient 0.5, $\dfrac{1\,0}{0}$

Repeating

$\dfrac{1}{3}$ becomes $3\overline{)1.00}$ with quotient $0.33\ldots$, $\dfrac{9}{10}$, $\dfrac{9}{}$

You can write a terminating decimal as a fraction by using the place value of the last digit.

$0.25 = \dfrac{25}{100}$ ← 5 is in hundredths' place.

$= \dfrac{1}{4}$

APPLYING THE BIG IDEAS

Big Idea 1
You compare fractions in **Steps 1–4.**

Big Idea 2
You add and subtract fractions in **Steps 1 and 3.**

Big Idea 3
You convert fractions to decimals in **Step 2.**

PROBLEM How can you use fractions to make a nameplate showing your first name?

STEP 1 Write your first name.

On a white piece of paper, write your first name in marker using the following guidelines.

- Each letters must be capitalized and in a rectangular box.
- The width of each box must be at least $\frac{3}{4}$ inch.
- All boxes must have the same height, but not necessarily the same width.
- The total width of all the boxes cannot be greater than $10\frac{1}{2}$ inches.

STEP 2 Cut out the letters.

Cut out the rectangular boxes that contain the letters of your name. Find the width of each box and then convert each width to a decimal. What is the width of the widest box?

STEP 3 Arrange the nameplate.

Choose a piece of 9 by 12 inch colored paper for the background of your nameplate. Space the boxes evenly on the colored paper. The space between the boxes should be at least $\frac{1}{4}$ inch and at most $\frac{5}{8}$ inch. Either tape or glue the boxes to the background.

STEP 4 Cut out the nameplate.

Cut out a uniform border of at least $\frac{1}{4}$ inch around your name.
Your nameplate should look similar to the nameplate shown.
What is the total length of your nameplate including the border?

Extending the Problem

Use your results from the problem above to complete the exercises.

1. What fraction of the total length of the nameplate is made up of boxes? Convert this fraction to a decimal.

2. What is the maximum number of letters you can have in your nameplate? *Explain.*

REVIEW KEY VOCABULARY

- fraction, *p. 75*
- equivalent fractions, *p. 75*
- simplest form of a fraction, *p. 75*
- least common denominator, *p. 80*
- multiplicative inverse, *p. 99*
- reciprocal, *p. 106*
- rational number, *p. 113*
- repeating decimal, *p.113*
- terminating decimal, *p. 113*

VOCABULARY EXERCISES

In Exercises 1–3, copy and complete the statement.

1. The product of the fractions $\frac{3}{5}$ and $\frac{5}{3}$ is 1, so the fractions are __?__ or __?__.

2. A number that can be written as $\frac{a}{b}$, where a and b are integers and $b \neq 0$, is a __?__.

3. The __?__ of $\frac{1}{3}$ and $\frac{1}{5}$ is 15.

4. **NOTETAKING SKILLS** Make a *process diagram* like the one on page 74 for dividing fractions and mixed numbers.

REVIEW EXAMPLES AND EXERCISES

2.1 Simplifying Fractions

pp. 75–79

Gr 6 NS 2.4

EXAMPLE

Write $\frac{48}{72}$ in simplest form.

Write the prime factorization of each number.

$48 = 2 \cdot 2 \cdot 2 \cdot 2 \cdot 3$
$72 = 2 \cdot 2 \cdot 2 \cdot 3 \cdot 3$

The GCF of 48 and 72 is $2 \cdot 2 \cdot 2 \cdot 3 = 24$.

$\frac{48}{72} = \frac{48 \div 24}{72 \div 24}$ **Divide numerator and denominator by GCF.**

$= \frac{2}{3}$ **Simplify.**

EXERCISES

SEE EXAMPLES 1 AND 4
on pp. 75–77
for Exs. 5–8

Write the fraction in simplest form.

5. $\frac{15}{45}$

6. $\frac{12}{80}$

7. $\frac{9ab}{27a}$

8. $\frac{18n^3}{54n}$

2.2 Comparing Fractions and Mixed Numbers

pp. 80–84

NS 1.1

EXAMPLE

Compare $\frac{11}{18}$ and $\frac{3}{4}$.

The least common multiple of 18 and 4 is 36, so the least common denominator is 36. Write each fraction using the LCD.

$$\frac{11}{18} = \frac{11 \cdot 2}{18 \cdot 2} = \frac{22}{36} \qquad\qquad \frac{3}{4} = \frac{3 \cdot 9}{4 \cdot 9} = \frac{27}{36}$$

▶ **Answer** Because $\frac{22}{36} < \frac{27}{36}$, you can write $\frac{11}{18} < \frac{3}{4}$.

EXERCISES

SEE EXAMPLES 1, 2, AND 3 on pp. 80–82 for Exs. 9–17

Copy and complete the statement with <, >, or =.

9. $\frac{79}{16} \underline{\ ?\ } \frac{35}{8}$

10. $6\frac{2}{3} \underline{\ ?\ } \frac{81}{12}$

11. $-\frac{161}{9} \underline{\ ?\ } -17\frac{8}{9}$

12. $\frac{223}{15} \underline{\ ?\ } 14\frac{4}{5}$

Order the numbers from least to greatest.

13. $\frac{7}{11}, \frac{2}{3}, \frac{5}{8}$

14. $-9\frac{1}{2}, -\frac{29}{3}, -\frac{37}{4}$

15. $5\frac{7}{8}, \frac{53}{9}, \frac{17}{3}$

16. $\frac{25}{6}, \frac{49}{12}, 4\frac{1}{10}$

17. GARDENING Joe picked $4\frac{7}{8}$ cups of green beans and Sarah picked $\frac{29}{6}$ cups. Who picked more beans?

2.3 Adding and Subtracting Fractions

pp. 85–89

NS 1.2

EXAMPLE

Find the sum.

$$\frac{2}{9} + 3\frac{4}{9} = 3 + \left(\frac{2}{9} + \frac{4}{9}\right) \qquad \text{Group fractions.}$$

$$= 3\frac{6}{9} \qquad \text{Add fractions.}$$

$$= 3\frac{2}{3} \qquad \text{Simplify.}$$

EXERCISES

SEE EXAMPLES 1 AND 2 on pp. 85–86 for Exs. 18–21

Find the sum or difference.

18. $\frac{8}{9} + \frac{4}{9}$

19. $3\frac{5}{8} - 1\frac{7}{8}$

20. $\frac{3}{10} - \frac{7}{10} - \frac{9}{10}$

21. $\frac{4}{7} + \frac{2}{7} + \frac{6}{7}$

2.4 Using a Common Denominator

pp. 91–95

NS 1.2

EXAMPLE

Find the difference.

$$2\frac{9}{14} - \frac{6}{7} = 2\frac{9}{14} - \frac{12}{14}$$ Rewrite fractions using LCD of 14.

$$= 1\frac{23}{14} - \frac{12}{14}$$ Rename $2\frac{9}{14}$ as $1\frac{23}{14}$.

$$= 1 + \left(\frac{23}{14} - \frac{12}{14}\right)$$ Group fractions.

$$= 1\frac{11}{14}$$ Subtract inside parentheses.

EXERCISES

SEE EXAMPLES
1, 2, AND 3
on pp. 91–92
for Exs. 22–25

Find the sum or difference.

22. $\frac{3}{5} + \frac{1}{4}$ **23.** $3\frac{1}{3} - 1\frac{1}{4}$ **24.** $6\frac{2}{7} + \left(-7\frac{1}{8}\right)$ **25.** $\frac{8}{17} - \frac{1}{2}$

2.5 Multiplying Fractions

pp. 98–104

NS 1.2

EXAMPLE

Find the product.

$$3\frac{3}{5} \cdot \frac{4}{9} = \frac{18}{5} \cdot \frac{4}{9}$$ Write $3\frac{3}{5}$ as an improper fraction.

$$= \frac{18 \cdot 4}{5 \cdot 9}$$ Use rule for multiplying fractions.

$$= \frac{\overset{2}{\cancel{18}} \cdot 4}{5 \cdot \underset{1}{\cancel{9}}}$$ Divide out common factor.

$$= \frac{8}{5}, \text{ or } 1\frac{3}{5}$$ Multiply and write as a mixed number.

EXERCISES

SEE EXAMPLES
1 AND 3
on pp. 98–100
for Exs. 26–33

Find the product.

26. $-\frac{5}{8} \cdot \frac{2}{5}$ **27.** $-\frac{9}{5} \cdot \left(-\frac{11}{15}\right)$ **28.** $\frac{7}{2} \cdot \frac{2}{7}$ **29.** $\frac{3}{8} \cdot \left(-\frac{12}{13}\right)$

30. $8\frac{2}{3} \cdot (-3)$ **31.** $-7\frac{4}{9} \cdot \left(-\frac{1}{4}\right)$ **32.** $-6\frac{3}{7} \cdot 2\frac{1}{2}$ **33.** $4 \cdot \left(-3\frac{5}{12}\right)$

2.6 Dividing Fractions

pp. 106–111

NS 1.2

EXAMPLE

Find the quotient.

$$2\frac{1}{5} \div 2\frac{3}{4} = \frac{11}{5} \div \frac{11}{4}$$ Write $2\frac{1}{5}$ and $2\frac{3}{4}$ as improper fractions.

$$= \frac{11}{5} \cdot \frac{4}{11}$$ $\frac{11}{4} \cdot \frac{4}{11} = 1$, so the reciprocal of $\frac{11}{4}$ is $\frac{4}{11}$.

$$= \frac{\overset{1}{\cancel{11}} \cdot 4}{5 \cdot \underset{1}{\cancel{11}}}$$ Divide out common factor.

$$= \frac{4}{5}$$ Multiply.

EXERCISES

SEE EXAMPLES
1, 2, AND 3
on p. 107
for Exs. 34–41

Find the quotient.

34. $\dfrac{13}{18} \div \dfrac{5}{6}$ **35.** $5\dfrac{8}{11} \div \left(-\dfrac{3}{4}\right)$ **36.** $2\dfrac{3}{4} \div 1\dfrac{1}{3}$ **37.** $12\dfrac{1}{2} \div 4$

38. $\dfrac{5}{12} \div \dfrac{3}{4}$ **39.** $2\dfrac{1}{8} \div 3\dfrac{2}{5}$ **40.** $-6\dfrac{3}{7} \div 5$ **41.** $9 \div \dfrac{1}{2}$

2.7 Rational Numbers in Decimal Form

pp. 113–117

NS 1.5

EXAMPLE

Write 1.568 as a fraction.

$$1.568 = 1\frac{568}{1000}$$ 8 is in the thousandths' place.

$$= 1\frac{\overset{71}{\cancel{568}}}{\underset{125}{\cancel{1000}}}$$ Divide out common factor.

$$= 1\frac{71}{125}$$ Simplify.

EXERCISES

SEE EXAMPLES
1, 2, AND 3
on pp. 113–114
for Exs. 42–46

Write the fraction as a decimal or the decimal as a fraction or mixed number.

42. $\dfrac{3}{5}$ **43.** $-\dfrac{7}{8}$ **44.** -0.13 **45.** 3.45

46. A cord measures $1\dfrac{5}{8}$ feet. Write the length of the cord as a decimal.

VOCABULARY Copy and complete the statement.

1. A fraction is in __?__ form if its numerator and denominator have a greatest common factor of 1.

2. If the quotient of a fraction's numerator and denominator has a remainder of zero, the result is a(n) __?__.

Tell whether the fractions are equivalent.

3. $\dfrac{21}{24}, \dfrac{35}{40}$

4. $-\dfrac{10}{35}, -\dfrac{16}{56}$

5. $\dfrac{36}{45}, \dfrac{48}{62}$

6. $\dfrac{132}{228}, \dfrac{231}{399}$

Copy and complete the statement with <, >, or =.

7. $\dfrac{11}{12} \;\underline{\;?\;}\; \dfrac{41}{48}$

8. $4\dfrac{3}{6} \;\underline{\;?\;}\; \dfrac{9}{2}$

9. $8\dfrac{7}{16} \;\underline{\;?\;}\; \dfrac{17}{2}$

10. $\dfrac{35}{7} \;\underline{\;?\;}\; 5\dfrac{1}{7}$

Find the sum or difference. Then simplify if possible.

11. $4\dfrac{5}{11} - 2\dfrac{6}{11}$

12. $\dfrac{9}{16} - \left(-\dfrac{11}{16}\right)$

13. $-\dfrac{5}{6} + \dfrac{1}{8}$

14. $\dfrac{3}{7} + \left(-\dfrac{8}{21}\right) + \dfrac{2}{3}$

Find the product or quotient. Then simplify if possible.

15. $\dfrac{2}{9} \cdot (-4)$

16. $\dfrac{5}{2} \cdot \dfrac{4}{15}$

17. $3\dfrac{1}{2} \div 2$

18. $7\dfrac{3}{4} \div 2\dfrac{7}{12}$

Write the fraction as a decimal or the decimal as a fraction or mixed number.

19. $\dfrac{11}{20}$

20. $\dfrac{3}{40}$

21. 0.0082

22. 5.23

23. **CAKE** Three identical cakes are served at a party. Each cake is cut into a different number of equal-sized slices. After the guests leave, $\dfrac{1}{8}$ of the yellow cake, $\dfrac{3}{16}$ of the chocolate cake, and $\dfrac{1}{4}$ of the carrot cake remain. Which type of cake has the least amount left over? *Explain* your answer.

24. **HOMEWORK** Yesterday you spent $3\dfrac{1}{4}$ hours on homework. Today you will spend $1\dfrac{4}{5}$ hours. How many more hours did you spend yesterday?

25. **BOOK CLUB** You are reading a novel for your book club. You can read one chapter in $\dfrac{5}{12}$ hour. How many chapters can you read in $3\dfrac{3}{4}$ hours?

26. **EXAM** On a recent exam, $\dfrac{9}{10}$ of the class received 70% or higher. Of the students receiving 70% or higher, $\dfrac{1}{4}$ received 90% or higher. What fraction of all the students received 90% or higher?

27. **MILE RUN** The times for three students to complete a mile run in gym class are shown. Write each time as a mixed number.

Runner	Tim	Joe	Mark
Time (min)	6.4	6.25	6.15

STRATEGIES YOU'LL USE:
- SOLVE DIRECTLY
- ELIMINATE CHOICES

Standards
NS 1.1, NS 1.2

If you have difficulty solving a multiple choice problem directly, you may be able to use another approach to eliminate incorrect answer choices and obtain the correct answer.

PROBLEM 1

Four friends planted flower bulbs at the same time. The table shows the amount each person's plant grew in the first week. Whose plant grew the most?

Plant Growth (inches)			
Mark	**Julie**	**Brett**	**Sara**
$1\frac{3}{8}$	$\frac{7}{6}$	$\frac{17}{12}$	$1\frac{1}{4}$

(A) Mark's   (B) Julie's   (C) Brett's   (D) Sara's

Strategy 1   SOLVE DIRECTLY

The amounts each plant grew can be rewritten as improper fractions.

STEP 1 **Find** the LCM of 8, 6, 12, and 4. List the multiples of each number.

   8: 8, 16, **24**, 32, 40, 48, . . .
   6: 6, 12, 18, **24**, 30, 36, . . .
   12: 12, **24**, 36, 48, 60, . . .
   4: 4, 8, 12, 16, 20, **24**, . . .
   The LCD of the fractions is 24.

STEP 2 **Rewrite** as improper fractions

   Mark: $1\frac{3}{8} = \frac{11}{8} = \frac{11 \cdot 3}{8 \cdot 3} = \frac{33}{24}$

   Julie: $\frac{7}{6} = \frac{7 \cdot 4}{6 \cdot 4} = \frac{28}{24}$

   Brett: $\frac{17}{12} = \frac{17 \cdot 2}{12 \cdot 2} = \frac{34}{24}$

   Sara: $1\frac{1}{4} = \frac{5}{4} = \frac{5 \cdot 6}{4 \cdot 6} = \frac{30}{24}$

STEP 3 **Compare** the numerators: $28 < 30 < 33 < 34$.

Brett's plant grew the most.

The correct answer is C. (A) (B) (C) (D)

Strategy 2   ELIMINATE CHOICES

You can use estimation to eliminate answer choices.

STEP 1 **Note** that Mark's plant and Brett's plant grew relatively close to $1\frac{1}{2}$ inches. Julie's plant and Sara's plant grew noticeably less than $1\frac{1}{2}$ inches. Since you are looking for the plant with the greatest growth, you can eliminate choices B and D.

STEP 2 **Eliminate** one of choices A and C. To find which one is greater, compare the two numbers by finding the LCD, rewriting each number as an improper fraction, and comparing the numerators.

$$1\frac{3}{8} = \frac{11}{8} = \frac{33}{24}$$

$$\frac{17}{12} = \frac{34}{24}$$

Because $1\frac{3}{8} < \frac{17}{12}$, Brett's plant grew the most.

The correct answer is C. (A) (B) (C) (D)

PROBLEM 2

The table shows the results of a survey that asked students about their favorite type of vegetable. If $\frac{1}{4}$ of the students who said "Other" like carrots best, how many more students like broccoli than carrots?

Favorite Vegetable			
Corn	**Green beans**	**Broccoli**	**Other**
9	7	8	12

Ⓐ 2 　　　　Ⓑ 5 　　　　Ⓒ 9 　　　　Ⓓ 10

Strategy 1 **SOLVE DIRECTLY**

We know that $\frac{1}{4}$ of the students who chose "Other" like carrots.

STEP 1 **Find** the number of students surveyed that like carrots best.

$$\frac{1}{4} \cdot 12 = 3$$

STEP 2 **Subtract** the number of students who like carrots best from those that like broccoli best.

$$8 - 3 = 5$$

There were 5 more students who said they like broccoli best than students who said they like carrots best.

The correct answer is B. Ⓐ Ⓑ Ⓒ Ⓓ

Strategy 2 **ELIMINATE CHOICES**

In some cases, you can use the wording of a multiple choice question to eliminate choices.

STEP 1 **Observe** that 8 students chose broccoli. The answer must be less than or equal to the number of students that chose broccoli. Because 9 and 10 are greater than 8, you can eliminate choices C and D.

STEP 2 **Eliminate** one of choices A and B. If only 2 more students like broccoli than carrots, then 6 students like carrots. However, this would mean that $\frac{6}{12} = \frac{1}{2}$ of the students who said "Other" like carrots, which contradicts the given information. So, you can eliminate choice A.

The correct answer is B. Ⓐ Ⓑ Ⓒ Ⓓ

STRATEGY PRACTICE

Explain why you can eliminate the highlighted answer choice.

	Bar A	**Bar B**	**Bar C**	**Bar D**
Total calories	170	210	250	260
Protein calories	40	60	65	60

1. Use the table. What fraction of the total calories in bar B is from protein?

   Ⓐ $\frac{2}{9}$ 　　　　Ⓑ $\frac{2}{7}$ 　　　　Ⓒ $\frac{2}{5}$ 　　　　Ⓓ✕ $\frac{5}{7}$

2. Use the table. Which bar contains the greatest fraction of calories from protein?

   Ⓐ Bar A 　　　　Ⓑ Bar B 　　　　Ⓒ Bar C 　　　　Ⓓ✕ **Bar D**

1. Which fraction is not equivalent to $\frac{48}{140}$? **NS 1.1**

   A $\frac{4}{15}$

   B $\frac{60}{175}$

   C $\frac{12}{35}$

   D $\frac{84}{245}$

2. A round of golf consists of the front nine holes and the back nine holes for a total of 18 holes. After a round of golf, Steve had a total score of 74. What fraction of his total score was scored on the front nine holes? **NS 1.1**

Golf Score Card										
Hole	**1**	**2**	**3**	**4**	**5**	**6**	**7**	**8**	**9**	**T**
Front	4	6	3	4	3	3	4	4	3	34
Back	5	3	4	5	5	5	4	6	3	40

   A $\frac{17}{37}$

   B $\frac{17}{36}$

   C $\frac{1}{2}$

   D $\frac{20}{37}$

3. Last season, a softball team played $\frac{3}{4}$ of their games at night and $\frac{1}{4}$ of their games during the day. The team won $\frac{4}{5}$ of their night games and $\frac{1}{2}$ of their day games. What fraction of the season's games did the team win? **NS 1.2**

   A $\frac{5}{8}$

   B $\frac{29}{40}$

   C $\frac{31}{40}$

   D $\frac{17}{20}$

4. Which length is greater than the length of the flashlight? **NS 1.5**

   A $\frac{5}{16}$ m

   B $\frac{1}{3}$ m

   C $\frac{55}{162}$ m

   D $\frac{8}{23}$ m

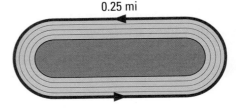

0.34 m

5. What is the value of $-1\frac{1}{2} \cdot \frac{9}{20}$? **NS 1.2**

   A $-1\frac{9}{20}$

   B $-1\frac{1}{20}$

   C $-\frac{27}{40}$

   D $-\frac{3}{10}$

6. How many times must you run around the track to run $3\frac{1}{2}$ miles? **NS 1.2**

   A 7

   B 9

   C 12

   D 14

0.25 mi

7. You are transplanting some houseplants. You buy an 8 quart bag of potting soil. You use $1\frac{1}{5}$ quarts for a spider plant, $2\frac{7}{8}$ quarts for an ivy plant, and $1\frac{3}{4}$ quarts for a fern. How much soil do you have left? **NS 1.2**

   A $1\frac{1}{2}$ quarts

   B $2\frac{7}{40}$ quarts

   C $2\frac{33}{40}$ quarts

   D $3\frac{37}{40}$ quarts

8. Which property is used to simplify $\frac{2}{3} \cdot \frac{3}{2} + \frac{5}{6}$ to $1 + \frac{5}{6}$? **AF 1.3**

   A Distributive Property

   B Inverse Property of Multiplication

   C Commutative Property of Addition

   D Associative Property of Multiplication

9. Which decimal is equivalent to $-\frac{7}{15}$? **NS 1.3**

   A -2.1

   B -0.7

   C -0.5

   D $-0.4\overline{6}$

10. What expression can you use to estimate $4\frac{1}{8} \cdot \frac{11}{20}$? **NS 1.3**

    A $4 \cdot 2$

    B $4 \cdot \frac{1}{2}$

    C $5 \cdot 2$

    D $5 \cdot \frac{1}{2}$

11. The table shows the fraction of free throws made by Ed, Al, Jay, and Jen during a competition. Which conclusion is reasonable according to the data? **NS 1.1, MR 2.4**

Name	Ed	Al	Jay	Jen
Fraction made	$\frac{7}{10}$	$\frac{3}{4}$	$\frac{3}{5}$	$\frac{9}{10}$

    A Al makes a greater fraction of his free throws than Ed does.

    B Ed and Al make fewer baskets than Jay and Jen make.

    C Jen makes 3 times as many free throws as Jay.

    D If Ed and Jen each try 15 free throws, either player could make more baskets.

12. On Pi Day, which is March 14, Ms. Steven's class had a pie party. At the end of the party, there were leftovers that included $\frac{1}{4}$ of the pumpkin pie, $\frac{3}{16}$ of the blueberry pie, $\frac{5}{24}$ of the coconut cream pie, and $\frac{3}{8}$ of the apple pie. How much pie was left? **NS 1.2**

    A 0

    B $1\frac{1}{48}$

    C $1\frac{7}{24}$

    D $1\frac{9}{16}$

13. The recipe shown is for 1 batch of pizza dough. You want to make 4 batches of dough for a pizza party. You have $12\frac{1}{2}$ cups of flour. How many more cups of flour do you need? **NS 1.2**

    A $\frac{1}{4}$

    B $\frac{1}{2}$

    C $\frac{3}{4}$

    D $1\frac{1}{2}$

    Pizza Dough
    $3\frac{1}{2}$ cups flour
    1 cup water
    2 tbsp. yeast
    $\frac{1}{2}$ cup olive oil
    $\frac{1}{2}$ tsp. salt

14. The height of the tallest player on a basketball team is $6\frac{1}{4}$ feet. The height of the third tallest player is $6\frac{1}{6}$ feet. What is a possible height for the second tallest player? **NS 1.1, MR 2.7**

    A $6\frac{1}{2}$ ft

    B $6\frac{3}{8}$ ft

    C $6\frac{5}{24}$ ft

    D $6\frac{3}{24}$ ft

Before

In previous chapters, you learned the following skills, which you'll use in Chapter 3:

- Performing operations with integers
- Performing operations with fractions
- Converting between fractions and decimals

Now

In Chapter 3 you'll study these

Big Ideas:

1. Performing operations with decimals

2. Converting between percents, fractions, and decimals

3. Using percents in real-life applications

Why?

So you can solve real-world problems about . . .

- Shot put, p. 140
- Dancing, p. 140
- Biology, p. 147
- Lava, p. 148
- Reptiles, p. 153
- Music, p. 159

Animated Math

at *classzone.com*

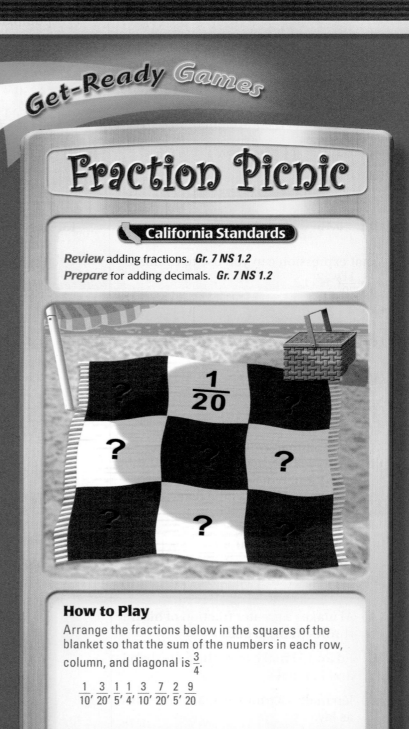

Get-Ready Games

Fraction Picnic

California Standards

Review adding fractions. *Gr. 7 NS 1.2*
Prepare for adding decimals. *Gr. 7 NS 1.2*

$\frac{1}{20}$

How to Play

Arrange the fractions below in the squares of the blanket so that the sum of the numbers in each row, column, and diagonal is $\frac{3}{4}$.

$$\frac{1}{10}, \frac{3}{20}, \frac{1}{5}, \frac{1}{4}, \frac{3}{10}, \frac{7}{20}, \frac{2}{5}, \frac{9}{20}$$

CALIFORNIA STANDARDS

- **Gr. 7 NS 1.2 Add, subtract, multiply, and divide rational numbers** (integers, fractions, and **terminating decimals**) and take positive rational numbers to whole-number powers. *(Lessons 3.2, 3.3)*

- **Gr. 7 NS 1.7 Solve problems that involve discounts, markups, commissions, and profit and compute simple and compound interest.** *(Lessons 3.6, 3.8)*

Deep Sea Math

California Standards

Review dividing fractions. **Gr. 7 NS 1.2**
Prepare for dividing decimals. **Gr. 7 NS 1.2**

How to Play

Play with a partner. The player with the greater score wins.

- Choose two fractions and find their quotient. A fraction cannot be used more than once.

- Add the quotient to your total score.

Games Wrap-Up

Draw Conclusions

Complete these exercises after playing the games.

1. **WRITING** In *Deep Sea Math*, how did you decide which fraction to use as your divisor and which to use as your dividend? *Explain.*

2. **REASONING** How can you use whole numbers to help you fill in the squares in *Fraction Picnic*? *Explain.*

Prerequisite Skills

California @*HomeTutor*
Prerequisite skills practice
at classzone.com

REVIEW VOCABULARY

- **simplest form of a fraction,** *p. 75*
- **equivalent fractions,** *p. 75*
- **rational number,** *p. 113*
- **terminating decimal,** *p. 113*
- **ratio,** *p. 732*

VOCABULARY CHECK

Copy and complete using a review term from the list at the left.

1. A(n) __?__ is a number that can be written as a quotient $\frac{a}{b}$ where a and b are integers and $b \neq 0$.

2. Fractions that represent the same number are __?__.

SKILL CHECK

Find the product or quotient. *(pp. 31, 36)*

3. $-125 \cdot 2$ 4. $-4 \cdot (-23)$ 5. $20 \cdot (-6)$ 6. $-8 \cdot (-7)$

7. $-39 \div 3$ 8. $-136 \div (-17)$ 9. $64 \div (-16)$ 10. $-27 \div (-9)$

Write the fraction in simplest form. *(p. 75)*

11. $\frac{4}{12}$ 12. $-\frac{35}{50}$ 13. $\frac{24}{52}$ 14. $-\frac{16}{96}$

Write two fractions that are equivalent to the given fraction. *(p. 75)*

15. $\frac{6}{14}$ 16. $\frac{7}{21}$ 17. $\frac{18}{24}$ 18. $\frac{24}{30}$

Notetaking Skills

NOW YOU TRY
Make a *cycle diagram* for writing a fraction as a decimal and writing a decimal as a fraction.

Focus on Graphic Organizers

You can use a *cycle diagram* to illustrate related processes, such as writing a mixed number as an improper fraction and writing an improper fraction as a mixed number.

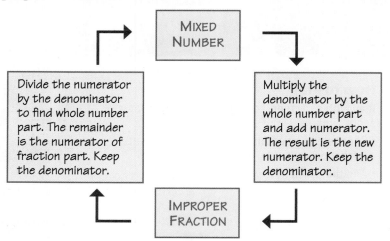

3.1 Comparing Decimals

Standards NS 1.1 Read, write, and compare rational numbers in scientific notation (positive and negative powers of 10), **compare rational numbers in general.**

Connect *Before* you converted fractions to decimals. *Now* you will compare decimals.

Math and **NATURE**
Example 1, p. 133

KEY VOCABULARY
• place value

You can use *place value* to compare two or more decimals. The **place value** of each digit in a decimal number depends on the digit's position relative to the decimal point. The chart below shows the names for the places in a decimal from millions to millionths. For instance, 5 is in the thousandths place, so its place value is $5 \times 0.001 = 0.005$.

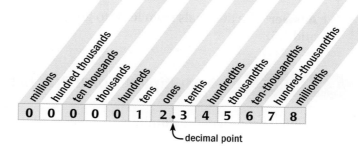

EXAMPLE 1 **Comparing Positive Decimals**

BIRDS An adult Calliope hummingbird has a length of 3.25 inches. An adult Costa hummingbird has a length of 3.5 inches. Which bird is longer?

SOLUTION

COMPARE NUMBERS
To make the comparison easier, it may be helpful to express 3.5 to the same number of decimal places as 3.25 by using 0 as a placeholder:
    3.5 = 3.50

METHOD 1 Look at the digits in corresponding places. Compare the digits in the place farthest to the left where the decimals have different digits.

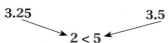

Because $2 < 5$, you know that $3.25 < 3.5$.

METHOD 2 Graph the decimals on a number line.

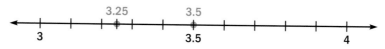

Because 3.25 lies to the left of 3.5, you know that $3.25 < 3.5$.

▶ **Answer** The Costa hummingbird is longer.

COMPARING POSITIVE AND NEGATIVE DECIMALS To compare positive and negative decimals, you can use a number line or you can compare corresponding place values of decimals. A negative decimal is always less than a positive decimal. The lesser of two negative decimals has the greater absolute value.

EXAMPLE 2 **Comparing Positive and Negative Decimals**

Order 0.7, −1.3, −0.4, 1.5, and −0.9 from least to greatest.

SOLUTION

Graph the decimals on a number line.

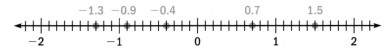

▶ **Answer** The decimals from least to greatest are −1.3, −0.9, −0.4, 0.7, and 1.5.

EXAMPLE 3 ◆ **Multiple Choice Practice**

Which list orders the numbers $\frac{27}{10}$, −0.5, $\left|-1\right|$, and −1 from least to greatest?

Ⓐ $-1, \left|-1\right|, -0.5, \frac{27}{10}$ Ⓑ $\left|-1\right|, -1, -0.5, \frac{27}{10}$

Ⓒ $-0.5, -1, \frac{27}{10}, \left|-1\right|$ Ⓓ $-1, -0.5, \left|-1\right|, \frac{27}{10}$

ELIMINATE CHOICES
An absolute value is always positive. Because $\left|-1\right| > -0.5$ and $\left|-1\right| > -1$, choices A and B can be eliminated.

SOLUTION

Graph the numbers on a number line. Note that $\frac{27}{10} = 2.7$ and $\left|-1\right| = 1$.

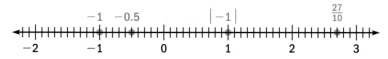

▶ **Answer** The correct answer is D. Ⓐ Ⓑ Ⓒ ●

✓ **GUIDED PRACTICE** for Examples 1, 2, and 3

Copy and complete the statement using <, >, or =.

1. 1.2 ? 1.5   **2.** 0.64 ? 0.68   **3.** 0.833 ? 0.83

Order the numbers from least to greatest.

4. −2.2, −1.1, −0.26, −0.19, −0.32   **5.** 0.81, $\left|-2\right|$, 0.2, −1, $-\frac{7}{9}$

3.1 EXERCISES

HOMEWORK KEY

◆ = **MULTIPLE CHOICE PRACTICE**
Exs. 15, 22, 45–47

○ = **HINTS AND HOMEWORK HELP**
for Exs. 11, 19, 41 at classzone.com

SKILLS • PROBLEM SOLVING • REASONING

1. **VOCABULARY** Copy and complete: The __?__ of each digit in a decimal number depends on the digit's position relative to the decimal point.

2. **WRITING** *Describe* how you can compare 1.49 and 1.479.

SEE EXAMPLE 1
on p. 133
for Exs. 3–15

COMPARING DECIMALS Copy and complete the statement using <, >, or =.

3. 7.1 _?_ 6.9
4. 8.5 _?_ 9.4
5. 2.8 _?_ 2.6
6. 3.4 _?_ 3.9
7. 12.0 _?_ 12
8. 1.21 _?_ 1.12
9. 8.7 _?_ 8.70
10. 4.40 _?_ 4.44
11. 2.746 _?_ 2.76
12. 5 _?_ 4.999
13. 6.253 _?_ 6.2513
14. 8.113 _?_ 8.1129

15. ◆ **MULTIPLE CHOICE** In what place is the digit 9 in the number 124.03976?

    A Thousandths   **B** Hundredths   **C** Hundreds   **D** Thousands

SEE EXAMPLE 2
on p. 134
for Exs. 16–22

ORDERING DECIMALS Order the decimals from least to greatest.

16. 5.34, 5.12, 5.43
17. −9.07, −9.06, −9.1
18. 4.3, 4.25, 4.31
19. 0.9, −1.1, −0.1, 1.5
20. −7.4, 7.9, 7, −6.9
21. 1.2, 1.05, −1.15, −0.98

22. ◆ **MULTIPLE CHOICE** Which list is ordered from least to greatest?

    A 0.4345, 0.3454, 0.3354, 0.3345   **B** 0.3354, 0.3345, 0.4345, 0.3454

    C 0.3345, 0.3354, 0.3454, 0.4345   **D** 0.3354, 0.3454, 0.3345, 0.4345

ERROR ANALYSIS *Describe* and correct the error in comparing two decimals.

23.
$$\times \quad -3.1 < -3.25$$

24.
× Three hundred twenty thousandths is greater than thirty-two hundredths.

COMPARING NUMBERS Copy and complete the statement using <, >, or =.

25. −4.29 _?_ −4.3
26. −1.1 _?_ −1.09
27. −0.4 _?_ $|-0.4|$
28. 5.3 _?_ $|-5.34|$
29. $-\frac{3}{4}$ _?_ −0.74
30. $-\frac{3}{4}$ _?_ −0.429
31. 0.3 _?_ $0.\overline{3}$
32. $\frac{11}{18}$ _?_ $|-0.6\overline{1}|$

SEE EXAMPLE 3
on p. 134
for Exs. 33–36

ORDERING NUMBERS Order the numbers from least to greatest.

33. $7\frac{4}{5}$, $7\frac{2}{3}$, 7.6, 7.71, $7\frac{8}{21}$

34. $9\frac{3}{4}$, 9.74, $9\frac{5}{7}$, 9.72, $9\frac{9}{13}$

35. 0.1, $\frac{5}{6}$, $\frac{3}{10}$, $-\frac{2}{7}$, $|-0.4|$

36. $-3.\overline{4}$, $-3.4\overline{2}$, $-|3.4|$, $-3\frac{3}{7}$

CONNECT SKILLS TO PROBLEM SOLVING Exercises 37–39 will help you prepare for problem solving.

37. The batting averages of two baseball players are 0.298 and 0.283. Which average is greater?

38. The average annual rainfall amounts for two cities are 45.03 inches and 45.2 inches. Which amount is greater?

39. The lengths of two pieces of wood are 8.27 inches and 8.4 inches. Which length is greater?

SEE EXAMPLES 2 AND 3 on p. 134 for Exs. 40–41

40. FROGS The table at the right shows the average lengths of four adult California frog species. Use a number line to order the lengths.

California **@HomeTutor** for problem solving help at classzone.com

Species	Length (cm)
California red-legged frog	12.7
Leopard frog	6.8
Foothill yellow-legged frog	5.9
Mountain yellow-legged frog	6.1

41. TEMPERATURE The average daily temperatures at McMurdo Station, Antarctica, for the months of October through March are $-18.9°C$, $-9.7°C$, $-3.4°C$, $-2.9°C$, $-9.5°C$, and $-18.2°C$. Order these temperatures from least to greatest.

California **@HomeTutor** for problem solving help at classzone.com

California red-legged frog

42. OPEN-ENDED Write three decimals between 1.5 and 1.6 with each decimal containing a different number of digits. Order your numbers.

43. CHALLENGE The table shows the qualifying speeds in miles per hour of five competitors in the 2004 Indianapolis 500. Of the competitors listed, who had the fastest qualifying speed?

Name	Speed
Adrian Fernandez	220.999
Buddy Rice	222.024
Dan Wheldon	221.524
Tony Kanaan	221.200
Vitor Meira	220.958

44. CHALLENGE Order the following decimals from least to greatest.

$$0.\overline{34}, \ 0.34, \ 0.\overline{346}, \ 0.343, \ 0.34\overline{3}, \ 0.3\overline{4}$$

◆ CALIFORNIA STANDARDS SPIRAL REVIEW

NS 1.3

45. Which decimal is equivalent to $5\frac{5}{8}$? *(p. 113)*

    Ⓐ 5.5   **Ⓑ** 5.55   **Ⓒ** 5.625   **Ⓓ** 5.675

NS 2.5

46. Which number has the greatest value? *(p. 12)*

    Ⓐ $|23|$ **Ⓑ** $|-24|$ **Ⓒ** 25   **Ⓓ** -26

AF 1.3

47. Three friends order sandwiches for \$3 each and drinks for \$2 each. Which expression could be used to find the total cost? *(p. 48)*

    Ⓐ $3(3) + 2$ **Ⓑ** $3(3 + 2)$ **Ⓒ** $2(3 + 3)$ **Ⓓ** $3 + 3(2)$

3.2 Adding and Subtracting Decimals

Standards NS 1.2 Add, subtract, multiply, and divide **rational numbers** (integers, fractions, and **terminating decimals**) and take positive rational numbers to whole-number powers.

Connect *Before* you ordered decimals. *Now* you will add and subtract decimals.

Math and
PERFORMING ARTS
Ex. 32, p. 140

KEY VOCABULARY
• front-end estimation

You can use a vertical format to add or subtract decimals. Begin by lining up the decimal points. Then add or subtract as with whole numbers. Be sure to include the decimal point in your answer.

EXAMPLE 1 Adding and Subtracting Positive Decimals

a. $2.4 + 0.86 + 6$

USE PLACEHOLDERS
You can write zeros after the last digit of a decimal number to help you line up the decimal points.

```
    1
  2.40
  0.86
+ 6.00
  9.26
```

CHECK Round decimals to whole numbers and add: $2 + 1 + 6 = 9$. The answer is reasonable.

b. $11.8 - 3.54$

```
  0 11 7 10
  1̶1̶.8̶0̶
-  3.54
   8.26
```

CHECK Add 8.26 and 3.54 to see if you get 11.8. It checks: $8.26 + 3.54 = 11.8$.

In Chapter 1, you learned rules for adding and subtracting positive and negative integers. You can apply the same rules to adding and subtracting positive and negative decimals.

EXAMPLE 2 Adding and Subtracting Negative Decimals

ADD AND SUBTRACT NUMBERS
For help with adding and subtracting integers, see pp. 18 and 24.

a. Find the sum $-2.9 + (-6.5)$.

Use the rule for adding numbers with the same sign.

$$-2.9 + (-6.5) = -9.4$$

— Add $|-2.9|$ and $|-6.5|$.

Both decimals are negative, so the sum is negative.

b. Find the difference $-25.38 - (-42.734)$.

First rewrite the difference as a sum: $-25.38 + 42.734$. Then use the rule for adding numbers with different signs.

$$-25.38 + 42.734 = 17.354$$

— Subtract $|-25.38|$ from $|42.734|$.

$|42.734| > |-25.38|$, so the sum has the same sign as 42.734.

EXAMPLE 3 Evaluating an Algebraic Expression

TEMPERATURE The Kelvin scale for temperature is used by chemists and other scientists. The formula $K = C + 273.15$ is used to convert from degrees Celsius C to kelvins K. A block of dry ice has a surface temperature of $-78.5°C$. What is this temperature in kelvins?

SOLUTION

To find the temperature in kelvins, substitute the Celsius temperature into the equation.

$K = C + 273.15$	**Original equation**
$K = -78.5 + 273.15$	**Substitute −78.5 for C.**
$K = 194.65$	**Add.**

▶ **Answer** The temperature in kelvins is 194.65 K.

✓ **GUIDED PRACTICE**   for Examples 1, 2, and 3

Find the sum or difference.

1. $8.93 + 0.367$ **2.** $-5.3 - 11.49$ **3.** $5.376 + (-0.8)$

4. TEMPERATURE What is 29°C in kelvins?

ESTIMATING You can estimate sums using **front-end estimation**. Add the front-end digits to get a low estimate. Then use the remaining digits to adjust the sum to a closer estimate.

EXAMPLE 4 Using Front-End Estimation

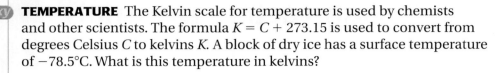

THEATER You want to estimate the cost of supplies for a play. Is the cost of the items shown (excluding tax) more or less than your $50 budget?

Play supplies	Cost
Cowboy hat	$18.95
Cotton fabric	$9.49
Rope	$3.49
Picnic basket	$16.05

SOLUTION

Use front-end estimation.

STEP 1
Add the **front-end digits**.

$18.95
$ 9.49
$ 3.49
$16.05
—————
$46

STEP 2
Estimate the sum of the remaining digits.

$18.95 —— $1
$ 9.49 ⟍
$ 3.49 ⟶ $1
$16.05 —— $0
—————
$2

STEP 3
Add the results.

$46
+ $ 2
—————
$48

▶ **Answer** The cost of the items is less than your $50 budget.

5. **GROCERIES** You buy the following items at a grocery store. Use front-end estimation to estimate your total cost.

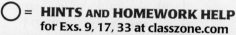

Grocery List

milk $3.12

bread $1.15

eggs $1.88

meat $8.46

fruit $1.32

3.2 EXERCISES

HOMEWORK
KEY

◆ = **MULTIPLE CHOICE PRACTICE**
Exs. 20, 21, 33, 41–43

○ = **HINTS** AND **HOMEWORK HELP**
for Exs. 9, 17, 33 at classzone.com

SKILLS • PROBLEM SOLVING • REASONING

1. **VOCABULARY** Copy and complete: You can get a low estimate of $13.56 + 11.42 + 25.94$ by adding the front-end digits __?__, __?__, and __?__.

2. **WRITING** *Explain* how to find the difference $-104.89 - 22.48$.

SEE EXAMPLES
1 AND 2
⋯⋯⋯⋯⋯⋯⋯⋯
on p. 137
for Exs. 3–21

EVALUATING EXPRESSIONS **Find the sum or difference.**

3. $30.193 + 7.91$

4. $2.507 + 0.586$

5. $-6.08 + 2.661$

6. $-0.37 + (-1.8)$

7. $6.8 + (-1.812)$

8. $-12.09 + 1.20$

9. $3.28 + (-4.91)$

10. $1.46 + (-1.564)$

11. $1.57 - 9.28$

12. $68.79 - 9.18$

13. $15.7 - (-6.4)$

14. $-0.99 - 0.304$

15. $25.885 - 6.9$

16. $29.1 - (-3.05)$

17. $-4.22 - 0.807$

ERROR ANALYSIS *Describe* and correct the error in the solution.

18.
$$\begin{array}{r} 10.43 \\ + \; 7.521 \\ \hline 8.564 \end{array}$$ ✗

19.
$$\begin{array}{r} 12.70 \\ - \; 4.53 \\ \hline 8.23 \end{array}$$ ✗

20. ◆ **MULTIPLE CHOICE** An item costs $9.87 plus sales tax of $.49. What is the total cost of the item?

(A) $8.38   (B) $9.36   (C) $9.38   (D) $10.36

21. ◆ **MULTIPLE CHOICE** What is the value of $12.9 + 3.1 - 7.6$?

(A) 2.2   (B) 8.4   (C) 17.4   (D) 23.6

22. **PUZZLE PROBLEM** Replace the question marks with digits to make the solution correct.

$$\begin{array}{r} 5.?4 \\ - \; ?.6? \\ \hline 3.21 \end{array}$$

SEE EXAMPLE 4
on p. 138
for Exs. 23–26

ESTIMATING SUMS **Use front-end estimation to estimate the sum.**

23. 2.32 + 6.69 + 8.50 + 4.46

24. 10.23 + 6.98 + 9.05 + 5.80

25. 5.62 + 4.89 + 3.44 + 9.98

26. 23.70 + 16.12 + 5.96 + 14.18

27. ⬡ **GEOMETRY** Plot the following points in a coordinate plane. Then connect the points to form a rectangle and find its perimeter.

$A(1.25, 3.5)$, $B(4.25, 3.5)$, $C(4.25, 6.75)$, $D(1.25, 6.75)$

CONNECT SKILLS TO PROBLEM SOLVING **Exercises 28–30 will help you prepare for problem solving.**

28. To pay for milk that costs $3.79, you hand the clerk a $5 bill. How much change should you receive?

29. You buy a pair of soccer shorts for $8.95 and a team shirt for $10.59. How much do you spend?

30. You run 400 meters in 58.01 seconds. What is the difference of your time and the school record of 55.49 seconds?

SEE EXAMPLE 1
on p. 137
for Exs. 31–32

31. **SHOT PUT** The world record for men's shot put is 23.12 meters. The Olympic record is 22.47 meters. The gold medal winning throw at the 2004 Summer Olympics was 21.16 meters.

   a. How much longer is the world record throw than the gold medal winning throw at the 2004 Olympics?

   b. How much longer is the Olympic record throw than the gold medal winning throw at the 2004 Olympics?

California @HomeTutor for problem solving help at classzone.com

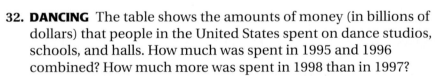

World record holder Randy Barnes

32. **DANCING** The table shows the amounts of money (in billions of dollars) that people in the United States spent on dance studios, schools, and halls. How much was spent in 1995 and 1996 combined? How much more was spent in 1998 than in 1997?

Money Spent on Dancing					
Year	1994	1995	1996	1997	1998
Dollars (billions)	0.906	0.947	1.046	1.08	1.138

California @HomeTutor for problem solving help at classzone.com

SEE EXAMPLE 3
on p. 138
for Ex. 33

33. ◆ **MULTIPLE CHOICE** The formula $K = \frac{5}{9}(F - 32) + 273.15$ converts degrees Fahrenheit to kelvins. The boiling point of water is 212°F. What is this temperature in kelvins?

   (A) 100 K   **(B)** 273.15 K   **(C)** 373.15 K   **(D)** 390.93 K

34. **REASONING** A city had 4.52 inches of rain in April, 5.23 inches of rain in May, and 3.41 inches of rain in June. During this three month period, did the city have more than 12 inches of rain? *Explain* why an estimate is sufficient to answer the question.

Space Shuttle On a space shuttle mission, astronauts are allowed 1.5 pounds of personal items. The table shows the weights of some possible items. A penny from space is a popular collectible.

Astronauts' Personal Items	
Item	**Weight (pounds)**
2 Rolls of pennies	0.55
5 Golf balls	0.506
Watch	0.09
College sweatshirt	0.750
Whistle	0.125
Camera	0.625

35. **Calculate** An astronaut decides to bring two rolls of pennies, a watch, and a college sweatshirt on the mission. What is the total weight?

36. **Calculate** Another astronaut brings five golf balls and a camera. How much weight allowance is left for an additional item?

37. **Open-Ended** A third astronaut wants to bring four different items from the table. Find four items that the astronaut could choose.

38. **Compare** List the items in this table in order from lightest to heaviest.

39. **CHALLENGE** Use the table shown.
    a. Copy and complete the table.
    b. Using the results of your table, what is another name for $0.\overline{9}$?

Fraction pair	$\frac{1}{3}, \frac{2}{3}$	$\frac{1}{6}, \frac{5}{6}$	$\frac{4}{9}, \frac{5}{9}$	$\frac{3}{11}, \frac{8}{11}$
Decimal pair	?	?	?	?
Fraction sum	?	?	?	?
Decimal sum	?	?	?	?

40. **CHALLENGE** One *mole* of hydrogen atoms has a mass of 1.0079 grams. One mole of oxygen atoms has a mass of 15.9994 grams. A mole of water is made up of 2 moles of hydrogen and 1 mole of oxygen. What is the mass of a mole of water?

◆ CALIFORNIA STANDARDS SPIRAL REVIEW

NS 1.1

41. Which decimal is less than 1.059? *(p. 133)*

   (A) 1.58   **(B)** 1.1   **(C)** 1.092   **(D)** 1.0073

NS 1.5

42. What is 2.352 written as a mixed number? *(p. 113)*

   (A) $2\frac{27}{200}$ **(B)** $2\frac{3}{10}$ **(C)** $2\frac{7}{20}$ **(D)** $2\frac{44}{125}$

NS 1.2

43. Toni jogged $\frac{3}{8}$ mile on Saturday and $\frac{1}{4}$ mile on Sunday. Which fraction represents the total distance Toni jogged over the weekend? *(p. 85)*

   (A) $\frac{7}{12}$ mi   **(B)** $\frac{5}{8}$ mi   **(C)** $\frac{3}{4}$ mi   **(D)** $\frac{5}{6}$ mi

3.3 Modeling Decimal Multiplication

MATERIALS · graph paper · colored pencils

Standards

NS 1.2 Add, subtract, **multiply,** and divide **rational numbers** (integers, fractions, and **terminating decimals**) and take positive rational numbers to whole-number powers.

QUESTION How can you model decimal multiplication?

You can use a 10 by 10 square drawn on graph paper to model multiplication of whole numbers or decimals.

EXPLORE 1 Use a model to find products

Use a model to find (a) 6 × 7 and (b) 0.6 × 0.7.

First, decide what amount the areas of the large square and each small square will represent. Then shade an appropriate number of rows and columns.

a. Let the area of the large square be 100. So, the area of each small square is 1. Shade 6 rows of the large square red and 7 columns blue.

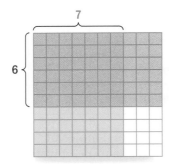

Because 42 small squares are doubly shaded, 6 × 7 = 42.

b. Let the area of the large square be 1. So, the area of each small square is $\frac{1}{100}$, or 0.01. Shade 6 rows of the large square red and 7 columns blue.

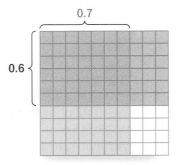

Because 42 small squares are doubly shaded, $0.6 \times 0.7 = \frac{42}{100} = 0.42$.

DRAW CONCLUSIONS Use your observations to complete these exercises

1. Use a model to find the products 0.3 × 0.8 and 0.5 × 0.9. What do you notice about the relationship between the number of decimal places in the factors and the number of decimal places in the product? Make a conjecture about this relationship.

2. **REASONING** Predict the value of the product 0.06 × 0.07. *Explain* your reasoning.

EXPLORE 2 **Use a model to find a product**

Use a model to find the product 1.3 × 2.5.

Use six 10 by 10 squares arranged in a rectangle, as shown. Let the area of each 10 by 10 square represent 1. So, the area of each small square is $\frac{1}{100}$, or 0.01. Shade 13 rows of the rectangle red and 25 columns blue.

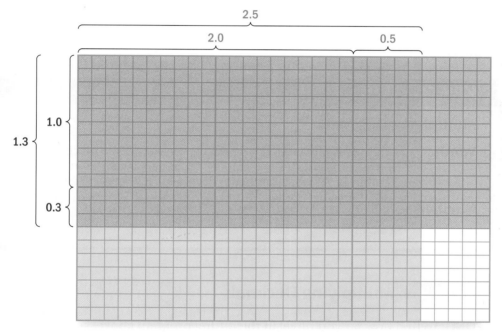

There are 100 + 30 + 100 + 30 + 50 + 15 = 325 small squares that are doubly shaded. Because 325 hundredths equals 3.25, 1.3 × 2.5 = 3.25.

DRAW CONCLUSIONS **Use your observations to complete these exercises**

3. Use a model to find the product 13 × 25. How does the product 13 × 25 compare with the product 1.3 × 2.5 from Explore 2?

4. In Explore 2, how do the numbers of decimal places in the factors 1.3 and 2.5 relate to the number of decimal places in the product 3.25?

Predict the number of decimal places in the product. Then check your answer by using a calculator to find the product.

5. 0.5 × 0.9

6. 1.25 × 1.8

7. 0.65 × 1.98

8. 3.45 × 2.37

9. 4.05 × 3.135

10. 2.981 × 1.43

3.3 Multiplying and Dividing Decimals

Standards NS 1.2 Add, subtract, **multiply, and divide rational numbers** (integers, fractions, and **terminating decimals**) and take positive rational numbers to whole-number powers.

Connect *Before* you added and subtracted decimals. *Now* you will multiply and divide decimals.

Math and RECREATION
Example 1, p. 144

KEY VOCABULARY
• leading digit

You travel downstream in a raft at a rate of about 4.3 miles per hour. How far will you travel in 2.5 hours? To answer this question, you need to multiply decimals.

KEY CONCEPT *For Your Notebook*

Multiplying Decimals

Words Multiply decimals as you do whole numbers. Then place the decimal point. The number of decimal places in the product is the total number of decimal places in the factors.

Numbers

2.25	×	8.9	=	20.025
2 places		1 place		3 places

EXAMPLE 1 Multiplying Decimals

REVIEW DISTANCE FORMULA
For help with the distance formula, see p. 732.

RAFTING To find how far you travel in the rafting problem above, substitute the given values into the distance formula: distance = rate • time.

$$d = rt$$
$$= 4.3 \cdot 2.5$$
$$= 10.75$$

$$\begin{array}{r} 4.3 \\ \times\ 2.5 \\ \hline 215 \\ 86 \\ \hline 10.75 \end{array}$$

1 decimal place
+ 1 decimal place

2 decimal places

▶ **Answer** You will travel about 10.75 miles.

CHECK A number's **leading digit** is its leftmost nonzero digit. To check for reasonableness, round each factor to its leading digit and multiply.

4.3 • 2.5   **Round factors to leading digit.** ➡ 4 • 3 = 12

✓ **GUIDED PRACTICE** for Example 1

Find the product. Check that the answer is reasonable.

1. 7.39 • 2.1   **2.** 19.62 • 5.07   **3.** 1.13 • 0.04   **4.** 0.85 • 8

Dividing Decimals

Words   When you divide by a decimal, multiply both the divisor and the dividend by the power of ten that will make the divisor an integer. Then divide.

Numbers $2.75\overline{)15.125}$ **Multiply by 100.** ➡ $275.\overline{)1512.5}^{\;5.5}$

EXAMPLE 2   **Dividing Decimals**

Animated Math

For an interactive example of dividing decimals, go to **classzone.com**.

To find the quotient $60.102 \div 6.3$, multiply the divisor and dividend by 10. Move the decimal points 1 place to the right.

$6.3\overline{)60.102}$ **Move decimal points.** ➡ $63.\overline{)601.02}$

$$63\overline{)601.02}^{\;9.54}$$ *Then divide.*

CHECK   To check that the quotient is reasonable, round the quotient and the divisor to the leading digit. Then multiply and compare to the dividend.

$9.54 \cdot 6.3$ **Round.** ➡ $10 \cdot 6 = 60 \approx 60.102$

AVOID ERRORS

Remember to use the *original* divisor, *not* the divisor you used after moving the decimal points when checking.

EXAMPLE 3   **Using Zeros as Placeholders**

To find some quotients, you may need to use zeros as placeholders.

Placeholder in Dividend   **Placeholder in Quotient**

$6 \div 1.2$ $0.0126 \div 1.8$

⬇   ⬇

 $1.2\overline{)6.0}$ ⟵ Zero as placeholder $1.8\overline{)0.0126}$

⬇   ⬇

$$\begin{array}{r} 5 \\ 12\overline{)60} \\ 60 \\ \hline 0 \end{array}$$

$$\begin{array}{r} 0.007 \\ 18\overline{)0.126} \\ 126 \\ \hline 0 \end{array}$$
  ⟵ Zeros as placeholders

✓   **GUIDED PRACTICE**   for Examples 2 and 3

Find the quotient. Check that the answer is reasonable.

5. $1.6 \div 0.04$ **6.** $0.632 \div 0.79$ **7.** $13 \div 0.65$

8. $4.365 \div 4.5$ **9.** $0.3744 \div 1.56$ **10.** $0.0108 \div 2.7$

WORKING WITH NEGATIVE DECIMALS In Chapter 1, you learned rules for multiplying and dividing positive and negative integers. You can apply the same rules to multiplying and dividing positive and negative decimals.

EXAMPLE 4 Multiplying and Dividing with Negative Decimals

REVIEW MULTIPLYING AND DIVIDING NUMBERS
For help with multiplying and dividing negative numbers, see pp. 31 and 36.

a. -4.2×-2.7

$$\begin{array}{r} -4.2 \\ \times\ -2.7 \\ \hline 294 \\ 84 \\ \hline 11.34 \end{array}$$

The decimals have the same sign, so the product is positive.

b. $2.1 \div (-0.24)$

$-0.24\overline{)2.1}\ \longrightarrow$

$$\begin{array}{r} -8.75 \\ -24\overline{)210.00} \\ 192 \\ \hline 180 \\ 168 \\ \hline 120 \\ 120 \\ \hline 0 \end{array}$$

The decimals have different signs, so the quotient is negative.

✓ **GUIDED PRACTICE** | for Example 4

Find the product or quotient. Check that the answer is reasonable.

11. $-1.5 \times (-2.3)$ **12.** -9.6×0.64 **13.** $-5.35 \div (-2.5)$ **14.** $-3.9 \div 5.2$

3.3 EXERCISES

HOMEWORK KEY
◆ = **MULTIPLE CHOICE PRACTICE**
Exs. 23, 26, 49, 58–60

○ = **HINTS AND HOMEWORK HELP**
for Exs. 3, 19, 49 at classzone.com

SKILLS • PROBLEM SOLVING • REASONING

1. VOCABULARY Copy and complete: In 0.0745, the leading digit is __?__ .

2. WRITING *Explain* when you need to include one or more zeros as placeholders in a quotient. Give an example.

SEE EXAMPLES 1, 2, 3, AND 4
on pp. 144–146
for Exs. 3–26

MULTIPLYING AND DIVIDING DECIMALS Find the product or quotient.
Check that the answer is reasonable.

3. $7.8 \cdot 2.6$ **4.** $3.75 \cdot (-0.4)$ **5.** $-8.2 \cdot 0.7$ **6.** $0.5 \div 1.25$

7. $25 \cdot 0.2$ **8.** $2.4 \cdot 0.3$ **9.** $13.2 \div 1.1$ **10.** $13.65 \cdot 1.1$

11. $4.8 \div 1.2$ **12.** $4.9 \div 0.07$ **13.** $-8 \div (-3.2)$ **14.** $5 \div (-0.1)$

15. $5.41 \div 0.35$ **16.** $4.844 \div 0.56$ **17.** $-0.57 \div 0.38$ **18.** $-2.687 \cdot (-9)$

19. $-37.41 \div 4.3$ **20.** $0.098 \cdot (-0.55)$ **21.** $6.025 \cdot 48.2$ **22.** $1.11 \div 0.925$

23. ◆ **MULTIPLE CHOICE** What is true of the quotient of -0.67 and 0.42?

(A) It is greater than 1. **(B)** It is between 0 and 1.

(C) It is between 0 and -1. **(D)** It is less than -1.

ERROR ANALYSIS *Describe* and correct the error in finding the product or quotient.

24.

$$
\times
\begin{array}{r}
9.78 \\
\times\ \ 3.4 \\
\hline
3912 \\
2934 \\
\hline
332.52
\end{array}
$$

25.

$$
\times \quad
\begin{array}{r}
0.24 \\
8\overline{)0.192} \\
\underline{16} \\
32 \\
\underline{32} \\
0
\end{array}
$$

26. ◆ **MULTIPLE CHOICE** What is the value of $(3.2)^3$?

    A −32.768   **B** 9.6   **C** 10.24   **D** 32.768

EVALUATING EXPRESSIONS Find the sum, difference, product, or quotient.

27. $-2.3 + 3.63$

28. $7.16 \times (-0.54)$

29. $6.87 - 2.514$

30. $28 \div (-1.6)$

31. $-9.49 - (-12.125)$

32. $15.282 + 7.78$

33. 1.628×0.61

34. $-8 \div (-6.8)$

35. -21.15×0.386

ESTIMATING QUOTIENTS Estimate each quotient. Then copy and complete the statement using < or >.

36. $105.4 \div 29.8 \ \underline{?}\ 20.4 \div 5.1$

37. $3.8 \div (-2.1) \ \underline{?}\ -1.8 \div 6.4$

EVALUATING EXPRESSIONS Evaluate the expression.

38. $(3.4)^3 + 5.1 \div 1.7 - 4.89$

39. $6.2(18.77 - 6.27) + (9.1)^2$

MULTIPLYING RATIONAL NUMBERS Find the product.

40. $\frac{1}{4} \times 0.62$

41. $\frac{1}{2}(28.1 - 14.27)$

42. $\frac{2}{5}\left[\frac{3}{8}(0.3 \times 5.4)\right]$

CONNECT SKILLS TO PROBLEM SOLVING Exercises 43–46 will help you prepare for problem solving.

43. What is the cost of 1.5 pounds of ground beef priced at $2.79 per pound?

44. What is the cost of 9 yards of fabric at $5.25 per yard?

45. What is the cost of 1 pound of potatoes if 5 pounds cost $1.89?

46. You pay $4.20 for 2.5 pounds of lunch meat. How much does 1 pound of the lunch meat cost?

SEE EXAMPLES 1 AND 2 on pp. 144–145 for Exs. 47–49

47. **BIOLOGY** A mother rhinoceros weighs 3600 pounds. Her baby weighs 0.038 of her weight.

    a. How much does the baby rhinoceros weigh?

    b. *Explain* how you can check whether your answer to part (a) is reasonable.

California @HomeTutor   for problem solving help at classzone.com

Rhinoceros

48. SHORT RESPONSE You have $75 to spend on daffodil bulbs.

    a. Boxes of bulbs cost $19.95 per box, including tax. How many boxes can you buy? Estimate to check that your answer is reasonable.

    b. Individual bulbs cost $1.20 each. How many bulbs can you buy with the money left over from purchasing the boxes of bulbs? *Explain.*

California @HomeTutor for problem solving help at classzone.com

(49.) ◆ **MULTIPLE CHOICE** You are buying balloons that cost $.89 per package, including tax. You have $14.75 to spend. How many packages of balloons can you buy?

    (A) 13.13   **(B)** 16   **(C)** 16.57   **(D)** 17

50. LOOK FOR A PATTERN Copy and complete the table by multiplying each number in the left column by the number at the top of each of the other columns. *Describe* the pattern.

x	1	0.1	0.01	0.001	0.0001
87	87	8.7	?	?	?
356	356	?	?	?	?
1200	?	?	?	?	?

SEE EXAMPLE 2
on p. 145
for Ex. 51

51. LAVA FLOWS A lava flow is a stream of molten rock that pours from an erupting vent of a volcano. A lava flow travels 15.5 miles down a steep slope in 2.5 hours. Find the average rate at which the flow travels. Write your answer in miles per hour. *Explain* why your answer is reasonable.

Kilauea volcano, Hawaii

52. REASONING Without evaluating, explain how you know that 3.5×0.2 and 0.35×2 are equivalent.

53. AIR TRAVEL A plane travels from Boston to London in 6.25 hours, a distance of about 3285 miles. The return trip takes 7.5 hours. How many miles per hour faster is the faster speed than the slower speed? How many times as fast?

54. POOLS A rectangular deck surrounds a swimming pool on all four sides. The deck has the dimensions shown. What is the area of the water?

55. CHALLENGE One micrometer is equal to 0.001 millimeter. A bacterium is 4 micrometers wide. How many times would you have to magnify the bacterium for it to appear 1 millimeter wide?

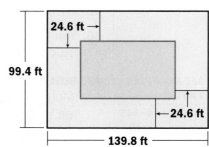

56. CHALLENGE One inch is equal to 2.54 centimeters. The volume of a cube is 8 cubic inches. What is the volume of the cube in cubic centimeters? Round your answer to the nearest tenth.

57. CHALLENGE You can write the expression $\frac{1.6}{2.4}$ as a quotient of integers by multiplying by $\frac{10}{10}$, a form of 1, to get $\frac{16}{24} = \frac{2}{3}$. Write each expression below as a quotient of integers and then in simplest form. Tell by what form of 1 you multiplied.

a. $\frac{0.5}{2}$ **b.** $\frac{1.75}{3.5}$ **c.** $\frac{0.75}{2.25}$ **d.** $\frac{4.8}{12}$

◆ CALIFORNIA STANDARDS SPIRAL REVIEW

NS 1.3

58. Which decimal is equivalent to $\frac{12}{5}$? *(p. 113)*

  A 0.4   **B** 1.2   **C** 2.4   **D** 3.2

NS 2.2

59. What is the value of $\frac{5}{17} - \frac{3}{7}$? *(p. 85)*

  A $-\frac{8}{17}$ **B** $-\frac{16}{119}$ **C** $\frac{15}{91}$ **D** $\frac{1}{5}$

NS 1.1

60. The table shows the times (in seconds) of four race car drivers qualifying for a race. The times are relative to the current leader. Each driver wants the lowest time. Which driver is the new leader? *(p. 137)*

Qualifying Results				
Driver	A	B	C	D
Time (sec)	+0.105	−0.098	+0.214	−0.108

  A Driver A   **B** Driver B   **C** Driver C   **D** Driver D

QUIZ *for Lessons 3.1–3.3*

Order the numbers from least to greatest. *(p. 133)*

1. $4.26, 4\frac{3}{8}, 4.024, \frac{29}{7}, 4\frac{11}{23}$ **2.** $1.244, -2.35, |-1.2|, -1\frac{6}{19}, \frac{13}{19}$

Find the sum or difference. *(p. 137)*

3. $-2.301 + 8.4$ **4.** $15.25 + 9.636$ **5.** $14.65 - 3.608$ **6.** $3.02 - (-0.255)$

Find the product or quotient. *(p. 144)*

7. -15.3×0.48 **8.** 3.88×0.9 **9.** $-0.162 \div (-2.7)$ **10.** $-2.07 \div 0.225$

11. EXERCISE You are exercising on a treadmill. You walk for 1.2 miles, jog for 3.7 miles, and then walk for another 0.9 mile. Your goal is to walk or jog for a total of 6 miles. How much farther must you walk or jog? *(p. 137)*

12. PHONE CARD Nancy uses her phone card to make a call and is charged $.84. How many minutes did she talk if the phone card rate is $.07 per minute? *(p. 144)*

3.4 Percents as Decimals and Fractions

Math and ECOLOGY
Example 2, p. 151

Standards NS 1.3 Convert fractions to decimals and percents and use these representations in estimations, computations, and applications.

Connect *Before* you wrote fractions as decimals. *Now* you will write percents as decimals and fractions.

KEY VOCABULARY
• percent

The word *percent* means "per hundred." A **percent** is a ratio whose denominator is 100. The symbol for percent is %.

The diagram below shows two ways to represent 20% using concepts from Lessons 2.1 and 2.7.

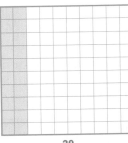

$$20\% = \frac{20}{100} = 0.20$$

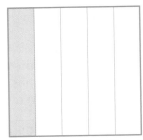

$$20\% = \frac{20}{100} = \frac{20 \div 20}{100 \div 20} = \frac{1}{5}$$

PERCENTS AND DECIMALS To write a percent as a decimal, you can divide by 100, because $p\% = \frac{p}{100} = p \div 100$. Recall that dividing by 100 is the same as moving the decimal point two places to the left.

EXAMPLE 1 Writing Percents as Decimals

a. $65\% = 65 \div 100 = .65 = 0.65$

b. $250\% = 250 \div 100 = 2.50 = 2.5$

c. $0.3\% = 0.3 \div 100 = .003 = 0.003$

d. $-125\% = -125 \div 100 = -1.25 = -1.25$

AVOID ERRORS
Add a zero on the left if necessary to move the decimal point two places to the left.

✓ GUIDED PRACTICE for Example 1

Write the percent as a decimal.

1. 98% **2.** 262% **3.** −22% **4.** 0.15%

5. −8% **6.** −0.2% **7.** 4.5% **8.** 0.05%

FINDING A PERCENT OF A NUMBER To find a percent of a number, first change the percent to a decimal or fraction. The word "of" translates to multiplication in percent problems. So, multiply the percent expressed as a decimal or fraction by the number. In general, $p\%$ of n is $\dfrac{p}{100} \times n$.

EXAMPLE 2 Finding a Percent of a Number

ECOLOGY A service club is planting seedlings as part of an erosion prevention project. The club has 240 seedlings to plant. Of the seedlings, 15% are laurel sumac. How many laurel sumac seedlings will the club plant?

SOLUTION

To find the number of laurel sumac seedlings the club will be planting, multiply 15% by 240.

$$15\% \times 240 = 0.15 \times 240 \qquad \text{Write 15\% as a decimal.}$$
$$= 36 \qquad \text{Multiply.}$$

▶ **Answer** The club will plant 36 laurel sumac seedlings.

✓ **GUIDED PRACTICE**   for Example 2

9. **WHAT IF?** In Example 2, suppose that 35% of the seedlings are laurel sumac. How many laurel sumac seedlings will the club plant?

PERCENTS AND FRACTIONS Since percent means per 100, to write $p\%$ as a fraction, use p as the numerator and 100 as the denominator. Then simplify.

EXAMPLE 3   Writing Percents as Fractions

COMMON EQUIVALENTS
For a list of common fraction, decimal, and percent equivalents, see p. 763.

a. $25\% = \dfrac{25}{100} = \dfrac{25 \div 25}{100 \div 25} = \dfrac{1}{4}$

b. $325\% = \dfrac{325}{100} = \dfrac{325 \div 25}{100 \div 25} = \dfrac{13}{4} = 3\dfrac{1}{4}$

c. $0.2\% = \dfrac{0.2}{100} = \dfrac{0.2 \times 10}{100 \times 10} = \dfrac{2}{1000} = \dfrac{1}{500}$

d. $-75\% = -\dfrac{75}{100} = -\dfrac{75 \div 25}{100 \div 25} = -\dfrac{3}{4}$

✓ **GUIDED PRACTICE**   for Example 3

Write the percent as a fraction.

10. 10%   **11.** −65%   **12.** 22%   **13.** 70.5%

14. **CALCIUM** One cup of fat-free milk supplies 30% of the Recommemded Daily Value of calcium. Write this percent as a fraction.

3.4 EXERCISES

HOMEWORK KEY

◆ = **MULTIPLE CHOICE PRACTICE**
Exs. 13, 20, 45, 48–50

○ = **HINTS AND HOMEWORK HELP**
for Exs. 11, 27, 45 at classzone.com

SKILLS • PROBLEM SOLVING • REASONING

1. VOCABULARY Copy and complete: Another way to say "25 songs out of 100" is to say "25 ？ of the songs."

2. WRITING *Describe* how to write a percent as a decimal.

SEE EXAMPLE 1
on p. 150
for Exs. 3–13

REWRITING PERCENTS **Write the percent as a decimal.**

3. 80%

4. 37.5%

5. −7.5%

6. 110%

7. 1.05%

8. −44.55%

9. −0.4%

10. 0.78%

11. 187.09%

12. 0.08%

13. ◆ MULTIPLE CHOICE Which of the following is equivalent to 12.5%?

Ⓐ 0.0125   Ⓑ 0.125   Ⓒ 1.25   Ⓓ 12.5

SEE EXAMPLE 2
on p. 151
for Exs. 14–20

FINDING PERCENTS OF NUMBERS **Find the percent of the number.**

14. What number is 25% of 200?

15. What number is 65% of 250?

16. What number is 45% of 245?

17. What number is 30% of 120?

18. What number is 520% of 150?

19. What number is 0.36% of 700?

20. ◆ MULTIPLE CHOICE What is 20% of $90?

Ⓐ $18   Ⓑ $20   Ⓒ $70   Ⓓ $72

SEE EXAMPLE 3
on p. 151
for Exs. 21–30

REWRITING PERCENTS **Write the percent as a fraction.**

21. 40%

22. 87%

23. −32.5%

24. 5%

25. −124%

26. 1%

27. −4.2%

28. 200.2%

29. −8.03%

30. 0.07%

ERROR ANALYSIS *Describe* and correct the error in the solution.

31. What number is 30% of 500?

$$30\% \times 500 = 30 \times 500$$
$$= 15,000$$

32. Write 75% as a fraction.

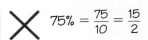

$$75\% = \frac{75}{10} = \frac{15}{2}$$

NUMBER SENSE **Copy and complete the statement using <, >, or =.**

33. 30% of 120 ？ 120% of 30

34. 20% of 80 ？ 40% of 50

35. 15% of 140 ？ 75% of 24

36. 25% of 80 ？ 125% of 12

37. 150% of 30 ？ 75% of 48

38. 10% of 400 ？ 25% of 160

39. OPEN-ENDED *Describe* a real-life situation in which a percent greater than 100% makes sense, and one where it does not make sense.

40. The price of a cat toy is $9.50. The sales tax is 8%. What is the amount of the sales tax?

41. You take a taxi ride. The fare is $22.50. You want to give a 15% tip. How much should your tip be?

42. Sixty athletes try out for the football team. Of the athletes, 80% will be selected for the team. How many athletes will be selected for the team?

SEE EXAMPLES 2 AND 3
on p. 151
for Exs. 43–45

43. GOLD 14 karat gold is 58.5% pure gold, and 18 karat gold is 75% pure gold. Write each percent as a fraction in simplest form.

California *@HomeTutor* for problem solving help at classzone.com

44. REPTILES The largest crocodiles alive today are 23 feet in length. Recently, researchers found bones of an ancient crocodile. It was 174% as long as today's longest crocodiles. How long was the ancient crocodile? Round to the nearest foot.

California *@HomeTutor* for problem solving help at classzone.com

Australian Saltwater Crocodile

45. ◆ **MULTIPLE CHOICE** A bicycle is on sale for 25% off the original price. The original price is $200. How much will you save?

Ⓐ $25   Ⓑ $50   Ⓒ $75   Ⓓ $100

46. CHALLENGE Is 50% of 30% of 120 the same as $\frac{3}{20}$ of 120? *Explain.*

47. CHALLENGE A worker gets a raise so that his pay is now 120% of what it was. Then the employer offers the worker the option of working less time but making only 80% of the new pay rate. Would choosing this option enable the worker to make *more, less,* or *the same amount* as before the raise? *Explain.*

◆ CALIFORNIA STANDARDS SPIRAL REVIEW

NS 1.5 **48.** Which of the following rational numbers is a repeating decimal? *(p. 113)*

Ⓐ $\frac{3}{4}$ Ⓑ 147.23   Ⓒ −20   Ⓓ $0.\overline{63}$

NS 1.2 **49.** What is the value of $2.4 \times 1.6 + 5.488 \div 1.4$? *(p. 144)*

Ⓐ 4.26   Ⓑ 7.76   Ⓒ 8.12   Ⓓ 8.68

NS 1.2 **50.** Kim uses $\frac{2}{3}$ pound of almonds to make 2 servings of trail mix. How many pounds of almonds does she need to make 6 servings? *(p. 98)*

Ⓐ $\frac{2}{5}$ lb   Ⓑ $1\frac{2}{3}$ lb   Ⓒ 2 lb   Ⓓ 4 lb

Multiple Choice Practice for Lessons 3.1–3.4

1. Which number is less than $|-0.3|$? **NS 1.1**

  (A) 0.038   **(B)** $\frac{1}{3}$

  (C) $|-0.34|$ **(D)** 0.3602

2. The table shows the top four finishers in the men's pommel horse finals for the 2004 Olympic games. A gold medal is awarded for first place, a silver medal for second, and a bronze medal for third. Who won the silver medal? **NS 1.1**

Score	Athlete
9.787	Kashima
9.825	Urzica
9.762	Cano
9.775	Huang

  (A) Kashima   **(B)** Urzica

  (C) Cano   **(D)** Huang

3. Your cell phone company charges $.10 per minute before 7:00 P.M. and $.05 per minute after 7:00 P.M. You make a phone call at 6:39 P.M. and talk for 18 minutes. At 7:15 P.M., you make another phone call and talk for 18 minutes. What is the difference in cost between the two calls? **NS 1.2, MR 2.7**

  (A) $.90   **(B)** $1.55

  (C) $1.80   **(D)** $2.10

4. What is 220% of 15? **NS 1.3**

  (A) 6.8   **(B)** 17.2

  (C) 25   **(D)** 33

5. Type O blood is the most common blood type. About 45% of the people in the United States have type O blood. If there are 1280 students in a U.S. school, about how many have type O blood? **NS 1.3**

  (A) 512   **(B)** 576

  (C) 704   **(D)** 768

6. What is the value of $4.34 - 2.083$? **NS 1.2**

  (A) −2.341   **(B)** 1.981

  (C) 2.157   **(D)** 2.257

7. What is the value of 6.015×4.82? **NS 1.2**

  (A) 2.89923   **(B)** 24.247

  (C) 28.9923   **(D)** 29.064

8. The perimeter of rectangle A is how many times as great as the perimeter of rectangle B? **NS 1.2**

  (A) 2.5   **(B)** 3

  (C) 3.5   **(D)** 4

9. What is 65.2% written as a fraction? **NS 1.3**

  (A) $\frac{13}{20}$ **(B)** $\frac{163}{250}$

  (C) $6\frac{13}{25}$ **(D)** $65\frac{1}{5}$

10. Water makes up about 95% of the weight of a watermelon. About how much of a 12 pound watermelon is *not* water? (*Note:* 1 lb = 16 oz.) **NS 1.3**

  (A) 6 oz   **(B)** 9.6 oz

  (C) 6 lb   **(D)** 11 lb 6 oz

11. The rectangular garden shown has an area of 8.96 square meters. What is the perimeter of the garden? **NS 1.2, MR 2.3**

  (A) 8 m

  (B) 12 m

  (C) 13.4 m

  (D) 14.2 m

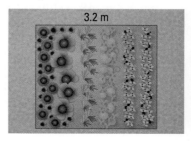

3.5 Decimals and Fractions as Percents

Math and SURVEYS
Ex. 42, p. 158

Standards NS 1.3 Convert fractions to decimals and percents and use these representations in estimations, computations, and applications.

Connect *Before* you wrote percents as decimals and fractions. *Now* you will write decimals and fractions as percents.

KEY VOCABULARY
• **percent,** *p. 150*

To write a decimal as a percent, you can multiply by 100. Note that multiplying by 100 is the same as moving the decimal point two places to the right.

EXAMPLE 1 Writing Decimals as Percents

Write the decimal as a percent.

a. $0.95 = (0.95 \times 100)\% = (095.)\% = 95\%$

AVOID ERRORS
Add a zero on the right if necessary to move the decimal point two places to the right.

b. $2.7 = (2.7 \times 100)\% = (270.)\% = 270\%$

c. $0.004 = (0.004 \times 100)\% = (000.4)\% = 0.4\%$

d. $-5.36 = (-5.36 \times 100)\% = (-536.)\% = -536\%$

✓ **GUIDED PRACTICE** for Example 1

Write the decimal as a percent.

1. 0.18 **2.** -0.682 **3.** 2.17 **4.** -1.705

FRACTIONS AND PERCENTS To write a fraction as a percent, write an equivalent fraction with a denominator of 100.

EXAMPLE 2 Writing Fractions as Percents

Write the fraction as a percent.

a. $\dfrac{40}{500} = \dfrac{40 \div 5}{500 \div 5} = \dfrac{8}{100} = 8\%$

b. $\dfrac{3}{5} = \dfrac{3 \cdot 20}{5 \cdot 20} = \dfrac{60}{100} = 60\%$

c. $\dfrac{35}{20} = \dfrac{35 \cdot 5}{20 \cdot 5} = \dfrac{175}{100} = 175\%$

d. $-\dfrac{17}{25} = -\dfrac{17 \cdot 4}{25 \cdot 4} = -\dfrac{68}{100} = -68\%$

ORDERING RATIONAL NUMBERS When ordering rational numbers given in different forms, first convert all of the numbers to the same form. Then order the numbers.

EXAMPLE 3 Ordering Rational Numbers

SURVEY A survey asking dog owners about where their dogs sleep had the following results: $\frac{9}{40}$ on owner's bed, 0.19 in a dog house, and 16.8% on the floor. Order the numbers from least to greatest.

Sleeping on floor: 16.8%

SOLUTION

METHOD 1 Write the numbers as percents.

$$\frac{9}{40} = \frac{9 \times 2.5}{40 \times 2.5} = \frac{22.5}{100} = 22.5\%$$

$$0.19 = (0.19 \times 100)\% = 19\%$$

$$16.8\% = 16.8\%$$

Compare the percents. **16**.8% < **19**% and **19**% < **22**.5%

METHOD 2 Write the numbers as decimals.

$$\frac{9}{40} = 0.225 \quad 0.19 = 0.190 \quad\quad 16.8\% = 0.168$$

Compare the decimals.

$$0.\mathbf{168} < 0.\mathbf{19}0 \text{ and } 0.\mathbf{19}0 < 0.\mathbf{2}25$$

CHECK Use a number line to order the decimals.

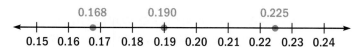

▸ **Answer** The numbers ordered from least to greatest are 16.8%, 0.19, and $\frac{9}{40}$.

✓ **GUIDED PRACTICE**   **for Examples 2 and 3**

Write the fraction as a percent.

5. $\frac{1}{5}$ **6.** $\frac{24}{25}$ **7.** $-\frac{1}{8}$ **8.** $\frac{528}{400}$

Order the numbers from least to greatest.

9. 41%, $\frac{9}{20}$, 0.389   **10.** $\frac{9}{10}$, 0.099, 95%   **11.** 1.5, 145%, $\frac{7}{5}$

CONCEPT SUMMARY   *For Your Notebook*

Decimals, Fractions, and Percents

Decimals, fractions, and percents are all different ways to represent the same number.

You can convert any representation of a number into another form for ease of use. The diagram at the right demonstrates the relationship between decimals, fractions, and percents.

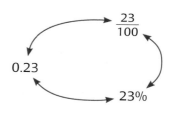

$\dfrac{23}{100}$

0.23

23%

3.5 EXERCISES

HOMEWORK KEY

◆ = **MULTIPLE CHOICE PRACTICE**
Exs. 13, 36, 43, 48–50

◯ = **HINTS** AND **HOMEWORK HELP**
for Exs. 11, 15, 43 at classzone.com

SKILLS • PROBLEM SOLVING • REASONING

1. **VOCABULARY** Copy and complete: To write a decimal as a percent, __?__ by 100.

2. **NOTETAKING SKILLS** Make a *cycle diagram* like the one on page 132 for writing a percent as a decimal and writing a decimal as a percent.

SEE EXAMPLE 1
on p. 155
for Exs. 3–14

REWRITING DECIMALS **Write the decimal as a percent.**

3. 0.09   4. 1.27   5. −0.7   6. 2.1   7. 4

8. −0.51   9. 0.003   10. −0.057   11. 0.039   12. 0.004

13. ◆ **MULTIPLE CHOICE** Which of the following is equivalent to 0.159?

  Ⓐ 0.159%   Ⓑ 1.59%   Ⓒ 15.9%   Ⓓ 159%

14. **ERROR ANALYSIS** *Describe* and correct the error in writing 0.001 as a percent.

$$\bcancel{\quad} \quad 0.001 = \dfrac{1}{100} = 1\%$$

SEE EXAMPLE 2
on p. 155
for Exs. 15–24

REWRITING FRACTIONS **Write the fraction as a percent.**

15. $\dfrac{5}{8}$ 16. $-\dfrac{3}{2}$ 17. $\dfrac{1}{80}$ 18. $\dfrac{3}{20}$ 19. $-\dfrac{31}{10}$

20. $\dfrac{4}{800}$ 21. $\dfrac{4}{50}$ 22. $-\dfrac{117}{200}$ 23. $-\dfrac{7}{16}$ 24. $\dfrac{11}{12}$

COMPARING **Copy and complete the statement using <, >, or =.**

25. $\dfrac{1}{4}$ _?_ 26%   26. 450% _?_ $\dfrac{9}{2}$ 27. $-\dfrac{13}{25}$ _?_ −0.5   28. 3.83% _?_ 0.383

29. **OPEN-ENDED** Write three different fractions that are equivalent to 60%. Then write each fraction as a decimal. What do you notice about the decimals? Will this always occur when you write equivalent fractions?

ORDERING NUMBERS **Order the numbers from least to greatest.**

30. $0.3, \frac{9}{40}, 22\%, 0.228, \frac{41}{125}$

31. $-6.5\%, \frac{9}{50}, 0.65, 66\%, -0.5$

32. $\frac{4}{7}, 0.058, 58, 58\%, 0.58\%$

33. $-212\%, -21.2, -\frac{21}{100}, -0.212, -\frac{21}{10}$

34. $-\frac{11}{15}, -0.73, -7.3\%, -\frac{75}{100}, -0.73\%$

35. $\frac{12}{25}, 480\%, 0.484, 4.84, 4.8\%$

36. ◆ **MULTIPLE CHOICE** Which numbers are in order from least to greatest?

(A) $0.25, 2.5\%, \frac{2}{7}$ (B) $2.5\%, 0.25, \frac{2}{7}$ (C) $0.25, \frac{2}{7}, 2.5\%$ (D) $2.5\%, \frac{2}{7}, 0.25$

37. **ERROR ANALYSIS** A student says that because $\frac{1}{4}$ equals 25% and 5 is greater than 4, $\frac{1}{5}$ must be greater than 25%. *Describe* and correct the error in the student's reasoning.

CONNECT SKILLS TO PROBLEM SOLVING **Exercises 38–40 will help you prepare for problem solving.**

Use the following information: In a recent year, a survey of U.S. high school students who studied a world language showed the following results: 0.69 studied Spanish, $\frac{1}{20}$ studied German, 0.18 studied French, and $\frac{2}{25}$ studied some other language.

38. Which language was studied by the most students?

39. What percent of the students studied French or German?

40. What percent of the students did not study Spanish?

41. **SLEEPING** You survey 48 people and find that 18 of them sleep eight hours a night. What percent sleep eight hours a night?

California *@HomeTutor* for problem solving help at classzone.com

42. **MULTI-STEP PROBLEM** A survey asked high school students how they prefer to spend their free time. Of the students surveyed, 140 said "with friends," 45 said "reading," 75 said "with family," 124 said "watching TV," and 16 said something other than these responses.

 a. How many students were surveyed?

 b. What percent of the students said "with friends"?

 c. What percent of the students said "with family" or "watching TV"?

California *@HomeTutor* for problem solving help at classzone.com

43. ◆ **MULTIPLE CHOICE** A football field is 100 yards long, excluding the end zones. Approximately what percent of a mile is a football field's length? (*Note:* 1 mile = 1760 yards.)

(A) 1.9% (B) 5.7% (C) 17.6% (D) 52.8%

44. **REASONING** If a fraction is greater than 1, what do you know about the equivalent percent? *Explain.*

45. **MUSIC** The table shows the results of a survey asking high school students to name the type of music they prefer. Write each decimal or fraction as a percent. Then order the types of music from least popular to most popular.

Music	Rock	Rap	R&B	Country	Other
Number	$\frac{63}{250}$	0.133	$\frac{53}{500}$	$\frac{13}{125}$	$\frac{81}{200}$

$\frac{63}{250}$ of students prefer rock music.

46. **CHALLENGE** In terms of n, what is $\frac{7n}{20}$ written as a percent?

47. **CHALLENGE** You conduct a survey about laundry detergent. Brand A is preferred by $\frac{2}{15}$ of the people. Brand B is preferred by $\frac{5}{12}$ of the people. Of the remaining people, 80% prefer brand C and the rest have no preference. What percent of all the people surveyed have no preference?

◆ CALIFORNIA STANDARDS SPIRAL REVIEW

NS 1.1

48. Which of the following numbers is between 0.25 and $\frac{27}{80}$? *(p. 133)*

    A 0.205   **B** $\frac{124}{500}$ **C** $\frac{36}{125}$ **D** 0.384

NS 1.2

49. What is the value of 16.7564 ÷ 3.26? *(p. 144)*

    A 4.604   **B** 5.14   **C** 5.287   **D** 5.3

NS 1.2

50. You are building a birdhouse from a piece of wood that is 56.25 inches long and 9.5 inches wide. You divide the wood lengthwise into 5 pieces of the same length. What are the dimensions of each of the five pieces? *(p. 144)*

    A 5.9 in. by 9.5 in.   **B** 9.5 in. by 9.5 in.

    C 11.25 in. by 9.5 in.   **D** 14 in. by 9.5 in.

QUIZ *for Lessons 3.4–3.5*

Write the percent as a decimal and as a fraction. *(p. 150)*

1. 28%   **2.** −10.5%   **3.** 122%   **4.** 0.48%

Write the decimal or fraction as a percent. *(p. 155)*

5. −0.634   **6.** 2.56   **7.** $\frac{17}{20}$ **8.** $-\frac{27}{10}$

9. CLOTHING SALES You save 40% on a shirt that originally cost $29. How much do you save? *(p. 150)*

10. EXAM George takes an exam with 60 questions and answers only 48 of the questions. What percent of the exam did he finish? *(p. 155)*

3.6 Discounts, Markups, Commissions, and Profit

Standards NS 1.7 **Solve problems that involve discounts, markups, commissions, and profit** and compute simple and compound interest.

Connect *Before* you wrote percents as decimals. *Now* you will use this skill to find discounts, markups, commissions, and profit.

Math and **MUSIC**
Example 1, p. 160

KEY VOCABULARY

- markup
- discount
- commission
- profit

KEY CONCEPT
For Your Notebook

Markups and Discounts

Markups

Retail stores buy items from manufacturers at wholesale prices and then sell the items to customers at retail prices. The retail price is obtained by adding a **markup** to the wholesale price.

$$\text{Retail price} = \text{Wholesale price} + \text{Markup}$$

Discounts

When an item is on sale, the sale price is obtained by subtracting the **discount** from the original price.

$$\text{Sale price} = \text{Original price} - \text{Discount}$$

EXAMPLE 1 Using a Discount to Find a Sale Price

GUITARS You are shopping for a guitar and find one with an original price of $160. The store is offering a 30% discount on all guitars. What is the sale price of the guitar?

ANOTHER WAY
For an alternative method for solving the problem in Example 1, turn to page 166 for the **Problem Solving Workshop**.

SOLUTION

STEP 1 **Find** the amount of the discount.

Discount = 30% of $160

     = 0.3(160)   **Write 30% as a decimal.**

     = 48   **Multiply.**

Guitar sale: 30% off

STEP 2 **Subtract** the discount from the original price.

160 − 48 = 112

▶ **Answer** The sale price of the guitar is $112.

EXAMPLE 2 Using a Markup to Find a Retail Price

CLOTHING A shirt has a wholesale price of $16. The percent markup is 120%. What is the retail price?

SOLUTION

STEP 1 **Find** the amount of the markup.

$$\text{Markup} = 120\% \text{ of } \$16$$
$$= 1.2(16) \qquad \text{Write 120\% as a decimal.}$$
$$= 19.2 \qquad \text{Multiply.}$$

STEP 2 **Add** the markup to the wholesale price.

$$16 + 19.2 = 35.2$$

▶ **Answer** The retail price of the shirt is $35.20.

AVOID ERRORS
Remember that the markup must be added to the wholesale price to find the retail price.

✓ **GUIDED PRACTICE** for Examples 1 and 2

Find the sale price or retail price.

1. Original price: $64
   Percent discount: 20%

2. Wholesale price: $35
   Percent markup: 110%

KEY CONCEPT   *For Your Notebook*

Commission

When a salesperson is paid a percent of his or her total sales, the amount of pay is called **commission**.

Commission = Percent commission × Total sales

EXAMPLE 3 Finding a Commission

SALES Angela works in a department store selling video equipment. She is paid a 12% commission on her sales. In January, her sales totaled $5850. Find the commission Angela earned for her January sales.

SOLUTION

Find the amount of the commission.

$$\text{Commission} = 12\% \text{ of } \$5850$$
$$= 0.12(5850) \qquad \text{Write 12\% as a decimal.}$$
$$= 702 \qquad \text{Multiply.}$$

▶ **Answer** Angela earned a commission of $702.

> **KEY CONCEPT**   *For Your Notebook*
>
> ## Profit
>
> The **profit** of a business is the difference of the income and expenses for the business.
>
> $$\text{Profit} = \text{Income} - \text{Expenses}$$

EXAMPLE 4 ◆ Multiple Choice Practice

> You run a fruit stand on weekends. This past weekend, you collected $127. Your expenses for the fruit products sold were $52. What is your profit?
>
> **(A)** $52   **(B)** $75   **(C)** $127   **(D)** $179

ELIMINATE CHOICES
Your total income was $127. The profit cannot be more than the income. So, choice D can be eliminated.

SOLUTION

$$\text{Profit} = \text{Income} - \text{Expenses}$$ **Write formula for profit.**

$$= 127 - 52$$ **Substitute.**

$$= 75$$ **Subtract.**

▶ **Answer** Your profit is $75. The correct answer is B.   Ⓐ Ⓑ Ⓒ Ⓓ

EXAMPLE 5   Finding a Profit

FUNDRAISER Your class is having a car wash to raise money for a class trip. Your expenses for towels, soap, window cleaner, and tire cleaner total $65. Your class washes 23 cars on Saturday and 35 cars on Sunday. The price per car wash is $5. Find the profit from the car wash.

Price per car wash: $5

SOLUTION

STEP 1 **Find** the income.

$$\text{Income} = 5 \cdot (23 + 35)$$ **Price per car wash times total cars washed**

$$= 290$$ **Simplify.**

STEP 2 **Identify** the expenses.

The expenses for the car wash total $65.

STEP 3 **Find** the profit by subtracting the expenses from the income.

$$\text{Profit} = 290 - 65 = 225$$

▶ **Answer** The profit from the car wash is $225.

3. Jeremy is paid a 15% commission on his sales. Last month, he sold $1745 worth of merchandise. Find his commission for the month.

4. **WHAT IF?** In Example 5, suppose your class charges $10 to wash each car and the expenses total $75. Find the profit from the car wash.

3.6 EXERCISES

HOMEWORK
KEY

 = **MULTIPLE CHOICE PRACTICE**
Exs. 17, 24, 31, 40–42

 = **HINTS AND HOMEWORK HELP**
for Exs. 3, 13, 33 at classzone.com

SKILLS • PROBLEM SOLVING • REASONING

1. **VOCABULARY** Copy and complete: To find the retail price, add the __?__ to the wholesale price.

2. **WRITING** *Explain* how to find the sale price of an item that had an original price of $60 and is now on sale for 20% off.

FINDING PRICES Find the sale price or retail price.

SEE EXAMPLES
1 AND 2
on pp. 160–161
for Exs. 3–10

3. Original price: $60
Percent discount: 15%

4. Original price: $28.50
Percent discount: 60%

5. Original price: $42
Percent discount: 30%

6. Wholesale price: $14.50
Percent markup: 140%

7. Wholesale price: $25
Percent markup: 65%

8. Wholesale price: $19
Percent markup: 110%

9. **ERROR ANALYSIS** A music store is offering a 25% discount on a $375 DVD cabinet. The clerk says that the cabinet costs $350 after applying the discount. *Describe* and correct the error in the clerk's reasoning.

10. **ERROR ANALYSIS** A musician is releasing a new CD. Each CD has a wholesale price of $7. The percent markup is 60%. Your friend, who works at a store that sells the CDs, says that the CDs will have a retail price of $2.80. *Describe* and correct the error in your friend's reasoning.

FINDING COMMISSION Find the commission.

SEE EXAMPLE 3
on p. 161
for Exs. 11–17

11. Total sales: $600
Percent commission: 10%

12. Total sales: $900
Percent commission: 12%

13. Total sales: $3250
Percent commission: 5%

14. Total sales: $770
Percent commission: 8%

15. Total sales: $2775
Percent commission: 13%

16. Total sales: $1100
Percent commission: 9%

17. ◆ **MULTIPLE CHOICE** Jason is paid an 8% commission on his sales. What is his commission if his weekly sales totaled $1600?

   A $128   **B** $160   **C** $200   **D** $225

SEE EXAMPLE 4
on p. 162
for Exs. 18–24

FINDING PROFIT Find the profit.

18. Income: $600
Expenses: $100

19. Income: $1900
Expenses: $225

20. Income: $2245
Expenses: $390

21. Income: $5270
Expenses: $575

22. Income: $2600
Expenses: $485

23. Income: $10,225
Expenses: $2340

24. ◆ **MULTIPLE CHOICE** On Saturday, several employees of a diving supplies shop gave 15 scuba diving lessons and collected $1125. The shop's owner estimated his expenses to be $225. What is his profit?

   A $75   **B** $900   **C** $1350   **D** $1500

CONNECT SKILLS TO PROBLEM SOLVING Exercises 25–27 will help you prepare for problem solving.

Determine the amount of profit.

25. Last summer, you earned $1200 mowing lawns. Your expenses totaled $145.

26. Your friend ran a lemonade stand on the weekend and collected $25. Your friend's expenses for sugar, lemons, and cups totaled $8.

27. Last week, a mechanic made 20 oil changes and collected $650. He estimated his expenses for the oil changes to be about $295.

**SEE EXAMPLES
1 AND 3**
on pp. 160–161
for Exs. 28–32

28. **REAL ESTATE** A real estate agent makes a 4% commission on property she sells. Find her commission for selling a house that costs $342,000.

   California @HomeTutor for problem solving help at classzone.com

29. **LAMP COSTS** A lamp that costs $25.75 is on sale for 10% off. What is the sale price?

   California @HomeTutor for problem solving help at classzone.com

30. **MAGAZINE SUBSCRIPTIONS** Ramon receives a 15% commission on magazine subscription sales. Last week, his total sales were $1080. Find his commission.

31. ◆ **MULTIPLE CHOICE** Your brother works part-time at an electronics store. His weekly salary is $100 plus an 8% commission on his total sales. What is his salary for a week when his total sales are $4000?

   A $100   **B** $320   **C** $420   **D** $4100

32. **EMPLOYMENT AGENCY** Your sister works at an employment agency. At the beginning of 2005, her supervisor asked her to reduce the agency's travel expenses by 10% in 2005 and another 10% in 2006. In 2004, the expenses were $100,000. What should the expenses be in 2005? in 2006?

SEE EXAMPLES
2, 4, AND 5
on pp. 161–162
for Exs. 33–35

33. **LUMBER** The Greenwood Lumber Company had an income of $7680 for one week in June. The company's expenses for that week were $2056. Find the company's profit for that week.

34. **CLOTHING** The wholesale price of a shirt is $15. A store marks up the price by 75%. When the shirts don't sell, the store offers a 20% discount. What is the sale price of the shirts?

35. **BIRDHOUSES** You want to make and sell birdhouses. You spend $500 to buy wood, paint, and other materials for the birdhouses. You sell each birdhouse for $20. What is your profit if you sell 40 birdhouses?

36. **REASONING** A store is having a sale on its coats. All coats are discounted 40%. One week later the store discounts the coats an extra 60%. Is the store giving away the coats for free? *Explain* your reasoning.

Discount on shirts: 20%

37. **ESTIMATION** The original price of an item is $42 and the percent of discount is 25%. *Explain* how to estimate the sale price.

38. **CHALLENGE** John works for the sales department of a furniture company. The table gives the percent commission he earns. For example, if John sells $2800 worth of furniture, his commission would be 0.12($2000) + 0.18($800), or $384. What is John's commission if he sells $3200 worth of furniture? $5450 worth of furniture? $7875 worth of furniture?

39. **CHALLENGE** A muffin recipe makes 35 muffins. The ingredients needed to make 35 muffins cost $7. You sell packages of 35 muffins for $24. *Explain* what happens to your profit and expenses when the sales of your muffins increase.

Employee Commission Breakdown	
Weekly sales	**Commission**
Up to $2000	12%
$2001–$4000	18%
$4001–$6000	20%
$6001 and up	24%

◆ CALIFORNIA STANDARDS SPIRAL REVIEW

NS 2.2

40. What is the value of $\frac{7}{12} + \frac{4}{15}$? *(p. 85)*

Ⓐ $\frac{1}{9}$ **Ⓑ** $\frac{19}{60}$ **Ⓒ** $\frac{11}{27}$ **Ⓓ** $\frac{17}{20}$

NS 2.5

41. Which value best describes the distance between the two points shown? *(p. 12)*

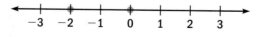

Ⓐ -2 **Ⓑ** 0 **Ⓒ** $|-2|$ **Ⓓ** $-|-2|$

NS 1.2

42. Janet earned $178, $229, and $274 during the last three weeks. What is Janet's mean weekly earnings? *(p. 36)*

Ⓐ $227   **Ⓑ** $274   **Ⓒ** $407   **Ⓓ** $681

Using ALTERNATIVE METHODS

Another Way to Solve Example 1, page 160

In Example 1 on page 160, you found the sale price of a guitar by subtracting the discount from the original price. You can also find the sale price by multiplying the original price by a percent.

PROBLEM

GUITARS You are shopping for a guitar and find one with an original price of $160. The store is offering a 30% discount on all guitars. What is the sale price of the guitar?

METHOD

Multiplication by a Percent An alternative approach is to multiply the original price by a percent.

STEP 1 **Find** the percent of the original price that you will pay. The store is offering a 30% discount off the price of the guitar. Because $100\% - 30\% = 70\%$, you will pay 70% of the original price.

STEP 2 **Calculate** the sale price of the guitar.

$$\text{Sale price of guitar} = 70\% \text{ of } \$160$$
$$= 0.7(160) \qquad \text{Write 70\% as a decimal.}$$
$$= 112 \qquad \text{Multiply.}$$

▶**Answer** The sale price of the guitar is $112.

PRACTICE

1. **COFFEEMAKERS** A store is offering a 10% discount on all coffeemakers. Find the percent of the original price you are paying for a coffeemaker.

2. **SURFBOARDS** A store is offering a 25% discount on all surfboards. Find the percent of the original price you are paying for a surfboard.

3. **WHAT IF?** In the problem above, suppose the store is offering a 22% discount off the price of guitars. What is the sale price of the $160 guitar? Solve this problem using two methods.

4. **SUNSCREEN** A store is offering a 15% discount on all sunscreen lotion. What is the sale price of a bottle of sunscreen lotion that originally cost $7.80? Solve this problem using two methods.

5. **FURNITURE** A furniture store is having a sale. All sofas are discounted 45%. What is the sale price of a sofa that normally sells for $1299? Solve this problem using two methods.

6. **VIDEO GAMES** A toy store is having a sale. All video games are discounted 20%. What is the sale price of a video game that normally sells for $50? Solve this problem using two methods.

3.7 Modeling Percent of Change

MATERIALS • graph paper • colored pencils

Standards

NS 1.6 **Calculate the percentage of increases** and decreases of a quantity.

QUESTION How can you model the percent of change in a quantity?

A *percent of change* shows how much a quantity has increased or decreased from the original amount.

EXPLORE Use an area model to find a percent of change

A figure has an area of 10 square units. You increase its area to 15 square units. By what percent does the area of the figure change?

STEP 1 **Define** the area of each square on your graph paper to be 1 square unit. Draw a figure that has an area of 10 square units, as shown at the right. Shade the 10 squares red.

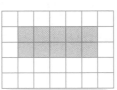

STEP 2 **Add** squares to the figure so that its area becomes 15 square units. Shade the added squares blue.

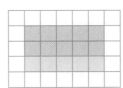

STEP 3 **Find** the ratio of the added area to the original area. Express the result as a percent. This percent is called the *percent of change*.

$$\frac{\text{Added area}}{\text{Original area}} = \frac{5 \text{ square units}}{10 \text{ square units}}$$

$$= 50\%$$

DRAW CONCLUSIONS Use your observations to complete these exercises

Use a model to find the percent of change in the area of the figure.

1. Original area: 12 square units
   New area: 18 square units

2. Original area: 5 square units
   New area: 7 square units

3. Original area: 3 square units
   New area: 6 square units

4. Original area: 6 square units
   New area: 8 square units

5. **REASONING** A figure has an area of 16 square units, and you increase its area to 20 square units. What percent of the original area is the new area? How is this percent related to the percent of change in the area?

3.7 Percent of Change

Math and **TOURISM**
Example 3, p. 169

Standards NS 1.6 Calculate the percentage of increases and decreases of a quantity.

Connect *Before* you calculated discounts, markups, commissions, and profit.
Now you will calculate percents of change.

KEY VOCABULARY
• percent of change
• percent of increase
• percent of decrease

A **percent of change** shows how much a quantity has increased or decreased from the original amount. When the new amount is greater than the original amount, the percent of change is positive and is called a **percent of increase**. When the new amount is less than the original amount, the percent of change is negative and its absolute value is called a **percent of decrease**.

KEY CONCEPT *For Your Notebook*

Percent of Change

Use the following equation to find a percent of change.

$$\text{Percent of change, } p\% = \frac{\text{New amount} - \text{Original amount}}{\text{Original amount}}$$

EXAMPLE 1 Finding a Percent of Increase

SCHOOL ENROLLMENT A school had 825 students enrolled last year. This year, 870 students are enrolled. Find the percent of increase to the nearest tenth.

SOLUTION

AVOID ERRORS
Make sure you use the original amount, not the new amount, in the denominator when finding a percent of change.

$p\% = \dfrac{870 - 825}{825}$ Write amount of increase and divide by original amount.

$= \dfrac{45}{825}$ Subtract.

≈ 0.0545 Write fraction as a decimal.

$= 5.45\%$ Write decimal as a percent.

▶ **Answer** The percent of increase is about 5.5%.

✓ **GUIDED PRACTICE** for Example 1

1. **WHAT IF?** In Example 1, suppose the enrollment this year is 990 students. Find the percent of increase to the nearest tenth.

EXAMPLE 2 Finding a Percent of Decrease

BEARS During the summer, a bear's heart rate is about 60 beats per minute, but it can drop to as low as 8 beats per minute during the winter. What is the percent of change in a bear's heart rate from the summer rate to the winter low rate?

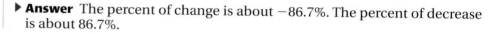

Summer heart rate: 60 beats/min

SOLUTION

$$p\% = \frac{8 - 60}{60}$$ Write amount of decrease and divide by original amount.

$$= \frac{-52}{60}$$ Subtract.

$$\approx -0.8667$$ Write fraction as a decimal.

$$= -86.67\%$$ Write decimal as a percent.

▶ **Answer** The percent of change is about -86.7%. The percent of decrease is about 86.7%.

FINDING A NEW AMOUNT If you know the original amount of a quantity and the percent of increase or decrease, you can find the new amount. First multiply the percent of increase or decrease by the original amount to find the amount of change. Then increase or decrease the original amount by the amount of change.

EXAMPLE 3 Using a Percent of Increase

NATIONAL PARK From January to February of one year, attendance at Joshua Tree National Park in California increased about 19.7%. There were 89,928 visitors in January. To the nearest hundred, how many people visited in February?

SOLUTION

STEP 1 Find the amount of increase.

Amount of increase = **19.7%** of 89,928

$$= \mathbf{0.197}(89{,}928)$$ Write 19.7% as a decimal.

$$\approx 17{,}716$$ Multiply.

STEP 2 Add the amount of increase to the original amount.

New Amount $\approx 89{,}928 + 17{,}716 = 107{,}644$

▶ **Answer** About 107,600 people visited the park in February.

 GUIDED PRACTICE for Examples 2 and 3

2. **DEPRECIATION** A new car costs $14,500 and decreases in value by 15% after 1 year. What is its value after 1 year?

3.7 EXERCISES

SKILLS • PROBLEM SOLVING • REASONING

1. **VOCABULARY** Copy and complete: When the original amount is less than the new amount, the percent of change is called a(n) ? .

2. **WRITING** The original amount of a quantity is decreased by 20%. *Describe* how you can find the new amount.

SEE EXAMPLES 1 AND 2
on pp. 168–169
for Exs. 3–10

FINDING PERCENT OF CHANGE Tell whether the change is an *increase* or *decrease*. Then find the percent of change. Round to the nearest percent.

3. 10 rabbits to 16 rabbits

4. 360 pounds to 352 pounds

5. $33,300 to $31,080

6. 12,200 voters to 13,908 voters

7. 50 minutes to 45 minutes

8. 350 meters to 420 meters

9. ◆ **MULTIPLE CHOICE** An increase from 1 to 3 is what percent of increase?

   (A) 66.7%   (B) 100%   (C) 200%   (D) 300%

10. ◆ **MULTIPLE CHOICE** A decrease from 15 to 12 is what percent of decrease?

    (A) 3%   (B) 15%   (C) 20%   (D) 25%

SEE EXAMPLE 3
on p. 169
for Exs. 11–16

FINDING NEW AMOUNTS Find the new amount.

11. 1100 is increased by 4%.

12. 24,700 is decreased by 13%.

13. 8 is increased by 60%.

14. 65 is decreased by 30%.

15. 88,000 is decreased by 12.5%.

16. 26,000 is increased by 14.6%.

17. **ERROR ANALYSIS** Your friend says "Multiplying a number by 5 is a 500% increase." *Describe* and correct the error in your friend's reasoning.

18. **ERROR ANALYSIS** A friend says that multiplying a number by $\frac{1}{4}$ is a 25% decrease. *Describe* and correct the error in your friend's reasoning.

CONNECT SKILLS TO PROBLEM SOLVING Exercises 19–21 will help you prepare for problem solving.

Determine the amount of the increase or decrease.

19. A town has a population of 3500 people. In one year, the population increases by 10%.

20. Lisa earns $9.50 per hour working as a sales clerk in a pet store. This year she gets a 5% increase in her hourly wage.

21. A manufacturer spends $1150 a month on shipping charges. The manufacturer wants to cut monthly shipping costs by 15%.

SEE EXAMPLES
1 AND 3
on pp. 168–169
for Exs. 22–23

22. POPULATION In 1993, the population of the United States was about 260,255,000. In 2003, it was about 291,049,000. Find the percent of increase to the nearest tenth of a percent.

California @HomeTutor for problem solving help at classzone.com

23. SHORT RESPONSE Oregon produces about 99% of the hazelnuts grown in the United States. Its record harvest was in 1997. In 2004 about how many tons of hazelnuts were produced in Oregon? *Explain.*

California @HomeTutor for problem solving help at classzone.com

1997   2004

51% less than in 1997

HAZELNUTS
OREGON
46,650 tons

OREGON

24. ◆ MULTIPLE CHOICE A camera is on sale for 10% off $170, and you have a coupon for an extra 10% off. How much will this camera cost?

(A) $136   **(B)** $137.70   **(C)** $153   **(D)** $168.30

25. PHOTOGRAPHY You have a photograph that is 6 inches by 4 inches. You want to enlarge it so that these dimensions are increased by 50%. What will the new dimensions be? Will the increase in area be *greater than*, *less than*, or *equal to* 50%? *Explain.*

26. PUZZLE PROBLEM There were 25 passengers riding a bus. After the first stop, the number of passengers increased by 100%. After the second stop, the number of passengers decreased by 100%. How many passengers were on the bus after the second stop?

27. CHALLENGE A number increases by 50% and then decreases by 50%. What is the percent of change from the original number to the final number?

28. CHALLENGE From 1990 to 2000, the population of Sacramento, California, increased by about 3%. In 2000, the population was 407,018. At this growth rate, is 387,600 a reasonable estimate for the population of Sacramento in 1990? *Explain.*

◆ CALIFORNIA STANDARDS SPIRAL REVIEW

NS 2.2 | **29.** What is the value of $\frac{4}{5} - \frac{3}{10}$? *(p. 85)*

(A) $-\frac{1}{2}$ **(B)** $\frac{1}{5}$ **(C)** $\frac{1}{2}$ **(D)** $\frac{11}{10}$

NS 1.3 | **30.** Which of the following is approximately equivalent to $\frac{6}{7}$? *(p. 113)*

(A) 0.857%   **(B)** 8.57%   **(C)** 85.7%   **(D)** 857%

NS 1.7 | **31.** A CD is on sale for 15% off the original price of $13.97. What is the sale price of the CD? *(p. 160)*

(A) $11.23   **(B)** $11.87   **(C)** $14.56   **(D)** $14.97

3.8 Simple and Compound Interest

Math and SUMMER JOBS
Example 2, p. 173

Standards NS 1.7 Solve problems that involve discounts, markups, commissions, and profit and **compute simple and compound interest.**

Connect *Before* you calculated the percent of a number. *Now* you will use percents to calculate simple and compound interest.

KEY VOCABULARY
- interest
- principal
- simple interest
- annual interest rate
- balance
- compound interest

The amount earned or paid for the use of money is called **interest**. The amount of money deposited or borrowed is the **principal**. Interest that is earned or paid only on the principal is called **simple interest**. The percent of the principal earned or paid per year is the **annual interest rate**.

KEY CONCEPT
For Your Notebook

Simple Interest

Words To find simple interest I, find the product of the principal P, the annual interest rate r written as a decimal, and the time t in years.

Algebra $I = Prt$

EXAMPLE 1 ◆ Multiple Choice Practice

You deposit $500 in a savings account that pays a simple interest rate of 2.5% per year. How much interest will you earn after 18 months?

(A) $8.92   **(B)** $13.43   **(C)** $18.75   **(D)** $19.15

Animated Math

For an interactive example of finding simple interest, go to **classzone.com.**

SOLUTION

$I = Prt$ **Write formula for simple interest.**

$= (500)(0.025)(1.5)$ **Substitute values. 18 months = 1.5 years.**

$= 18.75$ **Multiply.**

You will earn $18.75 in interest.

▶ **Answer** The correct answer is C. (A) (B) (C) (D)

✓ **GUIDED PRACTICE** for Example 1

1. **WHAT IF?** In Example 1, suppose the simple interest rate is 3.5%. How much interest will you earn after 24 months?

BALANCE When an account earns interest, the interest is added to the money in the account. The **balance** A of an account that earns simple annual interest is the sum of the principal P and the interest Prt.

$$A = P + Prt \quad \text{or} \quad A = P(1 + rt)$$

EXAMPLE 2 Finding the Balance

BICYCLE REPAIR You repair bicycles during your summer vacation and save $900 of your pay. You deposit this money into a savings account that pays 3% simple annual interest. Find your account balance after 9 months.

SOLUTION

In the formula $A = P(1 + rt)$, t is the time in years. Write 9 months as $\frac{9}{12}$ year, or 0.75 year. Then solve for A after substituting values for P, r, and t.

$A = P(1 + rt)$ **Write formula for finding the balance.**

$= 900[1 + 0.03(0.75)]$ **Substitute values.**

$= 920.25$ **Simplify.**

▸**Answer** Your account balance after 9 months is $920.25.

✓ GUIDED PRACTICE   for Example 2

2. **WHAT IF?** In Example 2, suppose you save $1200. Find your account balance after 6 months.

3. **CREDIT CARD** On June 1, the balance on a credit card is $1600. The credit card company charges 18% simple annual interest. If no payment or purchases are made, what will the balance be on July 1?

COMPOUND INTEREST **Compound interest** is interest that is earned on both the principal and any interest that has been earned previously. Suppose you deposit $50 in a savings account that earns 2% interest compounded annually. The table shows the balance of your account after each of 4 years.

Year	Balance at start of year	Balance at end of year
1	50	$50(1 + 0.02) = 50(1 + 0.02)^1$
2	$50(1 + 0.02)^1$	$50(1 + 0.02)^1 \cdot (1 + 0.02) = 50(1 + 0.02)^2$
3	$50(1 + 0.02)^2$	$50(1 + 0.02)^2 \cdot (1 + 0.02) = 50(1 + 0.02)^3$
4	$50(1 + 0.02)^3$	$50(1 + 0.02)^3 \cdot (1 + 0.02) = 50(1 + 0.02)^4$

The table above suggests a formula, shown on the next page, for finding the balance of an account that earns interest compounded annually.

Compound Interest

When an account earns interest compounded annually, the balance A is given by the formula

$$A = P(1 + r)^t$$

where P is the principal, r is the annual interest rate (written as a decimal), and t is the time in years.

EXAMPLE 3 **Calculating Compound Interest**

SAVINGS ACCOUNT You deposit $500 in an account that pays 6% interest compounded annually. What is your balance at the end of 4 years?

SOLUTION

METHOD 1 Solve using a table.

The table shows the balance of your account after each of 4 years.

Year	Beginning balance	Interest	Ending balance
1	$500	$I = (500)(0.06)(1)$ $= \$30$	$A = 500 + 30$ $= \$530$
2	$530	$I = (530)(0.06)(1)$ $= \$31.80$	$A = 530 + 31.80$ $= \$561.80$
3	$561.80	$I = (561.80)(0.06)(1)$ $= \$33.71$	$A = 561.80 + 33.71$ $= \$595.51$
4	$595.51	$I = (595.51)(0.06)(1)$ $= \$35.73$	$A = 595.51 + 35.73$ $= \$631.24$

METHOD 2 Solve using the compound interest formula.

A more convenient way to solve this problem is to use the formula for calculating compound interest.

$A = P(1 + r)^t$ **Write formula for compound interest.**

$\quad = 500(1 + 0.06)^4$ **Substitute values.**

$\quad = 631.24$ **Simplify.**

▶ **Answer** Your account balance at the end of 4 years is $631.24.

✓ **GUIDED PRACTICE**   **for Example 3**

4. **SAVINGS ACCOUNT** You deposit $800 in an account that earns 4% interest compounded annually. What is the account balance after 5 years?

3.8 EXERCISES

SKILLS • PROBLEM SOLVING • REASONING

1. VOCABULARY Copy and complete: The amount of money deposited or borrowed is called the __?__.

2. WRITING *Describe* the difference between simple interest and compound interest.

SEE EXAMPLE 1
on p. 172
for Exs. 3–7

SIMPLE INTEREST Find the amount of simple interest earned.

3. Principal: $520
Annual rate: 2%
Time: 3 years

4. Principal: $620
Annual rate: 3%
Time: 20 months

5. Principal: $500
Annual rate: 1.8%
Time: 2 years

6. ◆ MULTIPLE CHOICE What is the simple interest owed on $300 borrowed for 4 months at an annual interest rate of 5%?

A $4 **B** $5 **C** $15 **D** $60

7. ERROR ANALYSIS A $2000 bond earns 6% simple annual interest. *Describe* and correct the error in finding the interest earned after 3 months.

$$\times \quad \begin{aligned} I &= Prt \\ &= (2000)(0.06)(3) \\ &= \$360 \end{aligned}$$

SEE EXAMPLE 2
on p. 173
for Exs. 8–10

8. ◆ MULTIPLE CHOICE You deposit $450 in an account that earns simple interest at an annual rate of 4.5%. Which expression could be used to find the balance in the account after 2 years?

A $450(0.045)(2)$ **B** $450(0.45)(2)$

C $450 + 450(0.045)(2)$ **D** $450 + 450(0.45)(2)$

BALANCE OF AN ACCOUNT For an account that earns simple annual interest, find the balance of the account.

9. $P = \$600$, $r = 4\%$, $t = 3.5$ years

10. $P = \$1400$, $r = 2.5\%$, $t = 10$ years

SEE EXAMPLE 3
on p. 174
for Exs. 11–14

COMPOUND INTEREST Find the balance of the account that earns interest compounded annually.

11. Principal: $800
Annual rate: 5%
Time: 3 years

12. Principal: $2200
Annual rate: 2.3%
Time: 4 years

13. Principal: $700
Annual rate: 6.2%
Time: 24 months

14. ERROR ANALYSIS You deposit $800 in an account that earns 2.5% interest compounded annually. *Describe* and correct the error in finding the balance at the end of 2 years.

$$\times \quad \begin{aligned} A &= P(1 + r)^t \\ &= (800)(1 + 2.5)^2 \\ &= (800)(3.5)^2 = \$9800 \end{aligned}$$

CONNECT SKILLS TO PROBLEM SOLVING Exercises 15–17 will help you prepare for problem solving.

Find the simple interest earned and the balance of the account.

15. $100 at 3% annual simple interest for 1 year

16. $400 at 5% annual simple interest for 3 years

17. $600 at 10% annual simple interest for 6 months

SEE EXAMPLES 1 AND 3
on pp. 172–174
for Exs. 18–21

18. SAVINGS ACCOUNT You deposit $500 in an account that earns an interest rate of 4% compounded annually. How much will you have in your account after 6 years?

California @*HomeTutor*   for problem solving help at classzone.com

19. INVESTING You have $2000 that you want to invest. A bank has several CDs (certificates of deposit) available. How much interest would you earn for each of the CDs shown at the right?

California @*HomeTutor*   for problem solving help at classzone.com

MONTEREY BANK

Available Certificate of Deposit Rates:

1 year CD	4.88%
2 year CD	5.02%
3 year CD	5.35%
4 year CD	5.45%

Interest rates compounded annually

20. REASONING Which interest payment is larger, simple interest of 10% per year after 1 year or simple interest of 1.8% per year after 6 years? *Justify* your answer.

21. SHORT RESPONSE You want to borrow $5000 to buy a used car. Your mother offers to lend you the money at 4% annual simple interest for 7 years. Your grandfather also offers to lend you the money at 8% annual simple interest for 3 years. Assuming you make no payments until the end of the loan period, on which loan would you pay less interest? *Explain.*

In Exercises 22–24, find the balance in an account after 2 years when $1000 is invested at the given interest rate.

EXTENSION   **Compound Interest**

The compound interest formula on page 174 is used when interest is compounded once per year. When an account pays interest compounded n times per year, the account balance A is given by the formula

$$A = P\left(1 + \frac{r}{n}\right)^{nt}$$

where P is the principal, r is the annual interest rate (written as a decimal), and t is the time in years. For example, suppose you deposit $1000 in an account that earns 4% annual interest compounded semiannually (twice per year). After 3 years, the account balance is:

$$A = 1000\left(1 + \frac{0.04}{2}\right)^{2(3)} = 1000(1.02)^6 = \$1126.16$$

22. 8% annual interest compounded quarterly

23. 6% annual interest compounded monthly

24. 3.24% annual interest compounded semiannually

25. **INTEREST RATE** You deposit $1200 in an account at a bank that pays 5.25% annual simple interest. After 4 months, the interest rate on your account increases to 5.65% annual simple interest. After 1 year from the original deposit, how much additional money have you earned from the increase in the interest rate?

26. **CHALLENGE** At the beginning of every month, you deposit $100 in a savings account that earns simple interest each month at an annual rate of 3%. What is the balance of the account 1 year after you make your first deposit, but before you make your thirteenth deposit?

27. **CHALLENGE** At the start of every year, you deposit $3000 in an account that earns 5% interest compounded annually.

   a. What is the balance at the end of the second year? the third year?

   b. Will you have enough money at the end of the fourth year to buy a car that costs $13,800? *Explain* your reasoning.

◆ CALIFORNIA STANDARDS SPIRAL REVIEW

NS 1.2 28. What is the value of $12 + (-7) - (-3)$? *(p. 12)*

   Ⓐ -8 Ⓑ -2 Ⓒ 2 Ⓓ 8

NS 1.5 29. Which decimal is equivalent to the fraction $\frac{6}{11}$? *(p. 113)*

   Ⓐ $0.3\overline{12}$ Ⓑ $0.\overline{54}$ Ⓒ 0.75 Ⓓ $0.\overline{8}$

NS 1.6 30. A company's stock was valued at $15 per share. After 1 year, the stock price decreased to $12 per share. By what percent did the stock price decrease? *(p. 168)*

   Ⓐ 3% Ⓑ 15% Ⓒ 20% Ⓓ 25%

QUIZ *for Lessons 3.6–3.8*

Tell whether the change is an *increase* or *decrease*. Then find the percent of change. *(p. 168)*

1. Original amount: $120
   New amount: $138

2. Original amount: 260 miles
   New amount: 169 miles

3. **RETAIL** A shirt that has a $20 wholesale price is marked up 50%. What is the retail price of the shirt? *(p. 160)*

4. **COMMISSION** Lisette works part time in a shoe store and receives a 12% commission on her total sales. Find her commission for a week when her total sales are $1500. *(p.160)*

5. **LOAN** You borrow $1200 from a bank that charges 9.5% simple annual interest. After 15 months, you pay back the loan. How much interest do you pay on the loan? What is the total amount that you pay the bank? *(p. 172)*

3.8 Compound Interest

Standards

NS 1.7 Solve problems that involve discounts, markups, commissions, and profit and **compute simple and compound interest.**

QUESTION How can you use a calculator to find the balance of an account that earns compound interest?

EXAMPLE Find an account balance

Mark deposits $2000 into an account that pays an annual interest rate of 3.5% compounded annually. He doesn't add or remove money from his account for 4 years. How much money will Mark have in 4 years?

SOLUTION

The balance of an account after a year can be found by multiplying the principal balance by the sum of 1 and the annual interest rate written as a decimal. Use the keystrokes below to find the amount of money in the account in 4 years. Round the answer only after the final year, not after each year.

Keystrokes

2000 $=$ $\times$ 1.035 $=$

Display

2070	In 1 year
2142.45	In 2 years
2217.43575	In 3 years
2295.046001	In 4 years

▸ **Answer** Mark will have $2295.05 in his account in 4 years.

PRACTICE

Find the balance of the account earning interest compounded annually.

1. Principal: $7000
   Annual rate: 2%
   Time: 4 years

2. Principal: $7000
   Annual rate: 4%
   Time: 2 years

3. Principal: $1995
   Annual rate: 6.5%
   Time: 10 years

4. **INTEREST RATES** You deposit $1500 into an account that pays an interest rate of 4% compounded annually. Your friend deposits $1500 into an account that pays a simple annual interest rate of 4%. *Compare* the balances of the two accounts after 5 years.

5. **COMPARE** You deposit $9000 into an account that pays an interest rate of 3.5% compounded annually. Your sister deposits $10,000 into an account that pays a simple annual interest rate of 2.5%. *Compare* the balances of the two accounts after 10 years.

MIXED REVIEW *of Skills and Problem Solving*

Multiple Choice Practice for Lessons 3.5–3.8

1. A sporting goods store originally places a 60% markup on the wholesale price of a basketball. The store later discounts the price so that a customer can buy the basketball at the wholesale price, shown below. By what percent must the store discount the basketball? **NS 1.7, MR 3.3**

Sports Pro Supplies
$16
Basketballs on sale at wholesale prices

Ⓐ 9.6%   Ⓑ 37.5%

Ⓒ 60%   Ⓓ 62.5%

2. You deposit $550 in an account that earns 2.9% interest compounded annually. Which expression could be used to find the balance of your account after 24 months? **NS 1.7**

Ⓐ $550(3.9)^{24}$ Ⓑ $550(1.029)^2$

Ⓒ $550(3.9)^2$ Ⓓ $550(1.029)^{24}$

3. A desk that cost $180 is on sale for 20% off. What is the sale price? **NS 1.7**

Ⓐ $36   Ⓑ $72

Ⓒ $132   Ⓓ $144

4. What is $\frac{1}{4}$ written as a percent? **NS 1.3**

Ⓐ 25%   Ⓑ 50%

Ⓒ 75%   Ⓓ 100%

5. Brad deposits $300 in a savings account that earns simple interest at an annual rate of 2.3%. What is his account balance after 30 months? **NS 1.7**

Ⓐ $317.25   Ⓑ $507.75

Ⓒ $617.25   Ⓓ $725.50

6. Which list of numbers is in order from least to greatest? **NS 1.1**

Ⓐ 40%, 0.04, $\frac{9}{20}$, 0.54, $\frac{1}{2}$

Ⓑ $\frac{1}{2}$, 0.04, $\frac{9}{20}$, 40%, 0.54

Ⓒ 0.04, 40%, $\frac{9}{20}$, $\frac{1}{2}$, 0.54

Ⓓ 0.04, $\frac{9}{20}$, 40%, $\frac{1}{2}$, 0.54

7. Yesterday, Ann sold the items listed at the right. She is paid a 15% commission on her sales. What is her commission? **NS 1.7**

```
    BAY VIEW
   APPLIANCES

Washer  $693.49
Dryer   $493.99
Oven    $949.88

Total $2,137.36

  Thank You!
```

Ⓐ $257.50

Ⓑ $294.40

Ⓒ $318.75

Ⓓ $320.60

8. What is 0.003 written as a percent? **NS 1.3**

Ⓐ 0.03%   Ⓑ 0.3%   Ⓒ 3%   Ⓓ 30%

9. What is $\frac{1}{5}$ written as a percent? **NS 1.3**

Ⓐ 0.02%   Ⓑ 0.2%   Ⓒ 2%   Ⓓ 20%

10. A survey asked students to name their favorite day of the week. The results for those who replied are shown in the table below. What percent of the students surveyed did *not* reply? **NS 1.3, MR 1.1**

Favorite Day of the Week			
Day	Wed.	Fri.	Sat.	Sun.
Number	0.009	$\frac{1}{4}$	0.6	$\frac{1}{10}$

Ⓐ 0%   Ⓑ 3.7%

Ⓒ 4.1%   Ⓓ 5%

BIG IDEAS
For Your Notebook

Big Idea 1

Performing Operations with Decimals

Operation	Procedure
Addition and Subtraction	• Use a vertical format. • Line up the decimal points and then add or subtract as you would with whole numbers.
Multiplication	• Multiply decimals as you would whole numbers. Then place the decimal point in the product. • The number of decimal places in the product is equal to the sum of the numbers of decimal places in the factors.
Division	• Use long division to divide a decimal by a whole number. Divide as you would with whole numbers and then line up the decimal points in the quotient and the dividend. • When you divide by a decimal, multiply both the divisor and the dividend by a power of ten that will make the divisor a whole number.

Big Idea 2

Converting Between Percents, Fractions, and Decimals

Conversion	Procedure	Example
Writing a percent as a decimal	Divide by 100.	$89.3\% \div 100 = 0.893$
Writing a percent as a fraction	Use the percent as the numerator and 100 as the denominator, then simplify.	$74\% = \dfrac{74}{100} = \dfrac{74 \div 2}{100 \div 2} = \dfrac{37}{50}$
Writing a decimal as a percent	Multiply by 100.	$0.55 = (0.55 \times 100)\% = 55\%$
Writing a fraction as a percent	Write an equivalent fraction with a denominator of 100.	$\dfrac{11}{25} = \dfrac{11 \times 4}{25 \times 4} = \dfrac{44}{100} = 44\%$

Big Idea 3

Using Percents in Real-Life Applications

Application	Calculation
Discount	Original price − Sale price
Markup	Retail price − Wholesale price
Commission	Percent commission × Total sales
Profit	Income − Expenses
Percent of Change	$\dfrac{\text{New amount} - \text{Original amount}}{\text{Original amount}}$
Simple Interest	Interest = Prt; Balance = $P(1 + rt)$
Compound Interest	Balance = $P(1 + r)^t$

APPLYING THE BIG IDEAS

Big Idea 1
You perform operations with decimals in **Steps 1–3.**

Big Idea 2
You convert between percents, fractions, and decimals in **Step 1.**

Big Idea 3
You use percents in real-life applications in **Steps 1–3.**

PROBLEM How can decimals and percents be used to prepare a budget for a school store?

STEP 1 Determine the cost of inventory.

As manager of a new school store, you are responsible for placing an order at the beginning of the school year for the items below. Begin filling out the form by contacting a local supply store or using the Internet to find the wholesale price of each item.

SCHOOL STORE Mon.–Fri. 7 A.M.–8 A.M.

Pens, Pencils, Markers, Blank CDs, Notebooks

You should order enough items so that $\frac{1}{4}$ of the student body could buy at least one of each item. Find the number of students in your school. Use a percent to determine the number of each item you will order, and calculate the total cost.

Item	Wholesale price	Number to buy	Cost
Pens	?	?	?
Pencils	?	?	?
Markers	?	?	?
Blank CDs	?	?	?
Notebooks	?	?	?
		Total Cost	?

STEP 2 Calculate the retail price.

Choose a percent markup that creates a reasonable profit for the store but maintains an affordable price for the students. Calculate the retail price for each item.

STEP 3 Calculate discounts.

With one month left in the school year, 10% of each item remains. To sell the remaining inventory, the store will have a sale. Choose a percent discount for the sale. Find the new retail price for each item.

Extending the Problem

Use your results from the problem above to complete the exercises.

1. Assuming all inventory has been sold, find the store's income.

2. Assuming all inventory has been sold, find the store's profit.

REVIEW KEY VOCABULARY

• place value, *p. 133*
• front-end estimation, *p. 138*
• leading digit, *p. 144*
• percent, *p. 150*
• markup, *p. 160*
• discount, *p. 160*

• commission, *p. 161*
• profit, *p. 162*
• percent of change, *p. 168*
• percent of increase, *p. 168*
• percent of decrease, *p. 168*
• interest, *p. 172*

• principal, *p. 172*
• simple interest *p. 172*
• annual interest rate, *p. 172*
• balance, *p. 173*
• compound interest, *p. 173*

VOCABULARY EXERCISES

Match the definition with the correct word at the right.

1. The amount of money that you borrow or deposit

2. The amount paid for the use of money

3. The percent of the principal that you pay or earn each year

A. Annual interest rate

B. Interest

C. Principal

In Exercises 4–7, copy and complete the statement.

4. The percent of a sale that is earned by a salesperson is called the __?__.

5. Interest that is earned or paid only on the principal is called __?__.

6. The difference between the retail price and the wholesale price of an item is the __?__.

7. For an item that is on sale, the difference between the original price and the sale price is the __?__.

8. **NOTETAKING SKILLS** Make a *cycle diagram* like the one on page 132 for writing a percent as a fraction and writing a fraction as a percent.

REVIEW EXAMPLES AND EXERCISES

3.1 Comparing Decimals

pp. 133–136

NS 1.1 **EXAMPLE**

Order 1.2, −0.8, 3.1, 0.8, and −1.3 from least to greatest.

Graph the decimals on a number line.

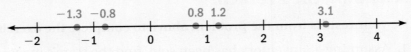

▶ **Answer** The decimals from least to greatest are −1.3, −0.8, 0.8, 1.2, and 3.1.

EXERCISES

SEE EXAMPLES
1, 2, AND 3
on pp. 133–134
for Exs. 9–12

Copy and complete the statement using <, >, or =.

9. 2.7 _?_ 2.2

10. 0.868 _?_ 0.89

11. −0.426 _?_ −0.31

12. BASEBALL The batting averages of three players on a baseball team are 0.336, 0.316, and 0.332. Write the averages in order from least to greatest.

3.2 Adding and Subtracting Decimals

pp. 137–141

NS 1.2

EXAMPLE

a. Find the sum of 14.02 and 9.81.

$$\begin{array}{r} 14.02 \\ +\ 9.81 \\ \hline 23.83 \end{array}$$

b. Find the difference of 20.5 and 3.764.

$$\begin{array}{r} 20.500 \\ -\ 3.764 \\ \hline 16.736 \end{array}$$

Use zeros as placeholders.

EXERCISES

SEE EXAMPLES
1 AND 2
on pp. 137–138
for Exs. 13–17

Find the sum or difference.

13. 1.2 + 0.67

14. 33.2 + 9.398

15. 3.16 − 1.845

16. 90.3 − (−7.81)

17. TEMPERATURE At 8 A.M., the temperature outside was 65.2°F. By noon, the temperature had increased by 8.5°F. At 6 P.M., the temperature was 5.1°F cooler than at noon. What was the temperature at 6 P.M.?

3.3 Multiplying and Dividing Decimals

pp. 144–149

NS 1.2

EXAMPLE

a. Find the product of 14.75 and 1.3.

$$\begin{array}{r} 14.75 \\ \times\ \ 1.3 \\ \hline 4\ 425 \\ 14\ 75 \\ \hline 19.175 \end{array}$$

2 decimal places
+ 1 decimal place

3 decimal places

b. Find the quotient of 21.726 and 4.26.

$$4.26\overline{)21.726} \longrightarrow 426\overline{)2172.6}$$ quotient 5.1

EXERCISES

SEE EXAMPLES
1, 2, 3, AND 4
on pp. 144–146
for Exs. 18–22

Find the product or quotient.

18. 6.24 • 0.375

19. 3.348 • (−0.9)

20. 66.96 ÷ (−2.7)

21. 18.91 ÷ 9.455

22. CATS A tiger at a zoo has a mass of 144.9 kilograms. This is 40.25 times the mass of a certain house cat. What is the mass of the house cat?

3.4 Percents as Decimals and Fractions

pp. 150–153

NS 1.3

EXAMPLE

Write 28% as a decimal and as a fraction.

$28\% = 28 \div 100 = .28 = 0.28$ Remove % sign. Move decimal point two places to the left.

$28\% = \dfrac{28}{100} = \dfrac{7}{25}$ Write as a fraction and simplify.

▶ **Answer** 28% can be written as 0.28 and as $\dfrac{7}{25}$.

EXERCISES

SEE EXAMPLES 1, 2, AND 3 on pp. 150–151 for Exs. 23–31

Write the percent as a decimal.

23. 74%   **24.** 3.8%   **25.** −16.8%   **26.** 130%

Write the percent as a fraction.

27. 18%   **28.** −35%   **29.** 228%   **30.** −28.5%

31. TRAVEL You survey 260 people and find that 55% of them like to travel. How many of the people surveyed like to travel?

3.5 Decimals and Fractions as Percents

pp. 155–159

NS 1.3

EXAMPLE

Write 0.67 and $\dfrac{3}{4}$ as a percent.

$0.67 = (067.)\% = 67\%$ Move the decimal point two places to the right and add % sign.

$\dfrac{3}{4} = \dfrac{3 \times 25}{4 \times 25} = \dfrac{75}{100} = 75\%$ Write an equivalent fraction with a denominator of 100. The numerator of the equivalent fraction is the percent.

▶ **Answer** 0.67 can be written as 67% and $\dfrac{3}{4}$ can be written as 75%.

EXERCISES

SEE EXAMPLES 1, 2, AND 3 on pp. 155–156 for Exs. 32–36

Write the decimal or fraction as a percent.

32. 0.93   **33.** −0.507   **34.** $\dfrac{3}{5}$ **35.** $-\dfrac{9}{20}$

36. Order the numbers from least to greatest: $\dfrac{3}{8}$, 37%, and 0.037.

3.6 Discounts, Markups, Commissions, and Profit

pp. 160–165

NS 1.7 **EXAMPLE**

A pair of shoes has an original price of $40. What is the sale price after a 15% discount?

$40 \times 0.15 = 6$ **Multiply to find discount.**

$40 - 6 = 34$ **Subtract discount from original price.**

▶ **Answer** The sale price of the shoes is $34.

EXERCISES

SEE EXAMPLES 1, 2, 4, AND 5 on pp. 160–162 for Exs. 37–39

Find the sale price or retail price.

37. Wholesale price: $30; Percent markup: 70%

38. Original price: $72; Percent discount: 18%

39. **MOWING LAWNS** Last week, you mowed 8 lawns for $25 each. Your expenses were $35. What was your profit?

3.7 Percent of Change

pp. 168–171

NS 1.6 **EXAMPLE**

Find the percent of increase in height of a plant 60 inches tall that grows to 84 inches.

$p\% = \dfrac{84 - 60}{60}$ **Write amount of increase and divide by original amount.**

$= \dfrac{24}{60}$ **Subtract.**

$= 0.4$ **Write fraction as a decimal.**

$= 40\%$ **Write decimal as a percent.**

▶ **Answer** The percent of increase in height is 40%.

EXERCISES

SEE EXAMPLES 1 AND 2 on pp. 168–169 for Exs. 40–42

Find the percent of increase or decrease. Round to the nearest percent.

40. Original amount: 90; New amount: 220   **41.** Original amount: 50; New amount: 35

42. **WEIGHT** A moving van's load changes from 1000 pounds to 800 pounds after delivering an appliance. What is the percent of decrease?

3.8 Simple and Compound Interest

pp. 172–177

NS 1.7 **EXAMPLE**

You deposit $750 in a savings account that pays a simple interest rate of 2.8% per year. What is the account balance after 4 years?

$A = P(1 + rt)$ Write formula for finding simple interest balance.

$= 750[1 + 0.028(4)]$ Substitute values.

$= 834$ Simplify.

▶ **Answer** The account balance is $834 after 4 years.

NS 1.7 **EXAMPLE**

You deposit $600 in a savings account that pays 3.5% interest compounded annually. What is the account balance after 3 years?

$A = P(1 + r)^t$ Write formula for finding compound interest balance.

$= 600(1 + 0.035)^3$ Substitute values.

$= 665.23$ Simplify.

▶ **Answer** The account balance is $665.23 after 3 years.

EXERCISES

SEE EXAMPLES 1, 2, AND 3
on pp. 172–174
for Exs. 43–51

Find the amount of simple interest earned with an annual rate of 3.5%.

43. Principal: $350
Time: 5 years

44. Principal: $840
Time: 9 months

45. Principal: $1350
Time: 1.5 years

Find the balance of the account that earns interest compounded annually.

46. Principal: $2000
Annual rate: 5%
Time: 36 months

47. Principal: $750
Annual rate: 4.2%
Time: 8 years

48. Principal: $5000
Annual rate: 4%
Time: 3 years

49. INTEREST You borrow $700 at an annual simple interest rate of 4%. How much interest do you owe after 6 months?

50. LOAN You borrow $1200 from a bank that charges 9.5% simple annual interest. After 15 months you pay back the loan. How much interest do you pay on the loan? What is the total amount that you pay the bank?

51. BANKING You deposit $3000 in a savings account for college that pays 4.5% interest compounded annually. What is the balance of the account after 8 years?

VOCABULARY Copy and complete the statement.

1. The sum of the principal and earned interest in an account is the __?__.

2. A(n) __?__ shows how much a quantity has increased or decreased from the original amount.

Copy and complete the statement with <, >, or =.

3. 2.7 _?_ 2.69

4. 23.09 _?_ −3.1

5. 7.2 _?_ $\left|-7.24\right|$

6. 4.38 _?_ $\frac{22}{5}$

Find the sum or difference.

7. $6.2 - 5.984$

8. $2.608 + 12.93$

9. $15.68 - (-4.94)$

10. $-3.64 + 14.2$

Find the product or quotient.

11. $-34.69 \cdot 12.7$

12. $0.123 \cdot 4.53$

13. $0.7992 \div (-0.333)$

14. $3.7611 \div 0.597$

Write the percent as a decimal and as a fraction.

15. 0.7%

16. 419%

17. 8%

18. -7.8%

Write the decimal or fraction as a percent.

19. 1.65

20. -0.49

21. $\frac{7}{20}$

22. $-\frac{11}{4}$

Find the percent of change. Tell whether it is an increase or decrease.

23. Original amount: 40
    New amount: 36

24. Original amount: 225
    New amount: 324

25. Original amount: 258
    New amount: 6.45

BAGELS In Exercises 26 and 27, use the table. It shows the approximate supermarket sales of three types of bagels (in billions of dollars) in 2003.

Bagels	Sales (billions)
Frozen	$.086
Refrigerated	$.077
Fresh	$.43

26. How much greater were the sales for frozen bagels than the sales for refrigerated bagels?

27. What is the total amount of sales of all three types of bagels?

28. **OFFICE SUPPLIES** A store is offering a 25% discount on an office desk with an original price of $280. What is the sale price?

29. **CAR SALES** A car salesperson earns a 5% commission on each sale. What is the commission on the sale of a $23,500 car?

30. **SAVINGS ACCOUNT** You deposit $900 in an account that earns 4.2% interest compounded annually. What is the account balance after 5 years?

3 ◆ MULTIPLE CHOICE STRATEGIES

STRATEGIES YOU'LL USE:
• SOLVE DIRECTLY
• ELIMINATE CHOICES

Standards
NS 1.6, NS 1.7

If you have difficulty solving a multiple choice problem directly, you may
be able to use another approach to eliminate incorrect answer choices and
obtain the correct answer.

PROBLEM 1

Eric deposits $500 in a savings account that earns 3% simple annual
interest. How much money will he have in his account after 42 months?

Ⓐ $52.50   **Ⓑ** $54.50   **Ⓒ** $552.50   **Ⓓ** $1130

Strategy 1 SOLVE DIRECTLY

Use the formula for simple interest to find
the interest earned. Then add the interest
to the principal to find the balance of the
account.

STEP 1 **Find** the simple interest. For the
formula, time is in years. So, write
42 months as 3.5 years.

$$I = Prt$$
$$= (500)(0.03)(3.5)$$
$$= 52.50$$

Eric will earn $52.50 in interest.

STEP 2 **Add** the interest to the principal.

$$\text{Balance} = \text{Principal} + \text{Interest}$$
$$= 500 + 52.50$$
$$= 552.50$$

After 42 months, Eric will have $552.50 in
his account.

The correct answer is C. Ⓐ Ⓑ ● Ⓓ

Strategy 2 ELIMINATE CHOICES

You can eliminate choices by determining
the reasonableness of the answer choices.

Because Eric is earning interest on his
account, he will have more money in his
account after 42 months than he does now.
Both choice A and choice B are less than he
has now. So, you can eliminate choices A
and B.

Because choice D is more than twice Eric's
original deposit, you can eliminate choice D.

The correct answer is C. Ⓐ Ⓑ ● Ⓓ

PROBLEM 2

An increase from 40 to 90 is what percent of an increase?

(A) 55.5%   **(B)** 100%   **(C)** 110%   **(D)** 125%

Strategy 1   SOLVE DIRECTLY

Find the percent of increase by finding the amount of increase and dividing it by the original amount. Then write the decimal as a percent.

STEP 1   **Find** the amount of increase.

$$90 - 40 = 50$$

STEP 2   **Divide** the amount of increase by the original amount.

$$\frac{50}{40} = 1.25$$

STEP 3   **Write** the decimal as a percent.

$$1.25 = 125\%$$

An increase from 40 to 90 is an increase of 125%.

The correct answer is D.   **(A)** **(B)** **(C)** **(D)**

Strategy 2   ELIMINATE CHOICES

You can eliminate choices by determining the reasonableness of the answer choices.

When you double a number, the number is increased by 100%. If 40 is doubled, the result is 80. Because 40 is increased to 90, the percent increase is more than 100% since 90 is more than 80. Because 55.5% and 100% are not more than 100%, you can eliminate choices A and B.

Because 40 increased by 100% is 80 and 10% of 40 is 4, it follows that 40 increased by 110% is 84, not 90. So, you can eliminate choice C.

The correct answer is D.   **(A)** **(B)** **(C)** **(D)**

STRATEGY PRACTICE

Explain why you can eliminate the highlighted answer choice.

1. A magazine subscription has a regular price of $24.50. You pay $14.70 for your subscription. What is the percent discount?

   (A) 40%   **(B)** 60%   **(C)** 66.7%   **(D)** **166.7%**

2. Last month, a restaurant had an income of $12,346 and expenses of $6,723. What was the profit for the month?

   (A) **−$4,325**   **(B)** $3,467   **(C)** $5,623   **(D)** $12,346

3. A coat has a wholesale price of $52. The markup is 110%. What is the retail price of the coat?

   (A) $68.50   **(B)** **$89.75**   **(C)** $109.20   **(D)** $125.42

1. Which decimal would be graphed halfway between the two points shown? **NS 1.1**

   3.42   3.43

   Ⓐ 0.3425

   Ⓑ 3.4

   Ⓒ 3.425

   Ⓓ 3.451

2. A survey of people's preferences for writing tools found that 22.5% like pencils, $\frac{5}{11}$ like ballpoint pens, and 0.32 like felt-tipped pens. Which list gives these values in order from least to greatest? **NS 1.1, MR 1.1**

   Ⓐ $\frac{5}{11}$, 22.5%, 0.32

   Ⓑ 22.5%, $\frac{5}{11}$, 0.32

   Ⓒ 22.5%, 0.32, $\frac{5}{11}$

   Ⓓ 0.32, $\frac{5}{11}$, 22.5%

3. What is $\frac{17}{200}$ as a decimal? **NS 1.3**

   Ⓐ 0.085

   Ⓑ 0.125

   Ⓒ 0.17

   Ⓓ 0.225

4. Joan invested $100 in an account that pays 5% simple annual interest. What is the account balance after 5 years? **NS 1.7**

   Ⓐ $25

   Ⓑ $105

   Ⓒ $125

   Ⓓ $350

5. A pepper grinder holds 1.8 ounces of peppercorns. You buy 9 ounces of peppercorns. How many times can you completely fill the pepper grinder? **NS 1.2**

   Ⓐ 2

   Ⓑ 5

   Ⓒ 8

   Ⓓ 9

6. The table shows the points scored by four players on a team in an academic competition. What percent of the team total did player 2 account for? **NS 1.3**

Player	1	2	3	4
Points	94	150	186	120

   Ⓐ 25%

   Ⓑ $27.\overline{27}$%

   Ⓒ 33.3%

   Ⓓ $37.\overline{5}$%

7. An increase from 280 to 315 is what percent of an increase? **NS 1.6**

   Ⓐ $11.\overline{1}$%

   Ⓑ 12.5%

   Ⓒ 35%

   Ⓓ $88.\overline{8}$%

8. You have the rectangular patio shown below. What is the area of the patio? **NS 1.2**

   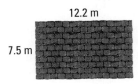

   12.2 m

   7.5 m

   Ⓐ 39.4 m^2

   Ⓑ 91.5 m^2

   Ⓒ 108.7 m^2

   Ⓓ 915 m^2

9. What is the value of 3.4 − 4.208? **NS 1.2**

(A) −0.808

(B) −0.192

(C) 0.192

(D) 0.808

10. Cindy wants to use a 10% discount coupon to buy a sweater and a 20% discount coupon to buy a coat. What would be the total cost of the items shown after using the coupons? **NS 1.7**

$36

$78

(A) $34.20

(B) $79.80

(C) $94.80

(D) $99.00

11. What is $\frac{18}{25}$ as a percent? **NS 1.3**

(A) 12%

(B) 25%

(C) 60%

(D) 72%

12. Your checking account has a beginning balance of $75.43. What is the ending balance after the transactions shown in the checkbook below? **NS 1.2, MR 1.3**

Date	Transaction	Deposit	Withdrawal
1/02	deposit	$50	
1/10	groceries		$75.35
1/16	bookstore		$12.95

(A) $37.13

(B) $50.08

(C) $63.03

(D) $113.73

13. What is the value of 8.253 ÷ 2.1? **NS 1.2**

(A) 2.96

(B) 3.12

(C) 3.83

(D) 3.93

14. An item with a wholesale price of $8.40 is marked up 60%. What is the retail price? **NS 1.7**

(A) $3.36

(B) $5.04

(C) $13.44

(D) $14.40

Use the following information to answer Exercises 15 and 16. The table shows the data for two sales at a computer store.

Computer Sales		
Sale number	1	2
Customer paid	$859	$1234
Store paid	$426	$675

15. What is the store's profit on sale 1? **NS 1.7**

(A) $129

(B) $406

(C) $433

(D) $859

16. Marion, a salesperson at the store, made sale 2. How much did he earn if he gets an 11% commission on the amount the customer paid? **NS 1.7**

(A) $46.86

(B) $74.25

(C) $94.49

(D) $135.74

Exponents and Irrational Numbers

Before

In previous chapters, you learned the following skills, which you'll use in Chapter 4:

- Raising rational numbers to whole-number powers
- Ordering decimals
- Evaluating algebraic expressions
- Comparing rational numbers

Now

In Chapter 4 you'll study these **Big Ideas:**

1 Understanding zero and negative exponents

2 Using square roots

3 Classifying real numbers

Why?

So you can solve real-world problems about . . .

- Population, p. 200
- Astronomy, p. 204
- State parks, p. 204
- Biology, p. 210
- Arts and crafts, p. 217
- Fire towers, p. 218
- Escape velocity, p. 223
- Box kites, p. 229

Animated Math

at *classzone.com*

Get-Ready Games

DETECTIVE DECODING

California Standards

Review using whole-number exponents. *Gr. 7 NS 1.2*
Prepare for using integer exponents. *Gr. 7 AF 2.1*

N	$3^2 \times 5^2$	H	$2 \times 2 \times 5 \times 5$
L	$2^3 \times 5^2$	O	$2 \times 2 \times 3 \times 5$
I	$2^2 \times 3^2$	E	$2^2 \times 3^2 \times 5$
U	$2^2 \times 3 \times 5^2$	W	$2^3 \times 3^3$
D	$3 \times 5 \times 5$	T	$2 \times 3 \times 3 \times 3$

| 216 | 100 | 60 | 75 | 300 | 225 | 36 | 54 |

How to Play

Evaluate each expression. Then match the letter associated with an expression with the value of the expression. Not every letter will be used.

The letters, written in the order of the values shown, give the name of a popular type of detective fiction.

CALIFORNIA STANDARDS

- **Gr. 7 NS 1.4** Differentiate between rational and irrational numbers. *(Lesson 4.6)*

- **Gr. 7 AF 2.1** Interpret positive whole-number powers as repeated multiplication and negative whole-number powers as repeated division or multiplication by the multiplicative inverse. Simplify and evaluate expressions that include exponents. *(Lessons 4.1, 4.3)*

MYSTERY · MATH

California Standards

Review using reasoning. **Gr. 7 MR 2.4**

Prepare for simplifying square roots. **Gr. 7 NS 2.4**

> I am a one digit number. I divide evenly into 27, but I do not divide into 30. **A**

> I am a two digit number. I can be divided evenly by 5. The sum of my two digits is 12. **B**

> I am a two digit number. My tens' digit is 7. I can be divided evenly by 12. **C**

> I am a two digit number. I can be divided evenly by 7. If you switch my digits, I grow by 18. **D**

A − 8   B − 67   C ÷ 9   D ÷ 5

How to Play

Use the clues to find the mystery numbers. Then use the mystery numbers to evaluate the expressions.

The values of the expressions, written in the order shown, give the year in which Sir Arthur Conan Doyle published the first Sherlock Holmes story.

Games Wrap-Up

Draw Conclusions

Complete these exercises after playing the games.

1. **WRITING** Without evaluating any expressions in *Detective Decoding*, how can you eliminate choices of letters to replace 216? *Explain* your reasoning.

2. **REASONING** Write two clues and two expressions, like those used in *Mystery Math*, that could be used to find the month and day of your birth.

Prerequisite Skills

California @HomeTutor
Prerequisite skills practice
at classzone.com

REVIEW VOCABULARY

- **power,** *p. 5*
- **exponent,** *p. 5*
- **base,** *p. 5*
- **integer,** *p. 12*
- **rational number,** *p. 113*

VOCABULARY CHECK

Copy and complete using a review term from the list at the left.

1. In the expression 2^6, 2 is called the __?__.

2. The expression 3^7 is a(n) __?__ of 3.

3. In the expression 5^4, 4 is called the __?__.

4. A number that can be written as a quotient $\frac{a}{b}$ where a and b are integers and $b \neq 0$ is called a(n) __?__.

SKILL CHECK

Evaluate the expression. *(p. 5)*

5. $3^2 \cdot 3$
6. $(2 + 3)^2$
7. $4^2 \div 4^2$
8. $(6 - 5)^7$
9. $3^2 + 4 \cdot 5$
10. $12 - 8 \div 2^2$
11. $7^2 - 3^3$
12. $6^2 \div 2^2$

Tell whether the number is included in each of the following number sets: *rational numbers, integers, whole numbers.* *(p. 113)*

13. 6
14. $-\frac{5}{2}$
15. 0
16. -4
17. $\frac{1}{7}$
18. 0.303
19. $-0.\overline{6}$
20. 13

Notetaking Skills

NOW YOU TRY
Make a *four square diagram* for the word *integer*.

Focus on Graphic Organizers

You can use a *four square diagram* to organize information about a vocabulary word, such as *power*.

Definition	Vocabulary
A product formed from repeated multiplication by the same number or expression	A power has a base and an exponent.

POWER

Examples	Non-Examples
3^2 25^6 x^3 $\left(\frac{1}{2}\right)^4$	$x + 1 = 3$ $45°$

4.1 Zero and Negative Powers of Ten

MATERIALS · paper and pencil

Standards

NS 2.1 Understand negative whole-number exponents. Multiply and divide expressions involving exponents with a common base.

QUESTION What does it mean for 10 to be raised to the power of zero or to a negative power?

You have used repeated multiplication to write a power of the form 10^n in standard form, where n is a positive integer. For example, $10^4 = 10 \times 10 \times 10 \times 10 = 10{,}000$. In this activity, you will evaluate powers of 10 where the exponent is zero or negative.

EXPLORE Use a pattern to raise 10 to a zero or negative power

STEP 1 **Copy** the table and complete the next two rows by evaluating 10^2 and 10^1.

Power	Standard form
10^3	1000
10^2	?
10^1	?
10^0	?
10^{-1}	?
10^{-2}	?
10^{-3}	?

STEP 2 **Look** at the rows you have completed. How does the standard form change each time the exponent decreases by 1?

STEP 3 **Use** the pattern you identified in Step 2 to complete the remaining rows in the table.

DRAW CONCLUSIONS Use your observations to complete these exercises

Write the power of 10 in standard form.

1. 10^4 **2.** 10^9 **3.** 10^{-4} **4.** 10^{-6}

5. REASONING Let n be a positive integer. How many zeros are there in the standard form of 10^n? in the standard form of 10^{-n}?

4.1 Integer Powers of Ten

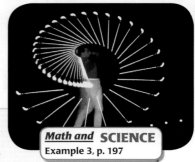

Standards

NS 1.1 Read, write, and compare rational numbers in scientific notation (positive and negative powers of 10), compare rational numbers in general.

NS 2.1 Understand negative whole-number exponents. Multiply and divide expressions involving exponents with a common base.

AF 2.1 Interpret positive whole-number powers as repeated multiplication and negative whole-number powers as repeated division or multiplication by the multiplicative inverse. Simplify and evaluate expressions that include exponents.

Math and **SCIENCE**
Example 3, p. 197

Connect *Before* you evaluated powers with positive exponents. *Now* you will evaluate powers with zero or negative exponents.

KEY VOCABULARY
• **power,** *p. 5*
• **multiplicative inverse,** *p. 99*

In this lesson, you will learn about powers of 10 that have a zero exponent or a negative integer exponent.

The table shows several powers of 10 in various forms. Note the following:

• Powers of 10 with positive integer exponents involve repeated multiplication by 10.

About the Standards

You observe patterns to develop rules for powers of 10 (MR 1.1) in this lesson.

• Powers of 10 with negative integer exponents involve repeated multiplication by $\frac{1}{10}$ (the multiplicative inverse of 10), or repeated division by 10.

• The power of 10 with an exponent of 0 equals 1.

Power	Repeated multiplication	Standard form
10^3	$1 \times 10 \times 10 \times 10$	1000
10^2	$1 \times 10 \times 10$	100
10^1	1×10	10
10^0	1	1
10^{-1}	$1 \times \frac{1}{10}$	0.1
10^{-2}	$1 \times \frac{1}{10} \times \frac{1}{10}$	0.01
10^{-3}	$1 \times \frac{1}{10} \times \frac{1}{10} \times \frac{1}{10}$	0.001

EXAMPLE 1 Write Powers of 10 in Standard Form

a. $10^3 = 10 \times 10 \times 10 = 1{,}000$

b. $10^{-5} = \frac{1}{10} \times \frac{1}{10} \times \frac{1}{10} \times \frac{1}{10} \times \frac{1}{10} = 0.00001$

✓ GUIDED PRACTICE for Example 1

Write the power of 10 in standard form.

1. 10^5 **2.** 10^6 **3.** 10^{-2} **4.** 10^{-7}

5. SCIENCE Scientists have created a microfabric using molded plastic. Its narrowest threads are 10^{-3} millimeter across. Write this number in standard form.

STANDARD FORM In Example 1, notice that the standard form of 10^3 is a 1 followed by 3 zeros. Also notice that the standard form of 10^{-5} is a decimal with $5 - 1 = 4$ zeros to the right of the decimal point, followed by a 1.

In general, if n is a positive integer, then the standard form of 10^n is a 1 followed by n zeros. The standard form of 10^{-n} is a decimal with $n - 1$ zeros to the right of the decimal point, followed by a 1.

EXAMPLE 2 **Write Numbers in Standard Form as Powers of 10**

a. $1,000,000,000 = 10^9$ There are 9 zeros after the 1 so the exponent is 9.

b. $0.000001 = 10^{-6}$ There are $5 = 6 - 1$ zeros after the decimal point, so the exponent is -6.

NEGATIVE POWERS OF 10 You can use the table on page 196 to write the following statements.

$$10^{-1} = \frac{1}{10^1} \qquad 10^{-2} = \frac{1}{10^2} \qquad 10^{-3} = \frac{1}{10^3}$$

This suggests a rule for any negative integer power of 10:

$$10^{-n} = \frac{1}{10^n}, \text{ where } n \text{ is a positive integer.}$$

EXAMPLE 3 **Using a Negative Exponent**

STROBE LIGHTS The picture of the golf ball was taken using a strobe light. Each flash of the strobe light lasts about 1 microsecond. Use a power of 10 to write this time in seconds.

SOLUTION

READING
The prefix *micro* means one millionth.

Each flash lasts 1 microsecond, or equivalently, $\frac{1}{1,000,000}$ second.

$$\frac{1}{1,000,000} = \frac{1}{10^6} \qquad \text{Write 1,000,000 as } 10^6.$$

$$= 10^{-6} \qquad \text{Use the fact that } \frac{1}{10^n} = 10^{-n}.$$

▶ **Answer** Each flash of the strobe light lasts about 10^{-6} second.

Time of flash: 1 microsecond

✓ **GUIDED PRACTICE** **for Examples 2 and 3**

6. Write the number 0.0001 as a power of 10.

7. **WHAT IF?** In Example 3, suppose each flash of the strobe light lasts one millisecond (or one thousandth of a second). Use a power of 10 to write this time in seconds.

EXAMPLE 4 ◆ **Multiple Choice Practice**

Which list of numbers is ordered from least to greatest?

(A) $10^2, 10^{-3}, 0.0001, 1, 10$ (B) $10^{-3}, 0.0001, 1, 10, 10^2$

(C) $0.0001, 10^{-3}, 1, 10, 10^2$ (D) $0.0001, 1, 10, 10^2, 10^{-3}$

ANOTHER WAY

You can also solve Example 4 by first writing each number as a power of 10. Then order the powers so that the exponents increase.

SOLUTION

Write each number in standard form. Then compare the numbers.

$10^2 = 100, 10^{-3} = 0.001, 0.0001, 1, 10$

The order of the numbers from least to greatest is $0.0001, 10^{-3}, 1, 10,$ and 10^2.

▶**Answer** The correct answer is C. (A) (B) (C) (D)

✓ **GUIDED PRACTICE** | **for Example 4**

Order the numbers from least to greatest.

8. $100, 10^{-2}, 1$ **9.** $0.01, 10^2, 1$ **10.** $10, 10^0, 10^{-1}, 10^2$

4.1 EXERCISES

HOMEWORK KEY

◆ = **MULTIPLE CHOICE PRACTICE**
Exs. 17, 22, 32, 46–48

○ = **HINTS AND HOMEWORK HELP**
for Exs. 5, 13, 39 at classzone.com

SKILLS • PROBLEM SOLVING • REASONING

1. VOCABULARY Copy and complete: The __?__ of 10 is $\frac{1}{10}$.

2. WRITING Let n be a positive integer. *Explain* how to write 10^n and 10^{-n} in standard form.

SEE EXAMPLE 1
on p. 196
for Exs. 3–10

STANDARD FORM Write the power of 10 in standard form.

3. 10^1 **4.** 10^{-14} **5.** 10^{10} **6.** 10^{-8}

7. 10^0 **8.** 10^{-3} **9.** 10^{-13} **10.** 10^{15}

SEE EXAMPLE 2
on p. 197
for Exs. 11–17

POWERS OF 10 Write the number as a power of 10.

11. 1000   **12.** 1   **13.** 100,000

14. 0.00001   **15.** 0.01   **16.** 0.0000000001

17. ◆ **MULTIPLE CHOICE** Which power of 10 is equal to 1000?

(A) 10^{-3} (B) 10^0 (C) 10^3 (D) 10^4

SEE EXAMPLE 4
on p. 198
for Exs. 18–22

ORDERING POWERS OF 10 **Order the numbers from least to greatest.**

18. $10, 0.0001, 10^2, 0.001$

19. $0.01, 10^0, 10^4, 0.000001$

20. $10^5, 10^{-5}, 0.001, 10^{-2}$

21. $10^0, \frac{1}{10}, 10^3, 10^{-2}, 0.0001$

22. ◆ **MULTIPLE CHOICE** Which list of numbers is ordered from least to greatest?

(A) $10^0, 10^1, 10^{-3}, 10^3$

(B) $10^4, 10^0, 0.001, 10^{-2}$

(C) $0.00001, 10^1, 10^3, 10^{-6}$

(D) $\frac{1}{10^4}, 10^{-3}, 0.01, 10^4$

23. **ERROR ANALYSIS** *Describe* and correct the error in writing 10^{-3} in standard form.

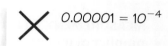

$$10^{-3} = -(10)(10)(10)$$
$$= -1000$$

24. **ERROR ANALYSIS** *Describe* and correct the error in writing 0.00001 as a power of 10.

$$0.00001 = 10^{-4}$$

REASONING **Tell whether each power of 10 is *less than*, *greater than*, or *equal to* 1.**

25. 10^0

26. 10^2

27. 10^{-1}

CONNECT SKILLS TO PROBLEM SOLVING **Exercises 28–31 will help you prepare for problem solving.**

Write each mass as a power of 10 expressed in grams.

28. The mass of a rock is 10,000 grams.

29. The mass of a paper clip is 1 gram.

30. The mass of a dust particle is 0.001 gram.

31. The mass of a car is 1,000,000 grams.

SEE EXAMPLE 3
on p. 197
for Exs. 32–34

32. ◆ **MULTIPLE CHOICE** What is the area of a rectangle with a length of 0.01 kilometer and a width of 0.001 kilometer?

(A) $10^{-6}\,\text{km}^2$ **(B)** $10^{-5}\,\text{km}^2$ **(C)** $10^{-4}\,\text{km}^2$ **(D)** $10^{-3}\,\text{km}^2$

California @HomeTutor for problem solving help at classzone.com

33. **BRIDGE** From the beginning of the West Bay Suspension Bridge to the end of the East Bay Cantilever Bridge, the Bay Bridge is 5410 feet long. In expanded form, this number can be written as

$$5 \times 1000 + 4 \times 100 + 1 \times 10 + 0 \times 1.$$

Write the length of the bridge in expanded form using powers of 10.

California @HomeTutor for problem solving help at classzone.com

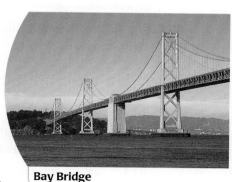

Bay Bridge

34. POPULATION In 2004, the population density of California was approximately 230.1 persons per square mile. In expanded form, this number can be written as

$$2 \times 100 + 3 \times 10 + 0 \times 1 + 1 \times 0.1$$

Write California's population density in expanded form using powers of 10.

REASONING Copy and complete the statement using *always, sometimes,* or *never. Explain* your reasoning.

35. A power of 10 with an exponent of zero is __?__ zero.

36. A power of 10 with a negative integer exponent is __?__ less than 1.

37. A power of 10 with a positive integer exponent is __?__ positive.

38. A power of 10 with a negative integer exponent is __?__ negative.

MEASUREMENT In Exercises 39–42, use the table. It shows the number of meters, written as powers of 10, that are equivalent to various metric measures. Write your answers in standard form.

Unit	Meter
decimeter	10^{-1}
centimeter	10^{-2}
nanometer	10^{-9}
picometer	10^{-12}
attometer	10^{-18}

39. How many picometers are in a decimeter?

40. How many attometers are in a picometer?

41. How many nanometers are in a decimeter?

42. How many attometers are in a centimeter?

43. REASONING *Explain* how you can use repeated division to determine that $10^0 = 1$.

44. CHALLENGE Use repeated multiplication to write the product $10^8 \times 10^6$ as a single power of 10. What do you notice? How do you think the product $10^{57} \times 10^{103}$ can be written as a single power of 10? *Explain.*

45. CHALLENGE In a vaccuum, light travels at a speed of approximately 299,790,000 meters per second. Write this speed in the form $c \times 10^n$ where $1 \le c$ and $c < 10$.

◆ **CALIFORNIA STANDARDS SPIRAL REVIEW**

AF 1.2

46. What is the value of $4(x - 7)$ when $x = 9$? *(p. 5)*

   A -8 **B** -2 **C** 8   **D** 16

NS 1.6

47. What is the percent of change from $50 to $75? *(p. 168)*

   A 25%   **B** 45%   **C** 50%   **D** 75%

NS 1.7

48. You deposit $600 into an account that earns 3.2% annual interest compounded annually. What is the account balance after 4 years? *(p. 172)*

   A $623.06   **B** $680.57   **C** $717.45   **D** $743.24

4.2 Scientific Notation

Math and ART
Example 1, p. 201

Standards NS 1.1 **Read, write, and compare rational numbers in scientific notation (positive and negative powers of 10)**, compare rational numbers in general.

Connect *Before* you evaluated powers of 10. *Now* you will read and write numbers in scientific notation.

KEY VOCABULARY
• scientific notation

One way to write very small numbers like the thickness of a soap bubble or very large numbers like the number of stars in a galaxy is to use powers of ten. This can be done by writing the numbers in *scientific notation*.

KEY CONCEPT *For Your Notebook*

Scientific Notation

A number is written in **scientific notation** if it has the form $c \times 10^n$ where $c \geq 1$, $c < 10$, and n is an integer.

Standard form	Product form	Scientific notation
325,000	$3.25 \times 100,000$	3.25×10^5
0.0005	5×0.0001	5×10^{-4}

EXAMPLE 1 Writing a Number in Scientific Notation

ART Joseph King used 110,000 toothpicks to make his Eiffel Tower model pictured above. To write 110,000 in scientific notation, use powers of 10.

AVOID ERRORS
When writing a number in scientific notation, the value you use for c is greater than or equal to 1 and less than 10.

Standard form	Product form	Scientific notation
110,000	$1.1 \times 100,000$	1.1×10^5
Move decimal point 5 places to the left.	5 zeros	Exponent is 5.

▶ **Answer** Joseph King used 1.1×10^5 toothpicks to make his model.

 GUIDED PRACTICE for Example 1

Write the number in scientific notation.

1. 4000

2. 7,300,000

3. 63,000,000,000

4. 230,000

5. 2,420,000

6. 105

7. REASONING Write the number 30×10^7 in scientific notation.

EXAMPLE 2 ◆ **Multiple Choice Practice**

The thickness of the wall of a soap bubble is about 0.000004 meter. What is the thickness written in scientific notation?

(A) 4×10^{-7} m   (B) 4×10^{-6} m

(C) 40×10^{-5} m   (D) 4×10^{7} m

Soap bubble wall thickness: 0.000004 meter

ELIMINATE CHOICES
A correct answer must be in the form $c \times 10^n$ where $c < 10$. Choice C is not in this form, so it can be eliminated.

SOLUTION

Standard form	Product form	Scientific notation
0.000004	4×0.000001	4×10^{-6}
Move decimal point 6 places to the right.		Exponent is -6.

The thickness of the wall of the bubble is about 4×10^{-6} meter.

▶ **Answer** The correct answer is B. (A) (B) (C) (D)

✓ **GUIDED PRACTICE**   for Example 2

Write the number in scientific notation.

8. 0.00475   **9.** 0.00000526   **10.** 0.0000000082

11. 0.0237   **12.** 0.000097   **13.** 0.0003041

STANDARD FORM A number in scientific notation can be written in standard form by using the exponent. Move the decimal point the appropriate number of places left or right, depending on the sign of the exponent.

EXAMPLE 3   **Writing Numbers in Standard Form**

Scientific notation	Product form	Standard form
a. 7.2×10^{5}	$7.2 \times 100{,}000$	720,000
Exponent is 5.		Move decimal point 5 places to the right.
b. 4.65×10^{-7}	4.65×0.0000001	0.000000465
Exponent is -7.		Move decimal point 7 places to the left.

✓ **GUIDED PRACTICE**   for Example 3

Write the number in standard form.

14. 3.5×10^{3} **15.** 2.48×10^{6} **16.** 5.1×10^{-4} **17.** 9.16×10^{-2}

4.2 EXERCISES

HOMEWORK KEY

◆ = **MULTIPLE CHOICE PRACTICE**
Exs. 12, 30, 39–41

◯ = **HINTS AND HOMEWORK HELP**
for Exs. 5, 15, 31 at classzone.com

SKILLS • PROBLEM SOLVING • REASONING

1. **VOCABULARY** Copy and complete: To write very small or very large numbers in terms of integer powers of 10, use __?__ notation.

2. **WRITING** *Explain* how to write 3.7×10^4 in standard form.

SEE EXAMPLES 1 AND 2
on pp. 201–202
for Exs. 3–13

SCIENTIFIC NOTATION Write the number in scientific notation.

3. 7900

4. 0.468

5. 0.0000671

6. 89,200,000,000

7. 8,100,000,000

8. 2,103,000

9. 0.03102

10. 0.000000415

11. 0.0000000342

12. ◆ **MULTIPLE CHOICE** What is 0.000000765 written in scientific notation?

A 7.65×10^{-9}
B 76.5×10^{-8}
C 7.65×10^{-7}
D 7.65×10^{-6}

13. **ERROR ANALYSIS** *Describe* and correct the error in writing the decimal 0.00076 as 7.6×10^4.

SEE EXAMPLE 3
on p. 202
for Exs. 14–21

STANDARD FORM Write the number in standard form.

14. 5.702×10^{-3}

15. 4.35×10^6

16. 9.6×10^7

17. 8.071×10^{-2}

18. 6.3537×10^{-6}

19. 1.76×10^{-9}

20. 4.1×10^9

21. 2.83×10^{12}

COMPARING Copy and complete the statement with <, >, or =.

22. 6.92×10^{11} __?__ 6.92×10^{12}

23. 3.4×10^{-20} __?__ 4.1×10^{-21}

24. **ERROR ANALYSIS** *Describe* and correct the error in comparing two numbers in scientific notation.

$$\times \quad 3 \times 10^{-6} < 3 \times 10^{-7}$$

25. **ORDERING** Order the numbers from least to greatest.

3.75×10^8 37,500,000 3.57×10^9 5.37×10^7

CONNECT SKILLS TO PROBLEM SOLVING Exercises 26–28 will help you prepare for problem solving.

26. A piece of paper has a thickness of about 0.0032 inch. Write this measurement in scientific notation.

27. An aircraft carrier weighs 75,000,000 pounds. Write this weight in scientific notation.

28. In the United States, 15,000,000 households use private wells for their water supply. Write this number in scientific notation.

SEE EXAMPLE 3
on p. 202
for Exs. 29, 31

29. ASTRONOMY The mass of Jupiter is about 1.9×10^{27} kilograms. Write this number in standard form.

California **@HomeTutor** for problem solving help at classzone.com

Jupiter's mass: 1.9×10^{27} kg

30. ◆ MULTIPLE CHOICE In 2000, there were approximately 281,000,000 people in the United States. Which of the following is *not* another way of expressing the number 281,000,000?

(A) 28.1 million   (B) 0.281 billion

(C) 28.1×10^7 (D) 2.81×10^8

California **@HomeTutor** for problem solving help at classzone.com

31. STATE PARKS The United States has a total of 1.2916×10^7 acres of land reserved for state parks. Write this number in standard form.

32. SCIENCE The masses of an oxygen atom and a hydrogen atom are shown below. Which atom has a greater mass?

Oxygen

mass $\approx 2.6561 \times 10^{-23}$ g

Hydrogen

mass $\approx 1.6735 \times 10^{-24}$ g

33. REASONING *Explain* how to compare numbers in scientific notation.

CHALLENGE Simplify. Write your answer in scientific notation.

34. $(3.2 \times 10^5) + (8.1 \times 10^3)$ **35.** $(5 \times 10^{-1}) + (9.8 \times 10^{-3})$

36. $(4.1 \times 10^8) - (7.7 \times 10^6)$ **37.** $(6.4 \times 10^4) - (5.9 \times 10^{-2})$

38. CHALLENGE A high-speed train travels approximately 6×10^3 centimeters in 1 second. About what distance in *meters* does the train travel in two hours? Write your answer in scientific notation.

◆ CALIFORNIA STANDARDS SPIRAL REVIEW

NS 1.1   **39.** What is 10^8 written in standard form? *(p. 196)*

(A) 0.00000001   (B) 1×10^8 (C) 100,000,000   (D) 1,000,000,000

NS 1.3   **40.** Which percent is equivalent to 14.5? *(p. 155)*

(A) 1.45%   (B) 14.5%   (C) 145%   (D) 1450%

NS 1.7   **41.** You borrow $300 at 10% annual simple interest for one year. If you make no payments, how much money do you owe at the end of the year? *(p. 172)*

(A) $30   (B) $270   (C) $330   (D) $390

4.2 Using Scientific Notation

Standards

NS 1.1 **Read, write**, and compare **rational numbers in scientific notation** (positive and negative powers of 10), compare rational numbers in general.

QUESTION How can you multiply or divide numbers in scientific notation using a calculator?

EXAMPLE Perform operations with numbers in scientific notation

The sun is about 1.5×10^8 kilometers from Earth, and Proxima Centauri is about 2.5×10^5 times as far from Earth as the sun is. How far is Proxima Centauri from Earth?

SOLUTION

To find how far Proxima Centauri is from Earth, multiply the distance between the Sun and Earth by 2.5×10^5.

Keystrokes

1.5 `EE` 8 `X` 2.5 `EE` 5 `=`

Display

3.75×10^{13}

The `EE` key on a calculator means "times 10 raised to the power of."

▶ **Answer** Proxima Centauri is approximately 3.75×10^{13} kilometers from Earth.

PRACTICE

Use a calculator to evaluate the expression. Write your answer in scientific notation.

1. $(3.19 \times 10^7) \times (8.5 \times 10^6)$

2. $(6.7 \times 10^{-3}) \times (1.12 \times 10^{15})$

3. $(3.3 \times 10^{-3}) \times (4.8 \times 10^{-9})$

4. $(7.1 \times 10^{-9}) \times (2.05 \times 10^6)$

5. $\dfrac{1.681 \times 10^{10}}{2.05 \times 10^3}$

6. $\dfrac{1.44 \times 10^{-15}}{1.2 \times 10^1}$

7. $\dfrac{8.241 \times 10^{-11}}{2.05 \times 10^{-4}}$

8. $\dfrac{6.25 \times 10^{-8}}{1.25 \times 10^{-12}}$

9. **WATER** About 110 billion gallons of water flow through Lake Erie each day. How many gallons of water flow through Lake Erie in a week? How many gallons of water flow through Lake Erie in a year? Write your answers in scientific notation.

4.3 Zero and Negative Exponents

Standards

NS 1.2 Add, subtract, multiply, and divide rational numbers (integers, fractions, and terminating decimals) and **take positive rational numbers to whole-number powers.**

NS 2.1 **Understand negative whole-number exponents.** Multiply and divide expressions involving exponents with a common base.

AF 2.1 Interpret positive whole-number powers as repeated multiplication and negative whole-number powers as repeated division or multiplication by the multiplicative inverse. Simplify and evaluate expressions that include exponents.

Math and **SCIENCE**
Ex. 44, p. 210

Connect *Before* you evaluated expressions with positive exponents. *Now* you will evaluate expressions with zero or negative exponents.

KEY VOCABULARY
• exponent, *p. 5*

In Lesson 4.1, you saw that $10^0 = 1$, and that $10^{-n} = \dfrac{1}{10^n}$ for any integer n. You can extend these definitions to powers with any nonzero base a.

KEY CONCEPT *For Your Notebook*

Definition of Zero and Negative Exponents

Let a be a nonzero number, and let n be an integer.

Words	**Algebra**	**Example**
a to the zero power is 1.	$a^0 = 1$	$5^0 = 1$
a^{-n} is the reciprocal of a^n.	$a^{-n} = \dfrac{1}{a^n}$	$2^{-3} = \dfrac{1}{2^3}$
a^n is the reciprocal of a^{-n}.	$a^n = \dfrac{1}{a^{-n}}$	$2 = \dfrac{1}{2^{-1}}$

EXAMPLE 1 Using Zero and Negative Exponents

a. $5^0 = 1$ **Definition of zero exponent**

b. $5^{-4} = \dfrac{1}{5^4}$ **Definition of negative exponent**

    $= \dfrac{1}{625}$ **Evaluate power.**

c. $\left(\dfrac{1}{2}\right)^{-3} = \dfrac{1}{\left(\dfrac{1}{2}\right)^3}$ **Definition of negative exponent**

    $= \dfrac{1}{\left(\dfrac{1}{8}\right)}$ **Evaluate power.**

    $= 8$ **Divide.**

EXAMPLE 2 Using Negative Exponents

SCIENCE A *half-life* is the amount of time that it takes for a radioactive substance to decay to one half of its original quantity.

Suppose radioactive decay causes 400 grams of a substance to decrease to 400×2^{-3} grams after 3 half-lives. Evaluate 400×2^{-3} to determine how many grams of the substance are left.

SOLUTION

$$400 \times 2^{-3} = 400\left(\frac{1}{2^3}\right) \qquad \text{Definition of negative exponent}$$

$$= 400\left(\frac{1}{8}\right) \qquad \text{Evaluate exponent.}$$

$$= 50 \qquad \text{Simplify.}$$

▶**Answer** There are 50 grams left of the substance.

✓ **GUIDED PRACTICE** for Examples 1 and 2

Evaluate the expression.

1. 7^{-2} 　　　　**2.** $(-2)^{-5}$ 　　　　**3.** $(-6)^0$ 　　　　**4.** $\left(\frac{1}{3}\right)^{-2}$

5. **WHAT IF?** In Example 2, suppose the substance has gone through 4 half-lives. Evaluate 400×2^{-4} to determine how many grams are left.

6. **REASONING** *Explain* why the expression 400×2^{-n} can be used to find the amount of the substance in Example 2 that remains after n half-lives.

EXAMPLE 3 Evaluating Algebraic Expressions

 Evaluate the expression when $x = 4$.

　　a. x^{-3} 　　　　　　　　　　　　**b.** 3^{-x}

AVOID ERRORS
In general,
$x^{-n} \neq n^{-x}$.

SOLUTION

a. $x^{-3} = 4^{-3}$ 　　　　　　　　　　**b.** $3^{-x} = 3^{-4}$

$\qquad = \frac{1}{4^3}$ 　　　　　　　　　　　$\qquad = \frac{1}{3^4}$

$\qquad = \frac{1}{64}$ 　　　　　　　　　　　$\qquad = \frac{1}{81}$

✓ **GUIDED PRACTICE** for Example 3

Evaluate the expression when $x = 2$.

7. x^{-4} 　　　　　　　**8.** 3^{-x} 　　　　　　　**9.** x^0

SIMPLIFYING EXPRESSIONS You can use definitions of zero and negative exponents to simplify algebraic expressions. An algebraic expression in simplified form contains only positive exponents.

EXAMPLE 4 **Simplifying Algebraic Expressions**

a. $-2n^0 = -2 \cdot n^0$ Zero exponent applies only to *n*.

$\qquad\quad = -2 \cdot 1$ Definition of zero exponent

$\qquad\quad = -2$ Multiply.

b. $8x^{-3} = 8 \cdot x^{-3}$ Exponent applies only to *x*.

$\qquad\quad = \dfrac{8}{x^3}$ Definition of negative exponent

---

✓ **GUIDED PRACTICE** for Example 4

Simplify the algebraic expression.

10. $3x^{-4}$ **11.** $7x^0$ **12.** $\dfrac{3}{x^{-1}}$ **13.** $\dfrac{9}{n^{-3}}$

4.3 EXERCISES

SKILLS • PROBLEM SOLVING • REASONING

1. VOCABULARY Copy and complete: For nonzero x, x^0 is equal to __?__.

2. WRITING *Explain* how to simplify the expression $2n^{-4}$.

EVALUATING EXPRESSIONS **Evaluate the expression.**

3. 3^{-4} **4.** 12^0 **5.** -2^{-4} **6.** $(-4)^{-3}$

7. $(-15)^0$ **8.** -8^0 **9.** 6^{-2} **10.** -5^{-3}

11. $\left(-\dfrac{4}{7}\right)^0$ **12.** $\left(\dfrac{1}{3}\right)^{-3}$ **13.** $\left(\dfrac{2}{5}\right)^{-2}$ **14.** $\left(-\dfrac{1}{4}\right)^{-3}$

ERROR ANALYSIS *Describe* and correct the error in evaluating the power.

15.

 $5^{-3} = (-5)(-5)(-5)$
$\quad = -125$

16.

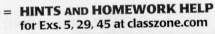 $(-3)^{-4} = \dfrac{-1}{3^4} = -\dfrac{1}{81}$

17. ◆ **MULTIPLE CHOICE** What is the value of $\left(\dfrac{2}{3}\right)^{-3}$?

(A) $-\dfrac{8}{27}$ **(B)** $\dfrac{8}{27}$ **(C)** $\dfrac{3}{8}$ **(D)** $\dfrac{27}{8}$

SEE EXAMPLE 3
on p. 207
for Exs. 18–25

XV **EVALUATING EXPRESSIONS** Evaluate the expression when $n = 3$.

18. n^{-2}

19. n^{-3}

20. 2^{-n}

21. -4^{-n}

22. n^0

23. $\dfrac{1}{n^{-1}}$

24. $\left(\dfrac{1}{2}\right)^{-n}$

25. $\left(\dfrac{2}{n}\right)^{-2}$

SEE EXAMPLE 4
on p. 208
for Exs. 26–34

XV **ALGEBRA** Simplify the algebraic expression.

26. x^{-4}

27. s^0

28. $9n^{-3}$

29. $-7x^{-5}$

30. $12b^{-4}$

31. $-3x^{-2}$

32. $\dfrac{3}{x^0}$

33. $\dfrac{8}{n^{-2}}$

34. ◆ **MULTIPLE CHOICE** What is the simplified form of $-3x^{-4}$?

(A) $-\dfrac{1}{3x^4}$

(B) $-\dfrac{3}{x^4}$

(C) $\dfrac{3}{x^{-4}}$

(D) $-\dfrac{3}{x^{-4}}$

REASONING Copy and complete the statement using *always, sometimes,* or *never*. *Explain* your reasoning.

35. A power with a nonzero base and an exponent of zero is __?__ positive.

36. A power with a positive base and a negative integer exponent is __?__ negative.

37. A power with a negative base and a positive integer exponent is __?__ positive.

CONNECT SKILLS TO PROBLEM SOLVING Exercises 38–41 will help you prepare for problem solving.

Write the measurement using only positive exponents.

38. One centimeter is equal to 10^{-2} meter.

39. One inch is equal to 6^{-2} yard.

40. One ounce is equal to 4^{-2} pound.

41. One fluid ounce is equal to 2^{-3} cup.

SEE EXAMPLE 4
on p. 208
for Ex. 42

42. PHYSICS The force used to move a large item up a ramp can be measured in *Newtons*. One Newton can be expressed as $1 \text{ kg} \cdot \text{m} \cdot \text{s}^{-2}$. Write this expression without negative exponents.

California @*HomeTutor*** for problem solving help at classzone.com

$1 \text{ N} = 1 \text{kg} \cdot \text{m} \cdot \text{s}^{-2}$

SEE EXAMPLE 2
on p. 207
for Ex. 43

43. MULTI-STEP PROBLEM Consider a quantity of a radioactive substance. The fraction of this quantity that remains after t half-lives can be found by using the expression 2^{-t}.

a. Simplify the expression 2^{-t}.

b. What fraction of the substance remains after 5 half-lives?

c. After how many half-lives does $\dfrac{1}{64}$ of the original quantity remain?

California @*HomeTutor*** for problem solving help at classzone.com

44. **BIOLOGY** Phytoplankton are tiny plants that live in the ocean. One type has a length of about 0.2 micrometer. A micrometer is 10^{-6} meter. What part of a meter is this phytoplankton? Use a positive exponent to write your answer.

45. ◆ **MULTIPLE CHOICE** What is the area of a rectangle with a length of 2^3 feet and a width of 4^{-2} foot?

Ⓐ $\frac{1}{2}$ ft^2 Ⓑ 2 ft^2 Ⓒ 4 ft^2 Ⓓ 128 ft^2

CHALLENGE **Find the missing exponent.**

46. $x^{(? - 4)} = 1$

47. $y^{-5(?)} = \dfrac{1}{y^{-25}}$

48. $17 + 20z^{(11 - ?)} = 37$

49. **CHALLENGE** Each edge of a cube-shaped trophy display case is x inches long. Show that the ratio of the number of square inches of surface area to the number of cubic inches of volume of the cube is $6x^{-1}$.

◆ CALIFORNIA STANDARDS SPIRAL REVIEW

NS 1.2   50. What is the value of $2.1(3.4 + 6.2)$? *(p. 144)*

Ⓐ 11.7   Ⓑ 13.34   Ⓒ 19.2   Ⓓ 20.16

NS 1.6   51. What is the percent of change from 25 to 30? *(p. 168)*

Ⓐ 20%   Ⓑ 83.3%   Ⓒ 125%   Ⓓ 250%

NS 1.1   52. The total area of the United States is about 3,800,000 square miles. What is this number in scientific notation? *(p. 201)*

Ⓐ 0.38×10^6 Ⓑ 3.8×10^5 Ⓒ 3.8×10^6 Ⓓ $3.8 \times 1,000,000$

QUIZ *for Lessons 4.1–4.3*

Write the power of 10 in standard form. *(p. 196)*

1. 10^3

2. 10^8

3. 10^{-2}

4. 10^{-8}

Write the number as a power of 10. *(p. 196)*

5. 10,000,000

6. 0.0001

7. 0.0000001

8. $\dfrac{1}{1000}$

Write the number in scientific notation. *(p. 201)*

9. 2000

10. 0.0201

11. 0.00006

12. 1,200,000

Evaluate the expression when $x = 4$. *(p. 206)*

13. x^{-1}

14. x^{-3}

15. 2^{-x}

16. -4^{-x}

17. **SCIENCE** One Fermi is equal to 10^{-15} meter. The radius of a proton is about 1.2 Fermis. Write the radius of a proton in meters in standard form. *(p. 201)*

EXTRA PRACTICE for Lesson 4.3, p. 750

ONLINE QUIZ at classzone.com

MIXED REVIEW of Skills and Problem Solving

Multiple Choice Practice for Lessons 4.1–4.3

In Exercises 1–4, use the table below showing the approximate land areas (in square kilometers) of several regions.

Region	Area (km^2)
Antarctica	14,000,000
Canada	10×10^6
Egypt	1,000,000
India	0.33×10^7
Russia	1.7×10^7
United States	9,600,000

1. What is Egypt's area as a power of 10? **NS 1.1**

   (A) $1.0^{-6} km^2$ (B) $10^5 km^2$

   (C) $10^6 km^2$ (D) $10^7 km^2$

2. Which region's area is expressed in scientific notation? **NS 1.1**

   (A) Canada   (B) Egypt

   (C) India   (D) Russia

3. What is Antarctica's area in scientific notation? **NS 1.1**

   (A) $1.4 \times 10^6 km^2$ (B) $1.4 \times 10^7 km^2$

   (C) $14 \times 10^6 km^2$ (D) $0.14 \times 10^8 km^2$

4. Which region has the greatest area? **NS 1.1**

   (A) Antarctica   (B) Canada

   (C) India   (D) Russia

5. Which measure, expressed in scientific notation, would most likely involve a negative exponent? **NS 2.1, MR 1.2**

   (A) The length in feet of a train

   (B) The age in years of a fossil

   (C) A quarterback's number of passing yards in a football game

   (D) The weight in pounds of a human hair

6. The teddy bear pictured below is only about 12 millimeters long. If one nanometer (nm) is 10^{-6} millimeter, how many nanometers long is the teddy bear? **NS 2.1**

   (A) 1.2×10^{-7} nm

   (B) 1.2 nm

   (C) 1.2×10^6 nm

   (D) 1.2×10^7 nm

7. What is the value of $(3 \cdot 12)^0$? **NS 1.2**

   (A) $\frac{1}{36}$ (B) 1

   (C) 3.6   (D) 36

8. What is the simplified form of $-4x^{-4}$? **AF 2.1**

   (A) $-\frac{1}{4x^4}$ (B) $4x^4$

   (C) $-\frac{4}{x^4}$ (D) $\frac{1}{256x^4}$

9. What is 100,000 written as a power of 10? **NS 1.1**

   (A) 10^4 (B) 10^5

   (C) 10^6 (D) 10×10^5

10. What is the value of x^{-3} when $x = -2$? **AF 2.1**

    (A) -8 (B) $-\frac{1}{8}$

    (C) $\frac{1}{8}$ (D) 8

11. The paperclip below has the indicated length. What is this length in standard form? **AF 2.1, MR 2.8**

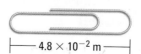

$\vdash\!\!-\!\! 4.8 \times 10^{-2} \text{ m} \!-\!\!\dashv$

   (A) 0.048 m   (B) 0.48 m

   (C) 4.8 m   (D) 4800 m

4.4 Using Area Models

MATERIALS · paper and pencil

Standards

NS 2.4 Use the inverse relationship between raising to a power and extracting the root of a perfect square integer; for an integer that is not square, determine without a calculator the two integers between which its square root lies and explain why.

QUESTION How can you find the side length of a square given the square's area?

EXPLORE Find side lengths of squares

Find the side lengths of squares with areas (in square units) of 1, 4, 9, 16, and 25.

STEP 1 Draw area models. The first three models are shown.

Area = 1   Area = 4   Area = 9

STEP 2 Copy and complete the table below.

You can count the number of units that represents the side length for each model you drew in Step 1.

Area of square (square units)	1	4	9	16	25
Side length (units)	1	2	3	?	?

DRAW CONCLUSIONS Use your observations to complete these exercises

1. Copy and complete the table below. Use area models to complete the table.

Area of square (square units)	36	49	64	81
Side length (units)	?	?	?	?

2. Without using area models, what is the length of each side of a square with an area of 100 square units? 400 square units? *Explain.*

3. **REASONING** *Describe* the length of a side of a square that has an area between 81 and 100 square units.

4.4 Finding and Approximating Square Roots

 Standards NS 2.4 Use the inverse relationship between raising to a power and extracting the root of a perfect square integer; for an integer that is not square, determine without a calculator the two integers between which its square root lies and explain why.

Connect *Before* you found squares of numbers. *Now* you will find and approximate square roots of numbers.

Math and
FARMING
Ex. 52, p. 217

KEY VOCABULARY
• perfect square
• radical expression
• square root

Numbers that are squares of integers, such as $4 = 2^2$, are called **perfect squares**. The inverse relationship of squaring a number is finding a *square root*.

About the Standards

You will learn rules for finding square roots (MR 3.2) in this lesson.

KEY CONCEPT   *For Your Notebook*

Square Roots

Words   A **square root** of a number n is a number m which, when multiplied by itself, equals n.

Numbers   The square roots of 16 are 4 and -4 because $4^2 = 16$ and $(-4)^2 = 16$.

Algebra   If $m^2 = n$, then m is a square root of n.

EXAMPLE 1   Finding Square Roots

a. You know that $9^2 = 81$ and $(-9)^2 = 81$. Therefore, the square roots of 81 are 9 and -9.

b. You know that $7^2 = 49$ and $(-7)^2 = 49$. Therefore, the square roots of 49 are 7 and -7.

✓ **GUIDED PRACTICE**   for Example 1

Find the two square roots of the number.

1. 100   **2.** 25   **3.** 169   **4.** 121

RADICAL EXPRESSIONS Every positive number has a positive square root and a negative square root. Zero has one square root, which is zero.

The symbol $\sqrt{}$ is called a *radical sign*. It is used to represent the positive square root. The symbol $-\sqrt{}$ represents the negative square root. A **radical expression** is an expression that involves a radical sign.

$\sqrt{25} = 5$ **Positive square root** $-\sqrt{25} = -5$ **Negative square root**

EXAMPLE 2 **Evaluating Square Roots**

a. $\sqrt{36} = 6$ because $6^2 = 36$. and $6 > 0$.

b. $-\sqrt{64} = -8$ because $(-8)^2 = 64$ and $-8 < 0$.

c. $\sqrt{\frac{4}{25}} = \frac{2}{5}$ because $\left(\frac{2}{5}\right)^2 = \frac{4}{25}$ and $\frac{2}{5} > 0$.

d. $\sqrt{0.81} = 0.9$ because $(0.9)^2 = 0.81$ and $0.9 > 0$.

APPROXIMATING SQUARE ROOTS Sometimes it is not possible to find the square root of a number exactly. However, you can approximate the square root using either mathematical reasoning or a calculator.

EXAMPLE 3 **Approximating a Square Root**

Between which two consecutive integers does $\sqrt{300}$ lie?

Make a list of numbers that are perfect squares: . . . 196, 225, 256, 289, 324, ...
Note that 300 is between 289 and 324. This statement can be expressed by the *compound inequality* $289 < 300 < 324$.

$289 < 300 < 324$ **Identify perfect squares closest to 300.**

$\sqrt{289} < \sqrt{300} < \sqrt{324}$ **Take positive square root of each number.**

$17 < \sqrt{300} < 18$ **Evaluate square root of each perfect square.**

▶ **Answer** The number $\sqrt{300}$ lies between 17 and 18.

EXAMPLE 4 ◆ **Multiple Choice Practice**

What is the value of $\sqrt{95}$ rounded to the nearest whole number?

   Ⓐ 8   Ⓑ 9   Ⓒ 10   Ⓓ 11

ELIMINATE CHOICES
You know that 95 is between 81 (or 9^2) and 100 (or 10^2), so $\sqrt{95}$ is between 9 and 10. Choices A and D can be eliminated.

SOLUTION

You can use a number line to approximate $\sqrt{95}$ to the nearest whole number. Because $\sqrt{95}$ is between 9 and 10, you need to decide whether $\sqrt{95}$ is closer to 9 or 10. Find $(9.5)^2$. You can calculate that $(9.5)^2 = 90.25$ and $(\sqrt{95})^2 = 95$.

$$\sqrt{81} \qquad \sqrt{90.25} \quad \sqrt{95} \quad \sqrt{100}$$

9   9.5   10

$9^2 = 81 \qquad 9.5^2 = 90.25 \qquad 10^2 = 100$

As shown on the number line, $\sqrt{95}$ is between $\sqrt{90.25}$ and $\sqrt{100}$, so it has a value between 9.5 and 10. Therefore, to the nearest whole number, $\sqrt{95} \approx 10$.

▶ **Answer** The correct answer is C. Ⓐ Ⓑ Ⓒ Ⓓ

Find the square root, or approximate it to the nearest integer.

5. $-\sqrt{36}$ **6.** $\sqrt{41}$ **7.** $\sqrt{\dfrac{25}{81}}$ **8.** $\sqrt{0.36}$

9. Between which two integers does $\sqrt{230}$ lie?

EXAMPLE 5   Using a Calculator

Evaluate the square root. Round to the nearest tenth if necessary.

   a. $-\sqrt{56.25}$ **b.** $\sqrt{8}$ **c.** $-\sqrt{1256}$

SOLUTION

	Keystrokes	Display	Answer
a.	(−) 2nd [√] **56.25** =	−7.5	−7.5
b.	2nd [√] **8** =	2.828427125	2.8
c.	(−) 2nd [√] **1256** =	−35.44009029	−35.4

EXAMPLE 6   Using a Square Root in Real Life

AMUSEMENT PARKS The model $s = 4.95\sqrt{r}$ gives the speed needed to keep riders pinned to the wall of an amusement park ride. In the model, s is the speed (in meters per second) and r is the radius of the ride (in meters). Find the speed necessary to keep riders pinned to the wall of a ride that has a radius of 2.61 meters.

Amusement park ride: radius = 2.61 meters

SOLUTION

$$s = 4.95\sqrt{r}$$ Write model for speed of the ride.

$$= 4.95\sqrt{2.61}$$ Substitute 2.61 for r.

$$\approx 4.95(1.62)$$ Approximate the square root using a calculator.

$$= 8.019$$ Multiply.

▶ **Answer** The speed should be about 8 meters per second.

✓ GUIDED PRACTICE   for Examples 5 and 6

10. Use a calculator to evaluate $\sqrt{236}$ to the nearest tenth.

11. WHAT IF? In Example 6, what is the speed necessary to keep riders pinned to the wall of a ride that has a radius of 3.55 meters? Round your answer to the nearest tenth of a meter per second.

4.4 EXERCISES

HOMEWORK KEY

◆ = **MULTIPLE CHOICE PRACTICE**
Exs. 15, 28, 52, 66–68

◯ = **HINTS AND HOMEWORK HELP**
for Exs. 13, 21, 55 at classzone.com

SKILLS • PROBLEM SOLVING • REASONING

1. **VOCABULARY** Copy and complete: A number b is a(n) __?__ of c if $b^2 = c$.

2. **NOTETAKING SKILLS** Make a *four square diagram* like the one on page 194 for the *square root*.

SEE EXAMPLE 1
on p. 213
for Exs. 3–10

FINDING SQUARE ROOTS Find the two square roots of the number.

3. 1
4. 64
5. 400
6. 225

7. $\frac{1}{4}$
8. $\frac{9}{16}$
9. $\frac{36}{25}$
10. $\frac{100}{49}$

SEE EXAMPLE 2
on p. 214
for Exs. 11–15

EVALUATING SQUARE ROOTS Find the square root.

11. $-\sqrt{1}$
12. $\sqrt{100}$
13. $\sqrt{144}$
14. $-\sqrt{16}$

15. ◆ **MULTIPLE CHOICE** What is the value of $\sqrt{289}$?

Ⓐ -19
Ⓑ -17
Ⓒ 17
Ⓓ 19

SEE EXAMPLE 3
on p. 214
for Exs. 16–19

APPROXIMATING SQUARE ROOTS Between which two consecutive integers does the square root lie?

16. $\sqrt{62}$
17. $\sqrt{280}$
18. $\sqrt{227}$
19. $\sqrt{1000}$

SEE EXAMPLE 4
on p. 214
for Exs. 20–28

APPROXIMATING SQUARE ROOTS Approximate the square root to the nearest whole number.

20. $\sqrt{33}$
21. $\sqrt{14}$
22. $\sqrt{117}$
23. $\sqrt{52}$

24. $\sqrt{74}$
25. $\sqrt{22}$
26. $\sqrt{48}$
27. $\sqrt{123}$

28. ◆ **MULTIPLE CHOICE** Which square root is closest to 13?

Ⓐ $\sqrt{165}$
Ⓑ $\sqrt{175}$
Ⓒ $\sqrt{185}$
Ⓓ $\sqrt{193}$

SEE EXAMPLE 5
on p. 215
for Exs. 29–32

USING A CALCULATOR Use a calculator to approximate the square root. Round to the nearest tenth if necessary.

29. $-\sqrt{34.6}$
30. $\sqrt{43.56}$
31. $\sqrt{2440}$
32. $-\sqrt{6204}$

REASONING Complete the statement with *always*, *sometimes*, or *never*.

33. Square roots are __?__ whole numbers.

34. A number __?__ has more than two square roots.

35. The square root of a number is __?__ less than the number.

ALGEBRA Evaluate the expression $\sqrt{a^2 - b^2}$ for the given values.

36. $a = 5, b = 5$
37. $a = 10, b = 8$
38. $a = 15, b = 12$

RATIONAL SQUARE ROOTS Find the square root.

39. $-\sqrt{\dfrac{1}{4}}$

40. $\sqrt{\dfrac{16}{25}}$

41. $-\sqrt{\dfrac{81}{100}}$

42. $\sqrt{\dfrac{144}{169}}$

43. $\sqrt{1.44}$

44. $\sqrt{1.96}$

45. $-\sqrt{0.25}$

46. $\sqrt{11.56}$

ERROR ANALYSIS *Describe* and correct the error in finding the square root.

47.
$$\sqrt{\dfrac{1}{4}} = \dfrac{1}{16} \quad \times$$

48.
$$\sqrt{0.81} = 0.09 \quad \times$$

CONNECT SKILLS TO PROBLEM SOLVING Exercises 49–51 will help you prepare for problem solving.

Find the side length of the object described.

49. A square greeting card whose area is 25 square inches

50. A square garden whose area is 900 square feet

51. A square tile whose area is 12.25 square inches

SEE EXAMPLES 2 AND 5
on pp. 214–215 for Exs. 52–53

52. ◆ **MULTIPLE CHOICE** You want to put a fence around a square plot of land that has an area of 6250 square yards. What is the length of a side of the plot, to the nearest tenth of a yard?

(A) 19.8 yd
(B) 79.0 yd
(C) 79.1 yd
(D) 625.0 yd

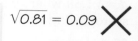 for problem solving help at classzone.com

53. **ARTS AND CRAFTS** You have a square piece of fabric for the front of a square pillow. The fabric has an area of 729 square inches. You use all the fabric. What is the length of one side of the pillow?

California @HomeTutor for problem solving help at classzone.com

54. **REASONING** *Explain* how to find the perimeter P of a square in terms of its area A.

55. **HOME DECORATING** A tablecloth measures 50 inches by 50 inches. Will it cover a square table with an area of 21.5 square feet? *Explain* your reasoning.

56. **ROADWAYS** A road that is 330 feet long joins two small, square parking lots, as shown. Each parking lot has an area of 576 square feet and sides of length w feet. Find the value of w. Then find the area of the road.

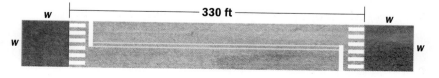

Fire Towers New Hampshire lookout towers were built in the early 1900s to spot forest fires. Mount Cardigan, which has a view of the 6288 foot tall Mount Washington, was built in 1924. Many towers were constructed over the next few decades. Sixteen towers are still in operation. Ideally, the distance d (in miles) that a person can see from a tower is given by the formula $d = \sqrt{1.5h}$ where h is the height (in feet) above the surrounding land.

Kearsarge North Fire Tower

SEE EXAMPLE 6 on p. 215 for Exs. 57–59

57. Calculate A ranger standing in the tower at Mount Cardigan is about 3100 feet above the surrounding land. How far can the ranger ideally see?

58. Reasoning A person standing in the fire tower of Mount Monadnock, which is no longer in use, could see 104 miles to Mount Washington. Mount Monadnock is about 3100 feet above the surrounding land. *Explain* how it is possible to see farther than the formula suggests.

59. Elevation A ranger at Mount Prospect tower can see about 57.6 miles. At about what height above the surrounding land is the ranger?

60. LOOK FOR A PATTERN Find the positive square roots of 0.36, 0.0036, 0.000036, and 0.00000036. What pattern do you notice? Using the pattern, predict the positive square root of 0.0000000036.

61. CHALLENGE *Explain* how to approximate the value of a square root to the nearest tenth if you do not have a calculator.

CHALLENGE Simplify the expression. Round to the nearest hundredth if necessary.

62. $\sqrt{\sqrt{625}}$ **63.** $-\sqrt{\sqrt{1296}}$ **64.** $-\sqrt{\sqrt{\sqrt{256}}}$ **65.** $\sqrt{\sqrt{\sqrt{4096}}}$

◆ CALIFORNIA STANDARDS SPIRAL REVIEW

AF 1.4   **66.** What is the variable in the expression $100 - 3x^2$? *(p. 5)*

     A -3 **B** 2   **C** 100   **D** x

NS 2.1   **67.** What is the value of $8 \cdot 2^{-3}$? *(p. 5)*

     A -64 **B** 1   **C** 8   **D** 64

NS 1.3   **68.** There is a 65% chance of rain today. Which fraction gives the chance of rain today? *(p. 150)*

     A $\frac{3}{10}$ **B** $\frac{3}{5}$ **C** $\frac{13}{20}$ **D** $\frac{3}{4}$

4.5 Simplifying Square Roots

Math and PHYSICS
Example 2, p. 220

Standards NS 2.4 **Use the inverse relationship between raising to a power and extracting the root of a perfect square integer**; for an integer that is not square, determine without a calculator the two integers between which its square root lies and explain why.

Connect *Before* you found square roots. *Now* you will simplify square root expressions.

KEY VOCABULARY
• simplest form of a radical expression

Compare the following pair of expressions.

$$\sqrt{4 \cdot 9} = \sqrt{36} = 6 \qquad \sqrt{4} \cdot \sqrt{9} = 2 \cdot 3 = 6$$

Notice that $\sqrt{4 \cdot 9} = \sqrt{4} \cdot \sqrt{9}$. This result suggests the product property of square roots.

KEY CONCEPT
For Your Notebook

Product Property of Square Roots

Algebra

$\sqrt{ab} = \sqrt{a} \cdot \sqrt{b}$, where $a \geq 0$ and $b \geq 0$

Numbers

$\sqrt{40} = \sqrt{4} \cdot \sqrt{10} = 2\sqrt{10}$

You can use the product property of square roots to simplify radical expressions. A radical expression is in **simplest form** when:

• The expression under the radical sign has no perfect square factors other than 1.

• There are no fractions under the radical sign, and no radicals appear in the denominator of a fraction.

EXAMPLE 1 Simplifying Radical Expressions

Write the radical expression in simplest form.

a. $\sqrt{250}$

b. $\sqrt{108}$

SOLUTION

a. $\sqrt{250} = \sqrt{25 \cdot 10}$ Factor out greatest perfect square factor.

$\qquad = \sqrt{25} \cdot \sqrt{10}$ Product property of square roots

$\qquad = 5\sqrt{10}$ Simplify.

b. $\sqrt{108} = \sqrt{36 \cdot 3}$ Factor out greatest perfect square factor.

$\qquad = \sqrt{36} \cdot \sqrt{3}$ Product property of square roots

$\qquad = 6\sqrt{3}$ Simplify.

EXAMPLE 2 **Using a Radical Expression in Real Life**

WALKING SPEED A person's maximum walking speed (in inches per second) can be approximated using the expression $\sqrt{384l}$ where l is the person's leg length (in inches).

  a. Write the expression in simplest form.

  b. Use the simplified expression to approximate the maximum walking speed of a person whose leg length is 29 inches.

ANOTHER WAY

For an alternative method for solving the problem in Example 2, turn to page 224 for the **Problem Solving Workshop**.

SOLUTION

  a. $\sqrt{384l} = \sqrt{64 \cdot 6l}$ **Factor out greatest perfect square factor.**

           $= \sqrt{64} \cdot \sqrt{6l}$ **Product property of square roots**

           $= 8\sqrt{6l}$ **Simplify.**

  ▶ **Answer** In simplest form, $\sqrt{384l} = 8\sqrt{6l}$.

  b. $8\sqrt{6l} = 8\sqrt{6 \cdot 29}$ **Substitute 29 for l.**

           $= 8\sqrt{174}$ **Multiply.**

           ≈ 106 **Approximate using a calculator.**

  ▶ **Answer** The person's maximum walking speed is approximately 106 inches per second.

EXAMPLE 3 **Simplifying a Product of Two Radicals**

Simplify the radical expression $\sqrt{5} \cdot \sqrt{10}$.

     $\sqrt{5} \cdot \sqrt{10} = \sqrt{50}$ **Product property of square roots**

               $= \sqrt{25 \cdot 2}$ **Factor out greatest perfect square factor.**

               $= \sqrt{25} \cdot \sqrt{2}$ **Product property of square roots**

               $= 5\sqrt{2}$ **Simplify.**

✓ **GUIDED PRACTICE**   **for Examples 1, 2, and 3**

Simplify the expression.

  1. $\sqrt{8}$ **2.** $\sqrt{27}$ **3.** $\sqrt{75}$

  4. $\sqrt{2} \cdot \sqrt{6}$ **5.** $\sqrt{3} \cdot \sqrt{6}$ **6.** $\sqrt{8} \cdot \sqrt{12}$

  7. WHAT IF? In Example 2, suppose that the person's leg length is 26 inches. Use the simplified radical expression to approximate the person's maximum walking speed.

QUOTIENTS Notice that $\sqrt{\dfrac{100}{4}} = \sqrt{25} = 5$, and $\dfrac{\sqrt{100}}{\sqrt{4}} = \dfrac{10}{2} = 5$. This result suggests the quotient property of square roots, shown below. This is another property that you can use to simplify radical expressions.

KEY CONCEPT *For Your Notebook*

Quotient Property of Square Roots

Algebra

$\sqrt{\dfrac{a}{b}} = \dfrac{\sqrt{a}}{\sqrt{b}}$, where $a \geq 0$ and $b > 0$

Numbers

$\sqrt{\dfrac{17}{9}} = \dfrac{\sqrt{17}}{\sqrt{9}} = \dfrac{\sqrt{17}}{3}$

EXAMPLE 4 Simplifying a Radical Expression

$\sqrt{\dfrac{7}{16}} = \dfrac{\sqrt{7}}{\sqrt{16}}$ **Quotient property of square roots**

$\qquad = \dfrac{\sqrt{7}}{4}$ **Simplify.**

✓ **GUIDED PRACTICE** for Example 4

Simplify the expression.

8. $\sqrt{\dfrac{3}{4}}$

9. $\sqrt{\dfrac{2}{9}}$

10. $\sqrt{\dfrac{5}{16}}$

4.5 EXERCISES

HOMEWORK KEY

◆ = **MULTIPLE CHOICE PRACTICE**
Exs. 23, 26, 31, 39–41

○ = **HINTS** AND **HOMEWORK HELP**
for Exs. 5, 17, 33 at classzone.com

SKILLS • PROBLEM SOLVING • REASONING

1. VOCABULARY Copy and complete: To simplify the radical expression $\sqrt{75}$, use the __?__ property of square roots.

2. WRITING *Explain* how you can tell whether the expression $\sqrt{\dfrac{15}{16}}$ is in simplest form.

SEE EXAMPLES 1 AND 3
on pp. 219–220
for Exs. 3–14

PRODUCT PROPERTY  Simplify the expression.

3. $\sqrt{50}$

4. $\sqrt{63}$

5. $\sqrt{80}$

6. $\sqrt{98}$

7. $\sqrt{243}$

8. $\sqrt{288}$

9. $\sqrt{3} \cdot \sqrt{8}$

10. $\sqrt{2} \cdot \sqrt{27}$

11. $\sqrt{6} \cdot \sqrt{12}$

12. $\sqrt{2} \cdot \sqrt{24}$

13. $\sqrt{10} \cdot \sqrt{20}$

14. $\sqrt{11} \cdot \sqrt{33}$

SEE EXAMPLE 4
on p. 221
for Exs. 15–22

QUOTIENT PROPERTY Simplify the expression.

15. $\sqrt{\dfrac{2}{81}}$ **16.** $\sqrt{\dfrac{11}{25}}$ **17.** $\sqrt{\dfrac{15}{64}}$ **18.** $\sqrt{\dfrac{33}{169}}$

19. $\sqrt{\dfrac{9}{49}}$ **20.** $\sqrt{\dfrac{16}{100}}$ **21.** $\sqrt{\dfrac{5}{36}}$ **22.** $\sqrt{\dfrac{121}{225}}$

23. ◆ **MULTIPLE CHOICE** Which radical expression is in simplest form?

A $\sqrt{\dfrac{2}{81}}$ **B** $\dfrac{\sqrt{7}}{\sqrt{121}}$ **C** $\sqrt{32}$ **D** $3\sqrt{6}$

ERROR ANALYSIS *Describe* and correct the error in writing the radical expression in simplest form.

24.

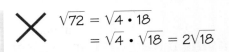

$\sqrt{72} = \sqrt{4 \cdot 18}$
$\quad = \sqrt{4} \cdot \sqrt{18} = 2\sqrt{18}$

25.

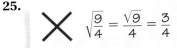

$\sqrt{\dfrac{9}{4}} = \dfrac{\sqrt{9}}{4} = \dfrac{3}{4}$

26. ◆ **MULTIPLE CHOICE** What is the simplified form of $\sqrt{\left(\dfrac{7}{25}\right)^2 + \left(\dfrac{24}{25}\right)^2}$?

A 1   **B** $\dfrac{\sqrt{31}}{5}$ **C** $\dfrac{31}{25}$ **D** $5\sqrt{31}$

CONNECT SKILLS TO PROBLEM SOLVING Exercises 27–29 will help you to prepare for problem solving.

Use the diagram of the rectangles.

27. Write an expression in simplified form for the area of the blue rectangle.

28. Write an expression in simplified form for the area of the green rectangle.

29. Write an expression in simplified form for the area of the red rectangle.

√3 ft   √5 ft
√8 ft
√15 ft

SEE EXAMPLES
2 AND 3
on p. 220
for Exs. 30–32

30. FALLING OBJECT The expression $\sqrt{\dfrac{10h}{49}}$ gives the time t (in seconds) it takes for a ball to drop from a height of h meters to the ground. Simplify this radical expression, then find the time it takes a ball dropped from a height of 10 meters to hit the ground.

California @HomeTutor for problem solving help at classzone.com

31. ◆ **MULTIPLE CHOICE** What is the area of a rectangle with a length of $\sqrt{10}$ feet and a width of $\sqrt{12}$ feet?

A $2\sqrt{30}$ ft^2 **B** $4\sqrt{10}$ ft^2 **C** $12\sqrt{5}$ ft^2 **D** $20\sqrt{5}$ ft^2

California @HomeTutor for problem solving help at classzone.com

32. REASONING Your friend simplified the radical expression $\sqrt{32}$ as shown below. Can the number of steps be reduced? *Explain* your reasoning.

$$\sqrt{32} = \sqrt{4} \cdot \sqrt{8} = 2\sqrt{8} = 2(\sqrt{4} \cdot \sqrt{2}) = 2(2\sqrt{2}) = 4\sqrt{2}$$

SEE EXAMPLE 2
on p. 220
for Exs. 33–35

33. **TREES** The expression $\sqrt{\dfrac{h}{16}}$ gives the time (in seconds) it takes a broken branch of a tree to fall to the ground from a height h (in feet).

   a. Write the expression in simplified form.

   b. Suppose a branch falls from a height of 150 feet. To the nearest second, how long does it take the branch to reach the ground?

34. **WHAT IF?** Suppose the branch in Exercise 33 fell from only half the height given in part (b). Would it take exactly half as long for the branch to reach the ground? *Explain.*

Jedediah Smith Redwoods State Park, California

35. **ESCAPE VELOCITY** The escape velocity of a planet is the speed required for an object to free itself from the planet's gravitational attraction. For a planet with gravitational acceleration g (in meters per second per second) and radius r (in meters), the escape velocity is given by the expression $\sqrt{2gr}$. Earth's radius is about 6,378,135 meters and its acceleration due to gravity is about 9.81 meters per second per second. Find Earth's escape velocity.

36. **PUZZLE PROBLEM** If $x^2 + y^2 = (kz)^2$, find the value of the expression $\sqrt{\dfrac{x^2}{z^2} + \dfrac{y^2}{z^2}}$ in terms of k.

37. **CHALLENGE** Find the next three numbers in the pattern:

$$\sqrt{3},\ \sqrt{6},\ 3,\ 2\sqrt{3},\ \sqrt{15},\ 3\sqrt{2},\ \ldots$$

38. **CHALLENGE** Physicians can calculate the body surface area (in square meters) of an adult using the expression $\sqrt{\dfrac{hw}{3600}}$ where h is the adult's height (in centimeters) and w is the adult's mass (in kilograms).

   a. Write the expression in simplest form.

   b. Write an expression in simplest form for the surface area of an adult who is 170 centimeters tall and has a mass of 70 kilograms. Then approximate the adult's surface area in square meters.

◆ CALIFORNIA STANDARDS SPIRAL REVIEW

NS 2.4

39. What is the value of $\sqrt{11}$ to the nearest whole number? *(p. 213)*

   Ⓐ 1   **Ⓑ** 2   **Ⓒ** 3   **Ⓓ** 4

NS 2.1

40. What is the value of 3^{-3}? *(p. 206)*

   Ⓐ $\dfrac{1}{27}$ **Ⓑ** $\dfrac{1}{9}$ **Ⓒ** 9   **Ⓓ** 27

NS 1.7

41. You deposit $350 in a savings account that earns 3.5% simple interest per year. How much interest will you earn after 15 months? *(p. 172)*

   Ⓐ $12.45   **Ⓑ** $15.31   **Ⓒ** $17.58   **Ⓓ** $19.24

Using ALTERNATIVE METHODS

Another Way to Solve Example 2, page 220

Standards
NS 2.4

Example 2 on page 220 was solved by first simplifying the expression for walking speed. This is helpful, especially if you are evaluating the expression for many different values of the variable. However, you can also solve the problem by evaluating the expression without first simplifying it.

PROBLEM

WALKING SPEED A person's maximum walking speed (in inches per second) can be approximated using the expression $\sqrt{384l}$ where l is the person's leg length (in inches). Approximate the maximum walking speed of a person whose leg length is 29 inches.

METHOD

Evaluating Without Simplifying You can evaluate the expression for walking speed by simply substituting for the variable.

STEP 1 **Substitute** 29 for l in the radical expression.

$$\sqrt{384l} = \sqrt{384 \cdot 29}$$
$$= \sqrt{11{,}136}$$

STEP 2 **Find** the approximate value by using a calculator.

$$\approx 106$$

▶ **Answer** The person's maximum walking speed is approximately 106 inches per second.

PRACTICE

1. **WHAT IF?** Suppose three of your friends have leg lengths of 27 inches, 28 inches, and 30 inches.

   a. Use the expression $\sqrt{384l}$ to approximate each friend's maximum walking speed.

   b. Use the simplified expression $8\sqrt{6l}$ to find the same approximations.

   c. *Explain* the advantage of using the simplified expression.

2. **REASONING** Simplify the expression $\sqrt{\dfrac{11}{144}}$. Then use a calculator to evaluate both the simplified and unsimplified expressions. *Compare* the results.

3. **VISUAL HORIZON** The *visual horizon* is the distance you can see before your line of sight is blocked by Earth's surface. If you are in a lighthouse, the visual horizon (in nautical miles) can be approximated by the expression $\sqrt{4h}$ where h is the vertical distance (in meters) from your eyes to the water's surface.

   a. Simplify the expression $\sqrt{4h}$.

   b. Suppose your eyes are 49 meters above the water's surface. Use the simplified expression from part (a) to find your visual horizon without a calculator.

4.6 Rational and Irrational Numbers

Standards NS 1.4 **Differentiate between rational and irrational numbers.**

Connect *Before* you investigated rational numbers. *Now* you will work with irrational numbers.

Math and SCIENCE
Example 4, p. 227

KEY VOCABULARY
• irrational number
• real number

Recall from page 113 that a rational number can be written as a quotient $\frac{a}{b}$ where a and b are integers and $b \neq 0$. An **irrational number** is a number that cannot be written as a quotient of two integers. If n is a positive integer and is not a perfect square, then $\sqrt{n}$ and $-\sqrt{n}$ are irrational numbers.

Together, rational numbers and irrational numbers make up the set of **real numbers**. The Venn diagram shows the relationships among numbers in the real number system.

REVIEW VENN DIAGRAMS
For help reviewing Venn diagrams, turn to p. 746.

Real Numbers

Rational numbers
Integers
Whole numbers

Irrational numbers
$\sqrt{2}$ π
0.1010010001...

The decimal form of a rational number is either terminating or repeating. The decimal form of an irrational number neither terminates nor repeats.

EXAMPLE 1 Classifying Real Numbers

Tell whether the number is *rational* or *irrational*.

a. $\frac{3}{4}$ **b.** $0.151515\ldots$ **c.** $\sqrt{3}$

SOLUTION

a. Because $\frac{3}{4}$ is a quotient of two integers (3 and 4), it is rational.

b. Because $0.151515\ldots$ is a repeating decimal, it is rational.

c. Because 3 is a positive integer and is not a perfect square, $\sqrt{3}$ is irrational.

Animated Math
For an interactive example of classifying numbers, go to **classzone.com.**

✓ **GUIDED PRACTICE** for Example 1

Tell whether the number is *rational* or *irrational*. *Explain* your reasoning.

1. $-\frac{5}{8}$ **2.** $\sqrt{7}$ **3.** $\sqrt{25}$ **4.** $0.020020002\ldots$

EXAMPLE 2 Comparing Real Numbers

Graph $\sqrt{\frac{1}{2}}$ and $\frac{1}{2}$ on a number line. Then copy and complete the statement $\sqrt{\frac{1}{2}}$ _?_ $\frac{1}{2}$ with <, >, or =.

SOLUTION

ANOTHER WAY

You can also use the quotient property to approximate the square root:

$\sqrt{\frac{1}{2}} = \frac{\sqrt{1}}{\sqrt{2}} \approx \frac{1}{1.41} \approx 0.71$

Use a calculator to approximate the square root. Graph the decimal forms of the numbers on a number line and compare.

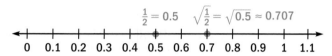

$\frac{1}{2} = 0.5$ $\sqrt{\frac{1}{2}} = \sqrt{0.5} \approx 0.707$

0   0.1   0.2   0.3   0.4   0.5   0.6   0.7   0.8   0.9   1   1.1

▶ **Answer** Because $\sqrt{\frac{1}{2}}$ is to the right of $\frac{1}{2}$, $\sqrt{\frac{1}{2}} > \frac{1}{2}$.

EXAMPLE 3 Ordering Real Numbers

Order the numbers $0.4\overline{7}$, $0.\overline{474}$, $0.\overline{47}$, and $\sqrt{0.23}$ from least to greatest.

SOLUTION

Animated Math

For an interactive example of ordering numbers, go to **classzone.com**.

STEP 1 Write each decimal out to six decimal places.

$0.4\overline{7} = 0.477777\ldots$

$0.\overline{474} = 0.474474\ldots$

$0.\overline{47} = 0.474747\ldots$

$\sqrt{0.23} = 0.479583\ldots$

Notice that the first two digits after the decimal point are the same for each number. Use the second pair of digits to order the decimals.

STEP 2 Write the decimals in order.

$0.474474\ldots$, $0.474747\ldots$, $0.477777\ldots$, and $0.479583\ldots$

▶ **Answer** From least to greatest, the order is $0.\overline{474}$, $0.\overline{47}$, $0.4\overline{7}$, and $\sqrt{0.23}$.

✓ **GUIDED PRACTICE** for Examples 2 and 3

Copy and complete the statement with <, >, or =.

5. 4 _?_ $\sqrt{8}$ **6.** $\frac{4}{5}$ _?_ $\sqrt{\frac{4}{5}}$ **7.** $\frac{1}{4}$ _?_ $\sqrt{\frac{1}{4}}$ **8.** $\sqrt{7}$ _?_ 3

Order the numbers from least to greatest.

9. $0.\overline{52}$, $0.\overline{525}$, $0.52\overline{5}$, and $\sqrt{0.276}$ **10.** 1.7, $\sqrt{1.7}$, $1.\overline{89}$, and $1.\overline{3}$

11. 1, $\sqrt{\frac{1}{10}}$, $\sqrt{\frac{1}{100}}$, and $\sqrt{\frac{101}{100}}$ **12.** $\sqrt{3}$, $1.\overline{71}$, $\sqrt{\frac{3}{2}}$, $\frac{3}{2}$

EXAMPLE 4 Using an Irrational Number in Real Life

WAVES For large ocean waves, the wind speed s (in knots) and the height h (in feet) of the waves are related by the model $s = \sqrt{\dfrac{h}{0.019}}$. If the waves are about 9.5 feet tall, what is the wind speed? (1 knot is equivalent to about 1.15 miles per hour.)

SOLUTION

$s = \sqrt{\dfrac{h}{0.019}}$ Write given model.

$\quad = \sqrt{\dfrac{9.5}{0.019}}$ Substitute 9.5 for h.

$\quad = \sqrt{500}$ Divide.

$\quad \approx 22.4$ Approximate square root.

▶ **Answer** The wind speed is about 22 knots.

Wave speed $s = \sqrt{\dfrac{h}{0.019}}$

✔ **GUIDED PRACTICE**   for Example 4

13. WHAT IF? In Example 4, suppose the waves grow to about 15 feet tall. What is the wind speed rounded to the nearest knot?

4.6 EXERCISES

HOMEWORK KEY

◆ = **MULTIPLE CHOICE PRACTICE**
Exs. 31, 33, 59, 70–72

◯ = **HINTS AND HOMEWORK HELP**
for Exs. 5, 27, 63 at classzone.com

SKILLS • PROBLEM SOLVING • REASONING

1. VOCABULARY Copy and complete: Together, rational and irrational numbers make up the set of __?__.

2. WRITING *Explain* how you can identify whether a number is rational.

SEE EXAMPLE 1
on p. 225
for Exs. 3–15

CLASSIFYING REAL NUMBERS **Tell whether the number is *rational* or *irrational*. *Explain* your reasoning.**

3. 0.682
4. $\sqrt{151}$
5. $0.\overline{2}$
6. 0.30311

7. $\sqrt{36}$
8. $\sqrt{62}$
9. $\sqrt{5}$
10. $\sqrt{144}$

11. $\dfrac{9}{46}$
12. $\sqrt{\dfrac{25}{49}}$
13. $\sqrt{\dfrac{100}{81}}$
14. $\dfrac{22}{31}$

15. WHICH ONE DOESN'T BELONG? Tell which number does not belong. *Justify* your reasoning.

A. $\sqrt{\dfrac{1}{4}}$
B. $\sqrt{\dfrac{1}{3}}$
C. $\sqrt{\dfrac{2}{5}}$
D. $\sqrt{\dfrac{5}{6}}$

SEE EXAMPLE 2
on p. 226
for Exs. 16–31

COMPARING REAL NUMBERS Graph the pair of numbers on a number line. Then copy and complete the statement with <, >, or =.

16. $\frac{5}{6}$? $\sqrt{\frac{5}{6}}$

17. $\sqrt{0.9}$? 0.9

18. $\sqrt{2.25}$? $\frac{3.5}{2.4}$

19. $\sqrt{4.6}$? 2.5

20. 2.6 ? $\sqrt{6.7}$

21. $\sqrt{\frac{8}{11}}$? $\frac{9}{10}$

CHOOSE A METHOD Copy and complete with <, >, or =. Tell whether you used *mental math, estimation,* or a *calculator.*

22. 0.81 ? $\sqrt{0.81}$

23. 5 ? $\sqrt{10}$

24. $\sqrt{\frac{64}{121}}$? $\frac{8}{11}$

25. $\sqrt{\frac{16}{3}}$? 5

26. $\sqrt{21}$? 7

27. -5 ? $-\sqrt{25}$

28. $\sqrt{9.9}$? 3.3

29. 1.3 ? $\sqrt{1.7}$

30. -0.4 ? $-\sqrt{1.6}$

31. ◆ **MULTIPLE CHOICE** Which statement is *not* true?

(A) $\sqrt{12} < 4$　　**(B)** $8 > \sqrt{16}$　　**(C)** $\sqrt{169} = 13$　　**(D)** $\sqrt{30} < 5$

SEE EXAMPLE 3
on p. 226
for Exs. 32–41

32. **GRAPHING REAL NUMBERS** Graph the numbers $-\sqrt{9}$, 8.69, $\sqrt{45}$, and $\frac{141}{25}$ on a number line. Then order the numbers from least to greatest.

33. ◆ **MULTIPLE CHOICE** Which list shows the numbers in order from least to greatest?

(A) $\sqrt{2}, \sqrt{5}, 1, 2, 3$

(B) $1, \sqrt{2}, \sqrt{5}, 2, 3$

(C) $1, \sqrt{2}, 2, \sqrt{5}, 3$

(D) $1, \sqrt{2}, 2, 3, \sqrt{5}$

ORDERING REAL NUMBERS Order the numbers from least to greatest.

34. $0.1\overline{3}, 0.\overline{131}, 0.\overline{13}, 0.133$

35. $0.\overline{26}, 0.266, 0.2\overline{6}, 0.\overline{262}$

36. $\sqrt{0.68}, 0.4\overline{5}, 0.455, 0.\overline{45}$

37. $0.3\overline{9}, \sqrt{0.17}, 0.\overline{39}, 0.399$

38. $1.5, \sqrt{8}, -4, -3.75$

39. $\sqrt{81}, 10.3, \sqrt{220}, -9$

40. $-\sqrt{12}, -\sqrt{\frac{1}{4}}, -3.5, -\frac{3}{4}$

41. $1.02, \sqrt{2.5}, \sqrt{1.25}, \frac{2}{5}$

ERROR ANALYSIS *Describe* and correct the error in the statement.

42. The number $\sqrt{64}$ is irrational because of the radical symbol.

43. The number $\sqrt{5}$ is rational because $\sqrt{5} = \frac{\sqrt{5}}{1}$.

44. The number $\sqrt{\frac{175}{7}}$ is irrational because neither 175 nor 7 is a perfect square.

ⓧⓨ **ALGEBRA** Evaluate when $a = 2$, $b = 4$, and $c = 9$. Round to the nearest tenth if necessary. Classify the result as *rational* or *irrational.*

45. $\sqrt{b + c}$

46. $\sqrt{c^2 - (a + b)}$

47. $\sqrt{a^2 - b + c}$

48. $\sqrt{bc + b + c}$

49. $\sqrt{c^2 - b^2 + 1}$

50. $\sqrt{ab + bc - a^2}$

51. REASONING Is $\sqrt{-4}$ a rational number? *Explain* your reasoning.

XY REASONING Determine whether the expression is *always, sometimes, or never* irrational for whole number values of x.

52. $\sqrt{x + 3}$ **53.** $\sqrt{x^2}$ **54.** $\sqrt{x} \div 4$

55. REASONING Is the sum of two irrational numbers *always, sometimes,* or *never* irrational? *Justify* your answer.

CONNECT SKILLS TO PROBLEM SOLVING Exercises 56–58 will help you prepare for problem solving.

Determine whether the number described is *rational* or *irrational*.

56. The incline of a ramp is $\sqrt{34}$ feet long.

57. A ladder leans against a building $\sqrt{48}$ meters above the ground.

58. The distance from the top of a flagpole to the end of its shadow is $\sqrt{144}$ feet.

SEE EXAMPLE 4
on p. 227
for Exs. 59–64

59. ◆ **MULTIPLE CHOICE** The area of a square judo mat is 400 square feet. What is *not* true about the perimeter?

  (A) It is rational.   **(B)** It is irrational.

  (C) It is an integer.   **(D)** It is a real number.

California @HomeTutor for problem solving help at classzone.com

Judo mat area = 400 ft²

60. FLOOR DIMENSIONS The floor of a square room has an area of 212 square feet. Are the dimensions of the room *rational* or *irrational*?

California @HomeTutor for problem solving help at classzone.com

61. WRITING Will a square carpet that has an area of 110 square feet fit in a bedroom that measures 10.5 feet by 11.2 feet? *Explain*.

62. DECORATING You are decorating your room. You have a square stencil that covers an area of 20.25 square inches. The wall you are decorating is $7\frac{1}{2}$ feet high. How many stencils fit between the floor and the ceiling?

63. BOX KITES To find the minimum wind speed required to fly a box kite, use the formula $m = 5\sqrt{\dfrac{w}{A}}$ where m is minimum speed (in miles per hour), w is the kite's weight (in ounces), and A is the area (in square feet) of the surface used to lift the kite. A box kite weighs 19.6 ounces and its surface area is 11.71 square feet. The wind is blowing at 6 miles per hour. Can you fly your kite?

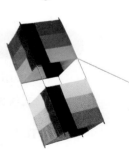

64. ⬡ **GEOMETRY** The radius r of a circle with area A is given by the formula $r = \sqrt{\dfrac{A}{\pi}}$. *Describe* the type of number the area needs to be for the radius to be an integer.

$w = 19.6$ oz,
$A = 11.71$ ft²

65. OPEN-ENDED Give an example of a rational number and an irrational number between 8 and 9.

66. REASONING Your friend gets a result of 2.645751311 on a calculator and says that it has to be an irrational number. Is your friend right? *Explain* your reasoning.

67. ⊘ **GEOMETRY** The figure is composed of one large square and four smaller squares. The smaller squares all have the same size. The area of the shaded region is 45 square centimeters. Is the side length of the large square *rational* or *irrational*? *Explain* your reasoning.

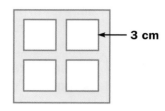 ← **3 cm**

68. CHALLENGE Find three rational numbers and three irrational numbers between $\frac{2}{3}$ and $\frac{3}{4}$. Can you write all of the rational numbers that are between these two numbers? *Explain* your reasoning.

69. CHALLENGE Describe the values of x for which $\sqrt{x^2} = -x$. Give an example to support your answer.

◆ CALIFORNIA STANDARDS SPIRAL REVIEW

NS 2.4

70. What is $\sqrt{16}$? *(p. 213)*

   A $\frac{1}{2}$ **B** 2   **C** 4   **D** 8

AF 2.1

71. Which of the following is equivalent to 10^4? *(p. 196)*

   A $10 \times 10 \times 10 \times 10$ **B** 10×4

   C $1 \times \frac{1}{10} \times \frac{1}{10} \times \frac{1}{10}$ **D** $1 \times \frac{1}{10} \times \frac{1}{10} \times \frac{1}{10} \times \frac{1}{10}$

NS 1.1

72. The weights of four steaks are given below. Which weight is the least? *(p. 133)*

   A $1\frac{1}{4}$ lb   **B** 1.2 lb   **C** $\frac{9}{8}$ lb   **D** 1.1 lb

---

QUIZ *for Lessons 4.4–4.6*

Simplify the expression.

1. $\sqrt{32}$ *(p. 219)*   **2.** $\sqrt{729}$ *(p. 213)*   **3.** $\sqrt{18} \cdot \sqrt{6}$ *(p. 219)*   **4.** $\sqrt{\frac{12}{36}}$ *(p. 219)*

Tell whether the number is *rational* or *irrational*. *(p. 225)*

5. $0.\overline{23}$ **6.** $\sqrt{18}$ **7.** $\sqrt{400}$ **8.** $\frac{2}{3}$

9. Between which two consecutive integers does $\sqrt{851}$ lie? Use a calculator to check your answer. *(p. 213)*

MIXED REVIEW of Skills and Problem Solving

Multiple Choice Practice for Lessons 4.4–4.6

1. Which number is irrational? **NS 1.4**

 (**A**) 0.13

 (**B**) 0.13030030003. . .

 (**C**) 0.13145673912

 (**D**) $0.1\overline{3}$

2. What is the value of $-\sqrt{225}$? **NS 2.4**

 (**A**) -25 (**B**) -15

 (**C**) 15   (**D**) 25

3. Martha bought a square rug with an area of 81 square feet to use in the room shown below. Without cutting the rug, what is the smallest width w of the room for which the rug will fit in the room? **NS 2.4**

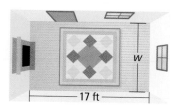

 (**A**) 8 ft   (**B**) 9 ft

 (**C**) 12 ft   (**D**) 81 ft

4. A fish slips out of an eagle's grasp at a height of 28 feet above a lake. It takes the fish $\sqrt{\dfrac{28}{16}}$ seconds to hit the water. What is the simplified form of this radical expression? **NS 2.4**

 (**A**) $\dfrac{\sqrt{7}}{8}$ (**B**) $\dfrac{\sqrt{7}}{4}$

 (**C**) $\dfrac{\sqrt{7}}{2}$ (**D**) $2\sqrt{\dfrac{7}{4}}$

5. The area of a square garden is 98 square meters. What is the side length of the garden in simplified form? **NS 2.4**

 (**A**) $2\sqrt{7}$ m   (**B**) 9.8 m

 (**C**) $7\sqrt{2}$ m   (**D**) $3\sqrt{11}$ m

6. A farmer wants to build a square pen with an area of 120 square feet. To the nearest foot, what should the value of s be in the farmer's diagram shown below? **NS 2.4, MR 2.3**

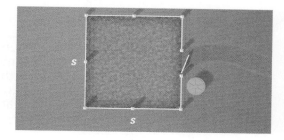

 (**A**) 10 ft   (**B**) 11 ft

 (**C**) 12 ft   (**D**) 30 ft

7. What is the simplified form of the expression $\sqrt{24} \cdot \sqrt{30}$? **NS 2.4**

 (**A**) $12\sqrt{3}$ (**B**) $12\sqrt{5}$

 (**C**) $24\sqrt{5}$ (**D**) $36\sqrt{5}$

8. A pinecone falls from a tree. Evaluate the expression $\dfrac{1}{4}\sqrt{h}$ for the number of seconds it takes the pinecone to reach the ground from a height of 81 feet. **NS 2.4**

 (**A**) $2\dfrac{1}{4}$ sec   (**B**) $4\dfrac{1}{2}$ sec

 (**C**) 10 sec   (**D**) $20\dfrac{1}{4}$ sec

9. Which of the following is an irrational number between 1.41 and 1.42? **NS 2.4**

 (**A**) 1.4010010001. . . (**B**) $1.4\overline{1}$

 (**C**) $\sqrt{2}$ (**D**) 1.42

10. The expression $5\sqrt{6}$ is the simplified form of which expression? **NS 2.4, MR 3.2**

 (**A**) $\sqrt{10} \cdot \sqrt{15}$ (**B**) $\sqrt{180}$

 (**C**) $\sqrt{5} \cdot \sqrt{36}$ (**D**) $\sqrt{15} \cdot \sqrt{20}$

BIG IDEAS
For Your Notebook

Big Idea 1

Understanding Zero and Negative Exponents

Topic	Rule	Examples
Zero and negative exponents	$a^0 = 1$ $a^{-n} = \dfrac{1}{a^n}$	$5^0 = 1$ $2^{-3} = \dfrac{1}{2^3} = \dfrac{1}{8}$
Scientific notation	A number is written in scientific notation if it has the form $c \times 10^n$ where $c \geq 1$, $c < 10$, and n is an integer.	**Standard form** **Scientific notation** $428{,}000 = 4.28 \times 10^5$ $0.00032 = 3.2 \times 10^{-4}$

Big Idea 2

Using Square Roots

Topic	Rule	Examples
Definition of square root	m is a square root of n if $m^2 = n$. If $n > 0$, then n has two square roots: $\sqrt{n}$ and $-\sqrt{n}$.	$\sqrt{16} = 4$ $-\sqrt{36} = -6$
Product property of square roots	$\sqrt{ab} = \sqrt{a} \cdot \sqrt{b}$	$\sqrt{27} = \sqrt{9} \cdot \sqrt{3} = 3\sqrt{3}$
Quotient property of square roots	$\sqrt{\dfrac{a}{b}} = \dfrac{\sqrt{a}}{\sqrt{b}}$	$\sqrt{\dfrac{11}{64}} = \dfrac{\sqrt{11}}{\sqrt{64}} = \dfrac{\sqrt{11}}{8}$

Big Idea 3

Classifying Real Numbers

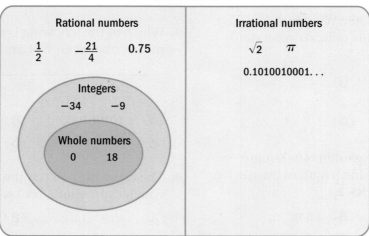

Real Numbers

Rational numbers

$\dfrac{1}{2}$ $-\dfrac{21}{4}$ 0.75

Integers

-34 -9

Whole numbers

0   18

Irrational numbers

$\sqrt{2}$ π

$0.1010010001\ldots$

CHAPTER PROBLEM

APPLYING THE
BIG IDEAS

Big Idea 1
You use negative exponents in **Step 5.**

Big Idea 2
You use square roots in **Step 3.**

Big Idea 3
You classify real numbers in **Step 4.**

PROBLEM How can you use square roots to calculate the reaction times of your classmates?

STEP 1 Conduct an experiment.

Work with a partner. Hold a yardstick vertically. Have your partner place his or her fingers near the lower end of the yardstick. Then drop the yardstick. Your partner should catch the yardstick as quickly as possible.

Measure the distance (in inches) that the yardstick fell. Repeat this process 10 times and then find the mean distance d.

STEP 2 Switch roles.

Switch roles with your partner and repeat Step 1.

STEP 3 Calculate reaction times.

Use the mean distances found in Steps 1 and 2 and the formula $t = \sqrt{\dfrac{d}{192}}$ to calculate the reaction time t (in seconds) for you and your partner.

STEP 4 Classify reaction times.

Classify both reaction times as rational or irrational numbers.

STEP 5 Use scientific notation.

Write both reaction times using scientific notation.

Extending the Problem

The table below shows drivers' approximate reaction times (in seconds) to things they see (visual stimuli) and hear (audio stimuli).

Age of driver	Reaction time to visual stimuli (sec)	Reaction time to audio stimuli (sec)
16	0.0196	0.0112
25	0.0194	0.0102
40	0.0208	0.0104

1. Write each reaction time in scientific notation.

2. Do drivers appear to react more quickly to visual stimuli or audio stimuli? *Explain.*

3. Write the radical expression used in Step 3 in simplest form. (*Hint:* find a fraction equivalent to $\dfrac{d}{192}$ with a perfect square denominator.)

REVIEW KEY VOCABULARY

- scientific notation, *p. 201*
- perfect square, *p. 213*
- square root, *p. 213*
- radical expression, *p. 213*
- simplest form of a radical expression, *p. 219*
- irrational number, *p. 225*
- real number, *p. 225*

VOCABULARY EXERCISES

In Exercises 1–3, copy and complete the statement.

1. The number 4.3×10^{21} is written in __?__ notation.

2. A number that is the square of an integer is a(n) __?__ .

3. The number 5 is a(n) __?__ of 25.

4. **NOTETAKING SKILLS** Make a *four square diagram* like the one on page 194 for *rational number*.

REVIEW EXAMPLES AND EXERCISES

4.1 Integer Powers of Ten
pp. 196–200

AF 2.1

EXAMPLE

Write the power of 10 in standard form.

a. $10^4 = 10 \cdot 10 \cdot 10 \cdot 10 = 10{,}000$

b. $10^{-3} = \dfrac{1}{10} \cdot \dfrac{1}{10} \cdot \dfrac{1}{10} = 0.001$

EXERCISES

SEE EXAMPLES
1 AND 2
on pp. 196–197
for Exs. 5–12

Write the power of 10 in standard form.

5. 10^3 **6.** 10^{10} **7.** 10^{-4} **8.** 10^{-10}

Write the number as a power of 10.

9. 0.001 **10.** 100 **11.** 10,000 **12.** 0.00000001

4.2 Scientific Notation
pp. 201–204

NS 1.1

EXAMPLE

Write the number in scientific notation.

a. $980{,}000 = 9.8 \times 100{,}000 = 9.8 \times 10^5$

b. $0.00012 = 1.2 \times 0.0001 = 1.2 \times 10^{-4}$

EXERCISES

SEE EXAMPLES 1, 2, AND 3 on pp. 201–202 for Exs. 13–19

Write the number in scientific notation.

13. 34,600,000,000

14. 0.0000009

15. 0.000000000502

Write the number in standard form.

16. 2.36×10^8

17. 1.5×10^3

18. 9.4×10^{-3}

19. ASTRONOMY There are over 300,000,000,000 stars in the Andromeda Galaxy. Write this number in scientific notation.

4.3 **Zero and Negative Exponents**

pp. 206–210

AF 2.1   **EXAMPLE**

Simplify the algebraic expression.

a. $-5n^0 = -5 \cdot n^0$
$= -5 \cdot 1 = -5$

b. $4x^{-2} = 4 \cdot x^{-2}$
$= \dfrac{4}{x^2}$

EXERCISES

SEE EXAMPLE 4 on p. 208 for Exs. 20–23

Simplify the algebraic expression.

20. b^0

21. c^{-3}

22. $5n^{-2}$

23. $-7s^{-4}$

4.4 **Finding and Approximating Square Roots**

pp. 213–218

NS 2.4   **EXAMPLE**

a. $-\sqrt{225} = -15$ because $(-15)^2 = 225$ and $-15 < 0$.

b. $\sqrt{\dfrac{9}{25}} = \dfrac{3}{5}$ because $\left(\dfrac{3}{5}\right)^2 = \dfrac{9}{25}$ and $\dfrac{3}{5} > 0$.

EXERCISES

SEE EXAMPLES 1, 2, AND 5 on pp. 213–215 for Exs. 24–28

Find or approximate the square root. Round to the nearest tenth if necessary.

24. $\sqrt{49}$

25. $-\sqrt{625}$

26. $\sqrt{77}$

27. $-\sqrt{40}$

28. ARCHITECTURE The area of the square base of a building is 2025 square feet. What is the length of one side of the base?

4.5 Simplifying Square Roots

pp. 219–223

NS 2.4 **EXAMPLE**

a. $\sqrt{6} \cdot \sqrt{10} = \sqrt{60}$

$= \sqrt{4} \cdot \sqrt{15}$

$= 2\sqrt{15}$

b. $\sqrt{\dfrac{5}{9}} = \dfrac{\sqrt{5}}{\sqrt{9}}$

$= \dfrac{\sqrt{5}}{3}$

EXERCISES

Simplify the expression.

SEE EXAMPLES
1, 3, AND 4
on pp. 219–221
for Exs. 29–32

29. $\sqrt{150}$

30. $\sqrt{14} \cdot \sqrt{21}$

31. $\sqrt{6} \cdot \sqrt{24}$

32. $\sqrt{\dfrac{13}{36}}$

4.6 Rational and Irrational Numbers

pp. 225–230

NS 1.4 **EXAMPLE**

Graph $\sqrt{7}$ and 3 on a number line. Then copy and complete the statement $\sqrt{7}$? 3 with <, >, or =.

Use a calculator to approximate the square root. Then graph the numbers on a number line and compare.

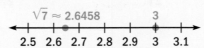

Because $\sqrt{7}$ is to the left of 3, $\sqrt{7} < 3$.

EXERCISES

SEE EXAMPLES
1 AND 2
on pp. 225–226
for Exs. 33–41

Tell whether the number is *rational* or *irrational*. *Explain* your reasoning.

33. $\sqrt{100}$

34. $0.\overline{6}$

35. $\dfrac{16}{25}$

36. $\sqrt{6}$

Graph the pair of numbers on a number line. Then copy and complete the statement with <, >, or =.

37. $\sqrt{31}$? 4

38. 7 ? $\sqrt{59}$

39. -9 ? $-\sqrt{81}$

40. $\sqrt{48}$? 6.3

41. **GEOMETRY** The length *d* of the diagonal of a square with area *A* can be found using the formula $d = \sqrt{2A}$. If a square has an area of 16 square feet, is the length (in feet) of its diagonal *rational* or *irrational*? *Explain* your answer.

VOCABULARY Copy and complete the statement.

1. The radical expression $7\sqrt{5}$ is in __?__ form.

2. Together, __?__ numbers and __?__ numbers make up the set of real numbers.

Write the power of 10 in standard form.

3. 10^4 4. 10^{-3} 5. 10^{-2}

Write the number as a power of 10.

6. 10,000   7. 1   8. 0.0001

Write the number in scientific notation.

9. 200,400   10. 0.000005126   11. 42,000

Write the number in standard form.

12. 7.72×10^6 13. 1.46×10^{-6} 14. 8.22×10^{-4}

Simplify the algebraic expression.

15. $m^8 \cdot n^{-3}$ 16. $\dfrac{x^7}{y^{-4}}$ 17. $(t + 1)^0$ 18. $\dfrac{p^3}{7^{-2}}$

19. $5x^{-3}$ 20. $\dfrac{2}{z^{-4}}$ 21. $25x^0$ 22. 5^{-2x}

Find or approximate the square root. Round to the nearest tenth if necessary.

23. $\sqrt{67}$ 24. $\sqrt{324}$ 25. $-\sqrt{49}$ 26. $\sqrt{500}$

Simplify the expression.

27. $\sqrt{45}$ 28. $\sqrt{6} \cdot \sqrt{18}$ 29. $\sqrt{\dfrac{13}{144}}$

Tell whether the number is *rational* or *irrational*. *Explain* your reasoning.

30. $\sqrt{16}$ 31. $\dfrac{23}{24}$ 32. $\sqrt{39}$ 33. $\sqrt{\dfrac{1}{4}}$

34. **WEIGHT** The western harvest mouse weighs approximately 1.5×10^{-3} kilograms at birth. Write this number in standard form.

35. **ZOOLOGY** A study of animal motion determined that an animal's maximum walking speed s (in feet per second) can be approximated by the formula $s = 5.66\sqrt{l}$ where l is the animal's leg length (in feet). What is the maximum walking speed for an ostrich with a leg length of 4 feet?

STRATEGIES YOU'LL USE:
• SOLVE DIRECTLY
• ELIMINATE CHOICES

Standards
NS 1.1, NS 2.4

If you have difficulty solving a multiple choice problem directly, you may be able to use another approach to eliminate incorrect answer choices and obtain the correct answer.

PROBLEM 1

The thickness of a United States dollar bill is about 0.000358 foot. What is the thickness written in scientific notation?

(A) 3.58×10^{-5} ft

(B) 0.358×10^{-3} ft

(C) 3.58×10^{-4} ft

(D) 3.58×10^{4} ft

Strategy 1 SOLVE DIRECTLY

Standard form 0.000358

Move decimal point 4 places to the right.

Product form 3.58×0.0001

Scientific notation 3.58×10^{-4}

Exponent is −4.

In scientific notation, 0.000358 is written as 3.58×10^{-4}.

The correct answer is C. (A) (B) (C) (D)

Strategy 2 ELIMINATE CHOICES

Use the definition of scientific notation and mathematical reasoning to eliminate answer choices.

The problem requires a number to be written in scientific notation. So, the answer must have the form $c \times 10^{n}$ where $c \geq 1$, $c < 10$, and n is an integer. Even if a choice has the correct value, that choice is not the correct answer if the value is not in scientific notation.

Because $0.358 < 1$, 0.358×10^{-3} is not written in scientific notation, choice B can be eliminated.

A number written in scientific notation is less than 1 when the exponent is negative. Because $0.000358 < 1$, n must be negative. Choice D can be eliminated.

Work backwards to eliminate the other choice. You can show that choice A is 0.0000358 when written in standard form. Choice A can be eliminated.

The correct answer is C. (A) (B) (C) (D)

PROBLEM 2

What is the simplified form of the radical expression $\sqrt{\dfrac{24}{324}}$?

(A) $\dfrac{\sqrt{24}}{18}$
(B) $\dfrac{2\sqrt{6}}{9\sqrt{4}}$
(C) $\dfrac{2\sqrt{6}}{18}$
(D) $\dfrac{\sqrt{6}}{9}$

Strategy 1 SOLVE DIRECTLY

Simplify the expression using properties of square roots.

$\sqrt{\dfrac{24}{324}} = \dfrac{\sqrt{24}}{\sqrt{324}}$ **Quotient property of square roots**

$= \dfrac{\sqrt{24}}{18}$ **Simplify.**

$= \dfrac{\sqrt{4 \cdot 6}}{18}$ **Factor using greatest perfect square factor.**

$= \dfrac{\sqrt{4} \cdot \sqrt{6}}{18}$ **Product property of square roots**

$= \dfrac{2\sqrt{6}}{18}$ **Simplify.**

$= \dfrac{\sqrt{6}}{9}$ **Simplify.**

The correct answer is D. (A) (B) (C) (D)

Strategy 2 ELIMINATE CHOICES

You can eliminate answer choices by using the definition of the simplest form of a radical expression.

The radical expression in choice A is not in simplest form because the number under the radical sign has a perfect square factor other than 1. So, choice A can be eliminated.

The radical expression in choice B is not in simplest form because there is a radical in the denominator. So, choice B can be eliminated.

The radical expression in choice C is not in simplest form because $\dfrac{2\sqrt{6}}{18}$ can be simplified to $\dfrac{\sqrt{6}}{9}$. So, choice C can be eliminated.

The correct answer is D. (A) (B) (C) (D)

STRATEGY PRACTICE

Explain why you can eliminate the highlighted answer choice.

1. What is the simplified form of the expression 11^0?

(A) ✗ **0**   (B) $\dfrac{1}{11}$ (C) 1   (D) 11

2. What is the simplified form of the radical expression $\sqrt{\dfrac{17}{81}}$?

(A) $\dfrac{\sqrt{17}}{9}$ (B) $\dfrac{\sqrt{17}}{\sqrt{81}}$ (C) ✗ $\dfrac{17}{9}$ (D) $9\sqrt{17}$

3. Jupiter, the largest planet in our solar system, has a radius of about 71,500 kilometers. What is Jupiter's radius (in kilometers) written in scientific notation?

(A) ✗ 7.15×10^{-4} (B) 71.5×10^3 (C) 7.15×10^4 (D) 71.5×10^4

4 ◆ MULTIPLE CHOICE PRACTICE

In Exercises 1 and 2, use the bar graph showing the approximate surface area of the bodies of water in three states.

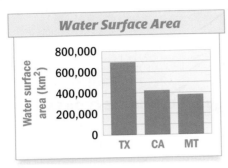

1. What is the largest area of water in scientific notation? **NS 1.1**

- **(A)** $6.96 \times 10^{-5} \text{ km}^2$
- **(B)** $696 \times 10^3 \text{ km}^2$
- **(C)** $69.6 \times 10^4 \text{ km}^2$
- **(D)** $6.96 \times 10^5 \text{ km}^2$

2. What is the area of water in California in scientific notation? **NS 1.1**

- **(A)** $4.24 \times 10^4 \text{ km}^2$
- **(B)** $424 \times 10^3 \text{ km}^2$
- **(C)** $4.24 \times 10^5 \text{ km}^2$
- **(D)** $4.24 \times 10^6 \text{ km}^2$

3. Between which two integers does $\sqrt{68}$ lie? **NS 2.4**

- **(A)** 6 and 7
- **(B)** 7 and 8
- **(C)** 8 and 9
- **(D)** 9 and 10

4. What is the simplified form of $\sqrt{\frac{24}{9}}$? **NS 2.4**

- **(A)** $\frac{2\sqrt{6}}{3}$
- **(B)** $2\sqrt{\frac{2}{3}}$
- **(C)** $2\sqrt{3}$
- **(D)** $6\sqrt{3}$

5. What is the simplified form of $\sqrt{14} \cdot \sqrt{42}$? **NS 2.4**

- **(A)** $\sqrt{588}$
- **(B)** $7\sqrt{12}$
- **(C)** $2\sqrt{147}$
- **(D)** $14\sqrt{3}$

6. Which procedure can be used to write 8.6×10^6 in standard form? **NS 1.1, MR 2.6**

- **(A)** Multiply 8.6 by 100,000.
- **(B)** Multiply 8.6 by 1,000,000.
- **(C)** Multiply 8.6 by 10,000,000.
- **(D)** Multiply 8.6 by 0.000001.

7. The table shows the approximate populations of three countries as powers of 10. What is the smallest of these populations in standard form? **NS 1.1**

Country	Population
India	10^9
Mexico	10^8
Hungary	10^7

- **(A)** 1,000,000
- **(B)** 10,000,000
- **(C)** 100,000,000
- **(D)** 1,000,000,000

8. Consider a square with a side length of s. Which value of s is irrational *and* results in an area of the square that is a rational number of square inches? **NS 1.4**

- **(A)** $\sqrt{7}$ in.
- **(B)** 3 in.
- **(C)** $3.\overline{4}$ in.
- **(D)** $\sqrt{16}$ in.

9. In 1891, Captain Dansey of the British Royal Artillery designed a kite for rescuing shipwreck victims. The kite was made from a square of fabric, as shown below. What is the perimeter of this square? **NS 2.4**

   Ⓐ 9 ft

   Ⓑ 18 ft

   Ⓒ 36 ft

   Ⓓ 162 ft

   $A = 81\ ft^2$

10. Which number is rational? **NS 1.4**

    Ⓐ $\sqrt{3}$

    Ⓑ $\sqrt{5}$

    Ⓒ 7.2020020002. . .

    Ⓓ $9.\overline{9}$

11. The diameter of a grain of sand is 2^{-4} millimeters. What is this measurement written without using a power? **NS 2.2**

    Ⓐ −16 mm

    Ⓑ $\frac{1}{16}$ mm

    Ⓒ $\frac{1}{8}$ mm

    Ⓓ 16 mm

12. What is the simplified form of $\sqrt{252}$? **NS 2.4**

    Ⓐ $6\sqrt{7}$

    Ⓑ $2\sqrt{63}$

    Ⓒ $3\sqrt{28}$

    Ⓓ $7\sqrt{6}$

13. Which number is irrational? **NS 1.4**

    Ⓐ $-\frac{10}{3}$

    Ⓑ $\sqrt{36}$

    Ⓒ $7.0\overline{7}$

    Ⓓ $\sqrt{145}$

14. The cell width of the bacterium below is 200^{-2} inches. What is this measurement written without using a power? **NS 2.1**

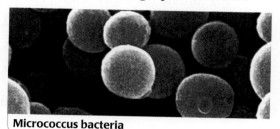

Micrococcus bacteria

    Ⓐ $\frac{1}{40,000}$ in.

    Ⓑ $\frac{1}{400}$ in.

    Ⓒ $\frac{1}{200}$ in.

    Ⓓ 0.2 in.

15. The table shows how many raffle tickets four schools sold. Which school's total can be written in a power of 10? **NS 1.1**

School	Total tickets sold
Washington Elementary	633
Garfield Middle School	1000
Kennedy Middle School	1152
Madison High School	1015

    Ⓐ Washington Elementary

    Ⓑ Garfield Middle School

    Ⓒ Kennedy Middle School

    Ⓓ Madison High School

16. Lynda says that 10×10^{-4} is not written in scientific notation. What number in scientific notation is equal to 10×10^{-4}? **NS 1.1, MR 1.1**

    Ⓐ 1.0×10^{-5}

    Ⓑ 10×10^{-5}

    Ⓒ 1.0×10^{-4}

    Ⓓ 1.0×10^{-3}

Evaluate the expression. *(p. 5)*

1. $8 + 6 \div 2$

2. $15 - 9 \div 3$

3. $3 \times (1.8 + 5 - 0.6)$

4. $9 \times 2^3 - 15$

5. $(2^5 + 8) \cdot 5^2$

6. $(18 \div 6)^3 + (11 - 4)^3$

7. $3(8 + 6)$

8. $5(7 - 3)$

9. $5 + 8 \cdot 4$

Use a number line to order the numbers from least to greatest.

10. $-15, 16, 1, -5, 4, 8$ *(p. 12)*

11. $40, -60, 98, -85, -6, 42$ *(p. 12)*

12. $2\frac{3}{10}, 2.32, \frac{11}{5}, 2.25, \frac{5}{2}$ *(p. 133)*

13. $0.45, \frac{3}{8}, 0.4, \frac{5}{12}, 0.46$ *(p. 133)*

Find the sum, difference, product, or quotient.

14. $29 + (-18)$ *(p. 18)*

15. $-8 - 9$ *(p. 24)*

16. $44 - (-11)$ *(p. 24)*

17. $-5(4)$ *(p. 31)*

18. $-12(-8)$ *(p. 31)*

19. $\frac{42}{-3}$ *(p. 36)*

20. $12\frac{1}{2} \cdot \frac{6}{25}$ *(p. 98)*

21. $\frac{13}{18} \div \frac{5}{6}$ *(p. 106)*

22. $5\frac{8}{11} \div \left(-\frac{3}{4}\right)$ *(p. 106)*

23. $16.7 \cdot (-3.2)$ *(p. 144)*

24. $43.4 \cdot 0.13$ *(p. 144)*

25. $3.434 \div 8.08$ *(p. 144)*

Evaluate the expression when $a = 4$, $b = -16$, and $c = 12$. *(p. 75)*

26. $\frac{-c}{a}$

27. $\frac{3b}{2c}$

28. $\frac{b}{-4a}$

29. $\frac{2abc}{abc}$

Write the fraction in simplest form. *(p. 75)*

30. $\frac{104}{39}$

31. $-\frac{32}{102}$

32. $\frac{200}{202}$

33. $-\frac{117}{13}$

Write the decimal or fraction as a percent. *(p. 155)*

34. 0.43

35. 0.003

36. $\frac{3}{10}$

37. $\frac{29}{20}$

38. 2.73

39. $\frac{7}{11}$

40. $\frac{25}{20}$

41. 0.05

Write the number in scientific notation. *(p. 201)*

42. $213,000$

43. 0.0000439

44. 978

Simplify the algebraic expression. *(p. 206)*

45. $7x^{-4}$

46. $a^{-6} \cdot b^4$

47. $\frac{8w^{-6}}{24w^0}$

48. $\frac{10}{5m^{-4}}$

49. **DOLPHINS** After swimming 22 miles, a dolphin changes speed and swims at a rate of 18 miles per hour. Use the expression $22 + 18t$, where t is the number of hours, to find the total distance traveled by the dolphin after 2.4 more hours. *(p. 5)*

50. **CHECKBOOK** The balance of a checkbook is $225. There are deposits of $80 and $40 and withdrawals of $100 and $25. What is the new balance of the checkbook? *(p. 18)*

51. **FALLING ROCK** A rock falls 144 feet from a ledge. The expression $-16t^2 + 144$ gives the height (in feet) of the rock after falling for t seconds. Evaluate the expression when t equals 2, 3, and 4 seconds. When does the rock hit the ground? What is the actual height of the rock after 4 seconds? *(p. 31)*

52. **RADIO** You are the disc jockey for a 15 minute radio show at your school. You must leave 3 minutes open for announcements, and you want to play 3 songs. Use the table at the right to determine the 3 songs you can play. *(p. 52)*

Song	A	B	C	D	E
Length (minutes)	6	4	3	5	6

BIOLOGY In Exercises 53 and 54, use the table. It shows approximate weights (in pounds) of several newborn animals. *(p. 137)*

53. How much more does the hippopotamus weigh than the gentoo penguin?

54. How much more does the polar bear weigh than the giant panda?

Newborn animal	Birth weight (lb)
Hippopotamus	66
Giant panda	0.25
Giraffe	150
Polar bear	1.32
Gentoo penguin	0.29

55. **ICEBERGS** When a rectangular iceberg broke free from Antarctica in May of 2002, it was about 34.5 miles long and about 11.5 miles wide. About how much area did the iceberg cover? *(p. 144)*

SURVEYS In Exercises 56–58, use the table. It shows the results of a survey of 300 students who were asked what they would choose for a final project. *(pp. 150, 155)*

56. What percent of students chose an oral report?

57. What fraction of students chose a visual project? Write the fraction in simplest form.

58. Which final project was chosen by 21% of the students?

Final project	
Visual project	105
Writing a paper	96
Taking a test	63
Oral report	36

59. **INTEREST** You invest $300 at a simple annual interest rate of 3.5% for one year. How much would you need to invest at a 2% simple annual interest rate to earn the same amount of interest that year? *(p. 172)*

60. **ENVIRONMENT** In the United States, approximately 120,000 aluminum cans are recycled each minute. Write this number in scientific notation. *(p. 201)*

5 Solving Equations and Inequalities

Before

In previous chapters, you learned the following skills, which you'll use in Chapter 5:

- Using the order of operations
- Using the distributive property
- Using properties of real numbers
- Evaluating expressions

Now

In Chapter 5 you'll study these
Big Ideas:

1. Writing and simplifying expressions
2. Writing and solving equations
3. Writing and solving inequalities

Why?

So you can solve real-world problems about . . .

- Movies, p. 250
- Television, p. 250
- Ice sculptures, p. 251
- Sea lions, p. 261
- Waterfalls, p. 267
- Basketball, p. 267
- Ski jumping, p. 286

Animated Math
at *classzone.com*

Get-Ready Games

EXPRESSION RACE

California Standards

Review evaluating expressions. **Gr. 7 AF 1.2**
Prepare for solving equations. **Gr. 7 AF 4.1**

Materials

- One *Expression Race* board
- One number cube
- One place marker for each player

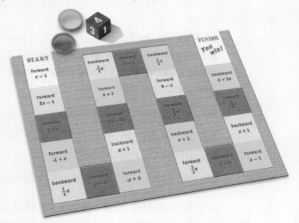

How to Play Each player should put a place marker on the Start space. Take turns following the steps on the next page.

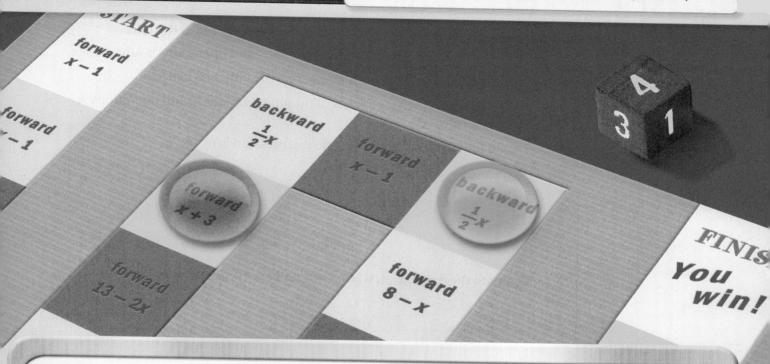

CALIFORNIA STANDARDS

• **Gr. 7 AF 4.1** Solve two-step linear equations and inequalities in one variable over the rational numbers, interpret the solution or solutions in the context from which they arose, and verify the reasonableness of the results. *(Lessons 5.5, 5.9)*

• **Gr. 7 AF 4.2** Solve multistep problems involving rate, average speed, distance, and time or a direct variation. *(Lesson 5.4)*

1 Roll the number cube.

2 Evaluate the expression on the space with your marker. Let the number you rolled equal *x*. Round any fraction to the nearest whole number.

3 Move your marker in the direction indicated by the space where it sits. The result of Step 2 is the number of spaces you should move.

How to Win Be the first player to land on the space marked Finish. Alternatively, be the player closest to Finish after a certain period of time.

Games Wrap-Up

Draw Conclusions

Complete these exercises after playing the game.

1. **WRITING** If your marker is on the space labeled "Forward 13 − 2*x*," what is the best number to roll? *Explain* your reasoning.

2. **REASONING** If you roll a 2 on every turn, would you ever reach Finish? *Explain* why or why not. What if you roll a 3 on every turn?

Prerequisite Skills

California @HomeTutor
Prerequisite skills practice
at classzone.com

REVIEW VOCABULARY

- **numerical expression,** *p. 6*
- **evaluate,** *p. 6*
- **variable,** *p. 7*
- **algebraic expression,** *p. 7*

VOCABULARY CHECK

Copy and complete using a review term from the list at the left.

1. An expression that consists of numbers and operations is a(n) __?__.

2. A symbol that represents one or more numbers is called a(n) __?__.

3. An expression that consists of numbers, variables, and operations is called a(n) __?__.

4. To find the value of a numerical expression is to __?__ it.

SKILL CHECK

Evaluate the expression. *(p. 36)*

5. $-3 - 2 + 8$

6. $3 - 7 + 2 - 1$

7. $-2(3 + 1) + 2$

8. $-5 \times 4 + 2$

9. $7(3 + 1) \div 2$

10. $-8 \div 2 + 4 \times 6$

Evaluate the expression when $s = 4$ and $t = 16$. *(p. 36)*

11. $(t - 9) + s$

12. $s(t - 5)$

13. $\frac{1}{4}t - 4$

14. $s^2 + 2t$

15. $\frac{1}{2}(s + t)$

16. $3s - t + 7$

Notetaking Skills

NOW YOU TRY
Use a *notetaking organizer* to write your notes about using the distributive property. You may want to use colored pencils.

Focus on Graphic Organizers

You can use a *notetaking organizer* to write your notes about a concept, such as evaluating an algebraic expression.

Write important vocabulary or formulas in the narrow column.

A variable is a letter (or other symbol) that represents a number.

Substitute a number for each variable.

Evaluate x(y + 2) for x = 2 and y = 3.

x(y + 2) = 2(3 + 2)
= 2(5)
= 10

Write your notes about evaluating an expression in the wide column.

How can you evaluate an expression like xyz, when there are no operators?

Write any questions you have about evaluating an expression at the bottom of the page.

5.1 Writing and Evaluating Expressions

Math and **RECREATION**
Example 2, p. 248

Standards AF 1.1 **Use variables and appropriate operations to write an expression,** an equation, an inequality, or a system of equations or inequalities **that represents a verbal description (e.g., three less than a number, half as large as area A).**

AF 1.2 **Use the correct order of operations to evaluate algebraic expressions** such as $3(2x + 5)^2$.

Connect *Before* you evaluated expressions. *Now* you will write expressions.

KEY VOCABULARY
- **variable,** *p. 7*
- **algebraic expression,** *p. 7*

You have already evaluated algebraic expressions. In this lesson, you will learn to write algebraic expressions. This involves translating verbal phrases into mathematical symbols.

Many words and phrases suggest mathematical operations. The following common words and phrases indicate addition, subtraction, multiplication, and division.

About the Standards
You will learn more about writing algebraic models (AF 1.1) later in Chapter 5 and in Chapter 6.

Addition	*Subtraction*	*Multiplication*	*Division*
plus	minus	times	divided by
the sum of	the difference of	the product of	the quotient of
increased by	decreased by	multiplied by	separate into
total	fewer than	of	equal parts
more than	less than	twice	
added to	subtracted from		

EXAMPLE 1 Translating Verbal Phrases

AVOID ERRORS
Order is important when translating subtraction and division expressions. The *difference of a number and 6* means $n - 6$, not $6 - n$. The *quotient of a number and 10* means $n \div 10$, not $10 \div n$.

Verbal Phrase	**Algebraic Expression**
The sum of a number and 9	$n + 9$
The difference of a number and 21	$n - 21$
The product of 6 and a number	$6n$
The quotient of 48 and a number	$\dfrac{48}{n}$
The square of a number, increased by 3	$n^2 + 3$

✓ **GUIDED PRACTICE**   **for Example 1**

Write the phrase as an algebraic expression. Let *x* represent the variable.

1. A number increased by 15

2. 8 times a number

3. 4 divided by a number, plus 3

4. 17 less than the cube of a number

VERBAL MODELS Before you write an algebraic expression, it may help to write a verbal model.

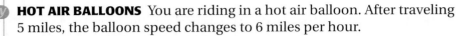

EXAMPLE 2 Writing an Algebraic Expression

HOT AIR BALLOONS You are riding in a hot air balloon. After traveling 5 miles, the balloon speed changes to 6 miles per hour.

a. Write an expression for the total distance after traveling for t hours at 6 mi/h.

b. What is the total distance if you travel for 2 hours at 6 mi/h?

SOLUTION

a. Write a verbal model.

| Original distance | $+$ | Speed | $\cdot$ | Time |

$$5 \quad + \quad 6 \quad \cdot \quad t$$

▸ **Answer** An expression for the total distance is $5 + 6t$.

b. Substitute for t to find the total distance traveled.

$$5 + 6(2) = 17 \qquad \text{Substitute 2 for } t.$$

▸ **Answer** You travel a total of 17 miles.

EXAMPLE 3 Writing an Expression with Two Variables

BASEBALL A baseball pitcher's earned run average (ERA) is calculated by multiplying the quotient of the number of earned runs and the number of innings pitched by 9.

a. Write an expression for a pitcher's ERA.

b. Los Angeles Dodger Derek Lowe gave up 89 earned runs in 222 innings pitched. What was his ERA?

Dodger Stadium in Los Angeles, California

SOLUTION

a. Write a verbal model. Let x be the number of earned runs and y be the number of innings pitched.

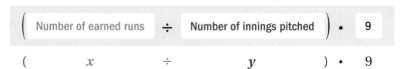

| (Number of earned runs | $\div$ | Number of innings pitched) | $\cdot$ | 9 |

$$(\quad x \quad \div \quad y \quad) \cdot 9$$

▸ **Answer** An expression for a pitcher's ERA is $(x \div y) \cdot 9$.

b. Substitute for x and y to find Derek Lowe's ERA.

$$(89 \div 222) \cdot 9 \approx 3.6 \qquad \text{Substitute 89 for } x \text{ and 222 for } y.$$

▸ **Answer** Derek Lowe's ERA is about 3.6.

5. **WHAT IF?** In Example 2, suppose the speed of the balloon changes to 8 mi/h after traveling 5 miles. Find the total distance if the balloon travels at this speed for 3 hours.

6. **CARNIVAL** At a carnival, the price of an adult ticket is $7 and the price of a child ticket is $4. Write an expression that gives the total cost of tickets for *a* adults and *c* children. Find the total cost of tickets for 3 adults and 4 children.

5.1 **EXERCISES**

HOMEWORK KEY
◆ = **MULTIPLE CHOICE PRACTICE**
Exs. 11, 14, 21, 29–31
○ = **HINTS AND HOMEWORK HELP**
for Exs. 5, 11, 21 at classzone.com

SKILLS • PROBLEM SOLVING • REASONING

1. **VOCABULARY** Copy and complete: An expression that consists of numbers, variables, and operations is called a(n) __?__ .

2. **WRITING** *Explain* why order is important when translating subtraction and division expressions.

SEE EXAMPLE 1
on p. 247
for Exs. 3–14

TRANSLATING VERBAL PHRASES Write the phrase as an algebraic expression. Let *x* represent the variable.

3. Two fifths of a number

4. A number subtracted from 10

5. 12 increased by a number

6. The quotient of a number and 7

7. The sum of a number and 11

8. A number decreased by 15

9. 5 less than 8 times a number

10. A number times 22, divided by *y*

11. ◆ **MULTIPLE CHOICE** Which algebraic expression represents the verbal phrase *the sum of the square of a number and 12*?

A $2x + 12$ **B** $2x - 12$ **C** $x^2 + 12$ **D** $x^2 - 12$

ERROR ANALYSIS *Describe* and correct the error in translating the verbal phrase to an algebraic expression.

12.
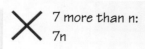
✗ 7 more than n:
7n

13.
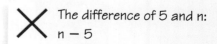
✗ The difference of 5 and n:
n − 5

14. ◆ **MULTIPLE CHOICE** Which algebraic expression represents the verbal phrase *2 minus the product of 6 and x*?

A $2 - 6x$ **B** $6x - 2$ **C** $2 - \dfrac{6}{x}$ **D** $2x - 6$

CONNECT SKILLS TO PROBLEM SOLVING Exercises 15–17 will help you prepare for problem solving.

15. A store sells CDs for $13 each. Write an expression for the store's total sales when x CDs are sold.

16. Your heart beats n times in 15 seconds. Write an expression for the number of times your heart beats in 1 minute.

17. The number c of people it takes to complete a construction job are separated into two equal groups. Write an expression for the number of people in each group.

SEE EXAMPLE 2
on p. 248
for Ex. 18

18. **MULTI-STEP PROBLEM** You buy a hat for $8 and DVDs for $12.80 each.
   a. Write an algebraic expression for the cost to buy a hat and m DVDs.
   b. Evaluate the expression when $m = 5$.

   California @HomeTutor for problem solving help at classzone.com

SEE EXAMPLE 3
on p. 248
for Exs. 19–20

19. **NUTRITION** Rice has 13 grams of protein per serving, beans have 15 grams per serving, and an orange has 2 grams per serving. Write an algebraic expression for the total grams of protein in x servings of rice, y servings of beans, and z oranges.

   California @HomeTutor for problem solving help at classzone.com

20. **MOVIES** At the movies, popcorn costs $2.75 and drinks cost $2.50. Write an expression to find the change you will receive from $20 if you buy p popcorns and d drinks. Find your change from $20 if you treat 3 people to popcorn and 4 people to drinks.

21. ◆ **MULTIPLE CHOICE** You are saving money to buy a bike that costs $152.88. You want to buy the bike in n weeks by saving the same amount of money each day. How much money should you save each day?

   (A) $\dfrac{152.88(7)}{n}$ (B) $\dfrac{152.88}{7n}$ (C) $\dfrac{152.88n}{7}$ (D) $\dfrac{152.88}{n}$

22. **MEASUREMENT** The vine shown below grows the same distance every week. Measure the vine's current length in centimeters. Write an algebraic expression for the length of the vine w weeks from now. Then estimate the vine's length in centimeters 19 weeks from now.

1 week from now   2 weeks from now

23. **TELEVISION** You watch x thirty-minute TV shows and y sixty-minute TV shows in one week, but you don't watch z three-minute commercial breaks during the shows. Write an algebraic expression representing the total number of minutes you spend watching television that week.

Ice Sculptures Ice sculptures can be beautiful additions to special parties and large celebrations. After 4 to 6 hours, a sculpture will begin to lose its detail. A 122-centimeter-thick ice sculpture would take about 192 hours at room temperature to melt completely. It melts at a constant rate of about 0.6 centimeter per hour.

Melting rate: 0.6 cm/h

24. Estimate How much does the sculpture described above melt in 3 hours? in 6 hours?

25. Write and Evaluate Write an expression for how long it would take a sculpture *x* centimeters thick to melt if it melts at the same rate. Then evaluate the expression when *x* = 64 centimeters. Round to the nearest hour.

26. Reasoning What factors might affect the melting rate of the ice sculpture?

27. CHALLENGE The perimeter of a rectangular swimming pool is 220 feet.

   a. Write an expression for the length of the pool in terms of the width *w*.

   b. Write an expression for the area of the pool in terms of the width *w*.

   c. Find the length and area of the pool when *w* = 35 feet.

28. CHALLENGE Jim's car gets 26 miles per gallon on the highway and 18 miles per gallon in city traffic. He has 22 gallons of gasoline in his tank and is going on a trip.

   a. Write an expression for the amount of gas Jim uses driving *h* highway miles and *c* city miles.

   b. Can Jim make a 480 mile trip consisting of 90 miles of city traffic without buying more gasoline? *Explain* your reasoning.

◆ CALIFORNIA STANDARDS SPIRAL REVIEW

NS 1.4 **29.** Which number is an irrational number? *(p. 225)*

   (A) $\frac{3}{4}$ **(B)** 2   **(C)** $\sqrt{5}$ **(D)** $\sqrt{36}$

NS 2.4 **30.** What is the simplified form of the expression $\sqrt{5} \cdot \sqrt{12}$? *(p. 219)*

   (A) $2\sqrt{3}$ **(B)** $\sqrt{15}$ **(C)** $2\sqrt{15}$ **(D)** $\sqrt{60}$

NS 1.7 **31.** A DVD has a wholesale price of $10. The percent markup is 120%. What is the retail price? *(p. 160)*

   (A) $12   **(B)** $18   **(C)** $22   **(D)** $26

5.2 Simplifying Expressions

Standards **AF 1.3** Simplify numerical expressions by applying properties of rational numbers (e.g., identity, inverse, distributive, associative, commutative) and justify the process used.

AF 1.4 Use algebraic terminology (e.g., variable, equation, **term**, **coefficient**, inequality, **expression**, constant) correctly.

Math and TOURISM
Example 4, p. 253

Connect *Before* you wrote algebraic expressions. *Now* you will simplify algebraic expressions.

KEY VOCABULARY
- **term**
- **coefficient**
- **like terms**
- **constant term**

The parts of an expression that are added together are called **terms**. In a term with a variable, the number multiplied by the variable is the **coefficient** of the variable. **Like terms** have identical variable parts with corresponding variables raised to the same power. A term that has no variable is a **constant term**. Constant terms are also like terms.

Coefficients are −1 and 4.   Constant term is 6.

$$-x + 4x + 6$$

$-x$ and $4x$ are like terms.

READING
Note that $-x$ has a coefficient of -1 even though the 1 is not written. Similarly, x has a coefficient of 1.

EXAMPLE 1   Identifying Parts of an Expression

Identify the terms, coefficients, like terms, and constant terms of the expression $5x + 2 - 7x - 3$.

SOLUTION

Write the expression as a sum: $5x + 2 + (-7x) + (-3)$.

Terms: $5x, 2, -7x, -3$ **Like terms:** $5x$ and $-7x$; 2 and -3

Coefficients: $5, -7$ **Constant terms:** $2, -3$

COMBINING LIKE TERMS The distributive property allows you to combine like terms that have variable parts. For example, $2x + 4x = (2 + 4)x = 6x$. An expression is simplified if it has no grouping symbols and if all of the like terms have been combined.

EXAMPLE 2   Combining Like Terms

REVIEW DISTRIBUTIVE PROPERTY
For help with using the distributive property, see p. 48.

a. $3x + 4x = (3 + 4)x$ **Distributive property**

$\qquad = 7x$ **Add inside grouping symbols.**

b. $-9y + 7y + 5z = (-9 + 7)y + 5z$ **Distributive property**

$\qquad\qquad = -2y + 5z$ **Add inside grouping symbols.**

EXAMPLE 3 Simplifying Expressions

a. $2(4 + x) + x = 8 + 2x + x$ **Distributive property**

              $= 8 + 3x$ **Combine like terms.**

b. $-5(3y - 6) + 7y = -15y + 30 + 7y$ **Distributive property**

                 $= -8y + 30$ **Combine like terms.**

✓ **GUIDED PRACTICE**   **for Examples 1, 2, and 3**

1. Identify the terms, coefficients, like terms, and constant terms of the expression $4x - 1 - 4y + 8x + y$.

2. Simplify the expression $17a + 3b - 4a - b$ by combining like terms.

3. Simplify the expression $2z - 3(6 + z)$.

EXAMPLE 4 Simplifying an Expression in Real Life

FIELD TRIPS A seventh grade class is planning a field trip. The students will visit the Monterey Bay Aquarium and the Monterey Museum of Art. The admission fees are $18.95 per student for the aquarium and $5 per student for the museum.

a. Write and simplify an expression for the total cost of admission to the aquarium and the museum.

b. Find the total cost of admission if there are 20 students in the class.

SOLUTION

a. Write a verbal model. Let n represent the number of students in the seventh grade class.

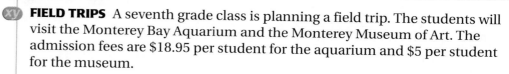

Aquarium admission fee	•	Number of students	+	Museum admission fee	•	Number of students

     $18.95 \cdot n + 5 \cdot n$ **Substitute.**

           $= 23.95n$ **Combine like terms.**

b. Substitute 20 for n to find the total cost of admission.

     $23.95(20) = 479$ **Substitute 20 for n and simplify.**

▶ **Answer** The total cost of admission is $479.

✓ **GUIDED PRACTICE**   **for Example 4**

4. **WHAT IF?** In Example 4, suppose the admission fee for the museum is $12 per student. Find the total cost of admission for 80 students.

5.2 EXERCISES

HOMEWORK KEY

◆ = **MULTIPLE CHOICE PRACTICE**
Exs. 3, 18, 24, 30–32

○ = **HINTS AND HOMEWORK HELP**
for Exs. 5, 11, 27 at classzone.com

SKILLS • PROBLEM SOLVING • REASONING

SEE EXAMPLE 1
on p. 252
for Exs. 1–3

1. **VOCABULARY** Identify the coefficient of the third term in the expression $7x - 3y - 6y + x + 2$.

2. **NOTETAKING SKILLS** Use a *notetaking organizer* like the one on page 246 to write your notes about simplifying an expression.

3. ◆ **MULTIPLE CHOICE** What is the constant term of the expression $6y - 9 + 10y$?

    (A) -9 **(B)** 6   **(C)** 9   **(D)** 10

SEE EXAMPLE 2
on p. 252
for Exs. 4–9

COMBINING LIKE TERMS Simplify the expression by combining like terms.

4. $r + 2s + 3r$

5. $11w + 9z + 3z + 5w$

6. $7a - 2a + 8b - 2b$

7. $3x + 2x + y + 2y - 3$

8. $-3x + 2x - 9y - 2x$

9. $r + 2s - (-3) - s$

SEE EXAMPLE 3
on p. 253
for Exs. 10–20

SIMPLIFYING EXPRESSIONS Simplify the expression.

10. $5(z + 2z) - 4z$

11. $2(2x + 1) + 3x - 5x$

12. $4(3c - 4) + 2 - 4c$

13. $8d - 2(3d - 5d)$

14. $3(a + 4) + b - 5 - a + 7(b - 3)$

15. $7(y - 1.3) + 2.4 - 5.3y$

16. $3.2(2z - 3x) + 4(1.1y + x) - 2z$

17. $5(x + 2) - 5(y + 3) - 2x + 5y$

18. ◆ **MULTIPLE CHOICE** Which expression is equivalent to $5(x + 7) - 2x$?

    (A) $3x + 7$ **(B)** $-5x + 7$ **(C)** $3x + 35$ **(D)** $-x + 35$

ERROR ANALYSIS *Describe* and correct the error in simplifying the expression.

19.
$$2x + 4y - 7x = 2x + 7x - 4y$$
$$= 9x - 4y$$ ✗

20.
$$4(3 + x) + x = 12 + x + x$$
$$= 12 + 2x$$ ✗

CONNECT SKILLS TO PROBLEM SOLVING Exercises 21–23 will help you prepare for problem solving.

21. You buy sandwiches and drinks for x people. Write an expression for the bill before tax if sandwiches cost $4 each and drinks cost $2 each.

22. You buy the same number x of sweaters as you do slacks. Write an expression for the total bill if sweaters cost $14 and slacks cost $17.

23. You drive x hours at a speed of 30 miles per hour and x more hours at a speed of 40 miles per hour. Write an expression for the total distance you drive.

SEE EXAMPLE 4
on p. 253
for Exs. 24–26

24. ◆ **MULTIPLE CHOICE** A recipe for fruit punch calls for two gallons of cranberry juice for every gallon of orange juice. Which expression represents the number of gallons of fruit punch made using x gallons of orange juice?

   A $3x$ **B** $2x$ **C** x **D** $2x^2$

California *@HomeTutor* for problem solving help at classzone.com

25. **GARDEN** You want to place a fence around your section of a community garden that has the dimensions shown in the diagram. Write and simplify an expression for the perimeter of your section of the garden. Find the perimeter when $x = 3$ ft.

California *@HomeTutor* for problem solving help at classzone.com

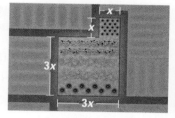

26. **EXERCISE** You are training for a triathlon. You swim at a speed of 2 miles per hour, bike at a speed of 25 miles per hour, and run at a speed of 8 miles per hour. Write and simplify an expression for the total distance you travel if you spend t hours training for each activity. Find the distance you travel if you spend a half-hour training for each activity.

27. **PUZZLE PROBLEM** You have twice as many nickels as pennies, and three times as many dimes as quarters in your pocket. Write and simplify an expression for the total number of coins in your pocket if you have m pennies and n quarters.

28. **CHALLENGE** Simplify the expression $7x^2[6yz^3 - 2z^3(y + 4)]$. Show and justify each step.

29. **CHALLENGE** You exercise for 45 minutes by walking and playing basketball. You burn 6 calories per minute walking and 9 calories per minute playing basketball. Write and simplify an expression for the total calories you burn while exercising if you spend w minutes walking. Then find the total number of calories burned if you walk for 20 minutes.

◆ CALIFORNIA STANDARDS SPIRAL REVIEW

NS 2.1   30. Which fraction is equivalent to $\left(\frac{3}{4}\right)^{-3}$? *(p. 206)*

   A $\frac{27}{64}$ **B** $\frac{9}{16}$ **C** $\frac{16}{9}$ **D** $\frac{64}{27}$

NS 2.2   31. What is the sum of $\frac{2}{3}$ and $\frac{1}{7}$? *(p. 91)*

   A $\frac{3}{10}$ **B** $\frac{11}{21}$ **C** $\frac{11}{14}$ **D** $\frac{17}{21}$

AF 1.1   32. Jane purchases 7 potted flowers and 2 bottles of plant food. Which expression gives the total cost of Jane's purchases if each potted flower costs x dollars and each bottle of plant food costs y dollars? *(p. 247)*

   A $7x + 2y$ **B** $2x + 7y$ **C** $9(x + y)$ **D** $7(x + 2y)$

5.3 Modeling One-Step Equations

MATERIALS · algebra tiles

Standards

AF 1.4 Use algebraic terminology (e.g., variable, **equation**, term, coefficient, inequality, expression, constant) **correctly**.

QUESTION   How can algebra tiles be used to solve addition equations?

To solve an *equation* such as $x + 3 = 8$, find the value of the variable that makes the equation true. You can do this using algebra tiles.

EXPLORE   Model and solve $x + 3 = 8$

| **STEP 1** | **Model** $x + 3 = 8$ using algebra tiles. |

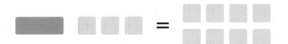

| **STEP 2** | **Remove** three 1-tiles from each side so the x-tile is by itself. |

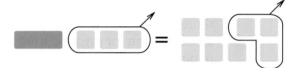

| **STEP 3** | **Write** the solution. The solution of the equation is 5. |

DRAW CONCLUSIONS   Use your observations to complete these exercises

Use algebra tiles to model each step. Draw a picture of each step.

1. **Step 1**   Model the equation $x + 5 = 7$.

   Step 2   Remove five 1-tiles from each side.

   Step 3   Find the solution.

2. **Step 1**   Model the equation $8 + x = 13$.

   Step 2   Remove eight 1-tiles from each side.

   Step 3   Find the solution.

Use algebra tiles to model and solve the equation.

3. $x + 4 = 9$ 4. $3 + x = 7$ 5. $6 = x + 2$ 6. $7 + x = 9$

7. **REASONING**   Consider an equation of the form $x + a = b$. *Explain* how to solve this equation without using algebra tiles.

5.3 Solving Equations Using Addition or Subtraction

Standards AF 1.1 **Use variables and appropriate operations to write** an expression, **an equation,** an inequality, or a system of equations or inequalities **that represents a verbal description** (e.g., three less than a number, half as large as area A).

AF 1.4 **Use algebraic terminology** (e.g., variable, **equation,** term, coefficient, inequality, expression, constant) **correctly.**

Math and **SPORTS**
Example 4, p. 259

Connect *Before* you added and subtracted integers. *Now* you will use addition and subtraction to solve equations.

KEY VOCABULARY
• equation
• solution of an equation
• equivalent equations
• inverse operation

An **equation** is a mathematical sentence formed by placing an equal sign (=) between two expressions. A **solution of an equation** with one variable is a number you can substitute for the variable to make the equation true.

For example, 3 is a solution of the equation $x + 2 = 5$ because when you substitute 3 for x, you obtain the true statement $3 + 2 = 5$.

EXAMPLE 1 Checking Solutions

Tell whether the value of the variable is a solution of $n - 8 = 20$.

a. $n = 12$

b. $n = 28$

SOLUTION

READING
The $\stackrel{?}{=}$ symbol means *are these values equal?* The $\neq$ symbol means *is not equal to.*

a. $n - 8 = 20$ **Write original equation.**

    $12 - 8 \stackrel{?}{=} 20$ **Substitute 12 for *n*.**

       $4 \neq 20$ ✗   **Simplify.**

▶ **Answer** 12 is not a solution.

b. $n - 8 = 20$ **Write original equation.**

    $28 - 8 \stackrel{?}{=} 20$ **Substitute 28 for *n*.**

      $20 = 20$ ✓   **Simplify.**

▶ **Answer** 28 is a solution.

✓ **GUIDED PRACTICE** for Example 1

Tell whether the value of the variable is a solution of the equation.

1. $a + 9 = 16$; $a = 7$ **2.** $\frac{88}{y} = 8$; $y = 8$ **3.** $7n = 13$; $n = 2$

4. $15 - n = 4$; $n = 11$ **5.** $8x = 32$; $x = 3$ **6.** $\frac{r}{12} = 4$; $r = 48$

EQUIVALENT EQUATIONS You can model and solve an equation by thinking of the equation as a "balanced" set of numbers, as shown below. In the model, removing three 1-tiles from each side of the scale keeps the scale in balance.

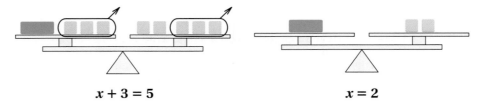

$$x + 3 = 5 \qquad\qquad x = 2$$

When you perform the same operation on each side of an equation, the result is a new equation that has the same solution. Equations that have the same solution are **equivalent equations**.

You solve an equation by using *inverse operations* to write equivalent equations. An **inverse operation** is an operation that "undoes" another operation. Addition and subtraction are inverse operations.

KEY CONCEPT *For Your Notebook*

Subtraction Property of Equality

Words   Subtracting the same number from each side of an equation produces an equivalent equation.

Numbers   If $x + 5 = 7$, then $x + 5 - 5 = 7 - 5$, or $x = 2$.

Algebra   If $x + a = b$, then $x + a - a = b - a$, or $x = b - a$.

EXAMPLE 2 Solving an Equation Using Subtraction

$$x + 8 = -15 \qquad \text{Original equation}$$
$$\underline{\;\;-8 \qquad -8\;\;} \qquad \begin{array}{l}\text{Subtract 8 from each side.}\\ \text{(Subtraction property of equality)}\end{array}$$
$$x \;\;\;\;= -23 \qquad \text{Simplify.}$$

▶ **Answer** The solution is -23.

CHECK
$$x + 8 = -15 \qquad \text{Write original equation.}$$
$$-23 + 8 \stackrel{?}{=} -15 \qquad \text{Substitute } -23 \text{ for } x.$$
$$-15 = -15 \checkmark \qquad \text{Solution checks.}$$

Animated Math

For an interactive example of solving an equation using subtraction, go to **classzone.com**.

✓ **GUIDED PRACTICE**   for Example 2

Solve the equation. Check your solution.

7. $x + 9 = 20$ **8.** $-10 = 3 + y$ **9.** $x + 12 = 18$

You can also use the *addition property of equality* to solve an equation.

KEY CONCEPT *For Your Notebook*

Addition Property of Equality

Words Adding the same number to each side of an equation produces an equivalent equation.

Numbers If $x - 2 = 6$, then $x - 2 + 2 = 6 + 2$, or $x = 8$.

Algebra If $x - a = b$, then $x - a + a = b + a$, or $x = b + a$.

EXAMPLE 3 **Solving an Equation Using Addition**

$$c - 4.5 = 13 \qquad \text{Original equation}$$

$$c - 4.5 + 4.5 = 13 + 4.5 \qquad \begin{array}{l}\text{Add 4.5 to each side.}\\ \text{(Addition property of equality)}\end{array}$$

$$c = 17.5 \qquad \text{Simplify.}$$

▶ **Answer** The solution is 17.5.

CHECK $17.5 - 4.5 \overset{?}{=} 13 \qquad$ Substitute 17.5 for *c* in original equation.

$$13 = 13 \checkmark \qquad \text{Solution checks.}$$

Animated Math

For an interactive example of solving an equation using addition, go to **classzone.com.**

EXAMPLE 4 **Using a Model**

 ROCK CLIMBING A cliff has a height of about 1500 feet. If you have already climbed 675 feet, how much farther do you have to climb to reach the top?

SOLUTION

Let *x* represent the distance left to climb.

$$1500 = x + 675 \qquad \text{Write an algebraic model.}$$

$$1500 - 675 = x + 675 - 675 \qquad \text{Subtract 675 from each side.}$$

$$825 = x \qquad \text{Simplify.}$$

▶ **Answer** You have about 825 feet left to climb.

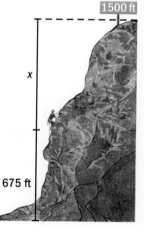

✓ **GUIDED PRACTICE** for Examples 3 and 4

10. Solve the equation $2 = z - 6.4$. Check your solution.

11. SEASHELLS Lucinda combines her 49 seashells with Jerry's seashells, for a total of 162. How many seashells did Jerry have?

5.3 EXERCISES

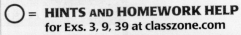
SKILLS • PROBLEM SOLVING • REASONING

1. VOCABULARY Name two inverse operations.

2. WRITING *Explain* why $7 = x + 9$ and $6 + x = 4$ are equivalent equations.

SEE EXAMPLE 1
on p. 257
for Exs. 3–8

CHECKING SOLUTIONS Tell whether the given value is a solution.

3. $35 - x = 21; x = 16$

4. $75 \div x = 5; x = 15$

5. $7x = 84; x = 14$

6. $x + 29 = 42; x = 13$

7. $15 + b = 28; b = 13$

8. $37 - d = 14; d = 21$

SEE EXAMPLES 2 AND 3
on pp. 258–259
for Exs. 9–24

SOLVING EQUATIONS Solve the equation. Check your solution.

9. $x + 10 = 16$

10. $12 = x - 8$

11. $43 = a - 21$

12. $23 = 6 + n$

13. $y - 15 = 9$

14. $2 + x - 4 = 12$

15. $d + 6(3) = -11$

16. $p + 3.4 = 4.4$

17. $1.76 = a - 2.94$

18. $\frac{2}{3} = d + \frac{1}{3}$

19. $y - \frac{3}{4} = \frac{1}{4}$

20. $3x - 2x + 8 - 10 = 7$

ERROR ANALYSIS *Describe* and correct the error in solving the equation.

21.
$$\times \quad \begin{aligned} x + 10 &= 50 \\ x + 10 + 10 &= 50 + 10 \\ x &= 60 \end{aligned}$$

22.
$$\times \quad \begin{aligned} -4 + x &= 10 \\ -4 + x + 4 &= 10 - 4 \\ x &= 6 \end{aligned}$$

23. ◆ **MULTIPLE CHOICE** Which equation has a solution of 5?

A $x - 5 = 10$ **B** $8 = x - 3$ **C** $13 + x = 18$ **D** $x + 5 = -10$

24. ◆ **MULTIPLE CHOICE** What is the solution of $-4 + x = 8$?

A -12 **B** -4 **C** 4 **D** 12

MODELING Write an equation to model the statement. Then solve for *n*.

25. The sum of a number *n* and twelve is twenty-five.

26. Thirty-five is the sum of a number *n* and eight.

27. Three less than a number *n* is negative sixteen.

GEOMETRY Write and solve an equation to find the missing side length.

28. Perimeter = 16 ft

2 ft
x
3 ft
6 ft

29. Perimeter = 97 cm

24 cm
k
38 cm
16 cm

30. Perimeter = 40 m

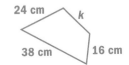
11 m
7 m
8 m
y

CONNECT SKILLS TO PROBLEM SOLVING Exercises 31–33 will help you prepare for problem solving.

Write a verbal model to represent the situation.

31. At 62 inches tall, you are 5 inches taller than your sister. What is your sister's height h?

32. An item that usually costs $2.29 will cost $1.79 with a coupon. What is the value c of the coupon?

33. The mean temperature for February 4 in Chicago is 3°F below the mean temperature of 27°F for all of February in Chicago. What is the mean temperature T for February 4?

SEE EXAMPLE 4 on p. 259 for Exs. 34–35

34. SCHOOL SUPPLIES You need to buy new school supplies. The price of the items is $54.99, but after the sales tax t is added, the cost is $58.29. Write and solve an equation to find the sales tax. Check your solution.

California @HomeTutor for problem solving help at classzone.com

35. ◆ MULTIPLE CHOICE Five less than the total number of students x is twenty-four. Which equation represents the statement?

(**A**) $5 - x = 24$ (**B**) $24 - 5 = x$ (**C**) $x + 24 = 5$ (**D**) $x - 5 = 24$

California @HomeTutor for problem solving help at classzone.com

36. SHORT RESPONSE *Explain* how to use inverse operations to solve equations of the form $x + a = b$ and $x - a = b$. Give two examples.

37. REASONING Without solving the equation $-10 + y = 5$, decide whether its solution is positive or negative. *Explain* your reasoning.

READING IN MATH Read the information below for Exercises 38–40.

Sea Lions Steller sea lions live in the North Pacific Rim, from central California to Japan. Pups are about 45 inches long at birth. Female sea lions reach their full adult size of about 104 inches in 7 years. Male sea lions reach their full size of about 128 inches in 12 years. These lengths (and also their weights) make the Steller sea lion the largest of all the eared seals.

38. Calculate Write and solve an equation to find the number of inches a female Steller sea lion grows between birth and adulthood.

39. Calculate Write and solve an equation to find the number of inches a male Steller sea lion grows between birth and adulthood.

Steller sea lions, common in California

40. Predict What is the average growth per year between birth and adulthood for a female and a male Steller sea lion? Round to the nearest inch. After five years, is a male or a female longer?

41. SHOPPING You spend a total of $11.09 at the store. You buy two bottles of water for $1.29 each, a magazine for $3.50, trail mix for $1.49, and a package of markers for m dollars.

   a. Write an equation for the situation. (Assume there is no sales tax.)

   b. Solve the equation to find the cost of the package of markers.

CHALLENGE Find the solutions of the equation.

42. $|x| - 3 = 14$ **43.** $|x| + 5 = 25$ **44.** $|x - 2| = 7$

45. CHALLENGE The cost b of a book bag is $3 more than the cost s of a pair of sneakers. The cost of the sneakers is $6 more than the cost c of a DVD, which is $8 less than the cost t of a T-shirt. The sneakers cost $18. Write and solve three equations to find the cost of the book bag, the DVD, and the T-shirt.

◆ CALIFORNIA STANDARDS SPIRAL REVIEW

AF 1.3   **46.** What is the simplified form of the expression $5x - 6x - 9y + x$? *(p. 252)*

    (A) $-2x - 9y$ **(B)** $-9y$ **(C)** $2x - 9y$ **(D)** $9y$

AF 1.2   **47.** What is the value of $\dfrac{3(c - p)}{p + 2}$ when $c = 4$ and $p = 1$? *(p. 5)*

    (A) -1 **(B)** $\dfrac{5}{4}$ **(C)** 2 **(D)** 3

AF 1.1   **48.** A CD player costs $35 and CDs cost $15 each. Which expression represents the total cost of the CD player and n CDs? *(p. 247)*

    (A) $35n + 15$ **(B)** $50 + n$ **(C)** $35 + 15n$ **(D)** $35 + \dfrac{15}{n}$

QUIZ *for Lessons 5.1–5.3*

Write the phrase as an algebraic expression. Let x represent the variable.
(p. 247)

  1. The difference of a number and 10   **2.** The quotient of 6 and a number

Simplify the expression. *(p. 252)*

  3. $7x - 4x$ **4.** $5y - x + 3x - y$ **5.** $3(x + y) - 3x - 2y$

Solve the equation. Check your solution. *(p. 257)*

  6. $x - 3 = 7$ **7.** $15 + x = 24$ **8.** $x - 7 - 4 = 13$

  9. $r + 2 = 7$ **10.** $-6 + m = 4$ **11.** $13 + t = 4$

12. COINS Jeremy has 25 coins. He combines his coins with Stephanie's coins to get a total of 105 coins. Write and solve an equation to find the number of coins Stephanie orginally had. *(p. 257)*

  EXTRA PRACTICE for Lesson 5.3, p. 751   🔍 **ONLINE QUIZ** at classzone.com

5.4 Solving Equations Using Multiplication or Division

Math and
ENTERTAINMENT
Ex. 44, p. 266

Standards   **AF 4.2** **Solve** multistep **problems involving** rate, average speed, distance, and time or **a direct variation**.

Connect   *Before* you solved equations using addition and subtraction. *Now* you will solve equations using multiplication and division.

KEY VOCABULARY

• **equivalent equations,** *p. 258*

• **inverse operations,** *p. 258*

Multiplication and division are inverse operations that can help you solve equations. You can use multiplication to undo division.

KEY CONCEPT   *For Your Notebook*

Multiplication Property of Equality

Words   Multiplying each side of an equation by the same nonzero number produces an equivalent equation.

Numbers   If $\frac{x}{3} = 4$, then $\frac{x}{3} \cdot 3 = 4 \cdot 3$, or $x = 12$.

Algebra   If $\frac{x}{a} = b$ and $a \neq 0$, then $\frac{x}{a} \cdot a = b \cdot a$, or $x = ab$.

EXAMPLE 1   Solving an Equation Using Multiplication

$$\frac{y}{3} = 5 \qquad \text{Original equation}$$

$$\frac{y}{3} \cdot 3 = 5 \cdot 3 \qquad \begin{array}{l}\text{Multiply each side by 3.}\\ \text{(Multiplication property of equality)}\end{array}$$

$$y = 15 \qquad \text{Simplify.}$$

▶ **Answer** The solution is 15.

CHECK ANSWERS
Remember to check your answer by substituting it in the original equation.

CHECK $\dfrac{y}{3} = 5$ **Write original equation.**

$\dfrac{15}{3} \stackrel{?}{=} 5$ **Substitute 15 for *y*.**

$5 = 5$ ✓   **Solution checks.**

✓ **GUIDED PRACTICE**   **for Example 1**

Solve the equation. Check your solution.

1. $21 = \dfrac{x}{9}$ **2.** $\dfrac{a}{8} = 4$ **3.** $\dfrac{x}{3.5} = 14$ **4.** $\dfrac{b}{12} = 3$

You can use division to solve equations involving multiplication.

KEY CONCEPT   *For Your Notebook*

Division Property of Equality

Words   Dividing each side of an equation by the same nonzero number produces an equivalent equation.

Numbers   If $2x = 24$, then $\frac{2x}{2} = \frac{24}{2}$, or $x = 12$.

Algebra   If $ax = b$ and $a \neq 0$, then $\frac{ax}{a} = \frac{b}{a}$, or $x = \frac{b}{a}$.

EXAMPLE 2 **Solving an Equation Using Division**

REVIEW DIVISION
For help with dividing negative numbers and decimal numbers, see pp. 36 and 144.

$-2.5x = 20$ **Original equation**

$\dfrac{-2.5x}{-2.5} = \dfrac{20}{-2.5}$ **Divide each side by -2.5. (Division property of equality)**

$x = -8$ **Simplify.**

EXAMPLE 3 **Writing and Solving an Equation**

 SPORTS Ninety basketball players show up for a tournament. Write and solve an equation to find how many five-person teams can be formed.

About the Standards

In Example 3, you reason mathematically using a variety of methods, including words, numbers, symbols, and models (MR 2.5).

SOLUTION

Let t be the number of five-person teams that can be formed.

Total number of people	=	Number per team	·	Number of teams

$90 = 5t$ **Write an algebraic model.**

$\dfrac{90}{5} = \dfrac{5t}{5}$ **Divide each side by 5.**

$18 = t$ **Simplify.**

▶ **Answer** Eighteen five-person teams can be formed.

Tournament: 90 players

✓ **GUIDED PRACTICE**   for Examples 2 and 3

Solve the equation. Check your solution.

5. $9x = 54$ **6.** $7y = 28$ **7.** $48 = -3x$ **8.** $4.2y = 21$

9. TEAM SIZE A teacher divided a class into four teams, with 6 students per team. Write and solve a division equation to find the class size.

REPEATING DECIMALS To write a repeating decimal as a fraction or mixed number, let the decimal equal x. Then form an equivalent equation by multiplying both sides of the original equation by 10^n, where n is the number of repeating digits. Finally, subtract the equations and solve for x.

EXAMPLE 4 **Writing a Repeating Decimal as a Fraction**

Write $0.\overline{48}$ as a fraction.

SOLUTION

STEP 1 Let $x = 0.\overline{48}$, or $0.484848\ldots$.

STEP 2 **Multiply** each side of the equation by 10^2, or 100, because the decimal has 2 repeating digits: $100x = 48.\overline{48}$, or $48.484848\ldots$.

STEP 3 **Subtract** x from $100x$.

$$
\begin{array}{r}
100x = 48.484848\ldots \\
-\ \ x = \ \ 0.484848\ldots \\
\hline
99x = 48.000000\ldots
\end{array}
$$

STEP 4 **Solve** for x and simplify. $\quad x = \dfrac{48}{99} = \dfrac{16}{33}$

▶ **Answer** The decimal $0.\overline{48}$ is equivalent to the fraction $\dfrac{16}{33}$.

✓ **GUIDED PRACTICE** for Example 4

Write the decimal as a fraction.

10. $0.\overline{7}$ **11.** $0.\overline{1}$ **12.** $0.\overline{25}$ **13.** $-0.\overline{36}$

5.4 EXERCISES

HOMEWORK KEY
◆ = **MULTIPLE CHOICE PRACTICE**
Exs. 27, 28, 45, 54–56
○ = **HINTS** AND **HOMEWORK HELP**
for Exs. 3, 11, 47 at classzone.com

SKILLS • PROBLEM SOLVING • REASONING

1. VOCABULARY Copy and complete: Multiplying each side of an equation by the same nonzero number produces a(n) __?__.

2. WRITING *Explain* why division is used to solve equations involving multiplication.

SEE EXAMPLES 1 AND 2
on pp. 263–264
for Exs. 3–28

INVERSE OPERATIONS *Describe* an inverse operation that will undo the given operation.

3. Multiplying by 5 **4.** Dividing by -9 **5.** Adding -6

6. Subtracting 10 **7.** Multiplying by -3 **8.** Subtracting -4

SOLVING EQUATIONS Solve the equation. Check your solution.

9. $\dfrac{p}{2} = 9$ **10.** $18 = 6g$ **(11.)** $3b = 39$ **12.** $44 = 4.4p$

13. $25 = \dfrac{h}{14}$ **14.** $14h = 35$ **15.** $\dfrac{r}{18} = 12$ **16.** $12m = -25.2$

17. $7 = \dfrac{k}{15}$ **18.** $-2.4k = 48$ **19.** $\dfrac{y}{-1.5} = 21$ **20.** $-21 = -0.7p$

21. $48 = 96z$ **22.** $\dfrac{z}{1.8} = 5$ **23.** $14 = \dfrac{x}{5}$ **24.** $12 = -2z$

ERROR ANALYSIS *Describe* and correct the error in solving the equation.

25.

$$20 = 5z$$
$$\dfrac{20}{5} = \dfrac{5z}{5}$$
$$20 = z$$ ✗

26.

$$\dfrac{x}{-7} = 56$$
$$\dfrac{x}{-7} \cdot 7 = 56 \cdot 7$$
$$x = 392$$ ✗

27. ◆ **MULTIPLE CHOICE** What is the solution of $-3 = 0.3a$?

   A -30 **B** -10 **C** 3 **D** 30

28. ◆ **MULTIPLE CHOICE** Which operation should you perform to solve the equation $4x = -2$?

   A Divide each side by 4.   **B** Multiply each side by 4.

   C Divide each side by -2.   **D** Multiply each side by -2.

SEE EXAMPLE 4
on p. 265
for Exs. 29–40

DECIMALS AS FRACTIONS Write the decimal as a fraction.

29. $0.\overline{8}$ **30.** $0.\overline{53}$ **31.** $0.\overline{21}$ **32.** $-0.\overline{6}$

33. $0.\overline{635}$ **34.** $-0.\overline{187}$ **35.** $-0.\overline{15}$ **36.** $4.\overline{025}$

37. $-0.\overline{3}$ **38.** $0.\overline{758}$ **39.** $-2.\overline{8}$ **40.** $9.6\overline{5}$

CONNECT SKILLS TO PROBLEM SOLVING Exercises 41–43 will help you prepare for problem solving.

Write an equation representing the situation.

41. Joanne drove for 3 hours at a constant speed of r miles per hour. She traveled a total of 174 miles.

42. Maria purchases 15 boxes of popcorn for a total of $45. Each box of popcorn costs x dollars.

43. Peanut butter contains an average of 45 peanuts per ounce. There are a total of x peanuts in 12 ounces of peanut butter.

SEE EXAMPLE 3
on p. 264
for Exs. 44–49

44. **THEATER** A movie theater has 1950 seats. Each row has 30 seats. Write and solve an equation to find how many rows of seats there are.

California @HomeTutor for problem solving help at classzone.com

◆ = **MULTIPLE CHOICE PRACTICE**   ○ = **HINTS AND HOMEWORK HELP** at classzone.com

45. ◆ **MULTIPLE CHOICE** A pizza shop cuts a pizza into 8 slices. One slice costs $1.10. Which equation can you use to find the cost x of the whole pizza?

A $1.10x = 8$ **B** $8x = 1.10$ **C** $\frac{x}{8} = 1.10$ **D** $x = \frac{1.10}{8}$

California @HomeTutor for problem solving help at classzone.com

WATERFALLS In Exercises 46–48, use the graph below. Write and solve an equation to find the unknown height. Use the graph to check whether your solution is reasonable.

46. The height of Skykje Falls in Norway is 1.25 times the height of Feather Falls in California.

47. The height of Comet Falls in Washington is $\frac{1}{5}$ the height of Takkakaw Falls in British Columbia.

48. The height of Angel Falls in Venezuela is 20 times the height of Niagara Falls in Canada and the United States.

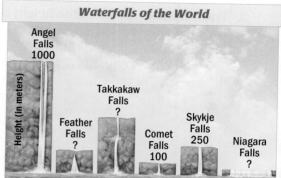

49. **BASKETBALL** A basketball team plays 20 games and averages 65 points per game. Write a verbal model involving division for finding the total number of points for the season. Write and solve a related equation. The team's goal for next season is to score 5 more points per game for 20 games. *Explain* how to adjust the equation to find the total number of points for next season. Then solve.

CHALLENGE Rewrite the formula so that the indicated varible is by itself.

50. $A = \frac{1}{2}bh$; $b = $ __?__ **51.** $V = \frac{1}{3}Bh$; $h = $ __?__ **52.** $V = \pi r^2 h$; $h = $ __?__

53. **CHALLENGE** The speed of a river's current is one-third the speed you row. You row with the current and travel 36 miles in 3 hours. What is the speed of the river's current?

◆ CALIFORNIA STANDARDS SPIRAL REVIEW

NS 2.2

54. What is the difference of $\frac{5}{6}$ and $\frac{2}{9}$? *(p. 91)*

A $\frac{1}{5}$ **B** $\frac{7}{15}$ **C** $\frac{11}{18}$ **D** 1

NS 1.5

55. Which decimal is equivalent to $\frac{2}{5}$? *(p. 113)*

A 0.2 **B** 0.4 **C** $0.\overline{4}$ **D** 2.5

NS 1.7

56. An MP3 player is on sale for 15% off $200. How much is deducted from the original price when you purchase the MP3 player? *(p. 160)*

A $10 **B** $20 **C** $30 **D** $40

Multiple Choice Practice for Lessons 5.1–5.4

1. What is the solution of $\frac{x}{12} = 6$? **AF 1.1**

   (**A**) 2   (**B**) 6

   (**C**) 36   (**D**) 72

2. The difference between the height of the CN Tower in Toronto, Canada, and the height of the Empire State building in New York is 565 feet. Which equation can you use to find the height C of the CN Tower? **AF 1.1, MR 1.1**

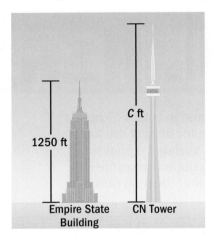

   (**A**) $C + 565 = 1250$

   (**B**) $C - 1250 = 565$

   (**C**) $1250 - C = 565$

   (**D**) $C + 1250 = 565$

3. A football team plays 16 games and averages 93 rushing yards per game. Which equation can you use to find the total number of rushing yards for the season? **AF 1.1**

   (**A**) $\frac{93}{16} = x$ (**B**) $93x = 16$

   (**C**) $\frac{16}{x} = 93$ (**D**) $\frac{x}{16} = 93$

4. Which expression is equivalent to $-4(x + 10) - 30$? **AF 1.3**

   (**A**) $-4x + 10$ (**B**) $-4x + 70$

   (**C**) $-4x - 70$ (**D**) $4x - 10$

5. Lola traveled from San Mateo to Palo Alto by train. The train traveled at an average speed of 35 miles per hour. The distance between the two cities is shown in the diagram. Approximately how many minutes did she spend on the train? **AF 4.2, MR 2.8**

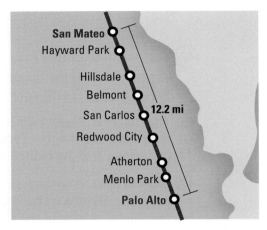

   (**A**) 12 min   (**B**) 21 min

   (**C**) 23 min   (**D**) 35 min

6. What is the solution of $x + 17 = 27$? **AF 1.1**

   (**A**) 7   (**B**) 10

   (**C**) 44   (**D**) 459

7. Which simplified expression represents the perimeter of the triangle below? **AF 1.3**

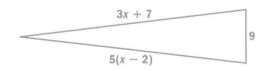

   (**A**) $8x + 6$ (**B**) $2x + 16$

   (**C**) $5x + 9$ (**D**) $8x + 29$

8. Which algebraic expression represents the verbal phrase *3 plus the quotient of 9 and x*? **AF 1.1**

   (**A**) $3 + \frac{9}{x}$ (**B**) $3 + \frac{x}{9}$

   (**C**) $9 + \frac{x}{3}$ (**D**) $3x + 9$

5.5 Modeling Two-Step Equations

MATERIALS · algebra tiles

Standards

AF 4.1 Solve two-step linear equations and inequalities **in one variable over the rational numbers,** interpret the solution or solutions in the context from which they arose, **and verify the reasonableness of the results.**

QUESTION How can algebra tiles be used to solve two-step equations?

A *two-step equation* is an equation you solve using two operations. You can use algebra tiles to model and solve two-step equations.

EXPLORE Model and solve $2x + 3 = 7$

STEP 1 **Model** the equation $2x + 3 = 7$.

STEP 2 **Remove** three 1-tiles from each side.

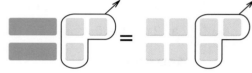

STEP 3 **Notice** there are two x-tiles, so divide the remaining tiles on each side into two identical groups.

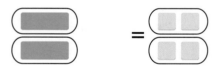

STEP 4 **Write** the solution. The solution is 2.

DRAW CONCLUSIONS Use your observations to complete these exercises

1. Model each step described below. Draw a picture of each step.

    Step 1 Use algebra tiles to model the equation $3x + 1 = 10$.

    Step 2 Remove one 1-tile from each side.

    Step 3 Divide the remaining tiles into three identical groups.

    Step 4 Solve the equation. Check your solution.

Use algebra tiles to model and solve the equation.

  2. $3x + 1 = 7$ **3.** $2x + 4 = 10$ **4.** $2x + 3 = 5$ **5.** $4x + 1 = 9$

  6. **REASONING** *Explain* what kinds of equations are difficult or impossible to solve using algebra tiles. Give an example.

5.5 Solving Two-Step Equations

Standards

AF 1.1 Use variables and appropriate operations to write an expression, **an equation**, an inequality, or a system of equations or inequalities **that represents a verbal description** (e.g., three less than a number, half as large as area A).

AF 4.1 Solve two-step linear equations and inequalities **in one variable over the rational numbers, interpret the solution or solutions in the context from which they arose, and verify the reasonableness of the results.**

Math and **READING**
Ex. 36, p. 274

Connect *Before* you solved one-step equations. *Now* you will solve two-step equations.

KEY VOCABULARY
• **equation,** *p. 257*
• **solution of an equation,** *p. 257*

In Lessons 5.3 and 5.4, you solved one-step equations by using a single inverse operation. Two-step equations involve two operations and therefore require using two inverse operations to solve.

EXAMPLE 1 **Solving Two-Step Equations**

 Solve the equation. Check your solution.

a. $2x + 1 = 5$ **b.** $3x - 4 = 11$

SOLUTION

a. $2x + 1 = 5$ Write original equation.

$2x + 1 - 1 = 5 - 1$ Subtract 1 from each side. (Subtraction property of equality)

$2x = 4$ Simplify.

$\dfrac{2x}{2} = \dfrac{4}{2}$ Divide each side by 2. (Division property of equality)

$x = 2$ Simplify.

▶ **Answer** The solution is 2.

CHECK $2(2) + 1 \overset{?}{=} 5$ Substitute 2 for *x*.

$5 = 5 ✓$ Solution checks.

b. $3x - 4 = 11$ Write original equation.

$3x - 4 + 4 = 11 + 4$ Add 4 to each side. (Addition property of equality)

$3x = 15$ Simplify.

$\dfrac{3x}{3} = \dfrac{15}{3}$ Divide each side by 3. (Division property of equality)

$x = 5$ Simplify.

▶ **Answer** The solution is 5.

CHECK $3(5) - 4 \overset{?}{=} 11$ Substitute 5 for *x*.

$11 = 11 ✓$ Solution checks.

1. Solve the equation $3x + 5 = 17$. Check your solution.

You can solve some problems by writing and solving two-step equations. You can use a verbal model to help you write a two-step equation.

EXAMPLE 2 ◆ **Multiple Choice Practice**

A zoo currently spends $1580 to feed its American flamingos. Next year its budget for feeding the flamingos will be $2370, and it will cost $395 to feed each additional flamingo the zoo buys. How many new flamingos can the zoo buy next year?

(A) 2   (B) 3   (C) 4   (D) 6

ANOTHER WAY

For an alternative method for solving the problem in Example 2, turn to page 276 for the **Problem Solving Workshop**.

SOLUTION

Write and solve a two-step equation to find the number of flamingos. Write a verbal model. Let n be the number of additional flamingos.

Budget available	=	Cost of each new flamingo	•	Number of new flamingos	+	Cost of existing flamingos

$$2370 = 395n + 1580 \qquad \text{Write an algebraic model.}$$
$$2370 - 1580 = 395n + 1580 - 1580 \qquad \text{Subtract 1580 from each side.}$$
$$790 = 395n \qquad \text{Simplify.}$$
$$\frac{790}{395} = \frac{395n}{395} \qquad \text{Divide each side by 395.}$$
$$2 = n \qquad \text{Simplify.}$$

The zoo can buy 2 new flamingos next year.

▶ **Answer** The correct answer is A. (A) (B) (C) (D)

EXAMPLE 3   **Solving with a Variable in the Numerator**

 Solve $\frac{x}{2} - 14 = 8$.

$$\frac{x}{2} - 14 = 8 \qquad \text{Write original equation.}$$
$$\frac{x}{2} - 14 + 14 = 8 + 14 \qquad \text{Add 14 to each side. (Addition property of equality)}$$
$$\frac{x}{2} = 22 \qquad \text{Simplify.}$$
$$\frac{x}{2} \cdot 2 = 22 \cdot 2 \qquad \begin{array}{l}\text{Multiply each side by 2.} \\ \text{(Multiplication property of equality)}\end{array}$$
$$x = 44 \qquad \text{Simplify.}$$

▶ **Answer** The solution is 44.

EXAMPLE 4 Solving with a Negative Coefficient

Solve $7 = 5 - 8x$.

$7 = 5 - 8x$	Write original equation.
$7 - 5 = 5 - 8x - 5$	Subtract 5 from each side. (Subtraction property of equality)
$2 = -8x$	Simplify.
$\dfrac{2}{-8} = \dfrac{-8x}{-8}$	Divide each side by -8. (Division property of equality)
$-\dfrac{1}{4} = x$	Simplify.

✓ **GUIDED PRACTICE** for Examples 2, 3, and 4

2. **FEEDING COSTS** It costs a zoo $1150 this year to feed tortoises. Each new tortoise costs $575 to feed. A zoo's budget for tortoise food next year is $2875. How many new tortoises can the zoo buy next year?

Solve the equation. Check your solution.

3. $13 = 11 + \dfrac{y}{3}$ 4. $\dfrac{z}{5} - 3 = 4$ 5. $-6x + 5 = 23$ 6. $6 = 16 - a$

5.5 EXERCISES

HOMEWORK KEY

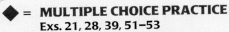

◆ = **MULTIPLE CHOICE PRACTICE**
Exs. 21, 28, 39, 51–53

◯ = **HINTS AND HOMEWORK HELP**
for Exs. 3, 17, 37 at classzone.com

SKILLS • PROBLEM SOLVING • REASONING

1. **VOCABULARY** Copy and complete: A number that you can substitute for a variable to make an equation true is a(n) __?__ of the equation.

2. **WRITING** Write two different two-step equations that each have a solution of 8.

SEE EXAMPLES 1, 3, AND 4 on pp. 270–272 for Exs. 3–23

SOLVING EQUATIONS Solve the equation. Check your solution.

3. $2x + 1 = 7$

4. $3y - 4 = 2$

5. $10 - 7z = 3$

6. $15 = -4p + 7$

7. $9 - 2k = 25$

8. $11 = \dfrac{h}{6} + 8$

9. $\dfrac{x}{9} - 4 = 5$

10. $6 + 2c = 15$

11. $29 = -5a + 4$

12. $7 + 5b = -23$

13. $100 - 7r = 44$

14. $20 - 6w = 14$

15. $-32 = -17 - \dfrac{d}{2}$

16. $\dfrac{c}{3} - 7 = 5.3$

17. $-7 + \dfrac{z}{4} = 5.2$

18. $\dfrac{3x}{5} = 12$

19. $\dfrac{2x}{3} = -8$

20. $-\dfrac{5m}{2} = 35$

21. ◆ **MULTIPLE CHOICE** What is the solution of the equation $21 = 3x + 9$?

    A -2 **B** 4 **C** 10 **D** 16

REASONING In Exercises 22 and 23, two methods for solving the equation $2(m + 3) = 18$ are shown. *Justify* each step of the solutions.

22.

$$2(m + 3) = 18$$
$$2m + 6 = 18$$
$$2m + 6 - 6 = 18 - 6$$
$$2m = 12$$
$$\frac{2m}{2} = \frac{12}{2}$$
$$m = 6$$

23.

$$2(m + 3) = 18$$
$$\frac{2(m + 3)}{2} = \frac{18}{2}$$
$$m + 3 = 9$$
$$m + 3 - 3 = 9 - 3$$
$$m = 6$$

WRITING AND SOLVING EQUATIONS Translate the statement into an equation. Then solve the equation.

24. The sum of 5 times a number and 4 is 9.

25. Seven subtracted from the quotient of a number and 2 is -6.

26. The sum of -2 times a number and 3.5 is 7.5.

27. Five less than the product of 2 and the absolute value of a number is 3.

28. ◆ **MULTIPLE CHOICE** The sum of twice a number and 5 is 13. Which equation represents this statement?

    A $2x + 5 = 13$ **B** $2x - 5 = 13$ **C** $x + 5 = 13$ **D** $5x + 13 = 2$

29. **ERROR ANALYSIS** *Describe* and correct the error in solving the equation.

$$\times \quad \begin{array}{l} 3x - 9 = 18 \\ 3x = 9 \\ x = 3 \end{array}$$

30. **ERROR ANALYSIS** *Describe* and correct the error in translating the statement into an equation.

The difference of 3 times a number and -2 is 4.

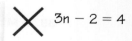 $3n - 2 = 4$

CONNECT SKILLS TO PROBLEM SOLVING Exercises 31–33 will help you prepare for problem solving.

Write an equation that can be solved to find x.

31. You and a friend buy a total of 18 apples. After eating x apples each, you and your friend have 14 apples remaining.

32. You subscribe to a magazine that costs $26 yearly. You make an initial payment of $5 and then make 3 equal payments of x dollars each.

33. A group orders 4 meals that cost x dollars each and leaves a $12 tip. The group spends a total of $76.

SEE EXAMPLE 1
on p. 270
for Exs. 34–35

34. **WALKING DOGS** You earn money by walking dogs in your neighborhood. Each neighbor pays you $5 per walk and you spend $4 per week on dog treats. If your goal is to earn $51 per week, how many walks do you need to do at $5 each? To answer this question, solve the equation $5w - 4 = 51$.

California @*HomeTutor* for problem solving help at classzone.com

Pay: $5 per walk

35. **SHORT RESPONSE** Students are cleaning up 11 miles of trails in a local park. After an hour, they have cleaned about 3 miles of trails. Solve the two-step equation $3h + 3 = 11$. *Explain* why the value of h is an estimate of the number of hours it will take to finish.

California @*HomeTutor* for problem solving help at classzone.com

SEE EXAMPLE 2
on p. 271
for Exs. 36–44

36. **READING** You want to find how many pages you need to read per week in order to finish several books in 6 weeks. The books have a total of 1244 pages. You have already read 500 pages. How many pages do you have to read per week?

37. **RUNNING TIME** How long will it take the dog to be 0.7 mile away from the owner? Use $d = 35t + 0.1$, where d is the distance (in miles) the dog is from the owner after t hours.

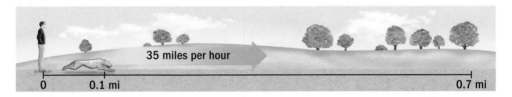

35 miles per hour

0   0.1 mi   0.7 mi

38. **PHONE CARD** You have $2.10 remaining on your phone card. You pay 7 cents for each minute of a call and a 75 cent charge for using a pay phone. If you make a call from a pay phone, what is the maximum whole number of minutes that you can talk? (*Hint:* The cost is the sum of the pay phone charge and 7 cents per minute for your call.)

39. ◆ **MULTIPLE CHOICE** A bicycle rental shop charges $5 per hour plus a fee of $10 each time you rent a bicycle. Which equation can you use to find the number of hours you can rent a bicycle for $45?

   (**A**) $5h + 10 = 45$ (**B**) $10h + 5 = 45$

   (**C**) $5 + h + 10 = 45$ (**D**) $15h = 45$

40. **HOURLY WAGE** In one week, you make a profit of $70 mowing lawns. You mow for 10 hours during the week and spend $20 on gasoline for your mower. How much do you earn each hour?

41. **PUZZLE PROBLEM** Ted has $12 more than Carla, and Carla has $8 more than Devon. Together they have $73. How much money does each person have?

42. RESTAURANT At a restaurant one day, 60 sandwiches were sold in all, some on rye bread and 28 on white bread. The number of sandwiches sold on rye bread was twice the number sold the day before. How many sandwiches on rye bread were sold the day before?

43. PARTY SUPPLIES You need 124 plastic forks for a party. At one store you buy the last 5 boxes, and each box contains 8 forks. At another store you find boxes that each contain 12 forks. How many of these boxes do you need to buy?

44. SHORT RESPONSE A taxicab costs $2 plus an additional $1.50 for every mile. Your ride cost $17 before the tip. How many miles did you go? Will it cost twice as much to go twice as far? *Explain.*

REASONING **Exercises 45 and 46 are missing information. Tell what information is needed to solve the problems.**

45. You jog for 5 minutes and then you run for 20 minutes. For each week after, you jog for 5 minutes, but increase the time that you run. After how many weeks will you be working out for a total of 85 minutes?

46. You have a job in which you make $6 per hour plus tips. You made a total of $34 yesterday. How much did you make in tips?

47. PUZZLE PROBLEM The length of a rectangle is 15 feet more than three times its width. The perimeter is 94 feet. Find the area of the rectangle.

$3w + 15$
w

CHALLENGE **Translate the statement into an equation. Then solve.**

48. The quotient of -36 and 9 exceeds 4 times a number n by 8.

49. The product of 8 squared divided by 16 and a number n is 24.

50. CHALLENGE Amanda takes her car to the repair shop. The mechanic starts working on her car at 10:30 A.M., takes a 45 minute lunch break, and then continues working into the afternoon. The parts to fix the car cost $350 and the labor costs $80 per hour. Amanda pays $730 in all. At what time did the mechanic finish the work?

◆ CALIFORNIA STANDARDS SPIRAL REVIEW

NS 1.4 | **51.** Which of the following is a rational number? *(p. 225)*

   A $\sqrt{\dfrac{4}{9}}$ **B** $\sqrt{\dfrac{25}{5}}$ **C** $\sqrt{18}$ **D** $\sqrt{45}$

NS 2.1 | **52.** What is the value of $10 \cdot 10^{-4}$? *(p. 206)*

   A 0.001   **B** 0.01   **C** 0.1   **D** 1000

AF 1.1 | **53.** You equally divide 32 dimes into 4 groups. Which equation can be solved to find the number x of dimes in each group? *(p. 263)*

   A $x - 4 = 32$ **B** $x + 4 = 32$ **C** $4x = 32$ **D** $\dfrac{x}{32} = 4$

Using ALTERNATIVE METHODS

Another Way to Solve Example 2, page 271

Standards
AF 4.1

In Example 2 on page 271, you solved a two-step equation using an algebraic method. You can also solve an equation using a table.

PROBLEM

A zoo currently spends $1580 to feed its American flamingos. Next year its budget for feeding the flamingos will be $2370, and it will cost $395 to feed each additional flamingo the zoo buys. How many new flamingos can the zoo buy next year?

(A) 2   (B) 3   (C) 4   (D) 6

METHOD

Using a Table One alternative approach is to use the *table* feature of a graphing calculator to solve the equation $2370 = 395n + 1580$ that you found in Example 2.

STEP 1 **Press** `Y=` and enter $y_1 = 395x + 1580$. Note that only the right side of the equation in Example 2 is entered and that the variable n is replaced by x.

STEP 2 **Set** up the table. Go to the TABLE SETUP screen. Use a starting value (TblStart) of 0 and an increment ($\triangle$Tbl) of 1.

STEP 3 **Display** the table by pressing `2nd` `TABLE`. Scroll down to find the value of x for which $y_1 = 2370$. This happens when $x = 2$.

```
TABLE SETUP
 TblStart=0
 ΔTbl=1
 Indpnt: Auto  Ask
 Depend: Auto  Ask
```

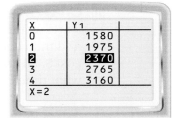

X	Y1
0	1580
1	1975
2	2370
3	2765
4	3160

X=2

The zoo can buy 2 new flamingos next year.

▶ The correct answer is A. (A) (B) (C) (D)

PRACTICE

1. **BUSINESS** A company has a payroll of $2.2 million. The budget allows for $2.5 million. How many new employees making $50,000 each can the company hire? Use a graphing calculator to solve the problem.

2. **WHAT IF?** Suppose the company in Exercise 1 will pay new employees $60,000 each. How many new employees can the company hire? Use algebra to solve the problem. Then check your answer using a graphing calculator.

5.6 Writing and Solving Proportions

Standards Preparation

Gr. 6 NS 1.3 Use proportions to solve problems (e.g., determine the value of N if $\frac{4}{7} = \frac{N}{21}$, find the length of a side of a polygon similar to a known polygon). **Use cross-multiplication as a method for solving such problems**, understanding it as the multiplication of both sides of an equation by a multiplicative inverse.

Math and NATURE
Example 1, p. 277

Connect *Before* you wrote and solved equations. *Now* you will write and solve proportions to prepare for Grade 7 Standard MG 1.2.

KEY VOCABULARY
- proportion
- cross products
- ratio, *p. 732*

A **proportion** is an equation stating that two ratios are equivalent. The proportion below is read "*a* is to *b* as *c* is to *d*."

$$\frac{a}{b} = \frac{c}{d}, b \neq 0, d \neq 0$$

EXAMPLE 1 Writing and Solving a Proportion

 RHINOCEROS BEETLES An adult rhinoceros beetle weighs 0.525 ounce but can carry about 446.25 ounces on its back. If a person were proportionately as strong as a rhinoceros beetle, how much weight could a 100 pound person carry?

SOLUTION

	Beetle	Person
Carries	446.25 oz	*x* lb
Weighs	0.525 oz	100 lb

Use a table to set up a proportion.

$$\frac{446.25}{0.525} = \frac{x}{100}$$

Write a proportion $\frac{\text{ounces}}{\text{ounces}} = \frac{\text{pounds}}{\text{pounds}}$.

$$\frac{446.25}{0.525} \cdot 100 = \frac{x}{100} \cdot 100$$

Multiply each side by 100.

$$85{,}000 = x$$

Simplify.

ANOTHER WAY
You can also use the following proportion in Example 1:

$$\frac{x}{446.25} = \frac{100}{0.525}$$

▶ **Answer** If human strength were proportional to that of a rhinoceros beetle, a 100 pound person could carry 85,000 pounds.

✓ GUIDED PRACTICE for Example 1

1. **WHAT IF?** Some ants weigh only 0.0001 ounce but can carry about 0.005 ounce. If a person were proportionately as strong as one of these ants, how much weight could a 100 pound person carry?

Solve the proportion.

2. $\dfrac{n}{12} = \dfrac{3}{4}$

3. $\dfrac{50}{20} = \dfrac{z}{16}$

4. $\dfrac{25}{3} = \dfrac{t}{51}$

VOCABULARY
The phrase *cross products* comes from the "X" shape formed by the diagonal numbers in the proportion.

CROSS PRODUCTS The proportion $\frac{a}{b} = \frac{c}{d}$ has **cross products** ad and bc.

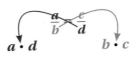

$$a \cdot d \qquad b \cdot c$$

You can use cross products to solve a proportion. You can also use cross products to check whether two ratios form a proportion.

KEY CONCEPT   *For Your Notebook*

Cross Products Property

Words   The cross products of a proportion are equal.

Numbers   Because 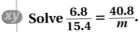 you know that $3 \cdot 12 = 4 \cdot 9$.

Algebra   If $\frac{a}{b} = \frac{c}{d}$, where b and d are nonzero numbers, then $ad = bc$.

EXAMPLE 2   **Using the Cross Products Property**

Solve $\frac{6.8}{15.4} = \frac{40.8}{m}$.

$\dfrac{6.8}{15.4} = \dfrac{40.8}{m}$	**Write original proportion.**
$6.8m = 15.4(40.8)$	**Cross products property**
$6.8m = 628.32$	**Multiply.**
$\dfrac{6.8m}{6.8} = \dfrac{628.32}{6.8}$	**Divide each side by 6.8.**
$m = 92.4$	**Simplify.**

CHECK You can check the solution by finding the cross products of the proportion. If the cross products are equal, the solution is correct.

$\dfrac{6.8}{15.4} \stackrel{?}{=} \dfrac{40.8}{92.4}$	**Substitute 92.4 for *m* in original proportion.**
$6.8(92.4) \stackrel{?}{=} 15.4(40.8)$	**Cross-multiply.**
$628.32 = 628.32 \checkmark$	**Solution checks.**

Animated Math
For an interactive example of using the cross products property, go to **classzone.com**.

✓ **GUIDED PRACTICE**   **for Example 2**

Solve the proportion. Check your solution.

5. $\dfrac{6}{c} = \dfrac{54}{99}$ **6.** $\dfrac{n}{14} = \dfrac{63}{84}$ **7.** $\dfrac{2.1}{0.9} = \dfrac{27.3}{y}$

8. $\dfrac{16.2}{67.4} = \dfrac{x}{134.8}$ **9.** $\dfrac{8}{a} = \dfrac{0.4}{0.62}$ **10.** $\dfrac{b}{1.8} = \dfrac{49.6}{14.4}$

EXAMPLE 3 ◆ Multiple Choice Practice

ELIMINATE CHOICES
Because you are finding the value of x for which the ratios are equal, the numerator, 30, should be less than the denominator, $2 + x$. This is not true for choice A, so it can be eliminated.

What is the solution of $\frac{30}{2 + x} = \frac{6}{7}$?

Ⓐ 23.7   **Ⓑ** 33   **Ⓒ** 35   **Ⓓ** 36

SOLUTION

$\frac{30}{2 + x} = \frac{6}{7}$	Write original proportion.
$30 \cdot 7 = (2 + x) \cdot 6$	Cross products property
$210 = 12 + 6x$	Multiply and use distributive property.
$198 = 6x$	Subtract 12 from each side.
$33 = x$	Divide each side by 6.

▶**Answer** The correct answer is B. Ⓐ **Ⓑ** Ⓒ Ⓓ

✓ **GUIDED PRACTICE** for Example 3

11. Solve the proportion $\frac{16}{x + 1} = \frac{8}{3}$. Check your solution.

5.6 EXERCISES

HOMEWORK KEY

◆ = **MULTIPLE CHOICE PRACTICE**
Exs. 15, 24, 31, 37–39

◯ = **HINTS AND HOMEWORK HELP**
for Exs. 3, 11, 33 at classzone.com

SKILLS • PROBLEM SOLVING • REASONING

1. **VOCABULARY** Copy and complete: An equation stating that two ratios are equivalent is a(n) __?__.

2. **WRITING** *Describe* how to use cross products to solve a proportion.

SEE EXAMPLE 2
on p. 278
for Exs. 3–15

USING CROSS PRODUCTS Solve the proportion.

3. $\frac{2}{3} = \frac{4}{z}$ 4. $\frac{6}{a} = \frac{3}{1}$ 5. $\frac{39}{13} = \frac{9}{d}$ 6. $\frac{-68}{12} = \frac{51}{p}$

7. $\frac{7.2}{m} = \frac{2.4}{1.8}$ 8. $\frac{256}{9.6} = \frac{-1.6}{g}$ 9. $\frac{67.2}{g} = \frac{16.8}{3.3}$ 10. $\frac{t}{29.4} = \frac{5.5}{4.2}$

CHECKING PROPORTIONS Tell whether the ratios form a proportion.

11. $\frac{3}{4} \overset{?}{=} \frac{6}{8}$ 12. $\frac{1}{2} \overset{?}{=} \frac{2}{5}$ 13. $\frac{14}{21} \overset{?}{=} \frac{26}{39}$ 14. $\frac{15}{45} \overset{?}{=} \frac{45}{135}$

15. ◆ **MULTIPLE CHOICE** What is the solution of $\frac{12}{15} = \frac{x}{25}$?

Ⓐ 7.2   **Ⓑ** 20   **Ⓒ** 22   **Ⓓ** 31.25

ERROR ANALYSIS *Describe* and correct the error in writing and solving a proportion for the situation.

16. You earn $40 in 5 hours. How much will you earn in 8 hours?

$$\frac{40}{5} = \frac{8}{d}$$
$$40d = 40$$
$$d = \$1$$

17. You run 2 miles in 15 minutes. How long will it take you to run 3 miles?

$$\frac{2}{15} = \frac{3}{t}$$
$$6 = 15t$$
$$0.4 \text{ min} = t$$

SEE EXAMPLE 3
on p. 279
for Exs. 18–24

SOLVING PROPORTIONS Solve the proportion.

18. $\frac{2}{x+2} = \frac{18}{27}$

19. $\frac{x-2}{8} = \frac{30}{40}$

20. $\frac{9}{5} = \frac{36}{x-3}$

21. $\frac{5}{x} = \frac{7}{x+4}$

22. $\frac{x}{5} = \frac{3x-4}{7}$

23. $\frac{3-5x}{4} = \frac{x+5}{9}$

24. ◆ **MULTIPLE CHOICE** Which equation shows the correct usage of the cross products property on the proportion $\frac{3}{5} = \frac{x-4}{35}$?

    (A) $3 + 35 = 5 + x - 4$ **(B)** $3 \cdot 5 = (x-4) \cdot 35$

    (C) $3 \cdot 35 = 5 \cdot (x-4)$ **(D)** $3 \cdot (x-4) = 5 \cdot 35$

MULTIPLE VARIABLES Find the value of each variable. Check your solution.

25. $\frac{4}{x-5} = \frac{3}{2x} = \frac{y}{21}$

26. $\frac{7}{b-36} = \frac{a}{72} = \frac{28}{b}$

27. $\frac{8}{p-10} = \frac{16}{p-5} = \frac{n+8}{p}$

CONNECT SKILLS TO PROBLEM SOLVING Exercises 28–30 will help you prepare for problem solving.

Write a proportion that can be used to solve the problem.

28. A car moving at a constant speed travels 88 feet in 2 seconds. How many feet does it travel in one minute?

29. You earn $54 mowing 3 lawns. You charge the same amount for each lawn. How much do you earn mowing 5 lawns?

30. A farmer advertises 12 ears of corn for $3. How much does it cost to buy 30 ears of corn?

SEE EXAMPLE 1
on p. 277
for Exs. 31–33

31. ◆ **MULTIPLE CHOICE** A teacher has 50 tests to grade. She can grade 4 tests in 6 minutes. How long will it take her to grade all of the tests?

    (A) 12.5 min   **(B)** 24 min   **(C)** 75 min   **(D)** 300 min

California @HomeTutor for problem solving help at classzone.com

32. **BEES** To produce one pound of honey, the bees from a hive fly over 55,000 miles and visit about 2 million flowers. About how many flowers are visited to make 19 ounces of honey?

California @HomeTutor for problem solving help at classzone.com

    ◆ = **MULTIPLE CHOICE PRACTICE**   ○ = **HINTS AND HOMEWORK HELP** at classzone.com

33. RUNNING SPEED At top speed, a greyhound, a roadrunner, and a cheetah can achieve the following distances in the given amounts of time. How far does each animal travel in 11 seconds?

330 ft in 5 sec

75 ft in 3 sec

198 ft in 2 sec

34. PUZZLE PROBLEM The ratio of Gary's age to Connie's age is $5:4$. In 6 years the ratio will be $6:5$. How much older is Gary than Connie?

35. CHALLENGE If $\frac{a}{b} = \frac{c}{d}$ where a, b, c, and d are nonzero numbers, is it true that $\frac{a}{c} = \frac{b}{d}$? Is it true that $\frac{d}{a} = \frac{c}{b}$? *Justify* your answers using algebraic properties or *counterexamples* (examples of when the statement is false).

36. CHALLENGE A 5 inch by 8 inch photo needs to be proportionally increased in size to fit a space whose width is 5 inches less than its length. Find the perimeter and area of the enlarged photo.

◆ CALIFORNIA STANDARDS SPIRAL REVIEW

NS 1.6

37. The value of a variable decreases from 42 to 35.7. What is the percent of decrease? *(p. 168)*

(A) 6.3%   (B) 10%   (C) 15%   (D) 25%

AF 1.4

38. Which expression has a coefficient of 2? *(p. 252)*

(A) $-2x^2 + 2$ (B) $x + 2$ (C) $2x^3$ (D) $3x^2$

AF 4.1

39. Henry paid $400 for painting supplies and earned $20 per painting. His profit was $560. How many paintings did he sell? *(p. 270)*

(A) 20   (B) 28   (C) 48   (D) 60

QUIZ *for Lessons 5.4–5.6*

Solve the equation.

1. $19r = 76$ *(p. 263)*   **2.** $\frac{y}{-1.4} = -5$ *(p. 263)*   **3.** $8 - 3x = -7$ *(p. 270)*

Solve the proportion. *(p. 277)*

4. $\frac{2}{3} = \frac{7}{x}$ **5.** $\frac{6}{8} = \frac{b}{28}$ **6.** $\frac{7}{4} = \frac{3-x}{10}$

7. BICYCLE Mary wants to buy a bicycle that costs $280. Her parents agree to pay $100. Mary will save $20 per week. Write and solve an equation to find how long it will take her to save enough money. *(p. 270)*

5.7 Solving Inequalities Using Addition or Subtraction

Standards

AF 1.1 Use variables and appropriate operations to write an expression, an equation, **an inequality,** or a system of equations or inequalities **that represents a verbal description** (e.g., three less than a number, half as large as area A).

AF 1.4 Use algebraic terminology (e.g., variable, equation, term, coefficient, **inequality,** expression, constant) **correctly.**

Connect *Before* you solved equations using addition and subtraction. *Now* you will solve inequalities using addition and subtraction.

Math and **SPORTS**
Example 3, p. 284

KEY VOCABULARY
- **inequality**
- **solution of an inequality**
- **equivalent inequalities**

In a game of disc golf, the target is beyond a pond, the far end of which is 300 feet away. Your first throw travels 134 feet. How long does your second throw have to be in order to clear the pond? You will use an inequality to answer this question in Example 3.

An **inequality,** such as $x \le 6$, is a statement formed by placing an inequality symbol between two expressions. A **solution of an inequality** is a number that you can substitute for the variable to make the inequality true. To translate sentences into inequalities, look for the following phrases:

Phrase	Symbol
is less than	$<$
is less than or equal to	$\le$
is greater than	$>$
is greater than or equal to	$\ge$

You can graph the solutions of an inequality using a number line. When graphing inequalities with $>$ or $<$, use an open circle. When graphing inequalities with $\ge$ or $\le$, use a closed circle.

EXAMPLE 1 Graphing Inequalities

REVIEW INEQUALITIES
For help with using inequality symbols, see p. 733.

Inequality	Graph	Verbal Phrase
a. $y < 7$	2 3 4 5 6 7 8	**All numbers less than 7**
b. $q \le 3$	$-2\ -1\ 0\ 1\ 2\ 3\ 4$	**All numbers less than or equal to 3**
c. $x > -5$	$-6\ \ -4\ \ -2\ \ \ 0$	**All numbers greater than -5**
d. $h \ge 2\frac{1}{2}$	0 1 2 3	**All numbers greater than or equal to $2\frac{1}{2}$**

SOLVING INEQUALITIES When you solve an inequality, you find all solutions of the inequality. Inequalities that have the same solutions are **equivalent inequalities.** You can solve some inequalities by adding or subtracting.

KEY CONCEPT *For Your Notebook*

Addition and Subtraction Properties of Inequality

Words   Adding or subtracting the same number on each side of an inequality produces an equivalent inequality.

Algebra   If $x - a > b$, then $x - a + a > b + a$, or $x > b + a$.

If $x + a > b$, then $x + a - a > b - a$, or $x > b - a$.

EXAMPLE 2   **Solving Inequalities**

Solve the inequality. Then graph the solution.

a. $x - 5 < 8$ **b.** $y - 7 \le -10$ **c.** $8 + m > 15$

SOLUTION

ANOTHER WAY
You can also write the solution of an inequality using *set notation*. For instance, the solution of the inequality in part (a) of Example 2 can be written as $\{x: x < 13\}$.

a.
$$x - 5 < 8$$ Write original inequality.
$$x - 5 + 5 < 8 + 5$$ Add 5 to each side. (Addition property of inequality)
$$x < 13$$ Simplify.

9 10 11 12 13 14 15

b.
$$y - 7 \le -10$$ Write original inequality.
$$y - 7 + 7 \le -10 + 7$$ Add 7 to each side. (Addition property of inequality)
$$y \le -3$$ Simplify.

−5 −4 −3 −2 −1 0 1

c.
$$8 + m > 15$$ Write original inequality.
$$8 - 8 + m > 15 - 8$$ Subtract 8 from each side. (Subtraction property of inequality)
$$m > 7$$ Simplify.

4 5 6 7 8 9 10

✔ **GUIDED PRACTICE**   for Examples 1 and 2

1. Graph and write a verbal phrase for the inequality $z \ge -1$.

Solve the inequality. Then graph the solution.

2. $x - 3 > -2$ **3.** $6 > t - 1$ **4.** $12 \ge p + 14$

EXAMPLE 3 Writing and Solving an Inequality

 DISC GOLF Using an inequality, you can find the distance the second throw must travel to clear the pond described on page 282. Let d be the distance of your second throw.

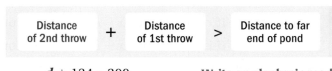

$d + 134 > 300$	Write an algebraic model.
$d + 134 - 134 > 300 - 134$	Subtract 134 from each side.
$d > 166$	Simplify.

▶ **Answer** Your second throw needs to travel more than 166 feet.

Disc golf basket

Animated Math

For an interactive example of writing and solving an inequality, go to **classzone.com**.

✓ **GUIDED PRACTICE** for Example 3

5. WHAT IF? In Example 3, suppose that your first throw went 155 feet. How far does your second throw have to go to clear the pond?

5.7 EXERCISES

HOMEWORK KEY

◆ = **MULTIPLE CHOICE PRACTICE**
Exs. 22, 23, 42, 50–52

○ = **HINTS AND HOMEWORK HELP**
for Exs. 3, 13, 41 at classzone.com

SKILLS • PROBLEM SOLVING • REASONING

1. VOCABULARY Copy and complete: $x < -2$ is a(n) __?__ .

2. WRITING *Explain* how to solve an inequality of the form $x + a > b$ where $a > 0$.

SEE EXAMPLE 1
on p. 282
for Exs. 3–12

MATCHING Match the inequality with its graph.

3. $x < -1$ **4.** $x \le 1$ **5.** $x \ge 1$ **6.** $x > -1$

A. ←——●——→ −2 −1 0 1 2

B. ←——●——→ −2 −1 0 1 2

C. ←——⊕——→ −2 −1 0 1 2

D. ←——⊕——→ −2 −1 0 1 2

WRITING INEQUALITIES Write the inequality and the verbal phrase represented by the graph.

7. ←——⊕——→ −3 −2 −1 0 1 2

8. ←——●——→ −10 −5 0 5 10 15

9. ←——●——→ −2 −1 0 1 2 3

10. ←——⊕——→ −2 0 2 4 6 8

11. ERROR ANALYSIS *Describe* and correct the error in graphing $m > 7$.

12. ERROR ANALYSIS *Describe* and correct the error in graphing $x \geq -6$.

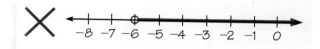

SEE EXAMPLE 2
on p. 283
for Exs. 13–27

SOLVING INEQUALITIES **Solve the inequality. Then graph the solution.**

13. $12 + p < 7$　　　　**14.** $k + 4 \leq 11$　　　　**15.** $n - 6 > 3$

16. $17 + r \geq 25$　　　**17.** $-8 \geq m - 19$　　　**18.** $-3.5 < w - 9$

19. $5.45 + b < -3.55$　　**20.** $\frac{2}{3} \leq p - 2\frac{1}{3}$　　　**21.** $t + \frac{1}{4} > 5$

22. ◆ MULTIPLE CHOICE Which inequality has 23 as a solution?

　A $x - 3 > 20$　　**B** $x - 3 \geq 20$　　**C** $x - 3 < 20$　　**D** $x + 3 \leq 20$

23. ◆ MULTIPLE CHOICE What is the solution of the inequality $-4 \leq s - 9.5$?

　A $s \leq -13.5$　　**B** $s \geq -13.5$　　**C** $s \leq 5.5$　　**D** $s \geq 5.5$

FINDING SOLUTIONS **Tell which positive integers less than 10 are solutions of the inequality.**

24. $-8 + x \leq 2$　　**25.** $x - 20 > -15$　　**26.** $10 \leq x + 4$　　**27.** $5 + x \leq 9$

OPEN-ENDED **Write two equivalent inequalities for the phrase. Then graph the solution.**

28. All real numbers less than 4　　　　**29.** All real numbers greater than -10

30. All real numbers greater than 19　　　**31.** All real numbers less than -7

32. REASONING Are the inequalities $x < 2$ and $2 > x$ equivalent? *Explain.*

CONNECT SKILLS TO PROBLEM SOLVING **Exercises 33–35 will help you prepare for problem solving.**

33. You run a race in 38 minutes. The record winning time is 32 minutes. Write an inequality that can be used to find the numbers of minutes you need to improve by to break the record.

34. You have a total of 279 points in your math class. You need at least 372 points to earn an A. Write an inequality that can be used to find the numbers of additional points you need to earn an A.

35. The trailer of a truck is loaded with 14,000 pounds of metal. The truck can tow at most 19,000 pounds. Write an inequality that can be used to find the weights that can be loaded on the trailer.

SEE EXAMPLE 3
on p. 284
for Exs. 36–38

36. MULTI-STEP PROBLEM On four tests you scored 90, 85, 98, and 87. To earn a B in math class, you need at least 425 points on five tests.

  a. Add your current scores.

  b. Let x represent the fifth score. Write and solve an inequality that represents the possible test scores you could get on your fifth test and still earn at least a B in the class.

  c. Graph the possible test scores.

  California @HomeTutor   for problem solving help at classzone.com

37. BANKING You have $33.96 in a savings account. At your bank, you must have a minimum balance of $50 in your account to avoid a fee. Write and solve an inequality to represent the amount of money you can deposit in order to equal or exceed the minimum balance.

  California @HomeTutor   for problem solving help at classzone.com

38 SKI JUMPING In a ski jumping competition, the top four jumpers perform as shown.

  a. Write and solve an inequality to find how much farther the fourth-place jumper needed to jump in order to place first.

  b. Graph the solution to part (a).

Name	Distance
Mitchell	93.5 m
Jason	91.5 m
Marisa	85 m
Cara	57 m

39. WRITING *Explain* why $x - 3 \geq 10$ and $x \geq 13$ are equivalent inequalities. Write a third inequality that is equivalent to the two given inequalities.

40. BIPLANE RIDE Your family bought your grandmother a biplane ride. The flight can last up to 1 hour 15 minutes.

The ride has 10 minutes of corkscrew rolls, 15 minutes of hammerheads, and 30 minutes of over-water flying. Write and solve an inequality to find how much time can be used for scenic flying without going over the time limit.

Biplane ride: 1 hour 15 minutes

41. PACKAGES A package that is mailed can weigh at most 70 pounds. The package of material you want to mail weighs 76.4 pounds.

  a. Write and solve an inequality to find the numbers of pounds of material you need to remove in order to mail your package.

  b. Graph the solution to part (a).

42. ◆ MULTIPLE CHOICE The frequency f of the human singing voice is between about 81 hertz and about 1100 hertz. Which statement is true?

  (A) $f \leq 81$ **(B)** $1100 \leq f$ **(C)** $81 \leq f$ **(D)** $f \geq 1100$

◆ = **MULTIPLE CHOICE PRACTICE**   ○ = **HINTS AND HOMEWORK HELP** at classzone.com

43. TIGER POPULATION The map shows the tiger population in India around 1900. The population dropped to below 2000 in 1972 but has rebounded since then, increasing by about 2200 animals. Based on the given information, find the minimum and maximum numbers of tigers today. Write two inequalities that together describe the possible numbers of tigers today.

Indian Tiger Population, 1900

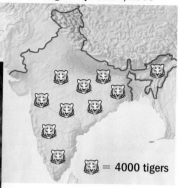

= 4000 tigers

Population increase: 2200

44. MULTI-STEP PROBLEM Lauren can spend at most $75 at the mall. She plans to buy a backpack for between $25 and $35. She'll spend the remaining money on gifts. Let x represent the cost of the gifts.

a. Write and solve an equation to find the least amount Lauren can spend on gifts.

b. Repeat part (a) to find the greatest amount Lauren can spend on gifts.

c. *Describe* possible values for x using inequalities.

CHALLENGE *Describe* the values of x that will make the statement true.

45. $|x| < 3$ **46.** $|x| > 2$ **47.** $|x| + 1 \le 5$ **48.** $|x| + 1 \ge 7$

49. CHALLENGE The *triangle inequality theorem* states that the sum of the lengths of any two sides of a triangle is greater than the length of the third side. A side of a triangle is 13 inches. Another side measures 6 inches. What values can the length x of the third side be? *Explain.*

◆ CALIFORNIA STANDARDS SPIRAL REVIEW

NS 1.1

50. Which fraction is greater than 0.36? *(p. 133)*

   A $\frac{8}{25}$ **B** $\frac{1}{3}$ **C** $\frac{53}{150}$ **D** $\frac{9}{22}$

AF 1.3

51. Which property is illustrated by $(m + 4) + 8 = m + (4 + 8)$? *(p. 41)*

   A Commutative property of addition

   B Associative property of addition

   C Distributive property

   D Identity property of addition

NS 2.4

52. You use a piece of wood to make a square sign that has an area of 576 square inches. What is the length of one side of the sign? *(p. 213)*

   A 23 in.   **B** 24 in.   **C** 25 in.   **D** 26 in.

5.8 Solving Inequalities Using Multiplication or Division

Standards **AF 1.1 Use variables and appropriate operations to write** an expression, an equation, **an inequality,** or a system of equations or inequalities **that represents a verbal description** (e.g., three less than a number, half as large as area A).

Connect *Before* you solved equations using multiplication and division. *Now* you will solve inequalities using multiplication and division.

Math and NATURE
Example 3, p. 289

KEY VOCABULARY
- inequality, *p. 282*
- solution of an inequality, *p. 282*
- equivalent inequalities, *p. 282*

Solving inequalities and solving equations have one important difference. Notice what happens when you multiply the inequality $3 > 1$ by -1.

$$3 > 1$$
$$3(-1) \underset{?}{\,} 1(-1)$$
$$-3 < -1$$

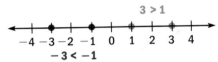

$$3 > 1$$

$$-3 < -1$$

From the number line you know that $-3 < -1$. So, when multiplying each side of an inequality by a negative number, you must *reverse the direction of the inequality symbol*. This is also true when dividing by a negative number.

KEY CONCEPT
For Your Notebook

Multiplication Properties of Inequality

Words	**Algebra**
Multiplying by a positive number Multiplying each side of an inequality by a *positive* number produces an equivalent inequality.	$4x < 10$ $\left(\dfrac{1}{4}\right)(4x) < \left(\dfrac{1}{4}\right)(10)$
Multiplying by a negative number Multiplying each side of an inequality by a *negative* number and *reversing the inequality symbol* produces an equivalent inequality.	$-5x < 10$ $\left(-\dfrac{1}{5}\right)(-5x) > \left(-\dfrac{1}{5}\right)(10)$

EXAMPLE 1 Solving an Inequality Using Multiplication

$$-\frac{1}{8}n \geq 2 \qquad \text{Original inequality}$$

$$-8 \cdot \left(-\frac{1}{8}n\right) \leq -8 \cdot 2 \qquad \begin{array}{l}\textbf{Multiply each side by } -8. \textbf{ Reverse inequality symbol.}\\ \textbf{(Multiplication property of inequality)}\end{array}$$

$$n \leq -16 \qquad \text{Simplify.}$$

KEY CONCEPT

For Your Notebook

Division Properties of Inequality

Words   **Algebra**

Dividing by a positive number Dividing each side of an $2x < 10$
inequality by a *positive* number produces an equivalent
inequality. $\dfrac{2x}{2} < \dfrac{10}{2}$

Dividing by a negative number Dividing each side of $-5x < 15$
an inequality by a *negative* number and *reversing the
inequality symbol* produces an equivalent inequality. $\dfrac{-5x}{-5} > \dfrac{15}{-5}$

EXAMPLE 2 Solving an Inequality Using Division

$15 > -3m$ **Original inequality**

$\dfrac{15}{-3} < \dfrac{-3m}{-3}$ **Divide each side by −3. Reverse inequality symbol.**
(Division property of inequality)

$-5 < m$ **Simplify.**

EXAMPLE 3 Using the Division Property of Inequality

BIOLOGY About 15,000 fruit-eating bats live on Barro Colorado Island. They eat up to 61,440,000 grams of fruit yearly. Write and solve an inequality to find up to about how many grams g of fruit each bat eats yearly.

SOLUTION

READING
Read the problem carefully to decide which inequality symbol to use. Because you know the bats eat "up to" 61,440,000 grams, then you know that the amount they eat is "≤" 61,440,000.

Number of bats	·	Grams each bat eats	≤	Maximum amount eaten yearly

$15,000g \le 61,440,000$ **Write an algebraic model.**

$\dfrac{15,000g}{15,000} \le \dfrac{61,440,000}{15,000}$ **Divide each side by 15,000.**

$g \le 4096$ **Simplify.**

▶ **Answer** Each bat eats up to about 4096 grams of fruit in a year.

✓ GUIDED PRACTICE for Examples 1, 2, and 3

1. Solve the inequality $\dfrac{t}{6} > 4$.   **2.** Solve the inequality $27 > -3t$.

3. BIOLOGY A bat that weighs about 25 grams can eat up to 2.5 times its body mass in figs in one night. Up to how many grams g of figs can it eat?

5.8 EXERCISES

HOMEWORK KEY

◆ = **MULTIPLE CHOICE PRACTICE**
Exs. 29, 30, 39, 46–48

○ = **HINTS AND HOMEWORK HELP**
for Exs. 5, 11, 39 at classzone.com

SKILLS • PROBLEM SOLVING • REASONING

1. **VOCABULARY** Copy and complete: When you multiply both sides of an inequality by a negative number, you need to __?__ the inequality symbol.

2. **WRITING** *Describe* how a number line can be used to decide when an inequality symbol should be reversed.

SEE EXAMPLES
1 AND 2
on pp. 288–289
for Exs. 3–30

PROPERTIES OF INEQUALITIES Tell whether you would reverse the inequality symbol when solving. Write *Yes* or *No*. Do not solve.

3. $\frac{1}{3}y < 18$

4. $-6x \geq 24$

5. $\frac{m}{-8} > 3$

6. $2b \leq -14$

MATCHING Solve the inequality. Match the inequality with the graph of its solution.

7. $\frac{1}{4}x \leq 8$

8. $-4x \geq 8$

9. $4x \geq -8$

10. $-\frac{1}{4}x \leq 8$

A. number line with points from −8 −6 −4 −2 0 2, filled dot at −4 going right

B. number line from −40 −32 −24 −16 −8 0, filled dot at −32 going right

C. number line from −8 −6 −4 −2 0 2, filled dot at −2 going left

D. number line from 0 8 16 24 32 40, filled dot at 32 going left

SOLVING INEQUALITIES Solve the inequality. Then graph the solution.

11. $\frac{1}{2}x < 4$

12. $\frac{m}{-7} \geq 6$

13. $9 \leq 3z$

14. $30 > -6p$

15. $\frac{1}{4}x > 1$

16. $-\frac{1}{7}t \geq -3$

17. $-\frac{1}{5}b \geq 72$

18. $\frac{1}{3}d < -33$

19. $4g < 24$

20. $12 \geq -3s$

21. $-9c \leq 54$

22. $5z < -15$

23. $7 > -\frac{1}{8}r$

24. $-6t \geq 36$

25. $-39 \leq 13k$

26. $-\frac{1}{6}a < -54$

ERROR ANALYSIS *Describe* and correct the error in solving the inequality.

27.
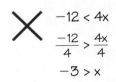
$-12 < 4x$
$\frac{-12}{4} > \frac{4x}{4}$
$-3 > x$

28.
$-7x \geq 35$
$\frac{-7x}{-7} \geq \frac{35}{-7}$
$x \geq -5$

29. ◆ **MULTIPLE CHOICE** Which inequality is represented by the graph?

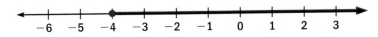

Ⓐ $2x \geq -8$ Ⓑ $3x < -12$ Ⓒ $\frac{1}{2}x > -2$ Ⓓ $\frac{x}{4} \leq -1$

30. ◆ MULTIPLE CHOICE What is the solution of the inequality $4x \le -36$?

(A) $x \le -9$ (B) $x \ge -9$ (C) $x \le 2$ (D) $\frac{x}{4} \ge 9$

NUMBER SENSE *Describe* all the numbers that satisfy both inequalities.

31. $\frac{n}{2} < 2$ and $-6n \le -6$

32. $3n < 48$ and $4n > 32$

CONNECT SKILLS TO PROBLEM SOLVING **Exercises 33–35 will help you prepare for problem solving.**

Write an inequality that models the situation.

33. Students want to raise at least $300 during a car wash. The profit is $5 per car. Let x be the number of cars washed.

34. You and 3 friends go out to eat. You decide to split the tip equally and contribute at least $3 each. Let t be the total amount of the tip.

35. A class is to be divided into 4 equal groups with at most 5 students per group. Let s be the number of students in the class.

SEE EXAMPLE 3
on p. 289
for Exs. 36–37

36. BORROWING MONEY You borrow $12 per week from your aunt.

    a. Write and solve an inequality to find when you will owe her more than $120.

    b. Graph the solution to part (a).

    California @HomeTutor for problem solving help at classzone.com

37. DANCE The student council must pay a disc jockey $275 to work at a dance. A ticket to the dance costs $5.50.

    a. Write and solve an inequality to find the numbers of tickets that can be sold to cover the cost of the disc jockey.

    b. Graph the solution to part (a).

    California @HomeTutor for problem solving help at classzone.com

Disc jockey fee: $275

38. REASONING A friend says that the solution of $-x < 0$ is all numbers greater than zero. Do you agree? *Explain.*

39. ◆ **MULTIPLE CHOICE** A science teacher weights the tests she gives by multiplying the total of each student's test scores by a percent x. John has test scores of 75, 84, 88, and 77. What is the lowest value of x for which the product of x and the total of John's scores is at least 32.4?

(A) 0.1%   (B) 5%   (C) 10%   (D) 15%

40. TICKETS Concert tickets are sold for $15 in advance and $20 at the door. Write and solve an inequality to find how many tickets must be sold at the door for total ticket revenue to be at least $4000 given that advance ticket sales totaled $1800.

41. MULTI-STEP PROBLEM An elevator can hold a maximum of 2000 pounds. The average weight of a person is 150 pounds. Let p be the number of people the elevator can hold.

    a. Write an inequality involving multiplication that models the situation.

    b. Solve the inequality.

    c. What does the solution of the inequality tell you about the number of people who can ride in the elevator?

42. BICYCLE RACING A bicycle racer trains by biking at least 50 miles a day. The racer bikes 15 miles in 1.5 hours. How long does the racer bike at this rate to complete the day's training shown below?

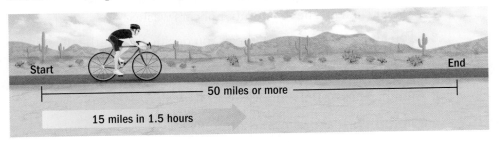

43. PUZZLE PROBLEM Joe has x baseball cards. If he had twice as many, he would have more than 20. If he had three times as many, he would have fewer than 36. Write and solve two inequalities to find how many baseball cards Joe has.

44. CHALLENGE Your neighbor is a real estate agent and earns a $50 commission for every $1000 in house sales, rounded to the nearest $1000. For what range of prices will the neighbor earn a commission between $4000 and $5000?

45. CHALLENGE Let a, b, c, and d be positive integers. Show that for fractions $\frac{a}{b}$ and $\frac{c}{d}$, if $ad > bc$, then $\frac{a}{b} > \frac{c}{d}$. Use this property to compare the fractions $\frac{3}{5}, \frac{5}{8}, \frac{7}{8}$, and $\frac{9}{11}$. If any of the integers are negative, is the statement still true?

◆ CALIFORNIA STANDARDS SPIRAL REVIEW

AF 1.2

46. What is the value of $3x - 5y + 2$ when $x = -2$ and $y = 3$? *(p. 5)*

    (A) -19 **(B)** -7 **(C)** 11 **(D)** 21

NS 2.5

47. Which has the greatest value? *(p. 12)*

    (A) $|-4|$ **(B)** $|4|$ **(C)** $-|5|$ **(D)** $|-5|$

NS 1.3

48. A car lost $\frac{1}{6}$ of its value last year. Which percent best approximates the decrease? *(p. 155)*

    (A) 1.67% **(B)** 6% **(C)** 16.7% **(D)** 167%

EXTRA PRACTICE for Lesson 5.8, p. 751   **ONLINE QUIZ** at classzone.com

5.9 Solving Two-Step Inequalities

Standards

AF 1.1 Use variables and appropriate operations **to write** an expression, an equation, **an inequality,** or a system of equations or inequalities **that represents a verbal description** (e.g., three less than a number, half as large as area A).

AF 4.1 Solve two-step linear equations and **inequalities in one variable over the rational numbers, interpret the solution or solutions in the context from which they arose, and verify the reasonableness of the results.**

Connect   *Before* you solved two-step equations and one-step inequalities. *Now* you will solve two-step inequalities.

Math and **SPORTS**
Ex. 31, p. 296

KEY VOCABULARY
- **like terms,** *p. 252*
- **inequality,** *p. 282*

ACTIVITY

Use a table to solve the inequality $x + 4 \geq 3x$.

STEP 1   **Copy** and complete the table.

STEP 2   **Find** the values of x that make the inequality true. What do you think is the solution of the inequality? *Explain* your reasoning.

x	$x + 4$	$3x$	Is $x + 4 \geq 3x$?
-1	3	-3	Yes
0	?	?	?
1	?	?	?
2	?	?	?
3	?	?	?
4	?	?	?

STEP 3   **Make** a similar table to find the solution of $4x > 9x - 10$. How is this solution different from the solution in Step 2?

STEP 4   **Determine** if the inequalities above are true when you substitute a number less than -1 for x. *Explain*.

In Lesson 5.5, you solved two-step equations algebraically. You can use many of the same steps to solve two-step inequalities.

EXAMPLE 1   Solving and Graphing a Two-Step Inequality

$10 + 4y < 18$	**Original inequality**
$10 + 4y - 10 < 18 - 10$	**Subtract 10 from each side.** **(Subtraction property of inequality)**
$4y < 8$	**Simplify.**
$\dfrac{4y}{4} < \dfrac{8}{4}$	**Divide each side by 4.** **(Division property of inequality)**
$y < 2$	**Simplify.**

Animated Math

For an interactive example of solving and graphing a two-step inequality, go to **classzone.com.**

```
<---+---+---+---+---+---+--->
    0   1   2   3   4   5
```

EXAMPLE 2 Combining Like Terms

$$3x - 14 < -x$$ Original inequality

$$3x - 14 - 3x < -x - 3x$$ Subtract 3x from each side. (Subtraction property of inequality)

$$-14 < -4x$$ Combine like terms.

$$\frac{-14}{-4} > \frac{-4x}{-4}$$ Divide each side by −4 and reverse the inequality symbol. (Division property of inequality)

$$\frac{7}{2} > x$$ Simplify.

AVOID ERRORS
Remember to reverse the inequality symbol when multiplying or dividing both sides of an inequality by a negative number.

EXAMPLE 3 ◆ Multiple Choice Practice

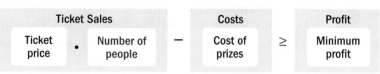

You are organizing a bowling night for charity. Each ticket costs $10 and includes shoe rental. Door prizes cost you $50. Which inequality describes the possible numbers x of people who need to attend for you to make a profit of at least $200?

Ⓐ $x \le 15$ Ⓑ $x \ge 15$ Ⓒ $x \le 25$ Ⓓ $x \ge 25$

ELIMINATE CHOICES
Because you want to make a profit of "at least $200", the answer choice should contain "$x \ge$". This is not true for choices A and C, so they can be eliminated.

SOLUTION

To find your profit, subtract the total costs from the total ticket sales. This amount should equal or exceed the minimum desired profit of $200.

Ticket Sales		Costs		Profit
Ticket price • Number of people	−	Cost of prizes	≥	Minimum profit

$$10x - 50 \ge 200$$ Write an inequality.

$$10x \ge 250$$ Add 50 to each side.

$$x \ge 25$$ Divide each side by 10.

▸ **Answer** The correct answer is D. Ⓐ Ⓑ Ⓒ Ⓓ

✓ **GUIDED PRACTICE** for Examples 1, 2, and 3

Solve the inequality. Then graph the solution.

1. $-7z + 15 \ge 57$ **2.** $11n + 40 < 3n$ **3.** $9y - 18 > -16$

4. WHAT IF? In Example 3, how many people need to attend for you to make a profit of at least $250?

5.9 EXERCISES

HOMEWORK KEY

◆ = **MULTIPLE CHOICE PRACTICE**
Exs. 16, 17, 32, 38–40

○ = **HINTS** AND **HOMEWORK HELP**
for Exs. 5, 17, 33 at classzone.com

SKILLS • PROBLEM SOLVING • REASONING

1. **VOCABULARY** *Describe* the meanings of the symbols $<$, $>$, $\leq$, and $\geq$.

2. **VOCABULARY** Copy and complete: Terms with identical variable parts with corresponding variables raised to the same power are called __?__.

3. **WRITING** How is solving a two-step inequality similar to solving a two-step equation? How is it different?

SEE EXAMPLES 1 AND 2
on pp. 293–294
for Exs. 4–19

SOLVING INEQUALITIES Solve the inequality. Then graph the solution.

4. $4a + 7 \geq 11$

5. $16 < 3b + 22$

6. $7 - 2p \geq -5$

7. $-3y + 2 < -16$

8. $-2w + 6 < 2w$

9. $26s \leq 3s + 69$

10. $12c + 12 > 48c$

11. $5x - 21 \leq 2x$

12. $-4z > 12 - z$

13. $10 \geq 15 + 5t$

14. $10 + 2n \leq 6$

15. $-3a - 6 < -3$

16. ◆ **MULTIPLE CHOICE** What is the solution of the inequality $-3b - 11b < 56$?

Ⓐ $b < -4$ Ⓑ $b > -4$ Ⓒ $b < 4$ Ⓓ $b > 4$

17. ◆ **MULTIPLE CHOICE** Which graph represents the solution of $13 \leq 4x - 3$?

Ⓐ [number line: 2, 2.5, 3 with point at 2.5]
Ⓑ [number line: 2, 2.5, 3]
Ⓒ [number line: 2, 3, 4, 5, 6 with point at 4]
Ⓓ [number line: 2, 3, 4, 5, 6 with shading]

ERROR ANALYSIS *Describe* and correct the error in solving the inequality.

18.
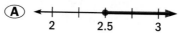

$$3x - 8 < -x$$
$$-8 < 2x$$
$$-4 < x$$
✗

19.

$$9 - 2x \leq 3$$
$$-2x \leq -6$$
$$\frac{-2x}{-2} \leq \frac{-6}{-2}$$
$$x \leq 3$$
✗

SOLVING INEQUALITIES Solve the inequality.

20. $\frac{4}{3} - \frac{1}{12}x < -\frac{3}{4}$

21. $\frac{2}{3}y + 13 \geq -\frac{4}{7}y$

22. $\frac{1}{2}k - 6 \geq -\frac{1}{6}k$

23. $\frac{1}{3}m - \frac{1}{2}m > -4$

24. $3.7z \leq 33.32 - 3.1z$

25. $-3.79 + 4.6y < 19.67$

26. $0.05a - 1.65a \leq -5.184$

27. $2.3x - 157.76 \leq -0.9x$

CONNECT SKILLS TO PROBLEM SOLVING Exercises 28–30 will help you prepare for problem solving.

Write an inequality that can be used to solve the problem.

28. Parking fees in a parking garage are $5 for the first hour and $1.50 for each additional hour x. You want to spend less than $10 on parking. How long can you park?

29. You have $50 and spend $8 for every hour x playing billiards. You want to have at least $10 left. How long can you play billiards?

30. Your printer takes 0.5 minute to print a plain copy and 2 minutes to print a color copy. You print x plain copies and x color copies. You want to print for at most 30 minutes. How many of each type can you print?

SEE EXAMPLE 3
on p. 294
for Exs. 31–34

31. **CHARITY** You agree to raise at least $2500 for charity to enter a race. You have already raised $925 by asking people to pledge $25 each. Use the verbal model to write and solve an inequality for the number p of additional $25 pledges that will satisfy the donation requirement. *Interpret* the solution.

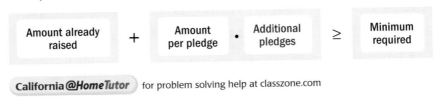

| Amount already raised | + | Amount per pledge | · | Additional pledges | ≥ | Minimum required |

California **@Home Tutor** for problem solving help at classzone.com

32. ◆ **MULTIPLE CHOICE** While at camp, you call your parents from a pay phone. The first minute costs you $.25 and each additional minute costs $.10. You have $1.65 in change. Solve the inequality $0.25 + 0.10m \le 1.65$ to find the number of additional minutes m you can talk.

(**A**) Less than 14   (**B**) No more than 14   (**C**) At most 19   (**D**) Fewer than 19

California **@Home Tutor** for problem solving help at classzone.com

33. **VIDEO GAMES** You are approaching the high score of 18,550 on a video game in which you have to catch discs for 150 points each. Your current score is 16,000. Use the verbal model to write and solve an inequality to find how many more discs you need to catch to have a new high score. *Interpret* the solution.

Your current score is 16,000.

| Current score | + | Points earned per disc | · | Discs caught | > | Current high score |

34. **REASONING** You and your sisters have $25 to spend at a baseball game. You buy 3 pretzels for $4 each and then use the rest for drinks that cost $3 each. You write and solve an inequality to find the number of drinks d you can afford. Tell why the solutions $d < 120$, $d \le 0$, and $d \ge 4$ *cannot* be correct.

35. WEATHER The minimum base height of a Cirro cloud is more than 3500 feet above 2.75 times the base height h of a Strato cloud. Solve the inequality $20,000 > 2.75h + 3500$. What does this solution say about the base height of a Strato cloud?

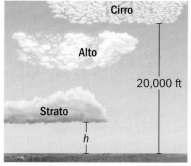

36. CHALLENGE Consider the inequality $ax + b < c$ where $a < 0$. Solve this inequality for x in terms of a, b, and c. *Justify* each step.

37. CHALLENGE It costs a magazine publisher $1.20 to produce each magazine. Overhead costs, such as salaries and office space, are $25,000 per month. The publisher sells the magazine for $3.95. How many magazines need to be sold each month in order to earn more than the production and overhead costs?

  a. Write a verbal model that represents this situation.

  b. Write and solve an inequality. *Interpret* the solution.

  c. If the magazine publisher cuts costs to $1.10 per magazine and $24,000 in overhead, what effect will this have? *Explain*.

◆ CALIFORNIA STANDARDS SPIRAL REVIEW

NS 1.5

38. Which fraction is less than 0.65? *(p. 113)*

  A $\frac{3}{5}$ **B** $\frac{13}{20}$ **C** $\frac{27}{40}$ **D** $\frac{7}{10}$

NS 2.2

39. What is the least common denominator of the fractions in the difference $\frac{7}{3} - \frac{7}{14}$? *(p. 91)*

  A 3   **B** 14   **C** 21   **D** 42

NS 1.7

40. Which discount results in the largest dollar decrease in the price of an MP3 player? *(p. 160)*

  A 20% off of $75   **B** 10% off of $140

  C 8% off of $200   **D** 3% off of $500

QUIZ *for Lessons 5.7–5.9*

Solve the inequality. Then graph the solution.

  1. $a + 9 \geq -1$ *(p. 282)*   **2.** $16 > y - 12$ *(p. 282)*   **3.** $\frac{x}{3} < -3$ *(p. 288)*   **4.** $-7x > 42$ *(p. 288)*

Solve the inequality. *(p. 293)*

  5. $-8a - 10 > 14$ **6.** $5b \geq 2b + 4.5$ **7.** $3z \leq 35 - 2z$ **8.** $19k - 16 \geq 3$

  9. CALLING CARD You have $9.50 to use for recharging your phone card. Write and solve an inequality to find how many minutes you can add to your phone card if each minute costs $.10. *(p. 288)*

5.9 Solving Two-Step Inequalities

Standards

AF 4.1 **Solve two-step linear** equations and inequalities in one variable over the rational numbers, interpret the solution or solutions in the context from which they arose, and verify the reasonableness of the results.

QUESTION How can a spreadsheet be used to solve two-step inequalities?

EXAMPLE Solve a two-step inequality

Use spreadsheet software to solve $3x < 2x - 8$.

STEP 1 **Enter** the integers -10 to 10 in column A. Column A contains possible solutions of the inequality.

B2	=3*A2			
	A	**B**	**C**	**D**
1	x-values	3x		
2	−10	−30		
3	−9	−27		
4	−8	−24		
5	−7	−21		

STEP 2 **Type** the formula "=3*A2" in cell B2. Use the fill down feature. Column B contains calculated values of the left side of the inequality.

STEP 3 **Type** the formula "=2*A2−8" in cell C2. Use the fill down feature. Column C contains values of the right side of the inequality.

A *truth function* compares values and returns *True* or *False*.

C2	=2*A2−8			
	A	**B**	**C**	**D**
1	x-values	3x	2x − 8	B < C?
2	−10	−30	−28	True
3	−9	−27	−26	True
4	−8	−24	−24	False
5	−7	−21	−22	False

STEP 4 **Type** the *truth function* "=B2<C2" in cell D2. Use the fill down feature. Column D tells whether the inequality is true or false for the x-value in that row.

▶ **Answer** The solution is all numbers less than -8.

PRACTICE

Use spreadsheet software to solve the inequality.

1. $13 - 3y > -2y$

2. $-2s < s - 9$

3. $2n - 10 \geq 12n$

4. $p + 16 \leq -3p$

5. $-2t + 9 > -5t$

6. $x - 4 < 5x$

7. **SHOPPING** Dani has at most $10 to buy school supplies. A notebook costs $1.50 and a pencil costs $.25. She needs two notebooks and some pencils. What are the possible numbers of pencils she can buy?

Multiple Choice Practice for Lessons 5.5–5.9

1. What is the solution of $\frac{7}{x-3} = \frac{3}{5}$? **Gr. 6 NS 1.3**

    (A) 1.2   **(B)** 4.8

    (C) 11   **(D)** $14.\overline{6}$

2. The Uniform Building Code requires at least 20 square feet of space for each student in a classroom. Which inequality models the number n of students that can legally be in the classroom below? **AF 1.1, MR 2.8**

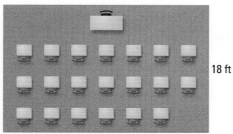

18 ft

28 ft

    (A) $\frac{n}{20} \le 504$ **(B)** $\frac{n}{20} \ge 504$

    (C) $20n \le 504$ **(D)** $20n \ge 504$

3. What is the solution of $5 - 4x = 23$? **AF 4.1**

    (A) -7 **(B)** -4.5

    (C) 4.5 **(D)** 7

4. Emma, Frank, and Megan are playing a game. The sum of Emma's score and Frank's score is less than Megan's score. Use the scores below. Which inequality models the number n of points that Emma has? **AF 1.1, MR 2.6**

Player	Score
Frank	30
Megan	75
Emma	n

    (A) $n + 30 < 75$

    (B) $n + 75 < 30$

    (C) $n - 30 < 75$

    (D) $n - 75 < 30$

5. What is the solution of $25a > -5a - 15$? **AF 4.1**

    (A) $a < -\frac{1}{2}$ **(B)** $a > -\frac{1}{2}$

    (C) $a < \frac{1}{2}$ **(D)** $a > \frac{1}{2}$

6. Mike and Rebecca plan to buy a gift for their parents. Mike contributes twice the amount Rebecca contributes. They need at least $27 for the gift. Which inequality describes the amount x (in dollars) that Rebecca must contribute? **AF 4.1**

    (A) $x \ge 9$ **(B)** $x \ge 18$

    (C) $x \le 9$ **(D)** $x \le 18$

7. What is the solution of $\frac{n}{2} = \frac{6}{5}$? **Gr. 6 NS 1.3**

    (A) $1.\overline{6}$ **(B)** 2.2

    (C) 2.4   **(D)** 12

8. Use the given information about the cost of using the city pool. Which equation can be used to find the number x of day passes for which the total cost is the same as purchasing a summer pass? **AF 1.1**

CITY POOL RATES

SUMMER PASS   **$100**
unlimited visits – including registration

DAY PASS   **$3**
additional $12 registration

    (A) $3x - 12 = 100$

    (B) $3x + 12 = 100$

    (C) $12x - 3 = 100$

    (D) $12x + 13 = 100$

9. What is the solution of $2n - 18 \ge 5n$? **AF 4.1**

    (A) $n \le -6$ **(B)** $n \ge -6$

    (C) $n \le 6$ **(D)** $n \ge 6$

CHAPTER SUMMARY

BIG IDEAS

For Your Notebook

Big Idea 1

Writing and Simplifying Expressions

When writing an expression, many common phrases can be translated into mathematical symbols, such as $+$, $-$, $\times$, or $\div$. To simplify an expression, combine like terms.

Addition	Subtraction	Multiplication	Division
plus	minus	times	divided by
the sum of	the difference of	the product of	the quotient of
increased by	decreased by	multiplied by	separate into equal parts
total	fewer than	of	
more than	less than	twice	
added to	subtracted from		

Big Idea 2

Writing and Solving Equations

You can solve equations by performing the same operation on each side using the same number.

Property	Words	Algebra
Addition Property of Equality	Add the same number to each side.	If $x - a = b$, then $x - a + a = b + a$, or $x = b + a$.
Subtraction Property of Equality	Subtract the same number from each side.	If $x + a = b$, then $x + a - a = b - a$, or $x = b - a$.
Multiplication Property of Equality	Multiply each side by the same number.	If $\frac{x}{a} = b$ and $a \neq 0$, then $\frac{x}{a} \cdot a = b \cdot a$, or $x = ab$.
Division Property of Equality	Divide each side by the same nonzero number.	If $ax = b$ and $a \neq 0$, then $\frac{ax}{a} = \frac{b}{a}$, or $x = \frac{b}{a}$.

Big Idea 3

Writing and Solving Inequalities

When solving an inequality, use rules similar to those above for solving equations, but remember to reverse the inequality symbol when multiplying or dividing each side by a negative number.

$3 - \dfrac{x}{5} > 8$	**Original equation**
$-\dfrac{x}{5} > 5$	**Subtract 3 from each side.**
$x < -25$	**Multiply both sides by -5. Reverse inequality symbol.**

APPLYING THE
BIG IDEAS

Big Idea 1
You write an expression in **Step 1.**

Big Idea 2
You write and solve an equation in **Step 2.**

Big Idea 3
You write and solve an inequality in **Step 3.**

PROBLEM How can you use expressions, equations, and inequalities to find the number of songs that you can download when you buy an MP3 player?

STEP 1 Write and evaluate an expression.

You can choose from four different MP3 players whose costs are $100, $180, $225, and $280. The cost of downloading one song from an online store is $.99.

Choose one of the MP3 players listed above. Write an expression to represent the total cost of buying the MP3 player and downloading n songs. What is the total cost when you download 25 songs?

STEP 2 Write and solve an equation.

You have $300 to buy an MP3 player and download songs. Write and solve an equation to find the maximum number of songs you can download when you buy the MP3 player you chose in Step 1.

STEP 3 Write and solve an inequality.

Suppose instead that you want to spend at most $350 on buying an MP3 player and downloading songs. Write and solve an inequality to find the numbers of songs you can download when you buy the MP3 player you chose in Step 1.

Extending the Problem

Use your results from the problem to complete the exercise.

1. Suppose you have $250 to buy an MP3 player and download songs. Choose a different MP3 player than the one chosen in Step 1. Write and solve an equation to find the maximum number of songs you can download when you buy this MP3 player.

2. The table at the right shows different accessories that you can buy for an MP3 player. Suppose you have $325 to spend. Choose one MP3 player and two accessories. Write and solve an inequality to find the numbers of songs you can download.

Accessory	Cost
Leather case	$10
Earphones	$40
Power adaptor	$35
Extra battery pack	$20
Radio transmitter	$45

REVIEW KEY VOCABULARY

• term, *p. 252*
• coefficient, *p. 252*
• like terms, *p. 252*
• constant term, *p. 252*
• equation, *p. 257*

• solution of an equation, *p. 257*
• equivalent equations, *p. 258*
• inverse operation, *p. 258*
• proportion, *p. 277*

• cross product, *p. 278*
• inequality, *p. 282*
• solution of an inequality, *p. 282*
• equivalent inequalities, *p. 282*

VOCABULARY EXERCISES

1. What does it mean for two inequalities to be equivalent? Give an example of equivalent inequalities.

Copy and complete the statement.

2. Two equations that have the same solution are __?__.

3. An equation stating that two ratios are equivalent is a(n) __?__.

4. A term that has no variable is a(n) __?__ term.

5. A number multiplied by a variable is the __?__ of the variable.

6. **NOTETAKING SKILLS** Use a *notetaking organizer* like the one on page 246 to write your notes about solving a proportion.

REVIEW EXAMPLES AND EXERCISES

5.1 Writing and Evaluating Expressions
pp. 247–251

AF 1.1 **EXAMPLE**

Verbal Phrase	Algebraic Expression
A number increased by 2	$x + 2$
A number decreased by 11	$x - 11$
Twice a number	$2x$
A number divided by 4	$\dfrac{x}{4}$

EXERCISES

SEE EXAMPLE 1
on p. 247
for Exs. 7–10

Write the phrase as an algebraic expression using the variable *x*.

7. 10 less than a number

8. A number increased by 4

9. The product of a number and 7

10. The square of a number divided by 2

5.2 Simplifying Expressions

AF 1.3

EXAMPLE

a. $3(5 + x) + x = 15 + 3x + x$ Distributive property

$= 15 + 4x$ Combine like terms.

b. $-2(5x - 8) + 4x = -10x + 16 + 4x$ Distributive property

$= -6x + 16$ Combine like terms.

EXERCISES

SEE EXAMPLES 2, 3, AND 4
on pp. 252–253
for Exs. 11–17

Simplify the expression.

11. $14x - 3y - 7x + y$ **12.** $4x - 11y + 2(1 - x)$ **13.** $5x + 2y - 9x - 8y$

14. $6a + 2a - 5b - 11a$ **15.** $9(4a - 2b) + 13a + 19b$ **16.** $-2(5 - y) + 11y + 12$

17. MOVIES You and two friends each purchase a ticket to a movie and a small bag of popcorn. Let x be the price of a ticket. The price of each bag of popcorn is one third the price of the movie ticket. Write and simplify an expression for the total amount of money your group spends.

5.3 Solving Equations Using Addition or Subtraction

AF 1.1

EXAMPLE

Solve the equation.

$x - 23 = 9$ Original equation

$x - 23 + 23 = 9 + 23$ Add 23 to each side.

$x = 32$ Simplify.

EXERCISES

SEE EXAMPLES 2 AND 3
on pp. 258–259
for Exs. 18–27

Solve the equation.

18. $c + 14 = 3$ **19.** $y - 31 = 11$ **20.** $7.7 = s - 4.3$

21. $29 = 40 + p$ **22.** $b + 3.09 = -5.91$ **23.** $v + 13 = 29$

24. $t - \frac{3}{7} = \frac{1}{7}$ **25.** $x + (-5) = -8$ **26.** $y - 3.9 = 10.9$

27. TREES Last year Marguerite had 12 elm trees in her yard. This year she has 17 elm trees. Write and solve an equation to find how many elm trees she planted this year.

Chapter Review   **303**

5.4 Solving Equations Using Multiplication or Division

pp. 263–267

AF 4.2

EXAMPLE

Solve the equation.

$$\frac{y}{4} = -8 \qquad \text{Original equation}$$

$$\frac{y}{4} \cdot 4 = -8 \cdot 4 \qquad \text{Multiply each side by 4.}$$

$$y = -32 \qquad \text{Simplify.}$$

$$-7x = -56 \qquad \text{Original equation}$$

$$\frac{-7x}{-7} = \frac{-56}{-7} \qquad \text{Divide each side by } -7.$$

$$x = 8 \qquad \text{Simplify.}$$

EXERCISES

SEE EXAMPLES
1 AND 2
on pp. 263–264
for Exs. 28–33

Solve the equation.

28. $\frac{m}{3} = 9$

29. $\frac{z}{-7} = 23$

30. $-5 = \frac{w}{-11}$

31. $-25x = 0$

32. $7 = 3.5t$

33. $-9.5m = -22.8$

5.5 Solving Two-Step Equations

pp. 270–275

AF 4.1

EXAMPLE

A catering company charges \$100 for setup plus \$15 per guest. How many guests can be served for a total cost of \$1000?

You can use a verbal model to write an equation involving the number n of guests.

$$\boxed{\text{Setup}} + \boxed{\begin{array}{c}\text{Cost per}\\\text{guest}\end{array}} \cdot \boxed{\begin{array}{c}\text{Number}\\\text{of guests}\end{array}} = \boxed{\begin{array}{c}\text{Total}\\\text{cost}\end{array}}$$

$$100 + 15n = 1000 \qquad \text{Write an algebraic model.}$$

$$15n = 900 \qquad \text{Subtract 100 from each side.}$$

$$n = 60 \qquad \text{Divide each side by 15.}$$

▶ **Answer** The number of guests that can be served is 60.

EXERCISES

SEE EXAMPLES
1, 3, AND 4
on pp. 270–272
for Exs. 34–39

Solve the equation. Check your solution.

34. $2p - 5 = 13$

35. $19 + 8v = 43$

36. $\frac{g}{9} + 6 = -2$

37. $\frac{c}{-10} + 26 = 46$

38. $-82 = 53 - 5t$

39. $-33 = -15t - 12$

5.6 Writing and Solving Proportions

pp. 277–281

Gr. 6 NS 1.3

EXAMPLE

Solve the proportion.

$$\frac{7.2}{9.4} = \frac{36}{x}$$ Original proportion

$$7.2 \cdot x = 9.4 \cdot 36$$ Cross products property

$$7.2x = 338.4$$ Multiply.

$$\frac{7.2x}{7.2} = \frac{338.4}{7.2}$$ Divide each side by 7.2.

$$x = 47$$ Simplify.

EXERCISES

SEE EXAMPLES 2 AND 3 on pp. 278–279 for Exs. 40–45

Solve the proportion.

40. $\dfrac{5}{13} = \dfrac{18}{c}$ **41.** $\dfrac{48}{54} = \dfrac{x}{6}$ **42.** $\dfrac{n}{12} = \dfrac{7}{8}$ **43.** $\dfrac{25}{b+1} = \dfrac{5}{2}$

44. EARNINGS You earn \$12 walking 3 dogs. You charge the same amount for each dog. How much do you earn for walking 5 dogs?

45. READING You can read 51 pages in 45 minutes. How many pages can you read in one hour?

5.7 Solving Inequalities Using Addition or Subtraction

pp. 282–287

AF 1.1

EXAMPLE

Solve the inequality. Then graph the solution.

$$x - 9 \le -4$$ Original inequality

$$x - 9 + 9 \le -4 + 9$$ Add 9 to each side.

$$x \le 5$$ Simplify.

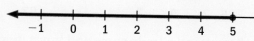

EXERCISES

SEE EXAMPLE 2 on p. 283 for Exs. 46–53

Solve the inequality. Then graph the solution.

46. $h - 12 > 12$ **47.** $-4 + k \le 6$ **48.** $7 < 15 + p$ **49.** $d + 11 \ge 5$

50. $m - 10 > 21$ **51.** $b + 13 \le 11$ **52.** $k - 8 \ge 2\frac{1}{2}$ **53.** $p - 2.5 < 7.7$

5.8 Solving Inequalities Using Multiplication or Division

AF 1.1

EXAMPLE

Solve the inequality.

$\frac{t}{7} > 2$	Original inequality
$\frac{t}{7} \cdot 7 > 2 \cdot 7$	Multiply each side by 7.
$t > 14$	Simplify.

$-12k \le 60$	Original inequality
$\frac{-12k}{-12} \ge \frac{60}{-12}$	Divide each side by -12. Reverse the inequality symbol.
$k \ge -5$	Simplify.

EXERCISES

**SEE EXAMPLES
1 AND 2**
on pp. 288–289
for Exs. 54–61

Solve the inequality.

54. $\frac{d}{6} \le 34$

55. $-\frac{1}{5}x \ge 20$

56. $-15b < 60$

57. $5c > 25$

58. $-4k \le -36$

59. $\frac{2}{3}y > -12$

60. $16z < 32$

61. $\frac{m}{5} \ge -11$

5.9 Solving Two-Step Inequalities

pp. 293–297

AF 4.1

EXAMPLE

$-5x - 45 \ge 30$	Original inequality
$-5x \ge 75$	Add 45 to each side.
$x \le -15$	Divide each side by -5 and reverse the inequality symbol.

EXERCISES

**SEE EXAMPLES
1, 2, AND 3**
on pp. 293–294
for Exs. 62–69

Solve the inequality.

62. $-5 < 3x + 16$

63. $-3m + 20 > -7$

64. $7 - g \le -8g$

65. $x - 10 < -x$

66. $2x + 5 \le -7$

67. $-y > y$

68. TRADE SHOW You pay $10 to attend a trade show and buy x items for $5 dollars each. You can spend no more than $55. Write and solve an inequality to find the numbers of items that you can buy.

69. FUNDRAISER The school chorus is selling $2 raffle tickets to raise money for a trip. The chorus already has $116 saved. How many tickets does the chorus need to sell in order to have at least $250 to help pay for the trip?

1. **VOCABULARY** Identify any like terms and coefficients in the expression $5x - 3y + 8y + x - 12$.

2. **VOCABULARY** Copy and complete: If $\frac{a}{b} = \frac{c}{d}$, then $ad = bc$ by the __?__ property.

Write the phrase as an algebraic expression using the variable x. Then evaluate the expression when $x = 12$.

3. A number times 3, subtracted from 20

4. The sum of 5 times a number and 14

Simplify the expression.

5. $3x + 4 - x + 1$

6. $2x - 3y + 5x - (-9y)$

7. $2(9x - 22y) + 4x$

Solve the equation.

8. $s - 6 = 39$

9. $x + 12 = -2$

10. $-236 = 29 - 5g$

11. $24v = 288$

12. $\frac{1}{9} = t + \frac{1}{9}$

13. $-9.8 = \frac{y}{-4.7}$

14. $5b - 7 = 120$

15. $14.6 = \frac{k}{2.5}$

Find the unknown dimension.

16. Perimeter = 62 in.

17. Area = 72 in.^{2}

18. Area = 200 cm^2

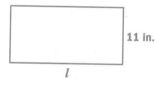

11 in.

l

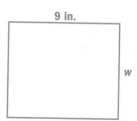

9 in.

w

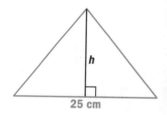

h

25 cm

Solve the proportion.

19. $\frac{12}{16} = \frac{18}{a}$

20. $\frac{15}{6} = \frac{d}{4}$

21. $\frac{9}{n} = \frac{21}{14}$

22. $\frac{t-3}{12} = \frac{11}{6}$

Solve the inequality.

23. $y + 78 < -124$

24. $-8.56 + k \geq 5.32$

25. $-8x < 64$

26. $-\frac{1}{6}x > 5$

27. $3x + 7 \leq 28$

28. $-\frac{1}{4}m - 3 \leq -2$

29. **HIKING** You go on a 10 mile hike. In the morning you hike 4.1 miles, and by 2:00 P.M. you have hiked 3.6 more miles. Write and solve an equation to find how many miles you have left to hike.

30. **LUNCH** You and a friend are having lunch together. You can spend no more than $30 on both meals. The total cost of your friend's meal is $14.78. Write and solve an inequality to determine how much you can spend on your meal.

If you have difficulty solving a multiple choice problem directly, you may be able to use another approach to eliminate incorrect answer choices and obtain the correct answer.

PROBLEM 1

A bus company charges $75 and an additional $2.50 for each student going on a field trip. The school has $180 set aside for the trip. What are all possible numbers of students that can go on the field trip?

Ⓐ $s \leq 20$　　Ⓑ $s \leq 30$　　Ⓒ $s \leq 42$　　Ⓓ $s \leq 72$

Strategy 1 SOLVE DIRECTLY

Write a verbal model that represents the situation. Then write and solve an inequality to find all possible numbers of students that can go on the field trip.

STEP 1 Write a verbal model.

| Bus cost | + | Cost per student | • | Number of students | ≤ | Total cost |

STEP 2 Write and solve an inequality. Let s represent the number of students.

$$75 + 2.5s \leq 180$$
$$75 - 75 + 2.5s \leq 180 - 75$$
$$2.5s \leq 105$$
$$\frac{2.5s}{2.5} \leq \frac{105}{2.5}$$
$$s \leq 42$$

At most 42 students can go on the field trip.

The correct answer is C. Ⓐ Ⓑ Ⓒ Ⓓ

Strategy 2 ELIMINATE CHOICES

Use the strategy work backwards to eliminate answer choices.

First find the amount of money remaining after the initial bus charge by subtracting the charge from the amount of money the school has set aside: $180 - 75 = 105$. There is $105 left for the cost of the students.

Because $72(2.5) = 180$, which is greater than 105, 72 students can not attend the field trip. So, you can eliminate choice D.

Note that $20(2.5) = 50$ and $30(2.5) = 75$, and that both of these numbers are less than 105. So, either 20 or 30 students can attend the field trip. Because $30 > 20$, you can eliminate choice A.

Because $42(2.5) = 105$, 42 students can attend the field trip. So, you can eliminate choice B since $42 > 30$. Because this cost equals $105, more than 42 students will not be able to go.

At most 42 students can go on the field trip.

The correct answer is C. Ⓐ Ⓑ Ⓒ Ⓓ

PROBLEM 2

Matt bought 104 hot dogs for a party. Hot dogs come in packages of 8. How many packages of hot dogs did Matt buy?

(A) 10 (B) 13 (C) 22 (D) 832

Strategy 1 | SOLVE DIRECTLY

Write a verbal model that represents the situation. Then write and solve an equation to find the number of packages of hot dogs that Matt bought.

STEP 1 Write a verbal model.

Hot dogs per package	·	Number of packages	=	Number of hot dogs

STEP 2 Write and solve an equation. Let p represent the number of packages of hot dogs.

$$8p = 104$$
$$\frac{8p}{8} = \frac{104}{8}$$
$$p = 13$$

Matt bought 13 packages of hot dogs.

The correct answer is B. (A) (B) (C) (D)

Strategy 2 | ELIMINATE CHOICES

You can eliminate choices of a multiple choice question by determining the reasonableness of the answer choices.

Because there is more than 1 hot dog in each package, the number of packages of hot dogs must be less than 104. So, you can eliminate choice D.

Think of multiples of 8 on either side of 104. For example, try 80 and 160.

$$80 < 104 < 160$$
$$10 < \frac{104}{8} < 20$$

Because the number of packages is strictly between 10 and 20, you can eliminate choices A and C.

The correct answer is B. (A) (B) (C) (D)

STRATEGY PRACTICE

Explain why you can eliminate the highlighted answer choice.

1. You are stuffing 560 envelopes for a school event. By 1:00 P.M., you have stuffed 140 envelopes. How many envelopes per hour do you need to stuff to finish by 5:00 P.M.?

   (A) ✗ **4 envelopes**
   (B) 84 envelopes
   (C) 105 envelopes
   (D) 420 envelopes

2. Your school earns $1.50 for every T-shirt sold. Find the minimum number of T-shirts you must sell to raise $500.

   (A) 333 (B) 334 (C) 500 (D) ✗ **750**

1. The area of the rectangle is 135 square centimeters. Which equation can you use to find the width w in centimeters? **AF 1.1**

15 cm

Ⓐ $15 = \frac{w}{135}$

Ⓑ $135 = 15w$

Ⓒ $135 = \frac{w}{15}$

Ⓓ $15 = 135w$

2. What is the solution of $5z < 65$? **AF 1.1**

Ⓐ $z > 13$

Ⓑ $z < 13$

Ⓒ $z > 60$

Ⓓ $z < 70$

3. Which algebraic expression represents the verbal phrase *the difference of 3 and $\frac{2}{3}$ of x*? **AF 1.1, MR 2.6**

Ⓐ $2 - x$

Ⓑ $\frac{2}{3}x - 3$

Ⓒ $3 - \frac{2}{3}x$

Ⓓ $3 - \frac{2}{3}x - x$

4. Jade works in a clothing store and earns $350 per week, plus $.20 for every dollar of clothing she sells. Which inequality represents how much she has to sell in one week to earn at least $500? **AF 1.1**

Ⓐ $350 + 0.2x \geq 500$

Ⓑ $350 + 0.2x > 500$

Ⓒ $350x + 0.2x \geq 500$

Ⓓ $350x + 0.2x > 500$

5. What is the solution of $y + 9 = 0$? **AF 1.1**

Ⓐ -9

Ⓑ 0

Ⓒ $\frac{1}{9}$

Ⓓ 9

6. What is the solution of $2y + 7 > 11$? **AF 4.1**

Ⓐ $y > 2$

Ⓑ $y > 4$

Ⓒ $y > 9$

Ⓓ $y > 18$

7. What is the solution of $3 + 3b \leq 5$? **AF 4.1**

Ⓐ $b \leq \frac{2}{3}$

Ⓑ $b \leq \frac{8}{3}$

Ⓒ $b \geq \frac{2}{3}$

Ⓓ $b \geq \frac{8}{3}$

8. You are driving to an interview downtown at a speed of 45 miles per hour. After driving for $\frac{2}{3}$ of an hour, you are forced to stop due to a traffic jam, as shown in the diagram. What is the distance x between your home and downtown? **AF. 4.1, MR 1.1**

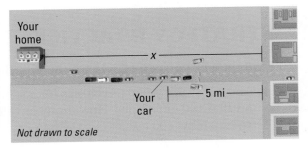
Your home
x
Your car
5 mi
Not drawn to scale

Ⓐ 25 mi

Ⓑ 30 mi

Ⓒ 35 mi

Ⓓ 40 mi

9. The weights of an empty basket and the same basket filled with tomatoes are shown below. Which statement is correct? **AF 1.1**

2 lb   More than 13 lb

(A) The tomatoes weigh more than 11 pounds.

(B) The tomatoes weigh exactly 11 pounds.

(C) The tomatoes weigh exactly 15 pounds.

(D) The tomatoes weigh at most 11 pounds.

10. A stage has the dimensions shown below. What are the values of x and y? **AF 4.1**

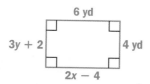

(A) $x = \frac{1}{2}$ yd; $y = 3$ yd

(B) $x = 2$ yd; $y = \frac{2}{5}$ yd

(C) $x = 4$ yd; $y = \frac{4}{3}$ yd

(D) $x = 5$ yd; $y = \frac{2}{3}$ yd

11. Which expression is equivalent to $2(x - 4) + 9x + 1$? **AF 1.3**

(A) $11x - 3$

(B) $11x - 7$

(C) $7x + 7$

(D) $10x - 7$

12. What is the solution of $\frac{d}{-11} \leq 6$? **AF 1.1**

(A) $d \leq 66$

(B) $d \geq 66$

(C) $d \leq -66$

(D) $d \geq -66$

13. The bill for the repair of a car is $560. The cost of parts is $440. The cost of labor is shown in the diagram. Which equation can you use to find the number h of hours of labor? **AF 4.1**

(A) $560 + 40h = 440$

(B) $40h - 560 = 440$

(C) $440 + 40h = 560$

(D) $440 - 40h = 560$

14. What is the solution of $216 = u - 129$? **AF 1.1**

(A) -345

(B) 2

(C) 87

(D) 345

15. What is the solution of $3x + 4 = 5$? **AF 4.1**

(A) $\frac{1}{3}$

(B) 3

(C) 9

(D) 12

16. Which algebraic expression represents the verbal phrase *seven minus the quotient of x and 4*? **AF 1.1**

(A) $\frac{x}{4} - 7$

(B) $7 - \frac{x}{4}$

(C) $\frac{7 - x}{4}$

(D) $\frac{x - 7}{4}$

6 Linear Equations and Graphs

Before

In previous chapters, you learned the following skills, which you'll use in Chapter 6:

- Solving equations in one variable
- Solving inequalities in one variable
- Graphing the solution of an inequality in one variable

Now

In Chapter 6 you'll study these **Big Ideas:**

1. Writing and graphing linear equations
2. Writing and graphing linear inequalities
3. Writing and solving systems of linear equations and inequalities

Why?

So you can solve real-world problems about . . .

- Skateboard wheels, p. 318
- Tides, p. 338
- Parachuting, p. 346
- Canoeing, p. 359
- Tennis, p. 366

Animated Math

at *classzone.com*

Get-Ready Games

SOCCER SCRAMBLE

California Standards

Review solving equations. *Gr. 7 AF 4.1*
Prepare for graphing equations. *Gr. 7 AF 3.3*

A $5x + 3 = -17$

T $3x + 15 = 18$

Q $-5x - 3 = 12$

S $20 = -14x - 8$

U $-2x + 3 = -1$

A $3x + 2 = -1$

K $-5x + 11 = -4$

Q $7 = -4x + 7$

How to Play

Find the name of an Eskimo game like soccer that was played on ice.

- Solve each equation.
- Order the solutions from least to greatest, and write the corresponding letters in the same order.

CALIFORNIA STANDARDS

• **Gr. 7 AF 3.3** Graph linear functions, noting that the vertical change (change in *y*-value) per unit of horizontal change (change in *x*-value) is always the same and know that the ratio ("rise over run") is called the slope of a graph. *(Lessons 6.2, 6.3, 6.4, 6.5)*

• **Gr. 7 AF 3.4** Plot the values of quantities whose ratios are always the same (e.g., cost to the number of an item, feet to inches, circumference to diameter of a circle). Fit a line to the plot and understand that the slope of the line equals the ratio of the quantities. *(Lesson 6.6)*

SOCCER CITY

California Standards

Review graphing ordered pairs. ***Gr. 5 AF 1.4***
Prepare for graphing lines. ***Gr. 7 AF 3.3***

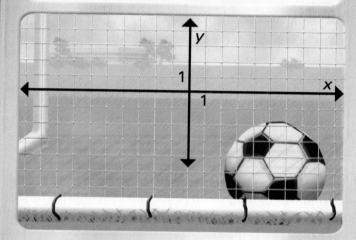

How to Play

Find the city in which the international organization that governs soccer (FIFA) was first formed.

• For each group of ordered pairs, plot and connect the points in the order given. Do not connect points from different groups.

1 (3, 2), (3, −2)

2 (−4, −2), (−3, 2), (−2, −2), (−2.5, 0), (−3.5, 0)

3 (−7, −2), (−7, 2), (−5, 2), (−5, 0), (−7, 0)

4 (7, 2), (5, 2), (5, 0), (7, 0), (7, −2), (5, −2)

5 (−1, −2), (−1, 2), (1, 2), (1, 0), (0, 0), (1, −2)

Games Wrap-Up

Draw Conclusions

Complete these exercises after playing the games.

1. WRITING While playing *Soccer Scramble*, a student says that the first step to solve the equation $5x + 3 = -17$, is to subtract $5x$ from both sides. *Describe* and correct the student's error.

2. REASONING Write instructions with ordered pairs, like those given in *Soccer City*, that would allow someone to write your name or the name of your town on a coordinate plane.

6 Getting Ready

Prerequisite Skills

REVIEW VOCABULARY

- **variable,** *p. 7*
- **coefficient,** *p. 252*
- **constant term,** *p. 252*
- **equation,** *p. 257*
- **solution of an equation,** *p. 257*
- **coordinate plane,** *p. 734*

VOCABULARY CHECK

Copy and complete using a review term from the list at the left.

1. In the expression $-5y$, y is the __?__ and -5 is the __?__.

2. A statement with an equal sign between two expressions is a(n) __?__.

3. The value of x that makes $2x + 5 = 12$ a true statement is a(n) __?__.

4. Ordered pairs like $(-2, 3)$ and $(4, 6)$ can be graphed in the __?__.

SKILL CHECK

Simplify the expression by combining like terms. *(p. 252)*

5. $7x + 4 - 3x$ 6. $-2x + 5x - x$

7. $x + 4 - 12x$ 8. $6x - 5 + x$

9. $15y + 9x - 6x - y$ 10. $-13y + 8x - 2x + 3y - 10$

Solve the equation. Check your solution. *(p. 293)*

11. $3 = 9x - 24$ 12. $7 - 8x = 3$ 13. $6x + 9 = -45$

14. $\frac{x}{4} - 1 = 6$ 15. $15 - x = -22$ 16. $-9 = \frac{x}{2} + 4$

Notetaking Skills

NOW YOU TRY
Make a *decision tree* for solving a one-step inequality. You may want to use colored pencils.

Focus on Graphic Organizers

You can use a *decision tree* to map out a procedure, such as solving a one-step equation. In a decision tree, each box represents a possible step that you can take in the process. Arrows branching from one box indicate a choice that you must make.

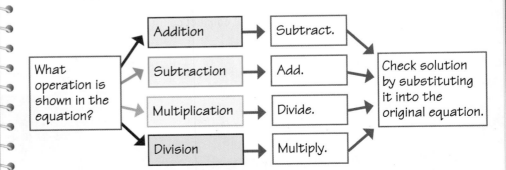

SOLVING A ONE-STEP EQUATION

314

6.1 Equations in Two Variables

Standards AF 4.2 Solve multistep problems involving rate, average speed, distance, and time or a direct variation.

Connect *Before* you found solutions of equations in one variable. *Now* you will find solutions of equations in two variables.

Math and SPORTS
Example 2, p. 316

KEY VOCABULARY

• solution of an equation in two variables

A **solution of an equation in two variables** is an ordered pair whose coordinates make the equation true. For example, (2, 3) is a solution of $x + y = 5$ because $2 + 3 = 5$.

EXAMPLE 1 Checking Solutions

Tell whether the ordered pair is a solution of the equation.

a. $x + 3y = 14$; (7, −6)

b. $4x − 2y = −28$; (−5, 4)

SOLUTION

a.
$$x + 3y = 14 \quad \text{Write original equation.}$$
$$7 + 3(-6) \stackrel{?}{=} 14 \quad \text{Substitute 7 for } x \text{ and } -6 \text{ for } y.$$
$$7 + (-18) \stackrel{?}{=} 14 \quad \text{Multiply.}$$
$$-11 \neq 14 \; \boldsymbol{X} \quad \text{Add. Solution does not check.}$$

▶ **Answer** The ordered pair (7, −6) is *not* a solution of $x + 3y = 14$. When you substitute 7 for x and −6 for y, the result is not a true equation.

b.
$$4x - 2y = -28 \quad \text{Write original equation.}$$
$$4(-5) - 2(4) \stackrel{?}{=} -28 \quad \text{Substitute } -5 \text{ for } x \text{ and 4 for } y.$$
$$-20 - 8 \stackrel{?}{=} -28 \quad \text{Multiply.}$$
$$-28 = -28 \; \checkmark \quad \text{Subtract. The solution checks.}$$

▶ **Answer** The ordered pair (−5, 4) is a solution of $4x - 2y = -28$. When you substitute −5 for x and 4 for y, the result is a true equation.

✓ GUIDED PRACTICE for Example 1

Tell whether the ordered pair is a solution of the equation.

1. $y = 3x - 7$; (6, 5)

2. $-2x - 4y = 12$; (−4, −1)

3. $y = -4x + 9$; (3, −3)

4. $6x - 5y = -27$; (−2, 3)

5. $y = -12 - x$; (−5, −17)

6. $-x + 8y = -27$; (−1, −7)

Generally, an equation in two variables has an infinite number of solutions. You can use substitution to find solutions.

EXAMPLE 2 Making a Table of Solutions

IN-LINE SKATES It costs $7 per hour to rent in-line skates and $10 for safety equipment. The total cost can be modeled by the equation $C = 10 + 7h$ where C is the total cost (in dollars) and h is the number of hours skated. Make a table that shows some possible total costs.

SOLUTION

STEP 1 **Substitute** several values of h into $C = 10 + 7h$ and solve for C.

h-value	Substitute for h.	Evaluate.	Solution (h, C)
$h = 1$	$C = 10 + 7(1)$	$C = 17$	$(1, 17)$
$h = 2$	$C = 10 + 7(2)$	$C = 24$	$(2, 24)$
$h = 3$	$C = 10 + 7(3)$	$C = 31$	$(3, 31)$
$h = 4$	$C = 10 + 7(4)$	$C = 38$	$(4, 38)$

STEP 2 **Make** a table of the solutions. Show the cost C for h hours.

Hours, h	1	2	3	4
Cost, C	$17	$24	$31	$38

> **CHOOSING VALUES**
> Because you cannot skate for a negative number of hours, choose only positive values to substitute for h.

SOLVING FOR Y When you are finding solutions of an equation, it may be helpful to first rewrite the equation by solving for y.

Not solved for y	Solved for y
$2x + y = 12$	$y = -2x + 12$

EXAMPLE 3 Finding Solutions of an Equation

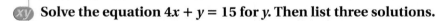

Solve the equation $4x + y = 15$ for y. Then list three solutions.

SOLUTION

STEP 1 **Solve** the equation for y.

$4x + y = 15$ **Write original equation.**

$y = 15 - 4x$ **Subtract 4x from each side.**

STEP 2 **Choose** several values to substitute for x. Then solve for y.

x-value	Substitute for x.	Evaluate.	Solution (x, y)
$x = -1$	$y = 15 - 4(-1)$	$y = 19$	$(-1, 19)$
$x = 0$	$y = 15 - 4(0)$	$y = 15$	$(0, 15)$
$x = 2$	$y = 15 - 4(2)$	$y = 7$	$(2, 7)$

▶ **Answer** Three solutions are $(-1, 19)$, $(0, 15)$, and $(2, 7)$.

7. **WHAT IF?** If the store in Example 2 charges $8 per hour to rent in-line skates, then the total cost can be modeled by $C = 10 + 8h$. Make a table of solutions for this equation.

List three solutions of the equation.

8. $y = -2x + 6$ 9. $y = 4.5x - 8$ 10. $3x + y = 4$

6.1 EXERCISES

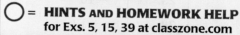

HOMEWORK KEY

◆ = **MULTIPLE CHOICE PRACTICE**
Exs. 10, 21, 38, 47–49

○ = **HINTS AND HOMEWORK HELP**
for Exs. 5, 15, 39 at classzone.com

SKILLS • PROBLEM SOLVING • REASONING

1. **VOCABULARY** Copy and complete: An ordered pair (x, y) whose coordinates make an equation such as $y = 9x + 5$ true is a(n) __?__ .

2. **WRITING** *Describe* the outcome when you substitute the coordinates of an ordered pair into an equation if the ordered pair is *not* a solution.

SEE EXAMPLE 1
on p. 315
for Exs. 3–10

CHECKING SOLUTIONS **Tell whether the ordered pair is a solution of the equation.**

3. $y = 4x + 2$; $(2, 10)$ 4. $2x + y = 5$; $(7, 5)$ 5. $y = 6 - x$; $(-3, 3)$

6. $x + 8y = 2$; $(10, -1)$ 7. $y = 6x + 7$; $(2, 21)$ 8. $3x - y = 26$; $(6, -8)$

9. **ERROR ANALYSIS** *Describe* and correct the error in deciding whether $(-5, 4)$ is a solution of $2x + 3y = -7$.

$$2x + 3y = -7$$
$$2(4) + 3(-5) \overset{?}{=} -7$$
$$8 + (-15) \overset{?}{=} -7$$
$$-7 = -7 \checkmark \quad \text{So, } (-5, 4) \text{ is a solution.}$$

10. ◆ **MULTIPLE CHOICE** Which ordered pair is a solution of $y = -3x + 11$?

    Ⓐ $(-2, 17)$ Ⓑ $(0, -11)$ Ⓒ $(2, 3)$ Ⓓ $(-1, -14)$

SEE EXAMPLE 2
on p. 316
for Exs. 11–13

CALCULATING Y-VALUES **Copy and complete the table for the equation.**

11. $y = x + 8$

12. $y = 4 - 3x$

13. $y = -20 + x$

x	−5	0	5	10
y	?	?	?	?

SEE EXAMPLE 3
on p. 316
for Exs. 14–33

FINDING SOLUTIONS **List four solutions of the equation.**

14. $3x + y = 13$ 15. $5x + y = 3$ 16. $16x + 24 = y$

17. $\frac{1}{5}x + 9 = y$ 18. $y = \frac{1}{2}x - 1$ 19. $y = -\frac{1}{3}x - 5$

20. ERROR ANALYSIS *Describe* and *correct* the error in finding a solution of the equation $y = -2x + 5$.

$$y = -2x + 5$$
$$y = -2\left(\frac{1}{2}\right) + 5$$
$$y = -1 + 5 = 4$$
So, $\left(4, \frac{1}{2}\right)$ is a solution. ✗

21. ◆ MULTIPLE CHOICE Which ordered pair is *not* a solution of $y + 8 = -2x$?

Ⓐ $(-2, -4)$ Ⓑ $(-1, 10)$

Ⓒ $(0, -8)$ Ⓓ $(1, -10)$

SOLVING FOR Y Solve the equation for *y*. Then list four solutions.

22. $x + y = 8$

23. $42 = 4x + y$

24. $33 = -3x + y$

25. $5x + y = 10$

26. $12 = 3x + y$

27. $19 = -2x + y$

28. $4y = 8x + 12$

29. $5y + 15x = 10$

30. $-32 = 4x - 12y$

31. $8y = 16x - 10$

32. $-6y + 3x = 9$

33. $42 - 7y = 15x$

CONNECT SKILLS TO PROBLEM SOLVING Exercises 34–36 will help you prepare for problem solving.

Use the following information: The distance *d* traveled by an object moving at speed *r* for time *t* is given by the equation $d = rt$.

34. Suppose Joe bicycles at a speed of 20 miles per hour. Write an equation that relates Joe's distance traveled and his time spent bicycling.

35. How far does Joe travel in 2 hours?

36. Joe travels 65 miles. How long does this take?

SEE EXAMPLES 2 AND 3 on p. 316 for Exs. 37–38

37. SKATEBOARD WHEELS You order new wheels for your skateboard that sell for $6 each. The charge for shipping and handling your order is $7.

a. Use the equation $C = 6n + 7$ where *C* is the total cost (in dollars) of your order and *n* is the number of wheels ordered. What is the total cost for 4 wheels?

b. The total cost of your order is $103. How many wheels did you purchase?

c. Suppose you double the number of wheels purchased in part (b). Will the total cost be $103 \times 2 = 206? *Explain.*

$6 per wheel,
$7 for shipping
any size order

California @*HomeTutor*   for problem solving help at classzone.com

38. ◆ MULTIPLE CHOICE You pay $25 to join a movie club and $3 to rent each movie. You can model this with the equation $C = 25 + 3m$ where *C* is the total cost (in dollars) and *m* is the number of movies you rent. If you can spend $60, what is the greatest number of movies you can rent?

Ⓐ 10   Ⓑ 11   Ⓒ 28   Ⓓ 205

California @*HomeTutor*   for problem solving help at classzone.com

39. **REASONING** *Explain* why it may be helpful to rewrite an equation by solving for y when finding solutions of the equation. Use several examples to show your reasoning.

40. **GLASS ELEVATOR** A glass elevator is at a height of 1200 feet. It is descending at a rate of 1000 feet per minute.

    a. Use the equation $h = 1200 - 1000t$ where h is the height (in feet) of the elevator and t is the time (in minutes). What is the height of the elevator after 1 minute?

    b. How long, in minutes and seconds, will it take the elevator to reach a height of 0 feet?

Descent rate:
1000 feet per minute

41. **SHORT RESPONSE** You want to buy x bottles of water and y bottles of sports drink. Each bottle of water costs \$1 and each bottle of sports drink costs \$2. The total cost C (in dollars) can be modeled by $C = x + 2y$. You have \$9. Can you buy 4 bottles of water and 3 bottles of sports drink? *Explain.*

42. **REASONING** In Example 3 on page 316, you solved the equation for y before substituting the x-values. Will you get the same solutions if you substitute the x-values before solving for y? *Justify* your reasoning.

43. **XY ALGEBRA** Solve the equation $ax + by = c$ for y.

CHALLENGE **Find the ordered pair that is a solution of both equations.**

44. $y = -2x + 3$
$y = 0.5x - 2$

45. $y = 6x - 10$
$y = -3x + 26$

46. **CHALLENGE** For a class project, you simulate a dog walking-and-feeding service. In week one, you charge \$2 per walk and \$4 per meal. In week two, you charge \$4 per walk and \$2 per meal. In week three, you charge \$4 per walk and \$4 per meal. You collect \$38, \$40, and \$52 respectively for the three weeks. Each week had the same number of walks and same number of meals. Find the numbers of walks and meals per week.

◆ CALIFORNIA STANDARDS SPIRAL REVIEW

NS 2.1   **47.** Which number equals $(3)^{-2}$? *(p. 196)*

    A -6 **B** $-\frac{1}{9}$ **C** $\frac{1}{9}$ **D** $\frac{1}{6}$

NS 2.4   **48.** Which square root is closest to 12? *(p. 213)*

    A $\sqrt{138}$ **B** $\sqrt{142}$ **C** $\sqrt{148}$ **D** $\sqrt{152}$

NS 1.1   **49.** In April of 2006, the population of the United States was approximately 299,000,000. Which choice shows the April 2006 population of the United States written in scientific notation? *(p. 201)*

    A 0.0299×10^{10} **B** 0.299×10^{9} **C** 2.99×10^{8} **D** 29.9×10^{7}

6.2 Graphs of Linear Equations

Math and
OCEANOGRAPHY
Ex. 42, p. 325

Standards   **AF 3.3 Graph linear functions**, noting that the vertical change (change in *y*-value) per unit of horizontal change (change in *x*-value) is always the same and know that the ratio ("rise over run") is called the slope of a graph.

Connect   *Before* you found solutions of equations in two variables. *Now* you will sketch the graphs of linear equations.

KEY VOCABULARY
• linear equation

ACTIVITY

You can graph an equation by plotting ordered pairs from a table.

STEP 1 **Copy** and complete the table of values for $y = 3x + 2$.

x	−4	−2	0	2	4
y	−10	?	?	?	?

STEP 2 **Plot** each ordered pair (x, y) from the table in a coordinate plane like the one shown.

$(-4, -10)$, $(-2, ?)$, $(0, ?)$, $(2, ?)$, $(4, ?)$

STEP 3 **Connect** the points. What pattern do you notice?

STEP 4 **Find** several more solutions of $y = 3x + 2$. Locate each solution in your coordinate plane. What do you notice?

REVIEW USING THE COORDINATE PLANE
For help using the coordinate plane, see p. 734.

STEP 5 **Make** a conjecture about the graph of all solutions of $y = 3x + 2$.

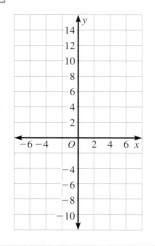

LINEAR EQUATIONS In the activity, you graphed solutions of a *linear equation*. A **linear equation** in two variables is an equation whose graph is a line or part of a line. The two variables appear in separate terms with each variable occurring only to the first power.

About the Standards

Equations like $y = x - 1$ are *linear functions*. You will learn about functions (AF 3.3) in Chapter 7.

Linear equations	Not linear equations
$y = x - 1$	$24 = rt$
$3p + 5q = 16$	$x^2 + y^2 = 25$
$s = 0.2t$	

The equation $24 = rt$ is not linear because it has two variables in the same term. The equation $x^2 + y^2 = 25$ is not linear because the variables are squared.

EXAMPLE 1 Graphing a Linear Equation

XY **Graph** $y = \frac{1}{2}x + 1$.

STEP 1 **Choose** several values to substitute for x. Then evaluate to find y and make a table of values.

x	−4	−2	0	2	4
y	−1	0	1	2	3

STEP 2 **List** the solutions as ordered pairs.

$(-4, -1), (-2, 0), (0, 1), (2, 2), (4, 3)$

STEP 3 **Plot** the ordered pairs and draw a line through them. The line is the graph of $y = \frac{1}{2}x + 1$.

Animated Math

For an interactive example of graphing a linear equation, go to **classzone.com.**

EXAMPLE 2 Using the Graph of a Linear Equation

XY **GROWTH RATE** Sue's hair is 3 inches long and grows $\frac{1}{2}$ inch per month. The length y (in inches) of her hair can be modeled by the equation $y = \frac{1}{2}x + 3$ where x is the time (in months). Use a graph to estimate how long it will take Sue to grow her hair to a length of $5\frac{1}{2}$ inches.

SOLUTION

Make a table of values and plot each solution. Draw a ray through the points. Then locate the point on the ray where $y = 5\frac{1}{2}$.

x	0	1	2	3
y	3	$3\frac{1}{2}$	4	$4\frac{1}{2}$

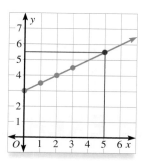

▶ **Answer** The graph shows that it will take about 5 months for Sue to grow her hair to a length of $5\frac{1}{2}$ inches.

AVOID ERRORS

In a real-world situation, be sure to choose x-values that make sense in the context of the problem. In Example 2, the x-values should include only nonnegative numbers.

✓ **GUIDED PRACTICE** for Examples 1 and 2

Graph the linear equation.

1. $y = x + 4$ **2.** $y = x + 6$ **3.** $y = \frac{1}{2}x - 7$ **4.** $y = -2x - 3$

5. **WHAT IF?** In Example 2, suppose Sue's hair is 4 inches long. The length y (in inches) of her hair can be modeled by the equation $y = \frac{1}{2}x + 4$ where x is the time (in months). Use a graph to estimate how long it will take Sue to grow her hair to a length of $7\frac{1}{2}$ inches.

VERTICAL AND HORIZONTAL LINES Some linear equations have only one variable. The graphs of these equations are vertical or horizontal lines.

> **KEY CONCEPT** *For Your Notebook*
>
> **Vertical and Horizontal Lines**
>
> The graph of $x = a$ is the vertical line passing through $(a, 0)$.
>
> The graph of $y = b$ is the horizontal line passing through $(0, b)$.

EXAMPLE 3 Graphing Vertical and Horizontal Lines

a. The graph of $x = -2$ is the vertical line through $(-2, 0)$.

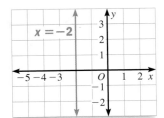

For all values of y, the x-value is -2.

b. The graph of $y = 4$ is the horizontal line through $(0, 4)$.

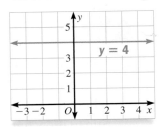

For all values of x, the y-value is 4.

✓ **GUIDED PRACTICE** for Example 3

Graph the equation.

6. $y = -4$ **7.** $x = \dfrac{3}{2}$ **8.** $y = 5.7$ **9.** $x = -1$

6.2 EXERCISES

HOMEWORK KEY

◆ = **MULTIPLE CHOICE PRACTICE**
Exs. 7, 25, 38, 47–49

○ = **HINTS AND HOMEWORK HELP**
for Exs. 15, 19, 43 at classzone.com

SKILLS • PROBLEM SOLVING • REASONING

1. VOCABULARY Copy and complete: The graph of a linear equation in two variables is a(n) __?__.

VOCABULARY Tell whether the equation is linear.

2. $3x + y = 8$ **3.** $2y - 5x = 10$ **4.** $9x^2 = y + 4$ **5.** $y = -4$

6. WRITING Your friend says that the graphs of $y = b$ and $x = a$ will always intersect at (b, a). Is your friend correct? *Explain.*

SEE EXAMPLE 1
on p. 321
for Exs. 7–17

7. ◆ MULTIPLE CHOICE Which equation's graph includes the point (0, 0)?

(A) $y = \frac{1}{2}x + 6$ **(B)** $2x + 3y = 6$ **(C)** $y = \frac{1}{2}x$ **(D)** $2x = 6 - 3y$

GRAPHING WITH TWO VARIABLES Graph the linear equation.

8. $y = x + 9$ **9.** $y = x - 14$ **10.** $y = x - 17$

11. $y = -2x + 1$ **12.** $y = -4x + 8$ **13.** $y = 8x$

14. $y = -3x$ **15.** $y = \frac{1}{2}x + 5$ **16.** $y = \frac{1}{4}x + 12$

17. ERROR ANALYSIS A student graphs the
equation $y = 4x + 1$ as shown at the
right. *Describe* and correct the error
in the student's graph.

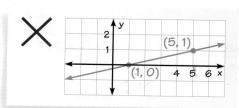

SEE EXAMPLE 3
on p. 322
for Exs. 18–28

GRAPHING WITH ONE VARIABLE Graph the vertical or horizontal line.

18. $x = 2$ **19.** $y = 6$ **20.** $y = -9$

21. $y = -1.5$ **22.** $x = 1.5$ **23.** $x = 3.5$

24. ERROR ANALYSIS A student graphs the
equation $y = 5$ as shown at the right.
Describe and correct the error in the
student's graph.

25. ◆ MULTIPLE CHOICE Which linear equation's
graph is a vertical line?

(A) $x = 7$ **(B)** $y = 8$

(C) $y = -5x$ **(D)** $y = 7x + 2$

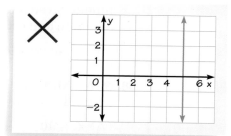

WRITING EQUATIONS Write an equation of the line.

26.
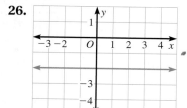

27.
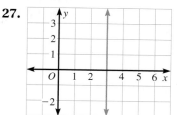

28.
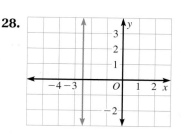

SOLVING FOR Y Solve the linear equation for y. Then graph the equation.

29. $16x - 4y = 8$ **30.** $9x + 3y = 18$ **31.** $10x = -2y$

32. COMPARING GRAPHS Graph the equations below in the same coordinate
plane. How are the graphs alike? How are they different?

$$y = x \qquad y = x + 7 \qquad y = x - 5 \qquad y = x - 9$$

CONNECT SKILLS TO PROBLEM SOLVING Exercises 33–35 will help you prepare for problem solving.

Graph the linear equation for each situation.

33. You earn $8 per hour raking leaves. The total amount y that you earn can be modeled by $y = 8x$ where x is the number of hours you work.

34. You drive 65 miles per hour. The total distance y that you travel can be modeled by $y = 65x$ where x is the number of hours you drive.

35. Admission to an amusement park costs $25 per person. One parking pass costs $8. The total cost y for one car full of visitors can be modeled by $y = 25x + 8$ where x is the number of visitors in the car.

SEE EXAMPLE 2
on p. 321
for Exs. 36–37

36. **PHOTOGRAPHY** You buy a digital camera using a payment plan that can be modeled by the equation $C = 10m + 50$ where C is the total cost (in dollars) and m is the number of months. Graph the equation and use your graph to estimate your cost for one year.

   California @*HomeTutor* for problem solving help at classzone.com

**Camera payment plan:
$50 deposit and
$10 per month**

37. **SAVINGS** Janet has $80 saved and plans to save $15.50 more each month. This situation can be modeled by the equation $y = 15.50x + 80$ where y is the amount of money saved and x is the number of months. Graph the equation and estimate when Janet will have $250.

   California @*HomeTutor* for problem solving help at classzone.com

38. ◆ **MULTIPLE CHOICE** A cell phone plan with unlimited minutes costs $40 a month. Which equation models the cost C of this plan for m months?

   A $C = 40$ **B** $m = 40$ **C** $C = 40m$ **D** $m = 40C$

READING IN MATH Read the information below for Exercises 39–41.

Temperature Temperature can be measured in degrees Fahrenheit or degrees Celsius. On the Fahrenheit scale, the difference between the freezing point and boiling point of water is 180°. On the Celsius scale, the difference is 100°. To convert from degrees Celsius C to degrees Fahrenheit F, you can use the formula $F = \frac{9}{5}C + 32$.

Common Temperatures	
Freezing point of water	32°F
Typical room temperature	70°F
Average body temperature	98.2°F
Boiling point of water	212°F

39. **Graph** Graph the equation that relates degrees Celsius to degrees Fahrenheit. Use $C = 0°$, 10°, 20°, 30°, and 40° in your table of values.

40. **Interpret** Use the Common Temperatures table and your graph. Approximate the average body temperature in degrees Celsius.

41. **Analyze** Is 10°C *warmer* or *colder* than typical room temperature? *Explain* how you can use your graph to answer this question.

◆ = **MULTIPLE CHOICE PRACTICE**   ◯ = **HINTS AND HOMEWORK HELP** at classzone.com

42. SHORT RESPONSE A deep-sea diver is 160 feet below the surface of the water. The diver ascends at a rate of 20 feet every 4 minutes.

Time (minutes)	4	8	12	16
Depth (feet)	?	?	?	?

   a. Copy and complete the table.

   b. Is the relationship between depth and time linear? *Explain.*

43. MULTI-STEP PROBLEM A local gym offers swimming lessons for beginners. The lessons start with 1 minute treading water, and 2 minutes are added each month. The time y (in minutes) spent treading water during a lesson can be modeled by $y = 2x + 1$ where x is the number of months.

   a. Graph the equation and estimate the number of months it will take for the students to tread water for 13 minutes during a lesson.

   b. Substitute your estimate from part (a) for x in $y = 2x + 1$ to verify that it is reasonable.

44. REASONING *Explain* how to find an equation of the line that is parallel to the x-axis and lies 8.6 units below it.

45. CHALLENGE Jared's age j is seven years more than his sister Karen's age k. Write and graph an equation in two variables to model this situation. *Explain* how to use your graph to find out how old they will be when Jared is twice as old as Karen.

46. CHALLENGE In this exercise, you will investigate the graph of $y = |x|$.

   a. Copy and complete the table for $y = |x|$.

x	−3	−2	−1	0	1	2	3
y	?	?	?	?	?	?	?

   b. Graph $y = |x|$ by plotting and connecting the points from the table.

   c. Is $y = |x|$ a linear equation? *Explain.*

◆ CALIFORNIA STANDARDS SPIRAL REVIEW

AF 2.1

47. What is 10^{-4} in standard form? *(p. 196)*

   (A) 0.01   **(B)** 0.001   **(C)** 0.0001   **(D)** 0.00001

NS 1.4

48. Which is an irrational number? *(p. 225)*

   (A) $\sqrt{3}$ **(B)** $\frac{7}{3}$ **(C)** $\sqrt{9}$ **(D)** 29

AF 4.1

49. You and a friend have $14.25 to spend at the movies. The total cost of admission for both of you is $12.50. Before the movie starts you plan to play arcade games. What is the maximum number of arcade games you can play if it costs $.50 per game? *(p. 315)*

   (A) 1   **(B)** 3   **(C)** 4   **(D)** 6

6.2 Graphing Linear Equations

Standards

AF 3.3 Graph linear functions, noting that the vertical change (change in *y*-value) per unit of horizontal change (change in *x*-value) is always the same and know that the ratio ("rise over run") is called the slope of a graph.

QUESTION How can you use a graphing calculator to graph a linear equation?

EXAMPLE Use a graphing calculator to graph an equation

Use a graphing calculator to graph $x - 2y = 6$.

STEP 1 **Solve** the equation for y: $y = \frac{1}{2}x - 3$. Use the following keystrokes on a graphing calculator to enter the equation:

Keystrokes

Display

STEP 2 **Use** the WINDOW feature to set the viewing window for the graph. Then view the graph by pressing the GRAPH button.

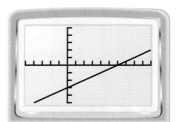

PRACTICE

Use a graphing calculator to graph the equation.

1. $y = 2x - 5$ **2.** $y = -x + 10$ **3.** $x - y = 11$ **4.** $x + y = 6$

5. $6x + 3y = 9$ **6.** $2x - 6y = 12$ **7.** $4x + 16y = 8$ **8.** $5x = -4y + 20$

Give an appropriate viewing window for the graph of the equation.

9. $y = 4x + 5$ **10.** $y = 2x + 14$ **11.** $y = -3x + 9$ **12.** $y = 10x - 1$

13. $y = \frac{1}{4}x + 7$ **14.** $y = -10x - 5$ **15.** $y = -82x + 1$ **16.** $y = 0.001x - 4$

6.3 Using Intercepts

Math and
RECREATION
Example 3, p. 328

Standards   **AF 3.3 Graph linear functions**, noting that the vertical change (change in
y-value) per unit of horizontal change (change in *x*-value) is always the same
and know that the ratio ("rise over run") is called the slope of a graph.

Connect   *Before* you graphed linear equations by making tables. *Now* you will use
x- and *y*-intercepts to graph linear equations.

KEY VOCABULARY
• *x*-intercept
• *y*-intercept

An **x-intercept** of a graph is the *x*-coordinate
of a point where the graph intersects the
x-axis. The graph of $2x + 3y = 12$ intersects
the *x*-axis at $(6, 0)$, so its *x*-intercept is 6.

A **y-intercept** of a graph is the *y*-coordinate of
a point where the graph intersects the *y*-axis.
The graph of $2x + 3y = 12$ intersects the *y*-axis
at $(0, 4)$, so its *y*-intercept is 4.

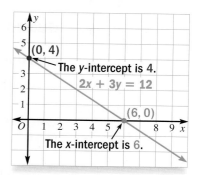

The *y*-intercept is 4.

$2x + 3y = 12$

The *x*-intercept is 6.

KEY CONCEPT   *For Your Notebook*

Finding Intercepts

x-intercept   To find the *x*-intercept of a line, substitute 0 for *y* into the
equation of the line and solve for *x*.

y-intercept   To find the *y*-intercept of a line, substitute 0 for *x* into the
equation of the line and solve for *y*.

EXAMPLE 1   Finding Intercepts

Find the intercepts of the graph of $y = \frac{1}{2}x - 5$.

STEP 1   Let $y = 0$ and solve for *x*
to find the *x*-intercept.

$$y = \frac{1}{2}x - 5$$

$$0 = \frac{1}{2}x - 5$$

$$5 = \frac{1}{2}x$$

$$10 = x$$

STEP 2   Let $x = 0$ and solve for *y*
to find the *y*-intercept.

$$y = \frac{1}{2}x - 5$$

$$y = \frac{1}{2}(0) - 5$$

$$y = 0 - 5$$

$$y = -5$$

▶ **Answer**   The *x*-intercept is 10 and the *y*-intercept is -5. The graph of the
equation crosses the *x*-axis at $(10, 0)$ and the *y*-axis at $(0, -5)$.

GRAPHING LINES The intercepts indicate the points where a line intersects the *x*-axis and the *y*-axis. You can use these points to graph a line.

EXAMPLE 2 Using Intercepts to Graph a Line

Graph the line with an *x*-intercept of −3 and a *y*-intercept of 2.

The *x*-intercept is −3, so plot the point (−3, 0). The *y*-intercept is 2, so plot the point (0, 2). Then draw a line through the two points.

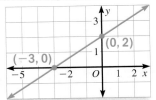

✓ **GUIDED PRACTICE** for Examples 1 and 2

Find the intercepts of the graph of the equation. Then graph the line.

1. $y = 2x - 10$ 2. $3x + y = -1$ 3. $5x + 3y = 18$

WRITING EQUATIONS In Chapter 5, you wrote equations in one variable to model given situations. Now you will write equations in two variables.

EXAMPLE 3 Writing an Equation in Two Variables

SACRAMENTO RIVER TRAIL Deena runs and walks with her dog for about 6 miles as shown below. She can run 6 miles per hour and walk 2 miles per hour. Write an equation in two variables that models the situation.

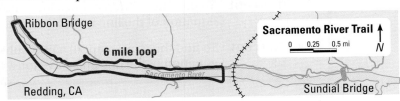

SOLUTION

STEP 1 Use a verbal model to represent the situation.

$$\boxed{\text{Distance Deena runs}} + \boxed{\text{Distance Deena walks}} = \boxed{\text{Total distance traveled}}$$

STEP 2 Represent the distance Deena runs as the product of her running rate and the number of hours *x* she runs: 6 mi/h • *x* h = **6*x*** mi.

STEP 3 Represent the distance Deena walks as the product of her walking rate and the number of hours *y* she walks: 2 mi/h • *y* h = **2*y*** mi.

STEP 4 Write the equation. The total distance, 6 miles, is equal to the sum of the distance Deena runs and the distance she walks:

$$6x \text{ mi} + 2y \text{ mi} = 6 \text{ mi} \quad \textbf{or} \quad \mathbf{6x + 2y = 6}$$

▶ **Answer** The equation $6x + 2y = 6$ models the situation described.

EXAMPLE 4 Using and Interpreting Intercepts

 SACRAMENTO RIVER TRAIL In Example 3, the equation $6x + 2y = 6$ models the amount of time Deena spends running and walking on the trail loop. Graph the equation. What do the intercepts represent?

SOLUTION

STEP 1 **Find** the x-intercept.

$$6x + 2y = 6$$
$$6x + 2(0) = 6$$
$$6x = 6$$
$$x = 1$$

STEP 2 **Find** the y-intercept.

$$6x + 2y = 6$$
$$6(0) + 2y = 6$$
$$2y = 6$$
$$y = 3$$

INTERPRET REASONABLENESS

In Example 4, the equation is graphed only in the first quadrant because negative values of x and y do not make sense in this situation.

STEP 3 **Graph** the equation. The x-intercept is 1 and the y-intercept is 3. So the points (1, 0) and (0, 3) are on the graph. Plot these points and draw a line segment joining them.

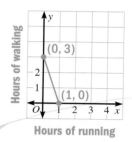

▶ **Answer** The x-intercept represents the number of hours it takes Deena to complete the trail loop if she runs the entire distance. The y-intercept represents the number of hours it takes Deena if she walks the entire distance.

✓ **GUIDED PRACTICE** for Examples 3 and 4

4. WHAT IF? In Examples 3 and 4, suppose Deena runs and walks 8 miles of trail. Write and graph an equation to represent this, where x is the number of hours she runs and y is the number of hours she walks. How are the intercepts affected by the change in distance traveled?

6.3 **EXERCISES**

HOMEWORK KEY

◆ = **MULTIPLE CHOICE PRACTICE**
Exs. 12, 24, 38, 45–47

○ = **HINTS** AND **HOMEWORK HELP**
for Exs. 7, 19, 39 at classzone.com

SKILLS • PROBLEM SOLVING • REASONING

VOCABULARY Copy and complete the statement.

1. The point where a line intersects the y-axis is the __?__ of the line.

2. Substitute 0 for y into the equation of a line and solve for x to find the __?__ of the line.

3. **WRITING** Is it possible for two linear equations in two variables to have different y-intercepts but the same x-intercept? *Explain*, using examples.

SEE EXAMPLE 1
on p. 327
for Exs. 4–13

IDENTIFYING INTERCEPTS Identify the *x*-intercept and the *y*-intercept.

4.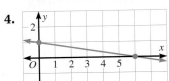

5.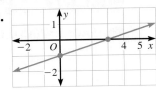

FINDING INTERCEPTS Find the intercepts of the graph of the equation.

6. $y = 6x - 3$

7. $x + 4y = 12$

8. $5x - 2y = 10$

9. $x + 9y = 18$

10. $4x + 5y = 20$

11. $7x - 9y = -63$

12. ◆ **MULTIPLE CHOICE** What is the *y*-intercept of the graph of $2x - y = 4$?

Ⓐ −4   Ⓑ −1   Ⓒ 2   Ⓓ 4

13. **ERROR ANALYSIS** *Describe* and correct the error in finding the intercepts of the graph of $4x - 3y = 12$.

$$4x - 3y = 12$$
$$4(0) - 3(0) \stackrel{?}{=} 12$$
$$0 \neq 12$$
There are no intercepts. ✗

SEE EXAMPLE 2
on p. 328
for Exs. 14–16

GRAPHING WITH INTERCEPTS Graph the line that has the given intercepts.

14. *x*-intercept: 9
   y-intercept: 4

15. *x*-intercept: −3
   y-intercept: 1

16. *x*-intercept: 6
   y-intercept: −10

**SEE EXAMPLES
1 AND 2**
on pp. 327–328
for Exs. 17–24

FINDING INTERCEPTS TO GRAPH Find the intercepts of the graph of the equation. Then graph the equation.

17. $y = 5x - 15$

18. $y = -2x + 7$

19. $8x + 10y = 30$

20. $7.5x + 3y = 19.5$

21. $-\frac{3}{4}x + y = -\frac{1}{2}$

22. $-\frac{1}{6}x + \frac{1}{3}y = \frac{1}{3}$

23. **ERROR ANALYSIS** *Describe* and correct the error in finding the *y*-intercept of the graph of $-3x + 2y = 6$.

$$-3x + 2y = 6$$
$$-3x + 2(0) = 6$$
$$-3x = 6$$
$$x = -2$$
✗ The y-intercept is −2.

24. ◆ **MULTIPLE CHOICE** Which equation's graph has an *x*-intercept of 5?

Ⓐ $x + 5y = 1$ Ⓑ $2x - 7y = 10$ Ⓒ $y = -5x$ Ⓓ $y = 5x + 15$

COMPARING INTERCEPTS Tell which intercept(s), if any, of the graphs of the two equations are equal.

25. $x + 2y = 5$
   $x - 2y = 5$

26. $3x - 2y = 6$
   $-3x - 2y = 6$

27. $7x + 5y = 35$
   $7x + 5y = -35$

FINDING INTERCEPTS Find the intercept(s) of the graph of the equation.

28. $y = 9$

29. $y = 14$

30. $x = 21$

◆ = **MULTIPLE CHOICE PRACTICE**   ◯ = **HINTS AND HOMEWORK HELP** at classzone.com

CONNECT SKILLS TO PROBLEM SOLVING Exercises 31–33 will help you prepare for problem solving.

Explain what the intercepts represent in each situation.

31. The equation $2x + 3y = 72$ represents the number of two-point baskets x and the number of three-point baskets y a basketball team made while scoring a total of 72 points.

32. The equation $0.5x + 0.6y = 3$ represents the number of apples x and the number of oranges y you bought for $3.

33. The equation $7x + 9y = 315$ represents the number of hours x you work at job A and the number of hours y you work at job B to earn $315.

SEE EXAMPLE 4
on pp. 329
for Exs. 34–36

34. **ENTERTAINMENT** You have $60 to spend. CDs are $12 each and videos are $10 each. The equation $12x + 10y = 60$ models this situation.

   a. Decide what x and y represent in the equation.

   b. Find the intercepts. Then graph the equation.

   c. *Explain* what the intercepts represent in this situation.

California @HomeTutor for problem solving help at classzone.com

35. **PRIZES** You need to buy 12 prizes for a school contest. T-shirts come in packs of 4, and DVD gift certificates come in packs of 2. The number of packs you can buy of each item is represented by the equation $4x + 2y = 12$. What does the x-intercept tell you in this situation?

California @HomeTutor for problem solving help at classzone.com

36. **SHORT RESPONSE** You are riding the bus home from school. After x minutes, the number of miles from home y is given by $2x + 3y = 18$. Find the intercepts. Then graph the equation. *Explain* what the points along the graph and the intercepts represent.

37. **WRITING** Do all graphs of linear equations have a y-intercept? *Explain* why or why not.

38. ◆ **MULTIPLE CHOICE** The equation $6x + 4y = 24$ represents the number x of adults and the number y of children that can attend a movie if a total of $24 is spent on admission tickets. What does the x-intercept represent?

Equation for bus ride:
$2x + 3y = 18$

   A Only adults attended.   **B** Only children attended.

   C Six adults attended.   **D** Six children attended.

SEE EXAMPLE 3
on p. 328
for Exs. 39–40

39. **EARNINGS** You earn $10 per hour regularly and $15 per hour for overtime. Write an equation that models how you can earn $450.

40. **ROAD TRIP** Al shares driving time on a 305 mile road trip with a friend. Al drives 55 miles per hour and Al's friend drives 65 miles per hour. Write an equation that models this situation.

41. REASONING The *x*-intercept of a line is positive and the *y*-intercept is negative. Does the line slant *up* or *down* from left to right? Through which quadrant(s) does the line pass? *Explain* your reasoning.

42. BANKING A bank offers a savings account with a 2% simple annual interest rate and a certificate of deposit with a 5% simple annual interest rate. Write an equation that models ways to earn $100 in interest in 1 year. What do the intercepts represent in this situation? *Describe* one way you can invest $3500 and earn exactly $100 interest.

43. CHALLENGE Find the intercepts of the graphs of $y = 0.5x$, $y = 3x$, and $y = -5x$. Using your results, write a conjecture about the intercepts of the graph of $y = kx$ where k is a nonzero number. *Justify* your reasoning.

44. CHALLENGE Consider the line with equation $ax + by = c$ where $a \neq 0$ and $b \neq 0$. Find the *x*- and *y*-intercepts of the line in terms of *a*, *b*, and *c*.

◆ CALIFORNIA STANDARDS SPIRAL REVIEW

AF 1.4

45. In the equation $4x - y = 12$, what is *x*? *(p. 5)*

    A A constant   **B** A variable   **C** A coefficient   **D** An inequality

AF 1.1

46. The difference of 3 times a number *n* and 5 is 13. Which equation shows this relationship? *(p. 247)*

    A $13 - 5 = 3n$ **B** $3n - 5 = 13$ **C** $5 - 3n = 13$ **D** $3(n - 5) = 13$

NS 1.6

47. The original price of a spring jacket was $38.90. It is on sale for 20% off. What is the sale price? *(p. 160)*

    A $29.18   **B** $31.12   **C** $33.07   **D** $35.01

QUIZ *for Lessons 6.1–6.3*

Solve the equation for *y*. Then list three solutions of the equation. *(p. 315)*

1. $7y + x = 21$ **2.** $-5x - 2y = -20$ **3.** $-3x + 9y = -18$

Graph the linear equation. *(p. 320)*

4. $y = 2x + 3$ **5.** $2y + x = 6$ **6.** $x = 3$

Find the intercepts of the graph of the equation. *(p. 327)*

7. $2.5x - y = 10$ **8.** $\frac{1}{5}x - 3y = 45$ **9.** $\frac{2}{3}x + \frac{1}{8}y = 3$

10. CAR WASH Your skating club holds a car wash to raise money. In 180 minutes, the club can wash *x* small vehicles and *y* large vehicles. It takes 10 minutes to wash one small vehicle and 15 minutes to wash one large vehicle. Write and graph an equation that models this situation. Find the intercepts. What do the intercepts represent? *(p. 327)*

6.4 Exploring Slope

MATERIALS · 5 books · 2 rulers

Standards

AF 3.3 Graph linear functions, noting that the vertical change (change in *y*-value) per unit of horizontal change (change in *x*-value) is always the same and **know that the ratio ("rise over run") is called the slope of a graph**.

QUESTION **How can slope help you describe the steepness of a ramp?**

A ramp's steepness is described by its slope, the ratio of the vertical rise to the horizontal run.

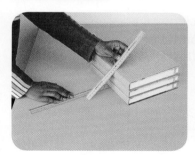

slope $= \dfrac{\text{rise}}{\text{run}} = \dfrac{1}{4}$

EXPLORE **Use slope to describe the steepness of a ramp**

| **STEP 1** **Make** a stack of books. Use one ruler as a ramp. Using the other ruler, measure and record the rise and the run of the ramp. Calculate and record the slope of the ramp. | **STEP 2** **Create** ramps with the same rise but three different runs by moving the lower end of the ruler. Measure and record the rise and the run of each ramp. Then calculate and record each slope. | **STEP 3** **Create** ramps with the same run but three different rises. Keep the lower end of the ruler in one spot. Add or subtract books to change the rise. Record the rise, the run, and the slope of each ramp. |

DRAW CONCLUSIONS **Use your observations to complete these exercises**

1. **WRITING** If one ramp is steeper than a second ramp, what is true about the slopes of the two ramps?

2. **WRITING** What is the relationship between the rise and the run of a ramp when the slope is 1? *Explain.*

3. **REASONING** What happens to the slope of a ramp when the rise increases and the run stays the same?

Rise	Run	Slope
3 in.	4 in.	$\frac{3}{4}$

6.4 Slope

Standards   **AF 3.3** Graph linear functions, noting that the vertical change (change in *y*-value) per unit of horizontal change (change in *x*-value) is always the same and know that the ratio ("rise over run") is called the slope of a graph.

Connect   *Before* you graphed linear equations. *Now* you will find and interpret slopes of lines.

Math and **ARCHITECTURE**
Ex. 34, p. 339

KEY VOCABULARY
- slope
- rise
- run
- average rate of change

The Mount Pilatus Railway in the Swiss Alps is the steepest cogwheel railway in the world. The track rises about 20 feet vertically for every 50 feet it runs horizontally. How can you describe the steepness of the track?

You can describe steepness using *slope*. The **slope** of a nonvertical line is the ratio of its vertical change, the **rise**, to its horizontal change, the **run**.

EXAMPLE 1   **Finding Slope**

 The diagram shows the rise and the run of the Mount Pilatus Railway described above. You can determine the slope of the railway by finding the ratio of the rise to the run.

Animated **Math**

For an interactive example of finding slope, go to **classzone.com**.

$$\text{slope} = \frac{\text{rise}}{\text{run}} = \frac{\overset{2}{\cancel{20\text{ ft}}}}{\underset{5}{\cancel{50\text{ ft}}}} = \frac{2}{5}$$

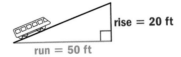
rise = 20 ft
run = 50 ft

▶ **Answer** The track has a slope of $\frac{2}{5}$.

✓   **GUIDED PRACTICE**   for Example 1

1. **RAMPS** Using slope, describe the steepness of a ramp that rises 6 feet vertically for every 18 feet it runs horizontally.

KEY CONCEPT   *For Your Notebook*

Formula for Slope

The slope *m* of a nonvertical line passing through the points (x_1, y_1) and (x_2, y_2) is:

$$m = \frac{\text{rise}}{\text{run}} = \frac{\text{change in } y}{\text{change in } x} = \frac{y_2 - y_1}{x_2 - x_1}$$

The slope of a line is the same no matter which two points on the line you choose to use in the formula.

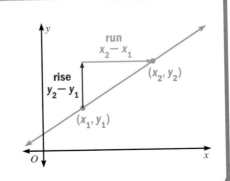

EXAMPLE 2 Positive and Negative Slope

xy Find the slope of the line.

a.

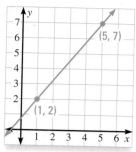

$$m = \frac{\text{rise}}{\text{run}} = \frac{y_2 - y_1}{x_2 - x_1}$$

$$= \frac{7 - 2}{5 - 1}$$

$$= \frac{5}{4}$$

b.

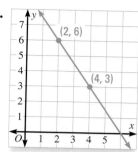

$$m = \frac{\text{rise}}{\text{run}} = \frac{y_2 - y_1}{x_2 - x_1}$$

$$= \frac{3 - 6}{4 - 2}$$

$$= \frac{-3}{2} \text{ or } -\frac{3}{2}$$

INTERPRETING SLOPE
The greater the absolute value of a slope, the steeper the line.

EXAMPLE 3 Zero and Undefined Slope

xy Find the slope of the line.

a.

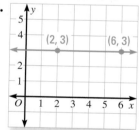

$$m = \frac{\text{rise}}{\text{run}} = \frac{y_2 - y_1}{x_2 - x_1}$$

$$= \frac{3 - 3}{6 - 2}$$

$$= \frac{0}{4}$$

$$= 0$$

b.

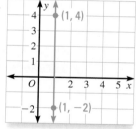

$$m = \frac{\text{rise}}{\text{run}} = \frac{y_2 - y_1}{x_2 - x_1}$$

$$= \frac{4 - (-2)}{1 - 1}$$

$$= \frac{6}{0}$$

The slope is undefined.

REVIEW RULES OF DIVISION
Remember that zero divided by any nonzero number is zero and that any number divided by zero is *undefined*.

✓ **GUIDED PRACTICE** for Examples 2 and 3

Find the slope of the line passing through the points.

2. $(2, 1)$, $(6, 4)$

3. $(0, 6)$, $(10, 0)$

4. $(-3, -4)$, $(5, 2)$

5. $(1, 5)$, $(-3, 5)$

6. $(1, 6)$, $(1, 2)$

7. $(-8, 3)$, $(8, 3)$

CONCEPT SUMMARY
For Your Notebook

Slope of a Line

A line with *positive* slope rises from left to right.

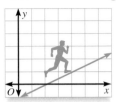

A line with *negative* slope falls from left to right.

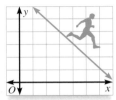

A line with *zero* slope is horizontal.

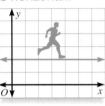

A line with *undefined* slope is vertical.

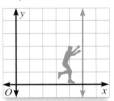

RATE OF CHANGE In real-world problems, slope is often used to describe a constant rate of change or an **average rate of change**. In such cases the slope has units of measure such as miles per hour or dollars per year.

EXAMPLE 4 ◆ Multiple Choice Practice

A class had 676 students in 2003 and 850 students in 2005. What was the average rate of change of the class size in students per year?

(A) 56 **(B)** 87 **(C)** 174 **(D)** 224

SOLUTION

You want to find the average rate of change of the class size per year. Let x represent the year and y represent the class size. Then the average rate of change per year is the change in y per change in x.

$$\text{Average rate of change} = \frac{\text{change in } y}{\text{change in } x}$$

You can write the data as the ordered pairs (2003, 676) and (2005, 850). The average rate of change is the slope of the line passing through these points.

$$\text{Average rate of change} = \frac{850 - 676}{2005 - 2003} = \frac{174}{2} = 87$$

▶ **Answer** The correct answer is B. Ⓐ **Ⓑ** Ⓒ Ⓓ

✓ **GUIDED PRACTICE**   *for Example 4*

8. **WHAT IF?** In Example 4, suppose the class size was 742 in 2003 and 684 in 2005. What was the average rate of change of the class size per year?

6.4 **EXERCISES**

HOMEWORK
KEY

◆ = **MULTIPLE CHOICE PRACTICE**
Exs. 16, 18, 32, 40–42

○ = **HINTS AND HOMEWORK HELP**
for Exs. 5, 13, 31 at classzone.com

SKILLS • PROBLEM SOLVING • REASONING

1. **VOCABULARY** Copy and complete: The horizontal change between two points is called the __?__ and the vertical change is called the __?__.

2. **WRITING** Are (1, 1), (4, 2), and (6, 4) on the same line? *Explain.*

SEE EXAMPLES 2 AND 3
on p. 335
for Exs. 3–18

SLOPE FROM A GRAPH Write the coordinates of the two given points on the line. Then find the slope of the line.

3.
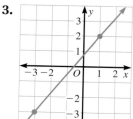

4.
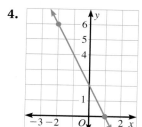

5.
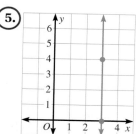

SLOPE FROM POINTS Find the slope of the line through the points.

6. $(-4, 8)$, $(6, 6)$ 7. $(1, 4)$, $(1, -7)$ 8. $(-5, 4)$, $(3, 4)$

9. $(-2, -4)$, $(4, 2)$ 10. $(-3, 1)$, $(-3, -2)$ 11. $(5, 8)$, $(0, 5)$

12. $(-6, -2)$, $(6, -7)$ 13. $(9, -8)$, $(15, -8)$ 14. $(12, 22)$, $(-20, 19)$

15. **ERROR ANALYSIS** *Describe* and correct the error in finding the slope of the line passing through $(1, -2)$ and $(3, 2)$.

$$\bcancel{\text{slope} = \frac{\text{rise}}{\text{run}} = \frac{y_2 - y_1}{x_2 - x_1} = \frac{2 - (-2)}{1 - 3} = -2}$$

16. ◆ **MULTIPLE CHOICE** A line includes $(-4, 0)$ and $(1, 2)$. What is the slope?

   (A) $-\frac{5}{2}$ (B) $-\frac{2}{5}$ (C) $\frac{2}{5}$ (D) $\frac{5}{2}$

17. **ERROR ANALYSIS** *Describe* and correct the error in finding the slope of the line shown at the right.

$$\bcancel{\text{slope} = \frac{\text{rise}}{\text{run}} = \frac{y_2 - y_1}{x_2 - x_1} = \frac{4 - 0}{0 - (-3)} = \frac{4}{3}}$$

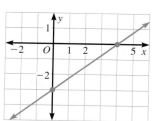

18. ◆ **MULTIPLE CHOICE** A line passing through $(-7, -3)$ has a slope of 0. Which point is *not* on the line?

(A) $(-3, 3)$ (B) $(-145, -3)$ (C) $(756, -3)$ (D) $\left(\frac{2}{9}, -3\right)$

19. REASONING Choose three different pairs of points on the line shown at the right, such as D and E, F and G, and E and H. Find the slope of the line using each pair. What conclusion can you draw from your results? *Explain.*

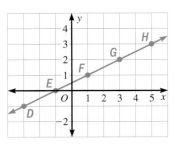

USING SLOPE **Find the unknown value using the given slope and points on the line.**

20. $m = 0$; $(0, 7)$, $(3, y)$ **21.** $m = -2.5$; $(w, 2)$, $(4, -3)$ **22.** $m = \frac{7}{4}$; $(x, -7)$, $(16, 0)$

CONNECT SKILLS TO PROBLEM SOLVING Exercises 23–25 will help you prepare for problem solving.

Find the slope of the object described.

23. A ramp rises 7 meters over a horizontal distance of 10 meters.

24. A ski slope rises 3240 feet over a horizontal distance of 6480 feet.

25. A slide falls 8 feet over a horizontal distance of 12 feet.

SEE EXAMPLE 1
on p. 334
for Exs. 26–29

BIRDHOUSE **Use the red line on the diagram of a birdhouse.**

26. What is the rise of the roof?

27. What is the run of the roof?

28. What is the slope of the roof?

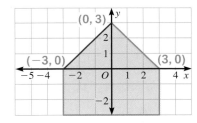

California *@HomeTutor* for problem solving help at classzone.com

29. TIDES A floating dock is shown below at low and high tide. Find the slope of the ramp in both images. When is the ramp steeper? *Explain.*

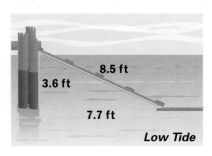

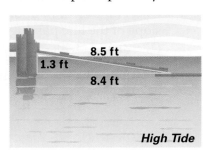

California *@HomeTutor* for problem solving help at classzone.com

30. WRITING Line A passes through $(1, 1)$ and $(3, 4)$. Line B passes through $(2, 5)$ and $(5, 8)$. Which line has a greater slope? *Explain* how you can tell by graphing the lines. *Explain* how you can tell by finding their slopes.

31. **REASONING** You have selected two points on a line to find its slope. Does it matter which point is (x_1, y_1) and which point is (x_2, y_2)? *Justify* your reasoning using examples.

32. ◆ **MULTIPLE CHOICE** A roof rises 6 feet over a horizontal distance of 14 feet. What is the slope of the roof?

   A −8   **B** $\frac{3}{7}$ **C** $\frac{7}{3}$ **D** 8

33. **SKIING** A ski slope has a starting altitude of 2800 meters and an ending altitude of 1886 meters. The horizontal length of the ski slope is about 3299 meters. Approximate its slope. Round to the nearest hundredth.

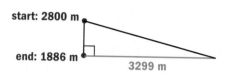

34. **WHEELCHAIR RAMP** The Americans with Disabilities Act requires that wheelchair ramps have a slope no greater than $\frac{1}{12}$. What is the minimum horizontal length a 2-foot-high ramp can have? *Explain.*

SEE EXAMPLE 4
on p. 336
for Exs. 35–36

35. **BAMBOO** On May 15, a bamboo cane is 47 inches tall. On May 27, it is 83 inches tall. What is the average rate of change in height per day?

36. **SPEED** At 2 P.M., you pass mile marker 171 on the highway. At 5 P.M., you pass mile marker 363. What is your average speed in miles per hour?

CHALLENGE **Find the unknown values using the given slope and points on the line.**

37. $m = \frac{1}{2}$; $(-8, 4)$, $(x, 2)$, $(6, y)$ **38.** $m = -4$; $(2, y)$, $(-1, 1)$, $(x, -19)$

39. **CHALLENGE** A highway off-ramp goes from the top of a bridge to a road 16 feet below. The ramp is $\frac{3}{4}$ of a circle that has a radius of 200 feet. For each foot that a car travels on the ramp, what is the car's average decrease in height? (*Hint:* The circumference of a circle is $2\pi r$ where r is the radius.)

◆ CALIFORNIA STANDARDS SPIRAL REVIEW

AF 4.1

40. What is the solution of the inequality $3x - 4 > 14$? (*p. 293*)

   A $x \le \frac{10}{3}$ **B** $x > 6$ **C** $x < -6$ **D** $x \ge 6$

NS 1.3

41. What is $\frac{123}{200}$ as a percent? (*p. 155*)

   A 12.3%   **B** 61.5%   **C** 123%   **D** 246%

AF 1.1

42. The sale price $28.57 of a soccer ball is $8.42 less than the original price x. What equation can be used to find the original price x? (*p. 257*)

   A $x - 8.42 = 28.57$ **B** $x + 8.42 = 28.57$

   C $28.57 - x = 8.42$ **D** $x + 28.57 = 8.42$

Multiple Choice Practice for Lessons 6.1–6.4

1. Which ordered pair is a solution of the equation $y = 5x - 3$? **AF 1.2**

  A $(0, 3)$ **B** $(-2, -13)$

  C $(1, -2)$ **D** $(3, 18)$

2. A hot-air balloon at a height of 5 feet above the ground begins rising at a rate of 2 feet per second. The height h (in feet) of the balloon can be modeled by the equation $h = 5 + 2t$ where t is the time (in seconds). How many seconds will it take for the balloon to reach 10 feet above the ground? **AF 4.2**

  A 2.5 sec   **B** 3.2 sec

  C 4 sec   **D** 4.5 sec

3. What is the x-intercept of the line shown below? **AF 3.3**

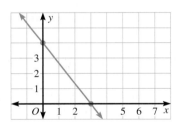

  A $-\dfrac{4}{3}$ **B** 0

  C 3   **D** 4

4. Dara spends 24 hours per month at ice skating lessons. In one month, she usually attends 12 individual lessons and 8 partner lessons. The lengths x and y of each type of lesson can be modeled by the equation $12x + 8y = 24$. What does the y-intercept represent in this situation? **AF 3.3**

  A Dara attending 3 partner lessons

  B Dara attending 2 individual lessons

  C Dara spending 3 hours per partner lesson

  D Dara spending 3 hours per individual lesson

5. A car moving at 8 feet per second begins increasing its speed by 4 feet per second each second. The speed s (in feet per second) is $s = 8 + 4t$ where t is the time (in seconds). Which table can be used to graph the equation? **AF 3.3, MR 2.5**

A

t	0	1	2
s	8	12	16

B

t	8	12	16
s	0	1	2

C

t	0	1	2
s	0	4	8

D

t	0	1	2
s	8	4	0

6. A line passes through $(5, -1)$ and $(x, 3)$ and has an undefined slope. What is the value of x? **AF 3.3**

  A -1 **B** 0

  C 3   **D** 5

7. What is the slope of the line passing through points $(0, 2)$ and $(5, 5)$? **AF 3.3**

  A $-\dfrac{5}{3}$ **B** $-\dfrac{3}{5}$

  C $\dfrac{3}{5}$ **D** $\dfrac{5}{3}$

8. Use the parasailing diagram below, where the boat is located at $(2, 0)$. At which location will the parasailer's tow rope have the greatest slope? **AF 3.3, MR 2.3**

  A $(4, 2)$

  B $(5, 4)$

  C $(6, 3)$

  D $(7, 5)$

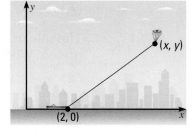

6.5 Slope-Intercept Form

MATERIALS · straightedge · graph paper

Standards

AF 3.3 Graph linear functions, noting that the vertical change (change in *y*-value) per unit of horizontal change (change in *x*-value) is always the same and know that the ratio ("rise over run") is called the slope of a graph.

QUESTION How can you find the slope and *y*-intercept of a line by looking at its equation?

You can find the slope and *y*-intercept of a line by looking at its equation in *slope-intercept form.*

EXPLORE Use a graph to find a slope and *y*-intercept

Graph $y = 4x + 3$. Identify the slope and *y*-intercept.

STEP 1 **Make** a table of values for the equation $y = 4x + 3$.

x	0	1	2
y	3	7	11

STEP 2 **Plot** the points and draw a line.

STEP 3 **Use** the graph to find the slope and *y*-intercept of $y = 4x + 3$.

$$\text{slope} = \frac{4}{1}$$

$$= 4$$

$$y\text{-intercept} = 3$$

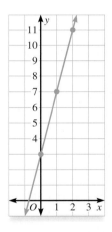

DRAW CONCLUSIONS Use your observations to complete these exercises

1. **LOOK FOR A PATTERN** Use the table.
   a. Copy and complete the table.
   b. Use your table to make a conjecture about how to use the equation of a line to find the slope and *y*-intercept of the line.

Equation	Slope	y-intercept
$y = 4x + 3$	?	?
$y = -2x - 1$	?	?
$y = 3x + 5$	?	?

2. **XY ALGEBRA** What does *m* represent in the equation $y = mx + b$? What does *b* represent in the equation $y = mx + b$?

6.5 Slope-Intercept Form

Math and **NATURE**
Example 4, p. 344

Standards **AF 3.3** Graph linear functions, noting that the vertical change (change in *y*-value) per unit of horizontal change (change in *x*-value) is always the same and know that the ratio ("rise over run") is called the slope of a graph.

Connect *Before* you graphed equations using intercepts. *Now* you will write and graph equations in slope-intercept form.

KEY VOCABULARY
• slope-intercept form

The activity on page 341 suggests that when an equation of a line is solved for *y*, you can use the equation to identify the slope and *y*-intercept.

KEY CONCEPT
For Your Notebook

Slope-Intercept Form

Words The linear equation $y = mx + b$ is written in **slope-intercept form**. The slope is *m*. The *y*-intercept is *b*.

Algebra $y = mx + b$ **Numbers** $y = 3x + 2$

EXAMPLE 1 Identifying Slopes and *y*-intercepts

 Find the slope and *y*-intercept of the graph of the equation.

a. $y = x - 3$

b. $-4x + 2y = 16$

SOLUTION

a. The equation $y = x - 3$ can be written as $y = 1x + (-3)$.

▶ **Answer** The line has a slope of 1 and a *y*-intercept of -3.

AVOID ERRORS
When you rewrite the equation in part (b) of Example 1, be sure to divide *both* terms of $4x + 16$ by 2.

b. Write the equation $-4x + 2y = 16$ in slope-intercept form.

$$-4x + 2y = 16 \qquad \text{Write original equation.}$$
$$2y = 4x + 16 \qquad \text{Add 4x to each side.}$$
$$y = 2x + 8 \qquad \text{Divide each side by 2.}$$

▶ **Answer** The line has a slope of 2 and a *y*-intercept of 8.

 GUIDED PRACTICE | **for Example 1**

Find the slope and *y*-intercept of the graph of the equation.

1. $y = 6x + 1$

2. $y = \frac{1}{4}x$

3. $-2x + 3y = 6$

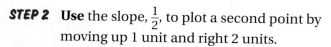

EXAMPLE 2 Graphing Using Slope-Intercept Form

Graph the equation $y = \frac{1}{2}x + 3$.

SOLUTION

STEP 1 **Use** the y-intercept, 3, to plot the point $(0, 3)$.

STEP 2 **Use** the slope, $\frac{1}{2}$, to plot a second point by moving up 1 unit and right 2 units.

STEP 3 **Draw** a line through the points.

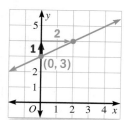

Animated Math

For an interactive example of graphing using slope-intercept form, go to **classzone.com.**

WRITING EQUATIONS Example 2 shows how to sketch a graph given an equation in the form $y = mx + b$. You can also write an equation in the form $y = mx + b$ given its graph.

EXAMPLE 3 ◆ Multiple Choice Practice

What is an equation of the line shown in the graph at the right?

(A) $y = -x + 6$

(B) $y = 6x - 1$

(C) $y = x + 6$

(D) $y = 4x + 6$

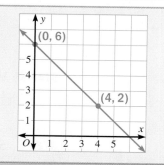

ELIMINATE CHOICES

Because the line crosses the y-axis at $(0, 6)$, $b = 6$. Choice B can be eliminated.

SOLUTION

STEP 1 **Find** the slope m using the labeled points.

$$m = \frac{2 - 6}{4 - 0} = \frac{-4}{4} = -1$$

STEP 2 **Find** the y-intercept b. The line crosses the y-axis at $(0, 6)$, so $b = 6$.

STEP 3 **Write** an equation of the form $y = mx + b$.

$$y = -x + 6$$

▶**Answer** The correct answer is A. Ⓐ Ⓑ Ⓒ Ⓓ

✓ **GUIDED PRACTICE** for Examples 2 and 3

Use the slope and y-intercept to graph the equation.

4. $y = 2x + 5$ **5.** $y = 7x$ **6.** $-x + y = 6$

Write an equation of the line passing through the given points.

7. $(0, 2)$ and $(2, 8)$ **8.** $(0, 0)$ and $(-5, 4)$ **9.** $(1, 4)$ and $(0, -8)$

MODELING REAL-LIFE SITUATIONS In real-life situations that can be modeled by an equation of the form $y = mx + b$, the value of m is the rate of change and the value of b is the initial, or starting, amount.

EXAMPLE 4 Writing an Equation

HIKING You are at the base of a trail on Mount Rainier in Washington. The temperature is 50.9°F. The temperature changes at a rate of −0.005°F per foot of elevation as you hike up. What is the temperature 1000 feet above the base?

Temperature change:
−0.005°F per foot

About the Standards

Example 4 shows how to solve for unknown quantities using algebraic techniques (MR 2.3).

SOLUTION

STEP 1 **Write** a verbal model to describe the situation.

| Temperature | = | Rate of temperature change | · | Increase in elevation | + | Initial temperature |

STEP 2 **Write** a matching algebraic model in slope-intercept form. Let y be the temperature and x be the increase in elevation.

$$y = mx + b \qquad \text{Write slope-intercept form.}$$

STEP 3 **Substitute** for m and b. The temperature changes at a rate of −0.005°F per foot, so $m = -0.005$. The initial temperature is 50.9°F, so $b = 50.9$.

$$y = -0.005x + 50.9 \qquad \text{Substitute −0.005 for } m \text{ and 50.9 for } b.$$

STEP 4 **Find** the value of y when $x = 1000$.

$$y = -0.005x + 50.9 \qquad \text{Write the equation.}$$
$$= -0.005(1000) + 50.9 \qquad \text{Substitute 1000 for } x.$$
$$= 45.9 \qquad \text{Simplify.}$$

▶ **Answer** The temperature 1000 feet above the base is 45.9°F.

✓ **GUIDED PRACTICE** for Example 4

10. **WHAT IF?** In Example 4, suppose the temperature at the base of the trail is 55.2°F. What is the temperature 2500 feet above the base?

11. **CHARITY EVENT** You are participating in a walk for charity. One donor will give you $4 for each mile you walk. Another donor gives you $25, a fixed amount that does not depend on how far you walk. How much money will you raise if you walk 6 miles?

6.5 EXERCISES

HOMEWORK KEY

◆ = **MULTIPLE CHOICE PRACTICE**
Exs. 6, 16, 39, 47–49

◯ = **HINTS** AND **HOMEWORK HELP**
for Exs. 9, 21, 41 at classzone.com

SKILLS • PROBLEM SOLVING • REASONING

1. **VOCABULARY** Copy and complete: For the graph of the linear equation $y = -5x + 7$, -5 is the __?__.

2. **WRITING** Is the equation $2y = 3x + 4$ in slope-intercept form? If not, explain how to rewrite it in slope-intercept form.

SEE EXAMPLE 1
on p. 342
for Exs. 3–16

REWRITING EQUATIONS Rewrite the equation in slope-intercept form.

3. $2x = y + 5$
4. $8x - 4y = 32$
5. $x - y = -2$

6. ◆ **MULTIPLE CHOICE** Which equation is *not* in slope-intercept form?

   (A) $y = 3x - 1$ (B) $y = -4x - 2$ (C) $3x + y = 5$ (D) $y = 2x - 9$

SLOPES AND Y-INTERCEPTS Find the slope and y-intercept of the graph of the equation.

7. $y = x + 3$
8. $y = 6 - x$
9. $1 = 2x - y$

10. $6x = 10 - y$
11. $y - 9 = -\frac{3}{4}x$
12. $\frac{2}{3}x - y = 3$

13. $2y - 6 = 0$
14. $y + 12x = 0$
15. $13x - 11y = 143$

16. ◆ **MULTIPLE CHOICE** What is the slope of the graph of $3x + y = 4$?

   (A) -4 (B) -3 (C) 3 (D) 4

SEE EXAMPLE 2
on p. 343
for Exs. 17–23

GRAPHING EQUATIONS Use the slope and y-intercept to graph the equation. Label the slope and y-intercept on your graph.

17. $y = x - 8$
18. $y = -x + 7$
19. $y = 3$

20. $2x - 2y = 1$
21. $-2x + 3y = -12$
22. $y = \frac{1}{5}x$

23. **ERROR ANALYSIS** *Describe* and correct the error in graphing the equation $y = -2x - 1$ using the slope and y-intercept.

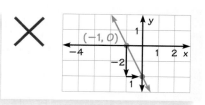

SEE EXAMPLE 3
on p. 343
for Exs. 24–27

INTERPRETING GRAPHS Write an equation of the line in slope-intercept form.

24.
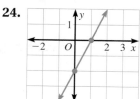

25.
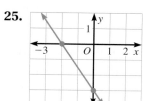

26.
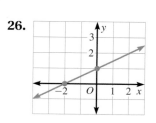

27. ERROR ANALYSIS A student determines that an equation of the line shown at the right is $y = 2x - \frac{2}{3}$. *Describe* and correct the error.

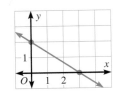

28. NUMBER SENSE Which equation has a steeper graph, $y = 3x - 1$ or $y = 2x - 1$? *Justify* your answer.

WRITING EQUATIONS Write an equation in slope-intercept form of the line with the given slope and y-intercept.

29. $m = 3; b = 0$

30. $m = -2; b = \frac{1}{3}$

31. $m = \frac{1}{2}; b = -4$

WRITING EQUATIONS Write an equation in slope-intercept form of the line that has the given slope and passes through the given point.

32. $m = -\frac{1}{2}; (-2, 2)$

33. $m = 0; (-5, 6)$

34. $m = 2; \left(\frac{1}{2}, 6\right)$

CONNECT SKILLS TO PROBLEM SOLVING Exercises 35–37 will help you prepare for problem solving.

Write an equation to represent the situation. Identify the slope and the y-intercept of the graph of the equation.

35. You buy x gallons of milk for $2.30 per gallon.

36. You have $500 in a savings account. You add $5 per week for x weeks.

37. A squirrel climbs down for x seconds from the top of a 37-foot tree at 1.5 feet per second.

SEE EXAMPLE 4
on p. 344
for Exs. 38–40

38. PARACHUTING The graph shows the altitude y (in feet) of a parachutist x seconds after opening the parachute. Find the slope and y-intercept of the graph. Write an equation for the altitude in slope-intercept form. What do the slope and y-intercept represent in this situation?

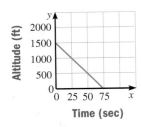

California @HomeTutor for problem solving help at classzone.com

39. ◆ MULTIPLE CHOICE You rent a canoe for $9 per hour. The cost for a ride back to the starting point is $12. Which equation models the total cost C (in dollars) of renting a canoe for h hours?

Ⓐ $C = 12h + 9$ Ⓑ $C = 9h + 12$ Ⓒ $h = 12C + 9$ Ⓓ $h = 9C + 12$

California @HomeTutor for problem solving help at classzone.com

40. MULTI-STEP PROBLEM You make and sell bracelets. You spend $28 for supplies and sell the bracelets for $3.50 each.

a. Write a verbal model to describe your profit or loss based on the number of bracelets sold.

b. Use the verbal model to write and graph an equation.

c. How many bracelets do you need to sell to exactly cover your expenses? to make a profit?

◆ = **MULTIPLE CHOICE PRACTICE**   ○ = **HINTS AND HOMEWORK HELP** at classzone.com

41. **SHORT RESPONSE** The number of chirps per minute y made by a cricket can be modeled by the equation $y = 4x - 156$, where x is the temperature in degrees Fahrenheit.

 a. Graph the equation.

 b. What does the slope mean in this situation?

 c. What does the y-intercept mean in this situation? Does it make sense? *Explain.*

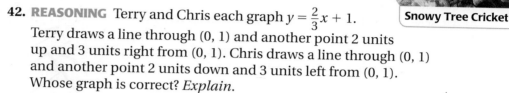

Snowy Tree Cricket

42. **REASONING** Terry and Chris each graph $y = \frac{2}{3}x + 1$. Terry draws a line through $(0, 1)$ and another point 2 units up and 3 units right from $(0, 1)$. Chris draws a line through $(0, 1)$ and another point 2 units down and 3 units left from $(0, 1)$. Whose graph is correct? *Explain.*

43. **OPEN-ENDED** *Describe* a real-world situation that can be represented by the graph at the right. What do the x- and y-intercepts mean in the situation?

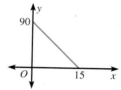

44. **MULTI-STEP PROBLEM** Use the equations $4x - 6y = -18$ and $-2x + 3y = 15$.

 a. Rewrite the equations in slope-intercept form. *Describe* any similarities.

 b. Graph the equations in the same coordinate plane. *Describe* how the graphs are related.

 c. Use your answers from parts (a) and (b) to make a conjecture about how the graphs of $y = -2x - 8$ and $y = -2x - 1$ are related. *Explain* your reasoning.

45. **CHALLENGE** Write an equation of the line containing the points $(x_1, mx_1 + b)$ and $(x_2, mx_2 + b)$ in slope-intercept form.

46. **CHALLENGE** The speed of a falling object can be modeled by a linear equation. Suppose a rock is falling 25 meters per second after 1 second and 44.6 meters per second after 3 seconds. Write an equation for the rock's speed y (in meters per second) after x seconds.

◆ CALIFORNIA STANDARDS SPIRAL REVIEW

AF 3.3

47. What is the slope of the line through $(-3, 5)$ and $(1, -3)$? *(p. 334)*

  Ⓐ -2 Ⓑ $-\frac{1}{2}$ Ⓒ 1 Ⓓ 4

AF 1.1

48. What is an expression for twice the sum of a number x and 9? *(p. 247)*

  Ⓐ $2x + 9$ Ⓑ $2(x + 9)$ Ⓒ $2(2x + 9)$ Ⓓ $2(x + 9)^2$

MG 2.1

49. You want the total area of the rectangular floor of a shed to be 58 square feet. Which of the following could be the dimensions of the floor? *(p. 98)*

  Ⓐ $8\frac{1}{2}$ ft by 7 ft Ⓑ $8\frac{1}{4}$ ft by 7 ft Ⓒ 8 ft by $7\frac{1}{2}$ ft Ⓓ 8 ft by $7\frac{1}{4}$ ft

6.6 Direct Variation

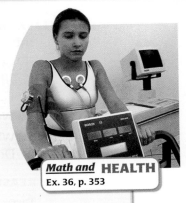

Standards AF 3.4 Plot the values of quantities whose ratios are always the same (e.g., cost to the number of an item, feet to inches, circumference to diameter of a circle). Fit a line to the plot and understand that the slope of the line equals the ratio of the quantities.

AF 4.2 Solve multistep problems involving rate, average speed, distance, and time or a direct variation.

Math and **HEALTH**
Ex. 36, p. 353

Connect *Before* you wrote and graphed linear equations of the form $y = mx + b$. *Now* you will write and graph direct variation equations of the form $y = kx$.

KEY VOCABULARY
- direct variation
- constant of variation

Two variables x and y show **direct variation** if $y = kx$ for some nonzero number k, called the **constant of variation**. The direct variation equation $y = kx$ can also be written in the form $\frac{y}{x} = k$. So, x and y show direct variation if the ratio of y to x is constant.

EXAMPLE 1 Identifying Direct Variation from an Equation

 Tell whether the equation represents direct variation.

a. $-2x + y = 0$ **b.** $-2x + y = 3$

SOLUTION

Solve each equation for y.

a. $-2x + y = 0$
$$y = 2x$$

The equation can be written in the form $y = kx$ where $k = 2$, so it represents direct variation.

b. $-2x + y = 3$
$$y = 2x + 3$$

The equation *cannot* be written in the form $y = kx$, so it does *not* represent direct variation.

EXAMPLE 2 Identifying Direct Variation from a Table

 Tell whether the table represents direct variation.

a.

x	1	2	3	4	5
y	6	10	14	18	22

b.

x	1	2	3	4	5
y	4	8	12	16	20

SOLUTION

For each table, determine whether the ratios of y to x are constant.

a. Because $\frac{6}{1} \neq \frac{10}{2}$, the ratios are *not* constant. So, the table does *not* represent direct variation.

b. Because $\frac{4}{1} = \frac{8}{2} = \frac{12}{3} = \frac{16}{4} = \frac{20}{5}$, the ratios are constant. So, the table represents direct variation.

EXAMPLE 3 Using Direct Variation

BUYING CDS At a music store sale, the amount y (in dollars) that you spend varies directly with the number x of CDs that you buy at the sale price. You pay $36 for 3 of the CDs on sale.

a. Write a direct variation equation for the situation that relates x and y.

b. Graph the equation from part (a). What does the slope represent?

c. Find the cost to buy 7 of the CDs on sale.

SOLUTION

a. Use the fact that $y = 36$ when $x = 3$ to write a direct variation equation.

$y = kx$ **Write direct variation equation.**

$36 = k(3)$ **Substitute 36 for *y* and 3 for *x*.**

$12 = k$ **Solve for *k*.**

▶ **Answer** A direct variation equation that relates x and y is $y = 12x$.

b. Make a table of values for the equation $y = 12x$.

x	0	1	2	3	4	5
y	0	12	24	36	48	60

Plot the points from the table, and draw a line through the points. The slope of the line is 12 and represents the cost (in dollars) per CD.

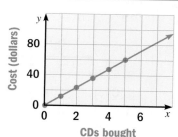

c. To find the cost of 7 CDs, substitute 7 for x in the equation from part (a).

$y = 12x$ **Write direct variation equation.**

$= 12(7)$ **Substitute 7 for *x*.**

$= 84$ **Simplify.**

▶ **Answer** The cost to buy 7 CDs is $84.

✓ **GUIDED PRACTICE**   for Examples 1, 2, and 3

Tell whether the equation or table represents direct variation.

1. $y = 3x$ **2.** $-x + y = 0$ **3.** $3x + y = 1$

4.

x	1	2	3	4
y	3	6	9	12

5.

x	1	2	3	4
y	8	9	10	11

6. WHAT IF? In Example 3, suppose you want to buy 9 of the CDs that are on sale. How much will this cost?

DIRECT VARIATION GRAPHS The graph of any direct variation equation $y = kx$ has the following properties.

Properties of Graphs of Direct Variation Equations

- The graph of a direct variation equation $y = kx$ is a line through the origin.

- The slope of the graph of $y = kx$ is k.

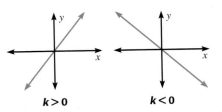

$k > 0$ $k < 0$

 EXAMPLE 4 ◆ **Multiple Choice Practice**

Which graph represents the direct variation equation $y = -5x$?

ELIMINATE CHOICES
The slope of the graph of the equation is -5. Choices A and B can be eliminated because the slopes of these graphs are positive.

Ⓐ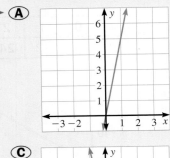

Ⓑ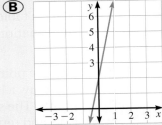

Ⓒ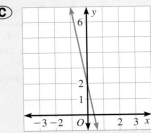

Ⓓ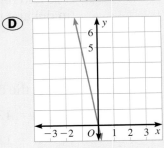

SOLUTION

The graph of $y = -5x$ passes through the origin and has a slope of -5.

▶ **Answer** The correct answer is D. Ⓐ Ⓑ Ⓒ ⬤

 GUIDED PRACTICE for Example 4

Graph the direct variation equation.

7. $y = -x$ **8.** $y = \frac{1}{2}x$ **9.** $y = -2x$

10. REASONING *Explain* why choice C can be eliminated as a possible correct answer in Example 4.

6.6 EXERCISES

HOMEWORK KEY

◆ = **MULTIPLE CHOICE PRACTICE**
Exs. 10, 15, 36, 39–41

○ = **HINTS AND HOMEWORK HELP**
for Exs. 5, 11, 35 at classzone.com

SKILLS • PROBLEM SOLVING • REASONING

VOCABULARY Copy and complete the statement.

1. Two variables x and y show __?__ if $y = kx$ for some nonzero number k.

2. The slope of a direct variation graph is equal to the __?__ .

3. NOTETAKING SKILLS Make a *decision tree* like the one on page 314 for determining whether a set of data represents direct variation.

SEE EXAMPLE 1
on p. 348
for Exs. 4–10

IDENTIFYING DIRECT VARIATION Tell whether the equation represents direct variation. If so, identify the constant of variation.

4. $y = x$ **5.** $y = 0$ **6.** $y = -7x$

7. $y + 6x = 1$ **8.** $y - 2x - 8 = 0$ **9.** $y = \frac{1}{6}x$

10. ◆ MULTIPLE CHOICE What is the constant of variation for the direct variation equation $y = 7x$?

(A) x **(B)** y **(C)** 0   **(D)** 7

SEE EXAMPLES 2 AND 3
on pp. 348–349
for Exs. 11–16

IDENTIFYING DIRECT VARIATION Tell whether the table represents direct variation. If so, write the direct variation equation.

11.

x	1	2	3	4
y	4	5	6	7

12.

x	1	3	5	7
y	-1	-3	-5	-7

13.

x	-4	-8	-12	-16
y	1	2	3	4

14.

x	3	4	5	6
y	2	3	4	5

15. ◆ MULTIPLE CHOICE Which table does *not* represent direct variation?

(A)

x	1	2	3
y	2	4	8

(B)

x	1	2	3
y	3	6	9

(C)

x	1	2	3
y	2	4	6

(D)

x	1	2	3
y	1	2	3

16. REASONING *Explain* why the graph of a direct variation equation must pass through the origin.

SEE EXAMPLE 4
on p. 350
for Exs. 17–23

IDENTIFYING DIRECT VARIATION Tell whether the graph represents direct variation. *Explain* your reasoning.

17.
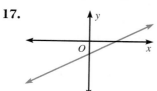

18.
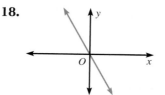

19.
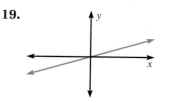

GRAPHING EQUATIONS Graph the direct variation equation.

20. $y = x$ **21.** $y = -3x$ **22.** $y = -0.5x$ **23.** $y = 9x$

ERROR ANALYSIS *Describe* and correct the error in determining whether direct variation is represented.

24.

$-4x + y = 0$
The equation does not show direct variation because it is not of the form y = kx.

25.

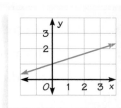

The graph is a line, so it shows direct variation.

CONNECT SKILLS TO PROBLEM SOLVING Exercises 26–31 will help you prepare for problem solving.

Use the following information: The total cost y of buying x units is given. Find k, the constant of variation. Then write a direct variation equation for the situation.

26. $y = \$5$, $x = 10$ pounds of apples   **27.** $y = \$24$, $x = 4$ softballs

28. $y = \$2.25$, $x = 9$ baseball cards   **29.** $y = \$3$, $x = 9$ permanent markers

30. $y = \$45$, $x = 3$ hours of tennis court time   **31.** $y = \$19.50$, $x = 3$ movie passes

SEE EXAMPLE 3
on p. 349
for Exs. 32–36

32. AVIATION NASA's Hyper-X aircraft set a world speed record for jets in 2004. It flew at an average speed of about 3.3 kilometers per second. The distance d (in kilometers) that the jet traveled varies directly with the time t (in seconds) flown at this speed. Write and graph a direct variation equation that relates t and d.

California @HomeTutor for problem solving help at classzone.com

Hyper-X flies from Edwards Air Force Base in California.

33. MEASUREMENT An object's length y in feet varies directly with its length x in inches. Write and graph a direct variation equation that relates x and y.

California @HomeTutor for problem solving help at classzone.com

34. REASONING Anthony is selling raffle tickets for $4 each.

    a. Write and graph a direct variation equation that represents the amount m of money Anthony will collect by selling t tickets.

    b. Suppose that Anthony also receives a $20 donation while he is selling the raffle tickets. Does m still vary directly with t? *Justify* your answer.

35. CIRCUMFERENCE The circumference, or the distance around a circle, is approximately 3.14 times the diameter of the circle. Write a direct variation equation that relates a circle's circumference C to its diameter d. Make a table and graph the direct variation equation. What does the slope represent? Find the circumference of a circle whose diameter is 100 feet.

36. ◆ **MULTIPLE CHOICE** The distance d (in miles) that you walk varies directly with the time t (in minutes) you spend on a treadmill. You walk 2 miles in 26 minutes. How far do you walk in 39 minutes?

   A 1 mi   **B** 3 mi   **C** 4 mi   **D** 13 mi

37. CHALLENGE In the direct variation equation $y = kx$, what happens to y when x is doubled? Is this true in general for a linear equation of the form $y = mx + b$? *Explain* why or why not.

38. CHALLENGE The table shows the average number a of team field goals attempted and the average number m of field goals made per game for all NCAA Division I women's basketball teams for 9 consecutive seasons.

a (attempts)	61.8	61.9	61.8	60.8	59.5	59.0	58.9	59.2	58.4
m (made shots)	25.7	25.6	25.6	25.2	24.5	24.6	24.5	24.3	24.0

Write a direct variation equation that relates a and m, rounding the constant of variation to the nearest tenth. Then estimate the number of field goals made by a team in a game in which they had 70 attempts.

◆ CALIFORNIA STANDARDS SPIRAL REVIEW

AF 4.1

39. What is the solution of the equation $3x - 4 = 11$? *(p. 270)*

   A 3   **B** 4   **C** 5   **D** 6

AF 3.3

40. What is the slope-intercept form of $3y - 12x = -6$? *(p. 342)*

   A $y = 4x - 2$ **B** $y - 4x = -2$ **C** $y + 2 = 4x$ **D** $y = 4x + 5$

NS 1.6

41. A bakery starts a day with 500 pounds of flour. That night there are 320 pounds of flour left. What is the percent of decrease? *(p. 168)*

   A 18%   **B** 22%   **C** 36%   **D** 64%

QUIZ *for Lessons 6.4–6.6*

Find the slope of the line passing through the points. *(p. 334)*

1. $(3, 4), (5, 7)$ **2.** $(-1, -3), (0, 0)$ **3.** $(-5, 3), (4, 3)$

Identify the slope and y-intercept of the graph of the equation. Then graph the equation. *(p. 342)*

4. $y = \dfrac{6}{5}x - 2$ **5.** $-5x - 5y = -20$ **6.** $y = -x$

7. DISTANCE Write a direct variation equation that relates kilometers x to miles y, given that 50 miles $\approx$ 80.45 kilometers. Los Angeles is 3900 kilometers from Cleveland. How far is this in miles? *(p. 348)*

6.7 Graphs of Linear Inequalities

Standards **AF 1.1 Use variables and appropriate operations to write** an expression, an equation, **an inequality,** or a system of equations or inequalities **that represents a verbal description** (e.g., three less than a number, half as large as area A).

Math and ART
Examples 3 and 4, p. 356

Connect *Before* you graphed linear equations. *Now* you will graph linear inequalities.

KEY VOCABULARY
- linear inequality in two variables
- solution of a linear inequality
- half-plane

ACTIVITY

You can use a graph to model linear inequalities.

STEP 1 **Sketch** the graph of $y = x - 1$.

STEP 2 **Plot** and label the following points:

$A(0, 0), B(-3, -2), C(4, -3), D(0, -4)$

STEP 3 **Draw** a circle around each point in Step 2 that makes the inequality $y < x - 1$ true. Draw a square around each point that makes the inequality $y > x - 1$ true.

STEP 4 **Make** an observation about the solutions of $y < x - 1$ and the solutions of $y > x - 1$.

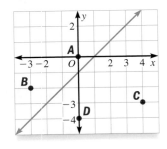

In the activity, you explored solutions of *linear inequalities*. A **linear inequality** in two variables x and y is an inequality that can be written in one of the following forms (where a, b, and c are constants):

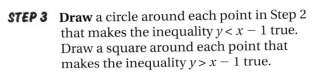

$$ax + by < c \qquad ax + by \le c \qquad ax + by > c \qquad ax + by \ge c$$

An ordered pair (x, y) is a **solution of a linear inequality** if the inequality is true when the values of x and y are substituted into the inequality.

EXAMPLE 1 Checking Solutions of a Linear Inequality

Tell whether the ordered pair is a solution of $3x - 4y \le -8$.

(x, y)	$3x - 4y$	$3x - 4y \overset{?}{\le} -8$	Conclusion
a. $(0, 0)$	$3(0) - 4(0) = 0$	$0 \nleq -8$	$(0, 0)$ is *not* a solution.
b. $(-1, 4)$	$3(-1) - 4(4) = -19$	$-19 \le -8$	$(-1, 4)$ is a solution.
c. $(4, 5)$	$3(4) - 4(5) = -8$	$-8 \le -8$	$(4, 5)$ is a solution.

Tell whether the ordered pair is a solution of $2x + 3y < 5$.

1. $(0, 0)$ **2.** $(-4, 2)$ **3.** $(5, -1)$ **4.** $(1, 1)$

GRAPHING LINEAR INEQUALITIES

The graph of a linear inequality in two variables is a **half-plane**. The shaded region includes all the solutions of the inequality.

A solid line indicates that points on the line *are* solutions of the inequality. A dashed line indicates that points on the line are *not* solutions.

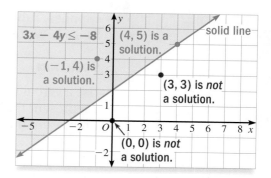

KEY CONCEPT   *For Your Notebook*

Graphing Linear Inequalities

STEP 1 **Change** the inequality symbol to "$=$". Graph the equation. Use a dashed line for $<$ or $>$. Use a solid line for $\leq$ or $\geq$.

STEP 2 **Test** a point in one of the half-planes to check whether it is a solution of the inequality.

STEP 3 **Shade** the half-plane that contains the test point if the point is a solution. Shade the other half-plane if the test point is *not* a solution.

EXAMPLE 2 **Graphing a Linear Inequality**

Graph $y - 2x > 3$.

STEP 1 **Change** $>$ to $=$ and write the equation in slope-intercept form.

$$y - 2x = 3 \qquad \text{Replace } > \text{ with } = \text{ sign.}$$

$$y = 2x + 3 \qquad \text{Add } 2x \text{ to each side.}$$

Graph the line with slope 2 and y-intercept 3. Because the inequality symbol is $>$, use a dashed line.

STEP 2 **Test** the point $(0, 0)$. Substitute the point into the original inequality.

$$y - 2x > 3$$

$$0 - 2(0) \overset{?}{>} 3$$

$$0 \not> 3 \qquad \text{(0, 0) is not a solution.}$$

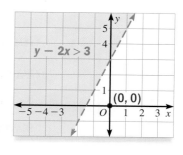

STEP 3 **Shade** the half-plane that does *not* contain $(0, 0)$.

WRITING INEQUALITIES In Chapter 5, you wrote inequalities in one variable. Now you will write inequalities in two variables.

EXAMPLE 3 Writing a Linear Inequality

ART SUPPLIES You can spend at most $40 on art supplies. Tubes of paint cost $6 each and brushes cost $4 each. Write an inequality to model the situation.

Tube of paint: $6
Brush: $4

SOLUTION

Use a verbal model to write the inequality. Let x represent the number of tubes of paint and let y represent the number of brushes.

Cost per tube of paint	·	Number of tubes of paint	+	Cost per brush	·	Number of brushes	≤	Amount you can spend
6	·	x	+	4	·	y	≤	40

▶ **Answer** The inequality $6x + 4y \le 40$ models the situation.

EXAMPLE 4 Using the Graph of a Linear Inequality

Graph the inequality in Example 3. How many tubes of paint and how many brushes can you buy?

SOLUTION

STEP 1 **Change** ≤ to = and write the equation in slope-intercept form: $y = -\frac{3}{2}x + 10$. Graph the equation using a solid line.

STEP 2 **Test** the point (0, 0): $6(0) + 4(0) \overset{?}{\le} 40$
$$0 \le 40 \checkmark$$

STEP 3 **Shade** the half-plane that contains (0, 0).

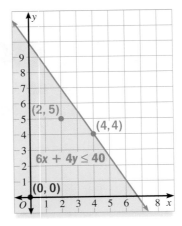

INTERPRET A GRAPH
All the points in the shaded region and on the line are solutions of the inequality. However, negative and fractional solutions do not make sense in this situation.

▶ **Answer** Many solutions are possible, such as (4, 4) and (2, 5). You could buy 4 tubes of paint and 4 brushes or 2 tubes of paint and 5 brushes.

✓ **GUIDED PRACTICE** for Examples 2, 3, and 4

Graph the inequality.

5. $y < x + 1$ **6.** $3x + y \ge 3$ **7.** $x - 2y \le -1$ **8.** $y > -2$

9. **WHAT IF?** In Example 3, suppose you can spend at most $36. Write and graph an inequality to model the situation. Find two possible solutions.

6.7 EXERCISES

HOMEWORK KEY

◆ = **MULTIPLE CHOICE PRACTICE**
Exs. 9, 28, 43, 52–54

◯ = **HINTS AND HOMEWORK HELP**
for Exs. 3, 11, 45 at classzone.com

SKILLS • PROBLEM SOLVING • REASONING

1. VOCABULARY Copy and complete: In the graph of $y < 2x + 1$, the dashed line divides the coordinate plane into two __?__.

2. WRITING You want to graph the inequality $y \leq x + 2$. Is $(3, 5)$ a good test point to use when deciding which half-plane to shade? *Explain.*

SEE EXAMPLE 1
on p. 354
for Exs. 3–9

CHECKING SOLUTIONS Tell whether the ordered pair is a solution of the inequality.

3. $5x + y \leq 17$; $(1, 2)$

4. $3x + 7y < 20$; $(-11, 2)$

5. $9x + 12y > 26$; $(3, -4)$

6. $11x + 18y \geq 31$; $(-6, -7)$

7. $-3x + 7y < 50$; $(1, 7)$

8. $-8x + 15y \leq 48$; $(-2, 2)$

9. ◆ MULTIPLE CHOICE Which ordered pair is a solution of $2x - 3y < -5$?

(A) $(-1, -2)$ **(B)** $(-1, 2)$ **(C)** $(1, -2)$ **(D)** $(1, 2)$

SEE EXAMPLE 2
on p. 355
for Exs. 10–27

GRAPHING INEQUALITIES Graph the inequality.

10. $y > 14 - 4x$

11. $y < x + 5$

12. $3x - 4 \geq y$

13. $y + 3 \geq 4x$

14. $-96 \leq -3x$

15. $6y > 36$

16. $y \geq 3x - 7$

17. $y \leq 4x - 12$

18. $y < 7x + 19$

19. $4x - 13 > y$

20. $y > 9 - 2x$

21. $22 < 2x$

22. $-2y \geq 74$

23. $4x - 3y \geq 12$

24. $-2x - 4y > 8$

25. $6x + 3y \leq -12$

ERROR ANALYSIS *Describe* and correct the error in graphing the inequality.

26. $y \leq 2x + 1$

27. $y \geq x - 2$

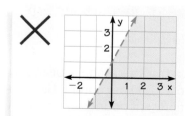

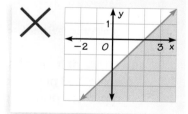

28. ◆ MULTIPLE CHOICE Which inequality describes the graph?

(A) $y \leq \frac{1}{2}x + 100$ **(B)** $y \geq \frac{1}{2}x + 100$

(C) $y \leq -\frac{1}{2}x + 100$ **(D)** $y \geq -\frac{1}{2}x + 100$

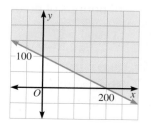

WRITING INEQUALITIES Write the sentence as an inequality. Then graph the inequality in a coordinate plane.

29. The sum of x and y is greater than 10.

30. y is no more than 15.

31. x is at least 20.

32. The difference of x and y is at most 15.

33. y is more than 2 times x.

34. x is no more than 3 times y.

REASONING Let a be a nonzero whole number. Tell whether a point of the given form is *always*, *sometimes*, or *never* a solution of the inequality.

35. $y \le 5x - a$; $(a, 2a)$

36. $3y > x + a$; $(a, a + 1)$

37. $10x > a - 2y$; $(-a, 5a)$

38. REASONING If you graph the inequalities $y < x + 3$ and $y > x + 3$, are there any points in the coordinate plane that are *not* solutions of either inequality? *Explain* your reasoning.

CONNECT SKILLS TO PROBLEM SOLVING Exercises 39–42 will help you prepare for problem solving.

Complete with the correct inequality symbol to model the situation.

39. Apples cost $.59 per pound and bananas cost $.89 per pound. You can spend no more than $5: $0.59x + 0.89y \ \underline{?} \ 5$.

40. You are setting up benches that each seat 2 people and folding chairs that each seat 1 person. At least 15 people are coming: $2x + y \ \underline{?} \ 15$.

41. Notebooks cost $1.25 each and pencils cost $.25 each. You need to spend more than $20 to get a discount: $1.25x + 0.25y \ \underline{?} \ 20$.

42. A truck carries 12 pound stereos and 15 pound speakers. The truck must hold less than 1000 pounds: $12x + 15y \ \underline{?} \ 1000$.

**SEE EXAMPLES
3 AND 4**
on p. 356
for Exs. 43–46

43. ◆ MULTIPLE CHOICE Sonya can spend up to $125 on decorations for a school dance. A bag of balloons costs $4 and a roll of streamers costs $2. If x is the number of bags of balloons and y is the number of rolls of streamers, which inequality models the situation?

(A) $2x + 4y \le 125$ **(B)** $4x + 2y \le 125$ **(C)** $2x + 4y \ge 125$ **(D)** $4x + 2y \ge 125$

California @HomeTutor for problem solving help at classzone.com

44. TRAIL MIX You have $6.00 to spend on a trail mix made of peanuts that cost $2.00 per pound and raisins that cost $1.50 per pound. Use x to represent pounds of peanuts and y to represent pounds of raisins. Write and graph an inequality that models the situation. Find two combinations of pounds of peanuts and raisins that you could buy for your trail mix.

California @HomeTutor for problem solving help at classzone.com

45. CLOTHING You are buying clothes with a $50 gift card. Shirts are $7 and shorts are $9. Write and graph an inequality that models this situation. What are the possible numbers of shirts and shorts that you can buy?

46. CANOEING Suppose a canoe can travel 2 miles per hour when two people paddle. When four people paddle, the canoe travels an extra 1.6 miles per hour. You want to travel at least 8 miles.

a. Write an inequality to model the situation, where x is the number of hours two people paddle and y is the number of hours four people paddle.

b. Graph the inequality. Use your graph to estimate the minimum amount of time that four people must paddle when only two people paddle for 3 hours. *Explain* how you found your answer.

47. OPEN-ENDED Write an inequality whose graph is a half-plane shaded above a dashed line. Then write an inequality whose graph is a half-plane shaded below a solid line.

48. SHORT RESPONSE Write an inequality whose graph is the half-plane showing all the points that are *not* solutions of the inequality $5x + y \geq 2$. *Explain* your reasoning.

49. REASONING Suppose you use a linear inequality to model all the possible numbers of $3 magazines and $5 novels you can buy with $30. *Describe* a solution of the inequality that is *not* a valid solution in the context of the problem. *Explain* your reasoning.

50. CHALLENGE Graph $y < mx + b$ and $y > mx + b$ for various values of m and b. Use your graphs to explain how you can use the inequality symbol (< or >) to determine which half-plane to shade.

51. CHALLENGE A widescreen format for a movie or television show is one in which the ratio of the projected picture's width y to its height x is greater than 4 : 3. Write and graph an inequality describing the possible widths and heights of a widescreen television picture.

2 paddlers: 2 mi/h
4 paddlers: 1.6 mi/h faster

◆ CALIFORNIA STANDARDS SPIRAL REVIEW

NS 1.3 | **52.** Which of the following is equivalent to $\frac{7}{5}$? *(p. 113)*

(**A**) 0.7   (**B**) 0.75   (**C**) 1.2   (**D**) 1.4

NS 2.2 | **53.** What is the value of $\frac{4}{3} + \frac{1}{12}$? *(p. 91)*

(**A**) $\frac{1}{4}$ (**B**) $\frac{5}{12}$ (**C**) $\frac{17}{12}$ (**D**) $\frac{5}{3}$

AF 4.2 | **54.** The elevation g (in feet) of a mountain goat t minutes after starting to descend a mountain is given by $g = 9400 - 40t$. What is the elevation of the goat 1 hour after it started descending? *(p. 315)*

(**A**) 2400 ft   (**B**) 5400 ft   (**C**) 7000 ft   (**D**) 9360 ft

6.8 Systems of Equations and Inequalities

Math and SPORTS
Example 2, p. 361

 Standards **AF 1.1 Use variables and appropriate operations to write** an expression, an equation, an inequality, or **a system of equations or inequalities that represents a verbal description** (e.g., three less than a number, half as large as area A).

Connect *Before* you solved linear equations and inequalities. *Now* you will solve systems of linear equations and inequalities.

KEY VOCABULARY

- **system of linear equations**
- **solution of a system of linear equations**
- **system of linear inequalities**
- **solution of a system of linear inequalities**

A **system of linear equations** in two variables, also called a *linear system*, consists of two or more linear equations in the same variables. A **solution of a system of linear equations** in two variables is an ordered pair that is a solution of each equation in the system.

In the system of equations below, (2, 4) is a solution.

System of equations		Check
$2x + 3y = 16$	**Equation 1**	$2(2) + 3(4) = 4 + 12 = 16$ ✓
$6x - 5y = -8$	**Equation 2**	$6(2) - 5(4) = 12 - 20 = -8$ ✓

If the graphs of the equations in a system intersect at a point, then the point is the solution of the system.

EXAMPLE 1 **Solving a Linear System by Graphing**

 Solve the linear system.

$$x + y = 5 \quad \text{Equation 1}$$
$$y = 2x - 1 \quad \text{Equation 2}$$

SOLUTION

STEP 1 **Graph** both equations as shown.

STEP 2 **Estimate** the point of intersection using the graph. It appears that the point of intersection is (2, 3).

STEP 3 **Check** whether (2, 3) is a solution by substituting 2 for *x* and 3 for *y* in each of the equations.

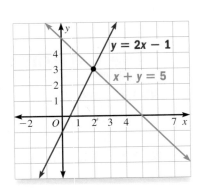

Equation 1	Equation 2
$x + y = 5$	$y = 2x - 1$
$2 + 3 \stackrel{?}{=} 5$	$3 \stackrel{?}{=} 2(2) - 1$
$5 = 5$ ✓	$3 = 3$ ✓

▶ **Answer** The solution is (2, 3).

EXAMPLE 2 ◆ **Multiple Choice Practice**

You can buy a skating park membership for a fee of $100. Each park visit costs members $8 and nonmembers $12. After how many visits will the total costs for a member and a nonmember be equal?

(A) 8   (B) 16   (C) 24   (D) 25

ELIMINATE CHOICES
You can see that for 8 visits, a nonmember will pay a total cost of $96. Because $96 is less than the $100 membership fee, choice A can be eliminated.

SOLUTION

STEP 1 **Use** verbal models to write equations representing each option.

Equation 1 (members)

| Total cost | = | Cost per visit | · | Number of visits | + | Membership fee |

$$y = 8x + 100$$

Equation 2 (nonmembers)

| Total cost | = | Cost per visit | · | Number of visits |

$$y = 12x$$

STEP 2 **Graph** the equations $y = 8x + 100$ and $y = 12x$ in only the first quadrant because negative values of x and y do not make sense in this situation.

STEP 3 **Estimate** the point of intersection. The graphs appear to intersect at (25, 300).

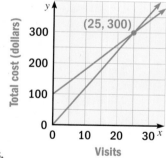

STEP 4 **Check** the solution.

$$300 = 8(25) + 100 ✓$$ **Equation 1 checks.**

$$300 = 12(25) ✓$$ **Equation 2 checks.**

After 25 visits, the total costs are equal.

▶ **Answer** The correct answer is D. (A) (B) (C) (D)

ANOTHER WAY
For an alternative method for solving the problem in Example 2, turn to page 368 for the **Problem Solving Workshop**.

✓ **GUIDED PRACTICE**   for Examples 1 and 2

Solve the linear system by graphing. Then check the solution.

1. $y = -x + 3$
    $y = x - 7$

2. $x - y = 2$
    $6x - 2y = 8$

3. $y = x - 5$
    $-3x + y = -3$

4. **WHAT IF?** In Example 2, suppose the membership fee is $60. After how many visits will the total costs for a member and nonmember be equal?

SYSTEMS OF INEQUALITIES A **system of linear inequalities** consists of two or more linear inequalities in the same variables. A **solution of a system of linear inequalities** is an ordered pair that is a solution of each inequality in the system.

In the system of inequalities below, $(2, -1)$ is a solution.

System of inequalities		Check
$x + y \leq 6$	**Inequality 1**	$2 + (-1) = 1 \leq 6$ ✓
$3x - y > 4$	**Inequality 2**	$3(2) - (-1) = 6 + 1 = 7 > 4$ ✓

To find solutions of a system of inequalities, graph each inequality in the system and identify the region where the graphs overlap.

EXAMPLE 3   Graphing a System of Linear Inequalities

Graph the system of inequalities.

$$y > -x - 3 \qquad \textbf{Inequality 1}$$
$$y \leq 2x + 1 \qquad \textbf{Inequality 2}$$

SOLUTION

STEP 1 **Graph** the first inequality in the system. Use **red** for $y > -x - 3$.

STEP 2 **Graph** the second inequality in the system. Use **blue** for $y \leq 2x + 1$.

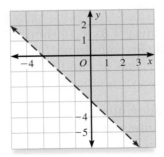

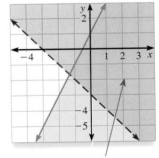

STEP 3 **Identify** the region that is common to both graphs. All ordered pairs in this region are solutions of the system of inequalities.

The graph of the system is the intersection of the red and blue regions, which is the purple region.

✓ **GUIDED PRACTICE**   **for Example 3**

Graph the system of inequalities.

5. $y < x + 2$
   $y \geq -2x - 1$

6. $x + y > 5$
   $y \leq 3x + 4$

7. $y \leq 4x - 2$
   $5x + y < 1$

8. REASONING Graph the system of inequalities consisting of $y > x + 3$ and $x - y > 2$. What does the graph tell you about the system's solutions? *Explain.*

EXAMPLE 4 Writing a System of Linear Inequalities

PHOTOGRAPHY You have $10 to spend on
reprints of a picture you took in Pfeiffer Big Sur
State Park. You would like to send one copy to
at least 12 friends. Small prints cost $.50 and
large prints cost $1. Write and graph a system
of inequalities to describe the situation. Then
determine two possible combinations of
print sizes you can buy.

Bixby Bridge in
Big Sur, California

SOLUTION

STEP 1 **Write** a system of inequalities where x is the number of small prints
and y is the number of large prints. The number of prints cannot be
negative, so you need to include the inequalities $x \geq 0$ and $y \geq 0$.

$x \geq 0$	The number of small prints cannot be negative.
$y \geq 0$	The number of large prints cannot be negative.
$x + y \geq 12$	You want to send prints to at least 12 friends.
$0.5x + y \leq 10$	You have $10 to spend on the prints.

STEP 2 **Graph** each inequality in the
system.

STEP 3 **Identify** the region that is
common to all of the graphs.
This region is shaded blue in the
graph shown at the right.

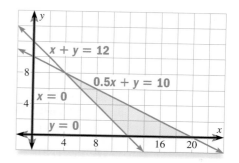

STEP 4 **Determine** how many of each
print size you can buy.

▶ **Answer** Several solutions are possible,
such as (10, 4) and (16, 2) as shown at
the right. You can buy 10 small prints
and 4 large prints, or 16 small prints
and 2 large prints.

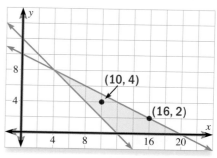

✓ **GUIDED PRACTICE** for Example 4

9. **WHAT IF?** In Example 4, suppose you are given an additional $5 to
spend on reprints. Graph the new system of inequalities and give two
new possible combinations of print sizes you can buy.

6.8 EXERCISES

HOMEWORK KEY

◆ = **MULTIPLE CHOICE PRACTICE**
Exs. 12, 13, 21, 31, 38–40

◯ = **HINTS AND HOMEWORK HELP**
for Exs. 11, 19, 29 at classzone.com

SKILLS • PROBLEM SOLVING • REASONING

1. VOCABULARY Copy and complete: Two or more linear inequalities in the same variables form a(n) __?__.

2. WRITING What must be true for an ordered pair to be a solution of a system of two linear equations?

SEE EXAMPLE 1
on p. 360
for Exs. 3–14

SYSTEMS OF EQUATIONS **Solve the linear system by graphing. Then check the solution.**

3. $y = x - 1$
$y = -x + 1$

4. $y = 2x + 1$
$y = x + 3$

5. $x + y = 4$
$y = x - 2$

6. $2x + y = 3$
$x + y = 5$

7. $y = 3x - 2$
$y = -3x + 4$

8. $4x + 2y = 6$
$-2x + y = 7$

9. $y = 4x + 4$
$2x + 2y = 8$

10. $6x - 3y = -6$
$-x + y = 4$

11. $x + 2y = 14$
$3x - y = 7$

12. ◆ MULTIPLE CHOICE Which system of equations is represented by the graph?

A $-x + y = 1$
$2x + y = 4$

B $x + y = 1$
$2x + y = 4$

C $-x + y = 1$
$-2x + y = 4$

D $x + y = 1$
$2x - y = 4$

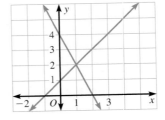

13. ◆ MULTIPLE CHOICE Which ordered pair is the solution of the system of equations given by $-x - 3y = 2$ and $9x + 3y = 6$?

A $(-1, 9)$ **B** $(2, 6)$ **C** $(1, -3)$ **D** $(1, -1)$

14. ERROR ANALYSIS *Describe* and correct the error in solving the linear system.

$x - y = 4$

$-\frac{1}{2}x + y = 1$

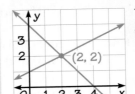

The solution of the system is (2, 2).

SEE EXAMPLE 3
on p. 362
for Exs. 15–23

SYSTEMS OF INEQUALITIES **Graph the system of inequalities.**

15. $y \geq -2$
$y \leq x + 1$

16. $y < 5$
$x + y > 5$

17. $y < 2x + 1$
$y > x - 4$

18. $y \geq -2x - 5$
$y \geq 4x - 3$

19. $-x + 2y < 10$
$x + 3y \geq 9$

20. $4x + 2y < 12$
$-x + 2y > -4$

21. ◆ **MULTIPLE CHOICE** Which system of linear inequalities includes the ordered pair $(2, -2)$ as a solution?

(A) $y < -x$
    $y < 2x + 1$

(B) $y \leq -x$
    $y > 2x + 1$

(C) $y < -2x + 3$
    $y \geq -x$

(D) $y \leq -x$
    $y > -3x + 4$

ERROR ANALYSIS *Describe* and correct the error in graphing the system of inequalities.

22. $y \geq -2$
    $x + y \geq 2$

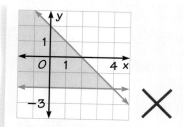

23. $y < x - 2$
    $2x + y > 3$

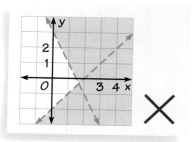

CONNECT SKILLS TO PROBLEM SOLVING Exercises 24–26 will help you prepare for problem solving.

Write a system of equations to represent the situation.

24. A shop rents in-line skates for $12 per day and bicycles for $25 per day. During one day, the shop collects $800 for 45 total rentals.

25. You are making a rectangular picture frame that is twice as long as it is wide. Its perimeter is 72 inches.

26. A business advertises in a newspaper and on the radio. A newspaper ad costs $500. A radio ad costs $300. The business has a monthly advertising budget of $32,000 and plans to run 70 ads each month.

SEE EXAMPLE 2 on p. 361 for Exs. 27–30

27. YOUTH CENTER It costs $100 for a yearly membership to a youth center. A session with a swimming coach costs $10 for members and $15 for nonmembers. Using the verbal models below, write and solve a system of equations to find the number of training sessions for which the total costs for a member and a nonmember are the same.

Members: $10/session
Nonmembers: $15/session

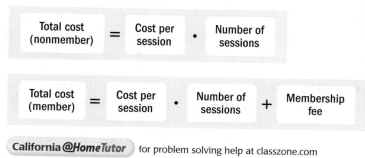

| Total cost (nonmember) | = | Cost per session | · | Number of sessions |

| Total cost (member) | = | Cost per session | · | Number of sessions | + | Membership fee |

California @HomeTutor for problem solving help at classzone.com

28. TENNIS A tennis club charges $110 for an eight month membership. Tennis court time costs $10 per hour for members and $20 per hour for nonmembers. For how many hours of court time will a member and a nonmember have equal total costs to play tennis?

California @*HomeTutor* for problem solving help at classzone.com

29. STORE DISPLAY A shoe store uses one wall to display court shoes and running shoes. There is enough room on the wall for 90 styles of shoes. Based on past sales, the store manager decides to display twice as many court shoes as running shoes. Write and solve a system of equations to find the number of each type of shoe displayed.

30. FUNDRAISING Your school invites a popular new musical act to play at a school fundraising event. Tickets cost $8 and the band agrees to be paid $600 plus $2 for every ticket sold.

  a. Write a system of equations modeling this situation.

  b. Use the graph of the system to determine the minimum number of tickets that must be sold for your school to collect more in ticket money than it pays the band.

Tickets: $8
Band fee: $600 plus $2 per ticket

31. ◆ MULTIPLE CHOICE In Exercise 30, suppose the band is paid $1 more per ticket sold. How does the minimum number of tickets that must be sold for the school to make a profit change?

  (A) It increases.

  (B) It decreases.

  (C) It remains constant.

  (D) Not enough information

SEE EXAMPLE 4
on p. 363
for Exs. 32–33

32. ART SUPPLIES A teacher is buying supplies for an art class of 12 students. The teacher has $36 to spend on brushes and wants at least one brush for each student. The table shows the two types of brushes the teacher wants to buy.

Type of brush	Cost per brush
Brush #5	$2
Brush #12	$3

  a. Write and graph a system of inequalities to describe the situation.

  b. Can the teacher buy four #5 brushes and ten #12 brushes? *Explain.*

33. SCHOOL GOVERNMENT Your school's student-teacher committee must have at least 4 members and at most 9 members. The committee also must have at least 2 teachers and at least 2 students.

  a. Write and graph a system of inequalities to describe the situation.

  b. Give two possible solutions for the numbers of teachers and students that can be on the committee.

◆ = MULTIPLE CHOICE PRACTICE   = HINTS AND HOMEWORK HELP at classzone.com

34. **REASONING** Write each equation in the linear system at the right in slope-intercept form. Graph the system. *Explain* why there is no solution.

$$x + y = 8$$
$$3x + 3y = 6$$

35. **REASONING** Write each equation in the linear system at the right in slope-intercept form. Graph the system. *Explain* why there are infinitely many solutions.

$$x - y = 4$$
$$-x + y = -4$$

36. **CHALLENGE** Write a system of linear equations that fits the given description.

    a. The system has exactly one solution.

    b. The system has no solutions.

    c. The system has infinitely many solutions.

37. **CHALLENGE** *Describe* how you could use a system of equations to solve $x + 2 = 3x - 4$.

◆ CALIFORNIA STANDARDS SPIRAL REVIEW

NS 1.5
38. What is $\frac{5}{6}$ written as a decimal? *(p. 113)*

    (A) 0.83   **(B)** 0.833   **(C)** $0.8\overline{3}$ **(D)** $0.\overline{83}$

AF 2.1
39. Which power of 10 is equivalent to 0.001? *(p. 196)*

    (A) 10^{-3} **(B)** 10^{-2} **(C)** 10^0 **(D)** 10^3

NS 1.7
40. You deposit $4200 into an account that earns 3% interest compounded annually. What is the balance after 5 years? *(p. 172)*

    (A) $668.95   **(B)** $4326   **(C)** $4862.03   **(D)** $4868.95

QUIZ *for Lessons 6.7–6.8*

Graph the inequality in a coordinate plane. *(p. 354)*

  1. $x \geq -3$ **2.** $2x + y < 5$ **3.** $-x + 2y > -10$

Solve the linear system. *(p. 360)*

  4. $y = 2x - 5$ **5.** $y = -x + 3$ **6.** $3x - y = 6$
      $y = x + 2$ $4x - 4y = -20$ $x + 3y = -8$

Graph the system of inequalities. *(p. 360)*

  7. $y > -x$ **8.** $x - y \geq 8$ **9.** $3x + 3y \leq 12$
      $y > 2x - 6$ $5x + y \leq 7$ $-x + 2y > -5$

10. **MOVIES** You have a $50 gift card to use at a movie theater. Matinees cost $6 and evening shows cost $10. Write an inequality for this situation and then sketch its graph. Give three possible combinations of matinees and evening shows you can attend. *(p. 354)*

Using ALTERNATIVE METHODS

Another Way to Solve Example 2, page 361

In Example 2 on page 361, you solved a system of linear equations by graphing. You can also solve a system of linear equations by using the *substitution method*.

PROBLEM

You can buy a skating park membership for a fee of $100. Each park visit costs members $8 and nonmembers $12. After how many visits will the total costs for a member and a nonmember be equal?

   A 8   **B** 16   **C** 24   **D** 25

METHOD

Using Substitution An alternative approach is to solve one of the equations for one of its variables (if necessary), substitute the resulting expression into the other equation, and find the values of the variables.

STEP 1 **Write** the cost equations for a member and a nonmember. Let x represent the number of visits and y represent the total cost. Notice that both equations are already solved for y.

Equation 1 (members)	Equation 2 (nonmembers)
$y = 8x + 100$	$y = 12x$

STEP 2 **Substitute** $12x$ for y (from Equation 2) in Equation 1 and solve for x.

$y = 8x + 100$ **Write Equation 1.**

$12x = 8x + 100$ **Substitute 12x for y.**

$4x = 100$ **Subtract 8x from each side.**

$x = 25$ **Divide each side by 4.**

STEP 3 **Substitute** the value of x you found into Equation 2 and solve for y.

$y = 12x$ **Write Equation 2.**

$y = 12(25)$ **Substitute 25 for x.**

$y = 300$ **Simplify.**

▶ **Answer** The solution is (25, 300). After 25 visits the member and nonmember costs will be the same. The correct answer is D. **Ⓐ Ⓑ Ⓒ ●**

PRACTICE

1. **GARDEN** A rectangular garden's length is three times its width. It takes 96 feet of fence to enclose the garden. Find the length and width using two methods.

2. **SOUVENIRS** A stand sells shirts for $9 and hats for $14. The stand sells 20 shirts and hats and collects $240. How many shirts and how many hats were sold?

MIXED REVIEW of Skills and Problem Solving

Multiple Choice Practice for Lessons 6.5–6.8

1. Paul is buying food at a basketball game. He has at most $10 to buy popcorn and drinks.

At most how many boxes of popcorn can he buy if he buys 2 drinks? **AF 1.1**

(A) 1   **(B)** 2

(C) 3   **(D)** 4

2. Which table does *not* represent direct variation? **AF 4.2**

(A)

x	1	2	3	4	5
y	2	4	6	8	10

(B)

x	1	2	3	4	5
y	4	7	10	13	16

(C)

x	4	5	6	7	8
y	20	25	30	35	40

(D)

x	1	2	3	4	5
y	1.8	3.6	5.4	7.2	9

3. An object's weight on Mars and its weight on Earth vary directly. A 150 pound man weighs about 57 pounds on Mars. About how many pounds does a 175 pound man weigh on Mars? **AF 4.2**

(A) 22 lb   **(B)** 66 lb

(C) 82 lb   **(D)** 461 lb

4. A system of four inequalities is graphed below. The shaded region represents the points that are solutions of the system. Which of the following is *not* one of the inequalities? **AF 1.1**

(A) $y < -\frac{1}{3}x + 2$

(B) $y > \frac{1}{3}x - 2$

(C) $y < \frac{2}{3}x - 3$

(D) $y < -\frac{2}{3}x + 3$

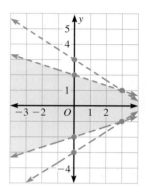

5. You buy sweet curry powder at $1.10 per ounce and hot curry powder at $1.30 per ounce. You want a total of 10 ounces of curry powder. Which of the following is an equation in slope-intercept form for the total cost y (in dollars) of the curry powder if x represents the number of ounces of sweet curry powder? **AF 1.1, MR 2.5**

(A) $y = \frac{13}{11}x$

(B) $y = 2.4x - 13$

(C) $y = -0.2x + 13$

(D) $y = 2.4x + 13$

6. The inequality $3.75x + 2y \le 30$ describes the weight x (in pounds) of strawberries, at $3.75 per pound, and the weight y (in pounds) of grapes, at $2.00 per pound, that can be bought with at most $30. Which combination of pounds of strawberries and grapes, written as an ordered pair (x, y), *cannot* be purchased with at most $30? **AF 1.1, MR 2.4**

(A) (3, 7)   **(B)** (10, 2)

(C) (5, 4)   **(D)** (2, 9)

BIG IDEAS

For Your Notebook

Big Idea 1

Writing and Graphing Linear Equations

A linear equation in two variables has the two variables in separate terms with each variable occurring only to the first power.

A linear equation $y = mx + b$ is written in slope-intercept form where m is the slope of the line and b is the y-intercept.

The graph of a linear equation such as $y = -2x + 3$ is the set of all points (x, y) that represent solutions of the equation.

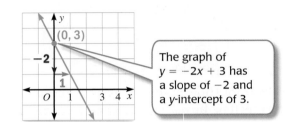

The graph of $y = -2x + 3$ has a slope of -2 and a y-intercept of 3.

Big Idea 2

Writing and Graphing Linear Inequalities

A linear inequality in two variables is an inequality that can be written in one of the following forms:

$y < ax + c$	$y > ax + c$	$y \le ax + c$	$y \ge ax + c$
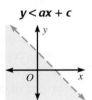			

Big Idea 3

Writing and Solving Systems of Linear Equations and Inequalities

A system of linear equations or inequalities in two variables consists of two or more linear equations or inequalities in the same variables.

A solution of a system of linear equations is any ordered pair that is a solution of each equation.

A solution of a system of linear inequalities is any ordered pair that is a solution of each inequality.

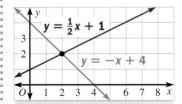

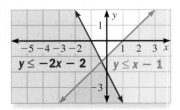

A point of intersection represents a solution of the system.

The region where the graphs overlap includes all the points that represent solutions.

APPLYING THE
BIG IDEAS

Big Idea 1
You write and graph linear equations in **Steps 1 and 2.**

Big Idea 2
You write and graph a linear inequality in **Step 3.**

Big Idea 3
You write and graph a system of linear inequalities in **Ex. 2.**

PROBLEM How can you use linear equations and inequalities to analyze profits from fundraisers?

STEP 1 Write and graph a linear equation.

Your class organizes a car wash to raise money for a field trip. It costs $23 for supplies. You charge $5 for each car. Write and graph a linear equation that represents the profit y (in dollars) from this fundraiser when you wash x cars.

STEP 2 Choose a second fundraiser.

Your class has four other ideas for fundraisers. Choose another fundraiser from the table below. Then write and graph a linear equation that represents the profit y (in dollars) from this fundraiser when you sell w items. Use the horizontal axis for the w-values.

Type of fundraiser	Cost of supplies	Amount charged
Selling bracelets with school logo	$21 for bracelets	$2.50 for each bracelet
Raffle for free yard work	$0	$.25 per ticket
Used book sale	$3 for fliers	$2 per donated book
Bean bag toss	$47 for prizes	$.50 per toss

STEP 3 Reach your goal.

Your class wants to raise at least $700 for the field trip. Write an inequality that describes the number of cars x from Step 1 and the number of items sold w from Step 2 that will allow your class to achieve this goal. Then graph your inequality. Use the horizontal axis for the x-values and the vertical axis for the w-values.

Extending the Problem

Use your results from the problem to complete the exercises.

1. Suppose your class washes 75 cars. What is the minimum number of items you must sell for the fundraiser you chose in Step 2 to reach your goal?

2. Write and graph a system of linear inequalities that gives the possible numbers of car washes and items sold if each fundraiser must be profitable. Use the inequality you wrote in Step 3 as one of the inequalities in the system.

REVIEW KEY VOCABULARY

• solution of an equation in two variables, *p. 315*
• linear equation, *p. 320*
• *x*-intercept, *p. 327*
• *y*-intercept, *p. 327*
• slope, *p. 334*
• rise, run, *p. 334*

• average rate of change, *p. 336*
• slope-intercept form, *p. 342*
• direct variation, *p. 348*
• constant of variation, *p. 348*
• linear inequality, *p. 354*
• solution of a linear inequality, *p. 354*

• half-plane, *p. 355*
• system of linear equations, *p. 360*
• solution of a system of linear equations, *p. 360*
• system of linear inequalities, *p. 362*
• solution of a system of linear inequalities, *p. 362*

VOCABULARY EXERCISES

In Exercises 1–3, copy and complete the statement.

1. An ordered pair whose coordinates make an equation in two variables true is a(n) __?__ of the equation.

2. The graph of a linear inequality in two variables is a(n) __?__.

3. The slope of a nonvertical line is the ratio of its __?__ to its __?__.

4. **NOTETAKING SKILLS** Make a *decision tree* like the one on page 314 for graphing a linear inequality.

REVIEW EXAMPLES AND EXERCISES

6.1 Equations in Two Variables
pp. 315–319

AF 4.2   **EXAMPLE**

List three solutions of the equation $y = 2x + 3$.

x-value	Substitute for *x*.	Evaluate.	Solution
$x = -2$	$y = 2(-2) + 3$	$y = -1$	$(-2, -1)$
$x = 0$	$y = 2(0) + 3$	$y = 3$	$(0, 3)$
$x = 2$	$y = 2(2) + 3$	$y = 7$	$(2, 7)$

EXERCISES

SEE EXAMPLE 3
on p. 316
for Exs. 5–6

5. List three solutions of the equation $x + 4y = 16$.

6. **TEMPERATURE** The temperature at the base of a mountain is 81°F. The temperature T (in degrees Fahrenheit) is approximated by $T = 81 - 0.005d$ where d is the vertical distance (in feet) above the base. What will the temperature be if a hiker climbs up 800 feet?

6.2 Graphs of Linear Equations

pp. 320–325

AF 3.3

EXAMPLE

Graph $y = 2x + 2$.

STEP 1 **Choose** several values to substitute for x. Then evaluate to find y and make a table of values.

x	-2	-1	0	1
y	-2	0	2	4

STEP 2 **List** the solutions as ordered pairs.

$(-2, -2), (-1, 0), (0, 2), (1, 4)$

STEP 3 **Plot** the ordered pairs and draw a line through them.

SEE EXAMPLES 1 AND 3
on pp. 321–322
for Exs. 7–10

EXERCISES

Graph the linear equation.

7. $y = x + 2$ **8.** $y = 8$ **9.** $y = -4x - 5$ **10.** $3x + 2y = -2$

6.3 Using Intercepts

pp. 327–332

AF 3.3

EXAMPLE

Find the intercepts of the graph of $y = 5x + 20$.

STEP 1 Let $y = 0$ and solve for x to find the x-intercept.

$0 = 5x + 20$

$-4 = x$

STEP 2 Let $x = 0$ and solve for y to find the y-intercept.

$y = 5(0) + 20$

$y = 20$

▶ **Answer** The x-intercept is -4 and the y-intercept is 20.

SEE EXAMPLES 1 AND 4
on pp. 327–329
for Exs. 11–12

EXERCISES

11. Find the intercepts of the graph of $-6x + 2y = 9$.

12. **TAXES** The approximate amount of taxes y (in billions of dollars) collected by the Internal Revenue Service from 1980 to 1990 can be modeled by $y = 53.1x + 505.7$ where x represents the number of years since 1980. What is the y-intercept of the graph of this equation? What does the y-intercept mean in this situation?

pp. 334–339

6.4 Slope

AF 3.3 **EXAMPLE**

Find the slope of the line passing through (0, 3) and (4, 6).

$$m = \frac{\text{rise}}{\text{run}} = \frac{y_2 - y_1}{x_2 - x_1} = \frac{6 - 3}{4 - 0} = \frac{3}{4}$$

EXERCISES

*SEE EXAMPLES
2 AND 3
....
on p. 335
for Exs. 13–15*

Write the coordinates of two points on the line. Then find the slope of the line.

13.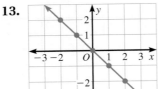

14.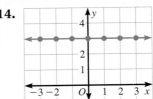

15. Find the slope of the line whose x-intercept is 5 and y-intercept is -2.

6.5 Slope-Intercept Form

pp. 342–347

AF 3.3 **EXAMPLE**

Find the slope and y-intercept of the graph of $-9x + 3y = 21$.

Write the equation $-9x + 3y = 21$ in slope-intercept form.

$-9x + 3y = 21$	**Write original equation.**
$3y = 9x + 21$	**Add 9x to each side.**
$y = 3x + 7$	**Divide each side by 3.**

▶ **Answer** The line has a slope of 3 and a y-intercept of 7.

EXERCISES

*SEE EXAMPLES
1 AND 2
....
on pp. 342–343
for Exs. 16–21*

Find the slope and y-intercept of the graph of the equation.

16. $y = 6x - 1$ **17.** $y = -\frac{2}{3}x + 4$ **18.** $y = 8$

Find the slope and y-intercept of the graph of the equation. Then graph the equation.

19. $y - 4x = 10$ **20.** $2y + 6 = x$ **21.** $-3x - 7y = 21$

6.6 Direct Variation

pp. 348–353

AF 4.2

EXAMPLE

Tell whether the equation $5x + y = 0$ represents direct variation. If so, identify the constant of variation.

$$5x + y = 0 \qquad \text{Write original equation.}$$

$$y = -5x \qquad \text{Subtract } 5x \text{ from each side.}$$

▶ **Answer** Because the equation $5x + y = 0$ can be rewritten in the form $y = kx$, it represents direct variation. The constant of variation is -5.

EXERCISES

SEE EXAMPLES 1 AND 3 on pp. 348–349 for Exs. 22–25

Tell whether the equation represents direct variation. If so, identify the constant of variation.

22. $\frac{1}{2}x + y = 0$

23. $-3x + y = 5$

24. $x + 4y = 0$

25. BICYCLING The number y of miles you ride your bicycle varies directly with the number x of hours that you ride it. In the first 2 hours of a bike ride, you go 20 miles. Write a direct variation equation for the situation that relates x and y. How many miles do you travel in 5 hours?

6.7 Graphs of Linear Inequalities

pp. 354–359

AF 1.1

EXAMPLE

Graph $y > -2x + 4$.

Graph $y = -2x + 4$, which has a slope of -2 and a y-intercept of 4.

Because the inequality is >, use a dashed line.

Use $(0, 0)$ as a test point:

$$0 \overset{?}{>} -2(0) + 4$$

$$0 \not> 4$$

Shade the half-plane that does *not* contain $(0, 0)$.

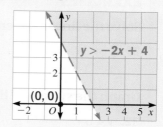

EXERCISES

SEE EXAMPLE 2 on p. 355 for Exs. 26–28

Graph the inequality.

26. $y < -\frac{3}{5}x - 3$

27. $3x - 7y \geq 21$

28. $4x + 8y \leq 32$

Systems of Equations and Inequalities

AF 1.1 **EXAMPLE**

Solve the linear system by graphing. Check your solution.

$$y = 2x - 3 \quad \text{Equation 1}$$
$$y = -x + 3 \quad \text{Equation 2}$$

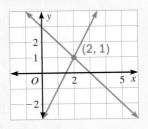

Graph both equations as shown. It appears that the point of intersection is (2, 1). Check whether (2, 1) is a solution by substituting 2 for x and 1 for y in each of the equations.

Equation 1	**Equation 2**	
$y = 2x - 3$	$y = -x + 3$	Write original equation.
$1 \stackrel{?}{=} 2(2) - 3$	$1 \stackrel{?}{=} -2 + 3$	Substitute 2 for x and 1 for y.
$1 = 1 \checkmark$	$1 = 1 \checkmark$	The solution checks.

▶ **Answer** The solution is (2, 1).

AF 1.1 **EXAMPLE**

Graph the system of linear inequalities.

$$y > -4 \quad \text{Inequality 1}$$
$$y \le x - 2 \quad \text{Inequality 2}$$

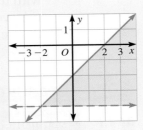

Graph each inequality in the same coordinate plane.

The region that is common to both graphs is the graph of the system. It is the blue region in the graph at the right. Each point in the blue region is a solution of the system.

EXERCISES

SEE EXAMPLES
1, 2 AND 3
on pp. 360–362
for Exs. 29–35

Solve the linear system by graphing. Check your solution.

29. $y = 3x$
$\quad\;\; y = x - 4$

30. $y = x - 3$
$\quad\;\; 2x + y = 6$

31. $x - y = 7$
$\quad\;\; 8x + 2y = 16$

Graph the system of linear inequalities.

32. $y < 6$
$\quad\;\; y \ge 2x - 5$

33. $x + y \le 8$
$\quad\;\; x \le 7$

34. $-6x + 2y < 12$
$\quad\;\; 3x + y > 4$

35. FUNDRAISING During a football game, the school's athletic booster club sells pretzels and popcorn to raise money. They charge $3 for a bag of popcorn and $2 for a pretzel. The club collects $312 from these sales during the game. They sell twice as many bags of popcorn as pretzels. How many bags of popcorn and how many pretzels do they sell?

VOCABULARY Copy and complete the statement.

1. A set of two or more linear equations with the same two variables is a(n) __?__ in two variables.

2. An equation in the form $y = mx + b$ is in __?__ form.

Tell whether the ordered pair is a solution of the equation $12x + 3y = 21$.

3. $(-1, 11)$ 4. $(-4, -9)$ 5. $(2, -15)$ 6. $(6, -17)$

Find the intercepts of the graph of the equation.

7. $y = 2x - 12$ 8. $8x - 3y = 24$ 9. $7 = -7x - 14y$

Find the slope and y-intercept of the graph of the equation. Then graph the equation.

10. $y = 6x + 3$ 11. $-5x - y = 1$ 12. $y = -\frac{1}{4}x$

Graph the inequality.

13. $y \geq -\frac{1}{2}x + 6$ 14. $7x - y \leq 49$ 15. $8x - 15y > 30$

Solve the system of equations or graph the system of inequalities.

16. $-x + 2y = 4$
    $4x - y = 5$

17. $2x + 3y = 9$
    $3x - y = 8$

18. $x - 3y > 3$
    $2x + y \leq 2$

For Exercises 19–21, use the diagram of a seesaw.

19. What is the run of the seesaw?

20. What is the rise of the seesaw?

21. What is the slope of the seesaw?

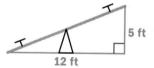
5 ft
12 ft

22. **YARD WORK** You have a job raking leaves. You charge $10 plus $.50 for each bag you fill with leaves. The equation $y = 0.50x + 10$ models this situation, where x is the number of bags and y is your total amount earned (in dollars). How many bags do you fill if you earn $17?

23. **FUEL USE** The distance d (in miles) that a scooter travels varies directly with the amount g (in gallons) of gas used. The scooter uses 2 gallons of gas to travel 120 miles. Write and graph an equation relating g and d. Predict the distance the scooter travels if it uses 12 gallons of gas.

24. **SOFTBALL** Your softball team must have at most 18 players. It must have at least 5 female and at least 5 male players. Write and graph a system of inequalities to describe the situation. Give two possible solutions for the numbers of female and male players.

STRATEGIES YOU'LL USE:
- **SOLVE DIRECTLY**
- **ELIMINATE CHOICES**

Standards
AF 1.1, AF 3.3

If you have difficulty solving a multiple choice problem directly, you may be able to use another approach to eliminate incorrect answer choices and obtain the correct answer.

PROBLEM 1

You have $45 to spend at a bookstore. Books cost $12 each and magazines cost $3 each. The inequality that model this situation is $12x + 3y \leq 45$ where x is the number of books purchased and y is the number of magazines purchased. Which of the following is *not* a solution of the inequality?

- **(A)** $(2, 3)$
- **(B)** $(2, 4)$
- **(C)** $(3, 3)$
- **(D)** $(3, 4)$

Strategy 1   SOLVE DIRECTLY

Check each possible solution (x, y) of the inequality by substituting x and y into the inequality.

(x, y)	$12x + 3y$	$12x + 3y \overset{?}{\leq} 45$
$(2, 3)$	$12(2) + 3(3)$	$33 \leq 45$ ✓
$(2, 4)$	$12(2) + 3(4)$	$36 \leq 45$ ✓
$(3, 3)$	$12(3) + 3(3)$	$45 \leq 45$ ✓
$(3, 4)$	$12(3) + 3(4)$	$48 \leq 45$ ✗

The ordered pair $(3, 4)$ is *not* a solution of the inequality. The combination of 3 books and 4 magazines could *not* be purchased.

The correct answer is D. Ⓐ Ⓑ Ⓒ **Ⓓ**

Strategy 2   ELIMINATE CHOICES

You can eliminate choices of a multiple choice question by checking the choices to see whether they are reasonable.

Because you are looking for the combination of books and magazines that could *not* be purchased, the correct answer is the combination of books and magazines whose total cost *exceeds* the $45 limit.

The number of books in choice A is the same as in choice B, but the number of magazines is less. The total cost of choice A will be less than the total cost of choice B. So, choice A can be eliminated.

The number of magazines in choice B is the same as in choice D, but the number of books is less. The total cost of choice B will be less than the total cost of choice D. So, choice B can be eliminated.

The number of books in choice C is the same as in choice D, but the number of magazines is less. The total cost of choice C will be less than the total cost of choice D. So, choice C can be eliminated.

The correct answer is D. Ⓐ Ⓑ Ⓒ **Ⓓ**

PROBLEM 2

A line with a slope of $\frac{5}{2}$ passes through $(-8, -3)$. What is the slope-intercept form of the equation of the line?

Ⓐ $y = -\frac{5}{2}x - 23$ **Ⓑ** $y = \frac{5}{2}x - 3$ **Ⓒ** $y = \frac{5}{2}x + 17$ **Ⓓ** $2y - 5x = 34$

Strategy 1 SOLVE DIRECTLY

Find the y-intercept of the line and then use slope-intercept form to write the equation.

STEP 1 **Find** the y-intercept by substituting the slope and the coordinates of $(-8, -3)$ into the equation $y = mx + b$.

$$y = mx + b$$
$$-3 = \frac{5}{2}(-8) + b$$
$$-3 = -20 + b$$
$$17 = b$$

The y-intercept is 17.

STEP 2 **Use** the slope and y-intercept to write the equation.

$$y = mx + b$$
$$y = \frac{5}{2}x + 17$$

The correct answer is C.   Ⓐ Ⓑ ⓒ Ⓓ

Strategy 2 ELIMINATE CHOICES

Use the definition of slope-intercept form to eliminate answer choices.

The slope of the line is $\frac{5}{2}$, but the slope of the line in choice A is $-\frac{5}{2}$. So, choice A can be eliminated.

You are looking for an equation in slope-intercept form. The equation in choice D is *not* written in slope-intercept form. So, choice D can be eliminated.

In choice B, the y-intercept of the line is -3. So, the line contains the point $(0, -3)$. If the line also contained the point $(-8, -3)$, it would be a horizontal line with a slope of 0. However, this is impossible because the slope of the line is $\frac{5}{2}$. So, choice B can be eliminated.

The correct answer is C.   Ⓐ Ⓑ ⓒ Ⓓ

STRATEGY PRACTICE

Explain why you can eliminate the highlighted answer choice.

1. What is the value of x if the line passing through $(-3, 5)$ and $(x, 8)$ has a slope of $\frac{1}{2}$?

   Ⓐ -9 **Ⓑ**✗ -3 **Ⓒ** 3   **Ⓓ** 9

2. Which ordered pair is a solution of $7x - 2y \le 5$?

   Ⓐ $(0, -3)$ **Ⓑ** $(0, 0)$ **Ⓒ** $(1, 0)$ **Ⓓ**✗ $(3, -5)$

1. What is the slope of the line? **AF 3.3**

Ⓐ $-\dfrac{3}{2}$

Ⓑ 0

Ⓒ 1

Ⓓ $\dfrac{3}{2}$

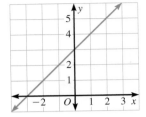

2. The height h of a stack of tires varies directly with the number n of tires in the stack. Based on the diagram below, how many tires are needed to make a stack with a height of 8 feet 3 inches? **AF 4.2**

3 ft

Ⓐ 5

Ⓑ 6

Ⓒ 11

Ⓓ 12

3. Which equation is *not* linear? **AF 3.3**

Ⓐ $y = -2x + 4$

Ⓑ $3x + 4y = 8$

Ⓒ $y = x^3 - 8$

Ⓓ $4x = 8 - 2y + 4$

4. Which ordered pair is a solution of $y = -6x - 3$? **AF 1.2**

Ⓐ $(1, -3)$

Ⓑ $(2, 9)$

Ⓒ $(-2, -15)$

Ⓓ $(-1, 3)$

5. Which equation is represented by the graph? **AF 3.3**

Ⓐ $y = \dfrac{1}{4}x + 3.5$

Ⓑ $y = -\dfrac{1}{4}x + 3.5$

Ⓒ $y = 4x + 3.5$

Ⓓ $y = -4x + 3.5$

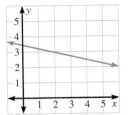

6. You earn money to go to the movies by babysitting for x dollars per hour. One weekend, you babysit for 9 hours and see 3 movies. Each movie costs y dollars. You have $12 left at the end of the weekend. Which equation models this situation in slope-intercept form? **AF 3.3**

Ⓐ $-3y = -9x + 12$

Ⓑ $x = \dfrac{1}{3}y + \dfrac{4}{3}$

Ⓒ $y = 3x + 4$

Ⓓ $y = 3x - 4$

7. You want to buy one gift each for at least 6 friends, choosing x pairs of earrings that cost $8 per pair and y belts that cost $12 each. You can spend at most $54. Which system of inequalities models the situation? **AF 1.1, MR 2.6**

Ⓐ $x + y \geq 6$, $12x + 8y \leq 54$, $x \geq 0$, and $y \geq 0$

Ⓑ $x + y \geq 6$, $8x + 12y \leq 54$, $x \geq 0$, and $y \geq 0$

Ⓒ $x + y \leq 6$, $8x + 12y \leq 54$, $x \geq 0$, and $y \geq 0$

Ⓓ $x + y \leq 6$, $12x + 8y \geq 54$, $x \geq 0$, and $y \geq 0$

8. What is the slope of the bottom section of the water slide shown? **AF 3.3**

Ⓐ $\dfrac{1}{4}$

Ⓑ $\dfrac{1}{3}$

Ⓒ 3

Ⓓ 4

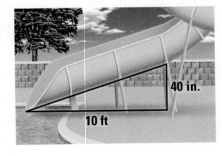

40 in.

10 ft

9. A line contains the points $(1, 2)$ and $(2, y)$ and has a slope of 0. What is the value of y? **AF 3.3**

(A) -1

(B) 2

(C) 3

(D) 5

10. Which inequality describes the graph? **AF 1.1**

(A) $y \geq \frac{1}{2}x$

(B) $y \leq \frac{1}{2}x$

(C) $y > 2x$

(D) $y \geq 2x$

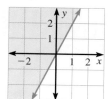

11. What is the x-intercept of $3x - 7y = 21$? **AF 3.3**

(A) -3

(B) $\frac{7}{3}$

(C) 3

(D) 7

12. You are running in a cross-country race. After x minutes, you are y miles from the finish line. This situation is modeled by $2x + 12y = 36$. How long is the race? **AF 3.3, MR 2.2**

(A) 3 mi

(B) 7 mi

(C) 10 mi

(D) 18 mi

13. What is the constant of variation for the equation $y = -4x$? **AF 4.2**

(A) -4

(B) -1

(C) 4

(D) There is no constant of variation.

14. A recreation center charges $240 for an annual membership. Raquetball court time costs $6 per hour for members and $14 per hour for nonmembers. After how many hours will the total costs for a member and a nonmember be equal? **AF 1.1**

(A) 26 h

(B) 30 h

(C) 35 h

(D) 42 h

15. You are saving money for a field trip. You have already saved $15 and plan on saving $10 more per week. This situation can be modeled by the equation $y = 10x + 15$ where y is the amount saved (in dollars) and x is the time (in weeks). Which table could be used to graph this equation? **AF 3.3**

(A)
x	1	2	3	4
y	20	25	30	35

(B)
x	1	2	3	4
y	15	30	45	60

(C)
x	1	2	3	4
y	25	35	45	55

(D)
x	1	2	3	4
y	20	35	60	85

16. Which system of inequalities describes the graph? **AF 1.1**

(A) $y \leq 2x$
$y > x + 1$

(B) $y \geq 2x + 3$
$y < -x + 1$

(C) $y \leq 2x + 3$
$y > -x + 1$

(D) $y \leq 2x + 3$
$y \geq -x + 1$

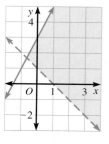

7 Exponents and Nonlinear Functions

Before

In previous chapters, you learned the following skills, which you'll use in Chapter 7:

- Evaluating powers
- Evaluating numerical expressions involving square roots
- Graphing ordered pairs
- Simplifying algebraic expressions

Now

In Chapter 7 you'll study these *Big Ideas:*

1 Applying properties of exponents

2 Representing relations and functions

3 Graphing nonlinear functions

Why?

So you can solve real-world problems about . . .

- Niagara Falls, p. 391
- Computers, p. 391
- Space exploration, p. 397
- Swimming, p. 403
- Recycling, p. 411

Animated Math
at *classzone.com*

Get-Ready Games

EQUATION SENSATION

California Standards

Review evaluating expressions with exponents. **Gr. 7 AF 1.2**

Prepare for using the rules of exponents. **Gr. 7 AF 2.1**

Materials

- One *Equation Sensation* board
- One number cube
- 30 place markers (15 each of two colors)

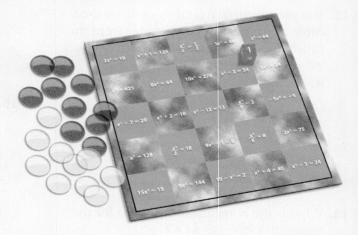

How to Play Play in pairs. Each player is given 15 markers of the same color. Players should take turns following the steps on the next page.

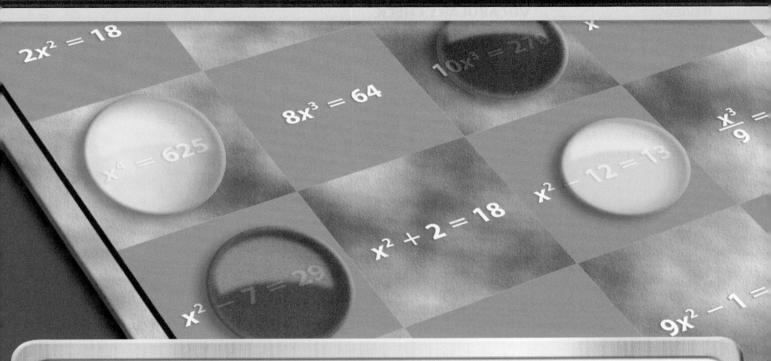

$2x^2 = 18$

$10x^3 = 270$

x

$8x^3 = 64$

$x^4 = 625$

$\frac{x^3}{9} =$

$x^2 - 12 = 13$

$x^2 + 2 = 18$

$x^2 - 7 = 29$

$9x^2 - 1 =$

1 **Roll** the number cube.

2 **Find** an equation on the board that is true when you substitute the number you rolled for x.

3 **Cover** the equation from Step 2 with a marker. No equation may be covered more than once.

How to Win Be the player with the most markers on the board when all the spaces are covered, or when a certain amount of time has passed.

Games Wrap-Up

Draw Conclusions

Complete these exercises after playing the game.

1. **WRITING** If the only spaces on the board that are not covered contain the equations $x^2 + 2 = 18$, $x^7 = 128$, and $3x^2 = 48$, what is the best number to roll? *Explain* your reasoning.

2. **REASONING** How many equations on the board have 5 as a solution? *Explain* how you found your answer.

Prerequisite Skills

California @HomeTutor

Prerequisite skills practice
at classzone.com

REVIEW VOCABULARY

- **power,** *p. 5*
- **exponent,** *p. 5*
- **base,** *p. 5*
- **simplest form of a fraction,** *p. 85*
- **square root,** *p. 213*
- **coordinate plane,** *p. 734*

VOCABULARY CHECK

Copy and complete using a review term from the list at the left.

1. The graph of the ordered pair $(-3, -2)$ appears in the third quadrant of the __?__.

2. In the expression x^5, x is the __?__ and 5 is the __?__.

3. The expression 4^7 can be read "4 to the seventh __?__."

SKILL CHECK

Solve the equation. Check your answer. *(p. 270)*

4. $2a + 6 = 14$	**5.** $8 - 4m = 20$	**6.** $-7 + 5c = -32$
7. $5x - 8 = 22$	**8.** $6d + 7 = 19$	**9.** $-12b + 4 = 52$

List four solutions of the equation. *(p. 315)*

10. $y = 3x - 5$	**11.** $y = -2x + 1$	**12.** $y = \frac{1}{2}x$
13. $y = -4x + 11$	**14.** $y = 5x - 6$	**15.** $y = 7 - 3x$

Notetaking Skills

NOW YOU TRY
Make an *information frame* for the distributive property. You may want to use colored pencils.

Focus on Graphic Organizers

You can use an *information frame* to organize information about a mathematical concept or property, such as the commutative property of addition.

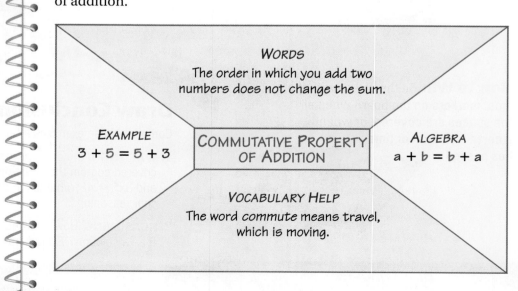

WORDS
The order in which you add two numbers does not change the sum.

EXAMPLE
$3 + 5 = 5 + 3$

COMMUTATIVE PROPERTY OF ADDITION

ALGEBRA
$a + b = b + a$

VOCABULARY HELP
The word *commute* means travel, which is moving.

Standards

AF 2.1 Interpret positive whole-number powers as repeated multiplication and negative whole-number powers as repeated division or multiplication by the multiplicative inverse. **Simplify and evaluate expressions that include exponents.**

7.1 Investigating Rules for Products and Powers

MATERIALS · paper and pencil

QUESTION How can you multiply powers with the same base?

EXPLORE 1 Find products of powers

Copy and complete the table.

Expression	Expression written using repeated multiplication	Number of factors	Simplified expression
$2^2 \cdot 2^4$	$(2 \cdot 2) \cdot (2 \cdot 2 \cdot 2 \cdot 2)$	6	2^6
$3^3 \cdot 3^5$	$(3 \cdot 3 \cdot 3) \cdot (3 \cdot 3 \cdot 3 \cdot 3 \cdot 3)$	?	$3^?$
$a^2 \cdot a^3$	?	?	?

EXPLORE 2 Find powers of powers

Copy and complete the table.

Expression	Expression written using repeated multiplication	Number of factors	Simplified expression
$(4^3)^2$	$(4^3)(4^3) = (4 \cdot 4 \cdot 4)(4 \cdot 4 \cdot 4)$	6	4^6
$(7^2)^3$	$(7^2)(7^2)(7^2) = (7 \cdot 7)(7 \cdot 7)(7 \cdot 7)$	?	$7^?$
$(x^5)^4$	?	?	?

DRAW CONCLUSIONS Use your observations to complete these exercises

1. **REASONING** In Explore 1, how are the exponents in the first and last columns of the table related?

2. Use your answer to Exercise 1 to simplify the product $10^8 \cdot 10^{12}$.

3. **REASONING** In Explore 2, how are the exponents in the first and last columns of the table related?

4. Use your answer to Exercise 3 simplify the product $(10^8)^3$.

7.1 Exponent Properties Involving Products

Math and NATURE
Ex. 52, p. 391

Standards   **NS 2.3** Multiply, divide, and simplify rational numbers by using exponent rules.

AF 2.1 Interpret positive whole-number powers as repeated multiplication and negative whole-number powers as repeated division or multiplication by the multiplicative inverse. **Simplify and evaluate expressions that include exponents.**

Connect   *Before* you evaluated powers. *Now* you will use exponent properties to simplify expressions involving products.

KEY VOCABULARY
- **power,** *p. 5*
- **exponent,** *p. 5*
- **base,** *p. 5*

A power is evaluated using repeated multiplication. Notice the pattern when you multiply powers with the same base.

$$a^4 \cdot a^2 = \underbrace{(a \cdot a \cdot a \cdot a)}_{\text{4 factors}} \cdot \overbrace{(a \cdot a)}^{\text{2 factors}} = a^6 = a^{4+2}$$
$$\underbrace{}_{\text{6 factors}}$$

This example suggests the following property of exponents.

KEY CONCEPT   *For Your Notebook*

Product of Powers Property

Words   To multiply powers with the same base, add their exponents.

Algebra $a^m \cdot a^n = a^{m+n}$ **Numbers** $5^6 \cdot 5^3 = 5^{6+3} = 5^9$

EXAMPLE 1   **Using the Product of Powers Property**

Simplify the expression.

REVIEW SIMPLIFYING
Recall from Lesson 4.3 that the simplified form of an expression must contain no negative exponents.

a. $7^8 \cdot 7^9 = 7^{8+9}$ **Product of powers property**

$ = 7^{17}$ **Add exponents.**

b. $x^7 \cdot x^4 = x^{7+4}$ **Product of powers property**

$ = x^{11}$ **Add exponents.**

c. $y^{-2} \cdot y^{-5} = y^{-2+(-5)}$ **Product of powers property**

$\phantom{y^{-2} \cdot y^{-5}} = y^{-7}$ **Add exponents.**

$\phantom{y^{-2} \cdot y^{-5}} = \dfrac{1}{y^7}$ **Definition of negative exponent:** $a^{-n} = \dfrac{1}{a^n}$

POWER OF A POWER Notice the pattern when you raise a power to a power.

$$(a^2)^3 = a^2 \cdot a^2 \cdot a^2 = (a \cdot a) \cdot (a \cdot a) \cdot (a \cdot a) = a^6 = a^{2 \cdot 3}$$

This example suggests the following property of exponents.

KEY CONCEPT   *For Your Notebook*

Power of a Power Property

Words   To simplify a power of a power, multiply exponents.

Algebra $(a^m)^n = a^{mn}$ **Numbers** $(5^4)^2 = 5^{4 \cdot 2} = 5^8$

EXAMPLE 2   **Using the Power of a Power Property**

Simplify the expression.

   a. $(6^4)^4$ **b.** $[(-0.3)^5]^2$ **c.** $(m^{-3})^4$ **d.** $(z^{-2})^{-2}$

SOLUTION

   a. $(6^4)^4 = 6^{4 \cdot 4}$ **Power of a power property**

         $= 6^{16}$ **Multiply exponents.**

   b. $[(-0.3)^5]^2 = (-0.3)^{5 \cdot 2}$ **Power of a power property**

         $= (-0.3)^{10}$ **Multiply exponents.**

   c. $(m^{-3})^4 = m^{-3 \cdot 4}$ **Power of a power property**

         $= m^{-12}$ **Multiply exponents.**

         $= \dfrac{1}{m^{12}}$ **Definition of negative exponent**

   d. $(z^{-2})^{-2} = z^{-2 \cdot (-2)}$ **Power of a power property**

         $= z^4$ **Multiply exponents.**

✓ **GUIDED PRACTICE**   **for Examples 1 and 2**

Simplify the expression.

   1. $4^4 \cdot 4^6$ **2.** $9^8 \cdot 9$ **3.** $b^6 \cdot b^9$

   4. $w^{-7} \cdot w^{-2}$ **5.** $(2^4)^2$ **6.** $(x^6)^5$

   7. $(p^{-3})^3$ **8.** $(x^{12})^4$ **9.** $[(-10)^2]^3$

10. WRITING *Explain* why you cannot use the product of powers property to simplify the expression $3^4 \cdot 5^2$.

POWER OF A PRODUCT Notice the pattern when you raise a product to a power.

$$(ab)^3 = (ab) \cdot (ab) \cdot (ab) = (a \cdot a \cdot a) \cdot (b \cdot b \cdot b) = a^3 b^3$$

The example above suggests the following property of exponents.

KEY CONCEPT *For Your Notebook*

Power of a Product Property

Words To simplify a power of a product, find the power of each factor and multiply.

Algebra $(ab)^m = a^m \cdot b^m$ **Numbers** $(5 \cdot 2)^4 = 5^4 \cdot 2^4$

EXAMPLE 3 Using the Power of a Product Property

Simplify the expression.

a. $(3x)^4$ **b.** $(ab)^7$ **c.** $(-4d)^{-3}$

SOLUTION

a. $(3x)^4 = 3^4 \cdot x^4$ Power of a product property

$\quad\quad\quad = 81x^4$ Evaluate power.

b. $(ab)^7 = a^7 \cdot b^7$ Power of a product property

$\quad\quad\quad = a^7 b^7$ Write without multiplication symbol.

c. $(-4d)^{-3} = (-4)^{-3} \cdot d^{-3}$ Power of a product property

$\quad\quad\quad = \dfrac{1}{(-4)^3} \cdot \dfrac{1}{d^3}$ Definition of negative exponent

$\quad\quad\quad = \dfrac{1}{-64} \cdot \dfrac{1}{d^3}$ Evaluate power.

$\quad\quad\quad = -\dfrac{1}{64d^3}$ Simplify.

✓ **GUIDED PRACTICE** for Example 3

Simplify the expression.

11. $(8y)^3$ **12.** $(pq)^{10}$ **13.** $(-2w)^5$ **14.** $(-5t)^{-2}$

PRODUCTS IN SCIENTIFIC NOTATION You can use the product of powers property to multiply two numbers written in scientific notation. This is demonstrated in Example 4.

EXAMPLE 4   Multiplying Numbers in Scientific Notation

REVIEW SCIENTIFIC NOTATION

For help with scientific notation, see p. 201.

AMAZON RIVER The Amazon River in South America contributes more water to Earth's oceans than any other river. Each second, it discharges about 4.2×10^6 cubic feet of water into the Atlantic Ocean. How much water does the Amazon River discharge in one year? There are approximately 3.15×10^7 seconds in one year.

Flow rate of Amazon:
4.2×10^6 ft³/sec

SOLUTION

To find how much water the river discharges in one year, evaluate the product $(4.2 \times 10^6) \times (3.15 \times 10^7)$.

$(4.2 \times 10^6) \times (3.15 \times 10^7)$

$= 4.2 \times 3.15 \times 10^6 \times 10^7$ **Commutative property of multiplication**

$= (4.2 \times 3.15) \times (10^6 \times 10^7)$ **Associative property of multiplication**

$= 13.23 \times 10^{13}$ **Product of powers property**

$= 1.323 \times 10^1 \times 10^{13}$ **Write 13.23 in scientific notation.**

$= 1.323 \times 10^{14}$ **Product of powers property**

▶**Answer** The Amazon River discharges about 1.323×10^{14} cubic feet of water in one year.

✓ **GUIDED PRACTICE**   for Example 4

15. AMAZON RIVER Look back at Example 4. How much water does the Amazon River discharge in one week (about 6.05×10^5 seconds)?

7.1 EXERCISES

HOMEWORK KEY

◆ = **MULTIPLE CHOICE PRACTICE**
Exs. 11, 20, 51, 59–61

○ = **HINTS AND HOMEWORK HELP**
for Exs. 9, 19, 53 at classzone.com

SKILLS • PROBLEM SOLVING • REASONING

1. VOCABULARY Copy and complete: Three is the __?__ of the power 3^4.

2. NOTETAKING SKILLS Make an *information frame* like the one on page 384 for the product of powers property.

SEE EXAMPLE 1
on p. 386
for Exs. 3–11

PRODUCT OF POWERS PROPERTY Simplify the expression.

3. $4^2 \cdot 4^4$ **4.** $3^2 \cdot 3^{-5}$ **5.** $a^5 \cdot a^7$ **6.** $u^{-7} \cdot u$

7. $7^{-2} \cdot 7^{-2}$ **8.** $v^2 \cdot v^{10}$ **9.** $(20.3)^{11} \cdot (20.3)^{-8}$ **10.** $(-4)^{-2} \cdot (-4)^3$

11. ◆ **MULTIPLE CHOICE** Which expression is equivalent to $y^5 \cdot y^3 \cdot y^{-2}$?

    Ⓐ y^{-30} Ⓑ y^6 Ⓒ y^{10} Ⓓ y^{13}

SEE EXAMPLE 2
on p. 387
for Exs. 12–20

POWER OF A POWER PROPERTY Simplify the expression.

12. $(7^3)^3$ **13.** $[(-3)^4]^{-2}$ **14.** $(t^4)^2$ **15.** $[(-2)^{-2}]^{-2}$

16. $(y^2)^2$ **17.** $[(0.71)^2]^{-9}$ **18.** $[(-x)^{-3}]^{-8}$ **⑲** $(d^{-2})^{-4}$

20. ◆ **MULTIPLE CHOICE** Which expression is equivalent to $(5^2)^4$?

    Ⓐ $\sqrt{5}$ Ⓑ 5^2 Ⓒ 5^6 Ⓓ 5^8

SEE EXAMPLE 3
on p. 388
for Exs. 21–28

POWER OF A PRODUCT PROPERTY Simplify the expression.

21. $(5z)^3$ **22.** $(-6x)^4$ **23.** $(4y)^{-2}$ **24.** $(-3w)^{-5}$

25. $(-dt)^4$ **26.** $(2m)^6$ **27.** $(-gh)^{-3}$ **28.** $(-7mn)^{-2}$

SEE EXAMPLE 4
on p. 389
for Exs. 29–34

SCIENTIFIC NOTATION Write the product in scientific notation.

29. $(3 \times 10^3) \times (2 \times 10^5)$ **30.** $(2 \times 10^{-6}) \times (4 \times 10^{-4})$

31. $(1.5 \times 10^{-2}) \times (3.9 \times 10^{-5})$ **32.** $(3.6 \times 10^8) \times (2.4 \times 10^5)$

33. $(2.6 \times 10^7) \times (4.1 \times 10^{-3})$ **34.** $(5.4 \times 10^5) \times (3.6 \times 10^{-9})$

ERROR ANALYSIS *Describe* and correct the error in simplifying.

35.

     ✗ $(3 \times 10^2) \times (1.2 \times 10^3)$
           $= (3 \times 1.2) \times (10^2 \times 10^3)$
           $= 3.6 \times 10^6$

36.

     ✗ $2^2 \cdot 2^4 = (2 \cdot 2)^{2+4}$
           $= 4^6$

⒳ ALGEBRA Find the number that makes the statement true.

37. $2^3 \cdot 2^? = 2^{11}$ **38.** $3^2 \cdot 3^? = 3^7$ **39.** $4^3 \cdot 4^? = 4^{-5}$ **40.** $9^5 \cdot 9^? = 9^{20}$

41. $4^? \cdot 4^{-5} = 4^{12}$ **42.** $5^4 \cdot ?^5 = 5^9$ **43.** $12^3 \cdot ?^{13} = 12^{16}$ **44.** $5^{-9} \cdot 5^? = 5^{-3}$

REASONING Tell whether the statement is *true* or *false*. If it is false, rewrite the right side of the equation to make it true.

45. $4^3 \cdot 4^2 = 4^6$ **46.** $10^5 \cdot 10^6 \cdot 10^7 = 10^{18}$ **47.** $a^2 \cdot a^3 \cdot a \cdot a^5 = a^{10}$

CONNECT SKILLS TO PROBLEM SOLVING Exercises 48–50 will help you prepare for problem solving.

48. Three square plots of land each measure 3 miles by 3 miles. Write a power that represents the total area of the land in square miles.

49. Write a simplified expression for the volume of a cube with edge length $2x$.

50. A city has a population of 7.3×10^5. Write an expression in scientific notation for the population if it doubles.

     ◆ = **MULTIPLE CHOICE PRACTICE**   ◯ = **HINTS AND HOMEWORK HELP** at classzone.com

SEE EXAMPLE 4
on p. 389
for Exs. 51–52

51. ◆ **MULTIPLE CHOICE** A white blood cell with a diameter of 6.0×10^{-4} centimeters is magnified by a microscope 1.0×10^3 times. What is the diameter of the magnified image?

Ⓐ 0.6×10^1 cm   Ⓑ 6.0×10^{-1} cm

Ⓒ 6.0×10^1 cm   Ⓓ 6.0×10^{20} cm

[California @HomeTutor] for problem solving help at classzone.com

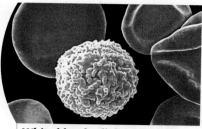

White blood cell diameter:
6.0×10^{-4} cm

52. **NIAGARA FALLS** At Niagara Falls, the American Falls in the United States and Horseshoe Falls in Canada have a combined average flow of about 1.0×10^5 cubic feet per second during the summer. How much water flows over these falls in one hour during the summer?

[California @HomeTutor] for problem solving help at classzone.com

53. **COMPUTERS** A friend's family first bought a computer in 1979. It had 2^3 kilobytes of memory. Your family's first computer, bought in 1987, had 64 times as much memory. How much memory did your family's computer have? Express your answer as a power of 2.

54. **CHECKING REASONABLENESS** It takes you 5^2 seconds to run x feet. If your speed remains constant, is it reasonable to say that it will take you 5^3 seconds to run $5x$ feet? *Justify* your answer.

CHALLENGE Find the value of x that makes the statement true.

55. $4^{2x} \cdot 4^{x-3} = 4^{12}$ 56. $5^{x-3} \cdot 5^{3x} = 5^{13}$ 57. $8^{3x+4} \cdot 8^x = 8^{12}$

58. **CHALLENGE** Use the product of powers property to prove the following two rules.

   a. $a^0 = 1$ (*Hint:* Write $a^m = a^{m+0}$.)

   b. $a^{-m} = \dfrac{1}{a^m}$ (*Hint:* Write $1 = a^0 = a^{m+(-m)}$.)

◆ CALIFORNIA STANDARDS SPIRAL REVIEW

NS 2.4

59. Between which two consecutive integers does $\sqrt{68}$ lie? (*p. 213*)

Ⓐ 6, 7   Ⓑ 7, 8   Ⓒ 8, 9   Ⓓ 9, 10

AF 1.3

60. Which statement is *not* always true for all nonzero values? (*p. 48*)

Ⓐ $y + (-y) = 0$ Ⓑ $k\left(\dfrac{1}{k}\right) = 1$

Ⓒ $4(x + y) = 4x + 4y$ Ⓓ $2x + y = 2y + x$

AF 4.2

61. You pay $100 plus a daily rental fee to rent a cottage. The total cost C (in dollars) for renting the cottage d days can be modeled by $C = 25d + 100$. What is the daily rental fee? (*p. 315*)

Ⓐ $25   Ⓑ $75   Ⓒ $100   Ⓓ $125

Standards

AF 2.1 Interpret positive whole-number powers as repeated multiplication and negative whole-number powers as repeated division or multiplication by the multiplicative inverse. **Simplify and evaluate expressions that include exponents.**

7.2 Investigating Rules for Quotients and Powers

MATERIALS · paper and pencil

QUESTION How can you simplify expressions involving quotients and powers?

EXPLORE 1 Find quotients of powers

Copy and complete the table.

Expression	Expression written using repeated multiplication	Simplified expression	Quotient as a power
$\dfrac{3^8}{3^3}$	$\dfrac{3 \cdot 3 \cdot 3 \cdot 3 \cdot 3 \cdot 3 \cdot 3 \cdot 3}{3 \cdot 3 \cdot 3}$	$3 \cdot 3 \cdot 3 \cdot 3 \cdot 3$	3^5
$\dfrac{6^5}{6^3}$	$\dfrac{6 \cdot 6 \cdot 6 \cdot 6 \cdot 6}{6 \cdot 6 \cdot 6}$	?	$6^?$
$\dfrac{a^7}{a^4}$	$\dfrac{a \cdot a \cdot a \cdot a \cdot a \cdot a \cdot a}{a \cdot a \cdot a \cdot a}$	?	?

EXPLORE 2 Find powers of quotients

Copy and complete the table.

Expression	Expression written using repeated multiplication	Multiply fractions	Quotient of powers
$\left(\dfrac{2}{3}\right)^4$	$\dfrac{2}{3} \cdot \dfrac{2}{3} \cdot \dfrac{2}{3} \cdot \dfrac{2}{3}$	$\dfrac{2 \cdot 2 \cdot 2 \cdot 2}{3 \cdot 3 \cdot 3 \cdot 3}$	$\dfrac{2^4}{3^4}$
$\left(\dfrac{-3}{y}\right)^3$	$\dfrac{-3}{y} \cdot \dfrac{-3}{y} \cdot \dfrac{-3}{y}$	$\dfrac{(-3)(-3)(-3)}{y \cdot y \cdot y}$	?
$\left(\dfrac{a}{b}\right)^5$	?	?	?

DRAW CONCLUSIONS Use your observations to complete these exercises

1. **REASONING** In Explore 1, how are the exponents in the first and last columns of the table related? Write the quotient $\dfrac{5^{12}}{5^9}$ as a power.

2. **REASONING** In Explore 2, how are the exponents in the first and last columns of the table related? Write $\left(\dfrac{10}{x}\right)^3$ as a quotient of powers.

7.2 Exponent Properties Involving Quotients

Standards NS 2.3 Multiply, **divide, and simplify rational numbers by using exponent rules.**

AF 2.1 Interpret positive whole-number powers as repeated multiplication and negative whole-number powers as repeated division or multiplication by the multiplicative inverse. **Simplify and evaluate expressions that include exponents.**

Connect *Before* you used exponent properties involving products. *Now* you will use exponent properties involving quotients.

Math and **SCIENCE**
Ex. 46, p. 398

KEY VOCABULARY
• **power**, *p. 5*
• **exponent**, *p. 5*
• **base**, *p. 5*

Notice the pattern when you divide powers with the same base.

$$\frac{a^5}{a^3} = \frac{\overbrace{a \cdot a \cdot a \cdot a \cdot a}^{\text{5 factors}}}{\underbrace{a \cdot a \cdot a}_{\text{3 factors}}} = \frac{a \cdot a \cdot \cancel{a} \cdot \cancel{a} \cdot \cancel{a}}{\cancel{a} \cdot \cancel{a} \cdot \cancel{a}} = \overbrace{a \cdot a}^{\text{2 factors}} = a^2 = a^{5-3}$$

This example suggests the following property of exponents.

KEY CONCEPT   *For Your Notebook*

Quotient of Powers Property

Words To divide two powers with the same nonzero base, subtract the exponent of the denominator from the exponent of the numerator.

Algebra $\dfrac{a^m}{a^n} = a^{m-n}, a \neq 0$ **Numbers** $\dfrac{4^7}{4^4} = 4^{7-4} = 4^3$

EXAMPLE 1 Using the Quotient of Powers Property

AVOID ERRORS
When using the quotient of powers property, be sure to subtract the exponents in the correct order. Always subtract the exponent of the denominator from the exponent of the numerator.

Simplify the expression.

a. $\dfrac{9^7}{9^3} = 9^{7-3}$ **Quotient of powers property**

$\phantom{\dfrac{9^7}{9^3}} = 9^4$ **Subtract exponents.**

b. $\dfrac{x^{12}}{x^7} = x^{12-7}$ **Quotient of powers property**

$\phantom{\dfrac{x^{12}}{x^7}} = x^5$ **Subtract exponents.**

c. $\dfrac{y^{-10}}{y^{-12}} = y^{-10-(-12)}$ **Quotient of powers property**

$\phantom{\dfrac{y^{-10}}{y^{-12}}} = y^2$ **Subtract exponents.**

POWER OF A QUOTIENT Notice what happens when you raise a quotient to a power.

$$\left(\frac{a}{b}\right)^4 = \overbrace{\frac{a}{b} \cdot \frac{a}{b} \cdot \frac{a}{b} \cdot \frac{a}{b}}^{\text{4 factors}} = \frac{a \cdot a \cdot a \cdot a}{b \cdot b \cdot b \cdot b} = \frac{a^4}{b^4}$$

This example suggests the following property of exponents.

KEY CONCEPT   *For Your Notebook*

Power of a Quotient Property

Words   To find the power of a quotient, find the power of the numerator and the power of the denominator, then divide.

Algebra $\left(\dfrac{a}{b}\right)^m = \dfrac{a^m}{b^m}, b \neq 0$ **Numbers** $\left(\dfrac{5}{8}\right)^6 = \dfrac{5^6}{8^6}$

EXAMPLE 2   Using the Power of a Quotient Property

Simplify the expression.

a. $\left(\dfrac{7}{-2}\right)^3 = \dfrac{7^3}{(-2)^3}$ **Power of a quotient property**

$= -\dfrac{343}{8}$ **Evaluate powers.**

b. $\left(\dfrac{3}{b}\right)^6 = \dfrac{3^6}{b^6}$ **Power of a quotient property**

$= \dfrac{729}{b^6}$ **Evaluate power.**

REVIEW NEGATIVE EXPONENTS
....
For help with negative exponents, see p. 206.

c. $\left(\dfrac{x}{5}\right)^{-2} = \dfrac{x^{-2}}{5^{-2}}$ **Power of a quotient property**

$= \dfrac{\frac{1}{x^2}}{\frac{1}{5^2}}$ **Definition of negative exponents**

$= \dfrac{1}{x^2} \cdot \dfrac{5^2}{1}$ **Multiply by reciprocal.**

$= \dfrac{25}{x^2}$ **Evaluate power and simplify.**

 GUIDED PRACTICE   for Examples 1 and 2

Simplify the expression.

1. $\dfrac{10^9}{10^6}$ **2.** $\dfrac{5^{-2}}{5^{-6}}$ **3.** $\left(\dfrac{5}{2}\right)^2$ **4.** $\left(\dfrac{a}{10}\right)^{-3}$

EXAMPLE 3 **Dividing Numbers in Scientific Notation**

AIRPORTS In 2004, about 2.29×10^7 people boarded planes at Los Angeles International Airport (LAX). That same year, about 5.19×10^6 people boarded planes at San Jose International Airport (SJC). The number of people who boarded planes at LAX was about how many times the number at SJC?

SOLUTION

Find the ratio of the number of people who boarded planes at LAX to the number at SJC.

$$\frac{2.29 \times 10^7}{5.19 \times 10^6} = \frac{2.29}{5.19} \times \frac{10^7}{10^6}$$ **Write quotient as product.**

$$\approx 0.441 \times 10^{7-6}$$ **Quotient of powers property**

$$= 0.441 \times 10^1$$ **Simplify exponent.**

$$= 4.41$$ **Write in standard form.**

▶**Answer** In 2004, the number of people who boarded planes at LAX was about 4.41 times the number of people who boarded planes at SJC.

✓ **GUIDED PRACTICE** **for Example 3**

5. **AIRPORTS** Use the information from Example 3. In 2004, about 6.53×10^8 people boarded planes at all United States airports. This is about how many times the number who boarded at SJC?

CONCEPT SUMMARY   *For Your Notebook*

Properties of Exponents

Let m and n be integers and let a and b be real numbers.

Property	Algebra	Example
Negative Exponent	$a^{-m} = \dfrac{1}{a^m},\ a \neq 0$	$5^{-2} = \dfrac{1}{5^2}$
Zero Exponent	$a^0 = 1,\ a \neq 0$	$(-49)^0 = 1$
Product of Powers	$a^m \cdot a^n = a^{m+n}$	$7^6 \cdot 7^3 = 7^{6+3} = 7^9$
Power of a Power	$(a^m)^n = a^{mn}$	$(6^3)^4 = 6^{3 \cdot 4} = 6^{12}$
Power of a Product	$(ab)^m = a^m \cdot b^m$	$(3y)^5 = 3^5 y^5$
Quotient of Powers	$\dfrac{a^m}{a^n} = a^{m-n},\ a \neq 0$	$\dfrac{10^8}{10^5} = 10^{8-5} = 10^3$
Power of a Quotient	$\left(\dfrac{a}{b}\right)^m = \dfrac{a^m}{b^m},\ b \neq 0$	$\left(\dfrac{3}{4}\right)^3 = \dfrac{3^3}{4^3}$

7.2 EXERCISES

HOMEWORK
KEY

◆ = **MULTIPLE CHOICE PRACTICE**
Exs. 19, 32, 43, 53–55

○ = **HINTS** AND **HOMEWORK HELP**
for Exs. 9, 27, 45 at classzone.com

SKILLS • PROBLEM SOLVING • REASONING

VOCABULARY Match the expression with the property used to simplify it.

1. $(x^2)^7$

2. $\dfrac{a^8}{a^5}$

3. $(2y)^5$

4. $3 \cdot x^4 \cdot x^5$

5. $\left(\dfrac{3}{w}\right)^3$

A. Product of powers property

B. Power of a power property

C. Power of a product property

D. Quotient of powers property

E. Power of a quotient property

6. WRITING *Describe* two ways to evaluate $\dfrac{6y^{10}}{3y^8}$ when $y = 5$. Evaluate the expression using both methods. Which method do you prefer? Why?

SEE EXAMPLE 1
on p. 393
for Exs. 7–19

QUOTIENT OF POWERS PROPERTY Simplify the expression.

7. $\dfrac{5^8}{5^4}$

8. $\dfrac{3^6}{3^{-2}}$

9. $\dfrac{d^8}{d}$

10. $\dfrac{x^{-5}}{x}$

11. $\dfrac{w^{-9}}{w^{-15}}$

12. $\dfrac{y^{20}}{y^{18}}$

13. $\dfrac{(-7)^7}{(-7)^{-4}}$

14. $\dfrac{(0.4)^{13}}{(0.4)^3}$

SIMPLIFYING EXPRESSIONS Simplify the expression.

15. $\dfrac{z^6 \cdot z^3}{z^4}$

16. $\dfrac{y^6 \cdot y^{13}}{y^9}$

17. $\dfrac{d^5}{d^{-4} \cdot d^6}$

18. $\dfrac{a^{-3} \cdot a^{14}}{a^{-5}}$

19. ◆ MULTIPLE CHOICE Which of the following expressions is equivalent to $\dfrac{a^9 \cdot a^6}{a^5}$?

A a^3

B a^5

C a^{10}

D a^{15}

SEE EXAMPLE 2
on p. 394
for Exs. 20–27

POWER OF A QUOTIENT PROPERTY Simplify the expression.

20. $\left(\dfrac{2}{3}\right)^3$

21. $\left(\dfrac{5}{3}\right)^2$

22. $\left(\dfrac{-2}{x}\right)^4$

23. $\left(\dfrac{3}{y}\right)^{-3}$

24. $\left(\dfrac{k}{g}\right)^5$

25. $\left(\dfrac{-m}{4}\right)^{-2}$

26. $\left(\dfrac{x}{-y}\right)^{-1}$

27. $\left(\dfrac{1}{-2}\right)^{-5}$

SEE EXAMPLE 3
on p. 395 for
Exs. 28–31

SCIENTIFIC NOTATION Evaluate. Write your answer in scientific notation.

28. $\dfrac{4.08 \times 10^6}{3.4 \times 10^2}$

29. $\dfrac{2.765 \times 10^{21}}{7.9 \times 10^9}$

30. $\dfrac{5.46 \times 10^{28}}{6.5 \times 10^{24}}$

31. $\dfrac{2.015 \times 10^7}{6.2 \times 10^3}$

32. ◆ MULTIPLE CHOICE Which expression is equivalent to $\left(\dfrac{x}{y^2}\right)^3$?

A $\dfrac{x}{y^2}$

B $\dfrac{x^3}{y^5}$

C $\dfrac{x^3}{y^2}$

D $\dfrac{x^3}{y^6}$

ERROR ANALYSIS *Describe* and correct the error in simplifying the expression.

33.

$$\times \quad \frac{x^{20}}{x^4} = x^{20/4} = x^5$$

34.

$$\times \quad \left(\frac{2a}{b}\right)^3 = \frac{2a^3}{b^3}$$

REASONING Tell whether the statement is *true* or *false*. If it is false, rewrite the right side of the equation to make it true.

35. $\dfrac{6^6}{6^4} = 6^{-2}$

36. $\dfrac{(-2)^7}{(-2)^2} = (-2)^5$

37. $\dfrac{8c^4}{8c} = c^4$

38. $\left(\dfrac{3x}{-5}\right)^{-3} = \dfrac{125}{9x^3}$

CONNECT SKILLS TO PROBLEM SOLVING Exercises 39–41 will help you prepare for problem solving.

39. The area of a rectangle is $3x^5$. The length of the rectangle is x^4. What is the width of the rectangle?

40. The volume of a small cube is $8x^3$. The volume of a large cube is $24x^6$. Write a simplified expression for the ratio of the volume of the small cube to the volume of the large cube.

41. The area of a rectangle is $32x^5$. The height is $8x^3$. What is the base?

SEE EXAMPLE 1
on p. 393
for Ex. 42

42. METRIC UNITS The metric system is a base-ten system. The number of meters in some metric measures can be written as powers of ten. There are 10^3 meters in a kilometer and 10^{15} meters in a petameter. How many kilometers are in a petameter? Write your answer as a power of ten.

California *@HomeTutor* for problem solving help at classzone.com

The historical standard
platinum iridium meter bar

SEE EXAMPLE 3
on p. 395
for Exs. 43–44

43. ◆ MULTIPLE CHOICE Blood vessels called arterioles have a width of about 1.0×10^{-3} meters. Blood vessels called venules have a width of about 2.0×10^{-5} meters. An arteriole is about how many times as wide as a venule?

(A) 0.02   **(B)** 0.2   **(C)** 5   **(D)** 50

California *@HomeTutor* for problem solving help at classzone.com

44. SPACE EXPLORATION The NASA spacecraft Deep Impact traveled about 1.55×10^6 miles per day to the comet Tempel 1, covering a total distance of 268 million miles. After the spacecraft traveled 128 million miles, about how many days of travel remained?

1.55×10^6 mi/day

45. **OPEN-ENDED** Write two expressions involving quotients that are equivalent to 9^6.

7.2 Exponent Properties Involving Quotients   **397**

46. **ANDROMEDA GALAXY** The distance from Earth to the Andromeda Galaxy is about 21 quintillion kilometers, which is 21 followed by 18 zeros. There are 10^9 meters in a gigameter. How many gigameters are in 21 quintillion kilometers?

READING IN MATH Read the information below for Exercises 47–49.

U.S. Currency Facts The United States Bureau of Engraving and Printing prints the nation's new money. In 2004, the bureau printed about 23.9 million bills daily with a face value of about $351 million. More than half of these were $1 and $5 bills. About 11.4 million were $1 bills and about 1.72 million were $5 bills.

The average life of a bill depends on its denomination. A $1 bill lasts an average of about 22 months, while a $100 bill lasts an average of about 8.5 years.

Currency printing press

47. **Calculate** About how many $1 bills were printed in one week? in one year? Write your answers in scientific notation.

48. **Calculate** About how many $5 bills were printed in one week? in one year? Write your answers in scientific notation.

49. **Compare** About how many times more $1 bills than $5 bills were printed daily? Use a quotient of numbers in scientific notation.

50. **REASONING** Use the definition of negative exponents and the product of powers property to show that the quotient of powers property is true.

51. **CHALLENGE** How many times as great as 2^n is 2^{n+1}?

52. **CHALLENGE** The surface area S and the volume V of a sphere are given by $S = 4\pi r^2$ and $V = \frac{4}{3}\pi r^3$ where r is the radius. Write a simplified expression for the ratio of the surface area to the volume of a sphere.

◆ CALIFORNIA STANDARDS SPIRAL REVIEW

AF 3.3 53. What is the y-intercept of the graph of $4x + 2y = 8$? *(p. 327)*

    (A) -4 **(B)** 2   **(C)** 4   **(D)** 8

AF 1.1 54. Which point represents a solution of the system of equations consisting of $2x - y = 0$ and $x + 4y = 9$? *(p. 360)*

    (A) (2, 4)   **(B)** (0, 0)   **(C)** (5, 1)   **(D)** (1, 2)

NS 1.1 55. The radius of the sun is 695,500 kilometers. What is the radius written in scientific notation? *(p. 201)*

    (A) 6.9×10^5 **(B)** 0.6955×10^6 **(C)** 6.955×10^5 **(D)** 695.5×10^3

7.3 Products, Quotients, and Roots of Monomials

Standards AF 2.2 Multiply and divide monomials; extend the process of taking powers and extracting square roots to monomials when the latter results in a monomial with an integer exponent.

Connect *Before* you applied properties of exponents to numerical expressions.
Now you will apply properties of exponents to monomials.

Math and SPORTS
Ex. 54, p. 403

KEY VOCABULARY
• **monomial**
• **square root,** *p. 213*
• **coefficient,** *p. 252*

A **monomial** is a number, a variable, or a product of a number and one or more variables with whole number exponents.

Monomials	Not monomials
$7 \quad 7x \quad 7x^4 \quad 7x^4y^3$	$7 + x \quad 7x - y \quad 7x^4y^{-1}$

To multiply and divide monomials, you can use the rules of exponents you learned in Lessons 7.1 and 7.2.

EXAMPLE 1 Finding Products of Monomials

 **Simplify the expression.**

a. $(2x^3)(-3x) = 2 \cdot x^3 \cdot (-3) \cdot x$ **Expand the expression.**

$= 2 \cdot (-3) \cdot x^3 \cdot x$ **Regroup factors.**

$= -6 \cdot x^3 \cdot x$ **Multiply coefficients.**

$= -6x^4$ **Product of powers property**

b. $(4mn^3)(6m^2n^4) = 4 \cdot m \cdot n^3 \cdot 6 \cdot m^2 \cdot n^4$ **Expand the expression.**

$= 4 \cdot 6 \cdot m \cdot m^2 \cdot n^3 \cdot n^4$ **Regroup factors.**

$= 24 \cdot m \cdot m^2 \cdot n^3 \cdot n^4$ **Multiply coefficients.**

$= 24m^3 \cdot n^3 \cdot n^4$ **Product of powers property**

$= 24m^3n^7$ **Product of powers property**

c. $(2a^3b^2)^3 = 2^3 \cdot (a^3)^3 \cdot (b^2)^3$ **Power of a product property**

$= 8 \cdot (a^3)^3 \cdot (b^2)^3$ **Evaluate power of coefficient.**

$= 8a^9 \cdot (b^2)^3$ **Power of a power property**

$= 8a^9b^6$ **Power of a power property**

✓ **GUIDED PRACTICE**   for Example 1

Simplify the expression.

1. $(5x)(2x^3)$ **2.** $(-2m)(6m^4)$ **3.** $(4cd^3)(-c^2d)$ **4.** $(3pq)^2$

EXAMPLE 2 **Finding Quotients of Monomials**

Simplify the expression.

a. $\dfrac{8a^4}{2a} = \dfrac{8}{2} \cdot \dfrac{a^4}{a}$ **Expand the expression.**

$= 4 \cdot \dfrac{a^4}{a}$ **Divide coefficients.**

$= 4a^3$ **Quotient of powers property**

b. $\dfrac{9x^3y}{3xy^2} = \dfrac{9}{3} \cdot \dfrac{x^3}{x} \cdot \dfrac{y}{y^2}$ **Expand the expression.**

$= 3 \cdot \dfrac{x^3}{x} \cdot \dfrac{y}{y^2}$ **Divide coefficients.**

$= 3 \cdot x^2 \cdot y^{-1}$ **Quotient of powers property**

$= \dfrac{3x^2}{y}$ **Definition of negative exponent**

c. $\left(\dfrac{m}{n^3}\right)^2 = \dfrac{m^2}{(n^3)^2}$ **Power of a quotient property**

$= \dfrac{m^2}{n^6}$ **Power of a power property**

EXAMPLE 3   **Using Properties of Exponents**

BIOLOGY Many birds drop shellfish onto rocks to break the shell so that they can eat the food inside. The distance d (in feet) that a dropped shellfish falls in t seconds is given by $d = 16t^2$. Describe how doubling the time affects the distance fallen.

A shellfish falls $16t^2$ ft in t sec.

ANOTHER WAY

For an alternative method for solving the problem in Example 3, turn to page 405 for the **Problem Solving Workshop**.

SOLUTION

Use a ratio to compare the distance the shellfish falls in $2t$ seconds with the distance it falls in t seconds.

$\dfrac{\text{Distance in } 2t \text{ seconds}}{\text{Distance in } t \text{ seconds}} = \dfrac{16(2t)^2}{16t^2}$ **Write ratio.**

$= \dfrac{16 \cdot 2^2 \cdot t^2}{16t^2}$ **Power of a product property**

$= \dfrac{64t^2}{16t^2}$ **Simplify numerator.**

$= 4 \cdot \dfrac{t^2}{t^2}$ **Divide coefficients.**

$= 4$ **Quotient of powers property**

▶ **Answer** When the time is doubled, the distance the shellfish falls is 4 times as great.

Simplify the expression.

5. $\dfrac{12x^6}{4x^2}$ 6. $\dfrac{3y}{6y^3}$ 7. $\dfrac{6ab^5}{2ab}$ 8. $\dfrac{5mn^3}{10m^2n}$

9. **WHAT IF?** In Example 3, describe how tripling the time affects the distance the shellfish falls.

SQUARE ROOTS In Lesson 4.5 you simplified numerical expressions involving square roots, such as $\sqrt{12}$. You can use the property below to simplify radical expressions involving variables.

SIMPLIFY RADICAL EXPRESSIONS

In this book, all variables in radical expressions represent nonnegative numbers.

KEY CONCEPT   *For Your Notebook*

Square Roots of Squared Expressions

Words   If a is a nonnegative number or expression, then the square root of a squared is a.

Algebra $\sqrt{a^2} = a,\ a \geq 0$ **Numbers** $\sqrt{5^2} = 5$

EXAMPLE 4   **Simplifying Square Roots**

Simplify the expression.

a. $\sqrt{9y^2} = \sqrt{3^2 \cdot y^2}$ Write 9 as 3^2.

$\phantom{\sqrt{9y^2}} = \sqrt{3^2} \cdot \sqrt{y^2}$ Product property of square roots

$\phantom{\sqrt{9y^2}} = 3y$ Simplify square roots of squared expressions.

AVOID ERRORS

In part (b) of Example 4, the final expression is written as $2s\sqrt{6}$ rather than as $2\sqrt{6}s$ to make it clear that the variable is *not* under the radical sign.

b. $\sqrt{24s^2} = \sqrt{2^2 \cdot 6 \cdot s^2}$ Factor greatest perfect square from 24.

$\phantom{\sqrt{24s^2}} = \sqrt{2^2} \cdot \sqrt{6} \cdot \sqrt{s^2}$ Product property of square roots

$\phantom{\sqrt{24s^2}} = 2 \cdot \sqrt{6} \cdot s$ Simplify square roots of squared expressions.

$\phantom{\sqrt{24s^2}} = 2s\sqrt{6}$ Commutative property

c. $\sqrt{x^4y^6} = \sqrt{(x^2)^2 \cdot (y^3)^2}$ Write x^4 and y^6 as squares of expressions.

$\phantom{\sqrt{x^4y^6}} = \sqrt{(x^2)^2} \cdot \sqrt{(y^3)^2}$ Product property of square roots

$\phantom{\sqrt{x^4y^6}} = x^2y^3$ Simplify square roots of squared expressions.

✓ **GUIDED PRACTICE**   for Example 4

Simplify the expression.

10. $\sqrt{x^4}$ 11. $\sqrt{16y^2}$ 12. $\sqrt{4x^8}$ 13. $\sqrt{12b^6}$

7.3 **EXERCISES**

HOMEWORK
KEY

◆ = **MULTIPLE CHOICE PRACTICE**
Exs. 24, 35, 53, 59–61

◯ = **HINTS AND HOMEWORK HELP**
for Exs. 11, 33, 55 at classzone.com

SKILLS • PROBLEM SOLVING • REASONING

1. **VOCABULARY** Copy and complete: A number, variable, or product of a number and one or more variables with whole number exponents is called a(n) __?__.

2. **WRITING** *Explain* why $-3x^2$ is a monomial but $3x^{-2}$ is not a monomial.

SEE EXAMPLE 1
on p. 399
for Exs. 3–25

MULTIPLYING MONOMIALS **Simplify the expression.**

3. $(-4x)(5x^3)$

4. $(-16t)(-3t^9)$

5. $(-x^2)(-3x)$

6. $(3s)(-2s^3)$

7. $(4x^2y)(2y^6)$

8. $(-3g^2h^3)(6g^3h^4)$

9. $(5x^4)(-5x^3)$

10. $(-2p^3q^4)(-7p^3q^6)$

11. $(-x^3y^5)(x^2y^8)$

APPLYING POWER PROPERTIES **Simplify the expression.**

12. $(x^2yz)^5$

13. $(2ab^6)^4$

14. $(2r^3)^3$

15. $(-3x^3y)^3$

16. $(4a^{12}b)^2$

17. $(10bh^2)^5$

18. $(ab^3)^2$

19. $(x^2y)^3$

20. $(-3a^2)^2$

21. $(3r^7s^5)^2$

22. $(m^2n^3)^2$

23. $(2x^4y^3)^3$

24. ◆ **MULTIPLE CHOICE** Which expression is equivalent to $(-2b^4)^3$?

   Ⓐ $-8b^{12}$ Ⓑ $-2b^{12}$ Ⓒ $-8b^7$ Ⓓ $-2b^7$

25. **REASONING** Find the simplified product of $5a^2b^3$ and $(4a^4b)^2$. *Justify* each step using properties.

SEE EXAMPLE 2
on p. 400
for Exs. 26–35

SIMPLIFYING EXPRESSIONS **Simplify the expression.**

26. $\dfrac{p^5q^6}{pq^8}$

27. $\dfrac{9m^9}{3m^5}$

28. $\dfrac{5n^{15}}{15n^5}$

29. $\dfrac{6xk^5}{24x^2k^3}$

30. $\dfrac{45r^2}{10r^9}$

31. $\dfrac{a^{11}b^7}{a^{10}b}$

32. $\left(\dfrac{x^2}{y}\right)^3$

33. $\left(\dfrac{2a}{b^3}\right)^2$

34. $\left(\dfrac{t^3}{3w^4}\right)^3$

35. ◆ **MULTIPLE CHOICE** Which of the following expressions is equivalent to $\dfrac{16x^2}{6x^5}$?

   Ⓐ $\dfrac{8}{3x^3}$ Ⓑ $\dfrac{3x^3}{8}$ Ⓒ $\dfrac{8}{3x^7}$ Ⓓ $\dfrac{8x^3}{3}$

SEE EXAMPLE 4
on p. 401
for Exs. 36–43

SIMPLIFYING SQUARE ROOTS **Simplify the expression.**

36. $\sqrt{25a^2}$

37. $\sqrt{49y^8}$

38. $\sqrt{36n^4}$

39. $\sqrt{27c^2d^2}$

40. $\sqrt{18x^2y^6}$

41. $\sqrt{48x^4y^2}$

42. $\sqrt{7x^8y^6}$

43. $\sqrt{32x^{10}y^{12}}$

ERROR ANALYSIS *Describe* and correct the error in simplifying the expression.

44.

$\times$ $(3x^3)^2 = 3x^{3 \cdot 2}$
$= 3x^6$

45.

$\times$ $\dfrac{x^{20}y^6}{x^5y^3} = x^4y^2$

XY ALGEBRA Simplify the expression when $x = 2$, $y = 3$, and $z = 4$.

46. $\dfrac{64a^z}{4a^y}$

47. $\dfrac{12m^{x+y}}{6m^{z-y}}$

48. $\dfrac{27n^{x+y}}{3n^x}$

CONNECT SKILLS TO PROBLEM SOLVING Exercises 49–52 will help you prepare for problem solving.

Write a simplified expression for the quantity described.

49. The area of a square with a side length of $6xy$

50. The area of a rectangle with side lengths of $3x^2y$ and $4x^3y^4$

51. The volume of a cube with an edge length of $2y^5$

52. The combined volume of three cubes, each with an edge length of $4m^7$

SEE EXAMPLE 3
on p. 400
for Exs. 53–56

53. ◆ **MULTIPLE CHOICE** The formula for the volume V of a sphere with radius r is $V = \dfrac{4}{3}\pi r^3$. The shot used in the shot put event is a metal sphere. The radius of a ball is twice the radius of a shot. The volume of the ball is how many times greater than the volume of the shot?

Ⓐ 1 Ⓑ 2 Ⓒ 4 Ⓓ 8

California @HomeTutor for problem solving help at classzone.com

54. **SWIMMING** The drag force F (in pounds) of water on a swimmer can be approximated using the equation $F = 1.35s^2$ where s is the swimmer's speed (in miles per hour). How does the drag force on a swimmer change when the swimmer's speed increases by 50%? *Justify* your answer algebraically.

California @HomeTutor for problem solving help at classzone.com

55. **BIOLOGY** The weight y (in pounds) of a rainbow trout x inches long can be approximated using the equation $y = 0.0005x^3$. *Compare* the weight of one rainbow trout with another that is three times as long.

56. **DECIBELS** A decibel (dB) is a measure of the intensity of sound. For each increase of 10 dB, the intensity is 10 times as great. You are trying to have a conversation at a stadium where the noise level is 110 dB. The noise level of your conversation is 60 dB. The intensity of the crowd noise is how many times the intensity of your conversation? *Explain* your reasoning.

Stadium noise: 110 dB

57. CHALLENGE One number consists of a nonzero digit x followed by b zeros. A second number consists of a nonzero digit y followed by b zeros, where $x > y$. The first number is how many times as great as the second number? *Explain* your reasoning.

58. CHALLENGE The power P (in watts) generated by an efficient windmill can be approximated by the equation $P = r^2 v^3$ where r is the radius of the propeller (in meters) and v is the wind speed (in meters per second). *Compare* the power generated by one windmill with the power generated by a second windmill that has three times the propeller radius and spins due to the force of wind that is blowing twice as fast.

◆ CALIFORNIA STANDARDS SPIRAL REVIEW

NS 1.4

59. Which number is irrational? *(p. 225)*

    A -3 **B** 0 **C** $\sqrt{9}$ **D** $\sqrt{22}$

NS 2.3

60. What is the product of $\frac{1}{9}$ and $\left(\frac{2}{3}\right)^2$? *(p. 98)*

    A $\frac{4}{81}$ **B** $\frac{4}{27}$ **C** $\frac{2}{9}$ **D** $\frac{4}{9}$

NS 1.6

61. In the first basketball game of the season, Jarod scored 39 points. In the second basketball game of the season, Jarod scored 44 points. What is the approximate percent of increase in the number of points Jarod scored from the first game to the second game? *(p. 168)*

    A 5%   **B** 10%   **C** 13%   **D** 17%

QUIZ for Lessons 7.1–7.3

Simplify the expression. *(pp. 386, 393)*

1. $b^2 \cdot b^4$ **2.** $c^5 \cdot c^{-2}$ **3.** $\dfrac{a^7}{a^2}$ **4.** $\dfrac{n^2}{n^3}$

Simplify the expression. *(p. 399)*

5. $(3t^4)(4t^2)$ **6.** $(2c^3)^4$ **7.** $(-2y^5)^2$ **8.** $\left(\dfrac{4x^2}{6y^3}\right)^3$

9. LAND AREA A square field has a side length of 3^5 meters. Find the area of the field. A larger square field has a side length that is 9 times that of the smaller field. Find the area of the larger field. *(p. 386)*

10. ASTRONOMY The diameter of the sun is approximately 1.39×10^6 kilometers. The diameter of Earth is approximately 1.28×10^4 kilometers. The diameter of the sun is how many times greater than the diameter of Earth? *(p. 393)*

11. METRIC UNITS There are 10^{24} meters in a yottameter and 10^{12} meters in a terameter. How many terameters are in a yottameter? *(p. 393)*

EXTRA PRACTICE for Lesson 7.3, p. 753   **ONLINE QUIZ** at classzone.com

Using ALTERNATIVE METHODS

Another Way to Solve Example 3, page 400

Standards
AF 2.2

In Example 3 on page 400, you used an equation and the properties of exponents to find how doubling the time a shellfish falls affects the distance fallen. You can also use a spreadsheet to discover how doubling the time affects the distance fallen.

PROBLEM

BIOLOGY Many birds drop shellfish onto rocks to break the shell so that they can eat the food inside. The distance d (in feet) that a dropped shellfish falls in t seconds is given by $d = 16t^2$. Describe how doubling the time affects the distance fallen.

METHOD

Using a Spreadsheet An alternative approach is to use a spreadsheet.

STEP 1 **Use** a spreadsheet to make a table with 3 columns as shown. Include the given formulas in cells A3, B2, B3, and C3.

	A	B	C
1	Time	Distance	Ratio of distances
2	1	=16*(A2)^2	
3	=2*A2	=16*(A3)^2	=B3/B2

STEP 2 **Use** the *fill down* feature to create more rows.

	A	B	C
1	Time	Distance	Ratio of distances
2	1	16	
3	2	64	4
4	4	256	4
5	8	1024	4

STEP 3 **Compare** the distances fallen for various times by using the ratio of distances. Notice that the ratio is always 4.

▶ **Answer** When time is doubled, the distance fallen is 4 times as great.

PRACTICE

1. **SURFACE AREA** The surface area of a sphere is $S = 4\pi r^2$ where r is the radius of the sphere. Use two methods to describe how tripling the radius affects the surface area of a sphere.

2. **VOLUME** The volume of a sphere is $V = \frac{4}{3}\pi r^3$ where r is the radius of the sphere. Use two methods to describe how tripling the radius affects the volume of a sphere.

MIXED REVIEW of Skills and Problem Solving

Multiple Choice Practice for Lessons 7.1–7.3

1. What is the simplified form of $(-3b)^3$? **AF 2.2**

   (A) $-9b^3$ (B) $\dfrac{b^3}{27}$

   (C) $-7b^3$ (D) $-27b^3$

2. The formula for the volume of a cube is given by $V = s^3$ where s is the edge length. The volume of cube B is how many times the volume of cube A? **AF 2.1, MR 1.3**

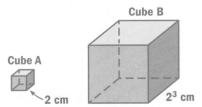

Cube B

Cube A

2 cm 2^3 cm

   (A) 16   (B) 32

   (C) 64   (D) 128

3. Olfactory receptor cells are located in the noses of mammals and help detect odors. A human has about 1.2×10^7 of these cells, while a bloodhound has about 4×10^9 of these cells. A bloodhound has about how many times as many olfactory receptor cells as a human? **NS 2.3**

   (A) 3.3×10^{-2} (B) 3.3

   (C) 33 (D) 3.3×10^2

4. What is the simplified form of $\left(\dfrac{2b}{-3}\right)^{-4}$? **AF 2.1**

   (A) $\dfrac{16b^{-4}}{81}$ (B) $\dfrac{81}{16b^4}$

   (C) $-\dfrac{81}{16b^4}$ (D) $-\dfrac{16b^4}{81}$

5. The average number of neurons in the human brain is about 1×10^{11}. The average mass of a neuron is 1.3×10^{-8} gram. About how much do the neurons in the human brain weigh? **NS 2.3, MR 2.1**

   (A) 1×10^{-88}g   (B) 1×10^{-3} g

   (C) 1×10^3 g   (D) 1×10^{19} g

6. What number makes the equation $4^{12} \cdot 4^? = 4^{-4}$ a true statement? **NS 2.3**

   (A) -16 (B) -8

   (C) 8 (D) 16

7. A field mouse has a mass of about 10^{-2} kilograms. A rhinoceros has a mass of about 10^3 kilograms. The mass of a rhinoceros is about how many times the mass of a field mouse? **NS 2.3**

10^3 kg 10^{-2} kg

   (A) 10^{-6} (B) 10^{-5}

   (C) 10^5 (D) 10^6

8. What is the simplified form of $\sqrt{49x^4y^6}$? **AF 2.2**

   (A) $7xy^3$ (B) $7xy$

   (C) $7x^2y^3$ (D) $7x^2y^2\sqrt{7}$

9. A square piece of fabric has a side length that is 3 times that of the square piece shown below. What is the area of the larger piece? **AF 2.1**

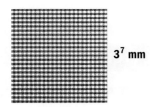

3^7 mm

   (A) 3^{14} mm^2 (B) 3^{16} mm^2

   (C) 3^{21} mm^2 (D) 3^{42} mm^2

406   Chapter 7   Exponents and Nonlinear Functions

7.4 Relations and Functions

Standards AF 1.5 Represent quantitative relationships graphically and interpret the meaning of a specific part of a graph in the situation represented by the graph.

Connect *Before* you graphed ordered pairs. *Now* you will use graphs to represent relations and functions.

Math and ZOOLOGY
Ex. 28, p. 412

KEY VOCABULARY
- relation
- domain
- range
- input
- output
- function
- linear function

The table below shows the ages and weights of five green sea turtles.

Age (years), x	2	2	3	3	4
Weight (lb), y	40	58	71	80	95

This table represents a *relation*. A **relation** is a pairing of numbers in one set, called the **domain**, with numbers in another set, called the **range**. Each number in the domain is an **input**. Each number in the range is an **output**. For a relation represented by a table of *x*- and *y*-values, the inputs are the *x*-values and the outputs are the *y*-values.

Four possible ways to represent a relation are ordered pairs, a table, a graph, or an equation.

EXAMPLE 1 Analyzing and Representing a Relation

Use the information in the table above that shows the ages and weights of five green sea turtles.

a. Identify the domain and the range of the relation.

b. Represent the relation using a graph.

SOLUTION

Green sea turtle

WRITE DOMAINS AND RANGES

When you specify a domain or range, you should list each repeated value only once. In part (a) of Example 1, for instance, the domain is 2, 3, 4, *not* 2, 2, 3, 3, 4.

a. The domain of the relation is the set of all inputs, or *x*-values.

   Domain: 2, 3, 4

   The range is the set of all outputs, or *y*-values.

   Range: 40, 58, 71, 80, 95

b. To represent the relation using a graph, write the ordered pairs given in the table.

   (**2**, 40), (**2**, 58), (**3**, 71), (**3**, 80), (**4**, 95)

   Graph the ordered pairs in a coordinate plane as shown. The graph shows that sea turtle weight tends to increase with age.

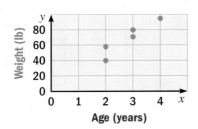

FUNCTIONS A relation is a **function** if for each input x in the domain there is *exactly one* output y in the range. In this case, you can say "*y is a function of x.*"

EXAMPLE 2 Identifying a Function

Tell whether the relation represented by the table of sea turtle ages and weights on page 407 is a function.

The input 2 has two outputs, 40 and 58, and the input 3 has two outputs, 71 and 80. Therefore, the relation is *not* a function. This makes sense, as two sea turtles of the same age do not necessarily weigh the same amount.

✔ GUIDED PRACTICE for Examples 1 and 2

For the relation, (a) identify the domain and range, (b) represent the relation using a graph, and (c) tell whether the relation is a function.

1. (1, 4), (2, 7), (3, 5), (5, 5), (7, 2)

2.

Input, x	−2	−1	0	−1	−2
Output, y	−1	0	3	3	1

EXAMPLE 3 ◆ Multiple Choice Practice

Which graph best represents the total cost of gasoline as a function of the number of gallons purchased?

ELIMINATE CHOICES
Eliminate choice A because the number of gallons should be on the x-axis.

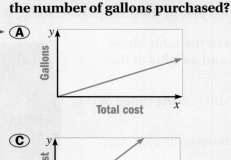

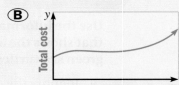

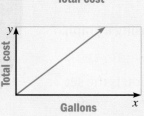

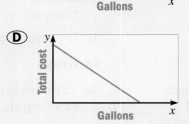

SOLUTION

Because total cost is a function of the number of gallons, the input values are the numbers of gallons. So, the x-axis should be labeled with *gallons*. In this situation, it also makes sense that the graph should include (0, 0) because 0 gallons of gasoline cost $0.

Choice C has the x-axis labeled with *gallons* and includes (0, 0).

▶ **Answer** The correct answer is C. Ⓐ Ⓑ ⓒ Ⓓ

LINEAR FUNCTIONS A **linear function** is a function whose graph is a line or a part of a line. For a linear function represented by a table of ordered pairs (x, y), constant changes in x correspond to constant changes in y. An equation that represents a linear function can be written in the form $y = mx + b$, where m is the slope of the graph of the function.

EXAMPLE 4 Writing a Linear Function Rule

ECOLOGY Yellow starthistle is an invasive weed spreading at a constant rate in California. The table shows the weed's approximate spread.

Time (years since 1998), x	Millions of acres covered, y
1	13.31
2	13.64
3	13.97
4	14.30

Yellow starthistle

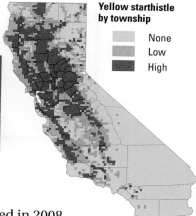
Yellow starthistle by township
None
Low
High

a. Write a linear function rule that relates x and y.

b. Predict the area of California covered by the weed in 2008.

SOLUTION

REVIEW RATE OF CHANGE
For help with finding an average rate of change, see p. 334.

a. To verify that a linear function models the data, show that the rate of change in the spread of yellow starthistle is constant from year to year.

$$\frac{13.64 - 13.31}{2 - 1} = 0.33 \qquad \frac{13.97 - 13.64}{3 - 2} = 0.33 \qquad \frac{14.30 - 13.97}{4 - 3} = 0.33$$

So the weed's spread can be modeled by a linear function $y = mx + b$ where the rate of change m is 0.33. To find b, substitute an ordered pair from the table, such as (**1**, **13.31**), into the equation $y = mx + b$.

$$\mathbf{13.31} = 0.33(\mathbf{1}) + b \qquad\Longrightarrow\qquad b = 13.31 - 0.33 = 12.98$$

▶ **Answer** A linear function rule that relates x and y is $y = 0.33x + 12.98$.

b. Because 2008 is 10 years after 1998, substitute 10 for x in the equation from part (a) to predict the area covered by the weed in 2008.

$$y = 0.33(\mathbf{10}) + 12.98 = 16.28$$

▶ **Answer** About 16.28 million acres of California will be covered by the weed in 2008.

Animated Math

For an interactive example of writing a linear function rule, go to **classzone.com**.

✓ **GUIDED PRACTICE** for Examples 3 and 4

3. Lisa is paid by the hour at her job. Sketch a graph that could show her total earnings as a function of the number of hours she worked.

4. **KUDZU** The table shows the length y of a kudzu vine as a function of time x. Write a function rule that relates x and y.

Time (days), x	1	2	3	4
Length (in.), y	16	26	36	46

Representing Relations

It may be possible to represent a relation in the following four ways:
ordered pairs, a table, a graph, or an equation.

Ordered pairs	Table	Graph	Equation

Ordered pairs

$(-2, 1)$
$(-1, 2)$
$(0, 3)$
$(1, 4)$
$(2, 5)$

Table

x	y
-2	1
-1	2
0	3
1	4
2	5

Graph

Equation

$y = x + 3$

7.4 EXERCISES

HOMEWORK KEY

◆ = **MULTIPLE CHOICE PRACTICE**
Exs. 21, 22, 32–34

○ = **HINTS AND HOMEWORK HELP**
for Exs. 11, 19, 29 at classzone.com

SKILLS • PROBLEM SOLVING • REASONING

1. **VOCABULARY** Copy and complete: For a relation, the set of all possible input values is its __?__ and the set of all possible output values is its __?__.

2. **WRITING** *Explain* how to tell whether a relation is a function.

SEE EXAMPLE 1
on p. 407
for Exs. 3–8

GRAPHING RELATIONS Identify the domain and range of the relation. Then represent the relation using a graph.

3. $(4, 5), (2, -3), (4, 9), (-2, -3)$
4. $(-3, 7), (3, 7), (7, 3), (-7, -3)$
5. $(2, 3), (1, -6), (5, 3), (-1, -6)$
6. $(-8, 10), (9, 2), (2, 11), (-8, -4)$
7. $(0, 6), (6, 1), (-2, -5), (2, -5)$
8. $(3, 1), (-2, -2) (-1, 4), (3, -1)$

SEE EXAMPLE 2
on p. 408
for Exs. 9–13

IDENTIFYING FUNCTIONS Tell whether the relation is a function. *Explain* your reasoning.

9. $(-3, 9), (-2, 4), (0, 0), (2, 4)$
10. $(4, 2), (4, -2), (2, 5), (5, -5)$

11.

Input, x	-1	0	1	2
Output, y	-3	-3	-3	-3

12.

Input, x	0	-1	0	-1
Output, y	-2	0	2	4

13. **ERROR ANALYSIS** A relation is represented by the following set of ordered pairs: $(-9, 81), (-4, 16), (0, 0), (4, 16), (-9, -81)$. Your friend says that the relation is a function. *Explain* your friend's error.

SEE EXAMPLE 3
on p. 408
for Exs. 14–16

GRAPHING **Sketch a graph that could relate the quantities described.**

14. The distance *y* traveled in *x* minutes when traveling at a constant speed

15. The number *y* of calories consumed by eating *x* ounces of grapes

16. The number *y* of mints left in a dish of 200 mints when *x* mints are eaten

SEE EXAMPLE 4
on p. 409
for Exs. 17–21

WRITING FUNCTION RULES **Write a linear function rule that relates *x* and *y*.**

17.

Input, x	−1	0	1	2
Output, y	5	6	7	8

18.

Input, x	0	1	2	3
Output, y	0	−5	−10	−15

19.

Input, x	1	2	3	4
Output, y	1	4	7	10

20.

Input, x	0	1	2	3
Output, y	2	1.5	1	0.5

21. ◆ **MULTIPLE CHOICE** Which equation relates *x* and *y* for the set of ordered pairs (3, 1), (6, 2), and (9, 3)?

A $y = \frac{1}{3}x$ **B** $y = 3x$ **C** $y = x - 2$ **D** $y = x - 6$

22. ◆ **MULTIPLE CHOICE** Which equation does *not* represent a function?

A $y = 5$ **B** $x = -4$ **C** $y = 7x - 3$ **D** $y = -13x$

23. **ERROR ANALYSIS** Steve says that if a table represents a linear function, the change in consecutive *y*-values must equal the corresponding change in consecutive *x*-values. Create an input-output table and write a related linear function rule to show that Steve is incorrect.

CONNECT SKILLS TO PROBLEM SOLVING **Exercises 24–26 will help you prepare for problem solving.**

Describe the situation using the phrase *is a function of.*

24. Alicia practices running the 100 meter dash every day. The faster she runs, the shorter her finishing time.

25. Students in a driver's education class study the night before a written exam. Students who study longer earn better exam scores.

26. At a city garage, it costs $6 to park for the first hour and $2.50 for each additional hour.

SEE EXAMPLE 4
on p. 409
for Exs. 27–28

27. **RECYCLING** A metal recycling company pays $.40 per pound for aluminum cans.

a. Write a linear function rule for this situation where *E* is the amount (in dollars) earned and *p* is the weight (in pounds) of cans that are recycled.

b. Make an input-output table to find the number of pounds of cans you need to recycle to earn $6.

Recycled aluminum: $.40 per pound

California @HomeTutor for problem solving help at classzone.com

28. **WHALES** A gray whale calf is nursed back to health with milk-based formula. The table shows the total number g of gallons of formula consumed over the course of f feedings. Use the table to write a function rule. Then use your function rule to find how much the whale consumes in 7 feedings.

Feedings, f	Gallons consumed, g
1	2
2	4
3	6
4	8

California @HomeTutor for problem solving help at classzone.com

29. **SPEED OF SOUND** The table shows the distance d (in miles) sound travels in sea water, where t is the time (in seconds).

t	1	2	3	4	5
d	0.9	1.8	2.7	3.6	4.5

Identify the domain and range, then graph the data. Does the graph represent a function? *Explain.*

30. **CHALLENGE** On a road trip, you stop every 90 minutes. You make a total of 4 stops and travel at various speeds between stops as shown below. Assume the car travels at a constant speed between stops.

a. Write a function rule that relates the speed x (in miles per hour) to the distance y (in miles) traveled between stops.

b. How long, in hours and minutes, would it take to complete the entire trip at 60 miles per hour with no stops?

31. **CHALLENGE** *Explain* why the height of a bouncing ball is a function of time. Sketch a possible graph of this situation.

◆ CALIFORNIA STANDARDS SPIRAL REVIEW

AF 2.2   32. Which expression is equivalent to $\sqrt{4x^6}$? *(p. 399)*

    A $2x$ **B** $2x^3$ **C** $4x^3$ **D** $4x^9$

AF 2.2   33. Which expression is equivalent to $\dfrac{10m^2n^3}{5mn^4}$? *(p. 399)*

    A $2mn$ **B** $\dfrac{2}{mn}$ **C** $\dfrac{2m}{-n}$ **D** $\dfrac{2m}{n}$

AF 1.1   34. A pet store has x pounds of dog food in stock. It sells 45 pounds and then receives 3x pounds in a new shipment. Which expression represents the number of pounds of dog food the store now has? *(p. 247)*

    A $-45 - 2x$ **B** $4x - 45$ **C** $45 - 2x$ **D** $-45 + 2x$

EXTRA PRACTICE for Lesson 7.4, p. 753   🔁 **ONLINE QUIZ** at classzone.com

7.5 Nonlinear Functions

Standards AF 3.1 Graph functions of the form $y = nx^2$ and $y = nx^3$ and use in solving problems.

Connect *Before* you graphed linear functions. *Now* you will graph nonlinear functions.

Math and **BIOLOGY**
Ex. 32, p. 419

KEY VOCABULARY
- nonlinear function
- vertical line test

A **nonlinear function** is any function whose graph is not a line or part of a line. A nonlinear function cannot be written in the form $y = mx + b$. One type of nonlinear function is a *quadratic function*. A function of the form $y = ax^2$, where a is a nonzero real number, is a quadratic function.

EXAMPLE 1 Graphing Quadratic Functions

UNDERSTAND
QUADRATIC FUNCTIONS
All quadratic functions can be written in the form $y = ax^2 + bx + c$ where a, b, and c are real numbers and a is nonzero. In this course, you will study only quadratic functions where b and c equal 0.

Graph the function using a table of values.

a. $y = x^2$

b. $y = -2x^2$

SOLUTION

To graph each function, make a table of values for the function. Then graph the ordered pairs and connect the points with a smooth curve.

a. STEP 1 Substitute x-values into $y = x^2$ to make a table.

x	y
−2	$(-2)^2 = 4$
−1	$(-1)^2 = 1$
0	$0^2 = 0$
1	$1^2 = 1$
2	$2^2 = 4$

STEP 2 **Graph** the ordered pairs and connect the points.

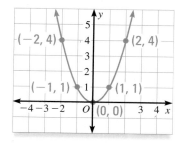

b. STEP 1 Substitute x-values into $y = -2x^2$ to make a table.

x	y
−2	$-2(-2)^2 = -8$
−1	$-2(-1)^2 = -2$
0	$-2(0)^2 = 0$
1	$-2(1)^2 = -2$
2	$-2(2)^2 = -8$

STEP 2 **Graph** the ordered pairs and connect the points.

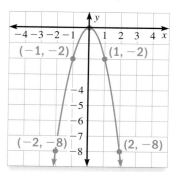

EXAMPLE 2 **Using the Graph of a Quadratic Function**

READING
The notation "ft/sec²"
is read "feet per second
squared."

SPEED SKIING A speed skier is accelerating at a rate of a ft/sec² for a period of t seconds. The function $d = \frac{1}{2}at^2$ models the distance d (in feet) traveled by the skier.

Graph the function that models an acceleration of 16 ft/sec². Use the graph to estimate the time it will take the skier to travel 100 feet.

Skier travels $\frac{1}{2}at^2$ feet in t seconds

SOLUTION

STEP 1 **Write** the function. Substitute 16 for a in the model $d = \frac{1}{2}at^2$.

$$d = \frac{1}{2}at^2 \qquad \text{Write model.}$$

$$d = \frac{1}{2}(16)t^2 \qquad \text{Substitute 16 for } a.$$

$$d = 8t^2 \qquad \text{Simplify.}$$

STEP 2 **Make** a table of values for the function. Then make a graph.

t	d
0	$8(0)^2 = 0$
1	$8(1)^2 = 8$
2	$8(2)^2 = 32$
3	$8(3)^2 = 72$
4	$8(4)^2 = 128$

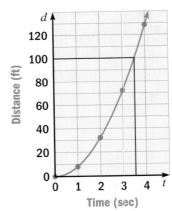

About the Standards

In Example 2, you estimate unknown quantities graphically (MR 2.3).

STEP 3 **Use** the graph. It appears that the skier will travel 100 feet after about 3.5 seconds.

▶ **Answer** It will take the skier about 3.5 seconds to travel 100 feet.

 GUIDED PRACTICE for Examples 1 and 2

Graph the function using a table of values.

1. $y = -x^2$

2. $y = \frac{3}{4}x^2$

3. $y = 2.5x^2$

4. **WHAT IF?** In Example 2, suppose the skier's acceleration is 12 ft/sec². Graph the function. Use the graph to estimate the time it will take the skier to travel 120 feet.

CUBIC FUNCTIONS Another type of nonlinear function is a *cubic function*. A function of the form $y = ax^3$ where a is a nonzero real number is a cubic function.

EXAMPLE 3 **Graphing Cubic Functions**

Graph the function using a table of values.

a. $y = x^3$

b. $y = \frac{1}{2}x^3$

SOLUTION

To graph each function, first make a table of values for the function. Then graph the ordered pairs and connect the points with a smooth curve.

a.

x	y
−2	$(-2)^3 = -8$
−1	$(-1)^3 = -1$
0	$0^3 = 0$
1	$1^3 = 1$
2	$2^3 = 8$

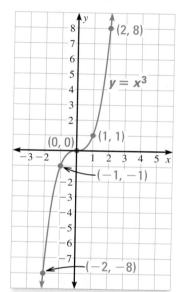

b.

x	y
−2	$\frac{1}{2}(-2)^3 = -4$
−1	$\frac{1}{2}(-1)^3 = -\frac{1}{2}$
0	$\frac{1}{2}(0)^3 = 0$
1	$\frac{1}{2}(1)^3 = \frac{1}{2}$
2	$\frac{1}{2}(2)^3 = 4$

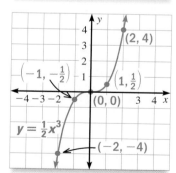

✓ **GUIDED PRACTICE** for Example 3

Graph the function using a table of values.

5. $y = -x^3$

6. $y = 2x^3$

7. $y = 0.1x^3$

VERTICAL LINE TEST You can use the **vertical line test** to tell whether the graph of a relation represents a function. If any vertical line intersects the graph at more than one point, then the graph does *not* represent a function. Otherwise, the graph *does* represent a function.

EXAMPLE 4 ◆ **Multiple Choice Practice**

Which blue graph does *not* represent a function?

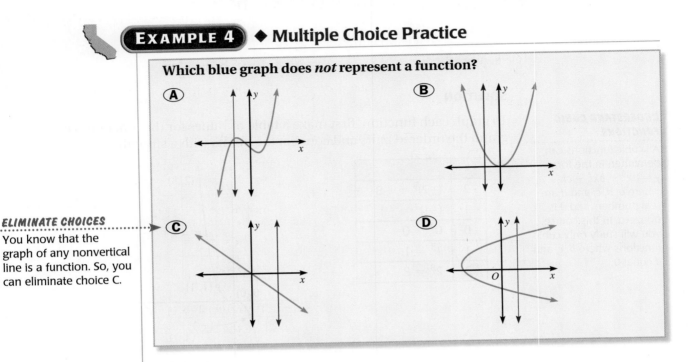

ELIMINATE CHOICES
You know that the graph of any nonvertical line is a function. So, you can eliminate choice C.

SOLUTION

For each graph, consider all possible vertical lines by passing a straightedge across the entire graph. If any vertical line intersects two or more points on the graph, then the graph does not represent a function.

Because no vertical line intersects the graphs in choices A, B, and C at more than one point, these graphs represent functions.

A vertical line intersects the graph in choice D at more than one point. So, the graph does *not* represent a function.

▶ **Answer** The correct answer is D. Ⓐ Ⓑ Ⓒ Ⓓ

✓ **GUIDED PRACTICE** | **for Example 4**

Tell whether the graph represents a function.

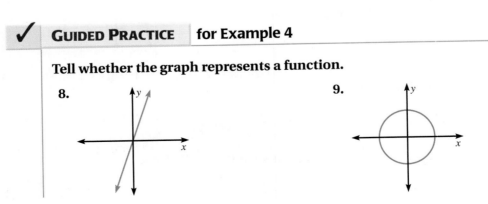

8.

9.

7.5 EXERCISES

HOMEWORK KEY

◆ = **MULTIPLE CHOICE PRACTICE**
Exs. 12, 30, 36–38

○ = **HINTS AND HOMEWORK HELP**
for Exs. 11, 23, 31 at classzone.com

SKILLS • PROBLEM SOLVING • REASONING

1. **VOCABULARY** Copy and complete: Any function whose graph is not a line or part of a line is a(n) __?__.

2. **WRITING** *Explain* how to use the vertical line test to determine whether the graph of a relation is a function.

SEE EXAMPLE 1
on p. 413
for Exs. 3–12

MATCHING In Exercises 3–5, match the equation with its graph.

3. $y = \frac{1}{4}x^2$

4. $y = -\frac{1}{2}x^2$

5. $y = 2x^2$

A.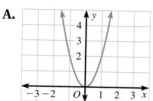

B.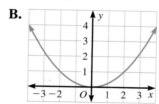

C.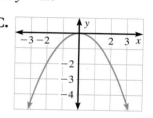

GRAPHING QUADRATIC FUNCTIONS Graph the function using a table of values that includes $x = -3, -2, -1, 0, 1, 2,$ and 3.

6. $y = 4x^2$

7. $y = -5x^2$

8. $y = 1.5x^2$

9. $y = \frac{2}{3}x^2$

10. $y = -0.2x^2$

11. $y = -\frac{3}{4}x^2$

12. ◆ **MULTIPLE CHOICE** Which is the graph of the function $y = \frac{1}{2}x^2$?

Ⓐ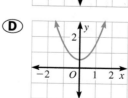

Ⓑ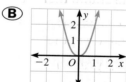

Ⓒ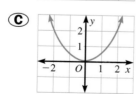

Ⓓ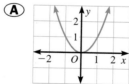

SEE EXAMPLE 3
on p. 415
for Exs. 13–16

GRAPHING CUBIC FUNCTIONS Graph the function using a table of values that includes $x = -3, -2, -1, 0, 1, 2,$ and 3.

13. $y = -3x^3$

14. $y = 4x^3$

15. $y = 2.5x^3$

16. $y = -\frac{1}{5}x^3$

SEE EXAMPLES 1, 2, AND 3
on pp. 413–415
for Exs. 17–20

USING GRAPHS TO ESTIMATE Use the graph of the function to estimate the value(s) of x for which $y = 7$.

17. $y = 5x^2$

18. $y = \frac{1}{3}x^2$

19. $y = -2x^3$

20. $y = \frac{1}{4}x^3$

ERROR ANALYSIS *Describe* and correct the error in graphing the function.

21. $y = -3x^2$

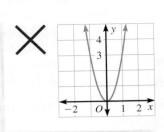

22. $y = \frac{1}{2}x^3$

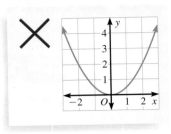

SEE EXAMPLE 4
on p. 416
for Exs. 23–25

VERTICAL LINE TEST Tell whether the graph represents a function.

(23.)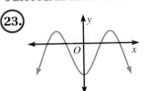

24.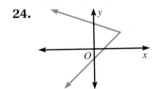

25.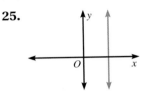

CONNECT SKILLS TO PROBLEM SOLVING Exercises 26–28 will help you prepare for problem solving.

Tell whether the equation giving y as a function of x is a *linear function*, a *quadratic function*, or a *cubic function*.

26. y is the area of a square with side length x.

27. y is the perimeter of a rectangle with side lengths x and $x + 3$.

28. y is the volume of a cube with edge length x.

SEE EXAMPLES 2 AND 3
on pp. 414–415
for Exs. 29–30, 32

29. FALLING COIN You drop a coin into a deep well. The distance d (in feet) the coin has fallen after t seconds in the air is given by $d = 16t^2$. Graph the function. If the water is 144 feet below the point where the coin was dropped, about how long will it take for the coin to hit the water?

California@HomeTutor for problem solving help at classzone.com

30. ◆ MULTIPLE CHOICE Carpeting costs $5 per square foot. Let x be the side length (in feet) of a square room, and let y be the cost (in dollars) to carpet the room. Use a graph to find which of the following square room sizes is the greatest that can be carpeted for less than $270.

(A) 6 ft by 6 ft   **(B)** 7 ft by 7 ft   **(C)** 8 ft by 8 ft   **(D)** 9 ft by 9 ft

California@HomeTutor for problem solving help at classzone.com

(31.) BALBOA PARK The length l and width w of the rectangular lily pond at Balboa Park in San Diego, California are $l = 195.5$ ft and $w = 42$ ft. The depth d (in feet) of the water is constant across the pond. The function $V = lwd$ models the volume (in cubic feet) of water in the pond. Write and graph a function that gives the cost C to fill the reflecting pond to depths up to 3.5 feet, if water costs $15.87 per 100 ft^3. Is the graph linear or nonlinear? *Explain.*

Balboa Park in San Diego, CA

32. BIOLOGY The model $A = 0.0779s^3$ can be used to relate an island's land area A (in square miles) to the number s of species of reptiles and amphibians the island can support. Graph the function for values of s from 0 to 100. Use the graph to approximate the number of species a 40,000 square mile island can support.

33. GRAPH AND COMPARE Graph the functions $y = 3x^3$ and $y = 3x^2$ using a table of values. Include negative and positive x-values in your table. *Describe* how the graphs are different.

34. CHALLENGE Write a function for the area of the rectangle shown. Find the length and width of the rectangle with the greatest area. *Explain* how you found your answers.

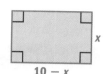

35. CHALLENGE Using tables of values, graph $y = (x - 7)(x + 4)$, $y = (x - 5)(x + 1)$, and $y = (x - 2)(x + 3)$. Use your three graphs to predict the x-intercepts of the function $y = (x - a)(x + b)$.

◆ CALIFORNIA STANDARDS SPIRAL REVIEW

AF 2.1   **36.** Which expression is equivalent to $x^6 \cdot x^2 \cdot x^{-3}$? *(p. 386)*

     Ⓐ x^{-36} **Ⓑ** x^5 **Ⓒ** x^7 **Ⓓ** x^{11}

AF 2.2   **37.** Which expression is equivalent to $(2d^5)^2$? *(p. 399)*

     Ⓐ $4d^7$ **Ⓑ** $2d^{10}$ **Ⓒ** $128d^7$ **Ⓓ** $4d^{10}$

AF 1.1   **38.** To buy a $190 camera, you pay $40 plus 4 equal payments. Which equation can you use to find the amount x of each payment? *(p. 270)*

     Ⓐ $190 = 44x$ **Ⓑ** $190 = 4 + 40x$

     Ⓒ $190 = 40 + 4x$ **Ⓓ** $190 = 40 + 4 + x$

QUIZ *for Lessons 7.4–7.5*

For the given relation, (a) identify the domain and range, (b) represent the relation using a graph, and (c) tell whether the relation is a function. *(p. 407)*

1. $(-3, 18), (-1, 2), (0, 0), (2, 8)$

2.

x	−5	−2	−2	2	5
y	2	3	−3	1	2

Graph the function using a table of values that includes $x = -3, -2, -1, 0, 1, 2$, and 3. *(p. 413)*

3. $y = -3x^2$ **4.** $y = 0.25x^2$ **5.** $y = 6x^3$ **6.** $y = -0.5x^3$

7. ENGINEERING The radius of a curved road is determined by the function $r = 0.334s^2$ where r is the radius (in feet) and s is the expected speed limit (in miles per hour). Graph the function. Estimate the expected speed limit on a curved road with a radius of 300 feet. *(p. 413)*

7.5 Graphing Nonlinear Functions

Standards

AF 3.1 Graph functions of the form $y = nx^2$ and $y = nx^3$ and use in solving problems.

QUESTION How can you graph nonlinear functions using a graphing calculator?

EXAMPLE Graph quadratic and cubic functions

Graph and compare the functions below using a graphing calculator.

$$y_1 = x^2 \qquad y_2 = 2x^2 \qquad y_3 = 3x^2 \qquad y_4 = 4x^2$$

Enter the functions into a graphing calculator. Use the keystrokes below.

Keystrokes

Display

	Keystrokes			
Y₁	Y=	X	x²	ENTER
Y₂	Y= 2	X	x²	ENTER
Y₃	Y= 3	X	x²	ENTER
Y₄	Y= 4	X	x²	

GRAPH

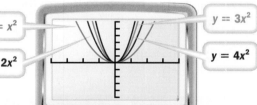

$y = x^2$ $y = 3x^2$ $y = 2x^2$ $y = 4x^2$

▶ **Answer** The graphs are curves, called *parabolas*, that pass through (0, 0). As the coefficient of x^2 increases, the curve gets narrower.

PRACTICE

Compare each graph to the graphs in the example above.

1. $y = -x^2$ **2.** $y = -2x^2$ **3.** $y = -3x^2$ **4.** $y = -4x^2$

5. REASONING Redo the example above using the following functions.

$$y_1 = x^3 \qquad y_2 = 2x^3 \qquad y_3 = 3x^3 \qquad y_4 = 4x^3$$

What happens to the graphs as the coefficient of x^3 increases? What would the graph of $y = 6x^3$ look like?

Multiple Choice Practice for Lessons 7.4–7.5

1. Which function rule relates x and y for the set of ordered pairs $(4, 1)$, $\left(6, \frac{3}{2}\right)$, $(8, 2)$? **AF 1.5**

  A $y = 4x$ **B** $y = x - 3$

  C $y = \frac{1}{4}x$ **D** $y = x - 6$

2. A function for the total cost C (in dollars) of an electric dryer is $C = 300 + 0.4h$ where h is the number of loads of laundry dried. Use an input-output table to find the number of loads of laundry it takes for the total cost to equal $500. **AF 1.5**

  A 80   **B** 200

  C 500   **D** 750

In Exercises 3 and 4, use the table, which shows the number of miles you run in the first four weeks of training for a 10 mile race.

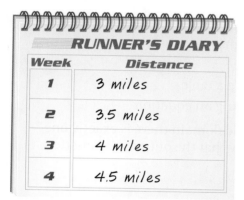

Week	Distance
1	3 miles
2	3.5 miles
3	4 miles
4	4.5 miles

3. What is a function rule for this situation? **AF 1.5, MR 2.6**

  A $d = w + 2$ **B** $d = 0.5w + 2.5$

  C $d = 2w + 0.5$ **D** $d = 3w$

4. Graph the function from Exercise 3. In what week do you run 10 miles? **AF 1.5**

  A Week 5   **B** Week 8

  C Week 9   **D** Week 15

5. Which best describes the graph shown? **AF 1.5**

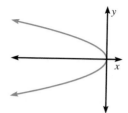

  A A linear function

  B Not a function

  C A nonlinear function

  D Not a relation

6. Use the graph of the function $y = -\frac{1}{3}x^3$ to determine which choice is the best estimate of the value of x when $y = 15$. **AF 3.1**

  A About -3.5 **B** About -2.5

  C About 3.1 **D** About 3.5

7. Which function rule relates x and y for the table below? **AF 1.5**

x	-1	1	3	5
y	4	6	8	10

  A $y = -4x$

  B $y = x - 5$

  C $y = -\frac{1}{4}x$

  D $y = x + 5$

8. You drop your keys off a tall bridge. The distance d (in feet) that the keys fall in t seconds is given by $d = 16t^2$. Use a graph of the function to choose the best estimate of the number of seconds it takes the keys to fall 300 feet. **AF 3.1, MR 2.3**

  A About 1.9 sec   **B** About 2.7 sec

  C About 4.3 sec   **D** About 5.1 sec

BIG IDEAS

For Your Notebook

Big Idea ①

Applying Properties of Exponents

Let m and n be integers and let a and b be real numbers.

Property	Definition	Example
Negative Exponent	$a^{-m} = \dfrac{1}{a^m}$, $a \neq 0$	$7^{-2} = \dfrac{1}{7^2}$
Zero Exponent	$a^0 = 1$, $a \neq 0$	$(-89)^0 = 1$
Product of Powers	$a^m \cdot a^n = a^{m+n}$	$5^6 \cdot 5^3 = 5^{6+3} = 5^9$
Power of a Power	$(a^m)^n = a^{mn}$	$(3^3)^4 = 3^{3 \cdot 4} = 3^{12}$
Power of a Product	$(ab)^m = a^m \cdot b^m$	$(2x)^5 = 2^5 \cdot x^5$
Quotient of Powers	$\dfrac{a^m}{a^n} = a^{m-n}$, $a \neq 0$	$\dfrac{6^8}{6^5} = 6^{8-5} = 6^3$
Power of a Quotient	$\left(\dfrac{a}{b}\right)^m = \dfrac{a^m}{b^m}$, $b \neq 0$	$\left(\dfrac{4}{7}\right)^3 = \dfrac{4^3}{7^3}$

Big Idea ②

Representing Relations and Functions

A *relation* is a pairing of numbers in one set, called the *domain*, with numbers in another set, called the *range*. It may be possible to represent a relation in the following four ways:

- Listing ordered pairs
- Drawing a graph
- Using a table
- Writing an equation

A relation is a *function* if for each input in the domain there is exactly one output in the range. In this case, you can say that the output is a function of the input.

Big Idea ③

Graphing Nonlinear Functions

A nonlinear function is any function whose graph is not a line or part of a line. Two types of nonlinear functions are shown in the table below.

	Quadratic Functions	Cubic Functions
General Equation	$y = ax^2$	$y = ax^3$
Graph	 $a > 0$	 $a > 0$

APPLYING THE BIG IDEAS

Big Idea 1
You apply properties of exponents in **Steps 1 and 2.**

Big Idea 2
You represent a function in **Step 3.**

Big Idea 3
You graph a nonlinear function in **Step 3.**

PROBLEM How can you compare the volumes of the planets in our solar system when given the radius of each planet?

STEP 1 Find the volume of each planet in our solar system.

Use the formula for the volume of a sphere, $V = \frac{4}{3}\pi r^3$, and the properties of exponents to find each planet's volume V (in cubic miles) given its radius r (in miles).

Planet	Radius (mi)
Mercury	$r = 1.5 \times 10^3$
Venus	$r = 3.8 \times 10^3$
Earth	$r = 4.0 \times 10^3$
Mars	$r = 2.1 \times 10^3$
Jupiter	$r = 4.4 \times 10^4$
Saturn	$r = 3.7 \times 10^4$
Uranus	$r = 1.6 \times 10^4$
Neptune	$r = 1.5 \times 10^4$

STEP 2 Compare volumes.

Write the volume of each planet in scientific notation. Then write the ratio of each planet's volume to Earth's volume. Use the rules of exponents to simplify each ratio.

STEP 3 Draw a graph.

Let x be a planet's radius (in thousands of miles) and let y be the volume (in billions of cubic miles). Plot ordered pairs (x, y) for Mercury, Venus, Earth, and Mars in the same coordinate plane. Does the graph represent a linear or nonlinear function? *Explain.*

Extending the Problem

Use your results from the problem to complete the exercises.

1. Use the results of Step 2 to list the planets whose volumes are at least 50 times Earth's volume.

2. In Step 3, why isn't it practical to also plot the ordered pairs (x, y) for Jupiter, Saturn, Uranus, and Neptune on the same graph?

3. The surface area S of a sphere is given by $S = 4\pi r^2$. Use a method similar to the one given in Steps 1 and 2 to compare the surface area of each planet with the surface area of Earth.

4. Use your results from Exercise 3 to list the planets whose surface areas are at least 50 times Earth's surface area.

5. *Explain* why the answers to Exercise 1 and Exercise 4 differ.

REVIEW KEY VOCABULARY

- monomial, *p. 399*
- relation, *p. 407*
- domain, *p. 407*
- range, *p. 407*
- input, *p. 407*
- output, *p. 407*
- function, *p. 408*
- linear function, *p. 409*
- nonlinear function, *p. 413*
- vertical line test, *p. 416*

VOCABULARY EXERCISES

In Exercises 1–4, copy and complete the statement.

1. The __?__ property states that $a^m \cdot a^n = a^{m+n}$.

2. A pairing of numbers in one set with numbers in another set is called a(n) __?__.

3. Quadratic functions and cubic functions are examples of __?__.

4. To tell whether a graph represents a function, you can use the __?__.

5. **NOTETAKING SKILLS** Make an *information frame* like the one on page 384 for the quotient of powers property.

REVIEW EXAMPLES AND EXERCISES

7.1 Exponent Properties Involving Products
pp. 386–391

AF 2.1 **EXAMPLE**

Simplify the expression.

a. $x^{-2} \cdot x^8 = x^{-2+8}$
   $= x^6$

b. $(5^6)^4 = 5^{6 \cdot 4}$
   $= 5^{24}$

c. $(xy)^5 = x^5 y^5$

EXERCISES

**SEE EXAMPLES
1, 2, 3, AND 4**
on pp. 386–389
for Exs. 6–18

Simplify the expression.

6. $3^2 \cdot 3^8$

7. $2^{-7} \cdot 2^6$

8. $y^{12} \cdot y^{-5}$

9. $x^{-4} \cdot x^4$

10. $d^{10} \cdot d^{-5}$

11. $(6^2)^3$

12. $(x^8)^7$

13. $(w^5)^{-9}$

14. $(z^{-2})^{-6}$

15. $(xz)^4$

16. $(x^{-2})^2$

17. $(-2x)^{-5}$

18. **OIL** In 2003, the United States imported about 5.1×10^2 gallons of crude oil per person. The population of the United States in 2003 was about 2.9×10^8. How many gallons of crude oil did the United States import in 2003?

7.2 Exponent Properties Involving Quotients

pp. 393–398

AF 2.1

EXAMPLE

Simplify the expression.

a. $\dfrac{x^5}{x^{11}} = x^{5-11} = x^{-6} = \dfrac{1}{x^6}$

b. $\left(\dfrac{a}{5}\right)^3 = \dfrac{a^3}{5^3} = \dfrac{a^3}{125}$

EXERCISES

SEE EXAMPLES
1, 2, AND 3
on pp. 393–395
for Exs. 19–23

Simplify the expression.

19. $\dfrac{7^4}{7^6}$

20. $\dfrac{(-x)^{14}}{(-x)^8}$

21. $\left(\dfrac{h}{6}\right)^4$

22. $\left(\dfrac{1}{n}\right)^{-3}$

23. ASTRONOMY Earth's galaxy has a radius of about 2.94×10^{17} miles, and its solar system has a radius of about 3.65×10^9 miles. The radius of Earth's galaxy is how many times the radius of its solar system?

7.3 Products, Quotients, and Roots of Monomials

pp. 399–404

AF 2.2

EXAMPLE

Simplify the expression $(x^3)(3x)^2$.

$(x^3)(3x)^2 = x^3(3^2 \cdot x^2)$ **Power of a product property**

$= x^3 \cdot 9 \cdot x^2$ **Evaluate the power.**

$= 9x^5$ **Product of powers property**

AF 2.2

EXAMPLE

Simplify the expression $\dfrac{6x^5y^3}{2xy^2}$.

$\dfrac{6x^5y^3}{2xy^2} = \dfrac{6}{2} \cdot \dfrac{x^5}{x} \cdot \dfrac{y^3}{y^2}$ **Expand the expression.**

$= 3 \cdot \dfrac{x^5}{x} \cdot \dfrac{y^3}{y^2}$ **Divide coefficients.**

$= 3x^4y$ **Quotient of powers property**

EXERCISES

SEE EXAMPLES
1, 2, AND 4
on pp. 399–401
for Exs. 24–27

Simplify the expression.

24. $(3y^3)(4y)^2$

25. $(-2a^2b)^3$

26. $\left(\dfrac{b^2}{2a}\right)^3$

27. $\sqrt{80a^{16}b^8}$

7.4 Relations and Functions

pp. 407–412

AF 1.5 **EXAMPLE**

Tell whether the relation is a function.

a. (3, 2), (5, 3), (5, 5), (6, 7)

b.

Input, x	−4	−3	−2	−1
Output, y	4	3	2	1

▶ **Answer** The relation is *not* a function because the input 5 has two outputs, 3 and 5.

▶ **Answer** The relation is a function because each input has exactly one output.

EXERCISES

SEE EXAMPLE 2 on p. 408 for Exs. 28–29

Tell whether the relation is a function. *Explain* your reasoning.

28. (0, 6), (2, 6), (4, 7), (0, 3), (2, 3)

29.

Input, x	0	1	2	3
Output, y	−8	−11	−14	−17

7.5 Nonlinear Functions

pp. 413–419

AF 3.1 **EXAMPLE**

Graph $y = -1.5x^2$.

STEP 1 **Choose** several x-values and make a table of values.

x	−2	−1	0	1	2
y	−6	−1.5	0	−1.5	−6

STEP 2 **Graph** the ordered pairs. Draw a smooth curve through the points, as shown.

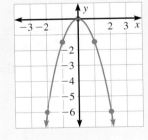

EXERCISES

SEE EXAMPLES 1, 2, AND 3 on pp. 413–415 for Exs. 30–34

Graph the function using a table of values.

30. $y = \dfrac{1}{5}x^2$

31. $y = 0.1x^2$

32. $y = -x^3$

33. $y = 3x^3$

34. ACORN The distance d (in feet) an acorn has fallen from a tree branch after t seconds in the air can be modeled by $d = 16t^2$. Graph the function. If the ground is 82 feet below the branch, about how long will it take the acorn to reach the ground?

VOCABULARY Copy and complete the statement.

1. A function has exactly one __?__ for each __?__ .

2. The expression $5x^2y^{11}$ is an example of a(n) __?__ .

Simplify the expression.

3. $3^5 \cdot 3^3$

4. $7^9 \cdot 7^{-2}$

5. $(-b)^{-7} \cdot (-b)^4$

6. $x^6 \cdot x^8$

7. $(6^4)^4$

8. $[(-2)^3]^2$

9. $(y^2)^{-5}$

10. $(a^{-6})^{-3}$

11. $\dfrac{3^7}{3^2}$

12. $\dfrac{6^3}{6^{-4}}$

13. $\dfrac{x^{10}}{x^6}$

14. $\dfrac{y^{-5}}{y^3}$

15. $(6m)^2$

16. $(2n)^5$

17. $(3x)^3$

18. $(-abc)^4$

19. $\dfrac{a^4 \cdot a^{-2}}{a^{-3}}$

20. $\dfrac{b^7}{b^{-4} \cdot b^{-3}}$

21. $\left(\dfrac{6}{7}\right)^2$

22. $\left(\dfrac{m}{n}\right)^6$

23. $(-6x^2)(-2x^4)$

24. $(5a^2b)(4a^3b^5)$

25. $\sqrt{36m^2}$

26. $\sqrt{121a^6b^{12}}$

Write the product in scientific notation.

27. $(3 \times 10^3) \times (4 \times 10^5)$

28. $(2 \times 10^{-2}) \times (6 \times 10^{-1})$

29. Identify the domain and range of the relation given by $(-2, -4)$, $(0, -2)$, $(1, -1)$, $(2, 0)$, $(2, 6)$, $(3, 1)$. Then graph the relation and tell whether it is a function. *Justify* your answer.

Graph the function using a table of values.

30. $y = -4x^2$

31. $y = 10x^2$

32. $y = -0.6x^3$

Tell whether the graph represents a function.

33.

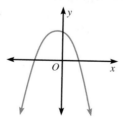

34.

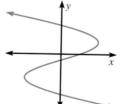

35.

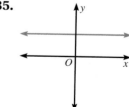

36. RECYCLED PAPER A sheet of recycled paper is 4.4×10^{-3} inch thick. The paper comes in packages of 500 sheets. Disregarding the package wrap, estimate the height of a stack of 25 packages.

37. APPLE PICKING The distance d (in meters) an apple has fallen from a branch after t seconds can be modeled by $d = 4.9t^2$. Graph the function. Use the graph to estimate the time it will take an apple falling from 10 meters above the ground to hit the ground.

STRATEGIES YOU'LL USE:
• SOLVE DIRECTLY
• ELIMINATE CHOICES

Standards
NS 2.3, AF 1.0

If you have difficulty solving a multiple choice problem directly, you may be able to use another approach to eliminate incorrect answer choices and obtain the correct answer.

PROBLEM 1

The nucleus of a human cell is about 7×10^{-6} meter in diameter. A ribosome, another part of a cell, is about 3×10^{-8} meter in diameter. A nucleus is about how many times as wide as a ribosome?

(A) -220 **(B)** 2   **(C)** 159   **(D)** 233

Strategy 1 SOLVE DIRECTLY

To compare the widths of a nucleus and a ribosome, divide the diameter of the nucleus by the diameter of the ribosome.

STEP 1 Write the quotient.

$$\frac{7 \times 10^{-6}}{3 \times 10^{-8}}$$

STEP 2 Apply the quotient of powers property.

$$\frac{7 \times 10^{-6}}{3 \times 10^{-8}} = \frac{7}{3} \times 10^2$$

STEP 3 Divide and write in standard form.

$$\frac{7}{3} \times 10^2 = 2.\overline{3} \times 100 \approx 233$$

The nucleus of a human cell is approximately 233 times as wide as a ribosome.

The correct answer is D. (A) (B) (C) (D)

Strategy 2 ELIMINATE CHOICES

You can use mathematical reasoning to eliminate answer choices.

To compare the widths of a nucleus and a ribosome, divide the diameter of the nucleus by the diameter of the ribosome.

The resulting quotient is:

$$\frac{7 \times 10^{-6}}{3 \times 10^{-8}}$$

The quotient cannot be negative because both the numerator and denominator in the quotient are positive. Choice A is negative, so it can be eliminated.

By the quotient of powers property, $\frac{7 \times 10^{-6}}{3 \times 10^{-8}} = \frac{7}{3} \times 10^2$.

Because $\frac{7}{3} > 2$, you know the following:

$$\frac{7}{3} \times 10^2 > 2 \times 10^2 = 200$$

So you can eliminate choices B and C, which are less than 200.

The correct answer is D. (A) (B) (C) (D)

PROBLEM 2

Which linear function relates x and y for the set of ordered pairs
$(1, 4)$, $(2, 6)$, $(3, 8)$, $(4, 10)$?

A $y = x + 3$ **B** $y = 3$ **C** $y = 2x + 2$ **D** $y = -4x + 3$

Strategy 1 SOLVE DIRECTLY

To find a linear function that relates x and y,
find the slope m and the y-intercept b of the
line. Then write the equation of the line in
slope-intercept form.

STEP 1 **Find** the slope m.

$$m = \frac{\text{change in } y}{\text{change in } x}$$

$$= \frac{6 - 4}{2 - 1} = 2$$

So, $y = 2x + b$.

STEP 2 **Substitute** one of the ordered pairs
into the equation to find b.

Let $(x, y) = (3, 8)$

$8 = 2(3) + b$

$2 = b$

The linear function is $y = 2x + 2$.

The correct answer is C. **A** **B** **C** **D**

Strategy 2 ELIMINATE CHOICES

Choice B represents a horizontal line where
the value of y is always 3. You can see that
this is not true for the given set of ordered
pairs. Choice B can be eliminated.

The slope of the line in choice D is negative.
When a line has a negative slope, the
y-values decrease as the x-values increase.
This is not true for the given set of ordered
pairs. Choice D can be eliminated.

Substitute ordered pairs into the remaining
choices.

Point	Choice A	Choice C
$(1, 4)$	$4 = 1 + 3$ ✓	$4 = 2(1) + 2$ ✓
$(2, 6)$	$6 = 2 + 3$ ✗	$6 = 2(2) + 2$ ✓

Eliminate choice A because it does not have
$(2, 6)$ as a solution.

The correct answer is C. **A** **B** **C** **D**

STRATEGY PRACTICE

Explain why you can eliminate the highlighted answer choice.

1. Which expression is equivalent to $y^9 \cdot y^3$?

A ✕ y^{-3} **B** y^3 **C** y^6 **D** y^{12}

2. Which expression is equivalent to $\left(\dfrac{x}{3y}\right)^2$?

A $\dfrac{x^2}{9y^2}$ **B** $\dfrac{9y^2}{x^2}$ **C** $\dfrac{2x}{6y}$ **D** ✕ $3y$

3. Your uncle uses a quadratic function to model the past sales of his business.
Which function could your uncle use?

A $y = 10x$ **B** ✕ $y = x^3$ **C** $y = 1500$ **D** $y = 2x^2 + 50$

1. The *Olympias* is a reconstruction of a trireme, a type of Greek galley ship used over 2000 years ago. The power P (in kilowatts) needed to propel the *Olympias* at a desired speed s (in knots) can be modeled by the following function:

$$P = 0.0289s^3$$

The fastest speed a volunteer crew of the *Olympias* was able to attain was about 7 knots. About how much power was the crew able to generate? **AF 3.1**

   (A) 0.202 kW

   (B) 1.42 kW

   (C) 9.91 kW

   (D) 343 kW

2. Which expression is equivalent to $\left(\dfrac{a^4}{b^3}\right)^{-2}$?
   AF 2.1

   (A) $\dfrac{a^8}{b^6}$

   (B) $\dfrac{a^2}{b}$

   (C) $\dfrac{b^3}{a^4}$

   (D) $\dfrac{b^6}{a^8}$

3. Which graph could be the graph of $y = -\dfrac{1}{7}x^2$? **AF 3.1**

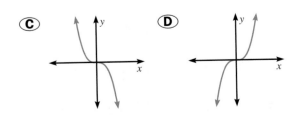

4. Which equation is represented by the graph? **AF 3.1**

   (A) $y = \dfrac{1}{4}x^3$

   (B) $y = 4x$

   (C) $y = 4x^2$

   (D) $y = 4x^3$

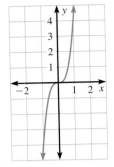

5. The volume V of a balloon with radius r can be approximated using the formula for the volume V of a sphere, $V = \dfrac{4}{3}\pi r^3$. Which expression can you use to approximate the volume of the balloon shown after the radius is tripled? **AF 2.2**

   (A) $\dfrac{4}{3}\pi r^3$

   (B) $4\pi r^3$

   (C) $36\pi r^3$

   (D) $36\pi r^9$

6. The energy E corresponding to the mass of an electron is given by the equation

$$E = mc^2$$

where c, the speed of light, is approximately 3×10^8 meters per second. The mass m of an electron is approximately 9.11×10^{-31} kilograms. What is the approximate amount of energy corresponding to the mass of one electron? (The unit of measure for energy is called a *joule*.) **AF 2.1**

   (A) 2.733×10^{-22} joules

   (B) 2.733×10^{-14} joules

   (C) 8.199×10^{-14} joules

   (D) 8.199×10^{48} joules

7. Which expression is equivalent to $(-3m^5)^3$? **AF 2.1**

  (A) $-27m^{15}$ **(B)** $-27m^8$

  (C) $-3m^8$ **(D)** $27m^{15}$

8. Which expression is equivalent to $(x^3)^{-2}$? **AF 2.1**

  (A) $\dfrac{1}{x^6}$ **(B)** x

  (C) x^5 **(D)** x^6

9. Which number makes $\dfrac{8^{12}}{8^?} = 8^3$ a true statement? **NS 2.3**

  (A) -9 **(B)** 3

  (C) 4 **(D)** 9

10. The power P (in watts) that a windmill generates can be modeled by $P = 0.015s^3$ where s is the wind speed (in miles per hour). Graph this function for values of s from 0 to 50. Use your graph to determine which of the following is the best estimate of the wind speed needed to generate 10 watts of power. **AF 3.1**

Windmill turbine at Altamont, CA

  (A) About 9 mi/h

  (B) About 19 mi/h

  (C) About 23 mi/h

  (D) About 31 mi/h

11. Which expression is equivalent to $\sqrt{18y^4}$? **AF 2.2**

  (A) $6y$ **(B)** $3y\sqrt{2}$

  (C) $6y^2$ **(D)** $3y^2\sqrt{2}$

12. It costs \$.42 per square foot to spread mulch in your garden. Write and graph a function to show the cost c to spread m square feet of mulch. Use values of m from 0 to 500. Use your graph to determine which of the following is the best estimate for the area that can be covered by \$75 worth of mulch. **AF 1.5, MR 2.3**

  (A) About 34 ft^2

  (B) About 101 ft^2

  (C) About 180 ft^2

  (D) About 200 ft^2

13. Which expression is equivalent to $\dfrac{8y^{-7}}{24y^{-4}}$? **AF 2.2**

  (A) $\dfrac{1}{3y^{11}}$

  (B) $\dfrac{1}{3y^3}$

  (C) $\dfrac{y^3}{3}$

  (D) $3y^3$

14. The graph below shows the length of a lemon shark at various ages.

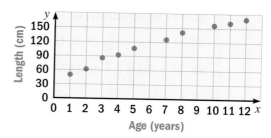

Which of the following statements is *not* true? **AF 1.5, MR 2.4**

  (A) The domain is 1, 2, 3, 4, 5, 7, 8, 10, 11, 12.

  (B) The shark's length at age 2 was about 60 centimeters.

  (C) The shark's length tends to increase with age.

  (D) The graph does *not* represent a function.

Evaluate the expression. *(p. 5)*

1. $66 - 11 \times 5$
2. $80 \div (35 + 5)$
3. $17 + (3 \times 4)^2$
4. $8 \times 6 \div 2^4$
5. $(11 - 3) + 5$
6. $(14 - 8) + 13$
7. $5(9 + 3)$
8. $2(6 - 1)$
9. $4 \times 7 + 10$

Find the sum, difference, product, or quotient.

10. $-55 + (-43)$ *(p. 18)*
11. $0 + (-144)$ *(p. 18)*
12. $-21 - 33$ *(p. 24)*
13. $-17 - (-67)$ *(p. 24)*
14. $-5(-16)$ *(p. 31)*
15. $3(-8)(10)$ *(p. 31)*
16. $\frac{-51}{-17}$ *(p. 36)*
17. $\frac{0}{-25}$ *(p. 36)*
18. $-\frac{19}{25} - \frac{11}{25}$ *(p. 85)*
19. $-9\frac{3}{4} + 4\frac{2}{3}$ *(p. 91)*
20. $3 - \frac{7}{9}$ *(p. 91)*
21. $\frac{9}{21} \cdot \frac{7}{5}$ *(p. 98)*
22. $5\frac{7}{5} \cdot \frac{3}{32}$ *(p. 98)*
23. $\frac{9}{14} \div \frac{4}{7}$ *(p. 106)*
24. $6\frac{3}{10} \div \left(-\frac{2}{5}\right)$ *(p. 106)*
25. $13.9 \cdot (-4.8)$ *(p. 144)*
26. $29.6 \cdot 1.21$ *(p. 144)*
27. $4.097 \div 12.05$ *(p. 144)*

Write the decimal or fraction as a percent. *(p. 155)*

28. 0.57
29. 0.012
30. $\frac{4}{25}$
31. $\frac{61}{50}$

Write the number in scientific notation. *(p. 201)*

32. $1{,}970{,}000$
33. 0.000275
34. 8831

Solve the equation or inequality.

35. $8 = b - (-6)$ *(p. 257)*
36. $9y = -63$ *(p. 263)*
37. $2c - 5 = 17$ *(p. 270)*
38. $d + 3.4 \le 9.1$ *(p. 282)*
39. $\frac{1}{3}x > -2$ *(p. 288)*
40. $7 - 2y \le 11$ *(p. 293)*
41. $-5x + 13 \ge 53$ *(p. 293)*
42. $6 - \frac{2}{3}a > 2$ *(p. 293)*
43. $-10 < 9x + 26$ *(p. 293)*

Graph the equation or inequality in a coordinate plane.

44. $y = -6x$ *(p. 320)*
45. $y = -3x + 4$ *(p. 320)*
46. $-\frac{1}{2}x + y = -3$ *(p. 327)*
47. $-10 \ge -2x$ *(p. 354)*
48. $y \le 2x - 5$ *(p. 354)*
49. $6x - 3y > 9$ *(p. 354)*

Simplify the expression.

50. $\left(11^3\right)^4$ *(p. 386)*
51. $\frac{x^{-8}}{x^{-3}}$ *(p. 393)*
52. $\frac{20x^5y^2}{5x^2y}$ *(p. 399)*

Graph the function using a table of values. *(p. 413)*

53. $y = -2.5x^2$
54. $y = \frac{2}{3}x^2$
55. $y = -2x^3$

56. CLOTHES A sweater costs $45 and a pair of jeans costs $35. You buy 3 sweaters and 2 pairs of jeans during a sale where sweaters are $10 off and jeans are $5 off. Evaluate the expression $3(45 - 10) + 2(35 - 5)$ for the total cost of the clothes. *(p. 5)*

57. TRIPLETS The weights in pounds of a set of newborn triplets are $4\frac{3}{4}$ pounds, $4\frac{5}{8}$ pounds, and $4\frac{7}{16}$ pounds. Order the weights from least to greatest. *(p. 80)*

58. VIDEO GAME A video game costs $39.50 and is on sale for 10% off. Find the sale price of the video game. *(p. 160)*

59. INTEREST You deposit $1500 in an account that pays 5% interest compounded annually. Find the account balance for the given time period. *(p. 172)*

    a. 4 years   **b.** 6 years   **c.** 24 months   **d.** 10 years

60. COURTYARD A square courtyard has an area of 6724 square feet. Write a relationship between the length of one side of the courtyard and the area of the courtyard. Then find its side length. *(p. 219)*

61. SAVING MONEY You have $80 today. You save $40 a week. How many weeks will it take to save enough to buy a camera that costs $320? How many weeks will it take if you save $35 a week? *(p. 270)*

62. PARTY You have $20 to spend on snacks for a party. Pretzels cost $1.50 per bag and trail mix costs $2.50 per bag. To find how much you can buy, graph the inequality $1.5x + 2.5y \le 20$ where x is the number of bags of pretzels and y is the number of bags of trail mix. Then find two possible combinations of bags of pretzels and bags of trail mix that you can buy for the party. *(p. 354)*

63. HEARTBEAT Consider a person whose heart beats approximately 70 times per minute and who lives to be 92 years old. Use scientific notation to estimate the number of times the person's heart beats during his or her life. Do not take leap years into account. *(p. 386)*

64. ASTRONOMY The star Canis Majoris is about 2.35×10^3 light years from Earth. A light year is about 5.88×10^{12} miles. About how many miles is Canis Majoris from Earth? *(p. 386)*

65. BAKE SALE The table shows the cost of cookies purchased at a bake sale, where x is the number of cookies purchased and y is the total cost. Write a function rule that relates x and y. Then predict the total cost of purchasing 15 cookies. *(p. 407)*

x	1	2	3	4	5
y	$.50	$1.00	$1.50	$2.00	$2.50

8 Measurements and Planar Figures

Before

In previous chapters, you learned the following skills, which you'll use in Chapter 8:

- Using units of measure
- Evaluating expressions involving exponents
- Simplifying square roots
- Solving equations

Now

In Chapter 8 you'll study these

Big Ideas:

1. Converting units of measure
2. Classifying plane figures
3. Finding areas of plane figures

Why?

So you can solve real-world problems about . . .

- Sewing, p. 442
- Babysitting, p. 447
- Gardening, p. 447
- Theater, p. 447
- Waterfalls, p. 452
- Wolverines, p. 453
- Optics, p. 458
- Hiking, p. 476

Animated Math
at *classzone.com*

Get-Ready Games

NUMBER STRUGGLE

California Standards

Review using exponents, powers, and roots. **Gr. 7 NS 2.0**

Prepare for using formulas for area. **Gr. 7 MG 2.1**

Materials

- One deck of *Number Struggle* cards

2^2

How to Play Play in pairs. Deal half of the cards to each player. Place your cards face down in a pile in front of you. On each turn, both players should follow the steps on the next page.

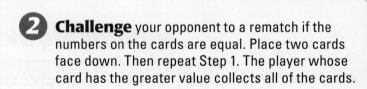

1 **Turn** over the top card in your pile. The player whose card has the greater value collects both cards and adds them to the bottom of his or her pile.

How to Win Collect all of the cards. Alternatively, be the player to have the greater number of cards after a certain period of time.

2 **Challenge** your opponent to a rematch if the numbers on the cards are equal. Place two cards face down. Then repeat Step 1. The player whose card has the greater value collects all of the cards.

Games Wrap-Up

Draw Conclusions

Complete these exercises after playing the game.

1. **WRITING** You turn over the card $2\sqrt{3}$ and your opponent turns over the card $\sqrt{20}$. *Explain* how to determine which card has the greater value without using a calculator.

2. **REASONING** Suppose you turn over the card 3^1. Is your opponent more likely to have a number that is greater than or less than yours? *Explain* your reasoning using the cards in the deck.

435

Prerequisite Skills

California @HomeTutor

Prerequisite skills practice
at classzone.com

**REVIEW
VOCABULARY**

- **simplest form of a
  fraction,** *p. 75*
- **point,** *p. 735*
- **ray,** *p. 735*
- **line,** *p. 735*
- **triangle,** *p. 736*
- **perimeter,** *p. 742*

VOCABULARY CHECK

In Exercises 1–3, identify the object using a review term from the list
at the left.

1. 　　　　　　　　　　　2. 　　　　　　　　　3.

4. Copy and complete using a review term from the list at the left:
   The distance around a figure is called its __?__ .

SKILL CHECK

Evaluate the expression. *(p. 5)*

5. $4^2 + 3^2$ 6. $14^2 - 5^2$ 7. $27^2 - 3^2$ 8. $2^2 + 6^2$

9. $6^2 - 3^2$ 10. $10^2 - 5^2$ 11. $5^2 + 6^2$ 12. $7^2 + 3^2$

Write the fraction in simplest form. *(p. 75)*

13. $\dfrac{15}{75}$ 14. $\dfrac{46}{69}$ 15. $\dfrac{35}{140}$ 16. $\dfrac{18}{36}$

17. $\dfrac{7}{28}$ 18. $\dfrac{38}{40}$ 19. $\dfrac{22}{55}$ 20. $\dfrac{42}{48}$

Notetaking Skills

NOW YOU TRY
Make a *concept map*
for the word *angle*.
You may want to use
colored pencils.

Focus on Graphic Organizers

You can use a *concept map* to organize ideas and words that relate to the
same concept, such as *triangle*.

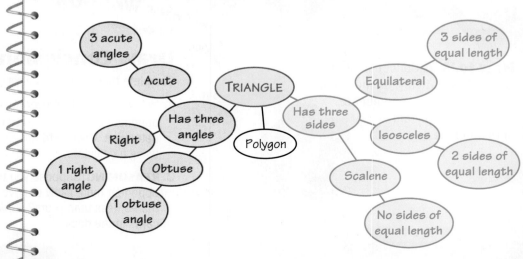

8.1 Comparing and Converting Measurements

Standards MG 1.1 Compare weights, capacities, geometric measures, times, and temperatures within and between measurement systems (e.g., miles per hour and feet per second, cubic inches to cubic centimeters).

Connect *Before* you used U.S. customary measures and metric measures. *Now* you will compare and convert U.S. customary measures and metric measures.

Math and
OCEANOGRAPHY
Exs. 54–56, p. 441

KEY VOCABULARY
• conversion factor
• unit analysis, *p. 53*

You can use equivalent measures to write a *conversion factor* when you convert from one measure to another. For a list of equivalent measures, see the Table of Measures on page 760.

KEY CONCEPT *For Your Notebook*

Conversion Factors

A **conversion factor** is a fraction equal to 1 that expresses the relationship between two different units of measure. For example, the statement 1 foot = 12 inches generates two conversion factors:

$$\frac{1 \text{ foot}}{12 \text{ inches}} \qquad \frac{12 \text{ inches}}{1 \text{ foot}}$$

EXAMPLE 1 Converting Within the Same Measurement System

Copy and complete the statement.

a. $9 \text{ c} = \underline{\ ?\ } \text{ fl oz}$ **b.** $5000 \text{ g} = \underline{\ ?\ } \text{ kg}$ **c.** $4.5 \text{ ft} = \underline{\ ?\ } \text{ in.}$

SOLUTION

CHOOSING A CONVERSION FACTOR
When you choose a conversion factor, the unit of measure you are converting *to* should be in the *numerator*.

a. $9 \text{ c} \times \dfrac{8 \text{ fl oz}}{1 \text{ c}} = \dfrac{9 \cancel{c} \times 8 \text{ fl oz}}{1 \cancel{c}} = 72 \text{ fl oz}$

b. $5000 \text{ g} \times \dfrac{1 \text{ kg}}{1000 \text{ g}} = \dfrac{\overset{5}{\cancel{5000 \text{ g}}} \times 1 \text{ kg}}{\underset{1}{\cancel{1000 \text{ g}}}} = 5 \text{ kg}$

c. $4.5 \text{ ft} \times \dfrac{12 \text{ in.}}{1 \text{ ft}} = \dfrac{4.5 \cancel{ft} \times 12 \text{ in.}}{1 \cancel{ft}} = 54 \text{ in.}$

✓ **GUIDED PRACTICE** for Example 1

Copy and complete the statement.

1. $21,120 \text{ ft} = \underline{\ ?\ } \text{ mi}$ **2.** $5.6 \text{ g} = \underline{\ ?\ } \text{ mg}$ **3.** $12 \text{ gal} = \underline{\ ?\ } \text{ pt}$

CONVERSIONS BETWEEN SYSTEMS To convert between metric and customary units, use the relationships shown below.

Quantity	Conversions	
Length	1 in. = 2.54 cm 1 mi ≈ 1.609 km	1 ft = 0.3048 m
Capacity	1 fl oz ≈ 29.573 mL 1 gal ≈ 3.785 L	1 qt ≈ 0.946 L
Weight/ Mass	1 oz ≈ 28.35 g	1 lb ≈ 0.454 kg

EXAMPLE 2 Converting Between Measurement Systems

Copy and complete the statement. Round to the nearest whole number.

a. 304 cm ≈ _?_ in. **b.** 1254 gal ≈ _?_ L **c.** 200 g ≈ _?_ oz

SOLUTION

Use the table above to find the appropriate conversion factors.

a. $304 \text{ cm} \times \dfrac{1 \text{ in.}}{2.54 \text{ cm}} = \dfrac{304 \text{ cm} \times 1 \text{ in.}}{2.54 \text{ cm}} \approx 120 \text{ in.}$

b. $1254 \text{ gal} \times \dfrac{3.785 \text{ L}}{1 \text{ gal}} = \dfrac{1254 \text{ gal} \times 3.785 \text{ L}}{1 \text{ gal}} \approx 4746 \text{ L}$

c. $200 \text{ g} \times \dfrac{1 \text{ oz}}{28.35 \text{ g}} = \dfrac{200 \text{ g} \times 1 \text{ oz}}{28.35 \text{ g}} \approx 7 \text{ oz}$

✓ GUIDED PRACTICE   for Example 2

Copy and complete the statement. Round to the nearest whole number.

4. 23 ft ≈ _?_ m **5.** 78 L ≈ _?_ qt **6.** 180 lb ≈ _?_ kg

EXAMPLE 3 Comparing Elapsed Times

ANOTHER WAY
You can also convert 150 hours to days and then compare.

$$150 \text{ h} \times \dfrac{1 \text{ d}}{24 \text{ h}}$$
$$= 6.25 \text{ d}$$

Because 6.25 < 20, the solar eclipse will occur first.

ASTRONOMY A solar eclipse will occur in 150 hours. A full moon will occur in 20 days. Which will occur first?

SOLUTION

Convert 20 days to hours:

$$20 \text{ d} \times \dfrac{24 \text{ h}}{1 \text{ d}} = \dfrac{20 \text{ d} \times 24 \text{ h}}{1 \text{ d}} = 480 \text{ h}$$

▶ **Answer** Because 150 hours is less than 480 hours, the solar eclipse will occur first.

Solar eclipse

AREA AND VOLUME You can use relationships between lengths to find conversion factors for converting between measures of area or volume.

EXAMPLE 4 Formulas for Converting Areas and Volumes

Derive a formula for converting between (a) square feet and square inches, and (b) cubic inches and cubic centimeters.

SOLUTION

a. You know that 1 ft = 12 in. You can use this fact and the figures below to conclude that $1 \text{ ft}^2 = 144 \text{ in.}^2$

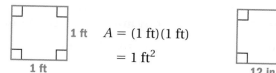

$$A = (1 \text{ ft})(1 \text{ ft})$$
$$= 1 \text{ ft}^2$$

$$A = (12 \text{ in.})(12 \text{ in.})$$
$$= 144 \text{ in.}^2$$

REVIEW VOLUME
For help reviewing volume, turn to p. 742.

b. You know that 1 in. = 2.54 cm. You can use this fact and the figures below to conclude that $1 \text{ in.}^3 \approx 16.4 \text{ cm}^3$.

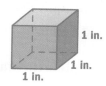

$$V = (1 \text{ in.})(1 \text{ in.})(1 \text{ in.})$$
$$= 1 \text{ in.}^3$$

$$V = (2.54 \text{ cm})(2.54 \text{ cm})(2.54 \text{ cm})$$
$$\approx 16.4 \text{ cm}^3$$

EXAMPLE 5 Converting Area and Volume Measures

Use a formula derived in Example 4 to copy and complete the statement. Round to the nearest whole number if necessary.

a. $5 \text{ ft}^2 = \underline{\ ?\ } \text{ in.}^2$

b. $165 \text{ cm}^3 \approx \underline{\ ?\ } \text{ in.}^3$

SOLUTION

a. $5 \text{ ft}^2 = 5 \text{ ft}^2 \times \dfrac{144 \text{ in.}^2}{1 \text{ ft}^2} = 720 \text{ in.}^2$

b. $165 \text{ cm}^3 \approx 165 \text{ cm}^3 \times \dfrac{1 \text{ in.}^3}{16.4 \text{ cm}^3} \approx 10 \text{ in.}^3$

✓ **GUIDED PRACTICE** for Examples 3, 4, and 5

7. Katia turns 13 in 20 days. Alex turns 13 in 500 hours. Who turns 13 first?

8. How many square feet are in 1 square mile?

9. Use your conversion from Exercise 8 to find the number of square feet in 30 square miles.

HOMEWORK
KEY

◆ = **MULTIPLE CHOICE PRACTICE**
Exs. 12, 22, 58, 67–69

◯ = **HINTS AND HOMEWORK HELP**
for Exs. 17, 31, 55 at classzone.com

SKILLS • PROBLEM SOLVING • REASONING

1. **VOCABULARY** Copy and complete: A fraction equal to 1 that expresses the relationship between two different units of measure is a(n) ? .

2. **WRITING** *Explain* why it would be unreasonable to use the conversion factor $\frac{1 \text{ min}}{60 \text{ sec}}$ to convert minutes to seconds.

SEE EXAMPLE 1
on p. 437
for Exs. 3–12

CONVERTING MEASUREMENTS Copy and complete the statement.

3. 12 ft = ? yd

4. 17 qt = ? pt

5. 2.75 m = ? cm

6. 3000 lb = ? ton

7. 18 qt = ? gal

8. 500 km = ? m

9. 8000 mg = ? g

10. 2.4 kL = ? L

11. 800 cm = ? m

12. ◆ **MULTIPLE CHOICE** How many ounces are equivalent to 16 pounds?

(A) 1 oz

(B) 16 oz

(C) 32 oz

(D) 256 oz

SEE EXAMPLE 2
on p. 438
for Exs. 13–22

CONVERTING MEASUREMENTS Copy and complete the statement. Round to the nearest whole number.

13. 31 lb ≈ ? kg

14. 26 m ≈ ? ft

15. 35 qt ≈ ? L

16. 250 g ≈ ? oz

17. 7.37 L ≈ ? gal

18. 7 in. ≈ ? cm

19. 8 oz ≈ ? g

20. 110 mL ≈ ? fl oz

21. 32 km ≈ ? mi

22. ◆ **MULTIPLE CHOICE** Which of the following measurements is greater than 1 yard?

(A) 1 meter

(B) 2.7 feet

(C) 34 inches

(D) 80 centimeters

SEE EXAMPLE 3
on p. 438
for Exs. 23–28

COMPARING TIMES Identify the greater time.

23. 350 seconds or 7 minutes

24. 276 hours or 12 days

25. 16 hours or 900 minutes

26. 52 weeks or 365 days

27. 130 minutes or 2 hours

28. 600 seconds or 11 minutes

**SEE EXAMPLES
4 AND 5**
on p. 439
for Exs. 29–39

CONVERTING AREAS AND VOLUMES Copy and complete the statement. Round to the nearest whole number if necessary.

29. $3 \text{ ft}^2 =$? in.^2

30. $81 \text{ ft}^2 =$? yd^2

31. $14 \text{ in.}^2 \approx$? cm^2

32. $72 \text{ ft}^2 \approx$? m^2

33. $49{,}000 \text{ cm}^2 \approx$? m^2

34. $8640 \text{ in.}^3 =$? ft^3

35. $0.25 \text{ m}^3 =$? cm^3

36. $7 \text{ m}^3 \approx$? ft^3

37. $5 \text{ km}^3 \approx$? mi^3

ERROR ANALYSIS *Describe* and correct the error in the conversion.

38. 288 in.^{2} = __?__ ft^2

$$288 \text{ in.}^2 \times \frac{1 \text{ ft}^2}{12 \text{ in.}^2} = \frac{\overset{24}{\cancel{288 \text{ in.}^2}} \times 1 \text{ ft}^2}{\cancel{12 \text{ in.}^2}_1}$$
$$= 24 \text{ ft}^2$$
So, 288 in.^{2} = 24 ft^2.   ✗

39. 3 yd^3 = __?__ ft^3

$$3 \text{ yd}^3 \times \frac{9 \text{ ft}^3}{1 \text{ yd}^3} = \frac{3 \cancel{\text{yd}^3} \times 9 \text{ ft}^3}{1 \cancel{\text{yd}^3}}$$
$$= 27 \text{ ft}^3$$
So, 3 yd^3 = 27 ft^3.   ✗

COMPARING MEASUREMENTS Copy and complete the statement with
<, >, or =.

40. 12,000 ft __?__ 2 mi

41. 3 yd __?__ 9 ft

42. 1 m __?__ 115 cm

43. 15 cm __?__ 2 in.

44. 900 mL __?__ 0.4 gal

45. 96 min __?__ 1.6 h

46. 100 cm^2 __?__ 1 m^2

47. 120 in.^{2} __?__ 0.5 m^2

48. 12,000 in.^{3} __?__ 1 m^3

CONNECT SKILLS TO PROBLEM SOLVING Exercises 49–51 will help you
prepare for problem solving.

The table shows the maximum dimensions of a postcard. Write the
conversion factor that is needed to find the indicated measure.

49. The maximum allowable height in
centimeters

50. The maximum allowable length in feet

51. The maximum allowable thickness in
centimeters

Dimension	Maximum measure
Height	4.25 in.
Length	6 in.
Thickness	0.016 in.

SEE EXAMPLE 1
on p. 437
for Exs. 52–56

52. WATER COOLER A water cooler holds 5 gallons of water. How many
quarts does the water cooler hold?

California @HomeTutor for problem solving help at classzone.com

53. BADGES A merit badge in the shape of an equilateral triangle has a side
length of 35 millimeters. Find the perimeter of the badge in centimeters.

California @HomeTutor for problem solving help at classzone.com

SUBMERSIBLES ALVIN is an underwater vehicle
used for research.

54. ALVIN weighs 35,200 pounds. What is its
weight in tons?

55. ALVIN can carry up to 1500 pounds. How
many tons can ALVIN carry?

56. What is ALVIN's depth limit in miles? Round
to the nearest tenth of a mile.

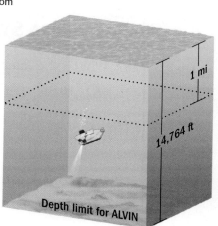

1 mi

14,764 ft

Depth limit for ALVIN

57. **HEIGHTS** The heights of four people are shown in the table at the right.

   a. Order the heights from least to greatest.

   b. Is it more convenient to convert all of the heights to metric units or to U.S. customary units? *Explain* your reasoning.

Heights of People	
John	1.5 meters
Amanda	63 inches
Myra	140 centimeters
Neil	1700 millimeters

58. ◆ **MULTIPLE CHOICE** A piece of chain is 3 feet long. Each link of the chain is about 3 inches long. About how many links make up the chain?

   (A) 4 **(B)** 9 **(C)** 12 **(D)** 36

SEE EXAMPLE 3
on p. 438
for Exs. 59–60

59. **ASTRONOMY** The length of a day on Saturn is 10.7 hours. The length of a day on Neptune is 966 minutes. Which planet has a shorter day?

60. **MARATHON** The two best finishing times for a marathon are 2.35 hours and 145 minutes. Which was the faster time?

61. **SEWING** You have 20 square yards of fabric. You need 60 square feet of fabric to make each blanket. How many blankets can you make?

62. **LANDSCAPING** You need to seed a rectangular portion of your yard that is 14 meters wide by 20 meters long. About how many bags of the grass seed shown do you need to seed this portion of your yard?

Grass Seed

Covers 600 ft²

63. **REASONING** The formula $F = \frac{9}{5}C + 32$ is used to convert from degrees Celsius to degrees Fahrenheit. *Explain* why a conversion factor cannot be used in this conversion.

64. **OPEN-ENDED** A car has a mass of 1.45×10^6 grams. Rewrite this mass using a more appropriate unit.

65. **CHALLENGE** Find the number of centimeters in 1 mile. Then use your answer to find the number of square centimeters in 1.6 square miles.

66. **CHALLENGE** Given that one milliliter of water has a mass of 1 gram, what is the weight of 1 gallon of water to the nearest tenth of a pound?

◆ CALIFORNIA STANDARDS SPIRAL REVIEW

NS 2.5

67. What is the value of $|9 - 4| + |5 - 8| \times |-5 + 1|$? *(p. 12)*

   (A) −8 **(B)** −7 **(C)** 17 **(D)** 32

AF 3.3

68. What is the slope of the graph of $y = 2 - 3x$? *(p. 342)*

   (A) −3 **(B)** $-\frac{2}{3}$ **(C)** $\frac{2}{3}$ **(D)** 2

NS 1.7

69. Which markup in price is *not* the result of a 20% increase? *(p. 160)*

   (A) $50 to $60 **(B)** $30 to $38 **(C)** $75 to $90 **(D)** $10 to $12

ONLINE QUIZ at classzone.com

8.2 Measures Involving Products and Quotients

Standards ▸ MG 1.3 Use measures expressed as rates (e.g., speed, density) and measures expressed as products (e.g., person-days) to solve problems; check the units of the solutions; and use dimensional analysis to check the reasonableness of the answer.

Connect ▸ *Before* you worked with rates. *Now* you will work with unit rates.

Math and THEATER
Ex. 36, p. 447

KEY VOCABULARY
• **unit rate**
• **rate,** *p. 732*

A rate is a ratio of two quantities that have different units. Two rates are equivalent if they have the same value. A **unit rate** is a rate that has a denominator of 1 unit. To write a unit rate, find an equivalent rate with a denominator of 1 unit.

EXAMPLE 1 Comparing Rates

RUNNING You can run 80 feet in 5 seconds. Your friend can run 90 feet in 6 seconds. Who runs faster?

SOLUTION

STEP 1 **Write** a rate of speed for each person.

You: $\dfrac{80 \text{ ft}}{5 \text{ sec}}$ Your friend: $\dfrac{90 \text{ ft}}{6 \text{ sec}}$

STEP 2 **Express** each person's speed as a unit rate.

You: $\dfrac{80 \text{ ft}}{5 \text{ sec}} = \dfrac{80 \div 5}{5 \div 5}$ **Divide numerator and denominator by 5 to get a denominator of 1 unit.**

$= \dfrac{16 \text{ ft}}{1 \text{ sec}}$ **Simplify.**

Your friend: $\dfrac{90 \text{ ft}}{6 \text{ sec}} = \dfrac{90 \div 6}{6 \div 6}$ **Divide numerator and denominator by 6 to get a denominator of 1 unit.**

$= \dfrac{15 \text{ ft}}{1 \text{ sec}}$ **Simplify.**

READING
When a unit rate is expressed as a verbal phrase, it often contains the word *per*, which means "for every."

▸ **Answer** You can run 16 feet per second and your friend can run 15 feet per second. So, you can run faster than your friend.

✓ GUIDED PRACTICE for Example 1

1. **WHAT IF?** In Example 1, suppose your friend can run 96 feet in 6 seconds. Who runs faster?

Write the rate as a unit rate.

2. $\dfrac{10 \text{ cm}}{2 \text{ min}}$ 3. $\dfrac{210 \text{ cal}}{3 \text{ oz}}$ 4. $\dfrac{5 \text{ dollars}}{2 \text{ lb}}$ 5. $\dfrac{3 \text{ runs}}{8 \text{ innings}}$

6. Write 60 miles per 4 hours as a unit rate.

EXAMPLE 2 ◆ **Multiple Choice Practice**

> Printer A prints 36 pages per minute, printer B prints 15 pages per 30 seconds, and printer C prints 35 pages per minute. Which is fastest?
>
> Ⓐ A   Ⓑ B   Ⓒ C   Ⓓ A and B

SOLUTION

STEP 1 **Write** a rate of printing for each printer.

Printer A: $\dfrac{36 \text{ pages}}{1 \text{ min}}$ Printer B: $\dfrac{15 \text{ pages}}{30 \text{ sec}}$ Printer C: $\dfrac{35 \text{ pages}}{1 \text{ min}}$

STEP 2 **Express** each printer's speed as a unit rate using the same unit of time. Convert the printing speed of printer B to pages per minute to match the units given for printers A and C.

Printer B: $\dfrac{15 \text{ pages}}{30 \text{ sec}} = \dfrac{15 \times 2}{30 \times 2} = \dfrac{30 \text{ pages}}{60 \text{ sec}} = \dfrac{30 \text{ pages}}{1 \text{ min}}$

STEP 3 **Compare** rates. In pages per minute, the speeds of printers A, B, and C are 36, 30, and 35, respectively. So, printer A prints the fastest.

▶ **Answer** The correct answer is A. Ⓐ Ⓑ Ⓒ Ⓓ

REVIEW RATES

For help reviewing rates, see p. 732.

UNITS THAT ARE PRODUCTS Some units of measure are products of quantities. An example of such a unit is a *person-day*. If a job takes 20 person-days to complete, then one person working alone would finish the job in 20 days. More generally, m people working at the job would finish the job in n days, where $mn = 20$. A *person-hour* is defined similarly.

EXAMPLE 3 **Using Units That Are Products**

TRANSPORTATION About 129,442,000 person-hours are saved annually by commuters in the Los Angeles area who use public transportation. An average of 6,812,737 people commute in the Los Angeles area by public transportation every day. About how many hours per year should the average commuter using public transportation expect to save?

L.A. public transportation: 6,812,737 commuters/day

SOLUTION

Let h represent the number of hours the average commuter will save by using public transportation. Write and solve an equation to find h.

$6{,}812{,}737 \cdot h = 129{,}442{,}000$ **Write an equation.**

$h \approx 19$ **Solve.**

▶ **Answer** The average commuter using public transportation will save about 19 hours per year.

UNDERSTAND RATES
If you can complete a job in 2 hours, your rate of work is $\frac{1 \text{ job}}{2 \text{ hours}}$, or $\frac{1}{2}$ job per hour.

WORK PROBLEMS To write an algebraic equation for work problems, you can use the formula below.

(Rate of work) • (Time worked) = (Part of job completed)

The rate of work per 1 unit of time is the part of a job that one person can do in one unit of time.

EXAMPLE 4 Using Rates to Solve a Work Problem

PAINTING Maria can paint a room in 3 hours. It takes Paul 4 hours to do the same job. How long would it take Maria and Paul to paint the room together?

SOLUTION

STEP 1 Find the rate of work for each person.

Maria can paint the room in 3 hours, so she can do $\frac{1}{3}$ of the job in 1 hour. So, her work rate is $\frac{1}{3}$. Similarly, Paul's work rate is $\frac{1}{4}$.

STEP 2 Find the work done by each person.

If Maria and Paul work together for the same amount of time t, you can write the part of the job completed by each person, as shown.

	Work rate ×	Time =	Part of job completed
Maria	$\frac{1}{3}$	t	$\frac{t}{3}$
Paul	$\frac{1}{4}$	t	$\frac{t}{4}$

STEP 3 Write an equation for the total work done. Then solve the equation.

Because the parts of the job completed by Maria and Paul make up one whole job, set the sum of the expressions equal to 1.

$$\frac{t}{3} + \frac{t}{4} = 1 \qquad \text{Write equation.}$$

$$4t + 3t = 12 \qquad \text{Multiply each side by the LCD, 12.}$$

$$t = \frac{12}{7} = 1\frac{5}{7} \qquad \text{Solve for } t.$$

▶ **Answer** Maria and Paul can paint the room in $1\frac{5}{7}$ hours.

✓ GUIDED PRACTICE   for Examples 2, 3, and 4

7. **WHAT IF?** In Example 2, suppose printer B prints 80 pages per 2 minutes and printer C prints 1 page per second. Which is fastest?

8. **CONSTRUCTION** A proposed construction job will take 30 person-days to complete. How long will it take 5 people to complete the job?

9. **WHAT IF?** In Example 4, suppose it takes Maria 5 hours to paint the room. How long would it take Maria and Paul to paint the room together?

8.2 EXERCISES

SKILLS • PROBLEM SOLVING • REASONING

1. **VOCABULARY** Copy and complete: A rate with a denominator of 1 unit is called a(n) __?__ rate.

2. **WRITING** *Explain* the difference between a rate and a unit rate.

SEE EXAMPLE 1
on p. 443
for Exs. 3–17

WRITING UNIT RATES Write the rate as a unit rate.

3. $\dfrac{220 \text{ mi}}{4 \text{ h}}$

4. $\dfrac{15 \text{ dollars}}{12 \text{ muffins}}$

5. $\dfrac{94.5 \text{ m}}{27 \text{ sec}}$

6. $\dfrac{4000 \text{ ft}}{15 \text{ sec}}$

7. $\dfrac{6.63 \text{ lb}}{3 \text{ kg}}$

8. $\dfrac{56.7 \text{ g}}{2 \text{ oz}}$

9. $\dfrac{10.16 \text{ cm}}{4 \text{ in.}}$

10. $\dfrac{8.05 \text{ km}}{5 \text{ mi}}$

COMPARING RATES Tell whether the rates are *equivalent* or *not equivalent*.

11. $\dfrac{32 \text{ calories}}{2 \text{ h}}, \dfrac{64 \text{ calories}}{4 \text{ h}}$

12. $\dfrac{60 \text{ words}}{3 \text{ min}}, \dfrac{25 \text{ words}}{1 \text{ min}}$

13. $\dfrac{8 \text{ lb}}{4 \text{ dollars}}, \dfrac{12 \text{ lb}}{3 \text{ dollars}}$

14. $\dfrac{42 \text{ visits}}{3 \text{ h}}, \dfrac{28 \text{ visits}}{2 \text{ h}}$

15. **ERROR ANALYSIS** *Describe* and correct the error in finding the price per DVD when paying $60 for 4 DVDs.

$\dfrac{4}{60} \approx 0.07$
$.07 per DVD ✗

16. ◆ **MULTIPLE CHOICE** Which rate is equivalent to 45 miles per 3 days?

Ⓐ $\dfrac{45 \text{ mi}}{1 \text{ d}}$

Ⓑ $\dfrac{15 \text{ mi}}{1 \text{ d}}$

Ⓒ $\dfrac{22.5 \text{ mi}}{2 \text{ d}}$

Ⓓ $\dfrac{15 \text{ mi}}{3 \text{ d}}$

17. **ERROR ANALYSIS** *Describe* and correct the error in finding the cost per book when paying $19.50 for 3 books.

$\dfrac{19.50}{3} = 6.50$
6.50 books per dollar ✗

SEE EXAMPLE 2
on p. 444
for Exs. 18–26

COMPARING SPEEDS Tell which speed is faster.

18. $\dfrac{2 \text{ steps}}{1 \text{ sec}}; \dfrac{180 \text{ steps}}{1 \text{ min}}$

19. $\dfrac{5 \text{ ft}}{1 \text{ min}}, \dfrac{200 \text{ ft}}{1 \text{ h}}$

20. $\dfrac{62 \text{ mi}}{1 \text{ h}}, \dfrac{65 \text{ mi}}{65 \text{ min}}$

COMPARING RATES Copy and complete the statement with <, >, or =.

21. $\dfrac{60 \text{ mi}}{2 \text{ h}} \; \underset{?}{} \; \dfrac{120 \text{ mi}}{3 \text{ h}}$

22. $\dfrac{4.5 \text{ dollars}}{1.5 \text{ pounds}} \; \underset{?}{} \; \dfrac{9 \text{ dollars}}{3 \text{ pounds}}$

23. $\dfrac{3 \text{ in.}}{10 \text{ sec}} \; \underset{?}{} \; \dfrac{1 \text{ ft}}{1 \text{ min}}$

24. $\dfrac{60 \text{ mi}}{1 \text{ h}} \; \underset{?}{} \; \dfrac{1 \text{ mi}}{1 \text{ min}}$

25. $\dfrac{70 \text{ lb}}{2 \text{ ft}^3} \; \underset{?}{} \; \dfrac{80 \text{ lb}}{2000 \text{ in.}^3}$

26. $\dfrac{10 \text{ m}^2}{1 \text{ d}} \; \underset{?}{} \; \dfrac{90{,}000 \text{ cm}^2}{25 \text{ h}}$

27. **REASONING** *Explain* how $\dfrac{35 \text{ mi}}{60 \text{ min}}$ can be converted to a unit rate.

CONNECT SKILLS TO PROBLEM SOLVING Exercises 28–31 will help you prepare for problem solving.

Find the unit price of each item.

28. A 12 ounce box of cereal costs $2.98.

29. A 20 ounce bottle of water costs $.90.

30. A 16 ounce can of soup costs $.85.

31. A 14 ounce box of cat food costs $2.50.

SEE EXAMPLES 1 AND 2
on pp. 443–444
for Exs. 32–33

32. BABYSITTING You earned $16 for babysitting $1\frac{2}{3}$ hours. What is your hourly rate?

California @HomeTutor for problem solving help at classzone.com

33. HUMMINGBIRDS On average, a ruby-throated hummingbird beats its wings about 3000 times in 60 seconds. A giant hummingbird beats its wings about 180 times in 15 seconds. Which bird beats its wings faster?

California @HomeTutor for problem solving help at classzone.com

Ruby-throated hummingbird

34. GARDENING You remove weeds in a local park. You earn $7.50 per hour. How much do you earn for working 7 hours?

35. ◆ **MULTIPLE CHOICE** On average, a car gets 20 miles per gallon of gasoline. At this rate, how many gallons of gasoline will the car use to travel 80 miles?

(A) 2.8 gal   **(B)** 3.5 gal   **(C)** 4 gal   **(D)** 4.6 gal

SEE EXAMPLE 3
on p. 444
for Exs. 36–37

36. THEATER It will take about 40 person-hours to build the set for a school play. How many hours will it take for 5 people to build the set?

37. BUSINESS A supervisor estimates that it will take 300 person-days to complete a large order.

a. If 20 workers are available, how many days will it take to complete the order?

b. The supervisor would like the job completed in 12 days. How many workers are necessary to complete the job in this amount of time?

38. ◆ **MULTIPLE CHOICE** The table shows the costs of oranges at four grocery stores. Which grocery store prices its oranges using a constant unit rate?

(A) Store A   **(B)** Store B

(C) Store C   **(D)** Store D

Amount	Cost of Oranges at Four Stores			
	A	B	C	D
10 lb bag	$11.70	$11.70	$12.00	$12.00
20 lb bag	$22.90	$23.40	$24.00	$22.00
30 lb bag	$33.60	$35.10	$35.00	$32.00

39. ELECTRICITY Your local electric company charges $.10 per kilowatt-hour. The power consumption of your stereo is 0.35 kilowatt. Use the verbal model below to find the number of hours you can play your stereo during a month so that the total cost of using the stereo is $6.

| Power consumption | • | Number of hours of use | • | Cost per kilowatt-hour | = | Total cost |

SEE EXAMPLE 4
on p. 445
for Exs. 40–41

40. PAINTING Joe and his sister Andrea are painting a garage. Joe estimates that he can paint the garage in 12 hours and that his sister can paint the garage in 10 hours. About how long will it take them to paint the garage if they work together?

41. PUZZLE PROBLEM You can complete a job in 1 hour. You work with a friend who is 80% as efficient as you are. How much time can you save by getting help from a third person whose efficiency is twice that of your friend?

42. CHALLENGE One third pound of chicken costs $2.15. How much does 2.5 pounds of chicken cost?

43. CHALLENGE Your family owns a horse ranch. The pasture is a rectangle $\frac{1}{2}$ mile wide and $\frac{3}{4}$ mile long. You want to provide enough grazing area for each horse on your ranch. The recommended grazing area is 3 acres for every 2 horses. There are 640 acres in 1 square mile. What is the maximum number of horses you should have in the pasture?

◆ CALIFORNIA STANDARDS SPIRAL REVIEW

AF 2.2

44. Which expression is equivalent to $(-16t)(-3t^9)$? *(p. 399)*

(A) $-48t^8$ (B) $48t^9$ (C) $48t^{10}$ (D) $48t^{11}$

AF 3.1

45. Which is the graph of $y = x^2$? *(p. 413)*

(A) 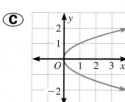   (B)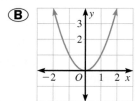

(C) 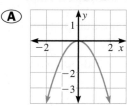   (D)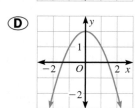

AF 4.1

46. The total cost to repair your car is $168. You pay $78 for parts and $45 for each hour of labor. How many hours did it take to repair the car? *(p. 270)*

(A) 1 h   (B) 1.5 h   (C) 2 h   (D) 3 h

8.3 Multi-Step Conversions

Standards

MG 1.1 Compare weights, capacities, geometric measures, times, and temperatures within and between measurement systems (e.g., miles per hour and feet per second, cubic inches to cubic centimeters).

MG 1.3 Use measures expressed as rates (e.g., speed, density) and measures expressed as products (e.g., person-days) **to solve problems; check the units of the solutions; and use dimensional analysis to check the reasonableness of the answer.**

Math and ASTRONOMY
Example 1, p. 449

Connect *Before* you converted measurements using one conversion factor. *Now* you will convert measurements using multiple conversion factors.

KEY VOCABULARY
- **unit rate,** *p. 443*
- **rate,** *p. 732*

To convert from one measure to another measure, you may need to multiply by more than one conversion factor. For example, you can convert 4 yards to inches as shown.

$$4 \text{ yd} \times \frac{3 \text{ ft}}{1 \text{ yd}} \times \frac{12 \text{ in.}}{1 \text{ ft}} = 144 \text{ in.}$$

EXAMPLE 1 Performing a Multi-Step Conversion

ASTRONOMY The time it takes for Saturn to orbit the sun is approximately 29.5 Earth years. About how long does it take Saturn to orbit the sun in seconds? Write your answer in scientific notation.

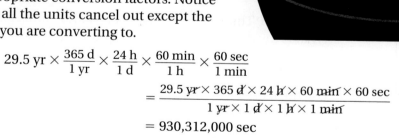

Sun
Earth
Saturn

SOLUTION

To convert years to seconds, use the appropriate conversion factors. Notice that all the units cancel out except the one you are converting to.

$$29.5 \text{ yr} \times \frac{365 \text{ d}}{1 \text{ yr}} \times \frac{24 \text{ h}}{1 \text{ d}} \times \frac{60 \text{ min}}{1 \text{ h}} \times \frac{60 \text{ sec}}{1 \text{ min}}$$

$$= \frac{29.5 \text{ yr} \times 365 \text{ d} \times 24 \text{ h} \times 60 \text{ min} \times 60 \text{ sec}}{1 \text{ yr} \times 1 \text{ d} \times 1 \text{ h} \times 1 \text{ min}}$$

$$= 930{,}312{,}000 \text{ sec}$$

$$\approx 9.3 \times 10^8 \text{ sec}$$

▶ **Answer** It takes Saturn about 9.3×10^8 seconds to orbit the sun.

✓ **GUIDED PRACTICE** for Example 1

Copy and complete the statement.

1. 9 d = __?__ min

2. 3 mi = __?__ in.

3. 50 c = __?__ gal

CHECK REASONABLENESS You can check the result of a conversion for reasonableness. Compare the original measurement and converted measurement to the measurements of real-life objects.

For example, the statement 11 ft = 95 cm is not reasonable because 11 ft is about the height of a basketball hoop, while 95 cm is about the length of a meter stick.

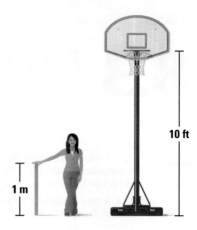

10 ft

1 m

EXAMPLE 2 ◆ Multiple Choice Practice

In a bicycle race, a participant's speed is 26.4 feet per second. What is the speed in miles per hour?

Ⓐ 0.3 mile per hour   Ⓑ 18 miles per hour

Ⓒ 25 miles per hour   Ⓓ 180 miles per hour

ELIMINATE CHOICES
A bicycle's speed should be less than the possible speed of a car. Because most cars cannot travel 180 miles per hour, it is not reasonable for a bicycle to travel 180 miles per hour. Eliminate choice D.

SOLUTION

To convert feet per second to miles per hour, use the appropriate conversion factors.

$$\frac{26.4 \text{ ft}}{1 \text{ sec}} \times \frac{1 \text{ mi}}{5280 \text{ ft}} \times \frac{60 \text{ sec}}{1 \text{ min}} \times \frac{60 \text{ min}}{1 \text{ h}} = \frac{95,040 \text{ mi}}{5280 \text{ h}} = \frac{18 \text{ mi}}{\text{h}}$$

So, the participant's speed is 18 miles per hour.

▶ **Answer** The correct answer is B. Ⓐ Ⓑ Ⓒ Ⓓ

EXAMPLE 3 Converting Density Measures

PLATINUM The density of platinum is 21.4 grams per cubic centimeter. What is the density of platinum in ounces per cubic inch?

SOLUTION

Use the fact that 1 oz ≈ 28.35 g and 1 in.^{3} ≈ 16.4 cm^3 to convert the density.

$$\frac{21.4 \text{ g}}{1 \text{ cm}^3} \times \frac{1 \text{ oz}}{28.35 \text{ g}} \times \frac{16.4 \text{ cm}^3}{1 \text{ in.}^3} = \frac{350.96 \text{ oz}}{28.35 \text{ in.}^3} \approx \frac{12.4 \text{ oz}}{1 \text{ in.}^3}$$

▶ **Answer** The density of platinum is about 12.4 ounces per cubic inch.

✓ **GUIDED PRACTICE**   for Examples 2 and 3

4. **WHAT IF?** In Example 2, suppose the participant's speed is only 9 miles per hour. What is the speed in feet per second?

5. Convert 7 grams per cubic centimeter to ounces per cubic inch.

8.3 EXERCISES

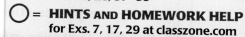

◆ = **MULTIPLE CHOICE PRACTICE**
Exs. 12, 28, 37–39

◯ = **HINTS** AND **HOMEWORK HELP**
for Exs. 7, 17, 29 at classzone.com

SKILLS • PROBLEM SOLVING • REASONING

1. **VOCABULARY** Copy and complete: A ratio of two quantities measured in different units is called a(n) __?__ .

2. **WRITING** *Explain* how you can use conversion factors to convert gallons to cups.

SEE EXAMPLE 1
on p. 449
for Exs. 3–12

CONVERTING MEASUREMENTS Copy and complete the statement. Round to the nearest whole number if necessary.

3. 14 yd = __?__ in.

4. 96 fl oz = __?__ qt

5. 2 km = __?__ mm

6. 500,000 mL = __?__ kL

7. 1,051,200 min = __?__ yr

8. 5200 mm ≈ __?__ ft

9. 915 g ≈ __?__ lb

10. 17 gal ≈ __?__ L

11. 3800 mL ≈ __?__ gal

12. ◆ **MULTIPLE CHOICE** How many miles are equivalent to 1,900,800 inches?

Ⓐ 12 mi
Ⓑ 30 mi
Ⓒ 36 mi
Ⓓ 360 mi

SEE EXAMPLE 2
on p. 450
for Exs. 13–16

CONVERTING RATES Copy and complete the statement. Round to the nearest whole number if necessary.

13. 20 inches per second = __?__ feet per minute

14. 3.3 meters per second ≈ __?__ kilometers per hour

15. 2 cents per second = __?__ dollars per hour

16. 10 millimeters per hour ≈ __?__ inches per day

SEE EXAMPLE 3
on p. 450
for Exs. 17–20

CONVERTING DENSITY MEASURES Copy and complete the statement. Round to the nearest whole number if necessary.

17. 14 grams per cubic centimeter ≈ __?__ ounces per cubic inch

18. 2 pounds per cubic inch ≈ __?__ grams per cubic centimeter

19. 11 ounces per cubic inch = __?__ pounds per cubic foot

20. 3000 kilograms per cubic meter ≈ __?__ ounces per cubic foot

ERROR ANALYSIS *Describe* and correct the error in the conversion.

21. 3 km ≈ __?__ ft

$$3 \text{ km} \times \frac{1 \text{ ft}}{1.609 \text{ km}} = \frac{3 \text{ km} \times 1 \text{ ft}}{1.609 \text{ km}}$$
$$\approx 1.86 \text{ ft}$$
So, 3 km ≈ 1.86 ft. ✗

22. 720 ft/h = __?__ in./min

$$\frac{720 \text{ ft}}{1 \text{ h}} \times \frac{1 \text{ in.}}{12 \text{ ft}} \times \frac{1 \text{ h}}{60 \text{ min}} = \frac{1 \text{ in.}}{1 \text{ min}}$$
So, 720 ft/h = 1 in./min. ✗

8.3 Multi-Step Conversions   **451**

CONNECT SKILLS TO PROBLEM SOLVING Exercises 23–25 will help you prepare for problem solving.

Write an expression that can be used to solve the problem.

23. You drive 1500 miles in 31 hours. How many minutes does it take you to drive 1500 miles?

24. The cost of cantaloupe is $1.12 per pound. What is the cost in cents per ounce?

25. A bear is running at a speed of 20 miles per hour. What is the bear's running speed in feet per second?

SEE EXAMPLES 1 AND 2
on pp. 449–450
for Exs. 26–28

26. WATERFALLS The two tallest waterfalls in California are Yosemite Falls and Snow Creek Falls. Their heights are 808 yards and 65,200 centimeters, respectively. Which waterfall is taller?

California @HomeTutor for problem solving help at classzone.com

27. FLYING SPEED An airplane travels at a speed of 500 miles per hour. About how fast does the airplane fly in meters per second?

California @HomeTutor for problem solving help at classzone.com

Yosemite Falls, California

28. ◆ MULTIPLE CHOICE A *light year* is the distance that light travels in one year. Light travels at a speed of about 186,000 miles per second. About how many miles are in one light year?

(A) 1.6×10^{10} mi   **(B)** 9.8×10^{10} mi   **(C)** 2.4×10^{11} mi   **(D)** 5.9×10^{12} mi

SEE EXAMPLE 3
on p. 450
for Exs. 29–31

METAL DENSITIES Convert the density of the metal to grams per cubic centimeter.

29. Silver   **30.** Copper   **31.** Gold

Density: 6.1 ounces per cubic inch

Density: 562 pounds per cubic foot

Density: 19,300 kilograms per cubic meter

32. TEMPERATURE The temperature of a substance increases by 10°C in 5 minutes. Write this as a unit rate. Then convert it to degrees Fahrenheit per hour.

33. REASONING Arriana claims that she can run 30 meters per second. Convert the speed to miles per hour to determine whether her claim is reasonable. *Explain* your reasoning.

34. **WOLVERINES** An adult male wolverine has a territory of about 386 square miles. An adult female wolverine has a territory of about 100,000,000 square meters. Does the male or female wolverine have the larger territory?

35. **CHALLENGE** The distance d (in inches) that a snail travels in t hours is given by the formula $d = 23t$. Write a new formula that gives the distance m (in miles) that a snail travels in t hours.

36. **CHALLENGE** The speed v (in meters per second) of a wave is given by $v = wf$ where w is the wavelength (in meters) and f is the frequency (in hertz). A sound wave with a wavelength of 0.85 meter has a frequency of 400 hertz. Approximate the speed of the sound wave in miles per hour.

Wolverine

◆ CALIFORNIA STANDARDS SPIRAL REVIEW

NS 2.2

37. Which of the following shows the next step in simplifying $\frac{9}{4} - \frac{3}{10}$ using the least common denominator? *(p. 91)*

(A) $\left(\frac{9}{4} \times \frac{5}{5}\right) - \left(\frac{3}{10} \times \frac{2}{2}\right)$ 　　　(B) $\left(\frac{9}{4} \times \frac{2}{2}\right) - \left(\frac{3}{10} \times \frac{5}{5}\right)$

(C) $\left(\frac{9}{4} \times \frac{3}{3}\right) - \left(\frac{3}{10} \times \frac{9}{9}\right)$ 　　　(D) $\left(\frac{9}{4} \times \frac{9}{9}\right) - \left(\frac{3}{10} \times \frac{3}{3}\right)$

AF 1.2

38. What is the value of $\frac{2^{x+y}}{3^{x+y}}$ when $x = 4$ and $y = 1$? *(p. 5)*

(A) $\frac{32}{243}$ 　　(B) $\frac{2}{3}$ 　　(C) $\frac{32}{27}$ 　　(D) $\frac{16}{9}$

MG 1.1

39. A train is 200 meters long. About how long is the train in feet? *(p. 437)*

(A) 61 ft 　　(B) 508 ft 　　(C) 600 ft 　　(D) 656 ft

QUIZ *for Lessons 8.1–8.3*

Copy and complete the statement. Round to the nearest whole number if necessary. *(pp. 437, 449)*

1. 31 yd = __?__ ft 　　　2. 91 g ≈ __?__ oz 　　　3. 5 in.^{2} ≈ __?__ cm^2

4. 3.5 qt = __?__ fl oz 　　5. 900 mm ≈ __?__ ft 　　6. 7.2 yr = __?__ h

Write the unit rate. *(p. 443)*

7. $\frac{2500 \text{ mi}}{5 \text{ h}}$ 　　　8. $\frac{99 \text{ cents}}{11 \text{ pencils}}$ 　　　9. $\frac{10.8°F}{3 \text{ h}}$

10. **WORK** A job takes about 150 person-hours to complete. To the nearest whole number, about how many 8 hour workdays will it take a staff of 6 workers to complete the job? *(p. 443)*

8.4 Segment and Angle Bisectors

Standards MG 3.1 **Identify** and construct **basic elements of geometric figures** (e.g., altitudes, **midpoints**, diagonals, **angle bisectors**, and **perpendicular bisectors**; central angles, radii, diameters, and chords of circles) by using a compass and straightedge.

Connect *Before* you identified line segments and angles. *Now* you will identify midpoints of segments and segment and angle bisectors.

Math and **RECREATION**
Ex. 25, p. 458

KEY VOCABULARY
- **congruent segments**
- **midpoint**
- **segment bisector**
- **perpendicular bisector**
- **congruent angles**
- **angle bisector**

Line segments that have the same length are called **congruent segments**. In the diagram at the right, you can say "the length of $\overline{AB}$ is equal to the length of $\overline{CD}$," which is written as $AB = CD$, or you can say "$\overline{AB}$ is congruent to $\overline{CD}$," which is written as $\overline{AB} \cong \overline{CD}$.

The **midpoint** of a segment is the point that divides the segment into two congruent segments. In the diagram below, M is the midpoint of $\overline{AB}$. So, $\overline{AM} \cong \overline{MB}$ and $AM = MB$.

EXAMPLE 1 Using a Midpoint

> **READING DIAGRAMS**
> In a diagram, tick marks indicate that segments are congruent.

Point M is the midpoint of $\overline{VW}$. Find the value of x.

SOLUTION

$\overline{VM} \cong \overline{MW}$	Definition of midpoint
$VM = MW$	Definition of congruent segments
$2x = 8$	Substitute.
$x = 4$	Divide each side by 2.

✓ **GUIDED PRACTICE** for Example 1

In Exercises 1–4, M is the midpoint of $\overline{AB}$. Find the value of x.

1. `12    3x` A M B

2. `2x − 1    25` A M B

3. `7x    35` A M B

4. `4x − 5    3x` A M B

5. Let M be the midpoint of $\overline{XY}$. If $XM = 5$ and $XY = 20t$, find the value of t.

REVIEW VOCABULARY
For help reviewing the terms *point, ray, line, segment,* and *plane,* see p. 735.

SEGMENT BISECTORS A **segment bisector** is a point, ray, line, line segment, or plane that intersects the segment at its midpoint. A segment bisector *bisects* a segment. A segment, ray, line, or plane that is perpendicular to a segment at its midpoint is called a **perpendicular bisector**.

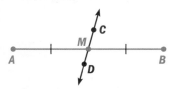

$\overleftrightarrow{CD}$ is a segment bisector of $\overline{AB}$.
So, $\overline{AM} \cong \overline{MB}$ and $AM = MB$.

$\overleftrightarrow{CD}$ is a perpendicular bisector of $\overline{AB}$.
So, $\overline{AM} \cong \overline{MB}$ and $AM = MB$.

EXAMPLE 2 **Identifying Segment Bisectors**

In the diagram, C is the midpoint of $\overline{AB}$. Tell whether the segment or line is a segment bisector of $\overline{AB}$, a perpendicular bisector of $\overline{AB}$, or neither.

a. $\overline{DE}$ **b.** $\overleftrightarrow{FG}$ **c.** $\overleftrightarrow{HJ}$

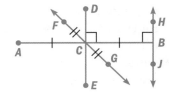

SOLUTION

a. Because $\overline{DE}$ intersects $\overline{AB}$ at its midpoint, and $\overline{DE}$ is perpendicular to $\overline{AB}$, $\overline{DE}$ is a perpendicular bisector of $\overline{AB}$.

b. Because $\overleftrightarrow{FG}$ intersects $\overline{AB}$ at its midpoint, and $\overleftrightarrow{FG}$ is not perpendicular to $\overline{AB}$, $\overleftrightarrow{FG}$ is a segment bisector of $\overline{AB}$.

c. $\overleftrightarrow{HJ}$ does not intersect $\overline{AB}$ at its midpoint, so $\overleftrightarrow{HJ}$ is not a bisector of $\overline{AB}$.

 GUIDED PRACTICE   **for Example 2**

6. In Example 2, C is the midpoint of $\overline{FG}$. Tell whether $\overline{AB}$ is a *segment bisector* of $\overline{FG}$, a *perpendicular bisector* of $\overline{FG}$, or *neither*.

READING DIAGRAMS
In a diagram, arcs indicate that angles are congruent.

CONGRUENT ANGLES Two angles are **congruent angles** if they have the same measure. In the diagram below, you can say "the measure of angle A is equal to the measure of angle B," which is written $m\angle A = m\angle B$. You can also say "angle A *is congruent to* angle B," which is written $\angle A \cong \angle B$.

ANGLE BISECTORS An **angle bisector** is a ray that divides an angle into two congruent angles. In the diagram at the right, $\overrightarrow{YW}$ bisects $\angle XYZ$.

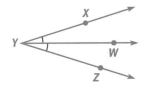

EXAMPLE 3 Using an Angle Bisector

REVIEW ANGLES
For help with classifying angles, turn to p. 736.

BASEBALL The foul lines of a baseball diamond form a right angle, $\angle ABC$, with vertex at home plate. The ray from home plate through second base, $\overrightarrow{BD}$, bisects $\angle ABC$. Find $m\angle ABD$.

SOLUTION

Because $\angle ABC$ is a right angle, it measures 90°.

$m\angle ABD = \frac{1}{2}(m\angle ABC)$ $\overrightarrow{BD}$ bisects $\angle ABC$.

$= \frac{1}{2}(90°)$ Substitute 90° for $m\angle ABC$.

$= 45°$ Simplify.

✓ **GUIDED PRACTICE**   for Example 3

7. Given that $\overrightarrow{RP}$ bisects $\angle SRT$, $m\angle PRT = (2x + 1)°$, and $m\angle SRP = (x + 20)°$, find the value of x.

8. **REASONING** Given that $\overrightarrow{AD}$ bisects $\angle BAC$ and $m\angle DAC = 75°$, is $\angle BAC$ *acute, right, obtuse,* or *straight? Explain.*

8.4 EXERCISES

HOMEWORK KEY

◆ = **MULTIPLE CHOICE PRACTICE**
   Exs. 11, 24, 30–32

○ = **HINTS AND HOMEWORK HELP**
   for Exs. 5, 17, 25 at classzone.com

SKILLS • PROBLEM SOLVING • REASONING

1. **VOCABULARY** Copy and complete: Point B is the __?__ of $\overline{AC}$ if B is on $\overline{AC}$ and $AB = BC$.

2. **VOCABULARY** Define *angle bisector*. Include a diagram in your answer.

3. **WRITING** *Explain* what it means to bisect a segment.

SEE EXAMPLE 1
on p. 454
for Exs. 4–11

MIDPOINTS In each diagram, M is the midpoint of the segment. Find the value of x.

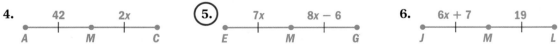

4.
```
   42        2x
A    M        C
```

5.
```
   7x      8x − 6
E     M       G
```

6.
```
  6x + 7     19
J     M        L
```

7.
```
  49     10x − 51
P    M       R
```

8.
```
  x + 15     35
S     M       U
```

9.
```
   73      5x − 22
X     M       Z
```

10. **ALGEBRA** Given that Y is the midpoint of $\overline{XZ}$, $XY = 5$, and $YZ = \frac{1}{2}x$, what is the value of x?

11. ◆ **MULTIPLE CHOICE** If M is the midpoint of $\overline{AB}$ and $MB = 12$, what is AB?

(A) 4   (B) 8   (C) 12   (D) 24

SEE EXAMPLE 2
on p. 455
for Exs. 12–15

SEGMENT BISECTORS In each diagram, J is the midpoint of $\overline{GH}$. Tell whether $\overleftrightarrow{CD}$ is a *segment bisector*, a *perpendicular bisector*, or *neither*.

12.

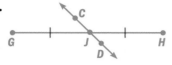

13.

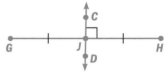

14.

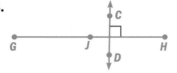

15.

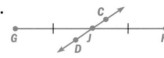

SEE EXAMPLE 3
on p. 456
for Exs. 16–17

ANGLE BISECTORS In each diagram, $\overrightarrow{BD}$ bisects $\angle ABC$. Find the value of x.

16.

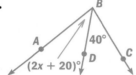

17.

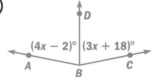

ERROR ANALYSIS *Describe* and correct the error in the statement.

18.

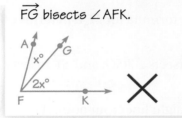

19.

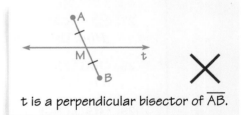

CONNECT SKILLS TO PROBLEM SOLVING Exercises 20–22 will help you prepare for problem solving.

In the diagram below, the post office is the midpoint of the segment formed by the school and the gym, and the gym is the midpoint of the segment formed by the school and the store. Find each distance.

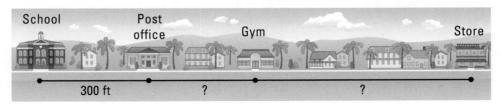

20. The distance between the gym and the post office

21. The distance between the post office and the store

22. The distance between the school and the store

23. OPTICS When light is reflected by a smooth surface, the *angle of incidence* equals the *angle of reflection*. In the diagram at the right, is $\vec{KR}$ an angle bisector of $\angle JKL$? *Explain.*

California **@HomeTutor** for problem solving help at classzone.com

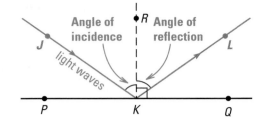

24. ◆ **MULTIPLE CHOICE** Your house, your friend's house, and your school are all on the same street. The distance between your house and your school is 0.8 mile. Your friend's house is the midpoint of the segment formed by your house and your school. On your way to school, you stop at your friend's house. How much farther do you have to walk?

(A) 0.4 mi   **(B)** 0.8 mi   **(C)** 1.6 mi   **(D)** 3.2 mi

California **@HomeTutor** for problem solving help at classzone.com

(25.) KITE In the kite, $\angle EKI$ is bisected by $\vec{KT}$ and $\angle ITE$ is bisected by $\vec{TK}$. Find the measures of $\angle EKI$ and $\angle ITE$.

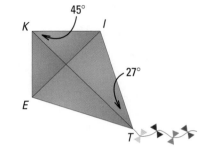

26. PUZZLE PROBLEM M_1 is the midpoint of $\overline{AB}$, M_2 is the midpoint of $\overline{M_1B}$, and in general M_n is the midpoint of $\overline{M_{n-1}B}$ where n is a positive integer greater than 1. Find M_7B if $AB = 1$.

27. ⟨XY⟩ **ALGEBRA** In Exercise 26, write a formula for M_nB in terms of n. (*Hint:* Use powers of 2.)

28. CHALLENGE $\vec{SQ}$ bisects $\angle RST$, $\vec{SP}$ bisects $\angle RSQ$, and $\vec{SV}$ bisects $\angle RSP$. If $m\angle VSP = 7°$, find $m\angle TSQ$.

29. CHALLENGE You are walking in a straight line from point A to point D. You walk to point B, which is the midpoint of $\overline{AD}$. You then walk one third of the remaining distance to point C. Find CD if $AD = 180$ yd.

◆ CALIFORNIA STANDARDS SPIRAL REVIEW

AF 4.1

30. What is the solution of $2x + 4 = -10$? *(p. 270)*

(A) -7 **(B)** -3 **(C)** 3 **(D)** 7

NS 2.3

31. What is the simplified form of $\dfrac{y^6 \cdot y^3}{y^9}$? *(p. 393)*

(A) 1 **(B)** y **(C)** y^2 **(D)** $2y$

AF 3.1

32. A particle accelerates at a rate of 12 m/sec^2. The equation $d = 6t^2$ models the distance d (in meters) traveled by the particle in t seconds. What is the distance that the particle travels in 1 minute? *(p. 413)*

(A) 6 m   **(B)** 72 m   **(C)** 360 m   **(D)** 21,600 m

8.4 Copy, Bisect, and Add Segments and Angles

MATERIALS · compass · straightedge

Standards

MG 3.1 Identify and **construct basic elements of geometric figures** (e.g., altitudes, **midpoints**, diagonals, **angle bisectors**, and **perpendicular bisectors**; central angles, radii, diameters, and chords of circles) **by using a compass and straightedge.**

QUESTION How can you copy, bisect, and add segments and angles?

A *construction* is a geometric drawing that uses a limited set of tools, usually a *compass* and *straightedge*.

EXPLORE 1 Copy a segment

Use the following steps to construct a segment that is congruent to $\overline{AB}$.

STEP 1	STEP 2	STEP 3

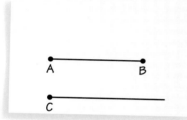 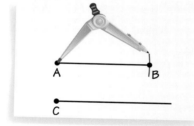 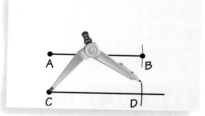

Draw a segment
Use a straightedge to draw a segment longer than $\overline{AB}$.

Measure length
Set your compass at the length of $\overline{AB}$.

Copy length
Mark point D on the new segment. $\overline{CD} \cong \overline{AB}$.

EXPLORE 2 Bisect a segment

Use the following steps to construct a perpendicular bisector of $\overline{AB}$.

STEP 1	STEP 2	STEP 3

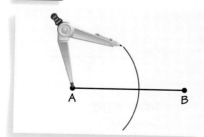 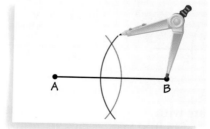 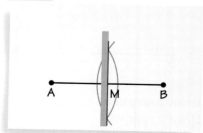

Draw an arc
Place the compass at A. Use a setting that is greater than one half of AB. Draw an arc.

Draw a second arc
Keep the same setting. Place the compass at B. Draw another arc as shown.

Bisect segment
Draw a segment through the two points of intersection. This is a perpendicular bisector.

EXPLORE 3 Add segments

Use the following steps to construct a segment with length $AB + CD$.

STEP 1

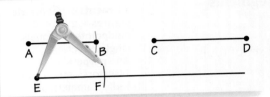

Measure and copy $\overline{AB}$
Use a straightedge to draw a segment
clearly longer than the sum of AB and CD.
Label point E on the new segment. Then
set your compass at the length of $\overline{AB}$. Place
the compass at E. Mark point F on the new
segment.

$EF = AB.$

STEP 2

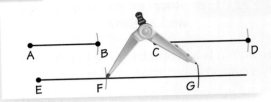

Measure and copy $\overline{CD}$
Set your compass at the length of $\overline{CD}$. Place
the compass at F. Mark point G on the new
segment.

$FG = CD.$
So, $EG = AB + CD.$

EXPLORE 4 Copy an angle

Use the following steps to construct an angle that is congruent to $\angle A$. In
this construction, the *radius* of an arc is the distance from the point where
the compass point rests (the *center* of the arc) to a point on the arc drawn
by the compass.

STEP 1

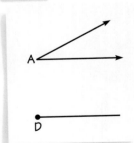

Draw a segment
Draw a segment.
Label point D on
the segment.

STEP 2

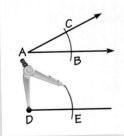

Draw arcs
Draw an arc with
center A. Using the
same radius, draw
an arc with center D.
Label B, C, and E.

STEP 3

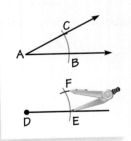

Draw arcs
Draw an arc with
radius BC and
center E. Label the
intersection of the
arcs F.

STEP 4

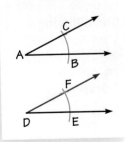

Draw a ray
Draw $\overrightarrow{DF}$.
$\angle EDF \cong \angle BAC.$

EXPLORE 5 · Bisect an angle

Use the following steps to construct a bisector of ∠A.

STEP 1

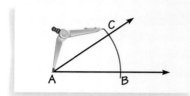

Draw an arc
Place the compass at *A*. Draw an arc that intersects both sides of the angle. Label the intersections *C* and *B*.

STEP 2

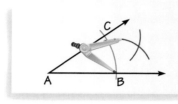

Draw arcs
Place the compass at *C*. Draw an arc. Then place the compass at *B*. Using the same radius, draw another arc.

STEP 3

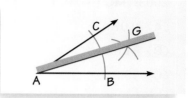

Draw a ray
Label the intersection *G*. Use a straightedge to draw a ray through *A* and *G*. $\overrightarrow{AG}$ bisects ∠*A*.

EXPLORE 6 · Add angles

Use the following steps to add ∠A and ∠G.

STEP 1

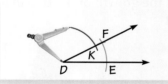

Copy angle and draw arc
Copy ∠*G* and name it ∠*FDE*. Set your compass to a radius of *AB*. Using this radius, draw an arc with center *D*. Label the intersection *K*.

STEP 2

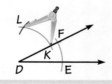

Draw arcs
Set your compass to a radius of *BC*. Keep this setting and draw an arc with center *K*. Label the intersection *L*.

STEP 3

Draw a ray
Draw $\overrightarrow{DL}$.

$m\angle LDE = m\angle A + m\angle G.$

DRAW CONCLUSIONS · Use your observations to complete these exercises

1. Draw $\overline{AB}$. Construct $\overline{CD}$ such that $CD = 2 \cdot AB$.

2. Draw ∠*XYZ*. Construct ∠*LMN* such that $m\angle LMN = 2 \cdot m\angle XYZ$.

3. **CHALLENGE** Construct an angle whose measure is 45°, without using a protractor.

Multiple Choice Practice for Lessons 8.1–8.4

1. Each person in the United States ate an average of about 1.1 pounds of Swiss cheese during 2003. On average, how many ounces of Swiss cheese did each person eat in 2003? **MG 1.1, MR 1.1**

   (A) 0.07 oz

   (B) 11 oz

   (C) 13.2 oz

   (D) 17.6 oz

2. Which number completes the statement 15 ounces per cubic inch = __?__ pounds per cubic foot? **MG 1.1**

   (A) 11.25   (B) 135

   (C) 1620   (D) 25,920

3. Alexis can wash her car in 10 minutes. It takes Leopold 15 minutes to do the same job. How long would it take them to wash the car together? **MG 1.3**

   (A) 5 min

   (B) 6 min

   (C) 8 min

   (D) 12.5 min

4. Which statement is *not* supported by the diagram? **MG 3.1, MR 2.5**

   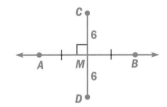

   (A) $\overleftrightarrow{AB}$ is a segment bisector.

   (B) $\overline{CD}$ is a perpendicular bisector.

   (C) The length of $\overline{MB}$ is 6.

   (D) The length of $\overline{CD}$ is 12.

5. In the diagram below, $\overrightarrow{BD}$ bisects $\angle ABC$. What is $m\angle DBC$? **MG 3.1**

   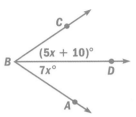

   (A) 5°   (B) 7°

   (C) 35°   (D) 70°

6. To the nearest whole number, which number completes the statement $39 \text{ cm}^2 \approx \underline{\ ?\ } \text{ in.}^2$? **MG 1.1**

   (A) 6

   (B) 15

   (C) 99

   (D) 252

7. A tree will grow as shown in the diagram. Which rate gives the growth of the tree in feet per year? **MG 1.3**

   (A) 2 ft/yr

   (B) 2.6 ft/yr

   (C) 20 ft/yr

   (D) 26 ft/yr

   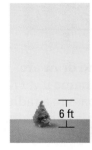

   6 ft

   26 ft

   10 years later

8. Which rate is equivalent to $\dfrac{\$520}{40 \text{ h}}$? **MG 1.3**

   (A) $\dfrac{\$50}{5 \text{ h}}$

   (B) $\dfrac{\$210}{20 \text{ h}}$

   (C) $\dfrac{\$13}{1 \text{ h}}$

   (D) $\dfrac{\$140}{10 \text{ h}}$

8.5 Triangles and Their Areas

Standards

MG 2.1 Use formulas routinely for finding the perimeter and area of basic two-dimensional figures and the surface area and volume of basic three-dimensional figures, **including** rectangles, parallelograms, trapezoids, squares, **triangles**, circles, prisms, and cylinders.

MG 3.1 Identify and construct **basic elements of geometric figures** (e.g., **altitudes**, **midpoints**, diagonals, angle bisectors, and perpendicular bisectors; central angles, radii, diameters, and chords of circles) by using a compass and straightedge.

Math and
RECREATION
Ex. 25, p. 467

Connect   *Before* you found areas of rectangles. *Now* you will find areas of triangles.

KEY VOCABULARY
- vertex
- altitude
- base
- height
- median of a triangle

A point where two sides of a triangle meet is called a **vertex** (plural *vertices*). A triangle has three vertices.

An **altitude** of a triangle is the perpendicular segment from a vertex to the side opposite the vertex, or to the line containing the opposite side. The length of an altitude is a **height** of a triangle. The side of the triangle that is perpendicular to an altitude is a **base**. A triangle has three altitudes and three bases associated with those altitudes.

The height of a triangle is the length of an altitude.

base

In an obtuse triangle, two altitudes are outside the triangle.

In the following activity, you will investigate how to use a base and height of a triangle to find the triangle's area.

ACTIVITY

About the Standards

You make and test conjectures (MR 2.4) in this activity.

STEP 1 **Copy** the diagram on graph paper.

STEP 2 **Cut** out the three pieces.

STEP 3 **Arrange** the pieces to make two equal-sized triangles.

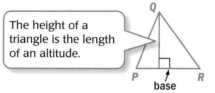

STEP 4 **Compare** the height of triangle 2 to the height of the original rectangle. What is the area of the rectangle? of triangle 2?

STEP 5 **Draw** your own triangle on graph paper so that its longest side is a side of a rectangle and the point where the two shorter sides of the triangle meet touches the opposite side of the rectangle. Find the triangle's area by following the steps above.

STEP 6 **Write** a formula for the area of a triangle.

Area of a Triangle

Words   The area of a triangle is one half the product of its base b and height h.

Algebra $A = \frac{1}{2}bh$ **Diagram**

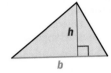

EXAMPLE 1   Area and Perimeter of a Triangle

REVIEW PERIMETER
For help with perimeter, see p. 742.

SAILBOATS Find the area and perimeter of the sail.

SOLUTION

$A = \frac{1}{2}bh$ $P = 171 + 159 + 159$

$\quad = \frac{1}{2}(159)(144)$ $= 489$

$\quad = 11{,}448$

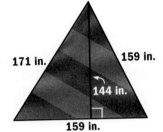

▶ **Answer** The area of the sail is $11{,}448$ in.^{2}, and the perimeter is 489 in.

EXAMPLE 2   Finding the Area of a Triangle

Find the area of the triangle.

SOLUTION

$A = \frac{1}{2}bh$ Write area formula.

$\quad = \frac{1}{2}(7)(16)$ Substitute values.

$\quad = 56 \text{ m}^2$ Multiply.

✓ **GUIDED PRACTICE**   for Examples 1 and 2

Find the area and perimeter of the triangle.

1.

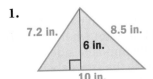

2.

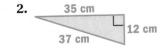

3.

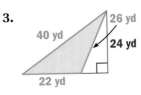

4. Draw a triangle with a height of 5 centimeters and a base of 10 centimeters. Find the area of the triangle.

MEDIAN OF A TRIANGLE A **median** of a triangle is a segment from a vertex to the midpoint of the opposite side. Unlike an altitude, a median is always contained entirely within the triangle.

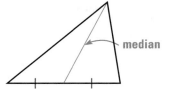 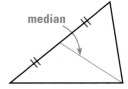 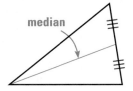

EXAMPLE 3 Naming Segments in Triangles

Tell whether the red segment is a *median*, *altitude*, or *both*.

a. 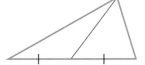 b. 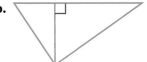 c.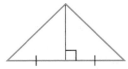

SOLUTION

a. The red segment intersects the opposite side at its midpoint, but it is not perpendicular. So, the segment is a median.

b. The red segment does not intersect the opposite side at its midpoint, but it is perpendicular. So, the segment is an altitude.

c. The red segment intersects the opposite side at its midpoint and it is perpendicular. So, the segment is both a median and an altitude.

✓ **GUIDED PRACTICE** for Example 3

Tell whether the red segment is a *median*, *altitude*, or *both*.

5.  6.  7.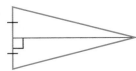

8.5 EXERCISES

HOMEWORK KEY ◆ = **MULTIPLE CHOICE PRACTICE**
Exs. 13, 23, 29–31

○ = **HINTS** AND **HOMEWORK HELP**
for Exs. 7, 11, 25 at classzone.com

SKILLS • PROBLEM SOLVING • REASONING

1. **VOCABULARY** Copy and complete: A segment whose endpoints are a vertex and the midpoint of the opposite side is a(n) ? of a triangle.

2. **WRITING** Can a median of a triangle also be an altitude? *Explain.*

**SEE EXAMPLES
1 AND 2**
on p. 464
for Exs. 3–9

FINDING AREA Find the area and perimeter of the triangle.

3.

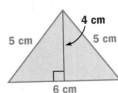
4 cm
5 cm   5 cm
6 cm

4.

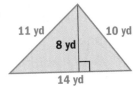
11 yd   10 yd
8 yd
14 yd

5.

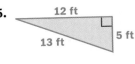
12 ft
13 ft   5 ft

6.

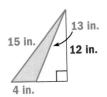
13 in.
15 in.   12 in.
4 in.

7.

10 mm
17 mm
8 mm
6 mm   9 mm

8.

55 m   9 m
48 m   73 m   80 m

9. ERROR ANALYSIS *Describe* and correct the error in finding the area of a triangle with a base of 5 inches and a height of 4 inches.

$$A = \frac{1}{2}(5 \text{ in.})(4 \text{ in.})$$
$$A = \frac{1}{2}(20 \text{ in.})$$
$$A = 10 \text{ in.}$$

SEE EXAMPLE 3
on p. 465
for Exs. 10–12

IDENTIFYING SEGMENTS Tell whether the red segment is a *median*, *altitude*, or *both*.

10.

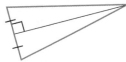

11.

12.

13. ◆ MULTIPLE CHOICE A triangle has an area of 182 square feet and a height of 13 feet. What is the length of the base?

  (A) 14 ft   **(B)** 25 ft   **(C)** 28 ft   **(D)** 32 ft

14. ❴xy❵ ALGEBRA A triangle has an area of 36 square meters, a height of 8 meters, and a base of $3x$ meters. What is the value of x?

REASONING *Describe* how the area of a triangle changes when the indicated change is made.

15. Double the height.

16. Double the base.

17. Double both the height and the base.

18. Change the triangle's shape, but not its base or height.

CONNECT SKILLS TO PROBLEM SOLVING Exercises 19–22 will help you prepare for problem solving.

    Find the area of the object described.

19. A triangular tile has a height of 4 inches and a base of 5 inches.

20. A triangular window has a height of 2.5 feet and a base of 3 feet.

21. A triangular sign has a base and height each measuring 7 feet.

22. A triangular pennant has a base of 8 inches and a height of 22 inches.

◆ = **MULTIPLE CHOICE PRACTICE**   ◯ = **HINTS AND HOMEWORK HELP** at classzone.com

SEE EXAMPLE 1
on p. 464
for Ex. 23

23. ◆ **MULTIPLE CHOICE** The flag of Puerto Rico is shown at the right. What fraction of the flag's area does the triangle cover?

14 in.

9 in.

21 in.

Ⓐ $\frac{3}{14}$ Ⓑ $\frac{7}{32}$

Ⓒ $\frac{1}{4}$ Ⓓ $\frac{9}{28}$

California @HomeTutor for problem solving help at classzone.com

24. **CHAIR DESIGN** The area of the triangular back of a chair is 216 square inches. The base of the triangular back is 2 feet. Find its height.

California @HomeTutor for problem solving help at classzone.com

25. **HANG GLIDER** The base of a triangular hang glider wing is 208 inches and the area is 16,848 square inches. What is the height of the wing?

26. **HONEYCOMB** A honeycomb is made up of regular *hexagons*, as shown at the right. Find the area and perimeter of one of the regular hexagons. All the triangles are congruent.

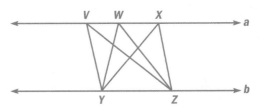

2 mm

1.732 mm

27. **CHALLENGE** Given points $A(0, 0)$, $B(0, 6)$, $C(8, 0)$, and $D(31, 6)$, explain why the area of triangle ABC is equal to the area of triangle ADC.

28. **CHALLENGE** In the diagram, $\overline{VX} \cong \overline{YZ}$, and the distance between lines a and b is constant. *Explain* why triangles VXZ, WYZ, and XYZ have the same area.

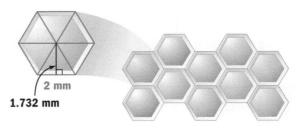

◆ CALIFORNIA STANDARDS SPIRAL REVIEW

NS 1.4

29. Which number is *not* a rational number? *(p. 225)*

Ⓐ $-\frac{7}{8}$ Ⓑ 1   Ⓒ $1\frac{2}{3}$ Ⓓ $\sqrt{5}$

AF 2.1

30. Which expression is equivalent to $\{(-2)^{-3}\}^4$? *(p. 386)*

Ⓐ -4096 Ⓑ $-\frac{1}{4096}$ Ⓒ $\frac{1}{4096}$ Ⓓ 4096

MG 1.3

31. A falcon is flying at a rate of 41 miles per hour, a hawk is flying at a rate of 50 feet per second, and an owl is flying at a rate of 6500 feet every two minutes. Which bird is flying the slowest? *(p. 449)*

Ⓐ Falcon   Ⓑ Hawk   Ⓒ Owl   Ⓓ Owl and hawk

8.5 Constructing Triangles

MATERIALS · compass · straightedge

Standards

MG 3.1 Identify and **construct basic elements of geometric figures** (e.g., **altitudes**, midpoints, diagonals, angle bisectors, and perpendicular bisectors; central angles, radii, diameters, and chords of circles) **by using a compass and straightedge.**

QUESTION How can you construct triangles and altitudes?

EXPLORE 1 Copy a triangle

Use the following steps to copy the triangle at the right.

| STEP 1 | STEP 2 | STEP 3 | STEP 4 |

 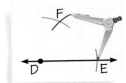 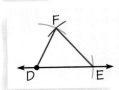

Copy $\overline{AB}$
Draw *D* on a line. Set the compass to the length of $\overline{AB}$. Place the compass at *D*. Mark *E*.

Copy $\overline{AC}$
Set the compass to the length of $\overline{AC}$. Place the compass at *D* and draw an arc as shown.

Copy $\overline{BC}$
Set the compass to the length of $\overline{BC}$. Place the compass at *E* and draw an arc. Label *F*.

Draw a triangle
Draw $\overline{DF}$ and $\overline{EF}$. Triangle *DEF* is congruent to triangle *ABC*.

EXPLORE 2 Construct an equilateral triangle

Use the following steps to draw an equilateral triangle.

| STEP 1 | STEP 2 | STEP 3 |

 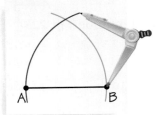 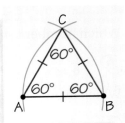

Draw an arc
Draw $\overline{AB}$. Place the compass at *A* and draw an arc that passes through *B*.

Draw a second arc
Place the compass at *B* and draw an arc through *A* that intersects the other arc.

Draw a triangle
The intersection of the arcs is point *C*. Draw $\overline{AC}$ and $\overline{BC}$ to form an equilateral triangle.

EXPLORE 3 **Construct an altitude of a triangle**

Use the following steps to construct an altitude from vertex *N* of the triangle at the right.

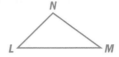

STEP 1	**STEP 2**	**STEP 3**	**STEP 4**
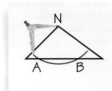	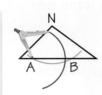		
Draw an arc Copy the triangle. Place the compass at *N* and construct *A* and *B* as shown.	**Draw an arc from *A*** Use a setting greater than half the length of $\overline{AB}$. Draw an arc as shown.	**Draw an arc from *B*** Keep the same compass setting. Place the compass at *B*. Draw another arc.	**Draw an altitude** Use the line through the intersections of the two arcs to draw the altitude from *N*.

EXPLORE 4 **Construct a right triangle**

Use the following steps to draw a right triangle.

STEP 1	**STEP 2**	**STEP 3**	**STEP 4**
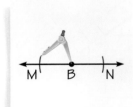	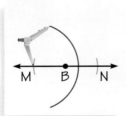	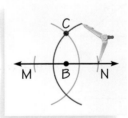	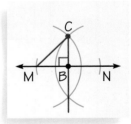
Draw a point Label *B* on a line. Place the compass at *B*. Use the same setting to construct *M* and *N*.	**Draw an arc** Place the compass at *M*. Use a compass setting greater than the length of $\overline{MB}$. Draw an arc.	**Draw a second arc** Keep the same compass setting. Place the compass at *N*. Draw an arc. Label *C* as shown.	**Draw a triangle** Draw $\overline{MC}$ and $\overline{BC}$ to form right triangle *MBC*.

DRAW CONCLUSIONS Use your observations to complete these exercises

1. Construct an isosceles triangle.

2. Construct an altitude of the triangle constructed in Exercise 1.

8.6 Modeling the Pythagorean Theorem

MATERIALS • graph paper

Standards

MG 3.3 Know and understand the Pythagorean theorem and its converse and use it to find the length of the missing side of a right triangle and the lengths of other line segments and, in some situations, **empirically verify the Pythagorean theorem by direct measurement.**

QUESTION   How can you use graph paper to find the length of a right triangle's *hypotenuse*, which is the side opposite the right angle?

EXPLORE   Find the length of the hypotenuse of a right triangle

Find the length of the hypotenuse of a right triangle whose other two sides are 3 units and 4 units long.

STEP 1 **Draw** the right triangle on graph paper. The sides of the triangle that form the right angle are called *legs*. For each leg, draw a square that has the leg as one side. What is the sum of the areas of these two squares?

STEP 2 **Measure** the hypotenuse using graph paper. If you draw a square with the hypotenuse as one side, what is its area?

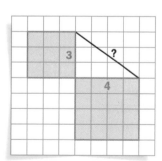

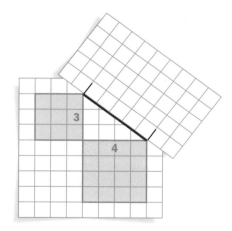

STEP 3 **Compare** the sum of the areas you found in Step 1 to the area you found in Step 2. What do you notice?

DRAW CONCLUSIONS   Use your observations to complete these exercises

Repeat Steps 1–3 for right triangles with legs of the given lengths.

1. 5, 12   2. 6, 8   3. 8, 15

4. **REASONING** Let the lengths of the legs of a right triangle be a and b, and the length of the hypotenuse be c. Write a conjecture about the relationship between a, b, and c.

8.6 The Pythagorean Theorem and Its Converse

Math and RECREATION
Ex. 35, p. 475

Standards MG 3.3 **Know and understand the Pythagorean theorem and its converse and use it to find the length of the missing side of a right triangle and the lengths of other line segments** and, in some situations, empirically verify the Pythagorean theorem by direct measurement.

Connect *Before* you found areas of triangles. *Now* you will use the Pythagorean Theorem to find unknown side lengths of right triangles.

KEY VOCABULARY
- leg
- hypotenuse
- Pythagorean Theorem
- converse

In a right triangle, the sides that form the right angle are called **legs**. The side opposite the right angle, which is always the longest side, is the **hypotenuse**. As you may have observed in the activity on page 470, the lengths of the legs and the hypotenuse are related by the **Pythagorean Theorem**.

KEY CONCEPT   *For Your Notebook*

Pythagorean Theorem

Words   For any right triangle, the sum of the squares of the lengths of the legs equals the square of the length of the hypotenuse.

$a = 3$ $c = 5$ $b = 4$

Algebra $a^2 + b^2 = c^2$ **Numbers** $3^2 + 4^2 = 5^2$

EXAMPLE 1 Finding the Length of a Hypotenuse

Find the length of the hypotenuse of a right triangle with a 15 inch leg and a 20 inch leg.

$$a^2 + b^2 = c^2 \qquad \text{Pythagorean Theorem}$$

$$15^2 + 20^2 = c^2 \qquad \text{Substitute 15 for } a \text{ and 20 for } b.$$

$$225 + 400 = c^2 \qquad \text{Evaluate powers.}$$

$$625 = c^2 \qquad \text{Add.}$$

$$\pm\sqrt{625} = c \qquad \text{Take square roots of each side.}$$

$$\sqrt{625} = c \qquad \text{Disregard negative square root.}$$

$$25 = c \qquad \text{Evaluate square root.}$$

INTERPRET RESULTS
Lengths cannot be negative, so disregard negative solutions.

▶ **Answer** The length of the hypotenuse is 25 inches.

INDIRECT MEASURE Some real-life measurements may be difficult to find directly. You may be able to find such measurements *indirectly*. For example, if you know the lengths of two sides of a right triangle, you can use the Pythagorean Theorem to find the length of the third side.

EXAMPLE 2 ◆ **Multiple Choice Practice**

You are parasailing as shown in the diagram at the right. After you get airborne and the boat reaches cruising speed, your position is 200 feet behind the boat. To the nearest foot, how high are you above the water?

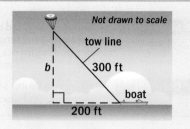
Not drawn to scale
tow line
300 ft
b
boat
200 ft

A −224 ft   **B** 224 ft

C 301 ft   **D** 361 ft

ELIMINATE CHOICES
Height is positive, so choice A can be eliminated.

SOLUTION

$$a^2 + b^2 = c^2$$ **Pythagorean Theorem**

$$200^2 + b^2 = 300^2$$ **Substitute 200 for *a* and 300 for *c*.**

$$40{,}000 + b^2 = 90{,}000$$ **Evaluate powers.**

$$b^2 = 50{,}000$$ **Subtract 40,000 from each side.**

$$b = \sqrt{50{,}000}$$ **Take positive square root of each side.**

$$b \approx 223.6$$ **Approximate square root.**

You are about 224 feet above the water.

▶ Answer The correct answer is B. Ⓐ Ⓑ Ⓒ Ⓓ

Animated **Math**

For an interactive example of using the Pythagorean Theorem, go to **classzone.com.**

EXAMPLE 3 **Finding the Length of an Altitude**

Find the length of the altitude shown. Round to the nearest tenth if necessary.

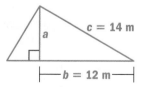
c = 14 m
a
b = 12 m

SOLUTION

Use the Pythagorean Theorem to find the length *a* of the altitude.

$$a^2 + b^2 = c^2$$ **Pythagorean Theorem**

$$a^2 + 12^2 = 14^2$$ **Substitute 12 for *b* and 14 for *c*.**

$$a^2 + 144 = 196$$ **Evaluate powers.**

$$a^2 = 52$$ **Subtract 144 from each side.**

$$a = \sqrt{52}$$ **Take positive square root of each side.**

$$a \approx 7.2$$ **Approximate square root.**

▶ Answer The length of the altitude is about 7.2 meters.

1. Find the length of the hypotenuse of a right triangle with a 28 inch leg and a 45 inch leg.

Find the unknown length. Round to the nearest tenth if necessary.

2. c $a = 7.5$ in.
   $b = 18$ in.

3. a $b = 8$ m
   $c = 16$ m

4. 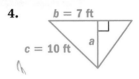 $b = 7$ ft
   $c = 10$ ft a

KEY CONCEPT   *For Your Notebook*

Converse of the Pythagorean Theorem

The Pythagorean Theorem can be written as an if-then statement with two parts.

Theorem If a triangle is a right triangle, then $a^2 + b^2 = c^2$.

When you reverse the parts of an if-then statement, the new statement is called the **converse** of the original statement.

Converse If $a^2 + b^2 = c^2$, then the triangle is a right triangle.

The converse of a *true* statement may or may not be true. The converse of the Pythagorean Theorem is true. You can use the converse of the Pythagorean Theorem to decide whether a triangle is a right triangle.

EXAMPLE 4   **Identifying Right Triangles**

About the Standards

You use the converse of the Pythagorean Theorem to make precise calculations (MR 2.8).

Tell whether the triangle with the given side lengths is a right triangle.

a. $a = 6, b = 8, c = 10$

$$a^2 + b^2 \stackrel{?}{=} c^2$$
$$6^2 + 8^2 \stackrel{?}{=} 10^2$$
$$36 + 64 \stackrel{?}{=} 100$$
$$100 = 100 \checkmark$$

▶ **Answer** A right triangle

b. $a = 10, b = 12, c = 16$

$$a^2 + b^2 \stackrel{?}{=} c^2$$
$$10^2 + 12^2 \stackrel{?}{=} 16^2$$
$$100 + 144 \stackrel{?}{=} 256$$
$$244 \neq 256$$

▶ **Answer** Not a right triangle

✓ **GUIDED PRACTICE**   for Example 4

Tell whether the triangle with the given side lengths is a right triangle.

5. 3 in., 4 in., 6 in.
6. 14 cm, 48 cm, 50 cm
7. 10 ft, 20 ft, 29 ft
8. 7 m, 8 m, 9 m
9. 0.3 in., 0.4 in., 0.5 in.
10. 16 mm, 30 mm, 34 mm

8.6 EXERCISES

HOMEWORK KEY

◆ = **MULTIPLE CHOICE PRACTICE**
Exs. 30, 36, 43–45

○ = **HINTS AND HOMEWORK HELP**
for Exs. 5, 19, 37 at classzone.com

SKILLS • PROBLEM SOLVING • REASONING

1. **VOCABULARY** Copy and complete: In a right triangle, the side opposite the right angle is called the __?__.

2. **WRITING** *Explain* what the converse of an if-then statement is.

SEE EXAMPLES 1 AND 2
on pp. 471–472
for Exs. 3–10

FINDING THE HYPOTENUSE Find the length of the hypotenuse.

3.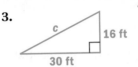

4.

5.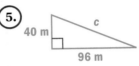

FINDING LEGS Find the length of the unknown leg. Round to the nearest tenth if necessary.

6.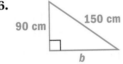

7.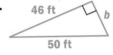

8. 46 ft, 50 ft, b

ERROR ANALYSIS *Describe* and correct the error in finding the missing length. Round to the nearest tenth of a foot.

9.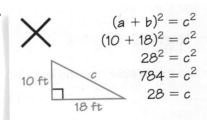

$$(a + b)^2 = c^2$$
$$(10 + 18)^2 = c^2$$
$$28^2 = c^2$$
$$784 = c^2$$
$$28 = c$$

10.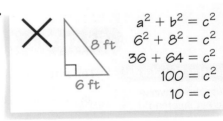

$$a^2 + b^2 = c^2$$
$$6^2 + 8^2 = c^2$$
$$36 + 64 = c^2$$
$$100 = c^2$$
$$10 = c$$

SEE EXAMPLE 3
on p. 472
for Exs. 11–13

FINDING LENGTHS OF ALTITUDES Find the length of the altitude. Round to the nearest tenth if necessary.

11.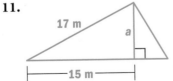

12.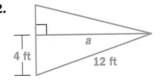

13.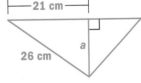

SEE EXAMPLE 4
on p. 473
for Exs. 14–19

CLASSIFYING TRIANGLES Tell whether the triangle with the given side lengths is a right triangle.

14. 4 m, 5 m, 7 m

15. 50 in., 64 in., 80 in.

16. 85 ft, 204 ft, 221 ft

17. 1.2 mi, 1.6 mi, 2 mi

18. 6.5 cm, 15.6 cm, 16.9 cm

19. 28.8 m, 8.4 m, 31 m

FINDING UNKNOWN LENGTHS Let *a* and *b* represent the lengths of the legs of a right triangle, and let *c* represent the length of the hypotenuse. Find the unknown length.

20. $a = 1.5$, $b = \underline{\ ?\ }$, $c = 2.5$

21. $a = \underline{\ ?\ }$, $b = 123$, $c = 139.4$

22. $a = 2.8$, $b = 4.5$, $c = \underline{\ ?\ }$

23. $a = 4.5$, $b = \underline{\ ?\ }$, $c = 7.5$

24. $a = \underline{\ ?\ }$, $b = 2$, $c = \sqrt{13}$

25. $a = \sqrt{8}$, $b = 1$, $c = \underline{\ ?\ }$

26. $a = \underline{\ ?\ }$, $b = 37.5$, $c = 42.5$

27. $a = 2.5$, $b = 6$, $c = \underline{\ ?\ }$

28. $a = 2$, $b = \sqrt{21}$, $c = \underline{\ ?\ }$

29. $a = \sqrt{6}$, $b = \underline{\ ?\ }$, $c = \sqrt{15}$

30. ◆ **MULTIPLE CHOICE** What is the perimeter of a right triangle whose leg lengths are 3.6 inches and 7.7 inches?

(A) 8.5 in.　　**(B)** 18.1 in.　　**(C)** 19.8 in.　　**(D)** 27.72 in.^{2}

31. **REASONING** An isosceles right triangle has a hypotenuse with a length of 6 feet. Find the length of each leg to the nearest hundredth of a foot.

CONNECT SKILLS TO PROBLEM SOLVING Exercises 32–34 will help you prepare for problem solving.

Find the distance between opposite corners of the object. Round to the nearest tenth.

32. A square checkerboard has side lengths of 18 inches.

33. A rectangular driveway is 8 feet wide and 20 feet long.

34. A rectangular basketball court is 50 feet wide and 94 feet long.

SEE EXAMPLE 1
on p. 471
for Ex. 35

35. **VOLLEYBALL NET** You are setting up a volleyball net using two 8 foot poles to hold up the net. You are going to attach each pole to a stake in the ground using a piece of rope. Each stake should be 4 feet from the pole. Assume that the ropes are stretched tight. How long should each rope be? Round to the nearest tenth of a foot.

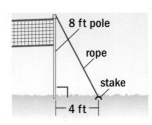

California@***HomeTutor*** for problem solving help at classzone.com

SEE EXAMPLE 2
on p. 472
for Exs. 36–37

36. ◆ **MULTIPLE CHOICE** A 13 foot ladder is leaning against a building. The bottom of the ladder is 5 feet from the building. How high up does the ladder meet the wall?

(A) 12 ft　　**(B)** 13.9 ft　　**(C)** 14 ft　　**(D)** 18 ft

California@***HomeTutor*** for problem solving help at classzone.com

(37.) **UTILITY POLES** A wire with a length of 23.8 meters is attached to a utility pole. The wire is anchored to the ground 9 meters from the base of the pole. How high above the ground is the wire attached to the utility pole? Round to the nearest tenth of a meter.

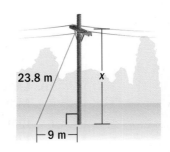

38. HIKING Eric is hiking from his campsite to a creek. He walks 3.5 miles directly south, 4 miles directly east, and then 1.5 miles directly south. Assume that the ground is flat. How much shorter is it to walk in a straight line than it is to take Eric's route?

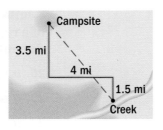
Campsite
3.5 mi
4 mi
1.5 mi
Creek

CHALLENGE Find the distance between the points.

39. (0, −12), (5, 0) **40.** (1, 6), (3, 4) **41.** (6, −3), (−5, −1)

42. CHALLENGE A rectangular room is 20 feet long, 12 feet wide, and 10 feet high. What is the maximum distance from one corner to another?

◆ CALIFORNIA STANDARDS SPIRAL REVIEW

NS. 1.5

43. Which number can be represented by a terminating decimal? *(p. 113)*

(A) $\frac{7}{12}$ (B) $\frac{11}{6}$ (C) $\sqrt{4.84}$ (D) $7.\overline{3}$

MG 1.1

44. Which speed is equivalent to 88,000 yards per hour? *(p. 443)*

(A) 20 yards per second   (B) 880 inches per second

(C) 4400 feet per second   (D) 52,800 feet per hour

AF 1.5

45. The graph shows the amount y of money you have after buying x trolley tickets. What does the x-intercept represent? *(p. 327)*

(A) The amount of money you start with

(B) The cost of 5 tickets

(C) The cost of each ticket

(D) The greatest number of tickets you can buy

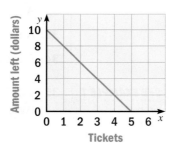
Amount left (dollars)
Tickets

QUIZ *for Lessons 8.4–8.6*

In Exercises 1–3, M is the midpoint of $\overline{AB}$. Find the value of x. *(p. 454)*

1. $AM = 2x$, $MB = 40$ **2.** $AB = 5x - 10$, $AM = 25$ **3.** $AB = 40$, $MB = \frac{5}{4}x$

4. What is the area of the triangle shown? *(p. 463)*

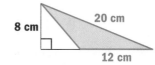
8 cm   20 cm   12 cm

5. Tell whether a triangle with side lengths 7, 24, and 25 units is a right triangle. *(p. 471)*

6. LANDMARKS You are standing 500 feet from the Washington Monument. Using a range finder on the ground, you measure the distance from your location to the top of the monument to be 747 feet. Find the height of the monument to the nearest foot. *(p. 471)*

8.7 Investigating Areas of Parallelograms

MATERIALS · paper · scissors

Standards

MG 2.1 Use formulas routinely for finding the perimeter and **area of basic two-dimensional figures** and the surface area and volume of basic three-dimensional figures, **including rectangles, parallelograms,** trapezoids, squares, triangles, circles, prisms, and cylinders.

QUESTION How can you find the area of a parallelogram?

A *parallelogram* is a four-sided figure with two pairs of parallel sides. The arrows in the diagram indicate that each pair of opposite sides is parallel.

A rectangle is a parallelogram with four right angles.

You have already learned that the area A of a rectangle is given by

$$A = bh$$

where b is the length of the base and h is the height.

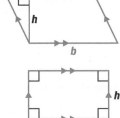

EXPLORE Change a parallelogram into a rectangle

| **STEP 1** Start with any parallelogram. | **STEP 2** Cut the parallelogram into two pieces, as shown. | **STEP 3** Move the triangle to form a rectangle. |

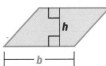 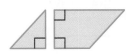 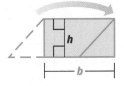

DRAW CONCLUSIONS Use your observations to complete these exercises

1. **REASONING** Make a conjecture about the relationship between the formula for the area of a rectangle and the formula for the area of a parallelogram.

Use your conjecture from Exercise 1 to find the area of a parallelogram with base b units and height h units.

2. $b = 10, h = 5$

3. $b = 2, h = 2$

4. $b = \frac{1}{2}, h = 16$

5. $b = 8, h = \frac{1}{8}$

6. $b = 0.25, h = 5$

7. $b = 100, h = 13$

8.7 Quadrilaterals and Their Areas

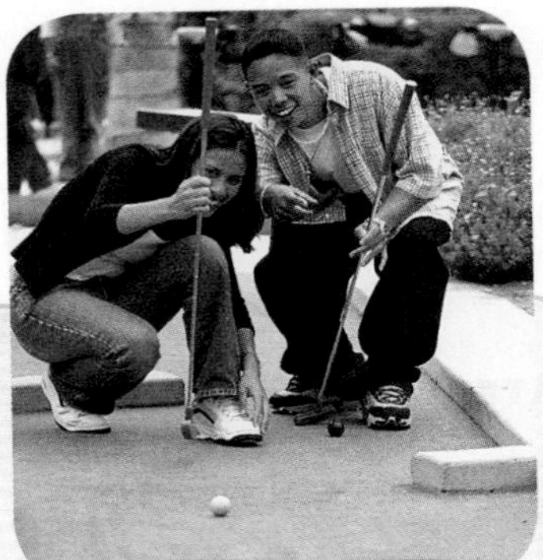

Standards MG 2.1 Use formulas routinely for finding the perimeter and area of basic two-dimensional figures and the surface area and volume of basic three-dimensional figures, **including rectangles, parallelograms, trapezoids, squares**, triangles, circles, prisms, and cylinders.

MG 2.2 Estimate and **compute the area of more complex or irregular two-** and three-**dimensional figures by breaking the figures down into more basic geometric objects.**

MG 3.1 **Identify** and construct **basic elements of geometric figures** (e.g., altitudes, midpoints, **diagonals**, angle bisectors, and perpendicular bisectors; central angles, radii, diameters, and chords of circles) by using a compass and straightedge.

Math and **SPORTS**
Ex. 57, p. 485

Connect *Before* you found areas of triangles. *Now* you will find areas of quadrilaterals.

KEY VOCABULARY
• quadrilateral
• trapezoid
• parallelogram
• rhombus
• diagonal

A **quadrilateral** is a closed plane figure with four sides that are line segments. The figures below are special types of quadrilaterals.

Special Quadrilaterals	Diagram
Trapezoid A **trapezoid** is a quadrilateral with exactly 1 pair of parallel sides.	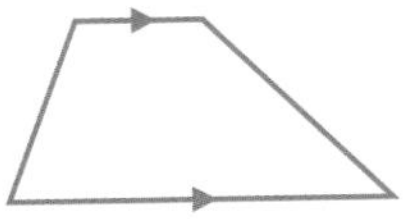
Parallelogram A **parallelogram** is a quadrilateral with 2 pairs of parallel sides.	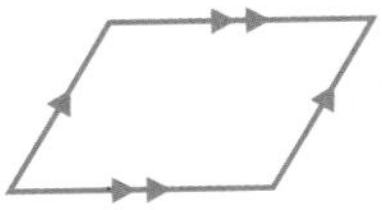
Rhombus A **rhombus** is a parallelogram with 4 sides of equal length.	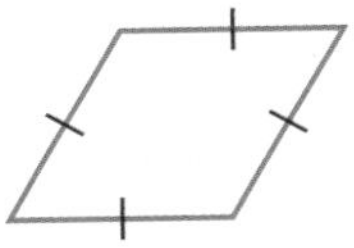
Rectangle A *rectangle* is a parallelogram with 4 right angles.	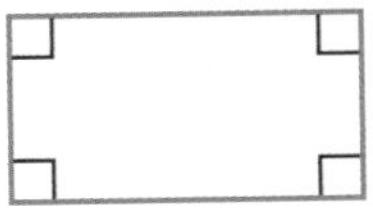
Square A *square* is a parallelogram with 4 sides of equal length and 4 right angles.	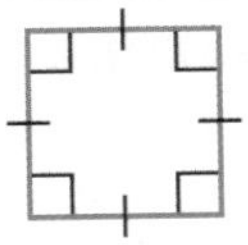

INTERPRETING A DIAGRAM In the diagrams above, the arrows indicate that pairs of line segments are parallel. When you are looking at a diagram with parallel lines or segments, you will either be told that two lines are parallel or it will be indicated by arrows, as in the diagrams above.

EXAMPLE 1 Classifying a Quadrilateral

Animated Math

For an interactive example of classifying quadrilaterals, go to **classzone.com.**

Classify the quadrilateral.

a.

The quadrilateral is a parallelogram with 4 sides of equal length. So, it is a rhombus.

b.

The quadrilateral is a parallelogram with 4 sides of equal length and 4 right angles. So, it is a square.

ANGLES IN A QUADRILATERAL A **diagonal** of a quadrilateral is a segment that joins two vertices of the quadrilateral but is not a side. You can use a diagonal of a quadrilateral to show that the sum of the angle measures in a quadrilateral is 360°.

Cut a quadrilateral along a diagonal to form two triangles.

The sum of the angle measures in each triangle is 180°.

The sum of the angle measures in a quadrilateral is 180° + 180° = 360°.

EXAMPLE 2 Finding an Unknown Angle Measure

Find the value of x.

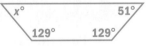

SOLUTION

$$x° + 51° + 129° + 129° = 360°$$ **The sum of the angle measures is 360°.**

$$x + 309 = 360$$ **Simplify.**

$$x = 51$$ **Solve for x.**

✓ GUIDED PRACTICE for Examples 1 and 2

Classify the quadrilateral.

1.

2.

3. In the diagram at the right, find the value of x.

BASE AND HEIGHT OF A PARALLELOGRAM Any side of a parallelogram can be considered the **base of the parallelogram**. The perpendicular distance between a base and the opposite side is the **height of the parallelogram**. The diagram below shows how to change a parallelogram into a rectangle with the same base, height, and area.

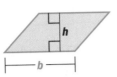

Start with any parallelogram.

Cut the parallelogram to form a right triangle and a trapezoid.

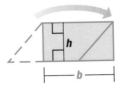

Move the triangle to form a rectangle.

As you may have observed in the activity on page 477, the area of a rectangle is the product of its base and its height, so the formula for the area A of a parallelogram is $A = bh$.

KEY CONCEPT   *For Your Notebook*

Area of a Parallelogram

Words   The area of a parallelogram is the product of the base and the height.

$h = 3$ cm
$b = 5$ cm

Algebra $A = bh$ **Numbers** $A = 5 \cdot 3 = 15$ cm^2

EXAMPLE 3   **Area and Perimeter of a Parallelogram**

FIND PERIMETER

In a parallelogram, opposite sides are always congruent. Use this fact to find the perimeter of a parallelogram.

Find the area and perimeter of the parallelogram.

SOLUTION

$A = bh$	$P = 2(8) + 2(11)$
$= 8 \cdot 10$	$= 16 + 22$
$= 80$	$= 38$

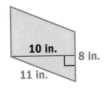

10 in.
8 in.
11 in.

▶ **Answer** The parallelogram has an area of 80 square inches and a perimeter of 38 inches.

✓ **GUIDED PRACTICE**   for Example 3

Find the area and perimeter of the parallelogram.

4.

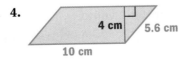

4 cm
5.6 cm
10 cm

5.

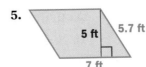

5 ft
5.7 ft
7 ft

READING

The bases of a trapezoid are labeled b_1 and b_2. You read these labels as "b sub one" and "b sub two."

TRAPEZOIDS The **bases of a trapezoid** are its two parallel sides. The perpendicular distance between the bases is the **height of the trapezoid**. The diagram below shows how two identical trapezoids with height h and bases b_1 and b_2 can form a parallelogram with height h and base $b_1 + b_2$.

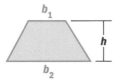 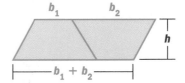

The area of the parallelogram is $(b_1 + b_2)h$, so the area of each trapezoid is $\frac{1}{2}(b_1 + b_2)h$.

KEY CONCEPT
For Your Notebook

Area of a Trapezoid

Words The area of a trapezoid is one half the product of the sum of the bases and the height.

$b_1 = 4$ m
$h = 3$ m
$b_2 = 8$ m

Algebra $A = \frac{1}{2}(b_1 + b_2)h$

Numbers $A = \frac{1}{2}(4 + 8)3 = 18$ m^2

EXAMPLE 4 Finding the Area of a Trapezoid

ANOTHER WAY

For an alternative method for solving the problem in Example 4, turn to page 488 for the **Problem Solving Workshop**.

ARCHITECTURE The Winslow House in River Forest, Illinois, was designed by Frank Lloyd Wright. The front part of the roof is a trapezoid, as shown. What is its area?

31 ft
25 ft
77 ft

Animated Math

For an interactive example of finding the area of a trapezoid, go to **classzone.com.**

SOLUTION

$A = \frac{1}{2}(b_1 + b_2)h$ Write formula for area of a trapezoid.

$= \frac{1}{2}(31 + 77)25$ Substitute values for b_1, b_2, and h.

$= 1350$ Simplify.

▶ **Answer** The front of the roof has an area of 1350 square feet.

✓ **GUIDED PRACTICE** for Example 4

Sketch the quadrilateral and find its area.

6. A trapezoid with bases of 14 feet and 17 feet and a height of 6 feet

7. A trapezoid with bases of 3 meters and 2 meters and a height of 4 meters

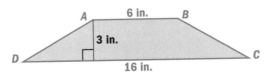

EXAMPLE 5 **Changing Dimensions**

The dimensions of trapezoid *ABCD* are shown below. How does the area change when the dimensions are doubled?

A   6 in.   *B*

3 in.

D ⌐_____ *C*
        16 in.

STEP 1 **Find** the area of trapezoid *ABCD* and the enlarged trapezoid.

$$A = \frac{1}{2}(b_1 + b_2)h \qquad\qquad A = \frac{1}{2}(b_1 + b_2)h$$

$$= \frac{1}{2}(6 + 16)3 \qquad\qquad = \frac{1}{2}(2 \cdot 6 + 2 \cdot 16)(2 \cdot 3)$$

$$= 33 \text{ in.}^2 \qquad\qquad = 132 \text{ in.}^2$$

STEP 2 **Compare** the areas: $\frac{132 \text{ in.}^2}{33 \text{ in.}^2} = 4$.

▶ **Answer** When the dimensions of trapezoid *ABCD* are doubled, the area becomes 4 times the original area.

✓ **GUIDED PRACTICE** for Example 5

8. **WHAT IF?** Suppose the dimensions of trapezoid *ABCD* in Example 5 are tripled. How does the area change?

8.7 EXERCISES

HOMEWORK KEY

◆ = **MULTIPLE CHOICE PRACTICE**
Exs. 15, 21, 56, 60–62

○ = **HINTS AND HOMEWORK HELP**
for Exs. 7, 19, 57 at classzone.com

SKILLS • PROBLEM SOLVING • REASONING

1. **VOCABULARY** Copy and complete: A segment that joins two vertices of a quadrilateral but is not a side is a(n) __?__.

2. **NOTETAKING SKILLS** Make a *concept map* like the one on page 436 for *quadrilateral*. Include information about the area of quadrilaterals.

WRITING *Explain* how to find the area of the polygon.

3. Parallelogram   4. Triangle   5. Trapezoid

SEE EXAMPLE 1
on p. 479
for Exs. 6–8

CLASSIFYING QUADRILATERALS Classify the quadrilateral.

6.

(7.)

8.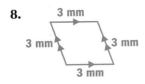

SEE EXAMPLE 2
on p. 479
for Exs. 9–17

XY **ALGEBRA** Find the value of *x*.

9.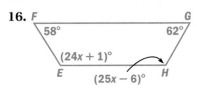

10.

11.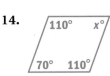

12.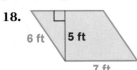

13.

14.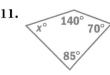

15. ◆ **MULTIPLE CHOICE** Classify the fourth angle of a quadrilateral that has three acute angles.

A Acute   **B** Right   **C** Obtuse   **D** Straight

XY **ALGEBRA** Find the value of *x* and the unknown angle measures.

16.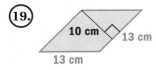

17.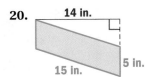

SEE EXAMPLE 3
on p. 480
for Exs. 18–29

FINDING AREA AND PERIMETER Find the area and perimeter of the parallelogram.

18.

19.

20.

21. ◆ **MULTIPLE CHOICE** What is the area of the parallelogram?

A 20 ft^2 **B** 25 ft^2

C 40 ft^2 **D** 50 ft^2

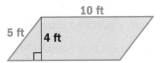

22. **ERROR ANALYSIS** *Describe* and correct the error in finding the area of the parallelogram.

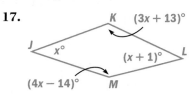

$A = bh$
$= 10 \cdot 7$
$= 70 \text{ in.}^2$

SKETCHING PARALLELOGRAMS Sketch a parallelogram with base *b* units and height *h* units. Then find its area.

23. $b = 12, h = 8$ 24. $b = 9, h = 14$ 25. $b = 10, h = 22$

26. $b = \sqrt{5}, h = \sqrt{10}$ 27. $b = \frac{1}{2}, h = \frac{1}{3}$ 28. $b = 3\frac{2}{5}, h = 5\frac{7}{8}$

29. **OPEN-ENDED** Sketch two parallelograms with equal areas but different perimeters.

SEE EXAMPLE 4
on p. 481
for Exs. 30–34

FINDING AREA Find the area of the trapezoid.

30.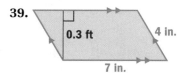
18 in.
12 in.
9 in.

31.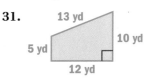
13 yd
10 yd
5 yd
12 yd

32.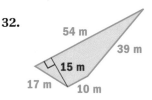
54 m
39 m
15 m
17 m   10 m

SKETCHING TRAPEZOIDS Sketch a trapezoid with bases b_1 units and b_2 units and height h units. Then find its area.

33. $b_1 = 13$, $b_2 = 7$, $h = 6$

34. $b_1 = 8$, $b_2 = 16$, $h = 11$

SEE EXAMPLE 5
on p. 482
for Exs. 35–38

CHANGING DIMENSIONS A parallelogram has a base of 5 units and a height of 8 units. How does the area of the parallelogram change when its dimensions are multiplied by the given factor k?

35. $k = 3$ **36.** $k = 5$ **37.** $k = \dfrac{1}{2}$ **38.** $k = \dfrac{1}{3}$

FINDING AREA AND PERIMETER Find the area and perimeter of the quadrilateral. Write your answers in terms of the larger unit.

39.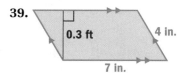
0.3 ft   4 in.
7 in.

40.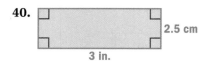
2.5 cm
3 in.

41.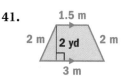
1.5 m
2 m   2 yd   2 m
3 m

FINDING AREA Find the area of the polygon.

42.
45 in.   37 in.
16 in.

43.
21 ft
9 ft
24 ft

44.
1 cm
2 cm
2 cm
3 cm

REASONING Tell whether the statement is *always*, *sometimes*, or *never* true. *Justify* your reasoning.

45. A rhombus is a parallelogram.   **46.** A rectangle is a square.

47. A trapezoid is a parallelogram.   **48.** A quadrilateral is a rectangle.

CONNECT SKILLS TO PROBLEM SOLVING Exercises 49–54 will help you prepare for problem solving.

Classify the quadrilaterals of each color in the design below.

49. Red   **50.** Purple   **51.** Yellow

52. Green   **53.** Light blue   **54.** Dark blue

SEE EXAMPLE 2
on p. 479
for Ex. 55

55. COMPASS ROSE A compass rose is a figure used on a map to show direction. The compass rose shown includes four red rhombuses. Find the value of x and the unknown angle measures.

California **@HomeTutor** for problem solving help at classzone.com

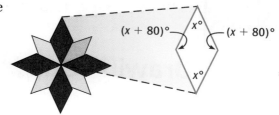

SEE EXAMPLES
3 AND 4
on p. 481
for Exs. 56–57

56. ◆ **MULTIPLE CHOICE** The front of an audio speaker is in the shape of a trapezoid. Its top edge is 14 inches wide, its bottom edge is 16 inches wide, and its height is 23 inches. What is the area of the front of the speaker?

(**A**) 173 in.^{2} (**B**) 345 in.^{2} (**C**) 368 in.^{2} (**D**) 5152 in.^{2}

California **@HomeTutor** for problem solving help at classzone.com

57. MINIATURE GOLF You are designing a putting green for a miniature golf course, as shown. What is the area of the green?

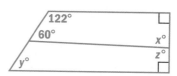

58. CHALLENGE The *midsegment of a trapezoid* is the segment that joins the midpoints of the legs (nonparallel sides) of the trapezoid. The length of the midsegment is one half the sum of the lengths of the bases.

a. Write a formula for the area of a trapezoid in terms of the length of the midsegment and the height.

b. *Compare* your answer from part (a) to the formula for the area of a parallelogram. What do you notice?

59. CHALLENGE Find the values of x, y, and z in the diagram. *Explain* your reasoning.

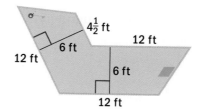

◆ **CALIFORNIA STANDARDS SPIRAL REVIEW**

MG 3.1

60. If $\overrightarrow{YW}$ bisects $\angle XYZ$, $m\angle XYW = 2x°$, and $m\angle XYZ = 80°$, what is the value of x? *(p. 454)*

(**A**) 20°   (**B**) 40°   (**C**) 80°   (**D**) 160°

AF 1.4

61. What is the coefficient of the expression $-23x$? *(p. 252)*

(**A**) −23   (**B**) 2   (**C**) x (**D**) 23

MG 1.3

62. It will take about 50 person-hours to complete landscaping for a new home. How long will it take 4 people to complete the job? *(p. 443)*

(**A**) 10 h   (**B**) 12.5 h   (**C**) 15 h   (**D**) 50 h

8.7 Drawing Quadrilaterals

MATERIALS · compass · straightedge

Standards

MG 3.1 Identify and construct basic elements of geometric figures (e.g., altitudes, midpoints, diagonals, angle bisectors, and perpendicular bisectors; central angles, radii, diameters, and chords of circles) **by using a compass and straightedge**.

QUESTION How can you construct a parallelogram and a rectangle using a straightedge and compass?

EXPLORE 1 Draw a parallelogram

Use the following steps to construct a parallelogram with sides congruent to the segments shown.

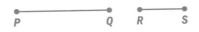

STEP 1

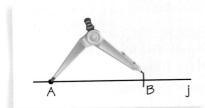

Measure length
Use a straightedge to draw line *j*. Label *A* on *j*. Set your compass at the length of $\overline{PQ}$. Place the compass at *A*. Mark point *B* on *j*.

STEP 2

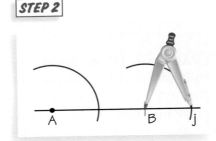

Draw arcs
Set your compass at the length of $\overline{RS}$. Place the compass at *A* and draw an arc. Keep the same setting. Place the compass at *B*. Draw a second arc.

STEP 3

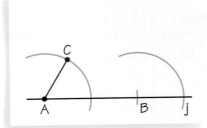

Draw a side
Choose a point *C* on the arc with center *A*. Draw $\overline{AC}$.

STEP 4

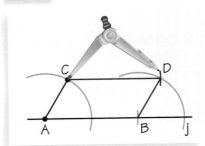

Draw remaining sides
Set your compass at the length of $\overline{AB}$. Place the compass at *C* and draw an arc. Label the intersection as *D*. Draw $\overline{CD}$. *ACDB* is a parallelogram.

EXPLORE 2 **Draw a rectangle**

Use the following steps to construct a rectangle with sides congruent to $\overline{TU}$ and $\overline{VW}$.

STEP 1

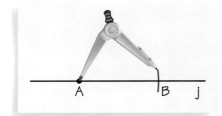

Measure length
Use a straightedge to draw line *j*. Label *A* on *j*. Set your compass at the length of $\overline{TU}$. Place the compass at *A*. Mark point *B* on *j*.

STEP 2

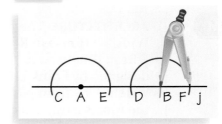

Draw arcs
Set your compass at the length of $\overline{VW}$. Place the compass at *A* and draw an arc. Label the intersections *C* and *E*. Keep the same setting. Place the compass at *B*. Draw a second arc. Label the intersections *D* and *F*.

STEP 3

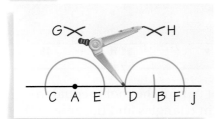

Draw arcs
Place the compass at *E*. Use a compass setting greater than the length of $\overline{AE}$. Draw an arc. Keep the same setting. Place the compass at *C*. Draw a second arc. Using the same setting, repeat this step with the compass placed at *F* and *D*. Label the intersections *G* and *H*.

STEP 4

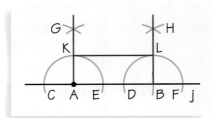

Draw sides
Draw $\overrightarrow{AG}$ and $\overrightarrow{BH}$. Label the intersections of the lines and arcs *K* and *L*. Draw $\overline{KL}$ to complete rectangle *AKLB*.

DRAW CONCLUSIONS **Use your observations to complete these exercises**

1. Draw a segment $\overline{AB}$. Construct a rhombus with sides congruent to $\overline{AB}$.

2. Draw a segment $\overline{QW}$. Construct a square with sides congruent to $\overline{QW}$.

Using ALTERNATIVE METHODS

Another Way to Solve Example 4, page 481

Standards
MG 2.2

In Example 4 on page 481, you found the area of the front part of a roof of a house by using the formula for the area of a trapezoid. You can also solve this problem by dividing the trapezoid into parts. Then find the sum of the areas of the parts.

PROBLEM

ARCHITECTURE The Winslow House in River Forest, Illinois, was designed by Frank Lloyd Wright. The front part of the roof is a trapezoid, as shown. What is its area?

METHOD

Divide the Trapezoid Into Parts You can also solve the problem by dividing the front part of the roof into a rectangle and two right triangles.

STEP 1 **Draw** a new diagram. If x is the length of the base of one of the right triangles, then $77 - (x + 31)$, or $46 - x$, is the length of the base of the other right triangle, as shown.

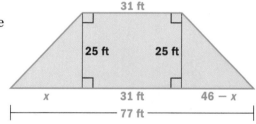

STEP 2 **Find** the area. The area of the front part of the roof is equal to the sum of the areas of the two right triangles and the area of the rectangle.

$$A = \frac{1}{2}bh + bh + \frac{1}{2}bh$$

$$= \frac{1}{2}(x)(25) + 31(25) + \frac{1}{2}(46 - x)(25)$$

$$= \frac{25x}{2} + 775 + 575 - \frac{25x}{2} = 1350$$

▶ The front of the roof has an area of 1350 square feet.

PRACTICE

1. **WHAT IF?** In the problem above, suppose the length of the shorter base is 35 feet. Find the area of the front part of the roof using two different methods.

2. **TRAPEZOID** Find the area of the trapezoid shown using two different methods.

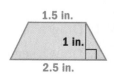

8.8 Circumferences and Areas of Circles

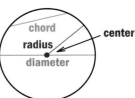

Standards

MG 2.1 **Use formulas routinely for finding the perimeter and area of basic two-dimensional figures** and the surface area and volume of basic three-dimensional figures, **including** rectangles, parallelograms, trapezoids, squares, triangles, **circles**, prisms, and cylinders.

MG 2.2 **Estimate and compute the area of more complex or irregular two-** and three-**dimensional figures by breaking the figures down into more basic geometric objects.**

MG 3.1 **Identify** and construct **basic elements of geometric figures** (e.g., altitudes, midpoints, diagonals, angle bisectors, and perpendicular bisectors; **central angles, radii, diameters, and chords of circles**) by using a compass and straightedge.

Math and
ENTERTAINMENT
Example 3, p. 490

Connect *Before* you found areas of quadrilaterals. *Now* you will find circumferences and areas of circles.

KEY VOCABULARY
- circle
- center
- radius, diameter
- chord
- central angle
- circumference

A **circle** is the set of all points in a plane that are the same distance from a fixed point called the **center**. A segment whose endpoints are the center and any point on the circle is a **radius**.

A **chord** is a segment whose endpoints are on a circle, and a **diameter** is a chord containing the center.

A **central angle** of a circle is an angle whose vertex is the center of the circle.

∠*ACB* is a central angle of the circle.

EXAMPLE 1 Identifying Parts of a Circle

READING
The terms radius and diameter also refer to the *lengths* of the respective segments.

Tell whether the figure is a *radius, chord, diameter,* or *central angle* of the circle.

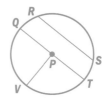

a. $\overline{RS}$ **b.** ∠*QPV*

c. $\overline{QP}$ **d.** $\overline{QT}$

SOLUTION

a. $\overline{RS}$ is a chord because its endpoints are on the circle.

b. ∠*QPV* is a central angle because its vertex, *P*, is the center of the circle.

c. $\overline{QP}$ is a radius because *P* is the center and *Q* is a point on the circle.

d. $\overline{QT}$ is a diameter because it is a chord that contains the center.

CLASSIFY NUMBERS
Although you can approximate π using the rational numbers 3.14 and $\frac{22}{7}$, π is an irrational number.

CIRCUMFERENCE The **circumference** of a circle is the distance around the circle. For every circle, the quotient of its circumference and its diameter is the same: about 3.14159. This constant is represented by π, the Greek letter *pi*. You can approximate π using 3.14, $\frac{22}{7}$, or the π key on a calculator.

KEY CONCEPT
For Your Notebook

Circumference of a Circle

Words The circumference of a circle is the product of π and the diameter, or the product of π and twice the radius.

$d = 2r$

Algebra $C = \pi d$ or $C = 2\pi r$

EXAMPLE 2   Finding the Circumference of a Circle

Find the circumference of a circle with a radius of 11 meters.

$C = 2\pi r$ **Circumference formula**

$\approx 2(3.14)(\mathbf{11})$ **Substitute 3.14 for π and 11 for r.**

$= 69.08$ **Multiply.**

▸ **Answer** The circumference is about 69.08 meters.

EXAMPLE 3   ◆ Multiple Choice Practice

A Ferris wheel has a circumference of about 423.9 feet. What is the approximate diameter of the Ferris wheel? Use 3.14 for π.

  (A) 13.5 ft   **(B)** 67.5 ft   **(C)** 135 ft   **(D)** 1350 ft

SOLUTION

Use the circumference formula that involves diameter.

$C = \pi d$ **Circumference formula**

$\mathbf{423.9} \approx 3.14d$ **Substitute 423.9 for C and 3.14 for π.**

$\dfrac{423.9}{3.14} = \dfrac{3.14d}{3.14}$ **Divide each side by 3.14.**

$135 = d$ **Simplify.**

The diameter is about 135 feet.

▸ **Answer** The correct answer is C. (A) (B) **(C)** (D)

✔ **GUIDED PRACTICE**   for Examples 1, 2, and 3

1. Draw and label a circle with a diameter of 32 inches. Find the circumference of the circle.

2. **WHAT IF?** In Example 3, suppose the circumference of the Ferris wheel is 462 feet. What is the diameter of the Ferris wheel? Use 3.14 for π.

AREA OF A CIRCLE To find the formula for the area A of a circle, you can first cut the circle into pieces. Arrange the pieces to form a shape resembling a parallelogram, as shown below. The approximate height h of the parallelogram is the radius r of the cricle, and the base b of the parallelogram is about half the circumference $2\pi r$. So, the circle's area A is:

$$A = bh = \left[\frac{1}{2}(2\pi r)\right]r = (\pi r)r = \pi r^2$$

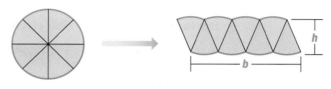

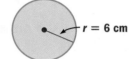

KEY CONCEPT

For Your Notebook

Area of a Circle

Words The area of a circle is the product of π and the square of the radius.

$r = 6$ cm

Algebra $A = \pi r^2$ **Numbers** $A = \pi(6)^2 = 36\pi$ cm^2

EXAMPLE 4 **Finding the Area of a Circle**

Find the area of the circle at the right.

Animated **Math**

For an interactive example of finding the area of a circle, go to **classzone.com.**

SOLUTION

Because the diameter is 10 in., the radius is $\frac{1}{2}$(10 in.) = 5 in.

$A = \pi r^2$ **Write formula for area.**

$\approx 3.14(5)^2$ **Substitute 3.14 for π and 5 for r.**

$= 78.5$ **Evaluate using a calculator.**

10 in.

▶ **Answer** The area is about 78.5 square inches.

EXAMPLE 5 **Finding the Radius of a Circle**

Find the radius of a circle that has an area of 530 square feet.

$A = \pi r^2$ **Write formula for area of a circle.**

$530 \approx (3.14)r^2$ **Substitute 530 for A and 3.14 for π.**

$168.79 \approx r^2$ **Divide each side by 3.14.**

$\sqrt{168.79} = r$ **Take positive square root of each side.**

$13 \approx r$ **Evaluate square root.**

AVOID ERRORS
Make sure you use the correct units when writing your answer. In Example 5, for instance, the units for radius are feet, not square feet.

▶ **Answer** The radius of the circle is about 13 feet.

EXAMPLE 6   Finding the Area of a Composite Figure

BASKETBALL The free throw region is outlined in white. Find its area.

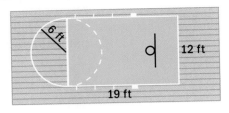

SOLUTION

STEP 1 Find the area of each shape.

Rectangle	Half circle
$A = lw$	$A = \frac{1}{2}\pi r^2$
$= 19 \cdot 12$	$\approx \frac{1}{2}(3.14)(6)^2$
$= 228$	$= 56.52$

STEP 2 Add the areas to find the total area: $228 + 56.52 = 284.52$.

▶**Answer** The area of the free throw region is about 285 square feet.

✓ **GUIDED PRACTICE**   for Examples 4, 5, and 6

Find the area of the circle with the given radius or diameter. Use 3.14 or $\frac{22}{7}$ for π. *Explain* your choice of approximation for π.

3. $r = 5$ cm
4. $r = 28$ in.
5. $d = 3$ km

6. What is the radius of a circle that has an area of 16π square feet?

7. What is the area of the figure at the right to the nearest square foot?

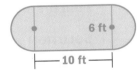

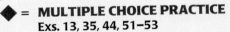

8.8 EXERCISES

SKILLS • PROBLEM SOLVING • REASONING

1. VOCABULARY Copy and complete: The circumference of a circle is the product of π and the __?__.

2. WRITING *Describe* how the diameter and circumference of a circle can be used to approximate π.

SEE EXAMPLE 1
on p. 489
for Exs. 3–6

IDENTIFYING PARTS OF A CIRCLE Tell whether the figure is a *radius*, *chord*, *diameter*, or *central angle* of the circle.

3. $\angle GFH$
4. $\overline{MJ}$
5. $\overline{HK}$
6. $\overline{GF}$

SEE EXAMPLES
2 AND 3
on p. 490
for Exs. 7–19

FINDING CIRCUMFERENCE Find the circumference of the circle with the given radius or diameter. Use 3.14 or $\frac{22}{7}$ for π.

7. $r = 10$ mm   **8.** $r = 3\frac{1}{2}$ ft   **9.** $d = 100$ cm

10. $r = 21$ ft   **11.** $d = 14$ in.   **12.** $d = 20$ mi

13. ◆ **MULTIPLE CHOICE** What is the circumference of a circle with a diameter of 4 feet? Use 3.14 for π.

   A 6.28 ft   **B** 12.56 ft   **C** 25.12 ft   **D** 50.24 ft

XY FINDING RADIUS OR DIAMETER Find the radius or diameter of the circle with the given circumference C. Use 3.14 or $\frac{22}{7}$ for π.

14. $C = 66$ in., $d = \underline{\ ?\ }$ **15.** $C = 3.14$ m, $r = \underline{\ ?\ }$ **16.** $C = 33$ km, $d = \underline{\ ?\ }$

17. $C = 628$ cm, $r = \underline{\ ?\ }$ **18.** $C = 9.42$ cm, $r = \underline{\ ?\ }$ **19.** $C = 330$ yd, $d = \underline{\ ?\ }$

SEE EXAMPLES
4 AND 5
on p. 491
for Exs. 20–31

USING DRAWINGS Find the area of the circle. Use 3.14 for π.

20.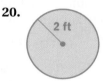

21.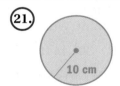

22.

FINDING AREA Find the area of the circle with the given radius or diameter. Use 3.14 or $\frac{22}{7}$ for π.

23. $r = 1.8$ cm   **24.** $d = \frac{7}{3}$ ft   **25.** $r = 10$ km

XY FINDING THE RADIUS Find the radius of the circle with the given area A. Use 3.14 for π.

26. $A = 28.26$ ft^2 **27.** $A = 3.14$ m^2 **28.** $A = 200.96$ yd^2

29. $A = 113.04$ in.^{2} **30.** $A = 12.56$ mm^2 **31.** $A = 254.34$ cm^2

XY ALGEBRA Find the area of the circle with the given circumference C. Use 3.14 for π.

32. $C = 18.84$ ft   **33.** $C = 81.64$ m   **34.** $C = 37.68$ cm

35. ◆ **MULTIPLE CHOICE** What is the approximate area of a circle with a circumference of 50.24 millimeters? Use 3.14 for π.

   A 8 mm^2 **B** 16 mm^2 **C** 200.96 mm^2 **D** 803.84 mm^2

ERROR ANALYSIS Use the circle to describe and correct the calculations in Exercises 36 and 37.

36.
$$C = 2 \cdot \pi \cdot r$$
$$\approx 2(3.14)(11)$$
$$= 69.08 \text{ yd}$$

37.
$$A = \pi^2 r$$
$$\approx (3.14)^2(5.5)$$
$$= 54.2278 \text{ yd}^2$$

SEE EXAMPLE 6
on p. 492
for Exs. 38–40

FINDING AREA Find the area of the shaded region. Use 3.14 for π.

38.
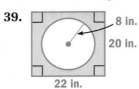
9 m
4 m

39.
8 in.
20 in.
22 in.

40.
4 km
7 km
10 km

CONNECT SKILLS TO PROBLEM SOLVING Exercises 41–43 will help you prepare for problem solving.

41. A dime has a radius of about 8.95 millimeters. Write expressions for the circumference and area of the dime.

42. A sprinkler rotates in a complete circle and sprays water 12 feet. Write expressions for the circumference and area of the yard that is watered.

43. A face-off circle on a hockey rink has a radius of 15 feet. Write expressions for the circumference and area of the face-off circle.

SEE EXAMPLE 2
on p. 490
for Ex. 44

44. ◆ **MULTIPLE CHOICE** The diameter of the U.S. Capitol Building's dome is 96 feet at its widest point. What is its approximate circumference?

(A) 150.72 ft   **(B)** 301.44 ft   **(C)** 473.26 ft   **(D)** 7234.54 ft

California **@HomeTutor**   for problem solving help at classzone.com

SEE EXAMPLE 6
on p. 492
for Exs. 45–48

45. TENNIS CENTER The ring-shaped roof of the New South Wales Tennis Center in Sydney, Australia, is shown at the right. The inner and outer edges of the roof are approximately circular. The inner diameter is about 65 meters, and the outer diameter is about 100 meters. What is the area covered by the roof? Use 3.14 for π.

California **@HomeTutor**   for problem solving help at classzone.com

New South Wales Tennis Center

READING *IN* MATH   Read the information below for Exercises 46–48.

Energy Savings The type of windows in a home affects heating costs. Double-paned windows will reduce the amount of heat lost during the winter. They cost about $1.50 more per square foot than single-paned windows. Double-paned windows offer an annual energy savings of $.60 per square foot.

46. Calculate You want to install the window shown. Find its area to the nearest square foot.

47. Calculate Find the additional cost of installing a double-paned window instead of a single-paned window.

48. Analyze After how many years is the extra cost of the double-paned window offset by the energy savings?

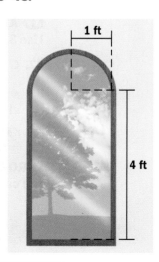

1 ft

4 ft

49. CHALLENGE In the diagram at the right, A is the center of the circle. Show that $y = 2x$.

50. CHALLENGE A car's wheel has a diameter of 26 inches. How many rotations will the wheel make if the car travels 6 miles? Round your answer to the nearest whole number.

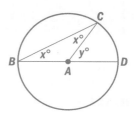

◆ CALIFORNIA STANDARDS SPIRAL REVIEW

NS 1.3

51. What is $\frac{7}{16}$ written as a percent? *(p. 155)*

    (A) 0.004375%   **(B)** 0.4375%   **(C)** 43.75%   **(D)** 437.5%

NS 2.3

52. What is $\left(\frac{6}{5}\right)^2 \times \left(-\frac{1}{3}\right)^3$? *(p. 98)*

    (A) $-\frac{972}{25}$ **(B)** $-\frac{4}{75}$ **(C)** $\frac{4}{75}$ **(D)** $\frac{972}{25}$

MG 2.2

53. The floor of a gazebo is shaped like the figure shown at the right. What is the area of the floor? *(p. 478)*

    (A) $12\sqrt{3}$ ft^2 **(B)** $16\sqrt{3}$ ft^2

    (C) $24\sqrt{3}$ ft^2 **(D)** $32\sqrt{3}$ ft^2

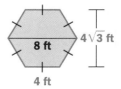

QUIZ *for Lessons 8.7–8.8*

Find the value of x or y. *(p. 478)*

1.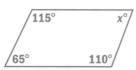

2.

3.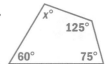

Find the area of the parallelogram or trapezoid. *(p. 478)*

4.

5.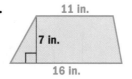

6.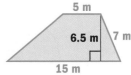

Find the circumference and area of the circle with the given radius or diameter. Use 3.14 or $\frac{22}{7}$ for π. *(p. 489)*

7. $r = 3.5$ in.   **8.** $d = 15$ m   **9.** $r = 84$ mm

10. BIG BEN The Great Clock of Westminster in London, England, rings the bell known as "Big Ben." The circumference of the clock face is about 72.25 feet. What is the approximate diameter of the clock face? *(p. 489)*

8.8 Constructions Involving Circles

MATERIALS • compass • straightedge

Standards

MG 3.1 Identify and construct basic elements of geometric figures (e.g., altitudes, midpoints, diagonals, angle bisectors, and perpendicular bisectors; central angles, radii, diameters, and chords of circles) by using a compass and straightedge.

QUESTION How can you construct a central angle, a chord, and the center of a circle?

EXPLORE 1 Construct a central angle with a measure of 60°

Use the following steps to construct a central angle with a measure of 60° for a circle.

STEP 1	STEP 2	STEP 3
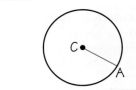	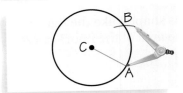	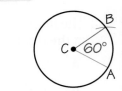

Draw a radius
Use a compass to draw a circle with center C. Then use a straightedge to draw radius $\overline{CA}$.

Draw an arc
Keep the same compass setting. Draw an arc centered at A that intersects the circle. Label the intersection B.

Draw a second radius
Draw radius $\overline{CB}$. ∠ACB a central angle of the circle with a measure of 60°.

EXPLORE 2 Construct a chord

Use the following steps to construct a chord congruent to a given segment.

STEP 1	STEP 2	STEP 3
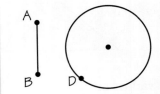	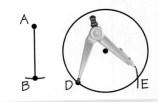	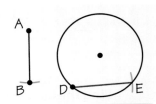

Construct a circle
Use a compass to draw a circle. Draw $\overline{AB}$ so that it is shorter than a diameter of the circle. Draw a point on the circle. Label the point D.

Draw an arc from D
Set your compass to the length of $\overline{AB}$. Draw an arc centered at D that intersects the circle. Label the intersection E.

Draw a chord
Draw chord $\overline{DE}$.
$\overline{DE} \cong \overline{AB}$.

EXPLORE 3 Use the perpendicular bisectors of two chords to find the center of a circle

Use the following steps to find the center of a circle by using the perpendicular bisectors of two chords.

STEP 1

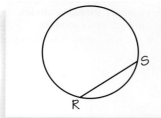

Draw a chord
Use a compass to draw a circle. Draw chord $\overline{RS}$.

STEP 2

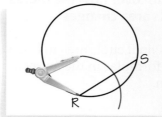

Draw an arc
Draw an arc centered at R whose radius is greater than half of the length of $\overline{RS}$.

STEP 3

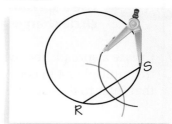

Draw a second arc
Keep the same compass setting. Draw an arc centered at S.

STEP 4

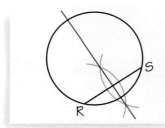

Draw the bisector
Draw a line through the points of intersection of the arcs. This is the perpendicular bisector of $\overline{RS}$.

STEP 5

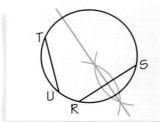

Draw a second chord
Draw a second chord. Label it $\overline{TU}$.

STEP 6

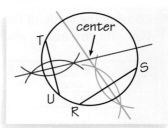

Find the center
Draw the perpendicular bisector of $\overline{TU}$. The center of the circle is the intersection of the perpendicular bisectors.

DRAW CONCLUSIONS Use your observations to complete these exercises

1. Construct a circle by placing a circular object on a piece of paper and tracing around its edge. Find the center of the circle.

2. Draw a circle. Construct its diameter.

3. **CHALLENGE** *Describe* how to construct a regular hexagon using a compass and a straightedge.

Technology **ACTIVITY** *Use after Lesson 8.8*

8.8 Comparing Radii of Circles

QUESTION How does the radius of a circle change when its area is multiplied by 4?

EXAMPLE Use a spreadsheet to discover how the radius of a circle changes when its area changes

Standards

MG 2.1 Use formulas routinely for finding the perimeter and **area of basic two-dimensional figures** and the surface area and volume of basic three-dimensional figures, **including** rectangles, parallelograms, trapezoids, squares, triangles, **circles,** prisms, and cylinders.

STEP 1 **Create** a spreadsheet with an original circle area in cell A1 and the multiplier 4 in cell A2. Enter formulas in the Area column that refer to these cells, as shown.

STEP 2 **Enter** formulas in the Radius column, as shown. The radius of a circle with area A is given by $\sqrt{\frac{A}{\pi}}$.

STEP 3 **Compare** the radii of the two circles by dividing the second radius by the first radius. Enter a formula for this quotient in the Ratio column.

	A	B	C
		Comparing Radii	
1	1	Original circle area	
2	4	Multiplier	
3			
4	Area	Radius	Ratio
5	=A1	=SQRT(A5/PI())	
6	=A5*A2	=SQRT(A6/PI())	=B6/B5

STEP 4 **Change** the value of the original circle area in cell A1 several times. What do you notice about the ratio of the radii?

	A	B	C
1	1	Original circle area	
2	4	Multiplier	
3			
4	Area	Radius	Ratio
5	1	0.564190	
6	4	1.128379	2

	A	B	C
1	5	Original circle area	
2	4	Multiplier	
3			
4	Area	Radius	Ratio
5	5	1.261566	
6	20	2.523133	2

	A	B	C
1	15	Original circle area	
2	4	Multiplier	
3			
4	Area	Radius	Ratio
5	15	2.185097	
6	60	4.370194	2

▶ **Answer** When the area of a circle is multiplied by 4, the radius is multiplied by 2.

PRACTICE

Determine how the radius of a circle changes when its area is multiplied by the given number.

1. 9   **2.** 16   **3.** 25   **4.** 36

5. REASONING How does the radius of a circle change when its *circumference* is doubled? tripled? *Explain.*

Multiple Choice Practice for Lessons 8.5–8.8

1. What is the area of the circle shown to the nearest square meter? **MG 2.1**

Ⓐ 25 m²

Ⓑ 47 m²

Ⓒ 50 m²

Ⓓ 201 m²

2. The diagram shows the measurements of a kite. What is the area of the kite to the nearest square inch? **MG 2.1**

Ⓐ 231 in.²

Ⓑ 287 in.²

Ⓒ 376 in.²

Ⓓ 462 in.²

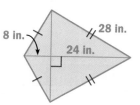

3. You are making a bookshelf, as shown below. What is the value of *x*, rounded to the nearest inch? **MG 3.3, MR 2.8**

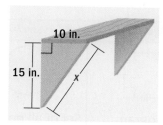

Ⓐ 18 in.   Ⓑ 25 in.

Ⓒ 43 in.   Ⓓ 63 in.

4. What is the area of the triangle shown? **MG 2.1**

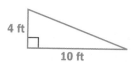

Ⓐ 15 ft²   Ⓑ 20 ft²

Ⓒ 25 ft²   Ⓓ 30 ft²

5. A rectangular house is built on a lot that is shaped like a trapezoid. The house is completely surrounded by a grass-covered lawn. The house is 55 feet long and 35 feet wide. The lot has base lengths of 75 feet and 125 feet, and a height of 65 feet. What is the area of the lot covered by grass? **MG 2.2**

Ⓐ 1925 ft²   Ⓑ 3476 ft²

Ⓒ 4575 ft²   Ⓓ 6500 ft²

6. What is the correct classification of the quadrilateral? **MG 2.1**

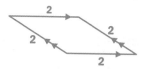

Ⓐ Rhombus

Ⓑ Square

Ⓒ Trapezoid

Ⓓ Rectangle

7. What is the approximate area of a circle with a circumference of 31 feet? **MG 2.1**

Ⓐ 5 ft²   Ⓑ 20 ft²

Ⓒ 24 ft²   Ⓓ 77 ft²

8. The diagram shows the dimensions of a track. What is the approximate perimeter of the track? **MG 2.1, MR 2.2**

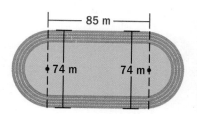

Ⓐ 318 m   Ⓑ 402 m

Ⓒ 550 m   Ⓓ 635 m

BIG IDEAS

For Your Notebook

Big Idea 1

Converting Units of Measure

To convert between metric and customary units, you can use the relationships in the table below. In some cases, you may need to multiply by more than one conversion factor.

Quantity	Conversions	
Length	1 in. = 2.54 cm 1 mi ≈ 1.609 km	1 ft = 0.3048 m
Capacity	1 fl oz ≈ 29.573 mL 1 gal ≈ 3.785 L	1 qt ≈ 0.946 L
Weight/Mass	1 oz ≈ 28.35 g	1 lb ≈ 0.454 kg

Big Idea 2

Classifying Plane Figures

Triangle	Trapezoid	Parallelogram
Closed figure with 3 straight sides that connect 3 points	Quadrilateral with 1 pair of parallel sides	Quadrilateral with 2 pairs of parallel sides

Rhombus	Rectangle	Square	Circle
Parallelogram with 4 sides of equal length	Parallelogram with 4 right angles	Parallelogram with 4 sides of equal length and 4 right angles	Set of all points in a plane that are the same distance from a fixed point

Big Idea 3

Finding Areas of Plane Figures

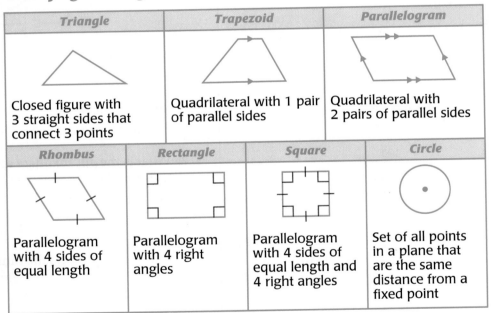

Triangle	Parallelogram	Trapezoid	Circle
$A = \frac{1}{2}bh$	$A = bh$	$A = \frac{1}{2}(b_1 + b_2)h$	$A = \pi r^2$

APPLYING THE BIG IDEAS

Big Idea 1
You convert units of measure in **Ex. 2.**

Big Idea 2
You classify plane figures in **Steps 1–3.**

Big Idea 3
You find the areas of plane figures in **Step 3.**

PROBLEM How can you use plane figures to make a prototype of a stained glass window?

STEP 1 Choose plane figures.

Create the design of your stained glass window by choosing several of the plane figures from the list below. Examples of windows are also shown.

Plane figures

parallelogram	rhombus
square	rectangle
trapezoid	triangle

STEP 2 Draw an outline of the stained glass window.

Using graph paper, a pencil, and a ruler, draw an outline of your stained glass window. Use the plane figures you chose in Step 1.

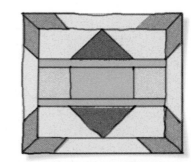

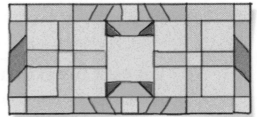

Examples of stained glass windows

STEP 3 Choose colors for the stained glass window.

You will use tissue paper to color your prototype stained glass window. Choose a different color of tissue paper for each shape. All figures with the same shape should have the same color. Find the combined area (in square inches) of all figures with the same shape to determine how much of each color of tissue paper you will need. Write the total area of each color on the chalkboard.

STEP 4 Finish the window.

Cut the necessary shapes from the colored tissue paper and glue them onto the graph paper. Then cut out the window.

Extending the Problem

Use your results from the problem to complete the exercises.

1. Suppose each sheet of tissue paper costs $.11 and has an area of 486 square inches. Find the approximate total cost of the tissue paper required for the entire class to make their windows.

2. Find the perimeter and area of your window in inches and square inches, respectively. What are the perimeter and area of your window in centimeters and square centimeters?

3. Find the perimeter of each figure in your window. Is the sum of the perimeters of the figures equal to the perimeter of the window?

REVIEW KEY VOCABULARY

- conversion factor, *p. 437*
- unit rate, *p. 443*
- congruent segments, *p. 454*
- midpoint, *p. 454*
- segment bisector, *p. 455*
- perpendicular bisector, *p. 455*
- congruent angles, *p. 455*
- angle bisector, *p. 455*
- vertex of a triangle, *p. 463*
- base of a triangle, *p. 463*
- height of a triangle, *p. 463*

- altitude, *p. 463*
- median of a triangle, *p. 465*
- legs of a right triangle, *p. 471*
- hypotenuse, *p. 471*
- Pythagorean Theorem, *p. 471*
- converse, *p. 473*
- quadrilateral, *p. 478*
- trapezoid, *p. 478*
- parallelogram, *p. 478*
- rhombus, *p. 478*
- diagonal, *p. 479*

- base of a parallelogram, *p. 480*
- height of a parallelogram, *p. 480*
- base of a trapezoid, *p. 481*
- height of a trapezoid, *p. 481*
- circle, *p. 489*
- center, *p. 489*
- radius, diameter, *p. 489*
- chord, *p. 489*
- central angle, *p. 489*
- circumference, *p. 489*

VOCABULARY EXERCISES

In Exercises 1–3, copy and complete the statement.

1. If point B lies on $\overline{AC}$ and $AB = BC$, then B is the __?__ of $\overline{AC}$.

2. In a right triangle, the side opposite the right angle is the __?__.

3. In a circle, a chord containing the center is called a(n) __?__.

4. **NOTETAKING SKILLS** Make a *concept map* like the one on page 436 for *circle*. Include information about circumference and area.

REVIEW EXAMPLES AND EXERCISES

8.1 Comparing and Converting Measurements
pp. 437–442

MG 1.1

EXAMPLE

How many inches are in 6.75 feet?

$$6.75 \text{ ft} \times \frac{12 \text{ in.}}{1 \text{ ft}} = \frac{6.75 \text{ ft} \times 12 \text{ in.}}{1 \text{ ft}} = 81 \text{ in.}$$

▶ **Answer** There are 81 inches in 6.75 feet.

EXERCISES

SEE EXAMPLES
1, 2, 4, AND 5
on pp. 437–439
for Exs. 5–10

Copy and complete the statement. Round to the nearest whole number if necessary.

5. 84 in. = __?__ ft

6. 22 pt = __?__ qt

7. 18 m ≈ __?__ ft

8. 75 lb ≈ __?__ kg

9. 432 in.^{2} = __?__ ft^2

10. 5 in.^{3} ≈ __?__ mm^3

8.2 Measures Involving Products and Quotients

pp. 443–448

MG 1.3 **EXAMPLE**

John swims 18 feet in 6 seconds. Stephanie swims 36 feet in 9 seconds. Who swims faster?

SOLUTION

STEP 1 **Write** a rate of speed for each person.

John: $\dfrac{18 \text{ feet}}{6 \text{ seconds}}$ Stephanie: $\dfrac{36 \text{ feet}}{9 \text{ seconds}}$

STEP 2 **Express** each person's speed as a unit rate.

John: $\dfrac{18 \text{ ft}}{6 \text{ sec}} = \dfrac{18 \div 6}{6 \div 6} = \dfrac{3 \text{ ft}}{1 \text{ sec}}$ **Divide numerator and denominator by 6 to get a denominator of 1 unit.**

Stephanie: $\dfrac{36 \text{ ft}}{9 \text{ sec}} = \dfrac{36 \div 9}{9 \div 9} = \dfrac{4 \text{ ft}}{1 \text{ sec}}$ **Divide numerator and denominator by 9 to get a denominator of 1 unit.**

▶ **Answer** John can swim 3 feet per second and Stephanie can swim 4 feet per second. So, Stephanie can swim faster than John.

EXERCISES

SEE EXAMPLES 1 AND 2 on pp. 443–444 for Exs. 11–13

Tell whether the rates are *equivalent* or *not equivalent*.

11. $\dfrac{32 \text{ sit-ups}}{2 \text{ min}}; \dfrac{84 \text{ sit-ups}}{4 \text{ min}}$

12. $\dfrac{12 \text{ miles}}{1 \text{ hour}}, \dfrac{24 \text{ miles}}{2 \text{ hours}}$

13. $\dfrac{30 \text{ words}}{2 \text{ min}}, \dfrac{60 \text{ words}}{4 \text{ min}}$

8.3 Multi-Step Conversions

pp. 449–453

MG 1.3 **EXAMPLE**

How many minutes are in 2 weeks?

$$2 \text{ wk} \times \dfrac{7 \text{ d}}{1 \text{ wk}} \times \dfrac{24 \text{ h}}{1 \text{ d}} \times \dfrac{60 \text{ min}}{1 \text{ h}} = 20{,}160 \text{ min}$$

▶ **Answer** There are 20,160 minutes in 2 weeks.

EXERCISES

SEE EXAMPLES 1 AND 2 on pp. 449–450 for Exs. 14–16

14. About how many millimeters are in 9 feet?

15. How many seconds are in 7 weeks?

16. **WEATHER** A storm is traveling 15 miles per hour. What is the speed of the storm in feet per second?

8.4 Segment and Angle Bisectors

pp. 454–458

EXAMPLE

Point *M* is the midpoint of $\overline{RT}$. Find the value of *x*.

SOLUTION

$\overline{RM} \cong \overline{MT}$	Definition of midpoint
$RM = MT$	Definition of congruent segments
$3x = 15$	Substitute.
$x = 5$	Divide each side by 3.

EXAMPLE

In the diagram, $\overrightarrow{SP}$ bisects $\angle RST$. Find the value of *x*.

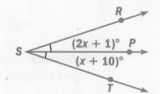

SOLUTION

Write and solve an equation. Because $\overrightarrow{SP}$ bisects $\angle RST$, you know that $\angle RSP \cong \angle PST$.

$\angle RSP \cong \angle PST$	Definition of angle bisector
$m\angle RSP = m\angle PST$	Definition of congruent angles
$2x + 1 = x + 10$	Substitute.
$x = 9$	Solve for *x*.

EXERCISES

SEE EXAMPLES
1 AND 3
on pp. 454–456
for Exs. 17–22

In each diagram, *M* is the midpoint of the segment. Find the value of *x*.

17.

18.

19. REASONING In Exercise 17, suppose *PM* is tripled. How does the value of *x* change if *M* is still the midpoint of $\overline{PQ}$?

In each diagram, $\overrightarrow{BD}$ bisects $\angle ABC$. Find the value of *x*.

20.

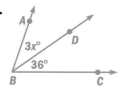

21.

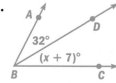

22. Given that $\overrightarrow{EG}$ bisects $\angle DEF$ and $m\angle DEG = 45°$, find $m\angle GEF$.

8.5 Triangles and Their Areas

pp. 463–467

MG 2.1

EXAMPLE

Find the area of the triangle.

SOLUTION

7 in.
6 in.

$A = \frac{1}{2}bh$ Write formula for area of a triangle.

$A = \frac{1}{2}(6)7$ Substitute 6 for b and 7 for h.

$A = 21$ Simplify.

▶ **Answer** The area of the triangle is 21 square inches.

EXERCISES

SEE EXAMPLES 1 AND 2 on p. 464 for Exs. 23–25

Find the unknown quantity for the triangle with base b, height h, and area A.

23. $b = 10$ cm, $h = 5$ cm, $A = \underline{\ ?\ }$ cm^2

24. $A = 45$ ft^2, $h = 10$ ft, $b = \underline{\ ?\ }$ ft

25. FLAG Find the height of a triangular flag with a base of 1 meter and an area of 1.5 square meters.

8.6 The Pythagorean Theorem and Its Converse

pp. 471–476

MG 3.3

EXAMPLE

Find the value of a in the diagram.

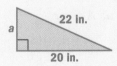
a
22 in.
20 in.

SOLUTION

$a^2 + b^2 = c^2$ Pythagorean Theorem

$a^2 + 20^2 = 22^2$ Substitute 20 for b and 22 for c.

$a^2 = 84$ Simplify.

$a \approx 9.2$ in.   Take positive square root of each side. Then approximate.

EXERCISES

SEE EXAMPLES 1 AND 2 on pp. 471–472 for Exs. 26–28

Let a and b represent the lengths of the legs of a right triangle, and let c represent the length of the hypotenuse. Find the unknown length.

26. $a = 2.4$, $b = 0.7$, $c = \underline{\ ?\ }$ **27.** $a = \underline{\ ?\ }$, $b = 24$, $c = 40$ **28.** $a = 8$, $b = \underline{\ ?\ }$, $c = 17$

Quadrilaterals and Their Areas   *pp. 478–485*

MG 2.1   **EXAMPLE**

Find the area of the trapezoid.

3 in.
4 in.
7 in.

$A = \frac{1}{2}(b_1 + b_2)h$ **Write formula for area of a trapezoid.**

$= \frac{1}{2}(7 + 3)4$ **Substitute 7 for b_1, 3 for b_2, and 4 for h.**

$= 20$ **Simplify.**

▶ **Answer** The area of the trapezoid is 20 square inches.

EXERCISES

SEE EXAMPLES
3 AND 4
·····················
on pp. 480–481
for Exs. 29–31

Find the area of the parallelogram or trapezoid.

29.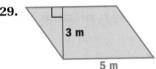
3 m
5 m

30.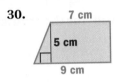
7 cm
5 cm
9 cm

31.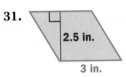
2.5 in.
3 in.

Circumferences and Areas of Circles   *pp. 489–495*

MG 2.1   **EXAMPLE**

Find the (a) area and (b) circumference of the circle. Use 3.14 for π.

6 cm

a. $A = \pi r^2$ **Write formula for area of a circle.**

$\approx 3.14(3)^2$ **Substitute 3.14 for π and $\frac{1}{2}(6) = 3$ for r.**

$= 28.26$ **Evaluate.**

▶ **Answer** The area of the circle is about 28.26 square centimeters.

b. $C = \pi d$ **Write formula for circumference of a circle.**

$\approx 3.14(6)$ **Substitute 3.14 for π and 6 for d.**

$= 18.84$ **Evaluate.**

▶ **Answer** The circumference of the circle is about 18.84 centimeters.

EXERCISES

SEE EXAMPLES
2 AND 4
·····················
on pp. 490–491
for Exs. 32–34

Find the area and circumference of the circle with the given radius r or diameter d.

32. $r = 5$ m   **33.** $d = 20$ ft   **34.** $r = 0.5$ mi

VOCABULARY Copy and complete the statement.

1. A rate that has a denominator of 1 unit is a(n) __?__ .

2. A parallelogram with 4 sides of equal length is a(n) __?__ .

Copy and complete the statement. Round to the nearest whole number if necessary.

3. 11 c = __?__ fl oz

4. 130 lb ≈ __?__ kg

5. 17.5 yd = __?__ in.

In Exercises 6–8, find an equivalent unit rate.

6. $\dfrac{336\ \text{mi}}{7\ \text{h}}$

7. $\dfrac{150\ \text{ft}}{12\ \text{sec}}$

8. $\dfrac{285\ \text{words}}{3\ \text{min}}$

9. Given that $\overrightarrow{PS}$ bisects $\angle QPR$, $m\angle RPS = (x + 16)°$, and $m\angle QPS = (2x - 8)°$, find the value of x.

Let a and b represent the lengths of the legs of a right triangle, and let c represent the length of the hypotenuse. Find the unknown length.

10. $a = 1.4$, $b = 4.8$, $c =$ __?__

11. $a =$ __?__ , $b = 3.2$, $c = 6.8$

Classify the quadrilateral.

12.

13.

14.

Find the area of the figure. If necessary, give your answer in terms of the larger unit. Use 3.14 for π.

15.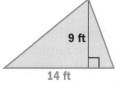
9 ft
14 ft

16.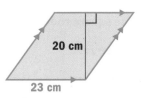
20 cm
23 cm

17.
17 m
19 m
2500 cm

18.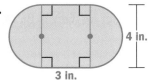
4 in.
3 in.

19.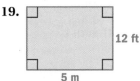
12 ft
5 m

20.
2 m
2 m
4 m

Find the area of the circle given its radius r or diameter d. Use 3.14 for π.

21. $r = 11$ cm

22. $d = 18$ yd

23. $r = 7$ mm

24. **UNIT COST** A medicine costs $42.50 per pound. What is the cost per ounce of the medicine?

STRATEGIES YOU'LL USE:
- SOLVE DIRECTLY
- ELIMINATE CHOICES

Standards
MG 1.1, MG 2.1

If you have difficulty solving a multiple choice problem directly, you may be able to use another approach to eliminate incorrect answer choices and obtain the correct answer.

PROBLEM 1

What is the area of the parallelogram in square meters?

A 9 yd^2 **B** 24 m^2

C 30 m^2 **D** 36 m^2

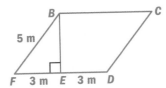

Strategy 1   SOLVE DIRECTLY

STEP 1   **Find** the height EB by using the Pythagorean Theorem.

$FE^2 + EB^2 = FB^2$ **Pythagorean Theorem**

$3^2 + EB^2 = 5^2$ **Substitute.**

$9 + EB^2 = 25$ **Evaluate powers.**

$EB^2 = 16$ **Subtract 9 from each side.**

$EB = \sqrt{16}$ **Take positive square root of each side.**

$EB = 4$ **Evaluate square root.**

STEP 2   **Find** the length of base $\overline{FD}$.

$FD = FE + ED$ **Segment addition**

$= 3 + 3 = 6$ **Substitute and simplify.**

STEP 3   **Use** the formula for the area of a parallelogram.

$A = bh$ **Parallelogram area formula**

$= FD \cdot EB$ **Name the base and height.**

$= 6(4) = 24$ **Substitute and simplify.**

The area of the parallelogram is 24 m^2.

The correct answer is B. Ⓐ **Ⓑ** Ⓒ Ⓓ

Strategy 2   ELIMINATE CHOICES

You can eliminate choices of a multiple choice question by determining the reasonableness of the answer choices.

In this problem, the formula for the area of the parallelogram is $A = FD \cdot EB$.

You know that $EB < FB$ because FB is the hypotenuse of the right triangle. So, $FD \cdot EB < FD \cdot FB$. Because $FD \cdot FB = 6(5) = 30$, the area of the parallelogram is less than 30 m^2. You can eliminate choices C and D.

Because the quantity 9 yd^2 is not written in terms of the required unit of measure, it is not a valid answer. You can eliminate choice A.

The correct answer is B. Ⓐ **Ⓑ** Ⓒ Ⓓ

PROBLEM 2

Which of the following rates is equal to $\frac{102 \text{ mi}}{1 \text{ h}}$?

(A) $\frac{5.3 \text{ ft}}{1 \text{ sec}}$ **(B)** $\frac{20 \text{ ft}}{1 \text{ sec}}$ **(C)** $\frac{149.6 \text{ ft}}{1 \text{ sec}}$ **(D)** $\frac{5675 \text{ ft}}{1 \text{ sec}}$

Strategy 1 SOLVE DIRECTLY

Use the appropriate conversion factors to convert the rate to feet per second.

$$\frac{102 \cancel{\text{mi}}}{1 \cancel{\text{h}}} \cdot \frac{5280 \text{ ft}}{1 \cancel{\text{mi}}} \cdot \frac{1 \cancel{\text{h}}}{60 \cancel{\text{min}}} \cdot \frac{1 \cancel{\text{min}}}{60 \text{ sec}} = \frac{102 \cdot 5280 \text{ ft}}{60 \cdot 60 \text{ sec}}$$

$$= \frac{538{,}560 \text{ ft}}{3600 \text{ sec}}$$

$$= \frac{149.6 \text{ ft}}{1 \text{ sec}}$$

The correct answer is C. **(A) (B) (C) (D)**

Strategy 2 ELIMINATE CHOICES

Use estimation and mathematical reasoning to eliminate answer choices.

Estimate how many miles you would travel in 1 hour traveling at a rate of 5.3 feet per second. Because there are 3600 seconds in 1 hour, you travel $(5.3)(3600) = 19{,}080$ feet in 1 hour. One mile is greater than 5000 feet, so in 1 hour, you will travel less than 4 miles.

Clearly this speed is less than $\frac{102 \text{ mi}}{1 \text{ h}}$. You can eliminate choice A.

Similarly, at a rate of 20 feet per second, you would travel less than 15 miles in 1 hour. You can eliminate choice B.

The rate of 5675 feet per second is greater than 1 mile per second, or 3600 miles per hour. Eliminate choice D.

The correct answer is C. **(A) (B) (C) (D)**

STRATEGY PRACTICE

Explain why you can eliminate the highlighted answer choice.

1. What is the area of the parallelogram?

   (A) 20 ft^2 **(B)** 24 ft^2

   (C) 30 ft^2 **(D)** 50 ft^2

2. Which of the following times is less than 2 hours?

   (A) 140 min   **(B)** $\sqrt{2}$ h   **(C)** 8000 sec   **(D)** 0.5 d

3. Which of the following measurements is greater than 3 pounds?

   (A) 750 g   **(B)** 2 tons   **(C)** 45 oz   **(D)** 1.5 kg

1. What is the volume of the cube shown to the nearest cubic meter? **MG 1.1**

   (A) 13 m^3

   (B) 42 m^3

   (C) 137 m^3

   (D) 15,880 m^3

   $V = 450$ ft^3

2. About how many hours are equivalent to 12 years? **MG 1.1**

   (A) 4000 h

   (B) 105,000 h

   (C) 263,000 h

   (D) 405,000 h

3. A basketball hoop has a circumference of about 56.5 inches. A basketball has a circumference of about 28.5 inches. What is the approximate difference between the diameter of the hoop and the diameter of the basketball? Use 3.14 for π. **MG 3.1**

   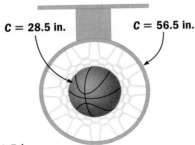

   C = 28.5 in.   C = 56.5 in.

   (A) 4.5 in.

   (B) 9 in.

   (C) 18 in.

   (D) 27 in.

4. What is the approximate area of the figure shown? **MG 2.2**

   (A) 201 ft^2

   (B) 256 ft^2

   (C) 356 ft^2

   (D) 457 ft^2

   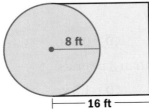

   8 ft

   16 ft

5. Freddy and Miranda share a newspaper route. The table below shows the times Freddy and Miranda take to deliver the newspapers on their own. What is the approximate time it would take them if they worked together? **MG 1.3, MR 1.1**

Freddy	35 minutes
Miranda	25 minutes

   (A) 14.6 sec

   (B) 30 min

   (C) 1 h

   (D) 875 sec

6. The density of a substance is 8 grams per cubic centimeter. What is the density of the substance to the nearest ounce per cubic inch? **MG 1.3**

   (A) 5 oz/in.^{3}

   (B) 131 oz/in.^{3}

   (C) 139 oz/in.^{3}

   (D) 3946 oz/in.^{3}

7. What is the area of the triangle? **MG 2.1**

   (A) 33 ft^2

   (B) 45 ft^2

   (C) 66 ft^2

   (D) 90 ft^2

   11 ft

   6 ft

   15 ft

8. Jess, Murphy, and Alexandria leave the mall at the same time. It takes 32 minutes for Jess to get home, 1860 seconds for Murphy to get home, and 0.6 hour for Alexandria to get home. Who arrives home first? **MG 1.1**

   (A) Jess

   (B) Murphy

   (C) Alexandria

   (D) All arrive at the same time.

9. In the diagram below, what are the diagonals of quadrilateral *ABCD*? **MG 3.1**

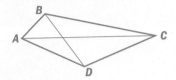

Ⓐ $\overline{AB}$ and $\overline{BD}$

Ⓑ $\overline{BC}$ and $\overline{AC}$

Ⓒ $\overline{AC}$ and $\overline{BD}$

Ⓓ $\overline{AD}$ and $\overline{BC}$

10. Jasmine and her friends set up a badminton net, as shown below. She ties a rope at the end of each pole to secure the net. Which is closest to the length of each rope? **MG 3.3**

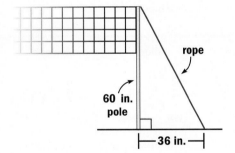

Ⓐ 10 in.

Ⓑ 48 in.

Ⓒ 70 in.

Ⓓ 96 in.

11. One circle has a radius of 10 feet. Another circle has a radius of 15 feet. About how much greater is the area of the second circle than the area of the first circle? **MG 2.1**

Ⓐ 10 ft^2

Ⓑ 25 ft^2

Ⓒ 39 ft^2

Ⓓ 393 ft^2

12. In the diagram below, the miniature golf course is the midpoint of the segment formed by the restaurant and the beach. How far is the restaurant from the beach? **MG 3.1**

Ⓐ 4 mi

Ⓑ 8 mi

Ⓒ 12 mi

Ⓓ 16 mi

13. Which reading speed is the fastest? **MG 1.3**

Ⓐ 4 words in 1 second

Ⓑ 252 words in 1 minute

Ⓒ 16,560 words in 1 hour

Ⓓ 39 words in 9 seconds

14. What is the value of *a* in the triangle shown? **MG 3.3**

Ⓐ 0.8 in.

Ⓑ 2 in.

Ⓒ 3.6 in.

Ⓓ 5 in.

15. The total area of the four congruent parking spaces below is 72 square meters. How long is each line dividing the spaces? **MG 2.1, MR 1.3**

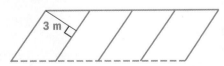

Ⓐ 3 m

Ⓑ 4 m

Ⓒ 6 m

Ⓓ 8 m

9 Congruence and Similarity

Before

In previous chapters, you learned the following skills, which you'll use in Chapter 9:

- Graphing points and lines in the coordinate plane
- Writing and solving proportions
- Multiplying fractions
- Finding angle measures and segment lengths

Now

In Chapter 9 you'll study these **Big Ideas:**

1. Using congruent and similar figures
2. Performing transformations in the coordinate plane
3. Using scale drawings and models

Why?

So you can solve real-world problems about . . .

- Soccer fields, p. 521
- Walkways, p. 526
- Telephone poles, p. 533
- Bookshelves, p. 539
- Space exploration, p. 544

Animated Math

at *classzone.com*

Get-Ready Games

Butterfly Challenge

California Standards

Review solving proportions. *Gr. 6 NS 1.3*
Prepare for reading scale models. *Gr. 7 MG 1.2*

Texan Crescent
$$\frac{3}{10} = \frac{?}{40}$$

Indian
$$\frac{2}{5} = \frac{?}{20}$$

Nymph
$$\frac{4}{7} = \frac{?}{35}$$

Buckeye
$$\frac{2}{9} = \frac{?}{18}$$

Empress
$$\frac{7}{8} = \frac{?}{24}$$

Silverspot
$$\frac{2}{3} = \frac{?}{15}$$

Red Rim
$$\frac{3}{7} = \frac{?}{14}$$

Morpho
$$\frac{3}{8} = \frac{?}{24}$$

Orion
$$\frac{1}{6} = \frac{?}{108}$$

How to Play

Find the butterfly name that means "sulfur."

- Solve each proportion.
- Order the solutions from least to greatest, and write the first letter of the corresponding names in the same order.

CALIFORNIA STANDARDS

- **Gr. 7 MG 3.2** Understand and use coordinate graphs to plot simple figures, determine lengths and areas related to them, and determine their image under translations and reflections. *(Lessons 9.2, 9.3, 9.4)*

- **Gr. 7 MG 3.4** Demonstrate an understanding of conditions that indicate two geometrical figures are congruent and what congruence means about the relationships between the sides and angles of the two figures. *(Lesson 9.1)*

GARDEN MIRROR

California Standards

Review graphing points. **Gr. 5 AF 1.4**
Prepare for images under reflections. **Gr. 7 MG 3.2**

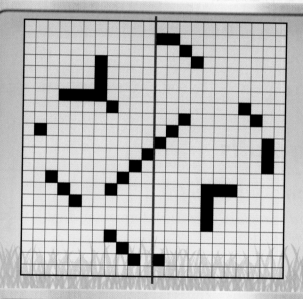

How to Play

The given drawing is incomplete. In the complete drawing, the red line acts as a mirror. The left and right sides of the red line are mirror images.

On a copy of the grid, complete the drawing by using the red line to shade the mirror image of each shaded square.

Games Wrap-Up

Draw Conclusions

Complete these exercises after playing the games.

1. **WRITING** *Describe* the procedure you used to complete the image in *Garden Mirror.*

2. **REASONING** Find one cross product for each proportion in *Butterfly Challenge.* Order the cross products from least to greatest. Write the last letters of the butterfly names in the same order to find the lifespan of the butterfly whose name you found in the puzzle.

Prerequisite Skills

California @HomeTutor
Prerequisite skills practice at classzone.com

REVIEW VOCABULARY

- **proportion,** *p. 277*
- **cross products,** *p. 278*
- **congruent segments,** *p. 454*
- **congruent angles,** *p. 455*
- **ratio,** *p. 732*
- **ordered pair,** *p. 734*

VOCABULARY CHECK

Copy and complete using a review term from the list at the left.

1. Line segments that have the same length are called __?__.

2. An equation stating that two ratios are equivalent is called a(n) __?__.

3. Two angles that have the same measure are called __?__.

SKILL CHECK

4. Write the ordered pair for each labeled point in the coordinate plane at the right. *(p. 734)*

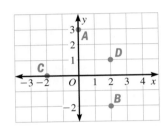

Plot the point in a coordinate plane. *(p. 734)*

5. $A(0, 4)$

6. $B(-2, 3)$

7. $C(5, -4)$

8. $D(-2, -3)$

Solve the equation. *(p. 263)*

9. $\frac{x}{7} = 3$

10. $\frac{x}{-2} = 4$

11. $-9x = 108$

12. $8x = 56$

13. $6x = 72$

14. $\frac{x}{4} = 8$

15. $-13x = 39$

16. $\frac{x}{-3} = 17$

Notetaking Skills

NOW YOU TRY
Make a *word triangle* for the word *ratio*.

Focus on Graphic Organizers

You can use a *word triangle* to organize information about a vocabulary word, such as *proportion*.

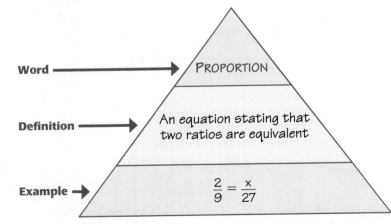

9.1 Investigating Similar Figures

MATERIALS · graph paper · protractor

Standards

MG 3.4 Demonstrate an understanding of conditions that indicate two geometrical figures are congruent and **what congruence means about the relationships between the sides and angles of the two figures.**

QUESTION How are similar figures related?

Two *similar* figures have the same shape, but not necessarily the same size. For example, a figure and its enlargement are similar figures.

EXPLORE Compare corresponding parts of a figure and its enlargement

STEP 1

Draw △*ABC* (read as "triangle *ABC*") so that $m\angle A = 90°$, $AB = 2$ units, and $AC = 4$ units. Find BC to the nearest 0.1 unit.

STEP 2

Draw △*DEF* so that $m\angle D = 90°$, $DE = 1.5 \cdot AB$, and $DF = 1.5 \cdot AC$. Find the side lengths of △*DEF*.

STEP 3

Use a protractor to find the measures of the angles of both triangles to the nearest degree.

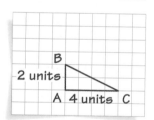

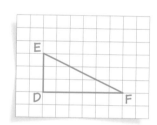

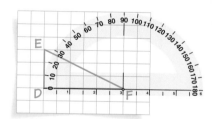

DRAW CONCLUSIONS Use your observations to complete these exercises

1. Copy and complete the tables.

Side of △ABC	Corresponding side of △DEF
$AB = 2$ units	$DE = ?$
$AC = 4$ units	$DF = ?$
$BC = ?$	$EF = ?$

Angle of △ABC	Corresponding angle of △DEF
$m\angle A = 90°$	$m\angle D = 90°$
$m\angle B = ?$	$m\angle E = ?$
$m\angle C = ?$	$m\angle F = ?$

2. Find the ratios of the corresponding side lengths of △*ABC* and △*DEF*. What do you notice about these ratios? What do you notice about the measures of the corresponding angles?

3. CONJECTURE Write a conjecture about the corresponding side lengths and the corresponding angle measures of similar figures.

4. Two figures are *congruent* if they have the same shape and the same size. What is the ratio of corresponding side lengths of two congruent figures?

9.1 Congruent and Similar Figures

Standards   **MG 3.4** Demonstrate an understanding of conditions that indicate two geometrical figures are congruent and what congruence means about the relationships between the sides and angles of the two figures.

Connect   *Before* you studied congruent segments and angles. *Now* you will study congruent and similar polygons.

Math and
TECHNOLOGY
Example 3, p. 518

KEY VOCABULARY
• congruent polygons
• corresponding parts
• similar polygons

Congruent polygons have the same shape and size. Polygons are congruent if their *corresponding* angles and *corresponding* sides are congruent. **Corresponding parts** are in the same position in different figures. To name congruent polygons, list their corresponding vertices in the same order.

KEY CONCEPT   *For Your Notebook*

Congruent Polygons

READING
The symbol △ is read as "triangle".

$\triangle KLM \cong \triangle PQR$

Corresponding angles are congruent.

$\angle K \cong \angle P \qquad \angle L \cong \angle Q \qquad \angle M \cong \angle R$

Corresponding sides are congruent.

$\overline{LM} \cong \overline{QR} \qquad \overline{KL} \cong \overline{PQ} \qquad \overline{KM} \cong \overline{PR}$

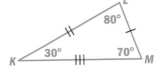

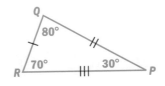

EXAMPLE 1   **Naming Corresponding Parts**

PICTURE FRAMES In the frame below, $ABCD \cong JKLM$. Name all pairs of corresponding angles and sides.

SOLUTION

Corresponding angles are congruent.

$\angle A, \angle J \qquad\qquad \angle B, \angle K$

$\angle C, \angle L \qquad\qquad \angle D, \angle M$

Corresponding sides are congruent.

$\overline{AB}, \overline{JK} \qquad\qquad \overline{BC}, \overline{KL}$

$\overline{CD}, \overline{LM} \qquad\qquad \overline{AD}, \overline{JM}$

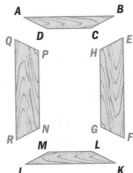

EXAMPLE 2 **Using Congruent Polygons**

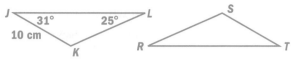

$\triangle JKL \cong \triangle TSR$. Find $m\angle S$.

SOLUTION

Corresponding angles are congruent.

REVIEW ANGLES OF TRIANGLES

For help with finding the sum of the angle measures of a triangle, see p. 740.

$\angle K$ and $\angle S$ are corresponding angles, so they have the same measure. Find $m\angle K$.

$m\angle J + m\angle K + m\angle L = 180°$	**Sum of angle measures is 180°.**
$31° + m\angle K + 25° = 180°$	**Substitute.**
$m\angle K + 56° = 180°$	**Add.**
$m\angle K + 56° - 56° = 180° - 56°$	**Subtract 56° from each side.**
$m\angle K = 124°$	**Simplify.**

▶ **Answer** Because $m\angle K = m\angle S$, you know that $m\angle S = 124°$.

✓ **GUIDED PRACTICE** **for Examples 1 and 2**

1. In Example 1, $EFGH \cong QRNP$. Name all pairs of corresponding angles and sides.

Find the value using the triangles in Example 2.

2. Length of $\overline{ST}$ 3. $m\angle T$ 4. $m\angle R$

SIMILAR POLYGONS **Similar polygons** have the same shape, but they can be different sizes. The symbol ~ means "is similar to." When you name similar polygons, list their corresponding vertices in the same order.

KEY CONCEPT *For Your Notebook*

Similar Polygons

$\triangle ABC \sim \triangle XYZ$

Corresponding angles are congruent.

$\angle A \cong \angle X$ $\angle B \cong \angle Y$ $\angle C \cong \angle Z$

The ratios of corresponding side lengths are equal. The corresponding side lengths are said to be proportional.

$\dfrac{AB}{XY} = \dfrac{BC}{YZ}$ $\dfrac{BC}{YZ} = \dfrac{AC}{XZ}$ $\dfrac{AC}{XZ} = \dfrac{AB}{XY}$

$\dfrac{8}{4} = \dfrac{6}{3} = 2$ $\dfrac{6}{3} = \dfrac{10}{5} = 2$ $\dfrac{10}{5} = \dfrac{8}{4} = 2$

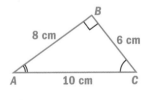

EXAMPLE 3 Identifying Similar Polygons

Tell whether the television screens are similar.

STEP 1 Decide whether corresponding angles are congruent. Each angle measures 90°.

$$\angle A \cong \angle E \qquad \angle B \cong \angle F$$
$$\angle C \cong \angle G \qquad \angle D \cong \angle H$$

REVIEW PROPORTIONS
For help with proportions, see p. 277.

STEP 2 Decide whether corresponding side lengths are proportional.

$$\frac{30 \text{ inches}}{18 \text{ inches}} \overset{?}{=} \frac{40 \text{ inches}}{24 \text{ inches}}$$

$$\frac{5 \cdot \cancel{6}}{3 \cdot \cancel{6}} \overset{?}{=} \frac{5 \cdot \cancel{8}}{3 \cdot \cancel{8}}$$

$$\frac{5}{3} = \frac{5}{3}$$

▶ **Answer** Yes, quadrilateral $ABCD \sim$ quadrilateral $EFGH$.

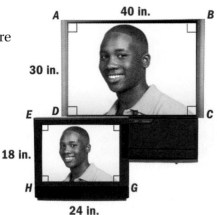

EXAMPLE 4 ◆ Multiple Choice Practice

In the diagram, $\triangle KLM \sim \triangle NPQ$. What is the length of $\overline{KL}$?

ELIMINATE CHOICES
Because $\triangle KLM$ is larger than $\triangle NPQ$, you know that the length of $\overline{KL}$ is greater than 12 m. So, you can eliminate choices A and B.

(A) 6 m   (B) 12 m

(C) 24 m   (D) 26 m

SOLUTION

Corresponding side lengths are proportional.

$$\frac{KL}{NP} = \frac{LM}{PQ} \qquad \text{Write a proportion.}$$

$$\frac{KL}{12 \text{ m}} = \frac{10 \text{ m}}{5 \text{ m}} \qquad \text{Substitute given values.}$$

$$KL = 24 \qquad \text{Solve the proportion.}$$

The length of $\overline{KL}$ is 24 meters.

▶ **Answer** The correct answer is C. (A) (B) (C) (D)

✓ **GUIDED PRACTICE** for Examples 3 and 4

5. The dimensions of rectangle $JKLM$ are 9 by 21. The dimensions of rectangle $EFGH$ are 3 by 7. Is rectangle $JKLM$ similar to rectangle $EFGH$?

6. At the right, $ABCD \sim FGHJ$. Find the value of x.

9.1 EXERCISES

HOMEWORK KEY

◆ = **MULTIPLE CHOICE PRACTICE**
Exs. 12, 27, 30–32

◯ = **HINTS AND HOMEWORK HELP**
for Exs. 5, 13, 27 at classzone.com

SKILLS • PROBLEM SOLVING • REASONING

1. **VOCABULARY** Copy and complete: Sides and angles that are in the same position in different figures are called __?__ .

2. **WRITING** *Explain* why all squares are similar, but not all rectangles are similar.

SEE EXAMPLES 1 AND 2
on pp. 516–517
for Exs. 3–5

USING CONGRUENT POLYGONS In the diagram, quadrilateral *KLMN* ≅ quadrilateral *SPQR*.

3. Name four pairs of congruent angles.

4. Find *m∠S*.

5. Find the length of $\overline{NK}$.

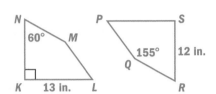

SEE EXAMPLE 2
on p. 517
for Exs. 6–12

MEASUREMENT Quadrilateral *ABEF* ≅ quadrilateral *DGHC*. Find the unknown measure.

6. *m∠C*   7. Length of $\overline{AF}$

8. *m∠A*   9. Length of $\overline{HC}$

10. *m∠B*   11. *m∠H*

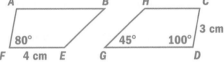

12. ◆ **MULTIPLE CHOICE** Polygon *ABCD* ≅ polygon *EFGH*. Find the value of *x*.

    (A) 10   **(B)** 12

    (C) 18   **(D)** 20

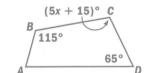

SEE EXAMPLE 3
on p. 518
for Exs. 13–14

IDENTIFYING SIMILAR POLYGONS Tell whether the polygons are similar. *Justify* your reasoning.

13.

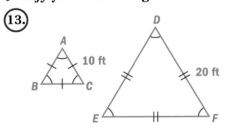

14.

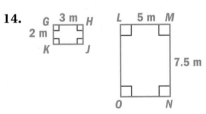

SEE EXAMPLE 4
on p. 518
for Exs. 15–16

USING SIMILAR POLYGONS Use the similar polygons to find the value of *x*.

15. △*ABC* ~ △*DEF*

16. *MNPQ* ~ *RSTV*

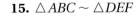

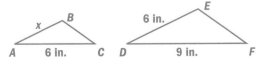

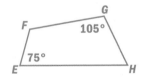

ERROR ANALYSIS In Exercises 17 and 18, use △*ABC* and
△*DEF* to describe and correct the error in the statement.

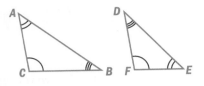

17. Triangle *ABC* is similar to triangle *DEF*.

18. Angle *A* is congruent to angle *D*.

In Exercises 19–20, tell how you know the polygons are congruent. *Justify*
your reasoning.

EXTENSION   Determining Whether Triangles are Congruent

You can use the special rules below to tell whether triangles are
congruent.

Side-Side-Side (SSS) If three sides of one triangle are congruent to three
sides of another triangle, then the triangles are congruent.

Side-Angle-Side (SAS) If two sides and the angle between them in one
triangle are congruent to two sides and the angle between them in
another triangle, then the triangles are congruent.

Angle-Side-Angle (ASA) If two angles and the side between them in
one triangle are congruent to two angles and the side between them in
another triangle, then the triangles are congruent.

Tell whether the triangles are congruent.

Because all three sides of △*ABC* are congruent to
all three sides of △*DEF*, △*ABC* ≅ △*DEF* by SSS.

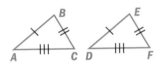

19.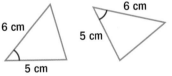

20.

CONNECT SKILLS TO PROBLEM SOLVING Exercises 21–23 will help you
prepare for problem solving.

A card and an envelope are similar. Write a proportion that can be
used to find the missing dimension *y* of the envelope.

21. The card is 5 in. × 5 in. The envelope is 6 in. × *y* in.

22. The card is 4 in. × 8 in. The envelope is 4.5 in. × *y* in.

23. The card is 6 in. × 4 in. The envelope is 7 in. × *y* in.

SEE EXAMPLE 4
on p. 518
for Ex. 24

24. ESTIMATION Rectangle *ABCD* is similar to rectangle *EFGH*. A friend says
that *EF* is about 8 meters. Is this estimate reasonable? *Explain.*

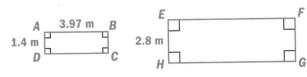

California @HomeTutor   for problem solving help at classzone.com

◆ = **MULTIPLE CHOICE PRACTICE**   ○ = **HINTS AND HOMEWORK HELP** at classzone.com

25. SOCCER FIELD In 1994, Michigan State University covered the floor of the Silverdome with natural grass for the World Cup Tournament. The pieces of sod were in the shape of regular hexagons. Two of these are pictured below. *Explain* how you know they are congruent.

Silverdome floor

California @*HomeTutor* for problem solving help at classzone.com

26. AREA The area of *ABCD* is 80 square inches. *ABCD* is similar to *WXYZ*. *Explain* how to find the length of side $\overline{XY}$.

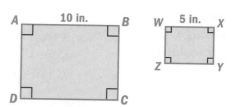

27. ◆ **MULTIPLE CHOICE** △*RST* is similar to △*VWX* where *RS* = 10 feet and *VW* = 30 feet. What is the ratio of the perimeters of △*RST* and △*VWX*?

(A) 1 : 3 **(B)** 1 : 4 **(C)** 1 : 9 **(D)** 1 : 12

28. CHALLENGE A golden rectangle is one whose length and width are in a ratio of about 8 to 5. A golden spiral is formed by drawing arcs centered at a corner of each square. These rectangles and spirals are often found in nature, art, and architecture. Name each golden rectangle at the right and measure its dimensions in millimeters. Are all of the golden rectangles similar? *Explain*.

29. CHALLENGE Trapezoid *ABCD* is similar to trapezoid *RSTU*. Base *AB* is 7 inches, and base *CD* is 3 inches longer than *AB*. The area of *ABCD* is 51 square inches. Base *RS* is 3.5 inches. Find the area of *RSTU*. *Explain* your method.

◆ CALIFORNIA STANDARDS SPIRAL REVIEW

MG 2.1 | **30.** Which is the radius of a circle whose area is about 314 inches? *(p. 489)*

(A) 0.01 in. **(B)** 0.1 in. **(C)** 10 in. **(D)** 100 in.

MG 2.1 | **31.** A triangle has an area of 12 square meters and a base of 8 meters. What is the height of the triangle? *(p. 463)*

(A) 1.5 m **(B)** 3 m **(C)** 4 m **(D)** 6 m

AF 3.3 | **32.** A roof rises 12 feet for every 16 feet of horizontal change. What is the slope of the roof? *(p. 334)*

(A) $\frac{3}{5}$ **(B)** $\frac{3}{4}$ **(C)** $\frac{4}{3}$ **(D)** $\frac{5}{3}$

9.2 Translations in the Coordinate Plane

Standards MG 3.2 Understand and use coordinate graphs to plot simple figures, determine lengths and areas related to them, and determine their image under **translations** and reflections.

Connect *Before* you graphed lines in a coordinate plane. *Now* you will translate the graph of a figure in a coordinate plane.

Math and TECHNOLOGY
Ex. 22, p. 526

KEY VOCABULARY
- **transformation**
- **image**
- **translation**

A **transformation** is an operation that changes a figure into another figure. The new figure created is called the **image**.

A **translation** is a transformation that moves each point of a figure the same distance in the same direction. The image is congruent to the original figure.

EXAMPLE 1 ◆ Multiple Choice Practice

In which figure is the red boat a translation of the blue boat?

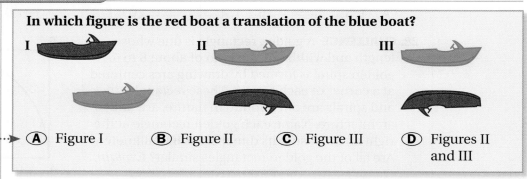

I   II   III

ELIMINATE CHOICES
Because translations move each point in the same direction, figure III is not a translation. So, you can eliminate choices C and D.

(A) Figure I   (B) Figure II   (C) Figure III   (D) Figures II and III

SOLUTION

Look for a figure in which every point moves the same distance in the same direction.

I   II   III

same distance,   different distances,   different distances,
same direction   same direction   different directions

▶ **Answer** The correct answer is A. (A) (B) (C) (D)

✓ GUIDED PRACTICE   for Example 1

1. **WHAT IF?** In Example 1, consider a transformation from the blue boat in figure II to the red boat in figure I. Is this a translation? *Explain.*

LABELING TRANSFORMATIONS You can label a point on an image by using the same letter as the corresponding point on the original figure followed by a prime symbol (′). For example, the image of point A is A'.

EXAMPLE 2 Translating a Figure

About the Standards

You will learn about reflecting figures in the coordinate plane in Lesson 9.3.

Rectangle $DEFG$ has vertices $D(-5, 4)$, $E(-2, 4)$, $F(-2, 2)$, and $G(-5, 2)$.

a. Graph $DEFG$. Then translate $DEFG$ 6 units to the right and 3 units down.

b. Find and compare the side lengths and areas of $DEFG$ and its image.

SOLUTION

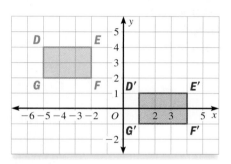

a. Graph $DEFG$ and its image.

b. Use your graph to find the side lengths and areas of $DEFG$ and $D'E'F'G'$.

$$DE = 3 = GF \qquad EF = 2 = DG$$
$$D'E' = 3 = G'F' \qquad E'F' = 2 = D'G'$$

Find the areas using $A = l \cdot w$.

The area of $DEFG$ is $3 \cdot 2$, or 6.

The area of $D'E'F'G'$ is $3 \cdot 2$, or 6.

The corresponding side lengths and the areas of the figures are equal.

To translate a figure in a coordinate plane, you find the coordinates of its image by using the guidelines below, assuming a and b are positive.

Slide to the right a units
$x \to x + a$

Slide up b units
$y \to y + b$

Slide to the left a units
$x \to x - a$

Slide down b units
$y \to y - b$

EXAMPLE 3 Using Coordinate Notation

$\triangle ABC$ has vertices $A(-4, 3)$, $B(-1, 4)$ and $C(0, 2)$. Translate $\triangle ABC$ using $(x, y) \to (x + 2, y - 5)$. Then describe the translation in words.

Animated Math

For an interactive example of using coordinate notation, go to **classzone.com**.

SOLUTION

Original		Image
(x, y)	$\to$	$(x + 2, y - 5)$
$A(-4, 3)$	$\to$	$A'(-2, -2)$
$B(-1, 4)$	$\to$	$B'(1, -1)$
$C(0, 2)$	$\to$	$C'(2, -3)$

Each point is translated 2 units to the right and 5 units down.

EXAMPLE 4 **Using Coordinate Notation in Real Life**

COMPUTER GRAPHICS In computer graphics, translations are used to create patterns and animations. Use coordinate notation to describe each translation.

a. From *A* to *B*   **b.** From *B* to *C*

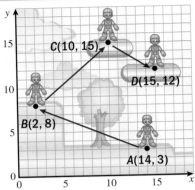
C(10, 15)
D(15, 12)
B(2, 8)
A(14, 3)

AVOID ERRORS
Make sure you incicate the correct direction of change. Use addition for points that slide to the right or up and subtraction for points that slide to the left or down.

SOLUTION

a. The character jumps from (14, 3) to (2, 8). So, each point moves 12 units to the left and 5 units up: $(x, y) \rightarrow (x - 12, y + 5)$.

b. The character jumps from (2, 8) to (10, 15). So, each point moves 8 units to the right and 7 units up: $(x, y) \rightarrow (x + 8, y + 7)$.

✓ **GUIDED PRACTICE**   **for Examples 2, 3, and 4**

2. The vertices of *ABCD* are *A*(0, 0), *B*(0, 2), *C*(2, 2), and *D*(2, 0). Graph *ABCD* and its image after a translation 1 unit to the left and 2 units up.

3. Graph the image of *ABCD* from Exercise 2 using $(x, y) \rightarrow (x + 3, y - 1)$.

4. In Example 4, use coordinate notation to describe the translation from *A* to *D*.

9.2 **EXERCISES**

HOMEWORK KEY

◆ = **MULTIPLE CHOICE PRACTICE**
Exs. 11, 14, 23, 26–28

○ = **HINTS AND HOMEWORK HELP**
for Exs. 9, 13, 23 at classzone.com

SKILLS • PROBLEM SOLVING • REASONING

1. VOCABULARY When a transformation changes a figure into another figure, what is the new figure called?

2. NOTETAKING SKILLS Make a *word triangle* for *translation* like the one on page 514. Include a sketch of an example.

SEE EXAMPLE 1
on p. 522
for Exs. 3–5

TRANSLATIONS **Tell whether the transformation shown is a translation.**

3.
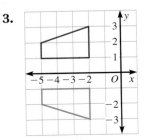

4.
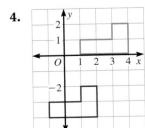

5.
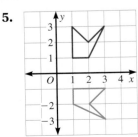

**SEE EXAMPLES
2 AND 3**
on p. 523
for Exs. 6–11

TRANSLATIONS In Exercises 6–9, graph △*LMN* with vertices *L*(2, 0), *M*(2, 3), and *N*(6, 0). Then graph the image after the given translation.

6. Translate 4 units to the left and 2 units down.

7. Translate 5 units to the left and 3 units up.

8. Translate using $(x, y) \rightarrow (x - 3, y - 4)$.

9. Translate using $(x, y) \rightarrow (x + 1, y + 1)$.

10. ERROR ANALYSIS *Describe* and correct the error in finding the coordinates of the endpoints of the image of $\overline{AB}$ after the translation $(x, y) \rightarrow (x - 6, y + 5)$.

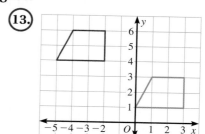

Original   Image
$A(-1, 3) \rightarrow A'(5, 8)$
$B(5, -4) \rightarrow B'(11, 1)$

11. ◆ MULTIPLE CHOICE What is the image of point $A(-3, -4)$ after the translation $(x, y) \rightarrow (x + 5, y - 4)$?

A $(1, -7)$ **B** $(2, 0)$ **C** $(-8, -8)$ **D** $(2, -8)$

SEE EXAMPLE 4
on p. 524
for Exs. 12–15

USING COORDINATE NOTATION Use coordinate notation to describe the translation from the blue figure to the red figure.

12.

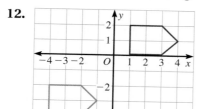

13.

14. ◆ MULTIPLE CHOICE Which translation transforms $A(4, -7)$ to $A'(1, 6)$?

A $(x, y) \rightarrow (x + 3, y + 13)$ **B** $(x, y) \rightarrow (x - 3, y + 13)$

C $(x, y) \rightarrow (x + 3, y - 1)$ **D** $(x, y) \rightarrow (x - 3, y + 1)$

15. ERROR ANALYSIS A point is translated 3 units to the right and 4 units down. *Describe* and correct the error in using coordinate notation to describe this translation.

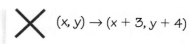

$(x, y) \rightarrow (x + 3, y + 4)$

16. REASONING You translate square *ABCD* using $(x, y) \rightarrow (x - 3, y - 4)$. The side length of *ABCD* is 5 units. Predict the side length of the image of *ABCD*.

CONNECT SKILLS TO PROBLEM SOLVING Exercises 17–20 will help you prepare for problem solving.

Use the following: You are standing at a corner. Use coordinate notation to describe the translation. The positive *y*-axis points north.

17. You walk east 5 blocks.   **18.** You walk south 4 blocks.

19. You walk east 2 blocks and north 3 blocks.   **20.** You walk west 1 block and south 3 blocks.

SEE EXAMPLE 2
on p. 523
for Ex. 21

21. MULTI-STEP PROBLEM The vertices of $\triangle RST$ are $R(-2, -1)$, $S(-5, -2)$, and $T(-4, 2)$.

   a. Graph $\triangle RST$.

   b. Find the vertices of the image of $\triangle RST$ after a translation 5 units to the right and 3 units up. Then graph the image of $\triangle RST$.

   California@*HomeTutor* for problem solving help at classzone.com

SEE EXAMPLE 4
on p. 524
for Exs. 22–23

22. WALKWAY The end of a moving walkway is 3 feet higher and 150 feet to the right of the start of the walkway. Use coordinate notation to describe the translation of a person who rides the moving walkway.

   California@*HomeTutor* for problem solving help at classzone.com

23. ◆ **MULTIPLE CHOICE** Translations are used to transform Figure 1 to Figure 2, Figure 2 to Figure 3, and so on, for a design on a quilt. Which translation could be used to transform Figure 1 to Figure 3?

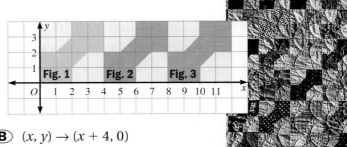

   A $(x, y) \rightarrow (x + 4, y)$ **B** $(x, y) \rightarrow (x + 4, 0)$

   C $(x, y) \rightarrow (x + 8, 0)$ **D** $(x, y) \rightarrow (x + 8, y)$

24. CHALLENGE Point $A(3, 2)$ is translated a units to the left and b units up to A'. Then A' is translated $3a$ units to the left and $0.5b$ units up to $A''(-5, 8)$. Find a and b. Then write a rule for each translation. Finally, write one rule that represents the combined effect of both translations.

25. CHALLENGE Translations can be used to create a *tessellation*. A tessellation is a repeating pattern of figures that covers a plane with no gaps or overlaps, as shown. Tessellations are often used to tile floors. Can a floor tile in the shape of a regular hexagon be used to form a tessellation? If so, describe how the hexagon is translated to form a tessellation.

◆ CALIFORNIA STANDARDS SPIRAL REVIEW

NS 2.4   **26.** Which expression has a value that is between 14 and 15? *(p. 213)*

     A $\sqrt{144}$ **B** $\sqrt{194}$ **C** $\sqrt{210}$ **D** $\sqrt{230}$

AF 4.1   **27.** What is the solution of $2x + 6 = 12$? *(p. 270)*

     A 3   **B** 6   **C** 9   **D** 12

MG 3.3   **28.** What is the length c in the triangle shown? *(p. 471)*

     A 32 in.   **B** 36 in.

     C 42 in.   **D** 45 in.

27 in. c

36 in.

 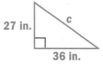

9.2 Translating Points

Standards

MG 3.2 **Understand and use coordinate graphs to plot simple figures,** determine lengths and areas related to them, **and determine their image under translations** and reflections.

QUESTION How can a spreadsheet be used to graph translations in a coordinate plane?

EXAMPLE Translate a point

Translate the point (3, 4) 1 unit to the left and 2 units up.

STEP 1 **Enter** the labels and the coordinates of the original point in rows 1 and 2.

STEP 2 **Enter** the labels and the numbers for the translation in rows 3 and 4.

	A	B
1	Original *x*	3
2	Original *y*	4
3	Translate left/right	−1
4	Translate up/down	2
5	Image *x*	=B1+B3
6	Image *y*	=B2+B4

STEP 3 **Enter** the labels and the formulas for the coordinates of the image in rows 5 and 6.

STEP 4 **Draw** the graph by selecting Insert, then Chart. Choose XY (Scatter) as the chart type, and click Next. Under the Series tab, enter "=Sheet1!$B$1" for X values and "=Sheet1!$B$2" for Y.

Then click Add and enter "=Sheet1!$B$5" for X values and "=Sheet1!$B$6" for Y. Click Next and make sure that both Major Gridlines boxes are checked under the Gridlines tab. Click Next, then Finish.

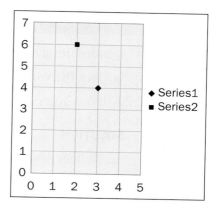

STEP 5 **Change** the numbers in cells B3 and B4 to produce other translations of the original point.

PRACTICE

Use a spreadsheet to translate the point (3, 4) as specified.

1. 3 units to the right and 6 units down

2. 2 units to the left and 7 units up

3. $(x, y) \rightarrow (x - 5, y - 2)$

4. $(x, y) \rightarrow (x + 1, y + 3)$

9.3 Reflections in the Coordinate Plane

Standards MG 3.2 Understand and use coordinate graphs to plot simple figures, determine lengths and areas related to them, and determine their image under translations and reflections.

Connect *Before* you translated figures. *Now* you will reflect figures and identify lines of symmetry.

Math and OPTICS
Ex. 23, p. 532

KEY VOCABULARY
• reflection
• line of reflection
• line symmetry

The photo above illustrates another type of transformation called a *reflection*. A **reflection** creates a mirror image of each point of a figure. The image is congruent to the original figure.

EXAMPLE 1 Identifying Reflections

Tell whether the red figure is a reflection of the blue figure.

a.

The figure is a reflection.

b.

The figure is *not* a reflection.

EXAMPLE 2 Reflecting in the *y*-Axis

Quadrilateral *ABCD* has vertices $A(1, 1)$, $B(2, 1)$, $C(2, -2)$, and $D(1, -2)$.

a. Plot the vertices and draw *ABCD*. Then reflect the figure in the *y*-axis.

b. Find and compare the side lengths and areas of *ABCD* and its image.

AVOID ERRORS
Because *ABCD* is being reflected in the *y*-axis, make sure the *y*-coordinates of *A′B′C′D′* remain the same.

SOLUTION

a. Reflect *ABCD* in the *y*-axis. The vertices of the image are $A'(-1, 1)$, $B'(-2, 1)$, $C'(-2, -2)$, and $D'(-1, -2)$.

b. Use your graph to find the side lengths and areas of *ABCD* and *A′B′C′D′*.

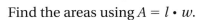

$AB = 1$	$CD = 1$	$A'B' = 1$	$C'D' = 1$
$BC = 3$	$AD = 3$	$B'C' = 3$	$A'D' = 3$

Find the areas using $A = l \cdot w$.

The area of *ABCD* is 3 • 1, or 3.

The area of *A′B′C′D′* is 3 • 1, or 3.

The corresponding side lengths and the areas of *ABCD* and its image are equal.

1. Tell whether the red arrow is a reflection of the blue arrow.

2. Graph the rectangle with vertices $J(0, 1)$, $K(0, 4)$, $L(5, 4)$, and $M(5, 1)$. Reflect the rectangle in the y-axis.

LINES OF REFLECTION When you reflect a figure in a line, the line is called the **line of reflection**. You may have noticed in Example 2 that when the line of reflection is the y-axis, the x-coordinate of each point is multiplied by -1.

KEY CONCEPT   *For Your Notebook*

Reflections in the *x*-axis

Words   To reflect a point in the x-axis, multiply its y-coordinate by -1.

Numbers $P(2, -3) \rightarrow P'(2, 3)$ **Algebra** $(x, y) \rightarrow (x, -y)$

Reflections in the *y*-axis

Words   To reflect a point in the y-axis, multiply its x-coordinate by -1.

Numbers $P(2, -3) \rightarrow P'(-2, -3)$ **Algebra** $(x, y) \rightarrow (-x, y)$

EXAMPLE 3   ◆ **Multiple Choice Practice**

ELIMINATE CHOICES
When you reflect a point in the x-axis, you multiply the y-coordinate by -1. So, you can eliminate choices A and B.

Reflect $\triangle PQR$ in the x-axis. What are the coordinates of the vertices of $\triangle P'Q'R'$?

(A) $(-1, 3), (-4, 4), (-5, 2)$

(B) $(1, 3), (4, 4), (5, 2)$

(C) $(1, -3), (4, -4), (5, -2)$

(D) $(-1, -3), (-4, -4), (-5, -2)$

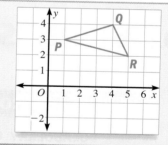

SOLUTION

Multiply each y-coordinate by -1.

Original		**Image**
(x, y)	$\rightarrow$	$(x, -y)$
$P(1, 3)$	$\rightarrow$	$P'(1, -3)$
$Q(4, 4)$	$\rightarrow$	$Q'(4, -4)$
$R(5, 2)$	$\rightarrow$	$R'(5, -2)$

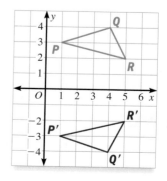

The coordinates of the vertices of $\triangle P'Q'R'$ are $(1, -3), (4, -4)$, and $(5, -2)$.

▶ **Answer** The correct answer is C. Ⓐ Ⓑ ● Ⓓ

LINE SYMMETRY A figure has **line symmetry** if one half of the figure is a mirror image of the other half. A *line of symmetry* divides the figure into two congruent parts that are mirror images of each other.

EXAMPLE 4 — Identifying Lines of Symmetry

How many lines of symmetry does the picture have?

Animated Math

For an interactive example of indentifying lines of symmetry, go to **classzone.com.**

a. One line of symmetry   **b.** Five lines of symmetry   **c.** No lines of symmetry

---

✓ **GUIDED PRACTICE**   for Examples 3 and 4

3. Graph the figure with vertices $S(-3, 2)$, $T(-1, 4)$, $U(-4, 5)$, and $V(-5, 3)$. Reflect the figure in the x-axis. Label the vertices of $S'T'U'V'$ with their coordinates.

4. How many lines of symmetry does a square have? a rhombus?

9.3 EXERCISES

HOMEWORK KEY   ◆ = **MULTIPLE CHOICE PRACTICE**
Exs. 12, 13, 26, 35–37
○ = **HINTS** AND **HOMEWORK HELP**
for Exs. 9, 13, 31 at classzone.com

SKILLS • PROBLEM SOLVING • REASONING

VOCABULARY Copy and complete the statement.

1. The transformation that creates a mirror image of the original figure is called a(n) __?__ .

2. If one half of a figure is a mirror image of the other half, then the figure has __?__ .

3. **WRITING** *Explain* how to determine whether two figures are reflections of one another in the y-axis.

SEE EXAMPLE 1
on p. 528
for Exs. 4–6

REFLECTIONS Tell whether the red figure is a reflection of the blue figure.

4.   **5.**    **6.**

SEE EXAMPLES 2 AND 3
on pp. 528–529
for Exs. 7–12

DRAWING REFLECTIONS **Graph the polygon and its reflection in the given axis.**

7. $A(3, 6)$, $B(6, 3)$, $C(5, 0)$, $D(1, 1)$; x-axis

8. $Q(-1, 3)$, $R(-3, 6)$, $S(-6, 4)$, $T(-6, 0)$; x-axis

9. $B(2, -1)$, $C(5, 0)$, $D(7, -2)$, $E(0, -6)$; y-axis

10. ERROR ANALYSIS *Describe* and correct the error in finding the coordinates of the vertices of the image of $\triangle ABC$ after a reflection in the x-axis.

Original:	Image:
A(4, 5)	A'(−4, 5)
B(2, 0)	B'(−2, 0)
C(6, 2)	C'(−6, 2)

11. TRANSFORMATIONS Consider quadrilateral $ABCD$ with vertices $A(-4, 2)$, $B(-1, 2)$, $C(-2, 0)$, and $D(-5, 0)$.

  a. Graph $ABCD$.

  b. Reflect $ABCD$ in the x-axis to form $A'B'C'D'$.

  c. Compare the areas of $ABCD$ and $A'B'C'D'$.

12. ◆ MULTIPLE CHOICE Which figure is a reflected image of Figure D?

  (A) Figure A   **(B)** Figure B

  (C) Figure C   **(D)** None

SEE EXAMPLE 4
on p. 530
for Exs. 13–15

13. ◆ MULTIPLE CHOICE How many lines of symmetry does Figure A have?

  (A) 0   **(B)** 1

  (C) 2   **(D)** 4

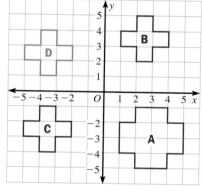

14. REASONING Draw and classify a quadrilateral with exactly two lines of symmetry. Draw the lines of symmetry. Is there more than one possible type of quadrilateral? If so, describe the quadrilateral(s).

15. ERROR ANALYSIS *Describe* and correct the error in determining the number of lines of symmetry.

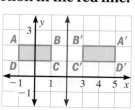

The letter Z has one line of symmetry.

REFLECTIONS **In a coordinate plane, you can reflect a figure in a line other than the x- or y-axis. In the diagram below, quadrilateral $ABCD$ is reflected in the red line. In Exercises 16–19, copy the coordinate plane, including the red line. Then graph the polygon and its reflection in the red line.**

16. $R(0, 0)$, $S(1, 3)$, $T(2, 0)$

17. $X(-2, 3)$, $Y(1, -2)$, $Z(-2, -3)$

18. $E(-3, 2)$, $F(1, 2)$, $G(1, -1)$, $H(-3, -1)$

19. $J(-4, 5)$, $K(-1, 5)$, $L(-1, 1)$, $M(-4, 1)$

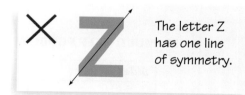

CONNECT SKILLS TO PROBLEM SOLVING Exercises 20–25 will help you
prepare for problem solving.

Name the type of transformation modeled by the action.

20. Riding a moving sidewalk

21. Making a fingerprint on paper

22. Going down a water slide

23. Looking in a mirror

24. Seeing the sun's image on a lake

25. Moving text by using the space bar

SEE EXAMPLE 3
on p. 529
for Ex. 26

26. ◆ **MULTIPLE CHOICE** $\triangle RST$ is reflected in the x-axis to form $\triangle R'S'T'$. The coordinates of point R are $(-4, 3)$. What are the coordinates of R'?

(**A**) $(4, 3)$ (**B**) $(4, -3)$ (**C**) $(-4, 3)$ (**D**) $(-4, -3)$

California @*HomeTutor* for problem solving help at classzone.com

SEE EXAMPLE 4
on p. 530
for Exs. 27–29

LINE SYMMETRY **How many lines of symmetry does the figure have?**

27.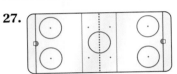

28.

29.

California @*HomeTutor* for problem solving help at classzone.com

30. **GEOMETRY** Graph the polygon with vertices $S(-6, 0)$, $T(0, 6)$, $V(6, 0)$, $W(2, -4)$, and $X(-2, -4)$. Reflect the polygon in the x-axis, graphing the image in the same coordinate plane used for the original figure. Does the original figure have more than one line of symmetry? *Explain.*

31. **GEOMETRY** Triangle ABC is congruent to triangle $A'B'C'$. Find a combination of translations and reflections that transform triangle ABC to triangle $A'B'C'$.

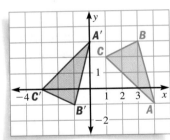

32. **MULTI-STEP PROBLEM** Use the table below.

Sides	3	4	5	6	8
Regular Polygon		?	?	?	?
Lines of Symmetry	?	?	?	?	?

  a. Sketch Copy the table and sketch a regular polygon with the given number of sides in each column. Draw all the lines of symmetry.

  b. Evaluate Count the lines of symmetry. Complete the table.

  c. Look for a Pattern How is the number of sides related to the number of lines of symmetry?

◆ = **MULTIPLE CHOICE PRACTICE** ◯ = **HINTS AND HOMEWORK HELP** at classzone.com

33. CHALLENGE A polygon has vertices $A(1, -2)$, $B(5, -1)$, $C(8, -4)$, $D(7, -7)$, and $E(4, -8)$. Reflect the polygon in the x-axis and find the coordinates of the vertices of its image. Then reflect the image in the y-axis. Is the third polygon a reflection of the original polygon? *Explain.*

34. CHALLENGE A telephone company wants to place a telephone pole along a street so that the combined length of wire from home A to the pole to home B is minimized. Using the graph shown, the company finds the reflection of A in the line of the street. Then they draw a line from A' to B. The intersection of this line and the line of the street is the location for the pole. Copy the graph and complete this process. Then use the Pythagorean Theorem to find the length of wire needed from each home to the telephone pole.

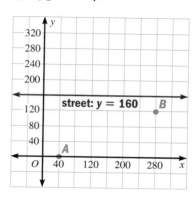

◆ CALIFORNIA STANDARDS SPIRAL REVIEW

MG 1.1

35. What number of grams is equal to 4.32 kilograms? *(p. 437)*

 Ⓐ 43.2 g   Ⓑ 432 g   Ⓒ 4320 g   Ⓓ 43,200 g

AF 2.2

36. What is the simplified form of $(x^9 y^3) \div (x^3 y^3)$? *(p. 399)*

 Ⓐ x^6 Ⓑ $x^6 y$ Ⓒ $x^3 y$ Ⓓ x^3

MG 3.4

37. The figure shows two views of a building. Quadrilateral $CDEF \cong$ quadrilateral $MLKJ$. What is $m\angle K$? *(p. 516)*

 Ⓐ 45°   Ⓑ 68°

 Ⓒ 96°   Ⓓ 112°

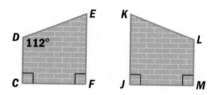

QUIZ *for Lessons 9.1–9.3*

In the diagram, $\triangle ABD \cong \triangle CDB$. *(p. 516)*

 1. Find $m\angle C$.   **2.** Find $m\angle ABD$.

 3. Find AD.   **4.** Find DC.

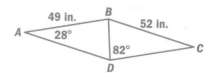

The vertices of $\triangle RST$ are $R(1, 2)$, $S(-1, 5)$, and $T(4, 1)$. Find the coordinates of the vertices of the image after the indicated transformation.

 5. Translation: $(x, y) \to (x + 4, y + 3)$ *(p. 522)*   **6.** Reflection in the y-axis *(p. 528)*

 7. Translation: $(x, y) \to (x - 5, y - 2)$ *(p. 522)*   **8.** Reflection in the x-axis *(p. 528)*

9. PHOTOGRAPH You enlarge a photograph that is 4 inches high and 6 inches long. The height of the enlarged picture is 6 inches. What is the length of the enlarged picture? *(p. 516)*

Multiple Choice Practice for Lessons 9.1–9.3

1. Which is the translation shown? **MG 3.2**

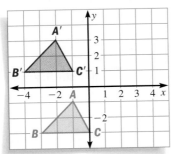

Ⓐ $(x, y) \rightarrow (x + 1, y - 4)$

Ⓑ $(x, y) \rightarrow (x - 4, y + 1)$

Ⓒ $(x, y) \rightarrow (x - 1, y + 4)$

Ⓓ $(x, y) \rightarrow (x + 4, y - 1)$

2. What is the image of $A(3, 2)$ after a reflection in the *x*-axis? **MG 3.2**

Ⓐ $A'(-3, 2)$ Ⓑ $A'(2, 3)$

Ⓒ $A'(-3, -2)$ Ⓓ $A'(3, -2)$

3. What is the image of $S(-3, 5)$ after a translation 6 units to the left and 4 units up? **MG 3.2**

Ⓐ $S'(3, 5)$ Ⓑ $S'(-9, 9)$

Ⓒ $S'(1, -1)$ Ⓓ $S'(-9, 1)$

4. Houses A and B are part of a housing complex composed of ten congruent houses. House A has a rectangular foundation that is 30 feet long and 24 feet wide. What is the length of the foundation of house B? **MG 3.4, MR 1.1**

Ⓐ 12 ft   Ⓑ 15 ft

Ⓒ 24 ft   Ⓓ 30 ft

5. Which action can be modeled by a reflection? **MG 3.2, MR 2.5**

Ⓐ Coasting downhill on a bike

Ⓑ A car traveling on a road

Ⓒ A gate swinging 180° on its hinges

Ⓓ A fish jumping out of water

6. In the figure, similar triangles are formed by Jared and his shadow and the tree and its shadow. What is the tree's height? **MG 3.4**

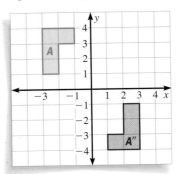

Ⓐ 10 ft   Ⓑ 11 ft

Ⓒ 12 ft   Ⓓ 30 ft

7. Which pair of transformations can be used to transform figure A to figure A″? **MG 3.2**

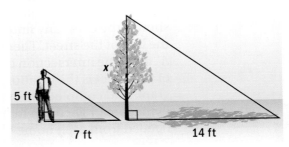

Ⓐ A reflection in the *x*-axis followed by a translation

Ⓑ A reflection in the *y*-axis followed by another reflection in the *y*-axis

Ⓒ A reflection in the *x*-axis followed by a reflection in the *y*-axis

Ⓓ A horizontal translation followed by a reflection in the *x*-axis

8. $\triangle ABC \cong \triangle DEF$. What is $m\angle A$? **MG 3.4**

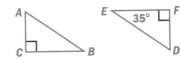

Ⓐ 35°   Ⓑ 55°

Ⓒ 65°   Ⓓ 75°

9.4 Dilations in the Coordinate Plane

Standards MG 3.2 **Understand and use coordinate graphs to plot simple figures, determine lengths and areas related to them,** and determine their image under translations and reflections.

Connect *Before* you transformed polygons using translations and reflections.
Now you will transform polygons using dilations.

Math and **DESIGN**
Example 3, p. 536

KEY VOCABULARY
- dilation
- scale factor

A **dilation** stretches or shrinks a figure. The image created by a dilation is similar to the original figure. The **scale factor** of a dilation is the ratio of a side length after the dilation to the corresponding side length before the dilation. In this lesson, the center of a dilation will always be the origin.

KEY CONCEPT
For Your Notebook

Dilations

Words To dilate a polygon, multiply the coordinates of each vertex by the scale factor k.

Numbers $P(4, 1) \rightarrow P'(8, 2)$ **Algebra** $P(x, y) \rightarrow P'(kx, ky)$

EXAMPLE 1 Dilating a Polygon

Rectangle $ABCD$ has vertices $A(-1, -1)$, $B(-1, 1)$, $C(2, 1)$, and $D(2, -1)$. Dilate $ABCD$ using a scale factor of 3. Then find the side lengths, perimeters, and areas of the two figures.

Graph $ABCD$. Then graph the image.

Original		**Image**
(x, y)	$\rightarrow$	$(3x, 3y)$
$A(-1, -1)$	$\rightarrow$	$A'(-3, -3)$
$B(-1, 1)$	$\rightarrow$	$B'(-3, 3)$
$C(2, 1)$	$\rightarrow$	$C'(6, 3)$
$D(2, -1)$	$\rightarrow$	$D'(6, -3)$

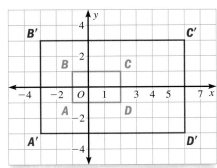

USING SCALE FACTOR
You can generalize the results in Example 1. If the scale factor for two similar figures is k, then the ratio of their perimeters is also k, and the ratio of their areas is k^2.

$AB = CD = 2$ $A'B' = C'D' = 6$
$BC = AD = 3$ $B'C' = A'D' = 9$

Perimeter of $ABCD = 2(3) + 2(2) = 10$
Perimeter of $A'B'C'D' = 2(9) + 2(6) = 30$

Area of $ABCD = 3 \cdot 2 = 6$
Area of $A'B'C'D' = 9 \cdot 6 = 54$

The side lengths of $A'B'C'D'$ are 3 times the corresponding side lengths of $ABCD$.

The perimeter of $A'B'C'D'$ is 3 times the perimeter of $ABCD$.

The area of $A'B'C'D'$ is 9 times the area of $ABCD$.

EXAMPLE 2 **Using a Scale Factor Less Than 1**

△*JKL* has vertices *J*(−6, 0), *K*(2, 8), and *L*(4, 6). Dilate △*JKL* using a scale factor of 0.5.

SOLUTION

UNDERSTANDING SCALE FACTOR

A scale factor greater than 1 results in an enlargement of the original figure. A scale factor between 0 and 1 results in a reduction of the original figure.

Graph the original triangle. Find the coordinates of the vertices of the image.

Original		**Image**
(*x*, *y*)	→	(0.5*x*, 0.5*y*)
J(−6, 0)	→	*J*′(−3, 0)
K(2, 8)	→	*K*′(1, 4)
L(4, 6)	→	*L*′(2, 3)

Graph △*J*′*K*′*L*′.

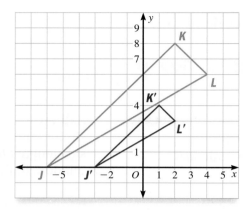

EXAMPLE 3 **Finding a Scale Factor**

PHOTOGRAPH A photographer uses a computer program to enlarge a photograph, as shown. What is the scale factor of the dilation?

About the Standards

Because the photograph is enlarged, the scale factor should be greater than 1. So, a scale factor of 3 is a reasonable solution (MR 3.1).

SOLUTION

Use the grid to find the width of the photographs. The width of the original photograph is 3 − 1 = 2 units. The width of the image is 9 − 3 = 6 units.

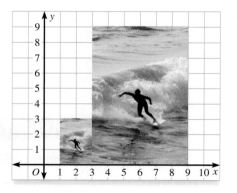

$$\text{Scale factor} = \frac{\text{Side length of dilated figure}}{\text{Side length of original figure}}$$ Definition of scale factor

$$= \frac{6}{2} = 3$$ Substitute and simplfiy.

▶ **Answer** The scale factor is 3.

✓ **GUIDED PRACTICE**   **for Examples 1, 2, and 3**

1. Graph △*RST* with vertices *R*(1, 1), *S*(3, 2), and *T*(2, 3). Then graph its image after a dilation using a scale factor of 2.

2. **WHAT IF?** In Example 2, suppose the scale factor of the dilation is $\frac{1}{4}$. Graph △*JKL* and its image using this scale factor.

3. $\overline{AB}$ has endpoints *A*(1, 3) and *B*(4, 3). $\overline{A'B'}$ has endpoints *A*′(1.5, 4.5) and *B*′(6, 4.5). Find the scale factor of the dilation.

9.4 EXERCISES

HOMEWORK KEY

◆ = **MULTIPLE CHOICE PRACTICE**
Exs. 11, 14, 24, 30–32

○ = **HINTS AND HOMEWORK HELP**
for Exs. 5, 15, 27 at classzone.com

SKILLS • PROBLEM SOLVING • REASONING

VOCABULARY Copy and complete the statement.

1. The ratio of corresponding side lengths is the __?__ of a dilation.

2. A polygon and its image after a dilation are always __?__.

3. **WRITING** A polygon is dilated using a scale factor of 1. Will the image be *larger than*, *smaller than*, or *identical to* the original polygon? *Explain.*

SEE EXAMPLES 1 AND 2
on pp. 535–536
for Exs. 4–12

GRAPHING DILATIONS Graph the polygon with the given vertices. Then graph its image after a dilation using a scale factor of k.

4. $W(2, 2)$, $X(0, 4)$, $Y(4, 6)$, $Z(6, 0)$; $k = 3$

5. $B(0, -2)$, $C(4, 2)$, $D(-2, 6)$, $E(-6, 6)$, $F(-4, 2)$; $k = \frac{1}{2}$

6. $R(8, 8)$, $S(-4, 4)$, $T(-4, -4)$; $k = \frac{3}{4}$

7. $L(2, -2)$, $M(4, 2)$, $N(-3, 2)$, $P(-1, -2)$; $k = 4$

8. $G(-2, -6)$, $H(-8, -8)$, $J(-6, -2)$, $K(0, 0)$; $k = 1.5$

9. $K(24, 6)$, $L(8, 10)$, $M(8, 0)$, $N(0, 18)$, $P(20, 22)$; $k = 1.75$

10. $Q(-3, 0)$, $R(3, 9)$, $S(6, -12)$; $k = \frac{2}{3}$

11. ◆ **MULTIPLE CHOICE** $\triangle A'B'C'$ is the image of $\triangle ABC$ after a dilation using a scale factor of 5. What are the coordinates of A'?

Ⓐ (25, 20)　　　Ⓑ (10, 10)

Ⓒ (15, −5)　　　Ⓓ (5, 5)

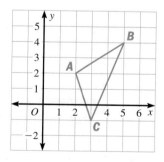

12. **ERROR ANALYSIS** A student is asked to graph the image of polygon $ABCD$ after a dilation using a scale factor of 3. *Describe* and correct the student's error.

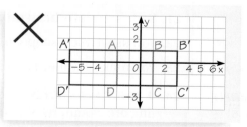

13. **ERROR ANALYSIS** $\triangle A'B'C'$ is the image of $\triangle ABC$ after a dilation. The length of $\overline{AB}$ is 3 and the length of $\overline{A'B'}$ is 6. A student says the scale factor of the dilation is $\frac{1}{2}$. *Describe* and correct the student's error.

SEE EXAMPLE 3
on p. 536
for Exs. 14–20

14. ◆ **MULTIPLE CHOICE** *EFGH* is the image of *ABCD* after a dilation. What is the scale factor?

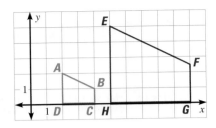

(A) 0.4   (B) 0.5

(C) 2   (D) 2.5

SCALE FACTORS Find the scale factor of the dilation.

(15.)

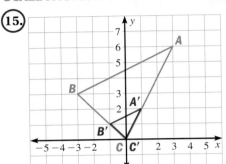

16.

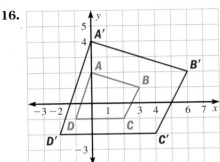

DILATIONS Graph the similar figures and find the scale factor.

17. △*ABC*: *A*(4, 6), *B*(8, 8), *C*(12, 4)
△*A'B'C'*: *A'*(2, 3), *B'*(4, 4), *C'*(6, 2)

18. *GHIJ*: *G*(1, 4), *H*(6, 4), *I*(6, 1), *J*(1, 1)
G'H'I'J': *G'*(3, 12), *H'*(18, 12), *I'*(18, 3), *J'*(3, 3)

19. *PQRS*: *P*(4, 8), *Q*(8, 8), *R*(8, 2), *S*(4, 2)
P'Q'R'S': *P'*(8, 16), *Q'*(16, 16), *R'*(16, 4), *S'*(8, 4)

20. **NAMING SIMILAR POLYGONS** Name two similar polygons in the diagram. Find the scale factor.

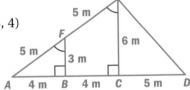

CONNECT SKILLS TO PROBLEM SOLVING Exercises 21–23 will help you prepare for problem solving.

Tell whether the scale factor is *greater than 1* or *between 0 and 1* for the situation.

21. You use an overhead projector for a presentation.

22. You use a microscope to view bacteria in science class.

23. You make a wallet-size photograph from an 8 in. × 10 in. photograph.

SEE EXAMPLE 3
on p. 536
for Exs. 24–25

24. ◆ **MULTIPLE CHOICE** The dimensions of a negative made from 35 mm film are 24 mm by 36 mm. If a 100 mm by 150 mm print is made from this negative, what is the scale factor?

(A) $\frac{6}{25}$ (B) $\frac{2}{3}$ (C) $\frac{3}{2}$ (D) $\frac{25}{6}$

California *@HomeTutor* for problem solving help at classzone.com

25. REASONING *EFGH* is the image of *ABCD* after a dilation. The vertices of *ABCD* and *EFGH* are *A*(−1, 2), *B*(3, 2), *C*(3, −1), *D*(−1, −1), *E*(−4, 8), *F*(12, 8), *G*(12, −4), and *H*(−4, −4). What is the scale factor? What are the perimeters of *ABCD* and *EFGH*? How is the ratio of the perimeters related to the scale factor?

California @*HomeTutor* for problem solving help at classzone.com

26. BOOKSHELF A friend buys the bookshelf shown below for her bedroom. The assembly instructions include the diagram shown below. Is the diagram a dilation of the bookshelf? *Justify* your reasoning.

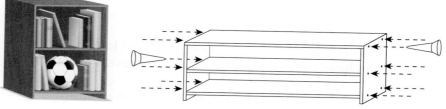

27. REASONING △*A'B'C'* is the image of △*ABC* after a dilation using a scale factor of $\frac{1}{2}$. △*A"B"C"* is the image of △*A'B'C'* after a dilation using a scale factor of 2. Is △*ABC* similar to △*A"B"C"*? If so, what is the scale factor? *Explain.*

28. CHALLENGE *Explain* why an 11 in. × 17 in. piece of paper is not a dilation of an 8.5 in. × 11 in. piece of paper.

29. CHALLENGE Draw a quadrilateral with vertices *A*(3, 2), *B*(8, 2), *C*(8, 5), and *D*(3, 6).

   a. Find the coordinates of the image *A'B'C'D'* after a dilation having a scale factor of −1. Draw the image.

   b. Reflect *ABCD* in the *x*-axis to obtain *A"B"C"D"*.

   c. Reflect *A"B"C"D"* in the *y*-axis to obtain *A'''B'''C'''D'''*.

   d. Use your results from parts (a) and (c) to make a conjecture about dilating using a scale factor of −1.

◆ CALIFORNIA STANDARDS SPIRAL REVIEW

AF 2.2

30. What is the simplified form of $\frac{36x^2y^4}{3xy^5}$? *(p. 399)*

   (A) $12xy$ **(B)** $\frac{18x}{y}$ **(C)** $\frac{12y}{x}$ **(D)** $\frac{12x}{y}$

AF 3.3

31. What is the slope of the graph of $y = -3x + 4$? *(p. 342)*

   (A) −3   **(B)** 0   **(C)** 3   **(D)** 4

MG 2.1

32. You need to replace the railing that goes around your circular swimming pool. The pool has a radius of 10 feet. What is the minimum length of railing that is needed? *(p. 489)*

   (A) 20 ft   **(B)** 20π ft   **(C)** 100 ft   **(D)** 100π ft

9.5 Making a Scale Model

MATERIALS • ruler • scissors • tape

Standards

MG 1.2 **Construct** and read drawings and models made to scale.

QUESTION How can you make a scale model of a classroom?

EXPLORE Make a scale model

Make a scale model of a rectangular classroom that is 24 feet long, 20 feet wide, and 10 feet high. In your model, let 1 inch represent 8 feet.

STEP 1 **Write** and solve proportions to find the length l, width w, and height h of the model classroom.

inches $\longrightarrow$
feet $\longrightarrow$

$$\frac{1}{8} = \frac{l}{24} \qquad \frac{1}{8} = \frac{w}{20} \qquad \frac{1}{8} = \frac{h}{10}$$

$$24 = 8 \cdot l \qquad 20 = 8 \cdot w \qquad 10 = 8 \cdot h$$

$$3 = l \qquad\quad 2.5 = w \qquad 1.25 = h$$

STEP 2 **Use** a ruler to create a scale drawing with the dimensions from Step 1. Your scale drawing should resemble the diagram shown below.

STEP 3 **Cut** out the scale drawing that you created in Step 2 along the solid lines. Fold along the dotted lines and use tape to assemble the model.

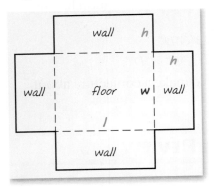

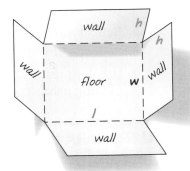

DRAW CONCLUSIONS Use your observations to complete these exercises

Make a scale model of the rectangular object. In your model, let 1 inch represent 8 feet.

1. Teacher's desk: $l = 6$ ft, $w = 4$ ft, $h = 4$ ft

2. Cabinet: $l = 12$ ft, $w = 4$ ft, $h = 4$ ft

3. **REASONING** Arrange the scale models from Exercises 1 and 2 inside the scale model of the classroom. *Explain* why this method might be used to decide how to arrange the furniture.

9.5 Scale Drawings and Models

Standards MG 1.2 Construct and **read drawings and models made to scale**.

Connect *Before* you found the scale factor of dilated figures.
Now you will use scale with drawings and models.

Math and ARCHITECTURE
Ex. 25, p. 544

KEY VOCABULARY
• scale drawing
• scale model
• scale

A **scale drawing** is a two-dimensional drawing that represents a real object. A **scale model** is a three-dimensional model that represents a real object.

The dimensions of a scale drawing or a scale model are proportional to the dimensions of the actual object it represents. The relationship between the drawing's or model's dimensions and the actual object's dimensions is called the **scale**.

For example, a map scale that reads "1 in. : 2 mi" or "1 in. = 2 mi" means that 1 inch on the map represents an actual distance of 2 miles.

EXAMPLE 1   Using a Scale Drawing

 WEST COAST On the map, the distance from Los Angeles to San Diego is 2 inches. What is the actual distance?

SOLUTION

ANOTHER WAY
For an alternative method for solving the problem in Example 1, turn to page 546 for the **Problem Solving Workshop**.

Let x represent the actual distance (in miles) between Los Angeles and San Diego. The ratio of the distance between the two cities on the map to the actual distance x is equal to the scale of the map. Write and solve a proportion using this relationship.

$\text{Scale} = \dfrac{\text{Distance on map}}{\text{Actual distance}}$ **Definition of scale**

$\dfrac{1 \text{ in.}}{60 \text{ mi}} = \dfrac{2 \text{ in.}}{x \text{ mi}}$ **Write proportion.**

$x = 60 \cdot 2$ **Cross products property**

$x = 120$ **Multiply.**

▶ **Answer** The actual distance from Los Angeles to San Diego is 120 miles.

✓ **GUIDED PRACTICE**   for Example 1

1. **WHAT IF?** Use a ruler and the map in Example 1 to find the distance (in miles) between Los Angeles and Oceanside.

EXAMPLE 2 Finding a Scale

BLUEPRINTS During construction of a building, electricians use detailed scale drawings, called blueprints, to determine where to install electrical outlets. Suppose a room in the building is to be 36 feet wide. An electrician is using a scale drawing of the room that is 18 inches wide. Find the drawing's scale.

SOLUTION

Write a ratio using corresponding side lengths of the scale drawing and the actual room in the building. Then simplify the ratio so the numerator is 1.

$$\frac{18 \text{ in.}}{36 \text{ ft}}$$ ← **Width of scale drawing**
← **Width of room in the building**

$$\frac{18 \text{ in.}}{36 \text{ ft}} = \frac{1 \text{ in.}}{2 \text{ ft}}$$ **Simplify.**

▶ **Answer** The drawing's scale is 1 in. : 2 ft.

SCALE FACTORS The scales in Examples 1 and 2 give the relationships between dimensions using units. A scale factor is a numeric value found by creating a scale without units. A scale can be written as a ratio without units if both measurements have the same unit. To write the scale from Example 2 without units, write 2 feet as 24 inches, as shown.

Scale with units   **Scale without units**

1 in. : 2 ft ⟶ $\frac{1 \text{ in.}}{2 \text{ ft}}$ ⟶ $\frac{1 \text{ in.}}{24 \text{ in.}}$ ⟶ 1 : 24

EXAMPLE 3 ◆ Multiple Choice Practice

Strawberry Point, Iowa, has a strawberry sculpture that is 180 inches tall. If the scale of this model is 120 : 1, how tall was the actual strawberry?

(A) 1.5 in.   **(B)** 15 in.   **(C)** 18 in.   **(D)** 180 in.

ELIMINATE CHOICES
According to the scale, the actual strawberry should be smaller than the sculpture. So, you can eliminate choice D.

SOLUTION

$$\text{Scale} = \frac{\text{Height of strawberry model}}{\textbf{Height of actual strawberry}}$$

$$\frac{120}{1} = \frac{180 \text{ in.}}{h \text{ in.}}$$ **Write a proportion.**

$$120h = 180$$ **Cross products property**

$$h = 1.5$$ **Divide each side by 120.**

The height of the actual strawberry was 1.5 inches.

180 in.

STRAWBERRY POINT

▶ **Answer** The correct answer is A.

2. **MAPS** On a map, 11 inches represents 275 miles. What is the scale?

3. **WHAT IF?** Suppose the scale in Example 3 was 100 : 1. What was the height of the actual strawberry?

9.5 EXERCISES

HOMEWORK KEY

◆ = **MULTIPLE CHOICE PRACTICE**
Exs. 7, 10, 20, 28–30

○ = **HINTS AND HOMEWORK HELP**
for Exs. 3, 9, 23 at classzone.com

SKILLS • PROBLEM SOLVING • REASONING

1. **VOCABULARY** Copy and complete: A two-dimensional drawing that represents a real object is a(n) __?__ .

2. **WRITING** *Describe* how to write a scale without units.

SEE EXAMPLE 1
on p. 541
for Exs. 3–7

USING SCALES The scale on a map is 1 cm : 4 km. Find the distance on the map for the actual distance given.

3. 16 km   4. 10 km   5. 52 km   6. 65 km

7. ◆ **MULTIPLE CHOICE** The scale on a map is 1 in. : 200 mi. The distance from A to B is 2.5 in. What is the actual distance from A to B?

Ⓐ 250 mi   Ⓑ 350 mi   Ⓒ 400 mi   Ⓓ 500 mi

SEE EXAMPLE 2
on p. 542
for Exs. 8–10

FINDING SCALES Find the scale.

8. Actual size: 12 meters
   Drawing size: 3 centimeters

9. Actual size: 45 feet
   Model size: 5 inches

10. ◆ **MULTIPLE CHOICE** A blueprint shows a width of 3 inches. The actual width is 108 inches. What is the scale of the blueprint?

Ⓐ 1 in. : 1 ft   Ⓑ 1 in. : 36 ft   Ⓒ 1 in. : 36 in.   Ⓓ 1 ft : 12 in.

ERROR ANALYSIS *Describe* and correct the error.

11. The scale is 1 cm : 100 m. What actual distance corresponds to 2 cm?

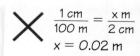

$$\times \quad \frac{1\,cm}{100\,m} = \frac{x\,m}{2\,cm}$$
$$x = 0.02\ m$$

12. Write the scale 1 in. : 10 yd without units.

$$\times \quad 1\ in. : 10\ yd = 1 : 10$$

SEE EXAMPLE 3
on p. 542
for Exs. 13–16

SCALE MODELS You use the scale 1 : 200 to make scale models of buildings. A building's actual height is given. Find the model's height.

13. $h = 100$ ft   14. $h = 240$ ft   15. $h = 316$ ft   16. $h = 545$ ft

CONNECT SKILLS TO PROBLEM SOLVING Exercises 17–19 will help you prepare for problem solving.

Find the scale of the drawing or model.

17. In a scale drawing, an object is 2 inches long. The actual object is 36 inches long.

18. In a scale model, an object is 2 feet tall. The actual object is 246 feet tall.

19. In a scale model, an object is 33 meters wide. The actual object is 3 meters wide.

SEE EXAMPLE 1
on p. 541
for Ex. 20

20. ◆ **MULTIPLE CHOICE** The scale on a map is $\frac{1}{4}$ in. : 20 mi. The distance from Montgomery, Alabama, to Atlanta, Georgia, is about 2 inches on the map. About how far is it from Montgomery to Atlanta?

(A) 20 mi   **(B)** 80 mi   **(C)** 160 mi   **(D)** 200 mi

California @HomeTutor for problem solving help at classzone.com

SEE EXAMPLE 2
on p. 542
for Exs. 21–22

21. **REASONING** The wingspan and length of a space shuttle orbiter model are shown. What additional information could be used to find the scale of the model? *Explain.*

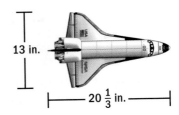

13 in.

$20\frac{1}{3}$ in.

California @HomeTutor for problem solving help at classzone.com

READING *IN* MATH Read the information below for Exercises 22–24.

Model Trains The San Diego Model Railroad Museum in Balboa Park features four models of California railroads as well as a toy train gallery. The railroad shown is an N-scale model of the Pacific Desert Lines railroad. N-scale models use a scale of 1 : 160. The Pacific Desert Lines railroad runs from San Diego to El Centro. It makes connections to the Atchison, Topeka, and Santa Fe Railway in San Diego and the Southern Pacific Railway in El Centro.

Scale is 1 : 160

22. **Scale** Write the scale of the Pacific Desert Lines railroad in feet to miles.

23. **Calculate** The length of the Pacific Desert Lines' mainline track is 33 miles. How long is the model railroad's mainline track?

24. **Calculate** A branch line of the model is 51 feet. How many miles is the actual branch line?

25. **SHORT RESPONSE** The Transamerica Building in San Francisco is 853 feet tall and is 145 feet wide at its widest point. You want to make a drawing of the building that has a scale of 1 in. : 80 ft. Will your drawing fit on a regular $8\frac{1}{2}$ in. × 11 in. sheet of paper? *Explain* your reasoning.

◆ = **MULTIPLE CHOICE PRACTICE**   ◯ = **HINTS AND HOMEWORK HELP** at classzone.com

26. CHALLENGE The width of an object is 12 feet. You make model A of the object using a scale factor of $\frac{1}{2}$. Then you make model B of model A using a scale factor of 3. Then you make model C of model B using a scale factor of $\frac{5}{6}$. What scale factor relates model C to the original object?

27. CHALLENGE A 5 in. × 8 in. photo needs to be proportionally increased in size to fit a space whose width is 5 inches less than its length. Find the perimeter and area of the enlarged photo.

◆ CALIFORNIA STANDARDS SPIRAL REVIEW

AF 2.2 **28.** What is the simplified form of $(4x^3)(-2x^2)$? *(p. 399)*

    (A) $2x$ **(B)** $-6x$ **(C)** $-8x^6$ **(D)** $-8x^5$

MG 3.3 **29.** The legs of a right triangle have lengths of 5 centimeters and 12 centimeters. What is the length of the hypotenuse? *(p. 471)*

    (A) 13 cm   **(B)** $\sqrt{191}$ cm   **(C)** $6\sqrt{7}$ cm   **(D)** 16 cm

AF 4.2 **30.** Your car gets 32 miles per gallon. Today, you plan on driving 152 miles. Tomorrow, you plan on driving 232 miles. What is the total amount of gas you should expect to use? *(p. 348)*

    (A) 8 gal   **(B)** 12 gal   **(C)** 22 gal   **(D)** 30 gal

QUIZ *for Lessons 9.4–9.5*

Graph the polygon with the given vertices. Then graph its image after a dilation using a scale factor of *k*. *(p. 535)*

1. $R(0, 2)$, $S(3, 6)$, $T(5, 1)$; $k = 3$

2. $F(-6, -6)$, $G(-9, 6)$, $H(6, 3)$, $J(9, -3)$; $k = \frac{1}{3}$

The scale on a map is 1 in. : 20 mi. Find the distance on the map for the actual distance given. *(p. 541)*

3. 60 mi   **4.** 15 mi   **5.** 45 mi   **6.** 125 mi

Find the scale. *(p. 541)*

7. Actual size: 110 centimeters
    Drawing size: 25 millimeters

8. Actual size: 3 yards
    Model size: 3 inches

9. PERIMETER Square A has a side length of 3 cm. It is dilated using a scale factor of 5. Find the perimeter of the image of square A. *(p. 535)*

10. STATUE A statue of a town's first mayor stands in front of town hall and is 111 inches tall. The scale of the statue is 1.5 : 1. How tall was the first mayor in feet and inches? *(p. 541)*

Using ALTERNATIVE METHODS

Another Way to Solve Example 1, page 541

Standards
MG 1.2

In Example 1 on page 541, you found the actual distance between Los Angeles and San Diego by finding the distance on a map and using the map's scale to set up a proportion. You can also find the actual distance between Los Angeles and San Diego by multiplying the original distance on the map by a scale factor.

PROBLEM

WEST COAST On the map, the distance from Los Angeles to San Diego is 2 inches. What is the actual distance?

METHOD

Using a Scale Factor The map is a dilation of the portion of California it shows. Let k be the scale factor of the dilation, and let x be the actual distance from Los Angeles to San Diego.

STEP 1 **Find** the scale factor k by writing the map's scale without units.

$$k = \frac{1 \text{ in.}}{60 \text{ mi}} \times \frac{1 \text{ ft}}{12 \text{ in.}} \times \frac{1 \text{ mi}}{5280 \text{ ft}} = \frac{1}{3,801,600}$$

STEP 2 **Write** and solve an equation to find the actual distance x. The product of k and x is the distance on the map (2 in.).

$$\frac{1}{3,801,600}x = 2 \text{ in.} \qquad\qquad x = 7,603,200 \text{ in.}$$

STEP 3 **Convert** the actual distance from inches to miles.

$$x = 7,603,200 \text{ in.} \times \frac{1 \text{ ft}}{12 \text{ in.}} \times \frac{1 \text{ mi}}{5280 \text{ ft}} = 120 \text{ mi}$$

▶ **Answer** The actual distance is 120 miles.

PRACTICE

1. **WHAT IF?** On the map, the distance from Oceanside to San Diego is 0.6 inch. What is the actual distance? Solve this problem using two methods.

2. **CAR** The length of a model car is 8 inches. The scale of the model is 1 in. : 2 ft. What is the actual length of the car?

3. **CONSTRUCTION** The length of a building on a blueprint is 20 inches. The scale on the blueprint is 1 in. : 25 ft. What is the actual length of the building?

4. **MURAL** A mural of an object has a scale of 1.5 m : 1 cm. In the mural, the object is 30 meters wide. What is its actual width?

MIXED REVIEW of Skills and Problem Solving

Multiple Choice Practice for Lessons 9.4–9.5

1. A scale model of the Chrysler Building in New York City has a scale of 1 in. : 200 ft. The height of the actual Chrysler Building is 1046 feet. The width of the model is 4.23 inches less than the height of the model. What is the width of the model? **MG 1.2, MR 2.1**

   (A) 1 in.
   (B) 5.23 in.
   (C) 1 ft
   (D) 200 ft

2. $\triangle DEF$ is the image of $\triangle ABC$ after a dilation. What is the scale factor? **MG 3.2**

   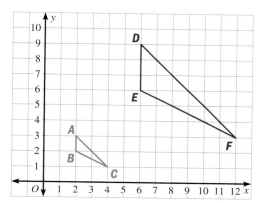

   (A) 2
   (B) 2.5
   (C) 3
   (D) 3.5

3. Quadrilateral $ABCD$ has vertices $A(-12, 8)$, $B(20, 16)$, $C(16, 4)$, and $D(-8, -16)$. What are the vertices of the image $JKLM$ when $ABCD$ is dilated using a scale factor of $\frac{1}{4}$? **MG 3.2, MR 2.6**

   (A) $J(-2, 3)$, $K(1, 4)$, $L(5, 5)$, $M(-7, -9)$
   (B) $J(-6, 4)$, $K(10, 8)$, $L(8, 2)$, $M(-4, -8)$
   (C) $J(-3, 2)$, $K(4, 4)$, $L(4, 2)$, $M(-2, -4)$
   (D) $J(-3, 2)$, $K(5, 4)$, $L(4, 1)$, $M(-2, -4)$

4. The actual length of an object is 84 feet. A scale drawing shows the length of the object as 6 inches. What is the scale of the drawing? **MG 1.2**

   (A) 1 in. : 14 in.
   (B) 1 ft : 14 ft
   (C) 14 in. : 1 ft
   (D) 1 in. : 14 ft

5. A map of a park has a scale of 1 in. : 3 yd. What do 7 inches on the map represent? **MG 1.2**

   (A) 7 yd
   (B) 21 yd
   (C) 42 yd
   (D) 63 yd

6. The rectangle shown is dilated using a scale factor of 4. What are the coordinates of C'? **MG 3.2**

   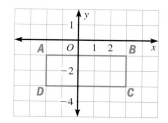

   (A) $(12, -12)$
   (B) $(12, -3)$
   (C) $(12, -4)$
   (D) $(12, -1)$

7. What is the scale 1 cm : 3 km without units? **MG 1.2**

   (A) 1 : 3000
   (B) 1 : 30,000
   (C) 1 : 300,000
   (D) 1 : 3,000,000

8. The model airplane shown was built using a scale of 1 : 40. What is the actual length of the airplane? **MG 1.2**

   6.65 in.

   (A) 22 ft 2 in.
   (B) 26 ft 6 in.
   (C) 40 ft
   (D) 266 ft

BIG IDEAS

For Your Notebook

Big Idea 1 — Using Congruent and Similar Figures

Congruent Figures	Similar Figures
Congruent polygons have the same size and shape. The corresponding angles and sides are congruent.	Similar polygons have the same shape, but they can be different sizes. The corresponding angles are congruent. The corresponding side lengths are proportional.
$\triangle PQR \cong \triangle STU$	$\triangle PQR \sim \triangle XYZ$

Big Idea 2 — Performing Transformations in the Coordinate Plane

A transformation is an operation that changes a figure into another figure called an image.

Translation	Reflection	Dilation
A translation moves each point of a figure the same distance in the same direction.	A reflection of a figure creates a mirror image of each point of the figure.	A dilation enlarges or shrinks a figure. The image is created by multiplying the coordinates of each point by a scale factor k.
A translation can be described by coordinate notation such as $(x, y) \rightarrow (x + a, y + b)$.	A reflection in the x-axis can be described as $(x, y) \rightarrow (x, -y)$. A reflection in the y-axis can be described as $(x, y) \rightarrow (-x, y)$.	A dilation can be described as $(x, y) \rightarrow (kx, ky)$.

Big Idea 3 — Using Scale Drawings and Models

The dimensions of a scale drawing or a scale model are proportional to the dimensions of the actual object it represents. The proportional relationship between the drawing's or model's dimensions and the actual object's dimensions is called the scale.

Scale with units   **Scale without units**

$$1 \text{ in.} : 2 \text{ ft} \longrightarrow \frac{1 \text{ in.}}{2 \text{ ft}} \longrightarrow \frac{1 \text{ in.}}{24 \text{ in.}} \longrightarrow 1 : 24$$

CHAPTER PROBLEM

Standards
MG 1.2, MG 3.2, MG 3.4

APPLYING THE BIG IDEAS

Big Idea 1
You use congruent and similar figures in **Step 1.**

Big Idea 2
You perform a transformation in the coordinate plane in **Ex. 4.**

Big Idea 3
You use a scale drawing in **Steps 1 and 2.**

PROBLEM How can you design a mall using a scale drawing?

STEP 1 Make a scale drawing.

Design a mall and make a scale drawing of the floor plan. Use the information below to make a scale drawing of your mall on graph paper.

Your mall should meet the following conditions:

- There must be at least 15 stores.
- Two walkways must intersect.
- Each store must be a minimum of 2000 square feet and a maximum of 10,000 square feet.
- The mall has to be at least 125,000 square feet.
- The front of each store has to be at least 30 feet wide.
- Each store's dimensions and square footage should be labeled.
- All mall entrances should be shown.
- Some stores should be congruent and some should be similar, but no more than four stores can be congruent.

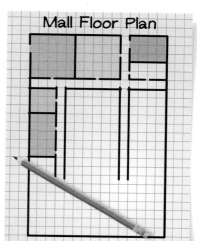

Mall Floor Plan

STEP 2 Add items to your scale drawing.

Add some of the following to your scale drawing:

- Color
- Shoppers
- Benches
- Parking lot

Extending the Problem

Use your results from the problem to complete the exercises.

1. What scale did you use? How did you determine your scale?

2. How many stores are congruent? Are any of the stores translations or reflections of each other?

3. How many stores are similar? Find the scale factor of any similar stores.

4. A pentagonal pool with a fountain will be built where the two walkways intersect. The fountain and pool bases are similar pentagons. On a coordinate plane, the fountain base has vertices (0, 4), (3, 1), (2, −4), (−2, −4), and (−3, 1) where each unit represents 1 foot.

    a. Graph the coordinates of the fountain base.

    b. Find and graph a possible set of vertices for the pentagonal pool that surrounds the fountain. *Explain* how you found your answer.

REVIEW KEY VOCABULARY

• congruent polygons, *p. 516*
• corresponding parts, *p. 516*
• similar polygons, *p.517*
• transformation, *p. 522*
• image, *p. 522*

• translation, *p. 522*
• reflection, *p. 528*
• line of reflection, *p. 529*
• line symmetry, *p. 530*
• dilation, *p. 535*

• scale factor, *p. 535*
• scale drawing, *p. 541*
• scale model, *p. 541*
• scale, *p. 541*

VOCABULARY EXERCISES

Match each word with the correct definition.

1. Transformation
2. Reflection
3. Translation
4. Dilation

A. A transformation that stretches or shrinks a figure

B. A transformation that slides a figure

C. A transformation that creates a mirror image of a figure

D. An operation that changes one figure into another figure

5. **NOTETAKING SKILLS** Make a *word triangle* like the one on page 514 for *reflection*. Include a sketch of an example.

REVIEW EXAMPLES AND EXERCISES

9.1 Congruent and Similar Figures
pp. 516–521

MG 3.4

EXAMPLE

Polygons *ABCD* and *FGHJ* are similar. Find the length of $\overline{BC}$.

$\dfrac{AB}{FG} = \dfrac{BC}{GH}$ Write a proportion.

$\dfrac{16}{20} = \dfrac{x}{15}$ Substitute.

$x = 12$ Solve for *x*.

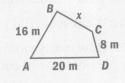
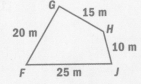

▶ **Answer** The length of $\overline{BC}$ is 12 meters.

EXERCISES

SEE EXAMPLE 4
on p. 518
for Exs. 6–7

6. $\triangle ABC$ is similar to $\triangle DEF$ with $AB = 4$, $BC = 7$, $AC = 8$, and $DE = 12$. Find the lengths of $\overline{EF}$ and $\overline{DF}$.

7. **BUILDING HEIGHTS** A 20 foot flagpole casts a shadow that is 25 feet long. At the same time, a building casts a shadow that is 60 feet long. The triangles formed are similar. How tall is the building?

9.2 Translations in the Coordinate Plane

pp. 522–526

MG 3.2

EXAMPLE

Graph △*KLM* with vertices *K*(3, 1), *L*(1, 4), and *M*(3, 3). Translate △*KLM* using $(x, y) \rightarrow (x - 5, y - 1)$.

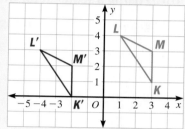

Original		Image
(x, y)	$\rightarrow$	$(x - 5, y - 1)$
$K(3, 1)$	$\rightarrow$	$K'(-2, 0)$
$L(1, 4)$	$\rightarrow$	$L'(-4, 3)$
$M(3, 3)$	$\rightarrow$	$M'(-2, 2)$

EXERCISES

SEE EXAMPLES 2 AND 3 on p. 523 for Exs. 8–10

Translate △*KLM* in the example above using the given rule.

8. $(x, y) \rightarrow (x - 2, y + 1)$

9. $(x, y) \rightarrow (x + 3, y - 3)$

10. 3 units to the right and 6 units down

9.3 Reflections in the Coordinate Plane

pp. 528–533

MG 3.2

EXAMPLE

Graph △*ABC* with vertices *A*(1, 3), *B*(4, 3), and *C*(3, 1). Then graph its reflection in the *x*-axis.

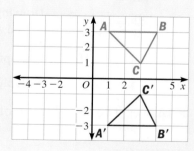

Original		Image
(x, y)	$\rightarrow$	$(x, -y)$
$A(1, 3)$	$\rightarrow$	$A'(1, -3)$
$B(4, 3)$	$\rightarrow$	$B'(4, -3)$
$C(3, 1)$	$\rightarrow$	$C'(3, -1)$

EXERCISES

SEE EXAMPLES 2 AND 4 on pp. 528–530 for Exs. 11–12

11. Graph the reflection of △*ABC* shown above in the *y*-axis.

12. Which of the 26 capital letters in the English alphabet have no line of symmetry? one line of symmetry? two lines of symmetry? more than two lines of symmetry?

MG 3.2   **EXAMPLE**

Quadrilateral *ABCD* has vertices $A(1, 1)$, $B(1, 3)$, $C(4, 2)$, and $D(4, 1)$. Dilate *ABCD* using a scale factor of 2.

Original		Image
(x, y)	$\rightarrow$	$(2x, 2y)$
$A(1, 1)$	$\rightarrow$	$A'(2, 2)$
$B(1, 3)$	$\rightarrow$	$B'(2, 6)$
$C(4, 2)$	$\rightarrow$	$C'(8, 4)$
$D(4, 1)$	$\rightarrow$	$D'(8, 2)$

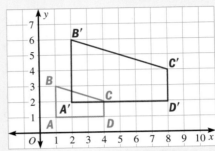

EXERCISES

SEE EXAMPLE 3
on p. 536
for Ex. 13

13. Rectangle *JKLM* is the image of rectangle *PQRS* after a dilation. *PQRS* has a length of 40 centimeters and a width of 10 centimeters. *JKLM* has a perimeter of 20 centimeters. Find the scale factor, then find the length and width of *JKLM*.

MG 1.2   **EXAMPLE**

The width of a house in a scale drawing is 15 inches. The scale on the drawing is 1 in. : 5 ft. Find the actual width of the house.

$$\frac{1 \text{ in.}}{5 \text{ ft}} = \frac{15 \text{ in.}}{x \text{ ft}} \qquad \begin{array}{l}\longleftarrow \text{ Drawing width} \\ \longleftarrow \text{ Actual width}\end{array}$$

$x = 5 \cdot 15$ **Cross products property**

$x = 75$ **Multiply.**

▶ **Answer** The actual width of the house is 75 feet.

EXERCISES

SEE EXAMPLES 1 AND 2
on pp. 541–542
for Exs. 14–16

Find the scale.

14. Actual size: 20 meters
Drawing size: 4 centimeters

15. Actual size: 80 feet
Model size: 4 inches

16. SCALE A map has a scale of 1 in. : 10 mi. The actual distance between two cities is 105 miles. Find the distance between the cities on the map.

1. **VOCABULARY** What type of transformation moves each point of a figure the same distance in the same direction?

2. **VOCABULARY** Copy and complete: A three-dimensional model that is proportional to the actual object it represents is a(n) __?__ .

Find the coordinates of the vertices of the image after the transformation. Then find and compare the areas of the figure and the image of the figure.

3. $\triangle PQR$: $P(1, 2)$, $Q(3, 4)$, $R(6, 2)$; translation: $(x, y) \rightarrow (x + 4, y - 2)$

4. $\triangle WXY$: $W(5, 1)$, $X(2, 6)$, $Y(5, 6)$; reflection in the y-axis

5. $PQRS$: $P(5, 2)$, $Q(5, 7)$, $R(1, 6)$, $S(1, 4)$; dilation using $k = 3$

Tell whether the line through the object is a line of symmetry.

6.

7.

8.

$\triangle A'B'C'$ is a dilation of $\triangle ABC$. Find the scale factor.

9. $\triangle ABC$: $A(2, 2)$, $B(-2, 3)$, $C(-1, -1)$
   $\triangle A'B'C'$: $A'(6, 6)$, $B'(-6, 9)$, $C'(-3, -3)$

10. $\triangle ABC$: $A(2, 6)$, $B(4, 2)$, $C(8, 10)$
    $\triangle A'B'C'$: $A'(1, 3)$, $B'(2, 1)$, $C'(4, 5)$

Find the scale.

11. Actual size: 5 meters
    Drawing size: 5 centimeters

12. Actual size: 18 inches
    Model size: 15 feet

13. **ALGEBRA** Write and solve an equation to find the value of x.

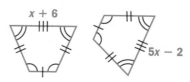

14. **GEOMETRY** The lengths of the sides of a triangle are 5 inches, 12 inches, and 15 inches. The shortest side of a similar triangle has a length of 12.5 inches. Find the lengths of the other two sides of the similar triangle.

15. **SHADOWS** Joe is 72 inches tall and casts a 108 inch shadow. At the same time, Martha casts a 96 inch shadow. The triangles formed by each person and his or her shadow are similar. How tall is Martha?

16. **MAPS** On a map, the road distance from Miami, Florida, to Columbia, South Carolina, is about 6.7 centimeters. The scale is 1 cm : 150 km. What is the actual distance from Miami to Columbia?

STRATEGIES YOU'LL USE:
- **SOLVE DIRECTLY**
- **ELIMINATE CHOICES**

Standards
MG 3.2, MG 3.4

If you have difficulty solving a multiple choice problem directly, you may be able to use another approach to eliminate incorrect answer choices and obtain the correct answer.

PROBLEM 1

Which graph shows the image of △ABC after a reflection in the y-axis followed by a translation using $(x, y) \rightarrow (x + 1, y + 3)$?

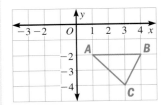

Ⓐ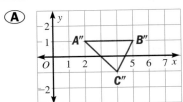

Ⓑ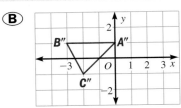

Ⓒ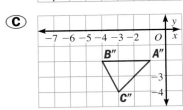

Ⓓ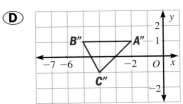

Strategy 1 SOLVE DIRECTLY

STEP 1 Identify the vertices of △ABC: $A(1, -2)$, $B(4, -2)$, and $C(3, -4)$.

STEP 2 Find the vertices of the image of △ABC. To reflect △ABC in the y-axis, multiply the x-coordinate of each vertex by −1. To translate each vertex after the reflection, add 1 to the x-coordinate and add 3 to the y-coordinate.

Original	Reflect in y-axis	Translate
$A(1, -2)$	$A'(-1, -2)$	$A''(0, 1)$
$B(4, -2)$	$B'(-4, -2)$	$B''(-3, 1)$
$C(3, -4)$	$C'(-3, -4)$	$C''(-2, -1)$

The vertices of the image of △ABC are $A''(0, 1)$, $B''(-3, 1)$, and $C''(-2, -1)$.

The correct answer is B. Ⓐ **Ⓑ** Ⓒ Ⓓ

Strategy 2 ELIMINATE CHOICES

You can perform the transformations on one vertex of the triangle to eliminate answer choices.

STEP 1 Reflect one of the vertices. To reflect $A(1, -2)$ in the y-axis, multiply the x-coordinate by −1 to obtain $A'(-1, -2)$.

STEP 2 Translate the reflected vertex. To translate $A'(-1, -2)$, add 1 to the x-coordinate and add 3 to the y-coordinate to obtain $A''(0, 1)$.

STEP 3 Eliminate choices A, C, and D because they do not contain $A''(0, 1)$.

The correct answer is B. Ⓐ **Ⓑ** Ⓒ Ⓓ

PROBLEM 2

In the diagram at the right, $\triangle ABC \sim \triangle DEF$. The area of $\triangle ABC$ is 24 square feet. What is the area of $\triangle DEF$?

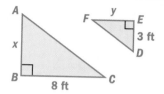

(A) $\frac{1}{2}$ ft^2

(B) 6 ft^2

(C) 24 ft^2

(D) 30 ft^2

Strategy 1 SOLVE DIRECTLY

The base of $\triangle ABC$ and the height of $\triangle DEF$ are given. Because the two triangles are similar, you know that their corresponding side lengths are proportional. Find the height x of $\triangle ABC$ and then write and solve a proportion to find the base y of $\triangle DEF$.

STEP 1 Find the height of $\triangle ABC$ using the area of $\triangle ABC$.

$$A = \frac{1}{2}bh \quad 24 = \frac{1}{2}(8)(x), \text{ so } x = 6.$$

STEP 2 Write a proportion to solve for y.

$$\frac{AB}{DE} = \frac{BC}{y} \quad \frac{6}{3} = \frac{8}{y}, \text{ so } y = 4.$$

STEP 3 Find the area of $\triangle DEF$ using y.

$$A = \frac{1}{2}bh \quad A = \frac{1}{2}(4)(3) = 6$$

The correct answer is B. **(A)** **(B)** **(C)** **(D)**

Strategy 2 ELIMINATE CHOICES

STEP 1 Find the height of $\triangle ABC$.

$$A = \frac{1}{2}bh \quad 24 = \frac{1}{2}(8)(x), \text{ so } x = 6.$$

$\overline{AB}$ and $\overline{DE}$ are corresponding sides of similar triangles, and the length of AB is greater than the length of DE. So, the area of $\triangle ABC$ is greater than the area of $\triangle DEF$. You can eliminate choices C and D.

STEP 2 Find the base of $\triangle DEF$ if its area is $\frac{1}{2}$.

$$A = \frac{1}{2}bh \quad \frac{1}{2} = \frac{1}{2}(y)(3), \text{ so } y = \frac{1}{3}.$$

This is not consistent with the value of y you get by solving a proportion:

$$\frac{AB}{DE} = \frac{BC}{y} \quad \frac{6}{3} = \frac{8}{y}, \text{ so } y = 4.$$

So, you can eliminate choice A.

The correct answer is B. **(A)** **(B)** **(C)** **(D)**

STRATEGY PRACTICE

Explain why you can eliminate the highlighted answer choice.

1. A person is standing next to a 20-foot-tall lamppost. The person casts a shadow 2 feet long and the lamppost casts a shadow 8 feet long. The triangles formed by the person and her shadow and by the lamppost and its shadow are similar. How tall is the person?

    (A) 4 ft
    (B) 5 ft
    (C) 6 ft
    (D) $\times$ 8 ft

2. A map has a scale of 1 in. : 25 mi. What distance on the map corresponds to an actual distance of 100 miles?

    (A) $\frac{1}{25}$ in.
    (B) $\frac{1}{4}$ in.
    (C) 4 in.
    (D) $\times$ 25 in.

1. *ABCDE* is shown on the coordinate grid below. *ABCDE* is reflected in the *y*-axis to form *A'B'C'D'E'*. What are the coordinates of *C'*? **MG 3.2**

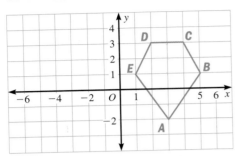

Ⓐ (−4, 3)

Ⓑ (4, −3)

Ⓒ (3, −4)

Ⓓ (−3, 4)

2. Triangle *LMN* is shown on the coordinate grid below. Triangle *LMN* is reflected in the *y*-axis to form triangle *L'M'N'*. What are the coordinates of *L'*? **MG 3.2**

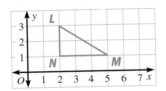

Ⓐ (−5, 3)

Ⓑ (−2, 3)

Ⓒ (2, −3)

Ⓓ (2, −1)

3. Elaine is tiling a floor. She uses the edge of a square floor tile to find a congruent length of molding. The edge of the floor tile is 18 inches long. How long is the congruent length of molding? **MG 3.4**

Ⓐ 12 in.

Ⓑ 18 in.

Ⓒ 24 in.

Ⓓ 1 yd

4. Triangle *ABC* has vertices *A*(2, 1), *B*(4, 3), and *C*(6, 2). Triangle *A'B'C'* is formed by reflecting triangle *ABC* in the *x*-axis. What are the coordinates of *B'*? **MG 3.2**

Ⓐ (−4, 3)

Ⓑ (4, −3)

Ⓒ (−4, −3)

Ⓓ (4, 3)

5. Triangle *ABC* is translated to form triangle *RST*. Two vertices of triangle *RST* are shown. What are the coordinates of *T*? **MG 3.2**

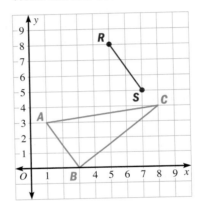

Ⓐ (14, 6)

Ⓑ (13, 8)

Ⓒ (12, 9)

Ⓓ (10, 10)

6. In the diagram below, triangle *LMN* is similar to triangle *PQR*. What is the value of *x*? **MG 3.4**

Ⓐ 6 ft

Ⓑ 8 ft

Ⓒ 9 ft

Ⓓ 10 ft

7. When you hit an air hockey puck, it moves across the table as shown in the diagram. The puck remains pointed in the same direction as it slides. Which transformation describes the movement of the puck? **MG 3.2, MR 2.5**

   Ⓐ Reflection in x-axis

   Ⓑ Reflection in y-axis

   Ⓒ Translation: $(x, y) \rightarrow (x + 24, y + 12)$

   Ⓓ Translation: $(x, y) \rightarrow (x + 12, y + 24)$

8. Triangle ABC is congruent to triangle DEF. Which procedure can be used to find the number of degrees in $\angle E$? **MG 3.4**

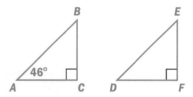

   Ⓐ Subtract 46 from 90.

   Ⓑ Subtract 46 from 180.

   Ⓒ Subtract 46 from 360.

   Ⓓ Subtract 136 from 360.

9. You are designing a model car that is a scale replica of a full-size car. The scale factor of the model to the actual car is $\frac{1}{24}$. The license plate on the model car is $\frac{1}{4}$ inch high and $\frac{1}{2}$ inch wide. What is the perimeter of the actual license plate? **MG 1.2**

   Ⓐ 24 in.

   Ⓑ 36 in.

   Ⓒ 48 in.

   Ⓓ 72 in.

10. Suppose you design a second model car that is $\frac{1}{4}$ the size of the model car you designed in Exercise 9. What is the perimeter of the license plate on the second model car? **MG 1.2, MR 3.2**

   Ⓐ $\frac{1}{4}$ in.

   Ⓑ $\frac{3}{8}$ in.

   Ⓒ $\frac{3}{4}$ in.

   Ⓓ 9 in.

11. The scale on a map is 1 in. : 24 mi. What distance on the map represents 168 miles? **MG 1.2**

   Ⓐ 4 in.

   Ⓑ 5 in.

   Ⓒ 6 in.

   Ⓓ 7 in.

12. The red figure is the image of the blue figure. Which diagram shows a reflection? **MG 3.2**

   Ⓐ A ∀

   Ⓑ B Ҍ

   Ⓒ C Ɔ

   Ⓓ D D

13. Which transformation makes the red figure the image of the blue figure? **MG 3.2**

   Ⓐ Reflection in x-axis

   Ⓑ A dilation

   Ⓒ $(x, y) \rightarrow (x + 3, y + 2)$

   Ⓓ $(x, y) \rightarrow (x - 3, y - 2)$

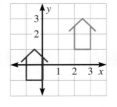

10 Surface Area and Volume

Before

In previous chapters, you learned the following skills, which you'll use in Chapter 10:

- Finding areas of two-dimensional figures
- Finding perimeters of two-dimensional figures
- Comparing similar figures

Now

In Chapter 10 you'll study these
Big Ideas:

1. Identifying solids and their components

2. Finding surface areas and volumes of solids

3. Comparing surface areas and volumes of similar solids

Why?

So you can solve real-world problems about . . .

- Origami, p. 565
- Cooking, p. 578
- Set design, p. 585
- Icicles, p. 585
- Swimming pools, p. 594
- Miniature City, p. 610

Animated Math
at *classzone.com*

Get-Ready Games

MEASURE MATCH

California Standards

Review finding areas and perimeters. **Gr. 7 MG 2.1**

Prepare for finding volume. **Gr. 7 MG 2.1**

Materials

- One deck of *Measure Match* cards

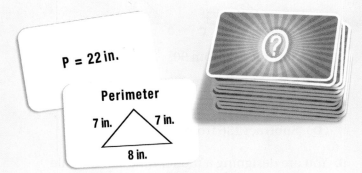

P = 22 in.

Perimeter

7 in.   7 in.

8 in.

How to Play There are 30 *Measure Match* cards. Fifteen of these cards show figures. The other 15 cards give a measure.

Shuffle the cards. Arrange the cards face down in five rows of six cards each. Players should take turns following the steps on the next page.

CALIFORNIA STANDARDS

• **Gr. 7 MG 2.1 Use formulas routinely for finding** the perimeter and area of basic two-dimensional figures and **the surface area and volume of basic three-dimensional figures, including** rectangles, parallelograms, trapezoids, squares, triangles, circles, **prisms, and cylinders.** *(Lessons 10.3, 10.4, 10.5, 10.6)*

• **Gr. 7 MG 3.6** Identify elements of three-dimensional geometric objects (e.g., diagonals of rectangular solids) and describe how two or more objects are related in space (e.g., skew lines, the possible ways three planes might intersect). *(Lessons 10.1, 10.2)*

Perimeter

7 in. 7 in.

8 in.

$P = 22$ in.

① **Turn** over two cards so that all players can see them.

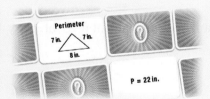

How to Win Be the player with the most cards when all matches have been found.

② **Decide** whether the cards are a match. A match shows a figure and a correct measure of the figure. If the cards match, place them in front of you and take another turn. Otherwise, return them to their original positions.

③ **Remember** where the cards are placed, so that you can find matches on future turns.

Games Wrap-Up

Draw Conclusions

Complete these exercises after playing the game.

1. **WRITING** A student claims that a card showing a circle with a radius of 2 inches matches with the measure $C \approx 6.28$ inches. *Describe* and correct the error.

2. **REASONING** If the cards showing area, perimeter, and circumference were all labeled with M, instead of A, P, or C, how could you tell which cards showed an area? *Explain.*

559

Prerequisite Skills

California @HomeTutor

Prerequisite skills practice
at classzone.com

VOCABULARY CHECK

Classify the figure using a review term from the list at the left.

1. Quadrilateral *ABCD*

2. $\overline{PQ}$

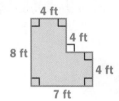

3. Quadrilateral *JKLM*

SKILL CHECK

Find the area of the shaded region. *(pp. 463, 478)*

4.

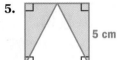

5.

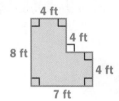

6.

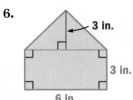

7. The scale on a map is 1 cm : 25 km. The distance on the map from A to B is 4.5 cm. What is the actual distance from A to B?

Notetaking Skills

Focus on Graphic Organizers

You can use an *information wheel* to organize details about a vocabulary word, such as *rectangle*.

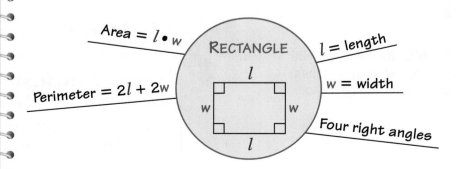

10.1 Lines and Planes

Math and ART
Ex. 24, p. 565

Standards MG 3.6 Identify elements of three-dimensional geometric objects (e.g., diagonals of rectangular solids) and **describe how two or more objects are related in space (e.g., skew lines, the possible ways three planes might intersect).**

Connect *Before* you related objects in two dimensions. *Now* you will relate objects in three dimensions.

KEY VOCABULARY
• coplanar
• skew lines
• plane, *p. 735*

A plane is a flat surface that extends without end in all directions. Points and lines that lie in the same plane are **coplanar**. In particular, a pair of intersecting lines or a pair of parallel lines are coplanar. Two lines are **skew lines** if they do not intersect and are not coplanar.

In the diagram, *A*, *B*, and *C* are planes, lines *m* and *n* are coplanar, and lines *k* and *m* are skew.

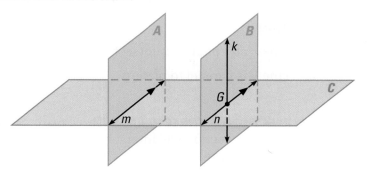

EXAMPLE 1 Relating Lines in Space

Use the diagram to name (a) a pair of coplanar, nonintersecting lines, (b) a pair of skew lines, and (c) a pair of coplanar, intersecting lines.

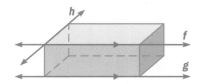

SOLUTION

a. Lines *f* and *g* are parallel, so they are coplanar, nonintersecting lines.

b. Lines *g* and *h* do not intersect and are not coplanar, so they are skew lines.

c. Lines *f* and *h* intersect, so they are coplanar, intersecting lines.

✓ **GUIDED PRACTICE** **for Example 1**

1. Use the diagram to name a pair of skew lines and a pair of coplanar lines.

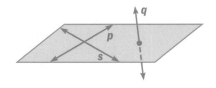

INTERSECTION OF TWO PLANES Two distinct planes that are parallel do not intersect. Two distinct planes that are not parallel intersect to form a line, as shown below.

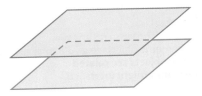

The planes are parallel, so they do not intersect.

The planes intersect to form a line.

EXAMPLE 2 Identifying Relationships Between Planes

Use the figure shown at the right.

a. Name a pair of intersecting planes.

b. Name a pair of parallel planes.

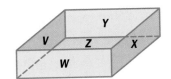

SOLUTION

a. Plane *Z* and plane *V* intersect.

b. Plane *V* is parallel to plane *X*.

INTERSECTION OF THREE PLANES Three distinct planes that have a common intersection will intersect to form a point or a line. Three distinct planes can also have no common point of intersection.

The planes intersect in a single point.

The planes intersect in a line.

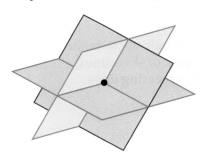

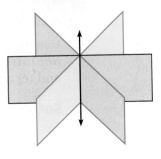

The planes have no common point of intersection.

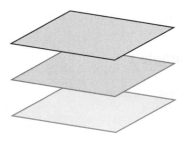

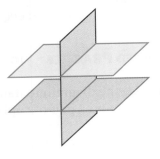

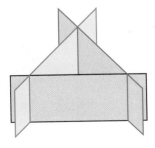

EXAMPLE 3 Identifying the Intersection of Three Planes

Name the point that is the intersection of the three planes outlined in red.

SOLUTION

You can see that the three planes intersect at point *C*.

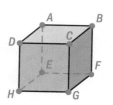

✓ **GUIDED PRACTICE** for Examples 2 and 3

2. In Example 2, describe the intersection of plane *W* and plane *X*.

3. In Example 3, name a point other than *C* that is the intersection of three planes.

10.1 EXERCISES

HOMEWORK KEY
◆ = **MULTIPLE CHOICE PRACTICE**
Exs. 11, 16, 25, 28–30

○ = **HINTS AND HOMEWORK HELP**
for Exs. 5, 15, 25 at classzone.com

SKILLS • PROBLEM SOLVING • REASONING

1. **VOCABULARY** Copy and complete: Points and lines that lie in the same plane are __?__ .

2. **WRITING** If two lines do not intersect, are they necessarily skew? *Explain.*

SEE EXAMPLES
1 AND 2
on pp. 561–562
for Exs. 3–15

SKEW LINES Determine whether the lines are skew. *Explain.*

3. *s* and *t*

4. *b* and *c*

5. *m* and *n*

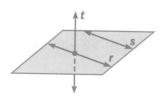

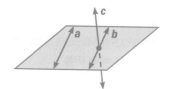

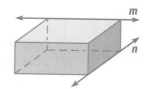

REASONING Copy and complete the statement with *sometimes, always,* or *never*. Sketch examples to justify your answers.

6. If two lines are coplanar, then they are __?__ parallel.

7. If two lines are skew, then they __?__ intersect.

8. If two lines are not coplanar, then they __?__ intersect.

9. Two planes that are not parallel __?__ intersect to form a line.

10. If two lines are parallel, then they are __?__ skew.

11. ◆ **MULTIPLE CHOICE** Which pair of lines are coplanar, nonintersecting lines?

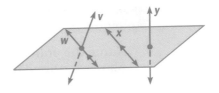

(A) v and w (B) v and x

(C) w and x (D) v and y

LINES AND PLANES **In Exercises 12–15, use the figure shown.**

12. Name a pair of coplanar lines.

13. Name a pair of skew lines.

14. Name a pair of parallel lines and the plane that contains them.

15. Name a pair of intersecting planes.

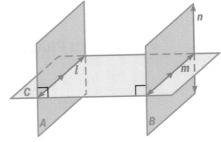

SEE EXAMPLE 3
on p. 563
for Exs. 16–17

16. ◆ **MULTIPLE CHOICE** Which does *not* describe a possible intersection of three distinct planes?

(A) A line   (B) A point   (C) A rectangle   (D) No intersection

ERROR ANALYSIS *Describe* and correct the error in the statement.

17.

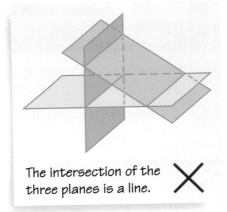

The intersection of the three planes is a line. ✕

18.

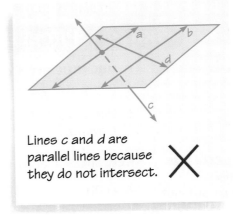

Lines c and d are parallel lines because they do not intersect. ✕

CONNECT SKILLS TO PROBLEM SOLVING **Exercises 19–22 will help you prepare for problem solving.**

Use the diagram of the aquarium.

19. Name a line that is parallel to line CD and passes through point B.

20. Name a line that is skew to line CD and passes through point B.

21. Name a plane parallel to the plane containing points C, D, and H.

22. Name all the planes that intersect the plane containing points C, D, and H.

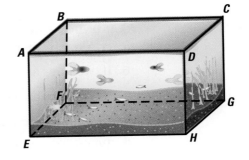

◆ = **MULTIPLE CHOICE PRACTICE**   ◯ = **HINTS AND HOMEWORK HELP** at classzone.com

SEE EXAMPLE 1
on p. 561
for Ex. 23

23. DESK Make a sketch of a table. Think of the legs as lines and the tabletop as a plane. Describe the relationship between any two of the legs.

California @HomeTutor for problem solving help at classzone.com

24. ORIGAMI You want to make an origami figure that consists of planes whose intersection is a point. What is the least number of planes needed to make the figure?

California @HomeTutor for problem solving help at classzone.com

SEE EXAMPLE 2
on p. 562
for Ex. 25

25. ◆ **MULTIPLE CHOICE** Which describes the intersection of the ceiling and a wall of a classroom?

A A line   **B** A point   **C** Two points   **D** Two lines

26. CHALLENGE In *spherical geometry,* you can think of the surface of a sphere as a plane and a *great circle,* which is a circle whose center is also the center of the sphere, as a line. On a globe of Earth, is a line of latitude *always, sometimes,* or *never* a great circle? Is a line of longitude *always, sometimes,* or *never* a great circle? *Explain* your answers.

27. CHALLENGE Draw lines *l, m,* and *n* so that *l* and *m* are skew, *l* and *n* are skew, and *m* and *n* are parallel.

◆ CALIFORNIA STANDARDS SPIRAL REVIEW

AF 3.3

28. What is the slope of the line passing through the points $(-2, 5)$ and $(1, 8)$? *(p. 334)*

A -1 **B** $-\frac{1}{3}$ **C** $\frac{1}{3}$ **D** 1

MG 3.1

29. What part of the circle at the right does *x* measure? *(p. 489)*

A Radius   **B** Diameter

C Chord   **D** Central angle

AF 1.5

30. The graph shows the cost of key chains. What does the point shown represent? *(p. 407)*

A Five key chains cost $5.

B Five key chains cost $6.

C Six key chains cost $5.

D Six key chains cost $6.

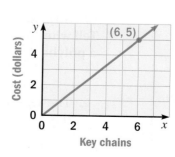

10.2 Three-Dimensional Figures

Standards

MG 3.5 Construct two-dimensional patterns for three-dimensional models, such as cylinders, prisms, and cones.

MG 3.6 Identify elements of three-dimensional geometric objects (e.g., diagonals of rectangular solids) and describe how two or more objects are related in space (e.g., skew lines, the possible ways three planes might intersect).

Math and **ARCHITECTURE**
Ex. 30, p. 570

Connect   *Before* you classified and sketched polygons. *Now* you will classify and sketch solids.

KEY VOCABULARY

- solid, polyhedron, face
- prism
- pyramid
- cylinder
- cone
- sphere
- edge, vertex, diagonal of a polyhedron

A **solid** is a three-dimensional figure that encloses a part of space. A **polyhedron** is a solid that is enclosed by polygons. A polyhedron has only flat surfaces. The polygons that form a polyhedron are called **faces**.

Classifying Solids

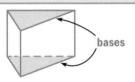

bases

A **prism** is a polyhedron. Prisms have two congruent bases that lie in parallel planes. The other faces are rectangles.

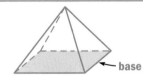

base

A **pyramid** is a polyhedron. Pyramids have one base. The other faces are triangles.

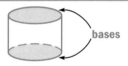

bases

A **cylinder** is a solid with two congruent circular bases that lie in parallel planes.

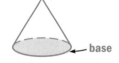

base

A **cone** is a solid with one circular base.

center

A **sphere** is all points in space that are the same distance from the center.

You can name a prism or pyramid using the shape of its base(s). For example, if the bases of a prism are pentagons, the solid is called a pentagonal prism.

EXAMPLE 1   Classifying Solids

Classify the solid. Tell whether it is a polyhedron.

a.

b.

Animated Math

For an interactive example of classifying solids, go to **classzone.com**.

a. The solid has two congruent circular bases that lie in parallel planes, so it is a cylinder. It is not a polyhedron, because circles are not polygons.

b. The solid has two congruent triangular bases that lie in parallel planes, so it is a prism. It is a polyhedron, because all of the faces are polygons.

PARTS OF A POLYHEDRON The line segments where faces of a polyhedron intersect are called **edges**. A **vertex** is a point where three or more edges meet. The plural of vertex is *vertices*. A **diagonal of a polyhedron** is any line segment connecting two vertices that do not lie in the same face.

EXAMPLE 2 Naming Parts of a Polyhedron

Name a face, edge, vertex, and diagonal of the rectangular prism.

SOLUTION

A face is any of the polygons that form a prism. So, *ABCD* is a face.

Faces *ABCD* and *ADFG* meet at $\overline{AD}$. So, $\overline{AD}$ is an edge.

Edges $\overline{AD}$, $\overline{AB}$, and $\overline{AG}$ meet at point *A*. So *A* is a vertex.

Vertices *G* and *C* do not lie in the same face. So, $\overline{GC}$ is a diagonal.

ADDITIONAL ANSWERS
There are several answers because a rectangular prism has 6 faces, 12 edges, 8 vertices, and 4 diagonals.

EXAMPLE 3 Counting Faces, Edges, and Vertices

Classify the solid. Then count the number of faces, edges, and vertices.

SOLUTION

The solid is a pentagonal pyramid.

6 faces

10 edges

6 vertices

Remember to include the base when counting faces.

Animated Math

For an interactive example of counting faces, edges, and vertices, go to **classzone.com**.

✓ **GUIDED PRACTICE**   for Examples 1, 2, and 3

Classify the solid. Then tell whether it is a polyhedron.

1.

2.

3.

4. Classify the solid. Name a face, edge, and vertex of the solid. Then count the number of faces, edges, and vertices.

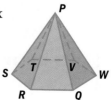

EXAMPLE 4 Sketching a Solid

OPTICS A triangular prism made of glass separates a light beam into the spectrum of visible light as shown at the right. Sketch a representation of the triangular prism.

ANOTHER WAY

For an alternative method of representing a triangular prism, turn to page 572 for the **Problem Solving Workshop**.

SOLUTION

STEP 1 **Sketch** two congruent bases.

STEP 2 **Connect** the vertices.

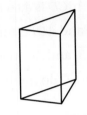

STEP 3 **Make** any hidden lines dashed.

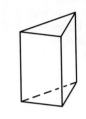

✓ **GUIDED PRACTICE** for Example 4

5. Sketch a rectangular pyramid.

10.2 EXERCISES

HOMEWORK KEY

◆ = **MULTIPLE CHOICE PRACTICE**
Exs. 6, 10, 31, 38–40

○ = **HINTS AND HOMEWORK HELP**
for Exs. 9, 11, 33 at classzone.com

SKILLS • PROBLEM SOLVING • REASONING

1. VOCABULARY Copy and complete: A polyhedron that has one base and whose other faces are triangles is called a(n) __?__ .

2. WRITING *Explain* the difference between a prism and a pyramid.

SEE EXAMPLE 1
on p. 566
for Exs. 3–6

CLASSIFYING SOLIDS **Classify the solid. Then tell whether it is a polyhedron.**

3.

4.

5.

6. ◆ MULTIPLE CHOICE Which describes the solid at the right?

(A) Rectangular prism

(B) Triangular prism

(C) Rectangular pyramid

(D) Triangular pyramid

SEE EXAMPLE 2
on p. 567
for Exs. 7–10

NAMING PARTS **Name a face, edge, vertex, and diagonal of the polyhedron, if possible.**

7.

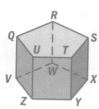

8.

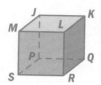

(9.)

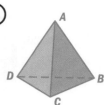

10. ◆ **MULTIPLE CHOICE** Which is a diagonal of the cube shown?

(A) $\overline{MQ}$ (B) $\overline{KL}$

(C) $\overline{QR}$ (D) $\overline{JL}$

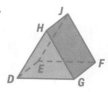

SEE EXAMPLE 3
on p. 567
for Exs. 11–14

COUNTING FACES, EDGES, AND VERTICES **Classify the solid. Then count the number of faces, edges, and vertices.**

(11.)

12.

13.

ERROR ANALYSIS *Describe* and correct the error in the statement.

14.

The base of this pyramid is a decagon, so the pyramid has 10 vertices.

15.

The polyhedron has two congruent bases that lie in parallel planes, so it is a rectangular prism.

SEE EXAMPLE 4
on p. 568
for Exs. 16–21

SKETCHING SOLIDS **Sketch the solid.**

16. Cube

17. Hexagonal prism

18. Cylinder

19. Rectangular prism

20. Cone

21. Square pyramid

22. **REASONING** *Explain* how a cylinder and a cone with congruent bases are alike and how they are different.

23. **REASONING** Does every polyhedron have at least one diagonal? *Justify* your answer with examples.

24. **OPEN-ENDED** Give an example of a cylinder, a cone, and a square prism in your classroom or at your home.

CONNECT SKILLS TO PROBLEM SOLVING Exercises 25–27 will help you prepare for problem solving.

Classify the highlighted brick in the pattern as a type of prism.

25.

26.

27.

SEE EXAMPLE 1
on p. 566
for Exs. 28–30

ARCHITECTURE Classify the solids that form the structure.

28.

29.

30.

California @HomeTutor for problem solving help at classzone.com

31. ◆ **MULTIPLE CHOICE** Which of the following solids is a polyhedron?

Ⓐ   Ⓑ   Ⓒ   Ⓓ

California @HomeTutor for problem solving help at classzone.com

32. **LOOK FOR A PATTERN** Copy and complete the table. Use the pattern to write a formula that gives the number of edges of a polyhedron in terms of the numbers of faces and vertices. This formula is called *Euler's formula*.

Figure	Number of faces F	Number of vertices V	Number of edges E	F + V
Pentagonal pyramid	6	6	10	12
Rectangular pyramid	?	?	?	?
Triangular prism	?	?	?	?
Rectangular prism	?	?	?	?
Hexagonal prism	?	?	?	?

33. **TRIANGULAR PYRAMID** Use your results from Exercise 32 to find the number of edges in a triangular pyramid.

34. CHALLENGE You are shipping an umbrella in a box shaped like a cube. Find the length *AB* of the longest umbrella that will fit in the box in terms of the edge length *s*.

CHALLENGE Classify the quadrilateral outlined in red, formed by the intersection of a cube and a plane.

35.   **36.**   **37.**

◆ CALIFORNIA STANDARDS SPIRAL REVIEW

AF 1.1

38. Four less than a number *n* is at most 5. Which equation or inequality represents the verbal description? *(p. 282)*

(A) $5 > n - 4$ **(B)** $5 \geq n - 4$ **(C)** $5 \geq 4 - n$ **(D)** $5 = 4 - n$

AF 4.1

39. What is the solution of $4x - 5 = 7$? *(p. 270)*

(A) $\frac{1}{3}$ **(B)** $\frac{1}{2}$ **(C)** 3   **(D)** $\frac{13}{4}$

MG 1.2

40. On a map, the distance from Dodger Stadium to Angel Stadium is 2.5 centimeters. The scale of the map is 1 cm : 12 mi. What is the actual distance? *(p. 541)*

(A) 6 mi   **(B)** 12 mi   **(C)** 24 mi   **(D)** 30 mi

QUIZ *for Lessons 10.1–10.2*

In Exercises 1–5, use the figure shown. *(p. 561)*

1. Name two pairs of coplanar, nonintersecting lines.

2. Name two pairs of skew lines.

3. Name a pair of parallel planes.

4. Name two pairs of intersecting lines.

5. Describe the intersection of plane *A* and plane *B*.

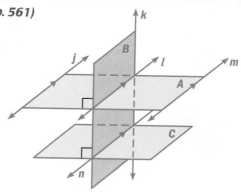

6. Classify the solid shown at the right. Then tell whether it is a polyhedron. *(p. 566)*

7. Sketch a pentagonal prism. Then count the number of faces, edges, and vertices. *(p. 566)*

Using ALTERNATIVE METHODS

Another Way to Solve Example 4, page 568

Standards
MG 3.5

In Example 4 on page 568, you saw how to represent a triangular prism with a sketch. You can also represent the prism by drawing different views of the solid.

PROBLEM

OPTICS A triangular prism made of glass can be used to split a beam of light into beams of different colors, as shown at the right. Sketch a representation of the triangular prism.

METHOD

Drawing Views Draw the top, front, and side views of the solid.

Top

Front

Side

PRACTICE

DRAWING VIEWS Draw the top, front, and side views of the solid.

1.

2.

3.

4.

5.

6.

SKETCHING SOLIDS Sketch the solid with the given views.

7.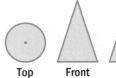

Top   Front   Side

8.

Top   Front   Side

10.3 Surface Areas of Prisms and Cylinders

Standards

MG 2.1 Use formulas routinely for finding the perimeter and area of basic two-dimensional figures and **the surface area and volume of basic three-dimensional figures, including** rectangles, parallelograms, trapezoids, squares, triangles, circles, **prisms, and cylinders.**

MG 3.5 Construct two-dimensional patterns for three-dimensional models, such as cylinders, prisms, and cones.

Connect *Before* you classified figures as prisms or cylinders. *Now* you will find surface areas of prisms and cylinders.

Math and DESIGN
Ex. 34, p. 579

KEY VOCABULARY
• net
• surface area
• lateral surface area

One way to represent a solid is to use a *net*. A **net** is a two-dimensional pattern that forms a solid when it is folded.

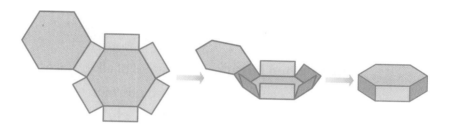

Each polygon of the net represents one face of the solid. For a given solid, several arrangements of these polygons are usually possible.

EXAMPLE 1 Drawing a Net

Draw a net of the triangular prism.

SOLUTION

METHOD 1
Draw one base with a rectangle adjacent to each side. Draw the other base adjacent to one of the rectangles.

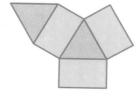

METHOD 2
For the rectangular faces, draw adjacent rectangles. Draw the bases on opposite sides of one rectangle.

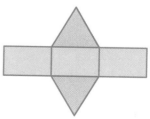

SURFACE AREA The **surface area** of a polyhedron is the sum of the areas of its faces. The surface area of a polyhedron is equal to the area of its net.

EXAMPLE 2 Using a Net to Find Surface Area

STORAGE CHEST You are painting a storage chest with the given dimensions. Find the surface area to be painted.

15 in.

30 in. 15 in.

ANOTHER WAY
Another way to draw a net for the storage chest is:

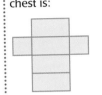

SOLUTION

STEP 1 **Draw** a net of the chest. There are 2 congruent square faces and 4 congruent rectangular faces.

STEP 2 **Find** the area of each square face.

15 in. • 15 in. = **225 in.²**

STEP 3 **Find** the area of each rectangular face.

30 in. • 15 in. = **450 in.²**

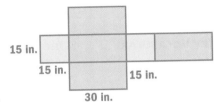

15 in.

15 in. 15 in.

30 in.

STEP 4 **Find** the sums of the areas of all the faces.

S = 2 • Area of a square face + 4 • Area of a rectangular face

= 2 • **225 in.²** + 4 • **450 in.²**

= 2250 in.²

▶ **Answer** The surface area of the storage chest is 2250 square inches.

In Example 2, note that the combined area of the sides of the chest is

$$2(30)(15) + 2(15)^2 = (2 \cdot 30 + 2 \cdot 15)(15) = Ph$$

where P is the perimeter of a base and h is the chest's height. To find the total surface area of the chest, you must add twice the area of a base to Ph.

KEY CONCEPT   *For Your Notebook*

Surface Area of a Prism

Words   The surface area of a prism is the sum of twice the area B of a base and the product of the base's perimeter P and the height h.

P   B

B

h

Algebra $S = 2B + Ph$

EXAMPLE 3 **Using a Formula to Find Surface Area**

Find the surface area of the triangular prism.

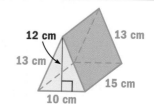

$$S = 2B + Ph$$

$$= 2\left(\frac{1}{2} \cdot 10 \cdot 12\right) + (13 + 13 + 10)15$$

$$= 660$$

CHECK FOR REASONABLENESS

Round each length to its leading digit. Then

$S \approx 2\left(\frac{1}{2}\right)(10^2) + 30 \cdot 20$

$= 100 + 600$

$= 700 \text{ cm}^2.$

▸**Answer** The surface area of the prism is 660 square centimeters.

✓ **GUIDED PRACTICE** for Examples 1, 2, and 3

Draw a net of the solid. Then find the surface area.

1.

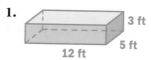

3 ft

5 ft

12 ft

2.

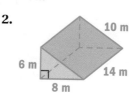

10 m

6 m

8 m

14 m

CYLINDERS The net of a cylinder has two circles for the bases. The curved surface of the cylinder becomes a rectangle in the net. The width of the rectangle is the height of the cylinder, and the length of the rectangle is the circumference of the base.

The **lateral surface area** of a three-dimensional figure is the surface area of the figure excluding the area of its bases.

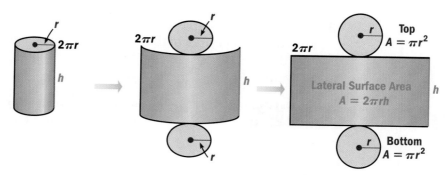

KEY CONCEPT *For Your Notebook*

Surface Area of a Cylinder

Words   The surface area of a cylinder is the sum of twice the area B of a base and the product of the base's circumference C and the height h.

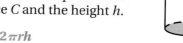

Algebra $S = 2B + Ch = 2\pi r^2 + 2\pi rh$

EXAMPLE 4 ◆ **Multiple Choice Practice**

What is the surface area of the can of sloppy joe sauce to the nearest square inch?

A 57 in.^{2} **B** 145 in.^{2}

C 369 in.^{2} **D** 2380 in.^{2}

10.7 cm

├── 8 cm ──┤

ELIMINATE CHOICES
Because a square centimeter is smaller than a square inch, you know that the answer in square inches must be less than the surface area in square centimeters (about 369 cm^2). So, choice D can be eliminated.

SOLUTION

The radius is one half the diameter, so $r = 4$ cm.

$S = 2\pi r^2 + 2\pi rh$ **Write formula for surface area.**

$= 2\pi(4)^2 + 2\pi(4)(10.7)$ **Substitute 4 for r and 10.7 for h.**

≈ 369.45 cm^2 **Evaluate using a calculator.**

The surface area of the can is about 369.45 square centimeters. Convert the answer to square inches. You know that 1 in. = 2.54 cm, so (1 in.)^2 = (2.54 cm)^2, or 1 in.$^2 \approx 6.45$ cm^2.

$$369.45 \text{ cm}^2 \times \frac{1 \text{ in.}^2}{6.45 \text{ cm}^2} \approx 57.3 \text{ in.}^2$$

The surface area of the can is about 57 square inches.

▶ **Answer** The correct answer is A. Ⓐ Ⓑ Ⓒ Ⓓ

✓ **GUIDED PRACTICE**   **for Example 4**

3. **WHAT IF?** In Example 4, suppose the height of the can is 18.3 centimeters. Find the surface area of the can to the nearest square inch.

10.3 EXERCISES

HOMEWORK KEY

◆ = **MULTIPLE CHOICE PRACTICE**
Exs. 13, 17, 29, 38–40

○ = **HINTS AND HOMEWORK HELP**
for Exs. 7, 15, 31 at classzone.com

SKILLS • PROBLEM SOLVING • REASONING

1. **VOCABULARY** Copy and complete: The net of a cylinder is made up of two __?__ and one __?__.

2. **WRITING** *Explain* how to use a net to find the surface area of a solid.

SEE EXAMPLE 1
on p. 573
for Exs. 3–5

DRAWING NETS **Draw a net of the prism.**

3.

4.

5.

SEE EXAMPLE 2
on p. 574
for Exs. 6–8

USING NETS Draw a net. Then use the net to find the surface area.

6.

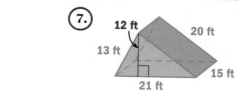

7.

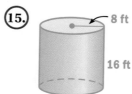

8.

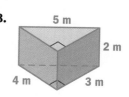

SEE EXAMPLE 3
on p. 575
for Exs. 9–13

USING FORMULAS Find the surface area of the prism with the given base area B, perimeter P, and height h.

9. $B = 4$ in.^{2}, $P = 8$ in., $h = 5$ in.

10. $B = 20$ cm^2, $P = 12$ cm, $h = 3$ cm

11. $B = 45$ yd^2, $P = 30$ yd, $h = 2.8$ yd

12. $B = 19.3$ m^2, $P = 16$ m, $h = 0.5$ m

13. ◆ **MULTIPLE CHOICE** What is the surface area of a rectangular prism that is 3 feet long, 2 feet wide, and 9 feet high?

(**A**) 14 ft^2 (**B**) 54 ft^2 (**C**) 61 ft^2 (**D**) 102 ft^2

SEE EXAMPLE 4
on p. 576
for Exs. 14–20

SURFACE AREA OF CYLINDERS Draw a net. Then find the surface area of the cylinder. Round to the nearest tenth.

14.

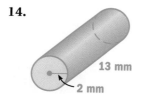

15.

16.

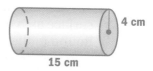

17. ◆ **MULTIPLE CHOICE** What is the surface area of the cylinder to the nearest square inch?

(**A**) 15 in.^{2} (**B**) 58 in.^{2}

(**C**) 74 in.^{2} (**D**) 478 in.^{2}

SKETCHING CYLINDERS Sketch a cylinder with radius r and height h. Then find its surface area and lateral surface area. Round to the nearest tenth.

18. $r = 6$ m, $h = 2$ m   **19.** $r = 1$ ft, $h = 7$ ft   **20.** $r = 10$ cm, $h = 20$ cm

ERROR ANALYSIS *Describe* and correct the error in finding the indicated measure.

21. Surface area

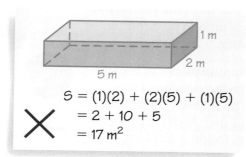

$$S = (1)(2) + (2)(5) + (1)(5)$$
$$= 2 + 10 + 5$$
$$= 17 \text{ m}^2$$

22. Lateral surface area

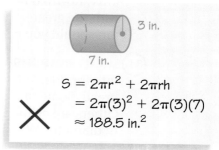

$$S = 2\pi r^2 + 2\pi rh$$
$$= 2\pi(3)^2 + 2\pi(3)(7)$$
$$\approx 188.5 \text{ in.}^2$$

23. REASONING Find the area of the figure shown. Will the figure form a solid when folded? If not, copy and complete the figure so it will form a solid.

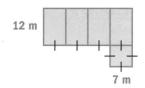

12 m

7 m

CONNECT SKILLS TO PROBLEM SOLVING Exercises 24–27 will help you prepare for problem solving.

Sketch the gift box that results after the net shown has been folded. Use the shaded face as the bottom of the box.

24.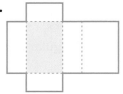

25.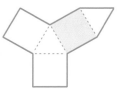

26.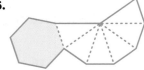

27.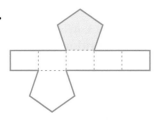

SEE EXAMPLES 2 AND 4 on pp. 574–576 for Exs. 28–30

28. CRYSTAL BRIDGE At the Myriad Botanical Gardens in Oklahoma City, a tropical conservatory bridges a small lake. The Crystal Bridge is a cylinder 224 feet long and 70 feet in diameter. Find the surface area of the Crystal Bridge, including bases. Round to the nearest tenth.

California *@HomeTutor* for problem solving help at classzone.com

Myriad Botanical Gardens

29. ◆ MULTIPLE CHOICE A cubic package has edge lengths of 8 inches. To the nearest square centimeter, what is the least amount of wrapping paper needed to wrap the package?

(A) 60 cm²   (B) 384 cm²   (C) 2477 cm²   (D) 4801 cm²

California *@HomeTutor* for problem solving help at classzone.com

30. COOKING You have to choose one of the two rolling pins shown to bake cookies. You want the rolling pin with the greater lateral surface area. Which rolling pin should you choose? *Explain.*

31. SHORT RESPONSE You are dipping pieces of bread into fondue. The fondue coats the outside of the bread. Some of the pieces of bread are 1 inch cubes. Others are cylinders that are 1 inch high and 1 inch in diameter. Which uses more fondue? *Explain.*

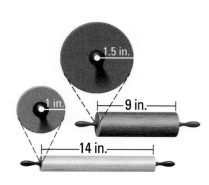

1.5 in.

1 in.

9 in.

14 in.

---

32. MULTI-STEP PROBLEM Use the rectangular prism shown.

   a. Find the surface area of the prism in square inches by first finding the surface area in square feet and then converting.

   b. Find the surface area of the prism in square inches by first converting the dimensions of the prism to inches.

   c. Use your results from parts (a) and (b) make a conjecture.

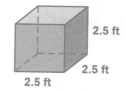

2.5 ft
2.5 ft
2.5 ft

33. Ⓧ **ALGEBRA** Each edge of a cube has length s. Write and simplify an expression for the surface area of the cube in terms of s.

34. DESIGN A company commissions the design of a parade float. The bottom of the float is to be a rectangular prism that is 14 feet long, 4 feet wide, and 2 feet tall. Violet flowers will be used to cover the lateral area of the prism so that 42 flowers cover 1 square foot. How many dozens of flowers will the designer need? *Explain* your answer.

35. OPEN-ENDED The height h of a cylinder is an integer. Give three possible values of the radius r for which the lateral surface area is also an integer. *Explain* how you found your answers.

36. CHALLENGE Does doubling the height of a prism or cylinder result in a doubling of the surface area? of the lateral surface area? *Explain*.

37. CHALLENGE Use the diagram of the backyard tent shown.

   a. Draw a net of the tent. *Explain* how to find the height h of the triangular bases.

   b. Write an expression in terms of l for the surface area of the tent.

   c. The surface area of the tent is $44\sqrt{3}$ square feet. What is the value of l?

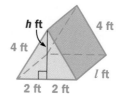

h ft
4 ft
4 ft
l ft
2 ft 2 ft

◆ CALIFORNIA STANDARDS SPIRAL REVIEW

AF 1.2   **38.** What is the value of $\frac{1}{2}(x+6)^2$ when $x = -2$? *(p. 5)*

   Ⓐ 4   Ⓑ 8   Ⓒ 16   Ⓓ 32

MG 3.4   **39.** Triangle $ABC \cong$ triangle DEF. What is the value of y? *(p. 516)*

   Ⓐ 4   Ⓑ 7

   Ⓒ 8   Ⓓ 19

8
B
F   y   E
A
7
D
4   C

AF 3.4   **40.** The graph of a line has a slope of 4. The graph is the relationship between which two units of measure? *(p. 348)*

   Ⓐ Feet and inches   Ⓑ Yards and feet

   Ⓒ Gallons and cups   Ⓓ Gallons and quarts

10.4 Surface Areas of Pyramids and Cones

Standards MG 2.1 Use formulas routinely for finding the perimeter and area of basic two-dimensional figures and **the surface area** and volume **of basic three-dimensional figures**, including rectangles, parallelograms, trapezoids, squares, triangles, circles, prisms, and cylinders.

MG 2.2 Estimate and compute the area of more complex or irregular two- and three-dimensional figures by breaking the figures down into more basic geometric objects.

MG 3.5 Construct two-dimensional patterns for three-dimensional models, such as cylinders, prisms, and **cones**.

Math and
ARCHITECTURE
Ex. 31, p. 586

Connect *Before* you found the surface areas of prisms and cylinders. *Now* you will find the surface areas of pyramids and cones.

KEY VOCABULARY
• slant height

For a pyramid, the faces other than the base are called *lateral* faces and meet at a point called the *vertex*. The perpendicular distance from the base to the vertex is the height h of the pyramid.

USING PYRAMIDS
In this lesson, all of the pyramids that appear are regular pyramids.

A *regular* pyramid has a regular polygon for its base and congruent isosceles triangles for its lateral faces. The **slant height** l of a regular pyramid is the height of each lateral face.

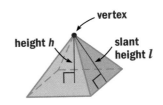

A regular pyramid with a square base is shown below, along with the pyramid's net.

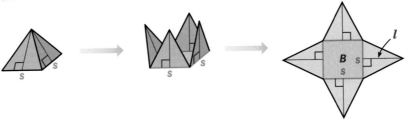

You can use the net of the pyramid and the following verbal model to find a formula for the pyramid's surface area.

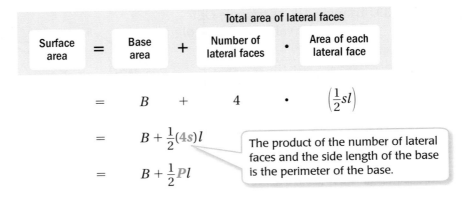

			Total area of lateral faces	
Surface area	=	Base area	+	Number of lateral faces • Area of each lateral face

$$= \quad B \quad + \quad 4 \quad \cdot \quad \left(\frac{1}{2}sl\right)$$

$$= \quad B + \frac{1}{2}(4s)l$$

$$= \quad B + \frac{1}{2}Pl$$

The product of the number of lateral faces and the side length of the base is the perimeter of the base.

The result at the bottom of the previous page can be generalized to *any* regular pyramid.

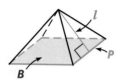
EXAMPLE 1   **Finding the Surface Area of a Pyramid**

**Find the surface area of the regular pyramid.
Round to the nearest tenth.**

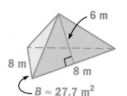

6 m
8 m   8 m
$B \approx 27.7 \text{ m}^2$

SOLUTION

STEP 1   **Find** the perimeter of the base.

$P = 8 + 8 + 8 = 24$

STEP 2   **Substitute** into the formula for surface area.

$S = B + \frac{1}{2}Pl$ **Write formula for surface area of a pyramid.**

$\approx 27.7 + \frac{1}{2}(24)(6)$ **Substitute 27.7 for B, 24 for P, and 6 for l.**

$= 99.7$ **Simplify.**

▶ **Answer** The surface area is about 99.7 square meters.

CONES You can use a net of a cone to find a cone's surface area. The curved, lateral surface of a cone is a section of a circle with radius l, which is the slant height of the cone. The area of this curved surface, called the lateral surface area of the cone, is $A = \pi rl$ where r is the radius of the cone's base.

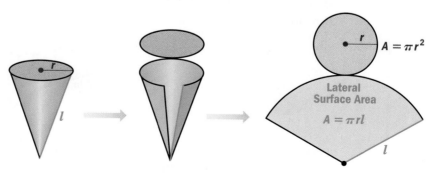

> # KEY CONCEPT
> *For Your Notebook*
>
> ## Surface Area of a Cone
>
> **Words**   The surface area of a cone is the sum of the area of the circular base with radius r and the product of π, the radius r of the base, and the slant height l.
>
>
>
> **Algebra** $S = B + \pi r l = \pi r^2 + \pi r l$

EXAMPLE 2   Finding the Surface Area of a Cone

Find the surface area of a cone with radius 4 meters and slant height 9 meters.

SOLUTION

$$S = \pi r^2 + \pi r l \qquad \text{Write formula for surface area of a cone.}$$

$$= \pi(4)^2 + \pi(4)(9) \qquad \text{Substitute 4 for } r \text{ and 9 for } l.$$

$$\approx 163.4 \qquad \text{Evaluate using a calculator.}$$

▶ **Answer** The surface area is about 163.4 square meters.

✓ GUIDED PRACTICE   for Examples 1 and 2

Draw a net of the pyramid. Then find the surface area. Round to the nearest tenth if necessary.

1.
12 ft
8 ft
8 ft

2. 10 in.
12 in.
12 in.
$B \approx 62.4 \text{ in.}^2$

3.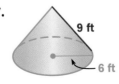
9 mm
6 mm

4. Find the lateral surface area of a square pyramid with a base side length of 12.5 centimeters and a slant height of 8.4 centimeters.

Draw a net of the cone. Then find the surface area and lateral surface area. Round to the nearest tenth.

5.
12 m
6 m

6.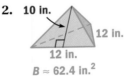
5 in.
16 in.

7.
9 ft
6 ft

COMPOSITE SOLIDS Composite solids are made up of two or more simpler solids, such as prisms, cylinders, and cones. You can find the surface area of a composite solid by finding the exposed surface area of each simpler solid.

EXAMPLE 3 **Finding the Surface Area of a Composite Solid**

STORAGE TANK The storage tank shown is composed of a cylinder and a cone. Find the surface area of the storage tank.

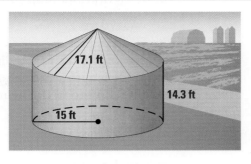

17.1 ft

14.3 ft

15 ft

About the Standards

To solve Example 3, you can break the problem into simpler parts (MR 1.3) by identifying which solids make up the composite solids.

SOLUTION

You do not need to include the top base of the cylinder, so the formula for the cylinder's surface area is $S = \pi r^2 + 2\pi rh$. You need to include only the lateral surface of the cone, so use the formula $S = \pi rl$.

$S =$ **Cylinder area** + Cone Area   **Break into simpler parts.**

$= (\pi r^2 + 2\pi rh) + \pi rl$ **Write equation for surface area.**

$= \pi(15)^2 + 2\pi(15)(14.3) + \pi(15)(17.1)$ **Substitute 15 for r, and 14.3 for h, and 17.1 for l.**

≈ 2860.4 **Approximate using a calculator.**

▶ **Answer** The surface area of the storage tank is about 2860.4 square feet.

✓ **GUIDED PRACTICE**   **for Example 3**

8. In Example 3, what is the surface area of the storage tank if you exclude *both* of the bases of the cylinder?

10.4 EXERCISES

HOMEWORK KEY

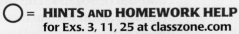

◆ = **MULTIPLE CHOICE PRACTICE**
Exs. 6, 13, 23, 36–38

○ = **HINTS AND HOMEWORK HELP**
for Exs. 3, 11, 25 at classzone.com

SKILLS • PROBLEM SOLVING • REASONING

1. VOCABULARY Draw a square pyramid with the height and slant height labeled.

2. WRITING *Describe* the difference between the *slant height* and the *height* of a pyramid.

SEE EXAMPLES 1 AND 2
on pp. 581–582
for Exs. 3–12

NETS AND SURFACE AREA Draw a net of the solid. Then find the surface area. Round to the nearest tenth if necessary.

 3.

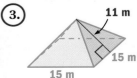

11 m

15 m

15 m

4.

10 cm

6 cm

5.

1.5 mm

1.5 mm

1.5 mm

6. ◆ **MULTIPLE CHOICE** What is the surface area of a square pyramid with a base side length of 7 meters and a slant height of 5 meters?

    A 70 m²   **B** 95 m²   **C** 119 m²   **D** 150.5 m²

FINDING SURFACE AREA Find the surface area of the square pyramid with base side length *s* and slant height *l*, or of the cone with radius *r* and slant height *l*. Round to the nearest tenth if necessary.

7. $s = 5$ cm
$l = 4.2$ cm

8. $s = 15$ yd
$l = 10$ yd

9. $r = 12$ m
$l = 6.5$ m

10. $r = 4$ mm
$l = 5.5$ mm

ERROR ANALYSIS *Describe* and correct the error in finding the surface area of the cone.

⑪.
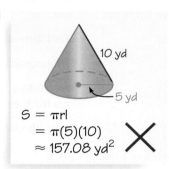

$$S = \pi rl$$
$$= \pi(5)(10)$$
$$\approx 157.08 \text{ yd}^2 \quad \times$$

12.
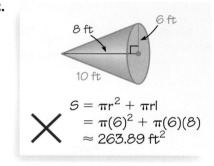

$$\times \quad S = \pi r^2 + \pi rl$$
$$= \pi(6)^2 + \pi(6)(8)$$
$$\approx 263.89 \text{ ft}^2$$

SEE EXAMPLE 3 on p. 583 for Exs. 13–15

13. ◆ **MULTIPLE CHOICE** What is the surface area of the composite object?

    A 48 cm²   **B** 49 cm²

    C 58 cm²   **D** 60 cm²

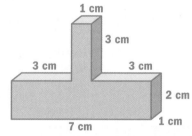

COMPOSITE SOLIDS The solids shown are composed of prisms and half-cylinders. Find the surface area of the solid. Round to the nearest tenth if necessary.

14.
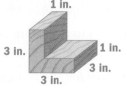

15.

SPHERES The surface area *S* of a sphere is $S = 4\pi r^2$ where *r* is the radius of the sphere. Find the surface area of the sphere. Round to the nearest tenth.

16.   —1.25 in.

17.   —8.8 in.

18.   —7 in.

     ◆ = **MULTIPLE CHOICE PRACTICE**   ◯ = **HINTS AND HOMEWORK HELP** at classzone.com

19. REASONING *Explain* how to find the slant height of the cone. Then find it and calculate the surface area of the cone. Round to the nearest tenth.

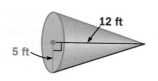

12 ft

5 ft

CONNECT SKILLS TO PROBLEM SOLVING Exercises 20–22 will help you prepare for problem solving.

Sketch the object described and label its dimensions. Match the sketch with the formula below needed to find its surface area.

20. A lamp shade in the shape of a square pyramid with an open bottom is 14 inches high, and the base has a side length of 14 inches.

21. A traffic cone with an open bottom is 24 inches high with a radius of 5 inches.

22. A paperweight in the shape of a cone is 5 centimeters tall with a radius of 1 centimeter.

A. $S = \pi r l$ **B.** $S = \frac{1}{2} Pl$ **C.** $S = \pi r^2 + \pi r l$

SEE EXAMPLES 1 AND 2
on pp. 581–582
for Exs. 23–28

23. ◆ **MULTIPLE CHOICE** What is the approximate lateral surface area of the ice cream cone shown?

1 in.

$4\frac{1}{4}$ in.

(A) 13.4 in.^{2} **(B)** 16.5 in.^{2}

(C) 26.7 in.^{2} **(D)** 39.3 in.^{2}

California *@HomeTutor*   for problem solving help at classzone.com

24. SET DESIGN Your school needs a square pyramid with a base for a play. Each side of the base will have a length of 10 feet. The slant height will be 15 feet. How many square feet of material are needed to build this pyramid?

California *@HomeTutor*   for problem solving help at classzone.com

ICICLES Icicles are shaped like cones. As they melt, icicles change size but stay cone shaped. Find the lateral surface area of an icicle with the given dimensions in terms of π.

25. $r = 1$ in., $l = 6$ in.   **26.** $r = 2$ in., $l = 12$ in.

27. $r = 3$ in., $l = 18$ in.   **28.** $r = 4$ in., $l = 24$ in.

29. LOOK FOR A PATTERN *Describe* the pattern developed in Exercises 25–28. Then use the pattern to predict the lateral surface area of an icicle with a radius of 5 inches and a slant height of 30 inches in terms of π.

30. NUMBER SENSE Predict which solid has a greater surface area: a *square pyramid* with a slant height of 12 units and a base side length of 10 units or a *cone* with a slant height of 12 units and a diameter of 10 units. *Explain* your reasoning. Then check your answer.

31. SHORT RESPONSE The Walter Pyramid in Long Beach, California, is a square pyramid with a height of 192 feet. Each side of its base measures 345 feet. *Explain* how to find the slant height. Then find the slant height and the lateral surface area of the pyramid.

CHALLENGE **The surface area S, base side length b, and slant height l of a square pyramid are given. Find the value of x.**

32. $S = 555$ m^2
$b = 15$ m
$l = (2x + 1)$ m

33. $S = 460$ cm^2
$b = 10$ cm
$l = (3x - 3)$ cm

34. $S = 125.6$ in.^{2}
$b = 5$ in.
$l = (x + 2)$ in.

35. CHALLENGE Find the surface area of the regular hexagonal pyramid. In the diagram of its base, all the triangles are equilateral and congruent. *Explain* how you found your answer.

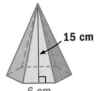
15 cm
6 cm

3 cm 3 cm

◆ CALIFORNIA STANDARDS SPIRAL REVIEW

NS 2.1

36. What is the value of x^{-2} when $x = 4$? *(p. 206)*

   A 0.0625   **B** 0.625   **C** 62.5   **D** 625

AF 1.3

37. Which operation will not change the value of a nonzero number? *(p. 31)*

   A Multiplying by 1   **B** Adding 1
   C Multiplying by 0   **D** Subtracting 1

MG 1.3

38. Which results in the fastest average speed? *(p. 443)*

   A Running 2 miles in 14 minutes   **B** Running 2.5 miles in 18 minutes
   C Running 5 miles in 32 minutes   **D** Running 4 miles in 28 minutes

QUIZ *for Lessons 10.3–10.4*

Find the surface area of the solid. Round to the nearest tenth if necessary.

1. *(p. 573)*
6 m
10 m
24 m

2. *(p. 573)*
7 yd
14 yd

3. *(p. 580)*
8 cm
5 cm

4. *(p. 580)*
11 cm
9 cm
9 cm

ONLINE QUIZ at classzone.com

Multiple Choice Practice for Lessons 10.1–10.4

1. The crystal below is composed of which two types of solids? **MG 3.6**

(A) Cone, cylinder

(B) Cylinder, prism

(C) Prism, pyramid

(D) Pyramid, cone

2. What is the approximate surface area of the triangular pyramid shown whose base has an area of about 15.6 square meters? **MG 2.1**

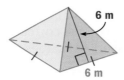

6 m

6 m

(A) 33.6 m^2 **(B)** 54 m^2

(C) 69.6 m^2 **(D)** 123.6 m^2

3. A cylinder has a height of 18 centimeters and a radius of 2 centimeters. What is the lateral surface area of the cylinder to the nearest tenth of a square centimeter? **MG 2.1, MR 2.7**

(A) 113.1 cm^2 **(B)** 226.2 cm^2

(C) 238.8 cm^2 **(D)** 251.3 cm^2

4. What is the least amount of wrapping paper needed to cover the gift box below? **MG 2.1**

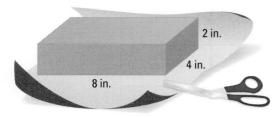

2 in.

4 in.

8 in.

(A) 56 in.^{2} **(B)** 64 in.^{2}

(C) 80 in.^{2} **(D)** 112 in.^{2}

5. Which solid has three rectangular faces and two triangular faces? **MG 3.6**

(A) Pentagonal prism

(B) Pentagonal pyramid

(C) Rectangular pyramid

(D) Triangular prism

6. Which is a true statement? **MG 3.6, MR 3.0**

(A) Three planes always intersect.

(B) Three planes cannot intersect in a line.

(C) Two planes can intersect in a line.

(D) Two planes can intersect in a point.

7. Which best describes the relationship of the lightning rod (line *AB*) and the gutter (line *CD*)? **MG 3.6**

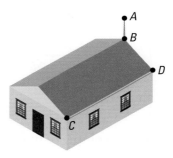

A

B

D

C

(A) Skew lines

(B) Intersecting lines

(C) Parallel lines

(D) Coplanar lines

8. You are making cone-shaped paper cups. A small cup has a radius of 1.2 inches and a slant height of 3.2 inches. A large cup has a radius of 1.5 inches and a slant height of 3.5 inches. About how much more paper does it take to make the large cup than the small cup? **MG 2.1**

(A) 1.09π in.^{2} **(B)** 1.41π in.^{2}

(C) 3.27π in.^{2} **(D)** 6.97π in.^{2}

10.5 Exploring Volume

MATERIALS • small cubes

QUESTION How do you find the volume of a prism?

The volume of a solid is a measure of how much space it occupies. Volume is measured in cubic units. One cubic unit is the amount of space occupied by a cube that measures one unit on each side. This cube is called a *unit cube*.

EXPLORE Find the volume of a rectangular prism

To find the volume of the prism shown, first build the prism using small cubes to represent unit cubes. Then count the number of cubes you used.

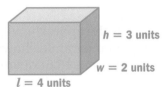

$h = 3$ units
$w = 2$ units
$l = 4$ units

STEP 1 **Make** the bottom of the prism using 8 cubes in 2 rows of 4.

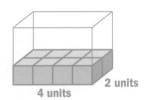

4 units
2 units

STEP 2 **Make** the prism the correct height by adding 2 layers of 8 cubes.

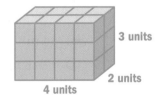

3 units
4 units
2 units

STEP 3 **Find** the volume of the prism. There were 24 cubes used. Because the volume of each cube is 1 cubic unit, the volume of the prism is 24 cubic units.

DRAW CONCLUSIONS Use your observations to complete these exercises

1. Copy and complete the table to find the volume of the rectangular prism with the given dimensions.

Dimensions of the prism	Cubes to cover the bottom of the prism	Layers of cubes to make the prism	Volume of the prism
$4 \times 2 \times 3$	8	3	24
$6 \times 1 \times 2$	?	?	?
$7 \times 5 \times 3$	?	?	?
$4 \times 2 \times 8$	?	?	?

2. **REASONING** Write a formula for the area B of the base of a rectangular prism. Then write a formula for the volume of the prism.

10.5 Volumes of Prisms and Cylinders

Math and **ECOLOGY**
Example 3, p. 591

Connect *Before* you found the surface areas of prisms and cylinders. *Now* you will find the volume of prisms and cylinders.

KEY VOCABULARY
• volume, *p. 742*

Recall that the volume of a solid is a measure of the amount of space it occupies. Volume is measured in *cubic units*. One cubic unit is the amount of space occupied by a cube that measures one unit on each side.

KEY CONCEPT   *For Your Notebook*

Volume of a Prism

Words   The volume of a prism is the product of the area B of the base and the height h.

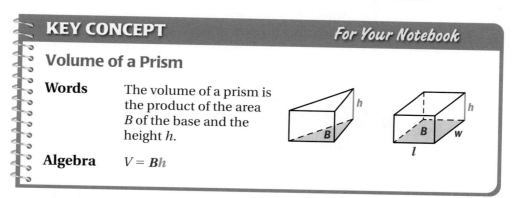

Algebra $V = Bh$

EXAMPLE 1   Finding Volumes of Prisms

AVOID ERRORS
When you find the volume of a triangular prism, be careful not to confuse the height of the prism with the height of the triangular base. In part (b) of Example 1, $h = 10$.

Find the volume of the prism.

a.
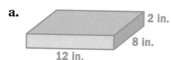
2 in.
8 in.
12 in.

$$V = Bh$$
$$= lwh$$
$$= 12(8)(2)$$
$$= 192$$

▶ **Answer** The volume is 192 cubic inches.

b.
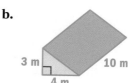
3 m
10 m
4 m

$$V = Bh$$
$$= \frac{1}{2}(4)(3)(10)$$
$$= 60$$

▶ **Answer** The volume is 60 cubic meters.

Animated Math

For an interactive example of finding the volume of a prism, go to **classzone.com.**

VOLUMES OF CYLINDERS As you discovered in the activity on page 588, the volume of a prism can be calculated by finding the number of square units in the base and multiplying by the height. The formula for the volume of a cylinder is similar to the formula for the volume of a prism.

REVIEW CYLINDERS
....
Remember, the base of a cylinder is a circle. So the area of the base is πr^2.

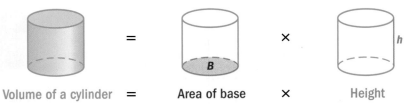

Volume of a cylinder = Area of base × Height

KEY CONCEPT   *For Your Notebook*

Volume of a Cylinder

Words   The volume of a cylinder is the product of the area B of the base and the height h.

Algebra $V = Bh$

              $= \pi r^2 h$

EXAMPLE 2   **Finding the Volume of a Cylinder**

Find the volume of the cylinder.

SOLUTION

The radius is one half the diameter, so $r = 3$ cm.

$V = Bh$	Write formula for volume of a cylinder.
$= \pi r^2 h$	The area of a circular base is πr^2.
$= \pi(3)^2(9)$	Substitute 3 for r and 9 for h.
$= 81\pi$	Simplify.
≈ 254.469	Evaluate using a calculator.

▶ **Answer** The volume is about 254 cubic centimeters.

✓   **GUIDED PRACTICE**   **for Examples 1 and 2**

Find the volume of the solid. Round to the nearest tenth if necessary.

1.
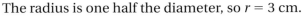
3 ft
11 ft
6 ft

2.
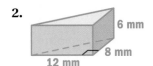
6 mm
8 mm
12 mm

3.

10 in.
$1\frac{1}{2}$ in.

EXAMPLE 3 **Comparing Capacities**

RECYCLING To decide which of the recycling bins shown on page 589 can hold more, find the volume of each bin.

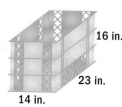
16 in.
23 in.
14 in.

9 in.
23 in.

READING
When the abbreviation for a unit of measure has an exponent of 3, you read the 3 as "cubic."
ft^3 means "cubic feet."
m^3 means "cubic meters."

$V = Bh$

$\quad = lwh$

$\quad = 23(14)(16)$

$\quad = 5152 \text{ in.}^3$

$V = Bh$

$\quad = \pi r^2 h$

$\quad = \pi(9)^2(23)$

$\quad \approx 5852.8 \text{ in.}^3$

▶ **Answer** The cylindrical recycling bin holds more.

EXAMPLE 4 **Finding the Volume of a Composite Solid**

The composite solid shown is composed of a rectangular prism and a triangular prism. Find the volume of the solid in cubic centimeters.

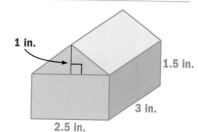
1 in.
1.5 in.
3 in.
2.5 in.

SOLUTION

STEP 1 **Find** the volume of the rectangular prism.

$\quad V = Bh$ Write formula for volume of rectangular prism.

$\quad\quad = 3(2.5)(1.5) = 11.25$ Substitute 3(2.5) for B and 1.5 for h. Then simplify.

STEP 2 **Find** the volume of the triangular prism.

$\quad V = Bh$ Write formula for volume of triangular prism.

$\quad\quad = \frac{1}{2}(2.5)(1)(3) = 3.75$ Substitute $\frac{1}{2}(2.5)(1)$ for B and 3 for h. Then simplify.

CONVERT MEASURES
Because 1 in. = 2.54 cm, you know that:
$(1 \text{ in.})^3 = (2.54 \text{ cm})^3$
$1 \text{ in.}^3 \approx 16.39 \text{ cm}^3$
Use this fact in Step 3 of Example 4.

STEP 3 **Calculate** the volume of the composite figure in cubic centimeters.

Find the sum of the volumes from Steps 1 and 2.

$\quad V = 11.25 + 3.75 = 15 \text{ in.}^3$

Then convert cubic inches to cubic centimeters.

$\quad 15 \text{ in.}^3 \times \frac{16.39 \text{ cm}^3}{1 \text{ in.}^3} \approx 245.9 \text{ cm}^3$

▶ **Answer** The volume of the solid is about 245.9 cubic centimeters.

EXAMPLE 5 Graphing a Volume Function

A rectangular prism has a fixed length of 3 centimeters and a fixed width of 2 centimeters. Graph the volume of the rectangular prism as a function of x where x represents the height of the prism.

SOLUTION

STEP 1 **Write** a formula for the volume of the prism.

$V = Bh$		**Write general formula for the volume of a prism.**
$= l \cdot w \cdot h$		**Write formula for the volume of a rectangular prism.**
$= 3 \cdot 2 \cdot x$		**Substitute.**
$= 6x$		**Simplify.**

STEP 2 **Make** a table.

x	1	2	3	4	5
V	6	12	18	24	30

STEP 3 **Graph** the ordered pairs. Draw a line through the points.

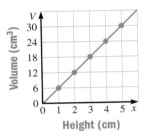

Notice that the graph represents a direct variation function. The volume varies directly with the height of the prism.

✓ **GUIDED PRACTICE** for Examples 3, 4, and 5

4. Which solid has the greater volume? *Explain* your reasoning.

Find the volume of the solid. Round to the nearest tenth.

5.

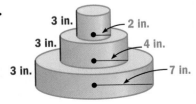

6.

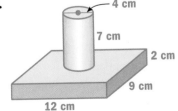

7. The base of a triangular prism has a fixed area of 10 square inches. Graph the volume of the triangular prism as a function of x where x represents the height of the prism.

10.5 EXERCISES

HOMEWORK KEY

◆ = **MULTIPLE CHOICE PRACTICE**
Exs. 26, 35, 45–47

○ = **HINTS** AND **HOMEWORK HELP**
for Exs. 3, 7, 35 at classzone.com

SKILLS • PROBLEM SOLVING • REASONING

1. **VOCABULARY** Copy and complete: The volume of a prism or cylinder is the product of the area of the __?__ and the __?__.

2. **NOTETAKING SKILLS** Make an *information wheel* like the one on page 560 for *cylinder*.

SEE EXAMPLE 1
on p. 589
for Exs. 3–6

VOLUMES OF PRISMS Find the volume of the rectangular prism with length *l*, width *w*, and height *h*.

3. $l = 6$ m, $w = 2$ m, $h = 11$ m

4. $l = 7$ in., $w = 7$ in., $h = 7$ in.

5. $l = 3.8$ cm, $w = 3$ cm, $h = 1.2$ cm

6. $l = 16$ ft, $w = 3$ ft, $h = 2\frac{1}{2}$ ft

SEE EXAMPLE 2
on p. 590
for Exs. 7–12

VOLUMES OF CYLINDERS Find the volume of the cylinder with radius *r* and height *h*. Round to the nearest tenth.

7. $r = 4$ ft, $h = 11$ ft

8. $r = 3$ cm, $h = 9$ cm

9. $r = 1.2$ m, $h = 4.5$ m

10. $r = 6.4$ in., $h = 12$ in.

11. $r = 7$ m, $h = 15$ m

12. $r = 8.3$ yd, $h = 1.6$ yd

*SEE EXAMPLES
1 AND 2*
on pp. 589–590
for Exs. 13–20

FINDING VOLUMES Find the volume of the solid. Round to the nearest tenth if necessary.

13.
2 yd, 4 yd, 8 yd

14.
12 cm, 2 cm

15.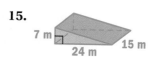
7 m, 24 m, 15 m

16.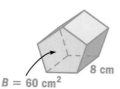
8 cm
$B = 60$ cm^2

17.
6 cm, 3 cm

18.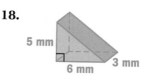
5 mm, 6 mm, 3 mm

ERROR ANALYSIS *Describe* and correct the error in finding the volume.

19.

$V = Bh$
$= 2\pi rh$
$= 2\pi(4)(5)$
≈ 125 m^3

✗

4 m, 5 m

20.

$V = Bh$
$= l \cdot w \cdot h$
$= (0.25)(2)(1)$
$= 0.5$ in.^{3}

✗

1 in., 2 in., 0.25 ft

SEE EXAMPLE 4
on p. 591
for Exs. 21–25

FINDING VOLUMES Find the volume of the solid. Round to the nearest tenth if necessary. Express your answer using the smaller units.

21.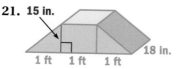
15 in., 18 in., 1 ft, 1 ft, 1 ft

22.
0.5 yd, 1.5 ft, 18 in.

23. 3 ft, 5 ft, 3 yd, 7 ft

VOLUMES OF COMPOSITE FIGURES **Find the volume. Round to the nearest tenth if necessary.**

24.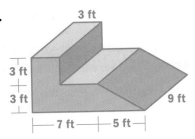

25.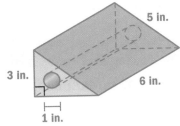

26. ◆ **MULTIPLE CHOICE** The volume of a solid is 6 cubic yards. What is the volume of the solid in cubic feet?

(A) 2 ft^3 (B) 18 ft^3 (C) 54 ft^3 (D) 162 ft^3

SEE EXAMPLE 5
on p. 592
for Exs. 27–28

GRAPHING VOLUME FUNCTIONS **In Exercises 27 and 28, make a table of values, then graph the volume V of the solid as a function of the variable dimension.**

27. A cylinder has a fixed height of 5 meters and a base with radius r.

28. A triangular prism has a fixed height of 8 inches and an equilateral triangle base with side length s. (*Hint:* To write the volume function, use the formula $A = \frac{1}{4}\sqrt{3}s^2$ for the area of an equilateral triangle.)

CONNECT SKILLS TO PROBLEM SOLVING **Exercises 29–32 will help you prepare for problem solving.**

Tell whether you would need to calculate *surface area* or *volume* to find the quantity.

29. The amount of wrapping paper needed to wrap a gift

30. The amount of cereal that will fit in a box

31. The amount of water needed to fill a bottle

32. The amount of paint needed to cover a chest of drawers

SEE EXAMPLE 3
on p. 591
for Exs. 33–34

33. **SWIMMING POOLS** A rectangular in-ground pool is 40 feet long, 16 feet wide, and 4 feet deep. A cylindrical above-ground pool is 6 feet deep and has a radius of 12 feet. Which pool holds more water? About how much more? *Explain*.

California **@HomeTutor** for problem solving help at classzone.com

34. **ERASERS** Find the volume of each eraser shown at the right to the nearest tenth. How many pencil-top erasers would you use in the time it takes you to completely use the larger eraser? *Explain* your reasoning.

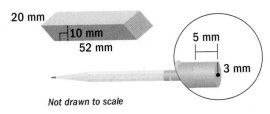

Not drawn to scale

California **@HomeTutor** for problem solving help at classzone.com

35. ◆ **MULTIPLE CHOICE** A cylindrical paint can is a 19 centimeters tall and 16 centimeters in diameter. What is its approximate volume?

(A) 955 cm³   (B) 3820 cm³   (C) 4536 cm³   (D) 15,281 cm³

SOLIDS In Exercises 36 and 37, sketch the solid formed by translating the plane figure the given distance along the line. Then find the volume of the solid. If necessary, round your answer to the nearest tenth.

EXTENSION   Translating to Form a Solid

Sketch the solid formed by translating the circle 8 centimeters along the line. Then find the volume of the solid.

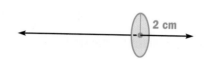

SOLUTION

STEP 1   **Draw** other possible locations where the circle could appear after being translated.

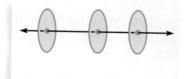

STEP 2   **Use** the drawings in Step 1 to sketch the solid formed by the translated circle.

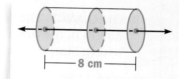

STEP 3   **Find** the volume of the cylinder.

$$V = \pi r^2 h$$
$$= \pi(2)^2(8) \approx 100.5 \text{ cm}^3$$

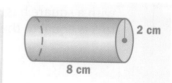

▶ **Answer** The volume of the cylinder is about 100.5 cubic centimeters.

---

36. 9 centimeters

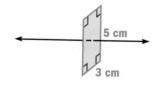

37. 4 inches

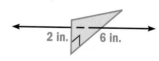

38. **OBLIQUE CYLINDER** In the extension above, the line of translation is perpendicular to the bases of the solid, so the solid is called a *right solid*. If the line is not perpendicular to the bases, then the solid is an *oblique solid*.

The volume of an oblique solid is given by $V = Bh$ where B is the area of a base and h is the height. The height is the perpendicular distance between the two parallel planes containing the bases. Find the volume of the oblique cylinder shown.

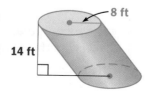

39. **SALT SHAKERS** You buy a cylindrical container of salt that has a diameter of 4 inches and a height of 6 inches. Your salt shaker is a rectangular prism that is $1\frac{1}{2}$ inches by $1\frac{1}{2}$ inches by 3 inches. Estimate how many times the salt container can fill the salt shaker.

40. **REASONING** Suppose two prisms have different surface areas, can they have the same volume? *Explain*.

41. **PUZZLE PROBLEM** A 4-centimeter-thick cylindrical slice of watermelon has a diameter of 24 centimeters. The rind is 2 centimeters thick. What percent of the slice is rind?

42. **MULTI-STEP PROBLEM** Use the cylinder at the right.

   a. What is the effect of tripling the radius on the surface area and volume of the cylinder?

   b. What is the effect of tripling the height on the surface area and volume of the cylinder?

   c. What is the effect of tripling *both* the radius and the height on the surface area and volume of the cylinder?

43. **CHALLENGE** The volume of a rectangular prism is 54 cubic inches. The length of the prism is twice its width. The height of the prism equals its width. Find the dimensions of the prism.

44. **CHALLENGE** Find the surface area S and volume V of the cube at the right. Give the dimensions of another prism with a square base such that the ratio of the surface area to S is equal to the ratio of the volume to V.

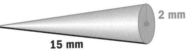

◆ CALIFORNIA STANDARDS SPIRAL REVIEW

MG 2.1

45. What is the approximate surface area of the cone? *(p. 580)*

   A 97.4 mm^2 **B** 100.5 mm^2

   C 106.8 mm^2 **D** 238.8 mm^2

MG 3.6

46. The structure shown is composed of which solids? *(p. 566)*

   A 1 pentagonal prism and 1 rectangular prism

   B 2 rectangular prisms

   C 2 pentagonal prisms

   D 2 trapezoidal prisms

MG 3.3

47. A rectangular pool is 20 feet wide and 40 feet long. You swim diagonally across the pool. To the nearest foot, how far did you swim? *(p. 471)*

   A 26 ft   **B** 30 ft   **C** 45 ft   **D** 54 ft

10.6 **Comparing Volumes**

MATERIALS · tape · scissors · thin cardboard · popcorn kernels

Standards

MG 3.5 Construct two-dimensional patterns for three-dimensional models, such as cylinders, prisms, and cones.

QUESTION How is the volume of a pyramid related to the volume of a prism with the same base and height?

EXPLORE Compare pyramids and prisms

STEP 1 **Draw** the nets shown on cardboard. Cut out and tape the nets to make an open square prism and an open square pyramid.

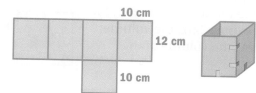
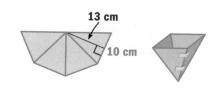

STEP 2 **Compare** the height and base of the prism to the height and base of the pyramid. What do you notice?

STEP 3 **Fill** the pyramid with popcorn kernels and pour the contents into the prism. Repeat until the prism is full. How many times did you have to empty the pyramid into the prism? Use this number to write the ratio of the volume of the pyramid to the volume of the prism.

DRAW CONCLUSIONS Use your observations to complete these exercises

Use the formula for the volume of a rectangular prism and the ratio found in the activity to find the volume of the square pyramid.

1.

4 cm
2 cm
2 cm

2.
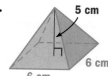
5 cm
6 cm
6 cm

3.

8 cm
3 cm
3 cm

4. Draw the nets shown on cardboard. Use the nets to make an open cylinder and an open cone. Repeat Steps 2 and 3 above using the cylinder and cone.

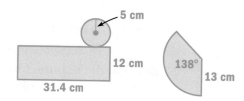
5 cm
12 cm
31.4 cm
138°
13 cm

10.6 Volumes of Pyramids and Cones

Standards **MG 2.1** Use formulas routinely for finding the perimeter and area of basic two-dimensional figures and the surface area and **volume of basic three-dimensional figures**, including rectangles, parallelograms, trapezoids, squares, triangles, circles, prisms, and cylinders.

MG 2.4 Relate the changes in measurement with a change of scale to the units used (e.g., square inches, cubic feet) and to conversions between units (1 square foot = 144 square inches or [1 ft.^{2}] = [144 in.^{2}]; 1 cubic inch is approximately 16.38 cubic centimeters or [1 in.^{3}] = [16.38 cm^3]).

Math and **HISTORY**
Example 3, p. 600

Connect *Before* you found the volumes of prisms and cylinders. *Now* you will find the volumes of pyramids and cones.

KEY VOCABULARY

• **pyramid,** *p. 580*
• **cone,** *p. 580*
• **volume,** *p. 742*

The volumes of a pyramid and a prism with the same base area and the same height are related. As you may have discovered in the activity on page 597, the volume of the pyramid is exactly one third the volume of the prism.

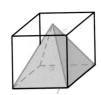

KEY CONCEPT   *For Your Notebook*

Volume of a Pyramid

Words   The volume *V* of a pyramid is one third the product of the area *B* of the base and the height *h*.

Algebra $V = \frac{1}{3}Bh$

EXAMPLE 1 Finding the Volume of a Pyramid

Find the volume of the square pyramid.

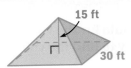

15 ft

30 ft

SOLUTION

$V = \frac{1}{3}Bh$ Write formula for volume of a pyramid.

$= \frac{1}{3}(30^2)(15)$ Substitute 30^2 for *B* and 15 for *h*.

$= 4500$ Evaluate using a calculator.

▶ **Answer** The pyramid has a volume of 4500 cubic feet.

Notice that the volume formula for pyramids does not require that the pyramid be regular, unlike the surface area formula.

EXAMPLE 2 **Finding the Volume of a Pyramid**

Find the volume of the pyramid in cubic inches.

12 cm
10 cm
24 cm

SOLUTION

STEP 1 Find the volume in cubic centimeters.

$$V = \frac{1}{3}Bh$$ **Write formula for volume of a pyramid.**

$$= \frac{1}{3}\left(\frac{1}{2} \cdot 24 \cdot 10\right)(12)$$ **The base is a triangle, so $B = \frac{1}{2}bh$.**

$$= 480 \text{ cm}^3$$ **Multiply.**

STEP 2 Convert to cubic inches. Because 1 in. = 2.54 cm, you know that
$(1 \text{ in.})^3 = (2.54 \text{ cm})^3$, or $1 \text{ in.}^3 \approx 16.39 \text{ cm}^3$.

$$480 \text{ cm}^3 \times \frac{1 \text{ in.}^3}{16.39 \text{ cm}^3} \approx 29.3 \text{ in.}^3$$

▶ **Answer** The pyramid has a volume of about 29.3 cubic inches.

 GUIDED PRACTICE   **for Examples 1 and 2**

Find the volume of the square pyramid with base side length *s* and height *h*.

1. $s = 4$ cm, $h = 5$ cm   **2.** $s = 6$ in., $h = 15$ in.   **3.** $s = 8$ mm, $h = 27$ mm

4. $s = 3$ yd, $h = 3$ yd   **5.** $s = 7$ m, $h = 9$ m   **6.** $s = 12$ ft, $h = 21$ ft

Find the volume of the pyramid given the area *B* of the base and the height *h*. Express your answer using the larger unit.

7. $B = 8$ cm^2, $h = 40$ mm   **8.** $B = 81$ in.^{2}, $h = 1$ ft   **9.** $B = 27$ ft^2, $h = 5$ yd

VOLUMES OF CONES The volume of a cone is related to the volume of a cylinder in the same way the volumes of a pyramid and a prism are related. That is, the volume of a cone is one third the volume of a cylinder that has the same base and height.

KEY CONCEPT   *For Your Notebook*

Volume of a Cone

Words   The volume *V* of a cone is one third the product of the area *B* of the base and the height *h*.

Algebra $V = \frac{1}{3}Bh = \frac{1}{3}\pi r^2 h$

h
B   *r*

EXAMPLE 3 Finding the Volume of a Cone

HISTORY Many Native American tribes built tepees that were similar to a cone in shape. A tepee has a height of 12 feet and a base diameter of 12 feet. Approximate the volume of the tepee.

12 ft

12 ft

Animated Math

For an interactive example of finding the volume of a cone, go to **classzone.com**.

SOLUTION

The radius is one half the diameter, so $r = 6$ feet.

$$V = \frac{1}{3}\pi r^2 h \qquad \text{Write formula for volume of a cone.}$$

$$= \frac{1}{3}\pi(6)^2(12) \qquad \text{Substitute 6 for } r \text{ and 12 for } h.$$

$$= 144\pi \qquad \text{Simplify.}$$

$$\approx 452.389 \qquad \text{Evaluate using a calculator.}$$

▶ **Answer** The tepee has a volume of about 452 cubic feet.

About the Standards

You can use estimation to check for reasonableness (MR 2.1).

CHECK Because $\frac{1}{3}\pi \approx 1$, $V \approx 36 \cdot 12 \approx 40 \cdot 10 = 400 \text{ ft}^3$. The answer is reasonable.

✓ **GUIDED PRACTICE** for Example 3

Find the volume of the cone with radius r and height h.

10. $r = 24$ m, $h = 18$ m   **11.** $r = 4$ in., $h = 16$ in.   **12.** $r = 15$ ft, $h = 28$ ft

10.6 **EXERCISES**

HOMEWORK KEY

◆ = **MULTIPLE CHOICE PRACTICE**
Exs. 19, 37, 46, 51–53

◯ = **HINTS AND HOMEWORK HELP**
for Exs. 7, 17, 47 at classzone.com

SKILLS • PROBLEM SOLVING • REASONING

1. VOCABULARY What formula can you use to find a pyramid's volume?

2. WRITING How is the formula for the volume of a cone related to the formula for the volume of a cylinder?

FORMULAS Match each solid with the *best* formula for its volume.

3. Prism   **4.** Cylinder   **5.** Pyramid   **6.** Cone

A. $V = \frac{1}{3}Bh$ **B.** $V = \pi r^2 h$ **C.** $V = \frac{1}{3}\pi r^2 h$ **D.** $V = Bh$

SEE EXAMPLES 1 AND 2
on pp. 598–599
for Exs. 7–15

VOLUME OF A PYRAMID Find the volume of the pyramid given the area B of the base and the height h.

7. $B = 9$ in.^{2}, $h = 4$ in.   **8.** $B = 12$ ft^2, $h = 15$ ft   **9.** $B = 1.5$ m^2, $h = 0.6$ m

VOLUME OF A SQUARE PYRAMID Find the volume of the square pyramid with base side length *s* and height *h*.

10. $s = 15$ m, $h = 4$ m

11. $s = 12$ yd, $h = 3$ yd

12. $s = 6$ in., $h = \frac{1}{2}$ in.

VOLUME OF A SOLID Find the volume of the solid. Round to the nearest tenth if necessary. Check that your answer is reasonable.

13.
20 m
24 m
16 m

14.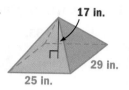
17 in.
29 in.
25 in.

15.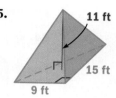
11 ft
15 ft
9 ft

SEE EXAMPLE 3
on p. 600
for Exs. 16–20

16.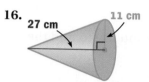
27 cm   11 cm

17.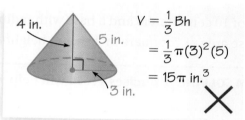
45 ft
45 ft

18.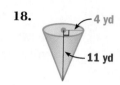
4 yd
11 yd

19. ◆ **MULTIPLE CHOICE** What is the volume of the cone?

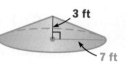
3 ft
7 ft

(A) 10π ft^3

(B) 21π ft^3

(C) 49π ft^3

(D) 147π ft^3

ERROR ANALYSIS *Describe* and correct the error in finding the volume.

20.

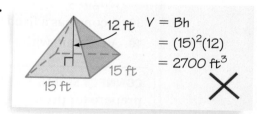
4 in.
5 in.
3 in.

$V = \frac{1}{3}Bh$

$= \frac{1}{3}\pi(3)^2(5)$

$= 15\pi$ in.^{3} ✗

21.

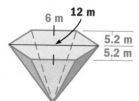
12 ft
15 ft
15 ft

$V = Bh$

$= (15)^2(12)$

$= 2700$ ft^3 ✗

VOLUME OF A CONE Find the volume of the cone with the given dimensions. If two units of measure are used, express your answer using the smaller unit. Round to the nearest tenth.

22. $r = 3$ in., $h = 7$ in.

23. $r = 11$ ft, $h = 4$ ft

24. $d = 1.2$ m, $h = 4.5$ m

25. $r = 83$ cm, $h = 2.8$ m

26. $d = 5$ m, $h = 492$ cm

27. $d = 3$ ft, $h = 10$ yd

VOLUME OF A PYRAMID Find the area of the base and the volume of the pyramid with the given height *h* and base shown.

28. $h = 1.8$ cm

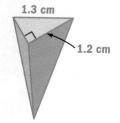
1.3 cm
1.2 cm

29. $h = 8$ m

6 m   12 m
5.2 m
5.2 m

30. $h = 18$ in.

6 in.
8 in.
16 in.
10 in.

XY ALGEBRA **Find the unknown dimension using the given information.**

31. Square pyramid
volume = 156 yd³
base side length = 6 yd
height = _?_

32. Cone
volume = 216π ft³
height = 8 ft
radius = _?_

33. Right triangular pyramid
volume = 28 in.³
legs = 3 in., 4 in.
height = _?_

FINDING VOLUME **Find the volume of the solid. Round to the nearest tenth.**

34.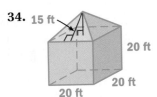
15 ft
20 ft
20 ft
20 ft

35.
10 cm
6 cm
14 cm

36.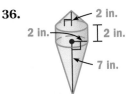
2 in.
2 in.
2 in.
7 in.

37. ◆ **MULTIPLE CHOICE** Which two formulas can you use to find the volume of the solid shown?

A $V = \frac{1}{3}Bh$ and $V = \pi r^2 h$

B $V = \pi r^2 h$ and $V = Bh$

C $V = \frac{1}{2}Bh$ and $V = Bh$

D $V = \frac{1}{3}Bh$ and $V = \pi rh$

GRAPHING VOLUME FUNCTIONS **In Exercises 38–40, graph the volume V of the solid as a function of the variable dimension.**

38. A square pyramid has a fixed height of 6 inches and a base with side length s.

39. A cone has a fixed height of 10 centimeters and a base with radius r.

40. A pyramid with a fixed base area of 15 square inches and height h.

CONNECT SKILLS TO PROBLEM SOLVING **Exercises 41–44 will help you prepare for problem solving.**

Find the volume of each item. If necessary, round your answer to the nearest tenth.

41. A cone shaped hat with a height of 8 inches and a radius of 3 inches

42. A square pyramid shaped candle with a height of 2 inches and a base with a side length of 3 inches

43. A cone shaped paper cup with a height of 4 inches and a radius of 1.5 inches

44. A pyramid shaped trophy with a height of 5 inches and a base with an area of 14 square inches

SEE EXAMPLE 3
on p. 600
for Ex. 45

45. **SPOTLIGHT** The light from a spotlight extends out in a cone shape from the bulb. The light of the beam extends 24 feet before it hits the floor directly under the spotlight and creates a circle with a radius of 10 feet. What is the volume of the space directly lit by the spotlight? Round to the nearest tenth.

California @HomeTutor for problem solving help at classzone.com

◆ = **MULTIPLE CHOICE PRACTICE**   ◯ = **HINTS AND HOMEWORK HELP** at classzone.com

SEE EXAMPLES 2 AND 3
on pp. 599–600
for Ex. 46

46. ◆ **MULTIPLE CHOICE** Each of four wooden models has a height of 6 inches. Which model has the greatest volume?

Ⓐ A square pyramid with base side length 8 in.

Ⓑ A rectangular pyramid with base side lengths 8 in. and 6 in.

Ⓒ A cylinder with diameter 8 in.

Ⓓ A cone with diameter 8 in.

California @HomeTutor for problem solving help at classzone.com

47. **REASONING** A rectangular prism-shaped hole 10 feet by 12 feet by 8 feet is dug into the ground. Which is the taller solid that can be formed with the excavated dirt: a *square pyramid* with a base side length of 10 feet or a *cone* with a radius of 5 feet? *Explain* your reasoning.

48. **MULTI-STEP PROBLEM** A diagram of an hourglass that measures 60 minutes is shown.

a. Find the volume of the cone-shaped pile of sand.

b. If this is an accurate hourglass, at what rate does the sand fall through the opening? Give your answer in cubic inches per minute.

3 in.

9 in.

49. **CHALLENGE** Find the volume of a regular hexagonal pyramid with a height of 6 meters and a base side length of 4 meters. Round to the nearest tenth.

50. **CHALLENGE** A cone-shaped cup has a height of 11 centimeters and a radius of 4 centimeters. You pour water into the cup until it is 2 centimeters from the top. Sketch the cone. How many fluid ounces of water are in the cup? Round to the nearest tenth. (*Hint:* Use similar triangles and the fact that $1 \text{ cm}^3 \approx 0.0338 \text{ fl oz.}$)

◆ CALIFORNIA STANDARDS SPIRAL REVIEW

MG 2.1

51. What is the volume of the triangular prism shown at the right? *(p. 589)*

Ⓐ 97 m^3 Ⓑ 100 m^3

Ⓒ 120 m^3 Ⓓ 238 m^3

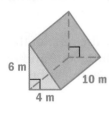

6 m   10 m   4 m

MG 3.6

52. Which two points in the diagram are collinear and in plane P? *(p. 561)*

Ⓐ A and B Ⓑ B and C

Ⓒ C and D Ⓓ A and D

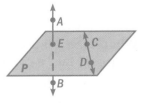

AF 4.2

53. The number y of screws a machine can make varies directly with the number x of hours the machine operates. A machine can make 6300 screws in 3 hours. Which equation relates x and y? *(p. 348)*

Ⓐ $y = 2100x$ Ⓑ $y = 3150x$ Ⓒ $y = 6300x$ Ⓓ $y = 18,900x$

10.7 Investigating Similar Solids

MATERIALS • spreadsheet software (optional)

Standards

MG 2.3 Compute the length of the perimeter, the surface area of the faces, and the volume of a three-dimensional object built from rectangular solids. **Understand that when the lengths of all dimensions are multiplied by a scale factor, the surface area is multiplied by the square of the scale factor and the volume is multiplied by the cube of the scale factor.**

QUESTION **How can you determine the relationship between the surface areas and volumes of similar solids?**

Two solids of the same type with equal ratios of corresponding linear dimensions, such as heights or radii, are called *similar solids*. Similar solids have the same shape but may be different sizes. The common ratio of corresponding linear dimensions of two similar solids is called the *scale factor*. All cubes are similar.

EXPLORE **Compare the surface areas and volumes of similar solids**

STEP 1 **Record** the edge lengths, surface areas, and volumes of the cubes at the right.

1 in.   2 in.   3 in.

	A	B	C	D	E	F
1	Edge length (in.)	Scale factor, k	Surface area (in.^{2})	Ratio of surface areas	Volume (in.^{3})	Ratio of volumes
2	1	?	6	?	1	?
3	2	?	24	?	8	?
4	3	?	54	?	27	?

STEP 2 **Calculate** the scale factor of each cube to a unit cube.

STEP 3 **Calculate** the ratio of the surface area of each cube to the surface area of a unit cube and the ratio of the volume of each cube to the volume of a unit cube.

PRACTICE

1. **REASONING** What is the relationship between the surface area ratios and the scale factors? Make a conjecture.

2. **REASONING** What is the relationship between the volume ratios and the scale factors? Make a conjecture.

3. Find the scale factor of two similar solids if the ratio of their surface areas is $\frac{25}{36}$.

10.7 Similar Solids

Standards MG 2.3 Compute the length of the perimeter, the surface area of the faces, and the volume of a three-dimensional object built from rectangular solids. Understand that when the lengths of all dimensions are multiplied by a scale factor, the surface area is multiplied by the square of the scale factor and the volume is multiplied by the cube of the scale factor.

Connect *Before* you found the surface areas and volumes of solids. *Now* you will determine whether solids are similar.

Math and
ARCHITECTURE
Example 4, p. 607

KEY VOCABULARY
• similar solids

Two solids of the same type with equal ratios of corresponding linear measures, such as heights or radii, are called **similar solids**. The common ratio is called the *scale factor*. Similar solids have the same shape, but their sizes may differ. Any two cubes are similar, as are any two spheres.

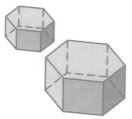

Similar

Similar

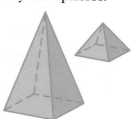

Not similar

EXAMPLE 1 Identifying Similar Solids

Tell whether the rectangular prisms in parts (a) and (b) are similar to the given prism.

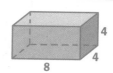

a.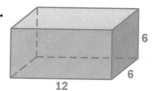

b.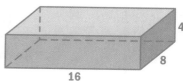

SOLUTION

COMPARE RATIOS
To compare the ratios of corresponding side lengths, write the ratios as fractions in simplest form.

a. **Ratio of lengths:** $\frac{12}{8} = \frac{3}{2}$ **Ratio of widths:** $\frac{6}{4} = \frac{3}{2}$ **Ratio of heights:** $\frac{6}{4} = \frac{3}{2}$

▶ **Answer** The prisms are similar because the ratios of the corresponding linear measures are equal. The scale factor is $3:2$.

b. **Ratio of lengths:** $\frac{16}{8} = 2$ **Ratio of widths:** $\frac{8}{4} = 2$ **Ratio of heights:** $\frac{4}{4} = 1$

▶ **Answer** The prisms are not similar because the ratios of the corresponding linear measures are not all equal.

KEY CONCEPT
For Your Notebook

Ratios of Measures of Similar Solids

If two solids are similar with a scale factor of k, then:

- the surface areas of the solids have a ratio of k^2
- the volumes of the solids have a ratio of k^3

EXAMPLE 2 **Comparing Surface Area and Volume**

The solids shown are similar with a scale factor of $1:2$, or $\frac{1}{2}$.
The surface area and volume of Solid A are given. Find
(a) the surface area and **(b)** the volume of Solid B.

Surface area of A = 14 in.^{2}
Volume of A = 3 in.^{3}

SOLUTION

a. The two solids are similar with a scale factor of $\frac{1}{2}$,
so the ratio of their surface areas is $\left(\frac{1}{2}\right)^2$ or $\frac{1}{4}$.

$\frac{1}{4} = \dfrac{14}{\text{Surface area of B}}$ **Write proportion using ratios of surface areas.**

$\text{Surface area of B} = 4(14)$ **Cross products property**

$\text{Surface area of B} = 56$ **Multiply.**

▶ **Answer** The surface area of Solid B is 56 in.^{2}

b. The two solids are similar with a scale factor of $\frac{1}{2}$, so the ratio of their
volumes is $\left(\frac{1}{2}\right)^3$, or $\frac{1}{8}$.

$\frac{1}{8} = \dfrac{3}{\text{Volume of B}}$ **Write proportion using ratios of volumes.**

$\text{Volume of B} = 8(3)$ **Cross products property**

$\text{Volume of B} = 24$ **Multiply.**

▶ **Answer** The volume of Solid B is 24 in.^{3}

✓ **GUIDED PRACTICE** **for Examples 1 and 2**

1. Determine whether a rectangular prism with dimensions 5 meters,
   5 meters, and 9 meters is similar to a rectangular prism with dimensions
   3 meters, 3 meters, and 6 meters.

2. **WHAT IF?** In Example 2, suppose the scale factor is $3:4$, the surface
   area of Solid A is 224 in.^{2}, and the volume of Solid A is 192 in.^{3} Find the
   surface area and volume of the Solid B.

EXAMPLE 3 ◆ **Multiple Choice Practice**

The dimensions of a prism are shown. A similar prism can be produced by multiplying each dimension by the same number. What happens to the volume when the dimensions are doubled?

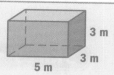

3 m

3 m

5 m

(A) The volume is cut in half. **(B)** The volume is multiplied by 2.

(C) The volume is multiplied by 4. **(D)** The volume is multiplied by 8.

Animated Math

For an interactive example of finding volume using a scale factor, go to **classzone.com.**

SOLUTION

Because the given dimensions are doubled, the scale factor of the new prism to the original prism is $\frac{2}{1} = 2$. So, the ratio of the volumes is $2^3 = 8$. Doubling the dimensions multiplies the volume by 8.

▶ **Answer** The correct answer is D. (A) (B) (C) ●

EXAMPLE 4 **Finding a Scale Factor**

LIGHTHOUSE The Old Point Loma Lighthouse in San Diego has a surface area of about 3,220 square feet. A scale paper model of the lighthouse has a surface area of about 0.389 square feet. Find the scale factor of the paper model to the actual lighthouse.

Paper model of Old Point Loma Lighthouse

SOLUTION

WRITE SCALE FACTORS

It is often useful to write the scale factor of a model to the actual object in the form $\frac{1}{n}$. In this form, the scale factor tells you that each dimension of the actual object is n times the corresponding dimension of the model.

Write and solve an equation to find the scale factor k.

$k^2 = \dfrac{0.389}{3220}$ k^2 equals the ratio of the surface areas.

$k = \sqrt{\dfrac{0.389}{3220}}$ Take positive square root of each side.

$k = \dfrac{\sqrt{0.389}}{\sqrt{3220}}$ Use quotient property of square roots.

$k \approx \dfrac{0.627}{56.74} \approx \dfrac{1}{91}$ Write scale factor in the form $\frac{1}{n}$.

▶ **Answer** The scale factor of the model to the lighthouse is about 1 : 91.

✓ **GUIDED PRACTICE** **for Examples 3 and 4**

3. If the dimensions of a prism are tripled what happens to the volume?

4. In Example 4, suppose the surface area of the paper model is 250 square inches. Find the scale factor of the paper model to the actual lighthouse.

10.7 EXERCISES

HOMEWORK
KEY

◆ = **MULTIPLE CHOICE PRACTICE**
Exs. 11, 17, 23, 34–36

○ = **HINTS AND HOMEWORK HELP**
for Exs. 3, 15, 23 at classzone.com

SKILLS • PROBLEM SOLVING • REASONING

1. **VOCABULARY** Copy and complete: Two solids of the same type with equal ratios of corresponding linear measures are called __?__.

2. **WRITING** *Explain* how to find the scale factor of two similar solids.

SEE EXAMPLE 1
on p. 605
for Exs. 3–6

IDENTIFYING SIMILAR SOLIDS Tell whether the solids are similar. *Explain your reasoning.*

3.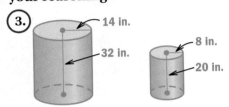

4.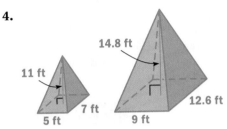

5.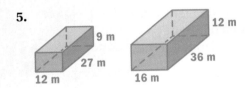

6.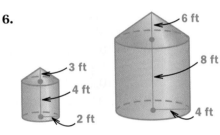

SEE EXAMPLE 2
on p. 606
for Exs. 7–10

USING SCALE FACTOR Solid A (shown) is similar to solid B (not shown) with the given scale factor of A to B. Find the surface area and volume of solid B.

7. Scale factor of 1 : 2

$S = 150\pi$ in.^{2}
$V = 250\pi$ in.^{3}

8. Scale factor of 3 : 1

$S = 18$ m^2
$V = 4$ m^3

9. Scale factor of 5 : 2

$S = 2356.2$ cm^2
$V = 7450.9$ cm^3

10. **ERROR ANALYSIS** The scale factor of two similar cones is 1 : 5. The volume of the smaller cone is 400 cubic inches. *Describe* and correct the error in writing a proportion to find the volume *V* of the larger cone.

$$\frac{400}{V} = \left(\frac{1}{5}\right)^2 \quad \times$$

SEE EXAMPLE 3
on p. 607
for Exs. 11–12

11. ◆ **MULTIPLE CHOICE** Cylinders A and B are similar. The dimensions of cylinder A are ten times those of cylinder B. The volume of cylinder A is how many times the volume of cylinder B?

(A) 0.001　　(B) 10　　(C) 1000　　(D) 10,000

12. ERROR ANALYSIS Fred said that if the dimensions of a prism are multiplied by 5, the surface area of the new prism equals the surface area of the original prism multiplied by 5. *Describe* and correct his error.

SEE EXAMPLE 4
on p. 607
for Exs. 13–17

FINDING SCALE FACTOR **In Exercises 13–16, solid A is similar to solid B. Find the scale factor of solid A to solid B.**

13.

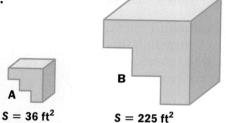

A
S = 36 ft²   B
S = 225 ft²

14.

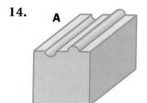

A
B
S = 224 m²   S = 8.75 m²

15.

A
B
S = 64 cm²   S = 36 cm²

16. A

B
S = 192 cm²   S = 108 cm²

17. ◆ MULTIPLE CHOICE You have two similar cones. The surface area of the smaller cone is 16 m². The surface area of the larger cone is 36 m². What is the scale factor of the smaller cone to the larger cone?

Ⓐ $\frac{4}{9}$ Ⓑ $\frac{2}{3}$ Ⓒ $\frac{3}{2}$ Ⓓ $\frac{9}{4}$

CONNECT SKILLS TO PROBLEM SOLVING **Exercises 18–20 will help you prepare for problem solving.**

Find the scale factor of the smaller object to the larger object.

18. The lengths of two similar baseball bats are 24 inches and 34 inches.

19. The heights of two similar coffee pots are 25 centimeters and 30 centimeters.

20. The widths of two similar MP3 players are 0.5 inch and 0.75 inch.

SEE EXAMPLE 4
on p. 607
for Ex. 21

21. SIGNS The surface areas of two similar business signs are 192 square inches and 1728 square inches. What is the scale factor of the smaller sign to the larger sign?

California @HomeTutor for problem solving help at classzone.com

22. STATUE OF LIBERTY You purchase a souvenir of the Statue of Liberty. The height of your souvenir is 1 foot, and the height of the actual Statue of Liberty in New York City is approximately 305 feet. Find the ratio of the surface area of your souvenir to the surface area of the Statue of Liberty.

California @HomeTutor for problem solving help at classzone.com

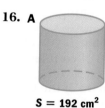

1 ft

23. ◆ **MULTIPLE CHOICE** Paperweights A and B are similar. The dimensions of paperweight A are four times those of paperweight B. The volume of paperweight A is how many times the volume of paperweight B?

A 0.4   **B** 4   **C** 16   **D** 64

READING IN MATH   **Read the information below for Exercises 24–27.**

Miniature City The Madurodam is a miniature city in Holland. Built on 5 acres, the city is an attraction that includes buildings, parks, canals, railroads, and much more. Every object is similar to an actual real-life object, and the scale factor is 1 : 25.

Madurodam in Holland

24. Calculate If a model of a boat in the Madurodam is 2 feet long, how long is the actual boat?

25. Calculate If you are 5 feet tall, how tall would a model of yourself be in the Madurodam?

26. Calculate If the volume of an actual fountain is 400 cubic feet, what would the volume of the model fountain be in the Madurodam?

27. Write *Explain* how to find what the dimensions of a model of your classroom would be in the Madurodam.

---

28. GRAPHING FUNCTIONS *Explain* why any two cubes are similar. Write and graph an equation giving the volume V of a cube as a function of its edge length x. Then use your equation to show that if the scale factor relating two cubes is k, then the ratio of the volumes of the cubes is k^3. (*Hint:* Let the edge lengths of the two cubes be x and kx.)

29. REASONING Would doubling the height or doubling the radius change the volume of a cone more? *Explain* your reasoning.

30. MULTI-STEP PROBLEM The similar solids shown at the right are composed of rectangular prisms.

  a. What is the scale factor of the larger solid to the smaller solid?

  b. Find the perimeters of the highlighted corresponding faces. Then find the ratio of the larger perimeter to the smaller perimeter. What do you notice?

  c. Find the sum of the edge lengths for each solid. Then find the ratio of the sum for the larger solid to the sum for the smaller solid. What do you notice?

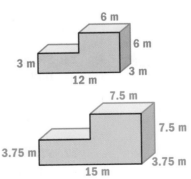

31. REASONING The ratio of the surface area of solid A to the surface area of solid B is 1 : 9. What is the ratio of the volume of solid A to the volume of solid B? *Explain.*

◆ = **MULTIPLE CHOICE PRACTICE**   ◯ = **HINTS AND HOMEWORK HELP** at classzone.com

32. CHALLENGE One sphere has a radius x, and a second sphere has a radius x^2. Find the ratio of their surface areas and the ratio of their volumes.

33. CHALLENGE A sand sculpture consists of three similar sand figures with lengths of 25 centimeters, 35 centimeters, and 45 centimeters. The smallest figure weighs 1.2 kilograms. Find the approximate total weight of the sand used to make the entire sculpture.

◆ CALIFORNIA STANDARDS SPIRAL REVIEW

MG 1.1

34. Approximately how many cubic centimeters are equal to 7 cubic inches? *(p. 437)*

    (A) 87.2 cm³   **(B)** 114.7 cm³   **(C)** 198.6 cm³   **(D)** 223.1 cm³

AF 3.3

35. What is the slope of the graph of $y = -\frac{1}{2}x - 4$? *(p. 342)*

    (A) -2 **(B)** $-\frac{1}{2}$ **(C)** $\frac{1}{2}$ **(D)** 2

MG 2.1

36. What is the approximate volume of the traffic cone? *(p. 598)*

    (A) 25.1 in.³   **(B)** 75.4 in.³

    (C) 113.1 in.³   **(D)** 201.1 in.³

8 in.

3 in.

QUIZ *for Lessons 10.5–10.7*

Find the volume of the solid. Round your answer to the nearest tenth, if necessary. *(pp. 589, 598)*

1.

32 yd

150 yd

2.

3 ft

3 ft

3.

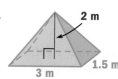

2 m

3 m 1.5 m

Tell whether the solids are similar. *Explain* **your reasoning.** *(p. 605)*

4.

1 m

0.5 m

1 m

2 m

5.

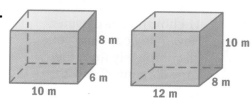

8 m

10 m 6 m

10 m

12 m 8 m

6. ACCESS RAMP How many cubic feet of concrete are needed to make the access ramp shown? *(p. 589)*

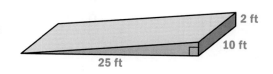

2 ft

10 ft

25 ft

Multiple Choice Practice for Lessons 10.5–10.7

1. What is the volume of the triangular prism? **MG 2.1**

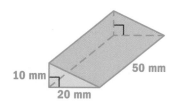

- **(A)** 2700 mm^3
- **(B)** 3333.3 mm^3
- **(C)** 5000 mm^3
- **(D)** 10,000 mm^3

2. What is the volume of a square pyramid with a base side length of 7 inches and a height of 18 inches? **MG 2.1**

- **(A)** 42 in.^{3}
- **(B)** 294 in.^{3}
- **(C)** 441 in.^{3}
- **(D)** 756 in.^{3}

3. What is the volume of the composite solid? **MG 2.1**

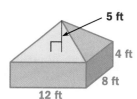

- **(A)** 384 ft^3
- **(B)** 544 ft^3
- **(C)** 864 ft^3
- **(D)** 1920 ft^3

4. You are filling cone-shaped paper cups with water. The dimensions of a cup are shown in the diagram. A larger container holds 41 cubic inches of water. How many cups can you fill completely from the large container? **MG 2.1**

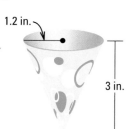

- **(A)** 2
- **(B)** 4
- **(C)** 6
- **(D)** 9

5. A company makes the two types of raisin containers shown below. Approximately, how much greater is the capacity of the cylindrical container? **MG 2.1, MR 2.7**

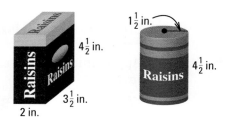

- **(A)** 0.2 in.^{3}
- **(B)** 0.3 in.^{3}
- **(C)** 1.2 in.^{3}
- **(D)** 2 in.^{3}

6. What is the surface area of the solid composed of rectangular prisms shown below? **MG 2.3**

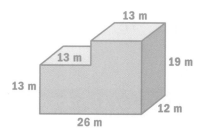

- **(A)** 956 m^2
- **(B)** 1912 m^2
- **(C)** 2068 m^2
- **(D)** 4992 m^2

7. The dimensions of a cylinder are shown below. A similar cylinder is produced by multiplying each dimension by 1.5. What happens to the volume? **MG 2.3, MR 1.2**

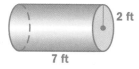

- **(A)** The volume is 1.5 times as great.
- **(B)** The volume is 2.25 times as great.
- **(C)** The volume is 3 times as great.
- **(D)** The volume is 3.375 times as great.

Standards

MG 2.1, MG 2.2, MG 2.3, MG 2.4, MG 3.5, MG 3.6, AF 3.2

BIG IDEAS

For Your Notebook

Big Idea ①

Identifying Solids and Their Components

Classifying Solids	
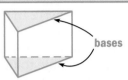 A prism is a polyhedron. Prisms have two congruent bases that lie in parallel planes. The other faces are rectangles.	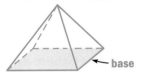 A pyramid is a polyhedron. Pyramids have one base. The other faces are triangles.
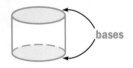 A cylinder is a solid with two congruent circular bases that lie in parallel planes.	 A cone is a solid with one circular base. 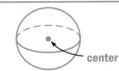 A sphere is all points in space that are the same distance from the center.

Big Idea ②

Finding Surface Areas and Volumes of Solids

Solid	Surface area formula	Volume formula
Prism	$S = 2B + Ph$	$V = Bh$
Cylinder	$S = 2B + Ch = 2\pi r^2 + 2\pi rh$	$V = Bh = \pi r^2 h$
Pyramid	$S = B + \frac{1}{2}Pl$	$V = \frac{1}{3}Bh$
Cone	$S = \pi r^2 + \pi rl$	$V = \frac{1}{3}Bh = \frac{1}{3}\pi r^2 h$

Big Idea ③

Comparing Surface Areas and Volumes of Similar Solids

Two solids of the same type with equal ratios of corresponding linear measures, such as heights or radii, are called similar solids. This common ratio is called the scale factor.

- If two solids are similar with a scale factor of k, then the surface areas of the solids have a ratio of k^2.

- If two solids are similar with a scale factor of k, then the volumes of the solids have a ratio of k^3.

APPLYING THE
BIG IDEAS

Big Idea 1
You identify a solid
and its components in
Step 2.

Big Idea 2
You find the surface
area and volume of a
solid in **Steps 3 and 4.**

Big Idea 3
You compare the
surface areas and
volumes of similar
solids in **Ex. 4.**

PROBLEM How can you use a single piece of construction paper to construct a solid with the greatest possible volume?

STEP 1 Build a solid.

Build a complete solid from a 9 inch by 12 inch piece of construction paper. You can cut, fold, and tape the paper any way you want as long as there are no holes. You must also be able to find the surface area and volume of the solid using the methods in this chapter. Try to build the solid with the greatest volume possible.

STEP 2 Make observations.

Identify the solid. If it is a polyhedron, count the number of faces, edges, and vertices.

STEP 3 Find the surface area.

Find the surface area of the solid in square inches. What percent of the area of the original piece of construction paper is the surface area?

STEP 4 Find the volume.

Find the volume of the solid in cubic inches.

STEP 5 Find a ratio.

Find the ratio of the surface area to the volume of the solid.

Extending the Problem

In Exercises 1–3, compare all of the solids made by the students in your class.

1. What type of solid had the greatest surface area?

2. What type of solid had the greatest volume?

3. What type of solid had the greatest ratio of surface area to volume?

4. Suppose you make a scale model of your solid in which all of the linear dimensions are four times as long. How does the surface area of the scale model compare to the surface area of the original solid? How does the volume of the scale model compare to the volume of the original solid?

5. Suppose your model must have a square base. How does your design change? How does the surface area of the model change? How does the volume of the model change?

10 CHAPTER REVIEW

California @HomeTutor
classzone.com
• Multi-Language Visual Glossary
• Vocabulary practice

REVIEW KEY VOCABULARY

- coplanar, *p. 561*
- skew lines, *p. 561*
- solid, *p. 566*
- polyhedron, *p. 566*
- face, *p. 566*
- prism, *p. 566*

- pyramid, *p. 566*
- cylinder, *p. 566*
- cone, *p. 566*
- sphere, *p. 566*
- edge, *p. 567*
- vertex, *p. 567*

- diagonal of a polyhedron, *p. 567*
- net, *p. 573*
- surface area, *p. 574*
- lateral surface area, *p. 575*
- slant height, *p. 580*
- similar solids, *p. 605*

VOCABULARY EXERCISES

Classify the solid.

1.

2.

3.

4.

5. **NOTETAKING SKILLS** Make an *information wheel* like the one on page 560 for a *square pyramid*.

REVIEW EXAMPLES AND EXERCISES

10.1 Lines and Planes
pp. 561–565

MG 3.6

EXAMPLE

Describe the intersection of planes *G* and *J* shown in the diagram.

SOLUTION

The intersection of plane *G* and plane *J* is line *b*.

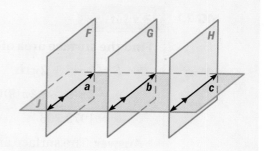

EXERCISES

SEE EXAMPLES 1, 2, AND 3
on pp. 561–563
for Exs. 6–8

In Exercises 6–8, use the diagram above.

6. Are lines *a* and *b* skew or coplanar? *Explain*.

7. *Describe* the intersection of planes *F* and *J*.

8. *Describe* the intersection of planes *F*, *G*, and *H*.

10.2 Three-Dimensional Figures

pp. 566–571

MG 3.6

EXAMPLE

Classify the solid. Then count the number of faces, edges, and vertices.

4 faces   6 edges   4 vertices

The solid has 4 triangular faces, so it is a triangular pyramid. It is a polyhedron.

EXERCISES

**SEE EXAMPLES
1 AND 3**
on pp. 566–567
for Exs. 9–12

Classify the solid. Then tell whether it is a polyhedron.

9.    10.   11.

12. Count the number of faces, edges, and vertices in the figure in Exercise 11.

10.3 Surface Areas of Prisms and Cylinders

pp. 573–579

MG 2.1

EXAMPLE

Find the surface area of the cylinder.

$S = 2\pi r^2 + 2\pi rh$ **Formula for surface area of a cylinder**

$= 2\pi(9)^2 + 2\pi(9)(26)$ **Substitute.**

≈ 1979.203 **Evaluate using a calculator.**

▶ **Answer** The surface area of the cylinder is about 1979 square centimeters.

EXERCISES

**SEE EXAMPLES
2, 3, AND 4**
on pp. 574–576
for Exs. 13–15

13. Find the surface area of the net. Identify the solid it forms.

14. Find the surface area of a rectangular prism with a length of 5 feet, a width of 2 feet, and a height of 9 feet.

15. Find the surface area of a cylinder with a radius of 5 meters and a height of 10 meters.

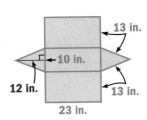

10.4 Surface Areas of Pyramids and Cones

pp. 580–586

MG 2.1

EXAMPLE

Find the surface area of the square pyramid.

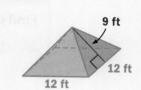

$$S = B + \frac{1}{2}Pl \qquad \text{Formula for surface area of a pyramid}$$

$$= 12^2 + \frac{1}{2}(4 \cdot 12)(9) \qquad \text{Substitute.}$$

$$= 360 \qquad \text{Evaluate.}$$

▶ **Answer** The surface area of the pyramid is 360 square feet.

EXERCISES

**SEE EXAMPLES
1 AND 2**
on pp. 581–582
for Exs. 16–18

16. Find the surface area of a square pyramid with a base area of 49 square meters and a slant height of 4 meters.

17. Find the surface area of a cone with a diameter of 20 feet and a slant height of 15 feet.

18. GIFTS You are wrapping a square pyramid puzzle. The base side length is 4 inches and the slant height is 5 inches. What is the minimum amount of wrapping paper needed?

10.5 Volumes of Prisms and Cylinders

pp. 589–596

MG 2.1

EXAMPLE

Find the volume of the prism.

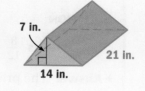

$$V = Bh \qquad \text{Formula for volume of a prism}$$

$$= \frac{1}{2}(14 \cdot 7)(21) \qquad \text{Substitute.}$$

$$= 1029 \qquad \text{Evaluate.}$$

▶ **Answer** The volume of the prism is 1029 cubic inches.

EXERCISES

**SEE EXAMPLES
1 AND 2**
on pp. 589–590
for Exs. 19–21

Find the volume of the solid. Round to the nearest tenth if necessary.

19.

20.
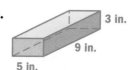

21.
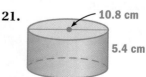

MG 2.1 **EXAMPLE**

Find the volume of the cone.

$$V = \frac{1}{3}(\pi r^2)h \qquad \text{Formula for volume of a cone}$$

$$= \frac{1}{3}\pi(7)^2(18) \qquad \text{Substitute.}$$

$$\approx 923.628 \qquad \text{Evaluate using a calculator.}$$

▶ **Answer** The volume of the cone is about 924 cubic feet.

EXERCISES

SEE EXAMPLES 1 AND 3
on pp. 598–600
for Exs. 22–23

22. Find the volume of a cone with a radius of 4 inches and a height of 8 inches.

23. CANDLES You have 12 cubic inches of candle wax. You have a mold for a square pyramid shaped candle that has a base side length of 3 inches and a height of 5 inches. Do you have enough wax to make this candle? *Explain.*

MG 2.3 **EXAMPLE**

Tell whether the prisms are similar.

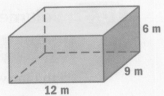

SOLUTION

Lengths $\frac{8}{12} = \frac{2}{3}$ Widths $\frac{6}{9} = \frac{2}{3}$ Heights $\frac{4}{6} = \frac{2}{3}$

▶ **Answer** The prisms are similar because the ratios of corresponding linear measures are equal.

EXERCISES

SEE EXAMPLE 1
on p. 605
for Exs. 24–25

Tell whether the solids are similar.

24.

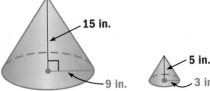

25.

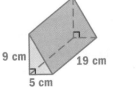

1. **VOCABULARY** *Describe* the difference between surface area and volume.

2. **VOCABULARY** What does it mean for two solids to be similar?

Tell whether the lines are skew. *Explain.*

3. *p* and *q*

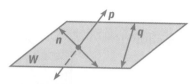

4. *e* and *f*

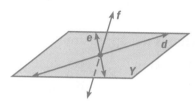

In Exercises 5–7, classify the solid. Then tell whether it is a polyhedron.

5.

6.

7.

8. Count the number of faces, edges, and vertices in the figure in Exercise 6.

Find the surface area and volume of the solid. Round to the nearest tenth if necessary.

9.

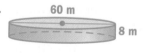

60 m

8 m

10.

16 in.

15 in.

15 in.

11.

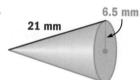

6.5 mm

21 mm

12. **VOLUME** Graph the volume *v* of a pyramid with a fixed base area of 20 square inches as a function of its height *h*.

Tell whether the solids are similar.

13.

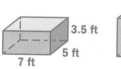

3.5 ft

5 ft

7 ft

6 ft

9 ft

10 ft

14.

4.5 in.

9 in.

6 in.

12 in.

15. **PAINTING** You plan to paint the 4 walls and ceiling of a rectangular room. The dimensions of the ceiling are 20 feet by 15 feet. The height of the room is 8 feet. You are going to paint the door, but not the window that is 3 feet by 4 feet. How many square feet are you painting?

STRATEGIES YOU'LL USE:
- SOLVE DIRECTLY
- ELIMINATE CHOICES

Standards
MG 2.1, MG 3.6

If you have difficulty solving a multiple choice problem directly, you may be able to use another approach to eliminate incorrect answer choices and obtain the correct answer.

PROBLEM 1

What is the approximate volume of the water cooler shown?

(A) 905 in.^{2} (B) 2036 in.^{3}

(C) 3054 in.^{3} (D) 8143 in.^{3}

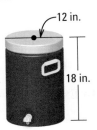

12 in.

18 in.

Strategy 1 SOLVE DIRECTLY

The cooler is in the shape of a cylinder. The diameter is 12 inches. The radius is one half of the diameter, so $r = 6$ inches.

$V = Bh$	Write formula for volume of a cylinder.
$= \pi r^2 h$	The area of a circular base is πr^2.
$= \pi(6)^2(18)$	Substitute 6 for r and 18 for h.
$= \pi(36)(18)$	Evaluate power.
$= 648\pi$	Multiply.
≈ 2036	Use a calculator.

The volume of the water cooler is about 2036 cubic inches.

The correct answer is B. (A) (B) (C) (D)

Strategy 2 ELIMINATE CHOICES

Use estimation and mathematical reasoning to eliminate answer choices.

You can eliminate choice A by observing units. Volume is expressed in cubic units. Because choice A involves square units, it can be eliminated.

You can estimate and compare to eliminate choices C and D. If the cooler were in a box, the volume of the box would be greater than the volume of the cooler since there would be additional space around the cooler.

Think of the box as a rectangular prism with the same height as the cooler. The length and width will be the same as the diameter of the cooler. So, the rectangular prism is 12 inches wide, 12 inches long, and 18 inches high and has a volume of 12(12)(18), or 2592 cubic inches. Since the cooler must have a smaller volume, choices C and D can be eliminated.

The correct answer is B. (A) (B) (C) (D)

PROBLEM 2

Which lines in the diagram are skew lines?

(A) *a* and *b*   **(B)** *a* and *c*

(C) *b* and *d*   **(D)** *c* and *d*

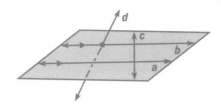

Strategy 1 SOLVE DIRECTLY

Lines that do not intersect and are not coplanar are skew lines.

You can see that line *c* and line *d* do not intersect and are not coplanar.

So, line *c* and line *d* are skew lines.

The correct answer is D. **(A) (B) (C) (D)**

Strategy 2 ELIMINATE CHOICES

Use the definitions of parallel lines and intersecting lines to eliminate answer choices.

You know that skew lines do not intersect and are not coplanar, so identify lines that intersect and lines that are coplanar to eliminate answer choices.

Lines *a* and *c* intersect, so they are not skew. Lines *b* and *d* intersect, so they are not skew. Choices B and C can be eliminated.

Lines *a* and *b* are coplanar, so they are not skew. Choice A can be eliminated.

The correct answer is D. **(A) (B) (C) (D)**

STRATEGY PRACTICE

Explain why you can eliminate the highlighted answer choice.

1. What is the approximate surface area of a cone whose radius is 7 centimeters and whose slant height is 14 centimeters?

    (A) 307.9 cm^2 **(B)** 461.8 cm^2 **(C)** ✕ **622.1 cm^3**   **(D)** 923.6 cm^2

2. Two lines are coplanar. What kind of lines must they be?

    (A) Intersecting   **(B)** ✕ **Skew**

    (C) Parallel   **(D)** Intersecting or parallel

3. What is the volume of the rectangular prism shown?

    (A) 19 in.^{3} **(B)** 90.25 in.^{3}

    (C) 100 in.^{3} **(D)** ✕ **147.25 in.^{3}**

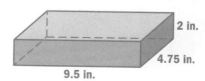

2 in.

4.75 in.

9.5 in.

1. Which pair of lines are coplanar, nonintersecting lines? **MG 3.6**

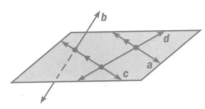

- **A** *b* and *c*
- **B** *a* and *c*
- **C** *a* and *b*
- **D** *b* and *d*

2. The solid below is composed of which two types of solids? **MG 3.6**
   - **A** Prism and cone
   - **B** Cylinder and pyramid
   - **C** Cylinder and cone
   - **D** Prism and sphere

3. How many vertices does a hexagonal pyramid have? **MG 3.1**
   - **A** 6
   - **B** 7
   - **C** 12
   - **D** 18

4. Leon weighs a log of firewood that is one foot long and one foot in diameter. He finds that it weighs 36 pounds. A cord of firewood is 128 cubic feet. His truck can carry up to 1200 pounds. Use the weight and volume of the log to find how many trips Leon must make to deliver a cord of split firewood. **MG 2.1, MR 1.3**

   - **A** 3
   - **B** 4
   - **C** 5
   - **D** 6

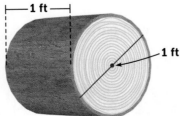

5. The prisms shown are similar with a scale factor of 1:2. The surface area of the smaller prism is given in the diagram. What is the surface area of the larger prism? **MG 2.3**

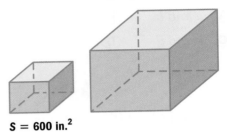

S = 600 in.²

- **A** 800 in.²
- **B** 1200 in.²
- **C** 1800 in.²
- **D** 2400 in.²

6. Which two figures describe the two possible ways three distinct planes can intersect? **MG 3.6**
   - **A** A point and a line
   - **B** A plane and a line
   - **C** A point and a plane
   - **D** No possible intersection

7. A candle maker produces two different shaped candles. One is a cylinder and the other is a triangular prism. The dimensions are given in the diagram. To the nearest tenth of a cubic inch, how much smaller is the cylinder's surface area? **MG 2.1**

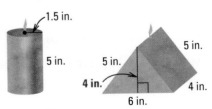

- **A** 17.4 in.²
- **B** 22.6 in.²
- **C** 26.7 in.²
- **D** 34.2 in.²

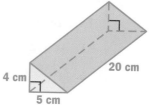

8. Gillian has two similar rectangular boxes. The dimensions of box A are three times those of box B. The volume of box A is how many times the volume of box B? **MG 2.3**

(A) 3

(B) 9

(C) 18

(D) 27

9. What is the surface area of the square pyramid below? **MG 2.1**

(A) 140 ft^2

(B) 160 ft^2

(C) 180 ft^2

(D) 200 ft^2

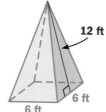

12 ft

6 ft

6 ft

10. A farmer is planning to paint the roof of the silo shown. What is the best estimate for the number of square feet the farmer must paint? **MG 2.2, MR 3.1**

(A) 250 ft^2

(B) 500 ft^2

(C) 750 ft^2

(D) 1000 ft^2

10 ft   Roof

8 ft

11. Jennifer wrapped a birthday present in the box below. What is the total surface area of the gift box? **MG 2.1**

(A) 420 in.^{2}

(B) 456 in.^{2}

(C) 566 in.^{2}

(D) 664 in.^{2}

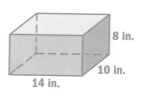

8 in.

10 in.

14 in.

12. What is the volume of the prism below? **MG 2.1**

(A) 200 cm^3

(B) 280 cm^3

(C) 350 cm^3

(D) 400 cm^3

4 cm

20 cm

5 cm

13. What is the volume of the cone below? Round your answer to the nearest whole number. **MG 2.1**

(A) 60 m^3

(B) 62 m^3

(C) 66 m^3

(D) 68 m^3

3 m

7 m

14. The surface area of a solid is 2.3 square meters. What is the surface area in square centimeters? **MG 2.4**

(A) 0.023 cm^2

(B) 0.23 cm^2

(C) 2300 cm^2

(D) 23,000 cm^2

15. What is the name of the solid with the given views? **MG 3.5**

top   front   side

(A) Triangle

(B) Triangular prism

(C) Triangular pyramid

(D) Rectangular pyramid

Evaluate the expression when $a = 3, b = -15, c = 15, x = 7,$ **and** $y = 5.$ *(p. 5)*

1. $3x + 2$

2. $30 - 2x$

3. $2c - y$

4. $8a - 3c$

5. $\dfrac{y + x}{x - y}$

6. $\dfrac{6b}{2c}$

7. $\dfrac{c}{-5a}$

8. $\dfrac{b^2}{a^2}$

Write the number in scientific notation. *(p. 201)*

9. 0.0672

10. $2,450,000$

11. 0.00000000314

12. $4,260,000,000,000$

13. 0.00000561

14. 345

Solve the equation or inequality. *(pp. 270, 293)*

15. $\dfrac{d}{5} + 13 = -10$

16. $17 = \dfrac{x}{12} - 31$

17. $-21 - \dfrac{t}{3} = -6$

18. $-6x + 2 = -10$

19. $4x - 8 = 11$

20. $-5x < 25$

21. $\dfrac{2}{3}h - 3 \geq 1$

22. $\dfrac{1}{2}x + 4 \leq 7$

23. $-\dfrac{3}{4}x - 10 \geq 8$

Use the slope and y-intercept to graph the equation. Label the slope and y-intercept on your graph. *(p. 342)*

24. $y = 3x + 5$

25. $y = -\dfrac{1}{2}x + 3$

26. $y = \dfrac{2}{5}x - 4$

27. $y = -\dfrac{3}{4}x - 9$

Tell whether the equation represents direct variation. If so, identify the constant of variation. *(p. 348)*

28. $y = 2x$

29. $y = -x$

30. $y = 9$

Simplify the expression. *(pp. 386, 393)*

31. $v^2 \cdot v^{-6}$

32. $w^0 \cdot w^{-3} \cdot w^3$

33. $\dfrac{4x^{-4}}{2x^8}$

34. $\dfrac{9y^{-5}}{27y^{10}}$

Simplify the expression. *(p. 399)*

35. $(3x^4)(-4x^{-3})$

36. $(-3p^3q^7)(-7p^5q^{-2})$

37. $(-5s^{-3}t^4)(2s^{-5}t^{-3})$

Find the area of the figure. Round to the nearest tenth if necessary.

38. *(p. 463)*

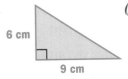

39. *(p. 478)*

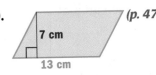

40. *(p. 463)*

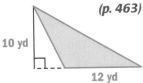

41. *(p. 478)*

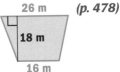

42. *(p. 489)*

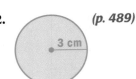

43. *(p. 489)*

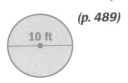

Find the volume of the figure. Round to the nearest tenth if necessary.

44.  *(p. 589)*

4 ft

7 ft

9 ft

45. 5 m *(p. 589)*

12 m

46. 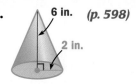 6 in. *(p. 598)*

2 in.

47. NUTRITION One serving of rice pilaf has 220 calories, including 35 calories from fat. One serving of soup has 70 calories, including 15 calories from fat. Write the calories from fat as a fraction of the total calories for each food. Which food has a greater fraction of calories from fat? *(p. 80)*

48. COINS A quarter's diameter is 0.955 inch. A dime's diameter is 0.705 inch. How much longer is a quarter? *(p. 137)*

49. INTEREST You invest $300 at a simple annual interest rate of 3.5% for one year. How much would you need to invest at a 2% simple annual interest rate to earn the same amount of interest that year? *(p. 172)*

50. DRIVING You are driving 2760 miles across the country. During the first 3 days of your trip, you drive 1380 miles. If you continue to drive at the same rate each day, how many additional days will it take you to complete the trip? *(p. 277)*

51. LADDER A ladder is placed against the side of a house. The ladder rises 16 feet over a horizontal distance of 8 feet. Find the slope of the ladder. *(p. 334)*

52. EXERCISE The graph at the right shows the distance between a dog and his owner as they play catch. *Describe* their game of catch as shown in the graph. *(p. 407)*

53. CLASSROOM A classroom is 25 feet by 40 feet and has seating for 28 students. Each student has a desk and chair that take up 9 square feet. There also is one large table that takes up 20 square feet. How many square feet of walking space does the classroom have? *(p. 478)*

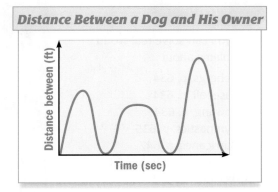

Distance Between a Dog and His Owner

Distance between (ft)

Time (sec)

54. CONTAINERS Two containers have the same volume. One container is a cylinder, and the other is a rectangular prism. The cylinder has a radius of 6 inches and a height of 7 inches. The prism has a length of 9 inches, a width of 8 inches, and a height of 11 inches. Which container uses less material? About how much less material? Round to the nearest tenth of a square inch. *(pp. 573, 589)*

Before

In previous courses, you learned the following skills, which you'll use in Chapter 11:

- Performing operations with whole numbers
- Interpreting bar graphs
- Finding a percent of a number

Now

In Chapter 11 you'll study these

Big Ideas:

1. Describing data using statistical measures
2. Representing information using data displays
3. Drawing conclusions from data displays

Why?

So you can solve real-world problems about . . .

- Icebergs, p. 634
- Baseball, p. 634
- Bowling, p. 634
- Gymnastics, p. 635
- Hurricanes, p. 647
- Amazon parrots, p. 653
- Basketball, p. 659

Animated Math

at *classzone.com*

Get-Ready Games

TARGET: ONE HUNDRED

California Standards

Review calculating with percents. *Gr. 7 NS 1.3*

Prepare for making circle graphs. *Gr. 7 SDAP 1.1*

Materials

- One deck of *Target: One Hundred* cards

75% of 48

How to Play Play in groups of three or four. Shuffle the deck of cards and deal two cards to each player. Players should not show each other their cards. Players should take turns following the steps on the next page.

CALIFORNIA STANDARDS

- **Gr. 7 SDAP 1.1** Know various forms of display for data sets, including a stem-and-leaf plot or box-and-whisker plot; use the forms to display a single set of data or to compare two sets of data. *(Lessons 11.2, 11.3, 11.4, 11.5, 11.6)*

- **Gr. 7 SDAP 1.3** Understand the meaning of, and be able to compute, the minimum, the lower quartile, the median, the upper quartile, and the maximum of a data set. *(Lesson 11.5)*

$\frac{3}{8}$ of 30

The solution of $\frac{14}{25} = \frac{28}{x}$

① Find the sum of the numbers on your cards. Do not share this sum with the other players.

The solution of $\frac{14}{25} = \frac{28}{x}$ $\frac{3}{8}$ of 30

② Take another card from the deck, only if you think it would bring the total sum of your cards closer to 100 without going over 100. Place the new card face up in front of you.

③ Continue taking cards until you think an additional card would make the total sum of your cards greater than 100. When all players have stopped taking cards, they should show all their cards and compare sums.

How to Win Have the sum closest to 100 without being greater than 100.

The solution of $\frac{14}{25} = \frac{28}{x}$ $\frac{3}{8}$ of 30   75% of 48

Games Wrap-Up

Draw Conclusions

Complete these exercises after playing the game.

1. **WRITING** *Explain* how you can use mental math to evaluate 10% of 9.

2. **REASONING** At what point in each round did you stop taking additional cards? *Explain* your reasoning.

627

Getting Ready

Prerequisite Skills

California @HomeTutor

Prerequisite skills practice
at classzone.com

VOCABULARY CHECK

Copy and complete using a review term from the list at the left.

1. Find the sum of the values in a set of data and then divide by the number of data values to find the __?__ of the data.

2. A(n) __?__ is an equation stating that two ratios are equivalent.

SKILL CHECK

Find the mean of the data set. *(p. 36)*

3. 23, 27, 13, 24, 19, 21, 25, 25, 12

4. 0.2, 0.35, 1.33, 1.32, 0.05, 0.5

Order the numbers from least to greatest. *(p. 133)*

5. $0, -0.25, \frac{1}{3}, \frac{12}{9}, -1.11, \frac{9}{8}$

6. $1.28, -\frac{7}{8}, \frac{1}{12}, \frac{10}{3}, -0.02, 0.34$

Find the percent of the number. *(p. 150)*

7. What is 25% of 180?

8. What is 8% of 72?

Solve the proportion. *(p. 277)*

9. $\frac{n}{20} = \frac{3}{5}$

10. $\frac{2}{3} = \frac{t}{18}$

11. $\frac{33}{60} = \frac{z}{20}$

12. $\frac{5}{6} = \frac{a}{138}$

13. $\frac{n}{57.6} = \frac{1.6}{3.2}$

14. $\frac{c}{4.5} = \frac{27.9}{40.5}$

Notetaking Skills

Focus on Graphic Organizers

You can use a *word magnet* to organize words and ideas that are related to the same word or term, such as *coordinate plane.*

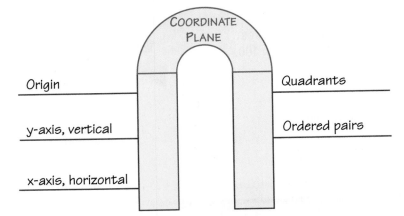

COORDINATE PLANE

Origin — Quadrants

y-axis, vertical — Ordered pairs

x-axis, horizontal

11.1 Collecting and Analyzing Data

MATERIALS · number cubes

Standards Preparation

Gr. 6 SDAP 1.1 Compute the range, mean, median, and mode of data sets.

QUESTION How can you represent a data set with one number?

You can collect data and find a number that represents the data. The *median* is the middle value when the values are written in order. The *mode* is the value that occurs most often. Recall that the mean of a set of data values is the sum of the values divided by the number of values.

EXPLORE 1 Collect data by rolling two number cubes to explore how often each sum occurs

STEP 1 **Roll** a pair of number cubes eleven times and record the sums.

$3 + 2 = 5$	$4 + 4 = 8$	$6 + 6 = 12$	$1 + 2 = 3$	$1 + 6 = 7$	$2 + 1 = 3$
$5 + 3 = 8$	$4 + 1 = 5$	$1 + 5 = 6$	$2 + 6 = 8$	$2 + 2 = 4$	

STEP 2 **Add** the sums together. Divide by the number of rolls to find the mean.

$$\frac{5 + 8 + 12 + 3 + 7 + 3 + 8 + 5 + 6 + 8 + 4}{11} = \frac{69}{11} \approx 6.3$$

STEP 3 **Order** the sums. Find the median and the mode.

3, 3, 4, 5, 5, 6, 7, 8, 8, 8, 12

middle number   most frequent number

The median is 6, and the mode is 8.

STEP 4 **Compare** your results with the results of other groups. Which sum occurs most often?

DRAW CONCLUSIONS Use your observations to complete these exercises

In Exercises 1–3, find the mean, median, and mode of the data.

1. 4.2, 6.1, 3.8, 4.1, 10.2, 9.6, 6.1, 7.3, 2.1, 2.4, 9.8

2. 105, 121, 42, 78, 77, 63, 108, 32, 33, 121, 64

3. 56.4, 25.1, 24.3, 56.4, 48.7, 59.2, 37.9

4. **WRITING** *Explain* why it is important to order the sums in Step 3 before you identify the median and the mode. *Continued on next page*

EXPLORE 2 Collect data about the number of letters in the last name of each student in your class

STEP 1 **Find** the shortest and longest names so you can make a *frequency table*.

STEP 2 **Count** the number of letters in each name. Make a tally mark for each name.

STEP 3 **Find** the mean number of letters in the last names.

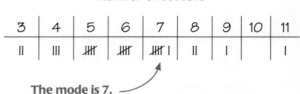

Cho = 3
Fitzpatrick = 11

Number of Letters

3	4	5	6	7	8	9	10	11
II	III	IIII	IIII	IIII I	II	I		I

$\begin{matrix}3 & 4 & 5 & 6 & 7 & 8\\ \times 2 & \times 3 & \times 5 & \times 5 & \times 6 & \times 2\end{matrix}$

6 + 12 + 25 + 30 + 42 + 16 + 9 + 0 + 11 = 151

You can multiply to count the number of letters for each column. Then add the column totals.

Divide by the number of students. The mean is $151 \div 25 \approx 6$.

STEP 4 **Find** the most frequent name length. This is the mode.

Number of Letters

3	4	5	6	7	8	9	10	11
II	III	IIII	IIII	IIII I	II	I		I

The mode is 7.

STEP 5 **Decide** whether it makes sense to use the mean to describe the average length of a last name in your class. Then decide whether it makes sense to use the mode. *Explain* your reasoning.

DRAW CONCLUSIONS Use your observations to complete these exercises

5. A new student whose last name has 16 letters joins your class. If you add "16" to your data set, how does this affect the mean and the mode? *Explain*.

6. **WRITING** You are designing a form to collect data. Students will write their last names in a row of small boxes with one letter per box. How many boxes do you think the form should provide? *Explain* your reasoning.

11.1 Mean, Median, Mode, and Range

Standards Preparation

Gr. 6 SDAP 1.1 Compute the range, mean, median, and mode of data sets.

Gr. 6 SDAP 1.4 Know why a specific measure of central tendency (mean, median) provides the most useful information in a given context.

Math and NATURE
Example 1, p. 631

Connect *Before* you used tables and graphs to analyze data sets. *Now* you will describe data sets to prepare for Grade 7 Standard SDAP 1.3.

KEY VOCABULARY
- statistics
- median
- mode
- range
- outlier
- mean, *p. 37*

Statistics are numerical values used to summarize and compare sets of data. Three common statistics called *averages* are the *mean, median,* and *mode*. In Lesson 1.6, you learned how to find the mean of a data set. Activity 11.1, on pages 629–630, explores the median and the mode.

In this lesson, you will use these averages to describe data sets. You will also learn how to choose which average best represents a data set.

KEY CONCEPT   *For Your Notebook*

Averages

The **mean** of a data set is the sum of the values divided by the number of values.

The **median** of a data set is the middle value when the values are written in numerical order. If a data set has an even number of values, the median is the mean of the two middle values.

The **mode** of a data set is the value that occurs most often. A data set can have no mode, one mode, or more than one mode.

EXAMPLE 1 Finding a Mean

BIOLOGY A marine biologist records the following locations of 6 deep sea jellyfish in relation to the ocean surface: -2278 feet, -1875 feet, -3210 feet, -2755 feet, -2407 feet, and -2901 feet. What is the mean location of the deep sea jellyfish?

$$\text{Mean} = \frac{-2278 + (-1875) + (-3210) + (-2755) + (-2407) + (-2901)}{6}$$

$$= \frac{-15{,}426}{6}$$

$$= -2571$$

▶**Answer** The mean location in relation to the ocean surface is -2571 feet.

RANGE AND OUTLIERS The **range** of a data set is the difference of the greatest value and the least value. The range measures how spread out the data are. An **outlier** is a value in a data set that is much greater or much less than the other values.

EXAMPLE 2 Finding Median, Mode, and Range

Find the median, mode(s), and range of the prices.

$7.20, $13.25, $14.94, $16.56, $18.74, $19.99, $19.99, $29.49

AVOID ERRORS
If the data are not ordered, you need to order the data to find the median.

Median: The data set has an even number of prices, so the median is the mean of the two middle values, $16.56 and $18.74.

$$\text{Median} = \frac{\$16.56 + \$18.74}{2} = \frac{\$35.30}{2} = \$17.65$$

Mode: The price that occurs most often is $19.99. This is the mode.

Range: Find the difference of the greatest and the least values.

$$\text{Range} = \$29.49 - \$7.20 = \$22.29$$

EXAMPLE 3 ◆ Multiple Choice Practice

Ten people try a new cereal and rate it on a scale of 1 to 20. The ratings are shown below. Which averages best represent the data?

1, 1, 2, 2, 2, 2, 3, 3, 4, 20

Ⓐ Mean and median   Ⓑ Mode and median

Ⓒ Mean and mode   Ⓓ Mean, median, and mode

ELIMINATE CHOICES
By inspection, you can see that the mode is 2 and does represent the data well. So, because choice A does not include the mode, it can be eliminated.

SOLUTION

Compare each average to the whole data set.

$$\textbf{Mean} = \frac{40}{10} = 4 \qquad \textbf{Median} = \frac{2+2}{2} = \frac{4}{2} = 2 \qquad \textbf{Mode: } 2$$

Because 20 is an outlier, the mean is greater than all but two ratings. It does not represent the data well. The mode and median best represent the data.

▶ **Answer** The correct answer is B. Ⓐ Ⓑ Ⓒ Ⓓ

✓ **GUIDED PRACTICE**   for Examples 1, 2, and 3

Find the mean, median, mode(s), and range of the data.

1. 14, 13, 20, 24, 15, 10, 22, 17, 18   **2.** 9, 7, 4, 9, 4, 10, 5, 14, 9, 4

3. WHAT IF? In Example 3, suppose another group tries the new cereal. Their ratings are: 1, 1, 1, 2, 3, 4, 4, 9, 10, 10. Which average or averages best represent the data?

11.1 **EXERCISES**

HOMEWORK KEY

◆ = **MULTIPLE CHOICE PRACTICE**
Exs. 12, 13, 22, 32–34

○ = **HINTS** AND **HOMEWORK HELP**
for Exs. 5, 15, 23 at classzone.com

SKILLS • PROBLEM SOLVING • REASONING

VOCABULARY In Exercises 1–3, use the data set 6, 12, 4, 15, 10, 6, 2, and 9.
Copy and complete the statement using *mean, median, mode,* or *range*.

1. The __?__ is 8.
2. The __?__ is 6.
3. The __?__ is 13.

4. **WRITING** *Explain* how to find the median of 23, 15, 12, 17, 43, and 56.

**SEE EXAMPLES
1 AND 2**
on pp. 631–632
for Exs. 5–13

FINDING AVERAGES AND RANGE In Exercises 5–9, find the mean, median,
mode(s), and range of the data.

5. Depths of fish: -71 in., -56 in., -62 in., -44 in., -56 in., -47 in.

6. Golf scores relative to par: $-2, 0, 3, 1, 0, -1, 2, -2, -3, 0, 4, 1$

7. Temperatures: $20°F$, $-11°F$, $72°F$, $-1°F$, $9°F$, $51°F$, $17°F$, $-5°F$

8.

Daily Hits at a Website						
Day	Mon.	Tues.	Wed.	Thur.	Fri.	Sat.	Sun.
Hits	164	157	289	185	225	208	240

9.

Daily Calories Consumed						
Day	Mon.	Tues.	Wed.	Thur.	Fri.	Sat.	Sun.
Cal.	2000	1628	1680	1920	2080	1675	1595

ERROR ANALYSIS *Describe* and correct the error in the solution.

10.
✗ 3, 6, 5, 2, 8, 9, 5, 8, 1, 5, 10, 8
The mode of the data set is 5.

11.
✗ 12, 8, 9, 13, 10, 6, 8, 11, 5
The median of the data set is 10.

12. ◆ **MULTIPLE CHOICE** Which has the same value as the median of the
following data set: 45, 56, 50, 43, 56, 64, 36?

(A) Mean   (B) Mode   (C) Range   (D) Outlier

13. ◆ **MULTIPLE CHOICE** What is the mean of 2, 2, 6, 7, 9, and 10?

(A) 2   (B) 6   (C) 6.5   (D) 7.2

EXAMINING OUTLIERS Find the mean, median, mode(s), and range of the
data with and without the number(s) in red. *Describe* the effect of the red
data value(s) on the averages and on the range.

14. 19, 16, 23, 35, 28, 20, 16, 36, **98**, 13, 26, 29, 31

15. 58, 67, 94, 85, 78, 76, **6**, 99, 100, 88, 76, **2**, 82, 81, 94, 98

16. 184, 192, 173, 181, **65**, 199, 200, 158, **25**, 165, 178, 150

CONNECT SKILLS TO PROBLEM SOLVING Exercises 17–19 will help you prepare for problem solving.

Tell which average(s) best represent the data.

17. The test scores of a student for the first semester of a history class:
100, 80, 90, 100, 100, 70, 80

18. The waiting times (in minutes) of several people at a doctor's office:
24, 19, 15, 20, 10, 22, 12, 10

19. The prices of 8 mountain bikes:
$250, $290, $200, $230, $210, $200, $260, $270

SEE EXAMPLES 1, 2, AND 3
on pp. 631–632
for Exs. 20–22

20. ICEBERGS An iceberg's depth can be 3 to 9 times its height above the water surface. The image below shows the distances (in meters) below the water surface that six icebergs reach. What is the mean distance below the water surface that these icebergs reach?

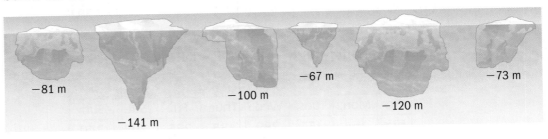

−81 m   −100 m   −67 m   −120 m   −73 m   −141 m

California @HomeTutor for problem solving help at classzone.com

21. BASEBALL The attendance for the 2001 World Series is shown in the table below. Find the mean, median, and mode(s) of the data. Which average do you think best represents the attendance data? *Explain.*

Game	1	2	3	4	5	6	7
Attendance	49,646	49,646	55,820	55,863	56,018	49,707	49,589

California @HomeTutor for problem solving help at classzone.com

22. ◆ MULTIPLE CHOICE The scores on a 20-point math quiz are 8, 9, 11, 12, 14, 14, 15, 16, 17, 17, 18, and 20. Which averages best represent the data?

(A) Mean and median

(B) Mode and median

(C) Mean and mode

(D) Mean, median, and mode

23. BOWLING You are bowling three games. In the first two games, you score 125 and 113 points. How many points do you need in the third game to have a mean score of 126 points?

24. MOVIE SURVEY Ten people rate a movie on a scale from 1 to 10. The ratings are 1, 7, 7, 8, 8, 8, 8, 8, 9, and 9. Find the outlier of the data. Then find the mean, median, and mode of the data with the outlier and without the outlier. Which average is most affected by the outlier? *Explain.*

25. OPEN-ENDED Write an example of a data set whose mode is greater than its mean.

◆ = **MULTIPLE CHOICE PRACTICE**   ○ = **HINTS AND HOMEWORK HELP** at classzone.com

Gymnastics At Ramsey High's last gymnastics meet, the Rams overran the competition once again. They were lead by their top three scorers on the rings. The scores for this event from each of the 6 judges are shown below. The final score for each gymnast is calculated by dropping the highest and lowest scores and taking the mean of the remaining 4 scores.

Gymnast on the rings

	Judge 1	Judge 2	Judge 3	Judge 4	Judge 5	Judge 6
Isaac	9.600	9.600	9.600	9.650	9.800	9.650
Carl	9.800	9.800	9.700	9.700	9.700	9.800
Kurt	9.550	9.400	9.800	9.750	9.800	9.600

26. Calculate Find the final score for each gymnast. Who was awarded first, second, and third places on the rings?

27. Investigate For each gymnast, find the mean of the 6 judges' scores. If these averages were used as the final scores, would the ranking of the gymnasts be the same? *Explain.*

CHALLENGE **Find a data set of five numbers with the given statistics.**

28. Mean: 11
Median: 12
Mode: 17
Range: 13

29. Mean: 16
Median: 15
Mode: 15
Range: 22

30. Mean: 5
Median: 1
Mode: −4
Range: 26

31. CHALLENGE Find a set of five data values with modes 0 and 2, median 2, and mean 2. *Explain* how you found your answer.

◆ CALIFORNIA STANDARDS SPIRAL REVIEW

MG 3.2

32. What is the image of point $A(-2, 5)$ after the translation $(x, y) \rightarrow (x - 3, y - 7)$? *(p. 522)*

Ⓐ $(-5, -2)$ Ⓑ $(-1, -2)$ Ⓒ $(1, 12)$ Ⓓ $(1, -2)$

MG 3.3

33. What is the perimeter of a right triangle whose leg lengths are 0.5 centimeter and 1.2 centimeters? *(p. 471)*

Ⓐ 1.3 cm   Ⓑ 3 cm   Ⓒ 3.38 cm   Ⓓ 3.4 cm

MG 2.1

34. A can of bread crumbs is a cylinder 8 inches tall and 4 inches in diameter. What is the volume of the can to the nearest cubic inch? *(p. 589)*

Ⓐ 50 in.³   Ⓑ 101 in.³   Ⓒ 128 in.³   Ⓓ 402 in.³

11.2 Bar Graphs and Circle Graphs

Standards SDAP 1.1 **Know various forms of display for data sets**, including a stem-and-leaf plot or box-and-whisker plot; **use the forms to display a single set of data or to compare two sets of data.**

Connect *Before* you described data sets using mean, median, mode, and range. *Now* you will use bar graphs and circle graphs to describe data sets.

Math and **SCIENCE**
Example 1, p. 636

KEY VOCABULARY
- bar graph
- double bar graph
- circle graph

A **bar graph** is a type of graph in which the lengths of bars are used to represent and compare data in categories. In previous lessons, you have interpreted bar graphs. The following example shows you how to make a bar graph.

EXAMPLE 1 Making a Bar Graph

VOLCANOES The table shows the numbers of historically active volcanoes in four countries. Make a bar graph of the data.

Country	Canada	Chile	Mexico	U.S.
Number of Volcanoes	20	116	45	171

Animated Math

For an interactive example of making a bar graph, go to **classzone.com**.

SOLUTION

STEP 1 **Decide** how far to extend the scale. Start the scale at 0. The greatest data value is 171, so end the scale at a value greater than 171, such as 180.

STEP 2 **Choose** the increments for the scale. Choose an increment that is easy to work with and compatible with 180. The scale at the right uses increments of 30.

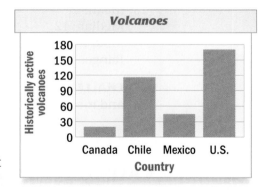

STEP 3 **Draw** and label the graph. Be sure to title your graph and label the scale.

✓ GUIDED PRACTICE for Example 1

1. Make a bar graph of the data.

Types of Books in a Home Library			
Type of book	Children's	Young adult	Adult fiction	Reference
Number of books	32	12	38	22

REVIEW INTERPRETING BAR GRAPHS

For help with reading bar graphs, see p. 743.

DOUBLE BAR GRAPHS A **double bar graph** shows two sets of data on the same graph. The two bars for each category are drawn next to each other using two colors. A key tells which set of data belongs to each color.

EXAMPLE 2 Making a Double Bar Graph

WILD ANIMALS Several classes of sixth and seventh grade students were asked to name their favorite wild animal. The results are shown in the table. Make a double bar graph of the data.

Favorite wild animal	Lion	Giraffe	Monkey	Elephant
Sixth grade	19	13	29	21
Seventh grade	24	6	26	28

SOLUTION

STEP 1 **Draw** one set of bars using the sixth grade data, as shown below. The greatest data value in the table for either grade is 29, so end the scale at 30.

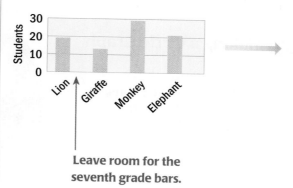

Leave room for the seventh grade bars.

STEP 2 **Draw** the seventh grade bars next to the sixth grade bars and shade them a different color. Add a title and a key.

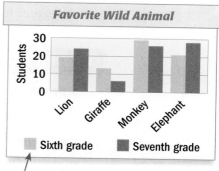

Make a key to show what each color represents.

✓ **GUIDED PRACTICE** for Example 2

2. **FAVORITE SPORTS** Make a double bar graph of the data.

Favorite Sports					
Sport	Basketball	Swimming	Gymnastics	Hockey	Track
Watching	593	260	370	175	250
Participating	570	319	97	197	209

CIRCLE GRAPHS A **circle graph** represents data as sections of a circle. Each section can be labeled with its data value or with the data value's portion of the whole written as a fraction, decimal, or percent. Because the graph represents all the data, the sum of the portions must equal 1, or 100%.

EXAMPLE 3 Interpreting a Circle Graph

AREAS OF OCEANS The circle graph shows the amount of Earth's surface (in millions of square kilometers) that is covered by each ocean.

a. Which ocean covers the least area?

b. Which ocean covers the greatest area?

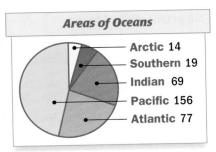

Areas of Oceans

- Arctic 14
- Southern 19
- Indian 69
- Pacific 156
- Atlantic 77

SOLUTION

a. To find which ocean covers the least area, find the smallest section of the circle graph. The section for the Arctic Ocean is the smallest, so the Arctic Ocean covers the least area.

b. To find which ocean covers the greatest area, find the largest section of the circle graph. The section for the Pacific Ocean is the largest, so the Pacific Ocean covers the greatest area.

MAKING A CIRCLE GRAPH To make a circle graph, first find the angle measure, to the nearest degree, that represents each data value's portion of the whole. The sum of all the angle measures must equal 360°, the number of degrees in a circle.

EXAMPLE 4 Making a Circle Graph

MARINE MAMMALS An aquarium has a yearly food budget of $10,000 for sea lions, $13,300 for harbor seals, and $40,000 for California sea otters. Make a circle graph to represent the data.

California sea otter

SOLUTION

STEP 1 Use a proportion to find the number of degrees you should use to represent each yearly food budget as a section of a circle graph. Note that the total budget is $10,000 + $13,300 + $40,000 = $63,300.

Sea lions	Harbor seals	Sea otters
$\dfrac{\$10{,}000}{\$63{,}300} = \dfrac{a}{360°}$	$\dfrac{\$13{,}300}{\$63{,}300} = \dfrac{b}{360°}$	$\dfrac{\$40{,}000}{\$63{,}300} = \dfrac{c}{360°}$
$a \approx 56.87° \approx 57°$	$b \approx 75.64° \approx 76°$	$c \approx 227.49° \approx 227°$

DRAW SECTIONS
In Example 4, you can draw the 57° and 76° angles first. Then the remaining section of the circle will have a measure of 227°.

STEP 2 Draw a circle. Show its center.

STEP 3 Use a protractor to draw the first angle measure. Label the section.

STEP 4 Draw and label the remaining sections. Include a title.

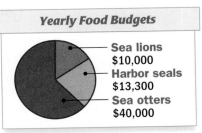

Yearly Food Budgets

- Sea lions $10,000
- Harbor seals $13,300
- Sea otters $40,000

EXAMPLE 5 Choosing a Data Display

Choose an appropriate display for the data.

a. The table shows the results of a survey that asked students if they are going on a trip during summer vacation.

Response	Percent
Yes	48%
No	37%
Don't know	15%

b. The table shows the results of a survey that asked students why they use the Internet.

Purpose	Percent
Research	62%
Shopping	34%
E-mail	45%
Browsing	18%

AVOID ERRORS
You can display data with a circle graph only if the categories don't overlap and the percents add up to 100%, as in part (a) of Example 5.

SOLUTION

a. The percents total 100%, so a circle graph is appropriate.

b. The percents total more than 100%. An appropriate display is a bar graph.

✓ **GUIDED PRACTICE** for Examples 3, 4, and 5

3. SHOES The results of a student survey on favorite shoes were as follows: *dress shoes*, 11; *sneakers*, 56; *sandals*, 11; and *boots*, 22. Make a circle graph of the data. Then find how many students do *not* prefer sneakers.

4. REASONING In Exercise 3, could you also display the results of the survey using a bar graph? *Explain*.

11.2 EXERCISES

HOMEWORK KEY

◆ = **MULTIPLE CHOICE PRACTICE**
Exs. 5, 21, 31, 37–39

○ = **HINTS AND HOMEWORK HELP**
for Exs. 3, 17, 31 at classzone.com

SKILLS • PROBLEM SOLVING • REASONING

1. VOCABULARY Copy and complete: In a(n) __?__, the lengths of bars are used to represent and compare data in categories.

2. WRITING *Explain* how to find the angle measures for the categories in a circle graph.

SEE EXAMPLE 1
on p. 636
for Exs. 3–6

BAR GRAPHS Make a bar graph of the data.

 3.

Mountain Ranges of the World	
Range	**Peaks (over 6000 m)**
Andes	102
Kunlun	228
St. Elias	1
Pamir	9

4.

Adults Surveyed Who Participate in Lawn and Garden Activities	
Activity	**Number**
Lawn care	47
Flower gardening	37
Vegetable gardening	26
Herb gardening	9

5. ◆ **MULTIPLE CHOICE** What is the best increment for the numerical scale of a bar graph showing the data values 53, 31, 25, 13, and 46?

(A) 1   (B) 10   (C) 40   (D) 50

6. **ERROR ANALYSIS** A student is making a bar graph showing the amounts of money raised by four students for a fundraiser. *Describe* and correct the error in choosing the scale for this bar graph.

> ✗ Kaitlin: $120   Jose: $256
> Terrell: $234   Mia: $287
>
> $287 \div 40 = 7.175$, which rounds to 7. So, use 40 intervals that represent increases of $7.

SEE EXAMPLE 2
on p. 637
for Exs. 7–9

DOUBLE BAR GRAPHS **Make a double bar graph of the data.**

7.

Cost of Food (cents per pound)		
Food	**1990**	**2000**
Apples	77	82
Chicken	86	108
Eggs	100	96
Ice cream	254	366
Spaghetti	85	88

8.

Major Indoor Soccer League National Conference 2000–2001		
Team	**Wins**	**Losses**
Detroit	13	27
Kansas City	14	26
Milwaukee	24	16
Toronto	21	19
Wichita	18	21

9. Use your graph from Exercise 7. Which food had the greatest price increase between 1990 and 2000?

SEE EXAMPLE 3
on p. 638
for Exs. 10–12

CIRCLE GRAPHS **The circle graph shows the numbers of seats available in a theater.**

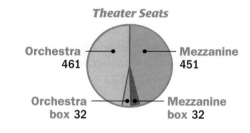

Theater Seats

Orchestra 461   Mezzanine 451
Orchestra box 32   Mezzanine box 32

10. How many seats are in the theater?

11. How many more orchestra seats than mezzanine seats are there?

12. How many mezzanine box tickets will be sold if a show sells out for 5 performances?

SEE EXAMPLE 4
on p. 638
for Exs. 13–21

FINDING ANGLES **Find the angle measure in a circle graph for the given ratio.**

13. 31%   14. $\frac{3}{8}$ 15. 14%   16. 27 out of 60

MAKING CIRCLE GRAPHS **A survey asked 200 students "How often do you snack during the day?" Make a circle graph of the survey data.**

17.

Answer	Students
Never	20
Rarely	90
Sometimes	70
Often	20

18.

Answer	Students
Never	0
Rarely	50
Sometimes	120
Often	30

19.

Answer	Students
Never	40
Rarely	20
Sometimes	85
Often	55

20. ERROR ANALYSIS A survey asked 75 students "Do you like the new lunch menu?" The responses were: *yes*, 50; *no*, 10; *undecided*, 15. *Describe* and correct the error in finding the angle measures for a circle graph of the data.

> Yes = 50%, or 180°
> No = 10%, or 36°
> Undecided = 360 − (180 + 36)
>   = 144°

21. ◆ MULTIPLE CHOICE You polled 30 students in your class about how much their families pay for Internet service. Twelve of the 30 pay more than $25 per month. Which proportion could you use to find the number of degrees in the section of a circle graph that represents these results?

A $\frac{12}{30} = \frac{x}{360}$ **B** $\frac{12}{30} = \frac{360}{x}$ **C** $\frac{12}{25} = \frac{x}{30}$ **D** $\frac{12}{25} = \frac{30}{x}$

SEE EXAMPLE 5
on p. 639
for Exs. 22–23

CHOOSING APPROPRIATE DISPLAYS Choose an appropriate display for the data. *Justify* your choice.

22.

Sport played	Percent
Baseball	22%
Basketball	30%
Soccer	10%

23.

Response	Percent
Yes	30%
No	45%
Undecided	25%

CONNECT SKILLS TO PROBLEM SOLVING Exercises 24–26 will help you prepare for problem solving.

Tell which type of display you would use for the data described. *Explain* your reasoning.

24. You record the percent of students in your class who play soccer, hockey, or tennis.

25. You ask 100 students which flavor of yogurt they prefer: *strawberry*, *vanilla*, or *blueberry*.

26. You record the grade levels of 200 students attending a high school basketball game.

**SEE EXAMPLES
1 AND 4**
on pp. 636–638
for Exs. 27–28

27. PISTACHIO ACREAGE The table shows California's 2003 pistachio acreage by county. Make a circle graph to represent the data.

County	Pistachio acreage
Kern	46,613
Madera	20,588
Tulare	9,647
Fresno	9,373
Kings	8,854
Merced	4,826
All others	5,292

California @HomeTutor for problem solving help at classzone.com

California pistachios

28. **MOVIES** The table shows the numbers of movies released in the United States from 2000 through 2003. Make a bar graph of the data. Then compare the values for different years to describe how they have changed.

California **@HomeTutor** for problem solving help at classzone.com

Year	Movies
2000	502
2001	477
2002	473
2003	492

MEDIA In Exercises 29–31, use the triple bar graph. It shows how many U.S. high schools (per 100 schools) have the given media activities.

29. Which of the given media did the greatest number of schools offer in each of the 3 years?

30. **SHORT RESPONSE** Which of the media saw the most growth from 1991 to 2002? *Explain* how you can tell that from the graph.

31. ◆ **MULTIPLE CHOICE** In 1998, how did the number of high schools with newspapers compare to the number of high schools with radio or TV stations?

    A About $\frac{1}{4}$ as many had newspapers.

    B About $\frac{1}{2}$ as many had newspapers.

    C About twice as many had newspapers.

    D About 4 times as many had newspapers.

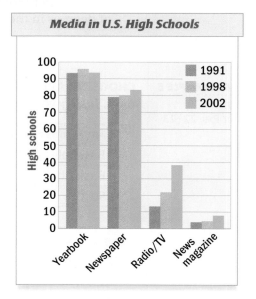

Media in U.S. High Schools

CHALLENGE Find the percent of a circle that corresponds to the given angle measure.

32. 30°   33. 98°   34. 172°   35. 220°

36. **CHALLENGE** A circle graph is used to represent a family's annual budget. If $9500 is spent on food and the angle measure for the food section of the graph is 72°, how much is the total budget?

◆ CALIFORNIA STANDARDS SPIRAL REVIEW

MG 1.1 37. Which rate is equivalent to 10 miles per hour? *(p. 449)*

    A 88 ft/min   **B** 880 ft/min   **C** 52,800 ft/min   **D** 3,168,000 ft/min

NS 1.7 38. A bicycle that costs $190 is on sale for 20% off. What is the sale price? *(p. 160)*

    A $38   **B** $152   **C** $190   **D** $228

AF 4.2 39. Kiesha earns $44 for 4 hours of work. At that rate, how long would she have to work to earn $495? *(p. 277)*

    A 20 h   **B** 35 h   **C** 45 h   **D** 60 h

11.3 Frequency Tables and Histograms

Connect *Before* you used bar graphs and circle graphs to analyze data sets. *Now* you will use frequency tables and histograms to analyze data sets.

**Math and
ENTERTAINMENT**
Example 1, p. 643

KEY VOCABULARY
• categorical data
• numerical data
• frequency table
• histogram

In Lesson 11.2, you made bar graphs and circle graphs to represent *categorical data*. **Categorical data** are data that consist of names, labels, or other nonnumeric values, such as types of animals or colors of hair. Data that consist of numbers, such as weights of animals or lengths of hair, are **numerical data**.

One way to organize numerical data is by using a *frequency table*. A **frequency table** is a display that groups data into intervals to show frequencies. The *frequency* of an interval is the number of data values in that interval.

EXAMPLE 1 Making a Frequency Table

ROLLER COASTERS The data show the heights (in meters) of some of the tallest roller coasters in the world. Make a frequency table of the data.

66.4, 94.5, 68.3, 115, 62.5, 97, 66.4, 126.5, 63.4, 74.7, 63.4,
70.1, 66.4, 64.9, 63.7, 79, 63.4, 63.1, 62.5, 61.9, 71.6

SOLUTION

AVOID ERRORS
Make sure that the intervals in a frequency table do not overlap.

STEP 1 **Choose** intervals of equal size for the data. The intervals should include numbers from 61.9 to 126.5.

STEP 2 **Tally** the data in each interval. Use tally marks to record each occurrence of a height in its interval.

STEP 3 **Write** the frequency for each interval by totaling the tally marks.

Height (m)	Tally	Frequency
60–69.9	JHIT JHIT III	13
70–79.9	IIII	4
80–89.9		0
90–99.9	II	2
100–109.9		0
110–119.9	I	1
120–129.9	I	1

HISTOGRAMS A **histogram** displays data from a frequency table. A histogram has one bar for each interval. The length of a bar indicates the frequency of the interval. There is no space between bars of a histogram. Because the intervals of a histogram have equal size, the bars have equal width.

EXAMPLE 2 Making a Histogram

Make a histogram of the data in the frequency table in Example 1.

STEP 1 **Draw** and label the horizontal and vertical axes. Start the vertical scale at 0 and end at a number greater than 13. Use equal increments.

STEP 2 **Draw** a bar to represent the frequency of each interval. The bars of neighboring intervals should touch.

STEP 3 **Write** a title for the histogram.

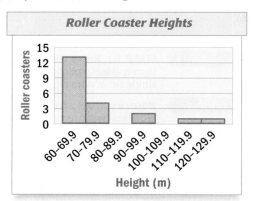

EXAMPLE 3 ♦ **Multiple Choice Practice**

The histogram below shows the distances (to the nearest thousand miles) traveled by 189 buses before their engines failed. About what percent of the buses experienced engine failure before traveling 100,000 miles?

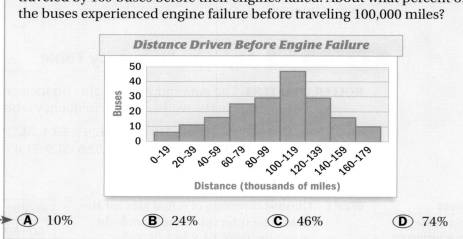

(A) 10%   (B) 24%   (C) 46%   (D) 74%

ELIMINATE CHOICES
Notice that 10% of the total number of buses is about 19 buses. By looking at the graph, you can see that more than 19 buses experienced engine failure before traveling 100,000 miles, so you can eliminate choice A.

SOLUTION

Add up the number of buses in the first 5 bars: $6 + 11 + 16 + 25 + 29 = 87$.

Then divide 87 by 189: $87 \div 189 \approx 0.46$, or 46%. So, about 46% of the buses experienced engine failure before traveling 100,000 miles.

▸**Answer** The correct answer is C. (A) (B) (C) (D)

✔ **GUIDED PRACTICE**   for Examples 1, 2, and 3

1. **WHAT IF?** Using the data from Example 1, make a new frequency table with 6 intervals. Then make a histogram from your frequency table.

2. **BUSES** In Example 3, about what percent of the buses traveled at least 120,000 miles before experiencing engine failure?

11.3 EXERCISES

HOMEWORK KEY

◆ = **MULTIPLE CHOICE PRACTICE**
Exs. 10, 12, 20, 29–31

◯ = **HINTS AND HOMEWORK HELP**
for Exs. 3, 7, 23 at classzone.com

SKILLS • PROBLEM SOLVING • REASONING

1. **VOCABULARY** Copy and complete: A histogram is a graph that shows data that are divided into equal __?__.

2. **NOTETAKING SKILLS** Make a *word magnet* like the one on page 628 for *histogram*.

SEE EXAMPLES 1 AND 2
on pp. 643–644
for Exs. 3–9

MAKING DATA DISPLAYS **Make a frequency table and a histogram of the data. Then identify the intervals that have the greatest frequency and the least frequency.**

3. Point values of a team's shots during the first half of a basketball game:
   2, 2, 1, 3, 2, 2, 1, 3, 2, 2, 1, 2, 3, 2, 2, 1, 2, 1, 2, 1, 1

4. Numbers of weeks class members attended summer camp:
   4, 0, 1, 2, 8, 2, 4, 4, 8, 5, 6, 4, 6, 6, 4, 0, 6, 8, 4, 4, 8, 4, 4, 4, 8, 4

5. Ages of dancers in a ballet class:
   5, 6, 10, 8, 8, 10, 12, 8, 7, 10, 10, 6, 15, 15, 16, 5, 6, 5, 10, 12, 10, 8, 5

6. Numbers of at-bats for the players on a women's softball team:
   2, 6, 6, 16, 19, 20, 20, 21, 22, 25, 26, 30

7. **MULTI-STEP PROBLEM** The data show the numbers of hours 30 students in a class spent on the Internet in a week.

   4, 2.5, 5.7, 1.8, 3.7, 5.4, 5.5, 11.6, 3.7, 6.5, 2, 10, 0.5, 4.5,
   5, 9.5, 2.1, 4.5, 7.5, 2.5, 8, 1, 9, 4.2, 8, 7, 3, 7, 5, 6

   a. **Make a Frequency Table** Make a frequency table of the data. Use 0–1.9 as the first interval.

   b. **Make a Frequency Table** Make a frequency table of the data. Use 0–2.9 as the first interval.

   c. **Compare** Does the frequency table in part (a) or part (b) give a clearer representation of the data? *Explain* your reasoning.

8. **ERROR ANALYSIS** *Describe* and correct the error in making the histogram using the frequency table below.

Interval	Tally	Frequency
0–2		0
3–5	III	3
6–8	IIII	5
9–11	IIII	4

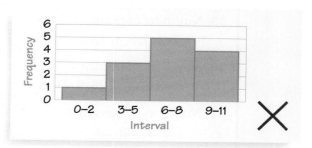

9. **ERROR ANALYSIS** Jack used the intervals 0–2, 3–6, 7–12, 13–15, and 16–22 to make a histogram. *Describe* the error Jack made.

SEE EXAMPLE 3
on p. 644
for Exs. 10–12

10. ◆ **MULTIPLE CHOICE** The histogram at the right shows the scores of 20 students on a history quiz. How many students have a score of at least 7?

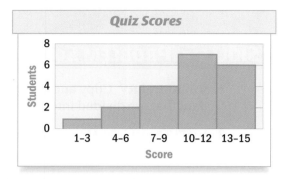

Ⓐ 3   Ⓑ 7

Ⓒ 13   Ⓓ 17

11. **MULTI-STEP PROBLEM** The data below are the number of medals the United States won in each of the Winter Olympic Games as of 2006.

     4, 7, 12, 4, 9, 11, 7, 10, 6, 7, 8, 10, 12, 8, 6, 11, 13, 13, 34, 25

   a. **Make Histograms** Make a histogram of the data with intervals of 5 and a second histogram with intervals of 10.

   b. **Interpret Histograms** Which histogram gives a clearer picture of how many medals you can expect the U.S. to win in future Winter Olympics? What might account for the 34 medals won?

12. ◆ **MULTIPLE CHOICE** The frequency table at the right shows the ages of students in the science club. What is the median of the ages?

Ⓐ 11.5   Ⓑ 12

Ⓒ 12.5   Ⓓ 13

Age	Tally	Frequency
11	III	3
12	IIII I	6
13	IIII	4
14	II	2

13. **REASONING** You want to collect data about the pets of students in your class. What data would you collect to make a histogram? What data would you collect to make a bar graph?

CONNECT SKILLS TO PROBLEM SOLVING Exercises 14–17 will help you prepare for problem solving.

List the intervals you would use to make a frequency table for the given data.

14. Numbers of cars in a parking lot at 11 A.M. for several days:
     150, 167, 181, 156, 168, 135, 146, 142, 166, 163, 155, 139, 148, 127

15. Numbers of books students in a class read during summer vacation:
     2, 3, 1, 5, 4, 4, 3, 1, 1, 2, 4, 3, 6, 2, 2, 3, 6, 5, 1, 4, 3, 6, 2

16. Numbers of minutes several people spent reading a newspaper in a day:
     7, 37, 13, 9, 25, 9, 21, 5, 17, 29, 7, 33, 11, 14, 8, 6, 5, 25, 10, 11, 35

17. Numbers of passing touchdowns for 16 quarterbacks:
     36, 31, 30, 29, 28, 27, 25, 22, 21, 19, 18, 16, 14, 12, 10, 9

◆ = **MULTIPLE CHOICE PRACTICE**   ○ = **HINTS AND HOMEWORK HELP** at classzone.com

SEE EXAMPLES 1 AND 2
on pp. 643–644
for Exs. 18–21

TEST SCORES In Exercises 18–20, use the frequency table. It shows the test scores for a math class.

18. Copy and complete the frequency table.

19. What is the increase in frequency from the interval 61–70 to the interval 71–80?

20. ◆ **MULTIPLE CHOICE** How many scores are less than 91?

   (A) 4   (B) 11   (C) 13   (D) 17

California @HomeTutor for problem solving help at classzone.com

Percent	Tally	Frequency
61–70	IIII	?
71–80	JHT II	?
81–90	JHT I	?
91–100	III	?

21. **MULTI-STEP PROBLEM** The data show the average numbers of meteors that fall per hour during 39 annual meteor showers. For example, in the first meteor shower, an average of 60 meteors fall each hour.

    60, 4, 1, 5, 5, 1, 40, 4, 5, 20, 2, 15, 8, 6, 21, 15,
    20, 30, 3, 15, 10, 62, 25, 26, 50, 12, 20, 12, 15,
    30, 10, 10, 20, 12, 12, 60, 10, 12, 20

a. **Frequency Table** Make a frequency table of the data. Use intervals of 10 starting with 0–9.

b. **Histogram** Make a histogram of the data from your frequency table.

c. **Compare** *Compare* the displays. Discuss one thing that is easier to tell about the data from each display.

California @HomeTutor for problem solving help at classzone.com

Meteor shower in Joshua Tree National Park, CA

SEE EXAMPLE 3
on p. 644
for Exs. 22–24

HURRICANES In Exercises 22–24, the histogram shows the numbers of hurricanes in the Atlantic Ocean from 1950 through 1999.

22. About how many years did 10–12 hurricanes occur?

23. Can you determine the number of years that 10 hurricanes occurred in the Atlantic Ocean? *Explain.*

24. During about how many years were there 6 or fewer hurricanes?

25. **OPEN-ENDED** Give an example of a set of data that can be displayed using a bar graph but not using a histogram.

26. **TRACK TEAM** The histogram shows the miles run in practice by members of a track team in September. Find the mean, median, and mode(s) of the data.

27. **CHALLENGE** *Explain* why a frequency table isn't appropriate to show the data 23, 97, 184, 551, 2097, 9143, and 12,221.

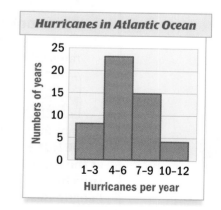

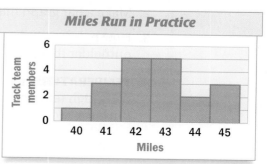

28. CHALLENGE In this exercise, you will examine the possible areas of rectangles with the same perimeter.

    a. On graph paper, draw all rectangles with perimeter 60 centimeters and with sides whose lengths are whole numbers.

    b. Find the area of each rectangle.

    c. Make a histogram of the areas. Start with the intervals 1–50, 51–100, and so on.

    d. Use the histogram you made in part (c) to make two statements about rectangles.

◆ CALIFORNIA STANDARDS SPIRAL REVIEW

NS 2.4

29. Which statement is *not* true? *(p. 213)*

    (A) $\sqrt{225} = 15$ **(B)** $\sqrt{81} < 10$ **(C)** $7 > \sqrt{64}$ **(D)** $\sqrt{49} > 6$

AF 1.4

30. Which two terms are like terms? *(p. 252)*

    (A) $2x, 2$ **(B)** $3x, 3y$ **(C)** $4y, -5$ **(D)** $2x, -x$

AF 4.2

31. The weight of 5 bricks is 18 pounds. Use a direct variation equation that relates the number x of bricks and the weight y (in pounds) of the bricks to find the weight of 23 bricks. *(p. 348)*

    (A) 6.4 lb   **(B)** 82.8 lb   **(C)** 115 lb   **(D)** 414 lb

QUIZ for Lessons 11.1–11.3

1. TORNADOES The table shows the numbers of tornadoes in the United States during the years 1998–2004. Find the mean, median, mode(s), and range of the data. *(p. 631)*

Year	1998	1999	2000	2001	2002	2003	2004
Tornadoes	1424	1342	1071	805	941	1376	1819

HOME RUNS In Exercises 2 and 3, use the table at the right. It shows the record number of home runs hit in a single season by position in Major League Baseball as of 2005. *(p. 636)*

Position	Home runs
Catcher	42
1st baseman	69
Pitcher	9
2nd baseman	42
Shortstop	57
3rd baseman	48
Outfielder	71

2. Make a bar graph that displays the data.

3. How many more home runs is the record for outfielder than for pitcher?

4. TEMPERATURE The data below give the average daily high temperatures (in degrees Fahrenheit) during a two week period of a certain city. Make a frequency table and a histogram of the data. *(p. 643)*

    32, 30, 28, 20, 35, 49, 22, 23, 34, 43, 36, 31, 24, 21

MIXED REVIEW of Skills and Problem Solving

Multiple Choice Practice for Lessons 11.1–11.3

In Exercises 1–4, use the following information.

The data below give the times (in minutes) that you spend instant messaging during several days.

18, 15, 7, 10, 32, 28, 15, 21, 94

1. What is the mean of the data? **Gr. 6 SDAP 1.1**

   (A) 15   **(B)** 18

   (C) 24   **(D)** 26.7

2. What is the median of the data? **Gr. 6 SDAP 1.1**

   (A) 9   **(B)** 15

   (C) 18   **(D)** 26.7

3. What is the mode of the data? **Gr. 6 SDAP 1.1**

   (A) 7   **(B)** 9

   (C) 15   **(D)** 18

4. What is the range of the data? **Gr. 6 SDAP 1.1**

   (A) 9   **(B)** 87

   (C) 94   **(D)** 101

In Exercises 5–7, use the following information.

The frequency table shows the heights of 30 students.

Height (inches)	Frequency
54–55.9	1
56–57.9	2
58–59.9	4
60–61.9	5
62–63.9	7
64–65.9	6
66–67.9	3
68–69.9	2

5. Which height interval has the most students? **SDAP 1.1**

   (A) 54–55.9   **(B)** 60–61.9

   (C) 62–63.9   **(D)** 68–69.9

6. How many students have a height in the range 58 inches through 63.9 inches? **SDAP 1.1**

   (A) 4   **(B)** 5

   (C) 7   **(D)** 16

7. How many students are less than 60 inches tall? **SDAP 1.1**

   (A) 2   **(B)** 4

   (C) 7   **(D)** 13

8. The circle graph below shows the number of wins, losses, and ties for a hockey team in one season. One third of the losses occurred in overtime. How many losses occurred in overtime? **SDAP 1.1, MR 2.8**

   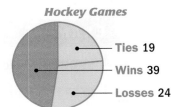

   Hockey Games

   Ties 19   Wins 39   Losses 24

   (A) 8   **(B)** 14

   (C) 24   **(D)** 27

9. The table shows the distances you traveled on your bike. You want to make a data display that shows which days you increased your miles biked from the previous week. Which data display would you choose for the data? **SDAP 1.1, MR 2.5**

Day of the week	Distance (miles)	
	Week 1	Week 2
Monday	2	5
Tuesday	0	2
Wednesday	5	0
Thursday	3	3
Friday	2	1

   (A) Circle graph   **(B)** Double bar graph

   (C) Histogram   **(D)** Venn diagram

11.4 Stem-and-Leaf Plots

Math and SPORTS
Example 1, p. 650

Standards SDAP 1.1 **Know various forms of display for data sets, including a stem-and-leaf plot** or box-and-whisker plot; **use the forms to display a single set of data or to compare two sets of data.**

Connect *Before* you organized data using bar graphs and histograms. *Now* you will make and interpret stem-and-leaf plots.

KEY VOCABULARY
• stem-and-leaf plot

Hurdlers entering the 200 meter hurdles at a track meet were ranked according to their qualifying times (in seconds) shown below.

28.6 29.2 28.1 27.5 29.8 28.7
30.2 29.3 28.3 28.9 29.9 28.4

How can the data be displayed to show the distribution of the times?

A **stem-and-leaf plot** is a data display that helps you see how data are distributed. A stem-and-leaf plot is useful for ordering large sets of data.

EXAMPLE 1 Making a Stem-and-Leaf Plot

SPORTS Make an ordered stem-and-leaf plot of the qualifying times above.

> **READING**
> In a stem-and-leaf plot, a stem can be one or more digits. A leaf is usually a single digit.

STEP 1 **Identify** the stems. The times range from 27.5 seconds to 30.2 seconds. Let the **stems** be the digits in the tens' and ones' places. Then the **leaves** are the tenths' digits.

STEP 2 **Write** the stems first. Then record each time by writing its tenths' digit on the same line as its corresponding stem. Include a key that shows what the stems and leaves represent.

STEP 3 **Make** an ordered stem-and-leaf plot.

> **Animated Math**
> For an interactive example of making a stem-and-leaf plot, go to **classzone.com.**

Unordered Plot

27	5
28	6 1 7 3 9 4
29	2 8 3 9
30	2

Key: 27 | 5 = 27.5

Ordered Plot

27	5
28	1 3 4 6 7 9
29	2 3 8 9
30	2

Key: 27 | 5 = 27.5

The leaves for each stem are listed in order from least to greatest.

✓ **GUIDED PRACTICE** for Example 1

1. **VIDEO GAMES** Make an ordered stem-and-leaf plot of the video game prices:

$40, $15, $19, $10, $24, $15, $39, $50, $35, $20, $43, $36, $30, $24, $27, $29

EXAMPLE 2   Interpreting a Stem-and-Leaf Plot

BIOLOGY The stem-and-leaf plot at the right shows the lengths (in millimeters) of fish in a tank. Use the stem-and-leaf plot to describe the data. What interval includes the most lengths?

Fish lengths

```
4 | 9
5 | 7 7 9
6 | 1 2 4 4 7 8 8 9
7 | 6 8
8 | 4        Key: 6 | 8 = 68
```

SOLUTION

The longest fish is 84 millimeters and the shortest fish is 49 millimeters. So the range of lengths is 35 millimeters. Most of the lengths are in the 60–69 interval.

DOUBLE STEM-AND-LEAF PLOTS A double stem-and-leaf plot can be used to compare two sets of data. You read to the left of the stems for one set of data and to the right for the other.

EXAMPLE 3   Making a Double Stem-and-Leaf Plot

TEST SCORES The data below show the test scores for Beth's class and Marisa's class. Overall, which class had the better test scores?

Beth's class: **95, 86, 79, 79, 58, 68, 90, 63, 71, 81, 82, 94, 64, 76, 77, 79, 83, 91, 83, 68, 74, 71**

Marisa's class: 95, 73, 76, 84, 84, 89, 67, 82, 88, 86, 93, 97, 96, 84, 60, 75, 91, 87, 89, 86, 76, 93

SOLUTION

You can use a double stem-and-leaf plot to compare the test scores.

Beth's Class		Marisa's Class
8	5	
8 8 4 3	6	0 7
9 9 9 7 6 4 1 1	7	3 5 6 6
6 3 3 2 1	8	2 4 4 4 6 6 7 8 9 9
5 4 1 0	9	1 3 3 5 6 7

Key: 0 | 9 | 1 represents 90 and 91

▶ **Answer** Marisa's class had better scores, because her class had more scores in the eighties and nineties.

✓ **GUIDED PRACTICE**   for Examples 2 and 3

2. **PHONE CALLS** Make an ordered double stem-and-leaf plot to compare the lengths (in minutes) of the last 15 phone calls made by two friends. In general, who made longer calls, Kenyon or Jason? *Explain.*

Kenyon: 8, 12, 8, 17, 5, 28, 16, 23, 29, 14, 21, 34, 16, 28, 31
Jason: 31, 16, 24, 28, 7, 12, 5, 11, 5, 13, 14, 6, 11, 19, 24

11.4 EXERCISES

HOMEWORK KEY

◆ = **MULTIPLE CHOICE PRACTICE**
Exs. 14, 15, 28, 35–37

◯ = **HINTS AND HOMEWORK HELP**
for Exs. 11, 17, 27 at classzone.com

SKILLS • PROBLEM SOLVING • REASONING

1. VOCABULARY Copy and complete: The key for a stem-and-leaf plot says $7 \mid 4 = 74$. In the plot, 7 is the __?__ and 4 is the __?__.

2. WRITING *Explain* why you need to include a key in a stem-and-leaf plot.

SEE EXAMPLE 1
on p. 650
for Exs. 3–13

STEMS AND LEAVES **Write the number as it would appear in a stem-and-leaf plot. Identify the stem and the leaf.**

3. 80   **4.** 117   **5.** 12.9   **6.** 4.6

STEM-AND-LEAF PLOTS **Make an ordered stem-and-leaf plot of the data. Identify the interval that includes the most data values.**

7. 45, 48, 65, 50, 67, 82, 74, 63, 52, 61, 84, 66, 40

8. 33, 12, 8, 14, 35, 9, 26, 37, 4, 6, 8, 20, 15, 32, 29

9. 108, 95, 89, 112, 109, 94, 103, 115, 105, 92

10. 461, 492, 439, 467, 501, 485, 475, 451, 510, 468, 494, 461

11. 20.2, 22.6, 18.3, 18.7, 22.5, 18.1, 18.6, 21.9, 18.4, 22.8

12. 5.1, 4.0, 5.3, 3.2, 5.7, 6.9, 5.3, 4.6, 5.2, 6.7, 4.9, 4.7, 5.5

13. ERROR ANALYSIS *Describe* and correct the error in making a stem-and-leaf plot for the data set:

115, 111, 108, 95, 91, 83

```
8 | 3
9 | 1 5
1 | 8 11 15   Key: 1 | 15 = 115    ✕
```

SEE EXAMPLE 2
on p. 651
for Exs. 14–15

14. ◆ MULTIPLE CHOICE What is the range of the data in the stem-and-leaf plot?

   A 3   **B** 3.7

   C 7   **D** 37

```
10 | 1 4
11 | 2 3 5 5 9
12 | 0 0
13 | 1 6 8 8    Key: 12 | 0 = 120
```

15. ◆ MULTIPLE CHOICE In the stem-and-leaf plot from Exercise 14, which interval has the most data values?

   A 100–109   **B** 110–119   **C** 120–129   **D** 130–139

SEE EXAMPLE 3
on p. 651
for Exs. 16–19

DOUBLE STEM-AND-LEAF PLOTS **Make an ordered double stem-and-leaf plot of the two sets of data.**

16. Set A: 16, 19, 8, 22, 18, 20, 32, 5
      Set B: 12, 8, 25, 42, 31, 15, 16, 9

17. Set C: 102, 98, 111, 70, 118, 92, 77
      Set D: 115, 88, 87, 102, 65, 95, 93

18. Set A: 24, 27, 28, 32, 58, 32, 32, 25
      Set B: 22, 31, 43, 22, 21, 55, 36, 29

19. Set C: 8.8, 9.8, 4.7, 6.3, 6.8, 8.0, 7.7
      Set D: 9.5, 6.8, 7.8, 10, 5.5, 9.1, 9.3

20. 5 | 0 0 1 6
6 | 5 9 9
7 | 1 1 2 4 4 4 8   Key: 5 | 0 = 50

21. 0 | 1 1
1 | 4 5 9
2 | 0 0 5 8 8
3 | 0 9   Key: 1 | 4 = 1.4

CONNECT SKILLS TO PROBLEM SOLVING Exercises 22–24 will help you prepare for problem solving.

List the stems for the given data set.

22. The weights (in pounds) of 15 pets owned by students:
25, 7, 8, 10, 13, 22, 10, 15, 12, 13, 9, 40, 15, 21, 14

23. Ages of 12 contestants that participated in a state talent show:
8, 10, 14, 9, 23, 16, 17, 11, 12, 10, 22, 15

24. The times (in seconds) of 7 runners in the 100 meter event:
12.3, 13.5, 11.2, 12.5, 13.2, 14.0, 12.7

SEE EXAMPLES 1 AND 2
on pp. 650–651
for Exs. 25–28

25. AMAZON PARROTS The average weights (in ounces) of several species of Amazon parrots are as follows:

11.0, 15.9, 11.5, 12.7, 11.3, 12.3, 13.4, 13.1

Make an ordered stem-and-leaf plot of the data.

California @HomeTutor for problem solving help at classzone.com

Amazon parrots

26. EXERCISE You surveyed 12 people at a gym about the number of miles they walk on the gym's treadmill. Your results are as follows:

4.1, 3.5, 5.7, 1.4, 3.9, 3.3, 1.8, 4.5, 3.0, 3.1, 2.9, 5.8

Make an ordered stem-and-leaf plot of the data.

California @HomeTutor for problem solving help at classzone.com

27. RESTAURANTS The stem-and-leaf plot at the right shows the average waiting times (in minutes) to be seated for fifteen restaurants. What are the shortest and longest waiting times? Which interval has the fewest number of waiting times?

0 | 5 6 9
1 | 2 5 5
2 | 0 0 5 8
3 | 2 8
4 | 0 5 5   Key: 2 | 5 = 25

28. ◆ MULTIPLE CHOICE The stem-and-leaf plot shows the ages of several people. What is the median age?

(A) 25
(B) 30
(C) 31
(D) 37

1 | 3 7 9
2 | 0 1 4 5
3 | 7 9
4 | 0 1 2 2 2   Key: 4 | 1 = 41

29. REASONING Can you make a stem-and-leaf plot from a frequency table? *Explain* why or why not.

30. MULTI-STEP PROBLEM The average monthly temperatures in degrees Fahrenheit (°F) for Los Angeles, California, are given below.

56.8, 57.6, 58.0, 60.1, 62.7, 65.7, 69.1, 70.5, 69.9, 66.8, 61.6, 56.9

a. **Display** Make an ordered stem-and-leaf plot of the data. What is the range of the data?

b. **Convert** Convert the data to degrees Celsius (°C) using the formula $C = \frac{5}{9}(F - 32)$. Round to the nearest tenth of a degree.

c. **Compare** Make an ordered stem-and-leaf plot of the converted data. *Describe* how the plots are alike and how they are different.

31. FOOTBALL The total points that the Cleveland Browns scored in each game of a recent season are given below. Red numbers represent wins, and blue numbers represent losses. Make an ordered double stem-and-leaf plot of the data. *Describe* the relationship between points scored and the outcome of the game.

6, **24**, 23, **20**, 14, **24**, 21, 12, **27**, 18, 15, 16, 10, 7, **41**, 7

CHALLENGE Make an ordered stem-and-leaf plot with data that have the given characteristics. The display should have at least 8 data values.

32. A range of 52 and a mode of 30

33. A mean of 10 and a median of 15

34. CHALLENGE For an awards banquet, you are making a highlight video that can last no more than 15 minutes. Use the following lengths, in minutes and seconds, of the video segments you would like to include.

2:30, 2:29, 2:14, 2:19, 1:49, 2:30, 2:57, 2:30, 2:01, 2:21, 1:53

Make an ordered stem-and-leaf plot of the data. *Explain* how you chose a key. What is the greatest and least number of segments that you can show without leaving time for another? *Justify* your reasoning.

◆ CALIFORNIA STANDARDS SPIRAL REVIEW

MG 2.1

35. What is the volume of the cylinder? *(p. 589)*

Ⓐ $\frac{27\pi}{4}$ cm³   Ⓑ 27π cm³

Ⓒ 36π cm³   Ⓓ 108π cm³

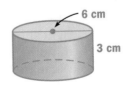
6 cm
3 cm

MG 3.2

36. Which transformation moves each point of a figure the same distance in the same direction? *(p. 522)*

Ⓐ Dilation   Ⓑ Reflection   Ⓒ Rotation   Ⓓ Translation

MG 3.3

37. You need to move a large square painting into a room. The doorway to the room is 84 inches tall and 36 inches wide. What is the maximum side length, to the nearest inch, of a square painting that will fit through the doorway? *(p. 471)*

Ⓐ 84 in.   Ⓑ 89 in.   Ⓒ 91 in.   Ⓓ 95 in.

11.5 Box-and-Whisker Plots

Standards

SDAP 1.1 Know various forms of display for data sets, including a stem-and-leaf plot or **box-and-whisker plot**; use the forms to display a single set of data or to compare two sets of data.

SDAP 1.3 Understand the meaning of, and be able to compute, the minimum, the lower quartile, the median, the upper quartile, and the maximum of a data set.

Math and
ENGINEERING
Example 1, p. 655

Connect *Before* you found the median and range of a data set. *Now* you will use these statistics to make and interpret box-and-whisker plots.

KEY VOCABULARY
• box-and-whisker plot
• lower quartile
• upper quartile
• lower extreme
• upper extreme
• interquartile range

A **box-and-whisker plot** is a data display that organizes data values into four parts. Ordered data are divided into lower and upper halves by the median.

The **lower quartile** is the median of the lower half of the data set. The median of the upper half of the data set is the **upper quartile**.

The **lower extreme**, or minimum, is the least data value. The **upper extreme**, or maximum, is the greatest data value.

EXAMPLE 1 Making a Box-and-Whisker Plot

BRIDGES The Golden Gate bridge, shown above, is one of the world's longest suspension bridges. The lengths (in meters) of the world's ten longest suspension bridges are listed below. Display the lengths in a box-and-whisker plot.

1280 1490 1991 1377 1298 1210 1624 1158 1385 1410

FIND QUARTILES
If a data set has an odd number of values, then the median is not included in either half of the data when finding the quartiles. For help with finding a median, see p. 631.

STEP 1 **Order** the data to find the median, the quartiles, and the extremes.

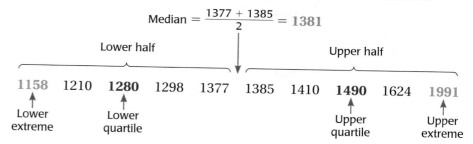

$$\text{Median} = \frac{1377 + 1385}{2} = 1381$$

Lower half: **1158** 1210 **1280** 1298 1377

Upper half: 1385 1410 **1490** 1624 **1991**

1158 — Lower extreme
1280 — Lower quartile
1490 — Upper quartile
1991 — Upper extreme

STEP 2 **Plot** these values below a number line.

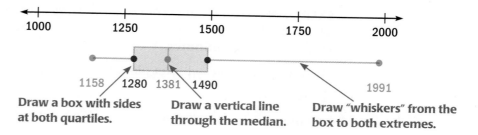

1158 1280 1381 1490 1991

Draw a box with sides at both quartiles.

Draw a vertical line through the median.

Draw "whiskers" from the box to both extremes.

Animated Math

For an interactive example of making a box-and-whisker plot, go to **classzone.com**.

INTERPRETING A BOX-AND-WHISKER PLOT A box-and-whisker plot shows how varied, or spread out, the data are. The points divide the data into four parts. Each part represents about one quarter of the data. The **interquartile range** is the difference of the upper quartile and the lower quartile.

The large box highlights the interquartile range. It represents **about half** of the data.

Each whisker represents **about one quarter** of the data.

You can use box-and-whisker plots to compare two or more data sets.

EXAMPLE 2 Interpreting Box-and-Whisker Plots

FOOD SCIENCE You are testing whether a fertilizer helps tomato plants grow. You divide the plants into two equal groups and give fertilizer to the plants in group 2, but not in group 1. The box-and-whisker plots show how much the plants grew (in centimeters) for each group of plants after two weeks.

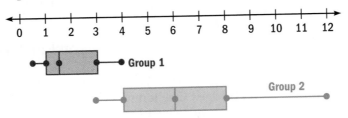

Tomato plant seedling

a. About what fraction of the unfertilized plants grew as much as any of the fertilized plants?

b. About what fraction of the fertilized plants grew 4 to 8 centimeters?

SOLUTION

a. The right whisker for group 1 overlaps the left whisker for group 2. So about one quarter of the unfertilized plants grew as much as any of the fertilized plants.

b. The large box in the plot for group 2 ranges from 4 to 8, so about one half of the fertilized plants grew 4 to 8 centimeters.

✓ **GUIDED PRACTICE** for Examples 1 and 2

EXERCISING Over a period of ten days, Ming exercised for 34, 27, 26, 15, 24, 21, 30, 23, 24, and 35 minutes. Chantelle exercised for 26, 33, 36, 21, 41, 36, 29, 25, 34, and 35 minutes.

1. Make a box-and-whisker plot of the data for each person.

2. Who usually exercised longer? *Explain.*

3. About how often did each person exercise for 25–35 minutes?

11.5 EXERCISES

HOMEWORK KEY

◆ = **MULTIPLE CHOICE PRACTICE**
Exs. 11, 19, 26–28

○ = **HINTS AND HOMEWORK HELP**
for Exs. 3, 9, 21 at classzone.com

SKILLS • PROBLEM SOLVING • REASONING

1. **VOCABULARY** Copy and complete: The median of the lower half of a data set is the __?__.

2. **WRITING** *Explain* how to determine the interquartile range for a data set.

SEE EXAMPLE 1
on p. 655
for Exs. 3–7

MAKING BOX-AND-WHISKER PLOTS **Make a box-and-whisker plot of the data.**

3. $67, $53, $41, $33, $52, $28, $70, $56, $54, $48, $65, $72, $44, $59, $62

4. 26 m, 389 m, 878 m, 144 m, 515 m, 404 m, 423 m, 357 m, 421 m, 593 m

5. 92 cm, 106 cm, 84 cm, 120 cm, 12 cm, 256 cm, 396 cm, 1024 cm, 297 cm

6. **ERROR ANALYSIS** You are analyzing the data set 23, 25, 29, 31, 33, 35. Your friend says that because the greatest data value is 35, the upper quartile is 35. *Describe* and correct the error made by your friend.

7. **ERROR ANALYSIS** You and your friend are analyzing the data set 4, 7, 9, 10, 13, 15, 16, 18, 22. Your friend says that 13 is the median and that the lower quartile is 9. *Describe* and correct the error made by your friend.

SEE EXAMPLE 2
on p. 656
for Exs. 8–11

INTERPRETING BOX-AND-WHISKER PLOTS **In Exercises 8–10, use the box-and-whisker plots below. They show the average monthly temperatures in degrees Fahrenheit (°F) for two cities.**

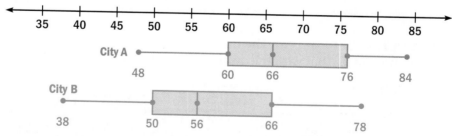

8. Compare the median, range, and interquartile range of the two cities.

9. For each city, about what percent of the average monthly temperatures are below 66°F?

10. Which city is generally warmer than the other? *Explain.*

11. ◆ **MULTIPLE CHOICE** About what percent of the data values in the box-and-whisker plot are *not* in the interval 15–25?

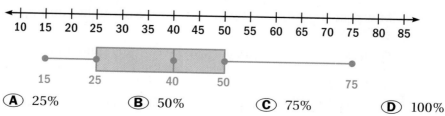

Ⓐ 25%   Ⓑ 50%   Ⓒ 75%   Ⓓ 100%

REASONING Tell whether the statement is *true* or *false*. *Justify* your reasoning.

12. The interquartile range includes about half of the data.

13. There are more data values from the lower extreme to the lower quartile than there are from the median to the upper quartile.

CONNECT SKILLS TO PROBLEM SOLVING Exercises 14–18 will help you prepare for problem solving.

Find the lower and upper quartiles for the given data set.

14. Ticket prices for 11 concerts:
$24, $36, $48, $32, $24, $27, $52, $42, $25, $39, $58

15. Numbers of pages in 10 books:
125, 96, 175, 152, 212, 68, 232, 148, 116, 320

16. Numbers of passing touchdowns in a year for 10 quarterbacks:
21, 22, 27, 31, 27, 28, 30, 29, 21, 27

17. Numbers of puppies born in 9 different litters:
5, 4, 6, 3, 4, 6, 2, 5, 7

18. Class sizes for 8 different grade levels:
220, 196, 234, 243, 221, 187, 206, 213

SEE EXAMPLES
1 AND 2
on pp. 655–656
for Exs. 19–21

19. ◆ **MULTIPLE CHOICE** The data below are the weights (in pounds) of 10 giant pumpkins. What is the upper quartile of the data?

853, 811.5, 785, 1020, 826.5, 789, 838, 810, 731, 822.5

(A) 789 **(B)** 810 **(C)** 817 **(D)** 838

California @*HomeTutor* for problem solving help at classzone.com

20. **MULTI-STEP PROBLEM** The table shows the running times (in minutes) of the movies that won the award for Best Picture from 1970 through 1999.

RUNNING TIMES OF BEST PICTURES
(MINUTES)

1970s	170	104	175	129	200	133	119	93	183	105
1980s	124	123	188	132	158	150	120	160	133	99
1990s	183	118	131	197	142	177	160	194	122	121

a. Graph Make a box-and-whisker plot of the data for each decade using the same number line.

b. Interpret Identify the median and the range of the running times for each decade.

c. Compare *Compare* and contrast the running times of the Best Pictures in the 1970s, the 1980s, and the 1990s.

California @*HomeTutor* for problem solving help at classzone.com

21. BASKETBALL The box-and-whisker plots show the points scored in several games for two players. What conclusions can you make about the players' performances? Which player is more consistent? *Explain.*

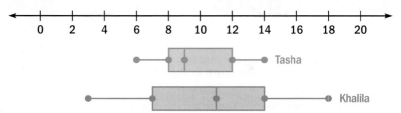

LAKE AREA In Exercises 22 and 23, use the following areas (in square kilometers) of the world's ten largest lakes: 371,000, 82,100, 69,500, 64,500, 59,600, 57,800, 32,900, 31,500, 31,300, 28,900.

22. Make a box-and-whisker plot of the data above. Which value is an outlier?

23. REASONING Remove the outlier and then make another box-and-whisker plot. *Describe* how an outlier affects a box-and-whisker plot.

24. CHALLENGE Change one value in the data set below so that the median of the data becomes 13, the lower quartile becomes 7, and the upper quartile becomes 17.

3, 4, 5, 7, 9, 11, 13, 15, 17, 18, 21

25. CHALLENGE The circle graph displays the age groups of 16 people in a tennis club. Make two sets of data that could be represented by the circle graph. The sets should have different medians and quartiles. Then make a box-and-whisker plot of each set.

Lake Huron has an area of 59,600 square kilometers.

Ages of Club Members

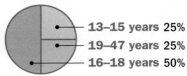

— 13–15 years 25%
— 19–47 years 25%
— 16–18 years 50%

◆ CALIFORNIA STANDARDS SPIRAL REVIEW

NS 2.3

26. Which rational number is equivalent to $\dfrac{4^{-2} \cdot 3^{-1} \cdot 2^4}{4^{-3} \cdot 3 \cdot 2}$? *(p. 393)*

   Ⓐ $\dfrac{2}{3}$ **Ⓑ** 2   **Ⓒ** $\dfrac{32}{9}$ **Ⓓ** $\dfrac{128}{3}$

MG 1.1

27. What is 30 miles per hour converted to feet per second? *(p. 449)*

   Ⓐ 44 ft/sec   **Ⓑ** 88 ft/sec   **Ⓒ** 96 ft/sec   **Ⓓ** 132 ft/sec

MG 2.1

28. A rectangular kitchen floor has the dimensions shown. A service charges $.25 per square foot to clean the tile portion of the floor. How much does it cost to clean the tile portion? *(p. 463)*

tile
12 ft
6 ft
16 ft

   Ⓐ $28.50   **Ⓑ** $36.00   **Ⓒ** $45.25   **Ⓓ** $52.00

11.6 Scatter Plots and Line Graphs

Math and SCIENCE
Example 1, p. 660

Standards **SDAP 1.1 Know various forms of display for data sets**, including a stem-and-leaf plot or box-and-whisker plot; **use the forms to display a single set of data** or to compare two sets of data.

SDAP 1.2 Represent two numerical variables on a scatterplot and informally describe how the data points are distributed and any apparent relationship that exists between the two variables (e.g., between time spent on homework and grade level).

Connect *Before* you found equations of lines given tables of values. *Now* you will make scatter plots and line graphs from tables.

KEY VOCABULARY
• scatter plot
• line graph

NASA's Crawler Transporter is a large vehicle that moves the space shuttle and its launch platform to the launch pad. The crawler uses about 126 gallons of fuel to travel 1 mile.

The table shows the amount of fuel (in gallons) that is used to travel different numbers of miles. How can you present this information using a graph?

Distance (miles)	1	2	3	4	5	6
Fuel used (gallons)	126	252	378	504	630	756

You can represent the information using a *scatter plot*. A **scatter plot** is a graph of a collection of ordered pairs.

EXAMPLE 1 Making a Scatter Plot

Make a scatter plot of the data given above.

ANOTHER WAY
For an alternative method for solving the problem in Example 1, turn to page 670 for the **Problem Solving Workshop**.

SOLUTION

STEP 1 Plot the ordered pairs from the table.

(1, 126), (2, 252), (3, 378),
(4, 504), (5, 630), (6, 756)

STEP 2 Label the horizontal and vertical axes.

Put *Distance (mi)* on the horizontal axis and *Fuel used (gal)* on the vertical axis.

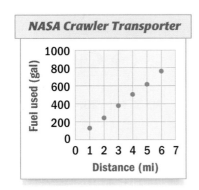

NASA Crawler Transporter

✓ **GUIDED PRACTICE**   for Example 1

Make a scatter plot of the data.

1.
c	−2	−1	0	1
d	−5	−4	−3	−2

2.
x	0	3	6	9
y	−2	−4	−6	−8

INTERPRETING SCATTER PLOTS Scatter plots show what kind of relationship, or *correlation*, exists between two variables.

Positive correlation	Negative correlation	Relatively no correlation
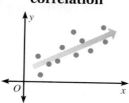	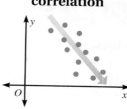	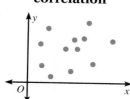
The *y*-coordinates tend to increase as the *x*-coordinates increase.	The *y*-coordinates tend to decrease as the *x*-coordinates increase.	No obvious pattern exists between the coordinates.

EXAMPLE 2 Interpreting a Scatter Plot

UNIT COST The table shows the cost per ounce *y* of breakfast cereal when you buy *x* ounces. Make a scatter plot of the data. Predict whether the cost per ounce for a 22 ounce box of cereal will be *more than* or *less than* $.22. Explain.

Number of ounces, x	9.6	11.4	18.2	18.3	24	25.5
Cost per ounce, y	$.44	$.33	$.25	$.22	$.17	$.16

SOLUTION

STEP 1 **Make** a scatter plot of the data.

STEP 2 **Describe** the relationship between the variables. The *y*-coordinates decrease as the *x*-coordinates increase. So, the quantities have a *negative correlation*.

▶ **Answer** Because a 22 ounce box weighs more than an 18.3 ounce box, the 22 ounce box should cost less per ounce. The cost per ounce for an 18.3 ounce box is $.22, so the cost per ounce for a 22 ounce box should be less than $.22.

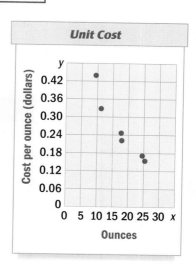

✓ GUIDED PRACTICE   for Example 2

Make a scatter plot of the data. Tell whether *x* and *y* have a *positive correlation*, a *negative correlation*, or *relatively no correlation*.

3.

x	0	1	2	3	4
y	3	6	12	15	20

4.

x	5	10	15	20	25
y	24	18	25	15	22

LINE GRAPHS A **line graph** uses line segments to connect data points. A line graph is often used to represent data that change over time.

EXAMPLE 3 Making and Interpreting a Line Graph

ENVIRONMENT The table shows the number of insect species on the United States endangered species list. Make a line graph of the data. What happened to the number of endangered species over time?

Year	1994	1996	1998	2000	2002	2004
Number	19	20	28	33	35	35

Karner blue butterfly

AVOID ERRORS
Make sure you choose the horizontal and vertical scales carefully so that the data are not distorted.

STEP 1 **Draw** and label the horizontal and vertical scales.

STEP 2 **Plot** a point for each data pair.

STEP 3 **Draw** line segments to connect the points. Include a title.

The graph shows an increase over time.

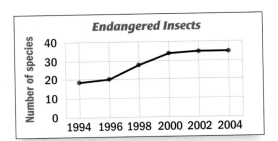

✓ **GUIDED PRACTICE** **for Example 3**

5. In Example 3, use the line graph to determine the time period when the number of insect species on the endangered species list increased the most. *Explain.*

CONCEPT SUMMARY   *For Your Notebook*

Using Appropriate Data Displays

Using appropriate data displays helps you analyze data.

📊 Use a *bar graph* to display data in distinct categories.

🔘 Use a *circle graph* to represent data as parts of a whole.

📊 Use a *histogram* to compare the frequencies of data that are grouped in equal intervals.

Use a *stem-and-leaf plot* to order a data set.

Use a *box-and-whisker plot* to show the data's distribution in quarters, using the median, quartiles, and extremes.

Use a *scatter plot* to see trends in paired numerical data.

Use a *line graph* to display data over time.

EXAMPLE 4 Choosing an Appropriate Display

WEATHER The data displays organize the daily high temperatures during a recent month in Boston, Massachusetts. Which display can you use to find the median high temperature?

```
3 | 6
4 | 0 1 4 5 7 8 9 9 9
5 | 3 3 3 4 6 6 6 8 8
6 | 0 0 2 3 5 5 7
7 | 2 3
8 | 4 5
Key: 3 | 6 = 36°F
```

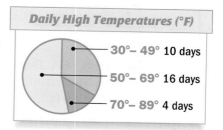

Daily High Temperatures (°F)

30°– 49° 10 days
50°– 69° 16 days
70°– 89° 4 days

SOLUTION

You can use the stem-and-leaf plot to find the median high temperature, 56°F, because it displays the individual temperatures in order. The circle graph does not display the individual temperatures.

✓ **GUIDED PRACTICE** for Example 4

6. **WEATHER** You record the temperature (in degrees Fahrenheit) at noon for seven days in a row. The data are listed below. Which data display would you use to show how the temperature changed during that time? Make the display.

Day	1	2	3	4	5	6	7
Temperature	50°F	42°F	30°F	32°F	45°F	55°F	50°F

11.6 EXERCISES

HOMEWORK KEY

◆ = **MULTIPLE CHOICE PRACTICE**
Exs. 14, 22, 24, 36–38

○ = **HINTS AND HOMEWORK HELP**
for Exs. 3, 7, 23 at classzone.com

SKILLS • PROBLEM SOLVING • REASONING

1. **VOCABULARY** Copy and complete: A graph that is used to display changes in a quantity over time is called a(n) ? .

2. **WRITING** Describe the difference between a *positive correlation* and a *negative correlation*.

SEE EXAMPLE 1
on p. 660
for Exs. 3–4

MAKING SCATTER PLOTS Make a scatter plot of the data.

 3.

x	1	2	3	4	5
y	5	3	−5	7	−1

4.

x	1	2	3	4	5
y	−2	−1	0	1	2

SEE EXAMPLE 2
on p. 661
for Exs. 5–10

IDENTIFYING RELATIONSHIPS Tell whether *x* and *y* have a *positive correlation*, a *negative correlation*, or *relatively no correlation*.

5.

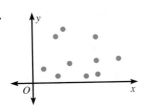

6.

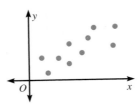

7.

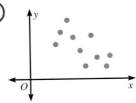

8. ERROR ANALYSIS *Describe* and correct the error in determining the correlation between the variables.

x	−4	−3	−2	−1	0	1
y	3	2	0	5	6	8

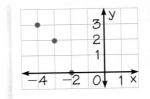

y decreases as x increases. There is a negative correlation.

INTERPRETING Make a scatter plot of the data. Tell whether *x* and *y* have a *positive correlation*, a *negative correlation*, or *relatively no correlation*.

9.

x	1	2	3	4	5
y	5	6	15	18	26

10.

x	3	4	5	6	7
y	11	9	7	4	1

REASONING Predict the type of correlation the data have. *Explain.*

11. The height of a student in 8th grade and a test score of the student

12. The size of a pizza and the price of a pizza

13. The amount of money you pay and the amount you still owe

14. ◆ MULTIPLE CHOICE The variables *m* and *n* have a positive correlation. What conclusion can you make?

(A) *m* is a function of *n*. **(B)** *n* is a function of *m*.

(C) *n* increases as *m* increases. **(D)** *n* increases as *m* decreases.

SEE EXAMPLE 3
on p. 662
for Exs. 15–17

MAKING LINE GRAPHS Make a line graph of the data.

15.

Day	Mon	Tue	Wed	Thu	Fri
Distance (mi)	480	400	355	330	402

16.

Year	2000	2001	2002	2003	2004
Rainfall (in.)	8.5	6.8	2.4	2.4	8.2

17. ERROR ANALYSIS *Describe* and correct the error in making a line graph of the data in the table.

x	1	2	3	5
y	5	2	4	6

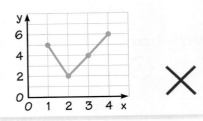

◆ = **MULTIPLE CHOICE PRACTICE**   ○ = **HINTS AND HOMEWORK HELP** at classzone.com

CONNECT SKILLS TO PROBLEM SOLVING Exercises 18–20 will help you prepare for problem solving.

Tell which type of display you would use for the data described. *Explain* your reasoning.

18. You record the temperature at noon every day for a month.

19. You record the attendance at several basketball games as the team progresses through the season.

20. You record the results of a survey that has 3 possible responses.

SEE EXAMPLES
1 AND 2
on pp. 660–661
for Exs. 21–22

21. **MULTI-STEP PROBLEM** The table shows the numbers of cookbooks sold at a bookstore in the first 6 years.

Year, x	1	2	3	4	5	6
Books, y	450	650	700	800	1100	1250

a. Make a scatter plot of the data.

b. Tell whether x and y have a *positive correlation*, a *negative correlation*, or *relatively no correlation*.

c. In year 9, would you expect to sell *more* or *fewer* than 1250 cookbooks?

California @HomeTutor for problem solving help at classzone.com

22. ◆ **MULTIPLE CHOICE** A scatter plot of the amount of bottled water sold each month from August through December shows a negative correlation. Which conclusion is valid based on the plot?

Ⓐ The most water is sold in July.

Ⓑ As months pass, less water is sold.

Ⓒ The most water is sold in December.

Ⓓ As months pass, more water is sold.

California @HomeTutor for problem solving help at classzone.com

SEE EXAMPLE 3
on p. 663
for Exs. 23–24

23. **BASEBALL** The table shows the height of a baseball over time after the baseball is hit. Make a data display that shows the change in the height of the baseball over time.

Time (sec)	0	0.5	1	1.5	2	2.5	3
Height (ft)	2	22.5	34	37.5	33	20.5	0

24. ◆ **MULTIPLE CHOICE** A house was worth $145,000 in 1990, $198,000 in 1995, $225,000 in 2000, and $300,000 in 2005. What data display would you choose to show the change in the house's value over that time?

Ⓐ Histogram Ⓑ Bar graph Ⓒ Line graph Ⓓ Circle graph

25. **CLASS STATISTICS** A preschool director wishes to compare the ages of the children in two classes. The director wants to display the ages of the oldest and the youngest child in each class, and the median of the ages. What type of display could the director use? *Explain.*

26. OPEN-ENDED *Describe* a real-world set of data that shows a positive correlation.

TELEPHONE SALES In Exercises 27–30, use the table showing the numbers (in thousands) of corded and cordless telephones sold to dealers from 1999 to 2004.

	1999	2000	2001	2002	2003	2004
Corded	34,486	29,670	24,957	23,813	21,918	20,051
Cordless	39,654	39,042	40,000	36,556	37,998	33,809

27. Make a double line graph showing these data. *Explain* how you chose the scale you used on the vertical axis.

28. Between which two consecutive years did the number of cordless telephones sold increase the most? Is this easier to tell from the *table* or the *graph*? *Justify* your answer.

29. What is the mean of the annual decreases in sales of corded telephones from 1999 to 2004?

30. INTERPRET What can you conclude about the trends in sales of each type of telephone? *Justify* your answer using the graph.

In Exercises 31 and 32, use a scatter plot and a trend line to estimate the value of the output when the input is 6.

EXTENSION Drawing Trend Lines

BASKETBALL The table relates the height of a basketball player and the average number of rebounds per game. Use a scatter plot to estimate the number of rebounds per game that a 78-inch-tall player makes.

Height (inches)	76	77	79	80	83	84
Average rebounds per game	4.2	4	5.2	5.4	6.8	10

SOLUTION

Plot the data as shown. There appears to be a positive correlation. Use a ruler to draw a line showing the trend in the data.

The line appears to pass through (78, 4.8). You can estimate that a 78-inch-tall player averages about 4.8 rebounds per game.

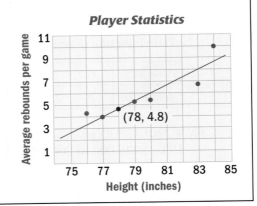

Player Statistics

(78, 4.8)

31.

Year	1	9	15	19	32
Mean winter temp. (°F)	21	25	24	28	30

32.

Week	1	3	4	5	7
Amount owed ($)	30	25	20	16	5

◆ = **MULTIPLE CHOICE PRACTICE**   ◯ = **HINTS AND HOMEWORK HELP** at classzone.com

33. REASONING A newspaper claims that there is a strong relationship between the weather on the day of an election and voter turnout. What do you think the newspaper means? Could the newspaper use a scatter plot to support its claim? If so, what would the labels on each axis be? *Explain.*

34. CHALLENGE Make an input-output table for $y = (-1)^x$. Use the domain 0, 1, 2, 3, 4, 5, and 6. Then make a scatter plot of the data. What do you think the value of y will be when $x = 500$? *Explain* your reasoning.

Storm Drenches City

A major storm rushed through downtown yesterday, affecting voter turnout. Electricity has been restored to sections that lost power for several hours.

35. CHALLENGE For the top eight teams during the regular season of the National Football League in 2004, there was a positive correlation between the average margin of victory (points scored − points allowed) and the number of wins. There was *no* correlation between points scored and number of wins. *Explain* how this is possible.

◆ CALIFORNIA STANDARDS SPIRAL REVIEW

MG 2.1

36. What is the surface area of a square pyramid with a base side length of 8 feet and a slant height of 6 feet? *(p. 580)*

   (A) 128 ft²   **(B)** 142 ft²   **(C)** 160 ft²   **(D)** 188 ft²

AF 4.2

37. You can read 7 pages in 5 minutes. At this rate, how many pages can you read in 2 hours? *(p. 443)*

   (A) 84   **(B)** 126   **(C)** 168   **(D)** 210

MG 3.4

38. Elena is 6 feet tall and casts a 9 foot shadow. Kelly is also 6 feet tall and casts a shadow next to Elena's. The triangles formed are congruent. What is the length of Kelly's shadow? *(p. 516)*

   (A) 6 ft   **(B)** 9 ft   **(C)** 12 ft   **(D)** 15 ft

QUIZ *for Lessons 11.4–11.6*

1. ATTENDANCE Make an ordered double stem-and-leaf plot of the ballpark attendance data below for April and June. Then make a pair of box-and-whisker plots of the data. Use the displays to compare April attendance to June attendance. *(pp. 650, 655)*

April: 1025, 1058, 1030, 997, 990, 1116, 1001, 995, 1122, 1099
June: 1056, 1125, 1151, 1048, 1123, 1097, 1042, 1164, 1125, 1131

2. FOOD Consumption of peanuts per person in the United States was as follows: 1999, 6 lb; 2000, 5.8 lb; 2001, 5.9 lb; 2002, 5.8 lb; 2003, 6.3 lb. Make a bar graph or a line graph of the data. *Explain* your choice. *(p. 660)*

11.6 Making Data Displays

QUESTION How can you create data displays using a graphing calculator?

EXAMPLE 1 Make a box-and-whisker plot

The list gives the ticket prices for 11 concerts that you attended. Make a box-and-whisker plot of the data using a graphing calculator.

$36, $42, $25, $56, $35, $76, $45, $30, $28, $40, $55

SOLUTION

STEP 1 **Enter** the data into list L1.

STEP 2 **Press** [WINDOW] and set appropriate values for Xmin, Xmax, Ymin, Ymax, and Xscl.

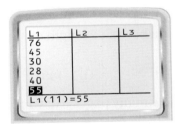

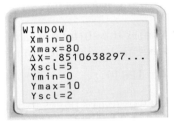

STEP 3 **Choose** the box-and-whisker display from the PLOT menu and set the Xlist to L1.

STEP 4 **Press** [GRAPH] to show the display you have chosen.

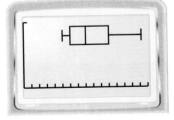

PRACTICE

1. Use a graphing calculator to make a box-and-whisker plot of the following data: 36, 42, 12, 39, 34, 71, 33, 32, 40, 32.

2. Use a graphing calculator to make a box-and-whisker plot of the following data: 82, 96, 71, 73, 89, 84, 82, 67, 68, 91, 85, 88, 94.

EXAMPLE 2 Make a scatter plot or a line graph

Minutes	Cost (dollars)
5	0.5
10	1
15	1.5
20	2
25	2.4
30	2.7

The table shows the cost (in dollars) of a phone call based on the length (in minutes) of the call. Make a scatter plot or a line graph using a graphing calculator.

SOLUTION

STEP 1 **Enter** the data into two lists.

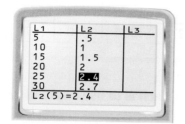

STEP 2 **Choose** maximums and minimums for the window.

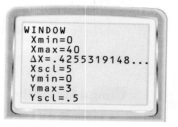

STEP 3 **Choose** a display from the PLOT menu and set the Xlist and Ylist.

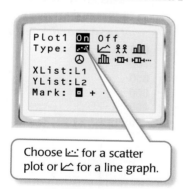

Choose ⊡⋰ for a scatter plot or ⟋ for a line graph.

STEP 4 **Press** GRAPH to show the display you have chosen.

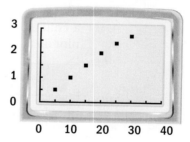

PRACTICE

In Exercises 3 and 4, use a graphing calculator to make a scatter plot and a line graph of the data.

3.

Year	2000	2001	2002	2003	2004	2005
Rainfall (in.)	21.4	39.8	34.5	26.1	44.9	38.7

4.

Altitude (mi)	1	2	3	4	5	6	7	8
Temperature (°F)	52	33	15	−4	−22	−41	−59	−78

Using ALTERNATIVE METHODS

Another Way to Solve Example 1, page 660

Standards
SDAP 1.0, SDAP 1.2

In Example 1 on page 660, you used pencil and paper to make a scatter plot showing the amount of fuel used by NASA's Crawler Transporter to travel various distances. You can also make a scatter plot using a spreadsheet.

PROBLEM

NASA Make a scatter plot of the data in the table. It shows the amount of fuel (in gallons) that is used by NASA's Crawler Transporter to travel different distances.

Distance (miles)	1	2	3	4	5	6
Fuel used (gallons)	126	252	378	504	630	756

METHOD

Using a Spreadsheet An alternative approach is to use a spreadsheet to make the scatter plot.

STEP 1 **Enter** the data into the first two columns of a spreadsheet. Highlight the cells A1:B6 and insert a chart. Select a scatter plot as the chart type.

	A	B
1	1	126
2	2	252
3	3	378
4	4	504
5	5	630
6	6	756

STEP 2 **Choose** chart options to label the title and axes and show the grid lines.

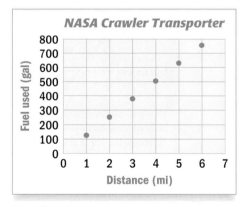

STEP 3 **Double-click** on a chart feature to change its formatting.

PRACTICE

Use a spreadsheet to make a scatter plot.

1.
x	1	2	3	4	5	6	7
y	45	90	135	180	225	270	315

2.
x	2	4	6	8	10	12	14
y	1070	995	920	845	770	695	620

3. **ANIMALS** At top speed, a cheetah can run approximately 102 feet per second. Make a table showing the distance a cheetah can run in 1 second, 2 seconds, . . . , 7 seconds. Make a scatter plot of the data. Then predict how long a cheetah running at top speed would take to run 1000 feet.

Multiple Choice Practice for Lessons 11.4–11.6

In Exercises 1 and 2, use the stem-and-leaf plot showing the number of home runs for each player on a softball team.

Home Runs

```
0 | 4 5 7 8
1 | 2 4 5 6 6 8
2 | 1 4 5
3 | 0            Key: 1|2 = 12
```

1. What is the range of the data? **SDAP 1.1**

Ⓐ 2.6   Ⓑ 3

Ⓒ 6   Ⓓ 26

2. Which interval includes the most data values? **SDAP 1.1**

Ⓐ 0–9

Ⓑ 10–19

Ⓒ 20–29

Ⓓ 30–39

3. What is the lower quartile of the data set? **SDAP 1.3**

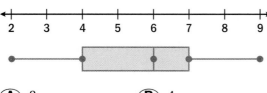

Ⓐ 2   Ⓑ 4

Ⓒ 6   Ⓓ 7

4. The stem-and-leaf plot shows the number of miles that each member of a track team ran last month. What is the mode? **SDAP 1.1**

Miles Run

```
4 | 3 5 8
5 | 2 5 5 9
6 | 0 0 0 6
7 | 2          Key: 5|9 = 59
```

Ⓐ 43   Ⓑ 56.25

Ⓒ 57   Ⓓ 60

5. If you were to make a scatter plot of the given variables, which would most likely show a negative correlation? **SDAP 1.2, MR 2.4**

Ⓐ x = weight of a car; y = price of a car

Ⓑ x = height of a car; y = price of a car

Ⓒ x = age of a car; y = price of a car

Ⓓ x = length of a car; y = price of a car

6. The box-and-whisker plots show the prices of gasoline for several weeks in two cities. Which statement is *not* true? **SDAP 1.3. MR 3.1**

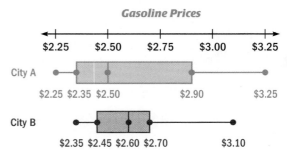

Ⓐ City A's prices were more consistent.

Ⓑ City B's median was higher.

Ⓒ City A's lower quartile was lower.

Ⓓ City B's lower extreme was higher.

7. The numbers of minutes that you and a friend played a video game are given below. Red numbers represent your times, and blue numbers represent your friend's times. Which data display is most appropriate for representing the data? **SDAP 1.1**

12, 10, 26, 22, 18, 17, 5, 20, 22, 18, 15, 8, 14, 19, 22, 23, 25, 8, 16, 20

Ⓐ Circle graph

Ⓑ Bar graph

Ⓒ Double stem-and-leaf plot

Ⓓ Scatter plot

BIG IDEAS

For Your Notebook

Big Idea 7

Describing Data Using Statistical Measures

Statistics are numerical values used to summarize and compare sets of data. Four common statistics are *mean*, *median*, *mode*, and *range*.

Mean	The *mean* of a data set is the sum of the values divided by the number of values.
Median	The *median* of a data set is the middle value when the values are written in numerical order. If a data set has an even number of values, the median is the mean of the two middle values.
Mode	The *mode* of a data set is the value that occurs most often. A data set can have no mode, one mode, or more than one mode.
Range	The *range* of a data set is the difference of the greatest value and the least value. The range measures how spread out the data are.

Big Idea 2

Representing Information Using Data Displays

Using appropriate data displays helps you analyze data.

- Use a *bar graph* to display data in distinct categories.
- Use a *circle graph* to represent data as parts of a whole.
- Use a *histogram* to compare the frequencies of data that are grouped in equal intervals.
- Use a *stem-and-leaf plot* to order a data set.
- Use a *box-and-whisker plot* to show the data's distribution in quarters, using the median, quartiles, and extremes.
- Use a *scatter plot* to see trends in paired numerical data.
- Use a *line graph* to display data over time.

Big Idea 3

Drawing Conclusions From Data Displays

You can draw conclusions about data from a graph used to display the data.

The line graph shows Jose's height from birth to 5 years old. In which year did Jose grow the most?

The graph is steepest from birth to age 1. So, Jose grew the most in his first year.

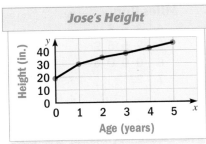

Jose's Height

PROBLEM How can you compare two players in your favorite sport?

STEP 1 Choose two players in a sport and a statistic to compare.

For example, you could choose two professional quarterbacks and compare their passing yards per game.

STEP 2 Find the data.

Use the Internet to find data for each player for a recent regular season. For example, you could use the official website of the National Football League to find the numbers of passing yards per game for the quarterbacks mentioned in Step 1. Make sure the data set for each player includes at least 10 values.

STEP 3 Calculate and interpret statistical measures.

Use your data from Step 2 to create a table like the one below.

Name of Player	Mean	Median	Mode	Range
?	?	?	?	?
?	?	?	?	?

Based on the three averages in your table, which player is the better performer? Based on the range, which player is more consistent?

STEP 4 Represent the information using data displays.

Choose and create one or more data displays to represent and compare your data sets. For example, data sets giving two quarterbacks' passing yards per game could be displayed in a double box-and-whisker plot or in two scatter plots of the ordered pairs (game number, passing yards). What conclusions can you draw from your display(s)?

Extending the Problem

Use your results from the problem above to complete the exercises.

1. For the two players you chose to compare, include their postseason data (if any) with their regular season data. Then repeat Steps 3 and 4. Which player is better in both the regular season and the postseason?

2. Choose another statistic and compare the two players again by repeating Steps 2–4. (For instance, if you are comparing two quarterbacks, you could choose touchdown passes thrown per game.) Which player is better in terms of this statistic?

California @*HomeTutor*
classzone.com
• Multi-Language Visual Glossary
• Vocabulary practice

REVIEW KEY VOCABULARY

- statistics, *p. 631*
- median, *p. 631*
- mode, *p. 631*
- range, *p. 632*
- outlier, *p. 632*
- bar graph, *p. 636*
- double bar graph, *p. 637*

- circle graph, *p. 637*
- categorical data, *p. 643*
- numerical data, *p. 643*
- frequency table, *p. 643*
- histogram, *p. 643*
- stem-and-leaf plot, *p. 650*
- box-and-whisker plot, *p. 655*

- lower quartile, *p. 655*
- upper quartile, *p. 655*
- lower extreme, *p. 655*
- upper extreme, *p. 655*
- interquartile range, *p. 656*
- scatter plot, *p. 660*
- line graph, *p. 662*

VOCABULARY EXERCISES

Copy and complete the statement.

1. A value that occurs most often in a data set is a(n) __?__.

2. A graph that uses bars to display data in distinct categories is a(n) __?__.

3. Data that consist of names, labels, or other nonnumerical values are called __?__.

4. A graph that shows data that are divided into equal intervals is a(n) __?__.

5. A data display that helps you see how data are distributed is a(n) __?__.

6. **NOTETAKING SKILLS** Make a *word magnet* like the one on page 628 for *box-and-whisker plot*.

REVIEW EXAMPLES AND EXERCISES

11.1 Mean, Median, Mode, and Range
pp. 631–635

Gr. 6 SDAP 1.1

EXAMPLE

Find the mean, median, mode(s), and range of the following ordered set of data.

$$4, 5, 6, 6, 7, 9, 11, 12$$

Mean: $\dfrac{4 + 5 + 6 + 6 + 7 + 9 + 11 + 12}{8} = \dfrac{60}{8} = 7.5$

Median: $\dfrac{6 + 7}{2} = \dfrac{13}{2} = 6.5$

Mode: 6

Range: $12 - 4 = 8$

EXERCISES

SEE EXAMPLES
1 AND 2
on pp. 631–632
for Exs. 7–11

Find the mean, median, mode(s), and range of the data set.

7. Temperatures (°C): −7, −1, 0, 8, 4, 2, −7, 2

8. Lengths of bike trails (kilometers): 7, 8.3, 17.1, 4.8, 3.9, 7, 4.8, 13.1

9. Thicknesses of books (inches): 2.4, 1, 3.7, 1.4, 1.3, 2.5, 2, 2.5

10. Prices of portable MP3 players (dollars): 70, 180, 110, 100, 200, 100, 80

11. Ages of houses in a neighborhood (years): 28, 20, 28, 26, 20, 63, 23, 24

11.2 Bar Graphs and Circle Graphs

pp. 636–642

SDAP 1.1

EXAMPLE

A survey indicates that 35% of students do not know who they will vote for in a school election, 38% will vote for Wong, and 27% will vote for Nelson. Display the data in a circle graph.

STEP 1 **Find** the number of degrees to use to represent each response as a section in a circle graph.

Not sure
$0.35(360°) = 126°$

Wong
$0.38(360°) \approx 137°$

Nelson
$0.27(360°) \approx 97°$

STEP 2 **Draw** a circle and use the angle measures to draw the sections.

Who Will You Vote For?

Not sure 35%
Wong 38%
Nelson 27%

EXERCISES

SEE EXAMPLES
2, 3, AND 4
on pp. 637–638
for Exs. 12–14

12. **SURVEY** The results of a student survey on favorite summer drinks were as follows: *iced tea*, 50%; *lemonade*, 25%; *limeade*, 10%; *other*, 15%. Display the data in a circle graph.

13. Use your graph from Exercise 12. Which drink was the students' second favorite drink?

14. **BASKETBALL** The table shows the number of shots made and shots attempted by three players on a basketball team. Make a double bar graph of the data.

Player	Shots made	Shots attempted
Kaye	14	15
Teva	8	13
Olivia	16	22

Frequency Tables and Histograms   *pp. 643–648*

SDAP 1.1   **EXAMPLE**

The list below shows the numbers of pledges that students in a class received for a walk-a-thon. Make a frequency table and a histogram of the data.

10, 37, 12, 20, 4, 16, 7, 32, 25, 3, 9, 11, 41, 2, 12, 4, 38, 8, 18, 19, 21

Pledges	Tally	Frequency
0–9	JHT II	7
10–19	JHT II	7
20–29	III	3
30–39	III	3
40–49	I	1

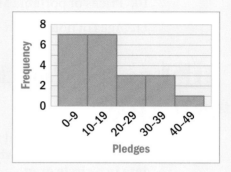

EXERCISES

SEE EXAMPLES
1 AND 2
·······
on pp. 643–644
for Exs. 15–16

15. **SHOPPING** The data below give the ages of people shopping at a clothing store. Make a frequency table and a histogram of the data.

16, 42, 26, 34, 22, 17, 35, 33, 19, 18, 38, 24, 21, 28, 23, 16, 18, 26

16. **FISHING** The data below are the weights (in ounces) of fish caught in a lake. Make a frequency table and a histogram of the data.

23, 19, 24, 33, 20, 25, 23, 23, 26, 21, 31, 20, 20, 21, 22, 21, 25, 24, 25, 17, 19

Stem-and-Leaf Plots   *pp. 650–654*

SDAP 1.1   **EXAMPLE**

Make a stem-and-leaf plot of the data below.

24, 29, 35, 32, 22, 20, 43, 27, 41, 31, 26

STEP 1   **Record** the data set in an unordered stem-and-leaf plot.

```
2 | 4 9 2 0 7 6
3 | 5 2 1
4 | 3 1
```

STEP 2   **Order** the leaves. Include a key.

```
2 | 0 2 4 6 7 9
3 | 1 2 5
4 | 1 3        Key: 4 | 1 = 41
```

EXERCISES

SEE EXAMPLES 1 AND 2
on pp. 650–651
for Exs. 17–20

In Exercises 17–19, make an ordered stem-and-leaf plot of the data. Identify the interval that includes the most data values.

17. 20, 25, 36, 16, 29, 32, 27, 42, 28, 31, 15, 19, 21, 37, 22

18. 11.2, 7.5, 15.1, 15.7, 15.0, 6.7, 11.3, 8.4, 7.3, 10.6, 9.2, 15.6, 11.9, 15.8

19. 81, 100, 94, 97, 86, 100, 97, 96, 84, 99

20. WIND SPEED The following wind speeds (in miles per hour) were recorded at an airport each day at noon for a two week period: 9, 15, 8, 19, 11, 18, 11, 24, 7, 14, 21, 7, 15, 12. Make an ordered stem-and-leaf plot of the data.

11.5 Box-and-Whisker Plots

pp. 655–659

SDAP 1.1

EXAMPLE

Make a box-and-whisker plot of the data below

70, 69, 75, 65, 64, 85, 61, 66, 73, 61, 84

STEP 1 **Order** the data to find the median, quartiles, and extremes.

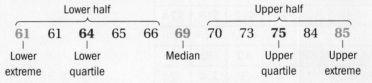

STEP 2 **Plot** these values below a number line.

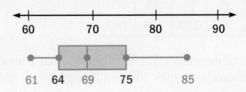

EXERCISES

SEE EXAMPLE 1
on p. 655
for Exs. 21–24

In Exercises 21–23, make a box-and-whisker plot of the data.

21. 5, 13, 9, 31, 25, 21, 25, 18, 23, 14, 32, 3, 22, 11, 16

22. 22, 7, 4, 30, 28, 15, 32, 25, 8, 12, 20, 19, 22, 18, 9, 14

23. 62, 41, 65, 76, 68, 83, 81, 80, 70, 85, 79, 42, 61, 74, 68

24. CHESS The prices of several chess sets are $15, $20, $38, $95, $60, $45, $40, $35, and $50. Make a box-and-whisker plot of the data.

SDAP 1.2 **EXAMPLE**

Make a scatter plot of the data in the table. Then describe the relationship between *x* and *y*.

x	−1	0	1	2
y	−6	−5	−4	−3

To make a scatter plot, plot the ordered pairs from the table.

$(-1, -6), (0, -5), (1, -4), (2, -3)$

The *y*-coordinates increase as the *x*-coordinates increase. So, the variables have a positive correlation.

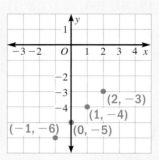

EXERCISES

SEE EXAMPLES 1, 2, AND 3
on pp. 660–662
for Exs. 25–29

In Exercises 25–27, make a scatter plot of the data. Then describe the relationship between the quantities.

25.

Muffins sold	12	24	36	48
Profit	$6	$12	$18	$24

26.

Speed (mi/h)	30	40	50	60
Time (h)	4	3	2.4	2

27.

Age	8	14	19	31
Bowling score	77	237	125	149

28. **INTERNET** The table shows the number of countries connected to the Internet for various years. Make a line graph of the data. Use it to estimate the number of countries connected in 1995.

Year	1988	1990	1992	1994	1996	1998	2000
Countries connected	8	22	43	81	165	200	214

29. **CATS** The table below shows the number of pet cats in the United States for various years. Make a line graph of the data.

Pet Cats in the United States					
Year	1993	1995	1997	1999	2001	2003
Cats (millions)	64	66	70	73	76	78

VOCABULARY Copy and complete the statement.

1. The median of the upper half of a data set is the __?__.

2. The sum of the values of a data set divided by the number of values of the data set is the __?__.

Make a stem-and-leaf plot of the data. Identify the interval that includes the most values. Then make a box-and-whisker plot of the data.

3. 46 kg, 70 kg, 21 kg, 136 kg, 55 kg, 60 kg, 72 kg, 104 kg, 52 kg, 96 kg, 43 kg, 59 kg, 88 kg, 56 kg

4. 12.1 in., 13.5 in., 12.8 in., 10 in., 7 in., 11.2 in., 12.9 in., 11.1 in., 12 in., 13.7 in., 8.2 in., 10.1 in., 13.3 in., 12.5 in., 11.7 in.

Use the circle graph. It shows student replies to *Which animal career would you most enjoy?*

5. Which animal career is the least favorite?

6. Which animal career is the most favorite?

7. If 300 students responded to this survey, how many students said they would most enjoy a career as a zookeeper?

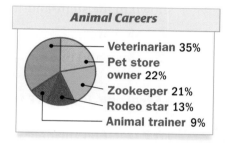

Animal Careers

- Veterinarian 35%
- Pet store owner 22%
- Zookeeper 21%
- Rodeo star 13%
- Animal trainer 9%

8. **SPORTS** In a survey, 3000 people in Japan were asked whether they participated in each of ten sports. The results for four sports are shown in the table. Make a bar graph of the data.

Sport	Participants
Gymnastics	1002
Bowling	996
Jogging	807
Swimming	717

9. **STUDYING** Last week, twelve students spent the following numbers of hours studying. Find the mean, median, mode(s), and range of the data.

2, 5, 3, 7, 10, 9, 8, 7, 6, 7, 6, 2

10. **CAMERA PRICES** The prices of several cameras are $180, $330, $230, $285, $400, $380, $300, $260, and $260. Order the list of prices from least to greatest. Then make a box-and-whisker plot of the data. What conclusions can you make?

11. **SOFTBALL** The table shows the number of runs scored in each inning of a seven inning softball game. Make a scatter plot of the data.

Inning	1	2	3	4	5	6	7
Runs	0	0	4	2	1	0	1

12. **NAMES** The list below shows the numbers of letters in student's names. Make a frequency table of the data.

6, 5, 4, 4, 5, 3, 9, 8, 6, 4, 3, 4, 7, 5, 4, 3, 8, 4, 9, 3

STRATEGIES YOU'LL USE:
• SOLVE DIRECTLY
• ELIMINATE CHOICES

Standards
SDAP 1.1

If you have difficulty solving a multiple choice problem directly, you may be able to use another approach to eliminate incorrect answer choices and obtain the correct answer.

PROBLEM

Your basketball team wins its first 7 games of the season. The stem-and-leaf plot at the right shows the margins of victory for each game. Which averages best represent(s) the data shown in the stem-and-leaf plot?

(A) Median

(B) Mode

(C) Mean and mode

(D) Median and mode

Margins of Victory

```
0 | 8 8 9
1 | 3 4
2 | 3
4 | 4
```
Key: 2 | 3 = 23

Strategy 1 · SOLVE DIRECTLY

STEP 1 **Order** the data values.

8 8 9 13 14 23 44

STEP 2 **Calculate** the averages.

Mean: $\dfrac{\text{Sum of values}}{\text{Number of values}} = \dfrac{119}{7} = 17$

Median: 8 8 9 **13** 14 23 44
The median is 13.

Mode: Because 8 occurs most, it is the mode.

STEP 3 **Compare** mean, median, and mode.

The mean is 17 which is greater than five of the seven data values.

The median represents the data well.

The mode is 8 which is less than five of the seven data values.

The median best represents the data.

The correct answer is A. (A) (B) (C) (D)

Strategy 2 · ELIMINATE CHOICES

Use mathematical reasoning to eliminate answer choices.

Notice that choices B, C, and D all contain the mode. So, you should check whether the mode represents the data first. If it doesn't, then you can eliminate three choices easily.

Looking at the data, you can see that the mode is 8. This value is less than five of the seven margins of victory. It does not represent the data well. So, choices B, C and D, which include the mode, can be eliminated.

The correct answer is A. (A) (B) (C) (D)

PROBLEM 2

The line graph shows the number of visitors (in millions) that visited California's national parks from 2000 to 2005. Between which two consecutive years was the increase in the number of visitors the greatest?

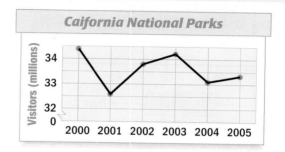

Caifornia National Parks

(A) 2000–2001

(B) 2001–2002

(C) 2002–2003

(D) 2004–2005

Strategy 1 SOLVE DIRECTLY

STEP 1 **Estimate** the number of visitors for each year.

2000: 34.4 million   2001: 32.6 million
2002: 33.8 million   2003: 34.2 million
2004: 33.1 million   2005: 33.4 million

STEP 2 **Find** the difference of the numbers of visitors for the consecutive years given in the answer choices.

2000–2001: $32.6 - 34.4 = -1.8$ million
2001–2002: $33.8 - 32.6 = 1.2$ million
2002–2003: $34.2 - 33.8 = 0.4$ million
2004–2005: $33.4 - 33.1 = 0.3$ million

The largest increase was 1.2 million, which occurred during 2001–2002.

The correct answer is B. (A) (B) (C) (D)

Strategy 2 ELIMINATE CHOICES

Use your understanding of slope and mathematical reasoning to eliminate answer choices.

By looking at the graph, you can see that there was a decrease between 2000 and 2001. So, you can eliminate choice A.

Looking at the graph, you can see that the slopes of the lines for the intervals 2002–2003 and 2004–2005 are less steep than the slope of the line for the interval 2001–2002. Because the steeper the slope of a line for an interval means a greater increase, you can eliminate choices C and D.

The correct answer is B. (A) (B) (C) (D)

STRATEGY PRACTICE

Explain why you can eliminate the highlighted answer choice.

1. The data set below shows the weights (in pounds) of 10 dogs. Which measure(s) of central tendency best represent(s) the data?

36, 39, 39, 39, 45, 50, 50, 72, 77, 107

(A) Mean   (B) Median   (C) ✗ **Mode**   (D) Mean and median

2. How many stems would you need to make a stem-and-leaf plot of the data in Exercise 1?

(A) ✗ 1   (B) 4   (C) 5   (D) 8

In Exercises 1 and 2, use the following information.

The double box-and-whisker plot shows the heights (in inches) of players on two basketball teams.

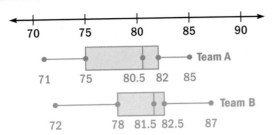

1. Which statement is *not* true? **SDAP 1.3**

   Ⓐ The shortest player is on team A.

   Ⓑ The upper extreme for team A is greater than the upper extreme for team B.

   Ⓒ The range for team B is greater than the range for team A.

   Ⓓ The median for team A is less than the median for team B.

2. What is the interquartile range of the data set for team A? **SDAP 1.3**

   Ⓐ 5

   Ⓑ 7

   Ⓒ 10

   Ⓓ 14

3. The results of a student survey about whether a school dance should be held in the gym are shown. In a circle graph, what angle measure should you use to represent the portion of students who said *Yes*? **SDAP 1.1**

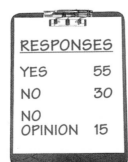

RESPONSES

YES 55

NO 30

NO OPINION 15

   Ⓐ 54°

   Ⓑ 108°

   Ⓒ 198°

   Ⓓ 225°

4. The stem-and-leaf plot shows the average fuel efficiency (in miles per gallon) for 8 cars. Which statistic is equal to 19? **SDAP 1.1**

Fuel Efficiency

2	3 7 9
3	0 2 3 8
4	2

Key: 2 | 3 = 23

   Ⓐ Mean

   Ⓑ Median

   Ⓒ Mode

   Ⓓ Range

5. The line graph shows a city's average high temperatures for the month of August from 2002 to 2007. Between which two consecutive years was the difference in high temperatures the greatest? **SDAP 1.1**

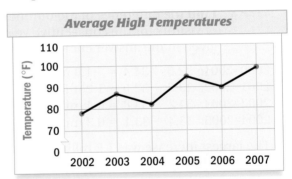

   Ⓐ 2002–2003

   Ⓑ 2003–2004

   Ⓒ 2004–2005

   Ⓓ 2006–2007

6. Which data set of people's ages has a range of 23, an upper quartile of 45, an interquartile range of 10, and a median of 41? **SDAP 1.3**

   Ⓐ 23, 25, 32, 36, 41, 42, 42, 45, 45, 46

   Ⓑ 23, 26, 32, 36, 41, 41, 33, 54, 54, 35

   Ⓒ 19, 25, 32, 31, 40, 42, 33, 24, 19, 35

   Ⓓ 55, 39, 43, 36, 44, 32, 33, 54, 45, 35

7. The scatter plot shows the price of ladders in relation to the length of the ladders. Which statement best describes the relationship shown? **SDAP 1.2, MR 2.4**

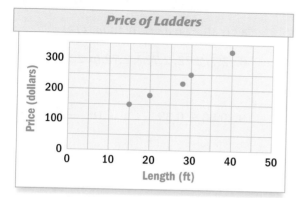

Price of Ladders

Price (dollars) vs Length (ft)

Ⓐ The price of ladders decreases as the length increases.

Ⓑ The price of ladders increases as the length increases.

Ⓒ The price of ladders first increases and then decreases as the length increases.

Ⓓ The price of ladders shows no relationship to the length.

8. Below are statistics for an exam in a history class.

Lower extreme	55
Lower quartile	61
Median	68
Upper quartile	74
Upper extreme	92

Suppose 6 students have scores ranging from 68 to 74. What is the best estimate for the number of students in the class?
SDAP 1.3, MR 3.3

Ⓐ 12 students

Ⓑ 18 students

Ⓒ 20 students

Ⓓ 24 students

9. The frequency table shows the heights (in inches) of several Douglas Fir trees in a nursery. About what percent of the trees are at most 44 inches tall? **SDAP 1.1**

Height (in.)	Frequency
33–36	8
37–40	6
41–44	5
45–48	2
49–52	5
53–56	3
57–60	1

Ⓐ 17%

Ⓑ 37%

Ⓒ 48%

Ⓓ 63%

10. The double bar graph shows the winning distances for the javelin throw in the Olympics. In what year was the difference between the distances of the men's and women's throws the least? **SDAP 1.1**

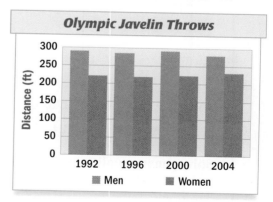

Olympic Javelin Throws

Distance (ft) by year: 1992, 1996, 2000, 2004. ■ Men ■ Women

Ⓐ 1992

Ⓑ 1996

Ⓒ 2000

Ⓓ 2004

Order the numbers from least to greatest.

1. $-45, 45, 43, -43, -43.5$ *(p. 12)*

2. $-25, |35|, -|20|, |-16|$ *(p. 12)*

3. $2\frac{3}{10}, 2.32, \frac{11}{5}, 2.25, \frac{5}{2}$ *(p. 113)*

4. $0.45, \frac{3}{8}, 0.4, \frac{5}{12}, 0.46$ *(p. 113)*

5. $0.\overline{18}, 0.1\overline{81}, 0.1\overline{88}, 0.188$ *(p. 225)*

6. $2.\overline{7}, 2.\overline{72}, 2.\overline{727}, 2.72$ *(p. 225)*

Find the sum or difference. *(p. 137)*

7. $7.92 + 6.5$

8. $28.012 + 94.3$

9. $0.88 - 0.39$

10. $-2.91 - 0.452$

Find the product or quotient. *(p. 144)*

11. 0.15×24

12. $0.26 \times (-9.58)$

13. $-133.6 \div 8$

14. $57.3 \div 0.003$

Find the sale price or retail price. *(p. 160)*

15. Original price: $110
    Percent discount: 25%

16. Wholesale price: $58
    Percent markup: 145%

Evaluate the expression $\sqrt{x^2 - y^2}$ for the given values. *(p. 213)*

17. $x = 5, y = 3$

18. $x = 10, y = 8$

19. $x = 15, y = 12$

Find the unknown dimension. *(p. 257)*

20. Perimeter = 48 in.

21. Area = 63 in.^{2}

22. Area = 198 cm^2

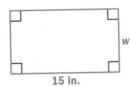

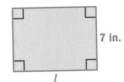

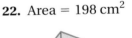
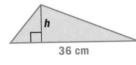

Solve the equation. *(p. 270)*

23. $2x + 9 = 21$

24. $7x - 15 = 27$

25. $\frac{y}{2} + 5 = 15$

26. $\frac{4}{5}m - 6 = 10$

Solve the inequality. *(pp. 282, 288)*

27. $3y < 12$

28. $m - 9 \geq 19$

29. $x + \frac{2}{5} > -\frac{1}{5}$

30. $\frac{2}{3}x > 18$

Simplify the expression. *(pp. 386, 393)*

31. $4^3 \times 4^6$

32. $\frac{(-5)^7}{(-5)^5}$

33. $m^4 \cdot m^{-5}$

34. $\frac{3^{-5} \cdot x^4 \cdot y^3}{3^{-7} \cdot x^2 \cdot y^4}$

Make a stem-and-leaf plot of the data. Tell which stem includes the most values. Then make a box-and-whisker plot. *(pp. 650, 655)*

35. 46 kg, 70 kg, 21 kg, 136 kg, 55 kg, 60 kg, 72 kg, 104 kg, 52 kg

36. 12.1 in., 13.5 in., 12.8 in., 10 in., 7 in., 11.2 in., 12.9 in., 11.1 in., 12 in., 13.7 in.

37. **WALKING** You take a break after walking $3\frac{3}{4}$ miles of a 5 mile trail. How much of the trail is left? You walk $\frac{1}{2}$ of the remaining portion of the trail, and then you run to the end of the trail because it starts to rain. How far did you run? *(pp. 91, 98)*

38. **INTEREST** You deposit $250 into a savings account that earns an interest rate of 4% compounded annually. How much will you have in your account after 2 years? *(p. 172)*

39. **LANDSCAPING** You are using a lawn cart to haul logs across your yard for a landscaping project. The cart can haul up to 300 pounds. Using 15 pounds as the average weight per log, write an inequality that models the situation. Solve the inequality and interpret the solution. *(p. 288)*

40. **PARTY MIX** You have $48 to spend. Almonds are $8 per package and raw cashews are $6 per package. The number of each item you can buy is modeled by the equation $8x + 6y = 48$. Graph the equation and explain what the intercepts represent. *(p. 327)*

41. **GROCERY SHOPPING** You have $20 to spend on peppers for a big pot of chili you are making. Jalapeno peppers cost $3.00 per pound and red bell peppers cost $4.00 per pound. The amount of each pepper you can buy is modeled by the inequality $3x + 4y \leq 20$ where x is the number of pounds of jalapeno peppers and y is the number of pounds of red bell peppers. Graph the inequality. *(p. 354)*

42. **BAKING** You want to make several cakes for your school bake sale. Flour comes in two containers. Container A is a cylinder with a radius of 6 inches and a height of 6 inches. Container B is a rectangular box with a length of 4 inches, a width of 4 inches, and a height of 10 inches. Which container holds more flour? *(p. 589)*

43. **ZOOLOGY** The table below shows the maximum life spans of various animals in captivity. Make a bar graph to represent the data. *(p. 636)*

Animal	Asian elephant	Giraffe	Lion	Monkey
Life Span (yr)	77	36	30	37

44. **TEMPERATURE** The record low temperatures in Miami, Florida, are given in the table. Display the data in an appropriate graph. *Justify* your choice of display. *(p. 660)*

Month	Ja	Fe	Mr	Ap	Ma	Jn	Jl	Au	Se	Oc	No	De
Temp (°F)	30	32	32	46	53	60	69	68	68	51	39	30

12 Polynomials: Review and Preview

Before

In previous chapters, you learned the following skills, which you'll use in Chapter 12:

- Simplifying algebraic expressions
- Evaluating expressions involving exponents
- Using the distributive property
- Multiplying monomials using the rules of exponents

Now

In Chapter 12 you'll study these **Big Ideas:**

1. Classifying and simplifying polynomials
2. Adding and subtracting polynomials
3. Multiplying polynomials

Why?

So you can solve real-world problems about . . .

- Baseball, p. 692
- Falling objects, p. 692
- Compound interest, p. 708
- Stage design, p. 708
- Swimming pools, p. 709
- Coasters, p. 711

Animated Math
at *classzone.com*

Get-Ready Games

Piñata Punch

California Standards

Review evaluating with exponents. *Gr. 7 NS 2.3*
Prepare for multiplying polynomials. *Alg. 1 10.0*

$$(11 - 5)^3 \cdot 2 \cdot (-6)^{-2}$$

$$\frac{4^7}{(9 - 5)^3}$$

$$3^{-3} \cdot 3^8 + 5$$

$$2^5 \cdot 7 \cdot 2^{-1}$$

$$\frac{(7 + 1)^6}{8^4}$$

18 12 248 112 256 64

How to Play

Find the best spot to hit the piñata so that it will break.

- Evaluate each expression.
- The part of the piñata that has a value not equal to the value of any of the expressions is where you should hit the piñata to break it.

686

CALIFORNIA STANDARDS

• **Gr. 5 AF 1.3** Know and use the distributive property in equations and expressions with variables. *(Lesson 12.1)*

• **Alg. 1 10.0** Students add, subtract, multiply, and divide monomials and polynomials. Students solve multistep problems, including word problems, by using these techniques. *(Lessons 12.2, 12.3, 12.4)*

UNMASKING EXPRESSIONS

California Standards

Review simplifying expressions. **Gr. 7 AF 1.3**
Prepare for adding polynomials. **Alg. 1 10.0**

$x - 4x + 3 + 9x$

$5(x - 6) + 10x - 3$

$-7x + 8 - 2(3x + 4)$

$8x - 3 - 4(2x + 3)$

$4 - (3x - 1) + x$

$17 - 4x - 13 + 2x$

John	Maria	Sam	Carol	Vincent	Sophie
$6x + 3$	$-2x + 4$	$-13x$	-15	$-2x + 5$	$15x - 33$

How to Play

Find the person wearing each mask.

• Match the expression beneath each mask with its simplified form.

• The name that is above the correct simplified expression belongs to the person wearing the mask.

Games Wrap-Up

Draw Conclusions

Complete these exercises after playing the games.

1. **WRITING** *Explain* the steps for simplifying the expression that is given under the mask worn by Sam in *Unmasking Expressions.*

2. **REASONING** Write an expression, using negative exponents, whose value would *not* allow you to break the piñata in *Piñata Punch.*

687

Prerequisite Skills

California @HomeTutor
Prerequisite skills practice
at classzone.com

**REVIEW
VOCABULARY**

- **base,** *p. 5*
- **exponent,** *p. 5*
- **coefficient,** *p. 252*
- **like terms,** *p. 252*
- **monomial,** *p. 399*

VOCABULARY CHECK

Copy and complete using a review term from the list at the left.

1. In the monomial $2x^3$, the ___?___ is 2 and the ___?___ is 3.

2. A number, a variable, or a product of a number and one or more variables with whole number exponents is a(n) ___?___.

3. Terms that have identical variable parts with corresponding variables raised to the same power are ___?___.

SKILL CHECK

Simplify the expression. *(p. 252)*

4. $6x - 4 + 4x - 3$

5. $-5(2x + 3) - 4x$

6. $7(3x - 5) - (-x)$

7. $-2x - (-5x)$

8. $-2(-4x - 8)$

9. $-3(3x) + 18x$

Simplify. Write the expression using only positive exponents. *(pp. 386, 393)*

10. $\dfrac{y^4}{y^6}$

11. $\dfrac{5^{37}}{5^{35}}$

12. $x^4 \cdot x^5$

13. $2x^3 \cdot 4x^6$

14. $\dfrac{a^7}{a}$

15. $5b^2 \cdot 6b^8$

Notetaking Skills

NOW YOU TRY

Make a *Y chart* that compares the product of powers property with the power of a power property.

Focus on Graphic Organizers

You can use a *Y chart* to compare two concepts, such as the formulas for the volume of a prism and the volume of a cylinder. Highlight similar characteristics in the branches. List similarities in the lower box.

FORMULAS FOR THE VOLUME OF A PRISM AND A CYLINDER

VOLUME OF A PRISM
Volume = Bh
B = area of base
h = height

VOLUME OF A CYLINDER
Volume = Bh
B = area of base
h = height
Volume = $\pi r^2 h$

SIMILARITIES
Volume = Bh
B = area of base, h = height

12.1 Polynomials

Math and SPORTS
Example 3, p. 690

Standards Review Gr. 5 AF 1.3 Know and use the distributive property in equations and expressions with variables.

Connect *Before* you perfomed operations on monomials. *Now* you will use monomials to review Grade 5 AF Standard 1.3.

KEY VOCABULARY
- polynomial
- binomial
- trinomial
- standard form of a polynomial
- monomial, *p. 399*

In Lesson 7.3, you were introduced to monomials. A **polynomial** is a monomial or a sum of monomials. Each monomial in a polynomial is called a *term*. Polynomials are classified by the number of their terms when they are in simplified form. If a polynomial has more than three terms, it is simply called a polynomial.

Monomial	**Binomial**	**Trinomial**
(1 term)	(2 terms)	(3 terms)
$-2x$	$3x - 2$	$-2a^2 + 3a + 1$
4	$-s^4 + 6s^3$	$3 + 5r - 7r^2$

A polynomial in one variable is written in **standard form** if the exponents of the variable decrease from left to right.

Standard Form	**Not Standard Form**
$3x^3 - 2x^2 + 4$	$3 + 5y$
$-2m^6 + 5m^3 - m$	$7t^4 - t^7 - 2t^2 + 3t$

EXAMPLE 1 Writing Polynomials in Standard Form

 Write the polynomial in standard form and classify it.

AVOID ERRORS
If you do not see an exponent with a variable, then the exponent of the variable is 1.
$$2x = 2x^1$$

a. $x - 9 + 5x^2 = x + (-9) + 5x^2$ Write subtraction as addition.

$\qquad\qquad = 5x^2 + x + (-9)$ Order terms with decreasing exponents.

▶ **Answer** The polynomial $5x^2 + x - 9$ has 3 terms, so it is a trinomial.

b. $2x - 3x^3 = 2x + (-3x^3)$ Write subtraction as addition.

$\qquad\quad = -3x^3 + 2x$ Order terms with decreasing exponents.

▶ **Answer** The polynomial $-3x^3 + 2x$ has 2 terms, so it is a binomial.

 GUIDED PRACTICE   for Example 1

Write the polynomial in standard form and classify it.

1. $4 + b^2 - 8b$ **2.** $11 + 2n^4 - 7n + 5n^2$ **3.** $-5 + 3x^2$

SIMPLIFYING POLYNOMIALS Remember that *like terms* are terms that have identical variable parts with corresponding variables raised to the same power. To simplify a polynomial, combine like terms by adding their coefficients.

EXAMPLE 2 Simplifying Polynomials

 Simplify the polynomial and write it in standard form.

a. $3x^2 - 2x + 4x^2 - 3 = 3x^2 + 4x^2 - 2x - 3$ Group like terms.

$= 7x^2 - 2x - 3$ Simplify.

> *REVIEW LIKE TERMS*
> For help with like terms, see page 252. Remember that $x^2 = 1x^2$.

b. $x^2 + 2 + 4(x^2 - 2x) = x^2 + 2 + 4(x^2) - 4(2x)$ Distributive property

$= x^2 + 2 + 4x^2 - 8x$ Multiply.

$= x^2 + 4x^2 + 2 - 8x$ Group like terms.

$= 5x^2 + 2 - 8x$ Simplify.

$= 5x^2 - 8x + 2$ Write in standard form.

EXAMPLE 3 Evaluating a Polynomial Expression

 SOFTBALL You hit a softall with an initial velocity of 80 feet per second. The height (in feet) of the softball after t seconds can be found using the polynomial $-16t^2 + 80t + 2$. Find the height of the softball after 2 seconds.

Softball height:
$-16t^2 + 80t + 2$

SOLUTION

$-16t^2 + 80t + 2 = -16(2)^2 + 80(2) + 2$ Substitute 2 for t.

$= -16(4) + 80(2) + 2$ Evaluate the power.

$= -64 + 160 + 2$ Multiply.

$= 98$ Add.

▶ **Answer** The softball's height after 2 seconds is 98 feet.

✓ **GUIDED PRACTICE**   for Examples 2 and 3

Simplify the polynomial and write it in standard form.

4. $7p + 5p^2 - 2 - 3p^2$ **5.** $2(a^2 + 3a - 1) + 2a^2$

6. SOFTBALL In Example 3, find the height of the softball after 3 seconds.

12.1 EXERCISES

HOMEWORK KEY

◆ = **MULTIPLE CHOICE PRACTICE**
Exs. 11, 20, 34, 38–40

○ = **HINTS** AND **HOMEWORK HELP**
for Exs. 5, 17, 35 at classzone.com

SKILLS • PROBLEM SOLVING • REASONING

1. **VOCABULARY** Copy and complete: The polynomial $x^2 + 3x - 7$ has 3 terms, so it is a(n) __?__ .

2. **WRITING** *Explain* what it means to write a polynomial in standard form.

SEE EXAMPLE 1
on p. 689
for Exs. 3–11

CLASSIFYING Write the polynomial in standard form and classify it.

3. $7 + 3m$

4. $8 - n + 2n^2$

5. $5n - 1 - n^2$

6. $4b - 4 + 6b^3$

7. $2 - 5y + y^2$

8. $z^3 + 4z^2 + 7z^7$

9. $-13x^3 + 4x^{10}$

10. $3 - r^4 + r + 2r^3$

11. ◆ **MULTIPLE CHOICE** Which is the correct classification of $3(x^3 - 2x^2)$?

   (A) Monomial   (B) Binomial   (C) Trinomial   (D) None of these

SEE EXAMPLE 2
on p. 690
for Exs. 12–22

SIMPLIFYING Simplify the polynomial and write it in standard form.

12. $2c^2 - c^2 + 5c$

13. $4q^3 - 7q^5 + 3q - q^3$

14. $g^3 - 10 + 2g^2 - 5g^3$

15. $1 + 12m^2 - 5m + 6m - 7$

16. $3x^2 + 5(x^2 - 3x + 6)$

17. $-6(2y^3 - 4y^2 + 1) + 10y^2$

18. $-4(t - 3t^2 + 8 - 4t) + 6t^2 - 5$

19. $-3(-s^4 + 2s - 6 - s) - 8s + s^4$

20. ◆ **MULTIPLE CHOICE** Which polynomial is the standard form of $5(x^2 - 2x - 3) - 9x^2$?

   (A) $4x^2 + 10x - 15$

   (B) $-4x^2 + 10x - 15$

   (C) $-4x^2 - 15x - 10x$

   (D) $-4x^2 - 10x - 15$

ERROR ANALYSIS *Describe* and correct the error in simplifying the polynomial and writing it in standard form.

21.

$$\begin{aligned} -4(5x + 1) - 3x^2 \\ = -20x - 4 - 3x^2 \\ = -23x - 4 \end{aligned}$$

22.

$$\begin{aligned} -3(7x + 2) + 4x^2 \\ = -21x - 6 + 4x^2 \end{aligned}$$

GEOMETRY Write an expression for the perimeter in standard form.

23.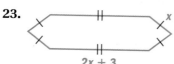
2x + 3

24.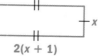
2(x + 1)

SIMPLIFYING POLYNOMIALS Simplify the polynomial.

25. $5a - 4(3b + 6) + 4b$

26. $-z^2 + 3z - 2(4y - 5z)$

27. $-3ab^2 + 2ab - 3ab^2 + 4ab$

28. $3xy + 2xy^2 - 5x^2y^2 + 3x^2y - 4xy$

CONNECT SKILLS TO PROBLEM SOLVING Exercises 29–32 will help you prepare for problem solving.

Use the following information: A player hits a baseball 88 ft/sec upward. Evaluate $-16t^2 + 88t + 2$ to find the ball's height (in feet) after the given number of seconds.

29. $t = 1.5$ **30.** $t = 2$ **31.** $t = 2.5$ **32.** $t = 3$

SEE EXAMPLE 3
on p. 690
for Exs. 33–34

33. FALLING OBJECTS You drop a pinecone from a bridge that is 150 feet high. The height (in feet) of the pinecone after falling for t seconds can be found using the polynomial $-16t^2 + 150$. Find the pinecone's height after 2 seconds.

(California @HomeTutor) for problem solving help at classzone.com

34. ◆ MULTIPLE CHOICE The height (in feet) of a pebble after t seconds of falling from a height of 45 feet can be found using the polynomial $-16t^2 + 45$. What is the pebble's height after 1.5 seconds?

A 9 ft   **B** 21 ft   **C** 24 ft   **D** 36 ft

(California @HomeTutor) for problem solving help at classzone.com

35. REASONING Tell whether the sum of a monomial and a binomial is *always*, *sometimes*, or *never* equal to a trinomial. *Justify* your reasoning.

36. CHALLENGE The amount of waste generated y (in millions of tons) can be modeled by $y = 0.00287x^4 - 0.139x^3 + 2.09x^2 - 5.16x + 149$ where x is the number of years since 1980. In what year were about 182 million tons of waste generated?

37. CHALLENGE Determine whether the equation $4g^2 + 3g = 7g^3$ is true for *all*, *some*, or *no* values of g. *Explain* your reasoning.

◆ CALIFORNIA STANDARDS SPIRAL REVIEW

MG 2.4

38. Two square feet is equal to how many square inches? *(p. 437)*

A 48 in.^{2} **B** 144 in.^{2} **C** 288 in.^{2} **D** 576 in.^{2}

SDAP 1.1

39. What is the range of the data in the stem-and-leaf plot? *(p. 650)*

A 0.26   **B** 2

```
2 | 1 5 7 9
3 | 2 6 9
4 | 0 7      Key: 2|1 = 21
```

C 6   **D** 26

MG 2.2

40. A rectangular canvas has the dimensions shown. The canvas is painted blue and white, and the white portion consists of two congruent isosceles triangles. How many square feet of the canvas are painted blue? *(p. 463)*

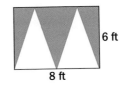

6 ft

8 ft

A 18 ft^2 **B** 24 ft^2 **C** 36 ft^2 **D** 48 ft^2

12.2 Adding and Subtracting Polynomials

Math and **DESIGN**
Example 4, p. 695

Standards Preview

Alg. 1 10.0 Students add, subtract, multiply, and divide **monomials and polynomials. Students solve multistep problems, including word problems, by using these techniques.**

Connect *Before* you simplified and classified polynomials. *Now* you will add and subtract polynomials to prepare for Algebra 1 Standard 10.0.

KEY VOCABULARY
- **opposite,** *p. 14*
- **like terms,** *p. 252*

ACTIVITY

You can model polynomial addition with algebra tiles.

x^2-tile   *x*-tile   1-tile

STEP 1 **Write** the two polynomials represented by the two groups of algebra tiles below.

STEP 2 **Group** *like* algebra tiles to model the sum of the polynomials. Draw your model. Write the polynomial that your drawing represents.

STEP 3 **Use** algebra tiles to model the sum of the polynomials below. Write the polynomial that your model represents.

   a. $(3x^2 + 6x + 1) + (x^2 + x)$ **b.** $(2x^2 + 3x + 1) + (4x^2 + x)$

In the activity, you used algebra tiles to add two polynomials. You add polynomials by combining like terms.

EXAMPLE 1 Adding Polynomials Vertically

Find the sum $(-4x^3 + x^2 - 3x - 1) + (4x^2 - 7x + 5)$.

$$
\begin{array}{r}
-4x^3 + x^2 - 3x - 1 \\
+ \qquad\quad 4x^2 - 7x + 5 \\
\hline
-4x^3 + 5x^2 - 10x + 4
\end{array}
$$

Write the second polynomial under the first.

Arrange like terms in columns.

Add like terms.

HORIZONTAL ADDITION In Example 1, you combined like terms vertically. You can also add polynomials by combining like terms horizontally. When you regroup terms, move a subtraction or addition sign with the term that follows it.

EXAMPLE 2 Adding Polynomials Horizontally

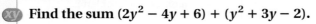 Find the sum $(2y^2 - 4y + 6) + (y^2 + 3y - 2)$.

SOLUTION

$$(2y^2 - 4y + 6) + (y^2 + 3y - 2)$$
$$= 2y^2 + y^2 - 4y + 3y + 6 - 2 \qquad \text{Group like terms.}$$
$$= 3y^2 - y + 4 \qquad \text{Combine like terms.}$$

Animated Math

For an interactive example of adding polynomials, go to **classzone.com**.

✓ **GUIDED PRACTICE** for Examples 1 and 2

Find the sum.

1. $(6x^2 - 3x + 1) + (3x^3 + 4x^2 - 5x)$ 2. $(5n^2 + 2n - 9) + (3n^2 - 4)$

3. $(y^2 - y + 1) + (-2y^2 + 2y - 1)$ 4. $(3p^2 - p - 1) + (p^2 + p - 4)$

SUBTRACTING POLYNOMIALS You can subtract a polynomial by adding its *opposite*. To find the opposite of a polynomial, multiply each of its terms by -1. You can subtract polynomials vertically or horizontally.

EXAMPLE 3 Subtracting Polynomials Vertically

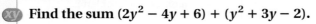 Find the difference $(4x^3 + 5x^2 - 2x - 5) - (3x^3 - 4x + 2)$.

SOLUTION

AVOID ERRORS
Be sure to write the opposite of every term in the second polynomial, not just the first term.

STEP 1 Find the opposite of the second polynomial.

$$-(3x^3 - 4x + 2) = -3x^3 + 4x - 2$$

STEP 2 Find the sum $(4x^3 + 5x^2 - 2x - 5) + (-3x^3 + 4x - 2)$.

$$\begin{array}{r} 4x^3 + 5x^2 - 2x - 5 \\ + \ -3x^3 \qquad\quad + 4x - 2 \\ \hline x^3 + 5x^2 + 2x - 7 \end{array}$$

Write the second polynomial under the first.
Arrange like terms in columns.
Add like terms.

✓ **GUIDED PRACTICE** for Example 3

Find the difference.

5. $(4r^2 - r + 8) - (r^2 + 6r - 1)$ 6. $(6m^2 + 2m - 3) - (7m^2 + 4)$

7. $(9x^2 + 4x - 3) - (-2x^2 + x)$ 8. $(-5y^2 + 2) - (2y^3 + y^2 - 6y)$

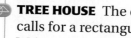 **Finding Geometric Measures**

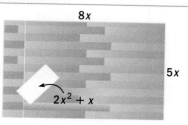

TREE HOUSE The design for a tree house calls for a rectangular hole in the floor. Write a polynomial expression for the area of the tree house floor.

SOLUTION

To find the area of the floor, use the area of the two rectangles.

Area of Large Rectangle

$$8x \cdot 5x = 40x^2$$

Area of Small Rectangle

$$2x^2 + x$$

| Area of floor | = | Area of large rectangle | − | Area of small rectangle |

 AVOID ERRORS
Be sure to write the second polynomial in parentheses when subtracting.

$$= 40x^2 - (2x^2 + x) \qquad \text{Substitute.}$$
$$= 40x^2 + (-2x^2 - x) \qquad \text{Add the opposite.}$$
$$= 38x^2 - x \qquad \text{Combine like terms.}$$

▶ **Answer** A polynomial expression for the area of the floor is $38x^2 - x$.

✓ **GUIDED PRACTICE** for Example 4

9. **WHAT IF?** Suppose the tree house in Example 4 has a length of $10x$ and a width of $6x$, and the area of the rectangular hole is $4x^2 - 2x$. Write a polynomial expression for the area of the tree house floor.

12.2 EXERCISES

HOMEWORK KEY

◆ = **MULTIPLE CHOICE PRACTICE**
Exs. 12, 22, 40, 48–50

○ = **HINTS AND HOMEWORK HELP**
for Exs. 7, 25, 43 at classzone.com

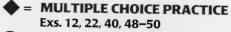 **SKILLS • PROBLEM SOLVING • REASONING**

1. **VOCABULARY** *Explain* how to find the opposite of a polynomial.

2. **WRITING** *Describe* the similarities and differences between adding and subtracting integers and adding and subtracting polynomials.

SEE EXAMPLES 1 AND 2
on pp. 693–694
for Exs. 3–12

ADDING POLYNOMIALS Find the sum.

3. $(8y + 5) + (4y - 3)$

4. $(x - 6) + (2x + 9)$

5. $(4x + 7) + (x - 3)$

6. $(-2a - 9) + (a + 4)$

 7. $(-g^2 + g + 9) + (7g^2 - 6)$

8. $(3z^2 - 2z + 1) + (4z^3 + 3z)$

9. $(2k^2 + 5k + 7) + (4k^2 - 5k - 2)$

10. $(6x^3 - 12x + 1) + (8x^2 - 4x + 2)$

11. **ERROR ANALYSIS** *Describe* and correct the error in finding the sum of the polynomials $(-4x^3 + 5x^2 - 7x + 2)$ and $(2x^3 - 6x + 10)$.

$$
\begin{array}{r}
-4x^3 + 5x^2 - 7x + 2 \\
+ \quad 2x^3 \quad - 6x + 10 \\
\hline
-2x^3 - \quad x^2 + 3x + 2
\end{array}
$$

12. ◆ **MULTIPLE CHOICE** What is the sum of the polynomials $(x^3 - 9x + 3)$ and $(-7x^3 + 4x^2 - 1)$?

Ⓐ $-6x^3 + 4x^2 - 9x + 2$　　　Ⓑ $-8x^3 + 4x^2 - 9x - 4$

Ⓒ $-6x^3 + 5x^2 + 2$　　　Ⓓ $-8x^3 - 5x^2 + 4$

SEE EXAMPLE 3
on p. 694
for Exs. 13–22

SUBTRACTING POLYNOMIALS **Find the difference.**

13. $(7x + 10) - (x - 2)$

14. $(4p + 1) - (p - 7)$

15. $(-5d - 1) - (5d + 6)$

16. $(7y + 1) - (3y - 2)$

17. $(6r^2 + 2r - 5) - (3r^2 - 9)$

18. $(-4b^3 - 9b + 2) - (b^3 - b + 3)$

19. $(5a^2 + 3a + 8) - (2a^2 - 2a - 9)$

20. $(4p^3 + p^2 - 8) - (7p^3 + 2p + 5)$

21. **ERROR ANALYSIS** *Describe* and correct the error in finding the difference $(8x^2 - 6x + 4) - (5x^2 + 2x - 1)$.

$$
\begin{array}{r}
8x^2 - 6x + 4 \\
+ \quad -5x^2 + 2x - 1 \\
\hline
3x^2 - 4x + 3
\end{array}
$$

22. ◆ **MULTIPLE CHOICE** What is the difference of the polynomials $(3x^3 + 6x + 9)$ and $(3x^3 - 2x^2 + 8x)$?

Ⓐ $-2x^2 + 2x - 9$　　　Ⓑ $2x^2 - 2x + 9$

Ⓒ $6x^3 - 2x^2 + 2x + 9$　　　Ⓓ $6x^3 + 4x + 9$

SIMPLIFYING EXPRESSIONS **Simplify the expression.**

23. $(4n - 3) + (9n + 5) - (n - 1)$

24. $(-8m + 1) - (2m - 6) + 5m$

25. $-2(5y + 3) - 9(y + 1)$

26. $4(-3s^2 + s - 4) + (5s^2 + s + 7)$

27. $3(q^2 - q) + 2(7q^2 - 2q)$

28. $6(t^3 - t^2 + 3t) - 4(5t^3 + t^2 - t)$

29. $5(4x^3 - 2x^2 + 1) + 3(7x^2 - 5x)$

30. $-7(2v^4 + 3v^2 - 1) - 5(-3v^3 - 6)$

SEE EXAMPLE 4
on p. 695
for Exs. 31–32

 GEOMETRY **Write a polynomial expression for the perimeter of the figure. Simplify the polynomial.**

31.

$-x^2 + 11x + 8$　　$x^2 + 3x - 4$

$2x^2 - x + 10$

32.

$2x^2 - 2x + 3$

$-x^2 + 10x + 1$

SOLVING EQUATIONS **Solve the equation.**

33. $(2x^2 - 3x + 4) - (x^2 - 3x + 13) = 0$

34. $(-6x^2 + 7x - 5) - (-6x^2 - 5x + 7) = 0$

35. $(-7x^2 + 6x - 2) + (8x^2 - 6x - 10) = 0$

36. $(4x^2 + 7x - 11) + (-4x^2 - 3x - 9) = 0$

CONNECT SKILLS TO PROBLEM SOLVING Exercises 37–39 will help you prepare for problem solving.

Use the following information: You use the length of your shoe to measure the perimeter of a rectangular rug. You know your shoe is *x* inches long. Write an expression in terms of *x* for the perimeter of the rug with the given measurements.

37. $l = 3$ shoe lengths and 2 inches, $w = 5$ shoe lengths and 4 inches

38. $l = 6$ shoe lengths less 3 inches, $w = 4$ shoe lengths less 2 inches

39. $l = 8$ shoe lengths and 3 inches, $w = 4$ shoe lengths less 5 inches

SEE EXAMPLE 4
on p. 695
for Exs. 40–41

40. ◆ **MULTIPLE CHOICE** The perimeter of the rectangle shown is 118 feet. What is the value of *x*?

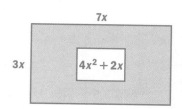
(3x + 4) ft
(2x + 5) ft

   A 10   **B** 21.8   **C** 29.5   **D** 38

California @HomeTutor for problem solving help at classzone.com

41. **SHORT RESPONSE** *Explain* how to find the area of wallboard needed to cover the wall shown, not including the window. Then find the area as a polynomial in standard form.

7x
3x
$4x^2 + 2x$

California @HomeTutor for problem solving help at classzone.com

READING IN MATH Read the information below for Exercises 42–44.

Basketball In 1891, Dr. James Naismith invented the game of basketball to occupy his students during gym class at a YMCA. He hung peach baskets on a railing and used a soccer ball instead of a basketball. Five years later, Stanford and Berkeley played the first women's intercollegiate game. The original rules resulted in a low-scoring game: Stanford 2, Berkeley 1.

Basketball continues to be a popular sport. During the period 1999–2004, the number of boys *B* and girls *G* who participated in high school basketball can be modeled by

$$B = -231.852t^3 + 2596.07t^2 - 9929.69t + 549{,}198$$
$$G = -436.611t^3 + 3809.26t^2 - 7920.65t + 456{,}676$$

where *t* is the number of years since 1999.

42. **Write** Write a polynomial expression for the total number of students that participated in high school basketball during the period 1999–2004.

43. **Write** Write a polynomial expression for the difference in boys and girls participation in high school basketball during the period 1999–2004.

44. **Evaluate** Approximately how many girls participated in high school basketball in 2003? How many boys participated that year?

Dr. James Naismith

45. ⚙ **GEOMETRY** You are constructing two wooden pyramids with square bases using the designs shown. Write a simplified polynomial expression for the total surface area of the two pyramids.

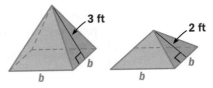
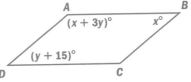

46. **CHALLENGE** Let A and B represent polynomial expressions. Find A and B in terms of z if $A + B = 5z - 4$ and $A - B = 3z + 10$.

47. **CHALLENGE** A tile is in the shape of a parallelogram, as shown. Find the values of x and y. (*Hint:* Opposite angles of a parallelogram are congruent.)

◆ **CALIFORNIA STANDARDS SPIRAL REVIEW**

MG 1.3

48. The density of water is 1 gram per cubic centimeter. The density of ice is 920,000 grams per cubic meter. Which statement is true? *(p. 449)*

    (A) Ice is denser than water.   **(B)** Water is denser than ice.

    (C) They have the same density.   **(D)** You cannot tell which is denser.

MG 3.5

49. The net shown represents which solid? *(p. 580)*

    (A) Cone   **(B)** Square pyramid

    (C) Cube   **(D)** Cylinder

MG 2.3

50. A store sells paint in two sizes of similar cylindrical cans. The smaller can has a volume of 50 cubic inches. The scale factor of the larger can to the smaller can is 2. What is the volume of the larger can? *(p. 605)*

    (A) 100 in.^{3} **(B)** 200 in.^{3} **(C)** 300 in.^{3} **(D)** 400 in.^{3}

QUIZ *for Lessons 12.1–12.2*

Simplify the polynomial and write it in standard form. *(p. 689)*

1. $5x^2 + 4x - 3x^2 - 11x$

2. $-5k^3 - 2(3k^3 + k - 4)$

Find the sum or difference. *(p. 693)*

3. $(6n^3 - 2n^2) + (n^3 + 7n^2 - 4n)$

4. $(4b^2 - 3b + 8) - (2b^2 - 6)$

5. $(x^2 + 6x + 1) - (2x^2 - 8x + 4)$

6. $(3m^2 + m - 9) + (7m^2 + 2m - 5)$

7. **LAWN** An L-shaped lawn has the dimensions shown. Write a polynomial expression for the perimeter of the lawn. *(p. 693)*

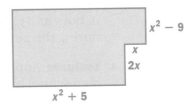

12.3 Multiplying Polynomials by Monomials

Standards Preview

Alg. 1 10.0 Students add, subtract, **multiply**, and divide **monomials** and **polynomials. Students solve multistep problems, including word problems, by using these techniques.**

Connect *Before* you added and subtracted polynomials. *Now* you will multiply polynomials by monomials to prepare for Algebra 1 Standard 10.0.

Math and **ENTERTAINMENT** Example 3, p. 700

KEY VOCABULARY
• **monomial,** *p. 399*
• **polynomial,** *p. 689*

You can use the distributive property and the properties of exponents to find the product of a monomial and a polynomial.

EXAMPLE 1 Using the Distributive Property

 Simplify the expression.

a. $2n(4n^2 - 5)$

b. $7y^3(6y^5 + 9y^4)$

SOLUTION

a. $2n(4n^2 - 5) = 2n(4n^2) - 2n(5)$ **Distributive property**

$= 8 \cdot n \cdot n^2 - 10 \cdot n$ **Multiply coefficients.**

$= 8n^3 - 10n$ **Product of powers property**

b. $7y^3(6y^5 + 9y^4) = 7y^3(6y^5) + 7y^3(9y^4)$ **Distributive property**

$= 42 \cdot y^3 \cdot y^5 + 63 \cdot y^3 \cdot y^4$ **Multiply coefficients.**

$= 42y^8 + 63y^7$ **Product of powers property**

EXAMPLE 2 Multiplying a Monomial and a Trinomial

 Simplify the expression.

a. $(x^3 - 3x + 8)3x^2$

b. $a^5(4a^3 - 2a^2 + a)$

About the Standards

The strategy used to simplify the expressions in Example 1 can also be used to simplify the more complex expressions in Example 2 (MR 2.2).

SOLUTION

a. $(x^3 - 3x + 8)3x^2$ **Write product.**

$= x^3(3x^2) - 3x(3x^2) + 8(3x^2)$ **Distributive property**

$= 3 \cdot x^3 \cdot x^2 - 9 \cdot x \cdot x^2 + 24 \cdot x^2$ **Multiply coefficients.**

$= 3x^5 - 9x^3 + 24x^2$ **Product of powers property**

b. $a^5(4a^3 - 2a^2 + a)$ **Write product.**

$= a^5(4a^3) - a^5(2a^2) + a^5(a)$ **Distributive property**

$= 4a^8 - 2a^7 + a^6$ **Product of powers property**

EXAMPLE 3 ◆ Multiple Choice Practice

A small outdoor music festival has reserved seats in a roped-off area in front of the main stage. The rectangular roped-off area is connected to the stage as shown below. Festival organizers have 70 feet of rope. Let l represent the length (in feet) of the roped-off area, and let w represent the width (in feet) of the roped-off area. What is a polynomial expression in terms of w that represents the area of the reserved seating?

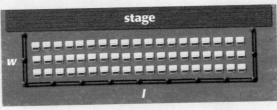

(A) $35l - \frac{1}{2}l^2$ **(B)** $70 - 2w$ **(C)** $35w - w^2$ **(D)** $70w - 2w^2$

ELIMINATE CHOICES
You know that the polynomial expression should be in terms of w. So, you can eliminate choice A.

SOLUTION

STEP 1 **Write** the equation given the length R of rope needed in terms of l and w. From the diagram, you can see that $R = l + 2w$. (Note that there is no rope along the side of the seating area that is adjacent to the stage.) Solve this equation for l after substituting 70 for R.

$R = l + 2w$ Write equation.

$70 = l + 2w$ Substitute 70 for **R**.

$70 - 2w = l$ Subtract 2**w** from each side.

STEP 2 **Find** the area in terms of w.

$A = lw$ Formula for area of a rectangle

$= (70 - 2w)w$ Substitute 70 − 2**w** for **l**.

$= 70w - 2w(w)$ Distributive property

$= 70w - 2w^2$ Product of powers property

The area can be represented by the polynomial $70w - 2w^2$.

▶ **Answer** The correct answer is D. Ⓐ Ⓑ Ⓒ ●

✓ **GUIDED PRACTICE**   for Examples 1, 2, and 3

Simplify the expression.

1. $p(2p + 3)$

2. $-2x^3(4x^2 + 2x - 7)$

3. **WHAT IF?** In Example 3, suppose the organizers have 100 feet of rope to rope-off the reserved seating area. Write a polynomial expression in terms of the width w that represents the area of the reserved seating.

SKILLS • PROBLEM SOLVING • REASONING

1. **VOCABULARY** Copy and complete: A monomial or a sum of monomials is called a(n) __?__ .

2. **NOTETAKING SKILLS** Make a *Y chart* like the one on page 688 that compares multiplying two monomials with multiplying a monomial and a polynomial.

SEE EXAMPLE 1
on p. 699
for Exs. 3–9

USING THE DISTRIBUTIVE PROPERTY **Simplify the expression.**

3. $2w(3w + 1)$

4. $-t(t^2 - 4)$

5. $-8x^2(x^5 + x)$

6. $(12 - k^5)3k^2$

7. $(3q + 6)4q^3$

8. $-7a^2(5a^3 - 9a)$

9. ◆ **MULTIPLE CHOICE** Which expression is equivalent to $-4x^2(x + 5)$?

Ⓐ $-4x^3 + 5$ Ⓑ $-4x^3 - 20x$ Ⓒ $-4x^3 + 20x^2$ Ⓓ $-4x^3 - 20x^2$

SEE EXAMPLE 2
on p. 699
for Exs. 10–16

MULTIPLYING A MONOMIAL AND A TRINOMIAL **Simplify the expression.**

10. $2(4x^2 + 3x + 1)$

11. $(3y^3 - 5y - 10)y$

12. $-3m(2m^2 + m + 7)$

13. $(5n^3 - 8n^2 + 3n)n^2$

14. $5a^2(-a^4 + 2a^2 + 9)$

15. $-2t^3(9t^3 - 4t^2 + t)$

16. ◆ **MULTIPLE CHOICE** Which expression is equivalent to $3b^2(-4b^2 - 5b - 7)$?

Ⓐ $-b^2 - 5b - 7$

Ⓑ $-12b^2 - 15b - 21$

Ⓒ $-12b^4 - 15b^3 - 21b^2$

Ⓓ $-12b^4 - 15b^2 - 21$

ERROR ANALYSIS *Describe* and correct the error in finding the product of a monomial and a polynomial.

17.
$$
\begin{array}{l}
\times \quad -x(x^2 + 7) \\
\quad = x \cdot x^2 + x \cdot 7 \\
\quad = x^3 + 7x
\end{array}
$$

18.
$$
\begin{array}{l}
\times \quad x^2(3x^2 + 2x - 8) \\
\quad = x^2 \cdot 3x^2 + 2x - 8 \\
\quad = 3x^4 + 2x - 8
\end{array}
$$

CONNECT SKILLS TO PROBLEM SOLVING Exercises 19–21 will help you prepare for problem solving.

Write a polynomial expression in terms of the given variable for the area of the object described.

19. The length of a rectangular room is 10 feet less than twice the width w.

20. The height of a triangular rug is 4 inches greater than the base b.

21. The length l of a rectangular table is 20 inches greater than the width.

22. PHOTO ALBUM You are making photo albums in different sizes. The photo area on each page is twice as long as it is wide and needs a 2 inch margin for binding. Write a polynomial expression for the total area of one page.

California @HomeTutor for problem solving help at classzone.com

2w

2 in.   w

23. SEAT CUSHION You need fabric for a window seat cushion that is in the shape of a trapezoid. The lengths of the bases of the trapezoid are $3b$ and b, and the height is $b - 6$. Write a polynomial expression for the area of the trapezoid.

California @HomeTutor for problem solving help at classzone.com

24. FLOOR AREA Write a polynomial expression for the area of the floor surrounding the rug in the diagram.

x

$2x$ $x - 3$

$3x$

25. ◆ **MULTIPLE CHOICE** You are using 20 feet of fence to make a rectangular dog pen that will be attached to your house. Let w represent the length (in feet) of the two sides of the pen that are perpendicular to the side of your house. What is a polynomial expression in terms of w for the area of the pen?

A $20w - 2w^2$ **B** $20w - 2w$ **C** $10 - w$ **D** $10w - w^2$

26. CHALLENGE Copy and complete the statement with a monomial:
$8a^6 + 64a^3 = \underline{\ ?\ } \cdot (a^3 + 8)$.

27. CHALLENGE The length of a rectangular kitchen is 3 feet more than the width w of the kitchen. There is a rectangular built-in kitchen island. Its width is one third of the kitchen's width, and its length is 15 feet less than the length of the kitchen. Write an expression in terms of w for the area of the kitchen floor, not including the area covered by the island.

◆ CALIFORNIA STANDARDS SPIRAL REVIEW

AF 2.2

28. Which expression is equivalent to $\sqrt{20x^4}$? *(p. 399)*

A $2x^2\sqrt{10}$ **B** $4x^2\sqrt{5}$ **C** $4x^2$ **D** $2x^2\sqrt{5}$

NS 1.4

29. Which of the following is an irrational number? *(p. 225)*

A 0.1014 **B** $0.\overline{3}$ **C** $\sqrt{16}$ **D** $\sqrt{32}$

AF 3.2

30. Which table represents the graph that shows the volume V of a cube-shaped crate with side length x? *(p. 413)*

A

x	1	2	3
V	1	8	27

B

x	1	8	27
V	1	2	3

C

x	1	2	3
V	1	2	3

D

x	1	8	27
V	1	8	27

Volume

20
10
0
0 1 2 3 x
Side length

12.3 Graphing Polynomial Functions

Standards Preview

Alg. 1 10.0 Students add, subtract, **multiply,** and divide **monomials and polynomials.** Students solve multistep problems, including word problems, by using these techniques.

QUESTION How can you use a graph to check your work with polynomials?

EXAMPLE Check a product of a monomial and a polynomial

Tell whether the product is correct.

a. $2x(3x - 1) \stackrel{?}{=} 6x^2 - 2x$

b. $-x(2x^2 + x - 4) \stackrel{?}{=} -2x^3 + x^2 + 4x$

SOLUTION

STEP 1 **Enter** the original expression in y_1. Enter the product in y_2.

a.

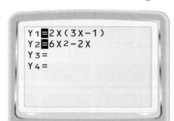

b.

STEP 2 **Select** a normal graph style for y_1. Select a thick graph style for y_2.

a.

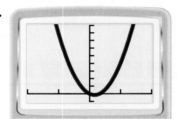

b.

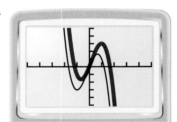

STEP 3 **Compare** the two curves in each graph. In graph (a), the thick curve coincides with the thin curve, so the product is correct. In graph (b), the thick curve does *not* coincide with the thin curve, so the product is incorrect.

PRACTICE

Tell whether the product is correct. Correct any incorrect answers.

1. $-x(4x - 9) \stackrel{?}{=} -4x^2 + 9x$

2. $2x(x^2 + 3) \stackrel{?}{=} 2x^3 + 3$

3. $3x(-x^2 + 4x - 4) \stackrel{?}{=} -3x^3 + 12x^2 - 12x$

4. $-4x(x^2 - 2x + 1) \stackrel{?}{=} -4x^3 - 8x^2 - 4x$

12.4 Multiplying Binomials

MATERIALS · algebra tiles

**Standards
Preview**

Alg. 1 10.0
Students add, subtract,
multiply, and divide
monomials and
polynomials. Students
solve multistep problems,
including word problems,
by using these
techniques.

QUESTION How can algebra tiles be used to multiply binomials?

You can model binomial multiplication with algebra tiles.

EXPLORE Model a product with algebra tiles

Model the product $(x + 3)(3x + 2)$ with algebra tiles.

STEP 1 **Model** each binomial
with algebra tiles. Arrange
the first binomial vertically
and the second binomial
horizontally, as shown.

STEP 2 **Notice** that the binomials
define a rectangular area
with length $(3x + 2)$ units
and width $(x + 3)$ units. Fill in
the region with the appropriate
tiles, as shown.

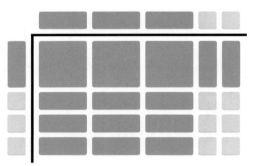

STEP 3 **Add** the areas of the rectangles on the inside of the model to see that
the total area is $3x^2 + 11x + 6$. This is the product of the binomials.

DRAW CONCLUSIONS Use your observations to complete these exercises

Find the product with algebra tiles. Draw your model.

1. $(x + 1)(x + 2)$ **2.** $(x + 4)(x + 4)$ **3.** $(x + 2)(2x + 2)$

Model the expression with algebra tiles. Arrange the tiles in a rectangle.
Find the two binomials that have this product.

4. $x^2 + 5x + 6$ **5.** $x^2 + 2x + 1$ **6.** $3x^2 + 8x + 4$

7. REASONING *Describe* how these models relate to the distributive property.

12.4 **Multiplying Binomials**

Standards Preview **Alg. 1 10.0** Students add, subtract, **multiply**, and divide monomials and **polynomials. Students solve multistep problems, including word problems, by using these techniques.**

Connect *Before* you multiplied polynomials by monomials. *Now* you will multiply binomials by binomials to prepare for Algebra 1 Standard 10.0.

Math and **PERFORMING ARTS** Ex. 37, p. 708

KEY VOCABULARY
- **polynomial,** *p. 689*
- **binomial,** *p. 689*

Visual models can be used to multiply binomials. The model below shows that $(x + 2)(3x + 1) = 3x^2 + 7x + 2$.

	x	x	x	1
x	x^2	x^2	x^2	x
1	x	x	x	1
1	x	x	x	1

$x + 2$

$3x + 1$

You can multiply two binomials using a vertical or horizontal method.

EXAMPLE 1 ◆ **Multiple Choice Practice**

ANOTHER WAY
For an alternative method for solving the problem in Example 1, turn to page 710 for the **Problem Solving Workshop**.

> **What is the product of $2x - 5$ and $3x + 4$?**
>
> **A** $5x - 1$ **B** $6x^2 - 7x - 20$
>
> **C** $6x^2 - 20$ **D** $6x^2 + 8x - 20$

SOLUTION

Find the product $(2x - 5)(3x + 4)$ and simplify.

$$
\begin{array}{r}
2x - 5 \\
\times \quad 3x + 4 \\
\hline
8x - 20 \\
6x^2 - 15x \\
\hline
6x^2 - 7x - 20
\end{array}
$$

Write the first binomial.

Write the second binomial.

Multiply 4 and $2x - 5$.

Multiply $3x$ and $2x - 5$. Line up like terms.

Add $8x - 20$ and $6x^2 - 15x$.

The product of $2x - 5$ and $3x + 4$ is $6x^2 - 7x - 20$.

▶ **Answer** The correct answer is B. Ⓐ **Ⓑ** Ⓒ Ⓓ

✓ **GUIDED PRACTICE** **for Example 1**

1. Use a vertical method to find the product of $3x + 1$ and $9x + 3$.

DISTRIBUTIVE PROPERTY Another way to multiply binomials is to use the distributive property to multiply the binomials horizontally.

EXAMPLE 2 Multiplying Binomials Horizontally

BANKING You deposit $1 into a savings account with interest compounded annually. The balance of the account after two years can be found using the expression $(1 + r)^2$ where r represents the annual interest rate. Expand this expression and simplify.

SOLUTION

To expand the expression, multiply two binomials.

$$(1 + r)^2 = (1 + r)(1 + r) \qquad \text{$(1 + r)^2$ means $(1 + r)(1 + r)$.}$$
$$= 1(1 + r) + r(1 + r) \qquad \text{Distributive property}$$
$$= 1 + r + r + r^2 \qquad \text{Distributive property}$$
$$= 1 + 2r + r^2 \qquad \text{Combine like terms.}$$
$$= r^2 + 2r + 1 \qquad \text{Write in standard form.}$$

THE FOIL METHOD The letters in the word FOIL can help you remember how to multiply binomials. The letters should remind you to multiply the First pair, Outer pair, Inner pair, and Last pair.

$$(a + b)\ (c + d) = ac + ad + bc + bd$$

EXAMPLE 3 Multiplying with the FOIL Method

Find the product $(2x + 3)(3x - 1)$ and simplify.

F		O		I		L	
First	+	Outer	+	Inner	+	Last	
$2x \cdot 3x$	+	$2x \cdot (-1)$	+	$3 \cdot 3x$	+	$3 \cdot (-1)$	Use FOIL.
$6x^2$	+	$(-2x)$	+	$9x$	+	(-3)	Multiply.
		$6x^2 + 7x - 3$					Combine like terms.

✓ **GUIDED PRACTICE** for Examples 2 and 3

Find the product and simplify.

2. $(x + 7)(x + 3)$ **3.** $(b - 4)(b - 3)$ **4.** $(3t - 4)(t + 2)$

5. $(d + 6)(d + 5)$ **6.** $(x - 3)(x - 1)$ **7.** $(5s + 3)(2s - 4)$

12.4 EXERCISES

HOMEWORK KEY

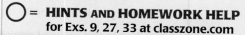

◆ = **MULTIPLE CHOICE PRACTICE**
Exs. 22, 23, 33, 43–45

◯ = **HINTS** AND **HOMEWORK HELP**
for Exs. 9, 27, 33 at classzone.com

SKILLS • PROBLEM SOLVING • REASONING

1. **VOCABULARY** Copy and complete: A polynomial with two terms is called a(n) __?__ .

2. **WRITING** How is finding the product of two binomials like finding the product of a monomial and a polynomial? How is it different?

SEE EXAMPLE 1
on p. 705
for Exs. 3–8

MULTIPLYING VERTICALLY Find the product by multiplying vertically. Simplify the result.

3. $(y - 4)(y + 1)$

4. $(g + 3)(g + 7)$

5. $(x - 4)(x + 4)$

6. $(2m + 3)(m - 7)$

7. $(3q - 1)(5q - 1)$

8. $(7b - 3)(9b + 4)$

SEE EXAMPLES 1, 2, AND 3
on pp. 705–706
for Exs. 9–27

MULTIPLYING BINOMIALS Find the product and simplify.

9. $(x + 9)(x - 2)$

10. $(x + 3)(x - 3)$

11. $(6r + 7)(r - 1)$

12. $(2m + 7)(3m + 1)$

13. $(t - 1)(-3t - 4)$

14. $(2g + 9)(2g - 9)$

15. $(3x + 1)(3x - 1)$

16. $(6z + 5)(6z + 5)$

17. $(7b - 3)(-2b + 5)$

18. $\left(\frac{1}{2}x + 2\right)(4x - 6)$

19. $(9b - 12)\left(\frac{1}{3}b - 6\right)$

20. $(n^2 - 2)(n^2 + 1)$

21. **ERROR ANALYSIS** *Describe* and correct the error in multiplying the binomials.

$$\times \quad (x + 3)(x + 6) = (x \cdot x) + (3 \cdot 6)$$
$$= x^2 + 18$$

22. ◆ **MULTIPLE CHOICE** What is the product $(x - 5)(x - 5)$?

Ⓐ $x^2 - 10x + 25$ Ⓑ $x^2 - 10x - 25$ Ⓒ $x^2 + 10x + 25$ Ⓓ $x^2 - 25$

23. ◆ **MULTIPLE CHOICE** What is the product $(x + 6)(x - 2)$?

Ⓐ $x^2 - 4x - 12$ Ⓑ $x^2 - 4x + 4$ Ⓒ $x^2 + 4x + 12$ Ⓓ $x^2 + 4x - 12$

24. **ERROR ANALYSIS** *Describe* and correct the error in multiplying the binomials.

$$(x + 2)(x - 4) = x \cdot x + x \cdot 4 + 2 \cdot x + 2 \cdot (-4)$$
$$\times \qquad = x^2 + 4x + 2x - 8$$
$$= x^2 + 6x - 8$$

MEASUREMENT Write the figure's area as a polynomial in standard form.

25.

$4x + 4$

$2x + 1$

26.

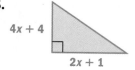

$x + 7$

$3x - 5$

27.

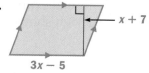

$x + 2$

$2x + 6$

$3x + 1$

CONNECT SKILLS TO PROBLEM SOLVING Exercises 28–30 will help you prepare for problem solving.

Write your answer as a polynomial in standard form.

28. What is the area of the shaded region?

29. What is the volume of the prism?

30. What is the surface area of the prism?

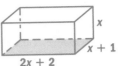

SEE EXAMPLE 2
on p. 706
for Exs. 31–32

31. COMPOUND INTEREST You deposit $50 into a savings account with interest compounded annually. The expression $50(1 + r)^2$, where r is the interest rate, gives the account balance after 2 years. Expand this expression and simplify. Find the account balance when $r = 0.03$.

> **California @HomeTutor** for problem solving help at classzone.com

32. ⬡ **AREA** The length of the side of a square tile is $x + 6$. Write a simplified polynomial for the area of the tile in terms of x. Find the area of the tile when $x = 4$.

> **California @HomeTutor** for problem solving help at classzone.com

㉝ ◆ **MULTIPLE CHOICE** You are framing your photo of Los Angeles. Which product gives the area of the photograph and frame?

ⓐ $(x + 18)(x + 8)$

ⓑ $(2x - 18)(2x - 8)$

ⓒ $(2x + 18)(2x + 8)$

ⓓ $(x - 18)(x - 8)$

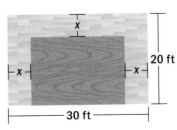

34. BASEBALL The middle of a baseball is a sphere made of cork and two layers of rubber with a radius of 0.6875 inch. Use the surface area formula $S = 4\pi r^2$ to write a polynomial expression in terms of x for the amount of leather needed to cover the ball. Expand the expression and simplify.

0.6875 in.

35. PUZZLE PROBLEM The base of a triangle is 6 inches less than twice a number n. The height of the triangle is 6 inches more than 6 times n. Write a simplified polynomial for the area of the triangle in terms of n.

36. REASONING *Describe* the pattern in the products of binomials like $(x - a)(x + a)$. Use the pattern to write $(x - 4)(x + 4)$ in standard form.

37. STAGE DESIGN You are building a platform on a 30 foot by 20 foot stage for a school talent show, as shown. Write and simplify a polynomial expression for the area of the platform using the design shown. Then find the area when x is 5 feet.

◆ = **MULTIPLE CHOICE PRACTICE**   ◯ = **HINTS AND HOMEWORK HELP** at classzone.com

CHALLENGE Copy and complete the statement with the correct binomial.

38. $x^2 + 8x + 7 = (\underline{})(x + 7)$

39. $x^2 + 6x + 8 = (x + 2)(\underline{})$

40. $x^2 - 9x + 14 = (\underline{})(x - 2)$

41. $x^2 - 7x - 18 = (x - 9)(\underline{})$

42. CHALLENGE A rectangular house is twice as long as it is wide. It is surrounded by a lawn that extends 15 feet from the house on all sides. There is a 3-foot-wide brick path from the street to the door.

   a. Find simplified expressions in terms of the house's width x (in feet) for the total area of the house and yard and for the area of the lawn.

   b. Suppose the house is 60 feet long. Find the area of the lawn.

◆ CALIFORNIA STANDARDS SPIRAL REVIEW

AF 4.1 **43.** What is the solution of the inequality $4x - 3 < 25$? *(p. 293)*

   (A) $x < 7$ **(B)** $x < 32$ **(C)** $x > 7$ **(D)** $x > 32$

MG 2.2 **44.** What is the area of the figure shown? *(p. 478)*

   (A) 24 cm^2 **(B)** 28 cm^2

   (C) 32 cm^2 **(D)** 34 cm^2

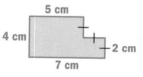

SDAP 1.2 **45.** A lifeguard monitors the number of people visiting a small beach and the high temperature each day for one week. The scatter plot shows the results. Which type of correlation do the data show? *(p. 660)*

   (A) Positive   **(B)** Negative

   (C) None   **(D)** Cannot be determined

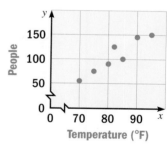

QUIZ *for Lessons 12.3–12.4*

Simplify the expression. *(p. 699)*

1. $y(y^2 + 4y + 7)$

2. $4m(2m^3 - m + 3)$

3. $2w^2(w^3 + 3w^2 - w)$

Find the product and simplify. *(p. 705)*

4. $(x + 9)(x - 1)$

5. $(b + 3)(4b - 3)$

6. $(4y + 5)(y - 2)$

7. $(a + 4)(a + 9)$

8. $(m - 2)(m - 8)$

9. $(3z - 2)(2z^2 - 7)$

10. SWIMMING POOL A swimming pool is surrounded by a walkway as shown. Write and simplify a polynomial expression for the area of the pool and walkway. *(p. 705)*

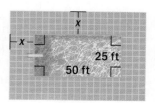

➡ **ONLINE QUIZ** at classzone.com

Using ALTERNATIVE METHODS

Another Way to Solve Example 1, page 705

Standards Preview

Alg. 1 10.0

In Example 1 on page 705, you found the product of two binomials using vertical multiplication. You can also multiply binomials using a table.

PROBLEM

What is the product of $2x - 5$ and $3x + 4$?

  Ⓐ $5x - 1$ Ⓑ $6x^2 - 7x - 20$

  Ⓒ $6x^2 - 20$ Ⓓ $6x^2 + 8x - 20$

METHOD

Using a Table An alternative approach is to use a table to find the product $(2x - 5)(3x + 4)$.

STEP 1 **Write** the terms of the first binomial on the left side of the table.

$2x$		
-5		

STEP 2 **Write** the terms of the second binomial above the table.

	$3x$	4
$2x$		
-5		

STEP 3 **Multiply** each term on the left of the table by each term above the table. Write the product in the corresponding cell of the table.

	$3x$	4
$2x$	$6x^2$	$8x$
-5	$-15x$	-20

STEP 4 **Add** the expressions in the table cells and combine like terms to find the product in standard form.

$$6x^2 + 8x - 15x - 20 = 6x^2 - 7x - 20$$

▸**Answer** The correct answer is B. Ⓐ Ⓑ Ⓒ Ⓓ

PRACTICE

1. **GEOMETRY** The side length of a square is $4x - 3$. Write a polynomial in standard form that represents the area of the square. Solve this problem using two methods.

2. **AREA** The height of a parallelogram is $x + 6$ and the base is $3x - 1$. Write a polynomial in standard form that represents the area of the parallelogram. Solve this problem using two methods.

3. **GARDEN** A rectangular garden has a length of $x + 5$ and a width of $x - 1$. Write a polynomial in standard form that represents the area of the garden.

4. **SWIMMING POOL** A circular swimming pool has a radius of $2x + 6$. Write a polynomial in standard form that represents the area of the swimming pool.

Multiple Choice Practice for Lessons 12.1–12.4

1. What is $(7x + 5) + (2x - 8)$? **Alg. 1 10.0**

   A $9x + 3$ **B** $5x + 3$

   C $9x - 3$ **D** $5x - 3$

2. The length of the longer side of a rectangle is 4 units greater than twice the length x of the shorter side. What is a polynomial expression for the perimeter of the rectangle? **Alg . 1 10.0**

   A $2x + 4$ **B** $3x + 4$

   C $4x + 8$ **D** $6x + 8$

3. Which expression is the simplified form of $3(x^2 - 4x) + 2x$? **Gr. 5 AF 1.3**

   A $3x^2 - 10x$ **B** $3x^2 - 14x$

   C $3x^2 - 6x$ **D** $3x^2 + 10x$

4. To make a set of coasters, you cut identical circles out of a piece of clay rolled into a flat square as shown. Which expression represents the area of clay that remains after you remove the circles? **Alg. 1 10.0, MR 2.2**

   A $4r^2 - 4\pi r^2$

   B $12r^2$

   C $16r^2 - 4\pi r^2$

   D $16r^2 - \pi r^2$

   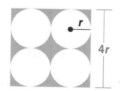

5. Which expression is the simplified form of $-x^2(5x^2 - 2x)$? **Alg. 1 10.0**

   A $-3x^3$ **B** $-5x^4 + 2x^2$

   C $4x^2 - 2x$ **D** $-5x^4 + 2x^3$

6. Which polynomial represents the area of the rug in square feet? **Alg. 1 10.0**

   $2x - 1$

   $x + 1$

   A $2x^2 - 1$ **B** $2x^2 - x + 1$

   C $2x^2 + x - 1$ **D** $2x^2 - x - 1$

7. The perimeter of a square office floor is 28 feet. The length of each wall is 1 foot more than twice the length x (in feet) of the desk. What is the length of the desk? **Alg. 1 10.0**

   A 3 ft **B** 7 ft

   C 12 ft **D** 25 ft

8. Three Coast Guard ships are searching for a lost fishing boat. The fishing boat is somewhere in the triangle formed by the three ships. The triangle is shown below. Which polynomial represents the number of square miles the Coast Guard has to search? **Alg. 1 10.0, MR 2.6**

   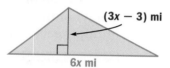

   $(3x - 3)$ mi

   $6x$ mi

   A $9x^2 - 9x$ **B** $18x^2 - 18x$

   C $9x^2 + 9x$ **D** $9x^2 - 3$

9. What is $(2x - 3) - (6x - 5)$? **Alg. 1 10.0**

   A $-4x - 8$ **B** $4x - 2$

   C $-4x - 2$ **D** $-4x + 2$

10. A smaller cube is removed from a larger cube, as shown. Which expression represents the surface area of the new solid including the interior? **Alg. 1 10.0**

    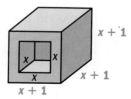

    $x + 1$

    x x

    x

    $x + 1$

    $x + 1$

    A $8x^2 + 8x + 4$ **B** $10x^2 + 12x + 6$

    C $3x^2 + 8x + 4$ **D** $5x^2 + 12x + 6$

11. What is $(x - 3)(6x + 1)$? **Alg. 1 10.0**

    A $6x^2 - 17x - 3$ **B** $7x - 2$

    C $-11x - 3$ **D** $6x^2 - 18x - 3$

BIG IDEAS

For Your Notebook

Classifying and Simplifying Polynomials

Monomial	Binomial	Trinomial
(1 term)	(2 terms)	(3 terms)
8	$2x + 9$	$x^2 + 2x^3 - x$

A polynomial in one variable is written in standard form if the exponents of the variable decrease from left to right.

Standard Form
$3x^3 + 4x - 3$

Not Standard Form
$4 - 3x^2 + 8x$

Adding and Subtracting Polynomials

You can add or subtract polynomials vertically or horizontally. To subtract a polynomial, add its opposite. To find the opposite of a polynomial, multiply each of its terms by -1.

To add polynomials vertically:	To add polynomials horizontally:
• Write the second polynomial under the first. • Arrange like terms in columns. • Add like terms.	• Group like terms. • Combine like terms.

Multiplying Polynomials

You can multiply polynomials vertically or horizontally.

To multiply polynomials vertically:	To multiply polynomials horizontally:
• Write the second polynomial under the first. • Multiply each term of the first polynomial by each term of the second polynomial. • Arrange like terms in columns. • Add like terms.	• Use the distributive property to multiply each term of the first polynomial by each term of the second polynomial. • Combine like terms.

To multiply binomials, you can also use the FOIL method.

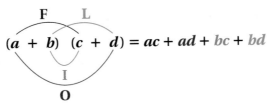

$$(a + b)(c + d) = ac + ad + bc + bd$$

APPLYING THE
BIG IDEAS

Big Idea 1
You classify polynomials in **Step 2** and you simplify polynomials in **Step 1**.

Big Idea 2
You add polynomials in **Step 1**.

Big Idea 3
You multiply polynomials in **Step 1**.

PROBLEM How can you use polynomials to express the dimensions, surface area, and volume of a gift box?

STEP 1 Write polynomials.

To make a gift box with no lid out of an 11 inch by 17 inch piece of cardboard, you would need to cut squares with side length x from each corner as shown. Then you would fold the sides up and tape them together.

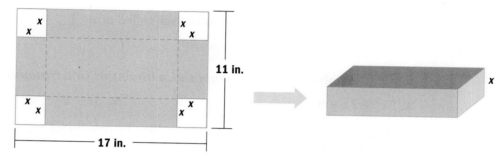

Write polynomials for the length, width, and height of the box. Then write polynomials for the surface area and volume of the box in standard form.

STEP 2 Classify polynomials.

Classify the polynomials you found in Step 1 based on their number of terms.

STEP 3 Make a gift box.

Make a gift box using an 11 inch by 17 inch piece of cardboard. Choose the size of the square that you will cut from each corner. Use a ruler to draw the squares, then cut out the squares using a pair of scissors. Fold up the four sides and tape them together.

STEP 4 Find the dimensions, surface area, and volume of your box.

Find the length, width, height, surface area, and volume of your box by substituting the value of x you used to make your box into the polynomials that you wrote in Step 1.

Extending the Problem

Use your results from the problem to complete the exercises.

1. Choose a different value of x than the value you used to make your box. Then find the length, width, height, surface area, and volume of the box using your new value of x. Which box has the greater volume?

2. Write an inequality that describes the possible positive values of x that can be used to make the box. *Explain* your answer.

REVIEW KEY VOCABULARY

- polynomial, *p. 689*
- binomial, *p. 689*
- trinomial, *p. 689*
- standard form of a polynomial, *p. 689*

VOCABULARY EXERCISES

Copy and complete the statement.

1. A monomial or a sum of monomials is called a(n) __?__.

2. The polynomial $x^3 - 2x + 1$ is a(n) __?__.

Classify the polynomial as a *monomial*, a *binomial*, or a *trinomial*.

3. $5x^3 + 2x + 3$ 4. $5a^3$ 5. $5y + 3$ 6. $-r + 3$

7. **NOTETAKING SKILLS** Make a *Y chart* like the one on page 688 that compares multiplying a monomial and a binomial with multiplying a binomial and a binomial.

REVIEW EXAMPLES AND EXERCISES

12.1 Polynomials

pp. 689–692

Gr. 5 AF 1.3

EXAMPLE

Simplify the polynomial $4x^2 - 5(x^2 - x + 3)$.

$4x^2 - 5(x^2 - x + 3)$

$= 4x^2 - 5x^2 + 5x - 15$ **Distributive property**

$= -x^2 + 5x - 15$ **Combine like terms.**

AF 1.2

EXAMPLE

A ball is hit upward at a rate of 75 mi/h, or 110 ft/sec. The height (in feet) of the ball t seconds after being hit can be found using the polynomial $-16t^2 + 110t + 3$. What is the ball's height after 3 seconds?

$-16t^2 + 110t + 3 = -16(3)^2 + 110(3) + 3$ **Substitute 3 for t.**

$= -16(9) + 110(3) + 3$ **Evaluate the power.**

$= -144 + 330 + 3$ **Multiply.**

$= 189$ **Add.**

▶ **Answer** The ball's height after 3 seconds is 189 feet.

EXERCISES

SEE EXAMPLES
1, 2, AND 3
on pp. 689–690
for Exs. 8–14

Simplify the polynomial and write it in standard form.

8. $8k + 1 + 3k + k^2 - 4$

9. $5w - 2w + 2w^2 - 8$

10. $6p^2 + 9(2p^3 + 3 + p^2)$

11. $3x^2 + 4(7 - x^2 + 4x)$

12. $-8(2s - 3s^2 + 7) + 4s^3$

13. $4(5y - 2y^2 + 11) - 2y^2$

14. HEIGHT The height (in feet) of an acorn t seconds after falling from a height of 70 feet can be found using the polynomial $-16t^2 + 70$. What is the acorn's height after 2 seconds?

12.2 Adding and Subtracting Polynomials

pp. 693–698

Alg. 1 10.0

EXAMPLE

Find the sum $(3x^2 - 2x + 7) + (5x - 9)$.

$$
\begin{array}{r}
3x^2 - 2x + 7 \\
+ \qquad 5x - 9 \\
\hline
3x^2 + 3x - 2
\end{array}
$$

Write the second polynomial under the first.
Arrange like terms in columns.
Combine like terms.

Alg. 1 10.0

EXAMPLE

Find the difference $(4x^2 + 7x - 6) - (2x^2 - 8)$.

STEP 1 **Find** the opposite of the second polynomial.

$$-(2x^2 - 8) = -2x^2 + 8$$

STEP 2 **Find** the sum $(4x^2 + 7x - 6) + (-2x^2 + 8)$.

$(4x^2 + 7x - 6) + (-2x^2 + 8)$

$= 4x^2 - 2x^2 + 7x - 6 + 8$ **Group like terms.**

$= 2x^2 + 7x + 2$ **Combine like terms.**

EXERCISES

SEE EXAMPLES
1, 2, AND 3
on pp. 693–694
for Exs. 15–19

Find the sum or difference.

15. $(10q^2 - 6) - (q^2 + 1)$

16. $(7y^2 + y - 4) + (y^2 - y - 1)$

17. $4(m^2 - 3m) + 5(2m^2 - m)$

18. $-2(v^3 - v^2 + v) - 3(v^3 + 4v^2)$

19. ⬢ **GEOMETRY** Write a polynomial expression for the perimeter of the quadrilateral. Simplify the polynomial.

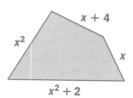

12.3 Multiplying Polynomials by Monomials

pp. 699–702

Alg. 1 10.0   **EXAMPLE**

Simplify the expression $3x(2x^2 - 6)$.

$$3x(2x^2 - 6) = 3x(2x^2) - 3x(6)$$ **Distributive property**

$$= 6 \cdot x \cdot x^2 - 18 \cdot x$$ **Multiply coefficients.**

$$= 6x^3 - 18x$$ **Product of powers property**

EXERCISES

*SEE EXAMPLES
1 AND 2*
on p. 699
for Exs. 20–25

Simplify the expression.

20. $x^2(5x - 7)$

21. $-3a(a^2 - 2a)$

22. $4x(3x^2 - 7x - 4)$

Write a polynomial expression for the area of the figure in standard form.

23.

2x

x + 4

24.

3x + 9   6x

25.

x − 5

4x

12.4 Multiplying Binomials

pp. 705–709

Alg. 1 10.0   **EXAMPLE**

Find the product $(x + 3)(x + 2)$ and simplify.

$$(x + 3)(x + 2) = x(x + 2) + 3(x + 2)$$ **Distributive property**

$$= x^2 + 2x + 3x + 6$$ **Distributive property**

$$= x^2 + 5x + 6$$ **Combine like terms.**

EXERCISES

*SEE EXAMPLES
1, 2, AND 3*
on pp. 705–706
for Exs. 26–31

Find the product and simplify.

26. $(t + 3)(t - 4)$

27. $(q - 7)(q - 9)$

28. $(2k - 9)(-4k - 1)$

Write a polynomial expression for the area of the figure in standard form.

29.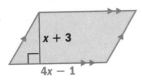

x + 3

4x − 1

30.

2x + 1

3x + 2

31.

x + 4

5x − 3

VOCABULARY Match the expression with the word that best describes it.

1. $-x^3 + 6$

2. $2x^2 - 3x + 12$

3. $4x$

    A. Monomial

    B. Binomial

    C. Trinomial

Simplify the polynomial and write it in standard form.

4. $10x - 7x + 4 + x^2 - 3x + 4$

5. $-y + 6(y^2 - y^3 + 1)$

Find the sum or difference.

6. $(3r^2 + 4r - 7) + (-r^2 - r + 11)$

7. $(4s^2 - 11s) - (s^2 - 6s + 21)$

8. $(4a^5 - a) + (-3a^5 + 1)$

9. $(-y^2 + 12) + (8y^2 - 10)$

10. $(5x^6 - 3x^2 + x) - (4x^2 + 2x)$

11. $(-7z^3 + z^2 - 5) - (z^3 - 3z^2 + 1)$

Write an expression for the perimeter of the figure in standard form.

12.

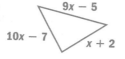

13.

14.

Find the product and simplify.

15. $m(3m + 8)$

16. $7n(n^2 - 2)$

17. $3p(2p^2 + 3p)$

18. $(2x + 7)(3x + 2)$

19. $(4y + 12)(y - 3)$

20. $(z - 9)(5z + 8)$

21. $(4k + 5)(2k + 8)$

22. $(7b + 9)(b - 4)$

23. $(t - 6)(3t + 12)$

Write a polynomial expression for the area of the figure in standard form.

24.

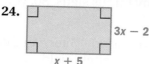

25.

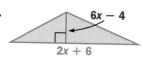

26.

27. APPLE PICKING An apple falls from a 28-foot-tall tree. The height (in feet) of the apple t seconds after it falls can be found using the polynomial $-16t^2 + 28$. Find the apple's height after 0.5 second.

28. GARDEN The length of a rectangular garden is 2 times the width. A 4-foot-wide stone walkway surrounds the garden as shown. Write a polynomial expression in standard form for the following.

a. The perimeter of the garden

b. The outside perimeter of the walkway

c. The area of the walkway

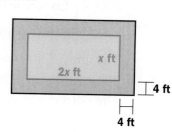

STRATEGIES YOU'LL USE:
- SOLVE DIRECTLY
- ELIMINATE CHOICES

Standards Preview

Alg. 1 10.0

If you have difficulty solving a multiple choice problem directly, you may be able to use another approach to eliminate incorrect answer choices and obtain the correct answer.

PROBLEM 1

A circular clock has a radius of $3x + 5$. Which polynomial represents the area of the clock?

3x + 5

(A) $9x^2 + 30x + 25$

(B) $9\pi x^2 + 30\pi x + 25\pi$

(C) $9\pi x^2 - 30\pi x - 25\pi$

(D) $6\pi x + 10\pi$

Strategy 1 SOLVE DIRECTLY

To find a polynomial expression for the area of the clock, substitute $3x + 5$ for r in the formula for the area of a circle. Then simplify the expression.

STEP 1 **Write** the formula for the area of a circle.

$$A = \pi r^2$$

STEP 2 **Substitute** $3x + 5$ for r.

$$A = \pi(3x + 5)^2$$

STEP 3 **Use** the distributive property to expand the expression.

$$A = \pi(3x + 5)(3x + 5)$$
$$= \pi(9x^2 + 15x + 15x + 25)$$
$$= 9\pi x^2 + 15\pi x + 15\pi x + 25\pi$$

STEP 4 **Combine** like terms.

$$A = 9\pi x^2 + 30\pi x + 25\pi$$

The area of the clock can be represented by $9\pi x^2 + 30\pi x + 25\pi$.

The correct answer is B. Ⓐ **Ⓑ** Ⓒ Ⓓ

Strategy 2 ELIMINATE CHOICES

Use the formula for the area of a circle and mathematical reasoning to eliminate answer choices.

Because the formula for the area of a circle, $A = \pi r^2$, has a factor of π, the polynomial that represents the area of the clock also has a factor of π. So, you can eliminate choice A.

Because there are no minus signs when you substitute $3x + 5$ for r in πr^2, the polynomial that represents the area of the clock does not have any minus signs. So, you can eliminate choice C.

Substituting $3x + 5$ for r in the formula for the area of a circle yields $\pi(3x + 5)^2$. When this expression is simplified, the exponent of the first term will be 2. So, you can eliminate choice D.

The correct answer is B. Ⓐ **Ⓑ** Ⓒ Ⓓ

PROBLEM 2

Which polynomial is the standard form of $5x^2(3x^2 - 5x + 6)$?

A $15x^4 - 25x^3 + 30x^2$

B $15x^4 + 30x^2$

C $15x^2 - 25x + 30$

D $15x^4 + 25x^3 + 30x^2$

Strategy 1 SOLVE DIRECTLY

Simplify the expression by applying the distributive property.

STEP 1 **Use** the distributive property.

$5x^2(3x^2 - 5x + 6)$

$= 5x^2(3x^2) - 5x^2(5x) + 5x^2(6)$

STEP 2 **Multiply** the coefficients.

$= 15 \cdot x^2 \cdot x^2 - 25 \cdot x^2 \cdot x + 30 \cdot x^2$

STEP 3 **Use** the product of powers property.

$= 15x^4 - 25x^3 + 30x^2$

The correct answer is A. **A** **B** **C** **D**

Strategy 2 ELIMINATE CHOICES

Use mathematical reasoning to eliminate answer choices.

When you simplify $5x^2(3x^2 - 5x + 6)$, you will end up with a polynomial having three terms. So, you can eliminate choice B.

After simplifying the expression, the exponent of the first term will be 4. So, you can eliminate choice C.

Because the product of $5x^2$ and $-5x$ is $-25x^3$, you can eliminate choice D.

The correct answer is A. **A** **B** **C** **D**

STRATEGY PRACTICE

Explain why you can eliminate the highlighted answer choice.

1. Which polynomial represents the area of a circle with a radius of $2x - 7$?

   A $4\pi x^2 + 49\pi$

   B $4\pi x^2 - 49\pi$

   C $4x^2 - 28x + 49$

   D $4\pi x^2 - 28\pi x + 49\pi$

2. Which polynomial represents the area of a circle with a radius of $4x + 6$?

   A $16\pi x^2 + 48\pi x + 36\pi$

   B $16\pi x^2 - 48\pi x + 36\pi$

   C $16x^2 + 48x + 36$

   D $16\pi x^4 + 48\pi x^2 + 36\pi$

3. Which polynomial is the standard form of $3x(4x^2 - 7)$?

   A $12x^2 - 21x$ **B** $12x^3 - 21x$ **C** $12x^3 - 7$ **D** $12x^3 + 7x^2 - 21x$

4. Which polynomial is the standard form of $4x^2(4x^2 + 7x - 5)$?

   A $16x^3 + 28x^2 - 20x$

   B $16x^4 + 8x^2$

   C $16x^4 - 28x^3 - 20x^2$

   D $16x^4 + 28x^3 - 20x^2$

1. Which polynomial is the standard form of $3a^2(4a + 1)$? **Alg. 1 10.0**

   Ⓐ $7a^2 + 3a$

   Ⓑ $7a^2 + 1$

   Ⓒ $12a^3 + 3a^2$

   Ⓓ $12a^3 + 3$

2. The doorway of a tent is in the shape of an isosceles triangle. Two of the sides have a length of $3x + 8$. The perimeter of the doorway is $11x + 11$. Which expression represents the length of the base of the doorway? **Alg. 1 10.0**

   Ⓐ $5x + 27$

   Ⓑ $5x - 5$

   Ⓒ $8x - 3$

   Ⓓ $8x + 17$

3. What is the product $(3x + 3)(2x - 2)$? **Alg. 1 10.0**

   Ⓐ $6x^2 + 6$

   Ⓑ $6x^2 - 6$

   Ⓒ $6x^2 + 6x - 6$

   Ⓓ $6x^2 - 6x + 6$

4. You are designing a rectangular park with a picnic grove. The park will have a walkway along two sides, as shown. Which expression represents the area of the picnic grove? **Alg. 1 10.0, MR 2.6**

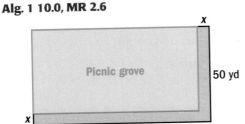

   Ⓐ 4500

   Ⓑ $x^2 - 140x + 4500$

   Ⓒ $x^2 + 4500$

   Ⓓ $x^2 + 140x + 4500$

5. The radius of a circular table is $2x - 3$. Which expression represents the circumference of the table? **Gr. 5 AF 1.3**

   Ⓐ $8\pi x^2 - 24\pi x + 18\pi$

   Ⓑ $8\pi x^2 + 24\pi x + 18\pi$

   Ⓒ $4\pi x - 3$

   Ⓓ $4\pi x - 6\pi$

6. What is the difference of $(-5n + 8)$ and $(2n - 11)$? **Alg. 1 10.0**

   Ⓐ $-7n - 3$

   Ⓑ $-3n - 3$

   Ⓒ $-7n + 19$

   Ⓓ $-3n + 19$

7. Which polynomial is the standard form of $2x(7x^2 - 3x + 8)$? **Alg. 1 10.0**

   Ⓐ $14x^3 - 3x + 8$

   Ⓑ $14x^2 - 6x + 16$

   Ⓒ $14x^3 - 6x^2 + 16x$

   Ⓓ $7x^3 - 3x^2 + 8x$

8. A farmer is enclosing a rectangular horse corral that connects to the side of a barn, as shown. The farmer uses 400 feet of fencing. Which polynomial expression in terms of the length l represents the area of the corral? **Alg. 1 10.0**

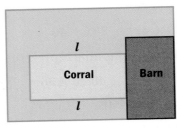

   Ⓐ $400 - 2l$

   Ⓑ $400l - 2l$

   Ⓒ $400l - 2l^2$

   Ⓓ $400l^2$

9. The height h of a cylinder is 4 more than its radius r. Which expression in terms of r represents the volume of the cylinder? **Alg. 1 10.0**

   (A) $\pi r^3 + 4$

   (B) $\pi r^3 + 4\pi r^2$

   (C) $36\pi h^3$

   (D) $144\pi h^3$

10. The wall shown has a rectangular window. Which expression represents the area of the wall not including the window? **Alg. 1 10.0**

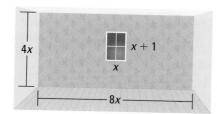

   (A) $x^2 + 13x$

   (B) $31x^2 - x$

   (C) $32x^2$

   (D) $33x^2 + x$

11. The height of a cone-shaped vase is 3 more than 6 times the radius r. Which expression represents the volume of the vase? **Alg. 1 10.0**

   (A) $6\pi r^3 + 3\pi r^2$

   (B) $2\pi r^3 + \pi r^2$

   (C) $2\pi r^3 + 3r^2$

   (D) $2\pi r^3 + 3$

12. Which polynomial is written in standard form? **Alg. 1 10.0**

   (A) $25 - m^2$

   (B) $n^2 + 21 - 3n$

   (C) $32 - 7x - x^2$

   (D) $-y^3 - 2y^2 + 6y$

13. Which expression represents the area of the rectangular parking lot? **Alg. 1 10.0**

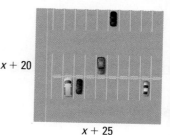

   (A) $2x + 45$

   (B) $4x + 90$

   (C) $x^2 + 500$

   (D) $x^2 + 45x + 500$

14. What is the sum of $(7y + 5)$ and $(4y - 9)$? **Alg. 1 10.0**

   (A) $11y - 4$

   (B) $11y + 14$

   (C) $11y - 14$

   (D) $3y - 4$

In Exercises 15 and 16, use the figure below.

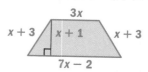

15. Which expression represents the perimeter of the trapezoid? **Alg. 1 10.0, MR 2.2**

   (A) $11x + 1$

   (B) $12x + 4$

   (C) $13x + 5$

   (D) $24x + 8$

16. Which expression represents the area of the trapezoid? **Alg. 1 10.0**

   (A) $x^2 + 4x + 3$

   (B) $5x^2 + 4x - 1$

   (C) $7x^2 + 5x - 2$

   (D) $10x^2 + 8x - 2$

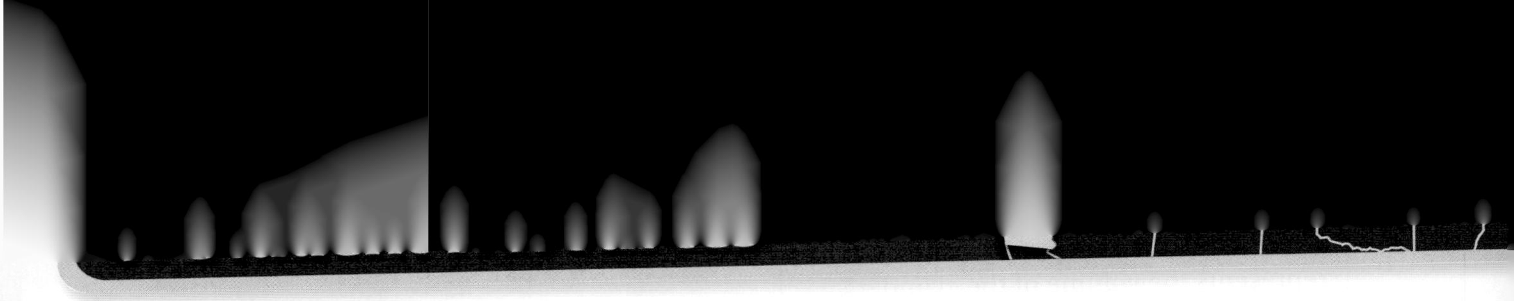

Standards Review Handbook

pp. 723–746

Extra Practice for Chapters 1–12

pp. 747–758

Tables

pp. 759–765

English-Spanish Glossary

pp. 767–794

Index

pp. 795–814

Credits

pp. 815–816

Selected Answers

pp. SA1–SA21

Rounding 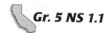 *Gr. 5 NS 1.1*

To **round** a number means to approximate the number to a given place value. When rounding, look at the digit to the right of that place value. If the digit to the right is less than 5 (0, 1, 2, 3, or 4), round down. If the digit to the right is 5 or greater (5, 6, 7, 8, or 9), round up.

EXAMPLE 1

Round the number to the place value of the red digit.

a. 6932

b. 45.674

SOLUTION

a. Because the 9 is in the hundreds' place, round 6932 to the nearest hundred. Notice that 6932 is between 6900 and 7000, so it will round to one of these two numbers.

```
          6932
     +----•--+------+
   6900   6950   7000
```
Notice that 6932 is closer to 6900 than to 7000.

The digit to the right of the 9 in the hundreds' place is the 3 in the tens' place. Because 3 is less than 5, round down.

▶ **Answer** 6932 rounded to the nearest hundred is 6900.

b. Because 6 is in the tenths' place, round 45.674 to the nearest tenth. Notice that 45.674 is between 45.6 and 45.7, so it will round to one of these two numbers.

```
            45.674
     +------•--+------+
   45.6   45.65   45.7
```
Notice that 45.674 is closer to 45.7 than to 45.6.

The digit to the right of the 6 in the tenths' place is the 7 in the hundredths' place. Because 7 is 5 or greater, round up.

▶ **Answer** 45.674 rounded to the nearest tenth is 45.7.

PRACTICE

Round the number to the place value of the red digit.

1. 1253
2. 57,309
3. 8.183
4. 32.76
5. 44,380
6. 12.535
7. 452.84
8. 998,543
9. 62.847
10. 640,796
11. 164.479
12. 1209.4

Divisibility Tests  *Gr. 4 NS 4.1*

When two nonzero whole numbers are multiplied together, each number
is a **factor** of the product. A number is **divisible** by another number if
the second number is a factor of the first. For example, $2 \times 5 = 10$, so 2
and 5 are factors of 10, and 10 is divisible by both 2 and 5. You can use the
following tests to determine whether a whole number is divisible by 2, 3, 4, 5,
6, 8, 9, and 10.

Divisible by 2: The last digit of the number is 0, 2, 4, 6, or 8.

Divisible by 3: The sum of the digits of the number is divisible by 3.

Divisible by 4: The number formed by the last two digits is divisible by 4.

Divisible by 5: The last digit of the number is 0 or 5.

Divisible by 6: The number is divisible by both 2 and 3.

Divisible by 8: The number formed by the last three digits is divisible by 8.

Divisible by 9: The sum of the digits of the number is divisible by 9.

Divisible by 10: The last digit of the number is 0.

EXAMPLE 1

Test the number for divisibility by 2, 3, 4, 5, 6, 8, 9, and 10.

a. 2736

b. 74,420

SOLUTION

a. The last digit of 2736 is 6, so it is divisible by 2 but not by 5 or 10. The sum
of the digits is $2 + 7 + 3 + 6 = 18$, so it is divisible by 3 and 9. The number
formed by the last two digits, 36, is divisible by 4, so 2736 is divisible by 4.
Because 2736 is divisible by both 2 and 3, it is divisible by 6. The number
formed by the last three digits, 736, is divisible by 8, so 2736 is divisible by 8.

▶ **Answer** 2736 is divisible by 2, 3, 4, 6, 8, and 9.

b. The last digit of 74,420 is 0, so it is divisible by 2, 5, and 10. The sum of the
digits is $7 + 4 + 4 + 2 + 0 = 17$, so it is not divisible by 3 or 9. The number
formed by the last two digits, 20, is divisible by 4, so 74,420 is divisible by
4. Because 74,420 is divisible by 2, but not by 3, it is not divisible by 6. The
number formed by the last three digits, 420, is not divisible by 8, so 74,420
is not divisible by 8.

▶ **Answer** 74,420 is divisible by 2, 4, 5, and 10.

PRACTICE

Test the number for divisibility by 2, 3, 4, 5, 6, 8, 9, and 10.

1. 34   **2.** 84   **3.** 285   **4.** 560   **5.** 972

6. 4210   **7.** 2815   **8.** 6390   **9.** 88,004   **10.** 75,432

Factors and Multiples  *Gr. 6 NS 2.4*

A **prime number** is a whole number that is greater than 1 and has exactly two whole number factors, 1 and itself. A **composite number** is a whole number that is greater than 1 and has more than two whole number factors.

Number	Product(s)	Factor(s)	Prime or composite?
1	1 · 1	1	Neither
2	1 · 2	1, 2	Prime
3	1 · 3	1, 3	Prime
4	1 · 4, 2 · 2	1, 2, 4	Composite
5	1 · 5	1, 5	Prime
6	1 · 6, 2 · 3	1, 2, 3, 6	Composite
7	1 · 7	1, 7	Prime
8	1 · 8, 2 · 4	1, 2, 4, 8	Composite
9	1 · 9, 3 · 3	1, 3, 9	Composite
10	1 · 10, 2 · 5	1, 2, 5, 10	Composite
11	1 · 11	1, 11	Prime
12	1 · 12, 2 · 6, 3 · 4	1, 2, 3, 4, 6, 12	Composite

When you write a composite number as a product of prime numbers, you are writing its **prime factorization**. You can use a **factor tree** to write the prime factorization of a number.

EXAMPLE 1

Write the prime factorization of 180.

Write 180 at the top of your factor tree. Draw two branches and write 180 as the product of two factors. Continue to draw branches until all the factors are prime numbers (shown in red). Here are two possible factor trees for 180.

Start with 180 = 3 · 60.

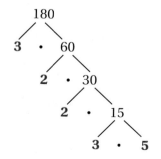

Start with 180 = 10 · 18.

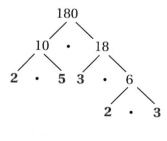

Both factor trees show that 180 = 2 · 2 · 3 · 3 · 5, or 180 = $2^2 \cdot 3^2 \cdot 5$.

▶ **Answer** The prime factorization of 180 is $2^2 \cdot 3^2 \cdot 5$.

For two or more nonzero whole numbers, a **common factor** is a whole number that is a factor of each number. The **greatest common factor (GCF)**, or greatest common divisor, of two or more nonzero whole numbers is the greatest of their common factors.

EXAMPLE 2

Find the greatest common factor of 60 and 280.

Write the prime factorization of each number. The GCF is the product of the common prime factors.

$$60 = 2 \cdot 2 \cdot 3 \cdot 5 \quad \text{and} \quad 280 = 2 \cdot 2 \cdot 2 \cdot 5 \cdot 7$$

The common prime factors are **2, 2,** and **5**. (Because 2 appears as a common factor twice, you must list it twice.) The GCF is the product $2 \cdot 2 \cdot 5 = 20$.

▶ **Answer** The greatest common factor of 60 and 280 is 20.

A **multiple** of a nonzero whole number is the product of the number and any nonzero whole number. A **common multiple** of two or more nonzero whole numbers is a multiple of each number. The **least common multiple (LCM)** of two or more nonzero whole numbers is the least of their common multiples.

EXAMPLE 3

Find the least common multiple of 54 and 252.

Write the prime factorization of each number using exponents. Circle the greatest power of each prime factor. The LCM is the product of these powers.

$$54 = 2 \cdot \boxed{3^3} \quad \text{and} \quad 252 = \boxed{2^2} \cdot 3^2 \cdot \boxed{7}$$

The LCM is the product $2^2 \cdot 3^3 \cdot 7 = 756$.

▶ **Answer** The least common multiple of 54 and 252 is 756.

PRACTICE

Write the prime factorization of the number if it is not a prime number. If the number is prime, write *prime*.

1. 28　　　　**2.** 96　　　　**3.** 11　　　　**4.** 49

5. 120　　　　**6.** 19　　　　**7.** 51　　　　**8.** 36

Find the greatest common factor and least common multiple of the numbers.

9. 12, 32　　　**10.** 42, 60　　　**11.** 36, 90　　　**12.** 96, 120

13. 14, 70　　　**14.** 48, 90　　　**15.** 72, 176　　　**16.** 3, 5

Mixed Numbers and Improper Fractions

Gr. 5 NS 1.5

A **fraction** is a number of the form $\frac{a}{b}$ ($b \neq 0$) where a is called the **numerator** and b is called the **denominator**.

The number $1\frac{3}{5}$, read as "one and three fifths," is a *mixed number*. A **mixed number** is the sum of a whole number part and a fraction part.

An **improper fraction**, such as $\frac{21}{8}$, is any fraction in which the numerator is greater than or equal to the denominator.

EXAMPLE 1

Write $3\frac{2}{5}$ as an improper fraction.

$$3\frac{2}{5} = \frac{15}{5} + \frac{2}{5} \qquad \text{1 whole} = \frac{5}{5}, \text{ so 3 wholes} = \frac{3 \times 5}{5}, \text{ or } \frac{15}{5}.$$

$$= \frac{17}{5} \qquad \text{Add.}$$

▶ **Answer** $3\frac{2}{5}$ is equivalent to the improper fraction $\frac{17}{5}$.

EXAMPLE 2

Write $\frac{13}{4}$ as a mixed number.

STEP 1 **Divide** 13 by 4.

$$\begin{array}{r} 3\text{R}1 \\ 4\overline{)13} \\ \underline{12} \\ 1 \end{array}$$

STEP 2 **Write** the mixed number. $\qquad 3 + \frac{1}{4} = 3\frac{1}{4}$

▶ **Answer** $\frac{13}{4}$ is equivalent to the mixed number $3\frac{1}{4}$.

PRACTICE

Copy and complete the statement.

1. $7\frac{3}{5} = \frac{?}{5}$
2. $3\frac{1}{6} = \frac{?}{6}$
3. $\frac{23}{4} = 5\frac{?}{4}$
4. $\frac{17}{7} = 2\frac{?}{7}$
5. $\frac{35}{8} = 4\frac{?}{8}$

Write the mixed number as an improper fraction.

6. $3\frac{1}{2}$
7. $1\frac{5}{6}$
8. $4\frac{3}{8}$
9. $8\frac{5}{7}$
10. $10\frac{3}{4}$

Write the improper fraction as a mixed number.

11. $\frac{11}{4}$
12. $\frac{15}{2}$
13. $\frac{25}{6}$
14. $\frac{17}{3}$
15. $\frac{33}{8}$

Solving Problems Using Addition, Subtraction, Multiplication, and Division

 *Gr. 6 NS 2.3*

A **sum** is the result when you add two or more numbers. A **difference** is the result when you subtract two numbers. Use the guidelines below to tell whether to use addition or subtraction to solve a word problem.

- Use addition to combine, find a total, or join.

- Use subtraction to separate, compare, take away, find how many are left, or find how many more are needed.

EXAMPLE 1

You have 36 stamps in your stamp collection. You plan to collect 18 more stamps. How many stamps will you have in all?

$36 + 18 = 54$ Because you need to combine, use addition.

▸ **Answer** You will have 54 stamps in your stamp collection.

EXAMPLE 2

Your total bill for lunch is $4.78. You pay with a $5 bill. How much change do you receive?

$5 - 4.78 = 0.22$ Because you need to take away, use subtraction.

▸ **Answer** You receive $.22 in change.

A **product** is the result when you multiply two or more numbers. A **quotient** is the result when you divide two numbers. Use the guidelines below to tell whether to use multiplication or division to solve a word problem.

- Use multiplication to find the total number of objects that are in groups of equal size or to find a fractional part of another number.

- Use division to find the number of equal groups or the number in each equal group.

EXAMPLE 3

You baked 48 muffins. You give $\frac{1}{3}$ of them to your friend. How many muffins did you give to your friend?

$48 \cdot \frac{1}{3} = 16$ Because you need to find the fractional part of another number, use multiplication.

▸ **Answer** You gave 16 muffins to your friend.

EXAMPLE 4

You bought 4 cans of soup for a total of $3.56. How much did you pay for each can of soup?

$3.56 \div 4 = 0.89$ **Because you need to find the amount in each equal group, use division.**

▶ **Answer** You paid $.89 for each can of soup.

A **verbal model** uses words to describe quantities in a word problem and uses math symbols to relate the words.

EXAMPLE 5

You have saved $27 to buy a $50 CD player. How much more do you need to save?

Write a verbal model and use it to solve the problem:

Amount needed	=	Cost of CD player	−	Amount saved

$$= \quad 50 \quad - \quad 27$$
$$= 23$$

▶ **Answer** You need to save $23 more.

PRACTICE

Write a verbal model to represent the situation. Then solve the problem.

1. You bought 8 packages of recordable CDs. If each package contains 16 CDs, how many CDs did you buy?

2. You have 900 minutes a month on your cell phone plan. You have used 652 minutes so far this month. How many minutes do you have left?

3. You paid $22.95 for the plates for your party. If you bought 9 packages of plates, how much did you pay for each package?

4. You have $149. You make $24 babysitting. How much money do you have now?

5. You bought a box of 96 pencils. You give 28 of the pencils to your friend. How many pencils do you have left?

6. You have 92 baseball cards. You give $\frac{1}{4}$ of your cards to your friend. How many cards did you give your friend?

7. You have 12 flats of flowers. If each flat contains 48 flowers, how many flowers do you have?

Using Estimation  *Gr. 4 NS 2.1*

To **estimate** a solution means to find an approximate answer. When you
round two numbers to estimate their sum or difference, you should round
the numbers to the same place value.

EXAMPLE 1

Estimate the sum or difference by rounding each number to the place
of its leading digit.

a.
$$
\begin{array}{r}
5284 \\
+ \, 2915
\end{array}
\quad\longrightarrow\quad
\begin{array}{r}
5000 \\
+ \, 3000 \\
\hline
8000
\end{array}
$$
Round each number to its leading digit.

▶ **Answer** The sum 5284 + 2915 is *about* 8000.

b.
$$
\begin{array}{r}
482 \\
- \, 218
\end{array}
\quad\longrightarrow\quad
\begin{array}{r}
500 \\
- \, 200 \\
\hline
300
\end{array}
$$
Round each number to its leading digit.

▶ **Answer** The difference 482 − 218 is *about* 300.

You can estimate a sum or difference more accurately by rounding to one
place to the right of the leading digit.

EXAMPLE 2

Estimate the sum or difference in Example 1 by rounding to one place
to the right of the leading digit.

a.
$$
\begin{array}{r}
5284 \\
+ \, 2915
\end{array}
\quad\longrightarrow\quad
\begin{array}{r}
5300 \\
+ \, 2900 \\
\hline
8200
\end{array}
$$
Round each number to one place to the
right of its leading digit.

▶ **Answer** The sum 5284 + 2915 is *about* 8200.

b.
$$
\begin{array}{r}
482 \\
- \, 218
\end{array}
\quad\longrightarrow\quad
\begin{array}{r}
480 \\
- \, 220 \\
\hline
260
\end{array}
$$
Round each number to one place to the
right of its leading digit.

▶ **Answer** The difference 482 − 218 is *about* 260.

The exact sum 5284 + 2915 is 8199. The exact difference 482 − 218 is 264.
So, rounding to one place to the right of the leading digit gave a more
accurate estimate than rounding to the leading digit.

One way to estimate a product or a quotient is to find a range for the product or quotient by calculating a low estimate and a high estimate. A low estimate and a high estimate can be found by using *compatible numbers,* which are numbers that make a calculation easier.

EXAMPLE 3

Find a low and high estimate for the product 56×35 using compatible numbers.

For a low estimate, round both factors *down.* $50 \times 30 = 1500$

For a high estimate, round both factors *up.* $60 \times 40 = 2400$

▶ **Answer** The product 56×35 is between 1500 and 2400.

EXAMPLE 4

Find a low and high estimate for the quotient $23,400 \div 45$ using compatible numbers.

When the divisor has more than one digit, round it.

For a *low* estimate, round the divisor *up* and choose a compatible dividend that is *lower* than the original dividend.

$$50\overline{)20,000}^{\,400}$$

For a *high* estimate, round the divisor *down* and choose a compatible dividend that is *higher* than the original dividend.

$$40\overline{)24,000}^{\,600}$$

▶ **Answer** The quotient $23,400 \div 45$ is between 400 and 600.

PRACTICE

Estimate the sum or difference by rounding each number to the place of its leading digit.

1. $935 + 887$

2. $4967 + 4802$

3. $5971 + 6032 + 7865$

4. $8891 - 4932$

5. $4373 - 2158$

6. $449,739 - 285,921$

Estimate the sum or difference by rounding each number to one place to the right of the leading digit.

7. $685 + 729$

8. $2394 + 3787$

9. $7462 + 9278 + 4851$

10. $5092 - 3946$

11. $12,704 - 10,363$

12. $743,156 - 678,492$

Find a low and high estimate for the product or quotient using compatible numbers.

13. 43×16

14. 359×28

15. 852×53

16. 734×76

17. $225 \div 6$

18. $2795 \div 7$

19. $17,934 \div 77$

20. $41,042 \div 92$

21. 625×28

22. 809×97

23. $742 \div 8$

24. $231 \div 38$

Ratios and Rates 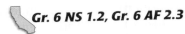 *Gr. 6 NS 1.2, Gr. 6 AF 2.3*

One way to compare numbers is to use a *ratio*. A **ratio** uses division to compare two numbers. You can write the ratio of a to b (where $b \neq 0$) as $\frac{a}{b}$, as $a : b$, or as "a to b."

EXAMPLE 1

There are 15 boys and 17 girls in a school band. Write the ratio of the number of boys to girls in the band in three ways.

$$\frac{\text{Number of boys}}{\text{Number of girls}} = \frac{15}{17} = 15 : 17 = 15 \text{ to } 17$$

▶ **Answer** The ratio can be written as $\frac{15}{17}$, as $15 : 17$, or as 15 to 17.

A **rate** is a ratio of two quantities that have different units, such as $\frac{150 \text{ miles}}{3 \text{ hours}}$.

Given a rate of speed and the time spent traveling at that speed, you can use the formula below to find the distance traveled.

$$\text{Distance} = \text{Rate} \times \text{Time, or } d = r \cdot t$$

EXAMPLE 2

A rabbit travels at a speed of 22 feet per second. How far can the rabbit travel in 12 seconds?

$d = r \cdot t$	**Write formula for distance traveled.**
$= 22 \cdot 12$	**Substitute 22 for r and 12 for t.**
$= 264$	**Multiply.**

▶ **Answer** The rabbit can travel 264 feet in 12 seconds.

PRACTICE

The table shows the numbers of boys and girls in Mr. Smith's class and in Ms. Jung's class. In Exercises 1–3, use the table to write the specified ratio in three ways.

1. Boys in Mr. Smith's class to girls in Mr. Smith's class

2. Boys in Mr. Smith's class to boys in Ms. Jung's class

3. Girls in Ms. Jung's class to girls in both classes

	Boys	Girls
Mr. Smith's class	13	12
Ms. Jung's class	17	11

4. You ski down a hill at a speed of 29 feet per second. How far do you ski in 30 seconds?

5. You drive at a constant speed of 52 miles per hour. How far do you travel in 4 hours?

Using Inequality Symbols 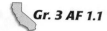 *Gr. 3 AF 1.1*

An **inequality** is a statement formed by placing an inequality symbol such as < or > between two numbers or expressions. Inequalities are written using the following inequality symbols.

Symbol	Meaning
<	is less than
>	is greater than
≤	is less than or equal to
≥	is greater than or equal to

EXAMPLE 1

Tell whether the statement is *true* or *false*.

a. $9 > 12$

b. $0 \leq 7$

SOLUTION

a. The statement says that 9 is greater than 12. This is false.

b. The statement says that 0 is less than or equal to 7. This is true.

EXAMPLE 2

Write an inequality to represent this situation: Children under 5 will be admitted to a movie at no charge.

▶ **Answer** Let a represent the age of a person. The inequality $a < 5$ represents the ages for which admission to the movie is free.

PRACTICE

Tell whether the statement is *true* or *false*.

1. $8 < 9$ **2.** $1 \geq 6$ **3.** $4 > 0$ **4.** $10 \leq 20$

Write an inequality to represent the situation.

5. You can save up to $10 on the purchase of a backpack.

6. Tina rides her bicycle for over 60 minutes.

7. The speed limit in a school zone is 20 miles per hour.

8. Your score on a math quiz is over 90 points.

9. The temperature is at least 80 degrees today.

10. You live less than 3 miles from your school.

The Coordinate Plane   *Gr. 5 AF 1.4*

A **coordinate plane** has a horizontal **x-axis** and a vertical **y-axis** that intersect at a point called the **origin** and divide the plane into four **quadrants**. The origin is labeled O.

Points in a coordinate plane are represented by **ordered pairs**, which have the form (x, y). The first number is the **x-coordinate** and the second number is the **y-coordinate**. The coordinates of the origin are $(0, 0)$. The point $P(-3, 1)$ is graphed at the right.

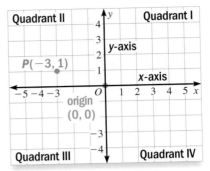

EXAMPLE 1

Give the coordinates of points A and B shown.

Point A is 3 units to the right of the origin and 2 units down, so the x-coordinate is 3 and the y-coordinate is -2.

▶ **Answer** The coordinates of point A are $(3, -2)$.

Point B is 0 units to the right or left of the origin and 1 unit up, so the x-coordinate is 0 and the y-coordinate is 1.

▶ **Answer** The coordinates of point B are $(0, 1)$.

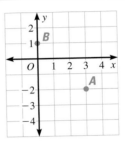

EXAMPLE 2

Plot $C(2, -1)$ and $D(-1, 1)$ in a coordinate plane.

To plot the point $C(2, -1)$, begin at the origin and move 2 units right, then 1 unit down.

To plot the point $D(-1, 1)$, begin at the origin and move 1 unit left, then 1 unit up.

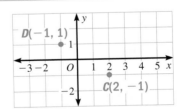

PRACTICE

Give the coordinates of the point.

1. A **2.** B **3.** C

4. D **5.** E **6.** F

Plot the point in a coordinate plane.

7. $N(2, -4)$ **8.** $P(0, -2)$ **9.** $Q(-2, -5)$

10. $R(-3, -2)$ **11.** $S(-1, -3)$ **12.** $T(4, 3)$

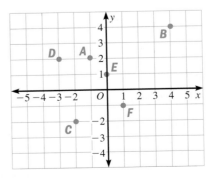

Points, Lines, and Planes   Gr. 5 MG 2.1

In geometry, a **point** is an object with no dimension that is usually represented by a dot labeled with an uppercase letter, such as *A* or *B*. Points are used to name *lines, rays,* and *segments*. A **plane** is a flat surface that extends without end in all directions. You can represent a plane by a figure that looks like a floor or a wall.

Words	Diagram	Symbols
A **line** extends without end in two *opposite* directions.	← X Y →	$\overleftrightarrow{XY}$ or $\overleftrightarrow{YX}$
A **ray** has one **endpoint** and extends without end in *one* direction.	X Y →	$\overrightarrow{XY}$
A **segment** has two endpoints.	X Y	$\overline{XY}$ or $\overline{YX}$

EXAMPLE 1

Identify and name the *line, ray,* or *segment*.

a. A ————— B

b. ← M N →

c. P ————— Q →

SOLUTION

a. The figure is a segment that can be named $\overline{AB}$.

b. The figure is a line that can be named $\overleftrightarrow{MN}$.

c. The figure is a ray that can be named $\overrightarrow{PQ}$.

PRACTICE

Match the name with the correct figure.

1. $\overline{CD}$

2. $\overleftrightarrow{CD}$

3. $\overrightarrow{CD}$

A. ← D   C →

B. C ————— D

C. ← C   D →

Identify the symbol using words.

4. $\overline{BC}$

5. $\overleftrightarrow{EF}$

6. $\overrightarrow{LM}$

In Exercises 7–10, use the diagram.

7. Name three points.

8. Name two rays.

9. Name two lines.

10. Name a segment that has *S* as an endpoint.

Classifying Angles and Triangles

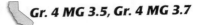

An **angle** is formed by two rays with the same endpoint. The endpoint is called the **vertex.** The symbol ∠ is used to represent an angle.

EXAMPLE 1

Name the angle shown in three ways.

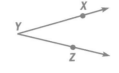

Name the angle by its vertex alone: ∠Y.

Name the angle by its vertex and two points, with the vertex as the middle point: ∠XYZ.

Name the angle by its vertex and two points, but reverse the order of the points: ∠ZYX.

▶ **Answer** The angle can be named ∠Y, ∠XYZ, or ∠ZYX.

An angle can be classified by its measure. The red mark in the right angle indicates that it is a right angle.

Name	Acute angle	Right angle	Obtuse angle	Straight angle
Example				180°
Measure	less than 90°	exactly 90°	greater than 90° and less than 180°	exactly 180°

EXAMPLE 2

Classify ∠A as *acute, right, obtuse,* or *straight.*

Compare the angle to the angles in the table above. The measure of the angle appears to be greater than 90° and less than 180°.

▶ **Answer** ∠A is obtuse.

Triangles can be classified by the measures of their angles and by their side lengths.

Classifying Triangles by Angle Measures		
An **acute triangle** has three acute angles.	A **right triangle** has one right angle.	An **obtuse triangle** has one obtuse angle.

Classifying Triangles by Side Lengths		
An **equilateral triangle** has three sides of equal length.	An **isosceles triangle** has at least two sides of equal length.	A **scalene triangle** has no sides of equal length.

EXAMPLE 3

a. Classify △XYZ by its angle measures.

b. Classify △XYZ by its side lengths.

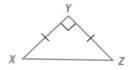

SOLUTION

a. The triangle has a right angle at Y. So, it is a right triangle.

b. The triangle has two sides of equal length. So, it is an isosceles triangle.

PRACTICE

Name the angle in three ways.

1.

2.

3.

4.

Classify the angle as *acute, right, obtuse,* or *straight*.

5.

6.

7.

8.

Classify the triangle by its angle measures.

9.

10.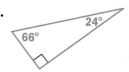

11.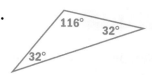

Classify the triangle by its side lengths.

12.

13.

14.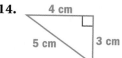

STANDARDS REVIEW HANDBOOK

Using a Protractor

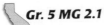 *Gr. 5 MG 2.1*

A **protractor** is a tool you can use to draw and measure angles. To measure an angle, place the center of the protractor on the vertex of the angle and line up one ray with the 0° line on one of the protractor's scales. Using the same scale, read the measure where the other ray crosses the protractor.

The measure of ∠*XYZ* is 135°. You can write this as *m*∠*XYZ* = 135°.

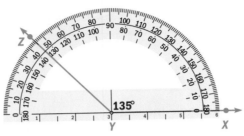

EXAMPLE 1

Use a protractor to draw an angle that has a measure of 48°.

STEP 1 **Draw** and label a ray.

STEP 2 **Place** the center of the protractor at the endpoint of the ray. Line up the ray with the 0° line. Then draw and label a point at the 48° mark on the inner scale.

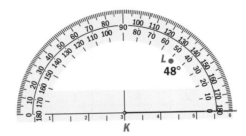

STEP 3 **Remove** the protractor and draw $\overrightarrow{KL}$ to complete the angle.

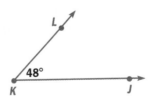

PRACTICE

Use a protractor to measure the angle.

1.

2.

3.

Use a protractor to draw an angle with the given measure.

4. 46°

5. 125°

6. 73°

Using a Compass  Gr. 5 MG 2.1

A **compass** is an instrument used to draw circles. A **straightedge** is any object that can be used to draw a segment.

EXAMPLE 1

Use a compass to draw a circle with radius 3 cm.

Recall that the *radius* of a circle is the distance between the center of the circle and any point on the circle.

Use a metric ruler to open the compass so that the distance between the point and the pencil is 3 cm.

Place the point on a piece of paper and rotate the pencil around the point to draw the circle.

3 cm

EXAMPLE 2

Use a straightedge and a compass to draw a segment whose length is the difference of the lengths of $\overline{PQ}$ and $\overline{MN}$.

M   N P   Q

SOLUTION

Use a straightedge to draw a segment longer than $\overline{PQ}$.

Open your compass to measure $\overline{PQ}$. Using this compass setting, place the point at the left end of your segment and make a mark that crosses your segment.

Then open your compass to measure $\overline{MN}$. Using this compass setting, place the point at the first mark you made on your segment and make another mark that crosses your segment to the left of the first mark.

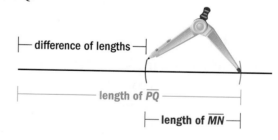
difference of lengths
length of $\overline{PQ}$
length of $\overline{MN}$

PRACTICE

1. Use a compass to draw a circle with radius 4 cm.

2. Use a straightedge and a compass to draw a segment whose length is the difference of the lengths of $\overline{AB}$ and $\overline{CD}$.

A   B
C   D

3. Draw a segment. Name it $\overline{XY}$. Use a compass to draw a circle whose radius is the length of $\overline{XY}$.

Polygons

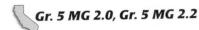 *Gr. 5 MG 2.0, Gr. 5 MG 2.2*

A **polygon** is a closed plane figure made up of three or more line segments, called sides, that each intersect exactly two other sides at their endpoints. In a **regular polygon**, all sides have the same length and all interior angles have the same measure. In a drawing of a polygon, tick marks indicate equal side lengths and arc marks indicate equal angle measures.

Polygons

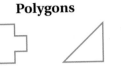

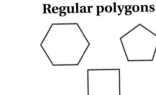

Regular polygons

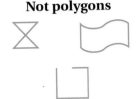

Not polygons

You classify a polygon according to the number of sides the polygon has.

Polygon	Triangle	Quadrilateral	Pentagon	Hexagon	Octagon
Number of sides	3	4	5	6	8

EXAMPLE 1

Classify the polygon and tell whether it is regular.

a.

b.

c.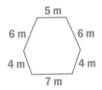

SOLUTION

a. Quadrilateral; the side lengths are not equal, so it is not regular.

b. Octagon; the side lengths are equal and the angle measures are equal, so it is a regular octagon.

c. Hexagon; the side lengths are not equal, so it is not regular.

A polygon with n sides is called an **n-gon**. The following expression gives the sum of the interior angle measures in an n-gon:

$$(n - 2) \cdot 180°$$

EXAMPLE 2

Find the sum of the interior angle measures in a octagon.

An octagon has 8 sides, so $n = 8$.

$$(n - 2) \cdot 180° = (8 - 2) \cdot 180° = 6 \cdot 180° = 1080°$$

▶ **Answer** The sum of the interior angle measures is $1080°$.

In a regular polygon, the measure of one interior angle is the sum of the angle measures divided by the number of sides. The following expression gives the measure of one interior angle of a regular *n*-gon:

$$\frac{(n-2) \cdot 180°}{n}$$

EXAMPLE 3

Find the measure of one interior angle in a regular pentagon.

A regular pentagon has 5 sides, so $n = 5$.

$$\frac{(n-2) \cdot 180°}{n} = \frac{(5-2) \cdot 180°}{5} \qquad \text{Substitute 5 for } n.$$

$$= \frac{540°}{5} \qquad \text{Simplify numerator.}$$

$$= 108° \qquad \text{Divide.}$$

▶ **Answer** The measure of one interior angle in a regular pentagon is 108°.

PRACTICE

Tell whether the figure is a polygon. If it is a polygon, classify it.

1. **2.** **3.**

Classify the polygon and tell whether it is regular. If it is regular, explain why.

4. **5.** **6.**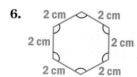

7. 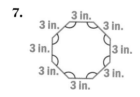 **8.** 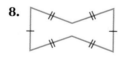 **9.**

Find the sum of the interior angle measures in the polygon.

10. Triangle **11.** Quadrilateral **12.** Hexagon

13. Polygon with 10 sides **14.** Polygon with 15 sides **15.** Polygon with 18 sides

Find the measure of one interior angle in the polygon. Round to the nearest degree if necessary.

16. Regular hexagon **17.** Regular quadrilateral **18.** Regular octagon

Perimeter, Area, and Volume

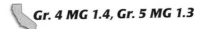 *Gr. 4 MG 1.4, Gr. 5 MG 1.3*

Perimeter is the distance around a figure. It is measured in units of length.

EXAMPLE 1

Find the perimeter of the figure.

a.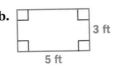

b.

c.

a. $P = 5 + 3 + 3 + 2$
$= 13$ units

b. $P = 2l + 2w$
$= 2(5) + 2(3) = 16$ ft

c. $P = 4s = 4(11)$
$= 44$ m

Area is the amount of surface covered by a closed figure. It is measured in square units.

EXAMPLE 2

Find the area of the rectangle or square.

a.

b.

a. $A = lw = 4(3) = 12$ m^2

b. $A = s^2 = 9^2 = 81$ ft^2

Volume is the amount of space a solid occupies. It is measured in cubic units.

EXAMPLE 3

Find the volume of the cube.

$V = s^3 = 2^3 = 8$ units^3

PRACTICE

Find the perimeter and area of the rectangle or square.

1.

2.

3.

4. Find the volume of a cube with an edge length of 4 inches.

Interpreting Bar Graphs and Tables

 *Gr. 4 SDAP 1.3*

Data are numbers or facts. One way to display data is in **bar graphs**, which use bars to compare quantities. Data may also be displayed in tables.

EXAMPLE 1

A group of students collected data on the number of students in each period's seventh grade math class at their school. The bar graph displays the data they collected.

a. Which class period has the most students?

b. Which class period has 15 students?

SOLUTION

a. The tallest bar in the bar graph represents class period 3, which has 25 students. So, class period 3 has the most students.

b. Look at the vertical scale and locate 15. Then find the bar that ends at 15. The bar that shows 15 students represents class period 5.

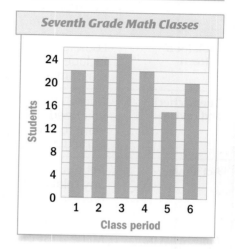

EXAMPLE 2

You collected data on the types of bagels sold in one hour at a bagel shop. What was the total number of bagels sold?

SOLUTION

To find the total number of bagels sold, add the numbers in the second column of the table.

$$12 + 7 + 4 + 10 + 11 = 44$$

▶ **Answer** A total of 44 bagels were sold.

Bagels Sold in One Hour	
Type of bagel	**Number sold**
Plain	12
Sesame	7
Rye	4
Cinnamon raisin	10
Egg	11

PRACTICE

In Exercises 1–3, use the bar graph in Example 1.

1. How many students are in class period 6?

2. Which two class periods have the same number of students?

3. Which class period has 24 students?

4. In Example 2, which type of bagel made up $\frac{1}{11}$ of the total sales?

Problem Solving Strategies  *Gr. 6 MR 1.0, Gr. 6 MR 2.0*

The following are strategies that you can use to solve problems.

Strategy	When to use	How to use
Draw a diagram	Draw a diagram when a problem involves any relationships that you can represent visually.	Draw a diagram that shows the given information. Label any unknowns in your diagram and look for relationships between givens and unknowns.
Look for a pattern	Look for a pattern when a problem includes a series of numbers or diagrams that you need to analyze.	Look for a pattern in any given information. Apply, extend, or generalize the pattern to solve the problem.
Guess, check, and revise	Guess, check, and revise when you need a place to start or you want to see what happens for a particular number.	Make a reasonable guess. Check to see if your guess solves the problem. If it does not, revise your guess and check again.
Act it out	Act out a problem that involves any relationships that you can represent with physical objects and movement.	Act out the problem, using objects described in the problem or other items that represent those objects.
Make a list or table	Make a list or table when you need to record, generate, or organize information.	Systematically list all possibilities. Look for relationships across rows or down columns within a table.
Solve a simpler or related problem	Solve a simpler or related problem when a problem seems difficult and can be made easier by using simpler numbers or conditions.	Think of a way to make the problem easier. Solve the simpler or related problem. Use what you learned to help you solve the original problem.
Work backward	Work backward when a problem gives you an end result and you need to find beginning conditions.	Work backward from the given information until you solve the problem. Work forward through the problem to check your answer.
Break into parts	Break into parts when a problem cannot be solved all at once, but can be solved in parts or stages.	Break the problem into parts and solve each part. Put the answers together to help you solve the original problem.

EXAMPLE 1

Andrew works out at the gym three times per week. He always starts with 15 minutes of stretching, followed by 50 minutes of cardiovascular exercise, and then 35 minutes of weightlifting. Andrew finishes a workout at 7:15 P.M. What time did he start his workout?

Work backward to determine the starting time of Andrew's workout.

$15 \text{ min} + 50 \text{ min} + 35 \text{ min} = 100 \text{ min} = 1 \text{ h } 40 \text{ min}$ **Find the total time.**

One hour before 7:15 P.M. is 6:15 P.M.,
and 40 minutes before 6:15 P.M. is 5:35 P.M. **Calculate the starting time.**

▶ **Answer** Andrew started his workout at 5:35 P.M.

1. Manny is stacking wooden crates to make a staircase, as shown. He keeps adding crates to increase the height of the staircase. Each crate has a height of 1 foot. How many crates will Manny use to make a staircase that reaches a height of 9 feet?

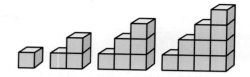

2. Justin, Bob, Kelly, Michelle, and Rebecca are all different heights. Kelly is taller than Michelle and Justin. Rebecca is shorter than Justin but taller than Michelle. Bob is the tallest of the five. List the students in order from tallest to shortest.

3. How many different rectangles are in the figure shown?

4. Marco and Ali deliver newspapers in the same neighborhood. Both start their paper routes at home. Marco's route takes him 2 blocks north, 3 blocks west, and then 5 blocks south. Ali's route takes her 4 blocks west, 3 blocks north, and then 5 blocks east. Marco lives 2 blocks north of Ali. How many times do their routes cross?

5. Ben has a $5 bill and a $10 bill. He decides to buy 2 souvenirs at an airport shop. The prices of various souvenirs are given at the right. Ben has $5.50 after his purchase. Which souvenirs did he buy?

Souvenir Price List

Pen $2.50

Keychain $4.75

Hat $6.25

6. The sum of two three-digit numbers is 534. Each number contains the digits 1, 2, and 3. What are the numbers?

$$\begin{array}{r} \boxed{?}\ \boxed{?}\ \boxed{?} \\ +\ \boxed{?}\ \boxed{?}\ \boxed{?} \\ \hline 5\ \ 3\ \ 4 \end{array}$$

7. At the beginning of the school year, your class was divided into seven equal groups. Later in the year, your group joined another group, and then two students left your group. Now there are four students in your group. How many students were in your class at the beginning of the year?

8. Jorie Middle School is having a slide show during the final assembly of the year. The slide show will have 200 photos of the sixth, seventh, and eighth graders taken throughout the year. The first photo will be of eighth graders, the second of sixth graders, the third of eighth graders, the fourth of seventh graders, the fifth of eighth graders, and so on. How many of the 200 photos will be of sixth graders?

9. Aisha runs every 3 days. She also does sit-ups every other day. If today is Tuesday and Aisha both ran and did sit-ups, on what day of the week did Aisha last do both activities on the same day?

Venn Diagrams and Logical Reasoning  *Gr. 6 MR 2.5*

A **Venn diagram** uses shapes to show how sets are related.

EXAMPLE 1

Draw and use a Venn diagram to complete parts (a)–(c).

a. Draw a Venn diagram of the whole numbers from 6 through 19 where set *A* consists of even numbers and set *B* consists of multiples of 5.

b. Is the following statement *true* or *false*? Explain. *No even whole number from 6 through 19 is a multiple of 5.*

c. Is the following statement *always, sometimes,* or *never* true? Explain. *A multiple of 5 from 6 through 19 is even.*

SOLUTION

a.

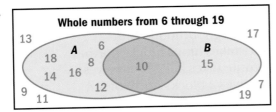

b. False. 10 is an even whole number that is a multiple of 5.

c. Sometimes. It is true that 10 is a multiple of 5 that is even, but 15 is a multiple of 5 that is odd.

PRACTICE

1. *Describe* the numbers in Example 1 that are in neither set *A* nor set *B*.

Draw a Venn diagram of the sets described.

2. Of the whole numbers less than 12, set *A* consists of numbers that are greater than 8 and set *B* consists of odd numbers.

3. Of the whole numbers less than 10, set *C* consists of multiples of 3 and set *D* consists of even numbers.

Use the Venn diagrams you drew in Exercises 2 and 3 to answer the question. Explain your reasoning.

4. Is the following statement *true* or *false*?
   There is only one odd number greater than 8 and less than 12.

5. Is the following statement *always, sometimes,* or *never* true?
   A whole number less than 10 is both a multiple of 3 and even.

Extra Practice

Chapter 1

1.1 Evaluate the expression.

1. $24 - (2^3 + 1) \cdot 2$

2. $6^3 \div (2 + 1)^2 + 3$

3. $(8 - 5)^4 + 7 \cdot 5^2$

Evaluate the expression when $r = 2$ and $s = 3$.

4. $10r + s$

5. $8rs$

6. $3(r + s)$

1.2 Use a number line to order the integers from least to greatest.

7. $3, -4, -2, 7, 9, -3$

8. $-2, 10, -5, -4, 5, 9$

Write the opposite and the absolute value of the integer.

9. -25

10. 467

11. 0

12. $|-2|$

1.3 Find the sum.

13. $342 + (-751)$

14. $-147 + 71$

15. $-89 + 268$

16. $-29 + (-51) + 36$

17. $-78 + 65 + 13$

18. $93 + (-57) + (-102)$

1.4 Find the difference.

19. $-12 - 4$

20. $10 - 13$

21. $34 - (-17)$

22. $-18 - (-17)$

23. $23 - 38$

24. $81 - (-16)$

25. $-9 - (-77)$

26. $-63 - 19$

27. $54 - 71$

1.5 Find the product.

28. $-7(-50)$

29. $25(-7)$

30. $-4(16)$

31. $-12(-21)$

32. $-95(0)(-58)$

33. $54(-1)(5)$

34. $8(-2)(-3)(5)$

35. $-14(4)(6)(9)$

36. $15(-82)(-4)(-9)$

1.6 In Exercises 37–40, find the quotient.

37. $\dfrac{96}{-8}$

38. $\dfrac{-48}{-12}$

39. $\dfrac{0}{4}$

40. $\dfrac{-80}{5}$

41. Find the mean of the data: $-8, 6, 3, -20, -9, 4$.

1.7 Evaluate the expression. *Justify* each step.

42. $-28 + (74 - 32)$

43. $7\left(2 \cdot \dfrac{3}{7}\right)$

44. $(-8 + 5) + (-5)$

1.8 Use the distributive property to evaluate or simplify the expression.

45. $-5(-3 + 8)$

46. $3(m - 4)$

47. $-1(4 + 9r)$

48. $8(-4j - 3)$

1.9

49. You do 5 hours of yard work each day for 4 days and earn $6 per hour. Then you buy 2 concert tickets for $12 each. Use the Problem Solving Plan to find how much money you have left.

Chapter 2

2.1 **Write the fraction in simplest form.**

1. $\frac{32}{64}$
2. $\frac{-15}{39}$
3. $\frac{-22}{77}$
4. $\frac{17}{51}$

5. $\frac{10}{45}$
6. $\frac{-16}{40}$
7. $\frac{-6}{4}$
8. $\frac{28}{7}$

Tell whether the fractions are equivalent.

9. $\frac{1}{2}, \frac{5}{8}$
10. $\frac{14}{16}, \frac{70}{80}$
11. $\frac{65}{90}, \frac{13}{18}$
12. $\frac{10}{15}, \frac{18}{20}$

Write two fractions that are equivalent to the given fraction.

13. $\frac{8}{12}$
14. $\frac{18}{32}$
15. $\frac{36}{54}$
16. $\frac{48}{96}$

2.2 **Copy and complete the statement with <, >, or =.**

17. $\frac{7}{8} \, \underline{?} \, \frac{9}{11}$
18. $3\frac{3}{5} \, \underline{?} \, \frac{11}{3}$
19. $\frac{17}{6} \, \underline{?} \, 2\frac{13}{18}$
20. $1\frac{10}{15} \, \underline{?} \, \frac{35}{21}$

21. $\frac{11}{10} \, \underline{?} \, 1\frac{1}{8}$
22. $\frac{4}{5} \, \underline{?} \, \frac{6}{11}$
23. $\frac{50}{9} \, \underline{?} \, 5\frac{2}{7}$
24. $\frac{63}{15} \, \underline{?} \, 4\frac{5}{12}$

Order the numbers from least to greatest.

25. $\frac{1}{2}, \frac{1}{3}, \frac{1}{4}, \frac{1}{5}$
26. $\frac{2}{3}, \frac{3}{4}, \frac{2}{5}, \frac{3}{7}$
27. $-\frac{1}{2}, -\frac{7}{8}, -\frac{11}{5}, -\frac{1}{4}$

28. $\frac{5}{4}, 1\frac{1}{5}, \frac{4}{3}, 1\frac{1}{2}$
29. $-3\frac{1}{3}, -\frac{24}{7}, \frac{29}{9}$
30. $3\frac{2}{5}, 2\frac{5}{6}, \frac{35}{12}, 3$

2.3 **Find the sum or difference.**

31. $\frac{7}{8} + \frac{5}{8}$
32. $5\frac{1}{5} - 3\frac{4}{5}$
33. $-\frac{11}{15} + \frac{1}{15}$
34. $-\frac{5}{9} - \frac{4}{9}$

2.4 **Find the sum or difference.**

35. $\frac{9}{10} - \frac{5}{6}$
36. $\frac{2}{5} - \frac{3}{7}$
37. $4\frac{1}{4} + 3\frac{7}{8}$
38. $-\frac{5}{12} + \frac{11}{16}$

2.5 **Find the product.**

39. $\frac{7}{8} \cdot \frac{3}{14}$
40. $5 \cdot \left(-3\frac{1}{4}\right)$
41. $-1\frac{3}{5} \cdot \left(-2\frac{1}{4}\right)$
42. $\frac{4}{5} \cdot \frac{2}{3} \cdot \frac{5}{4}$

2.6 **Find the quotient.**

43. $\frac{5}{9} \div 2$
44. $-\frac{7}{12} \div \frac{2}{3}$
45. $4\frac{1}{8} \div \left(-1\frac{1}{3}\right)$
46. $-2\frac{1}{2} \div (-10)$

2.7 **Write the fraction or mixed number as a decimal.**

47. $-\frac{48}{125}$
48. $4\frac{11}{12}$
49. $3\frac{7}{8}$
50. $-\frac{16}{250}$

Write the decimal as a fraction or mixed number.

51. -0.28
52. -1.72
53. 0.006
54. -8.34

Chapter 3

3.1 Copy and complete the statement with <, >, or =.

1. 5.7 ? 7.5

2. 0.84 ? 0.840

3. 17.98 ? 17.89

Order the numbers from least to greatest.

4. 0.90, 0.09, 0.99, 9.9

5. $-2.3, -2.12, -2.01, -2.1$

6. $-4.5, 4.05, -4.55, 4.15$

3.2 Find the sum or difference.

7. $7.21 + (-3.4)$

8. $-9.8 + (-3.7)$

9. $0.8 - (-12.3)$

10. $-8.78 + 3.9$

11. $3.28 - 11.395$

12. $-0.04 - 5.789$

3.3 Find the product or quotient.

13. $-8.32 \cdot (-0.47)$

14. $-20.51 \cdot 3.14$

15. $0.435 \div 0.29$

16. $2.072 \div (-0.74)$

17. $4.7 \cdot (-6.78)$

18. $0.224 \div 5.6$

3.4 Write the percent as a decimal.

19. 31%

20. 0.5%

21. 175%

22. 1.28%

Write the percent as a fraction.

23. 20%

24. 62%

25. 140%

26. 8%

3.5 Write the decimal or fraction as a percent.

27. 0.125

28. 0.08

29. $\frac{18}{25}$

30. $\frac{145}{200}$

3.6 In Exercises 31–33, find the sale price or retail price.

31. Original price: $40
Percent discount: 15%

32. Original price: $96
Percent discount: 10%

33. Wholesale price: $48
Percent markup: 40%

34. Terry receives a 12% commission on magazine subscription sales. Last week, his total sales were $1320. Find his commission.

3.7 Find the percent of increase or decrease. Round to the nearest percent.

35. Original amount: 25
New amount: 28

36. Original amount: 144
New amount: 126

37. Original amount: 56
New amount: 80

3.8 Find the amount of simple interest earned.

38. Principal: $420
Annual rate: 3%
Time: 2 years

39. Principal: $650
Annual rate: 2.5%
Time: 4 years

40. Principal: $1400
Annual rate: 4.25%
Time: 18 months

Find the balance of the account that earns interest compounded annually.

41. Principal: $900
Annual rate: 3.2%
Time: 2 years

42. Principal: $1250
Annual rate: 4.5%
Time: 5 years

43. Principal: $3200
Annual rate: 2.75%
Time: 12 months

Chapter 4

4.1 Write the power of 10 in standard form.

1. 10^7 **2.** 10^{-9} **3.** 10^0 **4.** 10^{-6}

Write the number as a power of 10.

5. 10,000 **6.** 0.000000001 **7.** 1 **8.** 1,000,000

4.2 Write the number in scientific notation.

9. 124,000 **10.** 0.0000005 **11.** 0.0000791 **12.** 32,100

Write the number in standard form.

13. 2.7×10^{-3} **14.** 9.09×10^2 **15.** 5.88×10^{11} **16.** 6.2×10^{-8}

4.3 Evaluate the expression.

17. $\left(\frac{2}{3}\right)^{-4}$ **18.** 20^{-2} **19.** $\frac{1}{3^{-5}}$ **20.** $\left(\frac{241}{7}\right)^0$

Simplify the algebraic expression.

21. $6k^{-1}$ **22.** $a^3 b^{-4}$ **23.** $271x^0$ **24.** $\frac{1}{t^{-6}}$

4.4 In Exercises 25–28, find or approximate the square root. Round to the nearest tenth if necessary.

25. $\sqrt{529}$ **26.** $-\sqrt{144}$ **27.** $\sqrt{70}$ **28.** $-\sqrt{52}$

29. Between which two integers does $\sqrt{461}$ lie?

4.5 Simplify the expression.

30. $\sqrt{80}$ **31.** $\sqrt{2} \cdot \sqrt{8}$ **32.** $\sqrt{\frac{20}{36}}$

33. $\sqrt{\frac{7}{49}}$ **34.** $\sqrt{10} \cdot \sqrt{1000}$ **35.** $\sqrt{\frac{36}{4}}$

4.6 Tell whether the number is *rational* or *irrational*. *Explain* your reasoning.

36. $\sqrt{400}$ **37.** $\sqrt{90}$ **38.** 0.373773777... **39.** $-\frac{4}{9}$

In Exercises 40–43, graph the pair of numbers on a number line. Then complete the statement with <, >, or =.

40. $\sqrt{18}$ _?_ 4 **41.** $\sqrt{\frac{9}{16}}$ _?_ $\frac{3}{4}$ **42.** -8 _?_ $-\sqrt{70}$ **43.** $\frac{2}{3}$ _?_ $\sqrt{\frac{1}{9}}$

44. Order the decimals 0.12, $0.\overline{1}$, $0.\overline{12}$, 0.123, and $0.\overline{123}$ from least to greatest.

45. Order the decimals 0.34, $0.\overline{3}$, $0.\overline{34}$, and 0.334 from least to greatest.

46. Order the numbers 1.35, $\sqrt{3.6}$, $\sqrt{1.4}$, and 1.98 from least to greatest.

47. Order the numbers $-\sqrt{15}$, -2.85, -3.7, and $-\sqrt{9.6}$ from least to greatest.

Chapter 5

5.1 Write the phrase as an algebraic expression. Let x represent the variable.

1. 4 more than the square of a number
2. Twice a number subtracted from 8
3. The quotient of a number cubed and 27
4. The sum of 17 and three times a number
5. The square of a number, decreased by 12

5.2 Simplify the expression.

6. $-x + 3y - 5y + 6x$
7. $2(3k - 6) + 4 + 5k$
8. $5a - 3(2a + b) - 7b$
9. $3(x + 2) + 4x$
10. $7y - 4(y - 5)$
11. $8(3a + 6) + a - 12$

5.3 Solve the equation. Check your solution.

12. $n - 3 = 5$
13. $36 = p + 20$
14. $-4 = h - 9$
15. $27 + z = 51$

5.4 Solve the equation. Check your solution.

16. $32 = \dfrac{x}{2}$
17. $11k = -55$
18. $76 = 19r$
19. $\dfrac{y}{-1.4} = -5$

5.5 Solve the equation. Check your solution.

20. $5a - 2 = 33$
21. $\dfrac{d}{3} + 8 = -6$
22. $-1 = 14 - 2h$
23. $84 - z = 96$

In Exercises 24–26, translate the statement into an equation. Then solve the equation.

24. Five less than the product of 6 and a number is 13.
25. The sum of 5 and the quotient of a number and 3 is -1.
26. The sum of -5 times a number and 7.5 is 22.5.

5.6 Solve the proportion. Then check your solution.

27. $\dfrac{x}{18} = \dfrac{25}{2}$
28. $\dfrac{4}{9} = \dfrac{5}{y}$
29. $\dfrac{3.6}{n} = \dfrac{4.8}{12.4}$
30. $\dfrac{m}{6} = \dfrac{35}{42}$

5.7 Solve the inequality. Then graph the solution.

31. $4 + j \geq -1$
32. $0 < m - 6$
33. $z + 4.5 \leq 2$
34. $-38 > t - 46$

5.8 Solve the inequality. Then graph its solution.

35. $5x < -25$
36. $3 \leq -\dfrac{1}{3}y$
37. $2 \geq \dfrac{s}{4}$
38. $-13k > -65$

5.9 Solve the inequality. Then graph its solution.

39. $19 - 8c > 3$
40. $14 + 2n \leq -10$
41. $10s + 3 \geq -7$
42. $20 - 11x \geq -2$
43. $4b - 12 > 20$
44. $-6y - 24 < 2y$

Chapter 6

6.1 **Tell whether the ordered pair is a solution of the equation.**

1. $y = -3x + 1$; $(-1, -2)$
2. $y = 9 - 2x$; $(6, -3)$
3. $y = \frac{2}{3}x + 5$; $(3, 7)$

4. $7 = 2x - y$; $(4, 1)$
5. $-19 = 3x + 5y$; $(6, -7)$
6. $5 = x - 8y$; $(23, 3)$

6.2 **Graph the linear equation.**

7. $y = x + 6$
8. $y = -2x + 3$
9. $y = -3x + 2$

10. $y = 1.5x - 4$
11. $y = 5x + 1$
12. $y = -\frac{1}{4}x - 2$

6.3 **Find the intercepts of the graph of the equation.**

13. $y = -2x + 4$
14. $y = 3x + 7$
15. $y = \frac{1}{2}x - 3$

16. $84 = -4x + 3y$
17. $10x - 2y = 100$
18. $-13x - 3y = -78$

6.4 **Find the slope of the line passing through the points.**

19. $(1, -8), (2, 8)$
20. $(7, 3), (1, 1)$
21. $(-2, 1), (-4, 4)$

22. $(-3, -8), (-3, 4)$
23. $(2, 1), (-2, 1)$
24. $(-4, 3), (0, -1)$

6.5 **Find the slope and the y-intercept of the graph of the equation.**

25. $y = -\frac{2}{9}x - 7$
26. $y = 8x + 5$
27. $12 = 4x - y$

28. $27 = 4x - 3y$
29. $36 = -5x + 6y$
30. $-2 = x - \frac{1}{3}y$

6.6 **Tell whether the equation represents direct variation. If so, identify the constant of variation.**

31. $y = -85x$
32. $y = 250x - 8$
33. $y = -\frac{3}{11}x$

34. $y = 7.333x$
35. $y = \frac{12}{11}x + \frac{11}{12}$
36. $y + 1 = x + 1$

6.7 **Tell whether the ordered pair is a solution of the inequality.**

37. $y > -x + 6$; $(-1, 5)$
38. $y \le 2x + 4$; $(3, 10)$
39. $5 \ge x - 3y$; $(1, -2)$

40. $4 < \frac{3}{4}x + \frac{1}{3}y$; $(4, 3)$
41. $21 \ge -9x + 2y$; $(-2, 1)$
42. $2 < -5x - 3y$; $(6, -9)$

6.8 **Solve the linear system by graphing. Then check the solution.**

43. $y = x - 2$
$\quad\;\; y = -2x + 1$

44. $4 = -x - 4y$
$\quad\;\; 3x + 2y = 8$

45. $3 = 2x - 3y$
$\quad\;\; -6 = 3x - y$

Graph the system of inequalities.

46. $y \ge 3x - 1$
$\quad\;\; y < -\frac{1}{2}x + 2$

47. $-5 \le 2x + y$
$\quad\;\; x + 4y > 8$

48. $-10 < 2x - 5y$
$\quad\;\; 2x + 3y \ge -6$

Chapter 7

7.1 **Simplify the expression. Write your answer using only positive exponents.**

1. $(-6)^5 \cdot (-6)^6$
2. $12^8 \cdot 12^{-2}$
3. $24^{-2} \cdot 24^{-2}$
4. $y^{-5} \cdot y^{-6}$
5. $(10^8)^7$
6. $[(-3)^{-7}]^3$
7. $(13^{-4})^{-5}$
8. $(x^3)^{-8}$
9. $(9y)^3$
10. $(2d)^{-5}$
11. $(bc)^8$
12. $(-5x)^{-2}$

Write the product in scientific notation.

13. $(4.1 \times 10^3) \times (1.6 \times 10^2)$
14. $(2.5 \times 10^6) \times (3.2 \times 10^{-4})$
15. $(1.8 \times 10^{-2}) \times (3.4 \times 10^{-4})$
16. $(5.4 \times 10^{-6}) \times (2.2 \times 10^7)$

7.2 **Simplify the expression. Write your answer using only positive exponents.**

17. $\dfrac{4^{11}}{4^{10}}$
18. $\dfrac{9^9}{9^4}$
19. $\dfrac{d^8}{d^5}$
20. $\dfrac{b^2}{b^{-3}}$
21. $\dfrac{w^{-9}}{w^{-7}}$
22. $\dfrac{12^{10}}{12^{16}}$
23. $\left(\dfrac{3}{2}\right)^3$
24. $\left(\dfrac{11}{-3}\right)^2$
25. $\left(\dfrac{2}{-x}\right)^4$
26. $\left(\dfrac{y}{7}\right)^{-3}$
27. $\left(\dfrac{-10}{-5}\right)^{-4}$
28. $\dfrac{m^{-3} \cdot m^{-5}}{m^7}$

7.3 **Simplify the expression.**

29. $(-4y^2)(5y^4)$
30. $(7a^2b)(2ab^9)$
31. $(-4c^3d)(-8c^5d)$
32. $(3m^8n)(5m^4n^4)$
33. $\dfrac{5b^6}{2b^3}$
34. $\dfrac{18cd^6}{24c^3d^2}$
35. $\left(\dfrac{y^2}{x}\right)^5$
36. $\left(\dfrac{5xw^2}{xw^3}\right)^3$
37. $\sqrt{49c^4}$
38. $\sqrt{4x^6}$
39. $\sqrt{52a^2b^8}$
40. $\sqrt{484w^4z^{10}}$

7.4 **Identify the domain and range of the relation and represent it using a graph. Then tell whether the relation is a function.**

41. $(1, 1), (2, -1), (3, 1), (4, -1), (5, 1)$
42. $(-1, 1), (0, 3), (1, 5), (2, 7), (-1, 2)$

43.

Input, x	-2	-1	0	1	-2
Output, y	3	4	5	6	7

44.

Input, x	0	1	2	3	4
Output, y	-4	-4	-4	-4	-4

Write a linear function rule relating x and y.

45.

Input, x	1	2	3	4	5
Output, y	-5	-7	-9	-11	-13

46.

Input, x	0	1	2	3	4
Output, y	1	6	11	16	21

7.5 **Tell whether the graph represents a function.**

47.

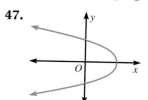

48.

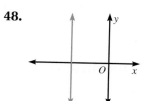

49.

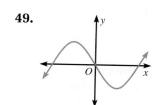

Chapter 8

8.1   **Copy and complete the statement.**

   1. 532 cm = __?__ m

   2. 3.5 tons = __?__ lb

   3. 5 qt = __?__ pt

   Identify the greater time.

   4. 20 days or 400 hours

   5. 135 seconds or 2 minutes

8.2   **Write the rate as a unit rate.**

   6. $\dfrac{80 \text{ km}}{2 \text{ h}}$

   7. $\dfrac{6 \text{ apples}}{3 \text{ dollars}}$

   8. $\dfrac{321 \text{ mi}}{5 \text{ h}}$

   9. $\dfrac{35 \text{ lb}}{2 \text{ gal}}$

   Tell whether the rates are *equivalent* or *not equivalent*.

   10. $\dfrac{8 \text{ pages}}{20 \text{ sec}}, \dfrac{10 \text{ pages}}{26 \text{ sec}}$

   11. $\dfrac{45 \text{ mi}}{3 \text{ h}}, \dfrac{185 \text{ mi}}{9 \text{ h}}$

8.3   **Copy and complete the statement. Round to the nearest whole number if necessary.**

   12. 12 dollars per hour = __?__ cents per day

   13. 270 kilometers per hour ≈ __?__ miles per minute

   14. 300 kilograms per cubic meter ≈ __?__ pounds per cubic foot

8.4   **In Exercises 15–17, M is the midpoint of $\overline{AB}$. Find the value of x.**

   15. $AB = 4x$, $AM = 10$

   16. $AM = 3x - 7$, $MB = 53$

   17. $AM = 8$, $MB = 5x - 92$

   18. If $\overrightarrow{BD}$ bisects $\angle ABC$ and $m\angle ABC = 42°$, what is $m\angle DBC$?

8.5   **Find the area of the triangle.**

   19.

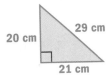

   20.

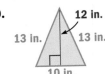

   21.

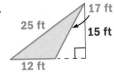

8.6   **Let a and b represent the lengths of the legs of a right triangle, and let c represent the length of the hypotenuse. Find the unknown length.**

   22. $a = 21$, $b = 28$, $c = $ __?__

   23. $a = $ __?__, $b = 63$, $c = 65$

   24. $a = 32$, $b = $ __?__, $c = 68$

8.7   **Sketch a parallelogram with base b units and height h units. Then find its area.**

   25. $b = 15$, $h = 13$

   26. $b = 9.4$, $h = 4.8$

   27. $b = 8\frac{1}{3}$, $h = 1\frac{1}{5}$

   Sketch a trapezoid with bases b_1 and b_2 and height h. Then find its area.

   28. $b_1 = 9$ m, $b_2 = 16$ m, $h = 18$ m

   29. $b_1 = 40$ yd, $b_2 = 28$ yd, $h = 10.5$ yd

8.8   **Find the circumference and area of the circle with the given radius r or diameter d. Use 3.14 for π.**

   30. $r = 18$ mi

   31. $d = 80$ in.

   32. $r = 2.9$ ft

   33. $d = 7.8$ in.

Chapter 9

9.1 In Exercises 1–4, $\triangle ABC \cong \triangle PQR$.

1. Name all pairs of congruent sides.

2. Name all pairs of congruent angles.

3. Find the measure of $\angle QPR$.

4. Find the length of $\overline{PQ}$.

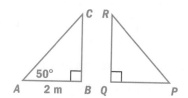

9.2 Tell whether the red figure is a translation of the blue figure.

5.

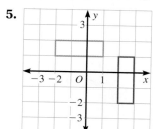

6.

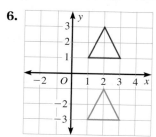

7.

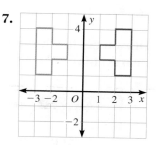

In Exercises 8–10, graph $\triangle ABC$ with vertices $A(-2, 4)$, $B(0, 2)$, and $C(-2, -6)$. Then graph its image after the given transformation.

8. Translate 3 units to the left and 1 unit up.

9. Translate using $(x, y) \rightarrow (x - 1, y + 4)$.

10. Translate using $(x, y) \rightarrow (x + 2, y - 3)$.

9.3 Graph the polygon with the given vertices and its reflection in the given axis.

11. $A(1, 1)$, $B(5, 1)$, $C(5, 4)$, $D(1, 4)$; y-axis

12. $E(0, 2)$, $F(2, 4)$, $G(-2, 4)$, $H(-4, 2)$; x-axis

13. $J(-1, 3)$, $K(-3, 3)$, $L(-5, -1)$, $M(-1, -1)$; y-axis

14. $P(3, -1)$, $Q(5, -3)$, $R(3, -5)$, $S(1, -3)$; x-axis

9.4 Graph the polygon with the given vertices. Then graph its image after a dilation using a scale factor of k.

15. $D(9, 9)$, $E(12, 6)$, $F(12, -3)$; $k = \dfrac{1}{3}$

16. $R(-1, 1)$, $S(-2, -2)$, $T(3, -2)$, $U(2, 1)$; $k = 2$

$\triangle A'B'C'$ is the image of $\triangle ABC$ after a dilation. Find the scale factor.

17. $A(1, 2)$, $B(-2, 3)$, $C(-1, 0)$
    $A'(3, 6)$, $B'(-6, 9)$, $C'(-3, 0)$

18. $A(14, -4)$, $B(-2, -4)$, $C(2, 6)$
    $A'(7, -2)$, $B'(-1, -2)$, $C'(1, 3)$

9.5 Find the scale.

19. Actual size: 27 feet
    Model size: 9 inches

20. Actual size: 16 meters
    Drawing size: 4 centimeters

Chapter 10

10.1 **In Exercises 1–4, use the figure shown.**

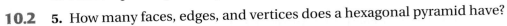

1. Name a pair of skew lines.

2. Name a pair of intersecting lines.

3. Name a pair of intersecting planes.

4. Name a pair of parallel planes.

10.2 5. How many faces, edges, and vertices does a hexagonal pyramid have?

6. Sketch a cylinder. Tell whether it is a polyhedron.

10.3 **Draw a net for the solid. Then find the surface area. Round to the nearest tenth if necessary.**

7.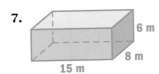

8.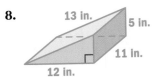

9.

10.4 **Find the surface area of the solid. Round to the nearest tenth if necessary.**

10. A square pyramid with base side length 12 m and slant height 9 m

11. A cone with radius 8 cm and slant height 9 cm

10.5 **Find the volume of the solid. Round to the nearest tenth if necessary.**

12. The prism in Exercise 7

13. The prism in Exercise 8

14. The cylinder in Exercise 9

10.6 **Find the volume of the solid. Round to the nearest tenth if necessary.**

15. A square pyramid with base side length 10 ft and height 8 ft

16. A cone with radius 18 m and height 6 m

17. The triangular pyramid shown at the right

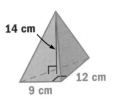

10.7 **In Exercises 18–20, solid A (shown) is similar to solid B (not shown) with the given scale factor of A to B. Find the surface area and volume of solid B. Round to the nearest tenth if necessary.**

18. Scale factor of 3 : 2

$S = 54$ in.^{2}
$V = 27$ in.^{3}

19. Scale factor of 3 : 4

$S = 21.51$ cm^2
$V = 16.76$ cm^3

20. Scale factor of 1 : 5

$S = 1608.50$ ft^2
$V = 4825.49$ ft^3

Chapter 11

In Exercises 1–4, find the mean, median, mode(s), and range of the data.

1. Finishing times for a race (in minutes): 24, 37, 57, 81, 31, 25, 43, 24, 39, 33, 40, 34, 65, 50, 24

2. Daily low temperatures: $-6°F$, $-7°F$, $-6°F$, 5°F, 3°F, 0°F, $-3°F$

3. Scores on quizzes: 93, 84, 100, 95, 89, 78, 78, 85, 83, 95

4. Elevations: 127 ft, -8 ft, 436 ft, 508 ft, -23 ft, 47 ft

11.2   5. Make a bar graph of the data below giving swimming speeds of fish.

Fish	Carp	Cod	Mackerel	Pike
Speed (km/h)	6	8	11	6

6. In a survey about favorite kinds of movies, 20 people chose dramas, 4 chose horror movies, 8 chose science fiction, and 18 chose comedies. Represent the data using a circle graph.

11.3   **The frequency table shows the heights (in inches) of 30 students.**

Height	56–57.9	58–59.9	60–61.9	62–63.9	64–65.9	66–67.9	68–69.9
Frequency	3	4	5	7	6	3	2

7. Make a histogram of the data shown in the frequency table.

8. Which height interval has the greatest number of students?

9. Can you use the histogram to determine the number of students who are between 60 and 69.9 inches tall? *Explain.*

In Exercises 10–12, use the following lengths (in inches) of alligators at an alligator farm: 140, 127, 103, 140, 118, 100, 117, 101, 116, 129, 130, 105, 99, 143.

11.4   10. Make an ordered stem-and-leaf plot of the data. Identify the interval that includes the most data values.

11. Find the median and the range of the data.

11.5   12. Make a box-and-whisker plot of the data. What conclusions can you make?

11.6   13. The table shows the age (in years) of seven used cars of the same model and the price (in hundreds of dollars) paid for the cars. Make a scatter plot of the data. *Describe* the relationship between age and price.

Age	4	5	3	5	6	4	7
Price	69	61	75	52	42	71	30

14. Make a line graph of the jogging data below.

Time spent jogging (sec)	0	10	20	30	40
Distance from start (m)	0	30	58	85	108

Chapter 12

12.1 In Exercises 1–8, simplify the polynomial and write it in standard form.

1. $3 + 5x - x^2 - 7x + 4$

2. $2t^4 + t^3 - 6 - 3t^3 + t^2$

3. $4(5 - k) + 4k - k^2 + 1$

4. $9 + 2x^2 + 4 + 7x^2 - 5x$

5. $6a^3 + 7a(3a^2 - a) - 10a^2$

6. $-5(2n - 4n^3 + 8n)$

7. $3(x^2 - 4x - 5) - 4x^2$

8. $-6(-s^3 + 2s^2 - s - 2) - 5s + 7s^2$

9. A squirrel drops a nut from a branch of a tree. The height (in feet) of the nut after t seconds can be found using the polynomial $-16t^2 + 90$. Find the height of the nut after 1.5 seconds.

12.2 Find the sum or difference.

10. $(3x^2 + 5x - 4) + (-2x^3 + x^2 + 9x)$

11. $(-8x^2 - x + 1) - (7x^2 - 5x + 1)$

12. $(4x^3 - 8x^2 + 2) - (x^3 + x^2 - 6x + 5)$

13. $(-x^2 - 3x + 7) + (x^2 + 4x - 9)$

14. $(2x^3 - 2x^2 + 1) + (-x^3 + 9x + 5)$

15. $(3x^2 - 5x - 10) - (5x^3 + x - 2)$

16. $(8x^2 + 4x - 2) + (-5x^2 - 3x - 7)$

17. $(9x^3 - 7x^2 + 10) - (2x^3 + 5x - 1)$

Write a polynomial expression for the perimeter of the figure. Simplify the polynomial.

18.

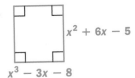
$x^2 + 6x - 5$
$x^3 - 3x - 8$

19.

$5x^2$ $3x$
$x^2 + 2x + 1$

12.3 Simplify the expression.

20. $-3n(2n - 5)$

21. $q^3(-q + 2)$

22. $-5a(6a^3 + 9a^2)$

23. $3x^2(2x^3 + 9x^2 - 4)$

24. $t^4(7t^6 - 8t^4 - t)$

25. $-r(2r^7 + 4r + 1)$

26. $7n^2(8n^4 + 5n^3 + n^2)$

27. $-11d^3(-4d^2 + 8d - 9)$

12.4 Find the product and simplify.

28. $(2x + 1)(x - 5)$

29. $(m - 3)(-m + 4)$

30. $(d + 6)(d + 4)$

31. $(4y - 3)(4y + 3)$

32. $(a - 8)(a - 7)$

33. $(5x + 2)(2x - 1)$

34. $(3n + 4)(n - 2)$

35. $(-7n + 3)(2b + 5)$

Write the figure's area as a polynomial in standard form.

36.

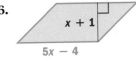
$x + 1$
$5x - 4$

37.

$3x + 3$ $2x + 4$

Tables

Table of Symbols

Symbol	Meaning	Page
4^3	$4 \cdot 4 \cdot 4$	5
$3 \cdot x$ $3(x)$ $3x$	3 times x	5, 7
$=$	equals, is equal to	5, 257
$\dfrac{14}{2}$	14 divided by 2	6
$(\ )$	parentheses—a grouping symbol	6
$[\ ]$	brackets—a grouping symbol	6
-3	negative 3	12
$\ldots$	continues on	12, 113
$\lvert a \rvert$	the absolute value of a number a	13
-3	the opposite of 3	14
$\approx$	is approximately equal to	53
26.10	decimal point	113
$1.1\overline{6}$	repeating decimal $1.16666\ldots$	113
$\%$	percent	150
$\sqrt{a}$	the positive square root of a number a where $a \geq 0$	213
$\overset{?}{=}$	is equal to?	257
$\neq$	is not equal to	257
$a : b, \dfrac{a}{b}$	ratio of a to b	277, 732
(x, y)	ordered pair	315, 734
$<$	is less than	354
$>$	is greater than	354

Symbol	Meaning	Page
$\leq$	is less than or equal to	354
$\geq$	is greater than or equal to	354
$\not\leq$	is not less than or equal to	354
$\overline{AB}$	line segment AB	454
AB	the length of $\overline{AB}$	454
$\cong$	is congruent to	454, 516
$\overleftrightarrow{AB}$	line AB	455
$\overrightarrow{AB}$	ray AB	455
$\llcorner$	right angle	455
$\angle A$	angle with vertex A	455
$m\angle B$	the measure of angle B	455
$^\circ$	degree(s)	456
$\pm$	plus or minus	471
$\rightleftarrows$	parallel lines	478
a_1	a sub 1	481
π	pi—an irrational number approximately equal to 3.14	489
$\triangle ABC$	triangle with vertices A, B, and C	516
$\sim$	is similar to	517
A'	the image of point A	523
$\rightarrow$	maps to	523

Table of Measures

60 seconds (sec) = 1 minute (min)
60 minutes = 1 hour (h)
24 hours = 1 day (d)
7 days = 1 week (wk)
4 weeks ≈ 1 month

$\left.\begin{array}{r}\text{365 days}\\ \text{52 weeks (approx.)}\\ \text{12 months}\end{array}\right\}$ = 1 year

10 years = 1 decade
100 years = 1 century

Metric

Length

10 millimeters (mm) = 1 centimeter (cm)

$\left.\begin{array}{r}\text{100 cm}\\ \text{1000 mm}\end{array}\right\}$ = 1 meter (m)

1000 m = 1 kilometer (km)

Area

$\left.\begin{array}{r}\text{100 square millimeters}\\ (mm^2)\end{array}\right.$ = 1 square centimeter (cm^2)

$10{,}000\ cm^2$ = 1 square meter (m^2)
$10{,}000\ m^2$ = 1 hectare (ha)

Volume

$\left.\begin{array}{r}\text{1000 cubic millimeters}\\ (mm^3)\end{array}\right.$ = 1 cubic centimeter (cm^3)

$1{,}000{,}000\ cm^3$ = 1 cubic meter (m^3)

Capacity

$\left.\begin{array}{r}\text{1000 milliliters (mL)}\\ \text{1000 cubic centimeters }(cm^3)\end{array}\right\}$ = 1 liter (L)

1000 L = 1 kiloliter (kL)

Mass

1000 milligrams (mg) = 1 gram (g)
1000 g = 1 kilogram (kg)
1000 kg = 1 metric ton (t)

United States Customary

Length

12 inches (in.) = 1 foot (ft)

$\left.\begin{array}{r}\text{36 in.}\\ \text{3 ft}\end{array}\right\}$ = 1 yard (yd)

$\left.\begin{array}{r}\text{5280 ft}\\ \text{1760 yd}\end{array}\right\}$ = 1 mile (mi)

Area

144 square inches $(in.^2)$ = 1 square foot (ft^2)
$9\ ft^2$ = 1 square yard (yd^2)

$\left.\begin{array}{r}\text{43,560 }ft^2\\ \text{4840 }yd^2\end{array}\right\}$ = 1 acre (A)

Volume

1728 cubic inches $(in.^3)$ = 1 cubic foot (ft^3)
$27\ ft^3$ = 1 cubic yard (yd^3)

Capacity

8 fluid ounces (fl oz) = 1 cup (c)
2 c = 1 pint (pt)
2 pt = 1 quart (qt)
4 qt = 1 gallon (gal)

Weight

16 ounces (oz) = 1 pound (lb)
2000 lb = 1 ton

Conversions Between Systems

Length	1 in. = 2.54 cm	1 ft = 0.3048 m	1 mi ≈ 1.609 km
Capacity	1 fl oz ≈ 29.573 mL	1 qt ≈ 0.946 L	1 gal ≈ 3.785 L
Mass/Weight	1 oz ≈ 28.35 g	1 lb ≈ 0.454 kg	

Table of Formulas

Geometric Formulas

Rectangle (p. 742)

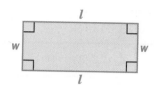

Area

$A = lw$

Perimeter

$P = 2l + 2w$

Square (p. 742)

Area

$A = s^2$

Perimeter

$P = 4s$

Triangle (p. 464)

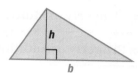

Area

$A = \frac{1}{2}bh$

Parallelogram (p. 480)

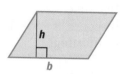

Area

$A = bh$

Trapezoid (p. 481)

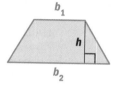

Area

$A = \frac{1}{2}(b_1 + b_2)h$

Circle (pp. 490, 491)

Area

$A = \pi r^2$

Circumference

$C = \pi d = 2\pi r$

Prism (pp. 574, 589)

Surface Area

$S = 2B + Ph$

Volume

$V = Bh$

Cylinder (pp. 575, 590)

Surface Area

$S = 2\pi r^2 + 2\pi rh$

Volume

$V = \pi r^2 h$

Pyramid (pp. 581, 598)

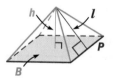

Surface Area

$S = B + \frac{1}{2}Pl$

Volume

$V = \frac{1}{3}Bh$

Cone (pp. 582, 599)

Surface Area

$S = \pi r^2 + \pi rl$

Volume

$V = \frac{1}{3}Bh = \frac{1}{3}\pi r^2 h$

Other Formulas

Temperature (p. 110)	$F = \frac{9}{5}C + 32$; $C = \frac{5}{9}(F - 32)$, where F is in degrees Fahrenheit and C is in degrees Celsius
Simple interest (p. 172)	$I = Prt$ where I = simple interest, P = principal, r = annual interest rate, and t = time in years
Pythagorean Theorem (p. 471)	In a right triangle, $a^2 + b^2 = c^2$ where a and b are the lengths of the legs and c is the length of the hypotenuse.

TABLES

Table of Properties

Property	Algebra	Example(s)
Identity Property of Addition (p. 19)	$a + 0 = a$	$7 + 0 = 7$
Identity Property of Multiplication (p. 32)	$a \cdot 1 = a$	$3 \cdot 1 = 3$
Inverse Property of Addition (p. 19)	$a + (-a) = 0$	$4 + (-4) = 0$
Inverse Property of Multiplication (p. 99)	$\dfrac{a}{b} \cdot \dfrac{b}{a} = 1; a, b \neq 0$	$\dfrac{2}{3} \cdot \dfrac{3}{2} = 1$
Closure Property of Addition (p. 19)	If a and b are integers, then $a + b$ is an integer.	Because 7 and 9 are integers, $7 + 9 = 16$ is an integer.
Closure Property of Multiplication (p. 32)	If a and b are integers, then $a \cdot b$ is an integer.	Because 3 and 5 are integers, $3 \cdot 5 = 15$ is an integer.
Multiplication Property of Zero (p. 32)	$a \cdot 0 = 0$	$6 \cdot 0 = 0$
Commutative Property of Addition (p. 41)	$a + b = b + a$	$-2 + 5 = 5 + (-2)$
Commutative Property of Multiplication (p. 41)	$ab = ba$	$3(-6) = -6(3)$
Associative Property of Addition (p. 42)	$(a + b) + c = a + (b + c)$	$(2 + 4) + 6 = 2 + (4 + 6)$
Associative Property of Multiplication (p. 42)	$(ab)c = a(bc)$	$(6 \cdot 2) \cdot 4 = 6 \cdot (2 \cdot 4)$
Distributive Property (p. 48)	$a(b + c) = ab + ac$ $a(b - c) = ab - ac$	$3(4 + 6) = 3(4) + 3(6)$ $2(8 - 5) = 2(8) - 2(5)$
Zero Exponent Property (p. 206)	$a^0 = 1; a \neq 0$	$4^0 = 1$
Negative Exponent Property (p. 206)	$a^{-n} = \dfrac{1}{a^n}; a \neq 0$	$3^{-2} = \dfrac{1}{3^2}$
Cross Products Property (p. 278)	If $\dfrac{a}{b} = \dfrac{c}{d}$, then $ad = bc$; $b, d \neq 0$	Because $\dfrac{3}{4} = \dfrac{6}{8}$, $3 \cdot 8 = 4 \cdot 6$.
Product of Powers Property (p. 386)	$a^m \cdot a^n = a^{m + n}$	$5^2 \cdot 5^3 = 5^{2 + 3} = 5^5$
Power of a Power Property (p. 387)	$(a^m)^n = a^{mn}$	$(2^5)^7 = 2^{5 \cdot 7} = 2^{35}$
Power of a Product Property (p. 388)	$(ab)^m = a^m \cdot b^m$	$(7 \cdot 8)^9 = 7^9 \cdot 8^9$
Quotient of Powers Property (p. 393)	$\dfrac{a^m}{a^n} = a^{m - n}$	$\dfrac{7^4}{7^2} = 7^{4 - 2} = 7^2$
Power of Quotient Property (p. 394)	$\left(\dfrac{a}{b}\right)^m = \dfrac{a^m}{b^m}; b \neq 0$	$\left(\dfrac{2}{5}\right)^3 = \dfrac{2^3}{5^3}$

Equivalent Fractions, Decimals, and Percents

Fraction	Decimal	Percent
$\frac{1}{10}$	0.1	10%
$\frac{1}{8}$	0.125	$12\frac{1}{2}\%$
$\frac{1}{5}$	0.2	20%
$\frac{1}{4}$	0.25	25%
$\frac{3}{10}$	0.3	30%
$\frac{1}{3}$	$0.\overline{3}$	$33\frac{1}{3}\%$
$\frac{3}{8}$	0.375	$37\frac{1}{2}\%$
$\frac{2}{5}$	0.4	40%
$\frac{1}{2}$	0.5	50%
$\frac{3}{5}$	0.6	60%
$\frac{5}{8}$	0.625	$62\frac{1}{2}\%$
$\frac{2}{3}$	$0.\overline{6}$	$66\frac{2}{3}\%$
$\frac{7}{10}$	0.7	70%
$\frac{3}{4}$	0.75	75%
$\frac{4}{5}$	0.8	80%
$\frac{7}{8}$	0.875	$87\frac{1}{2}\%$
$\frac{9}{10}$	0.9	90%
1	1	100%

Finding Squares and Square Roots

EXAMPLE 1   Finding a Square

Find 54^2.

Find 54 in the column labeled *No.* (an abbreviation for *Number*). Read across to the column labeled *Square*.

No.	Square	Sq. Root
51	2601	7.141
52	2704	7.211
53	2809	7.280
54	2916	7.348
55	3025	7.416

▶ **Answer** So, $54^2 = 2916$.

EXAMPLE 2   Finding a Square Root

Find a decimal approximation of $\sqrt{54}$.

Find 54 in the column labeled *No.* Read across to the column labeled *Sq. Root*.

No.	Square	Sq. Root
51	2601	7.141
52	2704	7.211
53	2809	7.280
54	2916	7.348
55	3025	7.416

▶ **Answer** So, to the nearest thousandth, $\sqrt{54} \approx 7.348$.

EXAMPLE 3   Finding a Square Root

Find a decimal approximation of $\sqrt{3000}$.

Find the two numbers in the *Square* column that 3000 is between. Read across to the column labeled *No.*; $\sqrt{3000}$ is between 54 and 55, but closer to 55.

No.	Square	Sq. Root
51	2601	7.141
52	2704	7.211
53	2809	7.280
54	2916	7.348
55	3025	7.416

▶ **Answer** So, $\sqrt{3000} \approx 55$. A more accurate approximation can be found using a calculator: 54.772256.

Table of Squares and Square Roots

No.	Square	Sq. Root	No.	Square	Sq. Root	No.	Square	Sq. Root
1	1	1.000	51	2601	7.141	101	10,201	10.050
2	4	1.414	52	2704	7.211	102	10,404	10.100
3	9	1.732	53	2809	7.280	103	10,609	10.149
4	16	2.000	54	2916	7.348	104	10,816	10.198
5	25	2.236	55	3025	7.416	105	11,025	10.247
6	36	2.449	56	3136	7.483	106	11,236	10.296
7	49	2.646	57	3249	7.550	107	11,449	10.344
8	64	2.828	58	3364	7.616	108	11,664	10.392
9	81	3.000	59	3481	7.681	109	11,881	10.440
10	100	3.162	60	3600	7.746	110	12,100	10.488
11	121	3.317	61	3721	7.810	111	12,321	10.536
12	144	3.464	62	3844	7.874	112	12,544	10.583
13	169	3.606	63	3969	7.937	113	12,769	10.630
14	196	3.742	64	4096	8.000	114	12,996	10.677
15	225	3.873	65	4225	8.062	115	13,225	10.724
16	256	4.000	66	4356	8.124	116	13,456	10.770
17	289	4.123	67	4489	8.185	117	13,689	10.817
18	324	4.243	68	4624	8.246	118	13,924	10.863
19	361	4.359	69	4761	8.307	119	14,161	10.909
20	400	4.472	70	4900	8.367	120	14,400	10.954
21	441	4.583	71	5041	8.426	121	14,641	11.000
22	484	4.690	72	5184	8.485	122	14,884	11.045
23	529	4.796	73	5329	8.544	123	15,129	11.091
24	576	4.899	74	5476	8.602	124	15,376	11.136
25	625	5.000	75	5625	8.660	125	15,625	11.180
26	676	5.099	76	5776	8.718	126	15,876	11.225
27	729	5.196	77	5929	8.775	127	16,129	11.269
28	784	5.292	78	6084	8.832	128	16,384	11.314
29	841	5.385	79	6241	8.888	129	16,641	11.358
30	900	5.477	80	6400	8.944	130	16,900	11.402
31	961	5.568	81	6561	9.000	131	17,161	11.446
32	1024	5.657	82	6724	9.055	132	17,424	11.489
33	1089	5.745	83	6889	9.110	133	17,689	11.533
34	1156	5.831	84	7056	9.165	134	17,956	11.576
35	1225	5.916	85	7225	9.220	135	18,225	11.619
36	1296	6.000	86	7396	9.274	136	18,496	11.662
37	1369	6.083	87	7569	9.327	137	18,769	11.705
38	1444	6.164	88	7744	9.381	138	19,044	11.747
39	1521	6.245	89	7921	9.434	139	19,321	11.790
40	1600	6.325	90	8100	9.487	140	19,600	11.832
41	1681	6.403	91	8281	9.539	141	19,881	11.874
42	1764	6.481	92	8464	9.592	142	20,164	11.916
43	1849	6.557	93	8649	9.644	143	20,449	11.958
44	1936	6.633	94	8836	9.695	144	20,736	12.000
45	2025	6.708	95	9025	9.747	145	21,025	12.042
46	2116	6.782	96	9216	9.798	146	21,316	12.083
47	2209	6.856	97	9409	9.849	147	21,609	12.124
48	2304	6.928	98	9604	9.899	148	21,904	12.166
49	2401	7.000	99	9801	9.950	149	22,201	12.207
50	2500	7.071	100	10,000	10.000	150	22,500	12.247

TABLES

English-Spanish Glossary

A

absolute value (p. 13) The absolute value of a number a is the distance between a and 0 on a number line. The absolute value of a is written $|a|$.

valor absoluto (pág. 13) El valor absoluto de un número a es la distancia entre a y 0 en una recta numérica. El valor absoluto de a se escribe $|a|$.

$$|4| = 4 \qquad |-7| = 7 \qquad |0| = 0$$

---

additive identity (p. 19) The number 0 is the additive identity because the sum of any number and 0 is the original number.

identidad de la suma (pág. 19) El número 0 es la identidad de la suma porque la suma de cualquier número y 0 es el número original.

$$-7 + 0 = -7$$
$$a + 0 = a$$

---

additive inverse (p. 19) The additive inverse of a number a is the opposite of the number, or $-a$. The sum of a number and its additive inverse is 0.

inverso aditivo (pág. 19) El inverso aditivo de un número a es el opuesto del número, o $-a$. La suma de un número y su inverso aditivo es 0.

The *additive inverse* of 6 is -6, so $6 + (-6) = 0$.

El *inverso aditivo* de 6 es -6, por lo tanto $6 + (-6) = 0$.

---

algebraic expression (p. 7) An expression that consists of numbers, variables, and operations.

expresión algebraica (pág. 7) Expresión compuesta de números, variables y operaciones.

$n - 3, \frac{2s}{t}$, and $x + 4yz + 1$ are *algebraic expressions*.

$n - 3, \frac{2s}{t}$ y $x + 4yz + 1$ son *expresiones algebraicas*.

---

altitude of a triangle (p. 463) The perpendicular segment from one vertex of the triangle to the opposite side or to the line that contains the opposite side.

altura de un triángulo (pág. 463) El segmento perpendicular que va desde uno de los vértices del triángulo hasta el lado opuesto o hasta la recta que contiene el lado opuesto.

---

angle bisector (p. 455) A ray that divides an angle into two angles that are congruent.

bisectriz de un ángulo (pág. 455) Una semirrecta que divide a un ángulo en dos ángulos congruentes.

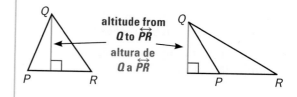

$\overrightarrow{YW}$ bisects $\angle XYZ$.
$\overrightarrow{YW}$ biseca a $\angle XYZ$.

---

annual interest rate (p. 172) In simple interest, the percent of the principal earned or paid per year.

tasa de interés anual (pág. 172) En interés simple, el porcentaje sobre el capital ganado o pagado por año.

See simple interest.

Véase interés simple.

average rate of change (p. 336) A comparison of a change in one quantity with a change in another quantity. In real-world situations, you can interpret the slope of a line as an average rate of change.

tasa de cambio promedio (pág. 336) Una comparación entre un cambio en una cantidad y un cambio en otra cantidad. En situaciones reales, puedes interpretar la pendiente de una recta como una tasa de cambio promedio.

You pay $7 for 2 hours of computer use and $14 for 4 hours of computer use. The *average rate of change* is

$$\frac{\text{change in cost}}{\text{change in time}} = \frac{14 - 7}{4 - 2} = 3.5$$

or $3.50 per hour.

Pagas $7 por usar la computadora durante 2 horas y $14 por usar la computadora por 4 horas. La *tasa de cambio promedio* es

$$\frac{\text{cambio en el costo}}{\text{cambio en el tiempo}} = \frac{14 - 7}{4 - 2} = 3.5$$

o $3.50 por hora.

B

balance (p. 173) The balance A of an account that earns simple annual interest is the sum of the principal and the interest Prt.

balance (pág. 173) El balance A de una cuenta que obtiene un interés anual simple es la suma del capital y el interés Prt.

$A = P + Prt$ or $A = P(1 + rt)$

$A = P + Prt$ o $A = P(1 + rt)$

---

bar graph (p. 636) A type of graph in which the lengths of bars are used to represent and compare data in categories.

gráfica de barras (pág. 636) Un tipo de gráfica en el que las longitudes de las barras se usan para representar y comparar datos clasificados en categorías.

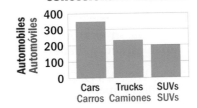

---

base of a parallelogram (p. 480) The length of any side of the parallelogram can be used as the base.

base de un paralelogramo (pág. 480) La longitud de cualquier lado del paralelogramo puede usarse como la base.

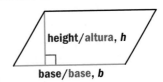

---

base of a power (p. 5) The number or expression that is used as a factor in a repeated multiplication.

base de una potencia (pág. 5) El número o la expresión que se usa como factor en una multiplicación repetida.

In the power 5^3, the *base* is 5.

La base de la potencia 5^3 es 5.

---

base of a triangle (p. 463) The length of any side of the triangle can be used as the base.

base de un triángulo (pág. 463) La longitud de cualquier lado de un triángulo puede usarse como base.

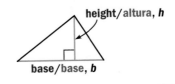

---

bases of a trapezoid (p. 481) The lengths of the parallel sides of the trapezoid.

bases de un trapecio (pág. 481) Las longitudes de los lados paralelos del trapecio.

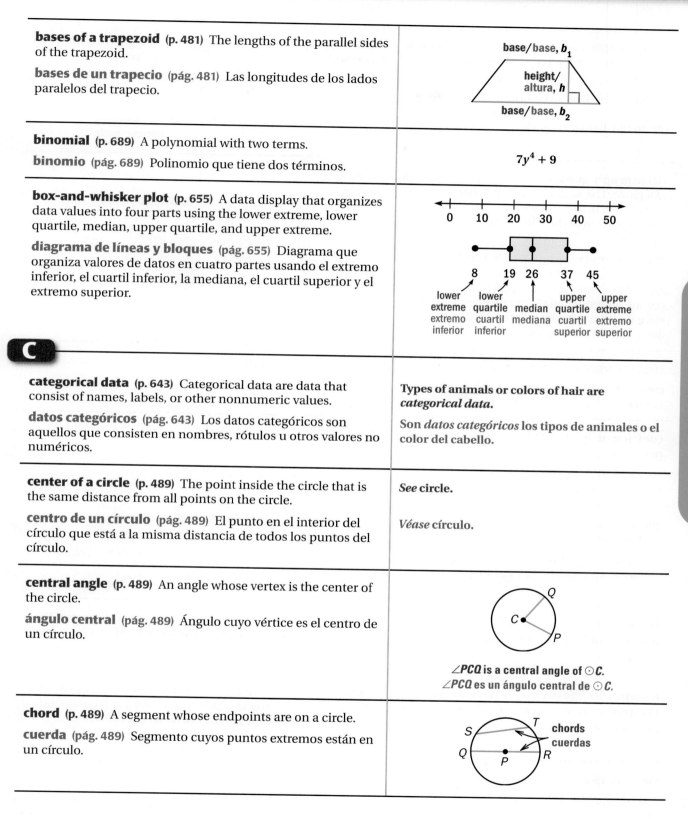

base/base, b_1
height/altura, h
base/base, b_2

binomial (p. 689) A polynomial with two terms.

binomio (pág. 689) Polinomio que tiene dos términos.

$$7y^4 + 9$$

box-and-whisker plot (p. 655) A data display that organizes data values into four parts using the lower extreme, lower quartile, median, upper quartile, and upper extreme.

diagrama de líneas y bloques (pág. 655) Diagrama que organiza valores de datos en cuatro partes usando el extremo inferior, el cuartil inferior, la mediana, el cuartil superior y el extremo superior.

0   10   20   30   40   50

8   19   26   37   45

lower extreme / extremo inferior
lower quartile / cuartil inferior
median / mediana
upper quartile / cuartil superior
upper extreme / extremo superior

C

categorical data (p. 643) Categorical data are data that consist of names, labels, or other nonnumeric values.

datos categóricos (pág. 643) Los datos categóricos son aquellos que consisten en nombres, rótulos u otros valores no numéricos.

Types of animals or colors of hair are _categorical data_.

Son _datos categóricos_ los tipos de animales o el color del cabello.

center of a circle (p. 489) The point inside the circle that is the same distance from all points on the circle.

centro de un círculo (pág. 489) El punto en el interior del círculo que está a la misma distancia de todos los puntos del círculo.

See **circle.**

Véase **círculo.**

central angle (p. 489) An angle whose vertex is the center of the circle.

ángulo central (pág. 489) Ángulo cuyo vértice es el centro de un círculo.

$\angle PCQ$ **is a central angle of** $\odot C$.
$\angle PCQ$ es un ángulo central de $\odot C$.

chord (p. 489) A segment whose endpoints are on a circle.

cuerda (pág. 489) Segmento cuyos puntos extremos están en un círculo.

chords
cuerdas

circle (p. 489) The set of all points in a plane that are the same distance, called the radius, from a fixed point, called the center.

círculo (pág. 489) El conjunto de todos los puntos en un plano que están a la misma distancia, llamada radio, de un punto fijo, llamado centro.

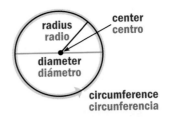

circle graph (p. 637) A circle graph displays data as sections of a circle. The entire circle represents all the data. Each section can be labeled with its data value or with the data value's portion of the whole written as a fraction, a decimal, or a percent.

gráfica circular (pág. 637) Una gráfica circular representa los datos como secciones de un círculo. El círculo completo representa todos los datos. Cada sección puede ser rotulada con su valor de los datos o con la porción del total que su valor de los datos representa, escrita en forma de fracción, de decimal o de porcentaje.

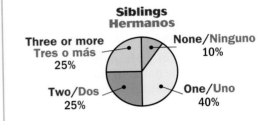

circumference (p. 489) The distance around a circle.

circunferencia (pág. 489) La distancia alrededor de un círculo.

See circle.

Véase círculo.

coefficient (p. 252) The number part of a term with a variable part.

coeficiente (pág. 252) La parte numérica de un término con una parte variable.

The *coefficient* of 7x is 7.

El *coeficiente* de 7x es 7.

commission (p. 161) The amount of pay when a salesperson is paid a percent of his or her total sales.

comisión (pág. 161) La cantidad pagada a un vendedor o vendedora cuando se le paga un porcentaje sobre sus ventas totales.

Commission = Percent commission × Total sales

Comisión = Porcentaje comisión × Ventas totales

compound interest (p. 173) Interest earned on both the principal and on any interest that has been earned previously.

interés compuesto (pág. 173) Interés que se gana sobre el capital y sobre cualquier interés que se ha ganado previamente.

You deposit $250 in an account that earns 4% interest compounded yearly. After 5 years, your account balance is:

$y = 250(1 + 0.04)^5 \approx \$304.16$

Depositas $250 en una cuenta que gana 4% de interés compuesto anualmente. Después de 5 años, el balance de tu cuenta es:

$y = 250(1 + 0.04)^5 \approx \$304.16$

cone (p. 566) A solid with one circular base.

cono (pág. 566) Un cuerpo geométrico que tiene una base circular.

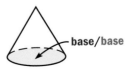

congruent angles (p. 455) Angles that have the same measure.	*See* **congruent polygons.**
ángulos congruentes (pág. 455) Ángulos que tienen medidas iguales.	*Véase* **polígonos congruentes.**
congruent polygons (p. 516) Polygons that have the same shape and size. For congruent polygons, corresponding angles are congruent and corresponding sides are congruent. **polígonos congruentes** (pág. 516) Polígonos semejantes que tienen la misma forma y el mismo tamaño. Para polígonos congruentes, los ángulos correspondientes son congruentes y los lados correspondientes son congruentes.	 $\triangle ABC \cong \triangle DEF$
congruent segments (p. 454) Segments that have the same length.	*See* **congruent polygons.**
segmentos congruentes (pág. 454) Segmentos que tienen igual longitud.	*Véase* **polígonos congruentes.**
constant of variation (p. 348) The nonzero constant k in a direct variation equation $y = kx$.	**The constant of variation in the direct variation equation $y = 7x$ is 7.**
constante de variación (pág. 348) La constante k no igual a cero, en una ecuación de variación directa $y = kx$.	**La constante de variación en la ecuación de variación directa $y = 7x$ es 7.**
constant term (p. 252) A term that has a number but no variable.	**In the expression $5y + 9$, the term 9 is a *constant term*.**
término constante (pág. 252) Un término que tiene un número pero no una variable.	**En la expresión $5y + 9$, el término 9 es un *término constante*.**
converse (p. 473) An if-then statement where the hypothesis and conclusion of the original statement have been reversed. **recíproco** (pág. 473) Un enunciado de tipo si-entonces en el cual la hipótesis y la conclusión del enunciado original se han intercambiado.	**Original: If you clean your room, then it will be neat.** *Converse*: **If your room is neat, then you will clean it.** **Original: Si ordenas tu habitación, entonces estará arreglada.** *Recíproco*: **Si tu habitación está arreglada, entonces la ordenarás.**
conversion factor (p. 437) A fraction equal to 1 that expresses the relationship between two different units of measure.	$\dfrac{1 \text{ foot}}{12 \text{ inches}}$ **and** $\dfrac{12 \text{ inches}}{1 \text{ foot}}$ **are conversion factors.**
factor de conversión (pág. 437) Una fracción igual a 1 que expresa la relación entre dos unidades diferentes de medidas.	$\dfrac{1 \text{ pie}}{12 \text{ pulg.}}$ **y** $\dfrac{12 \text{ pulg.}}{1 \text{ pie}}$ **son factores de conversión.**

coplanar (p. 561) Points and lines that lie in the same plane are coplanar.

coplanarios (pág. 561) Puntos y rectas sobre el mismo plano son coplanarios.

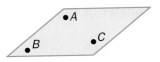

A, B, and C are coplanar.

A, B y C son coplanarios.

---

corresponding parts (p. 516) Pairs of sides and angles of polygons that are in the same relative position.

elementos correspondientes (pág. 516) Pares de lados y ángulos de polígonos que están en la misma posición relativa.

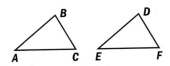

$\angle A$ and $\angle E$ are corresponding angles.
$\overline{AB}$ and $\overline{ED}$ are corresponding sides.

$\angle A$ y $\angle E$ son ángulos correspondientes.
$\overline{AB}$ y $\overline{ED}$ son lados correspondientes.

---

cross products (p. 278) For the proportion $\frac{a}{b} = \frac{c}{d}$, where $b \neq 0$ and $d \neq 0$, the cross products are ad and bc.

productos cruzados (pág. 278) Para la proporción $\frac{a}{b} = \frac{c}{d}$, donde $b \neq 0$ y $d \neq 0$, los productos cruzados son ad y bc.

The *cross products* of the proportion $\frac{2}{3} = \frac{4}{6}$ are $2 \cdot 6$ and $3 \cdot 4$.

Los *productos cruzados* de la proporción $\frac{2}{3} = \frac{4}{6}$ son $2 \cdot 6$ y $3 \cdot 4$.

---

cylinder (p. 566) A solid with two congruent circular bases that lie in parallel planes.

cilindro (pág. 566) Un cuerpo geométrico que tiene dos bases circulares congruentes que se ubican en planos paralelos.

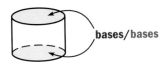

bases/bases

---

data (p. 37) Facts or numerical information that describes something.

datos (pág. 37) Hechos o información numérica que describen algo.

Numbers of cars sold annually at a dealership:
340, 350, 345, 347, 352, 360, 365

Número de carros que se venden anualmente en el concesionario:
340, 350, 345, 347, 352, 360, 365

---

diagonal (pp. 479, 567) A segment, other than a side or edge, that connects two vertices of a polygon or polyhedron.

diagonal (págs. 479, 567) Un segmento, distinto de un lado o arista, que conecta dos vértices de un polígono o de un poliedro.

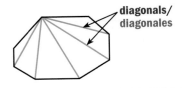

diagonals/
diagonales

---

diameter of a circle (p. 489) A chord containing the center of a circle.

diámetro de un círculo (pág. 489) Una cuerda que contiene el centro del círculo.

See circle.

Véase círculo.

dilation (p. 535) A transformation that stretches or shrinks a figure.

dilatación (pág. 535) Una transformación que estira o encoge una figura.

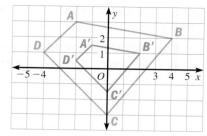

The scale factor is $\frac{1}{2}$.

El factor de escala es $\frac{1}{2}$.

---

direct variation (p. 348) The relationship of two variables x and y if there is a nonzero number k such that $y = kx$ or $k = \frac{y}{x}$.

variación directa (pág. 348) La relación entre dos variables x e y cuando hay un número k distinto de cero, de manera tal que $y = kx$ ó $k = \frac{y}{x}$.

$$y = 5x$$
$$y = kx$$

---

discount (p. 160) A decrease in the price of an item.

descuento (pág. 160) Una disminución en el precio de un artículo.

The original price of a pair of jeans is $42, but the store sells it for $29.99. The *discount* is $12.01.

El precio original de un par de pantalones es $42, pero la tienda los vende a $29.99. El *descuento* es $12.01.

---

domain of a relation (p. 407) The set of all possible input values for the relation.

dominio de una relación (pág. 407) El conjunto de todos los valores de entrada posibles para la relación.

See relation.

Véase relación.

---

double bar graph (p. 637) A bar graph that shows two sets of data on the same graph.

gráfica de doble barra (pág. 637) Gráfica de barras que muestra dos conjuntos de datos en la misma gráfica.

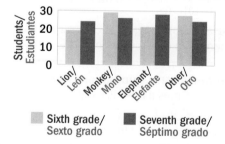

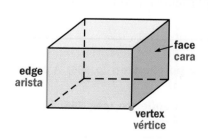

---

edge of a polyhedron (p. 567) A line segment where two faces of the polyhedron meet.

arista de un poliedro (pág. 567) Un segmento de recta donde se encuentran dos caras del poliedro.

equation (p. 257) A mathematical sentence formed by placing an equal sign between two expressions. **ecuación** (pág. 257) Un enunciado matemático que se forma al colocar un signo igual entre dos expresiones.	$3 \cdot 6 = 18$ and $x + 7 = 12$ are *equations*. $3 \cdot 6 = 18$ y $x + 7 = 12$ son *ecuaciones*.
equivalent equations (p. 258) Equations that have the same solution(s). **ecuaciones equivalentes** (pág. 258) Ecuaciones que tienen la misma solución o soluciones.	$2x - 6 = 0$ and $2x = 6$ are *equivalent equations* because the solution of both equations is 3. $2x - 6 = 0$ y $2x = 6$ son *ecuaciones equivalentes* porque la solución de ambas ecuaciones es 3.
equivalent expressions (p. 49) Numerical expressions that are equal, or algebraic expressions that are equal for all values of the variable(s). **expresiones equivalentes** (pág. 49) Expresiones numéricas que son iguales, o expresiones algebraicas que son iguales para todos los valores de la(s) variable(s).	$2 + 2$ and $3 + 1$ are *equivalent expressions* because the value of both expressions is 4. $2 + 2$ y $3 + 1$ son *expresiones equivalentes* porque el valor de ambas expresiones es 4.
equivalent fractions (p. 75) Fractions that represent the same number. Equivalent fractions have the same simplest form. **fracciones equivalentes** (pág. 75) Fracciones que representan el mismo número. Las fracciones equivalentes tienen la misma mínima expresión.	$\frac{6}{8}$ and $\frac{9}{12}$ are *equivalent fractions* that both represent $\frac{3}{4}$. $\frac{6}{8}$ y $\frac{9}{12}$ son *fracciones equivalentes* porque ambas representan $\frac{3}{4}$.
equivalent inequalities (p. 282) Inequalities that have the same solution. **desigualdades equivalentes** (pág. 282) Desigualdades que tienen la misma solución.	$3x \leq 12$ and $x \leq 4$ are *equivalent inequalities* because the solution of both inequalities is all numbers less than or equal to 4. $3x \leq 12$ y $x \leq 4$ son *desigualdades equivalentes* porque la solución de ambas desigualdades es todos los números menores que o iguales a 4.
evaluate (p. 6) To find the value of an expression with one or more operations. **hallar el valor** (pág. 6) Encontrar el valor de una expresión que tiene una o más operaciones.	$4(3) + 6 \div 2 = 15$
exponent (p. 5) A number or expression that represents how many times a base is used as a factor in a repeated multiplication. **exponente** (pág. 5) Un número o expresión que representa cuántas veces una base se usa como factor en una multiplicación repetida.	In the power 5^3, the *exponent* is 3. El *exponente* de la potencia 5^3 es 3.

F

face of a polyhedron (p. 566) A polygon that is a side of the polyhedron. **cara de un poliedro** (pág. 566) Un polígono que forma un lado del poliedro.	*See* edge of a polyhedron. *Véase* arista de un poliedro.

fraction (p. 75) A number of the form $\frac{a}{b}$ ($b \neq 0$) where a is called the numerator and b is called the denominator.

fracción (pág. 75) Un número de la forma $\frac{a}{b}$ ($b \neq 0$) donde a es el numerador y b es el denominador.

$\frac{5}{7}$ and $\frac{18}{10}$ are *fractions*.

$\frac{5}{7}$ y $\frac{18}{10}$ son *fracciones*.

---

frequency table (p. 643) A display that groups data into intervals to show frequencies.

tabla de frecuencias (pág. 643) Información que agrupa datos en intervalos que muestran frecuencias.

Interval Intervalo	Tally Marca	Frequency Frecuencia
0–9	II	2
10–19	IIII	4
20–29	IIII	5

---

front-end estimation (p. 138) A method for estimating the sum of two or more numbers. In this method, you add the front-end digits, estimate the sum of the remaining digits, and then add the results.

estimación por la izquierda (pág. 138) Un método para estimar la suma de dos o más números. En este método, se suman los dígitos de la izquierda, se estima la suma de los dígitos restantes y luego se suman los resultados.

To estimate 3.81 + 1.32 + 5.74, first add the front-end digits: 3 + 1 + 5 = 9.
Then estimate the sum of the remaining digits:
0.81 + (0.32 + 0.74) ≈ 1 + 1 = 2.
The sum is about 9 + 2 = 11.

Para estimar la suma de 3.81 + 1.32 + 5.74, suma primero los dígitos de la izquierda:
3 + 1 + 5 = 9.
Luego estima la suma de los dígitos restantes:
0.81 + (0.32 + 0.74) ≈ 1 + 1 = 2.
La suma es aproximadamente 9 + 2 = 11.

---

function (p. 408) A relation for which each input has exactly one output.

función (pág. 408) Una relación para la cual cada entrada tiene exactamente una salida.

Input/Entrada, *x*	1	2	3	4
Output/Salida, *y*	2	4	6	8

The input-output table above represents a *function*.

La tabla anterior de entrada y salida representa una *función*.

H

half-plane (p. 355) The graph of a linear inequality in two variables.

semiplano (pág. 355) La gráfica de una desigualdad lineal en dos variables.

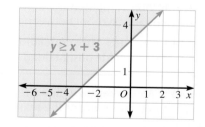

---

height of a parallelogram (p. 480) The perpendicular distance between the side whose length is the base and the opposite side.

altura de un paralelogramo (pág. 480) La distancia perpendicular entre el lado cuya longitud es la base y el lado opuesto.

See base of a parallelogram.

Véase base de un paralelogramo.

height of a trapezoid (p. 481) The perpendicular distance between the bases of the trapezoid.	*See* **bases of a trapezoid.**
altura de un trapecio (pág. 481) La distancia perpendicular entre las bases de un trapecio.	*Véase* **bases de un trapecio.**
height of a triangle (p. 463) The length of an altitude of a triangle.	*See* **base of a triangle.**
altura de un triángulo (pág. 463) La longitud de la altitud de un triángulo.	*Véase* **base de un triángulo.**

histogram (p. 643) A graph that displays data from a frequency table. A histogram has one bar for each interval of the frequency table. The length of the bar indicates the frequency of the interval.

histograma (pág. 643) Una gráfica que muestra datos de una tabla de frecuencias. Un histograma tiene una barra para cada intervalo de la tabla de frecuencias. La longitud de la barra indica la frecuencia para el intervalo.

Library Visitors on a Saturday / Visitantes a la biblioteca los sábados

hypotenuse (p. 471) The side of a right triangle that is opposite the right angle.

hipotenusa (pág. 471) El lado de un triángulo rectángulo que está opuesto al ángulo recto.

I

image (p. 522) The new figure formed by a transformation.	*See* **dilation, reflection,** *and* **translation.**
imagen (pág. 522) La figura nueva formada por una transformación.	*Véase* **dilatación, reflexión** *y* **traslación.**
inequality (p. 282) A mathematical sentence formed by placing an inequality symbol between two expressions.	$3 < 5$ and $x + 2 \geq -4$ are *inequalities.*
desigualdad (pág. 282) Un enunciado matemático formado colocando un símbolo de desigualdad entre dos expresiones.	$3 < 5$ y $x + 2 \geq -4$ son *desigualdades.*
input (p. 407) A number on which a relation operates. An input value is in the domain of the relation.	*See* **relation** *and* **function.**
entrada (pág. 407) Un número sobre el que opera una relación. Un valor de entrada está en el dominio de la relación.	*Véase* **relación** *y* **función.**

integers (p. 12) The numbers . . . , $-4, -3, -2, -1, 0, 1, 2,$ $3, 4, . . . ,$ consisting of the negative integers, zero, and the positive integers.

números enteros (pág. 12) Los números ..., $-4, -3, -2,$ $-1, 0, 1, 2, 3, 4, ...,$ que constan de los números enteros negativos, cero y los números enteros positivos.

-8 and 14 are *integers*.

$-8\frac{1}{3}$ and 14.5 are not *integers*.

-8 y 14 son *números enteros*.

$-8\frac{1}{3}$ y 14.5 no son *números enteros*.

---

interest (p. 172) The amount earned or paid for the use of money.

interés (pág. 172) La cantidad ganada o pagada por el uso de dinero.

See simple interest *and* compound interest.

Véase interés simple *e* interés compuesto.

---

interquartile range (p. 655) The difference between the upper and lower quartiles in a box-and-whisker plot.

rango entre cuartiles (pág. 655) La diferencia entre los cuartiles superior e inferior en un diagrama de líneas y bloques.

The *interquartile range* is $37 - 19$, or 18.

El *rango entre cuartiles* es $37 - 19$, ó 18.

---

inverse operations (p. 258) Operations that "undo" each other.

operaciones inversas (pág. 258) Operaciones que se "deshacen" mutuamente.

Addition and subtraction are *inverse operations*.

Multiplication and division are also *inverse operations*.

La suma y la resta son *operaciones inversas*.

La multiplicación y la división también son *operaciones inversas*.

---

irrational number (p. 225) A real number that cannot be written as a quotient of two integers. The decimal form of an irrational number neither terminates nor repeats.

número irracional (pág. 225) Un número real que no puede escribirse como un cociente de dos números enteros. La forma decimal de un número irracional no termina ni se repite.

$\sqrt{2}$ and $0.313113111...$ are *irrational numbers*.

$\sqrt{2}$ y $0.313113111...$ son *números irracionales*.

L

lateral surface area (p. 575) Surface area of a figure excluding the area of its base(s).

área de superficie lateral (pág. 575) Área de la superficie de una figura que excluye el área de su(s) base(s).

lateral surface
superficie lateral

base
base

leading digit (p. 144) The first nonzero digit in a number.	The *leading digit* of 725 is 7. The *leading digit* of 0.002638 is 2.
dígito dominante (pág. 144) El primer dígito distinto de cero en un número.	El *dígito dominante* de 725 es 7. El *dígito dominante* de 0.002638 es 2.
least common denominator (LCD) (p. 80) The least common multiple of the denominators of two or more fractions.	The *LCD* of $\frac{7}{10}$ and $\frac{3}{4}$ is 20, the least common multiple of 10 and 4.
mínimo común denominador (m.c.d.) (pág. 80) El mínimo común múltiplo de los denominadores de dos o más fracciones.	El *m.c.d.* de $\frac{7}{10}$ y $\frac{3}{4}$ es 20, que es el mínimo común múltiplo de 10 y 4.
legs of a right triangle (p. 471) The two sides of a right triangle that form the right angle.	*See* hypotenuse.
catetos de un triángulo rectángulo (pág. 471) Los dos lados de un triángulo rectángulo que forman el ángulo recto.	*Véase* hipotenusa.
like terms (p. 252) Terms that have identical variable parts with corresponding variables raised to the same power. (Two or more constant terms are considered like terms.)	In the expression $x + 4 - 2x + 1$, x and $-2x$ are *like terms*, and 4 and 1 are *like terms*.
términos semejantes (pág. 252) Términos que tienen partes variables idénticas con variables correspondientes elevadas a la misma potencia. (Dos o más términos constantes se consideran términos semejantes.)	En la expresión $x + 4 - 2x + 1$, x y $-2x$ son *términos semejantes* y 4 y 1 son *términos semejantes*.
linear equation (p. 320) An equation whose graph is a line or part of a line.	$7y = 14x + 21$ is a *linear equation*.
ecuación lineal (pág. 320) Una ecuación cuya gráfica es una recta o parte de una recta.	$7y = 14x + 21$ es una *ecuación lineal*.
linear function (p. 409) A function whose graph is a line or a part of a line.	
función lineal (pág. 409) Una función cuya gráfica es una recta o parte de una recta.	
linear inequality (p. 354) An inequality in which the variables appear in separate terms and each variable occurs only to the first power.	$y \leq 2x + 5$ is a *linear inequality*.
desigualdad lineal (pág. 354) Una desigualdad en la que las variables aparecen en términos separados y cada variable se eleva sólo a la primera potencia.	$y \leq 2x + 5$ es una *desigualdad lineal*.

line graph (p. 662) A type of graph in which points representing data pairs are connected by line segments. A line graph is used to show how a quantity changes over time.

gráfica lineal (pág. 662) Un tipo de gráfica en la que los puntos que representan pares de datos se conectan por segmentos de recta. Se usa una gráfica lineal para mostrar cómo una cantidad cambia en el tiempo.

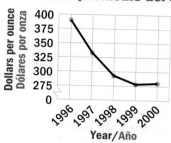

Average Price of Gold
Precio promedio del oro

---

line of reflection (p. 529) The line over which a figure is flipped when the figure undergoes a reflection.

línea de reflexión (pág. 529) La recta sobre la que se invierte una figura cuando dicha figura se refleja.

See reflection.

Véase reflexión.

---

line symmetry (p. 530) A figure has line symmetry if it can be divided by a line, called a line of symmetry, into two parts that are mirror images of each other.

simetría lineal (pág. 530) Una figura tiene simetría lineal si puede dividirse por una recta, llamada línea de simetría, en dos partes que son imágenes reflejas entre sí.

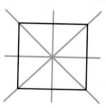

A square has 4 *lines of symmetry*.

Un cuadrado tiene 4 *líneas de simetría*.

---

lower extreme (p. 655) The least value in a data set; also called the *minimum*.

extremo inferior (pág. 655) El valor menor en un conjunto de datos; también llamado el *mínimo*.

See box-and-whisker plot.

Véase diagrama de líneas y bloques.

---

lower quartile (p. 655) The median of the lower half of a data set.

cuartil inferior (pág. 655) La mediana de la mitad inferior de un conjunto de datos.

See box-and-whisker plot.

Véase diagrama de líneas y bloques.

---

markup (p. 160) The increase in the wholesale price of an item.

margen (pág. 160) El aumento con respecto al precio de venta por mayor de un artículo.

The wholesale price of a loaf of bread is $1, but the store sells it for $1.59. The *markup* is $.59.

El precio de venta al por mayor de una hogaza de pan es de $1, pero la tienda la vende a $1.59. El *margen* es de $.59.

mean (pp. 37, 631) The sum of the values in a data set divided by the number of values.

media (págs. 37, 631) La suma de los valores en un conjunto de datos dividida por el número de valores.

The *mean* of the data set
$$85, 59, 97, 71$$
is $\frac{85 + 59 + 97 + 71}{4} = \frac{312}{4} = 78$.

La *media* del conjunto de datos
$$85, 59, 97, 71$$
es $\frac{85 + 59 + 97 + 71}{4} = \frac{312}{4} = 78$.

---

median of a data set (p. 631) The middle value in a data set when the values are written in numerical order. If the data set has an even number of values, the median is the mean of the two middle values.

mediana de un conjunto de datos (pág. 631) El valor que está en el medio de un conjunto de datos cuando los valores están escritos en orden numérico. Si el conjunto de datos tiene un número par de valores, la mediana es la media de los dos valores que están en el medio.

The *median* of the data set
$$8, 17, 21, 23, 26, 29, 34, 40, 45$$
is the middle value, 26.

La *mediana* del conjunto de datos
$$8, 17, 21, 23, 26, 29, 34, 40, 45$$
es 26, el valor que está en el medio.

---

median of a triangle (p. 465) A segment from one vertex of the triangle to the midpoint of the opposite side.

mediana de un triángulo (pág. 465) Segmento que va desde uno de los vértices del triángulo hasta el punto medio del lado opuesto.

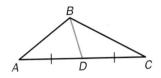

$\overline{BD}$ is a median of $\triangle ABC$.

$\overline{BD}$ es una mediana de $\triangle ABC$.

---

midpoint (p. 454) A point that divides a segment into two congruent segments.

punto medio (pág. 454) Punto que divide a un segmento separándolo en dos segmentos congruentes.

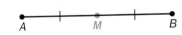

M is the midpoint of $\overline{AB}$.

M es el punto medio de $\overline{AB}$.

---

mode (p. 631) The value in a data set that occurs most often. A data set can have no mode, one mode, or more than one mode.

moda (pág. 631) En un conjunto de datos, el valor que ocurre con mayor frecuencia. Un conjunto de datos puede no tener moda, o puede tener una moda o más de una moda.

The *mode* of the data set
$$73, 42, 55, 77, 61, 55, 68$$
is 55 because it occurs most often.

La *moda* del conjunto de datos
$$73, 42, 55, 77, 61, 55, 68$$
es 55 porque es el valor que aparece más veces.

---

monomial (p. 399) A number, a variable, or a product of a number and one or more variables with whole number exponents.

monomio (pág. 399) Un número, una variable o un producto de un número y una o más variables con exponentes de números naturales.

$3xy$, $8x^2$, x, and 14 are *monomials*.

$3xy$, $8x^2$, x y 14 son *monomios*.

multiplicative identity (p. 32) The number 1 is the multiplicative identity because the product of any number and 1 is the original number. **identidad de la multiplicación** (pág. 32) El número 1 es la identidad de la multiplicación porque el producto de cualquier número y 1 es el número original.	$9 \cdot 1 = 9$ $a \cdot 1 = a$
multiplicative inverse (p. 99) The multiplicative inverse of a number $\frac{a}{b}$ ($a, b \neq 0$) is the reciprocal of the number, or $\frac{b}{a}$. The product of a number and its multiplicative inverse is 1. **inverso multiplicativo** (pág. 99) El inverso multiplicativo de un número $\frac{a}{b}$ ($a, b \neq 0$) es el recíproco de dicho número, es decir $\frac{b}{a}$. El producto de un número y su inverso multiplicativo es 1.	The *multiplicative inverse* of $\frac{3}{2}$ is $\frac{2}{3}$, so $\frac{3}{2} \cdot \frac{2}{3} = 1$. El *inverso multiplicativo* de $\frac{3}{2}$ es $\frac{2}{3}$, por lo tanto $\frac{3}{2} \cdot \frac{2}{3} = 1$.

N

negative integers (p. 12) The integers that are less than zero. **números enteros negativos** (pág. 12) Números enteros menores que cero.	The *negative integers* are $-1, -2, -3, -4, \ldots$. Los *números enteros negativos* son $-1, -2, -3, -4, \ldots$.
net (p. 573) A two-dimensional representation of a solid. This pattern forms a solid when it is folded. **red** (pág. 573) Representación bidimensional de un cuerpo geométrico. Este patrón forma un cuerpo geométrico cuando se dobla.	
nonlinear function (p. 413) Any function whose graph is not a line or part of a line. **función no lineal** (pág. 413) Cualquier función cuyo gráfico no es una recta o parte de una recta.	 The graph shows a *nonlinear function*. La gráfica muestra una *función no lineal*.
numerical data (p. 643) Data that consist of numbers. **datos numéricos** (pág. 643) Datos que consisten en números.	Weights of animals and lengths of hair are *numerical data*. Son *datos numéricos* el peso de los animales y la longitud del cabello.
numerical expression (p. 6) An expression consisting of numbers and operations. **expresión numérica** (pág. 6) Una expresión compuesta por números y operaciones.	$4(3) + 24 \div 2$

O

opposites (p. 14) Two numbers that are the same distance from 0 on a number line but are on opposite sides of 0.

opuestos (pág. 14) Dos números que están a la misma distancia de 0 en una recta numérica pero en lados opuestos de 0.

−3 and 3 are *opposites*.

−3 y 3 son *opuestos*.

---

order of operations (p. 6) A set of rules for evaluating an expression involving more than one operation.

orden de las operaciones (pág. 6) Conjunto de reglas para hallar el valor de una expresión que tiene más de una operación.

To evaluate $3 + 2 \cdot 4$, you perform the multiplication before the addition:
$$3 + 2 \cdot 4 = 3 + 8 = 11$$

Para hallar el valor de $3 + 2 \cdot 4$, haz la multiplicación antes que la suma:
$$3 + 2 \cdot 4 = 3 + 8 = 11$$

---

outlier (p. 632) A value that is much greater than or much less than the other values in a data set.

valor extremo (pág. 632) Un valor que es mucho mayor que o mucho menor que los otros valores en un conjunto de datos.

3 is an *outlier* in the data set
3, 11, 12, 13, 13, 14, 15, 15, 15, 15, 17.

3 es un *valor extremo* en el conjunto de datos
3, 11, 12, 13, 13, 14, 15, 15, 15, 15, 17.

---

output (p. 407) A number produced by evaluating a relation using a given input. An output value is in the range of the relation.

salida (pág. 407) Número producido al hallar el valor de una relación utilizando una entrada dada. Un valor de salida está dentro del rango de la relación.

See relation *and* function.

Véase relación *y* función.

P

parallelogram (p. 478) A quadrilateral with both pairs of opposite sides parallel.

paralelogramo (pág. 478) Un cuadrilátero que tiene dos pares de lados opuestos paralelos.

---

percent (p. 150) A ratio whose denominator is 100. The symbol for percent is %.

porcentaje (pág. 150) Razón cuyo denominador es 100. El símbolo de porcentaje es %.

$$\frac{17}{20} = \frac{17 \cdot 5}{20 \cdot 5} = \frac{85}{100} = 85\%$$

---

percent of change (p. 168) A percent that shows how much a quantity has increased or decreased in comparison with the original amount:

Percent of change, $p\% = \dfrac{\text{New amount} - \text{Original amount}}{\text{Original amount}}$

porcentaje de cambio (pág. 168) Porcentaje que muestra cuánto ha aumentado o disminuido una cantidad en comparación con la cantidad original:

Porcentaje de cambio, $p\% = \dfrac{\text{Nueva cantidad} - \text{Cantidad original}}{\text{Cantidad original}}$

The *percent of change* from 15 to 19 is:
$$p\% = \frac{19 - 15}{15} = \frac{4}{15} \approx 0.267 = 26.7\%$$

El *porcentaje de cambio* de 15 a 19 es:
$$p\% = \frac{19 - 15}{15} = \frac{4}{15} \approx 0.267 = 26.7\%$$

percent of decrease (p. 168) The percent of change in a quantity when the new amount of the quantity is less than the original amount.	*See* **percent of change.**
porcentaje de disminución (pág. 168) Porcentaje de cambio en una cantidad cuando el valor nuevo de una cantidad es menor que la cantidad original.	*Véase* **porcentaje de cambio.**
percent of increase (p. 168) The percent of change in a quantity when the new amount of the quantity is greater than the original amount.	*See* **percent of change.**
porcentaje de aumento (pág. 168) Porcentaje de cambio en una cantidad cuando el valor nuevo de una cantidad es mayor que la cantidad original.	*Véase* **porcentaje de cambio.**
perfect square (p. 213) A number that is the square of an integer.	**49 is a *perfect square* because 49 = $(\pm 7)^2$.**
cuadrado perfecto (pág. 213) Un número que es el cuadrado de un número entero.	**49 es un *cuadrado perfecto* porque 49 = $(\pm 7)^2$.**
perpendicular bisector (p. 455) A segment, ray, line, or plane that is perpendicular to a segment at its midpoint.	
mediatriz (pág. 455) Segmento, semirrecta, recta o plano que es perpendicular a un segmento en su punto medio.	
place value (p. 133) The value given to a digit in a number by virtue of the place the digit occupies relative to the decimal point.	**The *place value* of 3 in 4.532 is 3 hundredths.**
valor posicional (pág. 133) El valor dado a un dígito en un número en virtud del lugar que el dígito ocupa en el número en relación con el punto decimal.	**El *valor posicional* de 3 en 4.532 es tres centésimas.**
polyhedron (p. 566) A solid that is enclosed by polygons.	
poliedro (pág. 566) Cuerpo geométrico encerrado por polígonos.	
polynomial (p. 689) A monomial or a sum of monomials.	*See* **binomial, trinomial, monomial.**
polinomio (pág. 689) Un monomio o una suma de monomios.	*Véase* **binomio, trinomio, monomio.**
positive integers (p. 12) The integers that are greater than zero.	**The *positive integers* are 1, 2, 3, 4, ...**
números enteros positivos (pág. 12) Números enteros mayores que cero.	**Los *números enteros positivos* son 1, 2, 3, 4, ...**

power (p. 5) A product formed from repeated multiplication by the same number or expression. A power consists of a base and an exponent.

2^4 is a *power* with base 2 and exponent 4.
$2^4 = 2 \cdot 2 \cdot 2 \cdot 2 = 16$

potencia (pág. 5) Producto que se obtiene de la multiplicación repetida por el mismo número o expresión. Una potencia está compuesta de una base y un exponente.

2^4 es una *potencia* con base 2 y exponente 4.
$2^4 = 2 \cdot 2 \cdot 2 \cdot 2 = 16$

---

principal (p. 172) An amount of money that is deposited or borrowed.

See simple interest *and* compound interest.

capital (pág. 172) Una cantidad de dinero que se deposita o se solicita en préstamo.

Véase interés simple *e* interés compuesto.

---

prism (p. 566) A solid, formed by polygons, that has two congruent bases lying in parallel planes.

prisma (pág. 566) Cuerpo geométrico formado por polígonos, que tiene dos bases congruentes ubicadas en planos paralelos.

bases/bases
Rectangular prism / **Prisma rectangular**
Triangular prism / **Prisma triangular**

---

profit (p. 162) The difference of the income and expenses for a business.

Profit = Income − Expenses

ganancia (pág. 162) La diferencia entre el ingreso y los gastos en una actividad comercial.

Ganancia = Ingresos − Gastos

---

proportion (p. 277) An equation stating that two ratios are equivalent.

$\frac{3}{5} = \frac{6}{10}$ and $\frac{x}{12} = \frac{25}{30}$ are *proportions*.

proporción (pág. 277) Una ecuación que establece que dos razones son equivalentes.

$\frac{3}{5} = \frac{6}{10}$ y $\frac{x}{12} = \frac{25}{30}$ son *proporciones*.

---

pyramid (p. 566) A solid, formed by polygons, that has one base. The base can be any polygon, and the other faces are triangles.

pirámide (pág. 566) Cuerpo geométrico, formado por polígonos, que tiene una base. La base puede ser cualquier polígono y las otras caras son triángulos.

base/base

Pythagorean Theorem (p. 471) For any right triangle, the sum of the squares of the lengths a and b of the legs equals the square of the length c of the hypotenuse: $a^2 + b^2 = c^2$.

Teorema de Pitágoras (pág. 471) Para cualquier triángulo rectángulo, la suma de los cuadrados de las longitudes a y b de los catetos es igual al cuadrado de la longitud c de la hipotenusa: $a^2 + b^2 = c^2$.

25
15
20
$15^2 + 20^2 = 25^2$

quadrilateral (p. 478) A closed plane figure made up of four line segments, called sides, that intersect only at their endpoints; a polygon with four sides.

cuadrilátero (pág. 478) Figura plana cerrada formada por cuatro segmentos de recta, llamados lados, que se intersecan sólo en sus extremos; polígono de cuatro lados.

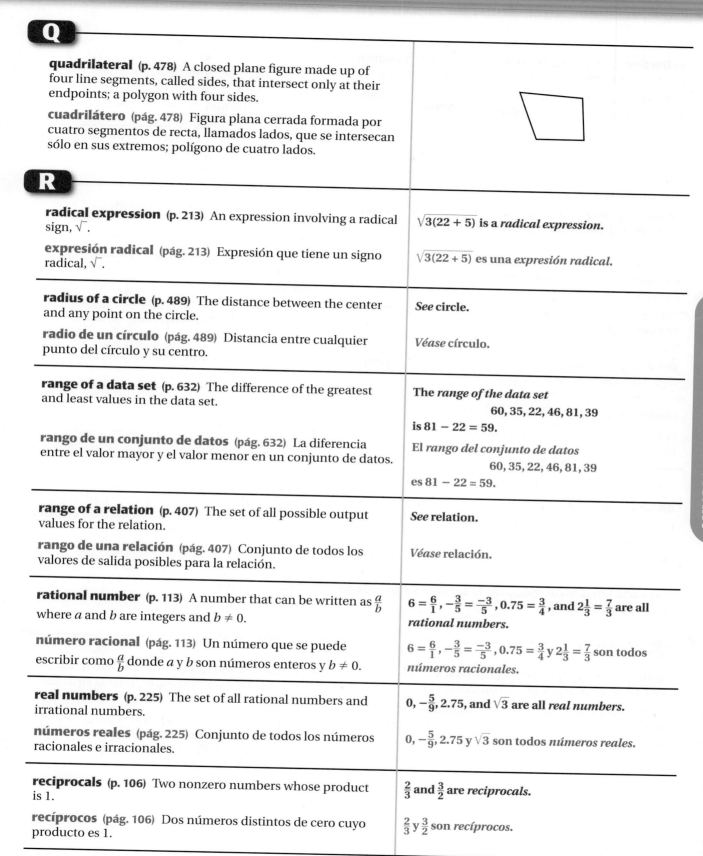

radical expression (p. 213) An expression involving a radical sign, $\sqrt{}$.

expresión radical (pág. 213) Expresión que tiene un signo radical, $\sqrt{}$.

$\sqrt{3(22 + 5)}$ is a *radical expression*.

$\sqrt{3(22 + 5)}$ es una *expresión radical*.

---

radius of a circle (p. 489) The distance between the center and any point on the circle.

radio de un círculo (pág. 489) Distancia entre cualquier punto del círculo y su centro.

See circle.

Véase círculo.

---

range of a data set (p. 632) The difference of the greatest and least values in the data set.

rango de un conjunto de datos (pág. 632) La diferencia entre el valor mayor y el valor menor en un conjunto de datos.

The *range of the data set*
$$60, 35, 22, 46, 81, 39$$
is $81 - 22 = 59$.

El *rango del conjunto de datos*
$$60, 35, 22, 46, 81, 39$$
es $81 - 22 = 59$.

---

range of a relation (p. 407) The set of all possible output values for the relation.

rango de una relación (pág. 407) Conjunto de todos los valores de salida posibles para la relación.

See relation.

Véase relación.

---

rational number (p. 113) A number that can be written as $\frac{a}{b}$ where a and b are integers and $b \neq 0$.

número racional (pág. 113) Un número que se puede escribir como $\frac{a}{b}$ donde a y b son números enteros y $b \neq 0$.

$6 = \frac{6}{1}, -\frac{3}{5} = \frac{-3}{5}, 0.75 = \frac{3}{4}$, and $2\frac{1}{3} = \frac{7}{3}$ are all *rational numbers*.

$6 = \frac{6}{1}, -\frac{3}{5} = \frac{-3}{5}, 0.75 = \frac{3}{4}$ y $2\frac{1}{3} = \frac{7}{3}$ son todos *números racionales*.

---

real numbers (p. 225) The set of all rational numbers and irrational numbers.

números reales (pág. 225) Conjunto de todos los números racionales e irracionales.

$0, -\frac{5}{9}, 2.75$, and $\sqrt{3}$ are all *real numbers*.

$0, -\frac{5}{9}, 2.75$ y $\sqrt{3}$ son todos *números reales*.

---

reciprocals (p. 106) Two nonzero numbers whose product is 1.

recíprocos (pág. 106) Dos números distintos de cero cuyo producto es 1.

$\frac{2}{3}$ and $\frac{3}{2}$ are *reciprocals*.

$\frac{2}{3}$ y $\frac{3}{2}$ son *recíprocos*.

reflection (p. 528) A transformation that creates a mirror image of each point of a figure.

reflexión (pág. 528) Transformación que crea una imagen refleja de cada punto de una figura.

reflection
reflexión
reflection in the y-axis
reflexión en el eje y

---

relation (p. 407) A pairing of numbers in one set, called the domain, with numbers in another set, called the range.

$(5, 7), (6, 5), (0, 5), (6, 0)$ is a *relation*.
Domain: 0, 5, 6
Range: 0, 5, 7

relación (pág. 407) La asociación en pares de números en un conjunto, llamado dominio, con números de otro conjunto, llamado rango.

$(5, 7), (6, 5), (0, 5), (6, 0)$ es una *relación*.
Dominio: 0, 5, 6
Rango: 0, 5, 7

---

repeating decimal (p. 113) A decimal that has one or more digits that repeat without end.

$0.7777\ldots$ and $1.\overline{29}$ are *repeating decimals*.

decimal periódico (pág. 113) Decimal que tiene uno o más dígitos que se repiten infinitamente.

$0.7777\ldots$ y $1.\overline{29}$ son *decimales periódicos*.

---

rhombus (p. 478) A parallelogram with four congruent sides.

rombo (pág. 478) Paralelogramo que tiene cuatro lados congruentes.

---

rise (p. 334) The vertical change between two points on a line.

See **slope.**

distancia vertical (pág. 334) El cambio vertical entre dos puntos en una recta.

Véase **pendiente.**

---

run (p. 334) The horizontal change between two points on a line.

See **slope.**

distancia horizontal (pág. 334) El cambio horizontal entre dos puntos en una recta.

Véase **pendiente.**

S

scale (p. 541) The relationship between a scale drawing's or scale model's dimensions and the actual object's dimensions.

In a scale drawing, the *scale* "1 in. : 10 ft" means that 1 inch in the drawing represents an actual distance of 10 feet.

escala (pág. 541) La relación de las dimensiones a escala de un dibujo o las dimensiones de un modelo a escala con las dimensiones reales.

En un dibujo a escala, la *escala* "1 pulg. : 10 pies" significa que una pulgada en el dibujo representa una distancia real de 10 pies.

---

scale drawing (p. 541) A two-dimensional drawing of an object in which the dimensions are in proportion to the actual dimensions of the object.

dibujo a escala (pág. 541) Un dibujo en dos dimensiones de un objeto cuyas dimensiones están en proporción con las dimensiones reales del objeto.

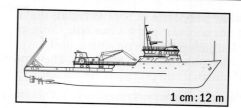

1 cm : 12 m

---

scale factor (p. 535) In a dilation, the ratio of a side length of the image to the corresponding side length of the original figure.

factor de escala (pág. 535) En una dilatación, la razón entre la longitud de un lado de la imagen y la longitud del lado correspondiente de la figura original.

See **dilation.**

Véase **dilatación.**

---

scale model (p. 541) A three-dimensional model of an object in which the dimensions are in proportion to the actual dimensions of the object.

modelo a escala (pág. 541) Un modelo en tres dimensiones de un objeto cuyas dimensiones están en proporción con las dimensiones reales del objeto.

A *scale model* of the White House appears in Tobu World Square in Japan. The scale used is 1 : 25.

En Tobu World Square, en Japón, hay un *modelo a escala* de la Casa Blanca. La escala utilizada es de 1 : 25.

---

scatter plot (p. 660) The graph of a set of ordered pairs (x, y), which is a collection of points in a coordinate plane.

diagrama de dispersión (pág. 660) La gráfica de un conjunto de pares ordenados (x, y), que es un grupo de puntos en un plano de coordenadas.

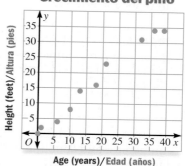

Pine Tree Growth
Crecimiento del pino

Height (feet)/Altura (pies)

Age (years)/Edad (años)

---

scientific notation (p. 201) A number is written in scientific notation if it has the form $c \times 10^n$, where c is greater than or equal to 1 and less than 10, and n is an integer.

notación científica (pág. 201) Un número está escrito en notación científica si tiene la forma $c \times 10^n$ donde c es mayor que o igual a 1 y menor que 10, y n es un número entero.

In *scientific notation*, 328,000 is written as 3.28×10^5, and 0.00061 is written as 6.1×10^{-4}.

En *notación científica*, 328,000 se escribe como 3.28×10^5 y 0.00061 se escribe como 6.1×10^{-4}.

---

segment bisector (p. 455) A point, ray, line, segment, or plane that intersects a segment at its midpoint.

bisectriz de un segmento (pág. 455) Un punto, una semirrecta, una recta, un segmento o un plano que interseca un segmento en su punto medio.

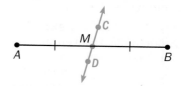

$\overleftrightarrow{CD}$ is a segment bisector of $\overline{AB}$.

$\overleftrightarrow{CD}$ es una bisectriz del segmento $\overline{AB}$.

similar polygons (p. 517) Polygons that have the same shape but not necessarily the same size. Corresponding angles of similar polygons are congruent, and the ratios of the lengths of corresponding sides are equal. The symbol ~ is used to indicate that two polygons are similar.

polígonos semejantes (pág. 517) Polígonos que tienen la misma forma pero no necesariamente el mismo tamaño. Los ángulos correspondientes de los polígonos semejantes son congruentes y las razones de las longitudes de los lados correspondientes son iguales. Se utiliza el símbolo ~ para indicar que dos polígonos son semejantes.

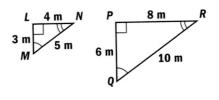

$$\triangle LMN \sim \triangle PQR$$

similar solids (p. 605) Two solids of the same type with equal ratios of corresponding linear measures, such as heights or radii.

cuerpos geométricos semejantes (pág. 605) Dos cuerpos geométricos del mismo tipo y con razones iguales en las medidas lineales correspondientes, como las alturas o los radios.

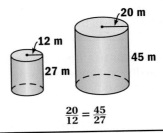

$$\frac{20}{12} = \frac{45}{27}$$

simple interest (p. 172) Interest that is earned or paid only on the principal. The simple interest I is the product of the principal P, the annual interest rate r written as a decimal, and the time t in years: $I = Prt$.

interés simple (pág. 172) El interés ganado o pagado sólo sobre el capital. El interés simple I es el producto del capital P, la tasa de interés anual r escrita en forma decimal y el tiempo t en años: $I = Prt$.

You deposit $700 in a savings account that pays a 3% *simple annual interest* rate. After 5 years, the interest is
$I = Prt = (700)(0.03)(5) = \$105$, and your account balance is $700 + $105 = $805.

Depositas $700 en una cuenta de ahorros que genera un *interés anual simple* del 3%. Después de 5 años, el interés es
$I = Prt = (700)(0.03)(5) = \$105$, y el saldo de tu cuenta es $700 + $105 = $805.

simplest form of a fraction (p. 75) A fraction is in simplest form if its numerator and denominator have a greatest common factor of 1.

mínima expresión de una fracción (pág. 75) Una fracción está en su mínima expresión si el máximo común divisor del numerador y del denominador es 1.

The *simplest form of the fraction* $\frac{6}{8}$ is $\frac{3}{4}$.

La *mínima expresión de la fracción* $\frac{6}{8}$ es $\frac{3}{4}$.

simplest form of a radical expression (p. 219) A radical expression is in simplest form when the expression under the radical sign has no perfect square factors other than 1, there are no fractions under the radical sign, and no radicals appear in the denominator of any fraction.

forma más simple de una expresión radical (pág. 219) Una expresión radical está en su forma más simple cuando la expresión bajo el signo radical no tiene más factores cuadrados perfectos que 1, no hay fracciones bajo el signo radical y ningún radical aparece en el denominador de una fracción.

$\sqrt{45}$ in simplest form is $3\sqrt{5}$.

$\frac{1}{\sqrt{16}}$ in simplest form is $\frac{1}{4}$.

$\sqrt{45}$ en su forma más simple es $3\sqrt{5}$.

$\frac{1}{\sqrt{16}}$ en su forma más simple es $\frac{1}{4}$.

skew lines (p. 561) Lines that do not intersect and are not coplanar.

rectas alabeadas (pág. 561) Rectas que no se cortan y que no son coplanarias.

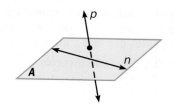

Lines *n* and *p* are skew lines.

Las rectas *n* y *p* son rectas alabeadas.

---

slant height (p. 580) The height of each lateral face of a regular pyramid.

altura inclinada (pág. 580) En una pirámide regular, la altura de cada cara lateral.

---

slope (p. 334) The slope of a nonvertical line is the ratio of the rise (vertical change) to the run (horizontal change) between any two points on the line.

pendiente (pág. 334) La pendiente de una recta no vertical es la razón entre la distancia vertical (cambio vertical) y la distancia horizontal (cambio horizontal) entre dos puntos cualesquiera de la recta.

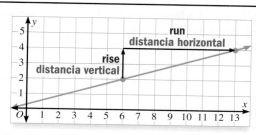

The *slope* of the line above is:

$$\text{slope} = \frac{\text{rise}}{\text{run}} = \frac{2}{7}$$

La *pendiente* de la recta anterior es:

$$\text{pendiente} = \frac{\text{distancia vertical}}{\text{distancia horizontal}} = \frac{2}{7}$$

---

slope-intercept form (p. 342) The form of a linear equation $y = mx + b$ where m is the slope and b is the y-intercept.

forma de pendiente e intersección (pág. 342) La forma de una ecuación lineal $y = mx + b$, donde m es la pendiente y b es la intersección en y.

$y = 6x + 8$ is in *slope-intercept form.*

$y = 6x + 8$ está en la *forma de pendiente e intersección.*

---

solid (p. 566) A three-dimensional figure that encloses a part of space.

cuerpo geométrico (pág. 566) Figura tridimensional que encierra una parte del espacio.

See **cone, cylinder, prism, pyramid,** *and* **sphere.**

Véase **cono, cilindro, prisma, pirámide** y **esfera.**

---

solution of an equation in one variable (p. 257) A number that makes the equation true when substituted for the variable in the equation.

solución de una ecuación con una variable (pág. 257) Número que hace verdadera la ecuación cuando sustituye la variable en la ecuación.

The *solution of the equation* $n - 3 = 4$ is 7.

La *solución de la ecuación* $n - 3 = 4$ es 7.

solution of an equation in two variables (p. 315) An ordered pair (x, y) whose coordinates make the equation true when the values of x and y are substituted into the equation.	$(3, 8)$ is a *solution* of $y = 3x - 1$.
solución de una ecuación con dos variables (pág. 315) Un par ordenado (x, y) cuyas coordenadas hacen verdadera la ecuación cuando se sustituyen los valores de x e y en la ecuación.	$(3, 8)$ es una *solución* de $y = 3x - 1$.
solution of an inequality in one variable (p. 282) A number that makes the inequality true when substituted for the variable in the inequality.	4 is a *solution of the inequality* $y + 2 > 5$.
solución de una desigualdad con una variable (pág. 282) Un número que hace verdadera la desigualdad cuando sustituyen la variable en la desigualdad.	4 es una *solución de la desigualdad* $y + 2 > 5$.
solution of a linear inequality in two variables (p. 354) An ordered pair (x, y) whose coordinates make the inequality true when the values of x and y are substituted into the inequality.	A *solution* of $y \geq 2x - 9$ is $(5, 1)$.
solución de una desigualdad lineal con dos variables (pág. 354) Un par ordenado (x, y) cuyas coordenadas hacen verdadera la desigualdad cuando los valores de x e y se sustituyen en la desigualdad.	La *solución* de $y \geq 2x - 9$ es $(5, 1)$.
solution of a system of linear equations in two variables (p. 360) An ordered pair (x,y) that is a solution of each equation in a system of linear equations.	The *solution of the system of linear equations in two variables* below is $(3, 3)$. $3y - x = 6$ $3y + 2x = 15$
solución de una ecuación lineal con dos variables (pág. 360) Un par ordenado (x,y) que es la solución de cada ecuación en un sistema de ecuaciones lineales.	La *solución de la ecuación con dos variables* que se presenta a continuación es $(3, 3)$. $3y - x = 6$ $3y + 2x = 15$
solution of a system of linear inequalities in two variables (p. 362) An ordered pair (x, y) that is a solution of each inequality in the system.	A *solution of the system of linear inequalities* below is $(-1, 1)$. $y > -2x - 5$ $y \leq x + 3$
solución de un sistema de desigualdades lineales con dos variables (pág. 362) Un par ordenado (x, y) que es una solución de cada desigualdad en el sistema.	Una *solución de un sistema de desigualdades lineales* es $(-1, 1)$. $y > -2x - 5$ $y \leq x + 3$
sphere (p. 566) A solid formed by all points in space that are the same distance from a fixed point called the center. **esfera** (pág. 566) Cuerpo geométrico formado por todos los puntos en el espacio que se encuentran a la misma distancia de un punto fijo llamado centro.	center centro

square root (p. 213) A square root of a number n is a number m which, when multiplied by itself, equals n.

raíz cuadrada (pág. 213) La raíz cuadrada de un número n es un número m, el cual, cuando se multiplica por sí mismo, es igual a n.

The *square roots* of 81 are 9 and -9 because $9^2 = 81$ and $(-9)^2 = 81$.

Las *raíces cuadradas* de 81 son 9 y -9 porque $9^2 = 81$ y $(-9)^2 = 81$.

---

standard form of a polynomial (p. 689) A polynomial written with the exponents of the variable decreasing from left to right.

forma estándar de un polinomio (pág. 689) Polinomio escrito con los exponentes de la variable en orden descendente de izquierda a derecha.

$3x^5 - 8x^3 + 5x^2 + x - 2$ is in *standard form*.

$3x^5 - 8x^3 + 5x^2 + x - 2$ está en *forma estándar*.

---

statistics (p. 631) Numerical values used to summarize and compare sets of data.

estadística (pág. 631) Valores numéricos usados para resumir y comparar conjuntos de datos.

See **mean, median, mode,** *and* **range.**

Ver **media, mediana, moda** *y* **rango.**

---

stem-and-leaf plot (p. 650) A data display that helps you see how data values are distributed. Each data value is separated into a leaf (the last digit) and a stem (the preceding digit or digits). In an ordered stem-and-leaf plot, the leaves for each stem are listed in order from least to greatest.

diagrama de tallo y hojas (pág. 650) Diagrama que muestra cómo se distribuyen los valores en un conjunto de datos. Cada valor está separado en una hoja (el último dígito) y un tallo (el o los dígitos precedentes). En un diagrama de tallo y hojas ordenado, las hojas para cada tallo están en orden de menor a mayor.

```
stems/tallos    leaves/hojas

    10        |   8
    11        |   2   2   5
    12        |   1   3
```

Key/Clave: 10 | 8 = 108

---

surface area of a polyhedron (p. 574) The sum of the areas of the faces of the polyhedron.

área de la superficie de un poliedro (pág. 574) La suma de las áreas de las caras del poliedro.

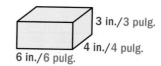

3 in./3 pulg.
4 in./4 pulg.
6 in./6 pulg.

Surface area
$$= 2(6)(4) + 2(6)(3) + 2(4)(3)$$
$$= 108 \text{ in.}^2$$

Área de la superficie
$$= 2(6)(4) + 2(6)(3) + 2(4)(3)$$
$$= 108 \text{ pulg.}^2$$

---

system of linear equations in two variables (p. 360) A set of two or more linear equations with the same variables.

sistema de ecuaciones lineales con dos variables (pág. 360) Un conjunto de dos o más ecuaciones lineales con las mismas variables.

$$3y - x = 6$$
$$3y + 2x = 15$$

system of linear inequalities in two variables (p. 362) A system consisting of two or more linear inequalities with the same variables.

sistema de desigualdades lineales con dos variables (pág. 362) Un sistema que consiste de dos o más desigualdades lineales con las mismas variables.

$$x + y \leq 8$$
$$4x - y > 6$$

T

terminating decimal (p. 113) A decimal that has a final digit.

decimal exacto (pág. 113) Decimal que tiene un dígito final.

0.4 and 3.6125 are *terminating decimals*.

0.4 y 3.6125 son *decimales exactos*.

---

terms of an expression (p. 252) The parts of an expression that are added together.

términos de una expresión (pág. 252) Las partes de una expresión que se suman entre sí.

The *terms* of $2x + 3$ are $2x$ and 3.

Los *términos* de $2x + 3$ son $2x$ y 3.

---

transformation (p. 522) An operation that changes a figure into another figure, called the image.

transformación (pág. 522) Operación que convierte una figura en otra figura, llamada imagen.

See **translation, reflection,** *and* **dilation.**

Véase **traslación, reflexión** y **dilatación.**

---

translation (p. 522) A transformation that moves each point of a figure the same distance in the same direction.

traslación (pág. 522) Transformación que mueve cada punto de una figura la misma distancia en la misma dirección.

---

trapezoid (p. 478) A quadrilateral with exactly one pair of parallel sides.

trapecio (pág. 478) Cuadrilátero que tiene exactamente un par de lados paralelos.

---

trinomial (p. 689) A polynomial with three terms.

trinomio (pág. 689) Polinomio que tiene tres términos.

$$3x^2 + 2x - 4$$

U

unit analysis (p. 53) Evaluating expressions with units of measure and checking that your answer uses correct units; also called *dimensional analysis*.

análisis de unidades (pág. 53) Hallar el valor de expresiones con unidades de medida y comprobar que la respuesta usa unidades correctas; también llamado *análisis de dimensiones*.

$$\frac{\text{miles}}{\text{hour}} \cdot \text{hours} = \text{miles}$$

$$\frac{\text{millas}}{\text{hora}} \cdot \text{horas} = \text{millas}$$

unit rate (p. 443) A rate that has a denominator of 1 unit.

tasa unitaria (pág. 443) Una tasa cuyo denominador es 1 unidad.

$\dfrac{\$9}{1\ \text{hour}}$ is a *unit rate*.

$\dfrac{\$9}{1\ \text{hora}}$ es una *tasa unitaria*.

---

upper extreme (p. 655) The greatest value in a data set; also called the *maximum*.

extremo superior (pág. 655) El valor mayor en un conjunto de datos; también llamado el *máximo*.

See **box-and-whisker plot.**

Véase **diagrama de líneas y bloques.**

---

upper quartile (p. 655) The median of the upper half of a data set.

cuartil superior (pág. 655) La mediana de la mitad superior de un conjunto de datos.

See **box-and-whisker plot.**

Véase **diagrama de líneas y bloques.**

V

variable (p. 7) A symbol, usually a letter, that is used to represent one or more numbers.

variable (pág. 7) Símbolo, usualmente una letra, que se usa para representar uno o más números.

In the expression $m + 5$, the letter m is the *variable*.

En la expresión $m + 5$, la letra m es la *variable*.

---

vertex of a polyhedron (p. 567) A point at which three or more edges of a polyhedron meet.

vértice de un poliedro (pág. 567) Punto en el que se juntan tres o más aristas de un poliedro.

See **edge of a polyhedron.**

Véase **arista de un poliedro.**

---

vertex of a triangle (p. 463) A point where two sides of a triangle meet.

vértice de un triángulo (pág. 463) El punto donde se encuentran dos lados de un triángulo.

---

vertical line test (p. 416) If any vertical line intersects a graph at more than one point, then the graph does not represent a function.

prueba de la línea vertical (pág. 416) Si una recta vertical interseca una gráfica en más de un punto, entonces la gráfica no representa una función.

Function
Función

Not a function
No es una función

X

x-intercept (p. 327) The x-coordinate of a point where a graph intersects the x-axis.

intersección en x (pág. 327) La coordenada x de un punto donde una gráfica interseca el eje x.

The x-intercept is **4**.
La intersección en x es **4**.

y-intercept (p. 327) The *y*-coordinate of a point where a graph intersects the *y*-axis.

intersección en y (pág. 327) La coordenada *y* de un punto donde una gráfica interseca el eje *y*.

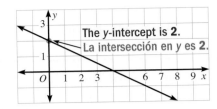

The *y*-intercept is **2**.
La intersección en *y* es **2**.

Index

INDEX

Congruent angles, 455
  angle bisectors and, 455–458
Congruent polygons, 515, 516–517,
  519, 548, 550
  tessellation and, 526
Congruent segments, 454
  constructing, 459
  creating by bisecting, 459
Conjecture, *See also* Draw
  conclusions
  making, exercises, 470, 515
Connections, *See* Applications
Connect Skills to Problem Solving,
  exercises, *Throughout. See for
  example,* 9, 15, 21, 27, 34, 39,
  44, 51, 56, 78, 83, 88
Constant term, in an algebraic
  expression, 252
Constant of variation, 348
Construction(s), 459–461, 468–469,
  486–487, 496–497
  add angles, 461
  add segments, 460
  altitude of a triangle, 469
  bisect an angle, 461
  chord congruent to a segment, 496
  circle with a given radius, 739
  copy an angle, 460
  copy a segment, 459
  copy a triangle, 468
  difference of two segments, 739
  draw a parallelogram, 486
  draw a rectangle, 487
  equilateral triangle, 468
  find the center of a circle, 497
  right triangle, 469
  segment bisector, 459
  sixty degree central angle, 496
**Converse of the Pythagorean
  Theorem,** 473
  using, 473–476
Converse of a statement, 473
Conversion, *See* Measurement
Conversion factor(s), 437
  multiple, 449–453
  using, 437–442
Coordinate notation
  reflection and, 528–533
  translation and, 523–526
Coordinate plane, 628, 734
  dilations in, 535–539, 548, 552
  graphs of cubic functions in, 415,
  417–420
  graphs of linear equations in,
  320–332, 341–353
  graphs of linear inequalities in,
  354–359, 371, 375
  graphs of linear systems in,
  360–361, 364–367, 371,
  376

graphs of quadratic functions in,
  413–414, 417–420
  graphs of relations in, 407–412
  half plane, 355
  origin, 734
  plotting ordered pairs in, 734
    game, 313, 513
  quadrants, 734
  reflections in, 528–533
  scatter plots in, 660–667, 678
  translations in, 522–527
  x-axis, 734
  y-axis, 734
Coplanar lines, 561
Coplanar points, 561
Copying
  an angle, 460
  a segment, 459
  a triangle, 468
Correlation
  negative, 661, 664–667
  positive, 661, 664–667
  relatively no, 661, 664–667
Corresponding angles, 516
Corresponding parts, 516
Corresponding sides, 516
Counterexample, 281
Critical thinking, *See* Reasoning
Cross multiplication, *See* Cross
  products
Cross products, 278
  to solve proportions, 278–281, 305,
  512
Cross products property, 278
  using, 278–281, 305, 512
Cube, volume of, 9, 742
Cubic function(s), 415, 417–420, 422,
  426
  form for, 415
Cubic unit, 588, 589, 591
Cumulative Review, 242–243,
  432–433, 624–625, 684–685
Customary units, *See also*
  Measurement
  converting among, 437–442, 500,
  501, 502
    multi-step conversions,
    449–453, 503
  converting to metric, 438,
  440–442, 500, 502
Cycle diagram, graphic organizer,
  132, 157, 182
Cylinder, 566, 613
  base of, 566, 575, 590
  height of, 575, 590
  lateral surface area of, 575, 577,
  578, 579
  net for, 575, 577, 597
  oblique, 595
    volume of, 595

surface area of, 575–579, 616
  formula, 575, 613
volume of, 590–596, 617, 620, 688
  formula, 590, 613

D

Data, 743, *See also* Statistics
  analyzing
    choose a representative average,
    630, 632, 634
    correlation, 661, 664–667
    effect of outliers, 632–635
    extremes, 655
    interquartile range, 656
    measures of central tendency,
    629–630, 672, 674–675, 680
    measures of dispersion,
    632–635, 655–659, 672, 678
    outliers, 632
    quartiles, 655
    range, 632–635
    slope, 333–339
    trend, 666
  categorical, 643
  collecting
    from an experiment, 233, 629
    from a survey, 630
  displaying
    in a bar graph, 636–637,
    639–642, 672, 675
    choosing a data display,
    639–642, 662, 663, 665–667,
    672
    in a circle graph, 638–642, 672,
    675
    frequency of an interval,
    643–648
    on a graphing calculator, 668,
    669
    in a histogram, 644–648, 676
    in a line graph, 662–667, 672
    in a scatter plot, 660–661,
    663–667, 672, 678
  numerical, 643
  organizing
    in a box-and-whisker plot,
    655–659, 672, 677
    in a concept map, 436, 482, 502
    in a cycle diagram, 132, 157,
    182
    in a decision tree, 314, 351, 372
    in a definition and examples
    chart, 4, 14, 62
    in a four square diagram, 194,
    216, 234
    in a frequency table, 643,
    645–648, 672, 676
    in an information frame, 384,
    389, 424

ordering, 80–84, 119, 122
percent and, 150–153, 155–159, 180, 181, 184, 763
reciprocals and, 106–111
repeating decimals and, 265, 266
simplest form, 75
simplifying, 75–79, 119, 121
subtracting
with a common denominator, 85–89, 119, 122
with different denominators, 90–95, 119, 120, 123
Frequency, of an interval, 643–648
Frequency table, 643
making, 643, 645–648, 676
Front-end estimation, 138–140
Function(s), 409, *See also* Linear equation(s); Linear function(s)
linear, 320–332, 341–353, 409–412
nonlinear, 413–420
cubic, 415, 417–420
quadratic, 413–414, 417–420
relations and, 408–412, 422, 426
vertical line test and, 416, 418
volume, 592, 594, 610

G

Games
algebra
evaluating expressions, 192, 244–245
simplifying expressions, 687
solving equations, 312, 382–383
solving proportions, 512
area and perimeter, 558–559
graphing ordered pairs, 313, 513
number sense
integer exponents, 686
number properties, 193
whole number exponents, 192, 434–435
operations
adding fractions, 131
integer, 72, 73
with percents, 626–627
whole number, 2, 3
Geometry, *See also* Applications; Area; Measurement; Surface area; Volume
angles
acute, 736
adding, construction, 461
bisecting, 455–458, 504
construction, 461
central, of a circle, 489
classifying, 736–737
classifying triangles by, 736–737
congruent, 455–458

copying, 460
corresponding, 516
degree measure for, 738
drawing, 515, 738
of incidence, 458
measure of one angle of a *n*-gon, 741
measuring to make circle graphs, 638–642
naming, 736
obtuse, 736
of refraction, 458
right, 736
straight, 736
sum of angle measures for a *n*-gon, 740–741
sum of measures for a quadrilateral, 479, 483–485
symbol for, 736
vertex of, 736
angle bisector, 455–458
chord, 489, 496, 497
circle, 489–495, 498, 500, 506
cone, 566, 613
net for, 581, 582, 583, 597
constructions, 459–461, 468–469, 486–487, 496–497
coplanar lines, 561
coplanar points, 561
corresponding parts, 515, 516
cube, 9
cylinder, 566, 575, 590, 613
net for, 575, 577, 597
oblique, 595
diagonals
of a polyhedra, 567
of a quadrilateral, 479
dilation, 535–539, 548
endpoint, 735
Euler's formula, 570
great circle, 565
half plane, 355
hexagon, 467, 740
lateral faces, 580
lines
coplanar, 561, 615
as intersection of three planes, 562
parallel, 478
skew, 561, 621
line segment, 454
midsegment, 485
oblique solid, 595
octagon, 740, 741
parallelogram, 477, 478, 480, 483, 486, 500
parallel planes, 562
pentagon, 740
planes, intersecting, 562–565
point, 735

polygons
classifying, 740–741
congruent, 515–517, 519, 548, 550
as faces of polyhedra, 566–571
regular, 740
polyhedra, 566–568, 616
Pythagorean Theorem, 471–476, 505
converse of, 473–476, 505
ray, 735
rectangle, 478, 487, 500, 560, 742
golden, 521
rhombus, 478, 479, 482, 500
segments, 735
congruent, 454, 459
similar polygons, 515, 517–521, 548, 550
similar solids, 604–611, 618
slant height, 580, 581
sphere, 566, 584, 613
spherical, 565
trapezoid, 478, 481, 484, 485, 500
triangle inequality theorem, 287
triangles
classifying, 736–737
constructions, 468, 469
right, 470–476, 505
Get Ready Games, *See* Games
Golden rectangle, 521
Graphic organizers
concept map, 436, 482, 502
cycle diagram, 132, 157, 182
decision tree, 314, 351, 372
definitions and examples chart, 4
four square diagram, 194, 216, 234
information frame, 384, 389, 424
information wheel, 560, 593, 615
notetaking organizer, 246, 254, 302
process diagram, 74, 121
word magnet, 628, 645, 674
word triangle, 514, 524, 550
Y chart, 688, 701, 714
Graphing
cubic functions, 415, 417–420, 422, 426
horizontal lines, 322, 323
inequalities, 282–286, 288, 290, 305
linear, 354–359, 375
two–step, 293–296
linear equations
direct variation, 349–353
using intercepts, 327–332
using ordered pairs, 320–325
using slope, 334–339
linear functions, 320–332, 341–353
linear systems, 360–361, 364–367, 376
nonlinear functions, 413–420, 422, 426

to solve equations, 263–267, 300, 304

to solve inequalities, 288–292, 306

to solve problems, 728–729

whole number, game, 2, 3

words indicating, 247, 300

Multiplication property of equality, 263

using, 263–267, 300, 304

Multiplication property of inequality, 288

using, 288–292, 300, 306

Multiplication property of zero, 32, 49, 60

using, 32–35

Multiplicative identity, 32

using, 32–35

Multiplicative inverse, 99

to divide fractions and mixed numbers, 106–111, 119, 124

negative powers and, 387–391

Multi-step problem

examples, *Throughout. See for example,* 13, 17, 37, 81, 138, 160, 161, 162, 169, 226, 265

exercises, *Throughout. See for example,* 10, 79, 94, 103, 110, 117

Negative correlation, 661, 663–667

Negative decimal(s), 134

adding, 137–141

comparing, 134–136

dividing with, 146–149

multiplying with, 146–149

subtracting, 137–141

Negative exponent, 206–210, 232, 235

Negative integer, 12

Negative powers of ten, 195–200

Negative slope, 335–339

Negative square root, 213

Net, 573

for a cone, 581, 582, 583, 597

for a cylinder, 575, 577, 597

for a prism, 573–574, 576, 578, 579, 597

for a pyramid, 580, 582, 583, 597

n **factorial,** 79

n-**gon,** 740

measure of one angle of, 741

sum of angle measures of, 740–741

Non-examples, *See* Examples and non-examples

Nonlinear function(s), 413–420, 422, 426

cubic functions, 415, 417–420, 422, 426

on a graphing calculator, 420

quadratic functions, 413–414, 417–420, 422, 426

Notetaking, *See* Chapter Summary; Concept Summary; Graphic organizers; Key Concept

Notetaking organizer, graphic organizer, 246, 254, 302

Number line

to approximate square roots, 214

to compare decimals, 133, 134, 156, 182

to compare fractions, 80, 81

distance between numbers on, 26, 27

to graph inequalities, 282–286, 288, 290, 293–296, 305

to model absolute value, 13, 60, 63

to model adding integers, 18

to model adding rational numbers, 92

to model history, 28

to order integers, 12, 13, 63

to order real numbers, 226, 228, 236

positive and negative integers on, 12

to round numbers, 723

to show distance, 58

Number(s)

absolute value of, 13, 60, 63

compatible, 731

composite, 725

factors, 724–726

greatest common factor (GCF), 75, 726

integers, 12–16, 18, 60, 63

irrational, 225–230, 232, 236

least common multiple (LCM), 726

mixed, 727

opposites, 14, 15, 16

perfect square, 213

prime, 725

prime factorization of, 75, 76, 121, 725–726

rational, 113, 225

reciprocals, 106

relationships among, 113, 225, 232

repeating decimals, 113–117

in scientific notation, 201–205, 232–235

Number sense, *See also* Approximation; Comparing; Estimation; Ordering; Pattern(s); Properties; Reasoning

absolute value, 13, 60, 63

additive identity, 19

additive inverse, 19

choose a representative average, 630, 632, 634

common factor, 75, 726

common multiple, 726

composite number, 725

divisibility tests, 724

exercises, 152, 291, 346, 585

exponents, 195–200, 201–205, 386–398

factors, 724–726

greatest common factor (GCF), 726

irrational numbers, 225–230, 232, 236

least common multiple, (LCM), 726

multiple, 726

multiplicative identity, 32

multiplicative inverse, 99

number relationships, 113, 225, 232

outliers, 632–635

perfect square numbers, 213

place value, 133

prime factorization, 75, 76, 121, 725–726

prime number, 725

repeating decimals, 113–117

rounding, 144, 145, 146, 723, 730

scientific notation, 201–205, 232–235

terminating decimals, 113–117

Numerator, 75, 727

Numerical data, 643

Numerical expression(s), 6, *See also* Algebraic expression(s)

absolute value, 15–16

exponential, 192, 206–210, 385–398

integer, 25–28

n factorial, 79

order of operations and, 6, 8–10

properties and, 41–45, 60, 61

radical, 213–214, 216, 219–224

rational, 87–90, 108–112

Oblique solid, 595

Obtuse angle, 736

Obtuse triangle, 736

Octagon, 740

sum of angle measures of, 741

One-step equation(s), 256–268

Online Quiz, *Throughout. See for example,* 10, 16, 23, 28, 35, 40, 45, 51, 58, 79, 84, 89

Open-ended problems, *Throughout. See for example,* 21, 27, 35, 57, 104, 136, 141, 152, 157, 230, 285, 347

to make a scatter plot, 670
to make a table, 405
solving two-step inequalities, 298
translating points, 527
Square, 478, 500
area of, 9, 742
perimeter of, 742
Square number(s)
finding, 764
perfect squares, 213
square root and, 212, 213, 764
table of, 765
Square root, 213, 232
approximating, 214–218, 235
on a calculator, 215, 216
equations, 215, 218
evaluating, 213–218
finding, 764
perfect squares and, 213
product property of, 219, 232
using, 219–224, 236
the Pythagorean Theorem and, 471–476
quotient property of, 221, 232
using, 221–223, 236
radical sign, 213
of a squared expression, 401–404, 425
square numbers and, 212, 213, 764
table of, 765
of zero, 213
Standard form
of a decimal, 195–205, 234
of a polynomial, 689, 712, 719
Standards Practice, SG2–SG23
Standards Review Handbook, 723–746
geometry
classifying angles and triangles, 736–737
using a compass, 739
points, lines, and planes, 735
polygons, 740–741
using a protractor, 738
graphing
in the coordinate plane, 734
interpreting bar graphs and tables, 743
logical reasoning, Venn diagrams and, 746
measurement, perimeter and area, 742
number sense
divisibility tests, 724
estimation strategies, 730–731
factors and multiples, 725–726
inequality symbols, 733
mixed numbers and improper fractions, 727

ratios and rates, 732
rounding, 723
operations, to solve problems, 728–729
problem solving strategies, 744–745
Statistics, 631, *See also* Data; Graphs
choosing a representative average, 630, 632, 634
extremes, 655–659
interquartile range, 656
measures of central tendency, 629–635, 672–675
measures of dispersion, 632–635, 655–659, 672
outliers, 632, 633, 634
quartiles, 655–659
range, 632–635
trend lines, 666
Stem-and-leaf plot, 650
choosing a data display, 662, 663, 665–667
double, 651–652, 654
interpreting, 651–654, 680
making, 650–654, 676–677
Stem(s), in a stem-and-leaf plot, 650
Straight angle, 736
Straightedge, 739
drawing with, 459–461, 468–469, 486–487, 496–497
Substitution
to check answers, 257–267, 270, 315, 354, 360, 361, 362
to find solutions of an equation in two variables, 316–317
to solve systems of linear equations, 368
Substitution method, for solving systems of linear equations, 368
Subtraction
decimal, 137–141, 180, 183
difference, 728
to divide powers, 392–398
with fractions, 85–95, 119, 120, 122, 123
integer, 24–28, 60, 64
game, 72, 73
as inverse of addition, 258–262
with mixed numbers, 86–89, 92–95, 122, 123
order of operations and, 6–10, 87
polynomial, 694–698, 712, 715
properties, 258, 283, 300
using properties of addition, 41, 42
to solve equations, 257–262, 300, 303
to solve inequalities, 283–287, 305
to solve problems, 728–729
whole number, game, 2, 3
words indicating, 247, 300

Subtraction property of equality, 258
using, 258–262, 300, 303
Subtraction property of inequality, 283
using, 283–287, 300, 305
Sum, 728
Surface area, 574
of a composite solid, 582–583, 584
of a cone, 581–586, 613, 617
of a cylinder, 575–579, 613, 616
of a prism, 573–579, 613, 616
of a pyramid, 580–586, 613, 617
of similar solids, 606–611, 613, 618
of a sphere, 584
Symbol(s)
absolute value, 13
angle, 736
equal angles, 740
equal side lengths, 740
grouping, 6
inequality, 282, 733
is not equal to, 257
is similar to, 517
line, 735
not less than or equal to, 354
parallel lines, 478
radical sign, 213
ray, 735
repeating digits, 113
segment, 735
table of, 759
Symmetry
line, 530, 532
line of, 530
System of linear equations, 360–361, 364–368, 370, 376
graphing, 360–361, 364–367, 371, 376
solution of, 360, 370
substitution method for solving, 368
writing, 361, 365–367, 371
System of linear inequalities, 362–367, 370, 376
graphing, 362–367, 376
solution of, 362, 370

T

Table of formulas, 761
Table of measures, 760
Table of properties, 762
Table(s)
frequency, 643, 645–648
on a graphing calculator, 276
to graph linear equations, 320–325, 341, 373
identifying direct variation from, 348–351
interpreting, 743

formula, 590, 613
   oblique, 595
functions, 592, 594
of a prism, 588–596, 617, 688
   formula, 589, 613
   modeling, 588
of a pyramid, 597–603, 618
   formula, 598, 613
   modeling, 597
of similar solids, 606–611, 613, 618

Weight, *See also* Mass
   converting between systems, 438,
      440–442, 502
   customary units of, converting
      among, 437–442, 500, 501, 502
What If? questions, *Throughout. See*
    for example, 7, 13, 42, 53, 54,
    93, 101, 107, 151, 163, 166,
    168
Which one doesn't belong?,
    exercises, 227
Word magnet, graphic organizer,
    628, 645, 674
Word triangle, graphic organizer,
    514, 524, 550
Work backward, problem solving
    strategy, 744–745
Work problems, 444–448
Writing, *See also* Communication;
    Verbal model
   equations
     addition and subtraction,
       259–262, 300, 303
     linear, 344, 346–347
     multiplication and division,
       264–267, 300, 304
     in two variables, 328, 329,
       331–332
   equivalent fractions, 75–79, 119,
     121
   expressions, 247–251, 300–303
   fractions as decimals, 113, 115
   inequalities, 284–287, 301, 733
     linear, 356, 358–359, 371
     two-step, 294, 296–297
   numbers
     in scientific notation, 201–205
     in standard form, 195–205
   percents, decimals, and fractions,
     150–153, 155–159
   powers, 5, 8
   proportions, 277–281, 305
   ratios, 732
   a rule for a linear function,
     409–412
   systems of linear equations, 361,
     365–367

x-**axis,** 734
   reflection in, 529–533
x-**coordinate,** 734
x-**intercept,** 327
   finding, 327, 330

Y

y-**axis,** 734
   reflection in, 528–533
Y chart, graphic organizer, 688, 701,
    714
y-**coordinate,** 734
y-**intercept,** 327
   finding, 327, 330
   slope intercept-form and, 341–347

Z

Zero
   division by, 36
   as an exponent, 195, 196, 206, 232,
    235
   as an integer, 12
   multiplicative inverse and, 99
   as a place holder, 137, 145
   square root of, 213
Zero slope, 335–339

Credits

Photography

Cover Chris Salvo/Salvo Shoots People

Authors, Teacher Advisors, and Reviewers

Aguilar Maritza Chang/Fantastic Shots; *Austin* Jostens Photography/Lifetouch; *Austin* Jostens Photography/Lifetouch; *Birbeck* Courtesy of Edie Birbeck; *Boswell* Robert C. Jenks, Jenks Studio; *Bryson* Margaret L. Kidd; *Carter* Lifetouch; *Chavez* Courtesy of Mark Chavez; *Cliffe* Timothy Cliffe; *Davis* Shawn Davis; *Duffy* Courtesy of Ellen Duffy; *Fox* Courtesy of Barry Fox ; *Kanold* McDougal Littell/Houghton Mifflin Co.; *Kohn* Sharon Kohn; *Kuykendall* Courtesy of Brent Kuykendall; *Larson* Meridian Creative Group; *Martinez* Courtesy of Chris Martinez; *Miyata* Courtesy of Greg Miyata; *Okamoto* Akiko Okamoto; *Pacheco* Nila Pacheco; *Phair* James F. Phair; *Sass* Courtesy of Rudy Sass; *Smith* Jessica Smith; *Stiff* Jerry Head Jr.; *Walker-Jennels* Courtesy of Gwendolyn Walker-Jennels.

TOC1 Royalty-Free/Corbis; **TOC2** Ambient Images Inc./Alamy; **TOC3** CrashPA/Alamy; **TOC4** Syracuse Newspapers/The Image Works; **TOC5** James A. Stewart/Shutterstock; **TOC6** Mike Fiala/epa/Corbis; **TOC7** David Young-Wolff/PhotoEdit; **TOC8** Bettmann/Corbis; **TOC9** Roger Ressmeyer/Corbis; **TOC10** Royalty-Free/Corbis; **TOC11** Rodolfo Arpia/Alamy; **TOC12** Diaphor Agency/Index Stock Imagery; **TOC13** Scott David Patterson/Shutterstock; **SG1** Royalty-Free/Corbis; **SG27** PhotoSpin; **SG27** McDougal Littell/Houghton Mifflin Co.; **2** Kelly-Mooney Photography/Corbis; **5** Greer & Associates, Inc/SuperStock; **9** David Young-Wolff/PhotoEdit; **10** ImageState/Alamy; **12** Rockwell/AP Images; **15** Andre Jenny/Alamy; **16** Goodshoot/Alamy; **18** Bob Daemmrich/Jupiter Images; **22** Gianni Dagli Orti/Corbis; **24** Tim Haske/Index Stock Imagery; **27** Jeff Hunter/The Image Bank/Getty Images; **28** Arthur Morris/Corbis; **31** Stephen Frink/Corbis; **35** Sean Millins/Shutterstock; **36** PhotoDisc/Getty Images; **39** Paul A. Souders/Corbis; **41** Steve Casimiro/Allsport Concepts/Getty Images; **44** *bottom right* Michael Newman/PhotoEdit; **48** Jim Schwabel/Index Stock Imagery; **52** Ted S. Warren/AP Images; **57** Jacky Chapman/Alamy; **61** Royalty-Free/Corbis; **72** *top* Royalty-Free/Corbis; *bottom* Wally McNamee/Corbis; *center* AFP Photo/Anatoly Maltsev/Corbis; **75** *top* Donna Day/Stone/Getty Images; *pearl* Eric Kamp/Index Stock Imagery, Inc.; *all others* Christie's Images; **80** Steve Miller/AP Images; **82** Konrad Wothe/Minden Pictures; **85** Flying Colors Ltd/Age Fotostock; **86** Photo by Shawn Lockhart, courtesy of Southwest Wisconsin Reptiles; **88** Xavier Pironet/Shutterstock; **89** David Madison/Stone/Getty Images; **91** Ryan McVay/PhotoDisc/Getty; **94** Todd Bissonette/AP Images; **98** Ruth Tomlinson/Robert Harding World Imagery/Getty Images; **100** Karin Lau/Shutterstock; **103** Gianni Cigolini/Image Bank/Getty Images; **106** Nicole Katano/age fotostock; **113** G.K. & Vikki Hart/The Image Bank/Getty Images; **114** Steve Maslowski/Photo Researchers, Inc.; **116** Tom Bean/Stone/Getty Images; **133** Joe McDonald/Corbis; **136** Bruce Watkins/Animals Animals; **137** Randy Snyder/AP Images; **138** Ken O'Donoghue/McDougal Littell/Houghton Mifflin Co.; **140** Patrick Hertzog/Staff, AFP/Getty Images; **144** Bruce Leighty/Index Stock Imagery, Inc.; **147**

Michael K. Nichols/National Geographic/Getty Images; **148** G. Brad Lewis/Imagestate; **150** Lee Celano/AP Images; **153** Kelvin Aitken/Peter Arnold, Inc.; **155** Richard Hutchings/PhotoEdit; **156** GK & Vikki Hart/Getty Images; **159** David Young-Wolff/PhotoEdit; **160** *top* Richard Heinzen/SuperStock; *bottom* Darrell Gulin/Stone/Getty Images; **162** Syracuse Newspapers/The Image Works; **165** Daniel Allan/Taxi/Getty Images; **168** Royalty-Free/Corbis; **169** PhotoDisc/Getty Images; **172** Steve Skjold/Alamy; **179** *left inset* Jorge Alban/McDougal Littell/Houghton Mifflin Co.; **196** M. Hans/Vandystadt/Photo Researchers, Inc.; **197** Roger Holden/Index Stock/JupiterImages; **199** James A. Stewart/Shutterstock; **201** 2001 Ripley Entertainment, Inc. "Believe It or Not!" is a registered trademark of Ripley Entertainment, Inc.; **202** Doug Campbell/Imagestate; **204** NASA; **206** Microfield Scientific LTD/Photo Researchers, Inc.; **209** Bonnie Kamin/PhotoEdit; **211** Frank Boxler/AP Images; **213** Ed Elberfeld/Index Stock Imagery, Inc.; **215** Eunice Harris/Photo Researchers, Inc.; **218** Jerry and Marcy Monkman/EcoPhotography.com/Alamy; **219** Royalty-Free/Corbis; **223** Frank Siteman/age fotostock; **225** Goran Stenberg/AP Images; **227** Nic Bothma/epa/Corbis; **229** *top* Tony Hopewell/Taxi/Getty Images; *bottom* Ken O'Donoghue/McDougal Littell/Houghton Mifflin Co.; **241** Visuals Unlimited/Corbis; **247** PunchStock; **248** Alex Carreño/Shutterstock; **251** Creatas/Jupiter Images; **252** Dave G. Houser/Post-Houserstock/Corbis; **257** Bobby Model/National Geographic/Getty Images; **261** Darryl Torckler/Stone/Getty Images; **263** G.D.T./The Image Bank/Getty Images; **264** Peter Hvizdak/The Image Works; **270** Gabe Palmer/Corbis; **274** Colin Young-Wolff/PhotoEdit; **277** Wolfgang Kaehler/Corbis; **282** Kurt Wittman/Corbis; **284** Ken O'Donoghue/McDougal Littell/Houghton Mifflin Co.; **286** Adrian Weinbrecht/Stone/Getty Images; **287** Anup Shah/Taxi/Getty Images; **288** Art Wolfe/Stone/Getty Images; **291** Pablo Corral V/Corbis; **293** George Blonsky/Alamy; **296** Brooklyn Productions/The Image Bank/Getty Images; **301** Jim Craigmyle/Corbis; **312** Royalty-Free/Corbis; **315** Merritt Vincent/PhotoEdit; **318** Ken O'Donoghue/McDougal Littell/Houghton Mifflin Co.; **319** FogStock LLC/Index Stock Imagery; **320** Royalty-Free/Corbis; **324** Antonio Mo/Taxi/Getty Images; **327** Myrleen Ferguson Cate/PhotoEdit; **331** Tom Stewart/Corbis; **333** *all* RMIP/Richard Haynes/McDougal Littell/Houghton Mifflin Co.; **334** Michael Newman/PhotoEdit; **338** Nancy R. Cohen/PhotoDisc Green/Getty Images; **342** RO-MA Stock/Index Stock Imagery; **344** David Frazier/PhotoEdit; **346** Ken O'Donoghue/McDougal Littell/Houghton Mifflin Co.; **347** John W. Bova/Photo Researchers, Inc.; **348** Gérard Villaréal/Photo Researchers, Inc.; **352** NASA Dryden Flight Research Center (NASA-DFRC); **354** Michael Booth/Alamy; **356** Ken O'Donoghue/McDougal Littell/Houghton Mifflin Co.; **359** Scott Spiker/Imagestate; **360** David Young-Wolff/PhotoEdit; **363** Michael Ludwig/Shutterstock; **365** Ryan McVey/Getty Images; **366** Jose Galvez/PhotoEdit; **371** *top right* Robert W. Ginn/PhotoEdit; **386** J. T. Lewis/Shutterstock; **391** Dr. Fred Hossler/Getty Images; **393** Royalty-Free/Corbis; **397** *top* H. Mark Helfer/National Institute for Standards & Technology; **397** *bottom* NASA; **398** SuperStock; **399** Pete Saloutos/Corbis; **400** Chris

Selected Answers

Chapter 1

1.1 Exercises (pp. 8–10) **1.** algebraic; numerical **3.** 9^2; 9 to the second power, or 9 squared **5.** 7^3; 7 to the third power, or 7 cubed **7.** 10^3; 10 to the third power, or 10 cubed **9.** x^2; x to the second power, or x squared **11.** a^5; a to the fifth power **13.** 1331 **15.** 64 **17.** 0 **19.** 121 **21.** 1000 **23.** 400 **25.** 12 **27.** 18 **29.** 6 **31.** 6 **33.** 109 **35.** 12 **37.** 4 **39.** 1 **41.** 3 **43.** 7^2 means $7 \cdot 7$ not $7 \cdot 2$; $7^2 = 49$. **45.** 28 **47.** 36 **49.** 16 **51.** 100 **53.** 4 **55.** 64 **57.** 23 **59.** 27 **61.** 3 **65.** 600 sheets **69.** $3 \cdot 2^4 = 48$ mi/h

1.1 Technology Activity (p. 11) **1.** 18 **3.** 19 **5.** 7 **7.** 1 **9.** 6 min

1.2 Exercises (pp. 14–16) **1.** opposites **3.** > **5.** < **7.** > **9.** > **11.** $-10, -6, -2, 3, 4, 5$ **13.** $-11, -8, -7, -5, -3, -2$ **15.** $-20, -10, 10, 40, 50, 60$ **19.** *Sample answer:* $-2 > -9$; $-9, -2, 0, 1, 3, 5$ **21.** 8; 8 **23.** 13; -13 **25.** 11; -11 **27.** 340; 340 **29.** -9 **31.** 5 **33.** -17 **35.** -4 **37.** $-|47|, -28, |-65|, -(-73), |95|$ **39.** $-14, -8, -|6|, |-1|, -(-5)$ **41.** Gieselmann Lake **43.** Gieselmann Lake **45.** Flight crew departs for launch pad; Pilot starts auxiliary power units; Main engine starts; Liftoff; Shuttle clears launch tower, and control switches to the Mission Control Center. **47.** $a > b$

1.3 Exercises (pp. 20–23) **1.** absolute values **3.** 2 **5.** -2 **7.** -3 **9.** 4 **11.** The absolute values of the integers were added instead of subtracting the lesser absolute value from the greater absolute value; $-8 + 5 = -3$. **15.** -112; Closure property of addition **17.** 0; Inverse property of addition, Closure property of addition **19.** -30; Closure property of addition **21.** -8; Closure property of addition **23.** -29; Closure property of addition **25.** 7; Closure property of addition **27.** -3; Inverse property of addition, Closure property of addition **31.** -51 **33.** 40 **35.** -64 **37.** 64 **39.** -1207 **41.** -999 **43.** Always; when adding integers with the same sign, keep the common sign. **45.** Sometimes; when adding integers with different signs, keep the sign of the integer with the higher absolute value, if the integer with the higher absolute value is negative, then the sum is negative. **47.** 1 **49.** -2 **51.** 4th floor **53.** Use the sign of the integer with the greater absolute value. **57.** 180 ft

1.4 Exercises (pp. 26–28) **1.** opposite **3.** -7 **5.** -4 **7.** 0 **9.** -8 **11.** -26 **13.** -10 **17.** The first step should have been to change the subtraction to addition of -5; $3 - 5 - (-9) = 3 + (-5) + 9 = 7$. **19.** -15 **21.** 5 **25.** 5 **27.** 11 **29.** -1000 **31.** -1550 **33.** 35°F **35.** Jurassic Period; $\frac{32}{93}$ **37.** 41°F

1.5 Exercises (pp. 33–35) **1.** multiplicative identity **3.** 28; closure property of multiplication **5.** -18; closure property of multiplication **7.** -17; identity property of multiplication, closure property of multiplication **9.** 0; multiplication property of zero, closure property of multiplication **11.** -18; closure property of multiplication **13.** 180; closure property of multiplication **15.** -6; closure property of multiplication **17.** 270; closure property of multiplication **19.** 60; closure property of multiplication **21.** -280; closure property of multiplication **23.** The product of two integers with the same sign is positive; $-8(-12) = 96$. **25.** 9 **27.** -16 **29.** -432 **31.** -1280 **33.** 63 **35.** -504 **37.** 81 **39.** 161 **41.** 74 **43.** 5184 **45.** -132 **47.** -90 **49.** 224 **51.** -126 **55.** 40 mi **57.** 150 ft **59.** 96 in. below the surface **63.** $-10, 100, -1000, 10,000, -100,000$; when the exponent is odd, the power is negative and when the exponent is even, the power is positive.

1.6 Exercises (pp. 38–40) **1.** mean **3.** -11 **5.** 9 **7.** 7 **9.** -9 **11.** 6 **13.** -7 **15.** Dividend is 0 so quotient is 0; $\frac{0}{3} = 0$. **17.** 1 **19.** 1 **21.** 13 **23.** 2 **25.** 9 **27.** -1 **29.** -52 **33.** 14 **35.** -4 **37.** 27 **39.** 19 **41.** A; the value of A is positive; the values of B, C, and D are all negative. **43.** 198 **45.** -9 students **47. a.** $9 **b.** $158 **49.** No. *Sample answer:* Not enough information is given about the range of temperatures.

1.7 Exercises (pp. 43–45) **1.** commutative **3.** 45; Commutative property of addition **5.** -290; Commutative property of multiplication **7.** 21; Associative property of addition **9.** -140; Commutative property of multiplication, Associative property of multiplication **11.** -900; Commutative property of multiplication, Associative property of multiplication **13.** $16 \cdot 54$ **15.** $(4 + 6) + 19$ **17.** $(16 + 8) + 2$ or $2 + (8 + 16)$ **19.** 69; $45 - (-68) - 44 = 45 + 68 + (-44)$ Change subtraction to addition $45 + (-44) + 68$ Commutative property of addition $1 + 68$ Add. 69 Add. **21.** 3; $(-26 + 33) + (-4) = [33 + (-26)] + (-4)$ Commutative property of addition $33 + [-26 + (-4)]$ Associative property of addition $33 + -30$ Add. 3 Add. **23.** 68; $(16 + 8) + 44 = (8 + 16) + 44$ Commutative property of addition $8 + (16 + 44)$ Associative property of addition $8 + 60$ Add. 68 Add. **25.** 420; $12 \cdot (7 \cdot 1 \cdot 5) = 12 \cdot (5 \cdot 7 \cdot 1)$ Commutative property of multiplication $(12 \cdot 5) \cdot (7 \cdot 1)$ Associative property of multiplication $60 \cdot 7$ Multiply. 420 Multiply. **27.** 57; $36 + 57 + (-36) = 36 + (-36) + 57$ Commutative property of addition $0 + 57$ Inverse property of addition, 57 Identity property of addition

29. 10; $24 + (-12 - 8) + 6 = 24 + 6 + (-12 - 8)$ Commutative property of addition $30 + (-20)$ Add. 10 Add. **31.** 88; $44 - 17 - 12 + 66 + 7 = 44 + (-17) + (-12) + 66 + 7$ Change subtraction to addition $44 + 66 + (-17) + 7 + (-12)$ Commutative property of addition $110 + (-10) + (-12)$ Add. 88 Add. **33.** -38; $58 - 39 - 48 - 11 + 2 = 58 + (-39) + (-48) + (-11) + 2$ Change subtraction to addition $58 + (-48) + (-39) + (-11) + 2$ Commutative property of addition $10 + (-50) + 2$ Add. -38 Add. **35.** $168{,}000$; $16(5 \cdot 2)(15 \cdot 7)(10) = (16 \cdot 5)(2 \cdot 15)(7 \cdot 10)$ Associative property of multiplication $80(30)(70)$ Multiply. $168{,}000$ Multiply. **39.** The negative sign should have stayed with the 8; $3 + (-8) = -8 + 3 = -5$. **41.** commutative property of multiplication **43.** *Sample answer:* hours/day $\cdot$ days $\cdot$ x wages $= 2(5)(8)$; $\$80$ **45.** 133 yards **47.** *Sample answer:* Write the sum as $(52 + 38) + (99 + 11) + 65$ to get $90 + 110 + 65$ and then as $200 + 65$ or 265. The commutative and associative properties of addition let you rearrange the order so you can pair numbers up that have a sum ending in zero.

1.8 Exercises (pp. 50–51) **1.** F **3.** D **5.** A **7.** C **9.** $4(7) + 4(8)$; 60 **11.** $-7(3) + (-7)(2)$; -35 **13.** $8(9) - 8(16)$; -56 **15.** $6(-5) + 6(10) + 6(2)$; 42 **17.** $-5(4) - (-5)(1) + (-5)(-9)$; 30 **19.** $9x - 27$ **21.** $-21 - 3x$ **23.** $155 + 5y$ **25.** $19w + 95$ **27.** $6 + 2x$ **29.** 136; $4(30) + 4(4) = 120 + 16$ **31.** 288; $24(10) + 24(2) = 240 + 48$ **33.** The 6 was not multiplied by 3; $6x + 18$. **35.** $2(15 + 8)$; $\$46$ **37.** $4(12 + 11)$; $\$92$

1.9 Exercises (pp. 55–58) **1.** unit analysis **3.** You know the cost of the lunch and the cost of the drink. You know how much money the customer gave you. You need to find out what the customer's change is. **5.** The 45 pictures already taken were not subtracted. So, $96 - 45 = 51$ pictures left to take the last 3 days, 51 should be divided by 3. $\frac{51}{3} = 17$; Daniel can take 17 pictures each day. **7.** $\$4$; "Each pack of pens contains 12 pens". **9.** $31x^2$, $39x^2$ **11.** You only have 4 days left; $\frac{60}{4} = 15$; you need to read 15 pages per day. **13.** Find the total cost of the tickets then the cost of the service charge. **15.** $15(4) + 2(2) = 64$ **17.** 5.5 hr **19.** 150 km **23.** 3 dimes and 7 quarters **27.** 9 mi

Chapter Review (pp. 62–66) **1.** numerical **3.** mean **7.** 1260 **9.** 144 ft **11.** $-10, -9, -6, -1, 3, 4$ **13.** 13; 13 **15.** -10; 10 **17.** -7; 7 **19.** 25; 25 **21.** -47 **23.** -65 **25.** -107 **27.** -87 **29.** 120 **31.** -77 **33.** -24 **35.** 33 **37.** -124 **39.** 112 **41.** 0 **43.** 1260 **45.** -60 **47.** 84 **49.** -36 **51.** -168 **53.** -13 **55.** 8 **57.** 4 **59.** 0 **61.** 0 **63.** 5 **65.** 8 **67.** 158; Commutative property of addition, associative property of addition **69.** 97; Associative property of addition, Inverse property of addition **71.** 0; Multiplication property of zero **73.** -56; Commutative property of addition, Associative property of addition, Inverse property of addition **75.** 47; Commutative property of addition, Associative property of addition, Identity property of addition **77.** $63 + 14y$ **79.** $72y - 48$ **81.** $20r + 25$ **83.** 16 tbsp

Chapter 2

2.1 Exercises (pp. 77–79) **1.** simplest form **3.** $\frac{3}{7}$ **5.** $\frac{2}{3}$ **7.** $\frac{-5}{8}$ **9.** $\frac{3}{4}$ **11.** $\frac{-7}{8}$ **13.** The numerator and denominator need to be multiplied by 2 not add 2; $\frac{6}{28}$. **15.** equivalent **17.** equivalent **19.** not equivalent **21.** equivalent **25.** *Sample answer:* $\frac{1}{2}, \frac{5}{10}$ **27.** *Sample answer:* $\frac{2}{5}, \frac{12}{30}$ **29.** $\frac{3}{x^2}; \frac{1}{3}$ **31.** $\frac{5}{y}; 1$ **33.** $\frac{-3xy}{4}; \frac{-45}{4}$ **35.** $\frac{2x^2}{7y^2}; \frac{18}{175}$ **37.** $\frac{9}{50}$ **39.** $\frac{8}{25}$ **41.** $\frac{17}{20}$ **45.** $\frac{1}{3}$; $8 + 12 = 20$ students voted for a car wash or a fair. A total of 30 students voted so $30 - 20 = 10$ students voted for a dance. The fraction of students who voted for a dance is $\frac{10}{30} = \frac{1}{3}$. **47.** *Sample answer:* No; the resulting fraction will only be in simplest form if you divide it by the GCF. $\frac{20}{30} = \frac{10}{15}$, but $\frac{10}{15}$ is not in simplest form.

2.2 Exercises (pp. 82–84) **1.** least common multiple **3.** 6 **5.** 24 **7.** 28 **9.** 120 **17.** $=$ **19.** $>$ **21.** $=$ **23.** $<$ **25.** The fractions do not have a common denominator; $\frac{3}{5} = \frac{21}{35}$ and $\frac{4}{7} = \frac{20}{35}$, so $\frac{3}{5} > \frac{4}{7}$.

27. $\frac{1}{8}, \frac{5}{16}, \frac{1}{2}, \frac{3}{4}$

29. $\frac{15}{16}, 1, \frac{5}{3}, 2\frac{2}{5}$

37. $>$ **39.** $<$ **41.** Juan **45.** The $10{,}200$ lb elephant; the heavier elephant is about 5000 lb heavier, but his trunk is only about 100 lb heavier. So, the lighter elephant has a comparably heavier trunk.

2.3 Exercises (pp. 87–89) **1.** denominator, numerator **3.** $\frac{2}{3}$ **5.** $-\frac{2}{5}$ **7.** $\frac{1}{5}$ **9.** $-8\frac{4}{7}$ **11.** $-1\frac{2}{7}$ **13.** $-8\frac{2}{5}$ **17.** $1\frac{1}{2}$ **19.** $1\frac{11}{18}$ **21.** $4\frac{1}{12}$ **23.** $-3\frac{3}{16}$ **25.** $-10\frac{2}{3}$ **27.** $-7\frac{1}{2}$ **29.** The student did not follow the order of operations; $\frac{6}{11}$. **31.** $18\frac{3}{4}$ in. **33.** 4 hr **35.** $2\frac{1}{2}$ mm **39.** 1 ft $8\frac{1}{2}$ in.

2.4 Exercises (pp. 93–95) **1.** least common denominator **3.** $\frac{5}{8}$ **5.** $-1\frac{7}{8}$ **7.** $-\frac{19}{60}$ **9.** $-\frac{1}{24}$ **11.** $13\frac{8}{35}$ **13.** $-4\frac{3}{7}$ **15.** $10\frac{1}{15}$ **17.** $-1\frac{53}{60}$ **19.** New fractions are not equivalent to the original fractions; $\frac{1}{3} = \frac{2}{6}, \frac{1}{2} = \frac{3}{6}$, so $\frac{1}{3} + \frac{1}{2} = \frac{2}{6} + \frac{3}{6} = \frac{5}{6}$. **23.** $-\frac{11}{28}$; rewrite with common denominator: $\frac{7}{28} - \frac{24}{28} + \frac{6}{28}$, evaluate: $-\frac{11}{28}$ **25.** $\frac{5}{18}$; rewrite using common denominator: $\frac{24}{18} - \frac{4}{18} - \frac{15}{18}$, evaluate: $\frac{5}{18}$ **27.** $1\frac{11}{18}$; rewrite using common denominator: $\frac{62}{18} - \frac{27}{18} - \frac{6}{18}$, evaluate: $\frac{29}{18}$, rewrite as a mixed number: $1\frac{11}{18}$ **29.** $7\frac{1}{4}$ ft **31.** $1\frac{5}{12}$ cups

35. no; $2\frac{1}{2} + 3\frac{1}{2} = 6$ **37. a.** $\frac{27}{50}$ **b.** West; the trip west is only $\frac{23}{50}$ of the distance around the equator.

2.5 Exercises (pp. 101–104) **1.** multiplicative inverse
5. $-1\frac{7}{8}$ **7.** 1 **9.** $\frac{1}{6}$ **11.** $-\frac{25}{72}$ **13.** $\frac{2}{9}$ **15.** $\frac{3}{4}$ **17.** $-10\frac{1}{4}$
19. -13 **21.** $-2\frac{4}{7}$ **23.** $\frac{11}{24}$ **25.** $1\frac{7}{8}$ in.^{2} **27.** $11\frac{113}{121}$ m^2
29. The student separated the mixed number and then multiplied; $2\frac{2}{3} \cdot 3\frac{3}{4} = \frac{8}{3} \cdot \frac{15}{4} = \frac{120}{12} = 10.$ **31.** $1\frac{3}{4}$
33. -54 **35.** 49 **37.** -15 **39.** $-4\frac{3}{4}$ **41.** $8\frac{1}{6}$ **43.** $3\frac{19}{120}$
45. $4\frac{3}{4}$ **47.** $\frac{1}{90}$ **49.** $-1\frac{46}{75}$ **51.** 196 ft **55.** 2, 3, 4
57. 12 years old **59.** $\frac{3}{20}$ of the employees

2.6 Exercises (pp. 108–111) **1.** $\frac{b}{a}$ **3.** 2 **5.** $-\frac{1}{8}$
7. 6 **9.** $-2\frac{1}{2}$ **11.** $\frac{7}{9}$ **13.** $-5\frac{4}{7}$ **15.** $\frac{5}{12}$ **17.** $-\frac{3}{20}$
21. Inverted the wrong fraction; $\frac{3}{10} \div \frac{4}{5} = \frac{3}{10} \cdot \frac{5}{4} = \frac{3}{8}.$
23. 8 **25.** $\frac{4}{9}$ **27.** $\frac{25}{36}$ **29.** 100 **31.** $2\frac{4}{49}$ **33.** $-7\frac{1}{12}$
35. $1\frac{3}{13}$ **37.** $3\frac{3}{5}$ **39.** $-1\frac{9}{14}$ **41.** $-5\frac{9}{10}$ **43.** $-\frac{3}{4}$
45. $1\frac{1}{15}$ **47.** $-1\frac{3}{7}$ **49.** $1\frac{7}{18}$ **51.** $2 \div \frac{4}{5}; 2\frac{1}{2}$ **53.** Yes; the c in the numerator and denominator will divide out.
55. Division, you are splitting $5\frac{1}{2}$ hours into $1\frac{3}{4}$ hours sections; $3\frac{1}{7}$ movies. **57.** Addition then division, you need a total distance, but then you need to split it into 3 sections; $8\frac{19}{36}$ ft.

2.6 Technology Activity (p. 112) **1.** $\frac{47}{55}$ **3.** $\frac{2}{3}$ **5.** $1\frac{1}{27}$
7. $\frac{2}{7}$ **9.** $11\frac{1}{5}$ **11.** $5\frac{1}{3}$ **13.** $374\frac{5}{8}$ lb

2.7 Exercises (pp. 115–117) **1.** repeating **3.** rational number, integer, whole number **5.** rational number, integer **7.** rational number **9.** rational number, integer
11. 0.6 **13.** -0.7 **15.** 0.75 **17.** -0.48 **19.** -10.16
21. 3.6875 **23.** $-0.\overline{42}$ **25.** $6.5\overline{3}$ **29.** $5\frac{1}{3} = \frac{16}{3}$ not $\frac{5}{3}$; $5.\overline{3}$
31. $-\frac{12}{25}$ **33.** $-2\frac{79}{100}$ **35.** $7\frac{253}{1000}$ **37.** $\frac{3}{2500}$ **39.** 3
41. 3 **43.** $44.50 **45.** $3.44 **49.** $\frac{3}{26}$; 0.1154
51. No; there are no digits or group of digits that repeat. So the number cannot be expressed as a fraction $\frac{a}{b}$.

Chapter Review (pp. 121–124) **1.** multiplicative inverses, reciprocals **3.** least common denominator
5. $\frac{1}{3}$ **7.** $\frac{b}{3}$ **9.** > **11.** = **13.** $\frac{5}{8}, \frac{7}{11}, \frac{2}{3}$ **15.** $\frac{17}{3}, 5\frac{7}{8}, \frac{53}{9}$
17. Joe **19.** $1\frac{3}{4}$ **21.** $1\frac{5}{7}$ **23.** $2\frac{1}{12}$ **25.** $-\frac{1}{34}$ **27.** $1\frac{8}{25}$
29. $-\frac{9}{26}$ **31.** $1\frac{31}{36}$ **33.** $-13\frac{2}{3}$ **35.** $-7\frac{7}{11}$ **37.** $3\frac{1}{8}$
39. $\frac{5}{8}$ **41.** 18 **43.** -0.875 **45.** $3\frac{9}{20}$

Chapter 3

3.1 Exercises (pp. 135–136) **1.** place value **3.** > **5.** >
7. = **9.** = **11.** < **13.** > **17.** $-9.1, -9.07, -9.06$
19. $-1.1, -0.1, 0.9, 1.5$ **21.** $-1.15, -0.98, 1.05, 1.2$
23. The numbers are negative, not positive; look on a number line, $-3.1 > -3.25$. **25.** > **27.** < **29.** < **31.** <
33. $7\frac{8}{21}, 7.6, 7\frac{2}{3}, 7.71, 7\frac{4}{5}$ **35.** $-\frac{2}{7}, 0.1, \frac{3}{10}, |-0.4|, \frac{5}{6}$
37. 0.298 **39.** 8.4 in. **41.** $-18.9°C, -18.2°C, -9.7°C, -9.5°C, -3.4°C, -2.9°C$

3.2 Exercises (pp. 139–141) **1.** 13, 11, 25 **3.** 38.103
5. -3.419 **7.** 4.988 **9.** -1.63 **11.** -7.71 **13.** 22.1
15. 18.985 **17.** -5.027 **19.** The hundredths place needs to be regrouped; 8.17. **23.** 22 **25.** 24
27.

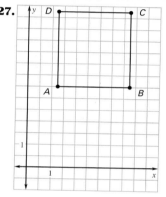

12.5 **29.** $19.54

31. a. 1.96 m **b.** 1.31 m **35.** 1.39 lb **37.** *Sample answer:* Watch, whistle, 5 golf balls, 2 rolls of pennies

3.3 Exercises (pp. 146–149) **1.** 7 **3.** 20.28 **5.** -5.74
7. 5 **9.** 12 **11.** 4 **13.** 2.5 **15.** 15.4571 **17.** -1.5
19. -8.7 **21.** 290.405 **25.** Zero needs to be used as a place holder; 0.024. **27.** 1.33 **29.** 4.356 **31.** 2.635
33. 0.99308 **35.** -8.1639 **37.** < **39.** 160.31 **41.** 6.915
43. $4.19 **45.** $0.38 per lb **47. a.** 136.8 lb
47. b. *Sample answer:* The mother's weight is about 4000 pounds and the baby's weight is about 100 pounds. $100 \div 4000 \approx 0.03$. **51.** 6.2 mi/h; $2.5 \approx 3, 3 \times 6 = 18$ which is close to 15.5. **53.** 87.6 mi/h; 1.2 times as fast

3.4 Exercises (pp. 152–153) **1.** percent **3.** 0.8
5. -0.075 **7.** 0.0105 **9.** -0.004 **11.** 1.8709 **15.** 162.5
17. 36 **19.** 2.52 **21.** $\frac{2}{5}$ **23.** $-\frac{13}{40}$ **25.** $-1\frac{6}{25}$ **27.** $-\frac{21}{500}$
29. $-\frac{803}{10,000}$ **31.** $30\% = 0.3$, not 30; $0.3 \times 500 = 150$.
33. = **35.** > **37.** > **41.** $3.38 **43.** $\frac{117}{200}; \frac{3}{4}$

3.5 Exercises (pp. 157–159) **1.** multiply **3.** 9%
5. -70% **7.** 400% **9.** 0.3% **11.** 3.9% **15.** 62.5%
17. 1.25% **19.** -310% **21.** 8% **23.** -43.75% **25.** <
27. < **31.** $-0.5, -6.5\%, \frac{9}{50}, 0.65, 66\%$ **33.** -21.2,
$-212\%, -\frac{21}{10}, -0.212, -\frac{21}{100}$ **35.** $4.8\%, \frac{12}{25}, 0.484, 480\%,$
4.84 **37.** $\frac{1}{5}$ is less than $\frac{1}{4}$, so $\frac{1}{5}$ is less than 25%. **39.** 23%
41. 37.5% **45.** 25.2%, 13.3%, 10.6%, 10.4%, 40.5%; Country, R&B, Rap, Rock, Other

3.6 Exercises (pp. 163–165) 1. markup **3.** $51
5. $29.40 **7.** $41.25 **9.** The clerk subtracted $25 from the original price instead of subtracting the discount; $0.25(\$375) = \$93.75$, $\$375 - \$93.75 = \$281.25$. **11.** $60
13. $162.50 **15.** $360.75 **19.** $1675 **21.** $4695
23. $7885 **25.** $1055 **27.** $355 **29.** $23.18 **33.** $5624
35. $300 **37.** 25% of $40 is $10, so estimate the sale price to be around $32.

3.7 Exercises (pp. 170–171) 1. increase **3.** increase; 60% **5.** decrease; -7% **7.** decrease; -10% **11.** 1144
13. 12.8 **15.** 77,000 **17.** Your friend did not add the increase to the original number. Multiplying a number by 5 and adding the product to the original number is a 500% increase. **19.** 350 people **21.** $172.50
25. 9 in. by 6 in.; the increase in area will be greater than 50%. The original area is 24 in^2. The area of the enlargement is 54 in^2. This is a 125% increase.

3.8 Exercises (pp. 175–177) 1. principal **3.** $31.20
5. $18 **7.** The time needs to be converted to years; $(2000)(0.6)(0.25) = \$30$. **9.** $684 **11.** $926.10
13. $789.49 **15.** $3, $103 **17.** $30, $630 **19.** $97.60, $205.84, $338.48, $472.96 **23.** $1127.16 **25.** $3.20

3.8 Technology Activity (p. 178) 1. $7577.03
3. $3744.89 **5.** $12,695.39; $12,500; you make $195.39 more.

Chapter Review (pp. 182–186) 1. C **3.** A
5. simple interest **7.** discount **9.** > **11.** < **13.** 1.87
15. 1.315 **17.** 68.6°F **19.** -3.0132 **21.** 2 **23.** 0.74
25. -0.168 **27.** $\frac{9}{50}$ **29.** $2\frac{7}{25}$ **31.** 143 people
33. -50.7% **35.** -45% **37.** $51 **39.** $165
41. 30% decrease **43.** $61.25 **45.** $70.88 **47.** $1042.32
49. $14 **51.** $4266.30

Chapter 4

4.1 Exercises (pp. 198–200) 1. multiplicative inverse
3. 10 **5.** 10,000,000,000 **7.** 1 **9.** 0.0000000000001
11. 10^3 **13.** 10^5 **15.** 10^{-2} **19.** 0.000001; 0.01; 10^0; 10^4
21. 0.0001; 10^{-2}; $\frac{1}{10}$; 10^0; 10^3 **23.** 10^{-3} means $\frac{1}{10^3}$ instead of a negative number; $10^{-3} = \left(\frac{1}{10}\right)\left(\frac{1}{10}\right)\left(\frac{1}{10}\right) = \frac{1}{1000}$.
25. equal to **27.** less than **29.** 10^0 g **31.** 15×10^6 g
33. $5 \times 10^3 + 4 \times 10^2 + 1 \times 10^1 + 0 \times 10^0$
35. Never; a power of 10 with an exponent of zero is 1.
37. Always; for the answer to be negative it must be multiplied by a negative number.
39. 100,000,000,000 **41.** 100,000,000

4.2 Exercises (pp. 203–204) 1. scientific
3. 7.9×10^3 **5.** 6.71×10^{-5} **7.** 8.1×10^9
9. 3.102×10^{-2} **11.** 3.42×10^{-8} **13.** The exponent should be negative since the decimal point must be moved to the left; 7.6×10^{-4}. **15.** 4,350,000
17. 0.08071 **19.** 0.00000000176
21. 2,830,000,000,000 **23.** > **25.** 37,500,000; 5.37×10^7; 3.75×10^8; 3.57×10^9 **27.** 7.5×10^7 lb
29. 1,900,000,000,000,000,000,000,000 kg
31. 12,916,000 acres **33.** *Sample answer:* First order by exponents. Then if any of the exponents are the same, order by the numbers.

4.2 Technology Activity (p. 205) 1. 2.7115×10^{14}
3. 1.584×10^{-11} **5.** 8.2×10^6 **7.** 4.02×10^{-7}
9. 7.7×10^{11} gal per wk; 4.004×10^{13} gal per yr

4.3 Exercises (pp. 208–210) 1. 1 **3.** $\frac{1}{81}$ **5.** $-\frac{1}{16}$
7. 1 **9.** $\frac{1}{36}$ **11.** 1 **13.** $\frac{25}{4}$ **15.** 5^{-3} means $\frac{1}{5^3}$;
$5^{-3} = \left(\frac{1}{5}\right)\left(\frac{1}{5}\right)\left(\frac{1}{5}\right) = \frac{1}{125}$. **19.** $\frac{1}{27}$ **21.** $-\frac{1}{64}$ **23.** 3 **25.** $\frac{9}{4}$
27. 1 **29.** $-\frac{7}{x^5}$ **31.** $-\frac{3}{x^2}$ **33.** $8n^2$ **35.** Always; when the exponent is zero, the answer is always one.
37. Sometimes; if the exponent is even, the answer is positive, but if the exponent is odd, the answer is negative. **39.** $\frac{1}{6^2}$ yd **41.** $\frac{1}{2^3}$ cup

4.4 Exercises (pp. 216–218) 1. square root **3.** $1, -1$
5. $20, -20$ **7.** $\frac{1}{2}, -\frac{1}{2}$ **9.** $\frac{6}{5}, -\frac{6}{5}$ **11.** -1 **13.** 12
17. 16, 17 **19.** 31, 32 **21.** 4 **23.** 7 **25.** 5 **27.** 11
29. -5.9 **31.** 49.4 **33.** sometimes **35.** sometimes
37. 6 **39.** $-\frac{1}{2}$ **41.** $-\frac{9}{10}$ **43.** 1.2 **45.** -0.5
47. The square of $\frac{1}{4}$ was found instead of the square root; $\sqrt{\frac{1}{4}} = \frac{1}{2}$. **49.** 5 in. **51.** 3.5 in. **53.** 27 in. **55.** No, the side length of the table is $\sqrt{21.5} \approx 4.6$ ft. The side length of the tablecloth is only $4\frac{1}{6}$ ft, and $4.6 > 4\frac{1}{6}$.
57. about 68.2 mi **59.** 2211.84 ft

4.5 Exercises (pp. 221–223) 1. product **3.** $5\sqrt{2}$
5. $4\sqrt{5}$ **7.** $9\sqrt{3}$ **9.** $2\sqrt{6}$ **11.** $6\sqrt{2}$ **13.** $10\sqrt{2}$ **15.** $\frac{\sqrt{2}}{9}$
17. $\frac{\sqrt{15}}{8}$ **19.** $\frac{3}{7}$ **21.** $\frac{\sqrt{5}}{6}$ **25.** The student did not take the square root of the denominator; $\sqrt{\frac{9}{4}} = \frac{\sqrt{9}}{\sqrt{4}} = \frac{3}{2}$.
27. $2\sqrt{10}$ ft^2 **29.** $5\sqrt{3} - 2\sqrt{10}$ ft^2 **33. a.** $\frac{\sqrt{h}}{4}$ **b.** 3 sec
35. 11,186.6 m/sec

4.6 Exercises (pp. 227–230) 1. real numbers
3. rational; terminating decimal **5.** rational; repeating decimal **7.** rational; square root of a perfect square
9. irrational; square root of a non-perfect square
11. rational; quotient of two integers **13.** rational; quotient of two integers **15.** A; A is rational, while B, C, and D are irrational. **17.** > **19.** < **21.** <
21–29. Sample methods are given. **23.** >, estimation
25. <, estimation **27.** =, mental math **29.** <, calculator
35. $0.\overline{262}, 0.2\overline{6}, 0.266, 0.2\overline{6}$ **37.** $0.\overline{39}, 0.399, 0.3\overline{9}, \sqrt{0.17}$
39. $-9, \sqrt{81}, 10.3, \sqrt{220}$ **41.** $\frac{2}{5}, 1.02, \sqrt{1.25}, \sqrt{2.5}$
43. $\sqrt{5}$ is irrational; $\sqrt{5}$ is irrational because 5 is not a perfect square. **45.** 3.6; irrational **47.** 3; rational
49. 8.1; irrational **51.** No; the number -4 is not a perfect square. **53.** never **55.** Sometimes.
Sample answer: $\sqrt{3} + \sqrt{3} = 2\sqrt{3}$, which is irrational; $\sqrt{3} + (-\sqrt{3}) = 0$, which is rational. **57.** irrational
63. no **67.** Rational; the area of the large square is the area of the shaded region plus the area of the four smaller squares. $A = 45 + 4 \cdot 9 = 81$ square centimeters. Since it is a square, the side length is 9 centimeters.

1. scientific
3. square root   **5.** 1000   **7.** 0.0001   **9.** 10^{-3} **11.** 10^4
13. 3.46×10^{10} **15.** 5.02×10^{-10} **17.** 1500
19. 3×10^{11} **21.** $\frac{1}{c^3}$ **23.** $-\frac{7}{s^4}$ **25.** -25 **27.** -6.3
29. $5\sqrt{6}$ **31.** 12   **33.** Rational; the square root of any
perfect square is a rational number.   **35.** Rational;
a quotient of two integers is a rational number.
37. >   **39.** =   **41.** irrational; $d = \sqrt{2A} = \sqrt{2 \cdot 16} = \sqrt{32}$,
32 is not a perfect square and the square root of a
non-perfect square is irrational.

Chapter 5

5.1 Exercises (pp. 249–251)   **1.** algebraic expression
3. $\frac{2}{5}x$ **5.** $12 + x$ **7.** $x + 11$ **9.** $8x - 5$
13. "The difference of 5 and n" means subtract n
from 5; $5 - n$.   **15.** $13x$ **17.** $\frac{c}{2}$ **19.** $13x + 15y + 2z$
23. $30x + 60y - 3z$ **25.** $\frac{x}{0.6}$; 107 h

5.2 Exercises (pp. 254–255)   **1.** -6 **5.** $16w + 12z$
7. $5x + 3y - 3$ **9.** $r + s + 3$ **11.** $2x + 2$ **13.** $12d$
15. $1.7y - 6.7$ **17.** $3x - 5$ **19.** The terms are $2x$, $4y$ and
$-7x$. The like terms are $2x$ and $-7x$, which combined is
$-5x$; $2x + 4y - 7x = 2x - 7x + 4y = -5x + 4y$.   **21.** $6x$
23. $70x$ **25.** $3x + 3x + 3x + x + x + x + 2x = 14x$; 42 ft

5.3 Exercises (pp. 260–262)   **1.** *Sample answer:*
Addition and subtraction, multiplication and division
3. no   **5.** no   **7.** yes   **9.** 6   **11.** 64   **13.** 24   **15.** -29
17. 4.7   **19.** 1   **21.** 10 should be subtracted from both
sides; $x + 10 - 10 = 50 - 10$, $x = 40$.   **25.** $n + 12 = 25$; 13
27. $n - 3 = -16$; -13 **29.** $24 + k + 16 + 38 = 97$; 19 cm
31. 62 is 5 more than h.   **33.** T is 3 less than 27.
37. Positive. *Sample answer:* When you undo subtraction
you add, adding a positive number to a positive number
makes the side without the variable positive.
39. $128 = 45 + n$ where n is the number of inches a male
Steller sea lion grows between birth and adulthood; 83 in.
41. a. $11.09 = 2(1.29) + 3.50 + 1.49 + m$ **b.** \$3.52

5.4 Exercises (pp. 265–267)   **1.** equivalent equation
3. dividing by 5   **5.** subtracting -6 **7.** dividing by -3
9. 18   **11.** 13   **13.** 350   **15.** 216   **17.** 105   **19.** -31.5
21. 0.5   **23.** 70   **25.** 20 divided by 5 is 4, not 20; $4 = z$.
29. $\frac{8}{9}$ **31.** $\frac{7}{33}$ **33.** $\frac{635}{999}$ **35.** $-\frac{5}{33}$ **37.** $-\frac{1}{3}$ **39.** $-\frac{26}{9}$
41. $3r = 174$ **43.** $\frac{x}{12} = 45$ **47.** $100 = \frac{1}{5}t$ where t is the
height of Takkakaw Falls; 500 m   **49.** 65 is the total
number of points for the season, p, divided by 20; $65 = \frac{p}{20}$,
1300 points; 70 is the total number of points for the
season, p, divided by 20; 1400 points.

5.5 Exercises (pp. 272–275)   **1.** solution   **3.** 3   **5.** 1
7. -8 **9.** 81   **11.** -5 **13.** 8   **15.** 30   **17.** 48.8   **19.** -12
23. equation; division property of equality; simplify;
subtraction property of equality; simplify
25. $\frac{x}{2} - 7 = -6$; 2   **27.** $2|x| - 5 = 3$; $-4, 4$ **29.** 9 should
have been added to both sides, not subtracted from one
side and added to the other side; $3x = 27$, $x = 9$.
31. $18 - 2x = 14$ **33.** $4x + 12 = 76$ **37.** $0.017 h$, or
about 1 min   **43.** 7 boxes   **45.** how much the time your
run increases each week

5.6 Exercises (pp. 279–281)   **1.** proportion   **3.** 6
5. 3   **7.** 5.4   **9.** 13.2   **11.** yes   **13.** yes   **17.** An error
was committed by computing the cross products
horizontally. Instead, cross products should be computed
diagonally; $2t = 45$, $t = 22.5$ min.   **19.** 8   **21.** 10   **23.** $\frac{1}{7}$
25. $x = -3$, $y = -10.5$ **27.** $n = 16$, $p = 15$
29. *Sample answer:* $\frac{54}{3} = \frac{x}{5}$ **33.** 726 ft; 275 ft; 1089 ft

5.7 Exercises (pp. 284–287)   **1.** inequality   **3.** C
5. B   **7.** $x > -2$; x is greater than -2.
9. $x \le 2$; x is less than or equal to 2.

11. The line should be highlighted to the right of the
circle instead of the left.

13. $p < -5$

17. $m \le 11$

25. 6 through 9   **27.** 1 through 4   **33.** $x + 32 > 38$
35. $x + 14{,}000 \le 19{,}000$ **37.** $x + 33.96 \ge 50$; $x \ge \$16.04$
41. a. $x + 70 \ge 76.4$;   **b.**
$x \ge 6.4$ lb

43. 2202 tigers, 4199 tigers; $T \le 4199$, $T \ge 2202$

5.8 Exercises (pp. 290–292)   **1.** reverse   **3.** No
5. Yes   **7.** $x \le 32$; D   **9.** $x \ge -2$; A

11. $x < 8$

13. $z \ge 3$

27. The inequality sign should not be reversed; $-3 < x$.
31. greater than or equal to 1 and less than 4
33. $5x \ge 300$ **35.** $\frac{s}{4} \le 5$ **37. a.** $5.5x \ge 275$; $x \ge 50$ tickets
b.

5.9 Exercises (pp. 295–297) **1.** less than; greater than; less than or equal to; greater than or equal to

5. $b > -2$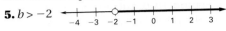

9. $s \le 3$

19. The inequality sign should have been reversed when dividing by -2; $x \ge 3$. **21.** $y \ge -10\frac{1}{2}$ **23.** $m < 24$
25. $y < 5.1$ **27.** $x \le 49.3$ **29.** $50 - 8x \ge 10$
31. $925 + 25p \ge 2500$; $p \ge 63$; you need at least 63 additional pledges to raise $2500. **33.** $16{,}000 + 150x > 18{,}550$; $x > 17$; you must catch more than 17 discs to beat the high score. **35.** $h < 6000$; the base height of a Strato cloud is less than 6000 feet.

5.9 Technology Activity (p. 298) **1.** $y < 13$ **3.** $n \le -1$
5. $t > -3$ **7.** $x \le 28$ pencils

Chapter Review (pp. 302 – 306) **1.** The solutions are the same. *Sample answer:* $x > 3$, $x - 1 > 2$ **3.** proportion
5. coefficient **7.** $x - 10$ **9.** $7x$ **11.** $7x - 2y$
13. $-4x - 6y$ **15.** $49a + b$ **17.** $3\left(x + \frac{1}{3}x\right)$; $4x$ **19.** 42
21. -11 **23.** 16 **25.** -3 **27.** $12 + t = 17$; 5 elm trees
29. -161 **31.** 0 **33.** 2.4 **35.** 3 **37.** -200
39. 1.4 **41.** $5.\overline{3}$ **43.** 9 **45.** 68 pages

49. $d \ge -6$

53. $p < 10.2$

55. $x \le -100$ **57.** $c > 5$

59. $y > -18$ **61.** $m \ge -55$ **63.** $m < 9$ **65.** $x < 5$
67. $y < 0$ **69.** $x \ge 67$ tickets

Chapter 6

6.1 Exercises (pp. 317–319) **1.** solution **3.** solution
5. not a solution **7.** not a solution **9.** The x and y values are switched; $2(-5) + 3(4) = -10 + 12 = 2$. That is not equal to -7, so $(-5, 4)$ is not a solution.
11. 3, 8, 13, 18 **13.** $-25, -20, -15, -10$
15–19. Sample answers are given. **15.** $(-1, 8)$, $(0, 3)$, $(1, -2)$, $(2, -7)$ **17.** $(-5, 8)$, $(0, 9)$, $(5, 10)$, $(10, 11)$
19. $(-3, -4)$, $(0, -5)$, $(3, -6)$, $(6, -7)$ **23.** $y = 42 - 4x$; $(-2, 50)$, $(-1, 46)$, $(0, 42)$, $(1, 38)$ **25.** $y = 10 - 5x$; $(-2, 20)$, $(-1, 15)$, $(0, 10)$, $(1, 5)$ **27.** $y = 19 + 2x$; $(-2, 15)$, $(-1, 17)$, $(0, 19)$, $(1, 21)$ **29.** $y = 2 - 3x$;
$(-2, 8)$, $(-1, 5)$, $(0, 2)$, $(1, -1)$ **31.** $y = 2x - 1\frac{1}{4}$;
$\left(-1, -3\frac{3}{4}\right), \left(0, -1\frac{1}{4}\right), \left(1, \frac{3}{4}\right), \left(2, 2\frac{3}{4}\right)$ **33.** $y = 6 - 2\frac{1}{7}x$;
$(-14, 36)$, $(-7, 21)$, $(0, 6)$, $(7, -9)$ **35.** 40 mi **37. a.** \$31
b. 16 wheels **c.** No, the total cost will be \$199. The total cost includes \$7, which is charged only once. The shipping and handling does not double when the number of orders doubles. **43.** $y = \dfrac{c - ax}{b}$ or $y = -\dfrac{ax}{b} + \dfrac{c}{b}$

6.2 Exercises (pp. 322–325) **1.** line **3.** linear **5.** linear

6.2 Exercises (pp. 322–325) **1.** line **3.** linear **5.** linear

15.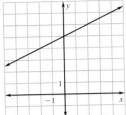

17. The x and y values are switched.

19.

27. $x = 3$ **29.** $y = 4x - 2$
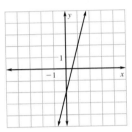

33.

37. in 11 months
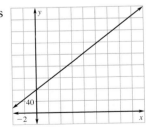

41. Colder. *Sample answer:* Using the graph or the table, 10°C is 50°F. Since room temperature is around 70°F, 10°C is colder.

6.2 Technology Activity (p. 326)

1. 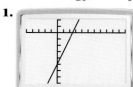   **3.**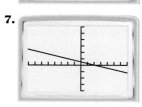

5. 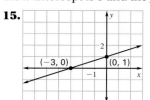   **7.**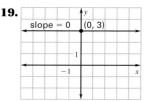

9–15. Sample answers are given.
9. X-min: 5; X-max: 5; Xscl = 1; Ymin = 5; Ymax = 5; Yscl = 1   **11.** X-min: 10; X-max: 10; Xscl = 1; Ymin = 10; Ymax = 10; Yscl = 1   **13.** X-min: 50; X-max: 20; Xscl = 10; Ymin = 20; Ymax = 20; Yscl = 10   **15.** X-min: 5; X-max: 5; Xscl = 1; Ymin = 100; Ymax = 100; Yscl = 1

6.3 Exercises (pp. 329 – 332)   **1.** y-intercept
5. x-intercept: 3; y-intercept: −1   **7.** x-intercept: 12; y-intercept: 3   **9.** x-intercept: 18; y-intercept: 2
11. x-intercept: −9; y-intercept: 7   **13.** Substitute $x = 0$ and $y = 0$ one at a time, and solve for the other variable; the x-intercept is 3 and the y-intercept is −4.

15.

17. x-intercept: 3; y-intercept: −15

19. x-intercept: 3.75; y-intercept: 3

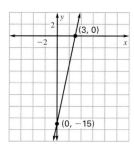

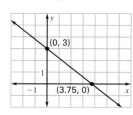

23. Substitute $x = 0$ to find the y-intercept; the y-intercept is 3.   **25.** x-intercepts   **27.** neither   **29.** x-intercept: none; y-intercept: 14   **31.** The x-intercept indicates how many 2 point baskets you need to shoot, with no 3 point shots, to get 72 points. The y-intercept indicates how many 3 point baskets you need to shoot, with no 2 point shots, to get 72 points.   **33.** The x-intercept indicates how many hours you must work at job A, without working any hours at job B, to earn \$315. The y-intercept indicates how many hours you must work at job B, without working any hours at job A, to earn \$315.

35. The x-intercept tells you how many packages of four t-shirts you need to buy to have 12 prizes.
39. $10x + 15y = \$450$ **41.** It slants up; it passes through Quadrants I, III, IV. *Sample answer:* Look at an example. If a line contains $(1, 0)$ and $(0, -1)$, it slants up from left to right and it goes through Quadrants I, III, and IV.

6.4 Exercises (pp. 337–339)   **1.** run, rise

3. $(1, 2)$, $(-3, -3)$; $\frac{5}{4}$ **5.** $(3,4)$, $(3, 0)$; undefined

7. undefined   **9.** 1   **11.** $\frac{3}{5}$ **13.** 0   **15.** Subtract $3 - 1$;
$\text{slope} = \dfrac{\text{rise}}{\text{run}} = \dfrac{y_2 - y_1}{x_2 - x_1} = \dfrac{2 - (-2)}{3 - 1} = 2$.   **17.** The x- and
y-coordinates are switched; $\text{slope} = \dfrac{\text{rise}}{\text{run}} = \dfrac{y_2 - y_1}{x_2 - x_1} =$
$\dfrac{0 - (-3)}{4 - 0} = \dfrac{3}{4}$.   **19.** The slope of the line is $\frac{1}{2}$; the slope of any two points on a given line is always the same as the slope of the line.   **21.** $w = 2$ **23.** $\frac{7}{10}$ **25.** $-\frac{2}{3}$ **27.** 3

29. $\frac{3.6}{7.7}$ or 0.47; $\frac{1.3}{8.4}$ or 0.15; the ramp is steeper at low tide because $0.47 > 0.15$.   **33.** 0.28   **35.** 3 in./day

6.5 Exercises (pp. 345–347)   **1.** slope   **3.** $y = 2x - 5$
5. $y = x + 2$ **7.** slope: 1; y-intercept: 3   **9.** slope: 2; y-intercept: −1   **11.** slope: $-\frac{3}{4}$; y-intercept: 9

13. slope: 0; y-intercept: 3   **15.** slope: $\frac{13}{11}$; y-intercept: −13

19.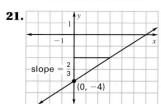

21.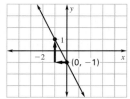

23. −1 is the y-intercept.

25. $y = -\frac{3}{2}x - 3$ **27.** The slope and y-intercept are switched; $y = -\frac{2}{3}x + 2$.   **29.** $y = 3x$ **31.** $y = \frac{1}{2}x - 4$
33. $y = 6$ **35.** $y = 2.3x$; slope: 2.3; y-intercept: 0
37. $y = -1.5x + 37$; slope: −1.5; y-intercept: 37

6.6 Exercises (pp. 351–353) **1.** direct variation **5.** no
7. no **9.** yes; $\frac{1}{6}$ **11.** no **13.** yes; $y = -\frac{1}{4}x$
17. No; it does no go through the origin. **19.** Yes; the graph is a line that goes through the origin.

21. 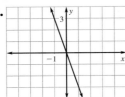 **23.**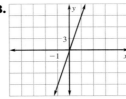

25. The graph does not go through the origin; the graph does not go through the origin so it does not show direct variation. **27.** $k = 6$; $y = 6x$ **29.** $k = \frac{1}{3}$; $y = \frac{1}{3}x$
31. $k = 6.5$; $y = 6.5x$

33. $y = \frac{1}{12}x$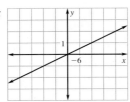

35. $C = 3.14d$; the slope represents pi; 314 ft.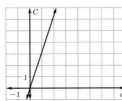

6.7 Exercises (pp. 357–359) **1.** half-planes
3. yes **5.** no **7.** yes

11. 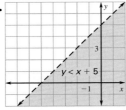 **13.**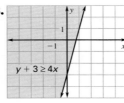

27. (0, 0) is a solution to the equation; the graph should be shaded on the other half-plane, such that (0, 0) is included.

29. $x + y > 10$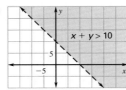

31. $x \geq 20$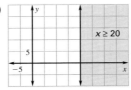

35. always **37.** never **39.** $\leq$ **41.** $>$
45. $7x + 9y \leq 50$. *Sample answer:* 3 shirts and 3 pairs of shorts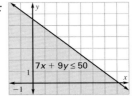

49. *Sample answer:* Any solution with a negative number is not a valid solution. A negative number of magazines or novels can not occur, so these solutions are invalid in the context of the problem.

6.8 Exercises (pp. 364–367) **1.** system
3. (1, 0)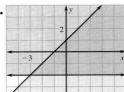

11. (4, 5)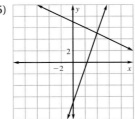

15. 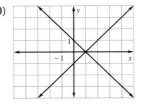 **19.**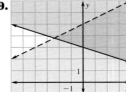

23. The solution is not shaded correctly.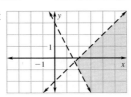

25. $y = 2x$, $2x + 2y = 72$ **27.** $C = 15n$, $C = 10n + 100$; 20 sessions **29.** $x + y = 90$, $2x = y$; 30 running shoes and 60 court shoes

33. a. $x + y \geq 4$, $x + y \leq 9$, $x \geq 2$, $y \geq 2$

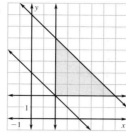

b. *Sample answer:* 3 students and 3 teachers or 4 teachers and 5 students

Chapter Review (pp. 372–376) **1.** solution **3.** rise, run
5. *Sample answer:* $(-4, 5)$, $(0, 4)$, $(4, 3)$

7. 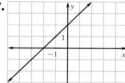 **9.**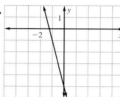

11. x-intercept: -1.5, y-intercept: 4.5

13. *Sample answer:* $(-1, 1)$, $(0, 0)$; -1 **15.** $\frac{2}{5}$

17. slope: $-\frac{2}{3}$, y-intercept: 4

19. slope: 4, y-intercept: 10;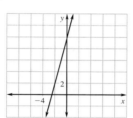

21. slope: $-\frac{3}{7}$, y-intercept: -3;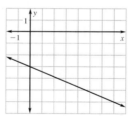

23. no **25.** $y = 10x$; 50 mi **27.**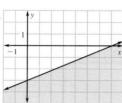

29. $(-2, -6)$ **31.** $(3, -4)$ **33.**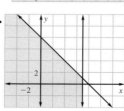

35. 78 bags of popcorn and 39 pretzels

Chapter 7

7.1 Exercises (pp. 389–391) **1.** base **3.** 4^6 **5.** a^{12}
7. $\frac{1}{7^4}$ **9.** $(20.3)^3$ **13.** $\frac{1}{(-3)^8}$ **15.** $(-2)^4$ **17.** $\frac{1}{0.71^{18}}$ **19.** d^8
21. $125z^3$ **23.** $\frac{1}{16y^2}$ **25.** d^4t^4 **27.** $-\frac{1}{g^3h^3}$ **29.** 6×10^8
31. 5.85×10^{-7} **33.** 1.066×10^5 **35.** The exponents of
10 were multiplied instead of added; 3.6×10^5.
37. 8 **39.** -8 **41.** 17 **43.** 12 **45.** false; 4^5 **47.** false; a^{11}
49. $8x^3$ **53.** 2^9 kilobytes

7.2 Exercises (pp. 396–398) **1.** B **3.** C **5.** E **7.** 5^4
9. d^7 **11.** w^6 **13.** $(-7)^{11}$ **15.** z^5 **17.** d^3 **21.** $\frac{25}{9}$
23. $\frac{y^3}{27}$ **25.** $\frac{16}{m^2}$ **27.** -32 **29.** 3.5×10^{11} **31.** 3.25×10^3
33. The exponents were divided instead of subtracted;
x^{16}. **35.** false; 6^2 **37.** false; c^3 **39.** $3x$ **41.** $4x^2$
47. 7.98×10^7; 4.1496×10^9 **49.** about 7 times more

7.3 Exercises (pp. 402–404) **1.** monomial **3.** $-20x^4$
5. $3x^3$ **7.** $8x^2y^7$ **9.** $-25x^7$ **11.** $-x^5y^{13}$ **13.** $16a^4b^{24}$
15. $-27x^9y^3$ **17.** $100{,}000b^5h^{10}$ **19.** x^6y^3 **21.** $9r^{14}s^{10}$
23. $8x^{12}y^9$ **25.** $(5a^2b^3)(4a^4b)^2 = (5a^2b^3)(16a^8b^2)$ (Power
of a power property) $= 80a^{10}b^5$ (Product of powers
property) **27.** $3m^4$ **29.** $\frac{k^2}{4x}$ **31.** ab^6 **33.** $\frac{4a^2}{b^6}$ **37.** $7y^4$
39. $3cd\sqrt{3}$ **41.** $4x^2y\sqrt{3}$ **43.** $4x^5y^6\sqrt{2}$
45. The exponents should be subtracted, not divided; $x^{15}y^3$.
47. $2m^4$ **49.** $36x^2y^2$ **51.** $8y^{15}$ **55.** It is 27 times
the weight.

7.4 Exercises (pp. 410–412) **1.** domain; range

3. domain: $-2, 2, 4$;
range: $-3, 5, 9$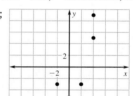

5. domain: $-1, 1, 2, 5$;
range: $-6, 3$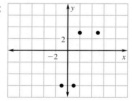

9. Yes; each input has exactly 1 output.
11. Yes; each input has exactly 1 output. **13.** The input
-9 has 2 output values: -81 and 81.

15. 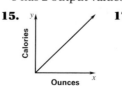 **17.** $y = x + 6$ **19.** $y = 3x - 2$

23. *Sample answer:* $y = 5x$

Input, x	1	2	3	4
Output, y	5	10	15	20

25. Exam scores are a function of study time.
27. a. $E = 0.40p$ **27. b.** 15 lb

29. domain: 1, 2, 3, 4, 5; range: 0.9, 1.8, 2.7, 3.6, 4.5; the graph represents a function since each input has exactly 1 output.

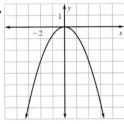

7.5 Exercises (pp. 417–419)   **1.** nonlinear function
3. B   **5.** A

11.

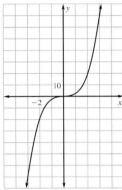

15.

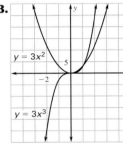

17. *Sample answer:* 1   **19.** *Sample answer:* -1.5

21. The negative sign was not considered when drawing the graph.

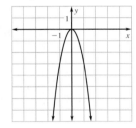

23. yes   **25.** no   **27.** linear function

29.

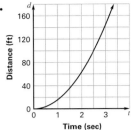

3 sec

31. $C = 1303.09d$, for $0 \leq d \leq 3.5$; linear; the graph is part of a line.

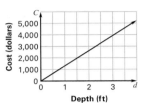

33.

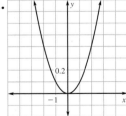

Sample answer: The graph of $y = 3x^3$ does not have a line of symmetry while the graph of $y = 3x^2$ does.

7.5 Technology Activity (p. 420)   **1.** It is the graph of $y = x^2$ reflected over the x-axis.   **3.** It is the graph of $y = 3x^2$ reflected over the x-axis.   **5.** The graph gets more narrow; it has the same general shape as the other functions but it is closer to the y-axis.

Chapter Review (pp. 424–426)   **1.** product of powers
3. nonlinear   **7.** $\frac{1}{2}$ **9.** 1   **11.** 6^6 **13.** $\frac{1}{w^{45}}$ **15.** x^4z^4

17. $\frac{1}{-32x^5}$ **19.** $\frac{1}{49}$ **21.** $\frac{h^4}{1296}$ **23.** about 8.05×10^7

25. $-8a^6b^3$ **27.** $4a^8b^4\sqrt{5}$ **29.** Function; each input has exactly one output.

31.

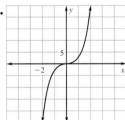

33.

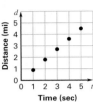

Chapter 8

8.1 Exercises (pp. 440–442) **1.** conversion factor
3. 4 **5.** 275 **7.** 4.5 **9.** 8 **11.** 8 **13.** 14 **15.** 33 **17.** 2
19. 227 **21.** 20 **23.** 7 min **25.** 16 h **27.** 130 min
29. 432 **31.** 90 **33.** 5 **35.** 250,000 **37.** 1
39. Multiplied 3 yd^3 by $\frac{9\,\text{ft}^3}{1\,\text{yd}^3}$ instead of by $\frac{27\,\text{ft}^3}{1\,\text{yd}^3}$;
$3\,\text{yd}^3\left(\frac{27\,\text{ft}^3}{1\,\text{yd}^3}\right) = 81\,\text{ft}^3$. **41.** = **43.** > **45.** = **47.** <
49. $\frac{2.54\,\text{cm}}{1\,\text{in.}}$ **51.** $\frac{2.54\,\text{cm}}{1\,\text{in.}}$ **53.** 10.5 cm **55.** 0.75 ton
57. a. 140 cm, 1.5 m, 63 in., 1700 mm **b.** Metric system;
3 heights are already in the metric system.
59. Saturn **61.** 3 blankets

8.2 Exercises (pp. 446–448) **1.** unit **3.** 55 mi/h
5. 3.5 m/sec **7.** 2.21 lb/kg **9.** 2.54 cm/in.
11. equivalent **13.** not equivalent **15.** The price must
go in the numerator and the number of DVDs
in the denominator; $\frac{60}{4} = \$15$ per DVD. **17.** The rate
is dollars per books; $6.50 per book. **19.** $\frac{5\,\text{ft}}{1\,\text{min}}$
21. < **23.** > **25.** < **27.** Rewrite 60 minutes as 1 hour.
29. $0.05 per oz **31.** $0.18 per oz **33.** ruby-throated
hummingbird **37. a.** 15 days **37. b.** 25 workers
39. about 171 h

8.3 Exercises (pp. 451–453) **1.** conversion factor
3. 504 **5.** 2,000,000 **7.** 2 **9.** 2 **11.** 1 **13.** 100 **15.** 72
17. 8 **19.** 1188 **21.** Instead of $\frac{1\,\text{ft}}{1.609\,\text{km}}$, it should be
$\frac{1\,\text{mi}}{1.609\,\text{km}} \times \frac{5280\,\text{ft}}{1\,\text{mi}} \approx 9845\,\text{ft}$. **23.** $\frac{1500\,\text{mi}}{31\,\text{h}} \times \frac{1\,\text{h}}{60\,\text{min}}$
25. $\frac{20\,\text{mi}}{1\,\text{h}} \times \frac{5280\,\text{ft}}{1\,\text{mi}} \times \frac{1\,\text{h}}{60\,\text{min}} \times \frac{1\,\text{min}}{60\,\text{sec}}$ **27.** 224 m/sec
29. 10.5 g/cm^3 **31.** 19.3 g/cm^3 **33.** 67 mi/h; this is not
reasonable; the speed limit on most highways is 65 miles
per hour, and a person cannot run faster than a car on a
highway.

8.4 Exercises (pp. 456–458) **1.** midpoint **5.** 6 **7.** 10
9. 19 **13.** perpendicular bisector **15.** segment bisector
17. 20 **19.** t does not intersect $\overline{AB}$ at a right angle, so it is
not perpendicular. t is a segment bisector. **21.** 900 ft
23. Yes; since , $m\angle JKR = m\angle RKL$, $\overrightarrow{KR}$ divides $\angle JKL$ into
congruent angles. **25.** $m\angle EKI = 90°$ and $m\angle ITE = 54°$
27. $\frac{1}{2^n}$

8.5 Exercises (pp. 465–467) **1.** median **3.** 12 cm^2, 16 cm
5. 30 ft^2, 30 ft **7.** 36 mm^2; 36 mm **9.** The units for area
should be square inches; 10 in.^{2} **11.** altitude **15.** The
area is twice as large. **17.** The area is 4 times as large.
19. 10 in.^{2} **21.** 24.5 ft^2 **25.** 162 in.

8.6 Exercises (pp. 474–476) **1.** hypotenuse **3.** 34 ft
5. 104 m **7.** 24.5 in. **9.** The formula is $a^2 + b^2 = c^2$,
not $(a + b)^2 = c^2$; $10^2 + 18^2 = c^2$, $100 + 324 = c^2$, $424 = c^2$,
20.6 ft. **11.** 8 m **13.** 15.3 ft **15.** no **17.** yes **19.** no
21. 65.6 **23.** 6 **25.** 3 **27.** 6.5 **29.** 3 **31.** 4.24 ft
33. 21.5 ft **35.** 8.9 ft **37.** 22.0 m

8.7 Exercises (pp. 482–485) **1.** diagonal **7.** rectangle
9. 109 **11.** 65 **13.** 65 **17.** $x = 40°$; $m\angle J = 40°$;
$m\angle K = 133°$; $m\angle L = 41°$; $m\angle M = 146°$
19. 130 cm^2; 52 cm

23. 96 units^2

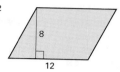

25. 220 units^2

31. 90 yd^2 **33.** 60 units^2

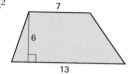

35. The area is 9 times as large. **37.** The area is $\frac{1}{4}$ as large.
39. area $\frac{7}{40}$ ft^2; perimeter $1\frac{5}{6}$ ft **41.** area about 4.1 m^2;
perimeter 8.5 m **43.** 360 ft^2 **45.** Always; opposite sides
are parallel. **47.** Never; a trapezoid has exactly
1 pair of parallel sides. **49.** square **51.** trapezoid
53. parallelogram **55.** $x = 50$; 50°, 130°, 50°, 130°
57. $121\frac{1}{2}$ ft^2

8.8 Exercises (pp. 492–495) **1.** diameter **3.** central
angle **5.** diameter **7.** 62.8 mm **9.** 314 cm **11.** 44 in.
15. 0.5 m **17.** 100 cm **19.** 105 yd **21.** 314 cm^2
23. 10.1736 cm^2 **25.** 314 km^2 **27.** 1 m **29.** 6 in.
31. 9 cm **33.** 530.66 m^2 **37.** The radius should be
squared, not π. $A = \pi r^2 = (3.14)(5.5)^2 = 94.985$ yd^2
39. 239.04 in.^{2} **41.** $C = 2(3.14)(8.95)$; $A = (3.14)(8.95)^2$
43. $C = 2(3.14)(15)$; $A = (3.14)(15)^2$ **45.** 4533.375 m^2
47. $15

8.8 Technology Activity (p. 498) **1.** The radius is
multiplied by 3. **3.** The radius is multiplied by 5.

Chapter Review (pp. 502–506) **1.** midpoint
3. diameter **5.** 7 **7.** 59 **9.** 3 **11.** not equivalent
13. equivalent **15.** 4,233,600 sec **17.** 9 **19.** It triples
from 9 to 27. **21.** 25 **23.** 25 **25.** 3 m **27.** 32
29. 15 m^2 **31.** 7.5 in.^{2} **33.** 314 ft^2; 62.8 ft

Chapter 9

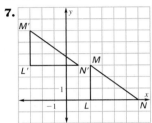
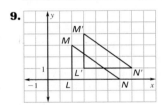
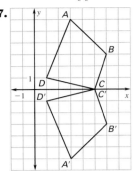
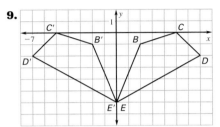
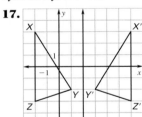
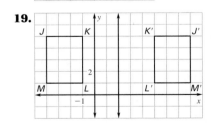

9.4 Exercises (pp. 537–539) **1.** scale factor

5.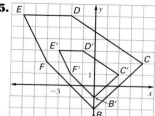

7.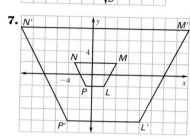

13. Scale factor $= \dfrac{\text{Side length of image}}{\text{Side length of original}} = \dfrac{\overline{A'B'}}{\overline{AB}} = \dfrac{6}{3} = 2$;
the scale factor of the dilation is 2. **15.** $\dfrac{1}{3}$

17. 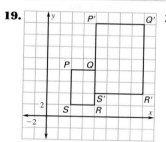 $\dfrac{1}{2}$

19. 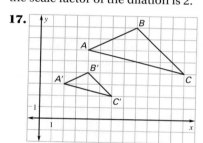 2

21. greater than 1 **23.** between 0 and 1

9.5 Exercises (pp. 543–545) **1.** scale model **3.** 4 cm
5. 13 cm **9.** 1 in.:9 ft **11.** The second proportion is
inverted; $\dfrac{1\,\text{cm}}{100\,\text{cm}} = \dfrac{2\,\text{cm}}{x\,\text{m}}$, $x = 200$ m. **13.** 0.5 ft
15. 1.58 ft **17.** 1:18 **19.** 11:1 **23.** 1089 ft

Chapter Review (pp. 550–552) **1.** D **3.** B **7.** 48 ft

9. 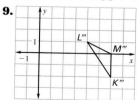 **11.**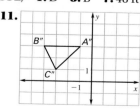

13. $\dfrac{1}{5}$; length: 8 cm, width: 2 cm **15.** 1 in.:20 ft

Chapter 10

10.1 Exercises (pp. 563–565) **1.** coplanar
3. Skew; *s* and *t* are not coplanar and do not intersect.
5. Skew; if you continue line *m* and line *n*, they do not
intersect and they are not coplanar.

7. never

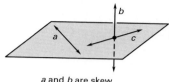

a and *b* are skew.
b and *c* are not skew.

9. always

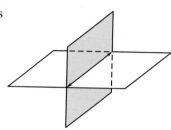

13. ℓ and *n* **15.** *Sample answer:* A and C, B and C
17. *Sample answer:* The three planes do not intersect at
one place, only pairs of planes intersect in the picture; the
intersection of two planes is a line. **19.** line *AB*
21. plane *ABFE* **23.** *Sample answer:* Each leg is parallel
to every other leg.

10.2 Exercise (pp. 568–571) **1.** pyramid **3.** sphere;
not a polyhedron **5.** cube; polyhedron **7.** *Sample
answer:* Faces: pentagons *QRSTU* and *VWXYZ*, rectangles
QRWV, *RSXW*, *STYX*, *TUZY*, and *QUZV*; edges: *QR*, *RS*,
ST, *TU*, *UQ*, *VW*, *WX*, *XY*, *YZ*, *ZV*, *QV*, *RW*, *SX*, *TY*, and *UZ*;
vertices: *Q*, *R*, *S*, *T*, *U*, *V*, *W*, *X*, *Y*, and *Z*; diagonals: *QX*, *QY*,
RY, *RZ*, *SZ*, *SV*, *TV*, *TW*, *UW*, and *UX* **9.** *Sample answer:*
Faces: *ABC*, *BCD*, *ABD*, and *ADC*; edges: *AB*, *AC*, *AD*, *BC*,
BD, *CD*; vertices: *A*, *B*, *C*, and *D*; no diagonals
11. rectangular pyramid; 5 faces, 8 edges, 5 vertices
13. octagonal prism; 10 faces, 24 edges, 16 vertices
15. The bases of the polyhedron are pentagons; the
polyhedron has two congruent bases that lie in parallel
planes, so it is a pentagonal prism.

19. **21.**

23. No; a triangular pyramid has no diagonals.
25. octagonal prism **27.** trapezoidal prism
29. cylinder, cone **33.** 6 edges

10.3 Exercises (pp. 576–579)   **1.** circles, rectangle

3.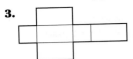

7. 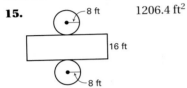   1062 ft^2

9. 48 in.^{2} **11.** 174 yd^2

15. 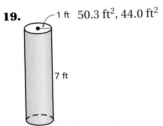   1206.4 ft^2

19. 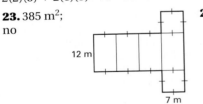 1 ft   50.3 ft^2, 44.0 ft^2

21. Each term needs to be multiplied by 2; $S = 2(1)(2) + 2(2)(5) + 2(1)(5) = 4 + 20 + 10 = 34$ m^2.

23. 385 m^2; no   **25.**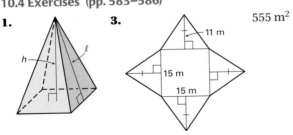

33. $S = 6s^2$

10.4 Exercises (pp. 583–586)

1. 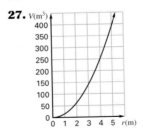   **3.** 555 m^2

5.    6.8 mm^2

7. 67 cm^2 **9.** 697.4 m^2 **11.** The formula used is for the lateral surface area; $S = \pi r^2 + \pi r\ell = \pi(5)^2 + \pi(5)(10) \approx 235.62$ yd^2.   **15.** 689.9 in.^{2} **17.** 243.3 in.^{2} **19.** Use the Pythagorean theorem to find the hypotenuse of the right triangle formed by the height of the cone and the radius of the cone; 13 ft, 282.7 ft^2.

21. 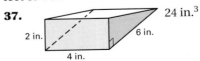 A   24 in.   5 in.

25. 6π in.^{2} **27.** 54π in.^{2} **29.** If the radius and slant height increase by the same factor, the lateral surface area increases by the square of that factor; 150π square inches.

10.5 Exercises (pp. 593–596)   **1.** base, height   **3.** 132 m^3
5. 13.68 cm^3 **7.** 552.9 ft^3 **9.** 20.4 m^3 **11.** 2309.1 m^3
13. 64 yd^3 **15.** 1260 m^3 **17.** 339.3 cm^3 **19.** *Sample answer:* The area of the base of the cylinder is πr^2, the student used the circumference of the base instead; $V = Bh = \pi r^2 h = \pi(4)^2(5) \approx 251$ m^3.   **21.** 6480 in.^{3}
23. 409.5 ft^3 **25.** 31.3 in.^{3}

27. V(m³) graph

29. surface area   **31.** volume   **33.** Cylindrical pool; 154 ft^3; the volume of each pool gives the amount of water it can hold. The rectangular pool holds 2560 cubic feet of water, the cylindrical pool holds about 2714 cubic feet of water.

37. 24 in.^{3} 2 in.   6 in.   4 in.

39. about 11 times

10.6 Exercises (pp. 600–603) **1.** $V = \frac{1}{3}Bh$ **3.** D **5.** A
7. 12 in.³ **9.** 0.3 m³ **11.** 144 yd³ **13.** 2560 m³
15. 247.5 ft³ **17.** 95,425.9 ft³ **21.** The formula for the
volume of a pyramid is $V = \frac{1}{3}Bh$; $V = \frac{1}{3}Bh = \frac{1}{3}(15)^2(12) =$
900 cubic feet. **23.** 506.8 ft³ **25.** 2,019,960.3 cm³
27. 70.7 ft³ **29.** 93.6 m², 249.6 m³ **31.** 13 yd **33.** 14 in.
35. 904.8 cm³

39.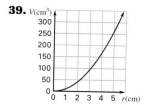

41. 75.4 in.³ **43.** 9.4 in.³ **45.** 2513.3 ft³ **47.** Cone.
Sample answer: There is 960 cubic feet of dirt to make
either solid. The square pyramid that has a side length of
10 feet and a volume of 960 cubic feet has a height of
28.8 feet. The cone that has a radius of 5 feet and a
volume of 960 cubic feet has a height of 36.7 feet.

10.7 Technology Activity (p. 604) **1.** *Sample answer:*
The surface area ratio is the scale factor squared. **3.** $\frac{5}{6}$

10.7 Exercises (pp. 608–611) **1.** similar solids **3.** Not
similar; the ratio of the radii is not the same as the ratio
of the heights. **5.** Similar; the ratios of the lengths,
widths, and heights are all equal. **7.** surface area:
600π in.², volume: 2000π in.³ **9.** surface area: 377 cm²,
volume: 476.9 cm³ **13.** 2:5 **15.** 4:3 **19.** 5:6 **21.** 1:3
25. 0.2 ft **27.** Multiply the dimensions of the classroom
by 25. **31.** 1:27; if the ratio of the surface areas is 1:9,
then the scale factor is 1:3, and the ratio of the volumes
is 1:27.

Chapter Review (pp. 615–618) **1.** triangular prism
3. rectangular pyramid **7.** line *a* **9.** triangular prism;
polyhedron **11.** pentagonal pyramid; polyhedron
13. 948 in.²; triangular prism **15.** about 471.2 m²
17. about 785.4 ft² **19.** 240 mm³ **21.** about 494.7
cm³ **23.** No; the candle needs 15 cubic inches of
wax. **25.** not similar

Chapter 11

11.1 Exercises (pp. 633–635) **1.** mean **3.** range
5. −56 in.; −56 in.; −56 in.; 27 in. **7.** 19°; 13°;
no mode; 83° **9.** $1796\frac{6}{7}$; 1680; no mode; 485
11. 10 is not the middle value when the numbers are
in numerical order; the median is 9. **15.** With red: 74,
81.5, 76 and 94, 98; without red: 84, 83.5, 76 and 94, 42;
with 2 and 6 removed, the mean gets much larger, the
range gets much smaller. The mode is unchanged, and
the median increases slightly. **17.** mean, median

19. mean, median **21.** 52,327; 49,707; 49,646; mean;
the mean takes into account the three dates with
higher attendance. **23.** 140 points **25.** *Sample
answer:* 5, 6, 8, 8 **27.** 9.650; 9.750; 9.650; no; Kurt and
Isaac would share second place.

11.2 Exercises (pp. 639–642) **1.** bar graph

3.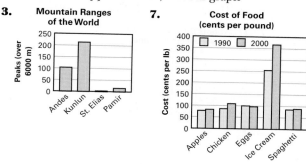
7.

9. ice cream **11.** 10 more seats **13.** 111.6° **15.** 50.4°

17.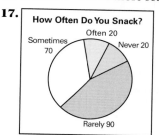

19.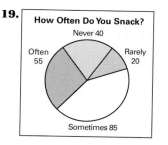

23. *Sample answer:* Circle graph; the data represents
parts of a whole. **25.** *Sample answer:* Circle graph;
since every student will have a response, the data
represents parts of a whole.

27. 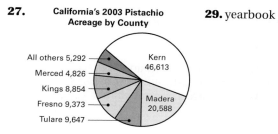 **29.** yearbook

11.3 Exercises (pp. 645–648)   **1.** intervals

3. *Sample:*

Interval	Tally	Frequency
1	ЖІ ІІ	7
2	ЖІ ЖІ І	11
3	ІІІ	3

greatest: 2;
least: 3

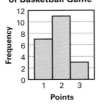

**Shots During First Half
of Basketball Game**

5. *Sample:*

Interval	Tally	Frequency
5–7	ЖІ ІІІ	8
8–10	ЖІ ЖІ	10
11–13	ІІ	2
14–16	ІІІ	3

greatest: 8–10;
least: 11–13

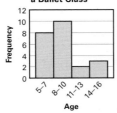

**Ages of Dancers in
a Ballet Class**

9. The intervals are not equal.   **15.** *Sample answer:* 1–2, 3–4, 5–6   **17.** *Sample answer:* 5–10, 11–16, 17–22, 23–28, 29–34, 35–40   **19.** 3   **23.** No; 10 is part of an interval, so the exact number cannot be determined.

11.4 Exercises (pp. 652–654)   **1.** stem, leaf

3. 8│0; stem: 8, leaf: 0   **5.** 12│9; stem: 12, leaf: 9

11.
18	1 3 4 6 7
19	
20	2
21	9
22	5 6 8

Key: 21│9 = 21.9

Interval with stem 18 has the most values.

13. The bottom row on the stem-and-leaf plot should be two rows with stems 10 and 11, and the key is incorrect; the key should be 11│5 = 115.

8	3
9	1 5
10	8
11	1 5

Key: 11│5 = 115

17.

Set C		Set D
	6	5
7 0	7	
	8	7 8
8 2	9	3 5
2	10	2
8 1	11	5

Key: 2│9│3 = 92 and 93

21. 2.0; 2.0; 0.1; 2.0 and 2.8   **23.** 0, 1, 2

25.
11	0 3 5
12	3 7
13	1 4
14	
15	9

Key: 15│9 = 15.9

27. 5 min, 45 min;
30-39 min interval

31.

	Wins		Losses
		0	6 7 7
	8	1	0 2 4 5 6
7 4 4 3 0		2	1
		3	
	1	4	

Key: 0│2│1 = 20 and 21

Sample answer: When the Browns scored less than 20 points, they usually lost. When they scored 20 or more points, they usually won.

11.5 Exercises (pp. 657–659)   **1.** lower quartile

3.

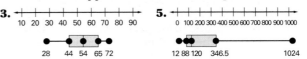

5.

7. *Sample answer:* The lower half is made up of the numbers 4, 7, 9, 10. The lower quartile is the mean of 7 and 9; the lower quartile is 8.   **9.** City A: 50%; City B: 75%   **13.** False. *Sample answer:* There is about one-quarter of the data between the lower extreme and the lower quartile. There is also about one-quarter of the data between the median and the upper quartile.   **15.** lower quartile: 116; upper quartile: 212   **17.** lower quartile: 3.5; upper quartile: 6   **21.** *Sample answer:* Khalila has a higher median score than Tasha, 11 points versus 9 points, but her performance is much more variable. For Khalila, it took an interval of 7, from 7 to 14, to contain half of her point totals, but for Tasha, it took only an interval of 4, from 8 to 12, to contain half of her point totals, so Tasha's scoring is more consistent. This is also shown by the fact that the extremes for Tasha are between the extremes for Khalila. Also, the range for Tasha is only 8 points, but the range is 15 points for Khalila.

23.

An outlier does not have much of an effect on the quartiles, but makes a box-and-whisker plot very long and this greatly increases the range.

11.6 Exercises (pp. 663–667)   **1.** line graph

3.

5. relatively no correlation   **7.** negative correlation

9.

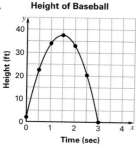

positive correlation

11. Relatively no correlation. *Sample answer:* A student's height is not related to the student's test score.
13. Negative correlation. *Sample answer:* If you have a loan, as you pay off the loan the amount you still owe goes down.

15.

17. The last ordered pair is (5, 6), the graph shows (4, 6).

19. *Sample answer:* Scatter plot; a scatter plot shows trends in the data.

23.

Height of Baseball

25. Box-and-whisker plot; this plot will show the median and the extremes.

27.

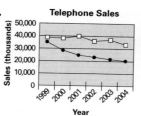

Telephone Sales

The vertical axis is marked off by 10,000's since the data range is 20,000 to 40,000.

29. 2887 telephones per year   **31.** *Sample answer:* 23

11.6 Technology Activity (pp. 668–669)

1.

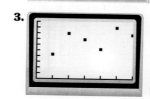

3.

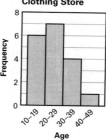

Chapter Review (pp. 674–678)   **1.** mode
3. categorical data   **5.** stem-and-leaf plot
7. 0.125; 1; −7 and 2; 15   **9.** 2.1; 2.2; 2.5; 2.7
11. 29; 25; 20 and 28; 43   **13.** lemonade

15. *Sample:*

Interval	Tally	Frequency
10–19	ⅢⅠ	6
20–29	ⅢⅡ	7
30–39	ⅢⅠ	4
40–49	Ⅰ	1

People Shopping at a Clothing Store

17.
```
1 | 5  6  9          20–29
2 | 0  1  2  5  7  8  9
3 | 1  2  6  7
4 | 2
```
Key: 4|2 = 42

21.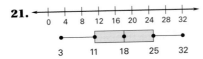

27. 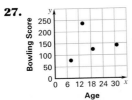 The scatter plot shows relatively no relationship between age and bowling score.

29.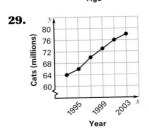

Chapter 12

12.1 Exercises (pp. 691–692)   **1.** trinomial
3. $3m + 7$; binomial   **5.** $-n^2 + 5n - 1$; trinomial
7. $y^2 - 5y + 2$; trinomial   **9.** $4x^{10} - 13x^3$; binomial
13. $-7q^5 + 3q^3 + 3q$ **15.** $12m^2 + m - 6$
17. $-12y^3 + 34y^2 - 6$ **19.** $4s^4 - 11s + 18$
21. $-20x$ and $-3x^2$ are not like terms; $-3x^2 - 20x - 4$.
23. $8x + 6$ **25.** $5a - 8b - 24$ **27.** $-6ab^2 + 6ab$
29. 98 ft   **31.** 122 ft   **33.** 86 ft   **35.** Sometimes; if the monomial and binomial have no like terms, the sum is a trinomial. If the monomial and binomial have like terms, the sum is a binomial.

12.2 Exercises (pp. 695–698)   **1.** Multiply each term by -1.   **3.** $12y + 2$ **5.** $5x + 4$ **7.** $6g^2 + g + 3$
9. $6k^2 + 5$ **11.** The terms were not aligned properly by degree, and unlike terms were combined; $-2x^3 + 5x^2 - 13x + 12$ **13.** $6x + 12$ **15.** $-10d - 7$
17. $3r^2 + 2r + 4$ **19.** $3a^2 + 5a + 17$ **21.** Only the first term of the second polynomial was subtracted. All three terms should be subtracted; $3x^2 - 8x + 5$.
23. $12n + 3$ **25.** $-19y - 15$ **27.** $17q^2 - 7q$
29. $20x^3 + 11x^2 - 15x + 5$ **31.** $2x^2 + 13x + 14$
33. $3, -3$ **35.** $2\sqrt{3}, -2\sqrt{3}$ **37.** $16x + 12$ **39.** $24x - 4$
43. $204.759t^3 - 1213.19t^2 - 2009.04t + 92,522$
45. $2b^2 + 10b$

12.3 Exercises (pp. 701–702)   **1.** polynomial
3. $6w^2 + 2w$ **5.** $-8x^7 - 8x^3$ **7.** $12q^4 + 24q^3$
11. $3y^4 - 5y^2 - 10y$ **13.** $5n^5 - 8n^4 + 3n^3$
15. $-18t^6 + 8t^5 - 2t^4$ **17.** The negative sign was not distributed; $x^2 \cdot 3x^2 + x^2 \cdot 2x - x^2 \cdot 8$; $-x^3 - 7x$.
19. $2w^2 - 10w$ **21.** $w^2 + 20w$ **23.** $2b^2 - 12b$

12.3 Technology Activity (p. 703)   **1.** yes   **3.** yes

12.4 Exercises (pp. 707–709)   **1.** binomial
3. $y^2 - 3y - 4$ **5.** $x^2 - 16$ **7.** $15q^2 - 8q + 1$
9. $x^2 + 7x - 18$ **11.** $6r^2 + r - 7$ **13.** $-3t^2 - t + 4$
15. $9x^2 - 1$ **17.** $-14b^2 + 41b - 15$ **19.** $3b^2 - 58b + 72$
21. Each term in the first binomial needs to be multiplied by each term in the second binomial; $(x \cdot x) + (x \cdot 6) + (3 \cdot x) + (3 \cdot 6)$, $x^2 + 9x + 18$.   **25.** $4x^2 + 6x + 2$
27. $4x^2 + 15x + 9$ **29.** $2x^3 + 4x^2 + 2x$
31. $50 + 100r + 50r^2$; $\$53.05$ **35.** $6n^2 - 12n - 18$
37. $600 - 70x + 2x^2$; 300 ft^2

Chapter Review (pp. 714–716)   **1.** polynomial
3. trinomial   **5.** binomial   **9.** $2w^2 + 3w - 8$
11. $-x^2 + 16x + 28$ **13.** $-10y^2 + 20y + 44$
15. $9q^2 - 7$ **17.** $14m^2 - 17m$ **19.** $2x^2 + 2x + 6$
21. $-3a^3 + 6a^2$ **23.** $2x^2 + 8x$ **25.** $4x^2 - 20x$
27. $q^2 - 16q + 63$ **29.** $4x^2 + 11x - 3$ **31.** $5x^2 + 17x - 12$

Standards Review Handbook

Rounding (p. 723)   **1.** 1300   **3.** 8.2   **5.** 40,000   **7.** 450
9. 62.8   **11.** 164.5

Divisibility Tests (p. 724)   **1.** 2   **3.** 3, 5   **5.** 2, 3, 4, 6, 9
7. 5   **9.** 2, 4

Factors and Multiples (p. 726)   **1.** $2^2 \cdot 7$ **3.** $2^3 \cdot 3 \cdot 5$
5. 4; 96   **7.** 14; 70

Mixed Numbers and Improper Fractions (p. 727)

1. 38   **3.** 3   **5.** 3   **7.** $\frac{11}{6}$ **9.** $\frac{61}{7}$ **11.** $2\frac{3}{4}$ **13.** $4\frac{1}{6}$ **15.** $4\frac{1}{8}$

Solving Problems Using Additions, Subtraction, Multiplication, and Division (p. 729)   **1.** Total CDs = Number of packages • CDs per package; 128 CDs
3. Cost per package = Total paid ÷ Number of packages; $\$2.55$ **5.** Pencils left = Total pencils − Pencils given away; 68 pencils   **7.** Total flowers = Number of flats • Flowers per flat; 576 flowers

Using Estimation (p. 731)   **1.** 1800   **3.** 20,000   **5.** 2000
7. 1420   **9.** 21,700   **11.** 3000   **13–23.** Sample estimates are given.   **13.** 400; 1000   **15.** 40,000; 54,000   **17.** 30; 40
19. 200; 300   **21.** 12,000; 21,000   **23.** 90; 100

Ratios and Rates (p. 732)   **1.** $\frac{13}{12}$, 13:12, 13 to 12   **3.** $\frac{11}{23}$,
11:23, 11 to 23   **5.** 208 mi

Using Inequality Symbols (p. 733)   **1.** true   **3.** true
5. $x \le \$10$ **7.** $s \le 20$ **9.** $t \ge 80$

The Coordinate Plane (p. 734)   **1.** $(-1, 2)$ **3.** $(-2, -2)$
5. $(0, 1)$

Points, Lines, and Planes (p. 735)   **1.** B **3.** A **5.** line
7. *Sample answer: R, U, V*   **9.** *Sample answer:* $\overrightarrow{UV}$, $\overleftrightarrow{RT}$

Classifying Angles and Triangles (p. 737) **1.** $\angle E$, $\angle DEF$, $\angle FED$, **3.** $\angle X$, $\angle WXY$, $\angle YXW$, **5.** right **7.** obtuse **9.** acute **11.** obtuse **13.** equilateral

Using a Protractor (p. 738) **1.** 110° **3.** 90°
5.

Polygons (p. 741) **1.** yes; pentagon **3.** yes; triangle **5.** quadrilateral; yes; all side lengths equal, all interior angle measures equal **7.** octagon; yes; all side lengths equal, all interior angle measures equal **9.** triangle; yes; all side lengths equal, all interior angle measures equal **11.** 360° **13.** 1440° **15.** 2880° **17.** 90°

Perimeter, Area, and Volume (p. 742) **1.** 48 m; 135 m² **3.** 32 yd, 64 yd²

Interpreting Bar Graphs and Tables (p. 743) **1.** 20 students **3.** period 2

Problem Solving Strategies (p. 745) **1.** 45 crates **3.** 18 rectangles **5.** 2 keychains **7.** 21 students **9.** Wednesday

Venn Diagrams and Logical Reasoning (p. 746) **1.** They are odd numbers that are not multiples of 5.
3.

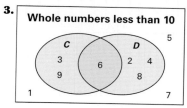

5. Sometimes. *Sample answer:* 6 is even and a multiple of 3, but 5 is neither.

Extra Practice

Chapter 1 (p. 747) **1.** 6 **3.** 256 **5.** 48 **7.** -4, -3, -2, 3, 7, 9 **9.** 25; 25 **11.** 0; 0 **13.** -409 **15.** 179 **17.** 0 **19.** -16 **21.** 51 **23.** -15 **25.** 68 **27.** -17 **29.** -175 **31.** 252 **33.** -270 **35.** -3024 **37.** -12 **39.** 0 **41.** -4
43. $7\left(2 \cdot \frac{3}{7}\right) = 7\left(\frac{3}{7} \cdot 2\right)$ [Commutative Property] =
$\left(7 \cdot \frac{3}{7}\right)2$ [Associative Property] = $3 \cdot 2$ [Inverse property of multiplication] = 6 [Multiplication] **45.** -25
47. $-4 - 9r$ **49.** $96

Chapter 2 (p. 748) **1.** $\frac{1}{2}$ **3.** $-\frac{2}{7}$ **5.** $\frac{2}{9}$ **7.** $-\frac{3}{2}$
9. not equivalent **11.** equivalent **13.** *Sample answer:* $\frac{4}{6}$; $\frac{16}{24}$ **15.** *Sample answer:* $\frac{2}{3}$; $\frac{4}{6}$ **17.** $>$ **19.** $>$ **21.** $<$

23. $>$ **25.** $\frac{1}{5}, \frac{1}{4}, \frac{1}{3}, \frac{1}{2}$ **27.** $-\frac{11}{5}, -\frac{7}{8}, -\frac{1}{2}, -\frac{1}{4}$
29. $-\frac{24}{7}, -3\frac{1}{3}, \frac{29}{9}$ **31.** $1\frac{1}{2}$ **33.** $-\frac{2}{3}$ **35.** $\frac{1}{15}$ **37.** $8\frac{1}{8}$
39. $\frac{3}{16}$ **41.** $3\frac{3}{5}$ **43.** $\frac{5}{18}$ **45.** $-3\frac{3}{32}$ **47.** -0.384
49. 3.875 **51.** $-\frac{7}{25}$ **53.** $\frac{3}{500}$

Chapter 3 (p. 749) **1.** $<$ **3.** $>$ **5.** $-2.3, -2.12, -2.1, -2.01$ **7.** 3.81 **9.** 13.1 **11.** -8.115 **13.** 3.9104 **15.** 1.5 **17.** -31.866 **19.** 0.31 **21.** 1.75 **23.** $\frac{1}{5}$ **25.** $1\frac{2}{5}$ **27.** 12.5% **29.** 72% **31.** $34 **33.** $67.20 **35.** 12% increase **37.** 43% increase **39.** $65 **41.** $958.52 **43.** $3288

Chapter 4 (p. 750) **1.** $10,000,000$ **3.** 1 **5.** 10^4 **7.** 10^0 **9.** 1.24×10^5 **11.** 7.91×10^{-5} **13.** 0.0027 **15.** $588,000,000,000$ **17.** $\frac{81}{16}$ **19.** 243 **21.** $\frac{6}{k}$ **23.** 271 **25.** 23 **27.** 8.4 **29.** 21 and 22 **31.** 4 **33.** $\frac{\sqrt{7}}{7}$ **35.** 3 **37.** Irrational; 90 is not a perfect square. **39.** Rational; fractions with an integer in the numerator and a nonzero integer in the denominator are rational.
41. $=$

43. $>$

45. $0.\overline{3}$, 0.334, 0.34, $0.\overline{34}$ **47.** $-\sqrt{15}$, -3.7, $-\sqrt{9.6}$, -2.85

Chapter 5 (p. 751) **1.** $x^2 + 4$ **3.** $\frac{x^3}{27}$ **5.** $x^2 - 12$ **7.** $11k - 8$ **9.** $7x + 6$ **11.** $25a + 36$ **13.** 16 **15.** 24 **17.** -5 **19.** 7 **21.** -42 **23.** -12 **25.** $5 + \frac{x}{3} = -1$; -18 **27.** 225 **29.** 9.3
31. $j \geq -5$
33. $z \leq -2.5$
35. $x < -5$
37. $s \leq 8$
39. $c < 2$
43. $b > 8$

Chapter 6 (p. 752) **1.** not a solution **3.** solution
5. not a solution

7. 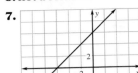 **9.**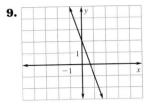

13. x-intercept: 2; y-intercept: 4 **15.** x-intercept: 6;
y-intercept: -3 **17.** x-intercept: 10; y-intercept: -50
19. 16 **21.** $-\dfrac{3}{2}$ **23.** 0 **25.** $-\dfrac{2}{9}$; -7 **27.** 4; -12 **29.** $\dfrac{5}{6}$; 6

31. direct variation; -85 **33.** direct variation; $-\dfrac{3}{11}$
35. not direct variation **37.** not a solution
39. not a solution **41.** solution

43. 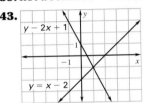 **45.**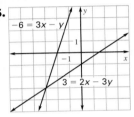

47.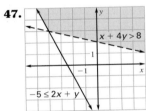

Chapter 7 (p. 753) **1.** $(-6)^{11}$ **3.** $\dfrac{1}{24^4}$ **5.** 10^{56} **7.** 13^{20}
9. $9^3 y^3$ **11.** $b^8 c^8$ **13.** 6.56×10^5 **15.** 6.12×10^{-6}
17. 4 **19.** d^3 **21.** $\dfrac{1}{w^2}$ **23.** $\dfrac{3^3}{2^3}$ **25.** $\dfrac{2^4}{x^4}$ **27.** $\dfrac{1}{2^4}$ **29.** $-20y^6$
31. $32c^8 d^2$ **33.** $\dfrac{5b^3}{2}$ **35.** $\dfrac{y^{10}}{x^5}$ **37.** $7c^2$ **39.** $2ab^4 \sqrt{13}$

41. domain: 1, 2, 3, 4, 5;
range: -1, 1; function

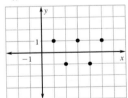

43. domain: -2, -1, 0, 1;
range: 3, 4, 5, 6, 7; not a
function

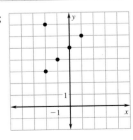

45. $y = -2x - 3$ **47.** not a function **49.** function

Chapter 8 (p. 754) **1.** 5.32 **3.** 10 **5.** 135 sec
7. 2 apples per dollar **9.** 17.5 lb per gal
11. not equivalent **13.** 3 **15.** 5 **17.** 20 **19.** 210 cm^2
21. 90 ft^2 **23.** 16

25. 195 units^2

27. 10 units^2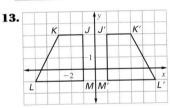

29. 357 yd^2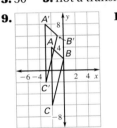

31. 251.2 in.; 5024 in.^{2} **33.** 24.492 in.; 47.7594 in.^{2}

Chapter 9 (p. 755) **1.** $\overline{AB} \cong \overline{PQ}$; $\overline{BC} \cong \overline{QR}$; $\overline{AC} \cong \overline{PR}$
3. 50° **5.** not a translation **7.** not a translation

9. 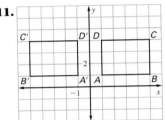 **11.**

13.

15.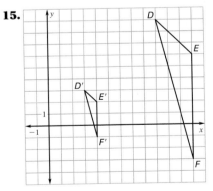

17. 3 **19.** 1 in. = 3 ft

Chapter 10 (p. 756) **1.** *Sample answer:* $\overrightarrow{PQ}$ and $\overleftrightarrow{RV}$
3. *Sample answer:* Plane PQR and plane PTW
5. 7 faces, 12 edges, 7 vertices

7. 516 m²

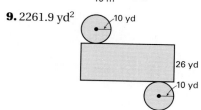

9. 2261.9 yd²

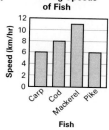

11. 427.3 cm² **13.** 330 in.³ **15.** 266.7 ft³ **17.** 252 cm³
19. 38.2 cm²; 39.7 cm³

Chapter 11 (p. 757) **1.** 40.5; 37; 24; 57 **3.** 88; 87; 78 and 95; 22

5.

Swimming Speeds of Fish

7.

Heights of 30 Students

9. Yes; add the number of students in each interval that is between 60 and 69.9. **11.** 117.5; 44

13. As the age of a car increases the price decreases.

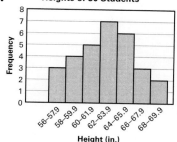

Car Age vs. Price

Chapter 12 (p. 758) **1.** $-x^2 - 2x + 7$ **3.** $-k^2 + 21$
5. $27a^3 - 17a^2$ **7.** $-x^2 - 12x - 15$ **9.** 54 ft
11. $-15x^2 + 4x$ **13.** $x - 2$ **15.** $-5x^3 + 3x^2 - 6x - 8$
17. $7x^3 - 7x^2 - 5x + 11$ **19.** $6x^2 + 5x + 1$
21. $-q^4 + 2q^3$ **23.** $6x^5 + 27x^4 - 12x^2$
25. $-2r^8 - 4r^2 - r$ **27.** $44d^5 - 88d^4 + 99d^3$
29. $-m^2 + 7m - 12$ **31.** $16y^2 - 9$ **33.** $10x^2 - x - 2$
35. $-14bn - 35n + 6b + 15$ **37.** $3x^2 + 9x + 6$